THE COMMON DENOMINATOR

Race boats, pleasure boats, luxury motor yachts, patrol boats, work boats and ferries. What do they have in common?

ARNESON SURFACE DRIVES™

Arneson Surface Drives provide all types of vessels with performance and reliability unmatched by any other propulsion system. The kind of performance and reliability that is far superior to conventional shafts, struts and rudders, stern drives or water jets. Arneson Surface Drives are technically advanced propulsion systems which use surface-piercing propellers. They are more efficient than conventional drive systems, thus producing greater speed and economy.

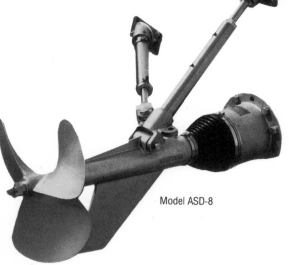
Model ASD-8

VOSPER 21 Metre

INTERCEPTOR 41'

Owners, designers and builders the world over specify Arneson Surface Drives because of their unique features:

- Excellent shallow water capability
- Higher top speed and increased efficiency
- Excellent maneuverability and steering control
- Flexibility of engine placement
- Maximum protection from electrolysis and corrosion
- Quick in-the-water propeller changes
- Ease of installation and alignment
- Eliminates cavitation
- Maximum reliability and minimum maintenance
- Vibration and noise minimized.

Arneson Surface Drives are manufactured in 14 different models to handle gas, diesel and turbine engines up to 5,000 HP on boats up to 150 feet.

If you want performance with reliability, get Arneson Surface Drives.

DENISON 80'

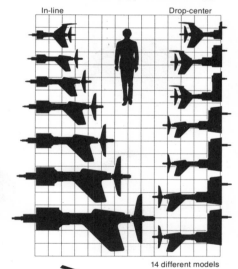
In-line   Drop-center

14 different models

COUGAR 41' Catamaran

ARNESON SURFACE DRIVES™
ARNESON MARINE, INC.

WATERMAN 56' Catamaran Passenger Ferry

15 Koch Road, Unit E
Corte Madera
CA 94925 USA
Tel: 415-927-1500
FAX: 415-927-1937

2850 N.E. 187th Street
North Miami Beach
FL 33180 USA
Tel: 305-935-1336
FAX: 305-932-4673

Via Coppino 345
55049 Viareggio
ITALY
Tel: 39-584-394602
FAX: 39-584-395701

JANE'S
HIGH-SPEED MARINE CRAFT
AND
AIR CUSHION VEHICLES
1988

JANE'S TRANSPORT PRESS

Jane's Publishing Company Limited, 238 City Road, London EC1V 2PU, England
Jane's Publishing Inc, 4th Floor, 115 Fifth Avenue, New York, NY 10003, USA

All the Defense Information you'll ever need

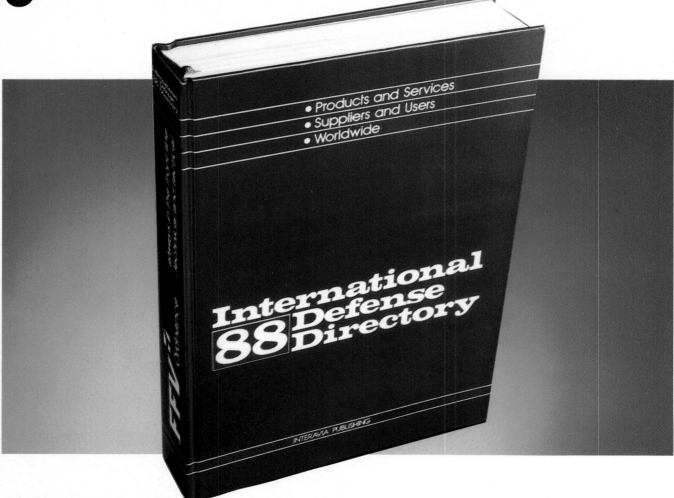

16,000 Companies, 6,000 Products, 1,200 Pages, 170 Countries
One Choice

To survive in this ever-changing market, you need accurate information *fast*.

Whether you manufacture, sell or buy, make sure you have a copy of IDD at your fingertips.

It's the only publication that gives you the names, addresses and contact details of virtually every organisation in the world involved in the manufacture, supply, purchase and procurement of all types of defense equipment.

There is no alternative—the International Defense Directory is absolutely essential for everyone in the world of defense.

For further information please contact

Jane's Publishing Inc. 1340 Braddock Place, Suite 300, Alexandria, VA 22314 USA Tel: 800 243 3852

Jane's Publishing Co. Ltd. Dept. DSM. 238 City Road London EC1V 2PU United Kingdom. Tel: 01-251 9281 Extension 65

[2]

[3]

Alphabetical list of advertisers

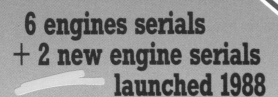

Classified list of advertisers

The companies advertising in this publication are involved in the fields of manufacture indicated below

Air cushion skirt systems
The Northern Rubber Company
Textron Marine Systems

Air cushion vehicles
Textron Marine Systems

Engines
Fiat
MTU
SACM UNI/Diesel

Guns and mountings
Breda Meccanica Bresciana

High-speed catamaran vessels
Cougar Holdings
Fairey Marinteknik
Fjellstrand A/S

High-speed mono-hull craft
Cougar Holdings
Fjellstrand A/S
Rodrìquez Cantieri Navali
Textron Marine Systems

Hydrofoil craft
Rodriquez Cantieri Navali

On-board generating sets
SACM UNI/Diesel

Surface-piercing propeller drives
Arneson Marine

RODRIQUEZ CANTIERE NAVALE S.p.A.
MESSINA – ITALY

SHOWN HERE ONE OF THE FOUR TYPES OF HYDROFOILS
BUILT TO FULFIL MODERN REQUIREMENTS FOR HIGH SPEED
WATERBORNE TRANSPORTATION:

— COMFORT
— LOW FUEL CONSUMPTION
— ECONOMICAL OPERATING COSTS

For further information, please contact:
Rodriquez Cantiere Navale S.p.A.
22, Via S. Raineri — 98100 Messina
Phone (090) 7765 — Cable Rodriquez
Telex 980030 RODRIK I

Our mark in the sky.

Our mark in the sea.

FIAT AVIAZIONE - AN OUTSTANDING, CONTINUING PRESENCE AT THE FOREFRONT OF AIRCRAFT AND MARINE ENGINE TECHNOLOGY:

AEROENGINES

RB 199 FOR THE ALL-WEATHER TORNADO

SPEY M.K. 807 FOR THE AMX LIGHT TACTICAL FIGHTER

T64-P4D FOR THE G 222 TRANSPORT PLANE

V2500 FOR SHORT-HAUL AIRCRAFT

PW 2037 FOR MEDIUM-HAUL AIRCRAFT

PW 4000 AND CF6-80C2 FOR LONG-HAUL AIRCRAFT

ENGINES FOR HELICOPTERS

PT6B-36

T700-CT7

MECHANICAL COMPONENTS FOR HELICOPTERS

SA 321 SUPER FRELON

SA 330 PUMA

SA 360/365 DAUPHIN

MARINE AND INDUSTRIAL TURBINES

LM 2500 IN THE 30,000 HP CLASS

LM 500 IN THE 6,000 HP CLASS

AUXILIARY POWER UNIT

FA 150 - ARGO

FIAT AVIAZIONE

The Holland Hovercraft Kolibrie 2000 *Capricorn 1* — a new challenger with a new design formula in the Deutz-powered multi-purpose
hovercraft market
(Foto Harry van Liempd Veghel)

JANE'S
HIGH-SPEED MARINE CRAFT
AND
AIR CUSHION VEHICLES

TWENTY-FIRST EDITION

EDITED BY
ROBERT L TRILLO, CEng, FIMechE, FRAeS, AFAIAA, AFCASI

1988

ISBN 0 7106-0851-9

JANE'S TRANSPORT PRESS
"Jane's" is a registered trade mark

In the USA and its dependencies
Jane's Publishing Inc, 4th Floor, 115 Fifth Avenue, New York, NY 10003, USA

COUGAR'S FLEET...
THE ULTRA-FAST. THE MULTI-ROLE.

THE ANSWER.

COUGAR'S CAT 900

In service for ten years and in more than a dozen countries, Cougar's CAT 900 is the ultimate in small, fast, multi-mission craft. Its deep tunnel GRP catamaran hull makes a stable work platform and is capable of speeds up to 55 Knots, dependent upon engines. In configurations including full cabin to open surveillance, armed or pure load carrier, CAT 900 is offered with twin Volvo Penta AQAD 41 inboard diesels, giving shallow draft operation at 42 Knots.

COUGAR'S 2100 SERIES

From its family of 18–33 Metre catamarans, Cougar has developed multi-role craft with speeds in excess of 50 Knots to meet the fast attack and support functions. With design ability to stay at sea for extended patrols and using the TAC project as a trial base, CAT 2100 offers a platform of comfort and stability for use as a patrol boat with full modern armament or as a payload or personnel carrier.

COUGAR'S ULTRA-FAST PATROL BOATS

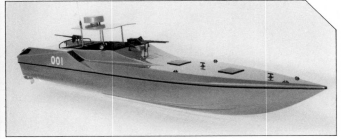

In GRP or aluminium, catamaran or monohull, Cougar's U.F.P.B. fleet are the ultimate pace setters. UFPB 1 is a 46 foot monohull, based on an offshore race proving regime and offered as a counter-insurgence patrol boat. Tested consistently to speeds in excess of 90 M.P.H. in civilian use, it and its UFPB variants are for authorities needing to move small personnel units with the minimum of delay and the maximum of surprise from speeds of 55 Knots.

KEVLAR

COUGAR HOLDINGS LIMITED
Cougar Quay, School Lane, Hamble, Hampshire SO3 5JD, England.
Tel: 0703 453513 Telex: 477229 COUGAR G Fax: 0703 453513.

COUGAR

Contents

Fairey
Marinteknik
Group

SETTING
THE STANDARDS
WORLDWIDE

☐ Priority to all technical and operational
criteria is of prime consideration in optimising the
final design and performance of each vessel.

☐ Development and investment in new technology,
operational experience linked with product support services
throughout the world, plus a workforce of skilled craftsmen,
qualified engineers, and enthusiastic management
provide a wealth of specialist knowledge and expertise.

☐ Excellence through design is the hallmark of
Fairey Marinteknik.

Fairey Marinteknik International Ltd., 33/F New World Tower, 16-18 Queen's Rd, Central Hong Kong. Tel: 5-218302/231054.
Fairey Marinteknik Shipbuilders (S) Pte. Ltd., 31 Tuas Road, Singapore 2263. Tel: (65) 8611706/7 or (65) 8616 271/2/3.
Fairey Marinteknik (UK) Ltd., Cowes Shipyard, Cowes, Isle of Wight, PO31 7DL. UK. Tel: (0983) 297111.
Marinteknik, Verkstads AB, PO Box 7, S-740 71 Oregrund, Sweden. Tel: (0) 173-30460.

FOREWORD

Industry change and growth

This is the twenty-first edition of a book that started in 1967 as *Jane's Surface Skimmer Systems*. The term 'surface skimmer' was coined to encompass all forms of craft or load carriers which were supported wholly or partially on air cushions or by hydrofoil surfaces. By 1967 the activity in this general field was increasing rapidly. Fast water-borne passenger transport had already been established in the 1950s by the hydrofoils. The 1960s saw the hovercraft moving into commercial and military realisation and, in parallel, the wider use of the air cushion as a suspension and lubricating support was being applied to overland vehicles and materials-handling devices. Many commentators have felt from time to time that certain craft types had 'come of age', had reached and passed their twenty-first birthdays but no such thing really happens. In fact we see a continual development in the whole area of high-speed marine transport so that all facets of development: operational requirements, economics, invention, vision, research, environment, money, traffic, politics, competition, physical restraints, etc, come together to evolve the changes. These ever-changing factors lead to specific craft types maturing and to the evolution of new or substantially new craft types. Looking back over the twenty-one years of this book it is interesting to note the following facts:

Of the ACV manufacturers listed (amphibious hovercraft and SES types which first entered service in 1962), nearly two-fifths are still engaged in manufacture and marketing:

British Hovercraft Corporation
Cushioncraft Ltd, now Air Vehicles Ltd
Hovermarine Ltd, now Hovermarine International Ltd
Bell Aerosystems Co, now Textron Marine Systems
Dobson Products Co
Mitsui Shipbuilding & Engineering Co
Krasnoye Sormovo A A Zhdanov Shipyard

Of the hydrofoil manufacturers listed, one-fifth are still engaged in manufacture and marketing:

Leopoldo Rodriquez Shipyard, now Rodriquez Cantieri Navali SpA
Hitachi Shipbuilding & Engineering Co
The Boeing Company, now Boeing Aerospace Company
Krasnoye Sormovo A A Zhdanov Shipyard

In this edition, there are now 43 manufacturers of commercial and military ACVs, 26 manufacturers of light/sports ACVs and approximately 12 manufacturers of hydrofoils, though the precise degree of activity in several of these organisations is unknown.

These figures should now be compared to the rise in the market for high-speed catamaran craft, a distinct type originally emerging from the hydrofoil builders Westermoen in 1970 and now being built by at least 23 companies worldwide with perhaps another seven or so soon to be more actively involved. It is clear that the catamaran is now the dominant craft type in the growth of the high-speed ferry business. Hydrofoils are still well established in the Mediterranean and the USSR for the very good reasons of craft suitability for the respective coastal and river conditions. It seems probable though that as traffic increases on Mediterranean routes (Italy, Greece, Gibraltar), requirements for larger craft capacities will provide an increasing opportunity for catamarans and high-speed mono-hull craft which will not suffer the hydrofoil's penalty of disproportionate increases in foil weight.

The apparent size of the ACV industry, as evidenced by the number of companies currently involved, is not always a reflection of corresponding production; more a reflection of a belief that the economic and technical problems of their craft are now being overcome and a recognition of how the specific characteristics of air cushion vehicles should be applied. Applications such as survey work over coastal and estuarine mud flats, tourist trips, communications along rivers with rapids, Coast Guard buoy maintenance, ice-breaking, as well as over-sand, over-ice and over-reef ferry services, are typical examples. The strongest ACV building activity at the moment is the Textron Marine Systems' LCAC (Landing Craft Air Cushion) for the US Navy, for which an eventual order of at least 90 (including some built by Lockheed) seems assured. Just prior to going to press, twelve of these 54- to 68-tonne payload craft had been delivered to bases at Camp Pendleton, just south of San Diego and to Little Creek, Virginia on the East coast. It is hoped that these 30- to 50-knot assault craft will never be used in action but they could be extremely useful in providing rapid response to natural disasters in coastal areas such as when earthquakes, hurricanes and flooding occur.

Air cushion vehicle development

The civil amphibious ACV has to evolve further if it is to gain a noticeable share of the market. Perhaps its amphibious capability should be concentrated upon. High-speed for amphibious hovercraft is attainable by a variety of craft types but the problem of ride behaviour for amphibious hovercraft has not yet been solved. Speed and amphibious capability combined are almost peculiar to the fully-skirted hovercraft concept. Where there are no harbours, where there are mud flats, reefs, exposed sand and ice to cross, then this type looks particularly worthy of consideration. The DSØ/SAS Copenhagen-Malmö AP1-88 hovercraft operation, started in June 1984, experienced two very severe winters during which frozen sea was crossed over the whole 13n mile-route, sometimes at very high speed over smooth ice or over skirt-tearing ice ridges. The service provides an effective and faster link than can be achieved by flying from Copenhagen's Kastrup airport to Malmö airport and then travelling by bus to Malmö, and is a good illustration of an appropriate application of the amphibious ACV. It is now some eight years since the AP1-88 design was first publicised and having established the basic viability of the 80 plus-seat diesel-powered amphibious hovercraft the time has perhaps come to update the configuration. The following features are some which could be improved: thrust to weight ratio can be increased to give better speed in over-wave operations for the typical seas which are encountered over coastal ferry routes, while at the same time noise can be reduced, both inside and outside; passenger visibility needs to be substantially improved; craft aerodynamic resistance can be substantially reduced helping performance, particularly in over-hump drag, headwind conditions; and aerodynamic design can certainly be integrated with aesthetic design. To take

advantage of over-rough ice capabilities the skirt must be extremely tough and this may not be compatible with low hydrodynamic resistance. Design improvements to avoid snatch loads due to segment snagging on obstacles is therefore worth continuing effort. Improvement in craft economics is always sought but design must not be heavily compromised to achieve simple cost savings; excellence in economics should accompany excellence in design.

In this edition, a newcomer appears in the smaller Deutz diesel-powered hovercraft range, the Holland Hovercraft Kolibrie 2000, an 18-seat craft, of similar form to the Air Vehicles, Griffon and Slingsby types. Holland Hovercraft has, however, carried the basic design of this category of craft a little further in a number of respects. In particular, the lift fans are driven by hydraulic motors with the fans situated in the 'wings' of the craft. As a result cabin noise levels are unusually low, further enhancing a craft with a high level of finish and design ingenuity. Specially designed air-conditioning is also fitted.

In May 1988 an Air Ride 102 air-lubricated-hull ferry with Arneson Surface Drive propulsion is due to be launched in the USA. This 356-seat, 36-knot Air Ride craft is the first to be built in the USA as a ferry, although it is understood that the *Air Ride Express*, a demonstration boat built in 1980 is now being converted to a ferry. A further Air Ride craft, a 25-metre yacht also with Arneson Surface Drive propulsion, is being built in Hong Kong by Cheoy Lee. Both these Air Ride craft have flexible cushion seals at the bow. As Air Ride craft enter service it will be interesting to observe if the principles of partial air support and lubrication employed in these designs will nudge forward the evolution of craft whose designers have broken free from 'a boat, is a boat, is a boat' philosophy. If flexible skirt elements prove to be essential, as on SESs, then here again there is further development needed both in terms of material wear properties and price reduction.

Fitting the market

There is often a tendency in the media to exaggerate what another country is doing in a particular line of work in order to induce the home government to consider making money available to enable a comparable effort to be mounted. Unfortunately the fiction of the exaggeration has a short life and if endlessly repeated without any evidence has no life at all. Similarly, the current popular use of the word 'threat' to generate a funding response for military craft is beginning to wear thin. If wastage and ill-conceived projects are to be avoided, expenditure whether by government or private means should be concentrated on real requirements, not those associated with prestige, national standing or the pressures of inflammatory comment. It is clear from an examination of the successful companies whose products are covered in this book that they have consistently provided what the market has asked for; they have not attempted to force on the market a product which is not attractive. Meeting market requirements requires response, constant evolution and change of direction. The highly successful Rodriquez production of hydrofoil craft is, for example, being followed by the development of a foil-stabilised mono-hull craft, the Mono-Stab, with a very interesting potential for improved ride and economics. Fjellstrand A/S has identified the need for far greater passenger comfort levels and is providing extremely attractive interior designs and very low passenger cabin noise levels, while International Catamarans Pty Ltd is forging ahead with its wave-piercing catamarans, a logical progression. Marinteknik Verkstads AB, having achieved success with the introduction of catamaran craft with waterjet propulsion (an initiative increasingly being followed in high-speed water-borne transport) has shown flexibility towards market requirements in responding to increasing orders for waterjet-propelled mono-hull craft. It is believed that none of these companies have received direct orders for craft from their governments (Italy, Norway, Australia, Sweden) while all have been very successful exporters and often to very great distances.

In the UK the construction of the first Marinteknik high-speed mono-hull ferry is proceeding at Fairey Marinteknik (UK) Ltd on the Isle of Wight. This 41-metre vessel is on order for Navigazione Libera del Golfo SpA and will seat 350 passengers with a maximum cruising speed of 28 knots, with waterjet propulsion from the new Swedish company MJP Marine Jet Power AB.

Surface effect ship progress

The continuing development of surface effect ships appears to contain a number of contradictions. More and more companies are coming into the business but the selling and overcoming of engineering problems does not seem to be keeping pace. The long-established builders, Hovermarine International and Textron Marine Systems (formerly Bell Halter) have not achieved noteworthy sales for SES over the past few years. Despite this, there are now new SES projects, for example, an SES ferry by Alfa/Naval in France, a 16·78m SES research craft by CHACONSA and Empresa Nacional Bazán in Spain, and in Australia an SES ferry by Precision Marine. The French are continuing SES development with DCN (Direction des Constructions Navales) leading studies for a naval SES project of 1000 tonnes and with Ateliers et Chantiers du Havre (ACH) and Constructions Mécaniques de Normandie (CMN) engaged on an inter-ministry programme for a 49·60m SES in both naval and civil versions. In addition, IFREMER (Institut Français de Recherche pour l'Exploitation de la Mer) has been engaged on design studies for a 22m SES for 100 to 120 passengers. Other continuing programmes are in the Netherlands where Le Comte-Holland are in the early stages of constructing a 26·9m SES and Royal Schelde and Wijsmuller Engineering are working on design proposals for a 32m 324-seat SES for naval and civil applications. And in Germany, studies for naval SES are in hand.

The Cirrus A/S design organisation in Norway continues its SES involvement, following the 32·2m Norcat design now successfully in service in Gabon (with a second to follow), with four 35·2m SES craft building at Brødrene Aa Båtbyggeri as well as an 18m SES, and it seems likely that Cirrus will also be involved in the design of ten mine-countermeasure SES for the Norwegian Navy.

Against this apparent high level of SES activity, the engineering problems of this craft type surfaced with the Karlskronavarvet Jet Rider 3400 SES vessels. The orders for two of these 244-passenger craft for the Sameiet Flaggruten service in Norway this year have now been cancelled due, it is understood, to difficulties in reaching contract speed (42 knots at full load) and with problems of air entering the waterjet intakes. A further two craft are, however, on order for JKL-Shipping A/S for 1989 service between Denmark and Sweden.

The apparent attraction of the SES over the catamaran is its lower power requirement at rather higher speeds in relation to work capacity. In addition, its ride motion in waves is rather more rapid, moving motion frequencies away from the band that induces seasickness. This characteristic may make coffee drinking more difficult but lessening or avoiding the risk of seasickness could be of rather greater interest. The development of ride control systems, as successfully demonstrated on the Textron Marine Systems SES-200, has provided a significant improvement in the potential for the SES. This advantageous over-wave behaviour, however, is heavily offset by the decrease in speed of the SES when operating in head seas with wave heights of 50% of cushion depth or greater. The air cushion system of the SES has a strong influence on craft layout and here there is a challenge

to the engineer to avoid machinery positioning that obstructs passengers' views, divides up passenger accommodation and generates totally unacceptable noise levels in cabin areas. The solutions are not easy, particularly in the smaller craft sizes.

Australia

The Australian drive and initiative in the high-speed craft industry is more than ever apparent in this edition with both craft builders and operators rapidly expanding their activities. Some 27 operators in Australia now operate a total of approximately 50 fast ferries with at least a further 10% on order for 1988 delivery. Apart from the long-established fleet of Rodriquez hydrofoil craft operated by the Urban Transit Authority of New South Wales, all the remaining craft are of Australian building and, with the exception of the NQEA AP1-88 hovercraft, are of Australian design. The Sydney to Manly operation of hydrofoils goes back to the mid-1960s but it was a long time before this high-speed craft initiative was followed. The real surge forward in the application of high-speed craft occurred with the formation of International Catamarans Pty Ltd in Hobart, Tasmania. While it now has the biggest share of craft in the Australian market and has successfully developed its wave-piercing concept from its basic form of catamaran, it is apparent that a diversity of types is beginning to appear in this market. After a long gestation period (not untypical for new ideas) the first two 41-seat air-lubricated-hull Stolkcraft are now in service with the Gold Coast Water Bus Company. Further north the Hover Mirage company is operating two NQEA AP1-88 70-seat hovercraft, linking Cairns International airport with Port Douglas over a 35n mile-route. As coastal airports are likely to become more common in the next decades due to air and road congestion, it seems more than likely that high-speed marine craft links with airports will offer many opportunities for amphibious and shallow-draught craft.

Waterjet progress

In this edition a new section appears covering gearboxes. Several manufacturers dominate the market but it is interesting to consider how the gearbox requirement will stand in future years. With waterjet propulsion now fully accepted and with it exceptionally good reverse thrust and manoeuvring capability, the need for a reverse gear has lapsed. Reverse flushing of a waterjet unit may be convenient when blockages occur but this function can hardly make the use of a gearbox essential. A reduction ratio between engine and waterjet may not always be required and this is an area which diesel engine and waterjet manufacturers together might profitably pursue. Remove that need and we are left with a clutch in the transmission line. With most mono-hull and catamaran craft the layout advantages of waterjet propulsion are substantial: the future offers prospects of greater simplicity.

Two new waterjet manufacturers appear in this edition, MJP Marine Jet Power AB of Sweden and Doen Jet Marketing International Pty Ltd of Australia. MJP is 50% owned by Marinteknik Verkstads AB and 50% by Osterbybruk Foundry. With Marinteknik's experience in the use of high-powered waterjet units going back nearly ten years, this new company may offer a formidable challenge to existing waterjet producers. The market, however, for these units is expanding so rapidly that excellent opportunities exist for all soundly based manufacturers offering units in the power range demanded and at competitive prices. MJP's first waterjets, two 600kW units, drive the Marinteknik 41m *Cinderella*, a highly economical passenger semi-fast ferry (22 knots) operating in the Stockholm archipelago. MJP designs are now available up to the 3500kW level which should well encompass present ideas for bigger and faster vessels.

The Australian waterjet company, Doen Jet Marketing International, has been in existence for some years, and although maintaining a quiet profile has a range of units on offer up to 1500kW. Doen Jet and MJP, together with KaMeWa, Riva Calzoni, CWF Hamilton and Castoldi, now offer six sources of supply of a device that the marine industry has until recently been very slow to adopt, despite a number of early applications in New Zealand, the USSR and the UK.

Safety

In compiling this book I am continuously reminded of the contrast between the highly detailed technical information available in the field of civil aircraft and the exact opposite in marine craft. To some extent this must be due to the far more exacting requirements in aviation, the potentially fatal consequences of error and the extreme level of competition. The technical information concerning the supporting element of an aircraft, the wing, is often published in great detail, the aerofoil section distribution, the twist, sweep angle, planform and dihedral or anhedral angle. In contrast, the supporting element of a boat, the hull, is seldom defined except by such expressions as deep-Vee forward, deadrise angle at stern, etc; the three-dimensional form is left undefined. Quoted performance is often rather vague, the term lightship is used, again without quantitative definition. Maximum speed is sometimes quoted for an empty craft, even with no fuel load carried! The term payload, the revenue-earning passenger and/or cargo load, is often incorrectly used to include fuel, crew and provisions, ie the disposable load, so that a false payload-carrying claim results. The discipline of aeronautical engineering could well be brought to bear on the marine world and a little more precision in definition would be welcome. Moving in this direction would accelerate development through the spread of greater knowledge and this in turn might well raise safety standards.

In the foreword to the 1987 edition I dwelt on the concern over safety of high-speed craft. Unlike conventional shipping, these craft have some of the aspects of commercial airliners (small volume per passenger, close proximity of passengers to engines and fuel) and they seemingly demand similar safety practices, and even those can be very considerably improved. In the March 1988 issue of the Australian magazine *Work and Patrol Boat World*, a detailed account is given of the fire which destroyed the high-speed catamaran, *Reef Link II*, in service on the run from Townsville to Magnetic Island, Queensland, on 5 July 1987; there were no injuries or loss of life. The fire occurred because of an estimated 800 litres of fuel that had been left lying in the bilge of the starboard engine room and when the craft accelerated to cruise this fuel came into contact with the engine flywheel, rapidly distributing some of it to hot engine parts at fuel-igniting temperature. Cable insulating plastics melted, short circuits occurred, spreading the fire forward. The deficiencies in the operation of the craft as determined by the Marine Board of Queensland are astonishing, but how many other operations contain the makings of a disaster?

Diversity

The Chinese Society of Naval Architecture and Marine Engineering are in November 1988 sponsoring an International High-Performance Vehicle Conference. The extent of Chinese work in this field is particularly evident in the Air Cushion Vehicle and Wing-in-Ground-Effect sections of this book, covering amphibious hovercraft, surface effect ships, low-speed air cushion platforms and power-assisted wing-in-ground-effect craft. The 45 papers to be presented include work on further advanced craft types and represent a wide international coverage.

As a world leader in advanced hull technology, one name stands out . . .

Textron Marine Systems

We're now an autonomous operating division of Textron Inc. Yet our heritage spans nearly 30 years. Formerly, as part of Bell Aerospace Textron, we pioneered the technological development of air cushioned vehicles and surface effect ships. Today, we continue the tradition. Our craft serve the U.S. Armed Forces, Coast Guard and commercial clients.

These traditions will continue to rewrite ship mission profiles like no other shipbuilder in the world, ushering in a new era of advanced marine vessels.
For further information, contact:

Textron Marine Systems
Division of Textron Inc.
6800 Plaza Dr., New Orleans, LA 70127-2596
Phone (504) 245-6600 Telex 6711199

A number of the papers are concerned with craft specifically intended for river use. This application will become of increasing interest in countries where land route and air traffic congestion already prevail and in other areas where long rivers exist and road and rail routes are limited. The USSR has for a long time used its rivers for high-speed passenger transport and has produced a series of hydrofoils successfully meeting this requirement. In addition, air cushion vehicles and air-lubricated-hull craft are in regular service on many rivers in the USSR. A relatively new Soviet river craft is the Polesye, a 53-passenger, 35-knot hydrofoil powered by a 810kW diesel. Designed to operate on foils in waves up to 0·5m height, or off foils, up to 1·2m in height, the Polesye has an extreme draught of only 0·4m. Another Soviet river craft is the Luch-1 waterjet-propelled sidewall air cushion vehicle which underwent first trials in 1983. Seats are provided for 51 passengers but on stages of one hour or less, an additional 15 passengers are allowed to stand. With a speed somewhat lower than the Polesye, Luch-1 is powered by a 346kW diesel giving a maximum speed of 23·75 knots. Luch-1 has an extreme draught of 0·65m and air draught of 0·65m. Such fast river craft will continue to appear in many forms to meet the exacting requirements of low draught (water and air), low wash, low noise and high manoeuvrability for both long distance and city services.

Finally, a mention must be made of the craft, all aluminium mono-hulls, being prepared for the attempts in July this year on the Atlantic Blue Riband record. The all-Italian 30·8m *Azimut Atlantic Challenger* is powered by four CRM BR-1/2000 diesels delivering maximum sprint power of 1850hp each and geared to drive two Riva Calzoni IRC DB2 DLX waterjets capable of producing 6·4 tonnes of thrust each at 45 knots. The tanks will contain 75 tonnes of fuel when the boat sets out with an initial speed of 29 knots, rising to approximately 55 knots at the end of the crossing as fuel is consumed.

In the UK two contenders have been constructed. At Vosper Thornycroft the 33·8m *Atlantic Challenger III*, also named *Gentry Eagle*, was launched in March 1988. Designed by Peter Birkett (designer of the 22m *Virgin Atlantic Challenger II* which had a 36·62-knot average speed for the record in 1982) for Tom Gentry of Hawaii, this vessel is powered by two MTU 16V 396 TB94 sequentially turbocharged marine diesels of 3480hp each, driving two KaMeWa 63 waterjet units. The second UK builder is Brooke Yachts International Ltd for which no details of the craft they are building for an American customer are available. Good luck to all the challengers!

Acknowledgements

A record number of replies have been received from the contributors making this enlarged 1988 edition possible. To all who have sent in material I give my sincere thanks and especially to the very many that I have not been able to write to and thank before now.

A special thanks too to those many correspondents who have kindly written from time to time helping me to update and track down information for the book.

Great assistance has been provided again this year by Ian Primrose who has looked after the mono-hull, engine and gearbox sections and by Ann Alexander who has handled the large amount of correspondence and the production of the bibliography and the comprehensive indexes; my thanks to both for their untiring but obviously tiring help!

Thanks too to the Jane's staff who have helped, Ken Harris, Alida Macchietto, David Rose and particularly to Chris Moss for her cheerful and continuous help in converting my copy into something that the printers, Netherwood Dalton, could so expertly convert to the printed page. I would also like to wish Chris all good fortune in her new career, as she is unfortunately unable to make the move with Jane's to their new offices in Coulsdon.

Robert L Trillo
Lymington, Hampshire
April 1988

PREFACE

SPEED/LENGTH COMBINATIONS

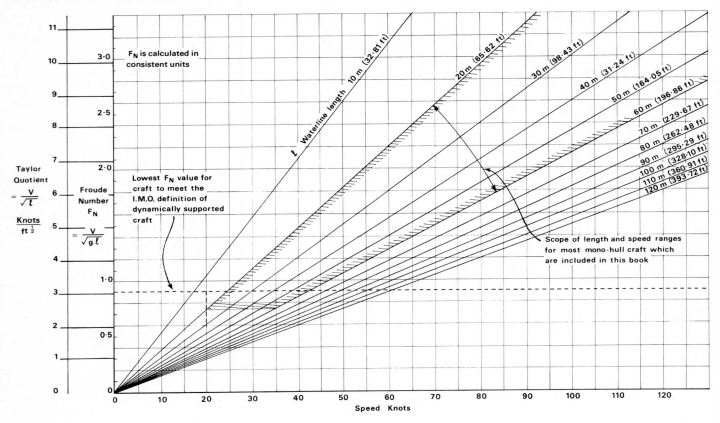

The accompanying chart is provided in order to help clarify the general term 'high-speed' in relation to water-borne craft. The basic plot shown is of Froude Number versus speed, Froude Number being the non-dimensional parameter which governs the ratio of the length of the wave made by the hull to the length of the hull, with this ratio determining the proportions of the major resistance components, skin friction and wave-making resistance.

$$F_N = \text{Froude Number} = \frac{V}{\sqrt{gl}}$$

where V = speed of craft relative to water
g = acceleration due to gravity
l = length of craft at the waterline

Since Froude Number is non-dimensional, it may be calculated in metric or English units.

Alongside the F_N scale on the chart there is a scale for the dimensional Taylor Quotient, $\frac{V}{\sqrt{l}}$, more commonly referred to as the 'speed-length ratio'. This is expressed in units of knots and feet, so has the dimensions $\frac{\text{knots}}{\text{ft}^{1/2}}$.

There is no precise definition for what constitutes high-speed but it is generally agreed to be around the condition where planing support takes over from buoyancy support and that this is in the region of Froude Numbers equal to 0·9 to 1·0. The International Maritime Organisation has set the minimum Froude Number for 'dynamically supported' craft at 0·9 though the displacement and engine power conditions (eg continuous or maximum) are undefined.

The chart shows the area of speed and length combinations for which mono-hull craft are included in this book. A minimum length of 20 metres is set simply to avoid attempting to cover the vast number of small high-speed mono-hull craft that exist in the world. A minimum speed of 20 knots is set and this then covers Froude Numbers down to 0·73.

DEFINITIONS OF SYMBOLS AND UNITS
Four of the seven base units of the SI (Système International d'Unités) which are used in this book are:

length	metre	m
mass	kilogram	kg
time	second	s
electric current	ampere	A

Decimal unit	Quantity	Formula
Pa (Pascal)	pressure or stress	N/m²
N (Newton)	force	kg.m/s²
W (Watt)	power	J/s
Hz (Hertz)	frequency	1/s (1 Hertz = 1 cycle per second in previous British practice)
V (Volt)	electric potential difference	W/A

Other units		Quantity
dB	(decibel)	sound pressure level, re 0·0002 microbar
dBA	(decibel)	sound level, A-weighted, re 0·0002 microbar

CONVERSIONS
Length
1 km = 0·6214 statute mile = 0·540 nautical mile
1 m = 3·281 ft
1 cm = 0·3937 in
1 mm = 0·0394 in
Area
1 ha (hectare = 10 000 m²) = 2·471 acres
1 m² = 10·764 ft²
Volume
1 m³ = 35·315 ft³
1 litre = 0·220 Imperial gallon = 0·264 US gallon
Velocity
1 km/h = 0·621 statute mile/h = 0·540 knots
1 m/s = 3·281 ft/s

[22]

Acceleration

$1 \text{ m/s}^2 = 3.281 \text{ ft/s}^2$

Mass

1 t (tonne) $= 1000 \text{ kg} = 0.9842 \text{ long ton} = 2204.62 \text{ lb} = 1.1023$ short tons

$1 \text{ kg} = 2.205 \text{ lb}$

1 g (gram) $= 0.002205 \text{ lb}$

Force

1 MN (meganewton) $= 100.36 \text{ long ton force}$

$1 \text{ kgf} = 2.205 \text{ lbf}$

1 kp (kilopond) $= 2.205 \text{ lbf}$

1 N (newton) $= 0.2248 \text{ lbf}$ (The Newton is that force which, applied to a mass of 1 kilogram, gives it an acceleration of 1 m/s^2.)

Moment of force (torque)

$1 \text{ Nm} = 0.7376 \text{ lbf.ft}$

Pressure, stress

1 atm (standard atmosphere) $= 14.696 \text{ lbf/in}^2$

1 bar (10^5 pascal) $= 14.504 \text{ lbf/in}^2$

1 kPa (kN/m^2) $= 20.885 \text{ lbf/ft}^2$

1 Pa (N/m^2) $= 0.020885 \text{ lbf/ft}^2$

Power

$1 \text{ metric horsepower}$ (ch, ps) $= 0.7355 \text{ kW} = 1.014 \text{ horsepower}$ (550 ft lb/s)

$1 \text{ kW} = 1.341 \text{ horsepower}$ (1 horsepower = 550 ft lb/s) $= 1.360$ metric horsepower

Nautical mile

The International Nautical Mile is equivalent to the average length of a minute of latitude and corresponds to a latitude of 45° and a distance of 1852 m = 6076.12 ft.

Fuel consumption

Specific fuel consumption, $1.0 \text{ g/kWh} = 0.001644 \text{ lb/hph}$ (hp = 550 ft lb/s)

$1.0 \text{ litre/h} = 0.220 \text{ Imperial gallon/h}$

$= 0.264 \text{ US gallon/h}$

Definitions of Sea Conditions: Wind and Sea for Fully Arisen Sea

Sea State	Description	(Beaufort) Wind force	Description	Range (knots)	Wind Velocity (knots)	Wave Height (ft) Average	Wave Height (ft) Significant	Wave Height (ft) Average of One-Tenth Highest	Significant Range Periods (sec)	Periods of Maximum Energy of Spectra $T_{max} = T_c$	Average Period T_z	Average Wave Length L_w (ft unless otherwise indicated)	Minimum Fetch (nautical miles)	Minimum Duration (hr unless otherwise indicated)
	Sea like a mirror	U	Calm	1	0	0	0	0	—	—	—	—	—	—
0	Ripples with the appearance of scales are formed, but without foam crests	1	Light airs	1-3	2	0.04	0.01 0.01	0.09	1.2	0.75	0.5	10 in	5	18 min
1	Small wavelets; short but pronounced crests have a glossy appearance, but do not break.	2	Light breeze	4-6	5	0.3	0.5	0.6	0.4-2.8	1.9	1.3	6.7	8	39 min
	Large wavelets; crests begin to break. Foam of glossy	3	Gentle	7-10	8.5	0.8	1.3	1.6	0.8-5.0	3.2	2.3	20	9.8	1.7
	appearance. Perhaps scattered with horses.		breeze		10	1.1	1.8	2.3	1.0-6.0	3.2	2.7	27	10	2.4
2	Small waves, becoming larger;	4	Moderate		12	1.6	2.6	3.3	1.0-7.0	4.5	3.2	40	18	3.8
					13.5	2.1	3.3	4.2	1.4-7.6	5.1	3.6	52	24	4.8
	fairly frequent white horses.		breeze	11-16	14	2.3	3.6	4.6	1.5-7.8	5.3	3.8	59	28	5.2
3					16	2.9	4.7	6.0	2.0-8.8	6.0	4.3	71	40	6.6
4	Moderate waves, taking a more	5	Fresh	17-21	18	3.7	5.9	7.5	2.5-10.0	6.8	4.8	90	55	8.3
					19	4.1	6.6	8.4	2.8-10.6	7.2	5.1	99	65	9.2
	pronounced long form; many white horses are formed (chance of some spray).		breeze		20	4.6	7.3	9.3	3.0-11.1	7.5	5.4	111	75	10
5	Large waves begin to form;	6	Strong	22-27	22	5.5	8.8	11.2	3.4-12.2	8.3	5.9	134	100	12
					24	6.6	10.5	13.3	3.7-13.5	9.0	6.4	160	130	14
	white crests are more extensive		breeze		24.5	6.8	10.9	13.8	3.8-13.6	9.2	6.6	164	140	15
6	everywhere (probably some spray).				26	7.7	12.3	15.6	4.0-14.5	9.8	7.0	188	180	17
	Sea heaps up, and white foam from breaking waves begins to be blown in streaks along the direction of the wind (Spindrift begins to be seen).	7	Moderate gale	28-33	28	8.9	14.3	18.2	4.5-15.5	10.6	7.5	212	230	20
					30	10.3	16.4	20.8	4.7-16.7	11.3	8.0	250	280	23
7					30.5	10.6	16.9	21.5	4.8-17.0	11.5	8.2	258	290	24
					32	11.6	18.6	23.6	5.0-17.5	12.1	8.6	285	340	27
7					34	13.1	21.0	26.7	5.5-18.5	12.8	9.1	322	420	30
	Moderate high waves of greater length; edges of crests break into spindrift. The foam is blown in well-marked streaks along the direction of the wind. Spray affects visibility.	8	Fresh gale	34-40	36	14.8	23.6	30.0	5.8-19.7	13.6	9.6	363	500	34
					37	15.6	24.9	31.6	6-20.5	13.9	9.9	376	530	37
					38	16.4	26.3	33.4	6.2-20.8	14.3	10.2	392	600	38
					40	18.2	29.1	37.0	6.5-21.7	15.1	10.7	444	710	42
8	High waves. Dense streaks of foam along the direction of the wind. Sea begins to roll. Visibility affected.	9	Strong gale	41-37	42	20.1	32.1	40.8	7-23	15.8	11.3	492	830	47
					44	22.0	35.2	44.7	7-24.2	16.6	11.8	534	960	52
					46	24.1	38.5	48.9	7-25	17.3	12.3	590	1110	57
	Very high waves with long overhanging crests. The resulting foam is in great patches and is blown in dense white streaks along the direction of the wind. On the whole, the surface of the sea takes on a white appearance. The rolling of the sea becomes heavy and shocklike. Visibility is affected.	10	Whole* gale	48-55	40	26.2	41.9	53.2	7.5-26	18.1	12.9	650	1250	63
					50	28.4	45.5	57.8	7.5-27	18.8	13.4	700	1420	69
					51.5	30.2	48.3	61.3	8-28.2	19.4	13.8	736	1560	73
9					52	30.8	49.2	62.5	8-28.5	19.6	13.9	750	1610	75
					54	33.2	53.1	67.4	8-29.5	20.4	14.5	810	1800	81
	Exceptionally high waves. Sea completely covered with long white patches of foam lying in direction of wind. Everywhere edges of wave crests are blown into froth. Visibility affected.	11	Storm*	56-63	56	35.7	57.1	72.5	8.5-31	21.1	15	910	2100	88
					59.5	40.3	64.4	81.8	10-32	22.4	15.9	985	2500	101
	Air filled with foam and spray. Sea white with driving spray. Visibility very seriously affected.	12	Hurricane*	64-71	>64	>46.6	74.5	94.6	10-35	24.1	17.2	—	—	—

* For hurricane winds (and often whole gale and storm winds) required durations and reports are barely attained. Seas are therefore not fully arisen.

BUILDERS

AIR CUSHION VEHICLES

AUSTRALIA

AIR CUSHION ENTERPRISES PTY LTD

PO Box 32, Manunda (near Cairns), Queensland 4870, Australia

Telephone: (070) 55 52 19

Management
A J Yuill, *Managing Director*
C Oliver
J Godfrey
J Foggin
R McCleod

Air Cushion Enterprises is a completely independent company which purchased all plant, equipment and design rights from Hovercraft Manufacturers (New Zealand) Ltd. The first of their designs to be built in Australia (to Det norske Veritas requirements) is the Surveyor 12 D and first launching was in early 1987.

SURVEYOR 12 D

An all new craft, the Surveyor 12 D has been designed for operation in extreme climatic conditions. Diesel power gives it greater economy, durability and reliability with important safety advantages.

The hull is of grp/foam sandwich construction with Kevlar in some areas. Side bodies are detachable. The lift system employs two axial flow fans, hydraulically driven.

ENGINE: One Deutz BF6L 913C
  120kW/2300rpm continuous
  142kW/2500rpm max
DIMENSIONS
Length, off cushion: 8·9m
  on cushion: 9·47m
Width, off cushion: 4·1m
  on cushion: 5·5m
Propeller dia: 1·21m
Cabin length: 3·70m
Cabin width: 2·26m
Cabin height: 1·42m
Hard structure clearance, bow: 0·65m
  stern: 0·57m
Shipping dimension: Dismantles to fit in 12·2m
  (40ft) container
WEIGHTS
Empty: 2200kg
Max: 3800kg
Useful payload: 1050kg
PERFORMANCE
Cruising speed: 45-65km/h
Max speed: 42 knots

Surveyor 12 D now in production in Australia with Air Cushion Enterprises Pty Ltd

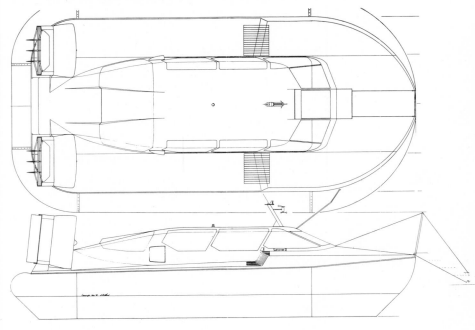

Surveyor 12 D

Fuel tank capacity: Two tanks, 55 litres each
Fuel consumption: approx 13 to 15 litres/h cruising
  approx 35 litres/h max

Cruising range: 240km not including reserve fuel
Accommodation: 15 passengers plus 1 pilot
Wave height limit: 1·5m

NQEA AUSTRALIA PTY LTD

36 Buchan Street, PO Box 1105, Portsmith, Cairns, Queensland 4870, Australia

Telephone: (070) 51 6600
Telex: 48087 AUS AA
Telefax: (070) 51 5520

D G Fry, *Chief Executive*
S C Grimley, *Managing Director*
G M Steene, *Executive Director, Marketing*
A Rankine, *Executive Director, Production*
R D Rookwood, *Senior Design Engineer*
S Cook, *Company Secretary*
A E G Mill, *Company Architect*

NQEA started activities in 1948 with the operation of general engineering agencies and later general engineering manufacture. In 1964 it entered the shipbuilding industry with the construction of dumb barges. This activity was followed by work on many types of vessels, including Australia's 'Attack Class' patrol boats, and the

The second and third NQEA AP1-88s to be built and in operation with Queensland Ferries Pty Ltd servicing Brisbane airport and Cairns
(Yon Ivanovic)

The first AP1-88 to be built by NQEA Australia Pty Ltd operating in Port Phillip Bay, Melbourne

(Yon Ivanovic)

construction of several medium-sized craft, including tug boats, fishing trawlers and 22 workboats for the Australian Defence Department.

In 1977, NQEA was the successful tenderer for 14 (of a total of 15) 42m 'Fremantle Class' patrol craft for the Australian Navy, the lead vessel being built in the UK by Brooke Marine. Taking 85 weeks to construct the craft, NQEA were delivering at a rate of one every 14 weeks.

More recently NQEA have been building a number of high-speed catamarans (International Catamarans type) and are building the British-designed AP1-88 under licence from British

Craft built	Name	Seats	Launched	Operator
BHC AP1-88	*Courier*	84	7 December 1986	Hovertravel Australia Ltd
BHC AP1-88	*Hover Mirage*	70	March 1987	Queensland Ferries Pty Ltd
BHC AP1-88	*Hover Mirage II*	70	April 1987	Queensland Ferries Pty Ltd
BHC AP1-88	—	—	Building 1987/88	—

Hovercraft Corporation, the first order having been received in February 1986. With three craft now completed and in operation along Australia's eastern coast, NQEA claims to be at the forefront of the high-speed vessel industry, offering prospec-

tive buyers in the ferry, patrol boat and general workboat fields the choice of mono-hull, catamaran and amphibious hovercraft.

Details of the AP1-88 hovercraft are given in the British Hovercraft Corporation entry.

BELGIUM

EUROSENSE TECHNOLOGIES NV

[OPERATOR]
J Van der Vekenstraat 158, B-1810 Wemmel, Belgium

Telephone: (02) 460 70 00
Telex: 26687
Telefax: (02) 460 49 58

E Maes, *Managing Director*
A Grobben, *Assistant Managing Director*

BEASAC II (DESIGN)

From 1985, Eurosense has been under contract with the Belgian Ministry of Public Works Coastal Services, for the constant monitoring of the navigational channels to the major Belgian seaports, and for the coverage of the coastal morphology. To do this, Eurosense has used aerial

remote sensing as well as hydrographic survey techniques. This diesel-powered hovercraft is the result of Eurosense's knowledge and experience with the BEASAC I (Belfotop Eurosense Acoustic-Sounding Air-Cushion) hovercraft (SR.N6 Mk 1S) in the field of hydrography.

The hovercraft can reach regions inaccessible to classic bathymetric vessels, eg the nearshore areas. The nearshore bathymetric surveys ensure an overlap with beach observations (executed by

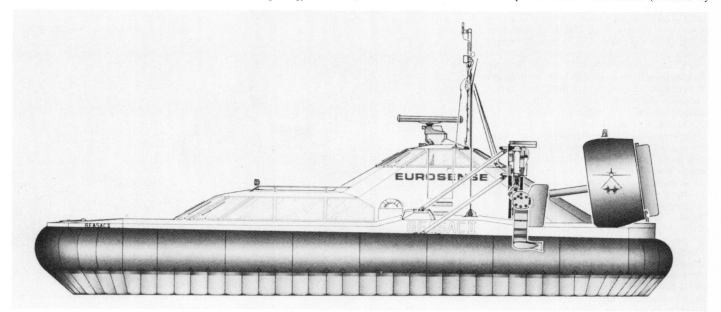

BEASAC II, a Eurosense Technologies NV design proposal for an amphibious hydrographic survey platform

aerial or terrestrial survey) thus enabling a complete coverage of the coast to be achieved.

This Eurosense design proposal for a new hydrographic survey platform enables bathymetric surveys to be effected, in coastal and offshore areas, at survey speeds up to 50km/h (27 knots), depending on weather conditions, resulting in measurements being obtained up to 4 times faster than those from classic hydrographic vessels.

The BEASAC II hovercraft will have an endurance of 10 hours and be able to work in wind forces up to Beaufort 6 and wave heights of 1·5m. With a cruise speed of 75km/h, remote areas up to 150km from base can be reached and surveyed the same day, still permitting 6 hours of operation on site.

The BEASAC II hydrographic platform is offered for sale, together with all the specially designed hydrographic surveying equipment, computers, sensors, shore-based data-processing and chart-plotting hardware and associated software.

LIFT AND PROPULSION: Motive power is supplied by four diesel engines. The large four-blade ducted propellers reduce internal and external noise to minimum levels. The propellers have variable pitch and low tip speed.

Propulsion is generated by two 313hp diesel engines. On each side of the craft two lift-fan units are installed, driven by 109hp diesel engines. In this way fully independent lift and propulsion is provided.

HULL: Welded marine aluminium. The central deck assembly comprises floor and buoyancy compartments with box members at bow and stern.
CONTROLS: Directional control is effected with multiple aerodynamic rudder vanes hinged at the aft end of the propeller ducts together with differential propeller thrust and with use of the skirt shift system. Differential pitch to the propellers augments the turning moment, and reverse thrust is possible by pitch control. These control systems make the craft highly manoeuvrable, able to turn in its own length and give optimum track-control, essential in hydrographic surveying.
SKIRT: Open loop/segmented type. Segments can be quickly changed without lifting the craft off its landing pads.
AUXILIARY POWER: Two 10kVA generators provide the electrical power supply for the onboard computers, sensors, hydrographic instruments, air-conditioning, etc.
HYDROGRAPHIC EQUIPMENT
Positioning systems: Several options are possible (eg Trisponder, Syledis, Toran, Motorola)
Depth measurement: Two hydraulically-retractable sensors are mounted on the sides of the craft. They bring the streamlined sword and fish in or out of the water. Two acoustic transducers (210 and 33kHz) are installed in each fish. Other sensors include a flux gate compass, gyroscope, heave compensator and air-cushion height detectors, permitting the simultaneous regis-

tration of all craft movements (eg roll, pitch, heading, etc)
Acquisition system: A powerful computer system is extended with interfacing networks to gather all sensor registrations. Adapted driver software interrogates, synchronises and memorises all sensor data together with depth and position. Special graphical navigation screens inform the pilot and surveyor of track, planimetry and quality control of the data
Shore-based data-processing: Special computer software and hardware enable easy and continuous chart production by the surveyor

DIMENSIONS	Length	Width	Height
Overall, on cushion	19·3m	8·2m	4·8m
Hard structure	18·0m	6·0m	3·9m
Pilot cabin	3·0m	2·0m	1·5m
Survey cabin	6·75m	3·0m	1·5m
Auxiliaries room	6·0m	3·0m	1·5m
Hoverheight	0·9m		

WEIGHTS
Equipped empty weight: 9500kg
Load (variable (crew, ballast), expendable (oil, payload): 3100kg
Usable fuel for 10 hours: 1400kg
Max weight: 14 000kg

PERFORMANCE
Max speed: 100km/h (54 knots)
Cruise speed: 75km/h (40 knots)
Survey speed: 50km/h (27 knots)
Max wave height: 1·5m
Max wind force: Beaufort 6

CANADA

ACV SALES INC

Box 11107 Royal Centre, 1400-1055 West Georgia Street, Vancouver, British Columbia V6E 3P3, Canada

Telephone: (604) 685 9824

Andrew Robertson, *President*

ACV Sales Inc builds the Amphibian hovercraft, designed to meet all-year-round climatic conditions in the Canadian north and other locations. It is suitable for a variety of commercial and military applications.

Amphibian was granted an Air Cushion Vehicle Type Design Certificate in April 1984 by the Air Cushion Vehicle Division of the Ship Safety Branch of the Canadian Coast Guard.

AMPHIBIAN (PROTOTYPE)
TYPE: Light amphibious multi-duty ACV capable of carrying an operator and up to four passengers or 454kg (1000lb) of freight.
LIFT AND PROPULSION: Integrated system powered by a single 340hp 253kW V8 Ford Type 429 CID water-cooled petrol engine. Mounted inboard the engine drives two centrifugal fans, type Chicago Blower 3000 SW Des 1902 mounted at the opposite ends of a split-transverse shaft. Air flow is ducted beneath the craft for lift and via port and starboard outlets aft for thrust. Recommended fuel is premium gasoline.
CONTROLS: Craft heading is controlled by multiple rudders in the thrust duct apertures or by the manipulation of port and starboard thrust duct gates. Driving controls comprise a steering wheel, thrust gate control switches, an electric starter switch and a throttle control for lift and thrust. Reverse thrust gates provide braking, stopping and manoeuvring capabilities.
HULL: Moulded glass-reinforced plastic and corrosion resistant aluminium construction. Buoyancy: 150 per cent.
ACCOMMODATION: Access to the enclosed cabin is via twin sliding doors, one port, one starboard.
DIMENSIONS
Length on cushion: 7·54m (24ft 9in)
Beam on cushion: 3·4m (11ft 2in)
Height on cushion: 2·67m (8ft 9in)

Amphibian light multi-duty ACV

Amphibian showing thrust duct apertures

WEIGHTS
Max gross weight limit: 2200kg
Empty weight: 1905kg
Payload: 454kg

PERFORMANCE
Max speed (land, water, ice and snow): 48km/h (30mph)
Range: 277km (172 miles)

Max gradient: 15°
Thrust: 300kg (660lb)
Cruise power: 210hp at 3800rpm

AMPHIBIAN (PRODUCTION VERSION)
ENGINE: GMC 454 CID, 410hp at 4500rpm, cruise rpm: 3200.

JONES KIRWAN & ASSOCIATES
Box 4406, Station 'D', Hamilton, Ontario L8V 4L8, Canada

Telephone: (416) 388 2929

D Jones, *President*

Jones Kirwan & Associates was responsible for the design of the Air Trek 140, as well as a number of other Canadian hovercraft. The company also designs air-cushion supported agricultural spray booms.

AIR TREK 140
Designed by Jones Kirwan & Associates for use in arctic conditions, this utility hovercraft carries up to 16 passengers or freight weighing up to 1360kg (3000lb). The main structure is built in marine-grade aluminium and is stressed to operate at 61km/h (38mph) in 0·9m (3ft) high seas. The craft received full certification from the Canadian Coast Guard in early 1984.

For several years the Air Trek 140 has been in use as an icebreaker capable of breaking ice 0·45m to 0·70m thick, in such applications as river mouth ice-clearing. Development of an ice-grooving tool to improve further the icebreaking capability of hovercraft is being undertaken by Jones Kirwan & Associates.

LIFT AND PROPULSION: Integrated system powered by a single 10·4-litre Caterpillar 3208 turbocharged, after-cooled, diesel rated at 360hp for 5 minutes and 350hp continuous. Thrust is supplied by a ducted, six-blade wooden propeller. Power is transmitted to two centrifugal lift fans behind the driver's and crewman's seats via an infinitely variable Eaton Hydrostatic drive system. The operator can select the fan speed to suit the terrain or wave conditions; the fans will then remain at that speed constantly irrespective of the main engine rpms.

CONTROLS: Multiple rudders operating in the propeller slipstream provide directional control and act as shut-off doors to modulate thrust. Louvres in the duct wall between the propeller and the rudders give reverse thrust.

SKIRT: HDL 'kneed' segments (96) in 542g/m² (16oz/yd²) neoprene coated fabric. Skirt may be reset from the craft deck while the craft is floating on water.

HULL: Marine-grade aluminium.

ACCOMMODATION: Cabin with independent diesel heater and heavily insulated for arctic conditions. Dual operating position.

DIMENSIONS
Length: 11·2m
Width: 5·73m

HULL: Kevlar 'S' glass and vinylester resin with a Termanto core.

ACCOMMODATION: Driver plus 8 passengers. Internal noise level to be less than 90dB. Cabin length: 2·39m; stretchers can be loaded athwartships.

CAPACITIES
Fuel tank: 303 litres (80 US gallons)

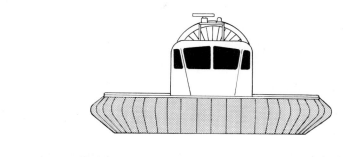

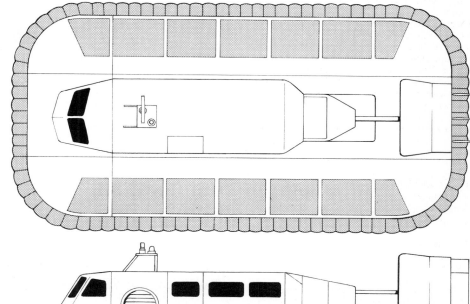

Air Trek 140 (early configuration)

Cabin, length: 3·93m
   width: 2·08m
   height: 1·83m
Freight area: 11·90m²

WEIGHTS
Max load: 1360kg
Fuel capacity: 363kg
Crew of two: 145kg
Craft weight: 4832kg
Max weight: 6700kg

WEIGHTS
Payload: 855kg
Empty weight: 1180-1270kg

PERFORMANCE
Speed, max: 30 knots, 0° yaw
   25 knots, 40° yaw
Fuel consumption: 26-38 litres/mile (7-10 US gallons/mile)

PERFORMANCE
Cruising speed, ice and water: 61km/h (38mph)
Cruising speed, ice: 72km/h (45mph)
Fuel duration at max cruising speed: 8 hours
Fuel consumption at max cruising speed: 45kg/h (100lb/h)

SIX-SEAT HOVERCRAFT (DESIGN)
Design of a new six-seat hovercraft started in the summer of 1987.

TRANSPORT CANADA
Transportation Development Centre (TDC)
[RESEARCH AND DEVELOPMENT ORGANISATION]
Complex Guy Favreau, 200 Dorchester West, Suite 601, West Tower, Montreal, Quebec H2Z 1X4, Canada

J E Laframboise, *Senior Development Officer*

Founded in Montreal in 1970, the Transportation Development Centre (TDC) is the research and development group within Transport Canada. TDC studies, promotes and directs the application of science and technology towards a more efficient and effective national transport system. Working in co-operation with the Can-

adian transport community, TDC conducts and commissions research projects covering all modes of transport.

AIR CUSHION TECHNOLOGY
TDC has investigated the application of air cushion technology to Canadian transportation since the early seventies, having acquired for evaluation the Bell Aerospace Textron Voyageur 002, since handed over to the Canadian Coast Guard.

TDC was also involved in a ship-to-shore supply operation in 1974-75 on the Quebec North Shore when Voyageur 004 was used to supply land-locked villages during the winter.

A number of research contracts dealing with air cushion stability and modelling were also granted

by TDC to the Air Cushion Group of the University of Toronto Institute of Aerospace Studies (UTIAS).

AEROBAC CONCEPT
As the major part of Canada consists of sparsely settled regions, with a prevalence of muskeg and other water-logged terrains, one of the domains of interest to TDC is off-road transportation. The Aerobac concept was developed following trials in the Canadian hinterland with air cushion trailers. These showed that while the air cushion itself was satisfactory over marshes and flat surfaces, it became a hindrance when dealing with hilly paths or rocky surfaces. Hence a vehicle was needed that could deal effectively with all surfaces, using air cushion for lift but able to revert to wheels or to

tracks, as local conditions dictated. Initially Aerobac trailers were considered, permitting the conventional off-road vehicles, to which they are coupled, to operate at their unladen foot-print pressure. Later amphibious self-propelled versions were developed. Tandem operation of the two versions is possible for increased payloads.

Commercial development of Aerobac vehicles does not come within the scope of TDC. A technology transfer agreement has been made between the Canadian government and VITRI Robots and Vehicles Inc (VRV) to market this vehicle concept. For description of the Aerobac family of vehicles see the VRV entry.

RECENT PROGRESS

During February and March 1987 TDC has co-operated with the Port of Chicoutimi (Quebec) in an icebreaking experiment on the Saguenay river, using the Air Trek 140 hovercraft to clear ice around a petroleum terminal, in order to ensure an early start to the shipping season. While the operation was experimental, it enabled three ship-loads to be delivered prior to the usual opening date of the terminal.

The Air Trek 140, operated by Ice Control Enterprise Inc, Hamilton, was able to break late winter-ice from 30 to 60cm thick. The Port of Chicoutimi is considering a permanent air cushion vehicle icebreaking operation to extend the terminal operations into late fall and leading, eventually, to year-round fuel delivery by ships.

VITRI ROBOTS AND VEHICLES INC (VRV)

[DESIGN, DEVELOPMENT AND MARKETING ORGANISATION]
238 De Brullon Street, Boucherville, Quebec J4B 2J8, Canada

Telephone: (514) 641 3914
Telex: (VIA USA) 750 846
Telefax: (514) 397 9494

Pierre F Alepin, *President*

VRV is involved in the development of products requiring the integration of diverse technologies. VRV works in conjunction with large organisations, providing them with needed entrepreneurial creativity developing from small organisations, and brings together individuals having the most appropriate background and experience for the task in hand.

The Aerobac concept, integrating air cushion technology with that of off-road vehicles, is being promoted by VRV for Canadian and world-wide applications.

VRV has acquired rights from Canadian Patents and Development Ltd, a Canadian Crown Corporation, for designs of the Aerobac family of vehicles developed by the Transportation Development Centre (TDC), of Transport Canada. VRV has also obtained a licence from Institut Français de Recherche pour l'Exploitation de la Mer (IFREMER) for the use of Bertin and SEDAM air cushion systems on hybrid vehicles using surface contacting propulsion and able to operate with or without the air cushion system.

VRV AEROBAC (DESIGN)

VRV vehicles are based on the designs licensed from TDC, comprising air cushion trailers and tracked self-propelled vehicles (AB-7), and on its own designs, based on a proposal to the US Air Force for an air cushion-assisted crash rescue vehicle (ACCRV), and developed as a family of wheeled cargo or passenger vehicles.

The designs are characterised by relatively high cushion pressures, 4 to 7kPa, and by a variable stiffness suspension system. A high stiffness is used for off cushion stability; when on cushion a low stiffness is desired in order to reduce shock load transfer to the structure. When on cushion the load on the wheels, or tracks, is kept at the minimum value compatible with guidance and traction requirements.

AEROBAC PCE (DESIGN)

In order to support a TDC evaluation programme, VRV has carried out a production cost evaluation (PCE) of an Aerobac AB-7 design (see Transport Canada entry in the 1986 edition), modified to a two-engine configuration, using cabin layout, transmission and tracks of a Bombardier B-10 muskeg vehicle. The air cushion fans are separately driven so that a breakdown of either engine systems still permits the vehicle to move off cushion, or to be towed, on cushion, to a repair depot.

As the TDC evaluation programme would involve testing as an airport rescue vehicle, a foam package can be installed on the PCE, with a capacity of 4500 litres. The transmission fitted on the PCE allows a speed of 60km/h to be attained, conditions permitting. The fire pump is driven by a power take-off from this transmission.

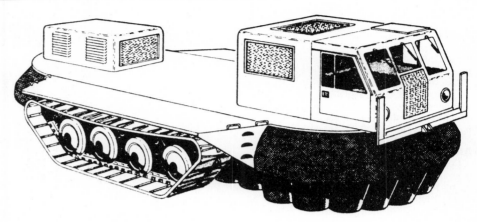

Aerobac PCE: design of prototype of tracked hybrid ACV with 7-tonne payload capability

LIFT AND PROPULSION
Traction system: Detroit 6V-92TA
  Power: 230kW
  Transmission: Clarke 28661
  Differential: Levy M-24
  Tracks: Muskeg 1m width
  Suspension: Oleo-pneumatic
Cushion system: Detroit 6V-92TA
  Power: 230kW
  Fans: Two VIM HCHB-040
  Total flow (at 7·5kPa): 20m³/s
SKIRT: SEDAM multicell.
DIMENSIONS
Length: 11·5m
Width: 6·2m
Height: 3·4m
Loading area: 20m²
WEIGHTS
Payload: 7 tonnes
Max weight: 21 tonnes
PERFORMANCE
Fuel capacity: 800 litres
Max speed: 60km/h
Max slope: 40%
Endurance (70% power): 8 hours
Ground pressure
  cushion only: 6·3kPa
  tracks only: 35·6kPa

AEROBAC CRV
FIRE PACKAGE
Water reservoir: 4500 litres
Foam agent: 600 litres
Fire pump: Hale 50FB
Power take-off: 75kW
Flow at 1·0MPa: 2500 litres/min

Roof turret: 2000 litres/min
Protection nozzles: 3 at 150 litres/min
Hose reel: 5cm, 50m

ACCRV (DESIGN)

In 1985 the US Air Force issued a request for proposals for a crash rescue vehicle with air cushion assist. In addition to a 4000-litre water capacity fire package this vehicle has to carry a rescue platform, extensible to 15m, and have a triage area able to receive three victims. It must be fully amphibious, protected against exploding ammunition on the ground, able to travel at 100km/h over smooth surfaces and able to negotiate rubble to 30cm height. As applicable to other US Air Force CRVs it must be made air transportable in a Lockheed C-130, within 15 minutes preparation time.

A VRV design study made use of a multicell air cushion (in order to provide high lateral stability), installed between the axles of the vehicle. Folding side bodies are fitted in order to meet the width requirement of the C-130. This design, with a maximum weight of 13·5 tonnes is illustrated in model form (for design data see VRV entry in 1987 edition).

AR-5 (DESIGN)

The basic vehicle design, without the ACCRV components, was transformed into a wheeled hybrid ACV, the AR-5. The use of air cushion vehicles over inland trails has been proposed at various times as a means of providing reasonably fast ground transportation in regions where population and traffic densities are too low to justify the cost of a conventional road. The

Aerobac CRV: design for a crash rescue vehicle PCE with a 4500-litre water capacity

Model of VRV proposed ACCRV design to a US Air Force requirement

Aerobac AR-5 design for an air cushion-assisted wheeled cargo vehicle with a 5-tonne payload capability

Terraplane BC-7 was developed by Bertin in 1965 for such a use (see *Jane's Surface Skimmers 1967-68*). If the trail, or hoverway, is relatively flat, wheeled propulsion is adequate resulting in a lighter vehicle. The AR-5, adapted from the ACCRV design retains removable side bodies to permit travel without restriction over public roads.

LIFT AND PROPULSION
Engine: KHD BF12L 413F
Power: 350kW (hydrostatic transfer to transmission and fans)
Fuel capacity: 600 litres
Fans: Two VIM HCHB 040
Total flow: 20m³/s (at 7·5kPa)
Max cushion pressure: 6kPa
DIMENSIONS
Length: 12·2m
Width: 4m (2·6m on road)
WEIGHTS
Max weight: 14 tonnes
Payload: 5 tonnes
PERFORMANCE
Max speed: 100km/h

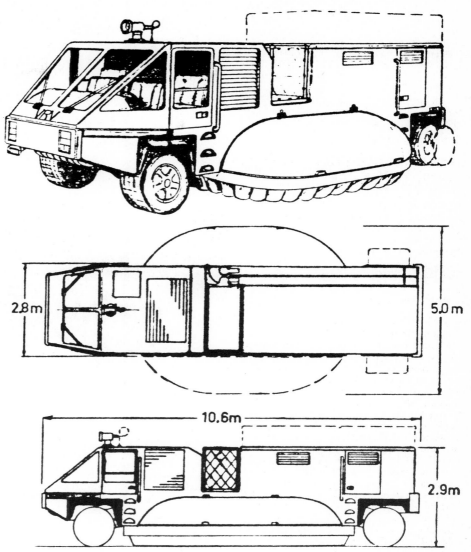

VRV proposed ACCRV design for US Air Force requirement

Speed, off road: 60km/h (roughness under 30cm)
 in water: 12km/h
Endurance: 8 hours

CHINA, PEOPLE'S REPUBLIC

MARINE DESIGN AND RESEARCH INSTITUTE OF CHINA (MARIC)

[DESIGN, RESEARCH AND DEVELOPMENT ORGANISATION]
346 Sichuan Road, Central, PO Box 3053, Shanghai, People's Republic of China

Telephone: 215044
Telex: 33029 MARIC CN

Liang Yun, *Deputy Chief Engineer, Director of Hovercraft Division*

The Marine Design and Research Institute of China (MARIC) has been responsible for much of the ACV research, development and design programmes on both amphibious and sidewall (SES) hovercraft which have been built in China. The following table summarises the more recent developments in ACVs in China.

Summary of craft built

Builder & craft	Designer	Seats/payload	Launched
Dagu Shipyard			
Tianjin			
Type 722 (Amphibious)	MARIC	15-ton payload	August 1979
Type 7203 (Sidewall)		81 seats	September 1982
Jinxiang (Sidewall)	MARIC	80 seats	1983
MARIC			
Shanghai			
Jing-Sah (Amphibious)	MARIC	0·84-ton payload	
Three-engined craft (Amphibious)	MARIC	(development craft, details in *Jane's Surface Skimmers 1985* and earlier editions)	
Shipbuilding and Marine Engineering Establishment			
Shanghai			
— (Amphibious)		2·8-ton payload	
Dong Feng Shipyard			
Hangzhou			
Type 717 II (Sidewall) *Ming Jiang*	MARIC	54-60 seats	October 1984
Type 717 III (Sidewall) *Chongqing*	MARIC	70 seats	September 1984
Type 7210 (Amphibious) two built	MARIC	0·8 tonnes	May 1985
Chaohu Shipyard			
Au-hui Province			
Type WR 901 (Sidewall) four built	Shanghai Ship and Shipping Research Institute & The Communications Bureau of Au-hui Province	40 seats	December 1980 (pre-production prototype)

Summary of craft built (contd)

Builder & craft	Designer	Seats/payload	Launched
Wuhu Shipyard			
Au-hui Province			
5-ton expl. craft (Sidewall)			1975
Type 719 (Sidewall)	MARIC	186 seats	1984
Shanghai Hu Dong Shipyard			
Type 716 II (Amphibious)	MARIC	32 seats or 2·5 tonnes	1985

CHINA AIR CUSHION TECHNOLOGY DEVELOPMENT CORPORATION (CACTEC)

[DESIGN, RESEARCH, DEVELOPMENT AND PRODUCTION ASSISTANCE ORGANISATION]

Head office: 9, Qi Xiang Nan Li, Bimhu Road, Tianjin, People's Republic of China

Telephone: 331859, 333339
Cable: 3333

Branch office: 171 Gaoxion Road, Shanghai, People's Republic of China

Telephone: 770539

Formed in 1984, CACTEC is a subsidiary of the China State Shipbuilding Corporation (CSSC) and is a specialised business corporation working jointly with MARIC on a wide variety of applications of the air cushion principle with emphasis on the research, development, design and production of amphibious and sidewall (SES) hovercraft. Craft operated by CACTEC are given in the *Operators* section of this edition.

DAGU SHIPYARD
Tianjin

TYPE 722

The largest ACV to be built in China, this 65-ton vehicle has been designed for a range of applications. The prototype has been under evaluation in the amphibious initial assault role, and a passenger/vehicle ferry version has been exhibited in model form.

Design was undertaken by MARIC and the craft was built at the Dagu Shipyard with the assistance of some 52 other specialist engineering and technical groups. Construction began in December 1977 and the craft was launched in August 1979. The initial trials programme began in September 1979.

The vehicle is described as being capable of operating over water, land, grasslands, marshlands, lakes, shallows and beaches. It can clear vertical obstacles 1m (3ft 3in) high and ditches up to 5m (16ft 4in) wide.

LIFT AND PROPULSION: Two 1850hp and two 1530hp engines drive three air propellers and six Type 4-73 centrifugal fans. Air for the engines appears to be drawn in through filtered roof intakes. Fan air, which is taken through three large filtered ducts each side of the superstructure, is discharged into the cushion via a continuous peripheral loop skirt with segmented fringes.

CONTROLS: It is believed that craft heading is controlled by swivelling a forward propeller pylon, operated in conjunction with the twin

Type 7203 fast ferry

aerodynamic rudders aft. Reverse thrust is applied for braking and reversing. Elevator provides pitch trim at cruising speed.

HULL: Riveted skin and stringer structure employing alloy sheet. Main hull is formed by a buoyancy raft based on a grid of longitudinal and transverse frames which form a number of flotation compartments. Two main longitudinal vertically stiffened bulkheads run the length of the craft separating the control load deck from the outer sidestructures which contain the lift fan engines, lift fans, transmissions and auxiliary power systems. The freight deck is reinforced to permit the carriage of heavy vehicles. A stern door and bow loading door/ramp provide a drive-on, drive-off through-loading facility. Separate side doors, port and starboard, give access to the two cabins which flank the load deck forward.

SKIRT: Loop and segment type tapered skirt, similar to that of the SR.N6, in coated nylon fabric.

DIMENSIONS
Length: 27·2m (89ft 3in)
Beam: 13·8m (45ft 3in)
Height: 9·6m (31ft 6in)
Cushion depth: 1·5m-1·8m (4ft 11in-5ft 11in)
WEIGHTS
Max weight: 65 tonnes
Useful load: 15 tonnes
PERFORMANCE
Speed, calm water: 55 knots

TYPE 7203

Derived from Types 713 and 717 (built in the 1970s), Type 7203 is a high-speed sidewall hovercraft passenger ferry for use on coastal and sheltered waters. Alternative applications include

coastguard patrol and port/harbour firefighting duties.

Built at the Dagu Shipyard, Tianjin, the prototype was launched in September 1982 and underwent trials on the Hai river and in Tang-Gu in late 1982.

LIFT AND PROPULSION: A multi-fan system improves seakeeping performance. Three centrifugal fans of different diameters are separately fitted in the bow, amidship and stern. Each feeds air to the bow and stern skirts and the air cushion at different volumes and pressures. Diameters of the bow, amidship and stern fans are 800mm, 1200mm and 450mm respectively. The lift system is powered by a single 12150C high-speed diesel rated at 300hp at 1500rpm. The lift engine directly drives the amidship and stern fans. The bow fan is driven via a hydraulic pump and motor. Total lift power is about 250hp. Disengaging the bow fan reduces lift power consumption to about 100hp in calm waters. When operating in waves the bow fan is required since it affects the craft's trim. Propulsive power is supplied by two 12150CZ watercooled, turbocharged, high-speed marine diesels, each rated at 450hp at 1450rpm. Each drives a three-bladed propeller via a V-type transmission.

CONTROLS: Craft direction controlled by twin rudders and by differential use of water propellers.

ACCOMMODATION: In standard configuration passenger cabin seats 81 passengers. If required, seating capacity can be increased to 100. Two aisles between seats are 800mm wide.

SKIRT: Loop and segment type in bonded natural rubber coated fabric.

DIMENSIONS
Length overall: 22·2m
Beam overall: 6·9m
Height overall: 5·2m
Height sidewalls: 1·1m
Draught, hullborne: 2·06m
Draught, on cushion: 1·22m
WEIGHT
Max: 35 tonnes
PERFORMANCE
Max speed: 30 knots
Cruising speed: 26 knots
Range: 180n miles

JINXIANG

An 80-seat sidewall passenger ferry, Jinxiang is a joint project of the Marine Design and Research Institute of China and the Dagu Shipyard, Tianjin. In July 1983 it successfully completed a 128km

Type 722 65-ton multi-duty hovercraft

MARIC-designed Type 7210 built by Dong Feng Shipyard

maiden voyage along the Yangtze river from Shanghai to Vantong in under three hours. The craft is diesel-powered and has a maximum speed of 55km/h.

HULL: High strength, corrosion-resistant aluminium alloy.

DIMENSIONS
Length: 22·2m
Beam: 6·9m
Height: 5·2m

DONG FENG SHIPYARD
Hangzhou
TYPE 7210

Two fully amphibious utility hovercraft type '7210' were completed in May 1985. They were designed by MARIC and constructed by Dong Feng Shipyard, Hangzhou. Built in medium-strength sea-water resistant aluminium alloy with riveted construction, the craft is powered by air-cooled marine diesels. Lift is provided by a Deutz BF6L 912 diesel engine driving via a gearbox a centrifugal aluminium fan. Thrust is supplied by another diesel, a Deutz BF6L 913 driving via a transmission shaft and elastic coupling, a 1·8m, five-blade, ducted air propeller built in grp. The skirt is of the bag-finger type in rubberised fabric, low-temperature resistant down to −20°C. The total skirt height is 500mm.

DIMENSIONS
Length overall: 9·85m
Beam overall: 3·40m
Overall height on landing pads: 2·80m
WEIGHTS
Max weight: 4·7 tons
Payload: 800kg

PERFORMANCE
Max water speed over calm water: 45km/h
Range: 250km

The first two craft were delivered to units of the oil industry for transporting people and equipment in offshore areas and marshes.

TYPE 717

This craft is a waterjet-propelled, rigid sidewall air cushion vehicle, designed by MARIC as a high-speed inland water passenger ferry for use on shallow water. The '717' series of the 1970s has been developed. The Type 717 II *Ming Jiang* passenger ferry hovercraft was completed in October 1984, and was delivered to the Changqing ship transportation company as a high-speed passenger ferry. The Type 717 *Chongqing* sidewall hovercraft was also completed in Dong Feng Shipyard, Hangzhou, in September 1984, and was delivered to the Chongqing ferry boat company as a high-speed passenger craft operating on the rapids of the Yangtze River.

LIFT AND PROPULSION: Integrated system powered by two 12V 150C marine diesels rated at 300hp continuous. Two engines are mounted aft and each drives a 600mm diameter centrifugal fan, Type 4-72 for lift, and via an elastic coupling, universal joint and transmission shaft, a mixed flow waterjet pump. Another bow fan is driven via a hydraulic pump and motor by the integrated power system.

STRUCTURE: The sidewalls are built in grp, but other parts of hull and superstructure are built in riveted, high-strength aluminium alloy.

DIMENSIONS	717 II	717 III
Length overall:	20·40m	21·20m
Beam overall:	4·54m	4·94m
Height overall:	3·80m	3·80m

MARIC Type 717 II

MARIC Type 717 III

MARIC Type 716 II 32-passenger ACV

WEIGHTS
Max weight:	21·2 tons	22·20 tons
Payload:	54-60 passengers	70 passengers

PERFORMANCE
Speed, max, calm water:	45km/h	42km/h
Range:	400km	250km

SHANGHAI HU DONG SHIPYARD
Shanghai

TYPE 716 II
Designed by MARIC, the amphibious hovercraft Type 716 II was completed in Shanghai Hu Dong Shipyard in 1985. The craft has undergone evaluation by the China Air Cushion Technology Development Corporation (CACTEC). The craft will operate in offshore areas, shallow water and marshes for transporting people and equipment.

HULL: Riveted skin and stringer structure employing high-strength aluminium alloy sheet. Main hull forms a buoyancy raft based on a grid of longitudinal and transverse frames which form a number of flotation compartments.

LIFT AND PROPULSION: One 428hp Deutz BF12L 413FC air-cooled marine diesel via a gearbox and transmission shaft drives a 2m diameter centrifugal fan. Two identical engines, via transmission shafts, drive directly two 2·3m diameter ducted air propellers.

CONTROLS: Directional control is by two sets of twin vertical aerodynamic rudders mounted on the rear of the propeller ducts.

DIMENSIONS
Length overall: 17·94m
Beam overall: 8·3m
Height on landing pads: 4·55m

WEIGHTS
Max weight: 18·6 tons
Payload: 2·5 tons (or 32 passengers)
PERFORMANCE
Max calm water speed: 39 knots
Range: 120n miles

WUHU SHIPYARD
Au-hui Province
TYPE 719
Designed by MARIC, and completed at Wuhu Shipyard, Au-hui Province, in 1984, the Type 719 sidewall hovercraft has undergone evaluation by the China Air Cushion Technology Development Corporation (CACTEC).

HULL: Main hull and sidewall are built in marine steel with welded construction, but superstructure is of grp construction.

LIFT AND PROPULSION: A 12180 four-stroke, water-cooled, turbocharged marine diesel rated at 900hp, via gearbox and transmission shaft, drives two 1·2m diameter twin air inlet type

Jing-Sah river test craft

centrifugal fans. Two identical diesels, via gearboxes and transmission shafts, drive two three-blade marine propellers.
CONTROLS: Craft direction controlled by twin rudders and by differential use of marine propellers.
SKIRT: Loop and segment type in bonded rubberised fabric.
DIMENSIONS
Length overall: 35·5m
Beam overall: 7·6m
Height overall: 8·5m
WEIGHTS
Max weight: 95 tons
Payload: 186 passengers
PERFORMANCE
Max calm water speed: 30 knots
Service water speed: 25 knots
Range: 500n miles

JING-SAH RIVER TEST CRAFT
Please see *Jane's Surface Skimmers 1985* for details of this craft.

MARIC Type 719G, 186-passenger sidewall hovercraft

SHIPBUILDING AND MARINE ENGINEERING ESTABLISHMENT
Shanghai
2·8-TONNE UTILITY HOVERCRAFT

A fully amphibious utility hovercraft was completed in 1980 by the Shipbuilding and Marine Engineering Establishment, Shanghai. Although intended primarily for seismic prospecting in offshore areas and marshes, it is suitable for a variety of other utility roles. Sturdily built in riveted aluminium alloy, it carries a driver and up to seven passengers at a speed of 23-33km/h.

Two craft of this type are reported to be in service with the Chinese onshore oil industry. See 1987 edition for photograph.

LIFT AND PROPULSION: Lift is provided by an 85hp BJ492Q-1 four-stroke automobile petrol engine driving, via a universal coupling and gearbox, a centrifugal aluminium fan. Thrust is supplied by a second engine of identical type driving, via a transmission shaft, elastic coupling, transmission gear and thrust bearing, a 1·4m, four-bladed, variable-pitch aircraft propeller built in grp. Range of pitch variation is from + 15 to − 15 degrees. When the vehicle is operating with the propeller at constant pitch, the rotational speed is charged through the adjustment of the engine throttle. Cushion pressure is $94\cdot5kg/m^2$ $(18lb/ft^2)$.

CONTROLS: Craft direction is controlled by twin aerodynamic rudders at the rear of the propeller duct.

HULL: Built in 919 medium strength seawater resistant aluminium alloy. Riveted construction.

SKIRT: Segmented bag-type fabricated in rubberised fabric. Height of fingers, 250mm, representing 50 per cent of the total skirt height. Tensile strength is 500 to 450kg/5cm width.

DIMENSIONS
Length: 9·19m
Width: 4·76m
Height: 3·32m
Deck area: $9m^2$
Cabin, internal height: 1·47m
Average draught: 0·22m

WEIGHTS
Fully loaded: 2769kg
Useful load (8 personnel at 75kg each = 600kg, fuel and water, 118kg): 718kg

PERFORMANCE
Max speed during tests, still water: 42km/h
Speed at wind scale 3: 23-33km/h
Vertical obstacle clearance: 0·5m

CHAOHU SHIPYARD
Au-hui Province
and
SHANGHAI SHIP AND SHIPPING RESEARCH INSTITUTE (SSSRI)
Head office: 200 Minsheng Road, Shanghai, People's Republic of China

Telephone: 840438
Telex: 33107 SSSRI CN

WR 901

The WR 901 is a waterjet-propelled, 40-seat, rigid sidewall hovercraft, designed for water-bus use on shallow rivers with a guaranteed depth of 0·8m.

The craft has been developed from a 5-ton experimental test craft designed by Shanghai Ship and Shipping Research Institute (SSSRI) built in Au-hui Province in 1975. The pre-production prototype was completed in December 1980. The design was jointly undertaken by the SSSRI and Communication Bureau of Au-hui Province and the craft was completed in the Chaohu Shipyard.

Official trials were completed in May 1981 on the river with depth of 0·8 to 1·2m. During a speed test over a measured mile with a full complement of passengers aboard, 38·5km/h (23·9mph) was attained.

Four of the first model of the WR 901 ACV were built.

LIFT AND PROPULSION: Integrated system powered by a main 12V 150Z diesel rated at 300hp

40-passenger SES

continuous mounted aft and a second 485Q diesel engine rated at 30hp continuous, mounted forward.

The main engine (210hp at 1400rpm) drives a 365mm diameter two-stage waterjet unit for propulsion and supplies 20hp to drive two 300mm diameter centrifugal fans for lift.

The second engine drives two 500mm diameter centrifugal fans for lift.

The air cushion is retained between rigid longitudinal sidewalls, and flexible bow and rigid stern seals. Cushion pressure is $240kg/m^2$.

CONTROLS: Helm operated surfaces located in the waterjet stream provide directional control. Thrust reversal is achieved by the use of waterflow deflectors.

HULL: Single shell glass-reinforced plastic moulding with sub-moulding, frames, bulkhead and cabin and base panels bonded together.

Materials used include expanded pvc foam, glass fibre, polyester resins and wood. The hull bottom, deck and superstructure top have longitudinal frames and the sidewall transverse frames.

Thickness of plating on the side hull bottom is 4·5mm (6mm in the bow section) and on the sidewall 5mm (up to 6mm in the bow section). Deck plates are 4mm thick and the top of the superstructure is in 2·5mm plating.

ACCOMMODATION: Seats are provided for a crew of two in a raised wheelhouse and for 40 passengers. Access to the passenger saloon is through single doors at the bow and stern.

The craft runs bow-on to flat sloping banks to embark and disembark passengers.

SYSTEMS, ELECTRICAL: One 1·2kW 24V dc engine-driven generator and batteries.

COMMUNICATION: Car radio in wheelhouse and speakers in passenger saloon.

DIMENSIONS
Length overall: 19·30m
Beam overall: 3·95m
Hull beam: 3·75m
Height of hull top wheelhouse: 3·90m
Height of sidewalls: 0·50m
Draught load: 0·65m
Draught cushionborne at bow: 0·1m
  at stern: 0·45m
WEIGHT
Max weight, with 40 passengers: 16 tons
PERFORMANCE
Service speed, normal: 33km/h

JING-SAH RIVER PASSENGER FERRY

This craft is diesel powered and propelled by waterscrews. It was built during 1969 and began trials in 1970. Please see *Jane's Surface Skimmers 1985* for details.

TAI HU PASSENGER FERRY

A 42-seat waterjet-propelled passenger ferry, this craft has been built for operation across Lake Tai. It was delivered during early 1983. Unconfirmed reports credit the craft with a speed of 40km/h and a range of 450km.

Jing-Sah river passenger ferry

Waterjet-propelled SES on Lake Tai

FINLAND

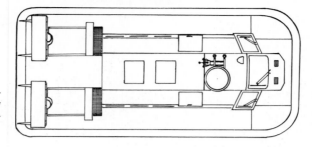

FINN-LEIJU KY

Rattipolku 7, 45360 Valkeala, Finland

Telephone: (9) 512 33321
Telex: 52004 KVOLA SF

J Hakanen, *Proprietor*

Builder of the successful Leiju 387 light hovercraft, this company has now developed a new design for a larger craft, diesel-powered, for over-ice use. The first craft will be completed in 1988.

FL 1010

LIFT AND PROPULSION: Two VM turbo-diesel engines, 130hp each at 4200rpm.
HULL: Diwinycell sandwich, spray-coated with polyurethane.
ACCOMMODATION: Seats for 15 to 20 passengers plus 2 crew.
DIMENSIONS
Length (hard structure), overall: 10·80m
Beam: 4·60m
WEIGHTS
Empty weight: 1800kg
Payload: 1500kg
PERFORMANCE
Speed, max: 35-45 knots
Fuel consumption: 40 litres/h

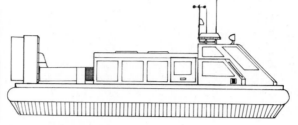
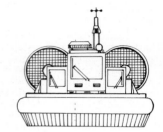

Finn-Leiju 1010 project

Weather restrictions
  Max, wind: 20 knots
  Max, wave height: 0·8m

OY WÄRTSILÄ AB

Helsinki Shipyard, PO Box 132, SF-00151 Helsinki 15, Finland

Telephone: 0 1941 (international)/90 1941 (national)
Telex: 121246 WHT SF
Telefax: 358 0 650 051

Pekka Laine, *President, Shipbuilding Division*
Martin Saarikangas, *Senior Vice President, Shipbuilding Division, and Managing Director, Wärtsilä, Helsinki Shipyard*
Robert Stenius, *President, Managing Director, Turku Shipyard*
Kaj Liljestrand, *Vice President, Marketing, Sales and R and D, Helsinki Shipyard*

Wärtsilä is one of the largest publicly quoted industrial companies in Finland. Group net sales for 1985 reached FIM 5500 million (approx US$ 1000 million). Exports and foreign operations together accounted for over 70 per cent of Group net sales. Wärtsilä also has several production plants outside Finland in Sweden, Norway, the Federal Republic of Germany, France, the USA and Singapore. The Group employs about 16 000 people, 3000 of whom work in the international units.

The Group is divided into six divisions. The largest one, the Shipbuilding Division comprises the Turku Shipyard, the Helsinki Shipyard, the Piikkiö factory for interior modules and the Ylivieska Factory for prefabricated pipe assemblies. Ship repairs are carried out at the repair yards in Turku and Kotka.

The traditional types of the Helsinki Shipyard are icebreakers, cruise ferries, cruise liners, cable layers and naval craft. The yard, which employs about 2000 people, has captured the greater part of the world market for icebreakers. By July 1986 it had delivered 54 icebreakers, ranging from smaller harbour icebreakers, shallow draught river icebreakers to arctic icebreakers of 26·5MW (36 000shp). Among four further icebreakers are two nuclear-powered shallow draught polar icebreakers of 38 200kW (52 000hp). The yard's research and development department is continuously engaged in feasibility studies and research on the development of ice-going tonnage and future transport needs in the Arctic and Antarctic areas.

The Wärtsilä Arctic Research Centre (WARC) has an ice model basin in which it is possible to test the behaviour of ships and other structures in several different kinds of simulated icefields. Research is also carried out for outside interests.

The Diesel Division is one of the world's leading manufacturers of medium-speed diesel engines. They are used as main and auxiliary engines in ships, on offshore rigs and to generate electricity in diesel power plants. The Division's production units are located in Finland, Sweden, Norway, France and Singapore.

Since 1976 Wärtsilä's Helsinki Shipyard has been applying the experience gained in its construction of icebreakers to the development of air cushion craft capable of negotiating the physical conditions encountered in cold regions. The prototype of the Polar Utility Craft PUC 22, a fully amphibious ACV mixed-traffic ferry with a 30-tonne capacity, is in service in Canada and a 70-tonne capacity ferry, the *Arctic Express*, is projected.

The company has also designed and built 14 TAV 40, 40-tonne capacity hover lighters to solve cargo transfer problems in the Arctic. A derivative of this design is the Vector 4, which is self-propelled and fitted with steerable outrigged

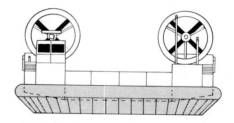

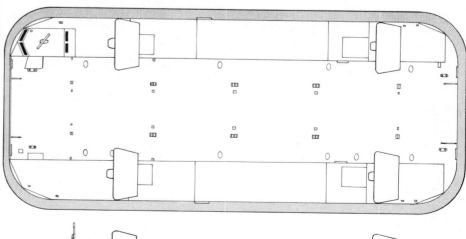

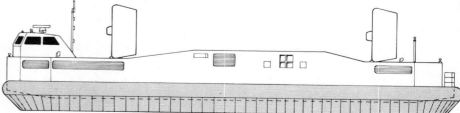

General Arrangement of Polar Utility Craft PUC 22

Wärtsilä air cushion vehicle *Larus* at its Tuktoyaktuk base, Northwest Territories   *(Ranson Photographers Ltd, Edmonton, Alberta)*

crawler tractor units fore and aft. Two recent additions to this range of self-propelled, year-round, heavy cargo transporters, are the Vector 75 and Vector 200.

Details of the TAV 40, Vector 4, Vector 75 and Vector 200 will be found in the *Low-Speed Air Cushion Platforms* section.

PUC 22

Larus, the prototype (new building 433) of this 30-tonne capacity amphibious mixed-traffic ferry, was ordered by the Finnish Board of Roads and Waterways from the Wärtsilä Helsinki Shipyard in January 1980 and was delivered in December 1981.

The craft was designed to carry winter traffic in the south west area of the Finnish archipelago where ice precludes the use of conventional ferries and has been used in the Gulf of Bothnia between Oulumsalo and the island of Hailuoto, completing winter service there in March 1985. The craft can carry up to 16 light motor vehicles or two buses or one heavy lorry and 50 passengers.

Although *Larus* has been developed for use as a ro-ro ferry, a variety of other applications have been under consideration. In 1985 a joint venture was formed between Wärtsilä Arctic Inc and Arctic Transportation (ATL) of Calgary, Canada, to bring *Larus* to Canada. See the *Civil Operators* section.

Changes to the craft were incorporated to ensure reliable operation in temperatures as low as −50°C. A paper by E Makinen on the operation of *Larus* in the Beaufort Sea is listed in the Bibliography section of this edition.

LIFT AND PROPULSION: Integrated system powered by four high-speed marine diesels, each rated at 650kW. The engines are mounted one forward and one aft in each of the two sidestructures. Each diesel drives, via a main gearbox, either one or two centrifugal fans and, via a bevel gear and vertical shaft, a four-bladed pylon-mounted ducted controllable-pitch propeller.

CONTROLS: Each propeller pylon rotates to provide both propulsion and directional control. The rotation is electro-hydraulically controlled from the wheelhouse or manually from the engine rooms. Each of the propeller pylons rotates 240°, 90° inwards and 150° outwards.

HULL: Built in marine grade aluminium. Buoyancy raft type structure with port and starboard longitudinal sidestructures. Each sidestructure contains two diesels, one forward, one aft, together with their associated fans, ducted propellers, transmission and auxiliary power systems. Hydraulically operated bow and stern loading ramps provide roll-on, roll-off through loading facilities.

SKIRT: 1m (3ft 3in) deep bag and segment type.

ACCOMMODATION: All controls are in a raised bridge well forward on the starboard superstructure. Passengers are seated amidships in two 25-seat cabins, one in each sidestructure.

PUC 22

DIMENSIONS
Length overall: 33m (108ft 3in)
 hull: 32m (105ft)
Beam overall: 14·7m (48ft 3in)
 hull: 13·5m (44ft 3½in)
Height overall: 8·2m (26ft 11in)
 hull side: 1m (3ft 3in)
Main deck: 25m × 7m (82ft × 23ft)
WEIGHT
Useful load: 25 tonnes
PERFORMANCE
Speed over water: 25 knots
Clearance height: 1m (3ft 3in)

ARCTIC EXPRESS (DESIGN)

Larger craft are under consideration employing a similar design configuration to the PUC 22 but capable of carrying much heavier loads. Arctic Express is a diesel-powered, mixed-traffic ferry with a payload capacity of 70 tonnes.

The hull is based on a buoyancy raft structure with port and starboard sidestructures. Each longitudinal structure contains two diesels, one forward driving the lift fan system, and one aft which drives a four-bladed, ducted controllable-pitch propeller.

All controls are in a raised bridge amidships above the starboard superstructure. Passengers are seated amidships in two cabins, one in each sidestructure.

The skirt is of bag and segment type, surrounded by an anti-spray apron.
DIMENSIONS
Length: 35m
Beam: 17m
Width across deck: 8·9m
WEIGHT
Payload: 70 tonnes
PERFORMANCE
Cruising speed: 34 knots, approx

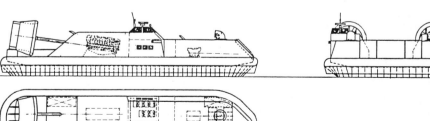

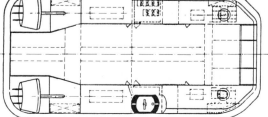

Arctic Express design

FRANCE

SOCIÉTÉ AEROPLAST sarl

Creux Redon de Cantadou, 34400 Lunel, France

Telephone: (67) 71 65 97

Guy Akerman, *Technical Director*

Aeroplast has developed over the past few years a range of light air cushion vehicles for sport and pleasure use which have led to a larger type, the ADOC 12, a 1·25-tonne payload utility craft supported in part by IFREMER.

ADOC 12

The ADOC 12 employs four very lightweight propulsion systems previously developed for much lighter craft. The same basic components are in use for Aeroplast one-, two-, three- and fourteen-seat craft allowing considerable flexibility in manufacture and reduced stocks of spare parts.

Two lift fans supply the air cushion, of the same Multiwing type as the four air propellers.

The frame of the craft is constructed in grp, Bureau Veritas controlled.

A diesel-powered version of the ADOC 12 was due to be produced in 1987.

ENGINES
Propulsion: Two 52hp two-stroke or four-stroke
Lift: Two 52hp two-stroke or four-stroke
ACCOMMODATION
Crew: 1 or 2
Passengers: 12
FUEL TANK
Capacity: 300 litres
DIMENSIONS
Length overall, rigid structure: 8·4m
  on cushion: 9·4m
Width overall, rigid structure: 4·4m
  on cushion: 5·4m
Height overall, rigid structure: 2·3m
  on cushion: 2·9m
Propellers, dia: 800mm
Fans, dia: 800mm
WEIGHTS
Weight, max: 3000kg
Payload: 1250kg
PERFORMANCE
Speed, max, calm water: 40 knots
Speed, cruising, calm water: 30 knots
Range at cruising speed: 210n miles
Obstacle clearance capability: 0·5m
Fuel consumption: 40 litres/h
WEATHER LIMITATIONS
Wind, max: 20 knots
Wave height, max: 1·0m

Aeroplast ADOC 12

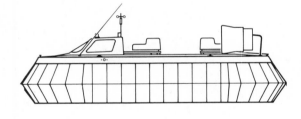
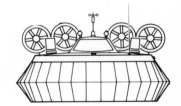

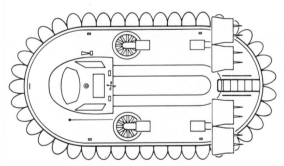

General Arrangement of ADOC 12

ALFA/NAVAL

ZP de Bregaillon, 83500 La Seyne, France

Telephone: (94) 94 54 44
Telex: 404631 F

Please see Addenda for SES design and production by this company.

Following the building of Alfa/Naval's first SES, powered by two 1070kW diesel engines, driving KMW 50S waterjet units, three further SES craft have been ordered, yard numbers 27-02, 27-03 and 27-04, powered by two 1500kW (2012bhp) engines driving KMW 56S waterjet units. The first of this batch was launched on 15 January 1988.

DIRECTION DES CON-STRUCTIONS NAVALES (DCN)

2 rue Royale, BP No 1, 75008 Paris, France

Telephone: (1) 260 33 30
Telex: 270734 F

The Délégation Générale pour l'Armement (DGA) is currently engaged in a research and development programme on surface effect ships. So as to be able to fulfil perceived naval requirements for 1995, DCN is studying an SES project of approximately 1000 tonnes for anti-submarine warfare (ASW) on the high seas. These studies are being conducted by the Service Technique des Constructions et Armes Navales (STCAN) under the aegis of a technical-operational working group, within the framework of a project named EOLES (light oceanic surface effect escort craft). The task lays down a requirement for an off cushion speed of 18 knots but with speeds in the order of 50 knots on cushion. Apart from its ASW armaments, the craft will be equipped with self-defence systems against air attack and surface ships.

Several stages of technology have to be passed through before this craft reaches the production phase. The experimental model, code-named MOLENES, has already largely been through its trials. In addition, DCN is involved in an inter-ministry programme aimed at developing the 200-tonne craft designed by STCAN. The NES (Navire à Effet de Surface) 200 SES experience will guide the operational and technological options arising from the EOLES project.

MOLENES (Modèle Libre Expérimental de Navire à Effet de Surface)

In 1980, DCN built under contract from DRET (Direction des Recherches Etudes et Techniques) a 5-tonne craft, which had its trials in 1981 in the Toulon area. MOLENES is a dynamic manned model capable of proving the NES concept of a high length/beam ratio, and confirmed results

MOLENES dynamic manned model of NES SES project

(STCAN-DOC)

obtained in the experimental tank and has provided data on sea-worthiness, performance and manoeuvrability, as well as acceleration levels and their effects on the structure, equipment and fittings.

LIFT AND PROPULSION: Propulsion is provided by two 55hp waterjet units. The air cushion is effected by two centrifugal fans on vertical axes, giving a pressure of 1800Pa (37·6lb/ft²) and a flow of 4m³/s (141ft³/s).

HULL: The timber side keels are joined together by a tubular pyramid structure of light aluminium alloy 7020.

DIMENSIONS
Length overall: 12·10m
Width overall: 3·43m
WEIGHT
Displacement: 5·5 tonnes

EOLES (Escorteur Océanique Léger à Effet de Surface) (DESIGN)

This project is being designed by STCAN under the control of a Technical Operational Group, commissioned with evaluating the capacity of EOLES to carry out the task of anti-submarine warfare. An operational research study has made it possible to compare EOLES with other solutions thought possible for future ASW.

The main advantage of this design is the combination of data available from the very low frequency sonar equipment with the availability of two on-board medium-weight helicopters, carried on an SES capable of high speed even in rough seas.

LIFT AND PROPULSION: Propulsion is provided by two waterjets driven by two TAG General Electric LM 2500 engines, each of 27 000hp.

Lift is provided by two centrifugal fans on vertical axes, driven by 5000hp diesel engines, which also provide propulsive power when operating off cushion.

ARMAMENT AND EQUIPMENT: Two medium helicopters, four missile launched torpedoes, 16 torpedoes launched from helicopters, four MM40 missiles, 16 SAAM missiles, 2 SATCP 'Sadral', ELW system.

DETECTION: ASW detection is effected by a towed linear antenna, EBTF, capable of being activated, and a dipping sonar (for use when stationary, with coverage being achieved by means of high-speed bounds). Air/surface detection is provided by SAAM radar, V15, DECCA and RODEO systems.

DIMENSIONS
Length overall: 89m
Width overall: 21·10m
Draught, off cushion: 3·60m
  on cushion: 1·60m
WEIGHT
Displacement, mean: 1200 tonnes
PERFORMANCE
Speed, off cushion: 18 knots
  on cushion: 50 knots
Range, off cushion: 1900n miles
  on cushion: 4400n miles

DIRECTION DES CONSTRUCTIONS NAVALES (DCN)

2 rue Royale, 75200 Paris Naval, France

and

ATELIERS ET CHANTIERS DU HAVRE (ACH)

BP 1390, 76066 Le Havre Cedex, France

Telex: 190322 F

and

CONSTRUCTIONS MÉCANIQUES DE NORMANDIE (CMN)

26 rue de Montevideo, 75116 Paris, France

Telephone: 45040877
Telex: 610097 F

NES 200 (DESIGN)

The NES 200 is being developed within the framework of an inter-ministry programme, in

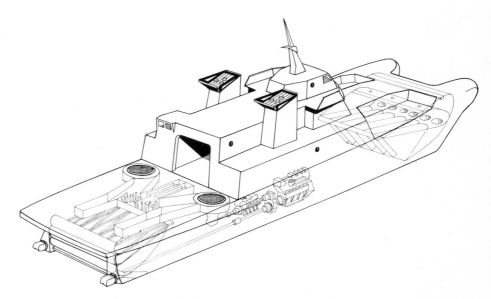

Arrangement of lift and propulsion systems in NES 200 SES design

which the following are participating: the Ministry of Defence, the Ministry of Research and the Ministry of Industry.

Involved in conducting the programme are La Direction des Recherches, Etudes et Techniques (DRET) and the Institute of France for Marine

Research and Exploitation of the Sea (IFREMER).

Industrial concerns involved are DCN, in respect of the project design, and ACH and CMN shipyards, in respect of the construction.

The project which is envisaged to produce a craft in the region of 200 tonnes, is being designed in the form of a basic air cushion platform for both civil and military versions.

The major components (propulsion system, lift fans etc) are all existing technology, and therefore require only a limited degree of development.

General specifications common to all the versions:

LIFT AND PROPULSION
Main propulsion: Two 4000hp (MTU 16V 538 TB 93 or SACM UD 33 M7) diesels driving two KaMeWa waterjet units
Lift: Two 1000hp (MTU 8V 396 TB 83 or SACM UD 20 M5) diesels driving two NEU centrifugal fans, 180 000m³ at 600kg/cm² off cushion, power transferable to the two KaMeWa waterjet units

DIMENSIONS
Length overall: 49·60m
  waterline: 44·80m
Width overall: 13·00m
Draught, off cushion: 3·00m
  on cushion: 1·10m

WEIGHT
Displacement, max: 260 tonnes

PERFORMANCE
Speed, off cushion: 15 knots
  on cushion: 40 knots

Anti-Surface Combat Version
Range, off cushion: 3200n miles at 12 knots
  1000n miles at 35 knots
Crew: 35
Weapon systems: one twin-barrel 30mm cannon or one Sadral
  two Exocet MM 40 missiles
  one Dauphin helicopter + radar
  two AS 15 heli-borne missiles
  two Protean decoy missiles
  one Triton S radar system
  one Totem optronic guidance system
  one DR 2000 Dalia

This design permits a combination of great mobility and over-the-horizon target definition by the helicopter on board the craft, giving full effect to the long-range MM 40 missiles.

In addition, its range when powered off cushion and the weapon capacity of the craft enable it to carry out interdiction tasks within sea-approaches.

Coast Guard Version/Commando Transport
Range off cushion: 3200n miles at 12 knots
  1000n miles at 35 knots
Crew: 26 + 12 passengers
Weapons: one single-barrel 40mm Bofors cannon
  two 12·7mm machine-guns
  one navigation radar

Fast Patrol Version
Range: 3200n miles at 12 knots
  1000n miles at 35 knots
Crew: 29
Weapon systems: one 57mm Bofors cannon
  one twin-barrel 30mm cannon
  two 4 MM 40 missiles
  one Sadral
  one Triton S radar

one Castor II B radar
two Protean decoy launchers
one DA 2000 Dalia

Passenger/car Ferry
Displacement, full load, approx: 260 tonnes
Disposable load, approx: 63 tonnes
Passengers: 250
Cars: 27

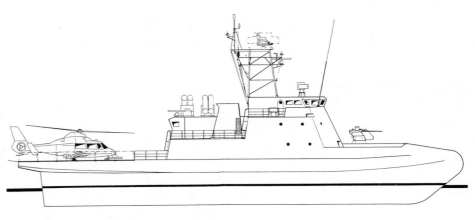

NES 200 design, anti-surface combat version

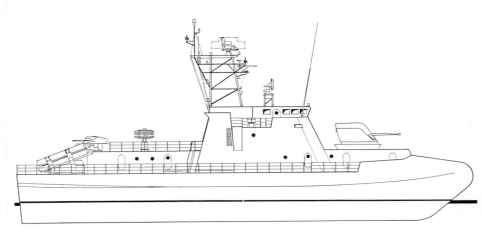

NES 200 design, fast patrol version

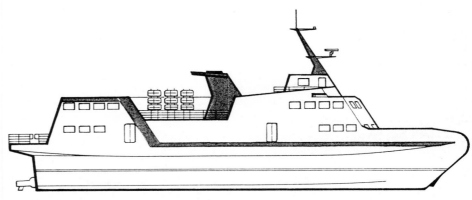

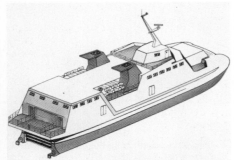

Isometric drawing of NES 200L passenger/car ferry

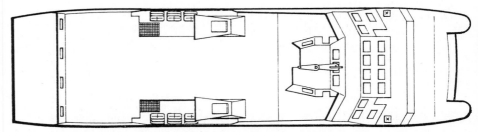

NES 200L passenger/car craft design

INSTITUT FRANÇAIS DE RECHERCHE POUR L'EXPLOITATION DE LA MER (IFREMER)

[DESIGN, RESEARCH AND DEVELOPMENT ORGANISATION]
Centre de Brest, BP 337, 29273 Brest Cedex, France

Telephone: (98) 22 40 40
Telex: 940627 OCEAN F

NES 24 (DESIGN)

This design is for a 22-metre surface effect ship which is being studied in collaboration with French shipyards.

POWER
Lift: Approx 350hp
Propulsion: Approx 1500hp
ACCOMMODATION
Passengers: 100 to 120
DIMENSIONS
Length: Approx 22m

Beam: Approx 6·5m
Draught, on cushion: Approx 0·2m bow, 0·7m stern
Draught, on hulls: Approx 1·4m
WEIGHTS
Weight, max: Approx 37 tonnes
Weight, empty: Approx 25 tonnes
PERFORMANCE
Speed, max, calm water: Above 35 knots
Speed, cruising: Above 30 knots
Range: Approx 240n miles

ITALY

TERMOMECCANICA ITALIANA/ CANTIERI STAIN Srl

TERMOMECCANICA ITALIANA
PO Box 341, Via Del Molo 1, I-19100 La Spezia, Italy

Telephone: (0187) 532111
Telex: 532267/270171 TMISP I

Piergiorgio Cominetta, *Vice Chairman and Managing Director*

CANTIERI STAIN Srl
Lungo Po Antonelli, Turin, Italy

Telephone: (011) 6497861/882403

TSES 8

A fast SES intervention craft first shown in prototype form at the Viareggio International Marine Show, May 1986. This 8-metre craft is a manned scale model prototype for a much larger project, the TSES 26.

TSES 26 (DESIGN)

This design is proposed for various applications including sea rescue, firefighting, civil protection, fast ferry, and military use for landing craft, patrol and coast guard.
HULL: To be built in peralluman, an aluminium alloy produced by the Alluminia company, EFIM Group.
MACHINERY
Main engines: Two Isotta Fraschini, 1600hp each
Auxiliary engines: Two VM (IRI, Finnmeccanica Group), 170hp each
Fans for cushion air: Termomeccanica
Ducted marine propellers: Termomeccanica
EQUIPMENT
Firefighting integral pump, water desalination units: Termomeccanica (capacity 2000 litres/day) powered by two 50kW diesel generators

Termomeccanica Italiana TSES 8 prototype SES   *(Milpress di Antonio O Ciampi & C Sas)*

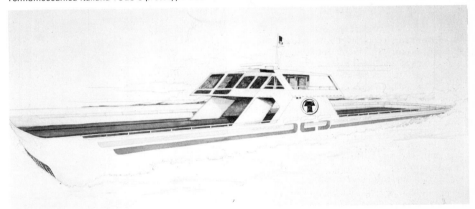
Termomeccanica Italiana design for a 26m SES, TSES 26   *(Milpress di Antonio O Ciampi & C Sas)*

DIMENSIONS
Length: 26·00m
Width: 7·00m
Draught at 40-tonne displacement, stationary: 0·95m

Draught at 40-tonne displacement, on-cushion: 0·45m
PERFORMANCE
Speed, max: 55 knots
Speed, operating on displacement vessel: 17 knots

JAPAN

MITSUI ENGINEERING & SHIPBUILDING CO LTD

6-4, Tsukiji 5-chome, Chuo-ku, Tokyo 104, Japan

Telephone: 544-3462
Telex: 22821 J, 22924 J

Kazuo Maeda, *Chairman*
Isshi Suenaga, *President*
Jiro Hoshino, *Executive Managing Director*
Hisashi Nemotoe, *Manager, Ship Sales Department*
Yoshio Yamashita, *General Manager, High-speed Craft Division*

Mitsui's Hovercraft Department was formed in May 1964, following the signing of a licensing agreement in 1963 with Hovercraft Development Ltd and Vickers Ltd, whose ACV interests were later merged with those of British Hovercraft Corporation.

The company has been developing Mitsui hovercraft independently after terminating the licensing agreement in March 1986. The company has built a new concept hovercraft, Mitsui Jet Hover, following a previous range of amphibious hovercraft types: two 11-seat MV-PP1s, 19 MV-PP5s; four MV-PP15s and two prototype MV-PP05As.

MV-PP1

The MV-PP1 is a small peripheral jet ACV built for river and coastal services and fitted with a flexible skirt. It seats a pilot and ten passengers and cruises at 40 knots.

The prototype, which was completed in July 1964 was designated RH-4, the first production model the PP1-01. The latter was sold to the Thai Customs Department for service in the estuary of the Menam Chao Phya and adjacent waters and has been named *Customs Hovercraft 1*. It has been in service with the Thai Customs Department since September 1967.

Details of construction, weights, performance, etc can be found in *Jane's Surface Skimmers 1970-71* and earlier editions.

MV-PP5

Mitsui's first large hovercraft, the 50-seat MV-PP5, is a gas-turbine powered craft intended primarily for fast ferry services on Japanese coastal and inland waters.
LIFT AND PROPULSION: All machinery is aft to minimise noise in the passenger cabin. A single IHI IM-100 gas turbine (licence-built General Electric LM100) with a maximum continuous rating of 1050hp at 19 500rpm drives the integrated lift/propulsion system. Its output shaft passes first to the main gearbox from which shafts extend sideways and upwards to two three-bladed Hamilton/Sumitomo variable-pitch propulsion propellers of 2·59m (8ft 6in) diameter. A further shaft runs forward to the fan gearbox from which a drive shaft runs vertically downwards to a 2·27m (7ft 7in) 13-bladed lift fan mounted beneath the air

intake immediately aft of the passenger saloon roof. The fan is constructed in aluminium alloy and the disc plate is a 40mm (1·5in) thick honeycomb structure.

To prevent erosion from water spray the propeller blades are nickel plated.

Fuel is carried in two metal tanks, with a total capacity of 1900 litres (416 gallons), located immediately ahead of the lift fan assembly.

CONTROLS: Twin aerodynamic rudders in the propeller slipstream and differential thrust from the propellers provide directional control. The rudders are controlled hydraulically from the commander's position.

A thrust-port air bleed system provides lateral control at slow speeds. The thrust ports are actuated by air extracted from the engine compressor and are located beneath the passenger doors, port and starboard.

HULL: Construction is primarily of high strength A5052 aluminium alloy suitably protected against the corrosive effects of sea water. The basic structure is the main buoyancy chamber which is divided into eight watertight sub-divisions for safety, and includes fore and aft trimming tanks. Two further side body tanks, each divided into three watertight compartments, are attached to the sides of the main buoyancy chamber. To facilitate shipment the side body tanks can be removed, reducing the width to 3·75m (12ft 4in).

The outer shell of the main buoyancy chamber, the machinery deck space, the forward deck and the passage decks around the cabin exterior are all constructed in honeycomb panels with aluminium cores.

The lift fan air intake, radar cover, part of the air conditioning duct, and inside window frames are grp.

SKIRT: The flexible skirt was designed by Mitsui following research conducted with aid of the RH-4 (MV-PP1 prototype). It is made of 0·8mm (1/32 in) thick chloroprene-coated nylon sheet. A fringe of finger type nozzles is attached to the skirt base at the bow and on both sides. At the stern a D-section bag skirt is used to avoid scooping up water.

Two transverse and one longitudinal stability bags are fitted.

ACCOMMODATION: The passenger cabin is sited above the forward end of the main buoyancy chamber. Seats for the two crew members are on a raised platform at the front of the cabin. All controls, navigation and radio equipment are

Craft built	Seats	Launched	Operator
Hakuchyo No 3	75*	June 1970	Oita Hoverferry Co Ltd
Hobby No 1	75*	May 1971	Oita Hoverferry Co Ltd
Hobby No 3	75*	September 1971	Oita Hoverferry Co Ltd
Hobby No 6	75*	October 1974	Oita Hoverferry Co Ltd
Angel No 2	51	June 1972	Oita Hoverferry Co Ltd
Angel No 5	75*	April 1975	Oita Hoverferry Co Ltd
Akatombo 52	51	—	Oita Hoverferry Co Ltd
Kamone (Sea Gull)	52	November 1971	

plus 11 others
*Converted to Mk II configuration.

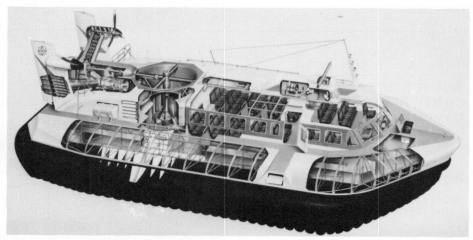

MV-PP5 showing integrated lift/propulsion system

MV-PP5 02 *Hakuchyo No 3*

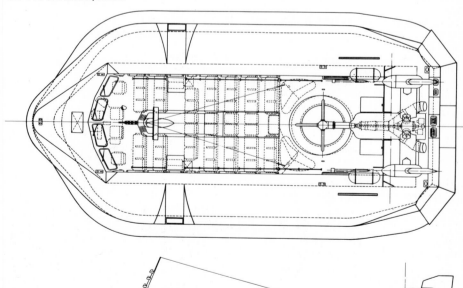

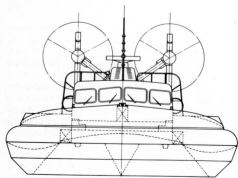

MV-PP5

concentrated around the seats. The windows ahead are of reinforced tempered glass and have electric wipers.

The two cabin entrance doors are divided horizontally, the lower part opening sideways, the top part upwards. The standard seating arrangement is for 42 passengers but ten additional seats can be placed in the centre aisle.

In accordance with Japanese Ministry of Transport regulations a full range of safety equipment is carried, including two inflatable life rafts, 54 life jackets, one automatic manually activated fire extinguisher for the engine casing and two portable fire extinguishers in the cabin. Other standard equipment includes ship's navigation lights, marine horn, searchlight and mooring equipment, including an anchor. The 12 side windows can be used as emergency exits and are made of acrylic resin.

SYSTEMS, ELECTRICAL: Two 2kW, 28·5V ac/dc generators driven by belts from the main gearbox. One 24V, 100Ah battery for engine starting.

PNEUMATIC SYSTEMS: A 4·7-7kg/cm² (56·8-99·5lb/in²) pneumatic system for thrust port operation.

COMMUNICATIONS AND NAVIGATION: Equipment includes a radio and radar.

DIMENSIONS
EXTERNAL
Length overall: 16m (52ft 6in)
Beam overall: 8·6m (28ft 2in)
Height overall on landing pad: 4·81m (15ft 9in)
Skirt depth: 1·2m (3ft 11in)
Draught afloat: 0·2m (8in)
Cushion area: 88m² (741ft²)
INTERNAL
Cabin
Length: 7·1m (23ft 4in)
Max width: 3·8m (12ft 6in)
Max height: 1·9m (6ft 3in)
Floor area: 26m² (280ft²)
Doors: Two 0·65 × 1·4m (2ft 1½in × 4ft 6in), one each side of cabin
Baggage-hold volume: 0·6m³ (21·2ft³)
WEIGHTS
Normal max: 16·3 tons
Normal payload: 4·3 tons
PERFORMANCE
Max speed, calm water: 102km/h (55 knots)
Cruising speed, calm water: 83km/h (45 knots)
Still air range and endurance at cruising speed: About 160n miles, 4 hours approx
Vertical obstacle clearance: 0·6m (2ft) approx

MV-PP5 Mk II

This is a stretched version of the MV-PP5 fast passenger ferry. Lift and propulsion systems and power arrangements are identical to those of the standard MV-PP5, but the hull has been lengthened by 2·18m (7ft 2in) raising the maximum passenger seating capacity from 52 to 76. Maximum speed in calm water is 52 knots. Endurance and cruising speeds are unaffected by the size increase.

MV-PP15 showing raised control cabin, pylon-mounted propellers, lift fan air intakes and thrust ports beneath passenger doors, port and starboard

Five PP5s have been converted to Mk II configuration and the original Mk II is in service with Japanese National Railways.
DIMENSIONS
Length overall: 18·18m (59ft 7in)
Beam overall: 8·6m (28ft 2in)
Height overall on landing pad to top of mast: 4·81m (15ft 9in)
Skirt depth: 1·2m (3ft 11in)
Draught afloat: 0·2m (8in)
Cushion area: 104m² (1120ft²)
WEIGHTS
Normal max: 19·3 tons
Normal payload: 7·2 tons
PERFORMANCE
Max speed, calm water: Approx 52 knots
Cruising speed, calm water: Approx 45 knots
Endurance at cruising speed: Approx 4 hours
Passenger capacity, max: 76

MV-PP15
(Four built)

Developed from the earlier PP5, the Mitsui MV-PP15 is designed for high-speed passenger-ferry services on coastal and inland waterways. Accommodation is provided for 155 passengers and a crew of five.

LIFT AND PROPULSION: Two Avco Lycoming TF25 gas turbines, each with a maximum continuous output of 2200hp at 15°C, drive the integrated lift/propulsion system. Each turbine drives a 2·3m (7ft 6in) diameter, 13-bladed centrifugal fan and a 3·2m (10ft 6in) diameter, four-bladed variable-pitch propeller. Power is transmitted via a main gearbox, propeller gearbox, fan gearbox and an auxiliary gearbox, all connected by shafting and flexible couplings. Auxiliary systems, such as hydraulic pumps for propeller pitch and lubricating oil pumps, are driven directly by auxiliary gears. Fuel is carried in two flexible tanks immediately ahead of the lift fan assemblies. Total volume of the fuel tanks is 0·6m³ (21·2ft³).

CONTROLS: Twin aerodynamic rudders in the propeller slipstream and differential propeller pitch provide directional control. The rudders are operated hydraulically by a wheel from the commander's position.

A thrust port air bleed system provides lateral control at slow speeds. Four ports are located beneath the passenger doors, port and starboard. A water ballast system is provided for longitudinal and transverse centre of gravity adjustment.

HULL: Construction is primarily in corrosion resistant aluminium alloy. The basic structure is the main buoyancy chamber which is divided into watertight sub-divisions for safety, and includes the fore and aft ballast tanks. Overall dimensions of the main buoyancy raft structure are 19·8m (64ft 10½in) long by 7·1m (23ft 3½in) wide by 0·7m (2ft 4in) high. Side bodies of riveted construction are attached to the sides of the main buoyancy structure. The outer shell of the main

Craft built	Seats	Launched	Operator
Tobiuo (Flying Fish)	66	March 1980	Japanese National Railways

MV-PP5 Mk II operated by Japanese National Railways

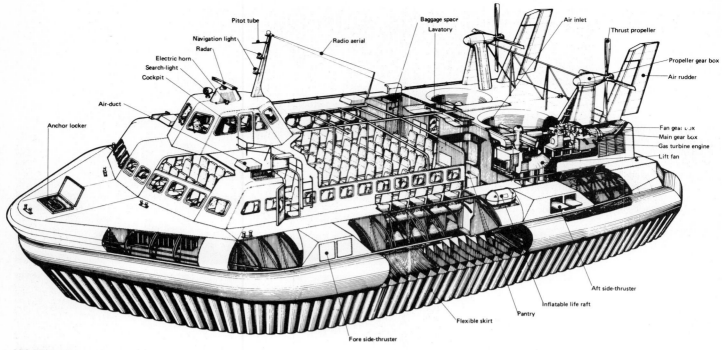

MV-PP15 cutaway

buoyancy chamber, machinery deck space, the forward deck and passageways around the cabin interior, are all constructed in honeycomb panels with aluminium cores. The lift fan air intake, inner window frames and hood for the electric motor that rotates the radar scanner are in glass fibre reinforced plastics.

Six rubber-soled landing pads are fitted to the hull base, together with jacking pads. Four lifting eyes for hoisting the craft are provided in the buoyancy chamber.

SKIRT: Tapered skirt of Mitsui design, fabricated in nylon-based sheet and coated both sides with synthetic rubber. Two transverse and one longitudinal stability bags are included in the skirt system to minimise pitch and roll.

ACCOMMODATION: The passenger cabin, containing 155 seats, is located above the forward part of the main buoyancy chamber. The seats are arranged in three groups and divided by two longitudinal aisles. Seats in the two outer sections are arranged in rows of three abreast, and in the centre section, six abreast.

The four cabin entrance doors, two port, two starboard, are divided horizontally, the top section opening upwards and the lower section opening sideways. A lavatory, toilet unit, pantry and luggage room are provided aft, and a second luggage room is located forward. Lockers are sited close to the forward entrance doors. The control cabin is located above the passenger cabin superstructure and provides a 360-degree view. It is reached from the passenger saloon by a companionway. An emergency exit is provided on the starboard side.

The cabin has a total of four seats, one each for the commander and navigator, plus two spare ones of the flip-up type. The wheel for the air rudders, the two propeller pitch-control levers, instrument panel and switches are arranged on a console ahead of the commander; and the radio, fuel tank gauge, water ballast gauge and fire warning system are arranged ahead of the navigator.

On the cabin roof are the radar-scanner, mast for navigation lights, a siren and a searchlight.

SYSTEMS, ELECTRICAL: 28·5V dc. Two 9kW generators are driven directly by the main engines. One 24V 175Ah battery is employed for starting, and another for control. Both are located in the engine room and are charged by the generators when the main engines are operating. A shore-based power source is used for battery charging when the main engines are not in use.

RADIO/NAVIGATION: Equipment includes one 25·4cm (10in) radar, compass, radio and one 22cm (9in), 250W searchlight.

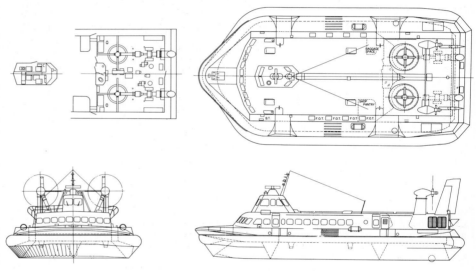

MV-PP15

AIR-CONDITIONING: Two air coolers, each with a capacity of 20 000 Kcal/h. Compressors are driven by belts from the auxiliary gearboxes and cooled air is supplied via air-conditioning ducts. Four ceiling ventilators are provided, each equipped with a 40W fan.

SAFETY: Remotely-controlled BCF or BTM fire extinguishers provided in the engine room. Portable extinguishers provided in the passenger cabin. Inflatable life boats, life jackets, automatic SOS signal transmitter and other equipment carried according to Japanese Ministry of Transport regulations.

DIMENSIONS

EXTERNAL

Length overall, on cushion: 26·4m (86ft 8in)
 on landing pads: 25·09m (82ft 4in)
Beam overall, on cushion: 13·9m (45ft 7in)
 on landing pads: 11·1m (36ft 5in)
Height, on cushion: 8·6m (28ft 3in)
 on landing pads to tip of propeller blade: 6·9m (22ft 8in)
Skirt depth, at bow: 2m (6ft 7in)
 at stern: 1·6m (5ft 3in)

INTERNAL

Passenger cabin including toilet, pantry and locker rooms
Length: 14·14m (46ft 5in)
Max breadth: 7·06m (23ft 2in)
Max height: 2·1m (6ft 11in)
Floor area: 93m² (1001ft²)

WEIGHT

Max: About 56 tons

PERFORMANCE

Max speed: About 60 knots
Cruising speed: About 50 knots
Fuel consumption: About 280g/shp/h at 15°C
Endurance: About 4 hours

MV-PP05A

(Two built)

The first MV-PP05A amphibious utility craft were delivered to the Japanese National Institute of Polar Research expedition in Antarctica early in 1981. The expansion of expeditions in Antarctica has led to a greater need for a safe and rapid means of surface transport, for personnel and supplies, over floating ice and crevassed areas. One consideration was that ACVs would be less expensive to operate than helicopters and also less affected by adverse weather conditions. A unique feature of the MV-PP05A is the provision of an auxiliary propulsion system thought to be used for climbing slopes and attaining high speeds.

The two prototypes are considered as research craft only, but they are expected to lead to the design of a larger machine which will combine the duties of cargo and personnel carrier.

LIFT AND PROPULSION: Integrated system powered by a single 1990cc Nissan GA 135 petrol engine rated at 90kW at 5000rpm. Power is transmitted to two transverse shafts at the

MV-PP05A polar terrain test craft

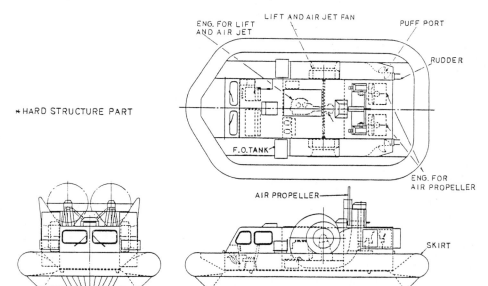

＊HARD STRUCTURE PART

MV-PP05A General Arrangement

opposite ends of which are two 13-blade centrifugal lift fans. Air is fed downwards into the cushion and backwards through airjet ducts for propulsion. Auxiliary propulsion is supplied by two pylon-mounted, fixed-pitch free-air propellers at the rear of the fan volutes. These are powered by two 1584cc Volkswagen VW 126A automotive engines, each rated at 33kW at 3600rpm.

CONTROLS: Craft heading is controlled by interconnected rudder vanes set in the airjet ducts aft. The airflow is deflected forwards for braking and reversing by reversible vanes.

SKIRT: Peripheral loop segment type, 0·6m (2ft) deep. Cushion pressure is about 130kg/m² (26·6lb/ft²).

DIMENSIONS

Length overall, hard structure: 7·1m (23ft 3½in)
    overall, skirt inflated: 8·1m (26ft 7in)

Beam: 4·8m (15ft 9in)
Beam overall, hard structure: 3·8m (12ft 5½in)
Height, on cushion: 3·5m (11ft 6in)

WEIGHTS

Max, with payload: 2·8 tonnes
Payload: 0·6 tonne

PERFORMANCE

Max speed, across ice: 55km/h (34mph)

JET HOVER

A new form of hovercraft has been developed by the Mitsui company, trials with the 10-metre prototype *Eaglet* having started in early 1986. The craft employs waterjet propulsion and is not therefore amphibious. The inlets for the two waterjet units are positioned on the underside of two skegs which extend on either side of the craft for a length of approximately one-third of overall craft length. Over this length the immersed areas of the skegs seal the air cushion; for the remainder of the cushion periphery a conventional loop and segment type skirt is employed. Unlike the sidewall hovercraft or surface-effect ships the craft is almost totally supported by its air cushion at cruising speed. The concept thus has the potential advantage of the fully skirted amphibious hovercraft for the attainment of high cruising speed with minimum hydrodynamic resistance (and, at speed, minimum wave generation), but in addition it also secures full directional control and the very minimum of noise and vibration, by the use of skeg-mounted Hamilton 771 waterjet propulsion units.

The craft is provided with a Mitsui motion control system exerting control over cushion air pressure variation and is fitted with fin stabilisers. The skirt/skeg combination is also found to give good ride comfort over waves through its soft response.

The Mitsui Jet Hover concept is aimed principally towards applications in shallow rivers, lakes and other smooth waters and for ultra-fast ferries for operation on coastal and inland sea routes.

EAGLET

ENGINES

Propulsion: Two 98hp (at 5000rpm) Nissan HA 120 marine petrol engines
Lift: Two Robin 22hp petrol engines

WATERJET UNITS: Two Hamilton 771 units.

AIR-CUSHION FANS: Two centrifugal.

HULL: Glass-reinforced plastic.

DIMENSIONS

Length overall: 10·90m
Breadth overall: 5·10m
Depth: 0·89m

PERFORMANCE

Speed, max: Approx 27 knots

Mitsui's Jet Hover experimental craft *Eaglet* fitted with Hamilton Jet waterjet units

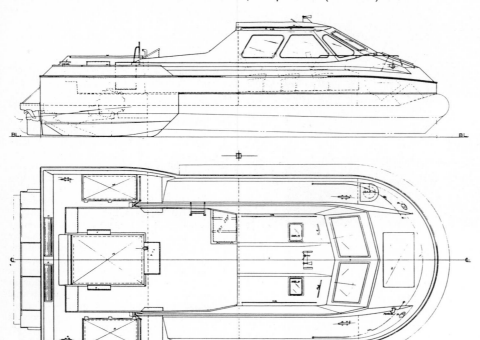

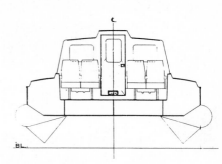

General Arrangement of Mitsui Jet Hover

KOREA, SOUTH

KOREA TACOMA MARINE INDUSTRIES LIMITED

Main office and shipyard: PO Box 339, 974-15 Yang duk-dong, Masan 610, South Korea

Telephone: (0551) 55-1181/8
Telex: 53662 KOTAMAI K
Telefax: (0551) 94-9449

Chong-Su Lee, *President*
Sung-Jin Lee, *Executive Managing Director*
Chae-Woo Lee, *Director*

Seoul office: CPO Box 4296, Seoul, South Korea

Telephone: (02) 777-0901/5
Telex: 53662 KOTAMAI K
Telefax: (02) 757 0884

Ever since its founding in 1971, Korea Tacoma Marine Industries Ltd (KTMI) has built a variety of fast patrol boats and high-speed passenger boats, and has concentrated its efforts on the development of high-speed SES and amphibious hovercraft for civil and paramilitary applications.

In 1977 KTMI began an ACV development programme, and the company designed and constructed a test surface effect ship in 1978.

KTMI named its first surface effect ship Turt II. This had a length of 8·2m, weight of 3·7 tons and capacity for 7 passengers. To date KTMI has developed and constructed five 18m SESs (90-passenger), one 11m SES (56-passenger), two 26m SESs (158-passenger), one 28m SES (200-passenger, modified 26m SES), a manned test amphibious hovercraft and a 12m diesel-powered prototype hovercraft.

TURT III

This fully-amphibious five-seater has an overall length of 7·65 metres and a maximum speed of 50 knots.
LIFT AND PROPULSION: Motive power for the lift system is a single 140hp engine. Thrust is supplied by a single 175hp engine driving a 1·35m diameter free-air propeller.
CONTROLS: Craft direction is controlled by twin aerodynamic rudders operating in the propeller slipstream.
HULL: Welded marine-grade aluminium.
SKIRT: Bag and segment type.

KTMI test hovercraft Turt III

ACCOMMODATION: Enclosed cabin with seats for driver and four passengers.
DIMENSIONS
Length overall: 7·65m
Beam: 4m
Height to tip of thrust propeller: 1·3m
  to top of cabin: 2·87m
WEIGHT
Loaded: 2·27 tonnes
PERFORMANCE
Max speed: 50 knots

8-METRE SES

This was the first of a projected series of multi-purpose surface effect craft.
LIFT AND PROPULSION: Motive power for

the lift system is provided by a single 80hp automotive engine. Thrust is supplied by two water propellers powered by twin outboards or diesel outdrive units of 80, 100 or 150hp.
CONTROLS: Craft direction is controlled by twin water rudders aft or rotation of the engine/propeller units.
HULL: Primary structure in welded marine aluminium alloy.
SKIRT: Segmented skirt at the bow and stern.
ACCOMMODATION: Choice of seating arrangements for five, ten or fifteen passengers.
DIMENSIONS
Length overall: 8·2m (26ft 11in)
Beam overall: 4·4m (14ft 5in)

KTMI 8m SES

Draught, hullborne: 0·6m (2ft)
  on cushion: 0·1m (4in)
WEIGHT
Normal max (according to power arrangements
  and passenger load): 3·5-4·5 tons
PERFORMANCE
Max speed, twin 80hp engines: 30 knots
  twin 100hp engines: 40 knots
  twin 150hp engines: 45 knots
Range: 120n miles

12-METRE SES

KTMI's 12m craft *Que-Ryoung* is a high-speed
waterbus delivered and launched on the Soyang
man-made lake near Seoul in 1982. The craft
is designed to run bow-on to flat sloping beaches and
river banks for the embarkation and off-loading of
passengers and freight.
LIFT AND PROPULSION: Power for the lift
fan is supplied by a single 72hp Volvo Penta MD
40A marine diesel. Propulsion engines are two
155hp Volvo Penta AQAD 40/280Bs, each incorporating stern-drive units.
CONTROLS: Both propeller units at the stern
rotate for steering. Additional control is provided
by the differential use of the water propellers.
HULL: The hull is built in welded marine alumin-
ium alloy and the deckhouse is constructed in
riveted marine aluminium alloy.
SKIRT: Flexible segmented skirt at the bow and
stern.
ACCOMMODATION: Air-conditioned accom-
modation for 4 crew members and 56 passengers.
DIMENSIONS
Length overall: 12·0m
Width: 4·6m
Height: 2·72m
WEIGHTS
Displacement, max: 11·5 tons
Payload: 5·5 tons
PERFORMANCE
Speed, max: 26·9 knots

Craft built	Seats	Owner	Route
Que-Ryoung	56	Dong-Bu Co Ltd	Soyang River – (Yang gu) to In Jae

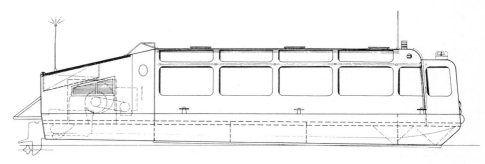

KTMI 12m SES waterbus *Que-Ryoung*

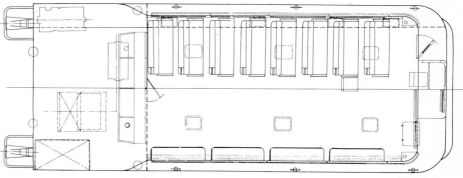

KTMI 12m SES

18-METRE SES

The 18m (59ft) design has buoyant catamaran-
type sidewalls almost identical in shape to those of
the smaller craft.
LIFT AND PROPULSION: Power for the lift
system is provided by a single marine diesel in the
400 to 500hp range. Power for the propulsion
system is provided by twin diesels of 650, 800 or
1300hp, each driving a water propeller via a
reversing gearbox and an inclined shaft.
CONTROLS: Twin water rudders aft, one on
each sidehull. Differential propeller thrust for
slow-speed manoeuvring.
HULL: Main structure built in welded marine
aluminium alloy.
SKIRT: Segmented skirt at the bow and stern.
ACCOMMODATION: Seating arrangements
for 60, 80 and 90 passengers according to route
requirements.
DIMENSIONS
Length overall: 18·1m (59ft 5in)
Beam overall: 9m (29ft 7in)
Draught, hullborne: 1·74m (5ft 8½in)
  on cushion: 1·08m (3ft 6½in)
WEIGHT
Normal max weight: 36 tons
PERFORMANCE
Max speed, twin 650hp diesels: 35 knots
  twin 800hp diesels: 40 knots
  twin 1300hp diesels: 50 knots

Craft built	Owner	Route
Air Ferry	Sae-Chang Haewoon	Pusan to Gejae Island
Cosmos	Ge-Jae Haewoon	Pusan to Gejae Island
Phinex	Ge-Jae Gaebal	Pusan to Gejae Island
Golden Star	Wha-Sung Haewoon	Pusan to Gejae Island
Tacoma II	KTMI	Masan to Gejae Island

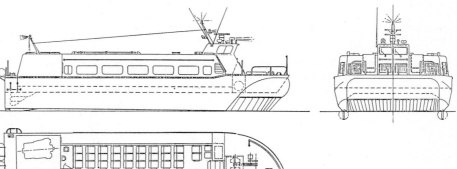

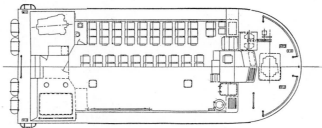

KTMI 18m SES

26-METRE SES

LIFT AND PROPULSION: The lift system is powered by a single General Motors Detroit Diesel Allison 12V-71TI rated at 510hp at 2100rpm. This engine directly drives a dual 1·075m diameter lift fan, to provide cushion air to the plenum chamber and, via toothed belts and hydraulic system, two secondary 0·61m diameter fans for stern skirt inflation. Propulsive power is supplied by two MTU 8V 396 TB 83 diesels, each rated at 1010hp at 1940rpm, each driving a water propeller via a reversing gearbox and an inclined shaft.

One GM 2-71 diesel generator, rated at 30kW 60Hz, 220V, is provided.

CONTROLS: Craft heading is controlled by twin balanced stainless steel rudders operated hydraulically by a steering wheel. Additional control is provided by differential use of the water propellers.

HULL: Main structure is built in welded marine aluminium alloy and the superstructure is constructed in riveted marine aluminium alloy.

SKIRT: The bow skirt consists of single bag and multi segments which are attached to the bag and connected to the underside of the hull by straps. The stern skirt is a multi-bag type consisting of three bag sections and is inflated to a pressure slightly above that of the cushion by two 0·61m fans on the deckhouse of the engine rooms.

ACCOMMODATION: Air-conditioning, audio system and airliner-type seating is provided for 10 crew members and 158 passengers. The bridge accommodates the commander, navigator and engineer.

DIMENSIONS
Length overall: 25·7m
Breadth: 10·2m
Depth: 2·7m
Draught, floating: 2·45m
    on cushion: 1·45m

WEIGHT
Displacement, max: 65 tons
Payload: 16·5 tons

PERFORMANCE
Speed, max: 35 knots
Range, full load: 250n miles

TURT IV

Builder of the first amphibious hovercraft in Korea, the Turt III type, a manned test craft launched in February 1981, KTMI followed it in December 1984 by the development of an amphibious utility hovercraft Turt IV type, the first diesel-powered amphibious hovercraft in Asia.

LIFT AND PROPULSION: The lift system comprises two single 1·075m fans driven by a Deutz air-cooled diesel engine rated at 320hp at 2300rpm. Thrust is supplied by a 422hp Deutz air-cooled diesel engine at 2300rpm driving a 2·75m ducted propeller.

CONTROLS: One rudder and one elevator positioned in the ducted propeller slipstream provide directional control and trim control respectively. Additional control in low speed is provided by two puff ports which are designed specially for turning and reversing and are supplied by cushion air.

HULL: The main hull is built in welded aluminium alloy 5086-H116 (plate) and 6061-T6 (extrusion), and the deck house is riveted.

SKIRT: The skirt is an open loop and segment type and anti-bouncing ties are built into the loop.

Outstanding ride quality and stability have been demonstrated during sea trials and the craft was safely operated in seas up to 2m maximum wave height.

DIMENSIONS
Length overall: 12·65m
Beam overall: 7·04m
Height, on cushion: 4·70m
    off cushion: 4·20m
Cushion height: 0·80m

WEIGHTS
Light weight: 8·10 tons
Payload: 1·50 tons

KTMI 18m SES

Craft built	Seats	Owner	Route
Young-Kwang I	158	Young Kwang Gaebal	Pusan to Gejae Island
*Young-Kwang II**	200	Young Kwang Gaebal	Pusan to Gejae Island
Tacoma III	158	Shin Young Shipbuilding and Engineering Co	Yeosu to Gemun Island

*Modified to 28m

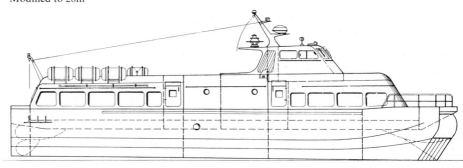

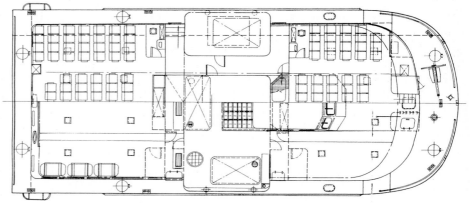

KTMI 26m SES

KTMI 26m SES

KTMI Turt IV type hovercraft *Eagle II*

PERFORMANCE
Speed, max: 55 knots
Speed, cruising: 40 knots
Range: 200n miles

TURT IV Mk 1

As a sea ambulance version, Turt IV Mk 1 is intended for quick transportation of patients from islands to land. The distinctive features of the craft compared with Turt IV are the twin propulsion units for increased manoeuvrability and the reduced lift power due to the developed skirt. Turt IV Mk 1 was under construction in 1987 and was delivered in April 1988.

LIFT AND PROPULSION: The lift system consists of two single 1·07m diameter fans driven by a Deutz air-cooled diesel engine rated at 272hp at 2300rpm. Thrust is supplied by two 272hp Deutz air-cooled diesel engines at 2300rpm driving two 2·0m diameter ducted propellers.

CONTROLS: Two rudders and two elevators positioned in each of the ducted propeller slip-streams provide directional control and trim control respectively. Additional control is provided by the differential thrust of the propellers. Directional control in low speed is provided by two puff ports which are designed specially for reversing and turning and are supplied by cushion air.

HULL: The main hull is built in welded aluminium alloy 5086-H116 (plate) and 6061-T6 (extrusion), and the deck house is riveted.

SKIRT: The skirt is an open loop and segment type and anti-bouncing ties are built into the loop.

DIMENSIONS
Length overall: 13·35m
Beam overall: 7·44m
Height, on cushion: 3·90m
    off cushion: 3·40m
Cushion height: 0·8m
WEIGHTS
Light weight: 11·3 tons
Payload: 1·5 tons
PERFORMANCE
Speed, max: 50 knots
Speed, cruising: 40 knots
Range: 150n miles
Weather restrictions: Operation in seas up to 2·0m
    max wave height

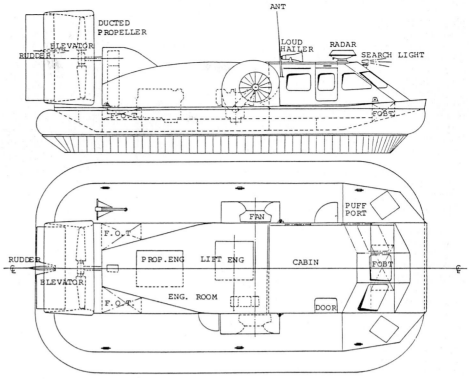

Layout of Turt IV

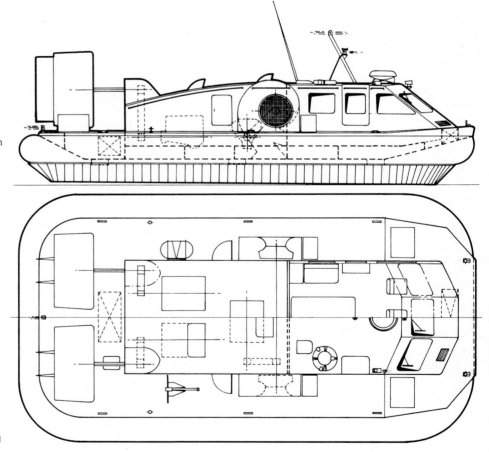

Layout of Turt IV Mk 1

THE NETHERLANDS

HOLLAND HOVERCRAFT vof

Industrieweg 2, 2921 LB Krimpen a/d Ijssel, The Netherlands
PO Box 733, 2920 CA Krimpen a/d Ijssel, The Netherlands

Telephone: (01807) 15975
Telex: 21571 HOCON NL
Telefax: (01807) 19956

Tom H van der Linden, *Technical Director*
William M Van Poelgeest, *Project Manager*

Holland Hovercraft is involved with the design, construction, leasing and sale of small hovercraft for 18 to 40 passengers. The company is also developing a hoverdock system for the transport of a 200- to 300-tonne cutter dredger over land. Following the 12-seat Kolibrie described below, an 18-seat craft was designed and built during 1987.

KOLIBRIE 1500

This prototype was built in 29 working days and completed in June 1986, the object being to test and perfect the techniques used. The craft is currently in use to instruct company staff and for demonstration to potential customers.

ENGINE: One Deutz BF6L 913C.

ACCOMMODATION: 12 passsenger seats, 2 crew.

EQUIPMENT: Radar, VHF radio, AP Navigator.

DIMENSIONS
Length overall: 8·25m
Beam: 3·90m
Height: 1·75m
Cabin length: 4·00m
Cabin width: 1·90m
PERFORMANCE
Speed, calm water, zero wind: 40 knots
Obstacle clearance height: 0·50m
Weather limitations: Force 5 Beaufort

18-PASSENGER HOVERCRAFT
Constructed 1987. Various cockpit options include hard-top, soft-top and open-top. Large items of cargo may be carried on the side decks.
ENGINE: One Deutz BF6L 913C, 190bhp at 2500rpm.
ACCOMMODATION: 16 passenger seats, 2 crew.
DIMENSIONS (off cushion)
Length overall: 10·60m
Beam: 4.60m
Beam, side bodies folded: 2·40m
Height: 1·80m
Cabin length: 5·50m
Cabin width: 2·00m

Holland Hovercraft Kolibrie 1500 12-seat craft

Cabin height: 1·50m
WEIGHTS
Weight, empty: 3000kg
Disposable load: 1500kg
PERFORMANCE
Speed, calm water, zero wind, max: 40 knots

Obstacle clearance: 0·5m
Fuel consumption: 35 litres/h, at max speed, 25 litres/h at cruise speed
Range, max: 200n miles
Weather limitations: Force 5 Beaufort wave height: 1·0m

LE COMTE-HOLLAND BV

Stuartweg 4, 4131 NJ Vianen, The Netherlands
Postbus 24, 4130 EA Vianen, The Netherlands

Telephone: (03473) 7 19 04
Telex: 40475 LECOM NL

A le Comte, *General Manager*

Le Comte-Holland BV Shipyard has developed a sidewall hovercraft design with a new seal system (patents were granted in 1982) based on an array of floating, hydrodynamically-shaped planing elements hinged on the wet deck of the craft. Each element operates independently and has restricted vertical movement. Tank tests at Wageningen have successfully demonstrated the hydrodynamic drag and sealing characteristics of this system, even in higher sea states.

The initial cost of the system is higher than that of a flexible skirt, but its long life expectancy will reduce maintenance costs. Front skirt element changes can be made without docking.

The segments are made from polyaramide reinforced polyester, which combines high impact

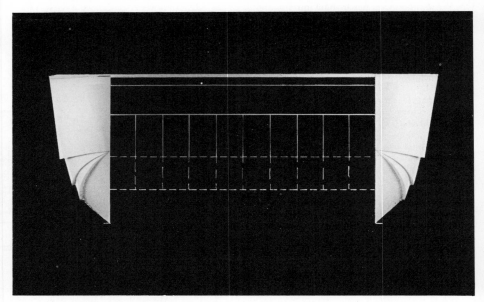

Le Comte bow form and segment arrangement

Various applications of Le Comte SES designs

strength with low weight. Low friction poly-ethylene plates the segments' sides, and assists vertical movement.

It is said that the immersion depth of the vessel does not affect the system, which rotates around the hinges until the lift forces are balanced by the internal restraining forces. The system is claimed to give a more accurate following of irregular incoming wave patterns and to be resistant to damage by floating objects. If the front seal elements are damaged, replacement can be under-taken without dry-docking the craft. A ride con-trol system is also being developed.

The project, which is backed by the Netherlands government, has undergone extensive model tests. Designs have been prepared for passenger ferries and patrol craft of 26·9, 32·1, 34·6 and 37·1 metres length. Construction of the first 26·9m SES started in late 1986.

26·9-METRE SES (DESIGN)

LIFT AND PROPULSION: For propulsion two MTU 12V 396 TB83 high-speed diesels are ins-talled giving a continuous power of 1150kW (1542bhp) each. Two 0·71m diameter fixed-pitch propellers are fitted. For lift two Mercedes-Benz OM 423 diesels are installed giving 261kW (350bhp) each. These engines power a hydraulic transmission system driving two cushion lift fans, one for supplying the stern cushion seal.

CONTROLS: NACA profile rudders control craft direction at high speed. Differential propeller thrust controls heading at low speed. An auto-matic roll stabilisation system is fitted.

HULL: Built in grp. Deck/wheelhouse is built in grp sandwich, including the bulkheads, for weight reduction and insulation against temperature differences. The deck is constructed of extruded aluminium alloy planking.

Patrol boat version of 26·9m Le Comte-Holland SES

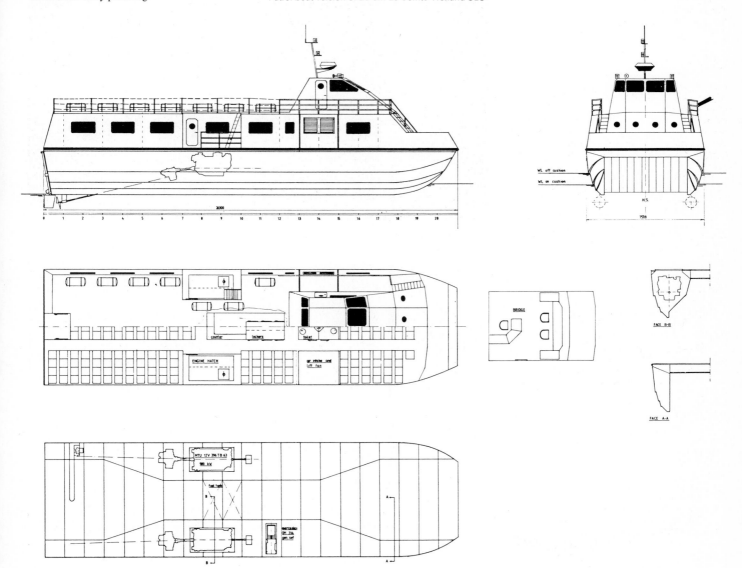

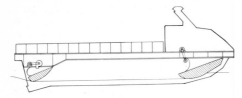

Le Comte-Holland SES air cushion seal system

SYSTEMS, ELECTRICAL: Auxiliary generating units and electrical systems available for 24V dc, 110V ac and/or 220V ac. One Mercedes-Benz OM 314, rated at 42hp at 1500rpm (50 cycles) or 51hp at 1800rpm (60 cycles).
ACCOMMODATION: Up to 200 passengers.
DIMENSIONS
Length: Approx 26·9m
Beam: Approx 7·8m
Depth: Approx 3·1m
Cushion height: Approx 2·5m
Draught, on cushion: Approx 1·5m
Draught, off cushion: Approx 2·2m
Deck area for patrol boat version: Approx 75m²
WEIGHTS/CAPACITIES
Max: 72 tonnes
Light ship: 54 tonnes
Fuel tank, patrol boat version: 6000 litres
Fuel tank, passenger boat version: 2000 litres

Le Comte hull mould which may be expanded in length, height and width dimensions to permit variations in moulding dimensions

PERFORMANCE
Speed, cruise, on cushion, Sea State 0: 40 knots, Sea State 3: 36 knots

Speed, cruise, off cushion, Sea State 0: 16 knots, Sea State 3: 13 knots

ROYAL SCHELDE
BV KONINKLIJKE MAATSCHAPPIJ DE SCHELDE
PO Box 16, 165 Glacisstraat, 4380 AA Vlissingen, Netherlands

Telephone: (1184) 83911
Telex: 37815 KMS NL
Telefax: (1184) 82686

A B A de Smit, *Chairman of the Managing Board*
C Hartog, *Vice Chairman of the Managing Board*
T C Bouwman, *Technical Director*

In the autumn of 1986 Royal Schelde announced that it was developing civil and military designs of a surface effect ship project in co-operation with Wijsmuller Engineering BV. The co-operation will cover design, training and operational stages of this development.
Extensive testing of hull and skirt designs has been carried out employing a manned test craft of 8 metres length. This craft has also been used to investigate ship motions. The hulls and superstructure construction may be in either aluminium or glass-reinforced plastic. The main deck is of modular aluminium construction, built in two sandwich layers, providing lightweight and ample reserve buoyancy. Each side hull is divided into the following watertight compartments: aft peak, general service room, main engine room/fuel tanks, auxiliary service room/fuel tanks, stores and fore peak.
Different versions of the SES are proposed, a civil 324-passenger craft, Seaswift 32, a multi-purpose military version, Seashark 32, a coast-guard version, Seaguard 32 and an offshore crew transport craft. Other applications in development are based on the same platform: luxury motor yachts, hydrographic research vessels, pilot vessels, etc.

SEASWIFT 32 (DESIGN)
This design is aimed at the ferry and cruise market.
ENGINES, PROPULSION AND LIFT SYSTEMS: Two high-speed diesel engines, delivering 2040kW (2736bhp) each, powering two waterjet units for propulsion and four centrifugal fans for lift. Each lift fan is powered separately. Cushion pressure max 5000N/m² (104lb/ft²).
ACCOMMODATION: 324 seats in two saloons. The second-class lower saloon for 270 passengers is designed with separate dining areas, a galley, a ship shop, lavatories, lockers and stairs to the upper deck. The first-class upper saloon is designed for 54 passengers and has access to the

Model of Royal Schelde/Wijsmuller Seaswift design   *(Atelier-Plein Negen)*

Model of Royal Schelde/Wijsmuller Seaguard 32 design   *(Atelier-Plein Negen)*

promenade deck being available for boarding and disembarkation.
ELECTRICAL SYSTEMS: Two 30kVA generating sets are installed in the auxiliary service rooms, giving ample spare capacity. In harbour conditions, electricity can be provided as well via a shore connection box.
DIMENSIONS
Length overall: Approx 32·00m
Beam overall: 10·30m
Depth midship: 3·75m
Draught, on cushion: 0·70m
    off cushion: 1·50m
WEIGHT
Displacement (full load): 145 tonnes

PERFORMANCE
Speed, max continuous: 46 knots
Speed, service: 40 knots
Range, at 46 knots: 150n miles
    at 40 knots: 165n miles

SEAGUARD 32 (DESIGN)

This version for paramilitary and government applications is based on the same platform as the Seaswift 32 type and has same main dimensions.
ENGINES, PROPULSION AND LIFT SYSTEMS: Two high-speed diesel engines, delivering 1600kW (2146bhp) each, powering two waterjet units for propulsion and four centrifugal fans for lift. Each lift fan is powered separately. Special

attention has been given to optimise off-cushion characteristics (catamaran mode) in order to obtain good seakeeping behaviour in combination with low fuel consumption, while drifting and manoeuvring. Cushion pressure max 5000N/m² (104lb/ft²). Displacement (full load) 128 tonnes.
ACCOMMODATION: For coastguard applications accommodation is envisaged for 15 crew members. A wardroom, mess, galley with stores complete a high living standard.
PERFORMANCE
Speed, max continuous: 44 knots
Speed, service: 38 knots
Range at 44 knots: 1500n miles
    at 38 knots: 1570n miles

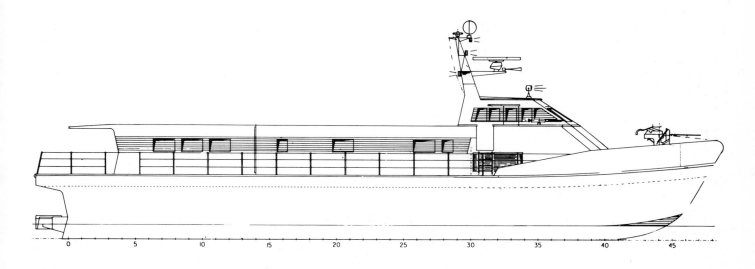

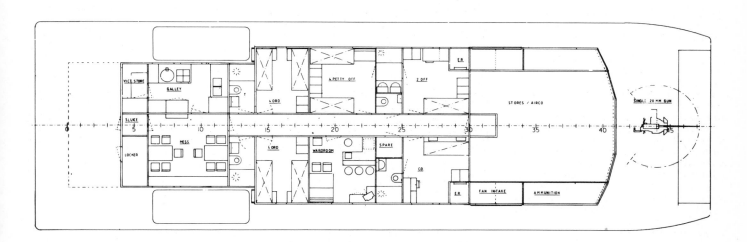

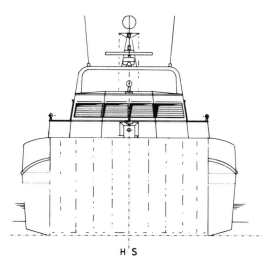

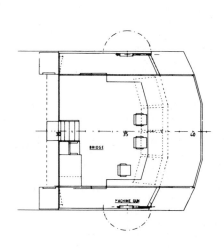

General Arrangement of Royal Schelde Seaguard 32 design

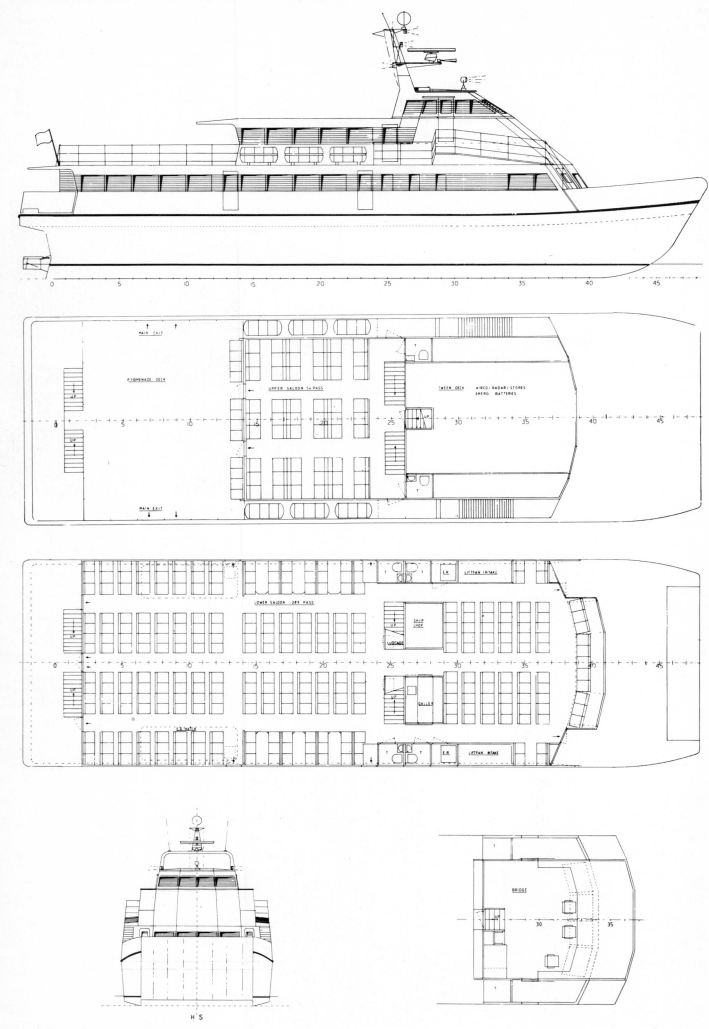

General Arrangement of Royal Schelde Seaswift 32 design

WIJSMULLER ENGINEERING BV

Office: Sluisplein 34, 1975 AG Ijmuiden, The Netherlands
PO Box 510, 1970 AM Ijmuiden, The Netherlands

Telephone: (02550) 62666
Telex: 41110 WIJSM NL
Telefax: (02550) 18695

S O Aarts, *Managing Director*
R J Valk, *Manager, Business Development*

Wijsmuller Engineering is co-operating with Royal Schelde in the development of civil and military versions of a surface effect ship project. Please see the Royal Schelde entry for details.

NEW ZEALAND

HOVERCRAFT MANUFACTURERS (NEW ZEALAND) LIMITED

PO Box 11095, 23 Watts Road, Christchurch, South Island, New Zealand

Telephone: 03 486 821
03 487 021
Telex: C/-4200

Ross McCleod, *Chief Designer*
Robert Walker, *Marketing Manager*

Manufacturing rights for the Airdash, Ranger 5 and Surveyor 12 D hovercraft were sold in January 1986 to a new Australian company, Air Cushion Enterprises Pty Ltd, which is manufacturing these craft in Cairns, Queensland, Australia. Hovercraft Manufacturers (New Zealand) Limited will manufacture components such as skirts for Air Cushion Enterprises, provide sales and service facilities in New Zealand and will continue to manufacture Riverland Surveyor 8 already established in New Zealand.

Demand for a larger craft has led the company to introduce the Surveyor 12 D. A larger payload and diesel power have made this craft a more attractive proposition for commercial applications.

The first of the new craft began service on Otago Harbour, Dunedin as a tourist machine. The second craft was delivered to Queensland, Australia. Most of the orders received to date have been from Australia and the Pacific region.

The Airdash is being re-introduced to the

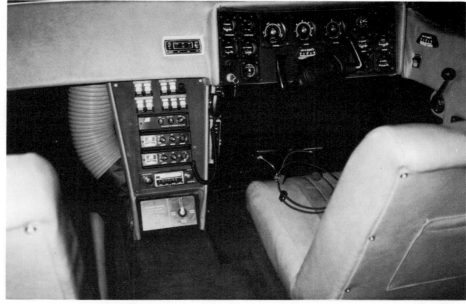
Driving position, Riverland Surveyor 8

market with improvements in aesthetics and performance. See Light/Sports Air Cushion Vehicles section.

RIVERLAND SURVEYOR 8

The size of this craft (length 6·7m) has made it particularly suitable for New Zealand's shingle rivers where manoeuvrability in relatively confined areas is important.

Craft built
		Operator
001	Riverland Surveyor 8 prototype (Chevrolet V8)	Bay of Islands Hovercraft Services
002	Riverland Surveyor 8 (Buick V6)	Hovercraft Adventures, Queenstown, New Zealand
003	Riverland Surveyor 8 (Buick V6)	Wanaka Lake Services Ltd, Wanaka, New Zealand
004	Surveyor 12 D	Harbour Cruises Dunedin Ltd, Dunedin, New Zealand
005	Surveyor 12 D	Queensland, Australia
006	Surveyor 12 D	Lake Taupo, New Zealand
007	Surveyor 12 D	Queensland, Australia

Riverland Surveyor 8

LIFT AND PROPULSION: Integrated system powered by a single 4·1-litre Buick V6 automotive engine. The engine room is pressurised to exclude dust and water when operating over dirty terrain or in salt water. Power is transmitted to the lift fan hydrostatically and to two four-bladed ducted fans by HTD belts and drive shafts. Fuel capacity is 120 litres. Larger tanks are optional.
CONTROLS: Craft heading is controlled by twin aerodynamic rudders attached to the rear of the twin thrust ducts. Elevators behind each thrust fan provide craft pitch and roll control.
HULL: Built in foam sandwich grp.
SKIRT: HDL bag and segment type in neoprene-coated nylon. Segments attached to the bag by quick-release nylon fasteners to facilitate servicing.
ACCOMMODATION: Bucket seats for driver and front passenger and normally two removable bench-type seats for passengers.
DIMENSIONS
EXTERNAL
Length: 6·7m
Beam: 3·44m
Height: 2m
INTERNAL
Cabin
Length: 2·45m
Width: 1·74m
Height: 1·25m
Door width: 0·87-1·09m
Door height: 1·28m
WEIGHTS
Empty: 1030kg
Max normal weight: 1800kg
Max overload weight: 2100kg
PERFORMANCE
Cruising speed: 35-60km/h
Max recommended speed: 80km/h
Max normal wave height: 1m
(Can be operated in surf up to 1·5m high)
Hard structure clearance: 0·5m
Fuel consumption: 18 to 32 litres/h
Noise level: 76dBA, peak reading, craft passing at 8m from instrument while cruising on water

NORWAY

BÅTSERVICE VERFT A/S

PO Box 113, 4501 Mandal, Norway

Telephone: (43) 61011
Telex: 21862 YARD N
Telefax: (43) 64580

Towards the end of 1987 it was announced that Båtservice Verft A/S, Veritas Marine Services, Kongsberg Albatross A/S and Cirrus A/S had been chosen by the Norwegian Ministry of Defence to produce ten mine countermeasure SESs for the Norwegian Navy. The order will comprise six minesweepers and four minehunters at a combined cost of NKr 2 billion. Contracts are to be placed in 1988 for final deliveries by 1996. The hulls will be of glass-reinforced plastic sandwich construction.

Artist's impression of mine countermeasures SES to be ordered by Norwegian Navy   (DnV)

BRØDRENE AA BÅTBYGGERI A/S

N-6780 Hyen, Norway

Telephone: 57 69 800
Telex: 42162 BRAA N

The Brødrene Aa boat building business started in 1947 with high-quality timber boat construction. Now working in grp/pvc core construction, over 95 people are employed in the Hyen yard and a second yard is now in operation, the Eikefjord division. Between 1984 and 1987 turnover was increased from NKr 30 million to NKr 60 million.

Brødrene Aa with Cirrus A/S have designed and developed a series of SES types for high-speed ferry services starting with the 32-metre CIRR 105P *Norcat* delivered in 1984 (now *Fjordkongen*) followed by the sister vessel *Ekwata* for Gabon and now followed by a larger 35-metre vessel, *Ekwata II*. The craft are built in glassfibre-reinforced plastic construction to DnV standards and may be classified as catamarans with the lift system being regarded as an auxiliary system.

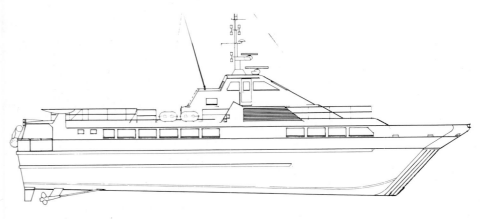

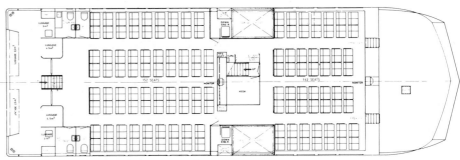

Outboard profile and passenger deck, *Fjordkongen*, showing original propeller installation

Brødrene Aa CIRR 105P *Fjordkongen* (ex *Norcat*)

Craft built or being built (SES)

	Yard No 169 CIRR 105P 32·2m Fjordkongen (ex Norcat)	Yard No 184 CIRR 105P 32·2m Ekwata	35·0m Ekwata II	Yard No 199	Yard No 200	Yard No 201	Yard No 202
LAUNCH/ LAUNCH PLANNED	June 1984	1986	1987	Aug 1988	Aug 1988	Jan 1989	Jan 1989
DIMENSIONS							
Length overall	32·20m	32·20m	35·25m				
Beam	11·00m	11·00m	11·50m				
Depth		3·23m	3·50m				
Draught							
on cushion		0·55m	0·70m				
off cushion		2·05m	2·15m				
GRT	290	290					
ACCOMMODATION							
Passengers	112 fwd saloon 152 aft saloon	112 1st class bow saloon 168 tourist aft saloon 10 VIP aft of wheelhouse	144 1st class bow saloon 136 toursit aft saloon 40 VIP aft of wheelhouse				
Total	264	290	320				
ENGINES							
Propulsion	two Detroit Diesel 16V-149 TIB 1195kW (1600bhp) each	two MWM TBD 604B V12 1728kW (1714bhp) each	two MWM TBD 604B V16 1715kW (2300bhp) each	two 1600kW (2146bhp) each			
Lift	two Detroit Diesel 8V-92 TA 298kW (400bhp)	two MWM TBD 234 V6 227kW (305bhp) each (also powering auxiliaries)	two MWM TBD 604B V6 298kW (400bhp)				
PROPULSION	KMW 56S waterjet units (originally fitted with propellers)	KMW 56S waterjet units	KMW 56S waterjet units	KMW 63S units	KMW 63S units	KMW 63S units	KMW 63S units
PERFORMANCE							
Service speed	36 knots		approx 45 knots				
Max speed	42 knots		approx 50 knots				
Fuel consumption	560 litres/h (15·5 litres/n mile)						
Time to accelerate		(0-40 knots) 45s					
OPERATOR	Troms Fylkes Dampskibsselskap	Gabon Ferry Services	Gabon Ferry Services				

Cirrus-designed CIRR 105P *Fjordkongen* (ex *Norcat*)

WESTAMARIN A/S

PO Box 143, 4501 Mandal, Norway

Telephone: 43 62222
Telex: 21514 WRIN N
Telefax: 43 62302

In 1986 Westamarin announced that it was outfitting under licence two Karlskronavarvet Jet Rider 3400 surface effect ships, grp sandwich construction being used in building of the hulls at Karlskronavarvet. The customer is Det Stavangerske Dampskibsselskab of Stavanger and the craft are to be operated by Sameiet Flaggruten. The vessels are equipped with ride control systems. Further details are given in the Karlskronavarvet entry, Karlskronavarvet being totally responsible for the design.

SES 3400

CLASSIFICATION: DnV + 1A1 R15 E0.
ACCOMMODATION: 244 seats, 6 cabins for crew.
ENGINES: Propulsion, two MTU 16V 396 TB 83, each 1540kW (2065bhp); lift, two Deutz/ MWM TBD 234 V12.
SYSTEMS
Reduction gears: ZF BU 750
Generators: Two Stamford MSC 334 A

Lift fans: Four, approx 100hp each
DIMENSIONS
Length overall: 33·40m
Length waterline: 28·20m
Beam: 10·50m
Depth, moulded: 3·25m
Draught, hullborne: 1·75m
Draught, on cushion: 0·80m
PERFORMANCE
Speed, service (full load): 42 knots

Craft built (SES 3400)

Yard No	Name	Completed	Seats	Operator	Route
427		1988	244	Sameiet Flaggruten	
428		1988	244	Sameiet Flaggruten	

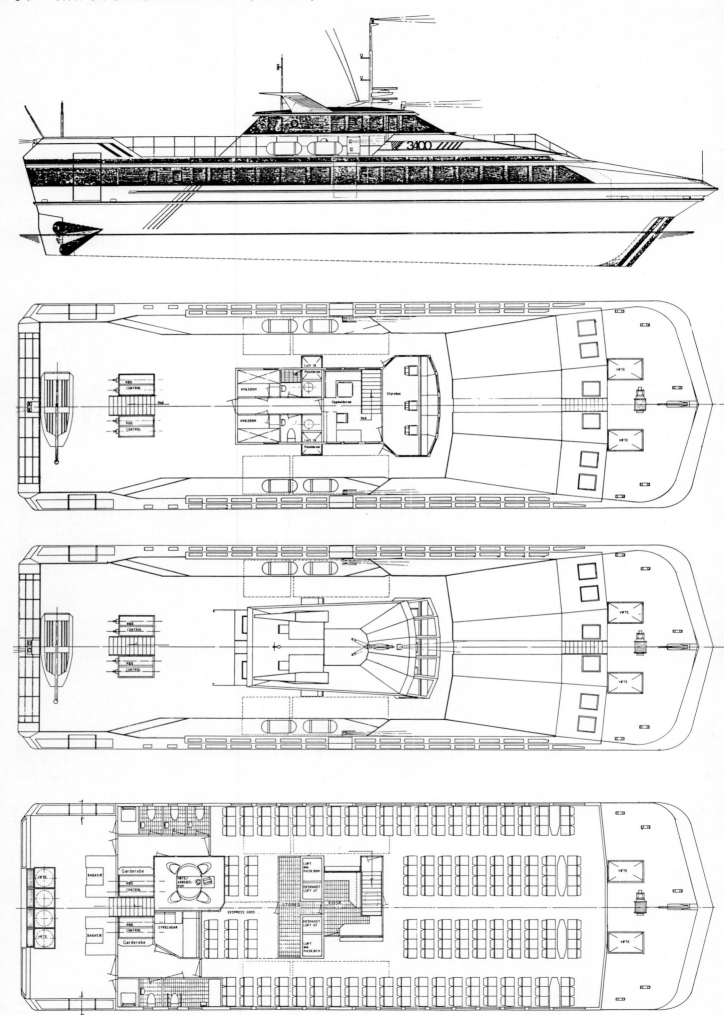

General Arrangement of Karlskronavarvet Jet Rider SES 3400 as completed by Westamarin

SES 3800

Announced in 1987 two of these vessels are to be built for JK Lindberg Shipping, Oslo, for delivery in Spring 1989.

ACCOMMODATION: Approx 400 seats.

ENGINES

Propulsion: Two MTU 16V 396 TB84, each 2040kW (2775bhp)

Lift and auxiliaries: Two 450kW (612bhp)

PROPULSION: Two KMW 71S62/6 waterjet units.

DIMENSIONS

Length overall: 37·80m
Breadth: 12·50m
Draught, on cushion: 0·40m
off cushion: 1·90m

PERFORMANCE

Speed, service: 45 knots
Speed, max: 51 knots
Fuel consumption: 23 litres/n mile at service speed
Range, at service speed: 390n miles

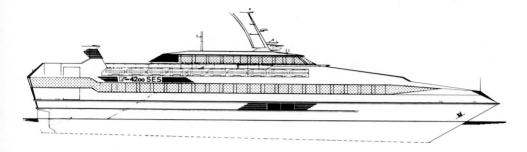
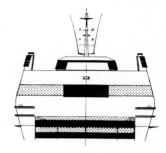
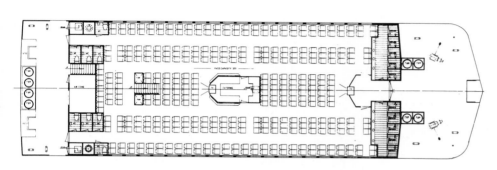
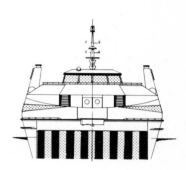
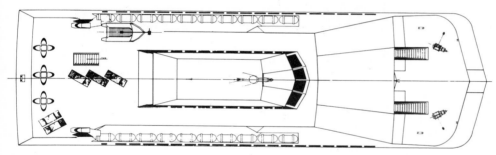

Westamarin SES 3800 design

SINGAPORE

SINGAPORE SHIPBUILDING AND ENGINEERING LTD

7 Benoi Road, Singapore 2262
PO Box 138, Jurong Town Post Office, Singapore 9161

Telephone: 8612244, 8616844
Telex: 21206 SINGA RS
Telefax: 8613028

TIGER 40

It was announced in November 1986 that Singapore Shipbuilding and Engineering Ltd was constructing the first Air Vehicles Tiger 40 air cushion vehicle carrier. The craft has been built for a leasing company in Singapore, SAL Leasing, which owns the craft. In 1987 this Tiger 40 was leased to the Singapore Navy. Details of the Tiger 40 are given in the entry for Air Vehicles Ltd. Tiger 40 craft are marketed in the Far East by Singapore Shipbuilding and Engineering Ltd.

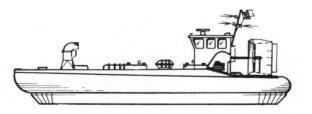

PROFILE

FRONT VIEW

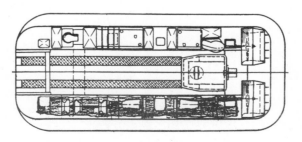

PLAN VIEW

Tiger 40 well-deck version

Air Vehicles Tiger 40 hovercraft built by Singapore Shipbuilding and Engineering Ltd (SSE)   *(J S Peach)*

Tiger 40 on trials for SAL Leasing

SPAIN

CHACONSA SA
COMPAÑIA HISPANO AMERICANA DE CONSTRUCCIONES CONSERVERAS SA
Mayor, 17-30006 Puente Tocinos, Apartado 419/30080, Murcia, Spain

Telephone: 68-230200; 238512; 230604
Telex: 67248 ABRO E

Carlos Ruiz Valero, *ACV Programme Manager*

CHACONSA launched its air cushion vehicle research programme in 1973. In 1976 it received a contract for the development of the VCA-36 from the Spanish Ministry of Defence. Design of the lift and propulsion system was aided by experiments with laboratory models. Two manned research models, the 750kg VCA-2 and the 5-tonne VCA-3, were later built to evaluate and refine the system.

In addition to its military programme, CHACONSA plans to build commercial hovercraft and is also examining industrial and agricultural applications of air cushion technology.

VCA-2
The first manned air cushion vehicle to be designed and built by CHACONSA, the VCA-2 has a maximum weight of 750kg. Like the VCA-3, described and illustrated below, it was employed as a test craft during the development of the lift system for the VCA-36 amphibious assault craft.

VCA-3
A 2·5 scale model of the VCA-36, the VCA-3, was built in 1978. Powered by two Porsche engines, it seats seven and has a maximum speed of 50 knots. At least one variant is likely to enter production.

VCA-2

VCA-3

LIFT AND PROPULSION: Integrated system powered by two 300hp Porsche 928-5 automotive engines. Each engine drives a centrifugal lift fan and a 2m diameter variable-pitch, two-bladed propeller for thrust.

CONTROLS: Craft heading is controlled by twin aerodynamic rudders operating in the propeller slipstream. At low speed direction control is by differential propeller pitch. A ballast system adjusts longitudinal and transverse trim.

HULL: Corrosion-resistant aluminium alloy. Buoyancy chamber includes compartments filled with plastic foam for reserve buoyancy. Six rubber landing pads are fitted to the hull base. Four lifting eyes are provided in the hull.

SKIRT: 0·53m deep, fingered-bag type of CHACONSA design, fabricated in nylon coated with synthetic rubber.

DIMENSIONS

EXTERNAL

Length overall, on cushion: 10·36m
Beam overall, on cushion: 4·45m
Height, on cushion: 4m
Skirt depth: 0·53m

INTERNAL

Cabin, max dimensions
Length: 4·1m
Width: 3·2m

WEIGHTS

Max: 5000kg
Payload: 1000kg

PERFORMANCE

Max speed: 50 knots
Cruising speed: 40 knots
Max gradient, continuous: 12%
Endurance: 3 hours

VCA-36

Designed to improve the rapid-lift capability of the Spanish armed forces, the VCA-36 will carry a 14-tonne payload, equivalent to three Land-Rovers and 70 fully-armed marines or infantrymen, to a beach landing zone at a speed of 60 knots. It could also be used for lighter-over-the-shore applications. Its dimensions will allow it to operate from the docking wells of a number of LSDs, and from ro/ro vessels with sufficient

CHACONSA VCA-36 on trials in 1986 *(CHACONSA)*

CHACONSA VCA-36 under construction showing fin mountings for the propeller shafts

headroom and suitable ramps. Lifting eyes in the hull will enable it to be hoisted on and off the decks of cargo ships. A removable roof above the cargo deck will permit the craft to be loaded alongside supply ships.

LIFT AND PROPULSION: Integrated system powered by two Avco Lycoming TF25 gas turbines, each with a maximum output of 2500hp. Each drives two centrifugal fans and a 4m diameter, five-bladed, variable-pitch propeller. Power is transmitted via two gearboxes with auxiliary outputs for lubrication, hydraulic pumps and generators. The combined epicyclic and bevel (splitter) gearbox (lower unit) transmits 1100hp from 14 500rpm to 1080rpm for the lift fans and 1900hp from 14 500rpm to 1988rpm for the pylon propulsion gearbox (upper unit). The pylon bevel gearbox reduces the speed from 1988rpm to the 1011rpm of the propulsion propeller.

CONTROLS: All controls are in a raised cabin, well forward on the starboard quarter and providing a 360-degree view. Directional control is by twin aerodynamic rudders and differential propeller pitch. A ballast system adjusts longitudinal and transverse trim.

HULL: Riveted aluminium structure based on a grid of longitudinal and transverse frames which form a number of watertight buoyancy compartments. Fuel, ballast tanks and bilge systems are contained within these compartments. Access to the cargo deck is via hydraulically-operated bow and stern ramps or the removable cargo deck roof. The central cargo deck is 18·65m long by 2·6m wide by 2·25m high. Two main longitudinal vertically stiffened bulkheads run the length of the hull. These separate the central vehicle/cargo deck from the sidestructures which contain the gas turbines, lift fans, transmissions, auxiliary power

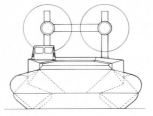
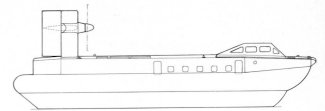
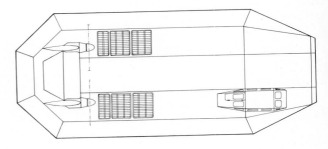

General Arrangement of VCA-36

systems and cabins. Marines or assault troops are accommodated in two 35-seat cabins, 7·4m long by 2·35m wide, one in the forward section of each sidestructure. Four landing pads are fitted to the hull base. Four lifting eyes are provided for hoisting the craft.

SKIRT: 1·4m deep, fingered-bag type of CHACONSA design in nylon coated with synthetic rubber.

SYSTEMS, ELECTRICAL: Two 15kVA generators driven by the main engines provide three-phase 50Hz at 380V for ac and dc supplies.

DIMENSIONS
Length overall, on cushion: 25·5m
Beam overall, on cushion: 11·04m
Height on cushion: 9·5m
Skirt depth: 1·4m
WEIGHTS
Max: 36 tonnes
Payload: 14 tonnes
PERFORMANCE
Max speed: 60 knots
Cruising speed: 50 knots
Endurance: 3 hours

CHACONSA BES-16 under construction, December 1987

BES

Early in 1987 it was announced that CHACONSA SA had teamed up with the Bazán yard (builder of naval fast craft) to develop a new surface effect ship, BES (Busque de Efecto Superfice). CHACONSA will work on the air cushion components at its El Carmeli factory while Bazán will be responsible for the hulls and engines, this work to be undertaken at its Cartagena yard. An initial investment of Ps160 million will be made by both companies. A prototype was expected to be finished by late 1987 or early 1988.

BES-16

At the end of 1984 CHACONSA established a 50/50 joint programme with Empresa Nacional Bazán for the study, analysis and development of SES craft technology in order to design and build these craft in the range of 50 to 500 tonnes, full load displacement.

The first craft to be built is the BES-16 research craft, launched in the first half of 1988.
HULL: Welded Al-Mg 4, 5 alloy.
PROPULSION: Two Isotta Fraschini diesel engines, 450hp each, two Castoldi 06 waterjet units.

LIFT: Two VM-HRI 492 diesel engines, 110hp each, six centrifugal lift fans.
DIMENSIONS
Length overall: 16·78m
Beam overall: 5·40m
Depth: 1·90m
Draught, mean: 0·75m
WEIGHT
Displacement: 14 tonnes

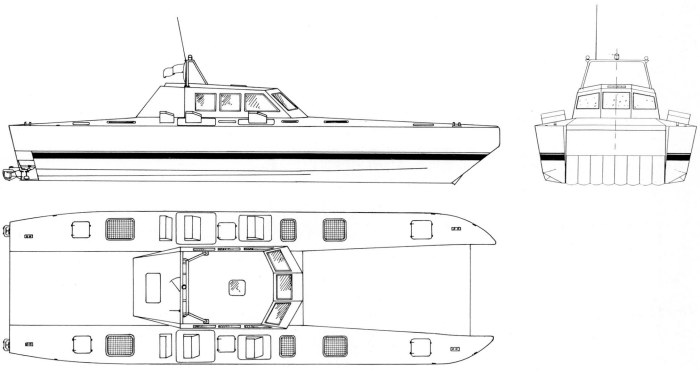

General Arrangement of CHACONSA BES-16

FM-AERODESLIZADORES

PO Box 1038, Alcalá de Henares, Madrid, Spain

Julián Martin Sanz, *Project Manager, Mechanical Engineer*
Joaquin Heras, *Electrical Engineer*

FM-HC-001 X

Successful trials of this craft began in the summer of 1979 when it was designated VAM-F1B. Employed as a research craft, it has an open cockpit and is fitted with a loop and segment skirt. During 1985 the craft was engaged in tests of systems and modifications.

LIFT AND PROPULSION: A single Volkswagen engine provides power for both the lift and propulsion systems, with a centrifugal clutch for the centrifugal lift fan. Thrust is supplied by a five-bladed axial fan driven by toothed belt.
CONTROLS: Craft direction is controlled by twin rudder vanes in the thrust fan slipstream and operated by a wheel.
HULL: Glass fibre structure, reinforced where necessary with aluminium tube.
SKIRT: Loop and segment type, fabricated in neoprene/nylon.
ACCOMMODATION: Open cockpit for driver and two passengers.
SYSTEMS, ELECTRICAL: 6V battery for starting and services.

DIMENSIONS
Length overall: 3·1m (10ft 2in)
Width, side bodies: 2·48m (8ft 1in)
  sides folded for transport: 1·04m (3ft 5in)
Height, skirt inflated: 1·26m (4ft 1½in)
PERFORMANCE
Max speed, estimated: 60km/h (37mph)

FM-HC-002

Please see Light/Sports Air Cushion Vehicles section for details of this craft.

FM-HC-003 (PROJECT DESIGN)

This is a design study for a high-speed amphibious two-seater powered by a 385hp gas turbine.
LIFT AND PROPULSION: Motive power is supplied by a single 385hp Allison 250B17 gas turbine. This drives two centrifugal lift fans and two ducted variable-pitch propellers for thrust.
HULL: Mixed fibreglass-reinforced plastics and aluminium construction.
CONTROLS: Craft direction is controlled by twin rudders aft of the propeller ducts. Pitch stability is provided by a horizontal stabiliser.
ACCOMMODATION: Enclosed cabin with two side-by-side seats.
SKIRT: Fingered-bag type.
DIMENSIONS
Length overall: 5·5m (18ft 2in)
Width: 2·85m (9ft 4in)
Max height: 2m (6ft 7in)
Skirt height: 0·53m (1ft 9in)
WEIGHTS
Total payload: 1150kg (2535lb)
Empty furnished: 590kg (1300lb)
Payload: 220kg (485lb)

FM-HC-001 X

FM-HC-004X

This craft is designed to be versatile and can operate without modifications in ambient air temperatures from −20°C to +70°C. Trials began in July 1986.

LIFT AND PROPULSION: Two 70hp BMW engines are used to drive the mechanically integrated lift and propulsion units, each engine positioned between a six-blade 800mm centrifugal lift fan and a six-blade ducted propeller. A centrifugal clutch is incorporated in each power unit and power transmission is by toothed belt/pulley arrangements.

CONTROLS: Craft direction is controlled by twin rudders positioned at the rear of the propeller ducts and operated by foot pedals. Three elevators are similarly positioned to provide control in pitch and roll and are operated by a hand wheel.

HULL: The craft is built in glass reinforced plastic and Plasticell. Sealed compartments provide reserve buoyancy.

SKIRT: Open loop segmented type. The rear segments are of conical form in order to avoid water scooping. The skirt is constructed of neoprene-coated nylon fabric.

ACCOMMODATION: The enclosed cabin has seating for one pilot and five passengers or one pilot, and co-pilot and a 400kg payload. A stretcher may be accommodated beside the pilot.

DIMENSIONS
EXTERNAL
Length, with inflated skirt: 6·11m
Width, with inflated skirt: 3·73m
Height, without inflated skirt: 1·975m
Cushion area: 14·63m²
INTERNAL (cabin)
Length: 1·75m
Width: 1·5m
Height: 1·25m

WEIGHTS
Empty: 900kg
Max payload plus fuel: 600kg

PERFORMANCE
Max speed over water: 75km/h
Max speed on land: 85km/h
Cruising speed: 65km/h
Gradient climbing capability: 1 in 7
Endurance: 5 hours
Max vertical obstacle clearance: 0·4m

VARIANTS: The design is adaptable for coastguard and patrol work and for search and rescue duties.

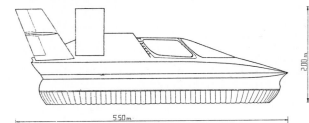
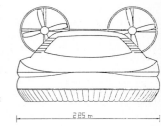
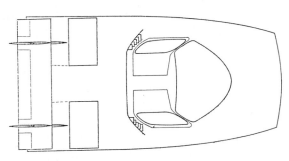

FM-HC-003 project design

FM-HC-004X

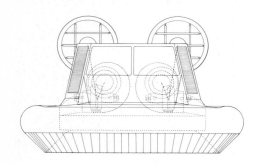
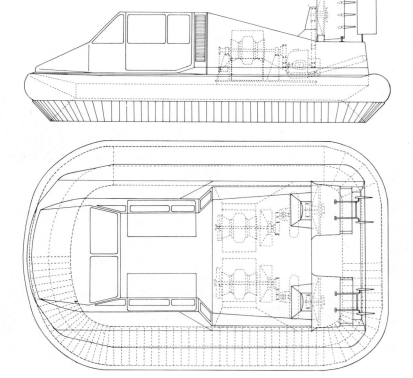

FM-HC-004X

FM-HC-005 HOVERBUS (PROJECT DESIGN)

A 48-seat diesel-powered project intended for fast ferry services, powered by two Deutz BF8L 513 air-cooled engines. The general features of the lift and thrust machinery installation are similar to the HC-004X craft scaled up and this machinery is housed in the two side bodies of the hull. The projected characteristics are as follows:

DIMENSIONS
EXTERNAL (without inflated skirt)
Length: 13·75m
Width: 6·5m
Height: 3m
INTERNAL (cabin)
Length: 11·5m
Width: 3m
Height: 1·7m
WEIGHTS
Empty: 8000kg

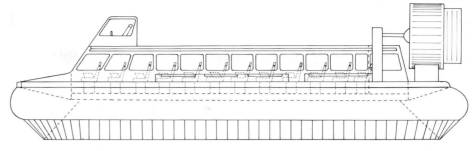

FM-HC-005 Hoverbus design

Max payload: 4800kg
PERFORMANCE
Max speed over calm sea: 70km/h

Max speed on land: 85km/h
Cruising speed: 60km/h
Obstacle clearance: 0·5m

NEUMAR SA

La Rinconada, B-6-28023 Madrid, Spain

Telephone: (91) 2071998/4582982

J M Isidro, *President*
M de la Cruz, *Technical Director*
J A Barbeta, *Manufacturing Manager*

Neumar SA was founded in 1983 as a consulting engineers and designers company for air cushion technology. The services it offers include research and development with an emphasis on lift systems; hovercraft design; project management, which can comprise construction subcontracting with collaborating shipyards; hovercraft skirt design and manufacturing; and technical and economic feasibility studies.

The company offers a range of hovercraft designs which are based on a new lift system that it has recently developed and patented. This has been called an Automatic Transversal Air Distribution (ATAD) lift system because of the main function it performs in providing very high stability with low power requirements and reduced manufacturing and maintenance costs. To prove the viability of this lift system, several two-dimensional models and a manned model/prototype have been built and tested.

ATAD LIFT SYSTEM

The ATAD lift system has been developed with the aim of obtaining high stability values with low lift power requirements. It is a pressure-stability, fully-segmented system that is based on a longitudinal flexible keel which has the inherent ability to increase the pressure difference between the two chambers into which it divides the air cushion, while keeping the pressure ratio between the air distribution duct and the air cushion at a very low level.

The stability keel has the same effect as a valve which is open to both air cushion chambers while the craft is level and which, when the craft heels, closes to the risen side while opening the air passage still further to the fallen side. This results in a very sharp rise of the pressure ratio between both cushion chambers even for very low duct-to-cushion pressure ratios. A second effect is that the lift air flow requirement is reduced in comparison to conventional systems. The keel is made of independently replaceable segments.

The peripheral skirt used with this lift system has been made fully segmented, each segment consisting of three independently replaceable sectors. It offers low drag over waves and low manufacturing and maintenance costs, and it has low geometrical stability in order to make any ride control system more effective.

A by-product of this lift system is a hull design which further increases the hovercraft seakeeping qualities. The hull bottom cross-section has the form of a 'W', both 'Vs' ending in conical surfaces which at the bow are prolonged upwards and forward forming a planing surface to prevent adverse consequences of any plough-in phe-

Neumaran NM-6 prototype approaching land *(Neumar)*

Trials of the Neumaran NM-6 prototype over mud and reeds *(Neumar)*

nomena. This hull form greatly reduces water impact loads and at the same time it has a high structural efficiency that in turn leads to a lower structure weight.

NEUMARAN NM-6

This three-/four-seat hovercraft has been designed for the pleasure boat market and for those other applications, for example coastal or inland water patrol and harbour policing, for which a high-speed small boat is required with the added advantage of its amphibious qualities. The design has sought a compromise between low cost and high performance, measuring the latter in terms of high speed, good manoeuvrability and very good seakeeping qualities for its size.

LIFT AND PROPULSION: The NM-6 features an integrated lift and propulsion system with a single engine driving twin 800mm diameter axial flow fans that provide the airflow required for both functions. The transmission consists of HTD toothed belts and pulleys. For the prototype a 120hp petrol engine has been chosen, but any engine from 100 to 150hp could be installed, depending on speed and payload requirements.
CONTROL: Yaw control is obtained by one aerodynamic rudder situated in the air outlet duct of each of the two fans. Top rudder deflection closes the outlet duct, directing the airflow forward through louvre nozzles at each side of the craft, thus producing a braking effect. Since each rudder can be independently deflected, a very

effective yaw control is obtained at all speeds. Roll
control is performed by two venting valves located
in the transom of the craft that discharge air from
each of the two chambers into which the air
cushion is divided.
HULL: The hull is made of moulded grp with
extensive use of sandwich structures. The hull
form is that described above for the ATAD lift
system, which greatly reduces water impact loads
while offering high structural efficiency.
SKIRT: The skirt design corresponds to the
ATAD lift system described before. All skirt
elements are made of neoprene-covered nylon
fabric.
ACCOMMODATION: The prototype provides
seating accommodation for three persons in a fully
enclosed cabin, but different superstructure and
cabin layouts are also possible and an open
cockpit with seating accommodation for four
persons is projected.
DIMENSIONS
Length, hard structure: 5·80m
Beam, hard structure: 2·05m
Height on cushion: 2·10m
Cushion depth, minimum: 0·40m
    mean: 0·52m
WEIGHTS
(With 120hp engine)
Displacement, light: 850kg
Useful load (including fuel): 350kg
Displacement, full load: 1200kg
PERFORMANCE
(With 120hp engine)
Speed, max, calm water: 42 knots
Speed, cruising: 30-35 knots
Gradient from standing start, max: 10%
Endurance at cruising power, max: 5 hours
Range, max: 150-175n miles
WEATHER LIMITATIONS
Waves: 1m
Wind: Beaufort 5

NEUMARAN NM-15 (DESIGN)

This amphibious assault landing craft design
followed a specific requirement, but other military
and civil variants can be derived from the basic
layout. Among the former, coastal patrol and
counter-insurgency missions can be mentioned,
while some of its possible civil applications would
be passenger ferry, crewboat or as a luxury
amphibious yacht. The design philosophy that has
been applied, which is based on the ATAD lift
system, leads to a cost-effective craft through the
use of diesel engines and a grp structure, while
craft performance can be adapted to each specific
requirement through the installation of the
adequate engine power.
LIFT AND PROPULSION: The basic design
has twin lift and propulsion integrated systems,
each consisting of a diesel engine that drives both a
centrifugal lift fan and a ducted variable-pitch
propeller. The proposed diesel engines are two
Deutz air-cooled units of the type BF12L 513 FC,
with a maximum rated power of 525hp each.
Transmission from the engines to fans and propellers is through toothed belts and pulleys.
CONTROL: Yaw control at high speed is obtained through three aerodynamic rudders located
in the slipstream of each propeller, and at low
speed, differential propeller pitch may be used.
Pitch control is by means of horizontal elevators
also situated in the propeller slipstreams. Pitch
trim is obtained through a fuel ballast system. Roll
control is performed by two venting valves installed in the transom of the craft as described for
the NM-6.
HULL: The hull is made of moulded grp using
sandwich structures with expanded pvc cores. For
special applications requiring maximum weight-
saving, Kevlar and carbon fibre reinforcements
could be used at an increased cost. The hull form is
as described above for the ATAD lift system.
SKIRT: The skirt design corresponds to the
ATAD lift system described before. All skirt
elements are made of neoprene-covered nylon
fabric.
ACCOMMODATION: The basic design
provides seating accommodation for 24 combat

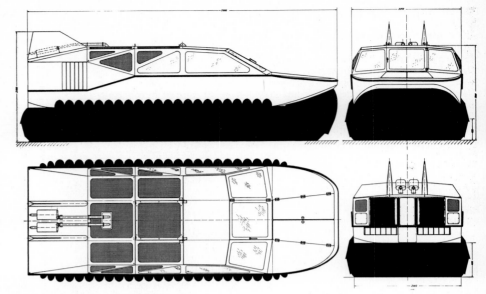

General Arrangement of Neumaran NM-6

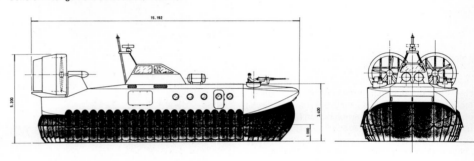

General Arrangement of Neumaran NM-15 design

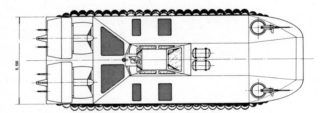

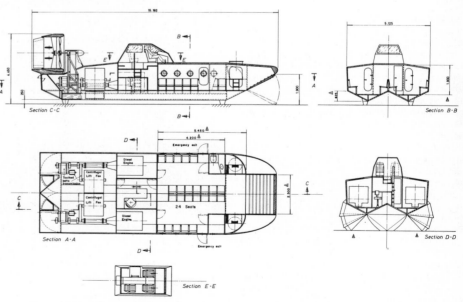

Internal Arrangement of Neumaran NM-15 design

troops. This layout is based on the requirement to
have an endurance of 8 hours, but if this figure is
reduced to 3 hours, 36 troops could be easily
seated in the main cabin. Access to this cabin takes
place through a bow ramp 2·50m wide. There are
also two emergency exits, one at each side of the
craft. Three seats can be installed in the raised
control cabin, which provides 360° visibility.

Access to this cabin is provided by a ladder from
the operations room below and there is also a door
that leads from the control cabin to the aft deck.
Two gunner wells have been allowed for in the
foredeck, where two 12·7mm or smaller calibre
machine guns could be installed. Direct access has
been provided from the main cabin to the two
gunner wells.

DIMENSIONS
EXTERNAL
Length, hard structure: 15·19m
Beam, hard structure: 5·13m
Height on cushion: 5·20m
Cushion depth, minimum: 1·00m
Cushion depth, mean: 1·31m
INTERNAL
Main cabin floor area: 22m²
Main cabin length: 5·40m
Main cabin width: 4·80m
Bow ramp width: 2·50m
WEIGHTS
Displacement, light: 11 300kg
Useful load (including fuel): 3700kg
Design fuel load (8 hours endurance): 1200kg
Design military load: 2500kg
Displacement, full load: 15 000kg
PERFORMANCE
Speed, max, calm water: 55 knots
Speed, cruising in Sea State 2: 40 knots
Gradient from standing start, max: 10%
Endurance with internal tanks at cruising power,
    max: 16 hours
Range at cruising speed, equivalent max: 640n
    miles
WEATHER LIMITATIONS
Waves: 2·5m
Wind: Beaufort 7

NEUMARAN NM-17 (DESIGN)

This design was carried out following a requirement for a low cost, relatively low-speed hovercraft for commuter passenger service on short routes. Low specific installed power (hp/ton) is therefore a special characteristic of this craft. The same hull design and general layout can be used for other higher performance applications if more powerful engines are installed. Other super-structure layouts, such as open deck versions, are also possible for vehicle carrying or utility purposes. Possible applications for the different versions of this design are largely the same as those mentioned before for the NM-15, with the added advantages in this case of its greater capacity and better seakeeping qualities. As for all Neumaran designs, the concepts applied are based on naval architecture considerations rather than on aeronautical technology. This has led to the use of diesel engines instead of gas turbines and of a grp hull which is based purely on naval technology.
LIFT AND PROPULSION: The basic design has twin lift and propulsion integrated systems, each consisting of a diesel engine that drives both a centrifugal lift fan and a ducted variable-pitch propeller. The proposed diesel engines are two Deutz air-cooled units of the type BF12L 513 FC, with a maximum rated power of 525hp each. For more powerful versions the lift fans would be driven separately by a third engine, in which case the propulsion propellers could be of the fixed-pitch type. In all cases the transmission is performed by means of toothed belts and pulleys.
CONTROL: The control system is of the same design as was described for the NM-15.
HULL: The hull design is also the same as for the NM-15.
SKIRT: The skirt design corresponds to the ATAD lift system described before. All skirt elements are made of neoprene-covered nylon fabric.
ACCOMMODATION: For short routes with high traffic density (typical commuter service) 56 seats can be installed in the main cabin with a seat width of 550mm and a row pitch of 825mm. Aisle width would be 600mm and the headroom at the aisles 2000mm. A separate compartment for the crew is located under the control cabin. A seat for a crew member has been provided in this compartment, and there is also more space available for stowage or for a small toilet.
The raised control cabin offers 360° visibility. Three seats would normally be installed here. Access to this cabin is by means of a ladder from the crew compartment below. There is also a door that leads from the control cabin to the aft deck. Passenger access to the main cabin is either through a bow ramp when the craft is on the ground, or through a stairway that leads from the

main cabin to the forward deck and which would be used when the craft is moored to a pier.

DIMENSIONS
EXTERNAL
Length, hard structure: 17·56m
Beam, hard structure: 6·15m
Height on cushion: 6·20m
Cushion depth, minimum: 1·20m
Cushion depth, mean: 1·57m
INTERNAL
Main cabin floor area: 36m²
Main cabin length: 7·00m
Main cabin width: 5·90m
Headroom: 2·00m
Max possible bow ramp width: 3·00m
WEIGHTS
Displacement, light: 16 500kg
Useful load (including fuel): 5500kg
Design fuel load (2 hours endurance): 400kg
Design payload: 5100kg
Displacement, full load: 22 000kg
PERFORMANCE
Speed, max, calm water: 45 knots
Speed, cruising in Sea State 2: 35 knots
Gradient from standing start, max: 7%
Range at cruising speed: 70n miles
Endurance with internal tanks at cruising power,
    max: 18 hours
Range at cruising speed, equivalent max: 630n
    miles

WEATHER LIMITATIONS
(for passenger service)
Waves: 2m
Wind: Beaufort 6

NEUMARAN NM-30 (DESIGN)

Two versions of this design are available: a passenger ferry and a military coastal patrol craft. From both versions different variants can in turn be derived, such as a mixed traffic ferry from the former and an amphibious assault craft from the latter. Both versions follow all the design concepts developed by Neumar around the ATAD lift system described earlier. These amphibious vessels offer very high stability characteristics and high speed with low power requirements and their design follows normal naval architecture practice, providing cost-effective craft with good sea-keeping qualities.
LIFT AND PROPULSION: The lift airflow is supplied by twin lift assemblies, each one consisting of a CRM diesel engine Type 12 D/S with a maximum power rating of 935hp, which drives two 1·22m diameter centrifugal fans through HTD toothed belts and pulleys. Propulsion is also by means of twin machinery groups, each of them incorporating a CRM diesel engine Type BR 1/2000 rated at 1815hp maximum power, which drives a ducted Hamilton Standard 3·60m diameter fixed-pitch propeller. Transmission is through two bevel gearboxes and the corresponding shafts.

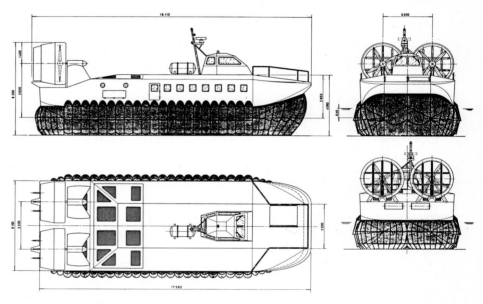

General Arrangement of Neumaran NM-17 design

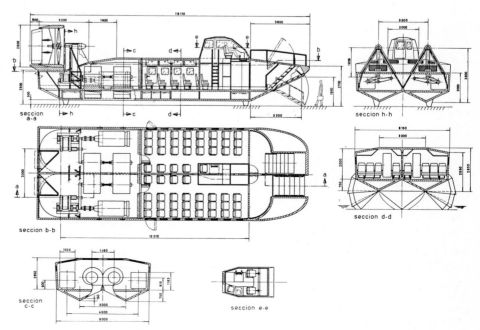

Internal Arrangement of Neumaran NM-17 design

Alternatively, if a higher speed is required the propulsion power can be provided by two groups of two CRM diesel engines Type 12 D/SS connected to twin-input, single-output reduction gears which would give a total maximum propulsion power of 5500hp.

CONTROL: Yaw control at high speed is obtained by means of three aerodynamic rudders located in the slipstream of each propeller, whereas at low speed differential power setting of the two propulsion groups is used. Pitch control is through four horizontal elevators also situated in the propeller slipstream. Longitudinal trim is obtained with a fuel ballast system. Roll control is performed by two venting valves installed either side near the stern of the craft, which also assist in turning, while transversal trim is obtained through differential power setting of the two lift engines.

HULL: The hull is made of moulded grp using sandwich structures with expanded pvc cores. For special applications requiring maximum weight saving, Kevlar and carbon fibre reinforcements could be used at an increased cost. The hull form is as described before for the ATAD lift system.

SKIRT: The skirt design corresponds to the ATAD lift system described earlier. All skirt elements are made of neoprene-covered nylon fabric.

ACCOMMODATION

Passenger ferry: The passenger ferry version is a double-deck design with a total capacity for 170 passengers divided into 98 seats on the main deck and 72 seats on the upper deck. A forward hold with access through the bow ramp offers space for luggage containers or trailers, or, depending on weight considerations, for two cars.

Coastal patrol craft: This design offers accommodation for the Commanding Officer, two officers, four petty-officers and six ratings, with a galley, messrooms and a wardroom to make living aboard possible for several days. This design has three decks: the main deck with the propulsion and lift machinery, crew quarters and galley, and a forward hold where a Land-Rover or freight could be carried; the upper deck with the operations room and the officers quarters; and the control cabin with four seats offering 360° visibility. An inflatable dinghy with its davit is carried on the aft deck and on the forward deck a twin 30mm gun mounting can be installed.

DIMENSIONS

Length, hard structure: 30·00m
Beam, hard structure: 10·25m
Height on cushion: 8·70m
Cushion depth, minimum: 2·00m
    mean: 2·63m
Bow ramp width: 2·50m

WEIGHTS

Displacement, light: 53 000kg
Useful load (including fuel): 22 000kg
Displacement, full load: 75 000kg

PERFORMANCE

Speed, max calm water: 60 knots
Speed, cruising in Sea State 2: 45 knots
Gradient from standing start, max: 10%
Endurance at cruising power
    Passenger ferry:
        10 hours with a payload of 13 tonnes
        4 hours with a payload of 18 tonnes
    Coastal patrol:
        20 hours with a military load of 5 tonnes
        12 hours with a military load of 12 tonnes

WEATHER LIMITATIONS

Civil applications: 2·5m waves, 7 Beaufort wind
Military use: 4m waves, 8 Beaufort wind

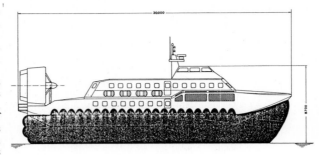
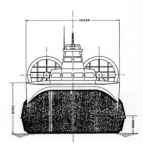
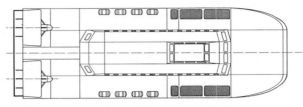

General Arrangement of Neumaran NM-30 design, ferry version

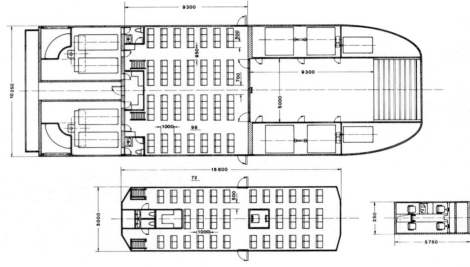

Interior layouts of cabins for NM-30 ferry design

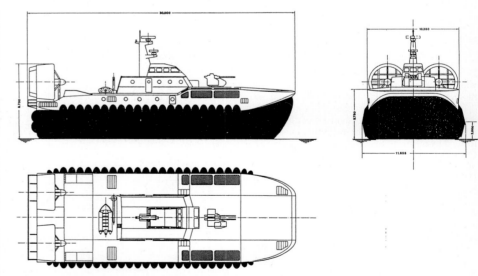

General Arrangement of Neumaran NM-30 design, military version

SWEDEN

KARLSKRONAVARVET AB

Box 1008, S-371 82 Karlskrona, Sweden

Telephone: 45519440
Telex: 8395018/8395028 KKRV S

JET RIDER SES 3400

Karlskronavarvet announced in 1985 the marketing of an SES ferry design, the 244-seat, 42-knot Jet Rider. This design emanates from a technology transfer agreement in 1984 between Karlskronavarvet and Textron Marine Systems (formerly Bell Aerospace Textron), the former company supplying grp sandwich technology to the US Navy Cardinal Class Mine Sweeper Hunter (MSH) programme (cancelled 1986) and the latter company supplying Karlskronavarvet with SES technology.

On 11 July 1986 Karlskronavarvet AB announced that it had received an order for two surface effect ships with an option for a third. The order is for a Norwegian group of three ferry companies: Det Stavangerske Dampskibsselskab, Sandnaes Dampskibs A/S and Hardanger Sunnhordlandske

Dampskipsselskab. The order is valued at about SKr50 million. The hulls will be built at Karls-kronavarvet and installation of machinery and outfitting will be undertaken by Westamarin A/S in Norway. The vessels were due for delivery at the end of 1987. A ride control system is installed in the vessels.

PROPULSION: Two MTU 16V 396 TB83 diesels, 2095hp each at 1940rpm, each driving KaMeWa 63/S62/6 waterjet unit.

CRUISING SPEED: 42 knots.

DIMENSIONS
Length overall: 34·05m
Length waterline: 27·65m
Beam overall: 10·50m
Depth moulded: 3·25m
Draught, hullborne: 1·65m
　on cushion: 0·80m

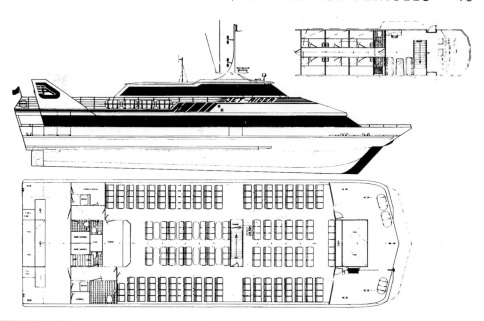

General Arrangement of Karlskronavarvet
Jet Rider design

TAIWAN

CHIVALRY UNIVERSAL COMPANY

PO Box 36-48 Taipei, Taiwan

Telephone: 02 6212197/7626110/7692511
Telex: 19113 FINFONG TP
Telefax: 7637106

C S Lee, *President*
H J Tsai, *Vice President, Research and Development*
T P Doo, *Vice President, Engineering*

Overseas Office: International Vehicle Research Inc, 14074 Nacogdoches Road, Suite No 322, San Antonio, Texas 78247, USA

Telephone: (512) 650 5188

Johnny Tseng-Pei Doo, *President*

Chivalry Universal produce both light sports and utility hovercraft. Details of the light models, CY-10 and CY-10 Mk II are to be found in the Light/Sports Air Cushion Vehicles section.

Chivalry is conducting the research and development, testing and design work in conjunction with the International Vehicle Research Inc, who also has the marketing responsibility for the CY-series hovercraft in the North American area.

CY-6

CY-6 Mk III is a five-/six-seater utility amphibian hovercraft. The production version is very similar to the prototype design in external dimensions but the internal transmission system and supporting structure has been redesigned for simpler maintenance procedures and lighter structure weight.

CY-6 Mk IV is a stretched version of the CY-6 Mk III. The fuselage is stretched 1·0m in length and the side panel widened 0·25m per side to provide additional payload capability, while the engine power is also increased to 145hp. The prototype was scheduled to be tested in January 1988.

LIFT AND PROPULSION: CY-6 Mk III has a single 120hp L20E engine with integrated transmission system which drives the lift and propulsion fan via toothed belts. Cushion air is supplied by two 0·53m diameter centrifugal fans. Thrust is provided by a 1·07m diameter axial flow ducted propeller. CY-6 Mk IV has a larger 145hp engine but utilises the same transmission system.

HULL: Glassfibre-reinforced plastic with close-cell form sandwich structure.

CONTROLS: Four rudder vanes at aft end of thrust fan duct provides heading control. Elevator

Chivalry CY-6 Mk II, prototype of the CY-6 Mk III　　　*(Chivalry)*

Chivalry CY-6 Mk III　　　*(Chivalry)*

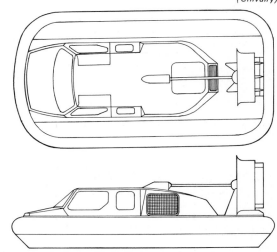

CY-6 Mk III

is added on the CY-6 Mk IV to provide trim control.
SKIRT: Bag-finger type.
ACCOMMODATION: Enclosed cabin for the pilot and five passengers for the CY-6 Mk III; seven passengers and the pilot for the CY-6 Mk IV.
SYSTEMS, ELECTRICAL: 12V dc system.
DIMENSIONS
Length,
  off cushion: 5·80m (Mk III); 6·80m (Mk IV)
  on cushion: 6·15m (Mk III); 7·15m (Mk IV)
Beam, off cushion: 3·30m (Mk III); 3·80m (Mk IV)
  on cushion: 3·75m (Mk III); 4·25m (Mk IV)
  side panel folded: 2·05m (Mk III and Mk IV)
Height,
  off cushion: 1·36m (Mk III); 1·46m (Mk IV)
  on cushion: 1·70m (Mk III); 1·90m (Mk IV)
WEIGHTS
Normal empty: 900kg (Mk III); 1150kg (Mk IV)
Gross: 1350kg (Mk III); 1750kg (Mk IV)
Payload: 450kg (Mk III); 600kg (Mk IV)
PERFORMANCE
Max speed: 40 knots
Cruising speed: 35 knots
Endurance: 3·5 hours

CY-12 (DESIGN)

Construction of the CY-12 project has been postponed due to budget restrictions but the design work is still continuing. The original CY-12 design has been revised to increase the payload capability from 3 tons to 3·8 tons, and the gross weight has been increased to 11·8 tons. The original version is named CY-12A, which will be the base for this family of utility hovercraft. Modular system and structural assemblies will facilitate modification and stretching for various applications.

The stretched version, which is 5 metres longer than the original version, is designated CY-12B and is designed to carry 5·5 tons of payload, giving a gross weight of 18·0 tons.
LIFT AND PROPULSION: CY-12A uses two 500hp diesel engines to drive two centrifugal fans for lift and two ducted propellers for thrust. CY-12B uses two 250hp engines to drive four centrifugal fans for lift and two 500hp engines to drive two ducted propellers for thrust.
CONTROLS: Aerodynamic rudders behind the ducted propellers provide heading control. Bow thrusters are mounted forward on the fuselage side structure.
HULL: Welded aluminium structure with glass-fibre-reinforced plastic sub-structure.
SKIRT: Bag-finger type, with independent cell for additional cushion stability.
ACCOMMODATION: Open deck, CY-12A has a 12·0 by 5·2m cargo area. CY-12B has a 17·0 by 5·2m cargo area. Wide bow and stern ramps simplify loading and unloading. Cabin can be added to 40 passengers for the CY-12A and 60 passengers for the CY-12B.
DIMENSIONS
Length overall: 15·2m (A); 20·2m (B)
Width overall: 10·4m (A); 10·4m (B)
Height, on landing pad: 4·6m (A); 4·6m (B)
  on cushion: 5·6m (A); 5·8m (B)
WEIGHTS
Max gross: 11·8 tons (A); 18·0 tons (B)
Payload: 3·8 tons (A); 5·5 tons (B)
PERFORMANCE
Max speed, calm water: 50 knots
Cruising speed: 40 knots
Endurance: 5 hours

CY-14 (DESIGN)

This is a 4·5-ton diesel-powered utility hovercraft designed to be an economical workhorse with 1100kg usable payload. The design has been in progress since January 1987. The prototype construction of CY-14 will begin in mid-1988. In addition, it is planned that this prototype will also serve as the test bed for the CY-12 project.
LIFT AND PROPULSION: A single 500hp diesel engine with integrated transmission system drives the lift and propulsion fans via toothed belts. Cushion air is supplied by two 0·67m

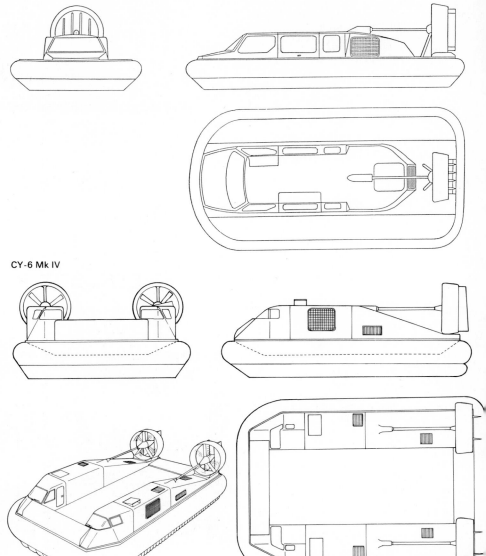

CY-6 Mk IV

Chivalry CY-12 design for utility craft

diameter double-inlet centrifugal fans. Thrust is provided by two 1·40m diameter axial flow ducted propellers.
HULL: Glassfibre-reinforced plastic with close-cell form sandwich structure.
CONTROLS: Two rudder vanes at aft end of each thrust fan ducts provides directional control.
SKIRT: Bag-finger type.
ACCOMMODATION: Enclosed cabin for pilot and 11 passengers.
SYSTEMS, ELECTRICAL: 12V dc system.

DIMENSIONS
Length: 9·8m
Beam: 4·5m
Height: 2·2m
WEIGHTS
Normal, gross: 4500kg
Payload: 1100kg
PERFORMANCE
Max speed: 38 knots
Cruising speed: 32 knots
Endurance: 3·5 hours

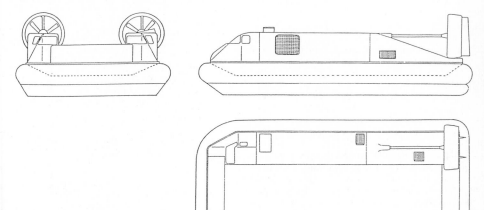

CY-14 design

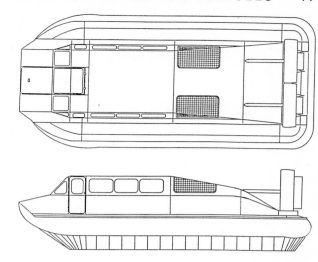

CY-12B design

UNION OF SOVIET SOCIALIST REPUBLICS

KRASNOYE SORMOVO SHIPYARD

Head Office and Works: Gorki, USSR

M Yuriev, *Shipyard Director*
Ivan Yerlykin, *Chief Hydrofoil Designer*

Export Enquiries: Sudotransport (V/O Sudo-import), 10 Uspenski Per, Moscow 103006, USSR

Telephone: 251 05 05/299 58 77/299 02 14
Telex: 411272/411387/411443 SUDO SU

This shipyard began work in the ACV field by building a five-passenger air cushion river craft, known as the Raduga, in 1962. Since then it has built the Sormovich, a 30-ton peripheral jet ACV for 50 passengers, and the Gorkovchanin, a 48-seat prototype sidewall craft for shallow, winding rivers. It is believed that the Gorkovchanin, Zarnitsa, Orion, Chayka and Rassvet were all designed by the Gorki Institute of Water Transport Engineers.

The production version of the Gorkovchanin, the Zarnitsa, of which more than 100 have been built, is employed on almost all the river navigation lines of the Russian Federative Republic as well as on the rivers of the Ukrainian, Moldavian, Byelorussian and Kazakhstan Soviet Socialist Republics.

The design of an 80-seat rigid sidewall ferry, the Orion, was approved by the Soviet Ministry of Inland Waterways in 1970. Construction of the prototype began in 1972 and trials were successfully undertaken in 1975. The craft has been in series production.

A third sidewall vessel is the Rassvet, designed to carry up to 80 passengers along local sea routes. Like Zarnitsa, the craft is able to run bow-on to flat sloping beaches and does not require piers or specially prepared moorings. Work is in hand aimed at evolving a substantially bigger sidewall ACV ferry which has been given the name, Turist. This craft has a design speed of 36 knots and is intended for shallow waterways unsuitable for hydrofoils. Two variants have been projected, a 300-seat passenger ferry and a mixed-traffic model for 15 cars and 100 to 120 passengers.

In 1969 prototypes of two fully-skirted hovercraft made their debut: the Briz, a light utility craft and the Skate, a 50-seat passenger ferry with an all-up weight of 27 tonnes and a cruising speed of 57mph. While there is no evidence of the Skate going into production, a military version, known in the West by the NATO code name Gus, is in service with the Soviet marine infantry and army. Gus was designed by a special Soviet Navy High-Speed Ship Design Bureau, in Leningrad, which was also responsible for the design of the Soviet Union's biggest skirted hovercraft, known in the West as Aist. More than 16 Aists are in service with the Soviet Navy as amphibious assault

landing craft. Aist can cross water, beaches and marginal terrain to deliver tanks, armoured transporters, equipment and personnel well beyond the shore line. Aist is generally similar in shape, size and performance to the BHC SR.N4 Mk 2.

Among military air cushion vehicles to enter production for the Soviet armed forces are a 90-tonne amphibious assault landing craft known by the NATO code name Lebed, a craft similar in size and overall appearance to the BH.7 and a successor to Gus.

Soviet air cushion vehicle activity is widely varied. Part of this activity is devoted to meeting Soviet military needs, but in the main it is devoted to the production of sidewall ACVs and to the development and construction of amphibious carriers and snowgoing and marshgoing vehicles capable of providing reliable year-round transport in the Soviet north and north-eastern regions where a number of vital development projects are under way including the Siberia-West Europe gas pipeline.

Only a small percentage of the freight required can be delivered to these areas by helicopter. Estimates of the Institute of Integrated Transport Problems, operating under the USSR Gosplan Institute, have indicated that the use of air cushion vehicles, apart from speeding up the construction of important facilities under difficult conditions, will enable haulage costs over difficult routes of the north and north-east to be reduced by one-third. As a result, savings in transport expenditure for the work volume forecast for the Eleventh Five-Year Plan will be 1200 to 1500 million roubles annually.

The use of amphibious ACVs in agricultural production enables operations including the application of fertilisers, herbicides and weeding to be conducted regardless of weather.

Large-load air-cushion platforms allow the movement of beet, potatoes and other crops from fields regardless of soil conditions. Expenditure for the chemical treatment of fields using self-propelled ACVs is half the cost of employing an AN-2 aircraft for this work and is one-third of the cost of an Mi-2 helicopter.

GORKOVCHANIN

The Gorkovchanin is a waterjet-propelled, 48-seat, rigid sidewall ACV, designed for water-bus services on secondary rivers with a guaranteed depth of 0·5m (1ft 8in). In view of the winding nature of these rivers, the craft operates at the relatively low speed of 30-35km/h (19-22mph). No marked reduction of speed is necessary in water up to 0·5m (1ft 8in) deep.

The craft has been developed from a ten-seat scale model built at the experimental yard of the Institute of Water Transport Engineers at Gorki in 1963, and the pre-production prototype was completed in September 1968. Design was undertaken by a team at the Volgobaltsudoproekt special design office.

Official trials were completed on the Sura river in May and June 1969. During speed tests over a measured mile with a full complement of passengers, 36·6km/h (22·75mph) was attained. The main engine developed 265hp of which approximately 30hp was used to drive the centrifugal fan.

The craft has covered the journey from Gorki to

Gorkovchanin

Summary of principal air cushion vehicle types built

Civil	Payload	No built	Year built	Designed by	Builders
Neva amphibious ACV	38 passengers	one			
Briz (Breeze)	6 passengers		1968		
Skate	50 passengers		1969		
Raduga amphibious ACV	5 passengers	one	1962		Krasnoye Sormovo Shipyard, Gorki
Sormovich amphibious ACV	50 passengers	one	1965		Krasnoye Sormovo Shipyard, Gorki
Gorkovchanin sidewall ACV	48 passengers	one	1969-70	Gorki Institute of Water Transport Engineers, Gorki	Krasnoye Sormovo Shipyard, Gorki
Zarnitsa sidewall ACV (based on Gorkovchanin)	48 passengers	over 100	1972	Gorki Institute of Water Transport Engineers, Gorki	Krasnoye Sormovo Shipyard, Gorki
Orion sidewall ACV	80 passengers		1973* 1975†	Gorki Institute of Water Transport Engineers, Gorki	Leningrad Shipyard
Chayka sidewall ACV	80 passengers	one		Gorki Institute of Water Transport Engineers, Gorki	Sosnovka Shipyard
Rassvet sidewall ACV	80 passengers	one		Gorki Institute of Water Transport Engineers, Gorki	Sosnovka Shipyard
Plamya sidewall ACV (based on Orion hull)	fire-fighting craft	one?		Central Design Bureau, Gorki	
Raduga-2 amphibious ACV	0·65 tonnes	n/a		Krasnoye Sormovo Shipyard, Gorki	
SAVR-1M amphibious ACV		one	1978		
SAVR-1 amphibious ACV	1·3 tonnes	production version of the 1M	1980	A M Gorki Memorial Marine Institute of Technology	
SAVR-2 amphibious ACV	2 tonnes		1982	A M Gorki Memorial Marine Institute of Technology	
SAVR-3 amphibious ACV	2 tonnes		1981	A M Gorki Memorial Marine Institute of Technology	
SAVR-5GD amphibious ACV	5 tonnes		1981 onwards	A M Gorki Memorial Marine Institute of Technology	
SAVR-40 amphibious ACV	50 tonnes		1987	A M Gorki Memorial Marine Institute of Technology	
MP-18 amphibious ACV	0·6 tonnes				
MPI-20 amphibious ACV	2- and 5-tonne versions				
Neptun AKVPR-001 amphibious ACV	research craft		1977	Neptun Central Design Bureau, Moscow	
Barrs-1 (Snow Leopard) amphibious ACV	0·65 tonnes or 7 passengers		1981	Neptun Central Design Bureau, Moscow	
Gepard (Cheetah)	5 passengers	quantity production	1981	Neptun Central Design Bureau, Moscow	
Taifun amphibious ACV	20 passengers or 3 tonnes			UFA Aviation Institute, Tyumen	
Klest amphibious ACV	4 seats?		1981	Vostok Central Design Bureau, Leningrad	
Luch sidewall ACV	66 passengers	reported in series production	1983 onwards		Astrakhan Shipyard
Puma	16 passengers	two prototypes		Neptun Central Design Bureau, Moscow	

* trials
† series production began

Military	Capacity	No built	First launched	Designed by	Builders
NATO Code name: **Gus** amphibious ACV	25 troops	31	1969, production ended 1979		
NATO Code name: **Aist** amphibious ACV	up to 100 tonnes	Possibly 16 in service	1970		Dekabristov Shipyard, Leningrad
NATO Code name: **Lebed** amphibious ACV	35 tonnes		1973	Soviet Navy's High-Speed Ship Design Bureau, Leningrad	
NATO Code name: **Pomornik**	—	—	1986?	—	—
Utenok Class	—	2	—	—	Feodosiya Shipyard
Tsaplya Class	40 tonnes	—	—	—	Feodosiya Shipyard

Moscow (1016km (622 miles)) and back in 31 and 27 running hours respectively at an average speed of approximately 35km/h (22mph) and has good manoeuvrability when running ahead and astern. In 1970 the Gorkovchanin was succeeded in production by a developed version, the Zarnitsa.

LIFT AND PROPULSION: Integrated system powered by a 3D6H diesel engine rated at 250hp continuous. The engine is mounted aft and drives a 960mm (3ft 1¾in) diameter six-bladed centrifugal fan for lift, and a 410mm (1ft 4½in) diameter single stage waterjet rotor for propulsion. Fan air is taken directly from the engine compartment. Skirts of rubberised fabric are fitted fore and aft. The bow skirt of production craft is of segmented type. Cushion pressure is 180kg/m^2.

The waterjet intake duct is 100mm (4in) below the displacement water level to prevent air entry, with a consequent reduction in the navigable draught.

CONTROLS: Vanes in the waterjet stream provide directional control. Thrust reversal is achieved by the use of waterflow deflectors.

HULL: The hull is built in riveted D16 corrosion resistant aluminium alloy. The hull bottom and sides have transverse frames and the sidewalls and superstructure top longitudinal frames. Thickness of plating on sides and bottom is 1·5mm (1/16in) (2·5mm (3/32in) in the bow section); and on the sidewalls 1mm (3/64in) (up to 5mm (13/64in) in the bow section). Deck plates are 1mm (3/64in) thick and the top of the superstructure is in 0·8mm (1/32in) plating.

Acoustic and thermal insulation includes 100mm (4in) thick foam polystyrene sheeting.

ACCOMMODATION: Seats are provided for a crew of two, who are accommodated in a raised wheelhouse, and 28 passengers. Access to the passenger saloon, which has airliner-type seats, is through a single door at the bow in the centre of the wheelhouse. The craft runs bow-on to flat sloping banks to embark and disembark passengers.

SYSTEMS, ELECTRICAL: One 1·2kW, 24V dc, engine-operated generator and batteries.

COMMUNICATIONS: Car radio in wheelhouse and speakers in passenger saloon.

DIMENSIONS
Length overall: 22·3m (73ft 2in)
Beam overall: 4·05m (13ft 3½in)
Hull beam: 3·85m (12ft 7⅝in)
Height of hull to top of wheelhouse: 3·3m (10ft 9⅘in)
Height of sidewalls: 0·45m (1ft 5¾in)
Draught afloat: 0·45m (2ft 1⅗in)
cushionborne: 0·65m (1ft 4⅘in)

WEIGHT
Max weight with 48 passengers, crew and fuel: 14·3 tons

PERFORMANCE
Normal service speed: 30-35km/h (19-22mph)
Distance and time from full ahead to full astern: 60m (197ft) and 14 seconds

ZARNITSA

Evolved from Gorkovchanin, the Zarnitsa is a 48 to 50-seat waterjet-propelled rigid sidewall ferry designed to operate on shallow rivers, some less than 0·7m (2ft 3in) deep. Series production is under way, and large numbers have been delivered.

The prototype was put into trial service on the Vyatka river, in the Kirov region, in the summer of 1972, and the first production models began operating on shallow, secondary rivers later in the year. During 1973-74, Zarnitsas entered service on tributaries of the Kama, Lena and Volga. More than 100 are employed on almost all the river navigation lines of the Russian Federative Republic as well as on the rivers of the Ukrainian, Moldavian, Byelorussian and Kazakhstan Soviet Socialist Republics.

LIFT AND PROPULSION, CONTROLS, HULL: Arrangements almost identical to those of the Gorkovchanin.

ACCOMMODATION: Seats are provided for two crew members, who are accommodated in the raised wheelhouse forward, and 48-50 passengers. Access to the passenger saloon is via a single door

Zarnitsa

Passenger saloon in Zarnitsa looking aft

at the bow in the centre of the wheelhouse. The craft runs bow-on to flat sloping banks to embark and disembark passengers.

DIMENSIONS
Length: 22·3m (72ft 3in)
Beam: 3·85m (12ft 8in)
Skeg depth: 0·45m (1ft 6in)
WEIGHTS
Light displacement: 9 tonnes
Max weight, with 48 passengers, crew and fuel: 15 tonnes
PERFORMANCE
Service speed: 33-35km/h (20-22mph)

LENINGRAD SHIPYARD
ORION-01

Design of the Orion, a rigid sidewall ACV with seats for 80 passengers, was approved in Moscow in autumn 1970. The prototype, built in Leningrad, began trials in October 1973 and arrived at its port of registry, Kalinin, in late 1974, bearing the serial number 01.

The craft is intended for passenger ferry services along shallow rivers, tributaries and reservoirs and can land and take on passengers bow-on from any flat sloping bank. It is faster than the Zarnitsa and its comfort and performance are less affected by choppy conditions. Cruising speed of the vessel, which is propelled by waterjets, is 53km/h (32·3mph). It belongs to the 'R' class of the Soviet River Register.

Several variants are under consideration, including a 'stretched' model seating 100 passengers on shorter routes, a mixed passenger/freight model, an all-freight model and an 'executive' version for carrying government officials.

Experimental operation of the Orion-01 was organised by the Port of Kalinin, Moscow River

Zarnitsa

Transport, the initial run being Kalinin—1 May Factory, a distance of 99km (61·5 miles), of which 45km (28 miles) is on the Volga, 42km (26 miles) on the Ivanov reservoir and 12km (7·5 miles) on the shallow waters of the Soz. The first weeks of operation showed that there was an insufficient flow of passengers on this particular route.

The vessel was then employed on public holidays only for carrying holiday makers and day trippers on such runs as Kalinin—Putlivo 31km (19 miles), Kalinin—Kokoshky 19km (12 miles) and Kalinin—Tarbasa 28km (17·3 miles), and subsequently on a regular schedule to Putlivo. Finally, Orion-01 was used on the Kalinin—Kimry run, a distance of 138km (85·7 miles), of which 70km (43·4 miles) passes through the

Ivanov reservoir and 68km (42 miles) on the Volga.

Particular attention was paid to skirt reliability. The side sections of the lower part of the bow skirt were badly chafed and split due to contact with the skegs when coming onto the shore. Upper parts of the skirt were not damaged. Problems were also experienced with the aft skirt made from a balloon type fabric. Layers of rubber in the aft part of the segments peeled off; chafing was caused by securing washers and splitting was experienced in the vicinity of the fastenings.

In order to reduce the time spent on repairs, sections of the stern skirt were attached to removable frames. Later a new stern skirt was introduced, based on panels made from a 12mm

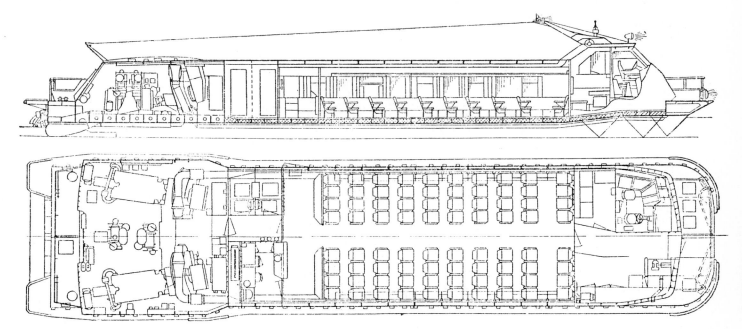

General Arrangement of Orion

ORION—Stopping and starting characteristics	Shallow water	Deep water
Distance run by vessel from Full Ahead to Stop		
Metres	136	120
Time in seconds	67	40
Distance run by vessel from Full Ahead to Full Astern		
Metres	84	65
Time in seconds	23	20
Distance necessary for attainment of Full Speed from Stop		
Metres	250	330
Time in seconds	60	80

(0·47in) thick conveyor belt. This enabled the stern draught, on cushion, to be reduced by 10cm (3·87in) and the speed to be increased by 1·5km/h (0·87mph). It also improved the reliability of the craft. During the 200 hours under way from the time the skirt was fitted until the end of the vessel's trials, there was no damage.

It was considered that, in the main, the Orion met the requirements of the Soviet operators for the rapid transport of passengers on 'R' class rivers and reservoirs. The elimination of the defects revealed during the experimental operation will improve the vessel's operational characteristics and increase its reliability.

Series production of this vessel is being undertaken at the Sosnovka Shipbuilding Yard in Kirovskaya Oblast.

LIFT AND PROPULSION: Integrated system powered by two 520hp 3D12N-520 diesels mounted in an engine room aft. Each engine drives a Type Ts 39—13 centrifugal fans for lift, and via a cardan shaft, a semi-submerged single-stage waterjet rotor for propulsion. Fan air is fed via ducts to the bow skirt, a transverse stability slot and to the fingered bag skirt aft. Casing of the waterjet system, which is removable, forms the stern section of the vessel. The waterjets are mounted on shock absorbers to reduce vibration.

HULL: Similar in overall appearance to Zarya and Zarnitsa types. All-welded structure in AlMg-61 aluminium-magnesium alloy. Lateral framing throughout hull with the exception of the bow and stern decks, where longitudinal frames have been fitted. Superstructure and wheelhouse are of welded and riveted duralumin construction on longitudinal framing.

ACCOMMODATION: Seats for operating crew of three, which is accommodated in a raised wheelhouse, a barman, two seamen and 80 passengers. At the aft end of the passenger saloon are two toilet/washbasin units and a bar. An off-duty cabin for the crew. Access to the passenger saloon is via a single door at the bow, in the centre of the wheelhouse. A ram-air intake provides ventilation while the craft is under way. Stale air is drawn out by the lift fans aft.

CONTROLS: Rudders located aft of the waterjet inlets and two waterjet deflectors control craft direction. Rudder and flap movement is by cables.

SYSTEMS, ELECTRICAL: Two G-73Z engine-driven generators, linked with two sets of STK-18M batteries, provide 28V, 1200W. One battery set is employed for engine starting, the other for supplying current for the ship's systems.

COMMUNICATIONS: Standard equipment comprises an R-809MZ radio-telephone, a Kama-3 UHF radio and an Unja cabin announcement system.

DIMENSIONS
Length overall: 25·8m (84ft 7¾in)
Beam overall: 6·5m (21ft 4in)
Height overall to mast top: 5·27m (17ft 3½in)
Height to top of wheelhouse: 3·97m (13ft ¼in)
Draught, displacement condition, fully loaded: 0·84m (2ft 9⅛in)
empty: 0·76m (2ft 5⅘in)
Draught, cushionborne, bow: 0·1m (4in)
stern: 0·5m (1ft 8in)
WEIGHTS
Loaded displacement: 34·7 tonnes
Light displacement: 20·7 tonnes
PERFORMANCE
Max speed: 60km/h (37·25mph)
Cruising speed, full load: 53km/h (33mph)

Max wave height on scheduled runs: 1·2m (4ft)
Range: 400km (249 miles)
Diameter of turn to port: 182m (597ft)
Time to complete turn with rudders at 33 degrees: 187 seconds
Time taken from start of berthing procedure to completion: 1 minute approx
Time taken to attain cruising speed from leaving berth: 2 minutes approx

SOSNOVKA SHIPYARD
Kirovskaya Oblast
RASSVET (DAWN) AND CHAYKA (GULL)

A waterjet-propelled sidewall passenger ferry, Rassvet is designed for local sea routes of limited water depth. It is an offshore counterpart to the Orion sidewall ACV. Plans call for the Rassvet to serve resort routes in the Crimea, on the Caspian and Baltic Seas as well as on large lakes and reservoirs. Like the Orion and Zarnitsa, its two predecessors, it can run bow-on to flat, sloping beaches to embark and disembark passengers. Landing on a beach is facilitated by an articulated gangway with a hydraulic drive.

Rassvet's features include shallow draught, good manoeuvrability and relatively simple construction.

The waterjet reversing/steering system is specially protected to enable the craft to moor alongside existing berths built originally for small conventional displacement ferries.

The Rassvet prototype, named Chayka-1 (Gull-1), is undergoing trials. The Chayka-1 was the first of thirty of its type to be built at the Sosnovka Shipyard in Kirovskaya Oblast for the Black Sea Shipping Line. In January 1976 it was stated that the vessel was the first seagoing passenger ACV to be built in the Soviet Union. The extent of the remote control, automation and monitoring provided for the powerplant and systems generally is sufficient to permit the craft to be operated by one person, with intermittent attendance to the machinery space.

Rassvet is designed to carry 80 passengers during daylight hours on coastal routes in conditions up to force 4. It complies with USSR Registration classification KM*II ① Passenger ACV Class.

LIFT AND PROPULSION: Power for the waterjet system is provided by two 3D12N-520 lightweight (3·54kg/kW) irreversible, high-speed four-cycle V-type marine diesels each with a gas-turbine supercharger and a rated power of 383kW at 1500rpm. Each powers a two-stage waterjet impeller. Water inlet scoops are arranged in the sidewalls and the pump parts, each of which comprises two rotors and two flow straightening devices, are installed in the sidewalls behind the transoms. Cushion air is generated by a single

Chayka-1

Chayka-1

110kW PD6S-150A diesel driving an NTs6 centrifugal fan via a universal joint and a torque-limited coupling.

CONTROLS: Craft direction is controlled by twin balanced rudders operating in the water discharged by each of the two waterjets. Reversal is achieved by applying rotatable deflectors to reverse the waterflow.

SKIRT: Double-row segmented type at bow; two-tier bag type skirt aft. Repair or replacement of sections of the bow skirt can be undertaken with the bow run on to a flat, gently sloping beach. The stern skirt is secured to special hinged sections which permit inspection and maintenance while still afloat.

HULL: Hull and superstructure are built in aluminium magnesium alloy. The hull is of all-welded construction in AlMg-61 and the decks, superstructure, pilot house and partitions are in AlMg-5 alloy. Hull, superstructure and pilot house have longitudinal frames. Single-piece pressed panels are employed for the lower sections of the sidewalls. Corrugated sheets are used for the hull bottom. Below the passenger deck the hull is sub-divided by transverse bulkheads into seven watertight compartments, access to which is via hatches in the passenger deck. The craft will remain afloat in the event of any one compartment flooding.

ACCOMMODATION: Rassvet seats 80 passengers in a single fully ventilated and heated saloon amidships. Airliner-type seats are provided, beneath each of which a life-jacket is located. Decks in the passenger cabin, pilot house and crew's off-duty cabin are covered with carpet and the floors of the companionways with pvc linoleum. Pavinol aircraft-type leather substitute decorates the deck-heads. Large windows give passengers a good view. At the aft end of the cabin are a small buffet and two toilets. At the forward end of the cabin are the wheelhouse, a duty crew restroom and a vestibule. The operating crew of six comprises captain, engineer, motorman, radio operator, seaman and one barman. Passenger embarkation at piers designed for the berthing of small ferries of the local services takes place across the section of open deck forward of the pilot house. Where conventional berthing facilities do not exist the craft runs bow-on to a flat sloping bank where

landing facilities are provided by an articulated gangway with a hydraulic drive.

SYSTEMS, ELECTRICAL: Power supply requirements are met by a 28V, KG-2·9kW generator driven by a power take-off shaft from the main engine and three 28V, 1·2kW G-732 charging generators mounted on the main engine. Two banks of storage batteries are installed. One, comprising two Type 6STK-180M storage batteries, supplies dc power when the craft is operating. The second bank, comprising four batteries of the same type, is employed for engine starting and for powering the diesel engine control circuits and emergency alarm systems. An inverter is installed for navigation and other equipment requiring ac supplies. An auxiliary circuit can be connected to shore systems for a 220V single-phase 50Hz ac supply.

SAFETY EQUIPMENT: PSN-10M and PSN-6M inflatable life rafts are installed in containers along each side of the craft. The number of rafts is designed to meet the requirements of all passengers and crew. Life raft release is remotely controlled from the landing positions at the bow and stern. Individual lifesaving devices, lifebelts and lifejackets are also provided.

FIREFIGHTING, HYDRAULICS, BILGE, BALLASTING, WATER SUPPLY: Complete systems installed as standard.

COMMUNICATIONS: Lastochka radio telephone transceiver for ship-to-shore and ship-to-ship communications; Kater uhf transceiver and Plot-M portable emergency transceiver. Ryabin passenger announcement and broadcast relay system. Omega radar for navigating along shorelines, in narrow waterways and in poor visibility.

ANCHOR: Single 100kg (220lb) Matrosov anchor operated by a hydraulic winch.

DIMENSIONS
Length overall: 26·7m (87ft 3in)
Beam, max: 7·1m (23ft 3in)
  amidship: 6m (19ft 8in)
Height overall, hull: 2·2m (7ft 3in)
  sidewall only: 1·5m (4ft 11in)
Draught hullborne: 1·27m (4ft 2in)
  cushionborne at bow: 0·1m (4in)
  stern: 0·8m (2ft 7½in)

WEIGHTS
Loaded displacement: 47·5 tonnes
Passenger capacity: 80 persons
PERFORMANCE
Cruising speed: 23 knots
Max speed: 29 knots
Range: 352km (190n miles)

PLAMYA (FLAME) ACV RIVER FIRETENDER

The Central Design Bureau at Gorki has developed a river-going firetender. The craft is based on the hull of the Orion sidewall-type passenger ferry, but the passenger cabin super-structure has been replaced by an open deck forward to accommodate a tracked or wheeled firefighting vehicle and its crew. Plamya is designed for the fast delivery of an off-the-road fire-fighting vehicle and its crew to points on lakes, reservoirs and major rivers near forest fires. The craft can be beached bow-on on the river bank and the firefighting vehicle or bulldozer off-loaded across the bow ramp.

Plamya meets the requirements of the Register of Shipping of the USSR and is constructed to class R in the RSFSR Inland Waterways Register. It is in service on the River Kama.

LIFT AND PROPULSION: Integrated system powered by two 520hp 3D12N-520 marine diesels. Each engine drives a Type Ts 39-13 centrifugal fan for lift and, via a cardan shaft, a semi-submerged single-stage waterjet rotor for propulsion.

CONTROLS: Rudders aft of the waterjet inlets and two waterjet deflectors control craft direction.

HULL: All-welded structure in AlMg-61 aluminium-magnesium alloy. Frames, plates, partitions and roof of superstructure in D16 alloy.

SKIRT: Bow, triple-row, fully segmented type; stern, fingered bag type.

ACCOMMODATION: As opposed to the 'Orion' class the Plamya's pilothouse is amidships, with a large cargo deck forward to facilitate the carriage of a firefighting vehicle or bulldozer and the crew. Alternative loads include an ATsL-3(66)-147 forest firefighting tracked vehicle, a VPL-149 firefighting cross-country vehicle, a truck with portable firefighting equipment and a crew of 18, or a bulldozer with a crew of three. Beneath the pilothouse superstructure are

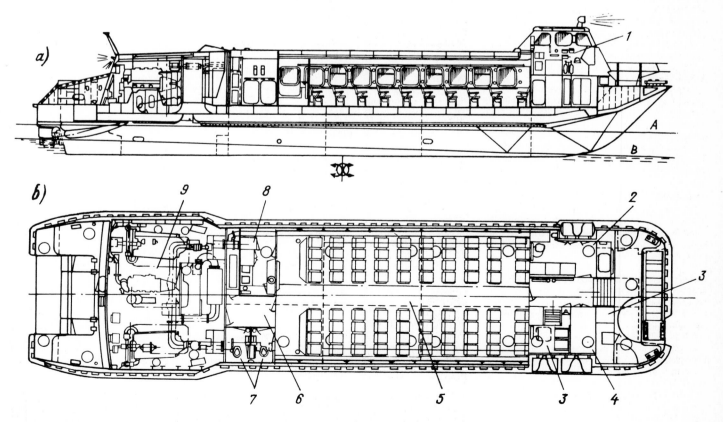

Longitudinal cross section (**a**) and passenger deck plan (**b**) of Chayka
(**A**) waterline in displacement condition; (**B**) waterline underway on air cushion; (**1**) pilot house; (**2**) crew's off-duty cabin; (**3**) storeroom; (**4**) baggage compartment; (**5**) passenger lounge; (**6**) companionway; (**7**) toilets; (**8**) buffet; (**9**) machinery space

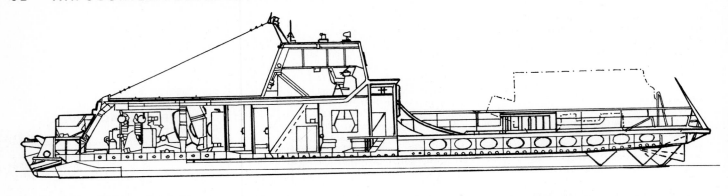

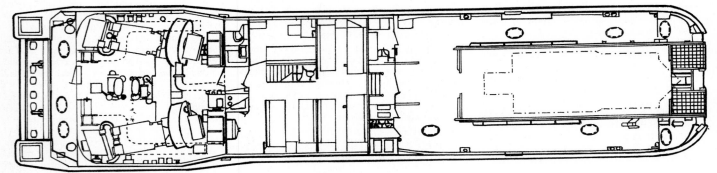

Inboard profile and deck plan of Plamya

storerooms for portable firefighting equipment, a lounge for the firefighting squad, an off-duty cabin for the crew of three and a toilet. Engine room is aft.

SYSTEMS, ELECTRICAL: 24V dc, supplied by two 1·2kW engine-driven generators linked with two sets of storage batteries.

COMMUNICATIONS: Kama-S UHF radio and PZS-68 passenger announcement system. Granit-M and Groza-2 transceivers for communication with firefighting team.

DIMENSIONS
Length overall: 26·1m (85ft 8in)
Beam: 6·5m (21ft 4in)
Height overall, amidship: 5·5m (18ft 2in)
Draught displacement condition: 0·88m (2ft 11in)
Draught, on cushion, at stern: 0·7m (2ft 4in)

WEIGHTS
Fully loaded: 34·5 tonnes
Cargo capacity: 7·3 tonnes

PERFORMANCE
Max speed: 50km/h (31mph)

Plamya

RADUGA-2

Little is known about this amphibious ACV, which was first reported in the Soviet press in late spring 1981. Designed at the Krasnoye Sormovo ship and ACV building facility at Gorki, Raduga-2, in common with the Gepard and Klest, is powered by an automotive engine, the Chayka. The 1962 Raduga was described in *Jane's Surface Skimmers 1985* and earlier editions.

SIDEWALL PASSENGER FERRIES

Details of two Soviet surface effect ship (SES) passenger ferry projects were published in Leningrad in late 1979, one seating 120 passengers, the other 150. Preliminary specifications of each are given below.

23·5-METRE SES PASSENGER FERRY

LIFT AND PROPULSION: Integrated system, powered by two 1000hp diesels.
CONTROLS: Craft heading is controlled by water rudders.
HULL: Welded marine aluminium.
ACCOMMODATION: 120 passengers.
DIMENSIONS
Length overall: 23·5m (77ft)
Max beam: 7m (23ft)
Sidewalls, height: 1·5m (4ft 11in)
    breadth: 1m (3ft 3in)
Air cushion, length: 20m (65ft 7in)
    breadth: 5m (16ft 4in)
    area: 100m² (1076ft²)

WEIGHTS
Empty: 15·3 tonnes
Max weight: 48·6 tonnes
Displacement tonnes/passenger: 0·406
PERFORMANCE
Max operating speed: 32 knots

25·6-METRE SES PASSENGER FERRY

LIFT AND PROPULSION: Integrated system, probably similar to that employed on Chayka and Turist, powered by two 1000hp marine diesels.
CONTROLS: Craft direction is controlled by water rudders.
HULL: Welded marine aluminium.
ACCOMMODATION: Seats are provided for 150 passengers.
DIMENSIONS
Length: 25·6m (84ft)
Max beam: 7m (23ft)
Air cushion, length: 22·5m (73ft 10in)
    breadth: 5m (16ft 5in)
    area: 110m² (1184ft²)
WEIGHTS
Empty: 18 tonnes
Max weight: 52·8 tonnes
Displacement tonnes/passenger: 0·354
PERFORMANCE
Max operating speed: 31 knots

TURIST DESIGN

The Central Scientific Research Institute has completed the design of a new sidewall ACV ferry,

the Turist. The vessel, which is based on extensive experience gained from the operation of the Zarnitsa, Orion and Rassvet, is virtually a scaled-up version of the latter. It has a design speed of 36 knots and is intended for use along shallow waterways unsuitable for hydrofoils. Propulsive thrust appears to be supplied by two gas turbine-driven waterjets, one in each sidewall. Two variants are projected, a 250- to 300-seat passenger ferry and a mixed traffic variant for 10 to 15 cars and 100 to 120 passengers. Turist is due to go into series production at the Nakhodka yard following the completion of shipbuilding facilities there.

Recent reports suggest that, as a result of detailed assessments undertaken in the Soviet Union over a period of years, a range of large sidewall hovercraft is being developed for the conveyance of freight. It appears that designs of 2000 to 4000 tons are under consideration.

ASTRAKHAN SHIPYARD
LUCH-1

A new sidewall ACV for river use was completed at the Astrakhan Shipyard and underwent State trials in September 1983. Designed to replace the twelve-year-old Zarnitsa, the craft, named Luch, Design No. 14351, carries two crew and up to 66 passengers, 15 standing. Of all-welded aluminium construction, it has a maximum operating weight of 22·6 tonnes and a top speed of 44km/h. The shallow on-cushion draught of just over 0·5m allows it to run bow-on to flat sloping river banks to embark and disembark passengers. A ladder is fitted at the bow.

New design features will permit operation on large rivers such as the Don, Kama, Oka and Volga, where high waves are encountered. However, the yard emphasises that it will be used primarily by oil and gas personnel and timber rafters who work on the banks of small rivers.

Among the basic design requirements were: that the Zarnitsa's general characteristics should be preserved; increased reliability; easier maintenance; increased service speed; widened operating potential and improved ride comfort.

Compared with the Zarnitsa, Luch has a more powerful diesel, the 380kW 81H12A, and uses a lighter form of construction. The overall dimensions of the craft permit rail transport to distant rivers and canals.

During trials before the commissioning of the first of the class it was demonstrated that its operating and technical performance is significantly superior to that of the Zarnitsa. The craft is built to the requirements of the 'R' class of the USSR's River Craft Registry. It is in series production and will be available for export in 1988.

LIFT AND PROPULSION: Power provided by single 81H12A marine diesel with normal service output of 346kW at 1500rpm. The engine is mounted aft and drives, via a transmission shaft, a centrifugal fan for lift and a waterjet rotor for propulsion. The waterjet rotor and its bearing can be replaced while the craft is in displacement condition without having to lift it out of the water.

CONTROLS: Twin rudder vanes in the waterjet stream control craft heading. Thrust reversal achieved by waterflow deflectors.

HULL: The buoyancy structure is built in welded AlMg-61 aluminium alloy. The superstructure is built in D16 alloy. Superstructure and bulkheads are riveted together. Pressed panels are employed throughout the hull to improve the external appearance and reduce the volume of assembly work necessary during construction.

SKIRT: Fingered type at bow, bag-type aft. Bow segments attached to an easily replaceable module.

ACCOMMODATION: Seats are provided for a crew of two, in a raised wheelhouse, and 51 passengers. On route sectors of 1 hour or less, the capacity can be increased to 66 by allowing 15 standing in the passenger cabin. The hull is divided into eight basic sections: a forward platform, the control cabin, service room, vestibule, passenger cabin, auxiliary rooms, engine room and stern platform. The bow platform has a gangway/ladder for embarkation and landing on unequipped stopping points, jetties and for mooring. The location of the control cabin at the bow simplifies handling on narrow waterways. A service room, aft of the control cabin, provides rest accommodation for the relief crew.

The lounge has 51 passenger seats, one seat for a

Gus

Gus

(Danish Defence)

guide and racks for small items of luggage. Large sliding windows ensure good visibility and ventilation. The lounge and crew rooms are air conditioned. The passenger cabin is separated from the engine room by a store room on the port side and a toilet on the starboard side, an arrangement which reduces the noise level. Mooring, refuelling, taking-on oil and water, discharging sewage and oil-contaminated waters to container vessels or shore based containers are all performed from the aft platform. A hatch on the aft platform gives access to the waterjet rotor.

SYSTEMS, ELECTRICAL: One 1·2kW 24V dc engine-operated generator and batteries. During prolonged night stops power can be supplied by a shore based 220V, 50Hz electrical supply.

COMMUNICATIONS: VHF, Kama 'R', marine transceiver. PA and crew command systems.

ENGINE
Type 81H12A diesel, max power: 380kW (510bhp)
Normal operating power: 346kW (464bhp)
DIMENSIONS
Length overall: 22·81m

Length, bp: 21·80m
Beam overall: 3·85m
Height overall: 3·35m
  side: 1·2m
  skegs: 0·45m
Depth: 1·25m
Guaranteed aft draught at water intake when travelling on air cushion at full displacement: 0·5m
Draught at full displacement, stationary: 0·65m
WEIGHTS
Max: 20·1 tonnes
Empty: 14·2 tonnes
Light displacement: 15·40 tonnes
Load displacement (cargo, 51 passengers and baggage): 21·2 tonnes
Extreme load displacement (cargo, 66 passengers and baggage): 22·6 tonnes
PERFORMANCE
Speed, max: 44km/h, 23·75 knots
Range, max fuel reserves: 300km
Endurance: 8 hours

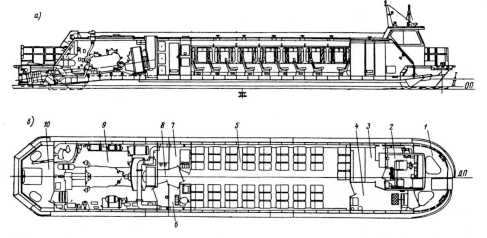

Inboard profile and plan of Luch: **(a)** longitudinal section **(b)** deck plan **(I)** waterline in displacement mode **(II)** waterline when cushionborne **(1)** fore deck **(2)** wheelhouse **(3)** duty compartment **(4)** vestibule **(5)** passenger saloon **(6)** toilet **(7)** storeroom **(8)** vestibule **(9)** engine room **(10)** aft deck

MILITARY CRAFT
GUS (NATO Code Name)

A variant of the Skate, which was designed as a 50-seat amphibious passenger ferry, but which was not put into production, Gus is now employed extensively by the Soviet Naval Infantry for river patrol, small-unit troop insertion and amphibious assault. The Soviet Navy's amphibious landing ship, the *Ivan Rogov*, can carry three amphibious assault ACVs of the Gus type. Each of these craft can carry a fully-armed platoon onto a landing beach at speeds of up to 60 knots. The prototype was launched in 1969 and it is thought that 31 of these 27-tonne vehicles are in service. Production of this class is thought to have been completed in 1979. A derivative with twin ducted propellers is under development.

LIFT AND PROPULSION: Motive power is provided by three 950hp TVD-10 marine gas turbines mounted aft. Two drive 3m (9ft 10in) diameter three-bladed variable and reversible-pitch propellers for thrust and the third drives an axial lift fan. Cushion air is drawn through a raised intake aft of the cabin superstructure.

CONTROLS: Craft direction is controlled by differential propeller pitch, twin aerodynamic rudders and forward and aft puff ports. Elevator provides pitch trim at cruising speed.

HULL: Hull and superstructure are in conventional corrosion-resistant marine light alloy. Basic structure comprises a central load-carrying platform which incorporates buoyancy tanks and outer sections to support the side ducts and skirt. The cabin, fuel tanks, lift fan bay engines and tail unit are mounted on the platform.

ACCOMMODATION: Air-conditioned cabin for up to 25 troops. Commander and navigator are seated in a raised wheelhouse. Battle crew of six, including two responsible for opening the two entry/exit doors forward and amidship, port and starboard.

DIMENSIONS

EXTERNAL
Length overall, power on: 21·33m (69ft 11½in)
Beam overall, power on: 7·8m (25ft 7½in)
Height to top of fin: 6·6m (21ft 8in)

WEIGHT
Normal operating: 27 tonnes

PERFORMANCE
Max speed: 60 knots
Cruising speed: 43 knots
Range: 200n miles

AIST (NATO Code Name)

The first large amphibious hovercraft to be built in the Soviet Union. Reports suggest that 16 have entered service to date. Built in Leningrad it is similar in appearance to the SR.N4 Mk 2 Mountbatten though giving the impression of being very much heavier than the British craft. It is likely that the bare weight, equipped but with no payload, crew or fuel, is as much as 170 tons. The prototype was launched in 1970 and production began in 1975.

Several variants have been built and differ externally in fin height, overall length, superstructure detail and defensive armament.

An Aist combat mission simulator has been introduced by the Soviet Navy to improve the ability of Aist commanders in operating the craft across sea and beach interfaces and Aist production facilities at Dekabristov, Leningrad, have been doubled.

Gus craft during exercise in eastern Baltic Sea

Training variant of Gus with raised second cabin for instructor

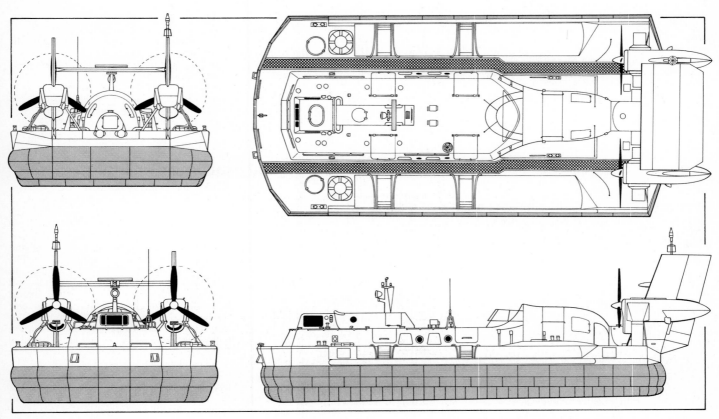
General Arrangement of Gus

A modified main engine air intake has been installed on all Soviet Navy Aists which are in service with the Baltic and Black Sea fleets. The intakes are believed to incorporate new filters to reduce the ingestion of salt water, sand and dust particles into Aist's engines and machinery, limiting the effects of salt corrosion and erosion. Due to high cushion pressure, Aist develops exceptionally heavy cushion spray, especially at low speeds.

Since delivery to the Soviet Navy, craft of this type have been employed largely as an amphibious assault landing and logistic supply craft, delivering naval infantry, its vehicles and weapons, mechanised infantry, self-propelled weapons, and main battle tanks to simulated beach-heads. Alternative military uses for amphibious craft of the Aist type would be mine countermeasures and fast patrol.

LIFT AND PROPULSION: Integrated system with motive power supplied by two NK-12MV marinised gas turbines, each of which is likely to be rated at 2400shp. Each gas turbine drives two 3·65m (12ft) diameter variable-pitch axial fans and two identical, pylon-mounted propellers, arranged in a facing pair, with the pusher propeller forward and the puller aft. The propellers, which are of the four-bladed variable- and reversible-pitch type are mounted so closely as to be virtually contraprops. Diameter of each propeller is thought to be about 6m (19ft 8¼in).

Modified engine air intakes are being installed on all Soviet Navy Aists. Several types are being tested. One modification involves the replacement of the original single, curved spine-like trunk above the longitudinal centreline by a mushroom sectioned box forward and a ribbed, shortened arch duct aft. The T-piece running athwartships across the stern superstructure between the twin fins has also been replaced by a ribbed arch duct. Alternative modifications include removing the athwartships T-piece and the shortened arch duct on the centreline leaving the mushroom sectioned box forward. Modified lift fans and new lift fan intakes are also being introduced.

Additional intakes appear to be sited in the sides of the superstructure towards the stern.

An auxiliary gas turbine is at the rear end of the combat information centre (CIC) at the back of the cabin superstructure.

CONTROLS: Deflection of twin aerodynamic rudders aft, differential propeller pitch and fore-and-aft thrust ports provide steering control. Rudders are controlled by a wheel and propeller pitch by levers. All controls are in a raised bridge well forward on the superstructure.

HULL: Built mainly in welded marine corrosion resistant aluminium alloys. Structure appears to follow standard practice for large amphibious ACVs. The main hull is formed by a buoyancy raft based on a grid of longitudinal and transverse frames which form a number of flotation compartments. Two main longitudinal vertically stiffened bulkheads run the length of the craft separating the central load deck from the outer or side-structures, which contain the gas turbines and their associated exhausts, lift fans, transmissions, auxiliary power systems and seating for half a company of troops in cabins in the forward port and starboard quarters.

Aist double bag skirt with finger fringe at base of lower loop

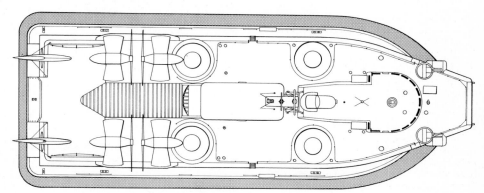

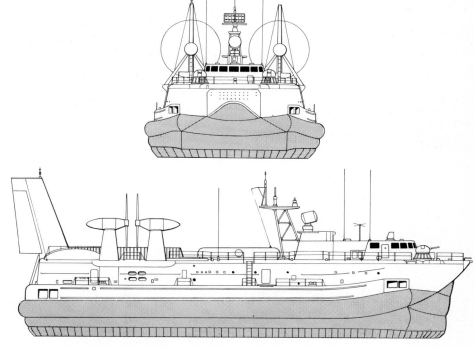

General Arrangement of Aist with modified main engine air intake

Aist in foreground has original main engine intake while second Aist has new split air intake

A full width ramp at the bow and a second at the stern, provide through loading facilities.

Typical vehicle loads include one or two T-62 or T-72 tanks or four PT-76 tanks; mobile radio trucks, armoured troop carriers, supply vehicles and ambulances.

ACCOMMODATION: Crew accommodation includes the control cabin or commander's cabin (Aist is described as being the sole warship type in the Soviet fleet in which the commander himself is responsible for steering), galley, radio room, sleeping and living quarters, engine mechanic's watch room and combat information centre (CIC). Naval infantrymen are seated in cabins on both sides of the central vehicle deck.

SKIRT: 2·5m (8ft 3in) deep double bag type in rubberised fabric with finger fringe beneath. Features include a high bow skirt line to protect the bow loading door against wave impact.

SYSTEMS, WEAPONS: Two twin 30mm fully-automatic dual-purpose mountings, controlled by Drum Tilt radar for close-in AA defence and by optical director and manual control for surface targets, including the suppression of LMG and rifle-fire during beach assaults.

DIMENSIONS (estimated)
Length overall, off cushion: 47·3m
Beam overall, off cushion: 17m
Height, control cabin: 1·98m
Length, control cabin: 10·5m
Width, bow ramp: 4·41m
    rear ramp: 4·87m
WEIGHTS (estimated)
Empty weight: 170 tons
Crew, fuel, AFVs or two main battle tanks and ½ company of naval infantry or troops: 90 tons
Max weight: 260-270 tons
PERFORMANCE (estimated)
Max speed: About 70 knots
Cruising speed: 50 knots
Endurance: About 5 hours
Range, cruising: 350n miles

Three-quarter view of Aist

Forward port quarter of Aist showing long bridge superstructure. Emblem in centre indicates amphibious ship, second insignia is combat efficiency award for operational readiness, rating craft an 'outstanding ship of the Soviet Navy'

Aist

LEBED (NATO Code Name)

Primary roles of this multi-duty hovercraft are as an amphibious initial assault landing craft and high-speed vehicle for LOTS (Logistics-over-the-shore) operations, providing Soviet naval infantry with a rapid lift capability to move personnel and equipment from the well decks of landing ships across water, beaches and marginal terrain to assembly points well above the shore line.

Smaller than both the US Navy's Jeff (A) and (B) and the Royal Navy's Vosper Thornycroft VT 2, Lebed has an overall length of about 24·4m, a gross weight of 86 tonnes and a maximum speed of 70 knots.

Two Lebeds or three Gus-type craft can be carried in the well deck of the Soviet Navy's LPD, the 13 100-ton *Ivan Rogov*, which also accommodates up to a battalion of naval infantry, 40 tanks and a range of supporting vehicles. Two Lebeds were demonstrated in South Yemen when the vessel called there on the way to the Soviet far east in 1979. The first of the 'Lebed' class was launched in 1973 and the craft entered production in 1976-77. If production rates have been similar to those of Gus (two to four units per year), it is likely that some 18 to 19 units are now operational. For use in the initial assault role, Lebeds would be pre-loaded before the *Ivan Rogov* sailed. Typical vehicle payloads include two PT-76 light amphibious tanks, two BMP-1 armoured personnel carriers, mobile radio trucks or supply vehicles up to a total weight of 35 tonnes. Design of Lebed is thought to have been undertaken by the Soviet Navy's High-Speed Ship Design Bureau in Leningrad.

LIFT AND PROPULSION: Integrated system powered by two marinised gas turbines mounted one each side of the cargo deck aft. Engines are two AI-20s, each rated at 4150shp continuous. Air for the two main engines appears to be drawn in through two rectangular, filtered intakes then fed aft through a curved spine-like trunk above the longitudinal centreline and terminating between the two fins. The intakes for the axial-flow lift fans are outboard of the two gas turbine air intakes. Each engine drives via a main gearbox and shaft a variable-pitch axial lift fan in light alloy. The fans deliver air to the cushion via a continuous peripheral loop skirt with segmented fringes. A second shaft from each main gearbox transmits power via bevel gears to a pylon-mounted four-bladed variable-pitch propulsion fan. The two propulsion fans are contained within aerodynamically shaped ducts which are partly submerged in the hull sidestructures. Apart from attenuating noise the ducts protect the fans from accidental damage. Exhaust covers are provided for both gas turbines aft at the rear of the port and starboard sidestructures.

CONTROLS: Control cabin is well forward above the port sidestructure and provides a 360-degree view. Directional control at normal operating speeds is by twin aerodynamic rudders aft of the thrust fan ducts and operating in the fan slipstreams. Differential pitch to the propulsion units augments the turning moment provided by rudder operation. Reverse thrust is applied for

Lebed   (Danish Defence)

Lebed unloading PT-76 tank

Lebed showing details of skirt at bow

Two Lebeds leave floodable well deck of Soviet Navy LPD, *Ivan Rogov*

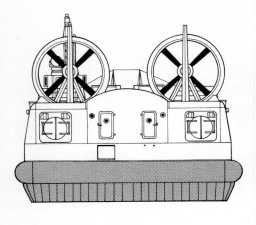

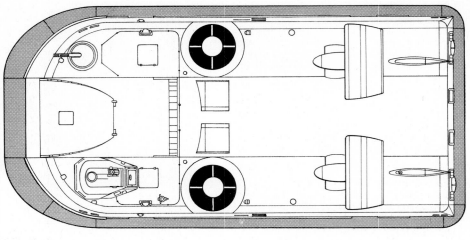

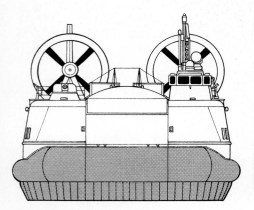

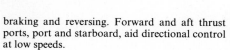

General Arrangement of Lebed

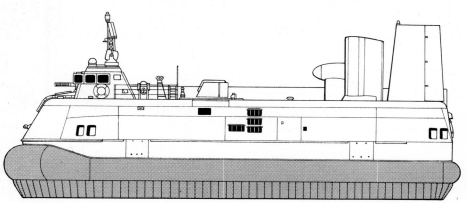

braking and reversing. Forward and aft thrust ports, port and starboard, aid directional control at low speeds.

HULL: Riveted skin and stringer structure employing alloy sheet. Structure follows standard practice for large and medium size amphibious ACVs. The main hull is formed by a buoyancy raft based on a grid of longitudinal and transverse frames which form a number of flotation compartments. Two main longitudinal vertically stiffened bulkheads run the length of the craft separating the 4·8m (15ft 9in) central load deck from the outer sidestructures which contain the gas turbines and their associated exhausts, lift fans, transmissions and auxiliary power systems. The freight deck is reinforced for the carriage of tanks, armoured troop carriers, self-propelled guns, rocket launchers and heavy vehicles. Drive-on, drive-off loading facility is provided by a full-width hydraulically-operated bow door/loading ramp. This is hinged from the base and has an overlapping hatch cover. Personnel doors are provided aft. Photographs suggest that six landing pads are built into the craft's undersurface.

SKIRT: Loop and segment type with raised hinge line at bow.

ARMAMENT: One remotely-controlled six-barrel Gatling-action 30mm cannon in barbette on forward quarter of the starboard sidestructure. Employed in conjunction with fire-control radar for close-in anti-aircraft and anti-missile defence and with optical sighting and manual control for surface targets including suppressing LMG and rifle fire during beach assaults.

It is reported that a new gun is being installed on Soviet 'Lebed' class medium air cushion landing craft. It has a 54cm long tapered barrel, with a 50mm external muzzle diameter and a 100mm diameter base at the gunhouse. As with the previous arrangement, the gun is mounted on a circular barbette on the starboard bow. A periscopic sighting device is fitted for manual operation and the gun can be elevated from about 13 degrees negative to 90 degrees vertical. The gun house is 134cm in diameter and 63cm high.

DIMENSIONS
Length overall: 24·4m (79ft 9¾in)
Beam overall: 10·8m (35ft 5¼in)

Lebed

WEIGHTS
Max all-up weight: 86 tonnes
Max payload: 35 tonnes

PERFORMANCE
Max speed, calm conditions: 70 knots
Cruising speed, calm conditions: 50 knots

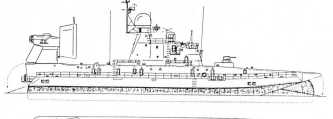

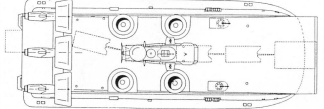

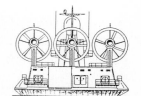

General Arrangement of Pormornik

Pomornik   *(West German Defence Ministry)*

POMORNIK (NATO Code Name)
A new Soviet hovercraft which appeared in the Baltic in the first half of 1986.
ENGINES: Three gas turbines for propulsion, two for lift fans.
DIMENSIONS
Length: 57·00m
Beam: 22·00m
Bow and stern ramps (stern on port side) at either end for roll-on, roll-off working
Propeller duct diameter: Approx 6·0m

WEIGHTS
Displacement: 350 tonnes, probably full operational condition
Disposable load: 100 tonnes estimated

UTENOK
A 70-tonne ACV powered by a single gas turbine. Two propellers give the craft a speed of 65 knots. Two Utenok-class ACVs have been built, 1982.

DIMENSIONS
Length: 26·30m
Beam: 13·00m

TSAPLYA
A 105-tonne ACV powered by two gas turbines with total power of 8000bhp, built 1982.
DIMENSIONS
Length: 26·00m
Beam: 13·00m

Pormornik   *(Federal German Navy)*

FURTHER CIVIL CRAFT

THE A M GORKI MEMORIAL MARINE INSTITUTE OF TECHNOLOGY

Mariinskiy, Iosha-Ola, USSR

S F Kirkin, *Chief Manager*

The student design group at the Mariinsky Institute of Technology has been involved in ACV development since 1970. It specialises in designing amphibious hovercraft for operation in the less accessible areas of the Soviet Union and has successfully built and tested craft commissioned by the Soviet Union's oil, gas and fisheries authorities. It has also adapted hovercraft for forestry and agricultural roles and for use in establishing communication networks.

Further studies include an investigation into soil damage caused by agricultural machines crossing farmland. The findings are likely to result in the wide scale use of hovercraft for Soviet agriculture. The Institute claims that conventional agricultural machinery is too heavy, and compacts the soil when crossing fields, whether on wheels or tracks. The subsequent disintegration of the soil structure results in a reduction in fertility and a loss of yield. It has been recommended that the size of these vehicles should be greatly reduced and, in some cases, they may be taken out of service.

Extensive use of hovercraft is seen as the answer, since their low pressure on the soil prevents any damage to its structure.

SAV SERIES
SAVR-1M
In 1977 the Institute was awarded a contract by the Soviet Gas Industry for a small snowmobile/hovercraft to carry a driver and two passengers, plus 500kg of cargo, over snow, ice and water. It also was required to travel over mud to ensure year-round operation on rivers. The first stage of the programme was the design and construction of an experimental model, designated SAVR-1.

LIFT AND PROPULSION: Separate lift and propulsion systems enable the craft to be operated at its maximum clearance height and speed depending on the surface and weather conditions. Two engines are fitted, the propulsion engine, which develops 72kW and the lift engine, developing 3kW. The propulsion engine drives a two-bladed airscrew and the lift engine an axial fan ahead of the cockpit.

WEIGHTS
Total weight: 1·8 tonnes
Load capacity: 0·8 tonnes
PERFORMANCE
Max speed, across snow: 70km/h
      across water: 40km/h

SAVR-1
Built in 1980, this production version of the SAVR-1M is intended for high-speed ferrying of personnel and urgent cargoes of up to 1·3 tonnes over roadless areas all year round.

LIFT AND PROPULSION: Cushion air is supplied by a 72kW (97hp) car engine driving two standard centrifugal fans. A clutch between the engine and fans allows the fans to be disconnected during engine startup and idling. Thrust is supplied by a 118kW (158hp) engine, aft, which drives a 2m diameter propeller. Distribution of power between cushion and thrust is varied according to terrain conditions.

CONTROLS: Directional control is by two air rudders operating in the slipstream.

HULL: Built in duralumin sheet. Buoyancy chamber of honeycomb construction.

DIMENSIONS
Length: 7·5m
Beam: 3·8m
Height, with propeller vertical: 3·3m
WEIGHTS
Total weight: 2·9 tonnes
Max useful load: 1·3 tonnes
PERFORMANCE
Cruising speed, across snow: 65km/h
      across water: 60km/h

SAVR-2
SAVR-2 made its appearance in 1982. It was designed and built to a specification prepared by the Soviet Ministry of Fisheries for a craft to serve the inaccessible water regions of North and West Siberia.

LIFT AND PROPULSION: Lift is provided by a single petrol engine aft of the crew cabin driving, via a split transverse shaft, two centrifugal fans. Thrust is supplied by a single 294kW (394hp) Ivchenko AI-14ChR air-cooled radial piston engine driving an AV-14 3-blade variable-pitch propeller. Fuel is carried in two 400-litre tanks, one for each engine. Fuel employed is standard automotive petrol. Engine compartment separated from the cabin by thermo-insulating and soundproofing partition.

CONTROLS: Craft heading is controlled by twin vertical aerodynamic rudders aft operating in the propeller slipstream. Reverse propeller pitch is employed for braking and reversing. A horizontal stabiliser is mounted between the twin rudders to adjust pitch trim. By altering its incidence angle

SAVR-1

SAVR-2

the centre of gravity can be moved along the longitudinal axis should an uneven load distribution cause it to move.

HULL: Believed to be a composite light alloy and glass fibre structure. Flotation compartments and basic raft structure filled with plastic foam make hull unsinkable.

ACCOMMODATION: Cabin seats driver with a passenger on each side. Interior lined with layer of polyurethane and pvc for thermal insulation. Passenger module seating 14 to 16 can be fitted on cargo platform aft of lift fan system.

SKIRT: Segmented skirts fore and aft. Bag-type skirts at sides. An experimental model of the SAVR-2 has two flexible side skids replacing the conventional skirt. The skids consist of a number of right-angled plates, hinged together, and fitted with removable stainless steel or polyethylene soles. The plates are fixed to the hull by lever suspension and spring shock absorbers. The area between skid and hull is covered with rubberised fabric. Flexible skids reduce to a minimum the air escaping from the cushion when travelling over rough ground, so reducing the power required from the lift system, as they follow the ground contours more accurately. When the craft is supported by the skids the pressure of the air cushion can be considerably reduced. Flexible skids provide lateral stability when the craft is stationary and when travelling over snow, ice and mud, and surfaces covered in a thin layer of water.

The least cushion pressure is required over damp, muddy terrain or land covered with a thin layer of water. To cross open water the pressure must be increased from 1000 to 1200Pa (70 to 80 per cent maximum) and over dry soil and ploughland it has to be increased to the maximum, 1400Pa.

DIMENSIONS
Length: 9·8m
Beam: 4·5m
Height: 3·7m
WEIGHTS
Total: 5900kg
Payload: 2 tonnes
PERFORMANCE
Fully laden, max speed: 50km/h
Range: 200km

SAVR-3
In 1981 the Ministry of Oil and Gas approved a programme for the construction of trackless modes of transport, building machines and pipe-laying equipment for muddy soils. Within this programme, which spans the period 1981-1985, the Institute was constructing three new transport hovercraft with the following load capacities: SAVR-3, 2 tons; SAVR-5, 5 tons; SAVR-40, 40 tons.

The SAVR-3 has the following characteristics:
ENGINE: 380kW (510hp) nominal rating, 300kW (402hp) cruise.

WEIGHT
Disposable load capacity: 3000kg
PERFORMANCE
Speed, max, over snow: 75km/h
Speed, max, over water: 50km/h
Slope (gradient) capability, sustained: 10°
   short duration: 25°

At the end of 1986 a decision was taken to build a working batch of SAVR-3 craft. In the spring of 1985 and 1986 early top dressing of winter crops with granulated fertilisers and sowing of wheat and barley in damp soil were undertaken with the first SAVR-3.

SAVR-5

Developed by the Institute in 1983 for freight transport of year round construction of pipelines on swamps. Road tests began in the first half of 1987.

The SAVR-5 is propelled by caterpillar tracks from T54B tractors, driven by a series-produced diesel as is the fan for the air cushion system. Maximum vehicle weight is 10 tonnes.

SAVR-40

A 40-tonne load-capacity air cushion vehicle for similar duties to the SAVR-5. Building of an experimental SAVR-40 was due to start at the end of 1987.

MPI-20

Impression of enlarged derivative of MPI-20

Reference: Development and Test Results of Air Cushion Vehicles Designed by The A M Gorki Mari Polytechnical Institute by S F Kirkin. Canadian Air Cushion Technology Society Conference, Montreal, October 1987.

MP-18

This snowmobile/amphibious hovercraft is designed to carry a 600kg load across snow, water and swamps. Air is fed into the cushion by a forward-mounted engine driving an axial lift fan. Cushion air is contained by a flexible polyethylene skirt forward, by a control flap aft and by rigid skids at the two sides. When partially cushion-borne, craft heading is controlled by movable front skids. Once contact with the supporting surface has ceased, steering is by an air rudder aft of the two-bladed propeller.
WEIGHTS
Payload: 600kg
Total weight: 1·2 tons
PERFORMANCE
Max speed: 75km/h

MPI-20

This cargo/passenger hovercraft was built in response to specifications prepared by the Ministry for Gas and a Siberian organisation, Sibribprom.

Built in modular form, the craft comprises fore and aft components linked by a coupling unit. It is supplied in two versions with load capacities of 3 and 5 tons.

PROJECTS

Current projects at the Institute include the design of new propellers to provide greater thrust and braking power when negotiating steeper inclines, and ride control systems to reduce heave motions when crossing undulating terrain at speed. It is also planned to build a modular hovercraft which can be built up from towed passenger and cargo platforms to suit traffic requirements.

NEPTUN CENTRAL DESIGN BUREAU
Moscow, USSR

Igor Alexandrovich Martynov, *Head of Design Bureau*
G Andreyev, *Chief Engineer*
Alexander Sergeyevich Kudryavtsev, *Chief Designer, AKVPR Project*
Valeriy V Protsenko, *Designer*
Alexander V Rubinov, *Test Engineer*

The Neptun Central Design Bureau is concerned primarily with the design of small launches, yachts and runabouts for leisure and commercial applications on Soviet inland and coastal waters.

The AKVPR-001 airjet-propelled amphibious ACV, Neptun's first attempt at designing and building a hovercraft, is intended for research only. Several variants are under development including the Barrs-1 which is destined for service in Siberia and other underdeveloped areas of the Soviet Union. A 20-seat derivative has been suggested and the bureau has a four-seater, the Gepard, on the drawing board.

AKVPR-001

This multi-purpose amphibious five-seater is being considered for use in geological expeditions, to provide communications in the Soviet far north and Siberia, in river rescue services and for emergency services when ice is forming and breaking up on inland waterways. The nomenclature AKVPR signifies 'Amphibious Air Cushion Craft, Airjet, Rivergoing'. A film of the craft taken during trials in the winter of 1977 and spring of 1978 showed the craft successfully operating across broken ice, negotiating ice hummocks at speed and crossing boggy terrain and marshes.
LIFT AND PROPULSION: Integrated lift/propulsion system. Power is supplied by a single automotive engine, aft of the cabin. Power is transmitted via a gearbox to two transverse shafts at the opposite ends of which are axial fans. Air is fed downwards into the cushion and through circular thrust outlets aft for propulsion.
CONTROLS: Craft heading is controlled by interconnected rudder vanes set in the airjet ducts aft and operated by a wheel. Airflow for braking and reversing is provided by deflecting thrust air upwards and through forward facing roof apertures.
HULL: Built mainly in corrosion resistant light alloy. Basic structure is the main hull which is divided into watertight sub-divisions for safety.
PERFORMANCE: Has achieved 50km/h (31mph) across calm water over a measured mile.

AKVPR-001

BARRS-1 (SNOW LEOPARD)

The prototype of this enlarged variant of the AKVPR-001 seats a driver and seven passengers. A cargo version carries a load of 650kg (1433lb).

A feature of the design is the use of a Kamov Ka-26 helicopter piston engine to power the integrated lift/propulsion system. The engine, the M-14V-26, has a rigidly-prescribed operational life and its use in Barrs-1 is the outcome of a search to find a terrestrial application for it once it had reached the end of its airborne career.

Barrs-1 is designed for year-round operation and can be used as a light passenger ferry, light freighter or as a service crews' launch on routes in remote and scarcely-developed regions of western and eastern Siberia, the far north and the far east, which have a thinly developed network for year-round transport of domestic goods.

Trials have shown that Barrs-1 can operate safely in wave heights of up to 0·6m (2ft) and can clear obstacles of up to 0·5m (1ft 8in) in height. It is said to 'ride superbly over sand and snow-covered ice'. During long runs it normally operates with a six-degree bow-up trim. It meets the requirements of Class 'L' in the Inland Waterway Register of the Russian Soviet Federated Socialist Republic (RSFSR).

LIFT AND PROPULSION: Integrated system powered by a single Vedeneev M-14V-26 air-cooled petrol-driven four-stroke piston engine developing 325hp at 2800rpm. Power is transmitted via a gearbox to two transverse shafts at the opposite ends of which are axial fans. Air is fed downwards into the cushion and through rectangular thrust outlets aft for propulsion. Cushion pressure, 115kg/m².

CONTROLS: Craft heading is controlled by interconnected rudder vanes set in the airjet ducts aft and operated by a wheel. Airflow for braking and reversing is provided by deflecting thrust air upwards and through forward-facing roof apertures.

HULL: Light metal alloy structure. Main hull divided into watertight sub-divisions for safety. Designed for mass production.

DIMENSIONS, EXTERNAL
Length overall: 7·43m (24ft 6in)
Width: 3·95m (13ft)
Height: 2·43m (8ft)
Draught, off cushion: 0·15m (6in)

DIMENSIONS, INTERNAL (CABIN)
Length: 3m (10ft)
Width: 2·6m (8ft 7in)
Height: 1·3m (4ft 4in)

WEIGHT
Loaded: 2·15 tons

PERFORMANCE
Max speed: 80 km/h (49·6mph)
Cruising speed: 50-60km/h (31-37·2mph)
Endurance: 5 hours

Barrs-1, an AKVPR-001 variant

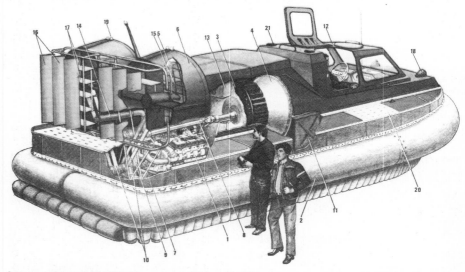

Cutaway of Gepard: (**1**) ZMZ-53 powerplant (**2**) bag skirt (**3**) fan (**4**) fan air scoop (**5**) thrust fan (**6**) duct (**7**) main (cardan) shaft (**8**) fan drive (cardan) shaft (**9**) fan transmission belts (**10**) airscrew transmission belts (**11**) fuel tank (**12**) deck cabin (**13**) water and oil radiators (**14**) exhaust pipe (manifold) (**15**) fan duct (**16**) vertical rudders (**17**) elevators (**18**) headlights (**19**) navigation and landing lights (**20**) drainage plate (**21**) ventilator heads

GEPARD (CHEETAH)

A multi-role five-seater introduced in 1981, Gepard has been designed to provide convenient, reliable and inexpensive transport in remoter areas of the Soviet Union. Specialist professions in those areas were questioned about their transport needs before finalising the design. Early in 1983 a Gepard successfully underwent trials at Andreyevskoye Lake, near the centre of the Tyuman Oblast. Gepard is due to go into quantity production.

The craft is designed to operate in an ambient air temperature range from −40°C to +40°C.

The following service life trials have been carried out:
Moscow to Lake Seleger and back: about 1000km
Along small rivers to the city of Vyshnii Volochek and back: about 1000km
Moscow by the Volga-Baltic route to Leningrad: about 2000km
Moscow to Volgograd on the lower Volga River: about 3500km

LIFT AND PROPULSION: Integrated system, powered by a 120hp ZMZ-53 lorry engine (a widely used engine), aft of the cabin. Output is transmitted to a centrifugal lift fan (0·97m diameter with grp blades) and a duct-mounted, multi-bladed 0·95m diameter glass-fibre propeller for thrust, the blade leading edges being protected with stainless steel sheaths. Power transmission is by toothed-belt drives, and a clutch is provided between the engine and propeller and fan drives.

CONTROLS: Directional control by interconnected rudder vanes hinged to the rear of the

The five-seat, 42-knot Gepard powered by a single 120hp ZMZ-53 petrol engine

Puma twin petrol-engine hovercraft designed by the Neptun Central Design Bureau, Moscow

thrust fan ducts and operated by a wheel. Horizontal vane surfaces are also provided.
HULL: Corrosion-resistant light alloy hull. Moulded pigmented glass-fibre cabin superstructure.
DIMENSIONS
Length overall: 7·30m
Width overall: 3·80m
Height overall: 2·80m

Cabin width: 1·50m
Cabin height: 1·40m
WEIGHT
Loaded weight: 1·7 tons?
PERFORMANCE
Max speed, fully loaded, calm water: 77km/h, 42 knots
Endurance: 5 hours
Rise height: 0·40m

PUMA
On the basis of experience with the Gepard type air cushion vehicle, the Neptun Central Design Bureau has developed the Puma, with two ZMZ-53 120hp petrol engines. Three versions are planned: an ambulance/first aid craft, a 16-seat passenger version and a craft for harbour officials. Prototypes of the first two versions have been built and trials conducted.

UFA AVIATION INSTITUTE
Tyumen, USSR

F Nuriakhmetov, *Head of Propulsion Systems Group*
I Shalin, *Design Engineer*
S Komarov, *Candidate of Science (Technical)*

Designers at the UFA Aviation Institute have been active in ACV development since the mid-1960s when they exhibited an experimental craft, named Skat, with a circular planform at the USSR National Economy Achievements Exhibition in Moscow.

TAIFUN
A multi-duty amphibious vehicle designed for all-weather, 24-hour operation. Please see *Jane's High-Speed Marine Craft and Air Cushion Vehicles 1987* for details.

VOSTOK CENTRAL DESIGN BUREAU
Leningrad, USSR

V D Rubtsov, *Chief Designer*
B V Baymistruk
Ye A Meschchanov
S F Gorbachevskiy

KLEST
Development of this small utility hovercraft began at the Vostok Central Design Bureau in 1979. Trials of the prototype, named *Metan 1*, were undertaken in the Gulf of Finland and at Bolshaya Nevka, Leningrad in summer 1981. An integrated lift/propulsion system is employed, powered by a single Volga Automotive Plant (VAZ) automotive engine. Power is transmitted to two ducted propulsion fans and a single lift fan. The fans are scaled-down and modified versions of conventional industrial fans used in Soviet coalmines. Parts for the engine and servicing can be provided by any Zhiguli service station, a network of which now exists in the Soviet Union. Series

Klest

production is proposed. Maximum speed is 80km/h (50mph).

UNITED KINGDOM

AIR VEHICLES LIMITED
Head Office and Factory: Unit 4, Three Gates Road, Cowes, Isle of Wight, England

Telephone: (0983) 293194
Telex: 86513 HVWORK G
Telefax: (0983) 294704

C D J Bland, *Director*
C B Eden, *Director*
A Mosely, *Director*

Air Vehicles Limited was founded in 1968 and has concentrated on the development of small commercial hovercraft and various systems and special equipment for larger craft.

The company's main products are the Tiger 4, Tiger 16 and Tiger 40; customers include the British, French and Canadian Ministries of Defence, the People's Republic of China, the Nigerian Police, the Bahrain Ministry of the Interior and the Republic of Singapore Navy.

Air Vehicles Limited is approved by the Civil Aviation Authority and undertakes modifications

to larger craft. These have included flat-deck freight conversions of the BHC SR.N5 and SR.N6 hovercraft, power-assisted rudder packs for both types, and the conversion of an SR.N6 Mk 1S for high-speed hydrographic surveying.

The company is a leader in the application of low-speed ducted propeller systems and following the success of the propeller duct fitted to an SR.N6, two duct units were supplied to the USA for a military hovercraft.

Air Vehicles Limited worked with British Hovercraft Corporation and Hovertravel Limited to produce the diesel amphibious hovercraft, the AP1-88. In the second half of the 1970s Air Vehicles produced a conceptual feasibility study for a four-engined diesel-powered hovercraft to meet the requirements of Hovertravel Ltd. The eventual requirement of Hovertravel led to the design of the BHC AP1-88 for which Air Vehicles undertook much of the detail design work.

Hydrographic Survey Craft

An SR.N6 Mk 1S has been modified for high-speed hydrographic surveying. The cabin is fitted with an air-conditioned computer room, and a control area for the survey crew. External modifications are flat side decks to ease crew movement; two 12·5kVA generators and two hydraulically operated 'fish', fitted with depth transducers, which are lowered into the water when taking depth measurements. The craft can operate at 25 knots while measuring depth and records its position by means of a Trisponder system.

A similar conversion has also been provided on a Tiger 12 craft. The cabin is converted to carry the recording instruments and is fully air-conditioned. A 2·5kW power supply is provided and the single transducer is mounted on a hydraulically deployed 'fish' at the front of the craft. Positioning is again by Trisponder and surveying is carried out at speeds up to 20 knots.

Operations from the shore in shallow areas are easily undertaken without requiring any prepared docking facilities.

TIGER 4

The Tiger 4 is a lightweight four-seat hovercraft which can operate at speeds of up to 30 knots over a wide variety of surfaces. Costing about the same as a four-seat all-wheel-drive vehicle or shallow water powerboat, it can often take the place of both, and operates economically in areas where neither can go.

The Tiger 4 was first introduced in 1973 by Michael Pinder, and the concept has proven itself worldwide in a variety of military and private uses. The latest design has a unique inflatable hull,

Hydraulically-operated transducer carrier for high-speed hydrographic survey on SR.N6 Mk 1S

patented skirt, high power engine with electric start, high thrust ducted fan, low noise level, spacious and comfortable cockpit and many detailed refinements.

LIFT AND PROPULSION: The integrated lift and propulsion system has a single axial fan operating in a glass-fibre duct and driven by a high torque, toothed belt transmission. The 493cc twin cylinder, air-cooled 2-stroke engine has a high power-to-weight ratio and an excellent reputation for reliability.

CONTROLS: The simple, centrally-mounted controls can be operated by either front seat occupant.

HULL: The four-compartment inflatable hull is made from Hypalon/nylon material. As well as

providing massive peripheral buoyancy which gives a stable working platform, it also acts as an impact absorbing fender.

COCKPIT: The spacious cockpit has comfortable seats which can be laid flat for sleeping or removed for carrying goods. The wrap-around windscreen gives good protection and is made of unbreakable polycarbonate.

SKIRT: The latest type of loop/segment skirt gives good stability, long life and excellent sealing with minimum drag on all types of surface. There are 100 separate segments which are easily attached and quickly replaced in the event of wear or damage. The possibility of damage is reduced by the weak link attachments. The neoprene/nylon material is suitable for all climatic conditions and has excellent wear and tear characteristics.

DIMENSIONS
Length: 5·10m
Width: 2·38m
Transport width: 2·36m
Height: 1·27m

WEIGHTS
Empty: 225kg
Max: 550kg
Disposable load: 325kg

PERFORMANCE
Max speed, over water: 30 knots
  over land: 28 knots
Fuel consumption, average: 11 litres/h

TIGER 12

The standard production craft has 12 seats (including the driver's) and the non-structural cabin top can be removed to suit various requirements. Fully amphibious, the craft can operate over a variety of surfaces such as mud, ice, sand and shallow water.

LIFT AND PROPULSION: Motive power for the integrated lift/propulsion system is provided by a single AMC 5900cc (360in³) petrol engine delivering 180hp at 3600rpm. The engine output is transferred to a 12-blade centrifugal lift fan and a 1·37m (4ft 6in) diameter, four-blade, ducted propeller through a toothed belt system. Normal fuel capacity is 213 litres (47 Imperial gallons).

CONTROLS: Multiple rudders hinged at the aft end of the propeller duct provide directional control. Elevators provide trim and, when raised fully, assist braking by reducing thrust. A water ballast system is used to adjust trim in pitch for varying load states.

HULL: Superstructure and all bulkheads are of marine grade aluminium sheet welded to form a strong rigid box structure. Side members are inflatable, giving additional buoyancy and protection for the craft when mooring. By deflating the side members the vehicle can be trailed behind any

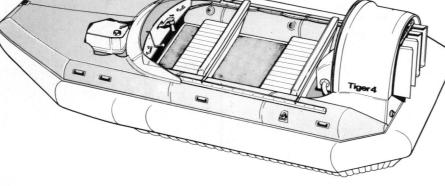

Tiger 4 hovercraft

Tiger 4

large car or small truck. Built-in jacking system provided for loading and maintenance.

ACCOMMODATION: Enclosed cabin for driver and up to 11 passengers. Access via sliding doors, one port, one starboard. Driver's seat forward right; navigator's forward left. Adequate space for radar, radios and navigation equipment ahead of these positions.

SKIRT: Pressurised bag type with separate segments. Inflatable sides and skirt attached to craft with quick-release piano hinges.

SYSTEMS, ELECTRICAL: 12V dc, negative earth, with engine driven 35A alternator and 60Ah battery.

DIMENSIONS
Length: 8·0m (26ft 2in)
Width, inflated: 3·85m (12ft 6in)
Transport width: 2·44m (8ft)
Height, off cushion: 2·26m (7ft 5in)
Hoverheight: 50-55cm (20-22in)
Cabin, length: 3·9m (12ft 9in)
    width: 1·8m (6ft)

WEIGHTS
Empty: 1910kg (4200lb)
Max: 2865kg (6300lb)
Disposable load: 910kg (2000lb)

PERFORMANCE
Max speed: 65km/h (35 knots)
Cruise speed: 46km/h (25 knots)
Fuel consumption, cruise: 27-45 litres/h (6-10 Imperial gallons/h)
    max: 70 litres/h (15·5 Imperial gallons/h)

WEATHER LIMITATIONS
Max conditions: 46km/h (25 knot) wind
    1·25m (4ft) sea

TIGER 16

The Tiger 16 is a fully amphibious hovercraft capable of carrying 16 people over a variety of terrain including shallow water, sand, mud and ice. The first craft was completed at the end of 1985.

LIFT AND PROPULSION: Various engine options are available according to duty and include the Deutz BF6L 913C air-cooled diesel rated at 190hp at 2500rpm and the Deutz BF8L 513. The engine power is transmitted via a toothed belt drive system to a 12-blade centrifugal lift fan and a 1·5m diameter four-blade ducted propeller. The propeller duct is designed to give efficient air entry and the outlet is shaped to provide for larger control surfaces. The propeller is designed to give high thrust per horsepower with low noise and is fitted with full length stainless steel leading edge protection.

CONTROLS: Four large rudders fitted at the propeller duct outlet provide directional control. Five elevators control pitch trim and when fully

Crash rescue Tiger 12 fitted with six 36-man life rafts

Tiger 12 with high-speed, hydrographic 'fish' deployed in the water

One of two Tiger 12s operated by British Army

Tiger 16 with forward cabin and open well-deck

raised shut off the thrust. A skirt shift system provides rapid control of trim in pitch and roll.

BALLAST AND FUEL SYSTEM: A fuel ballast system adjusts the craft trim in pitch, transferring fuel to the bow or stern of the craft. The main engine fuel tank is positioned amidships and is linked to the ballast system via a manually operated valve so that ballast fuel can be used to increase duration.

CAPACITIES

Engine fuel tank: 340 litres (75 Imperial gallons)
Ballast system normal: 225 litres (49 Imperial gallons)
Ballast system full: 450 litres (98 Imperial gallons)
Max long range capacity: 790 litres (173 Imperial gallons)

HULL AND ACCOMMODATION: The hull is a fully welded, light but robust, aluminium structure and offers a variety of options in the cabin layout. Seat mounting/load tie down rails allow easy conversion of the cabin for passenger or load carrying duties. The cabin options give any combination from fully trimmed and enclosed to a simple open workboat.

Rigid side bodies provide a convenient work platform when surveying and a carrying area for long loads. For transportation the side decks are easily removed.

An inflatable ring around the periphery of the craft provides for coming alongside and a 'soft edge' when working off the side decks.

SKIRT SYSTEM: An open loop and segment skirt is fitted. The skirt assembly is attached to the craft using an aluminium piano hinge. Segments are individually and easily replaced. A skirt shift system is fitted.

ELECTRICAL SYSTEM: 24V dc negative earth with engine-driven 45A alternator and 90Ah batteries.

DIMENSIONS

Length: 11·27m
Width: 4·1m
Transport width: 2·3m
Height, static to top of mast: 3·2m
Hoverheight: 0·65m
Cabin, length: 5·00m
        width: 1·80m

WEIGHTS

Empty: 2500kg
Payload: 1500kg

PERFORMANCE

Max speed: 33 knots
Cruise speed: 25 knots
Fuel consumption, cruise: 45 litres/h (10 Imperial gallons/h)
        max: 65 litres/h (15 Imperial gallons/h)

WEATHER LIMITATIONS

Max weather conditions: 46km/h (25 knot) wind 1·25m (4ft) sea

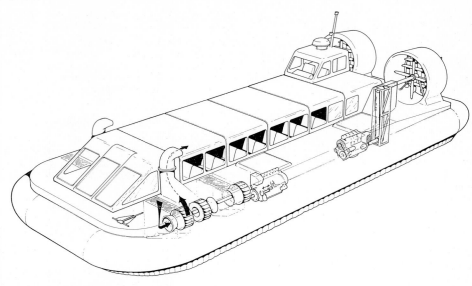

Tiger 40 passenger ferry design

TIGER 40

The Tiger 40 project is a development of the Tiger 12 and Tiger 16. It uses the same design approach and incorporates many of the features and components of the smaller craft.

The propulsion and lift machinery are fitted in the side bodies leaving the centre of the craft clear for a variety of layouts thus ensuring a well balanced craft at any load state. Different cabin modules fit the craft for a number of roles, ranging from workboat and patrol craft to cargo carrying and passenger transport.

LIFT SYSTEM: The lift system supplies pressurised air to lift the craft and power the bow thruster. Power is supplied by two air-cooled diesel engines mounted in the hull side bodies each driving three co-axial, centrifugal fans via a toothed-belt transmission system. The front fan delivers air to the bow thruster only and the rear two supply the skirt system. The fans are 0·84m diameter and manufactured in aluminium alloy and are all similar except with regard to direction of rotation.

Two BF6L 913C air-cooled, turbocharged and intercooled diesel engines supply the lift system power. Each engine has a capacity of 6·9 litres (421in³) and is rated at 141kW (190hp) at 2500rpm. Both engines and the complete lift fan assembly are rubber mounted.

BOW THRUSTERS: Bow thrusters at the forward end of the craft augment the directional control system. The rotatable thruster ducts are situated one on each side of the craft and are supplied with air from the forward fans. Each fan is driven by, but is isolated from, its respective lift system. Each duct is operated by a dc servo motor controlled from the pilot's position by a simple rotary switch. The bow thrusters can be operated ahead or astern and are provided with isolation switches.

THRUST SYSTEM: The thrust system is powered by two air-cooled diesel engines each driving a Robert Trillo Ltd 1·83m (6ft) diameter four-blade, fixed-pitch, ducted propeller via a toothed-belt transmission system. The engines and transmission frames are mounted in the hull side bodies and the ducted propeller assemblies are mounted on top of the athwartship beam at the rear of the craft.

Two BF8L 513 air-cooled, turbocharged diesel engines supply the thrust system power. Each engine has a capacity of 12·7 litres (779in³) and is rated at 235kW (315hp) at 2300rpm. Both engines and the thrust system assemblies including the propeller ducts are rubber mounted. Four rudder blades at the rear of each propeller duct provide main directional control. Three elevator blades inside each propeller duct give rapid control of craft pitch trim.

CONTROLS: Multiple rudders hinged at the aft end of the twin propeller ducts provide directional control. Elevators provide rapid pitch trim and the bow thruster units provide reverse thrust, a righting moment when cornering or in a beam wind, and accurate control at slow speed. The bow thrusters also supplement the forward thrust at speed.

Tiger 40 well-deck version as constructed by Singapore Shipbuilding and Engineering Ltd

HULL: The hull is in three sections, two side bodies and a central deck, all constructed in welded marine grade aluminium alloy. The two side bodies form the main longitudinal beams and house the engines, transmission assemblies, lift fans and propulsion units. The central deck assembly comprises floor and buoyancy compartments, with box members at the bow and stern.

ACCOMMODATION: The Tiger 40 layout gives complete flexibility for any duty. The clear deck allows various configurations without major changes in the basic structure, from a simple open workboat to a full passenger cabin. Cabin modules can be isolated from the primary structure to reduce cabin noise levels.

SKIRT SYSTEM: A tapered, open loop, segmented skirt is fitted. The hoverheight at the bow is 1m (3·28ft) and segment changes and skirt

maintenance are all easily carried out without lifting the craft.

BALLAST AND FUEL SYSTEM: A four-tank, diagonally-linked ballast system adjusts the trim in pitch and roll for various loads or weather conditions. The system uses diesel fuel and is linked to the engine fuel tanks to give extended duration if required.

The engine fuel system consists of two tanks fitted amidships, one port and one starboard. Each tank supplies the lift and propulsion engine on the same side.

CAPACITIES

Engine fuel tanks: Two 450 litres each (99 Imperial gallons each)

Ballast system normal: 450 litres (99 Imperial gallons)

Ballast system full: 900 litres (198 Imperial gallons)

Max long range capacity: 1800 litres (396 Imperial gallons)

DIMENSIONS

Length: 16·5m (54ft 3in)
Width: 6·0m (19ft 8in)
Height (off cushion) to top of mast: 5·24m (17ft)
Hoverheight, average: 0·8m (2ft 9in)

WEIGHTS

Payload: 3000kg (6615lb)

PERFORMANCE

Max speed: 38-40 knots
Endurance: 5 hours at cruising speed

WEATHER LIMITATIONS

Max weather conditions: 46km/h (25 knot) wind 1·5m (5ft) sea

BRITISH HOVERCRAFT CORPORATION (BHC)

(A Division of Westland Aerospace, East Cowes, Isle of Wight, England)

Telephone: (0983) 294101
Telex: 86761 G
Telefax: (0983) 291006

C C Gustar, *Managing Director, Westland Aerospace*
P Starke, *General Manager*

The roots of the Corporation extend back to the world's first hovercraft, the SR.N1, which was built by Saunders Roe Limited in 1959, just prior to its being taken over by Westland.

BHC was formed in 1966, uniting the hovercraft interests of Westland and Vickers and also involving NRDC.

The corporation deals with a wide variety of applications of the air cushion principle, the emphasis being on the development and production of amphibious hovercraft.

The world's first full-scale hovercraft production line was established at East Cowes in 1964.

Since then BHC has produced 10- to 17-ton SR.N6 craft, 50-ton BH.7 craft and 200- to 300-ton SR.N4 craft. The 39-ton AP1-88 is the current production craft.

Six SR.N4 class craft are in service, as passenger/car ferries on the Dover to Boulogne/Calais routes, with Hoverspeed, the cross-Channel operator, formed as the result of the merger between Hoverlloyd Limited and Seaspeed in October 1981.

Four of the craft are to Mk 2 standard and two have been converted from Mk 1 to Mk 3 (Super 4) standard. By the end of 1987 the SR.N4's had carried 30 million passengers.

One BH.7 has been in service with the Royal Navy and six with the Iranian Navy. Four of the Iranian BH.7s have been refurbished by BHC at Cowes.

Latest variant of the BH.7 is the Mk 20 which has been 'stretched', re-engined and incorporates the latest skirt technology. Power is supplied by an Allison marinised gas turbine flat rated to give 6000shp at ambient temperatures up to 40°C. Mine countermeasures, fast strike, patrol and logistics variants are available.

Military and general duty variants of the SR.N6 hovercraft are now in service with the Egyptian

Navy, Iraqi Navy, Iranian Navy, and the Canadian and Saudi Arabian Coast Guard.

SR.N6's have been operated in Africa, Canada, Denmark, Finland, India, South America and the Middle and Far East, logging well over 250 000 operating hours.

Commercial variants of the SR.N6 are in service with the Department of Transport, Canada, and Hoverwork Limited. The SR.N6 has also been used for general-purpose roles including hydrographic and seismic survey, freighting and search and rescue duties.

The latest addition to the BHC range is the AP1-88 diesel-powered, general-purpose hovercraft. Built in welded aluminium alloy employing shipbuilding techniques, it combines a 10-ton payload with a performance equal to that of the SR.N6. AP1-88's are in passenger ferry service in Australia, between Denmark and Sweden, in Norway and in the UK.

SR.N4 Mk 2

The SR.N4 is the world's largest commercial hovercraft and is designed for passenger/vehicle ferry operations on stage lengths of up to 185km (100n miles) on coastal water routes.

LIFT AND PROPULSION: Power is supplied

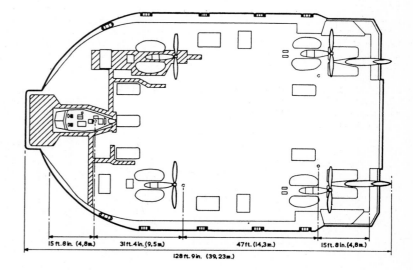

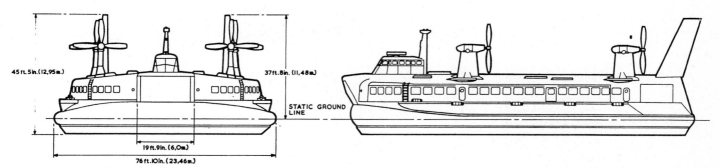

General Arrangement of the BHC SR.N4

by four 3400shp Rolls-Royce Marine Proteus free-turbine, turboshaft engines located in pairs at the rear of the craft on either side of the vehicle deck. Each has a maximum rating of 4250shp but usually operates at 3400shp when cruising. Each engine is connected to one of four identical propeller/fan units, two forward and two aft. The propulsion propellers, made by Hawker Siddeley Dynamics (now part of British Aerospace), are of the four-bladed, variable and reversible pitch type, 5·79m (19ft) in diameter. The lift fans, made by BHC, are of the 12-bladed centrifugal type, 3·5m (11ft 6in) in diameter.

Since the gear ratios between the engine, fan and propeller are fixed, the power distribution can be altered by varying the propeller pitch and hence changing the speed of the system, which accordingly alters the power absorbed by the fixed pitch fan. The power absorbed by the fan can be varied from almost zero shp (ie boating with minimum power) to 2100shp, within the propeller and engine speed limitations. A typical division on maximum cruise power would be 2000shp to the propeller and 1150shp to the fan; the remaining 250shp can be accounted for by engine power fall-off due to the turbine rpm drop, transmission losses and auxiliary drives.

The drive shafts from the engine consist of flanged light-alloy tubes approximately 2·28m (7ft 6in) long supported by steady bearings and connected by self-aligning couplings. Shafting to the rear propeller/fan units is comparatively short, but to the forward units is approximately 18·27m (60ft).

The main gearbox of each unit comprises a spiral bevel reduction gear, with outputs at the top and bottom of the box to the vertical propeller and fan drive shafts respectively. The design of the vertical shafts and couplings is similar to the main transmission shafts, except that the shafts above the main gearbox are of steel instead of light alloy to transmit the much greater torque loads to the propeller. This gearbox is equipped with a power take-off for an auxiliary gearbox with drives for pressure and scavenge lubricating oil pumps, and also a hydraulic pump for the pylon and fin steering control.

The upper gearbox, mounted on top of the pylon, turns the propeller drive through 90 degrees and has a gear ratio of 1·16:1. This gearbox has its own self-contained lubricating system.

Engines and auxiliaries are readily accessible for maintenance from inside the craft, while engine, propellers, pylons and all gearboxes can be removed for overhaul without disturbing the main structure.

The fan rotates on a pintle which is attached to the main structure. The assembly may be detached and removed inboard onto the car deck without disturbing the major structure.

CONTROLS: The craft control system enables the thrust lines and pitch angles of the propellers to be varied either collectively or differentially. The fins and rudders move in step with the aft pylons. The pylons, fins and rudders move through ±35 degrees, ±30 degrees and ±40 degrees respectively.

Demand signals for pylon and fin angles are transmitted electrically from the commander's controls. These are compared with the pylon or fin feed-back signals and the differences are then amplified to actuate the hydraulic jacks mounted at the base of the pylon or fin structure. Similar electro-hydraulic signalling and feed-back systems are used to control propeller pitches.

The commander's controls include a rudder bar which steers the craft by pivoting the propeller pylons differentially.

For example, if the right foot is moved forward, the forward pylons move clockwise, viewed from above, and the aft pylons and fins move anti-clockwise, thus producing a turning movement to starboard. The foregoing applies with positive thrust on the propellers, but if negative thrust is applied, as in the case of using the propellers for braking, the pylons and fins are automatically turned to opposing angles, thus maintaining the turn. A wheel mounted on a control column enables the commander to move the pylons and

Craft built	Yard No	Operator	Route
BHC SR.N4 Mk 1 *Swift* (GH 2004) in service 1969 modified to Mk 2 in 1973	002	Hoverspeed Ltd	Dover to Calais and Boulogne
BHC SR.N4 Mk 1 *Sure* (GH 2005) in service 1969 modified to Mk 2 in 1974	003	Hoverspeed Ltd	Dover to Calais and Boulogne
BHC SR.N4 Mk 1 *Sir Christopher* (GH 2008) in service 1972 modified to Mk 2 in 1974	005	Hoverspeed Ltd	Dover to Calais and Boulogne
BHC SR.N4 Mk 2 *The Prince of Wales* (GH 2054) in service 1977	006	Hoverspeed Ltd	Dover to Calais and Boulogne

SR.N4 Mk 2 *Swift*, a conversion of the Mk 1

SR.N4 Mk 2 *The Prince of Wales*

SR.N4 Mk 2 *Sure*

fins in unison to produce a drift to port or starboard as required. The control of the distribution of power between each propeller and fan is by propeller pitch lever. The pitch of all four propellers can be adjusted collectively over a limited range by a fore-and-aft movement of the control wheel.

HULL: Construction is primarily of high strength, aluminium-clad, aluminium alloy, suitably protected against the corrosive effects of sea water.

The basic structure is the buoyancy chamber, built around a grid of longitudinal and transverse frames, which form 24 watertight sub-divisions for safety. The design ensures that even a rip from end-to-end would not cause the craft to sink or overturn. The reserve buoyancy is 175%, the total available buoyancy amounting to more than 550 tons.

Top and bottom surfaces of the buoyancy chamber are formed by sandwich construction panels bolted onto the frames, the top surface being the vehicle deck. Panels covering the central 4·9m (16ft) section of the deck are reinforced to carry unladen coaches, or commercial vehicles up to 9 tons gross weight (maximum axle load 5900kg (13 000lb)), while the remainder are designed solely to carry cars and light vehicles (maximum axle load 2040kg (4500lb)). An articulated loading ramp 5·5m (18ft) wide, which can be lowered to ground level, is built into the bows, while doors extending the full width of the centre deck are provided at the aft end.

Similar grid construction is used on the elevated passenger-carrying decks and the roof, where the panels are supported by deep transverse and longitudinal frames. The buoyancy chamber is joined to the roof by longitudinal walls to form a stiff fore-and-aft structure. Lateral bending is taken mainly by the buoyancy tanks. All horizontal surfaces are of pre-fabricated sandwich panels with the exception of the roof, which is of skin and stringer panels.

Double curvature has been avoided other than in the region of the air intakes and bow. Each fan air intake is bifurcated and has an athwartships bulkhead at both front and rear, supporting a beam carrying the transmission main gearbox and the propeller pylon. The all-moving fins and rudders behind the aft pylons pivot on pintles just ahead of the rear bulkhead.

The fans deliver air to the cushion via a peripheral fingered bag skirt.

The material used for both bags and fingers is nylon, coated with neoprene and/or natural rubber, the fingers and cones being made from a heavier weight material than the trunks.

ACCOMMODATION: The basic manning requirement is for a commander, an engineer/radio operator and a radar operator/navigator. A seat is provided for a fourth crew member or a crew member in training. The remainder of the crew, ie those concerned with passenger service or car handling, are accommodated in the main cabins. The arrangement may be modified to suit individual operator's requirements.

The control cabin, which provides nearly 360-degree vision, is entered by one of two ways. The normal method, when the cars are arranged in four lanes, is by a hatch in the cabin floor, reached by a ladder from the car deck. When heavy vehicles are carried on the centre section, or if for some other reason the ladder has to be retracted, a door in the side of the port forward passenger cabin gives access to a ladder leading onto the main cabin roof. From the roof a door gives access into the control cabin.

The craft currently in service carry 282 passengers and 37 cars.

The car deck occupies the large central area of the craft, with large stern doors and a bow ramp providing a drive-on/drive-off facility.

Separate side doors give access to the passenger cabins which flank the car deck. The outer cabins have large windows which extend over the full length of the craft. The control cabin is sited centrally and forward on top of the superstructure to give maximum view.

DIMENSIONS
EXTERNAL
Overall length: 39·68m (130ft 2in)
Overall beam: 23·77m (78ft)
Overall height on landing pads: 11·48m (37ft 8in)
Skirt depth: 2·44m (8ft)
INTERNAL
Passenger/vehicle floor area: 539m² (5800ft²)
Vehicle deck headroom-centre line: 3·43m (11ft 3in)
Bow ramp door aperture size (height × width): 3·51 × 5·48m (11ft 6in × 18ft)

SR.N4 Mk II forward passenger cabin, starboard side   *(Hoverspeed Ltd)*

Craft built	Yard No	Operator	Route
BHC SR.N4 Mk 1 *The Princess Margaret* (GH 2006) in service 1968, modified to Mk 3 in 1979	001	Hoverspeed Ltd	Dover to Calais and Boulogne
BHC SR.N4 Mk 1 *The Princess Anne* (GH 2007) in service 1969, modified to Mk 3 in 1978	004	Hoverspeed Ltd	Dover to Calais and Boulogne

SR.N4 Mk 3 (Super 4), *The Princess Anne*

SR.N4 Mk 3 (Super 4), *The Princess Anne*

Stern door aperture size (height × width): 3·51 × 9·45m (11ft 6in × 31ft)
WEIGHT/CAPACITY
Normal gross: 200 tons
Fuel capacity: 20 456 litres (4500 Imperial gallons)
PERFORMANCE (at normal gross weight at 15°C)
Max water speed over calm water, zero wind (cont power rating): 70 knots
Average service water speed: 40-60 knots
Normal stopping distance from 50 knots: 480m (525 yards)

Endurance at max cont power on 2800 Imperial gallons: 2·5 hours
Negotiable gradient from standing start: 1 : 11

SR.N4 Mk 3 (SUPER 4)
The Super 4 differs from earlier Marks of the SR.N4 primarily in that it is 16·76m (55ft) longer, increasing the overall length to 56·38m (185ft) with a beam of 28·04m (92ft).

Modification of an SR.N4 Mk 1 to Super 4 standard necessitates adding a new 16·76m (55ft) section amidships, widening the existing superstructure and strengthening the original bow and stern halves to accept the increased stresses resulting from the 40 per cent increase in length. The propeller pylons are raised to allow 6·4m (21ft) diameter propellers to be fitted, the transmission systems are realigned and four uprated 3800shp Rolls-Royce Marine Proteus gas turbines are installed.

A more efficient low-pressure-ratio skirt system with larger fingers is fitted, giving a mean air cushion depth of 2·7m (9ft). Passenger cabin trim and seating have been completely revised and sound-proofing increased.

Compared with the SR.N4 Mk 1, the Super 4 has a 70 per cent greater revenue earning capability, but costs only about 15 per cent more to operate. The increased length and advanced skirt system give both a higher performance in adverse weather and greatly improved ride comfort for the passengers.

Craft handling and skirt behaviour have proved completely satisfactory over the entire weight range from 212 to 300 tons in sea conditions up to Force 8 to 9. Measurements taken in the passenger cabins of acceleration forces show a three-fold improvement in ride comfort over the SR.N4 Mk 2. The uprated Rolls-Royce Proteus gas turbines have been trouble-free and the new propellers have substantially reduced external noise when operating into and out of hovercraft terminals.

Super 4 has a payload of 418 passengers and 60 vehicles, a laden weight of 300 tons and a top speed in excess of 65 knots.

LIFT AND PROPULSION: Motive power is supplied by four Rolls-Royce Marine Proteus Type 15M/529 free-turbine turboshaft engines, located in pairs at the rear of the craft on either side of the vehicle deck. Each engine is rated at 3800shp continuous under ISA conditions and is connected to one of four identical propeller/fan units, two forward and two aft. The propellers, made by British Aerospace Dynamics, are of four-bladed, controllable-pitch type D258/485A/2. The lift fans, made by BHC, are of 12-bladed centrifugal type, 3·5m (11ft 6in) in diameter. Maximum fuel tankage, 28·45 tonnes; normal fuel allowing for ballast transfer, 18·29 tonnes.

AUXILIARY POWER: Two Lucas turboshaft engines driving 55kVA 200V, 400Hz Lucas alternators.

DIMENSIONS

Length overall: 56·38m (185ft)

Beam, hardstructure: 23·16m (76ft)

Height overall, on landing pads: 11·43m (37ft 6in)

Vehicle deck, SR.N4 Mk 3 (Super 4)

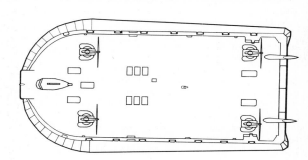

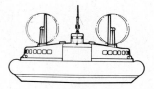

General Arrangement of SR.N4 Mk 3 (Super 4)

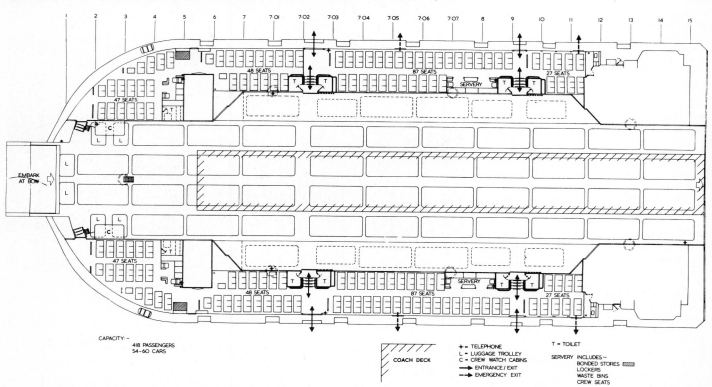

CAPACITY:-
418 PASSENGERS
54-60 CARS

COACH DECK

+ - TELEPHONE
L - LUGGAGE TROLLEY
C - CREW WATCH CABINS
→ ENTRANCE / EXIT
--→ EMERGENCY EXIT

T - TOILET

SERVERY INCLUDES:-
BONDED STORES
LOCKERS
WASTE BINS
CREW SEATS

Layout of vehicle deck and passenger cabins on SR.N4 Mk 3 (Super 4)

Bow ramp door aperture size,
  Height: 3·5m (11ft 6in)
  Width: 5·48m (18ft)
Stern door aperture size,
  Height: 3·51m (11ft 6in)
  Width: 9·45m (31ft)
Car deck area: 631m² (6790ft²)
WEIGHTS
Max laden: 300 tons
Max disposable load: 112 tons
Typical fuel load: 20 tons
Payload: 54-60 cars, 418 passengers
PERFORMANCE
Typical cruise water speeds:
Calm (2ft waves, 5 knots wind): 60-65 knots
Moderate (5ft waves, 20 knots wind): 50-55 knots
Rough (8ft waves, 27 knots wind): 35-45 knots
Endurance per ton of fuel: 0·23 hour

SR.N6

Craft built

SR.N6 Mk's 1 to 5	42
SR.N6 Mk 6	7
SR.N6 Mk 8	8

Designed primarily as a fast ferry for operation in sheltered waters, the SR.N6 Mk 1 can accommodate either 38 passengers or 3 tons of freight.

Fully amphibious, it can operate from relatively unsophisticated bases above the high water mark, irrespective of tidal state.

Directional control is achieved by twin rudders and a thrust port system. Two manually actuated elevators provide pitch trim at cruising speed.

SR.N6's have been in regular civil operations since 1965. Operators include Hoverwork Limited and the Canadian Coast Guard.

Military variants are in service with the Egyptian Navy, Iraqi Navy (type Mk 6C), Iranian Navy and the Saudi Arabian Frontier Force and Coast Guard.

LIFT AND PROPULSION: Power for the integrated lift/propulsion system is provided by a Rolls-Royce Marine Gnome gas turbine with a maximum continuous rating at 15°C of 900shp. This drives a BHC 12-blade centrifugal 2·13m (7ft) diameter lift fan, and a Dowty Rotol four-blade variable pitch 2·74m (9ft) diameter propeller for propulsion.

DIMENSIONS
EXTERNAL
Overall length: 14·8m (48ft 6in)
Overall beam, skirt inflated: 7·7m (25ft 4in)
Overall height on landing pads: 3·8m (12ft 6in)
Overall height, hovering: 5m (16ft 6in)
Skirt depth: 1·22m (4ft)
INTERNAL
Cabin size (length × width): 6·62 × 2·34m (21ft 9in × 7ft 8in)
Cabin headroom-centre line: 1·83m (6ft)
Door aperture size (height × width): 1·75 × 0·99m (5ft 9in × 3ft 3in)
WEIGHT
Max: 10 tons
PERFORMANCE (at normal gross weight at 15°C)
Max water speed over calm water, zero wind, (continuous power rating): 96km/h (52 knots)
Average service water speed in sheltered coastal waters: 55-65km/h (30-35 knots)
Endurance at max continuous power rating on 265 Imperial gallons of fuel: 3·6 hours

SR.N6 Mk 1S

In 1972 a 'stretched' version of the SR.N6 passenger craft known as SR.N6 Mark 1S was introduced, increasing the seating capacity from 38 to 58.

The Mark 1S is 3 metres longer than the Mark 1 and has additional baggage panniers on the rear sidedecks. To maintain performance the rating of the Rolls-Royce Gnome gas turbine is increased by 100 to 1000shp.

Three Mark 1S craft have been built.

SR.N6 Mk 6 GENERAL PURPOSE

The SR.N6 Mk 6 is the most recent development in the successful SR.N6 series and represents

Control cabin of Super 4

SR.N6 Mk 6 general purpose hovercraft showing twin-propeller arrangement and tapered skirt

significant steps forward in terms of all-weather performance and increased manoeuvrability, especially in high winds and at low speeds. There is also a significant reduction in the external noise level.

These advances have been achieved by the introduction of twin propellers, a more powerful

engine and a redesigned skirt. The tapered skirt, which is deeper at the bow than the stern, cushions the effect of operating over larger waves and surface obstacles and enables the craft to operate in winds of up to Beaufort Scale 8 and waves of up to 3·04m (10ft).

The cabin is the same size as on the SR.N6 Mk

IS and can accommodate 55 passengers or between 5 and 6 tons of equipment. Options include
air-conditioning and VIP interior trim.

LIFT AND PROPULSION: Motive power is
supplied by a single 1125hp Rolls-Royce Marine
Gnome GN 1301 gas turbine driving a single
2·13m (7ft) diameter BHC lift fan and two 3·05m
(10ft) diameter Dowty Rotol variable-pitch
propellers.

DIMENSIONS
Length overall: 18·80m
Beam overall: 7·92m
Height overall, on landing pads: 4·00m
  on cushion: 5·5m
WEIGHT
Max operating: 17 010kg (37 500lb)
PERFORMANCE
Max speed over calm water: 60 knots

SR.N6 Mk 8

The latest military variant of the single-
propeller SR.N6, the Mk 8 has the same overall
measurements as the SR.N6 Mk 6 twin-propeller
model.

In the logistic support role the Mk 8 can carry
up to 55 fully-equipped troops or loads of up to 6
tons. Access to the cabin, which measures 9·5 ×
2·3m (31ft 2in × 7ft 7in), is via a bow door. The
floor is fitted with tie-down points for stores and
equipment. Loads up to ½ ton which are too long
for the cabin may be carried externally on the sidedecks.

In the coastal patrol role, the operational
flexibility of the SR.N6 is greatly improved by its
ability to work from beaches and other
unprepared sites and to navigate freely in shallow
water. At the same time the craft is seaworthy and
can operate in most weather conditions by day or
night.

LIFT AND PROPULSION: Integrated system
powered by a single Rolls-Royce GN 1451 marine
gas turbine rated at 1080shp at 15°C. Auxiliary
power is supplied by a Lucas SS923 gas turbine
driving a three-phase alternator. Main fuel tank
capacity is 1204 litres (265 Imperial gallons).
Long-range tanks are incorporated, giving an
additional capacity of 1818 litres (400 Imperial
gallons).

ARMAMENT: Either a ring-mounted machine
gun (0·5in or 7·62mm) or short range wire-guided
surface-to-surface missiles mounted on the sidedecks.

DIMENSIONS
Length overall: 17·78m
Beam overall: 7·97m
Height overall on cushion: 6·32m
PERFORMANCE
Max speed, calm water: 50 knots
Endurance, on main tanks: 2·4 hours
  on long-range tanks: 6 hours
A further 1·8 hours endurance can be obtained by
using the fuel carried in the craft's trim system
giving a maximum endurance of 7·8 hours.

BH.7

BH.7 is a 56-tonne hovercraft which was designed specifically for naval and military roles. The
prototype, designated BH.7 Mk 2, has been in
service with the Royal Navy since 1970 where it
has been evaluated in a number of roles including
fishery protection, ASW and MCM work.

In 1982/83 the RN craft was equipped with an
operational mine hunting fit comprising: Plessey
193M and 2048 Speedscan sonar equipment and a
Racal Decca NAV/AIO system. Using this equipment the craft completed a very successful series of
trials, operating from the Royal Navy Air Station
at Portland.

The second and third craft, designated Mk 4,
and a further four Mk 5As, are in service with the
Iranian Navy.

LIFT AND PROPULSION: Power for the integrated lift propulsion system on the Mk 2 and
Mk 4 is provided by a Rolls-Royce Marine
Proteus 15M/541 gas turbine with a maximum
rating at 23°C of 4250shp. On the Mk 5A, a 15M/
549 is installed with a maximum rating of 4250shp.
In both types the engine drives, via a light alloy

SR.N6 operated by Canadian Coast Guard hovercraft units

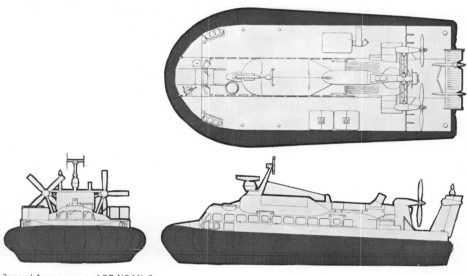

General Arrangement of SR.N6 Mk 6

SR.N6 Mk 8s

driveshaft and bevel drive gearbox, a BHC 12-
blade, centrifugal 3·5m (11ft 6in) diameter lift fan
and a British Aerospace Dynamics four-blade,
variable-pitch pylon-mounted propeller. Propeller
diameter on the Mk 4 is 5·79m (19ft) and 6·4m
(21ft) on the Mk 2 and Mk 5A. Normal fuel
capacity is up to 3000 Imperial gallons (13 635
litres).

CONTROLS: Craft direction is controlled by
swivelling the propeller pylon angle by a footpedal. Thrust ports are fitted at each quarter to
assist directional control at low speed, and a
hydraulically-operated skirt-lift system helps to
bank the craft into turns, thereby reducing drift.

Fuel is transferred between forward and aft
tanks via a ring main to adjust fore and aft trim.

HULL: Construction is mainly of corrosion resistant light alloy. Extensive use is made of components which were designed for the N4. The bow
structure is a Plasticell base covered with glass
fibre.

SKIRT: The fan delivers air to the cushion via a
continuous peripheral fingered bag skirt made in
neoprene-coated nylon fabric. The skirt provides
an air cushion depth of 1·68m (5ft 6in). The
cushion is divided into four compartments by a
full length longitudinal keel and by two transverse
keels located slightly forward of amidships.

ACCOMMODATION: The raised control cabin,
located slightly forward of amidships on the hull
centre line, accommodates a crew of three, with
the driver and navigator/radar operator in front

and the third crew member behind. The driver sits on the right, with the throttle and propeller pitch control lever on his right, and the pylon angle pedal and skirt-lift column in front.

The navigator, on the left, has a Decca radar display (Type 914 on the Mk 5) and compass in front and Decometers in an overhead panel.

The large main cabin area permits a variety of operational layouts. In a typical arrangement, the operations room is placed directly beneath the control cabin and contains communication, navigation, search and strike equipment and associated displays.

The craft has an endurance of up to 11 hours under cruise conditions but this can be extended considerably as it can stay 'on watch' without using the main engine.

Provision can be made for the crew to live aboard for several days.

SYSTEMS, ELECTRICAL: Two Rover IS/90 APUs provide, via two 55kVA generators, three-phase 400Hz ac at 200V for ac and dc supplies.

DIMENSIONS

EXTERNAL

Length overall: 23·9m
Beam overall: 13·8m
Overall height on landing pads: 10·36m
Cushion depth: 1·76m

INTERNAL (Main Cabin)

Cabin length: 13·2m
Cabin width: 4·17m
Headroom (on centre line): 2·38m

WEIGHTS

Max: 56 tonnes
Disposable load, incl role equipment: 18·3 tonnes

PERFORMANCE (at max operating weight at 15°C)

Max continuous calm water speed: 58 knots

BH.7 Mk 2

Craft built

One for the British Royal Navy, P235

BH.7 Mk 5A as supplied to Iranian Navy

BH.7 Mk 4 LOGISTIC SUPPORT VERSION

Craft built

Two BH.7 Mk 4s for the Iranian Navy

ACCOMMODATION: In this role, the main hold floor area of 56m² (600ft²) of the Mk 4 provides an unobstructed space suitable for loading wheeled vehicles, guns and military stores.

Two side cabins, fitted with paratroop-type seats, can accommodate up to 60 troops and their equipment.

Access at the bow is through a 'clamshell' door.

Machine guns can be fitted in gun rings on the roof on either side of the cabin and provision can be made for armour plating to protect personnel, the engine and vital electrical components.

TYPICAL MILITARY LOADS: 170 fully equipped troops or three field cars and trailers plus 60 troops or two armoured scout cars or up to 20 NATO pallets.

BH.7 Mk 5A COMBAT/LOGISTICS VERSION

Craft built

Four BH.7 Mk 5As for the Iranian Navy

Designed for coastal defence operations, the BH.7 Mk 5A carries medium-range surface-to-surface missiles, such as Exocet, on its sidedecks. Secondary armament consists of two roof-mounted 20mm guns.

The main central cabin, employed on the BH.7 Mk 4 for load-carrying, is equipped as an operations and fire-control room. The bow door is retained providing a dual missile/logistic capability. Since it is fully amphibious, the BH.7 can be operated from relatively unprepared bases on beaches and can head directly towards its target on interception missions regardless of the tidal state and marginal terrain. Also, since none of its solid structure is immersed, it is invulnerable to underwater defences such as acoustic, magnetic and pressure mines and to attack by torpedoes.

A full range of electronic navigational aids permits the craft to operate by day or night.

BH.7 Mk 20 (DESIGN)

During recent years various 'stretched' versions of the BH.7 have been projected and are described in earlier editions of *Jane's Surface Skimmers*. The most recent design proposal is the BH.7 Mark 20.

The maximum weight has been increased to 94 tonnes, more than doubling the disposable load relative to the earlier BH.7 craft. This has been possible by lengthening the craft by three structural bays (approximately 7·3 metres) and installing a more powerful gas turbine, the Allison 571-K. Other significant changes include a deeper, low-pressure-ratio skirt similar to the type fitted on the SR.N4 Mark 3, increased fuel tankage and a larger control cabin. The bow ramp and cutaway side cabins are retained as on the Mark 5A, allowing the craft to be adapted to a number of military roles, as listed below.

LIFT AND PROPULSION: Power for the integrated lift and propulsion system is provided by an Allison 571-K gas turbine, flat rated to give 6000shp at up to 40°C ambient air temperature. The propeller is a British Aerospace Dynamics, 4-blade controllable-pitch 6·4m diameter, and the lift fan is a BHC fixed-pitch 12-blade centrifugal type, 3·5m in diameter. Fuel capacity is 36 700 litres.

CONTROLS: As for earlier versions.

HULL: Construction as for earlier versions.

SKIRT: As for earlier versions but mean cushion depth is increased to 2m.

ACCOMMODATION: Similar to earlier versions but larger control cabin and overall length increased due to craft length increase of 3·0m. Crew: minimum of 3.

AUXILIARY POWER UNITS: Two Lucas SS923 gas turbines driving 60kVA, 200V, 400Hz, 3-phase Plessey alternators.

DIMENSIONS

Length (over hard structure): 30·54m
Beam (over hard structure): 12·0m

Royal Navy BH.7 Mk 2 equipped for minehunting with Plessey 193M sonar immersed

BH.7 Mk 2 with retracted Plessey 193M sonar tube

Beam (skirt inflated): 15·6m
Height (on landing pads): 12·5m
Cushion depth (mean): 2·0m
Main cabin length: 17·5m
Main cabin width: 4·1m
Main cabin height: 2·4m
WEIGHTS
Basic equipped weight: 54 tonnes
Disposable load: 40 tonnes
Max weight: 94 tonnes
Max fuel (tanks full): 30·8 tonnes
PERFORMANCE (at 0·8m max wave height)
Logistic: 30 tonnes for 240n miles
    8 tonnes for 1160n miles
Minehunting*: 30 hours at 2-5 knots (search)
    15 hours at 10-12 knots (speedscan)
Minesweeping*: 15 hours at 12 knots towing wire
    sweep
Route*: 16 hours at 16-20 knots
Surveillance: Towing sidescan sonar
Fast attack: Range 930n miles
Anti-submarine*: 20 hours on-task on typical
    dunk-dash cycle
* Quoted at 100n miles from base

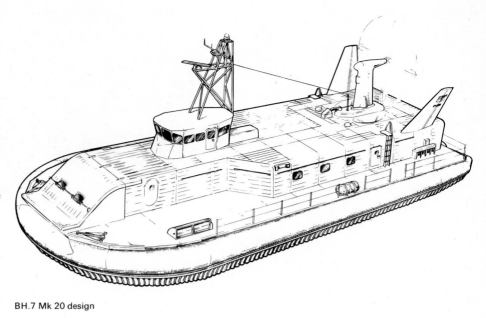

BH.7 Mk 20 design

Logistic Support/Amphibious Assault Role

In this role the craft can be equipped to carry troops and/or vehicles or freight. The bow ramp and large load-carrying capacity make it an excellent re-supply vehicle.

In addition, its amphibious capability enables stores to be unloaded directly ashore without the delays associated with conventional assault operations. The spacious main cabin enables very bulky loads to be carried either on pallets or netted down. Wheeled vehicles, such as Land-Rovers, having a maximum axle loading of 2000kg, can also be carried.

Anti-submarine Role

For this role the craft is equipped with a dunking ASW sonar, magnetic anomaly detector (MAD) and submarine attack torpedoes carried in twin sidedeck launchers. A 20 to 30mm gun is also mounted at the bow. An integrated navigation system is fitted, air/surface surveillance radar, plus electronic support measures (ESM) and chaff/IR launchers if required.

There is ample interior space for an operations room, galley and crew accommodation.

Mine Countermeasures Role

For minehunting the craft is fitted with an integrated NAV/AIO system and Plessey 193M

and 2048 (Speedscan) sonars deployed beneath the craft by means of a retractable 'stalk'. If required, a remotely-controlled mine disposal system (eg PAP104) can also be carried, or alternatively, mines can be destroyed by divers.

In the minesweeping role the craft can tow the lightweight sweeps developed for use by helicopters.

For fast route surveillance the craft can tow a sidescan sonar.

The interior accommodation includes an operations room and full crew facilities.

Fast Attack Role

For fast attack and escort duties the craft can be equipped with a variety of weapons including surface-to-surface and surface-to-air missiles and anti-aircraft guns. A typical fit could comprise:
    four SSMs (eg Harpoon, Exocet, Sea Skua)
    Sea Javelin SAM system
    two 30mm guns (eg Oerlikon)
In addition, the craft carries comprehensive navigation and surveillance equipment, fire control systems, electronic counter-measures (ECM), etc.

Interior accommodation includes a command information centre and crew facilities.

AP1-88

Major advances in hovercraft technology in recent years enabled British Hovercraft Corporation to offer a 7-tonne payload craft with a performance equal to that of the well-proven SR.N6. Built in welded aluminium alloy AP1-88 is powered by air-cooled marine diesels. Not only is it substantially cheaper in first and operating costs than the SR.N6 but it is considerably more robust than many earlier generation craft of this size. Most of its components are commercially available. AP1-88 has low crew and maintenance requirements, footprint pressure and noise levels.

The craft can be employed in a wide variety of commercial, military and para-military roles including:
    Passenger Ferrying
    Search and Rescue
    Hydrographic Surveying
    Anti-smuggling
    Firefighting
    Logistic Support
    Counter Insurgency
    Mine Counter-measures
    Anti-submarine Warfare
    Minelaying
In its civil passenger configuration it can seat up

One of BHC AP1-88s on the DSØ Malmö to Copenhagen route, winter 1985/86

to 101 passengers and as a troop carrier up to 90 fully-kitted troops. In a logistics role the AP1-88 will carry two Land-Rovers, a BV202 tracked vehicle and trailer unit or about 10 000kg of stores.

The first two AP1-88s *Tenacity* and *Resolution* began operating with Hovertravel between Ryde and Southsea in 1983. In 1985 *Resolution* was chartered to the US Navy as an LCAC trainer and a third 80-seater *Perseverance* was built to replace it on the Ryde-Southsea route. These three craft are built to the 2·4m shorter/80 configuration with Deutz 278kW (373bhp) BF10L 413F lift engines and Deutz 367kW (429bhp) BF12L 413FC propulsion engines.

During 1984 two of the production standard craft entered service with A/S Dämpskibsselskabet Øresund (DSØ) of Denmark on a route linking Copenhagen's Kastrup airport and Malmö.

Three AP1-88s have been built under licence in Australia by North Queensland Engineers and Agents (NQEA) (see entry) at Cairns and operate ferry services in the areas of Brisbane, Cairns and Melbourne.

A half well-deck variant has entered service with the Canadian Coast Guard undertaking search and rescue, navaid maintenance and icebreaking tasks on the St Lawrence River. The new hovercraft replaces the Voyageur ACV of the Coast Guard.

The craft is of a half well-deck configuration with accommodation for up to 12 crew members or technicians and up to 12 tons of cargo. This AP1-88 is equipped with a hydraulic crane, capstan and winch to facilitate the conduct of a variety of specialised coast guard tasks.

The design and construction of the AP1-88 comply with the BHSR, IMO and DnV standards and the craft is cleared to operate in winds up to 30 knots mean, 40 knots gust and in wave heights up to 2·4m (1·5m significant).

ENGINES: The AP1-88/100 craft is powered by four Deutz BF12L 513FC 12-cylinder air-cooled diesels each rated at 386kW (517hp) maximum (2300rpm) and 336kW (450hp) continuous (2200rpm).

LIFT AND PROPULSION: Two of the engines, housed in the side box structures, power the lift and bow thruster systems. On each side of the craft one engine drives three 0·84m diameter double-entry centrifugal fans, two of which supply air to the cushion via the skirt system and the third supplies air to the rotatable bow thruster. The well-deck version for the Canadian Coast Guard has four 0·885m diameter fans for the lift system with two 0·84m fans for the bow thrusters.

Propulsion is by two 2·74m diameter 4-blade Hoffman ducted propellers each driven by one of the diesels via a toothed belt. On craft 001, 103, 003, 004 and 005 the propellers are of fixed-pitch type, but ground adjustable through ±5°. Craft 002 and 006 have variable-pitch propellers, type HO-V-254P2DFR/D275. The belt-drive reduction ratio is 1:0·6.

FUEL/BALLAST SYSTEM: Fuel is carried in four tanks, one at each bow corner and two on the centre line at the stern. Fuel can be transferred between tanks for trimming purposes.
Total tank capacity: 4500 litres
Normal usable fuel capacity: 1800 litres

CONTROLS: Directional control is provided by two sets of triple aerodynamic rudder vanes mounted on the rear of the propeller ducts, differential propeller thrust and by swivelling bow thrusters. In the straight-aft position, the bow thrusters contribute to forward thrust. Trim is controlled by fuel ballast transfer.

STRUCTURE: Basic hull is formed by a buoyancy tank made almost entirely of very wide aluminium alloy extrusions, one extrusion being used for the I-beams forming the transverse frames and a second for the integrally stiffened planking used for the bottom and deck. The remainder of the rigid structure is built from smaller welded extrusions and plating, with the exception of the roof, made from riveted light gauge corrugated panels. The propeller ducts are a composite structure of light alloy and Kevlar

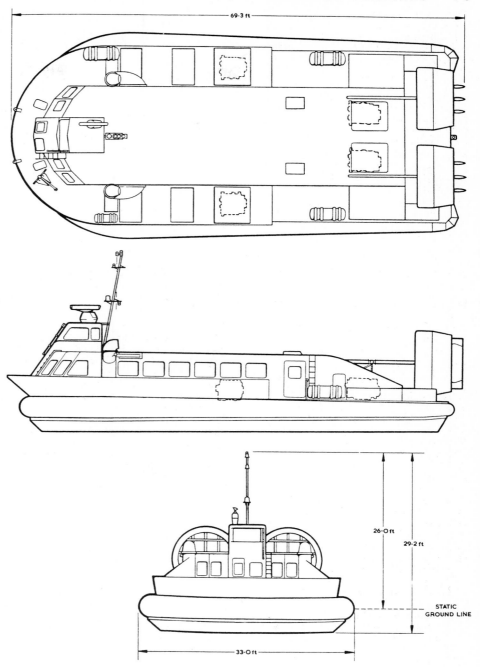

General Arrangement of AP1-88/80 hovercraft

AP1-88 (half well-deck) search and rescue craft building for the Canadian Coast Guard, autumn 1986

reinforced plastic. Marine alloys are used, including N8 plate and HE30 extrusions. In general, plate thicknesses are 2 or 3mm except for the light gauge roof plating. The structure is welded throughout to eliminate mechanical fastenings which can be sources of corrosion. Detachable panels give easy access for engine and fan removal and facilitate the inspection of ventilation ducting and tail control cable runs. Lifting, for the inspection of the craft underside and skirts, is achieved by three jacks which are fitted and operated from inside the craft.

SKIRT: Low-pressure ratio tapered skirt based on that of the Super 4. Mean cushion depth 1·37m.

ACCOMMODATION: The superstructure is divided into four main components: a large central accommodation area forward of a propulsion machinery bay and two side bodies containing the lift system machinery. A control cabin is mounted on top of the main cabin. In addition to the full-cabin and half well-deck versions, full well-deck variants are also available. The commercial full-cabin version seats a maximum of 101 passengers with the seats arranged in rows of seven across the cabin. The rows are divided by two gangways 600mm wide which separate the seats into a 2-3-2 configuration. Two doors, one port and one starboard, are at the aft end of the cabin. Doorways are 1·75 by 0·9 metres. An emergency door 1·06 by 0·9 metres is at the forward end of the passenger cabin. Craft built to standard include a cabin heating and ventilation system adequate for operation in temperate climates. Requirements for more elaborate air-conditioning will result in a reduced disposable load. A full air-conditioning system, complete with an APU installation, can be added with a disposable load penalty of approximately 1000kg.

There are two sets of four luggage panniers on the sidedecks aft of the cabin doors. Total volume of the eight panniers is approximately 6·6 cubic metres.

COMMUNICATIONS: A Sailor RT 145 VHF international marine band radio or similar equipment.

RADAR: Racal-Decca 914C. Antenna turning unit and transceiver on control cabin roof. Display unit mounted in control cabin on port side. Display is north-up stabilised by gyrocompass.

NAVIGATION: Remote reading gyrocompass; a Lambda T.12 spherical compass. Optional range of automatic and semi-automatic navigational aids.

DIMENSIONS
EXTERNAL
Length overall: 24·4m (80ft)
Beam overall: 11·0m (36ft 1½in)
Height on cushion: 9·5m (31ft 2½in)
Mean cushion depth: 1·37m (4ft 6in)
INTERNAL
Cabin, length: 14·4m (47ft 3in)
Beam: 4·8m (15ft 9in)
Headroom: 1·95m (6ft 4⅔in)
WEIGHTS
Basic equipped craft: 29 480kg (65 000lb)
Max disposable load (crew, fuel, provisions, fresh water, freight, passengers): 11 340kg (25 000lb)
Max weight: 40 820kg (90 000lb)
PERFORMANCE
Max calm water speed: 50 knots (93km/h)
Total fuel consumption at continuous power (full throttle): 368 litres/h (81 Imperial gallons/h)

P AP1-88/200
WABAN-AKI
This craft entered service with the Canadian Coast Guard in 1987.

LIFT AND PROPULSION: Four Deutz BF12L 513CP air-cooled turbocharged diesels, 441kW (591bhp) each, at 2300rpm. Two Hoffman 2·75m diameter variable-pitch propeller type HO-V-254P2DFR/D275, ducted. Four centrifugal lift fans 0·885m diameter. Two bow thrusters, centrifugal fans 0·840m diameter.

The following details are specifically applicable to Waban-Aki.

COMMUNICATIONS: VHF radio FM Wulfsberg RT 7200, VHF radio AM King KY 196 Silver Crown, HF King KHF 990.

Craft built (in UK)	Reg No	Serial No	No of seats	Name	Launched	Operator
AP1-88/80	GH 2087*	001	80	*Tenacity*	1983	Hovertravel Ltd
AP1-88/80	GH 2088*	002	80	*Resolution*	1983	US Navy (on charter from Hovertravel Ltd)
AP1-88/80	GH 2100*	103	80	*Perseverance*	1985	Hovertravel Ltd
API-88/100	GH 9029†	003	81	(ex *Expo Spirit*)	1984	Hovertransport A/S**
API-88/100	GH 9030‡	004	81	*Freja Viking*	1984	A/S Dämpskibsselskabet Øresund
API-88/100	GH 9031	005	81	*Liv Viking*	1984	A/S Dämpskibsselskabet Øresund
API-88/200 half well-deck	CH-C-CG	006	12	*Waban-Aki*	1986	Canadian Coast Guard

* hulls built at Fairey Allday Marine and fitted out by Hovertravel Ltd at Bembridge, Isle of Wight
† leased by BHC for five months (May to September) in 1986 to Hoverwest Ferry Services Inc, Canada and named *Expo Spirit*. The craft operated a service from Victoria, Vancouver Island to Canada Place at the Expo '86 site, Vancouver, BC
‡ hull built by Fairey Allday Marine and fitted out by BHC
** this craft was leased to Hovertransport A/S in 1987

AP1-88/100

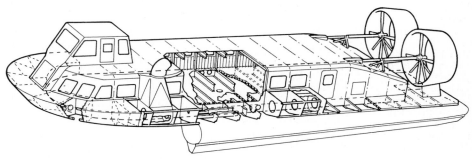

AP1-88/100 structure

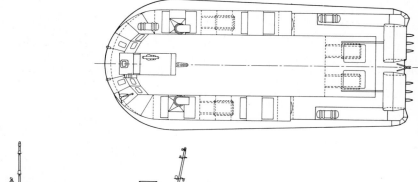

General Arrangement of AP1-88/100 hovercraft

NAVIGATION
Radar: Decca RM 914C, VHF (FM/AM)
ADF: OAR Type ADFS-347EH, HF ADF
Sitex 511 AADF

Navigator Plotter: Loran 'C' with RS 200 Shipmate colour track plotter, Gyromagnetic compass: AIM system
ELECTRICAL SYSTEM: Main system 28V dc;

auxiliary system 240/120V ac 60Hz single phase. Dc supply: four Bosch Type T1, 28V, 120A-17 generators. Ac supply: diesel engine auxiliary power unit, 12kW output. Batteries: start/service S1 two 12V, 143Ah; start/service S2 two 12V, 143Ah; essential service two 12V, 143Ah.

FUEL SYSTEM: Engine fuel and ballast transfer for adjustment of craft trim; fuel type: marine gas oil LS to BS 2869 1970 A1 (Canadian Grade CAN 2-3-6-M83); max tank capacities: four 1138-litre (250 Imperial gallons, 300 US gallons), two 680-litre (150 Imperial gallons, 180 US gallons), total 5900-litre (1298 Imperial gallons, 1558 US gallons).

HYDRAULIC SYSTEMS: Power assistance to rudders; control of variable pitch propellers; auxiliary hydraulic components.

DIMENSIONS
Length overall: 24·50m
Beam, rigid structure: 4·40m
    on cushion: 11·20m
Height at rest on ground, to top of radar scanner: 5·90m
    on cushion, to top of mast: 10·00m

WEIGHTS
Max weight: 47 150kg
Max disposable load: 12 450kg

PERFORMANCE
Speed, max: 50 knots
Endurance, normal max: 10 hours approx

AP1-88 TYPE 25 PATROL CRAFT
(DESIGN)

The Type 25 is designed to work from temporary bases on beaches and river banks. It can operate hullborne at sea or remain on land, monitoring water traffic with radar or visual aids. Interception is made at speeds up to 50 knots. Boarding vessels is aided by the air-filled peripheral skirt which acts as a fender.

The amphibious capability of the Type 25 design enables it to work where the terrain makes defence force operations difficult or impossible. Weapons up to 30mm, missiles, flare launchers, specialised radar and radio-equipment can be fitted.

AP1-88 ASSAULT/LOGISTICS CRAFT
(DESIGN)

Military logistic versions of the AP1-88 would feature a bow ramp for driving vehicles on and off. Troops can also disembark quickly in the landing zone. The logistic support variant has a deck 15 metres long by 4·8 metres wide which can accommodate light vehicles and logistic loads. Equipped to military standards, the full-cabin version seats 70 fully-armed troops. In the half-cabin version there are full mess and accommodation facilities for a crew of ten or, alternatively, 42 troops could be seated.

AP1-88 MINE COUNTER-MEASURES
(MCM) (DESIGN)

The AP1-88s inherently low underwater signatures and invulnerability to underwater weapons make it an ideal platform for mine counter-measures in coastal waters. Complete sonar and positioning system suites have been developed based on the Plessey 193 sonar.

General Arrangement of P AP1-88/200 as delivered to the Canadian Coast Guard, 1987

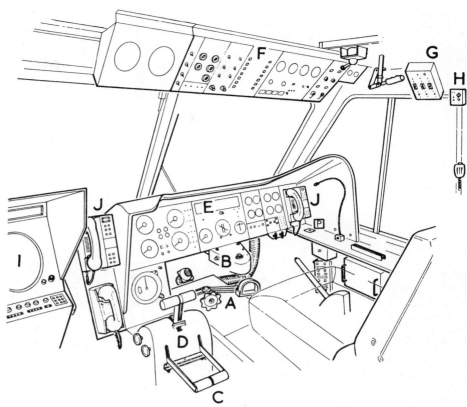

Controls of AP1-88/100 (A) rudder control pedals (B) bow thruster control panel (C) lift engine throttle levers (D) propulsion engine throttle levers (E) main instrument panel (F) overhead instrument panel (G) fire control panel (H) electrical bay smoke detector warning panel (I) Kelvin Huges 1600 radar display (J) vhf radio (2 sets)

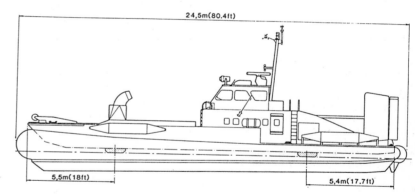

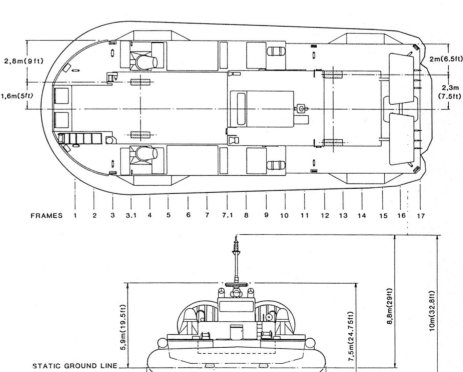

BHC P AP1-88/200 prior to delivery to the Canadian Coast Guard, 1987

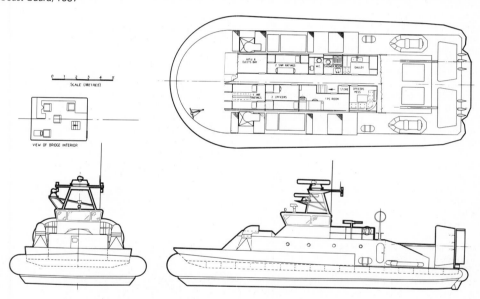

SCALE (METRES)

VIEW OF BRIDGE INTERIOR

AP1-88 Type 25 patrol craft design

GRIFFON HOVERCRAFT LIMITED

Head Office: Carlton House, Ringwood Road, Woodlands, Southampton SO4 2HT, England

Telephone: (0703) 813461
Telex: 47423 GIFTEK G
Telefax: (0703) 813462

D R Robertson, *Director*
E W H Gifford, *Director*
J H Gifford, *Director*

Founded in 1976, Griffon Hovercraft has concentrated on the design and development of small amphibious hovercraft.

The company's first design, Griffon, used a four-blade ducted propeller for propulsion with a centrifugal fan for lift, both driven by a Jaguar automobile engine. This craft was subsequently put into production as the Skima 12, built by Pindair Limited under licence from Griffon Hovercraft Ltd. Many of this type of craft have been in service throughout the world in a variety of roles.

The initial choice of a petrol engine was due to

its superior power-to-weight ratio, although the advantages of the diesel engine were recognised. The development of the turbocharged air-cooled diesel led to the company's decision, early in 1982, that a small commercial diesel-powered hovercraft would be feasible and would carry a useful payload.

Construction of the Griffon 1000 TD prototype began in June 1982. Performance trials began in May 1983 and exceeded expectations. The prototype is now with the company's US licensees, Frank W Hake Inc of Eddystone, Pennsylvania and is at present being operated by the Maryland Department of Natural Resources Marine Police, for patrol and rescue. Operating hours are in excess of 1500. Three production craft of this type have been supplied to Geophysical Surveys Inc of Dallas, USA, for use in an oilfield survey on the Yellow River, China. Due to the intensive nature of these operations, thousands of operating hours have been accumulated with minimal maintenance, proving the inherently rugged nature of the design. In 1987, a 1000 TD was supplied to the Water and Power Development Authority of Pakistan for survey work. Various features were added to the craft to meet the customer's particular requirements.

The success of the 1000 TD has led to a range of craft being developed with 1- to 4-tonne payloads, using similar machinery units and control systems. The company intends to concentrate on the requirements for a low-cost easily maintained craft for use in workboat, patrol and ferry applications.

All Griffon hovercraft are designed to comply with the IMO, the British CAA and the Canadian Coast Guard Regulations. The 1000 TD and 1500 TD have CAA Type approval, the 2500 TD is approved by the US and the Canadian Coast Guard. The company's design and manufacturing philosophy is such that customers' individual requirements, both as modifications to the company's standard range or complete special design projects, can be met on a cost effective basis.

Sales and marketing for the company's products on a worldwide basis are being carried out by Hovercraft Sales and Marketing, PO Box 7, Sarisbury Green, Southampton, Hants SO3 6YS, UK. Tel: (042 121) 3547; Telex: 477164 HOVSAM G.

Craft built

By licensed builder: 16
By Griffon Hovercraft Ltd: 12

1000 TD

The smallest craft in the range, the 1000 TD carries a payload of 1000kg or 10 passengers. The craft is powered by a single diesel engine and is available with a variety of superstructures. Folding sidedecks enable it to be loaded onto its purpose-built trailer and towed behind a small truck. It can also be fitted into a 20-foot container, after removal of bow and stern sections.

Craft built   Owner

001	Maryland Department of Natural Resources Police, USA, 1984-1987
002	Geophysical Surveys Inc, USA for Yellow River, China, 1984
003	Geophysical Surveys Inc, USA for Yellow River, China, 1984
004	Geophysical Surveys Inc, USA for Yellow River, China, 1984
008	Water and Power Development Authority (WAPDA), Pakistan (GH 9456)

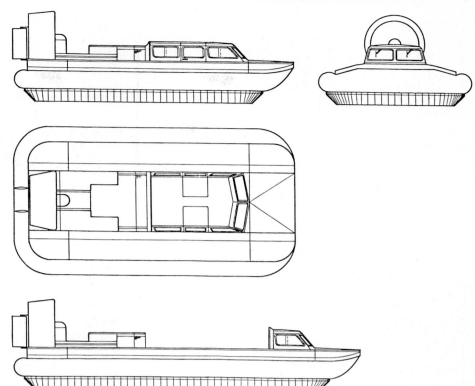

Above: 1000 TD with hard top cabin; below: 1500 TD with open deck

LIFT AND PROPULSION: Integrated lift/propulsion system powered by a single Deutz BF6L 913C air-cooled six-cylinder, in-line, turbocharged and intercooled diesel rated at 190hp (140kW) at 2500rpm. A 760mm diameter centrifugal lift fan is driven from the front of the crankshaft, via an HTD toothed belt. Power for the 1·37m diameter, four-blade Robert Trillo propeller is transmitted from the back of the engine via an automotive clutch to another HTD toothed belt transmission. Enclosed within a pylon, the belt drive is protected from the weather. The engine, transmission, duct and pylon are mounted on a welded aluminium alloy subframe attached to the hull via resilient mounts. On the latest craft, a simple system allows vertical movement of both pylon and duct, enabling very quick and accurate transmission belt adjustment to be made.

Cooling air for the engine passes through a Knitmesh filter to remove spray and is drawn into the front of the engine bay by the engine cooling fan before passing over the cylinders and being drawn out from the rear of the engine bay by the propeller.

CONTROLS: Triple rudders in the grp duct provide directional control. Elevators within the duct provide a degree of fore and aft trim, augmented by a fuel ballast system. The craft is fitted with an HDL-type skirt shift system, operated by a small electric winch, which provides responsive control on roll trim, offsets cross wind effects and banks the craft into turns.

HULL: Main hull and side structures are of welded, riveted and bonded marine grade aluminium. Side bodies fold upward for transport and they are locked into the running position by five struts on each side. Removable bow and stern sections reduce the length of the 1000 TD to 5·6m (18ft 6in) for shipment.

ACCOMMODATION: Seats forward for driver and passenger/navigator. A four-person inward facing bench-type seat is positioned on each side. Front seats and controls are behind a grp cabin with the front left-hand seat for driver. Radar can be fitted in front of right-hand seat. Options for remaining accommodation space are: grp cabin top, pvc cover over aluminium frame, open area, without cover.

SKIRT: HDL open loop/segment type, with similar segments at bow and sides. Cones are fitted at the stern. Segments are fitted to the loop with stainless-steel bolts and the inner ends are attached to the hull using plastic shackles. All skirt maintenance can be done without lifting the craft.

SYSTEMS: Electrical system is 24V as standard with a 12V option, 35A alternator, two 75 Ah, 12V batteries.

DIMENSIONS (hard structure)
Length: 8·40m
Width: 3·82m
Height: 2·68m
Hoverheight: 46·0cm
Cabin,
Length: 3·20m
Width: 1·80m
Height: 1·42m

Griffon 1000 TD as supplied to the Pakistan Water and Power Development Authority

WEIGHTS
Empty: 2000kg
Payload: 1000kg
PERFORMANCE
Max speed: 35 knots
Cruise speed: 28 knots
Max operating conditions: wind, 25 knots; waves,
     1m
Fuel consumption, max: 31·8 litres/h
     cruise: 22 litres/h

1500 TD

This variant is 1·8 metres longer than the 1000 TD, but with identical machinery. Capacity is increased to 1·5 tonnes or 16 persons. Bow and stern sections are not removable but folding side-decks allow transportation within a 40ft container.

Road transport of the 16-seat Griffon 1500 TD

Craft built	Owner
005	Griffon 1500 TD, Clements, Solomon Islands (GH-9452), 1987
006	Chiriqui Hovercraft, Panama, November 1985 to 1987
007	Griffon Hovercraft demonstrator (GH 2102)

These craft have been sold for tourism, survey work and pilot duties.

Details of this craft are as for the 1000 TD with the following exceptions:
DIMENSIONS
Overall length: 10·15m
Cabin length: 5·00m
WEIGHTS
Empty: 2300kg
Payload: 1500kg
PERFORMANCE
Max speed: 33 knots
Cruising speed: 27 knots
Fuel consumption, max: 31·8 litres/h
     cruise: 26 litres/h

1500 TD with modified cabin for film contract in Italy

1500 TDX (DESIGN)

Due to the flexible design and construction approach, the company now offer the larger 1500 TDX complete with the Deutz BF8L 513 power unit, a 330hp engine instead of the standard engine in the 1500 TD size hovercraft. This craft is primarily designed to keep performance up in adverse conditions.

All systems and cabin details are as before with the following exceptions:
Length: 11·00m
Empty weight: 2·9 tonnes
Max speed: 40 knots plus

2500 TD

This craft uses two identical machinery units from the smaller craft and has a payload of either 32 passengers or 2·5 tonnes of freight. Seating can be provided with either forward-facing aircraft type seats or sideways-facing bench seats.

The workboat version can be either supplied open with only the two-person cab, or with a portion of the deck covered.

A bow-loading ramp is also available to enable a vehicle (such as a long wheel-base Land-Rover) to be carried.

Two 2500 TD craft have been built for ferry/tourist operations. The first one was launched in November 1985 and having completed its trials and with Canadian Coast Guard Certification, started passenger carrying at Expo '86 in Vancouver. The craft ran a 10-hour day, seven-day week shuttle service for the duration of Expo '86 operating off a floating pontoon in Canada Place along a 7-mile route to alongside a pier in the Expo '86 site.

LIFT AND PROPULSION: Two separate lift and propulsion systems, mechanically integrated, each identical to that of the single engine craft.

CONTROLS: Similar systems to the single engine craft are employed with duplication in some areas. Triple rudders in each duct operated by a steering

Craft built	Name	In service	Owner
001 Griffon Hovercraft 2500 TD	*Rain Dance*	January 1986	Hover Systems Inc, USA, (1986 Canadian registration CH-FHI)
002 Hover Systems Husky G-2500 TD	*Bravo*	May 1986	Hover Systems Inc, USA, (Pennsylvania registration PA 2994 X)

Griffon 1500 TD deploying Vikoma anti-oil pollution equipment in shallow water

Griffon 2500 TD *Rain Dance* at the Canada Pavilion base, Expo '86, Vancouver, Oct 1986

yoke via stainless steel cables provide directional control. Fore and aft trim is achieved by a liquid ballast system whilst lateral trim is provided by an electrically operated skirt shift system. Twin engine throttles are mounted near to the driver's left hand whilst two clutch pedals (operated by the driver's feet) are provided for the propellers. By using only one propeller at low speed together with the rudder and skirt shift, the craft is highly man-oeuvrable. Control systems are powerful enough to allow the craft to be operated and controlled by only one engine, although at a much reduced speed.

HULL: The main hull is of welded marine grade aluminium alloy providing a very cost effective light and durable structure, consisting of four longitudinal box sections linked fore and aft by two transverse box sections. Side bodies, also in light alloy, can fold upward reducing width for road and sea transportation.

ACCOMMODATION: Superstructure can be to the customer's specification. The standard passenger cabin is constructed in light alloy with grp mouldings at the front and back. A great emphasis has been placed on passengers having good visibility and big windows and narrow pillars are featured. Also a portion of the roof is transparent. Forward-facing aircraft seats are provided as standard with four seats to a row with an aisle either side. In this configuration, up to 32 seats can be fitted. Air conditioning and heating systems can be provided and toilet/galley facilities can also be fitted if seating capacity is reduced.

CREW CABIN: A raised crew cabin is provided offering 360° visibility for two crew, although for most operations only one operator is required. Radio and radar can also be fitted.

SKIRT: HDL open loop/segment type with similar segments at bow and sides. Cones fitted at stern. Segments attached to outer loop with stainless steel bolts. All skirt maintenance can be carried out without lifting the craft.

DIMENSIONS
Length: 14·40m
Width: 5·78m
Height: 2·87m
Cabin length: 8·05m
Cabin width: 3·30m

PERFORMANCE
Max speed: 31 knots
Cruise speed: 26 knots
Hoverheight: 600cm
Max disposable load, crewboat version: 3·8 tonnes
Fuel consumption, max: 63 litres/h
  cruise: 45 litres/h
Fuel capacity (standard): 568 litres (125 Imperial gallons)
Max operating conditions: 25 knots wind
  1·25m wave height

2500 TDX (DESIGN)

During 1986 a new version of the 2500 TD was added to the range. This version is identical to the previous model except that the engines have been changed to Deutz BF8L 513, together with a corresponding increase in size of lift fans, propellers and transmission.

The specification is as for the 2500 TD except for:
DIMENSIONS
Craft length: 15·10m
PERFORMANCE
Max speed: 40 knots
Cruise speed: 38 knots
Max disposable load, crewboat version: 4·9 tonnes
Max operating conditions: 30 knots wind

4000 TD (DESIGN)

The 4000 TD is basically a stretched version of the 2500 TD with larger engines. The largest craft in the range, the 4000 TD can carry up to 50 passengers or 5·4 tonnes of cargo at speeds of up to 40 knots.

HULL: The main hull is identical in cross-section to the proven 2500 TD but 4m longer. The side bodies are also of similar construction but wider.

ACCOMMODATION: This is again of similar construction to the 2500 TD but has a wider,

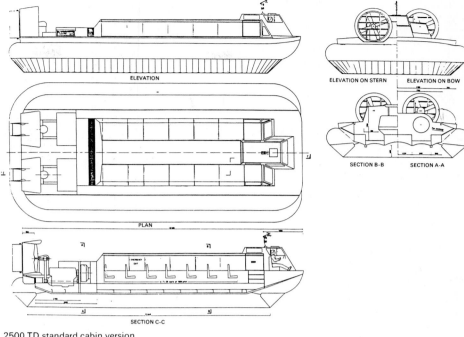
2500 TD standard cabin version

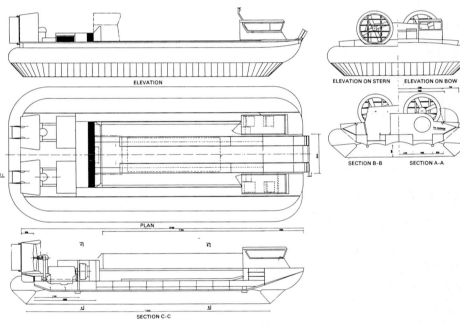
2500 TD workboat version design

Griffon 2500 TD

longer and higher cabin offering seating of five per row arranged 1-3-1 with up to five rows. Ventilation is provided and roof level stowage racks for passenger hand luggage.

Air conditioning and heating systems can be provided and toilet/galley facilities can be fitted if seating capacity is reduced.

CREW CABIN: A raised crew cabin is provided offering 360-degree visibility for the two-man crew. Radio and radar can also be fitted.

SKIRT: HDL open loop/segment type with similar segments at bow and sides. Cones fitted at stern. Segments attached to outer loops with stainless steel bolts. All skirt maintenance can be carried out without lifting the craft.

LIFT AND PROPULSION: The same twin-engined concept as the 2500 TD is used but with additional power. Two Deutz BF10L 513 engines each drive a 0·91m diameter lift fan and a 1·98m diameter ducted propeller. Transmission is the same as for the smaller craft.

CONTROLS: As for the 2500 TD.

DIMENSIONS
Length: 18·00m
Width: 6·68m
Height: 3·60m
Cabin,
Length: 9·50m
Width: 4·00m
Height: 1·83m
PERFORMANCE
Max speed: 38 knots
Cruise speed: 35 knots
Hoverheight: 0·85m
Max disposable load, crewboat version: 6·56 tonnes
Fuel consumption: 112 litres/h
Fuel capacity: 568 litres (125 Imperial gallons)
Max wave height: 1·5m
Max wind: 30 knots

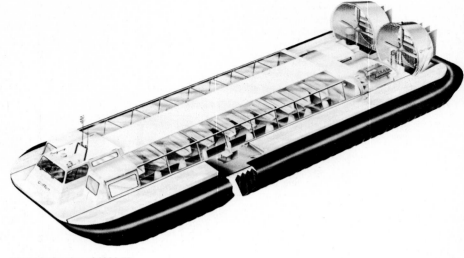

Isometric drawing of 4000 TD

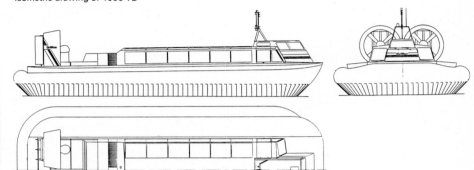

4000 TD standard cabin design

HOVERCRAFT DEVELOPMENT LIMITED (HDL)

[PATENT HOLDING AND LICENSING ORGANISATION]
101 Newington Causeway, London SE1 6BU, England

Telephone: 01-403 6666
Telex: 894397 G

M L Martin, *Chairman*
D J Veasey, *Director*
J Williams, *Secretary*

Hovercraft Development Limited (HDL) was formed in January 1959 by the National Research Development Corporation (NRDC) which is now part of the British Technology Group. The company uses its portfolio of patents as the basis of licensing agreements with hovercraft manufacturers in the UK and overseas. HDL or British Technology Group, may, in certain cases, provide financial backing to assist project development.

HDL's principal patents concern craft with segmented skirts. These skirt systems are now used by all major manufacturers of hovercraft. The skirt is a series of pockets arranged around the craft which when inflated seal against each other. The skirt is flexible and conforms to the contours of the surface over which it passes, and has a low drag characteristic both in calm water and waves. Should an individual segment be lost, the performance is not substantially affected.

Also included in the patent portfolio is the HDL skirt shift system.

Licences are available to all companies in the industry.

HOVERMARINE INTERNATIONAL LTD

Itchen Works, Hazel Road, Woolston, Southampton, Hampshire SO2 7GB, England

Telephone: (0703) 443122
Telex: 47141 G
Telefax: (0703) 444429

P J Hill, *Director and Joint General Manager*
E G Tattersall, *Director and Joint General Manager*

Hovermarine has sold over 100 surface effect ships (SES) to 31 countries and is one of the most experienced designers and builders of these craft. Hovermarine has its yard at Woolston, Southampton with an undercover area of more than 2300m².

Production designs are the 200 and 500 series craft. The 200 series comprises the HM 216 (16m, 60-seat) and HM 218 (18m, 84- to 103-seat) passenger ferries, 28 of which have been delivered to the Hongkong and Yaumati Ferry Company; the HM 218 multi-role harbour craft, four of which have been delivered to the Port of Rotterdam Authority; the HM 218 crewboat for the oil industry; the HM 221 (21m) fireboat; the HM 221

(21m) 112- to 135-seat passenger ferry and the HM 221 (21m) crewboat. Other variants of the 200 series craft are offered for hydrographic survey, coastguard and patrol duties. The HM 216 is no longer in production. The HM 500 series includes the Series 2 (27m, 256-seat) passenger ferry. Other designs (also 27m) are available for the following roles: naval fast strike and patrol craft, crewboat, hydrographic survey and coastguard patrol. All craft are type-approved in the UK by the Civil Aviation Authority and for operating permits issued by the Department of Transport. The craft have also been certified by Lloyds' Register of Shipping.

HM 216 HYDROGRAPHIC SURVEY VESSEL

One of these variants was delivered to the Belgian Ministry of Public Works in 1972 for survey work on the River Scheldt. The HM 216 is no longer in production.

POWERPLANTS
Lift: One 206bhp Cummins V-555-M marine diesel
Propulsion: Two 445bhp General Motors Detroit Diesel Allison 8V-92TI marine diesels
DIMENSIONS
Length overall: 15·24m (50ft)
Beam overall: 5·8m (19ft)

Height overall: 4·1m (13ft 4in)
Draught floating, loaded: 1·49m (4ft 10in)
on cushion, loaded: 0·87m (2ft 10in)
Bridge/cabin length: 4·3m (14ft)
beam: 4·3m (14ft)
height: 2m (6ft 6in)
WEIGHTS
Max: 19 300kg (42 500lb)
Normal disposable payload: 5600kg (12 300lb)
PERFORMANCE
Cruising speed: 35 knots
Standard range at cruising speed: 250n miles

HM 218 FERRY

The HM 218 ferry represents a 40 per cent improvement in payload over the earlier HM 216 ferry for only a 15 per cent increase in operating costs. It can carry 84 to 103 passengers at cruising speeds of up to 35 knots. An extended bow skirt permits passenger operations in up to 1·5m (5ft) waves. A computerised roll stabilisation system can be fitted to customer order.

The first HM 218 ferry went into service in 1976. A major operator of the type is the Hongkong and Yaumati Ferry Company, which has 24 in commuter service within Hong Kong and on an 100n mile international route to Kwang-Chow (Canton) in the People's Republic of China. Other HM 218 ferries operate in Brazil, the People's Republic of China, Indonesia, Japan, Kuwait, Malaysia, Singapore and Venezuela.

LIFT AND PROPULSION: Two General Motors Detroit Diesel Allison 8V-92TI V, eight-cylinder marine diesels, each developing 445bhp at 2300rpm, provide propulsive power. A single Cummins 90-degree V, eight-cylinder V-555-M marine diesel rated at 206bhp at 2800rpm drives the 0·6m (24in) diameter centrifugal lift fans.

The lift engine drives two pairs of forward fans through toothed belts and one aft fan through a hydraulic system. Air for the forward fans is drawn through inlets at each forward cabin quarter and in the base of the wheelhouse structure. Air for the aft fan is drawn through an inlet in the rear companionway.

The two propulsion engines each drive a 0·45m (18in) diameter aluminium bronze three-bladed propeller through a reversing gearbox and 1:1 ratio vee box. Fuel is carried in stainless steel tanks, two beneath the aft companionway and one under the main lift fans. Electrical power for instruments, radio, radar, lighting and air conditioning is supplied by ac/dc alternators driven by the lift and propulsion engines.

CONTROLS: Craft direction is by twin balanced stainless steel rudders operated hydraulically by a steering wheel. Additional control is by differential use of the water propellers.

HULL: Built in grp mouldings and various types of sandwich panels. The mouldings consist of the main deck, deck and superstructure centre section, forward intakes and wheelhouse, inner sidelinings, aft companionway and engine bay cowlings. The first three are joined by a system of transverse frames. The floor panels are bonded to the frames and to the longitudinal intercostal members.

The outer shell of the hull, including the bottom between the sidewalls and under the bow, is moulded in one piece, gunwale to gunwale. The hull moulding incorporates local thickening of the laminate to meet the design load requirements and to facilitate the incorporation of fittings and apertures. Frames and bulkheads are manufactured from sandwich panels of expanded pvc foam covered with grp. All frames and bulkheads are laminated into the hull.

ACCOMMODATION: The HM 218 ferry can be operated by a crew of two. Controls are in an elevated wheelhouse, with a 360-degree view, at the forward end of the passenger saloon. The saloon can be fitted out with up to 84 aircraft-type seats or 92 to 103 utility seats. These are normally arranged three abreast in banks of three. Toilet and baggage compartments are located aft. Up to six luggage containers, able to hold a total of 1500kg (3307lb), may be carried on the saloon roof.

Passenger access to the saloon is via a double width door aft. Crew and emergency access is forward via two hatch doors, one on each side of the wheelhouse. Knock-out emergency windows are fitted in the passenger saloon. Safety equipment includes life rafts, life jackets under the seats, fire detectors and extinguishers.

SKIRTS: The extended bow skirt consists of a single loop extending from the bow chine to a line just below the base of the main hull. 32 segments are attached to the main loop and connected to the underside of the hull by terylene ropes. An inner loop overlaps the fan volute outlet and causes the bow skirt to inflate.

The rear seal consists of a membrane and loop which is suspended front and rear by transverse continuous sheets of material. It is inflated to a pressure slightly above that of the cushion by the rear fan in the starboard propulsion engine room.

DIMENSIONS
Length overall: 18·29m (60ft)
Beam overall: 6·1m (20ft)
Height overall: 4·88m (16ft)
Draught floating, loaded: 1·72m (5ft 6in)
  on cushion, loaded: 1·07m (3ft 5in)
Saloon length: 9·75m (32ft)
  beam: 4·88m (16ft)
  height: 1·93m (6ft 4in)
WEIGHTS
Max: 27 900kg (61 520lb)

One of over 20 HM 218s operated by Hongkong and Yaumati Ferry Company

HM 218 operated by Shell Eastern Petroleum Ltd in Singapore

HM 218 for Touristic Enterprises Co, Kuwait

Normal disposable payload: 7154kg (15 775lb)
Normal fuel capacity: 1455 litres (320 Imperial gallons)
PERFORMANCE
Cruising speed: 34 knots
Acceleration 0-30 knots: 45 seconds
Standard range at cruising speed: 200n miles
Standard endurance at cruising speed: 4 hours

HM 218 CREWBOAT

Since 1979 three HM 218 crewboats have been operating in Venezuela, transporting crew to-and-from oil rigs on Lake Maracaibo. Five more have been delivered to Shell (Eastern) in Singapore. The crewboat is based on the HM 218 passenger ferry but has a substantially reinforced hull to withstand the buffeting which the craft receives alongside offshore installations.

A bow-loading technique has been developed; rollers are fitted to the bow allowing the craft to approach installations and transfer crew over the bow. This is safer than the conventional stern transfer system as the captain can view the whole operation.

Luggage containers (grp) may be fitted above the superstructure for extra baggage. An alternative version of the HM 218 crewboat accommodates 25 passengers, with a well-deck for 3 tonnes of cargo.

LIFT AND PROPULSION: Two General Motors 8V-92TI marine diesels driving fixed pitch propellers through Capitol reversing gearboxes and BPM V-drive gearboxes. Lift is by one Cummins V-555-M marine diesel driving two pairs of forward fans through toothed belts and one aft fan through a hydraulic system.

HULL: Shell mouldings, sub-mouldings, frames, bulkheads and major attachments in grp, using polyester resins and pvc foam. Construction is to Lloyds' survey requirements.

ACCOMMODATION: Air-conditioned accommodation for up to 99 passengers in airline-type seats. Toilet compartment in stern.

DIMENSIONS
Length overall: 18·29m (60ft)
Beam overall: 6·1m (20ft)
Height (underside of propeller to top of mast light): 7·4m (24ft 4in)
Draught, off cushion: 1·72m (5ft 8in)
  on cushion: 1·07m (3ft 6in)

PERFORMANCE
Max speed (fully loaded, calm water): 34 knots
Endurance (max continuous power, half load): 200n miles

HM 218 MULTI-ROLE HARBOUR CRAFT

Four HM 218 multi-role harbour craft were delivered to the Port of Rotterdam Authority in 1979-80. The design retains the standard HM 218 passenger ferry hull fitted with two superstructure modules to house port-monitoring and emergency-service equipment.

LIFT AND PROPULSION: Two General Motors 8V-92TI marine diesels drive fixed pitch propellers through reversing gearboxes and V drive gearboxes. The lift engine, which doubles as a pump engine for firefighting duties, is a Cummins V-504-M marine diesel. Engine transmission incorporates clutches for on-cushion lift, via four mechanically-driven and one hydraulically-driven centrifugal fans, or fire pump drive. Propulsion, lift and pumping machinery are controlled remotely from the wheelhouse. Engines are electrically started.

ACCOMMODATION: Utility standard accommodation for crew of commander, navigator, fire-control officer, medical attendant and one seaman. Crew's mess cabin with bunk and galley area is forward and medical room and toilet are aft. There are fan-assisted heaters.

EQUIPMENT: Firefighting equipment capable of delivering seawater, aspirated protein foam, high-pressure fog and dry powder. A remote control monitor with foam and seawater nozzles

HM 218 multi-role harbour craft

has a range of 46m (151ft) and flow rate of 2270 litres/minute (500 gallons/minute) for water or water/foam mix. The two deck hydrants can be supplied with water or water/foam mix. Each has four low-pressure outlets and one high-pressure outlet for fog generation.

Hull and superstructure are protected by a waterskirt drenching system. Other ancillary equipment includes wind speed and direction meters, explosive gas detection apparatus, water temperature monitoring and compressed air breathing equipment. For emergencies requiring medical aid, they are equipped with racks for four stretchers, oxygen respiratory equipment and a resuscitation unit.

The HM 218 port patrol boat can be operated on patrol by the commander and a navigating officer. For full duties, there are manning positions for a fire officer, traffic control officer and a working crew of four. Dimensions and power-plants are similar to the HM 218 ferry.

FENDERING: Fitted at the gunwale with three diagonals from gunwale level to below the waterline around both sidewalls and transom.

DIMENSIONS
Length overall: 18·29m (60ft)
Beam overall: 6·1m (20ft)

Height (including radar, mast, above water, off cushion): 6·5m (21ft 4in)
Draught, off cushion: 1·52m (5ft)
  on cushion: 0·91m (3ft)

LOGISTICS
Fresh water storage: 91 litres (20 gallons)
Fuel storage: 2500 litres (550 gallons)
Firefighting protein foam storage: 2545 litres (559·9 gallons)

PERFORMANCE
FULLY LOADED, CALM WATER
Max speed: 30 knots
Endurance (max speed): 280n miles

HM 221 FIREFIGHTING CRAFT

Two HM 221 firefighting craft were ordered by the city of Tacoma, Washington, USA in 1978. The first of these was delivered in May 1982 and the second late in 1982. They are fitted with a comprehensive range of firefighting, rescue, navigation and communications equipment.

LIFT AND PROPULSION: Two General Motors 8V-92TI marine diesels drive fixed pitch propellers via direct-drive reversing gearboxes and V-drive gearboxes. Lift power is from one General Motors 6V-92TI marine diesel which is also used as a pump engine. A second pump engine is

Craft built	In service	Operator
HM 221 *Defiance* (Fireboat No 5)	December 1982	City of Tacoma Fire Department
HM 221 *Commencement* (Fireboat No 15)	February 1983	City of Tacoma Fire Department

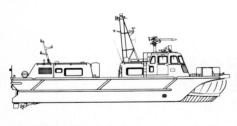
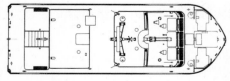
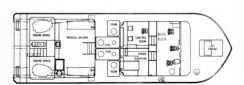

HM 218 multi-role harbour craft

HM 221 Tacoma fireboat on trials

provided by a General Motors 6V-92TI marine diesel. Propulsion, lift and pumping machinery is controlled from the wheelhouse. All engines electrically started.

ACCOMMODATION: Utility-standard crew accommodation comprises six-berth cabin with cooker, sink and toilet compartment.

EQUIPMENT: Two remotely-controlled bow-mounted monitors each of 9400 litres/minute water flow rate; one wheelhouse-mounted monitor of 20 800 litres/minute water flow rate; two under-wharf monitors of 9400 litres/minute water flow rate and one remotely-controlled 5600 litres/minute foam/water monitor fitted to the telescopic end of a high-level (10·5m) ladder which doubles as a crane. The monitors are remotely controlled for rotation and elevation from a console in the wheelhouse. The ladder is controlled from its base. All fire monitors, except the wheelhouse monitor, can be controlled from a straight stream to 90-degree fog.

FENDERING: Hardwood fendering fitted to the gunwale.

DIMENSIONS
Length overall: 20·9m (68ft 7in)
Beam overall: 6·1m (20ft)
Height above water, off cushion: 6·3m (20ft 9in)
Draught, off cushion: 1·55m (5ft 1in)
    on cushion: 1·1m (3ft 8in)
LOGISTICS
Fresh water storage: 90 litres (19·7 gallons)
Fuel storage: 2950 litres (649 gallons)
Allowance for miscellaneous firefighting equipment: 500kg
Firefighting AFFF foam: 1136 litres (249·9 gallons)
PERFORMANCE
FULLY LOADED, CALM SEA
Max speed: 30 knots
Endurance, max speed: 120n miles, including 5½ hours continuous pumping at rated capacity, plus a fuel allowance of 426 litres for station-keeping

HM 221 CREWBOAT

The HM 221 crewboat is based on the 21-metre HM 221 fireboat hull. Designed for offshore oil industry, it has a flat cargo-deck area aft. Rollers are fitted to the bow for passenger transfer.

LIFT AND PROPULSION: Two 510bhp General Motors 8V-92MTI marine diesels, driving fixed pitch propellers through reversing gearboxes and V-drive gearboxes, provide the main propulsion. Lift power is provided by one 356bhp General Motors 6V-92MTI marine diesel. The lift and propulsion engines are controlled from the wheelhouse. The engines are electrically started. Fuel capacity is 3·4 tonnes (900 Imperial gallons).

ACCOMMODATION: Air-conditioned accommodation for 28 passengers and crew. Crew accommodation comprises cabins for captain, engineer and crew, galley and two toilets.

DIMENSIONS
Length overall: 21·4m (70ft 3in)
Beam overall: 6·1m (20ft 1in)

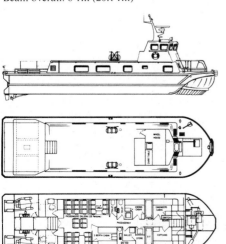

HM 221 crewboat for 28 passengers

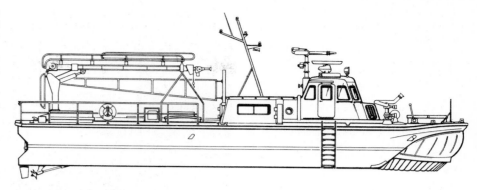

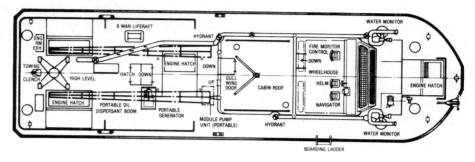

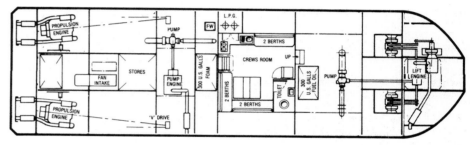

HM 221 firefighting craft

Height (wheelhouse top): 5·35m (17ft 7in)
Draught, off cushion: 1·75m (5ft 9in)
    on cushion: 1·06m (3ft 6in)
LOGISTICS
Fresh water storage: 1·35 tonnes

Fuel storage: 3·4 tonnes (900 Imperial gallons)
PERFORMANCE
FULLY LOADED, CALM CONDITIONS
Max speed: 30 knots
Endurance: 400n miles

Craft built	In service	Operator
HM 221 *Grayspear*	1982-1985	—

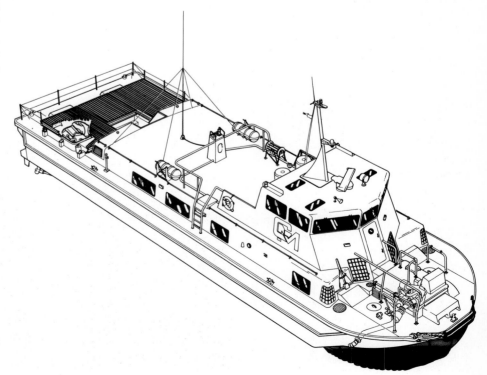

HM 221 PASSENGER FERRY

Based on the HM 221 (21-metre) hull, this variant seats 112 to 135 passengers depending on route requirements and has a continuous speed in excess of 31 knots in calm conditions and a range of 140n miles. The structure is designed to Lloyds Register Classification +Class ACV, Group 2, +LMC, CCS.

LIFT AND PROPULSION: Power for the lift system is provided by a single Cummins VT-555-M-BC marine diesel with a continuous rating of 270bhp at 2800rpm. Propulsive power is supplied by two General Motors 8V-92TI marine diesels, each rated at 490bhp at 2300rpm continuous. Power outputs correspond to ambient air temperature of 29°C and sea water temperature of 27°C. Lift and propulsion systems are mechanically controlled from the wheelhouse. Fuel capacity is 1450 litres when 95 per cent full.

HULL: Single shell grp mouldings, with submouldings, frames, bulkheads and other attachments bonded together.

ACCOMMODATION: Within the saloon of the 112-seat variant there are two toilet compartments, each with a WC and washbasin. Seats have a depth of 420mm, breadth of 430mm and a seat pitch of 460mm. Aisle width is a minimum of 470mm. Saloon and wheelhouse are air-conditioned. The air-conditioning plant is belt driven off the lift engine. Design conditions, internal 29·4°C dry bulb not greater than 65% relative humidity with ambient temperature of 34·4°C dry bulb 65% relative humidity.

CONTROLS: Power assisted manual/hydraulic system operating twin rudders with a hard over angle of 30°-0-30° when set with a zero rudder divergence. Hydraulic pump mechanically operated from the lift engines.

SYSTEMS
Electrical voltage: 24V dc nominal negative earth
Generation/charging equipment: Two propulsion engine driven ac/dc alternators rated at 27·5V, 100A. One lift engine driven ac/dc alternator rated at 27·5V, 100A
Batteries: Two 24V lead acid batteries, each with sufficient capacity to provide six starts for each engine
Lighting: Normal: 18W fluorescent tubes supplied from 24V dc system via invertors; Emergency: 24V incandescent fittings sited throughout craft
Communications: PA system between wheelhouse and passenger saloon; External: one VHF(FM) Sailor RT146/C401 radio telephone, frequency range 155·4 to 162·6MHz. Output 25/1W
Navigation: One Marinex Meteor transmitting magnetic compass. One emergency magnetic compass, Smith's type E2B. One Firebell Blipper radar reflector on mast. One Furono relative motion radar. One Vistar 301 night vision unit, comprising camera, main control and slave display

HM 221 crewboat

Craft built	Seats	Built	Operator
HM 221	112	1985	Donau-Dampfschiffahrts-Gesellschaft (DDSG)

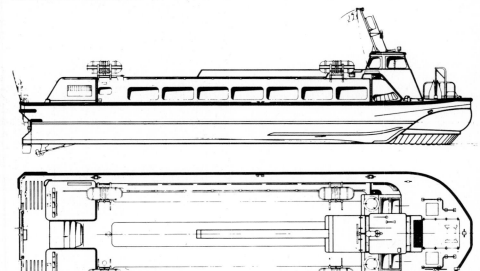

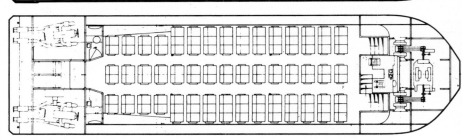
HM 221 ferry

HM 221 in operation with Donau-Dampfschiffahrts-Gesellschaft

Containers: Four grp luggage containers

Heating: Recirculating warm air heating system employing propulsion engine hot coolant

Bow loading: Flush foredeck, guardrails and bow polyethylene fenders arranged for bow loading of passengers

DIMENSIONS

Length overall: 21·19m

Beam overall: 5·91m

Height (underside of propeller to top of mast anchor light): 7·47m

Draught, off cushion: 1·76m
   on cushion, aft, loaded: 1·21m

WEIGHTS

Passengers, 112 at 66kg: 7392kg

Baggage, 112 at 9kg: 1008kg

Crew, 3 at 66kg: 201kg

Oil fuel: 1100kg

Payload: 8400kg

PERFORMANCE

Cruising speed, calm conditions, full payload, half fuel: 33 knots

Endurance: 140n miles

HM 527 SERIES 1 FERRY

The prototype HM 527 was launched in January 1982. It carries 200 passengers at a cruising speed of 36 knots and has been designed to operate on coastal and inland waters in wave heights of up to 3m (9ft 10in) with a payload of 21 000kg (20·7 tons). Normal range is 200n miles. A computerised roll stabilisation system is fitted as standard. The first four craft, ordered by Sealink Ferries Limited, were delivered before the end of 1983. Other designs based on the HM 527 hull include a hydrographic survey vessel and all-passenger crewboats and mixed payload supply boats for the offshore oil industry.

LIFT AND PROPULSION: The marine diesels are in two amidships engine rooms. Both accommodate one lift engine, one propulsion engine and one auxiliary power unit. The lift engines are General Motors Detroit Diesel Allison 8V-92TIs rated at 332kW at 2300rpm. Each drives a lift fan, via a gearbox, to provide plenum air and, via a hydraulic pump and hydraulic motors, two secondary fans for skirt inflation. The propulsion engines are MTU 12V 396 TB83 diesels rated at 1050kW at 1800rpm. Each incorporates a ZF BW 455 reverse-reduction gearbox and drives a single three-bladed propeller via transmission shafting inclined at 13 degrees. The outward rotating propellers operate at up to 900rpm. Two Perkins 4·236M marine diesels rated at 27·2kW, 50Hz, 220V drive the ac alternators and compressors for the air-conditioning system.

Fuel is carried in two tanks in the transom bay, in-line athwartships. Fuel capacity is 4·2 tonnes. Separate salt-water ballast tanks are provided with a capacity of 5 tonnes.

CONTROLS: Vessel heading is controlled by power-operated twin water rudders. Additional control is provided by differential use of the propellers. An automatic roll-stabilisation system operates through inclined independent rudders.

HULL: Single shell grp moulding with sub-moulding, frames, bulkheads and cabin sole panels bonded together. Materials used include expanded pvc foam, glass fibre, polyester resins, wood and aluminium alloy.

ACCOMMODATION: The bridge normally accommodates the commander, navigator and engineer. Passenger access is via doors port and starboard in the forward saloon and rearward double door for aft saloon. Emergency exits are located in both saloons. Four toilet/washbasin units are provided plus luggage space. Eight luggage containers can be mounted on the roof of the craft. Safety equipment includes life rafts, inflatable life jackets, lifebuoys and line-throwing apparatus.

SKIRTS: Main plenum chamber receives air from two lift fans via ducts located amidships port and starboard. Bow and stern skirts receive air from port and starboard fans, driven hydraulically by lift engine gearbox pumps, via ducts forming part of the superstructure.

Bow skirt is made up of two tailored neoprene/

Craft built	No of seats	In service	Operator
HM 527 *Tejo*	200	1983	Sealink Ferries Ltd, Hong Kong
HM 527 *Douro*	200	1984	Sealink Ferries Ltd, Hong Kong
HM 527 *Sado*	200	1984	Sealink Ferries Ltd, Hong Kong
HM 527 *Mondego*	200	1984	Sealink Ferries Ltd, Hong Kong

Shipment of first HM 527, *Tejo*, to Hong Kong

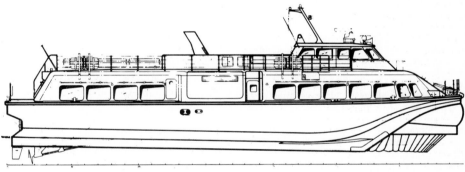

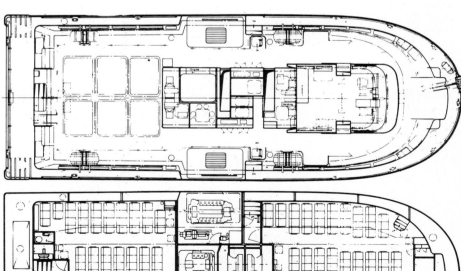

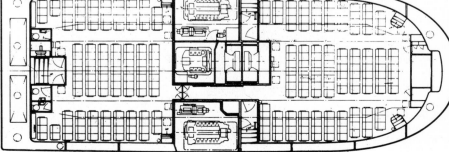

HM 527 Series 2 passenger ferry

nylon loops suspended in 180-degree arcs sidewall to sidewall and joined at their lower edges to form an irregularly shaped inflatable compartment. When inflated, the loops support 20 single fabric segments, attached at the loop joint line, and absorb wave impact shock to a degree. Four additional corner segments are attached on each side by ropes and shackles.

Three similar tailored loops are suspended under the stern. These are joined to form a single inflatable compartment.

DIMENSIONS
Length overall: 27·2m (89ft 3in)
Beam overall: 10·2m (33ft 5in)
Height overall: 4·9m (16ft)
Draught floating, loaded: 2·55m (8ft 4in)
　on cushion, loaded: 1·7m (5ft 6in)
Standard passenger capacity, forward saloon: 84
　aft saloon: 116
WEIGHT
Max gross: 87 000kg

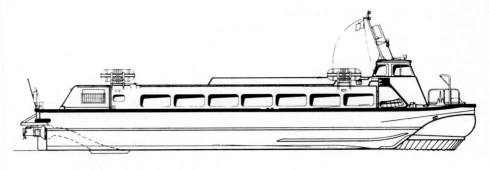

HM 527 SERIES 2 FERRY (DESIGN)

The refinements incorporated into this variant of the HM 527 result from experience gained with the Series 1 craft. With only a single diesel 332kW (445bhp) lift engine and carrying 56 more seats than the HM 527 Series 1 type the Series 2 offers greater economy with the same performance levels.

LIFT AND PROPULSION: Power is supplied by three marine diesels amidship in separate engine rooms in-line athwartships. The two outer engine rooms each accommodate one propulsion engine and one auxiliary power unit, the central engine room housing the lift engine. Lift is provided by a 550kW MTU 6V 396 TB53 driving, via a flexible coupling and Cardan shaft, two 1·22m (48in) diameter HEBA B centrifugal fans and, via a hydrostatic system, a secondary fan for aft skirt inflation. The propulsion engines are MTU 12V 396 TB83 diesels rated at 1150kW at 1800rpm continuous. Each incorporates a ZF BW 455 reverse-reduction gearbox and drives a single three-bladed propeller via transmission shafting inclined at 13 degrees. The outward rotating propellers operate at up to 900rpm. Fuel is carried in two tanks in the transom bay and fuel capacity is 4·2 tonnes. Machinery is monitored by a programmable controller and visual display.

CONTROLS: Lift and propulsion machinery controls in the wheelhouse meet Lloyds' requirements for unmanned machinery spaces. All diesel engines are electrically started. A plug-in portable unit provides bridge wing control of the propulsion gearbox clutches. Craft heading is by power-operated twin water rudders with a hard-over angle of 26°-0-26° when set with a zero rudder divergence. Additional control is by differential use of the propellers. Provision is made for emergency control from the aft deck. A Marconi Avionics automatic roll-stabilisation system operates through inclined independent rudders.

HULL: Grp structure comprising shell mouldings, sub-mouldings, frames, bulkheads and major attachments built from glass fibre weaves and mats using polyester resin matrix. Frame and bulkhead cores are end grain balsa or polyvinyl chloride foam.

ACCOMMODATION: Seats for 256 passengers in two saloons, forward and aft. Passenger access via doors, port and starboard, aft of forward saloon and double door at rear of aft saloon. Two emergency exits in both saloons. Bridge normally accommodates commander and navigator/engineer. Each passenger saloon has three hinging seats with safety belts for stewards/stewardesses. Safety equipment includes life rafts, inflatable life jackets, lifebuoys and line-throwing apparatus.

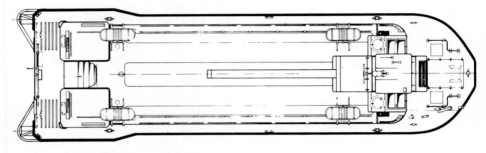

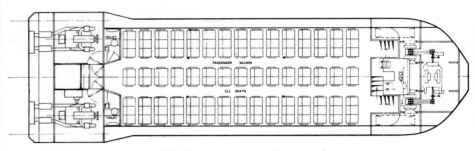

Design for Hovermarine International HM 221 waterjet-propelled passenger ferry

VENTILATION: Fresh air ventilation for passenger saloons, wheelhouse and toilet.

HEATING: Warm air heating.

FIRE SAFETY: Engine rooms: fire detection and extinguishing systems. Wheelhouse: two CO_2 portable fire extinguishers. Passenger areas: four AFFF portable fire extinguishers.

SYSTEMS, ELECTRICAL: Ship's service electrical plant comprises two diesel-driven, brushless, air-cooled ac generators rated at 45kVA, 36kW at 0·8 power factor lagging. Each machine can supply the normal running load. Medium voltage supply is 220V, 3-phase 50Hz, 3 wire. Supply for engine starting, essential services and exit point illumination is provided by 24V batteries.

COMMUNICATIONS
INTERNAL: Two-way amplified speech between wheelhouse, navigation positions, machinery compartments and steward's positions. Public address system.
EXTERNAL: One vhf (fm) radio telephone Type 145. Frequency range 155 to 163·2 MHz. Power output 25/1W. One Marconi Marine Survivor 3 emergency portable radio.

NAVIGATION
RADAR: Racal Decca RM 1216 relative motion radar with combined antenna/transceiver unit and one 12-inch master and one 9-inch slave displays.
COMPASS: Marinex transmitting magnetic compass with tape repeater and input to navigation radar displays. Smiths Type E2B emergency compass.
LOG: Chernikeeff Aquacatch EM Log with transducer and master unit.

DIMENSIONS
Length overall: 27·2m (89ft 3in)
Beam overall: 10·2m (33ft 5in)

Height (wheelhouse top): 4·9m (16ft)
Draught, off cushion: 2·7m (8ft 10in)
　on cushion: 1·7m (5ft 7in)
WEIGHTS
Oil fuel: 3500kg (7718lb)
Passengers and baggage, 256 at 75kg (165lb):
　19 200kg (42 240lb)
Crew, 7 at 75kg: 525kg (1158lb)
Fresh water: 180kg (396lb)
Total payload: 23 405kg (51 512lb)
PERFORMANCE
Max speed (fully loaded, zero wave height, zero wind speed): 36 knots
Speed, 85% continuous power: 28·5 knots
Endurance (at 85% continuous power and one generator running at 70% rated load): 300n miles

PROJECT DESIGNS

Hovermarine has drawn up a number of craft designs for particular applications based on the basic HM 218, HM 221 and HM 527 hulls. These designs include the following:
HM 527 SERIES 2 CREWBOAT
HM 527 SERIES FAST PATROL CRAFT
HM 527 SERIES STRIKE CRAFT

Details are given in *Jane's Surface Skimmers 1985* under Vosper Hovermarine Ltd entry.

A larger project design, the HM 700, with a displacement of 700 tonnes and a speed of over 50 knots is described in *Jane's Surface Skimmers 1983* (Vosper Hovermarine Ltd).

In 1987 a version of the HM 221 fitted with waterjet units was announced, length overall 21·90m, beam overall 6·60m, draught off cushion 1·21m.

RTK MARINE LIMITED

In mid-1987 Air Vehicles Ltd took over the complete marketing of Tiger hovercraft; full details of these craft are given under the entry for Air Vehicles Ltd.

SLINGSBY AVIATION LIMITED

Head Office: Kirkbymoorside, Yorkshire YO6 6EZ, England

Telephone: 0751 32474
Telex: 57597 SLINAV G

Hovercraft Division Office: Guild House, 151 Albert Road South, Southampton SO1 1FR, England

Telephone: 0703 37412
Telex: 477795 KRACON G
Telefax: 0703 32572

P G Pollock, *Chairman*
J S Tucker, *Chief Executive and Managing Director*
R Dobson, *Financial Director*
S A Cooper, *Contract Director*
M R Mobbs
Dr R Stanton Jones
Sir Peter Wykeham
A F White, *General Manager, Hovercraft*

Craft built	Name	Seats	Operator
SAH 2200 001			
SAH 2200 002			1987 Swedish military evaluation
SAH 2200 003	*Challenger No 1*	22	1987 Hover Travel Sdn Bhd
SAH 2200 004			1987 Maryland Natural Resources Police

Slingsby 2200 logistic support version

Slingsby 2200 passenger version

Formed in the 1930s as Slingsby Sailplanes, the company has grown over the years to its present size with around 200 employees, working on a site with covered factory space of 13 935m².

In the last 15 years the company has specialised in the fabrication of composite material structures and products for both marine and aviation markets. Work has been undertaken for the Royal Navy, Royal Air Force, Royal Marines, British Army, Airship Industries (UK) Ltd and oil companies. In addition a training aircraft, the Firefly, is produced, which is fully certificated by the CAA.

The company has full CAA approval and is also approved under MoD defence standard 05-21. Work is undertaken to meet Lloyds' and other marine regulatory authorities' standards.

The Hovercraft division was formed in 1984, to design and manufacture a 1500kg payload amphibious hovercraft in composite materials in order to complement Slingsby's existing product range.

In 1985 Slingsby Hovercraft operated a charter contract for an oil exploration company and has operated and maintained two hovercraft in the Middle East carrying out port maintenance and pollution duties from August 1985. The commercial department can arrange lease, charter or outright purchase to meet customer requirements and the product support department will offer substantial after sales service for customers worldwide.

In 1987 Slingsby Aviation became a member of the ML Holdings plc group of companies.

SAH 2200 (formerly SAH 1500)

In May 1986 the first SAH 1500, UK Registration No GH 9651, was delivered to the trials site in Southampton. Extensive trials and evaluation were carried out up to November 1986 when the craft was shipped overseas. Performance evaluation trials proved the craft exceeded all design criteria with a 14% increase in speed, 47% increase in payload and 2% decrease in weight. As a result the craft has been re-designated the SAH 2200 and the specification altered accordingly.

Since November 1986 when the first craft was shipped overseas, craft have been delivered and are operating in Europe, the Far East, the United States, the Caribbean, the Middle East and the UK. A sale of note was the craft purchased by the Department of Natural Resources (DNR) Police, Maryland. The craft's duties include search and rescue, medical evacuation, icebreaking and coastguard liaison. DNR Police had been leasing a hovercraft for over 18 months prior to purchasing the SAH 2200.

Slingsby 2200 interior views

The SAH 2200 is an amphibious hovercraft capable of carrying 23 passengers or 2200kg of disposable load. The design is such that rapid changes between cargo and passenger versions can be made. Diesel power has been chosen to reduce operating costs and maintenance time to a minimum. The composite plastics structure offers high strength, good fatigue characteristics and avoidance of corrosion for long life and low maintenance.

LIFT AND PROPULSION: Integrated system. A single Deutz BF6L 913C air-cooled diesel, rated at 190bhp at 2500rpm, drives a centrifugal lift fan and a Hoffman variable-pitch ducted propeller. The engine is mounted on resilient attachments and all machinery components are easily accessible for maintenance.

CONTROLS: Aerodynamic rudders mounted in the propeller slipstream provide directional control; similarly mounted elevators provide fore and aft trim. A fuel ballast system and roll control system is incorporated to counteract adverse loading and to improve craft performance in high wind and sea states. A controllable-pitch propeller allows variable thrust both in forward and reverse giving enhanced control particularly over land and in difficult downwind sea conditions.

HULL: Heavy duty composite plastics structure strengthened with Kevlar in high load areas. Heavy duty landing skids are provided. Four marine bollards on the deck form lifting rig attachments and guides for the integral jacking system. Sidedecks are rigid and enable large, bulky items to be carried outside the main load space. The sidedecks fold to allow transport of the craft by road vehicles or shipping within a 40ft flat rack container.

SKIRT: Loop and segment type.

SYSTEMS: 24V electrical supply is standard. Provision is made for optional extras such as radar, air conditioning, heating and searchlights.

ACCOMMODATION: Seats forward for commander and passenger/navigator are in a self-contained wheelhouse. The load space is flexible in

A Slingsby SAH 2200 as supplied to the Department of Natural Resources Police, Maryland, USA

layout and two quick-release composite canopies allow conversion to three versions:

PASSENGER VERSION: Bench seating running fore and aft providing a total of 23 passenger seats. Access is port and starboard through sliding doors mounted in canopies.

SUPPLY BOAT VERSION: Covered accommodation for eight passengers with open load space with capacity for up to 1400kg of cargo.

LOGISTIC SUPPORT VERSION: With canopies and seats removed, integral cargo lashing rails are provided to enable a disposable load of up to 2200kg to be carried.

In addition to the above, purpose designed pods to fit the load space can be manufactured to carry specialist equipment.

ACCOMMODATION
Disposable load: 2200kg
Seats: 24

SHIPPING INFORMATION
Can be airlifted, trailed or shipped within a 40ft flat rack. Packed dimensions with duct removed:
Length: 12·0m
Height: 2·0m
Beam: 2·4m
Weight: 3 tonnes
DIMENSIONS
Length: 10·60m
Beam: 4·20m
Height (off cushion): 2·60m
PERFORMANCE
Speed, max: 74km/h (40 knots)
Fuel consumption, average: 23 litres/h (5 gallons/h)
Range, max: 930km (500n miles)
Obstacle clearance: 0·50m

SAH 4000 (DESIGN)
A new project started in 1987.

UNITED STATES OF AMERICA

AIR CUSHION TECHNOLOGIES INTERNATIONAL INC (ACT-I)

10530 47th Street North, Clearwater, Florida 33520, USA

Telephone: (813) 579 0300

Henry G Saylor Jr, *President*
Mike January, *Vice President*
Mina K Saylor, *Secretary/Treasurer*

Air Cushion Technologies International was founded in 1981 by Henry G Saylor Jr, who had previously started Alaska Hovercraft Inc. The company is concentrating on the development of the 9-metre Corsair and 6·4-metre Falcon III amphibious multi-duty hovercraft. In 1986 Air Cushion Technologies International moved from Alaska to Florida.

Craft built
12 Maverick (ex Alaska Hovercraft Inc)
18 Falcon III
5 Corsair Mk I

CORSAIR Mk 1

Corsair is a fully-amphibious eight-seater (2 crew, 6 passengers) designed specifically for operations in arctic terrain. It can carry a payload of up to 1132kg (2500lb) and has a maximum speed of 48 knots.

LIFT AND PROPULSION: Lift is provided by a single GMC industrial engine driving, via a cog belt, two 0·76m (2ft 6in) diameter centrifugal fans generating a flow of 67 000cfm. Thrust is supplied by a GMC 454 marine engine driving, via a cog belt, a 1·87m (6ft 2in) diameter two-bladed propeller. Total fuel capacity is 189·26 litres (50

US gallons). Long-range tanks can be provided with a capacity for a further 189·26 litres (50 US gallons). Both engines run on standard petrol or 80·87 aviation fuel. Fuel consumption is 48·5 litres/h (12·8 US gallons/h).

HULL: Marine-grade aluminium.

CONTROLS: Heading is controlled by triple vertical rudders operated by a steering wheel. An elevator, mounted between two fixed vertical stabilisers, provides longitudinal trim.

SKIRT: Loop and segment type by Air Cushion Equipment Limited.

DIMENSIONS
EXTERNAL
Length overall: 8·99m (29ft 6in)
Length hull: 7·62m (25ft)
Hull width: 3·5m (11ft 6in)

Hull width, prepared for transport: 2·84m (9ft 4in)
Height, on cushion: 3·07m (10ft 1in)
  off cushion: 2·66m (8ft 9in)
INTERNAL
Cabin height: 1·829m (6ft)
Cabin width: 1·93m (6ft 4in)
Cabin length: 3·2m (10ft 6in)
WEIGHTS
Max weight: 3691kg (8150lb)
Disposable load: 1132kg (2500lb)
Empty weight: 2514kg (5550lb)
PERFORMANCE (zero wind, standard craft)
Max speed over land: 45 knots
  over water: 45 knots
Cruising speed over land: 35 knots
  over water: 30 knots
Vertical obstacle clearance: 406mm (1ft 4in)

Corsair Mk 1

Standard fuel consumption, zero wind: 12·8 US gallons/h

Max range, standard tanks, no reserve: 225km (140 miles)

Max range, long-range tanks, no reserve: 450km (280 miles)

FALCON III

This addition to the Air Cushion Technologies International range is designed to compete in size, payload and price with 20ft waterjet-powered speedboats. Falcon III seats five and has a top speed in calm water of 45mph. An automatic cushion relief system developed by the company is said to give a smooth ride, even in rough water.

LIFT AND PROPULSION: Integrated system powered by a single GMC 350 V8 marine petrol engine. Lift and thrust power are controlled independently by an automotive clutch which engages the thrust propeller and drives a 30-inch diameter centrifugal lift fan from the front of the engine crankshaft. Lift power is developed via a vernier control that adjusts the foot throttle to raise craft to full hoverheight with the propeller disengaged. Total fuel capacity is 40 US gallons. Long-range tanks give an extra capacity of 24 US gallons. The engine runs on standard petrol or 80·87 aviation fuel. Standard fuel consumption, in zero wind conditions, is 7 US gallons/h.

CONTROLS: Craft heading is by twin vertical rudders operated by a steering wheel. An elevator mounted between the two fixed vertical stabilisers provides longitudinal trim.

HULL: Welded marine-grade 5086 aluminium hull with glass fibre canopy.

SKIRT: Loop and segment type.

ACCOMMODATION: Enclosed cabin seats driver and four passengers.

DIMENSIONS

Length overall: 6·1m (20ft)
  hull: 5·7m (19ft)

Hull width, prepared for transport: 2·6m (8ft 6in)

Height, on cushion: 2·54m (8ft 4in)
  off cushion: 2·1m (7ft)

WEIGHTS

Max weight: 1630kg (3600lb)

Disposable load: 566kg (1250lb)

Empty weight: 1064kg (2350lb)

PERFORMANCE

Max speed, zero wind, over water: 72·4km/h (45mph)

Cruising speed, zero wind, over water: 48km/h (30mph)

Max range, standard tank, no reserve: 180 miles

Obstacle clearance: 0·3m (1ft)

SEA LION

A new 4-seat, 5·18m amphibious hovercraft, designed for recreational use, the Sea Lion was completed in autumn 1985.

LIFT AND PROPULSION: Single GMC Marine V6 petrol engine. Two ducted propellers for thrust.

SKIRT: Loop/finger type.

ACCOMMODATION: Driver plus four passengers.

DIMENSIONS

Length: 5·18m

Width: 2·44m

Height, off cushion: 1·78m
  on cushion: 2·08m

WEIGHTS

Max weight: 1019kg

Payload: 362kg

PERFORMANCE

Max speed: 64km/h

Cruise speed: 48km/h

Range at cruise speed: 130 miles with reserve

Fuel consumption: 5·2 US gallons/h

Obstacle clearance: 0·3m

Max wind limit: 40 km/h

LACV-5 (Light Air Cushion Vehicle, five-ton)

A US Army classification for a new ACT-I project. The first craft, Pegasus, will be the first USCG certified air cushion vehicle manufactured in the USA.

Falcon III

Falcon III

New ACT-I Sea Lion

LIFT AND PROPULSION: Single Deutz air-cooled BF8L 413F diesel for lift and two for thrust. Fuel tank capacity: 200 US gallons. Propellers: two three-blade.

CONTROLS: Two rudders mounted behind the vertical fixed fins. Twin elevators for trim.

SKIRT: Loop and finger type.

DIMENSIONS
EXTERNAL
Length: 12·2m
Width, on cushion: 6·4m
   off cushion: 5·49m
   (for C-130 transport): 2·95m
Height, on cushion: 4·17m
   off cushion: 3·25m
   (for C-130 transport): 2·74m
Cushion depth: 0·91m
Cargo deck area (side bodies): 12·2m × 1·22m
INTERNAL
Cargo area: 5·79m × 2·13m × 1·88m
Cargo volume: 23·09m³

WEIGHTS
Max weight: 12 002kg
Disposable load: 4529kg
Empty weight: 7473kg

PERFORMANCE
Cushion pressure at max weight: 43·5lb/ft²
Range, cruise: 210 miles

ACT-I LACV-5 Pegasus

Endurance: 12 hours
Fuel consumption: 30 US gallons/h

BERTELSEN INC

Head Office and Plant: 113 Commercial Street, Neponset, Illinois 61345, USA

Telephone: (309) 594 2041

William R Bertelsen, *Chairman of the Board, Vice President and Director of Research*
William C Stein, *President and Treasurer*
Charles A Brady, *Secretary*

Dr William R Bertelsen, a general practitioner and talented engineer, was one of the first to build and drive an air cushion vehicle.

Dr Bertelsen designed his first Aeromobile air cushion vehicle in 1950, and has since built and tested 16 full-scale vehicles, ranging from simple plenum craft to ram-wings. The 5·4m (18ft) long Aeromobile 200-2 was a star exhibit at the US Government's Trade Fairs in Tokyo, Turin, Zagreb and New Delhi in 1961. Descriptions of the Aeromobile 14 and 15 can be found in *Jane's Surface Skimmers 1980* and earlier editions.

Dr Bertelsen's two earliest vehicles, the Aeromobile 35 and the Aeromobile 72, were acquired by the Smithsonian Institution's National Air and Space Museum in January 1981.

During 1984 the company concentrated on improving the operating efficiency of the Mercury V6 150hp outboard engines in a 40in diameter duct driving a new computer-designed 12-blade axial lift/propulsion fan. The lift fan has been designed by the Turbo Machinery Engineering Faculty at the University of Illinois to produce 581lb thrust at 2900rpm or at a 2 : 1 reduction from engine rpm of 5800 at 150hp.

The company is developing an ACV crawler tractor which overcomes the problems of hill climbing, steering and obstacle clearance. It is designed to carry substantial loads at very low ground pressures.

AEROMOBILE 16

Interest in this 7·82m (25ft 8in) long utility vehicle, the largest to be constructed by Bertelsen, is being shown by potential customers throughout the USA and Canada. It employs a lift, propulsion and control system similar to that of the earlier Aeromobile 15. The craft is being retrofitted with 1·01m (40in) diameter spun aluminium ducted fans powered by two 150hp Mercury outboard engines for increased thrust and efficiency. The icebreaking capabilities of the A-16 were demonstrated during the winter of 1978-79. The craft can operate on cushion with one engine only, the other being employed for full propulsion and steering. It

Aeromobile 16 lift/propulsion unit under test

Aeromobile 16

is one of the few air cushion vehicles capable of sidehill operation.

LIFT AND PROPULSION: Power is supplied by two duct-mounted, 150hp, 122in³ displacement Mercury V-6 outboard engines, each driving a 1·01m (40in) diameter axial fan fabricated in spun aluminium. Each duct is spherical and gimbal-mounted at its centre so that it can be tilted and rotated in any direction. When the fan shaft is vertical the total airflow is discharged into the cushion. By tilting the gimbal the operator allows air from the fan to escape across the stern to provide propulsive thrust.

The thrust force is instantly available throughout 360 degrees and, metered finely by degree of tilt, provides propulsion, braking or yaw torque. The maximum available force is equal to 100 per cent of the propulsion force.

Under test is a variant with new HTD belt drive. Fan tip speed will be only 121·9m/second (400ft/

second). Thrust is expected to be 1162lb per unit, nearly double that of the earlier system. About 30 per cent of this is employed for lift at 90 degrees tilt.

Fuel is carried in two 90-litre (24-US gallon) tanks, one behind the forward engine and one forward of the aft engine. Type of fuel recommended is regular automobile petrol. Fuelling points are on deck above tanks.

HULL: Basic structure built in mild steel tubing. Designed to carry 907kg (2000lb) payload. Total buoyancy 6803kg (15 000lb).

ACCOMMODATION: Enclosed cabin with driver's seat forward and midship and rear bench seats behind, each seating three to four passengers. Access is via two doors, one each side. Seats are removable should the craft be required to undertake light utility roles. Cabin may be heated or air conditioned.

SYSTEMS, ELECTRICAL: Two 12V alternators and two 12V storage batteries.

Aeromobile 16

DIMENSIONS

EXTERNAL

Length overall, power off: 7·44m (24ft 5in)
    skirt inflated: 7·82m (25ft 8in)
Beam overall, power off: 4·31m (14ft 2in)
    skirt inflated: 5·48m (18ft)
Structure width, power off, folded: 2·28m (7ft 6in)
Height overall, on landing pads: 1·82m (6ft)
    skirt inflated: 2·23m (7ft 4in)
Cushion area: 24·15m² (260ft²)
Cushion height (hardstructure clearance): 406mm (1ft 4in)

INTERNAL

Cargo bay
Length: 3·35m (11ft)
Max width: 1·82m (6ft)
Max depth: 0·68m (2ft 3in)
Deck area total: 27·78m² (299ft²)

WEIGHTS

Normal empty: 1587kg (3500lb)
Normal max weight: 2268kg (5000lb)
Normal payload: 680kg (1500lb)

PERFORMANCE

Max speed, calm water, max power: 97km/h (60mph)
Cruising speed, calm water: 80km/h (50mph)
Turning circle diameter at 30 knots: 152m (500ft) estimated
Max wave capability: 1·2m (4ft)
Max survival sea state: 1·8m (6ft) waves
Still air endurance at cruising speed: 8 hours
Max gradient, static conditions: 10 degrees
Vertical obstacle clearance: 406mm (1ft 4in)

HOVER SYSTEMS INC

1500 Chester Pike, Eddystone, Pennsylvania 19013, USA

Telephone: (215) 876 8241
Telex: 62914561 (Easylink)

James D Hake, *President and Treasurer*
Joseph J Nestel, *Executive Vice President*
Frank W Hake, II, *Vice President*

Hover Systems Inc has design, manufacturing and test facilities located at Eddystone, Pennsylvania to supply and support hovercraft and other air cushion handling equipment.

In 1980 the company designed and built D-PAAC, a 50-ton payload, diesel-powered air cushion amphibious barge. Details of this vehicle are given in the Low-Speed Air Cushion Platforms section of this book. A subsidiary company, Air Cushion Equipment Ltd, in the UK designed and built a light hovercraft, the two-seat Hoversport 200 and details of this craft are given in the Light/ Sports Air Cushion Vehicles section of this book.

HUSKY G-1000, G-1500 AND G-2500 TD

In 1984 Hover Systems Inc concluded an agreement with Griffon Hovercraft Ltd of Southampton, UK as the exclusive US licensee for the construction and marketing of the Griffon G-1000 TD, G-1500 TD and G-2500 TD. The first of these craft, re-named Husky 1000 was delivered to the State of Maryland Natural Resources Police in May 1984. The craft has been successfully operated in many roles including search and rescue, emergency medical and icebreaking operations.

All US-built Husky TD Models are built to comply with rigid US Coast Guard Regulations and will carry US Coast Guard certification.

A Griffon 2500 TD hovercraft obtained Canadian Coast Guard certification and was in regular scheduled service at Expo '86 in Vancouver, British Columbia. The craft operated from a floating pontoon adjacent to the Canada Harbour Place section of the exposition along a seven-mile

Ducted propeller arrangement on Hover Systems Husky G-2500 TD *Bravo*

	G-1000 TD	G-1500 TD	G-2500 TD
Payload	978kg	1497kg	2494kg
Weight, empty	1995kg	2300kg	6757kg
Speed, max (no wind)	35 knots	33 knots	31 knots
Speed, cruise	28 knots	27 knots	26 knots
Standard seating	10 persons	16 persons	24-32 persons
Crew	1	1	2
Obstacle clearance	38cm	38cm	38cm
Weather limitations:			
Max wind	25 knots	25 knots	25 knots
Max wave height	1·0m	1·0m	1·0m
Engine	One BF6L 913C	One BF6L 913C	Two BF6L 913C
	190hp at 2500rpm	190hp at 2500rpm	190hp at 2500rpm
Length, overall	8·41m	10·15m	13·99m
Beam, hard structure	3·81m	3·81m	5·78m
Beam, side bodies removed	2·26m	2·26m	4·24m
Height, off cushion	2·68m	2·68m	2·87m
Cabin length	3·20m	5·00m	8·05m
Cabin width	1·80m	1·80m	3·29m

route to the main Expo '86 site. This craft operated 7 days a week and 10 hours a day throughout the Expo '86 period.

A second G-2500 TD was manufactured at the Hover Systems Inc facility in Eddystone, Pennsylvania, USA and thus meets the requirements of the Jones Act for commercial transportation service in the US. This craft has completed US Coast Guard trials in the Delaware River and Atlantic Coast areas and has made numerous trips through the Chesapeake Bay and in the Atlantic Ocean between Cape May, New Jersey and New York City. This craft is US Coast Guard certified.

The G-2500 TD hovercraft is fabricated from riveted and welded marine-grade aluminium. The primary structure consists of four longitudinal members enclosing multiple welded watertight compartments forming the main hull. Separate bow and stern sections are also fabricated from welded aluminium and bolted to the main hull. Secondary structural side bodies are attached to the hull with struts permitting the side bodies to be hinged upwards for transportation. The flexible neoprene-coated nylon loop and segment skirt is attached to the two side bodies and also to a skirt shift linkage to provide a lateral trim capability. All skirt maintenance can be performed without lifting the craft. Thrust is provided by two ducted propellers powered by two 190hp Deutz air-cooled turbocharged diesel engines. Commercial vehicle type clutches are fitted at the aft end of each engine which allow the propeller drive to be disconnected for hovering and independent control of each propeller. The clutch output shafts are fitted with sprockets to transmit power via toothed belts to the fixed-pitch four-bladed propellers mounted in aerodynamically shaped ducts. Lift fans are driven via toothed belts and pulleys from the forward end of each engine. In addition to the lateral trim control, longitudinal trim is provided by a fuel transfer system.

The control station includes seating for two crew members and is raised to provide good all-round visibility. Only one crew member is required to operate the craft, rudders in each duct are

Craft built	Name	Date completed
Husky G-2500 TD, Reg No PA 2994X	*Bravo*	1986
Husky G-2500 TD	—	1987

The first Hake-built Husky G-2500TD *Bravo*, operating on the Delaware River

controlled by a steering yoke, the propeller clutches are operated with foot pedals. A full instrumentation layout and switches for craft control and engine monitoring are provided and circuits are protected by circuit breakers. The 24V dc electrical system is supplied by two engine-driven alternators. The passenger cabin provides good visibility and accommodation and includes four abreast aircraft type seating for up to 32 passengers. The passenger cabin is ventilated by an offtake of cushion air distributed from an overhead duct and warm air is provided by a heater installed behind the rear bulkhead of the passenger compartment. A workboat version of this craft

can be provided with an open or closed deck area and with a bow loading ramp.

HUSKY 2500 TDX (DESIGN)

A modified version of the G-2500 TD craft is available. This craft is identical to the G-2500 TD except that the engines have been replaced with Deutz BF8L 513 engines capable of developing 320hp each at 2300rpm. In addition, the craft has larger ducts and propellers than the G-2500 TD and the hull length has been increased, resulting in predicted increased speed and operating capability of a maximum speed of 40 knots and a cruise speed of 38 knots.

LOCKHEED SHIPBUILDING COMPANY

Gulfport Marine Division, Gulfport, Mississippi, USA

LOCKHEED ADVANCED MARINE SYSTEMS

PO Box 4000, Santa Clara, California 95054, USA

P J Mantle, *Director, Advanced Ship Business Development*

Lockheed Marine Systems Group was reorganised in April 1986 and its activities are now undertaken by the Lockheed Shipbuilding Company. The organisation was originally awarded

a second source production contract on 30 September 1985, starting with two Textron Marine Systems (TMS) landing craft, air cushion (LCAC).

A new facility, Gulfport Marine Division, in Gulfport, Mississippi was acquired for Lockheed's production of LCACs. Production activities began on 30 May 1986 and delivery is planned for mid-1988, for the first Lockheed-produced LCAC which will be LCAC-18, to be followed by LCAC-21. Lockheed are contracted to produce seven further LCACs.

Four LCACs can be carried aboard the Whidbey Island Class dock-landing ships (LSDs). Lockheed Shipbuilding Company is the lead contractor on three LSD-41 Class ships. The LCACs are capable of carrying the M-1 tank and associated

equipment or 100 troops, from ship to shore and over the beach having a cargo deck area of 178m². The craft has amphibious capability, good manoeuvrability, better seakeeping than conventional displacement or planing hulls and is able to operate at speeds greater than 40 knots. The air cushion provides an excellent insulator from the water surface enhancing the craft's performance, minimising acoustic transmission and reducing vulnerability to mines and debris.

The new facility is on 9·92 hectares of prime property in a modern industrial part in Gulfport, Mississippi. Existing improvements include a 8733m² assembly plant, with an attached office suite, particularly suited for LCAC production, a large concrete apron and attendant service facilities. Lockheed also has an option on an

First production structures by Lockheed for LCAC-18 showing corner module and stern ramp (fixed part) (November 1986)   *(P J Mantle)*

additional 11·75 hectares of unimproved property directly east and adjoining the site. Both properties are on the Industrial Seaway that has direct access to the Gulf of Mexico. A craft tether test facility and a launch and recovery ramp to the seaway are under construction. The existing plant is being enlarged from the original 8733m² to 10 823m² by the addition of a 2090m² assembly building. This building will be further expanded to 4181m² to accommodate expected future production of LCACs and other air cushion craft. The plant is equipped with modern numerically controlled plasma burner, automatic seam welder and other equipment necessary for the production of LCACs.

TEXTRON MARINE SYSTEMS (TMS)

Division of Textron Inc
6800 Plaza Drive, New Orleans, Louisiana 70127-2596, USA

Telephone: (504) 245 6600
Telex: 6711199 BELLHAL

John J Kelly, *President*
Joseph J Halisky, *Vice President, Operations*
L W Frank, *Vice President, Manufacturing*
Frank P Higgins, *Vice President, Product Reliability and Support*
D F Bobeck, *Program Director, LCAC*
William M Rickett, *Program Director, SES*
J D O'Bryan, *Program Director, Lighterage ACVs*
James W Kratzer, *Vice President, Finance and Administration*
Larry N Hairston, *Executive Director of Marketing*

Bell Aerospace Textron began its air cushion vehicle development programme in 1958. In 1969, the New Orleans Operations was established to develop air cushion vehicles and surface effect ships for military and commercial markets. On 1 July 1986, Bell New Orleans Operations was renamed Textron Marine Systems (TMS). TMS now operates as a separate company independent of the other Bell Aerospace Divisions.

The company has rights to manufacture and sell in the USA machines employing the hovercraft principle through a licensing arrangement with the British Hovercraft Corporation and Hovercraft Development Ltd.

Craft which have been built by the company range in size from the SES-100B to the LCAC (Landing Craft, Air Cushion) currently in production for the US Navy. A total of 12 LCACs were delivered to the US Navy by the end of 1987 and 12 further craft are in production.

On 6 June 1986, LCAC-3, the third craft in the series, travelled over open water from New Orleans, Louisiana, to Panama City, Florida, at an average speed in excess of 40 knots. The voyage, which coincided with the 42nd anniversary of the World War II invasion of Normandy, marked the longest single trip ever made by a US air cushion assault landing craft. During 1987, the LCACs successfully completed a series of amphibious exercises with the US Fleet, and LCAC-4 participated in operations in Okinawa, Japan, marking the first entry of the craft on foreign soil.

Earlier work on air cushion vehicles which has led to current TMS developments may be summarised as follows:

In January 1969 the US Surface Effect Ships Project Office awarded TMS a contract for the detailed design of a 100-ton surface effect ship test craft. Construction began in September 1969 and a test and evaluation programme began in February 1972.

In March 1971 the company was awarded a Phase II contract by the US Navy to start work on a programme covering the detail design, construction and test of an experimental 160-ton AALC (amphibious assault landing craft), designated JEFF(B). Built at the NASA Michoud Assembly Facility, New Orleans, the craft was later transferred to the Naval Coastal Systems Center, Panama City, Florida. After preliminary testing the craft was delivered to the US Navy's Experimental Trials Unit at Panama City for crew training and operational trials.

Full details of the JEFF(B) are given on pp 93-94 of *Jane's High-Speed Marine Craft and Air Cushion Vehicles 1987*.

In January 1974 the company announced the successful completion of tests by the SES-100B, which confirmed the suitability of the design technology required for a 2000-ton ocean-going surface ship.

Principal craft built—Textron Marine Systems

SESs

SES-100B	surface effect ship test craft (see *Jane's Surface Skimmers 1984* and earlier editions)	on trials February 1972
Model 210A (110 Mk I)	demonstration SES, became USCG *Dorado* (WSES-1)	launched 1978 September 1980
Model 730A	became Model 730A, US Navy SES-200, with 15·24m (50ft) extension, USS *Jaeger*	
Model 720A	*Rodolf*—hydrographic survey boat for US Army Corps of Engineers	delivered 1980
Model 212A (110 Mk II)	crewboats: *Speed Command* *Swift Command*	delivered February 1981 delivered July 1981
Model 522A (110 Mk II)	'Seabird' class: *Sea Hawk* (WSES-2) *Shearwater* (WSES-3) *Petrel* (WSES-4) } US Coast Guard, Key West, Florida	October 1982 June 1983
Model 212B	Model 212A *Speed Command* and *Swift Command* converted to become Model 212B crewboats: *Margaret Jill* (chartered by GAC Offshore, UK, for Gulf or Suez service) *Speed Tide* (chartered by Tidewater Inc)	1985 1985

AMPHIBIOUS AIR CUSHION VEHICLES

AALC JEFF(B)	amphibious assault landing craft	completed March 1977
LACV-30	lighter, air cushion vehicle. 24 completed by 1986 for US Army Troop Support Command (18 completed by February 1985)	first ones delivered 1981
LCAC	Landing Craft, Air Cushion	twelve delivered by end of 1987, twelve more in production

The seventh Landing Craft, Air Cushion (LCAC) built by Textron Marine Systems and delivered 18 March 1987, operating on Lake Borgne, Louisiana, during trials

In July 1974 the Naval Materiel Command awarded TMS a US $36 million 18-month contract to conduct an advanced development programme for a 2000-ton, high-speed, ocean-going operational warship, the 2KSES. The company continues to support surface effect ship development through studies in advanced systems in lift and propulsion.

In autumn 1979 Bell Aerospace Textron signed a US $21 million contract with the US Army Mobility Equipment R & D Command (MERADCOM) for the first four of twelve LACV-30s (lighter, air cushion vehicle, 30 short ton payload) with the first deliveries made in 1981. In January 1981 an additional four craft were ordered and in autumn 1982 a further 12. A total of 26 production craft have been delivered, and the programme has been transferred from Bell Aerospace Niagara Frontier Operations to Textron Marine Systems.

In 1984, TMS entered into a joint venture with Avon Industrial Polymers Ltd, a British rubber company, to form Bell Avon. Bell Avon, located in Picayunen, Mississippi, manufactures skirts for TMS air cushion craft as well as other products.

The Textron Marine shipyard is located on a 10·1-hectare (25-acre) site in eastern New Orleans, Louisiana, and has direct access to the Intercoastal Waterway, the Mississippi River, and the Gulf of Mexico. Vessels built at the shipyard are in service with the US Army, the US Army Corps of Engineers, the US Navy, the US Coast Guard, and the commercial sector, and have accumulated many thousands of hours of service.

LCAC
(LANDING CRAFT, AIR CUSHION)

Craft built	Delivered to US Navy
LCAC-1	December 1984
LCAC-2	February 1986
LCAC-3	June 1986
LCAC-4	August 1986
LCAC-5	October 1986
LCAC-6	November 1986
LCAC-7	March 1987
LCAC-8	May 1987
LCAC-9	June 1987
LCAC-10	August 1987
LCAC-11	October 1987
LCAC-12	November 1987

Textron Marine Systems LCAC in well-deck of landing ship

On 5 June 1981 TMS signed a US $40 million contract with the US Navy for the detail design and long-lead materials for an amphibious assault landing craft designated by the Navy as the LCAC (Landing Craft, Air Cushion). The LCAC is the production version of the JEFF craft. The contract contained two options for the later construction of six craft. In February 1982 the US Navy exercised the first option for the production of three lead craft and in October 1982 it ordered a further three craft.

In March 1984 TMS was awarded a contract to build six more LCACs, with an option to construct an additional 12 craft. TMS, by December 1986, held contracts to produce a total of 14 LCACs. The LCACs are being assembled at the Bell Halter shipyard in eastern New Orleans, Louisiana.

In September 1985 Lockheed was awarded the second source construction contract for the LCAC programme, the total order between TMS and Lockheed to be raised to 108 craft. See Lockheed Shipbuilding Company entry.

On 5 December 1986 TMS announced that building had started on two more LCACs. On 1 July 1987, the US Navy awarded a US $187 million contract to TMS to construct another 10 LCACs. This contract marked the start of full production for the LCAC programme.

The LCAC is a high-speed, ship-to-shore, and over-the-beach amphibious landing craft, capable of carrying a 60-ton payload. It can transport equipment, personnel, and weapons systems (including the main battle tank) from ships located at increased stand-off distances, through the surf zone, and across the beach to hard landing points beyond the waterline. The craft is supported on a pressurised cushion of air and travels at much higher speeds than are presently possible with current conventional landing craft. Over-the-horizon launches are made possible by the high transit speeds of the LCAC.

The LCAC is capable of travelling over land and water. Compared to conventional landing craft, the percentage of the world's shorelines suitable for landing is increased from 17 to 70 per cent. The LCACs will operate from well-deck-equipped amphibious ships.

MACHINERY

Propulsion System

    Engines: Four Avco Lycoming TF40B gas turbines, 3955shp each, max continuous

    Fuel: Diesel marine (MIL-F-16884) or JP-5 (MIL-T-5624)

    Propellers: Two Dowty Rotol 3·582m (11ft 9in) diameter four-blade, variable and reversible pitch, ducted

    Lift fans: Four double-entry centrifugal type, diameter 1·60m

DIMENSIONS

Length overall, on cushion: 26·82m

Beam, on cushion: 14·33m

LCAC-1 crossing coastal scrub land

One of the bow thrusters on the LCAC which provide up to 10% of total thrust

Height, on cushion: 7·22m
Draught, off cushion:
    Hard structure: 0·71m
    Landing rails: 0·91m
Draught, on cushion:
    Cargo space: 20·43 × 8·23m
    Cargo deck area: 168 m²
WEIGHTS
Light-ship displacement: 92·5 tonnes
Design combat displacement: 103·1 tonnes
Payload
    design: 54·3 tonnes
    overload: 67·9 tonnes
PERFORMANCE (Combat weight)
Speed, max calm water: 50 knots
Speed, in Sea State 2: Over 40 knots
Speed, in Sea State 3: Over 30 knots

LACV-30 (LIGHTER, AIR CUSHION VEHICLE, 30 SHORT TONS PAYLOAD) MODEL 7467

This stretched version of the Voyageur has been designed to meet the US Army's requirements for a high-speed amphibious vehicle for logistics-over-the-shore operations.

In 1975 Bell Aerospace Textron built two prototypes as a joint development between the company's Niagara Frontier Operations near Niagara Falls, New York and Bell Aerospace Canada Textron at Grand Bend, Ontario. The prototypes, owned by the US Army, have been upgraded to production craft configuration by Bell. Delivery of the 26 production craft was completed in 1986. The programme has since been transferred to Textron Marine Systems.

The chief modifications are a 3·35m (11ft) lengthening of the deck ahead of the raised control cabin to facilitate the carriage of additional ISO containers and wheeled and tracked vehicles.

The LACV-30 is employed by the US Army as an amphibious lighter for efficient cargo removal

Craft built	Owner
LACV-30-1	US Army
LACV-30-2	US Army
LACV-30-3	US Army
LACV-30-4	US Army
LACV-30-5	US Army
LACV-30-6	US Army
LACV-30-7	US Army
LACV-30-8	US Army
LACV-30-9	US Army
LACV-30-10	US Army
LACV-30-11	US Army
LACV-30-12	US Army
LACV-30-13	US Army
LACV-30-14	US Army
LACV-30-15	US Army
LACV-30-16	US Army
LACV-30-17	US Army
LACV-30-18	US Army
LACV-30-19	US Army
LACV-30-20	US Army
LACV-30-21	US Army
LACV-30-22	US Army
LACV-30-23	US Army
LACV-30-24	US Army
LACV-30-25	US Army
LACV-30-26	US Army

First LCAC as delivered to the US Navy

Stern of LCAC

Bow ramp of LCAC

LACV-30

from ship to shore and inland when no port facilities exist. Capable of travelling up to 62mph (99km/h), it can operate over water, land, snow, ice, marshes, swamps and low brush, through 2·5m (8ft) surf and over 1·2m (4ft) obstacles. The craft can carry a variety of containerised cargo, wheeled and tracked vehicles, engineer equipment, pallets and barrels.

The craft can be used on 70 per cent of beaches compared to the 17 per cent accessible to conventional lighterage craft, permitting dry landings of cargo. As for many air cushion vehicles, its air cushion makes it an effective icebreaker. The LACV-30 can operate in harsh environments, from arctic to tropical conditions, including sand beaches and salt water and has achieved the best productivity per craft of all the US Army lighterage systems. In the last three years, a number of these craft have participated in major US Department of Defense training exercises on both the Atlantic and Pacific Coasts and in the Gulf of Mexico.

The LACV-30 can be carried, fully assembled, on containerships and break-bulk cargo ships, and all other US flag cargo ships. Not requiring dock or berthing facilities, it can be launched by its crew and readied for service in a few hours.

Endurance at cruising speed depends on the configuration role in which the craft is used. For the drive-on cargo and ISO cargo roles, the craft can carry payloads of 27·22 tonnes (30 short tons) with an endurance from 5 to 9 hours. With 33·57 tonnes (37 short tons) maximum payload, it can operate effectively in its lighterage role.

The craft is also suitable for a number of secondary roles such as coastal, harbour and inland waterway patrol, search and rescue, medical evacuation, water and fuel supply, vehicle, personnel and troop transport, augmentation of fixed ports, pollution and fire control.

In addition, a commercial equivalent, the Voyageur/AL-30, is offered with similar craft characteristics, including the 30-ton payload capability.

LIFT AND PROPULSION: Integrated system, powered by two Pratt and Whitney ST6T Twin-Pac gas turbines mounted aft, one at each side of the raised control cabin. Each engine is rated at 1800shp maximum and 1400shp at normal output. The output of each is absorbed by a three-bladed Hamilton Standard 43D50-367 reversible-pitch 2·74m (9ft) propeller and a 2·13m (7ft) diameter, twelve-blade, fixed-pitch light aluminium alloy, BHC centrifugal lift fan.

FUEL: Recommended fuel is standard aviation kerosene-Jet A-1, JP4, JP5, JP8 or light diesel fuel oil. Main usable fuel capacity is 8600 litres (2272 US gallons). Fuel ballast/emergency fuel capacity 5795 litres (1531 US gallons).

SYSTEMS, ELECTRICAL: Starter generators: four gearbox-driven, brushless, 28V dc, 200A each. One ac generator, gearbox driven, 400Hz, 115V. Batteries: two nickel cadmium, 28V dc, 40Ah each.

DIMENSIONS
Length overall, on cushion: 23·3m (76ft 6in)
Beam overall, on cushion: 11·2m (36ft 8in)
Height overall, on cushion: 7·52m (24ft 8in)
    off cushion: 6·56m (21ft 6in)
Skirt height, nominal: 1·21m (4ft)
Height, cargo deck, off cushion: 1·16m (3ft 10in)
Cargo deck: 15·69 × 9·9m (51ft 6in × 32ft 6in)

LACV-30

LACV-30-10

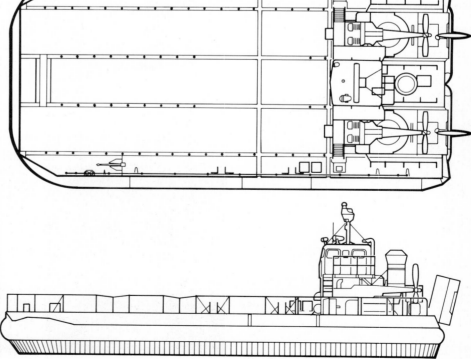

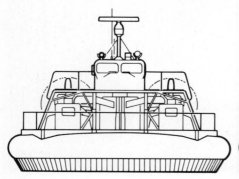
General Arrangement of the TMS Model 7467 LACV-30

An LACV-30 being carried by a Marine Travelift modified Model 70 BFM

(Marine Travelift Inc)

WEIGHTS
Light condition: 25 397kg (56 000lb)
Design max: 52 154kg (115 000lb)
Operating max: 53 515kg (118 000lb)
Max: 56 689kg (125 000lb)
Payload, max: 22·7 to 27·2 tonnes (25-30 short tons)

PERFORMANCE (estimated)
Standard day, zero wind, calm water, at gross weight of 52 154kg (115 000lb):
Normal rating: 74km/h (46mph), 40 knots
Max rating: 99km/h (62mph), 54 knots
Estimated fuel consumption during lighterage missions: 984 litres/h (260 US gallons/h)

Operation
Reference: The LACV 30 in Service by R W Helm, Canadian Aeronautics and Space Journal, Vol 33, No 1, March 1987.

MODEL 720A HYDROGRAPHIC SURVEY BOAT
(RODOLF)

Rodolf was built in 1979 and delivered to the US Army Corps of Engineers (Portland District) in early 1980.

The vessel operates as a displacement catamaran at low speeds and as an air-cushion-assisted planing catamaran at high speeds. With the lift system shut down, speeds in excess of 24km/h (15mph) are possible, with the sidehulls supporting 100 per cent of the weight through a combination of buoyancy and planing forces. The lift system can be employed at any speed to support part of the weight of the boat. At high speeds, up to 85 per cent of the weight can be supported by the air cushion, with a resulting increase of lift-to-drag ratio from 5 to approximately 11. The maximum speed is thereby increased to 56·32km/h (35mph). Over the complete speed range, from 24 to 56km/h (15 to 35mph) approximately, total power requirements, and hence fuel consumption, can be reduced by selecting the appropriate lift fan rpm settings.

LIFT AND PROPULSION: The lift system is powered by a single Detroit Diesel 4-53N rated at 105shp at 2600rpm. Propulsive thrust is supplied by twin Detroit Diesel Allison 8V-92N marine diesels rated at 360hp at 2100rpm, each driving a propeller via a standard Allison M reduction gear with a ratio of 1·52:1. Fuel is carried in four tanks, each with a capacity of 1325 litres (350 US gallons).
CONTROLS: Directional control is provided by twin water rudders aft, one on each sidehull, in addition to the differential use of propeller thrust for slow speed manoeuvring.
HULL: Primary structure is built of welded marine aluminium alloy 5086. The structure is of catamaran configuration and consists of two sidehulls, separated by decks and the cabin structure. The sidehull shell plating varies between ⅛ and ¼in thick, depending on local pressures, and is stiffened by T-section longitudinals. Sidehull shape is maintained by frames and bulkheads, spaced generally at 0·91 to 1·52m (3 to 5ft), that support the hull longitudinals.

Three watertight bulkheads are used in each sidehull and across the centre section between the hulls. Two are at the forward and aft ends of the cabin and one is forward of the helmsman's platform. The latter also forms a collision bulkhead. The bulkheads provide transverse bending and torsional continuity to the hull structure. There are also longitudinal watertight bulkheads running the full length of the craft aft of the collision bulkhead.
SKIRT: Flexible skirts at bow and stern. The bow seal consists of six fingers, each approximately 3·96m (13ft) long, 0·6m (2ft) wide and 1·95m (6ft 6in) high. All fingers are identical.

The stern seal has a constant cross-section and consists of two inflated lobes of coated-fabric material, with a horizontal diaphragm to sustain pressure loads. End caps, which bear partly on the sidehulls, contain the air at the ends of the seal. Principal dimensions of the stern seal are length 2·13m (7ft) and height 1·21m (4ft). Each lobe has a radius of approximately 304mm (1ft).
ACCOMMODATION: Deckhouse structure contains pilothouse, cabin and lift system housing. Pilothouse is in forward portion with pilothouse deck slightly higher than weather deck elevation. Main cabin deck is recessed below weather deck between sidehulls. Main cabin profile is lower than pilothouse to allow visibility directly aft through rear-facing pilothouse windows. Two interior stairways lead from main cabin deck level; one to pilothouse level and one to the aft section of weather deck. Provision is made for complement of seven crew and/or observers.
DIMENSIONS
EXTERNAL
Length overall: 14·63m (48ft)
Beam overall: 7·31m (24ft)
Height overall: 4·72m (15ft 6in)
Draught, max static: 1·6m (5ft 3in)
Skirt depth, bow: 1·82m (6ft)
      stern: 1·21m (4ft)
Cushion area: 62·92m² (677ft²)
INTERNAL
Length: 7·01m (23ft)
Max width: 3·65m (12ft)
Max height: 2·13m (7ft)
Floor area: 25·64m² (276ft²)
WEIGHTS
Normal empty: 18·6 long tons
Survey equipment: 1·2 long tons
Fuel capacity: 4·4 long tons
Normal gross: 24·2 long tons
SURVEY ELECTRONICS: Decca Survey Systems, Inc, Integrated Electronic Surveying System; Del Norte Trisponder electronic positioning; Ross Laboratories Digitising Fathometer; Houston Instruments X-Y Plotter; Digital Equipment

Hydrographic survey boat, *Rodolf*

computer and terminal; Digital Equipment magnetic and punch tapes; Decca Survey Interfaces, software, and left/right indicators.

PERFORMANCE

Max speed over calm water, max continuous power: 33 knots (29°C (85°F))

Cruising speed, calm water: 23 knots

Water speed in 1·22m (4ft) waves and 15 knot headwind: 24 knots

Still air range and endurance at cruising speed: 1090n miles and 50 hours

Max speed, over calm water, hullborne at 18·7 long tons displacement: 17 knots

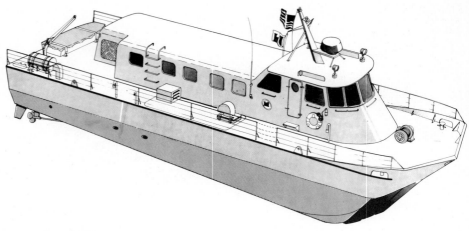

Model 415A utility boat or fishing vessel design

MODEL 415A UTILITY OR FISHING VESSEL (DESIGN)

The Model 415A is a derivative of the Model 410A, with overall length increased to 19·8m (65ft) for added payload capacity. The vessel has a wide range of applications, including harbour security and hydrographic survey, when more equipment and/or personnel are required. A version can be offered as a charter fishing vessel and, in comparison with conventional boats, improvements include reduced travel time to fishing grounds, improved ride, larger deck area and greater stability on site.

PROPULSION: Two 8V-92TI Detroit Diesel marine engines, rated at 430hp, each driving two 635mm (25in) diameter, four-bladed, stainless steel propellers.

LIFT: One 4-53T Detroit Diesel marine engine, rated at 155hp, driving one TMS 838mm (33in) diameter centrifugal fan.

SYSTEMS, ELECTRICAL

Generators: Two Onan, 15kW

DIMENSIONS

Length overall: 19·8m (65ft)

Beam overall: 7·92m (26ft)

Depth moulded: 2·92m (9ft 7in)

Draught, off cushion: 1·82m (6ft)
  on cushion: 1·21m (4ft)

WEIGHTS

Displacement, light ship: 28 086kg (62 000lb)

Payload: 3171kg (7000lb)

Fuel capacity: 1950 US gallons

Displacement, full load: 37 146kg (82 000lb)

PERFORMANCE

Speed: 32 knots

Range: 1000n miles

Model 110 Mk I demonstration SES

MODEL 210A (110 Mk I) DEMONSTRATION SES

Launched in late 1978, the Model 110 demonstration boat has undergone extensive successful testing by both commercial operators and the US Coast Guard. The basic hull and machinery layout permits modification of the deckhouse and arrangement of the deck space for a number of alternative applications, from crewboat and 275-seat passenger ferry to fast patrol boat.

In September 1980 the US Navy purchased the Demonstration SES (110 Mk I) to be used in a joint US Navy/US Coast Guard programme. The US Coast Guard, designating the boat the USCG *Dorado* (WSES-1), conducted an operational evaluation of the craft for the first six months of the programme. The craft was modified to conform to US Coast Guard requirements for an operational evaluation vessel. The US Coast Guard has completed its evaluation and a 15·24m (50ft) hull extension was added to the boat for the US Navy to assess the performance of a higher length-to-beam vessel. The craft has been designated the SES-200 by the US Navy (see later sub-entry for Model 730A).

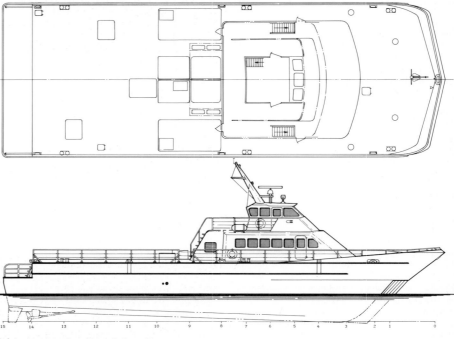

Original outboard profile and plan of Model 110 Mk I demonstration SES

MODEL 522A US COAST GUARD SES

In June 1981 the US Coast Guard awarded a contract for the purchase of three Model 522A (110 Mk II) high-speed cutters, the first two of which were delivered in October 1982.

The craft, known as the 'Seabird' class, are designated *Sea Hawk* (WSES-2), *Shearwater* (WSES-3) and *Petrel* (WSES-4). *Petrel* was delivered in June 1983. These vessels are based at Key West, Florida, at a new Coast Guard facility, and are being used to intercept drug runners

USCG *Dorado* (WSES-1), formerly Model 110 Mk I demonstrator SES before conversion by lengthening to become the SES 200

operating in the Gulf of Mexico and in the Caribbean Sea.

LIFT AND PROPULSION: Cushion lift is provided by two Detroit Diesel Allison 8V-92N marine diesels each driving a double-inlet centrifugal fan. Motive power for the propulsion system is furnished by two GM 16V-149TIB marine diesels each rated at 1800hp at 1900rpm. Each drives a 1·06m (42in) diameter three-blade, fixed-pitch propeller. Maximum fuel load is 34 050 litres.

CONTROLS: Craft direction is controlled by twin rudders, one aft on each sidehull. Differential propeller thrust is employed for slow-speed manoeuvring. The steering system is electro-hydraulic and can be operated from any of the control stations in the pilothouse and the wing bridges.

HULL: Primary structure is built in welded marine aluminium alloy 5086. The structure is of catamaran configuration and consists of two sidehulls separated by decks and transverse bulkheads. The sidehull shell plating varies between ¼ and ½in depending on local pressures, and is stiffened by T-section longitudinals. The spacing of the longitudinals is 457mm (1ft 6in) on the bottom plating and 381mm (1ft 3in) on the side plating. Sidehull shape is maintained by bulkheads spaced generally at 2·44m (8ft) which support the hull longitudinals. Bulkheads have ⅛in webs with T-section and flat bar stiffening and flat bar caps sized appropriately for each bulkhead.

Six of the bulkheads in each sidehull and also across the centre section between the hulls are watertight. Two are in the accommodation area, and one is forward of the deckhouse. The latter also forms a collision bulkhead. The bulkheads provide the transverse bending and torsional continuity to the hull structure.

The cabin superstructure consists of T-section frames fabricated from flat bars and spaced as the frames on the hull. T-stiffened plate is welded to the framing.

SKIRT: The bow seal consists of eight equally spaced fingers, each of which is attached to the underside of the centre hull. The stern seal, which has a constant cross section, consists of inflated horizontal lobes of coated-fabric material.

ACCOMMODATION: Deckhouse superstructure contains pilothouse at 01 level with communications and navigation equipment. Auxiliary control stations are provided plus additional controls on each wing bridge. Main deckhouse contains ship's office, armory, captain's stateroom, quarters for three officers and three men. Second deck accommodation includes galley and additional quarters for 12 crew.

ARMAMENT: Two 50-calibre machine guns on the foredeck.

DIMENSIONS

EXTERNAL

Length overall: 33·52m (110ft)
Beam overall: 11·88m (39ft)
Height, on cushion: 12m (39ft 5in)
    off cushion: 10·26m (33ft 8in)
Draught, on cushion: 1·67m (5ft 6in)
    off cushion: 2·51m (8ft 3in)
Skirt depth, bow: 2·28m (7ft 6in)
    stern: 1·52m (5ft)

INTERNAL

Control cabin
Length: 4·57m (15ft)
Max width: 3·35m (11ft)
Max height: 2·13m (7ft)
Main cabin
Length: 8·53m (28ft)
Max width: 9·14m (30ft)
Max height: 2·13m (7ft)
Floor area: 78·04m² (840ft²)

WEIGHTS

Max displacement: 150 long tons
Normal displacement: 134 long tons
Light ship displacement: 105 long tons

PERFORMANCE

Speed	Sea State 0	Sea State 3
on cushion:	30 knots	28 knots
hullborne:	19 knots	16 knots

RANGE

Sea State 0: 1550n miles
Sea State 3: 1250n miles

US Coast Guard cutter *Petrel*

Sea Hawk and *Shearwater*, the first two Model 522A cutters to be delivered to US Coast Guard

MODEL 212B (110 Mk II)

The Model 212B is a conversion of the Model 212A. The two craft converted are the *Margaret Jill* (ex *Speed Command*) and *Speed Tide* (ex *Swift Command*).

HULL MATERIALS: 5086 Aluminium.

MACHINERY

Main engines: Two Detroit Diesel Allison 16V-149TIB engines, diesel, turbocharged, intercooled, heat exchanger cooled, air start–1650bhp at 1900rpm

Gears: Two ZF BW 455 reduction gears. Input shafts–identical rotation, output shafts–opposite rotation (2:1 ratio)

Lift engines: Two GM 8V-92 engines, diesel, heat exchanger cooled, air start–350shp at 2100rpm

Lift fans: Two TMS 42-inch welded aluminium centrifugal fans

Generators: Two GM 3-71 65kVA heat exchanger cooled, one air start, one hydraulic start

UNDERWATER GEAR

Propeller shafts: 4-inch diameter 17-4 PH stainless steel

Bearings: 4-inch BJ Byplex rubber bearings

Propellers: 3-blade stainless

Rudders: Stainless steel built-up blades with 5-inch diameter stainless rudder stocks

Bearings: 5-inch BJ Byplex rubber bearings

Model 212B, *Margaret Jill*

ACCOMMODATION

Passenger accommodation: 119 4-inch thick cushioned bench seats on two deck levels. Two passenger heads provided.

Crew accommodation: Six in two single and two two-person cabins with hanging lockers. Two crew heads with showers provided. Mess area for six adjoins galley.

DIMENSIONS

Length, moulded: 33·25m

Breadth, moulded: 11·89m

Depth, moulded: 4·62m

Max draught

　Normal hullborne: 2·52m

　Loaded hullborne: 2·82m

　Normal cushionborne: 1·68m

CAPACITIES

Fuel capacity: 20 212 litres

Freshwater capacity: 3081 litres

Deck cargo: Up to 26 light tons

PERFORMANCE

Cruise speed: 31 knots in calm water

MODEL 340
PASSENGER FERRY (DESIGN)

The Model 340 is a derivative of the Model 210 crewboat, with an extended superstructure and seating for 276 passengers on the main deck. Second deck spaces can be used as passenger lounges, snack bars, or game rooms, according to customer requirements.

The overall dimensions are the same as those of the Model 210, and the same machinery could be used providing speed performance in the 30- to 32-knot range. Higher power diesels and variable-pitch propellers can be installed to provide cruising speeds between 40 and 50 knots.

MODEL 730A (USN SES-200)
HIGH LENGTH-TO-BEAM RATIO TEST CRAFT

The original 110ft SES demonstration boat is now owned by the US Navy. The boat was modified by adding a 50ft (15·24m) hull extension. The hull was cut amidships; the lift fans and engines remaining in the bow and the main engines remaining in the stern. Bow and stern sections were then moved apart and a 50ft (15·24m) plug section inserted between them. All major systems remained the same as they were in the original vessel, including the GM 16V-149TI engines.

In this configuration, the vessel has a 60 per cent greater disposable load than the demonstration boat, while its maximum speed is only reduced by 3 to 4 knots. At intermediate speeds, the power requirements are lower than for the shorter vessel, despite the greater displacement.

The engine rooms of the SES-200 can accommodate larger diesels, or CODOG/CODAG arrangements of diesels and gas turbines, to extend the speed capability up to the 50-knot range. Simple modifications can be made to

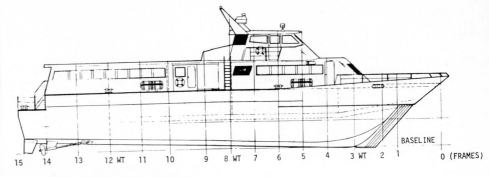

Outboard profile of Model 340 passenger ferry design

PERFORMANCE	3200hp diesels	CODOG (GE LM500 or Allison 570-KF)
Speed,		
calm:	39 knots	54 knots
Sea State 3:	32 knots	45 knots
Sea State 5:	27 knots	38 knots
RANGE		
High speed:	1140n miles	860n miles
Low speed:	1420n miles	1500n miles

reinforce the aft deck for helicopter operations. In this configuration, the beam of the vessel and the forward location of the superstructure results in a flight deck as large as those normally found on multi-thousand-ton naval combatants.

In 1986, the SES-200 successfully completed an eight-month series of joint technical and operational trials. The trials, which were conducted in Britain, Spain, France, Germany, Sweden, Norway and Canada, provided each host nation opportunities for direct evaluation of the high length-to-beam SES in their own waters.

ENGINES

Propulsion: Two GM 16V-149TI, 1600bhp each (driving 1·016m dia fixed-pitch propellers)

Lift: Four GM 8V-92TI, 435bhp each (driving 1·067m dia Bell centrifugal fans)

ELECTRICAL SYSTEM: GM diesel generator, 85kW plus 55kW back-up driven off one lift engine.

DIMENSIONS

Length overall: 48·7m (160ft)

Beam overall: 11·88m (39ft)

Height, on cushion: 12m (39ft 5in)

Depth, moulded: 4·63m

Draught, off cushion: 2·83m

Draught, on cushion: 1·67m

Wet deck height: 2·29m

Cushion length: 40·62m

Cushion beam: 9·63m

Cushion length/beam ratio: 4·25:1

WEIGHTS

Displacement, light ship: 127 tonnes

Fuel capacity: 80 128 litres (17 630 US gallons)

Displacement, full load: 207 tonnes

PERFORMANCE

Speed, max: 28 knots

　in 2·5m Significant Wave Height: 18-22 knots (max safe)

Time to accelerate to max speed: 60 seconds

Range, Sea State 0: 2950n miles at 30 knots

　3850n miles at 20 knots

Range, Sea State 3: 2400n miles at 25 knots

　2900n miles at 20 knots

Reference: The United Kingdom Trials of the SES 200 by B J W Pingree, B J Russell and J B Wilcox. Paper given at the Fourth International Hovercraft Conference, 6-7 May 1987

MODEL 511A
FAST PATROL CRAFT (DESIGN)

The Model 511A fast patrol craft uses the basic hull form of the 110ft SES but the overall length is increased to 45·72m (150ft). Construction is of welded 5086 marine aluminium, with T-stiffened plating for the exterior shell and bulkheads. The hull is divided into seven watertight compartments for safety in the event of hull damage. The second deck provides accommodation for a ship's complement of 28 officers and crew, together with wardroom, galley and mess facilities. A wide range of weapons systems, electronic warfare and countermeasures can be accommodated on the main deck. A high degree of computerised control and integration of the weapons systems with the ship systems can be provided.

US Navy SES-200, USS *Jaeger* (lengthened conversion of the 110 Mk I) showing spray discharging from the ride-control vent on the deck aft of the wheelhouse

DIMENSIONS
Length overall: 45·72m (150ft)
Beam overall: 11·88m (39ft)
Draught, on cushion: 1·82m (6ft)
    off cushion: 2·74m (9ft)

SES 1500 MEDIUM DISPLACEMENT COMBATANT CRAFT (DESIGN)

Textron Marine is continuing its research to extend the design technology of its existing range of surface effect ships to the 1000- to 1500-ton class ocean going naval combatant. The vessel would be of high length-to-beam configuration and would use high displacement sidehulls for efficient operation in the hullborne mode. The propulsion system would use partially submerged supercavitating propellers driven by CODOG machinery for high efficiency at all speeds. The vessel is fully air capable, with flight deck and hangar accommodation for two LAMPS helicopters.

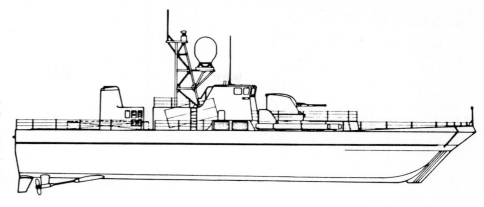

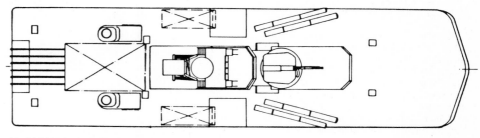

Model 511A fast patrol craft design

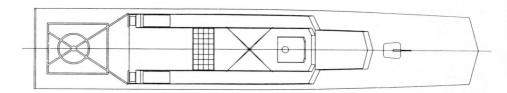

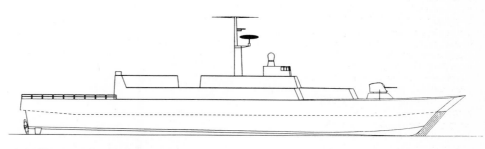

SES 1500-ton medium displacement combatant design

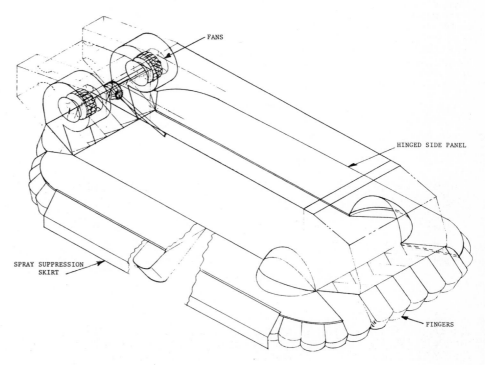

Components of the air cushion system of ACCRV

AIR CUSHION CRASH RESCUE VEHICLE (ACCRV) (DESIGN)

News of this combined air cushion and wheel-supported project was first announced on 18 March 1986. A 15-month design contract for $290 000 was placed with Bell Aerospace Textron, the design engineers working with the US Air Force Engineering and Services Center (AFESC) at Tyndall AFB, Florida, and with the Air Force Flight Dynamics Laboratory at Wright-Patterson AFB, Dayton, Ohio. A feasibility analysis and preliminary design has been undertaken by the Flight Dynamics Laboratory, funded by HQ AFESC/RDCF, Fire Research, Tyndall AFB, Florida. A 272kg scale model has been constructed by Textron Marine Systems for stability evaluation with the Flight Dynamics Laboratory whirling arm facility. The total development programme is expected to extend to four or five years. Full scale development began in the latter part of 1987.

A paper describing the preliminary design of the vehicle is listed in the bibliography section of this edition of *High-Speed Marine Craft and Air Cushion Vehicles*.

The approach adopted was to develop a multi-surface crash rescue vehicle incorporating a retractable air cushion system and with a performance comparable to the US Air Force Crash/Fire/Rescue (CFR) vehicle, the latest Class I Major Fire Fighting Vehicle, the P-19. Under most conditions, the air cushion skirt system would be retracted but over soft surfaces or rough terrain, the air cushion system would be deployed. In addition to propelling the vehicle while operating on a hard surface, the tyres will be used to stabilise and propel it while operating on air cushion over adverse terrain and water (waves not exceeding 0·3m in height), where a co-axial 'paddle track' gives additional propulsion.

PRINCIPAL PARTICULARS (PRELIMINARY DESIGN)

MATERIALS
Craft body structural material: Aluminium honeycomb sandwich

MACHINERY
Engine: Detroit Diesel 8V-92TA
Gearbox: HT-7500R 5-speed
Air cushion system: Skirt with open 50·8cm (20in) wide segments (knuckle shaped), 43° outer angle to ground, air cushion length: 8·74m air cushion width: 4·57m
Cushion pressure: 0·035kg/cm² (71·5lb/ft²)
Fans: Two 61mm (2·4in) dia, 25·5m³/s (900ft³/s) at 3400rpm
Air gap: 23mm (0·92in)

DIMENSIONS
Not to exceed (for C-130 aircraft loading):
Length: 10·67m
Width: 2·82m
Height: 2·67m
Weight: 13 605kg
Firefighting water and/or foaming agent: 3785 litres (1000 US gallons)
Rescue boom, extended length: 13·56m
Boom platform, max height: 15·55m at 9·375m from front of cab

Artist's impression of the US Air Force air cushion crash rescue vehicle

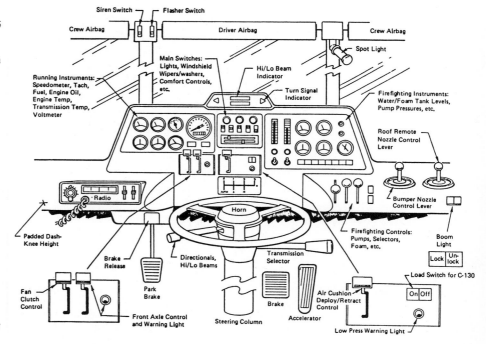

Proposed driver's controls and instruments for ACCRV

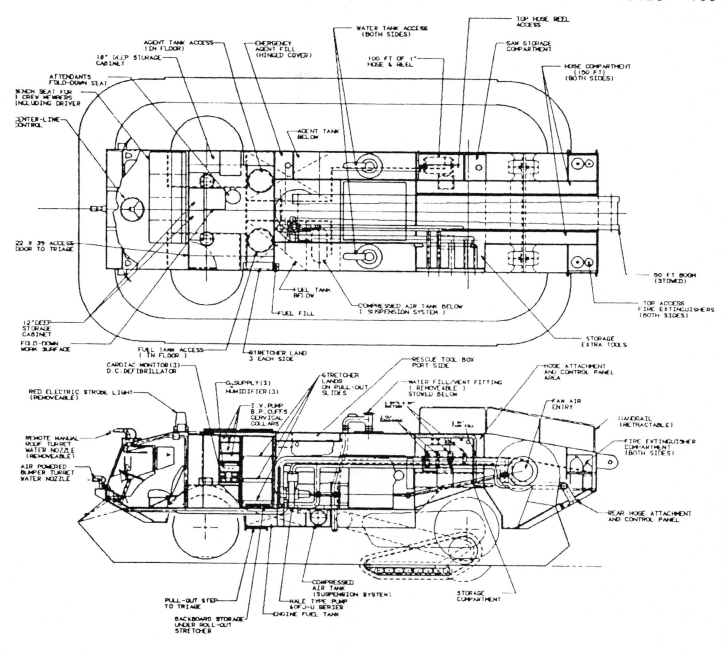

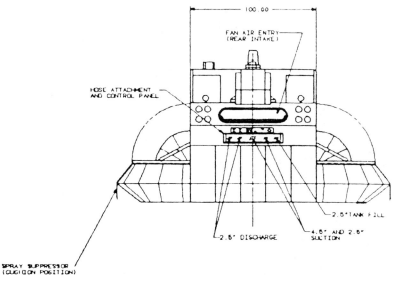

General Arrangement of ACCRV

LAMP-H (DESIGN)

The movement of large quantities of military supplies from ship to shore has historically proven to be a difficult task when piers are not available. Until recently, this logistics-over-the-shore (LOTS) mission has used either shallow draught landing craft that get as close to the beach as possible before discharging cargo, or amphibious craft that combine a crude boat hull with either wheels or tracks for overland operation. Both types of lighterage craft are severely limited in sea conditions, beach profile, and littoral terrain that can be accommodated.

The successful introduction of the LACV-30 into full Army service has demonstrated the potential of air cushion systems to improve the operational efficiency of the LOTS mission. Accordingly, the US Army initiated a programme to develop a heavier lift air cushion lighter, known as the LAMP-H (Lighter, Amphibious-Heavy). In May 1987, Textron Marine Systems (TMS) was awarded a US $250 000 study contract to develop the conceptual design. The study requires TMS to perform design, operational and cost analyses in support of vehicle configuration development, with the objective of making the most effective use of available technology in support of the overall mission objectives.

A broad parametric study has been completed by TMS, which has identified a number of candidate configurations capable of meeting the mission requirements. All are in the 100-ton payload class, and use either diesel or gas turbine engines for power. A number of propulsion options are being evaluated, and deck arrangements are being explored.

The study was scheduled to be completed in October 1987 with a report prepared for the US Army. It is anticipated that a request for proposal (RFP) for design and construction of a prototype craft will be released during 1988, and a contract could be awarded in early 1989.

EAGLE (DESIGN)

Announced on 10 April 1987 the Eagle (available in two sizes) is a new versatile air cushion vehicle that can be adapted to a variety of military and commercial missions and is capable of carrying cargo and crew over terrain inaccessible or inconvenient to land vehicles, watercraft, or helicopters and clearing obstacles of less than 0·6m in height. Because of its design, size and weight, the craft can be easily transported to a point of operation by truck, aircraft, trailer, helicopter, or other conventional means.

The craft is capable of performing surveillance, infiltration, target detection and interdiction, mapping and geodetic surveys, command and control, tactical mobility, or other mission requirements. In the commercial arena, the Eagle is well suited for servicing oil and gas production equipment, for seismic survey, police and customs work, pollution control, and search and rescue operations.

Because the craft uses a simplistic design and common equipment, personnel can become quickly proficient in operating the vehicle with minimal training. Maintenance can be accomplished with readily available, off-the-shelf materials and equipment.

There are several Eagle models available and each can be tailored to meet specific operational requirements.

PRINCIPAL PARTICULARS

	EAGLE MODEL 1200	EAGLE MODEL 2000
Hard structure dimensions		
length overall	6·50m	8·84m
beam	3·35m	4·27m
depth	0·30m	0·61m
Payload	545kg	4082kg
Seats	4	6
Propulsion and lift	150 to 180hp petrol engine	190hp Deutz diesel for thrust 50hp diesel for lift
Cushion area	13·75m²	28·61m²
Shipment	can be transported in CH-47 helicopter	can be transported in C-130 aircraft

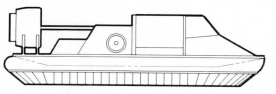

Eagle design Model 1200

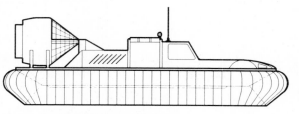
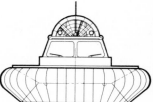

Eagle design Model 2000

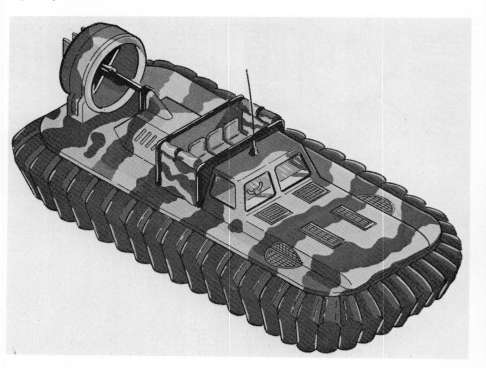

Artist's impression of the TMS Eagle Model 2000

LIGHT/SPORTS AIR CUSHION VEHICLES

AUSTRALIA

TURBO HOVERCRAFT PTY LIMITED

91 Pitt Street, Eltham, Victoria 3095, Australia

Telephone: (03) 439 9727

Paul Moody, *Director*
Owen Ellis, *Director*

Turbo Hovercraft Pty Limited was formed in 1983 by two engineers with extensive experience in hovercraft design and construction in Australia. The aim of the company is to develop a series of practical, 'state-of-the-art' craft to suit harsh Australian conditions. The first craft, the 225 Wedge, was released for sale in May 1984 and an uprated version, the 235 Superwedge first sold in kit form in June 1986. The company supplies kits, components and commercial craft on a 'one-off' basis. The design has been certified for commercial use by the Marine Authorities in certain states.

Turbo Hovercraft Nos 12, 18, 19, 20 and 25

TURBO 225 WEDGE

This craft was designed as a plan set for the home builder. Approximately 60 of these craft have been built but this model has now been substantially superseded by the 235 Superwedge model. Details of the 225 Wedge are given in the 1986 edition.

TURBO 235 SUPERWEDGE

This model was developed after extensive experience of the variety of conditions met by the 225 Wedge. A more powerful and reliable engine and a larger fan allow the craft to tackle almost any conditions.

LIFT AND PROPULSION: A Yamaha 485cc, 51bhp, twin-cylinder, two-stroke petrol engine drives, via a toothed belt, a 12-bladed, ducted Multiwing fan for both lift and propulsion, an aerodynamically integrated system. The engine, transmission, fan and duct are flexibly mounted to the hull, isolating the hull from vibration and the fan from shocks. Very fine tip clearances are maintained, giving good fan efficiency. The engine is in a fully enclosed engine bay, designed to reduce contamination of the engine air supply.

CONTROLS: Directional control is by five aerodynamic rudders in the fan slipstream, controlled by handlebars forward of the seat. Engine control is via a twist grip throttle on the handlebars.

HULL: The hull is a plywood monocoque construction, using 'stitch and glue' and sandwich panel techniques. A unique method of folding plywood allows sophisticated shapes to be made easily. An enclosed buoyancy tank around the hull periphery provides positive buoyancy and excellent floating stability in most sea states. There are storage compartments under the longitudinal seat and in the engine bay. A 23-litre marine fuel tank is located under the seat at the centre of mass of the craft.

SKIRT: The neoprene-coated nylon skirt uses an individually fed extended segment system. A skirt development programme is underway to improve the dynamic stability, increase the life and reduce the first cost of the skirt.

DIMENSIONS
Length: 3·52m
Width: 1·98m
Height: 1·22m
Hard structure clearance: 245mm
Prop/fan dia: 840mm
WEIGHTS
Empty: 180kg
Payload: 235kg (3 adults)

Yamaha engine installation in Turbo 235 Superwedge

Turbo Hovercraft 235 Superwedge

PERFORMANCE
Speed, max (ideal conditions): 100km/h
Speed, cruise (50-70% max engine rpm): 50km/h
Lift off: 45% engine speed
Rise height: 23cm
Climbing ability, static: 1 in 6 gradient
   dynamic: 1 in 3 gradient
Fuel consumption: 7 litres/h

FUTURE DEVELOPMENT
A programme is currently underway to develop a new craft incorporating modular design using high modulus composite technology and employing a new, unique construction technique.

This craft will be based on the Turbo Superwedge, utilising its proven technology and significantly up-grading it with a high strength, lightweight plastic hull. The hull will be constructed from vacuum-formed epoxy/fibreglass pvc foam sandwich with additional Kevlar and carbonfibre reinforcement. Use of a modular design concept will ultimately allow the craft to be supplied in various configurations, suiting a range of applications. For convenience and reduced freight costs, it is anticipated that the craft will be supplied in 'knock-down' form, allowing rapid assembly by individual customers or local dealers.

BRAZIL

DECORFIBRA INDUSTRIAL LIMITADA

Rua Guaianésia, 410-Chácaras Reunidas, Caixa Postal 381, São José dos Campos-SP, Brazil

Telephone: (0123) 31-2103

W Baere, *President*
Mª Emilia F M Lima, *Sales and Marketing Director*
R Baere, *Production Director*
F J X Carvalho, *Engineering and Consultancy Director*

Decorfibra Industrial Ltda is a company engaged in the development of high technology composite materials and their applications and for the past 20 years has supplied these materials for all aircraft produced by EMBRAER, Empresa Brasileira de Aeronautica.

GLM-S

The development of this two-seat craft started in 1984. A 12-blade propeller, 0·79m diameter, supplies both thrust and air for the lift system, air being ducted to the air cushion via six ducts.
ENGINE: 24hp, 2-cylinder, 2-stroke.
HULL: Fibreglass/Kevlar.
DIMENSIONS
Length: 3·50m
Width: 2·00m
PERFORMANCE
Speed, max: 43 knots, 80km/h
Rise height: 0·18m

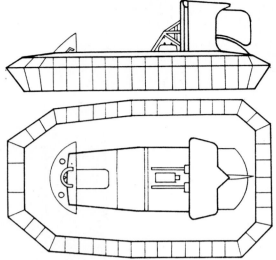

General Arrangement of Decorfibra GLM-S

Decorfibra GLM-S

CANADA

SPACE BOATS INC

746 Warden Avenue Unit 3, Toronto, Ontario M1L 4A2, Canada

Telephone: 755 2703

D Soutar, *President*

STARSHIP TX 500
SEATS: 1-4.
ENGINE: Air-cooled two-stroke Fuji Robin.
DIMENSIONS
Length: 3·96m
Width: 2·18m

WEIGHT
Empty: 175kg

Space Boats Starship TX 500

ULTRALIGHT HOVERCRAFT

PO Box 478, Carleton Place, Ottawa, Ontario
K7C 3P, Canada

Telephone: (613) 257 5219/224 5875

Ron Fishlock, *Director*
David Harwood, *Director*

Formed in 1984, Ultralight Hovercraft has to date concentrated its efforts in the design, development and testing of its Canair series of fully amphibious two-seat ACVs. An information package and a comprehensive set of plans are available to home builders. The company is working towards being able to supply less readily available items such as fans, timing belts, pulleys, glassfibre fan ducts, skirt material and studs.

Ultralight Hovercraft is presently developing a kit version of the Canair series, which will include every part necessary to assemble the craft. Other developments currently being worked on are a stretched version of the Canair 500, increasing its overwater payload to over 400kg as either a two-seater plus cargo and/or a four-seater craft. Another development is the addition of a central wheel that can be deployed when operating over road ways to reduce side slip.

Canair's special features include high manoeuvrability with variable lift air flow and a controllable reverse system, all of which are operated through one central control joystick; comfortable side-by-side seating on a movable seat used for pitch trim control; buoyant folding sides that can carry a useful payload and only take 5 minutes to fold up or deploy; and if fitted with an HDL/Fishlock loop segmented skirt offers low drag, smooth ride, low spray levels, low vulnerability to wear and tear, plus snap-on standard segments.

A single engine and Multiwing fan installation is used and when fitted with a current production snowmobile silencer system will result in an ACV with low noise emission.

CANAIR 340/440/500

TRANSMISSION: 50·8mm wide toothed belt.
CONTROLS: Single joystick, operates forward turning, reverse, throttle and variable lift flow.
STARTER: Hand pull.
FUEL: Petrol (82 Octane mix).
OIL: 2-cycle mix.
NOISE: Modern snowmobile level.
DIMENSIONS
Length: 3·84m
Width, on hover: 2·18m
Width, side folded: 1·22m
Hoverheight: 25cm

	Type 340	440	500
Engine, Snowmobile, 2-cycle: 2-cylinder, air-cooled:	340cc 28hp	440cc 36hp	503cc 45hp
Fan: Single axial, 800mm diameter:	10 blades	20 blades	20 blades
Empty weight:	158kg	172kg	181kg
Payload, normal:*	340kg	425kg	510kg
Payload, max:	181kg	226kg	272kg
Speed, max over water, calm, no wind:*	25mph	32mph	40mph
max over flat smooth ice:*	36mph	45mph	50mph
Endurance, on 19 litres of petrol:	3 hours	2·5 hours	1·5 hours

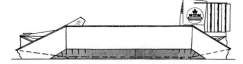
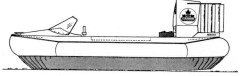
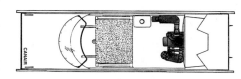
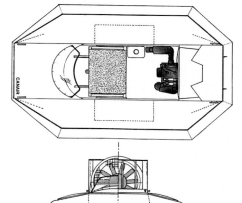
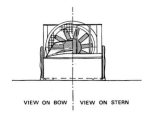

VIEW ON BOW | VIEW ON STERN

VIEW ON BOW | VIEW ON STERN

Canair craft with sides retracted for easy transport

General Arrangement of Canair Type 340

Ultralight Hovercraft Canair 500 *(Bill Sargeant)*

Ultralight Canair craft *(Bill Sargeant)*

CANAIR 500/2

Trials of the stretched Canair started in August 1987. This craft is one of the original two-seater prototypes, having been cut in half and a 1·14m mid-section added. The original 503cc engine has remained for the first phase of the trials.

WEIGHTS
Normal payload: 295kg
Max payload: 332kg
PERFORMANCE
Speed over water (max) calm sea, no wind, normal
  payload: 26 knots (55·5km/h)

The second trial phase will evaluate the craft fitted with a 60hp to 70hp rated engine.

The high length-to-beam ratio Canair 500/2 showing the reverse-thrust foil system

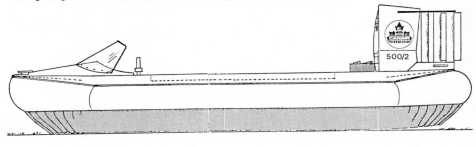

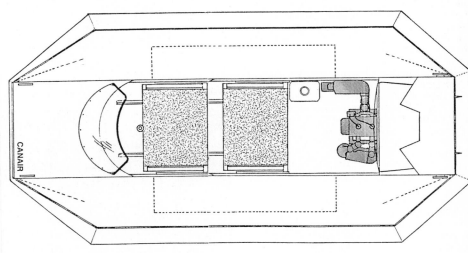

Layout of Canair 500/2

FINLAND

FINN-LEIJU KY

Rattipolku 7, 45360 Valkeala, Finland

Telephone: (9) 51233321
Telex: 52004 KVOLA SF

J Hakanen, *Director*

Designer and manufacturer of light hovercraft.

LEIJU 387

LIFT AND PROPULSION: Cushion air is supplied by a 9·5hp Solo engine, driving a 0·56m diameter 5-blade Multiwing 2H or 32C fan. Thrust is supplied by a Rotax 503, or 427 (liquid-cooled) engine driving, via a toothed belt, one 0·75m diameter Multiwing 5 ZL fan, ducted.
CONTROLS: Rudders set in propeller slipstream for directional control.
HULL: Built in moulded glassfibre with expanded polyurethane with some parts in sandwich construction.
SKIRT: Loop plus 72 segments in 227g/m² polyurethane-coated nylon.
ACCOMMODATION: Two seats in tandem; if enclosed 45kg extra weight.
DIMENSIONS
Length: 3·80m
Beam: 2·02m

Father Christmas arriving by a Finn-Leiju 387

WEIGHTS
Empty weight: 310kg
Payload: 290kg (over water)
PERFORMANCE
Speed, max, over water: 75 to 80km/h, 40 to 43
   knots, over ice and snow: 15% higher
Fuel consumption: 8 to 14 litres/h
Hoverheight: 0·25m

Finn-Leiju 387

FRANCE

JACQUES M THILLOY

20 rue Alexander Fleming, F-28600 Luisant,
France

Telephone: (37) 28 24 90

Since 1979 this company has offered a range of
three light amphibious hovercraft in kit form for
home building or ready to use. Other businesses
may manufacture the Rov' Air range under
licence. The two-seat Lestes 03 is designed for
cruising on inland waterways, the single-seat Rov'
Air for use in junior competitive events and Rov'
Air Mk 2 for European Formula 3 racing, or other
leisure applications.

With Rov' Air, this company introduces a new
concept in hovercraft construction: micro-hovercraft or microcraft.

LESTES 03

This was the first craft from the company,
completed in July 1979. The front fan delivers lift
air to the cushion via a peripheral fingered bag
skirt, which insures a better trim over rough
surfaces and allows high speed over water. The
single-seat Lestes 03 is ideal for cruising or
exploration.
LIFT AND PROPULSION: A single JLO 198cc
engine, rated at 7·3bhp at 4500rpm, drives a
600mm diameter, five-bladed Multiwing axial lift
fan. Blades have 30-degree pitch. A single Hirth
twin-cylinder 438cc engine rated at 32bhp at
5600rpm is employed for propulsion and drives,
via a toothed belt, a 1·1m diameter two-bladed
ducted propeller. Cushion pressure of the loaded
craft is 45kg/m² (9lb/ft²). The craft can carry 30
litres of fuel for cruising.
CONTROLS: A throttle lever controls the lift
engine and a twist-grip throttle controls the
propulsion engine. Twin aerodynamic rudders,
operated by handlebar, provide directional control. Electric starter is available on propulsion
engine.
HULL: All-wooden hull built in 4mm marine
plywood with wooden stringers. The fuel tank and
battery are under the seat. Closed compartments
along each side of the hull, packed with polyurethane foam, provide 150% buoyancy.
SKIRT: Bag and segments system. Skirt fabric is
neoprene-coated nylon.
ACCOMMODATION: Although designed as a
single-seater, the craft is capable of carrying two
persons in tandem. In single-seater form, there is
room enough for equipment such as extra fuel
tanks, tent and food containers.
DIMENSIONS
Length overall: 3·6m

Lestes 03

Width overall: 1·9m
Height overall, hovering: 1·75m
   at rest: 1·5m
WEIGHTS
Empty: 160kg
Max weight, one person: 245kg
Total disposable load: 140kg
PERFORMANCE
Max speed: 80km/h
Cruising speed: 40km/h
Endurance: 2 hours
Cruising range: 160km
Obstacle clearance: 0·25m

ROV' AIR

A new concept aimed at achieving a small-sized
amphibious hovercraft, easy to carry, and able to
travel at speed, this new micro-hovercraft is

suitable for river cruising and runabout trips,
fishing or exploring marginal terrain. This
2·4-metre single-seater is a low-cost craft of simple
design, easy to operate and to maintain. Rov' Air
is available in kit form for home building and can
also be supplied as a partially- or fully-assembled
structure. A wide range of completed components
is offered from the engine mounting to the skirt
system.
LIFT AND PROPULSION: Integrated system.
An 8hp Rowena Solo two-stroke engine, rated at
4200rpm drives directly a 600mm diameter ducted
axial fan. Air from this unit is used for lift and
thrust. The engine frame is rubber-mounted to
reduce vibration and entry to the fan duct is
covered by a heavy mesh safety guard.
CONTROLS: For simplicity only two controls
are provided: a lever control for the engine throttle

Rov' Air single-seater

is mounted on the control column, which operates a single aerodynamic rudder.

HULL: Marine grade 4mm plywood construction. Hull has full hydrodynamic surfaces. Polystyrene foam within the hull floor and side bodies provides buoyancy. Highly stressed areas are strengthened with glassfibre.

SKIRT: Either a simple bag skirt made from polyurethane nylon fabric or a pressure-fed segmented skirt in neoprene-coated nylon can be fitted. Each option gives about 0·17m obstacle clearance.

ACCOMMODATION: Open cockpit with single seat for driver. A removable 10-litre fuel tank, and dead-man switch are standard.

DIMENSIONS
Length overall: 2·4m
Width: 1·4m
Height on landing pads: 0·75m

WEIGHTS
Empty: 60kg
Payload: 75kg

PERFORMANCE
Max speed over calm water: 32km/h
Hard structure clearance: 0·17m
Endurance: 1 hour

Rov' Air Mk 2

ROV' AIR MK 2

Rov' Air Mk 2 is a single-seat microcraft designed for racing, following British and European Club Formula 3 regulations (engine capacity under 250cc). It can also be used for cruising in sheltered waters for various leisure applications. Microcraft Rov' Air Mk 2 is available as a kit or as a fully-assembled structure.

LIFT AND PROPULSION: Integrated system powered by a single 249cc Robin two-stroke engine running at 5500rpm. Power is transmitted via a toothed-belt to a 600mm diameter axial fan. Engine frame is rubber-mounted to reduce vib-

ration and to ease dismantling. This microcraft can be fitted with any suitable light powerful two-stroke engine.

CONTROLS: A handlebar, incorporating the engine throttle, operates a large single aerodynamic rudder.

HULL: Built in 3mm marine grade plywood. Base of the hull and stressed areas are reinforced with grp. Polystyrene foam within hull floor provides buoyancy.

SKIRT: Pressure-fed segmented type in neoprene-coated nylon material, with separate air-feed to every segment.

ACCOMMODATION: Open cockpit with a

single seat for driver. 10-litre removable fuel tank beneath driver's seat, dead-man switch and a set of tools are standard.

DIMENSIONS
Length overall: 2·6m
Beam overall: 1·6m
Height, off cushion: 0·7m

WEIGHTS
Empty: 65kg
Payload: 85kg

PERFORMANCE
Speed over calm water: 35-40km/h
Clearance: 0·2m
Endurance: 1 hour

SOCIÉTÉ AEROPLAST sarl

Creux Redon de Cantadou, 34400 Lunel, France

Telephone: (67) 71 65 97

Guy Ackerman, *Technical Director*

Aeroplast have developed over the past few years a range of light air cushion vehicles for sport and pleasure use and have also entered the utility vehicle market with their 1250kg payload ADOC 12 design in association with IFREMER. The ADOC 12 is described in the ACV Builders section of this book.

ADOC SPORT

This craft is offered in kit form by Aeroplast, a kit which takes about 30 to 40 hours to assemble. The hull is constructed in reinforced polyester.

ENGINE: 20 or 50hp.

DIMENSIONS
Length: 3·05m
Width: 1·85m
Height: 1·10m

WEIGHTS
Empty: 95kg
Payload: 90kg

MINI ADOC

A compact, high-performance, single-seat craft, the hull being of monocoque glass-reinforced polyester moulded construction with a polyurethane foam-sandwich bottom.

CONTROLS: Twist grips on handlebar for rudders and throttle.

SKIRT: French made bi-conical segment type.

ENGINE: Rotax two-cylinder two-stroke 25hp.

WEATHER LIMITATIONS
Wind, max: Beaufort 3 to 4
Wave height, max: 0·4m

FUEL TANK: 20 litres.

DIMENSIONS
Length: 3·0m
Width: 1·8m

ADOC Sport   (Aeroplast)

Mini ADOC   (Aeroplast)

Height: 1·15m
Prop/fan dia: 800mm
WEIGHTS
Weight, empty: 130kg
Payload: 120kg
PERFORMANCE
Speed, max: 70km/h
Speed, cruising: 40km/h
Gradient capability, from static: 5°
Gradient capability, at speed: 45°
Obstacle clearance: 0·20m
Fuel consumption: 8-10 litres/h

ADOC 3S TRIPLACE

A three-seat craft for touring, exploration and surveying. Built-in buoyancy 150%. Aerodynamically integrated lift and thrust.
ENGINE: Rotax 50hp.
DIMENSIONS
Length: 3·6m
Width: 1·8m
Height: 1·2m
Prop/fan dia: 800mm
WEIGHTS
Weight, empty: 150kg
Payload: 240kg
PERFORMANCE
Speed, max: 80km/h
Speed, cruising: 40km/h
Gradient capability, from static: 5°
Gradient capability, at speed: 45°
Obstacle clearance: 0·20m
Fuel consumption: 8-10 litres/h

ADOC 6 (DESIGN)

This design of a diesel-powered amphibious hovercraft was to be produced in 1987.
POWER
Lift: 22hp
Propulsion: 43hp
DIMENSIONS
Length: 5·60m
Width: 2·80m
Height, on cushion: 1·93m
Rise height: 0·35m
Cushion area: 14·0m²
WEIGHTS
Weight, max: 900kg
Weight, empty: 400kg
Disposable load: 500kg
PERFORMANCE
Thrust, static forward: 104kg
Thrust, static reverse: 42kg

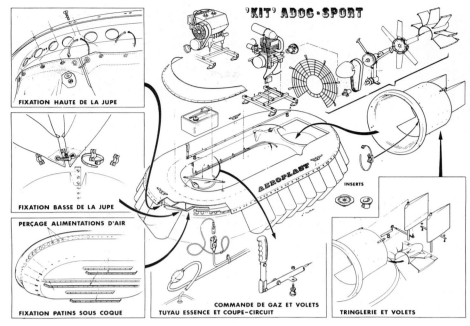

ADOC Sport kit of parts

ADOC 3S Triplace   *(Aeroplast)*

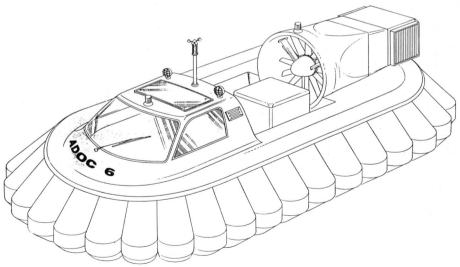

Design for ADOC 6 prototype

GERMANY, FEDERAL REPUBLIC

BUDERUS SELL GmbH

Head office and main works: Hüttenweg, Postfach 1161, D-6348 Herborn 1, Federal Republic of Germany

Telephone: 02772-710-325
Telex: 873413 D
Telefax: 02772-710-230

Hartmut Stiegler, *General Manager and Chief Designer*
Otto Fischer, *Production Manager and Test Engineer*

The company specialises in sports and commercial high-speed, lightweight hovercraft and is concentrating on the production of the Air Rider Junior and the Air Rider Hunter.

AIR RIDER HUNTER

Buderus Sell GmbH has developed a fast 2- to 3-seat hovercraft, the Air Rider Hunter, capable of over 100km/h (54 knots). Though intended primarily as a 2-seat craft to meet the need of enthusiasts and sportsmen for a powerful lightweight hovercraft, the Air Rider Hunter is also suitable for a variety of light commercial and utility roles (coast guard, military patrol, etc). The

Buderus Sell Air Rider Hunter

craft is fully amphibious and highly manoeuvrable over land, water, mud and snow and is to be put on sale in many versions.

LIFT AND PROPULSION: Aerodynamically integrated system powered by a 70hp air-cooled 4-stroke two-cylinder horizontally opposed engine (BMW type). Power is transmitted via five V-belts and a flexible coupling to a single five-blade 1·10m diameter ducted fan. The blades are adjustable. The primary airflow is ducted aft for propulsion while the secondary airflow is ducted into the plenum below for cushion lift. Fuel capacity is 60 litres (13·2 Imperial gallons). Fuel consumption is 10 litres/h.

CONTROLS: Craft direction is controlled by one aerodynamic rudder hinged to the rear of the propeller duct and operated by a wheel. A hand lever is provided for engine throttle control. Reverse thrust gates at both sides of the duct provide braking, stopping and manoeuvring capabilities.

HULL: Self-coloured carbon-Kevlar-glass-reinforced polyester plastic structure built in two halves, upper and lower, and bonded together around craft periphery. Spaces between the two hull shells are fitted with polystyrene foam. Reinforced areas are provided for four lifting points, three landing pads, one towing point and four for the engine mounting. The fan duct is also manufactured in crp. The craft has an enclosed cabin. Considerable attention has been paid to the aerodynamic lines of the craft. Tools and spares compartment provided.

SKIRT: Open loop and segment type fabricated in polyurethane-coated nylon fabric.

DIMENSIONS
Length: 4·20m
Beam: 2·20m
Height off cushion: 1·90m
Cushion inflated: 2·20m

WEIGHTS
Weight, empty: 350kg
Payload: 250kg
Fuel: 60 litres (13·2 Imperial gallons), 50kg
Max operating weight: 650kg

PERFORMANCE
At normal gross weight, calm water
Cruising speed: 90km/h (48·5 knots)
Max speed: 110km/h (59·4 knots)
Range: 450km
Endurance: 5 hours

AIR RIDER JUNIOR

The Air Rider Junior is primarily designed as a one-seat recreational craft. A powerful version of this craft is also suitable for hovercraft rallies.

LIFT AND PROPULSION: Aerodynamically integrated system powered by a 30hp air-cooled 2-stroke two-cylinder horizontally opposed aircraft engine (KFM Type 107 Maxi). Power is transmitted via a toothed belt to a single six-blade 0·74m diameter ducted fan. The blades are adjustable. The primary airflow is ducted aft for propulsion while the secondary airflow is ducted into the plenum below for cushion lift. Fuel capacity is 15 litres (3·3 Imperial gallons). Fuel consumption is 8·3 litres/h. The lift and propulsion system is designed for maximum reliability with simple maintenance.

CONTROLS: Craft heading is controlled by triple aerodynamic rudders operating in the propeller slipstream. A lever control for the engine throttle is mounted on the control column which operates the three rudders.

HULL: Self-coloured glass-reinforced polyester plastic structure built in two halves, upper and lower, and bonded together around craft periphery. Spaces between the two hull shells are fitted with polystyrene foam. Reinforced areas are provided for two lifting points, two landing pads, one towing point and one for the engine mounting. The fan duct is also manufactured in grp. The craft has an optional open or enclosed cockpit. Tools and spares compartment provided.

SKIRT: The craft is either supplied with a bag skirt or with a finger skirt fabricated in polyurethane-coated nylon fabric.

DIMENSIONS
Length: 2·97m
Beam: 1·55m
Height off cushion: 1·36m
Cushion inflated: 1·56-1·76m

WEIGHTS
Empty weight: 126kg
Payload: 100kg
Fuel: 15 litres (3·3 Imperial gallons), 12·5kg
Max operating weight: 240kg

PERFORMANCE
At normal gross weight, calm water
Cruising speed: 60km/h (32·4 knots)
Max speed: 90km/h (48·5 knots)
Range: 150km (93·2 miles)
Endurance: 2 hours

Buderus Sell Air Rider Junior

JAPAN

YAHIYU AIRCRAFT CORPORATION

2-15-3 Chofugaoka Chofu, Tokyo 182, Japan

Telephone: 0424 87 1162

Yasuhito Kaneko, *Director, Hovercraft Division*

Yahiyu Aircraft Corporation supplies amateur hovercraft builders with plans and components. It has introduced and is marketing in kit form a single-seat craft, the K-1.

K-1

An amphibious single-seat runabout, the K-1 has an empty weight of 88kg and a maximum speed of 56·3km/h.

LIFT AND PROPULSION: Aerodynamically integrated system powered by a 250cc, 2-cycle, single-cylinder air-cooled petrol engine. Power is transmitted to a 580cm diameter, 5-bladed ducted fan which supplies air to the lift and propulsion systems. Cushion area is 3·7m² and cushion pressure is 40kg/m².

CONTROLS: Craft direction is controlled by a column operating twin rudders in the propulsion duct and incorporating a twist-grip engine throttle.

SKIRT: Bag type, 20cm deep.

ACCOMMODATION: Open cockpit with single seat.

DIMENSIONS
Length: 2·9m
Beam: 1·6m
Height, off cushion: 0·84m
 on cushion: 1·04m

WEIGHT
Empty: 88kg
Max load: 90kg

PERFORMANCE
Max speed, over water: 40km/h
    over sand: 56km/h
Max gradient: 18%

K-1S

A more powerful version of K-1 equipped with a 53hp petrol engine.
LIFT AND PROPULSION: Aerodynamically integrated system powered by a 440cc, 2-cycle, 2-cylinder air-cooled petrol engine. Fan diameter 590cm, 10 blades.
SKIRT: Bag type, 20cm deep.
Cushion area: 3·7m²
Cushion pressure: 43kg/m², one occupant
    58kg/m², two occupants
ACCOMMODATION: Open cockpit, two seats.
DIMENSIONS
Length: 2·9m
Beam: 1·6m
Height: 0·84m
WEIGHTS
Empty: 100kg
Thrust, max: 44kg
Payload, max: 120kg
PERFORMANCE
Speed, max, over water: 60km/h

K-1

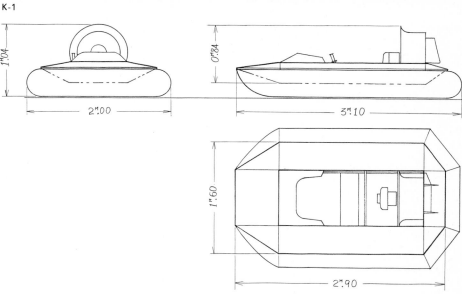

General Arrangement of Yahiyu K-1

K-1S

K-1S

NEW ZEALAND

HOVERCRAFT MANUFACTURERS (NEW ZEALAND) LIMITED

PO Box 11095, 23 Watts Road, Christchurch, South Island, New Zealand

Telephone: 03 486 821
          03 487 021
Telex: C/-4200

Robert Walker, *Marketing Manager*

AIRDASH

TYPE: Fully-amphibious two-seater for sports and light-utility applications, including surveying, weed spraying and rescue missions.
LIFT AND PROPULSION: Integrated system

Airdash

powered by 34kW (46hp) air-cooled, twin-cylinder two-stroke. Power is transmitted via a toothed drive belt to a 780 mm (2ft 7in) diameter ducted polypropylene fan with replaceable blades. Fuji Robin electric start motor. Fuel capacity is 33 litres (7·28 gallons) and recommended fuel is 96 octane oil pre-mix. Fuel consumption is 8 to 11·3 litres/h (1·75 to 2·75 gallons/h).

HULL: Monocoque construction in fibreglass. Deck, cockpit, seat and duct system moulded in one-piece grp. Hull base is moulded separately in one piece using core-mat/grp laminate. This is bonded to the top moulding to form a one-piece, lightweight, impact-resistant structure.

SKIRT: Fully-segmented type in pvc or neoprene-coated nylon. Segments individually replaceable using quick-release clips and nylon ties.

DIMENSIONS
Length: 3·45m (11ft 6in)
Width: 1·78m (5ft 9in)

WEIGHTS
Empty: 148kg (326lb)
Payload: 165kg (364lb)

PERFORMANCE
Max recorded speed, over land: 90km/h (56mph)
Max speed, still air, over water: 77km/h (48mph)
Normal cruising speed over water with full load: 48km/h (30mph)
Max wave height: 0·5-0·6m (20-24in)
Basic colour optional with order.

SPAIN

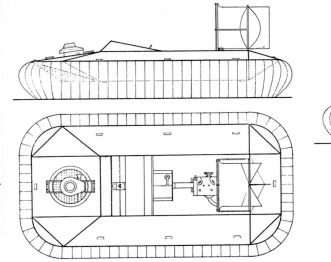

ALBERTO GIMENEZ DE LOS GALANES

Reyes 7, Madrid 8, Spain

Telephone: (1) 231 5289

Jorge Gomez Gomez, *Director*
Eduardo Sanchiz Garrote, *Director*

After several years of studying the theoretical aspects of hovercraft at the Escuela Tecnica Superior de Ingenieros Aeronauticos in Madrid, a group of aeronautical engineers decided in September 1979 to verify their technical predictions by constructing a small craft. The craft, named Furtivo I, is being used to provide confirmation of earlier theoretical studies, but a design is being developed which is likely to incorporate certain improvements such as the HDL Skirt Shift system. Furtivo I performed its first flight in February 1980.

FURTIVO I

LIFT AND PROPULSION: Lift is provided by a single Kyoritsu KEC 225cc two-stroke driving a 550mm (1ft 10in) diameter Multiwing axial fan. Cushion pressure is 10lb/ft². Thrust is provided by a single 38·5hp Rotax 640 two-stroke, air-cooled engine driving a 710mm (2ft 4in) diameter ducted

General Arrangement of Furtivo I

axial fan filled with Multiwing blades. The fan provides forward or reverse thrust.

CONTROLS: Craft heading is controlled by a centrally-located column which operates a single aerodynamic rudder. The throttle control for the

thrust engine is mounted on the stick. Another small column in the cockpit operates the thrust reversal mechanism.

HULL: Plywood structure with grp skin.

SKIRT: Fully-segmented type in neoprene-coated nylon.

ACCOMMODATION: Side-by-side seating for two in an open cockpit.

DIMENSIONS
Length overall, power off: 4m (13ft 1½in)
Beam overall, power off: 2m (6ft 6¾in)
Height overall, skirt inflated: 1·58m (5ft 2¼in)
Draught afloat: 8·5cm (3¼in)
Cushion area: 7·78m² (84ft²)
Skirt depth: 0·3m (12in)

WEIGHTS
Normal empty: 203kg (448lb)
Normal payload: 183kg (403lb)
Max payload: 197kg (434lb)

PERFORMANCE
CALM CONDITIONS
Max speed: 78km/h (48·5mph)
Gradient capability: 1 : 7
Vertical obstacle clearance: 0·3m (12in)

Furtivo I

FM-AERODESLIZADORES

PO Box 1038, Alcalá de Henares, Madrid, Spain

Julián Martin Sanz, *Mechanical Engineer*
Joaquin Heras, *Electrical Engineer*

FM-HC-002

The construction of this two-seat hovercraft began in October 1986.

LIFT AND PROPULSION: Aerodynamically integrated; two Multiwing prop/fans, type 560/9/4Z.

ENGINE: One Rotax, type 503, 52hp, 497cc, two carburettors.

HULL: Grp/sandwich construction.

SKIRT: Segmented.

DIMENSIONS
Length: 4·00m
Width: 2·00m
Height: 0·72m

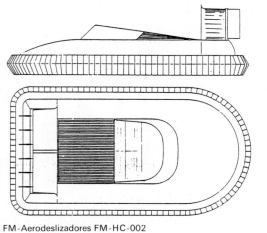

FM-Aerodeslizadores FM-HC-002

WEIGHT
Max: 300kg

PERFORMANCE
Speed, max: 70km/h

TAIWAN

CHIVALRY UNIVERSAL COMPANY LIMITED

PO Box 36-48 Taipei, Taiwan

Telephone: 02 6212197/7692511
Telex: 19113 FINFONG TP
Telefax: 02 7637106

C S Lee, *President*
H J Tsai, *Vice President, Research and Development*
T P Doo, *Vice President, Engineering*

Overseas Office: International Vehicle Research Inc, 14074 Nacogdoches Road, Suite 322, San Antonio, Texas 78247, USA

J T Doo, *President*

With the success of the CY-6 Mk III utility hovercraft, the development work of CY-6 Mk IV, a stretched version of CY-6 Mk III, was launched in early 1987 and testing started in early 1988. CY-6 Mk IV is 1·0m longer in comparison with the previous version CY-6 Mk III and carries 8 passengers or 600kg of payload.

The schedule for the CY-12 project has been extended due to funding delays, although the design work is still in progress. The payload capability of the CY-12 has been increased and the design for the stretched version, CY-12B, has also been initiated.

The design work of a 4·5-ton utility amphibian hovercraft CY-14 was initiated in January 1987, and the prototype construction is scheduled to start mid-1988. The prototype will also serve as an experimental test bed to verify some of the CY-12 design variables.

Chivalry Universal Co is conducting the research and development, testing and design work in conjunction with the International Vehicle Research Inc in the United States, which also has the marketing responsibility for the CY-series hovercraft in the North American area.

Chivalry CY-10 Mk II

SIREN CY-10

A highly manoeuvrable light ACV, the CY-10 is intended for recreational use. The design combines an frp hull with an integrated lift/propulsion system and a fully segmented skirt.

LIFT AND PROPULSION: Integrated system powered by a single 40hp Hirth 276R 3E two-stroke. This drives, via a toothed belt, a 12-blade ducted fan which provides air for lift and propulsion.
CONTROLS: Twin rudders at rear of thrust duct, in conjunction with cg movement, control craft heading.
HULL: Fibreglass reinforced plastic structure filled with polyurethane and pvc foam.
SKIRT: Nylon (coated) segmented skirt.
ACCOMMODATION: Open tandem seat for driver and passenger.
SYSTEMS, ELECTRICAL: 12V dc with engine-driven 123W magneto generator and 40Ah battery for engine starting and navigation lights.

DIMENSIONS
Length overall: 3·7m
Beam: 1·9m
Height: 1·3m
WEIGHTS
Empty: 190kg
Payload: 150kg
PERFORMANCE
Speed, max: 35 knots

CY-10 MK II

The latest version of the CY-10 series recreational hovercraft. A new cushion air distribution system improves the cushion stability and efficiency and also helps to prevent the plough-in phenomenon. In addition, a more aerodynamically efficient propeller duct with four rudders improves the acceleration and directional control.

LIFT AND PROPULSION: Aerodynamically integrated system powered by a single Rotax 503, 43hp, two-stroke engine which drives, via a toothed belt, a 12-blade ducted fan which provides air for propulsion and lift.
CONTROLS: Four rudders at rear of thrust duct, in conjunction with cg movement, control craft heading.
HULL: Fibreglass reinforced plastic structure filled with polyurethane and pvc foam.
SKIRT: Nylon (coated) segmented skirt.
ACCOMMODATION: Open tandem seat for driver and passenger.
SYSTEMS, ELECTRICAL: 12V dc with engine-driven 123W magneto generator and 40Ah battery for engine starting and navigation lights.
DIMENSIONS
Length overall: 3·7m
Beam: 1·9m
Height: 1·3m
WEIGHTS
Empty: 190kg
Payload: 150kg
PERFORMANCE
Speed, max: 35 knots

Siren CY-10

UNITED KINGDOM

AIR CUSHION EQUIPMENT (1976) LIMITED

15/35 Randolph Street, Shirley, Southampton SO1 3HD, England

Telephone: 0703 776468
Telex: 477537 G

J D Hake, *Chairman (US)*
R C Gilbert, *General Manager*
R R Henvest, *Factory Manager*

HOVERSPORT 200

A multi-purpose light sports hovercraft, Hover-sport 200 combines a top speed of 80km/h over land or water with a simple control system which enables any adult to operate it with complete safety after instruction. The fibreglass hull is fitted with a three-compartment inflatable surrounding structure. Additional buoyancy chambers are fitted within the hull to meet the United States National Marine Manufacturers Association (NMMA) requirements.

LIFT AND PROPULSION: Integrated system powered by a 500cc Rotax engine. Power is transmitted, via a gear, to a multiple-bladed axial-flow fan which is duct-mounted. Flow is divided to provide thrust and the air cushion. Fuel capacity is 23 litres. Fuel is petrol/two-stroke mixture.
CONTROLS: Three rudder vanes mounted on the duct are operated by handlebars to provide directional control. Engine speed is controlled by a handlebar-mounted twistgrip.
HULL: Grp sandwich construction with two inflated buoyancy bags inside hull and compartmented inflation collar around hull. Meets NMMA (US) boat safety requirements.
ACCOMMODATION: Open cockpit with seat for one or two persons.

DIMENSIONS
Length: 3·1m
Beam: 1·93m
Height off cushion: 1·18m
Height on cushion: 1·42m
WEIGHTS
Unladen: 205kg
Max payload: Two adults
PERFORMANCE
Cruising speed over land and water: 56km/h
Max speed over land and water: 80km/h
Noise level at cruising power: 82dB at 25m
Fuel consumption, average: 13·4 litres/h

Air Cushion Equipment Hoversport 200

BILL BAKER VEHICLES LIMITED (BBV)

Quarry Road, Hornton, Near Banbury, Oxon
OX15 6DF, England

Telephone: 0295 810624

W R L Baker, *Managing Director*
R V H Baker, *Director*

Bill Baker Vehicles Limited designs and manufactures multi-purpose hovercraft and also supplies components. The latter include tapered roller-bearing fan hubs, nylon pulleys and other items for racing and two-seat integrated cruising craft. Hirth, Rotax and Solo motors, Multiwing and Truflo fans are also available.

Since 1979 a range of craft has been developed for manufacture by the company or to be made under licence by suitable UK or foreign manufacturers. This has enabled the company to develop products such as a cab and cab heater for use in sub-zero conditions, tests being undertaken in Finland, Norway, Sweden and the USA on various winter surfaces to monitor performance.

The company supports the Hoverclub of Great Britain and international race meetings. Development of racing hovercraft is felt to be important for overall improvement of products from small-engined, integrated pleasure craft to larger four-seater craft.

BBV-1 (THE GNAT)

The smallest craft in the range is a low-price single-seater suitable for a beginner. It has a bag skirt and an 18hp Robin engine. It can also be fitted with the larger 48hp Rotax engine making it highly competitive in European Formula 'S' racing events. (Single engine, any size, single duct of 800mm maximum.) BBV-1 can be carried on a roof rack.
DIMENSIONS
Length: 3·0m (10ft)
Beam: 1·8m (6ft)
WEIGHTS
20hp motor: 85kg (187lb)
40-50hp motor: 110kg (242·5lb)
PRICE: Kit form, approximately £1000; complete craft, £1850 (1985). A photograph of this craft appears in *Jane's Surface Skimmers 1985*.

BBV-1-S

This racing craft, derived from the BBV-1, features a pressure-fed, segmented skirt and a full 800mm duct. Engines of between 20 and 80hp can be installed.
PRICE (dependent on engine type): Kit form, approximately £1900; complete craft, £2500 (1985)

BBV-2

This two- to three-seat craft has been designed for easy construction by the inexperienced kit builder. The main hull consists of a top and bottom moulding with a captive foam block set in the floor. The top and bottom outer edge is first bonded together and then riveted through an aluminium angle which gives considerable stren-

BBV-2

gth to the edge of the craft as well as providing a uniform attachment for the skirt.

The bottom moulding is constructed shiny side outwards, allowing all skirt location points to be moulded in for easy drilling. Four aluminium channel sections fit over moulded-in ribs, giving the craft a rigid, hard wearing bottom.

The craft uses an 8-bladed 915mm diameter fan supplying air for both lift and thrust which is highly efficient, giving more than adequate thrust from engines of over 40hp. The drive system has been designed so that should it be necessary the fan blades or drive belt can be easily changed. The bottom pulley hub uses sealed high-speed bearings and is driven through a flexible coupling. This design permits small automobile engines to be used, in addition to the standard range of 40 to 80hp two-cycle engines, without changing the thrust system.

The craft is fitted with spray dodger and windscreen, which coupled with optional side-by-side or pillion seating ensures a degree of comfort not normally found on a small craft. The segmented skirt design has evolved from BBV craft racing experience, giving a good stable performance even in adverse conditions. The ease of maintenance is a standard feature on all craft in the BBV range.
ENGINE
40hp 440cc two-stroke Hirth or
48hp 496cc two-stroke Rotax (petrol/oil mixture)

DIMENSIONS
Length: 3·83m
Beam: 2·0m
Hoverheight: 20cm
WEIGHTS/CAPACITIES
Empty weight: 145kg
Payload: 180kg
Fuel tank: 22·75 litres
PERFORMANCE
Speed: 45-50km/h
Fuel consumption: 10-16 litres/h
PRICE: Kit form, approximately £2200 (1985); complete craft, £2950 (1985)

BBV CRUISING CRAFT

More efficient hulls and the better matching of fans to installed power has improved the performance of BBV designs over the last few years.

Two- to three-seat hulls are available which take a variety of engines with outputs of between 40 to 100hp. These cruising hovercraft can be bought with or without engines.

BBV-2 + 2

This is a lengthened version of the BBV-2, and is fitted with electric start and four seats, plus further refinements as standard. Kits from £2500, finished craft, £3550 (1985). Details as for BBV-2 except length: 4·57m; beam: 2·0m; payload: 300kg.

BBV-2 + 2

BBV-4

This is a new craft embodying a great deal of both racing and cruising experience. The craft is available with two- or four-stroke engines of 80 to 100hp. Air from both 838mm diameter fans is used for lift and thrust. A full cabin is available giving good visibility and passenger comfort. With this craft a considerable reduction in noise has been achieved, whilst substantially improving the performance. A number of options are available, including a longer version if required. The hull and cab are made of self-coloured grp. Prices from £8500 (1985).

ENGINES
Subaru 80hp four-cycle
Fuji-Robin (Polaris) 85hp two-cycle
Rotax 530 80hp two-cycle
SKIRT: Fully segmented neoprene/nylon.
DIMENSIONS
Length: 5·11m
Beam: 2·34m
Hoverheight: 28cm

BBV-4

BBV-1-F1 RACING HOVERCRAFT

Winner of the 1984 European Formula One Championship, this craft uses the same hull shape and skirt design as the BBV-1-S, and BBV has also drawn on the experience gained during the development of its earlier Formula One racing craft, the BBV-11. The 9hp Solo lift engine drives a 558mm, 5-blade fan, and the Rotax 48-60hp engine drives two 645mm thrust fans, giving 110 to 140kg of thrust.
CONTROLS: Craft heading is controlled by twin rudders, one hinged to the rear of each thrust duct. Handlebars control rudder movement.
HULL: Two-part grp construction with foam buoyancy and a motorcycle-type seat moulded-in.

BBV-1-F1

Hull has full hydrodynamic surfaces and internal-skirt feed ducts.
SKIRT: Pressure-fed segmented system in neoprene-coated nylon.
DIMENSIONS
Length: 2·95m

Beam: 1·82m
WEIGHT
Unladen: 145kg
PERFORMANCE
Max speed, calm conditions: 88·51km/h
PRICE (approx): £3200 (1985)

GP VEHICLES LTD

Unit 7, Worton Hall, Worton Road, Isleworth, Middlesex TW7 6ER, England

Telephone: 01-568 4711/4664
Telex: 477019 GP G

John Jobber, *Managing Director*
Gary Bradley, *General Manager*

HOVER HAWK

This four-seat utility ACV is intended for survey and patrol duties as well as the leisure industry. Orders have been placed by countries throughout the world including North and South America, Europe, Scandinavia, South Africa, Australia, the Middle and the Far East. The price of the Hover Hawk in 1986 was £6700, and a car trailer for carrying the craft was £320.
LIFT AND PROPULSION: Integrated system. A single 1835cc Volkswagen VW4 air-cooled engine drives, via a belt, a ducted fan aft. Propulsion air is expelled rearwards and lift air is ducted into the plenum below. Fuel capacity is 28 litres (6 Imperial gallons). Fuel recommended 93 octane.
CONTROLS: Single control column operates a single rudder hinged to the rear of the fan duct. Column incorporates a twist-grip throttle for the engine.
HULL: Moulded glassfibre reinforced plastics structure.
SKIRT: Fully-segmented type in neoprene-coated nylon, with 68 air bag segments.
ACCOMMODATION: Open cockpit with seating for driver and up to three passengers.
DIMENSIONS
Length overall: 4·12m (13ft 6in)
Width: 2·5m (8ft)
Height, on cushion: 1·27m (4ft 2in)
WEIGHTS
Empty: 200kg (440lb)
Payload: 249kg (550lb)
PERFORMANCE
Max speed: Over 40 knots
Gradient capability: 1:7 from static hover
Obstacle clearance: 0·3m (12in)
Endurance, max: 3 hours
Fuel consumption, average: 7·8km/litre (22mpg)

Hover Hawk

Hover Hawk

HOVERCRAFT (INVESTMENTS) LIMITED

Registered office: Felbridge Hotel, East Grinstead, West Sussex RH19 2BH, England

Telephone: 0342 26992
Telex: 95156 G

Works: Unit 5D, Vallance-Byways, Lowfield Heath Road, Charlwood, Surrey, England

Telephone: 0293 862378

R L Fowler, *Managing Director*
P M Browne, *Director*

Hovercraft (Investments) Limited specialises in the manufacture of amphibious leisure/utility hovercraft and is now producing two models, Freedom 6 and Freedom 3. These hovercraft descend from a line which began in 1971 with the Cyclone, the first amphibious light hovercraft to be put into production. It was also the first to cross the English Channel and won the British Racing Championship for eight consecutive years.

Freedom 6 and Freedom 3 have been designed as fast open cruising hovercraft or as work craft where conventional transport is unsuitable.

FREEDOM 6

A replacement for Light Hovercraft Company's Phantom, Freedom 6 is a six-seater sports/utility hovercraft. Design features are reliability, ease of maintenance and quiet operation. The craft is easily manhandled onto a trailer for towing. It has also been designed to pull a water skier.

LIFT AND PROPULSION: Integrated system powered by a single 155bhp Rover V8, 3·5-litre SD1 engine. Power is transmitted by toothed belts and shafts to two ducted axial fans, air from which is used for both lift and propulsion. Thrust, approximately 180kg (400lb). Fuel capacity, 90 litres (20 gallons).

CONTROLS: Twin aerodynamic rudders hinged at the rear of each thrust duct control heading operated by a steering wheel. Trim is set by lever-operated elevons at the back of each duct.

HULL: Glassfibre reinforced plastic monocoque structure with sealed polyurethane block at base of craft for buoyancy. Storage compartments provided for tools and spares.

SKIRT: HDL loop segment type in neoprene-coated nylon.

DIMENSIONS
Length: 5·5m (18ft)
Beam: 2·75m (9ft)
WEIGHT
Payload capacity (approx): 550kg (1210lb)
PERFORMANCE
Max speed over land and water: 85km/h (45 knots)
Cruising speed: 55km/h (30 knots)
Hard structure clearance: 0·3m (1ft)
Endurance: 4 hours plus

Freedom 6

FREEDOM 3

This three-seater is powered by a single 40bhp Reliant engine and is suitable for cruising and sport and leisure activities.

LIFT AND PROPULSION: Integrated system powered by a single fully-enclosed 40bhp 850cc 4-cylinder 4-stroke, driving a ducted 735mm (29in) diameter polypropylene-bladed axial fan, air from which is used for both lift and propulsion. Thrust, 80kg (180lb). Fuel capacity, 46 litres (10 Imperial gallons).

CONTROLS: Heading is controlled by twin aerodynamic rudders hinged to rear of thrust duct and operated by steering wheel. Variable lift controlled by lever.

HULL: Glassfibre reinforced plastic monocoque construction with sealed polyurethane buoyancy block at base. Large storage compartment provided under seat.

SKIRT: Segmented type, 0·396m (1ft 4in) deep, neoprene-coated nylon.

DIMENSIONS
Length: 4·1m (13ft 6in)
Beam: 1·93m (6ft 4in)
WEIGHT
Payload: 250kg (550lb) plus
PERFORMANCE
Max speed over land and water: 65km/h (35 knots)
Cruising speed: 40km/h (22 knots)
Hard structure clearance: 0·23m (9in)
Endurance: 3 hours plus

Freedom 3

HOVERSERVICES SCARAB HOVERCRAFT

24 Hazel Grove, Wallingford, Oxon OX10 0AT, England

Telephone: 0491 37455
Telex: 859224 FLEXON G

Graham Nutt, *Proprietor*

Hoverservices was formed in 1972 to market Scarab hovercraft plans and components. The company now offers a range of light hovercraft plans for the single-seat Scarab 16 and two-seat Scarab II, in addition to plans for other racing craft such as the Snoopy II, Eccles and Cyclone II. All of these plans are marketed world-wide.

The company has a wide range of fans, grp ducts, skirt material and other components in stock and provides a complete engineering service.

SCARAB II (Plans)

Scarab II is a two-seater light hovercraft designed for cruising in calm coastal or sheltered estuarial waters. With its larger size it will accept a variety of engines for lift and propulsion.

LIFT AND PROPULSION: A typical lift engine for this craft would be a 5bhp Briggs & Stratton, driving a 558mm (22in) diameter axial lift fan fitted with Multiwing blades. For propulsion the craft could use various powerplants up to 42bhp driving either 609mm (24in) or 762mm (30in) diameter ducted Multiwing fans.

CONTROLS: Employs a single rudder positioned in the thrust duct which is activated by a joystick in the open cockpit. A twist grip throttle is used for the thrust engine and a quadrant type lever for lift.

HULL: This is made from triangular plywood boxes upon a framework of pine with grp tape for additional strength for joints etc. A full flow loop skirt is fitted.

ACCOMMODATION: Side-by-side seating for driver and one passenger in open cockpit.

DIMENSIONS
Length: 3·5m (11ft 6in)
Width: 1·83m (6ft)
Hoverheight: 228mm (9in)
WEIGHTS
Empty: 113kg (250lb)
Normal payload: 181kg (400lb) (two people)
Max weight: 295kg (650lb)
PERFORMANCE
Over land and water Scarab II craft, with propulsion units of 35-42bhp, can achieve speeds of 48-56km/h (30-35mph)

SCARAB 16 (Plans)

A development of the Scarab 14 (see 1986 edition) and built to comply with British and European Formula 3 racing regulations for craft with engines up to 250cc. Building plan sets are available.

LIFT AND PROPULSION: Aerodynamically integrated lift and propulsion system powered by a Robin EC25, Rotax 248 or Yamaha RD 250 engine.

HULL: Extremely lightweight hull built in triangulated box sections formed in epoxy-saturated 4mm ply, bonded with epoxy foam and grp tape.

SKIRT: Pressure fed segmented.

DIMENSIONS
Length: 3·04m
Width: 1·82m
Rise height: 0·23m

WEIGHTS
Weight, empty: 79kg
Payload: 79kg

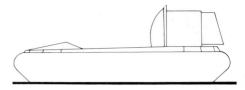
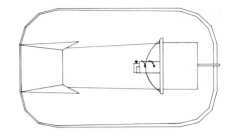

Scarab 16

INGLES HOVERCRAFT ASSOCIATES LIMITED/ MISSION AVIATION FELLOW-SHIP

Ingles Manor, Castle Hill Avenue, Folkestone, Kent CT20 2TN, England

Telephone: 0303 41356

S Sendall-King, *General Director*
D G Staveley, *UK Director*
T J R Longley, *Design Consultant*

Ingles Hovercraft Associates Limited administers the design and patent rights relating to the hovercraft developed by the Mission Aviation Fellowship (MAF).

MAF's first craft was the Missionaire, a general purpose amphibious five-seater. This was succeeded by the six-seat River Rover. Following evaluation trials by the Naval Hovercraft Trials Unit, the River Rover was chosen by the 1978-79 British Joint Services Expedition to Nepal. For a period of four months, two Mk 2 craft were successfully used over a 60-mile stretch of the turbulent Kali Gandaki river in support of a medical aid programme.

One of these craft is now in regular use by a mission in Irian Jaya, Indonesia, on the Baliem river and its tributaries, three are in service on the upper reaches of the Amazon in Peru; one with the Taiwanese Police and one with the Australian Army on tidal flats in South Australia.

RIVER ROVER

Designed as a water-borne counterpart to the Land Rover utility vehicle, River Rover is a sturdily constructed, six-seat cabin hovercraft which has proved its usefulness and reliability in many parts of the world where navigation by conventional boats is difficult or impossible.

The four main requirements for such a craft are:
Low cost, both of manufacture and of operation;

Positive control characteristics, enabling the craft to follow safely the course of a narrow, winding river with the minimum of sideways skidding;

Simple bolt-together unit construction, facilitating transport and simplifying maintenance and repair;

River Rover Mk 3

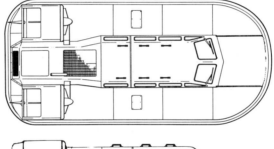
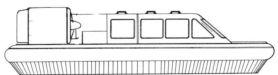
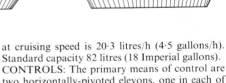

General Arrangement of River Rover Mk 3

An efficient and reliable skirt system, combining good wear resistance with ease of repair.

The following information refers to the River Rover Mk 3.

LIFT AND PROPULSION: Motive power is provided by a single 100bhp Renault R-20TS automotive engine. This drives a 630mm (25in) diameter lift fan, and two 710mm (28in) thrust fans mounted on either side of the lift fan. Power is transmitted via three Uniroyal HTD toothed belts and pulleys enclosed in streamlined fairings. All three fans are housed in grp ducts. Air from the lift fan is channelled through 90 degrees down beneath the craft via the skirt bag. Fuel consumption

at cruising speed is 20·3 litres/h (4·5 gallons/h). Standard capacity 82 litres (18 Imperial gallons).

CONTROLS: The primary means of control are two horizontally-pivoted elevons, one in each of the two square-sectioned ducts immediately aft of the thrust fans. Movement of foot pedals rotates the elevons jointly or differentially. Employed together, craft longitudinal trim is adjusted and, when rotated fully, braking is achieved. Used differentially, small deflections of the elevons enable the craft to be banked into a turn, thereby reducing sideways skidding. Greater pedal movement progressively closes the duct on the 'inside' of the turn, the outside duct remaining open. Thus differential thrust is added to the bank initially applied to the craft. Conventional vertically-pivoted aerodynamic rudders, controlled by a steering yoke, are fitted immediately aft of the elevons. These are used during operation in crosswinds, in conjunction with the elevons.

HULL: Aluminium alloy angle frame covered with 6mm (¼in) marine grade plywood panels. Engine bay bulkheads and sides are in aluminium alloy sheet. Structure is bolted together for ease of repair and simplicity of breakdown and reassembly. The entire hull is surrounded by an inflatable collar at deck level, providing all-round fendering and additional reserve buoyancy. The sliding cabin canopy is of moulded grp.

One of three River Rovers employed by 1982 British Joint Services Expedition to Peru

ACCOMMODATION: Three bench-type seats. These can be folded flat to provide sleeping accommodation for two persons, or, with cushions removed, for the carriage of freight. Alternatively, a stretcher can be carried aft on the port side of the cabin.

SKIRT: HDL-type loop and segment skirt in neoprene-coated nylon.
DIMENSIONS
Length: 6·19m (20ft 3¾in)
Width: 2·62m (8ft 7½in)
Height, off cushion: 1·45m (4ft 9½in)

WEIGHTS
Empty: 780kg (1716lb)
Total weight: 1230kg (2711lb)
PERFORMANCE
Max speed: 55km/h (34·3mph)
Cruising speed: 40km/h (25mph)

OSPREY HOVERCRAFT LIMITED

PO Box 34, Crawley, West Sussex RH10 4TF, England

Telephone: 04446 45791

P V McCollum, *Director*
D McCollum, *Director*

This company produces a range of four craft, Kestrel, Kestrel GT, Falcon and Cormorant. These craft recently underwent a modification programme which increased their performance by about 30 per cent. Osprey Hovercraft has also developed the Goshawk, its first model to be specifically designed for Formula I racing.

Osprey Hovercraft has constructed and tested a four- to six-seat sidewall design which will be in single engine integrated form or with twin engines. It is envisaged that the sidewall design could become a leisure product and that it could fulfil specialist roles, including shallow-water surveying.

CORMORANT

This addition to the Osprey range originated as a one-off craft to meet a particular customer requirement. After trials it was decided to include the design in the standard range. The chief difference between the Cormorant and the Falcon is the departure from the integrated lift/propulsion system of the latter by the introduction of a separate lift engine and fan. This arrangement has resulted in a craft with a greater payload capacity and generally increased all-round performance.
LIFT AND PROPULSION: A 10hp one-cylinder two-stroke engine mounted ahead of the cockpit drives a 560mm (22in) diameter polypropylene-bladed axial fan for lift. Thrust is furnished by a 49hp air-cooled twin-cylinder two-stroke driving a ducted 737mm (29in) polypropylene, nine-bladed axial fan via a heavy-duty toothed belt. Fuel capacity is 27 litres (6 Imperial gallons). Consumption is 9-16 litres/h (2-3·5 gallons/h).
CONTROLS: Craft heading is controlled by twin aerodynamic rudders hinged to the rear of the thrust duct and operated by a handlebar.
HULL: Monocoque construction in self-coloured glassfibre. Pre-formed sealed polyurethane block at base of craft for buoyancy. Tools and spares compartment provided.
SKIRT: Segmented type in neoprene-coated nylon material.
DIMENSIONS
Length: 3·8m (12ft 6in)
Width: 1·83m (6ft)
Height: 1·22m (4ft)

Falcon

WEIGHTS
Empty: 181kg (400lb)
Normal payload: 227kg (500lb)
PERFORMANCE
Speed over land and water: 88km/h plus (55mph plus)
Cruising speed: 32-40km/h (20-25mph)
Max continuous gradient, standing start: 1 : 8
Max short gradient, at speed: 1 : 4
Vertical hard obstacle clearance: 200mm (8in)

FALCON

Though intended primarily as a two-seat recreational craft, the Falcon is also suitable for a variety of light commercial and utility roles. Two of the craft are used by the Central Electricity Board on a land-reclamation scheme. A keynote of the design is its simplicity. All maintenance can be undertaken by a competent mechanic or handyman.

Some 50 per cent of Falcons sold are being employed for utility purposes. Several have been purchased as standby emergency craft in tidal areas and one Falcon is employed in Scotland for harvesting 9·65km (6 miles) of salmon nets. This craft is in use twice daily and is often required to operate at night. One Falcon is being evaluated by the West German Army.

A 'stretched' version, with a central driving position forward and a bench seat for two passengers aft, is in the planning stage. This arrangement will increase its ability to carry a larger payload when operating as a utility craft.

LIFT AND PROPULSION: Integrated system powered by a single 49hp air-cooled twin-cylinder two-stroke. This drives, via a heavy-duty toothed belt, a 737mm (29in) diameter polypropylene-bladed ducted fan, air from which is used for both lift and propulsion. Fuel capacity is 27 litres (6 Imperial gallons). Fuel recommended is 93 octane, oil mix 25 : 1. Consumption is 11-16 litres/h (2·5-3·5 gallons/h).
HULL: Monocoque construction in self-coloured glassfibre. All components and fasteners are made from marine quality material. Preformed sealed polyurethane block at base of craft for buoyancy. Tools and spares compartment provided.
SKIRT: Segmented skirt in neoprene-coated nylon material.
DIMENSIONS
Length: 3·8m (12ft 6in)
Beam: 1·83m (6ft)
Height: 1·22m (4ft)
WEIGHTS
Empty: 172kg (380lb)
Normal payload: 204kg (450lb)
Max payload: 295kg (650lb)
PERFORMANCE
Cruising speed: 32-40km/h (20-25mph)
Speed over land and water: 72km/h plus (45mph plus)
Max continuous gradient, standing start: 1 : 8
Max short gradient, at speed: 1 : 2 (45 degrees)
Vertical hard obstacle clearance: 200mm (8in)

KESTREL GT

Based on a standard Kestrel hull but fitted with the Falcon's engine and fan system, the Kestrel GT has been designed to meet the need of enthusiasts for a powerful lightweight hovercraft for sport and competitive racing. It is the fastest selling craft in the Osprey range. Due to its high power/weight ratio, it is particularly agile and can negotiate relatively steep slopes with comparative ease.
LIFT AND PROPULSION: Integrated system powered by a single 49hp air-cooled twin-cylinder two-stroke. This drives, via a heavy-duty toothed belt, a 737mm (29in) diameter polypropylene-bladed ducted fan, air from which is used for both lift and propulsion. Also available as a twin-engine model. Fuel capacity is 20·25 litres (4·5 Imperial gallons). Fuel recommended is 93 octane, oil mix 25:1.
CONTROLS: Twin aerodynamic rudders, operated by a handlebar, control craft heading. Engine throttle mounted on handlebar.

Cormorant

HULL: Monocoque construction in self-coloured glassfibre. Pre-formed sealed polyurethane block at base of craft for buoyancy. Tools and spares compartment provided.
SKIRT: Fully-segmented type in neoprene-coated nylon.
ACCOMMODATION: Open cockpit for driver.
DIMENSIONS
Length: 3·2m (10ft 6in)
Width: 1·83m (6ft)
Height: 1·22m (4ft)
WEIGHTS
Empty: 164kg (360lb)
Normal payload: 113kg (250lb)
PERFORMANCE
Speed across land and water: 80km/h plus (50mph plus)
Cruising speed: 32-40km/h (20-25mph)
Max continuous gradient, standing start: 1 : 6
Max short gradient, at speed: 1 : 2 (45 degrees)
Vertical hard obstacle clearance: 200mm (8in)

KESTREL

Designed as a single-seater this fully-amphibious recreational craft has nevertheless operated many times on inland waterways with two aboard in force 5 winds, gusting to force 6. Built on a base of solid foam it will not sink even if badly damaged. Recent modifications to the craft have made it a Formula III competitor.
LIFT AND PROPULSION: Integrated system with a single 22hp air-cooled one cylinder two-stroke driving one 737mm (29in) polypropylene-bladed ducted fan aft. Fuel capacity is 27 litres (6 Imperial gallons). Recommended fuel, 93 octane/oil mix 25 : 1. Consumption, 6·75 to 9 litres/h (1·5-2 gallons/h).
CONTROLS: Twin aerodynamic rudders controlled by handlebars. Engine throttle mounted on handlebars.
HULL: Self-coloured glassfibre structure based on a rigid foam block for strength and buoyancy. Built-in tools and spares compartment.
SKIRT: Segmented system in neoprene-coated nylon.
DIMENSIONS
Length: 3·2m (10ft 6in)
Beam: 1·83m (6ft)
Height: 1·00m (3ft 3in)
WEIGHTS
Empty: 127kg (280lb)
Normal payload: 114kg (250lb)
Max payload: 136kg (300lb)
PERFORMANCE
Cruising speed: 24-40km/h (15-25mph)
Speed across land and water: 56km/h plus (35mph plus)
Max continuous gradient, standing start: 1 : 7
Max short gradient, at speed: 1 : 2 (45 degrees)
Vertical hard obstacle clearance: 200mm (8in)

GOSHAWK

TYPE: Formula I racing craft.
LIFT AND PROPULSION: A 10hp one-cylinder two-stroke engine drives a 560mm (22in) diameter fan for lift. Powered by a 49hp twin-cylinder two-stroke driving two 686mm (27in) diameter polypropylene fans via a flexible coupling driving a toothed belt.
CONTROLS: Twin aerodynamic rudders in each fan duct controlled by handlebars. Engine throttles mounted on handlebars.
HULL: Monocoque construction in self-coloured glassfibre based on a rigid foam block for strength and buoyancy.
SKIRT: Fully-segmented in neoprene-coated nylon.
DIMENSIONS
Length: 3·5m (11ft 6in)
Beam: 1·85m (6ft 2in)
Height: 1·5m (5ft)
WEIGHT
Empty: 81kg (400lb)
PERFORMANCE
Speed across land and water: 96km/h plus (60mph plus)

Kestrel GT

Kestrel

Goshawk showing ducted propulsion fans and skirt detail

Goshawk

UNITED STATES OF AMERICA

DOBSON PRODUCTS CO

32901 Morrison Place, Lake Elsinore, California 92330, USA

Telephone: (714) 546 3646/678 4534

Franklin A Dobson, *Director*

Dobson Products Co was formed by Franklin A Dobson in 1963 to develop and market small ACVs either in complete, factory built form, or as kits for private use. His first model, the Dobson Air Dart, won the first ACV race in Canberra in 1964.

The first Dobson craft designed for quantity production was the Model H. Since good results have been obtained with the Dobson six-bladed variable-pitch propeller and more positive control is desirable at low and negative speeds, Model K has been developed using two side-by-side ducted thrust units. This gives powerful yaw control at all speeds in addition to a very considerable increase in positive as well as negative thrust together with low noise level.

Jane's Surface Skimmers 1985 contains full details of various Air Car models.

Dobson Air Car Model H

AIR CARS, MODELS A to F (1963 to 1970)

These are similar designs using an integrated system with a large slow-turning fan and vents for thrust and control. The central body acts as a splitter, giving good roll stability. The craft have coverings of fabric or lightweight plastic, supported by curved side members, and flexible skirts made up of combined hinged and flexible members. They have been sold in large numbers as plans and kits.

One was used by Boston Museum for demonstration and display; another won the first ACV race at Canberra. The company's Model F two-seater was described and illustrated in *Jane's Surface Skimmers 1973-74* and earlier editions.

Length: 3·66m
Width: 2·1m
Power: 7-12hp
Empty weight: 43-59kg
Max weight: 136-181kg
Performance: 25-30mph

AIR CAR, MODEL D (1969)

Two-place integrated design, generally similar to Models A–F.

Length: 4·27m (14ft)
Width: 2·1m (7ft)
Power: 15hp
Empty weight: 91kg (200lb)
Max weight: 226kg (500lb)
Performance: 30mph
Ten of these have been sold in kit form.

AIR CAR, MODEL H (1972)

This is a single-engined design using a variable-pitch ducted fan for thrust and braking, with a separate lift fan driven through a long shaft and right-angle gearbox. There are several variants, one using a fixed-pitch thrust fan with thrust reverser. The flexible skirt is supported by hinged floats.

Length: 3·35m
Width: 2·89m
Power: 18hp
Empty weight: 104kg (230lb)
Gross weight: 272kg (600lb)
Performance: 40mph

AIR CAR, MODEL K (1980)

A single-engined design, using two variable-pitch ducted fans for thrust, control and braking, with a lift fan driven through shaft and gearbox. The segmented skirt is supported by removable floats. The engine is controlled by a governor. The craft has excellent control in forward or backward flight and a very low noise level.

Length: 3·69m
Width: 2·89m

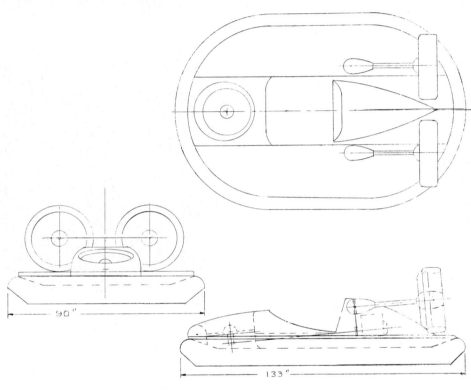
Air Car Model K

Air Car Model K (modified)

Power: 18hp Briggs and Stratton 2 cylinder 4-stroke engine
Empty weight: 127kg (280lb)
Gross weight: 272kg (600lb)
Performance: 35mph

AIR CAR, MODEL K (modified)

This is similar in general design to the Model K but is lighter and more streamlined. There is an additional lift fan at the rear, pulling air past the engine for cooling, thus allowing use of a totally-enclosed engine. It has a conical segment skirt, supported on removable floats.

Power: 22hp Chaparral engine
Empty weight: 118kg (260lb)
Otherwise similar to Model K.

HERMES

A new lightweight, single-engine two-place folding model combining the unusual feature of being able to operate at reduced clearance without a skirt if necessary. The lift fan is driven through a constant velocity universal joint which is quieter and lighter than gearboxes used in former designs.

A new control system is incorporated in this model. The 0·813m diameter Multiwing thrust propeller operates in a duct of roughly elliptical cross-section. Around the duct and extending aft from it are two curved streamlined covers hinged on a vertical axis near the rear and held against the duct by springs. There are two rudders which normally operate together when the control stick is moved sideways. If the control stick is pulled back the rudders turn outward, forcing the air against the covers which then open, exposing turning vanes which direct the thrust air forward for reverse thrust and control.

The Hermes uses a forward-facing 0·61m diameter Multiwing lift fan and a splitter body as on some earlier Dobson craft. A new type of skirt is employed made up of four interchangeable sections with Velcro attachment. The fan and skirt combination give reduced momentum drag, resulting in improved performance. Cushion pressure is 46·4kg/m² (9·5lb/ft²).
ENGINE: Chaparral G25A, 22hp at 7000rpm.
DIMENSIONS
Length: 3·96m (13ft)
Width: 2·44m (8ft)
Width, folded: 1·22m (4ft)
Cushion area: 5·1m² (55ft²)
Obstacle clearance: 203mm (8in)
WEIGHTS
Weight, empty: 102kg (225lb)
Weight, max: 238kg (525lb)
Payload: 136kg (300lb)
PERFORMANCE
Thrust, forward: 34·0kg (75lb)
Thrust, reverse: 13·6kg (30lb)
Drag, at hump: 12·1kg (28lb)

Dobson Hermes prototype

Dobson Hermes prototype

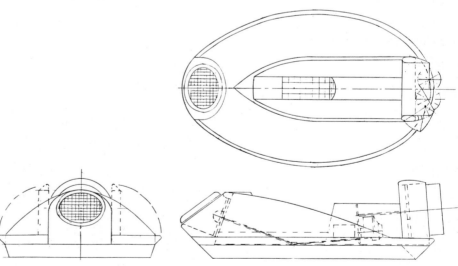

General Arrangement of Dobson Hermes

HOVERCRAFT INDUSTRIES INC

11352 Space Boulevard, Orlando, Florida 32821, USA

Telephone: (305) 857 4343

SUNRIDER I
ENGINE: Rotax Model 277, two-stroke 27hp, petrol/oil 40:1 mix, hand start.
SKIRT: Neoprene-coated nylon, segmented.
DIMENSIONS
Length: 3·2m (10ft 6in)
Beam: 1·83m (6ft)

Height, max: 1·22m (4ft)
Prop/fan dia: 0·737m (2ft 5in)
WEIGHT
Empty: 141kg (310lb)
PERFORMANCE
Rise height: 203mm (8in)
Tank capacity: 30·3 litres (8 US gallons)
Speed, max: 48km/h (30mph)

SUNRIDER II
ENGINE
Lift: 12hp, single-cylinder, 2-cycle
Thrust: 50hp, two-cylinder in line, 2-cycle, electronic start

CONTROLS: Two rudders, control column operated; thrust engine throttle, foot operated; lift engine throttle, hand operated.
DIMENSIONS
Length: 4·06m (13ft 4in)
Beam: 1·98m (6ft 6in)
Height: 1·12m (3ft 8in)
WEIGHTS
Empty: 299kg (660lb)
Payload: 200kg (440lb)
PERFORMANCE
Obstacle clearance height: 229mm (9in)
Tank capacity: 37·9 litres (10 US gallons)
Gradient capability from static hover: 1:8

NEOTERIC—USA—INC

Fort Harrison Industrial Park, Terre Haute, Indiana 47804, USA

Telephone: (812) 466 2303

J Christopher Fitzgerald, *President*
Donald Brown, *Secretary*

Neoteric—USA—Incorporated was formed in 1975 by three of the founders of Neoteric Engineering Affiliates Pty Ltd, Melbourne, Australia. The Neova range of two-seat ACVs, which is now being manufactured and marketed by Neoteric USA, was first introduced by the Australian associate. The fully amphibious Neova is available in kit or ready-built form. Other businesses may manufacture the Neoteric range under licence.

In 1986 Neoteric introduced its largest craft in the range, the four-seat, 5·95m Neova 6 and also the Neova IV a slightly smaller four-seat craft.

NEOVA II

A highly-manoeuvrable light ACV, the Neova is an amphibious two-seater intended primarily for recreational use. Neova II is supplied in kit form in two versions, Standard and Super. The Standard model comprises four basic modules: the fibreglass base, machinery, ducts and controls and skirt system. The Super model includes two additional modules: fibreglass-moulded upper hull and hatch and a trailer. Individual components are also supplied, enabling the homebuilder to assemble any part of the complete vehicle.

The overall dimensions of the machine—2·13 × 4·27m (7 × 14ft)—allow it to be transported by road on a flat trailer.

LIFT AND PROPULSION: Integrated system powered by a 1600cc, 46hp, 124A or 126A Volkswagen engine. The company has developed a new timing belt drive transmission. The new drive features a centrifugal clutch and an all-aluminium pod structure. Maintenance is reduced substantially and the life of the drive is increased. In addition assembly time is further reduced. Assembly time of the complete kit is 350 hours. Airflow is ducted into the plenum for lift and two outlets aft for thrust. The power module, comprising engine, transmission and axial-flow fans, is mounted on a rubber-seated frame, secured to the main hull by three bolts and is totally enclosed for safety. A large hatch provides ready access to the engine and all components. Fuel consumption, full throttle is 13·6 litres/h (3·6 US gallons/h).

SKIRT: Multi-cell jupe type.

CONTROLS: Back and forward movement of a dual stick control column operates two thrust buckets which vary the power and the direction of the thrust. The column is pulled back for reverse thrust and moved ahead for forward thrust. Differential use of the two columns, with one stick forward and the other back, is used for changing craft direction. The aerodynamic rudders at the rear of the propulsion ducts are normally used only for small corrections in heading at cruising speeds.

HULL: Fibreglass structure with solid foam buoyancy. Safety skids beneath. An integral siphon system prevents the collection of excessive water within the hull. Buoyancy is 150%. The skirt module is removable as two single units.

ACCOMMODATION: Side-by-side seating for two.

DIMENSIONS
Length overall: 4·27m (14ft)
Beam overall: 2·13m (7ft)
Height overall, skirt inflated: 1·4m (4ft 7in)
WEIGHTS
Empty weight: 341kg (750lb)
Payload, max: 196kg (430lb)
PERFORMANCE
Speeds: 48-96km/h (30-60mph)
Hard, beach: 56km/h (35mph)
Water: 51km/h (32mph)
Land: 48km/h (30mph)
Ice: 72km/h (45mph)
Firm snow: 65km/h (41mph)
Max gradient from standing start: 1 : 10

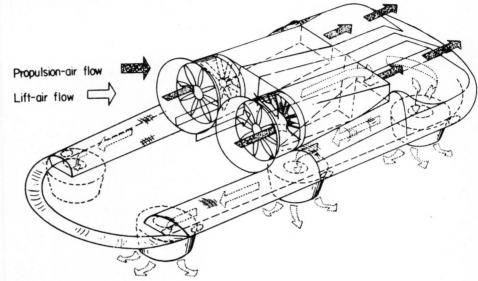

Neova II two-seater

Air flow system of Neova II

Neova II's propulsion transmission arrangement

Vertical obstacle clearance: 0·2m (8in)
Fuel consumption: 3·6 US gallons/h (13·6 litres/h)
Endurance on full power: 3 hours with 34-litre tank
Range with 34-litre (9-US gallon) tank: 128km (80 miles)

EXPLORER

The Explorer, previously known as the Lémere, is an all-terrain, two-seater built in glassfibre and pvc foam. It is not yet available in kit form. Maximum speed is about 64km/h (40mph). The craft can be towed behind a standard car on a single axle.

LIFT AND PROPULSION: Lift is provided by a single 8hp Briggs & Stratton type 319cc Series 190702 (reduction ratio: 31:74) four-cycle petrol engine driving an axial flow fan type 0·609m diameter Multiwing 32 Delrin. Thrust is supplied by a single 55hp Fuji Robin EC34PL or 50hp EC44PM liquid-cooled two-cycle engine driving a ducted fan type 0·609m diameter Multiwing 42 PAG, reduction ratio: 58:74.

HULL: Composite structure in glassfibre and pvc foam.

SKIRT: Bag type in neoprene/nylon material, riveted construction, 16oz/yd^2.

ACCOMMODATION: Side-by-side seating for two.

DIMENSIONS
Length, hardstructure: 3·5m (11ft 6in)
Width, hardstructure: 2·03m (6ft 8in)
Height, on landing pads: 0·91m (3ft)
WEIGHTS
Empty: 188kg (415lb)
Payload: 227kg (500lb)
PERFORMANCE
Range: 64km (40 miles)
Obstacle clearance height: 0·15m (6in)
PRICE: US $8995 (1986) including all options.

RACER

Introduced in late 1984 for hoverclub racing and cruising events, the Racer is a glassfibre hulled two-seater powered by a 50hp Fuji engine and capable of 80km/h. It is available in kit or ready-built form.

LIFT AND PROPULSION: Integrated system powered by 39·5kW (53hp) Fuji 44 2PM 1000 air-cooled, two-cycle engine. Alternative engines of similar output are acceptable on craft built from kits. Fuel capacity is 25·7 litres. Recommended fuel is two-cycle mix, 40:1. Fan: 609mm diameter Multiwing 4Z PAG, 9 blades, reduction ratio: 31:58.

CONTROLS: Handlebar operates rudders at rear of propulsion duct. Throttle on handlebar.

HULL: Composite structure in glassfibre and pvc foam.

SKIRT: Bag type in neoprene-coated nylon material, glued construction or 20cm deep segment type.

ACCOMMODATION: Seating for two in tandem.

DIMENSIONS
Length: 3·50m
Width: 2·03m
Height, off cushion: 0·94m
WEIGHTS
Empty: 137kg
Payload: 227kg
PERFORMANCE
Speed: 80km/h

Explorer 2- to 3-seater

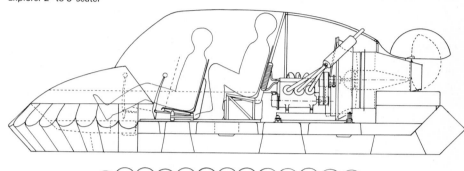

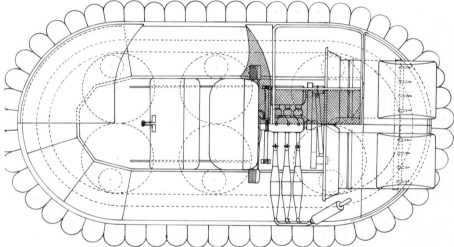

Layout of Neoteric Neova IV

Hoverheight: 20cm (7·9in)
Range: 64km (40 miles) good weather
PRICE: Nov 1986, US $4725

NEOVA IV

A four-seat variant of the Neova II, the latter having been marketed successfully for the past 12 years. Neova IV was released to the market in July 1986.

ENGINE: 90hp Fuji EC60 PL-01 or two 55hp Fuji EC44PM-1000s.

SKIRT: Segmented with inner jupes if additional stability required.

DIMENSIONS
Length: 4·27m
Width: 2·13m
WEIGHTS
Empty: 272kg
Payload: 365kg
PERFORMANCE
Speed, max: 80km/h (50mph)
Fuel consumption: 22·7 litres/h (6 US gallons/h)
Tank capacity: 64·3 litres (17 US gallons)
Operating temperature range: −30°C to +32°C
Obstacle clearance height: 25cm

NEOVA 6

The largest craft of the Neoteric range, the first one being built in 1986 and engaged in October 1986 on trials for the US Army Corps of Engineers. The Neova 6 is a four-seater built in pvc foam, 4lb/ft^2 density, and polyurethane foam 2lb/ft^3 density with 10oz/yd^2 fibreglass cloth and polyester resin. Eight fibreglass-coated wooden skid pads are provided on the hull underside. The craft is fitted with a Hadees Model 356 heater.

LIFT AND PROPULSION: The powerplant is a Chrysler LH 318 (87-312) 4-cycle petrol engine fitted with a California Turbo 40120 muffler. Fans for lift and propulsion are Multiwing, 91·44cm

80km/h Neoteric Racer

dia, 16 blades, type 16-4Z-45 deg. Power transmission is by toothed belts, type 8M-2000-85, 48-tooth drive shaft pulley, 75-tooth fan shaft pulley, drive ratio 1·563:1.

CONTROLS: Reverse thrust bucket, rudders and throttle all operated by Morse Red Jacket cables.

SKIRT: The skirt is constructed of 16oz/yd² nylon-reinforced neoprene rubber. There are eight jupes surrounded by 62 segments.

DIMENSIONS

Length overall: 5·95m off cushion
    6·17m on cushion
Width: 2·59m off cushion
    2·97m on cushion
Height: 1·76m off cushion
    2·07m on cushion

WEIGHTS

Weight, empty: 862kg ±45kg
Payload: 363kg normal
    455kg max

PERFORMANCE

Speed, max: 72km/h (45mph)
Speed, cruising, 2500rpm: 48km/h (30 mph)
Range: 201km (125 miles)
Tank capacity: 94·6 litres (25 US gallons)
Obstacle clearance: 30·5cm
Operational temperature range: −34·4°C to 43·3°C (−30°F to +110°F)
Weather restrictions: Wave height, max, 0·6m wind speed, 48km/h (30mph)

PRICE: US $40 000 (1986)

Neova IV

Neoteric Neova 6

SCAT HOVERCRAFT INC

10621 N Kendall Drive, Suite 208, Miami, Florida 33176, USA

Telephone: (305) 274 7228
Telex: 293894 SCAT

Ron Molina, *President and Chief Executive*

Sam Rosenblatt, *Director of Marketing*
Helmut Thompson, *Chief Engineer*

SCAT II

Designed by P V McCollum of Osprey Hovercraft Ltd, UK, the Scat two-seat hovercraft has been in production since June 1985. In February 1986 the Scat company completed a US$3·5 million public offering of shares and warrants, enabling it to expand significantly its marketing and production capabilities. The craft is built in a 4645m² plant in Miami and is sold through 250 dealer outlets. Approximately 4000 craft have been built to date and 1988 production is forecast at 4000. New models, 3·66m and 4·27m overall length, will be produced in 1988.

LIFT AND PROPULSION: A 26hp (6200rpm) Rotax two-stroke 277cc engine drives a 6-blade axial-flow fan, two thirds of the air going to thrust and one third to the cushion. A 22·7-litre (6-US gallon) fuel tank is fitted

CONTROLS: Throttle and handlebar-steered single rudder.

HULL: Glassfibre upper surfaces available in six colours, foam-filled deck, high impact ABS bottom.

SKIRT: Neoprene-coated nylon fabric, 64 segments.

DIMENSIONS

Length: 2·90m
Width: 1·83m
Height: 1·27m

WEIGHTS

Empty: 159kg
Payload, normal: 159kg
Payload, max: 181kg

PERFORMANCE

Speed, max: 30·5 knots (35mph)
Rise height: 20cm
Sea state capability: 0·6m
Stopping distance: 18m from 30·5 knots
Fuel consumption: 5·68 litres/h (1·5 US gallons/h)
Sound level, full throttle at 15·25m: 80dBA

PRICE

November 1987: Under US$6000

The Scat II with gear drive transmission

SEVTEC INC

PO Box 846, Monroe, Washington 98272, USA

Telephone: (206) 794 7505

Barry Palmer, *Owner*

Sevtec Inc was formed to research and market hovercraft technology. Emphasis has been placed on low operating costs and low noise levels for these craft. Consulting services are available and a home construction programme for hovercraft ranging from a 7hp one-seat craft, a four-seat 40hp craft through to an 80hp eight-seat craft.

The 18hp, two-seat prototype for the home builders' programme is a distillation of design efforts over the past 15 years in which prototypes from a 4hp vehicle capable of going over still deep water, still air hump drag conditions with 72·5kg aboard to a 56hp craft are capable of successfully carrying 8 adults.

The prototype homebuilders' programme specifications are:

Length: 4·24m
Width: 1·83m
Power: Briggs and Stratton 18hp at 3600rpm (13·23kW)
Empty weight: 175kg
Normal payload: 168kg
Max payload over hump: 227kg
Top speed, smooth water: 48km/h
Fuel consumption, 39km/h cruise: 5·3 litres/h
All specifications are for still deep water, still air.

A direct-drive 0·66m diameter, six-blade lift fan is located directly under the engine, and a Vee-belt drive turned through a right angle is used to drive, via a pair of idlers, an aluminium 0·122m diameter two-blade propeller.

The ducted propeller version of the craft has been abandoned in favour of the wire-guarded, open propeller version for improvement in both handling and straight line performance.

The hull of the four-seat craft is a 61cm stretch of the basic hull and craft empty weight is about the same as the prototype due to the replacement of the 18hp industrial engine with a lightweight snowmobile engine. Maximum planeout payload weight is expected to be over 364kg and top speed well over 64km/h. Essential parts kits consisting of rotors, drive components and skirt material are available from Sevtec Inc.

Hull construction is of wood with foam positive flotation. Glassfibre covers both sides of the wood in areas where moisture absorption or rot can cause damage and the deck is covered with aircraft fabric, providing a structure that can be stored outdoors.

The skirt is of 745g/m² vinyl, formulated for cold weather use and bonded together with vinyl contact cement. Skirt configuration is similar to the bag type except that two curtain type skirts cross the craft at the bow and about 30% behind the bow, compartmenting the 6·7m² base area into 1·67m² and 5·0m² fore and aft cushions. Forward cushion pressure can be controlled from the operator's position to aid in stopping and turning the craft. Foam flotation is placed on the skirt so that, together with a good drain system, skirt water purge problems normally associated with bag type skirts have been eliminated.

Propellers and fans can be built of wood by the homebuilder or purchased in aluminium from Sevtec Inc. A 61cm lift fan and 122cm 2-blade propeller (ducted) are used on machines of 7 to 18hp and 76cm lift fan and 152cm 2-blade propeller are used on the machines above 18hp.

A larger version of the basic 18hp craft has been built as a home construction project entirely from Sevtec plans. Performance was as predicted despite the fact that no prototype was built. The craft is a 4/3 scaled-up version of the basic 18hp craft hull, with an automotive engine mounted above the deck. The hull is of composite foam and polyester resin-fibreglass construction. Vee-belt drives are used to drive the rotors. A single 0·96m diameter twelve-blade aluminium axial-flow fan,

Wire guard protection on latest Sevtec craft (B Palmer)

New twin-propeller Sevtec craft

which is located aft directly under the engine, provides cushion air, while a pair of 1·52m diameter two-blade aluminium propellers provide thrust.

PRINCIPAL PARTICULARS
Length: 5·65m
Width: 2·44m

Engine: Datsun 1600cc, 66hp (84·3kW) at 3900rpm max, geared to rotors
Empty weight: 495kg
Normal, max payload: 518kg (6 persons)
Top speed, smooth water: 39 knots (72km/h)
Fuel consumption at 56km/h, 3300rpm, normal cruise: 12·2 litres/h

UNIVERSAL HOVERCRAFT

1204 3rd Street South, Box 281, Cordova, Illinois 61242, USA

Telephone: (309) 654 2588

R J Windt, *Director*

Formed in 1969, this company has designed and built over 80 different sports and utility ACV prototypes, ranging from an ultra-light single-seater to the 12-seat UH-26S powered by a 225hp automotive engine. Plans for some of these designs are available to homebuilders. The company has developed three new single-engined amphibious craft: a 3·65m (12ft) two-seater, a 3·96m (13ft) four-seater and a 5·48m (18ft) six-seater.

Work has also been undertaken on air cushion vehicles propelled by waterjets, outboard motors and sails.

Descriptions of the UH-10C, UH-11S and UH-11T will be found in *Jane's Surface Skimmers 1980* and earlier editions.

UH-10T

Designed specifically for amateur hovercraft builders, UH-10T can be built in between 90 and 180 hours at a cost of approximately US $150 (1984).

LIFT AND PROPULSION: A single 2·5 to 5hp vertical-shaft lawnmower engine, mounted ahead of the open cockpit, drives the lift fan. Thrust is supplied by a 5 to 8hp horizontal-shaft lawnmower engine driving a two-bladed propeller direct.

CONTROLS: A single rudder hinged to the rear of the propeller guard provides directional control.

HULL: Frame built from fir ribs and stringers and covered in 3·1mm (⅛in) plywood.

ACCOMMODATION: Open cockpit with seat for driver.

DIMENSIONS
Length: 3·32m (10ft 11in)
Beam: 1·93m (6ft 4in)

WEIGHTS
Empty: 102-132kg (225-290lb)
Payload, max: 125kg (275lb)

PERFORMANCE
Max speed over water: 32-48km/h (20-30mph)
Max speed over snow and ice: 40-56km/h (25-35mph)
Max gradient: 8-16%
PRICE: Complete set of plans for homebuilding, US $10. Full-size rib outlines US $4 (1984)

UH-12S

This lightweight two-seater is capable of carrying two adults and their camping or fishing equipment at 56·32km/h (35mph) over water.

LIFT AND PROPULSION: A single JLO 340 or 440 engine drives the lift fan and the thrust propeller via a V-belt system. The 0·61m (2ft) diameter fan turns at a maximum of 3500rpm, while the 1·21m (4ft) diameter thrust propeller turns at 2200rpm at full throttle.

CONTROLS: Three aerodynamic rudders behind the propeller provide directional control.

HULL: Construction is of fir ribs and stringers and 3·1mm (⅛in) plywood covering. Fibreglass applied to all joints and edges.

ACCOMMODATION: Tandem arrangement with passenger seated behind driver on a sliding seat.

DIMENSIONS
Length: 3·91m (12ft 10in)
Width: 1·82m (6ft)
Height: 1·52m (5ft)
WEIGHTS
Empty: 147kg (325lb)
Normal payload: 159kg (350lb)
Max payload: 204kg (450lb)
PERFORMANCE
Max speed, over land: 72km/h (45mph)
    over water: 56km/h (35mph)
Gradient at 450lb weight: 23%
PRICE: Plans US $15 (1984)

UH-12T2

This two- to three-seat easily constructed craft is powered by standard lawnmower engines. The low rpm of these engines ensures quiet operation and a long engine life. Construction costs range from US $200 to $500, depending on the quality of the engines and the materials used.

LIFT AND PROPULSION: Lift is supplied by a 5hp Briggs and Stratton engine driving a 0·6m (24in) diameter, 0·3m (14in) pitch four-bladed wooden fan at 3000rpm. Maximum cushion pressure is 11lb/ft². Thrust is provided by a 10hp Briggs and Stratton engine driving a 1·06m (42in) diameter, 40cm (16in) pitch two-bladed propeller aft. Total fuel capacity is 6·15 litres (1·5 US gallons).

CONTROLS: Triple rudders hinged to the rear of the propeller guard control craft handling.

HULL: Wooden structure built from pine ribs and struts and covered with 3·1mm (⅛in) plywood skin. The structure is designed to survive a 64km/h (40mph) plough-in in choppy water.

SKIRT: 177mm (7in) deep, 304mm (12in) diameter bag skirt, in 16oz/yd² neoprene-coated nylon.

ACCOMMODATION: Enclosed cabin seating driver and two passengers on a movable tandem seat.

DIMENSIONS
EXTERNAL
Length overall, power off: 3·93m (12ft 11in)
Beam overall, power off: 1·82m (6ft)
    skirt inflated: 2·03m (6ft 8in)
Cushion area: 6·03m² (65ft²)
Skirt depth: 177mm (7in)
INTERNAL
Cabin length: 1·21m (4ft)
Max width: 0·6m (2ft)
WEIGHTS
Normal empty: 136kg (300lb)
Normal gross: 272kg (600lb)
Normal payload: 136kg (300lb)
Max payload: 181kg (400lb)
PERFORMANCE
Max speed, calm water: 56km/h (35mph)
Max wave capacity: 0·3m (12in) chop
Max gradient, static conditions: 12 degrees at 600lb
Vertical obstacle clearance: 152mm (6in)
PRICE: Plans US $15 (1984)

UH-12T3

The UH-12T3, twin-engine light ACV is intended primarily for the first-time builder. It has side-by-side seating with room for storage or a seat for a child. Payload is 136-226kg (300-500lb), depending on power installed.

LIFT AND PROPULSION: Lift is supplied by a 5hp four-cycle lawnmower engine driving a four-bladed wooden fan. Thrust is provided by any suitable four-cycle horizontal-shaft lawnmower

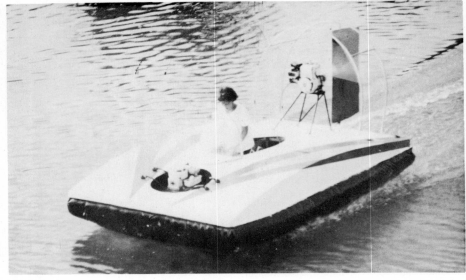
UH-10T

UH-12S amphibious two-seater

UH-12T2

UH-12T3

engine in the 8 to 16hp range or a two-cycle engine of up to 440cc with a maximum weight of 34kg (75lb).

CONTROLS: Twin rudders hinged to the rear of the propeller guard control craft direction.

HULL: Wooden structure built from pine ribs and struts and covered with 3·1mm (⅛in) plywood skin.

ACCOMMODATION: Open cockpit with side-by-side seating for two in front with room for child's seat behind.

DIMENSIONS
Length: 3·93m (12ft 11in)
Beam: 1·98m (6ft 6in)

WEIGHTS
Empty: 136-181kg (300-400lb)
Payload: 136-226kg (300-500lb)

PERFORMANCE
Max speed over water: 40-72km/h (25-45mph)
Max speed over land, snow and ice: 48-80km/h (30-50mph)

PRICE: Complete plans, US $12·75. Full-size rib outline, US $5·75 (1984)

UH-13SA

The prototype of this craft was built in 1974 from 25mm (1in) thick urethane foam fibreglass laminate. This type of construction proved too difficult for the homebuilder and so the craft was redesigned for wooden construction. The structure is built in fir or pine ribs and stringers, covered with 3·1mm (⅛in) plywood. An integrated lift/propulsion system is employed. Once engine speed is above idling the correct amount of lift is automatically maintained throughout the entire engine speed range by a patented system.

LIFT AND PROPULSION: Motive power is provided by a single JLO 440 driving a 0·63m (2ft 1in) diameter four-bladed lift fan and a 1·21m (4ft) diameter propeller via a V-belt reduction drive.

CONTROLS: Craft heading is controlled by twin rudders behind the propeller.

HULL: Construction is similar to that of UH-12T.

ACCOMMODATION: Two bench-type seats for two adults and two children.

DIMENSIONS
Length: 4·21m (13ft 10in)
Width: 1·98m (6ft 6in)

WEIGHTS
Empty: 181kg (400lb)
Normal payload: 181kg (400lb)
Max payload: 272kg (600lb)

PERFORMANCE
Max speed, over land, snow, ice: 96·56km/h (60mph)
over water: 80km/h (50mph)
Max gradient: 26%

PRICE: Complete plans, US $9. Full-scale outline US $3 extra (1984)

UH-13T

This derivative of the UH-13 employs the same basic hull as the UH-13S, but exchanges its automatic lift system for a separate lift engine.

The 13T can carry 136-181kg (300-400lb) even when powered by 10 to 16hp four-cycle lawn-mower engines.

LIFT AND PROPULSION: Recommended engines: lift, 8hp four-cycle vertical shaft mower engine or equivalent; thrust, two-cycle 20-55hp (295-760cc) or 10-16hp four-cycle engine weighing under 45kg (100lb).

DIMENSIONS
Length: 4·21m (13ft 10in)
Beam: 1·98m (6ft 6in)
Hoverheight: 203mm (8in)

WEIGHTS
Payload: 317kg (700lb)
Empty: 192-215kg (425-475lb)

PERFORMANCE
Max speed over water: 64-96km/h (40-60mph)
land, ice and snow: 72-112km/h (45-70mph)
Max gradient: 15-33%

UH-14B

An amphibious four-seater, the UH-14B has a maximum payload capacity of over 363kg (800lb). Employment of a large slow-turning propeller for

UH-13SA

UH-13T

UH-14B

thrust permits high-speed cruising while generating very little noise.

LIFT AND PROPULSION: A JLO 230 two-cycle engine turns a four-bladed fan for lift. Alternatively, an 8hp vertical shaft lawnmower engine may be used for lift. Thrust is supplied by a JLO 440 two-cycle engine driving a 1·21m (4ft) diameter propeller through a V-belt speed reduction system.

CONTROLS: Heading is controlled by multiple aerodynamic rudders aft of the propeller.

HULL: Construction is of fir or pine ribs and stringers, which are covered with 3·1mm (⅛in) plywood.

DIMENSIONS
Length: 4·52m (14ft 10in)
Width: 2·13m (7ft)
Height off cushion: 1·52m (5ft)

WEIGHTS
Empty: 204kg (450lb)
Normal payload: 227kg (500lb)
Max payload: 363kg (800lb)

UH-15P which won Canadian National Championships Rally in 1983 and 1984

UH-15P

PERFORMANCE
Max speed, over land, snow, ice: 97km/h (60 mph)
   over water: 89km/h (55mph)
Max gradient at 650lb weight: 28%
PRICE: Complete plans US $14. Full-scale
outline US $5 (1984)

UH-15P

A high-speed derivative of the UH-13, the UH-15P has an arrow-head planform which reduces air drag. It is one of the fastest craft in the Universal Hovercraft range and has attained 83mph during test runs. Roll and pitch stability are about the same as on the UH-13T. Some experimental work is being undertaken with ducted propellers employing the UH-15P as a test vehicle. The craft won the Canadian National Championships Rally in 1983 and 1984.
LIFT AND PROPULSION: Recommended engines: lift, 8 to 10hp four-cycle vertical shaft mower engine weighing 18·1 to 22·6kg (40 to 50lb) or equivalent; thrust, 10 to 20hp four-cycle mower engine for direct drive, or 20 to 60hp two-cycle for belt drive, high-performance application.
CONTROLS: Heading is controlled by triple aerodynamic rudders aft of the propeller.
ACCOMMODATION: Open cockpit for driver and up to two passengers.
HULL: Structure is of fir or pine ribs and stringers, covered with 3·1mm (⅛in) ply. Drainage system incorporated.
DIMENSIONS
Length: 4·82m (15ft 10in)
Width: 1·98m (6ft 6in)
Hoverheight: 0·2m (8in)
WEIGHTS
Empty: 159-204kg (350-450lb)
Payload: Up to 363kg (up to 800lb)
PERFORMANCE
Across water: 64-112km/h (40 to 70mph)
   ice, snow and land: 72-134km/h (45 to 83mph)
Max gradient: 15-40%
PRICE: Complete plans, US $15. Full-size rib outline, US $6 (1984)

UH-16S

First introduced in 1980, the UH-16S seats five to six and has a maximum speed over land, snow and ice of 104km/h (65mph).
LIFT AND PROPULSION: Integrated system, employing the same type of automatic lift control as fitted to the 13S, 18S and 26S. Motive power is by a 1500cc or larger Volkswagen, Corvair or any other four-cylinder water-cooled automotive engine weighing less than 150kg (350lb). Thrust, 68 to 158kg (150 to 350lb).
CONTROLS: Heading is controlled by triple-aerodynamic rudders aft of the propeller.
ACCOMMODATION: Enclosed cabin seating five to six.

UH-15P

UH-15Ps fitted with ducted propellers

UH-16S light amphibious hovercraft

DIMENSIONS
Length: 5·15m (16ft 11in)
Width: 2·28m (7ft 6in)

WEIGHTS
Empty: 340-453kg (750-1000lb)
Payload: 340kg (750lb) with 1500cc VW engine
   and over 454kg (1000lb) with 2300cc four-cylinder Ford engine

PERFORMANCE
Speed over water: 89km/h (55mph)
   land, snow and ice: 104km/h (65mph)
Clearance height: 0·18 to 0·3m (7-12in)
Gradient: 15-25%

UH-17S
Please see *Jane's High-Speed Marine Craft and Air Cushion Vehicles 1987* for details of this craft.

UH-17T

This latest Universal Hovercraft design is provided with seating for six large adults: 1815kg of buoyancy is provided.

LIFT AND PROPULSION: For lift, an 11 to 18hp vertical shaft mower engine can be fitted. For thrust a 50 to 100hp 4-cylinder automobile petrol engine may be employed, under 135kg weight. Thrust available: 110 to 200kg depending upon engine chosen.

ACCOMMODATION: Two bench seats for total six adults, enclosed cabin.

DIMENSIONS
Length: 5·34m
Width: 2·35m
WEIGHTS
Empty: 410-440kg
PERFORMANCE
Speed, on water, 60hp for thrust: 50 knots
Climb gradient: 11% to 30% depending upon load and engine

UH-18S

Please see *Jane's Surface Skimmers 1985* for details. Plans are no longer available for this craft.

UH-18T

Please see *Jane's High-Speed Marine Craft and Air Cushion Vehicles 1987* for details of this craft.

UH-19P

This new design is similar to the UH-15P but is larger. It has slightly less stability in roll than a craft with a rectangular hull, but has greater pitch stability and lower drag, giving it higher speeds. Seating is three in the front and two in the aft of the open cockpit. With an enclosed cabin the craft can attain 90mph across ice and snow. Construction time is approximately 200 to 350 hours. Cost is between US $1000 to $2000 (1984).

The craft has been employed in attempts to establish a new water craft speed record between New Orleans and St Louis, a distance of 1027 miles along the Mississippi.

Two attempts had been made up to November 1984 on the present record of 23 hours 9 minutes. One was foiled by a storm which damaged the craft, the second was completed in 25 hours. Difficulties encountered on the journey are rough water created by up to 150 barges encountered, each creating several miles of rough water; bad weather and the avoidance of obstacles at night. Further attempts were to be made during the summer of 1985.

LIFT AND PROPULSION: Motive power for the lift system is provided by an 18hp Briggs & Stratton vertical shaft mower engine driving an axial fan. Thrust is supplied by almost any

Universal Hovercraft UH-17T at National Rally in Troy, Ohio, June 1987

automobile engine of up to 1600cc, weighing less than 300lb. The craft would still be very fast with the smaller 1100cc Datsun and Toyota engines.

DIMENSIONS
Length: 5·91m (19ft 5in)
Width: 2·28m (7ft 6in)
WEIGHTS
Empty: 935lb (424kg)
Payload: 1000lb (454kg)
PERFORMANCE
Max speed, ice and snow, with closed cabin: 144km/h (90mph)

Max speed, calm water: 128km/h (80mph)
Max gradient capability: 30°-45°
Clearance height: 0·2m (8in)

UH-19S

This is a single-engine version of the UH-19P. The fan axis is set at 45 degrees to the horizontal and is driven by a variable automatic lift system similar to that used in the UH-18S. The engine is a Chevrolet Citation type of about 115hp. Estimated maximum speed is 144km/h (90mph), cruise 112km/h (70mph).

UH-19P

UH-19P

Bob Windt and Mike Kiester at speed in the UH-19S, a modified UH-19P

In 1985 this craft was used to set a speed record on the Mississippi from New Orleans to St Louis in 21 hours 47 minutes, beating the old record by 1 hour 22 minutes.

UH-26S

This 12- to 16-seat ACV is the largest homebuilt craft available. Ribs and stringers are in fir and pine and covered with a 6·3mm (¼in) plywood skin. The driver's seat is placed high and forward for good visibility. The passenger compartment can seat 16 or eight plus 544kg (1200lb) of cargo. The craft may also be equipped for touring with sleeping space for four to seven persons. In the hands of its designer, Bob Windt, the UH-26S completed a 4409km (2740 mile) trip from Cordova, Illinois to New Orleans, Louisiana and back in three weeks.

LIFT AND PROPULSION: Integrated system. Power supplied by a standard V-8 283-400in³ automobile engine driving a 1·06m (3ft 6in) diameter, four-bladed fan for lift and a 2·43m (8ft) diameter two-bladed propeller for thrust. Maximum recommended installed power is 225hp.

The lift fan is driven off the pulley end of the engine, employing a double Auto-lift system, drive shaft and right-angle drive gearbox. The two-

UH-26S

bladed propeller is belt-driven from the flywheel end of the engine.

DIMENSIONS
Length: 7·92m (26ft)
Width: 3·65m (12ft)
Hoverheight: 0·35m (14in)
WEIGHTS
Empty: 1134kg (2500lb)

Payload: 1134kg (2500lb)
Max weight capacity: 1359kg (3000lb)
PERFORMANCE
Max speed, over land: 105km/h (65mph)
over water: 89km/h (55mph)
Max gradient: 25%
PRICE: Complete set of plans available US $45.
Full size rib outline $10 (1984)

LOW-SPEED
AIR CUSHION PLATFORMS

CANADA

VITRI ROBOTS AND VEHICLES INC (VRV)

238 De Brullon Street, Boucherville, Quebec
J4B 2J8, Canada

Telephone: (514) 641 3914
Telex: (Via USA) 750 846
Telefax: (514) 397 9496

Pierre F Alepin, *President*

Please see ACV Builders section for background on company and VRV air cushion vehicles and trailers.

AEROBAC TRAILER (DESIGN)
Muskeg type tracked vehicles have light footprint pressure allowing them to move over marshes and other waterlogged terrains typical of the northern regions of Canada. An air cushion trailer will permit an increase in cargo load without an increase in tractor footprint pressure thus reducing surface damage. The trailer is equipped with wheels, able to carry the full load of the trailer, and is attached to the tractor with a fifth-wheel pin, as on conventional road equipment.

AT-20 TRAILER (DESIGN)
Length: 15m (17·5m to pin)
Width: 6m (reduced to 3m on-road)
Payload: 20 tonnes
Weight: 35 tonnes
Engine: Detroit 8V-92TA
Power: 310kW
Cushion pressure, max: 5kPa
Fans: Two VIM HCHB-050
Total flow: 36m³/s (at 6kPa)

AT-10 TRAILER (DESIGN)
Length: 12m (14·5m to pin)
Width: 4·6m (reduced to 2·6m on-road)
Payload: 10 tonnes
Weight: 20 tonnes
Engine: Detroit 6V-92TA
Power: 230kW
Cushion pressure, max: 5kPa
Fans: Two VIM HCHB-040
Total flow: 25m³/s (at 6kPa)

AT-5 TRAILER (DESIGN)
Length: 9m (11·5m to pin)

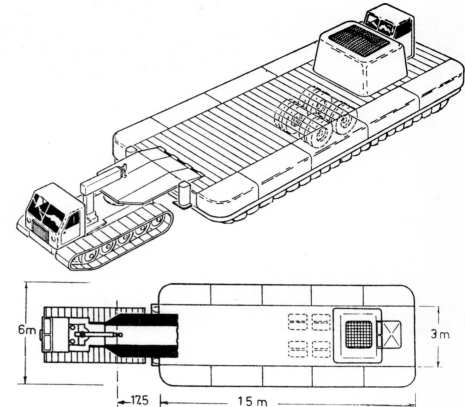

Aerobac AT-20 hybrid trailer design for 20-tonne payload

Width: 3·5m (reduced to 2·6m on-road)
Payload: 5 tonnes
Weight: 11 tonnes
Engine: Deutz (KHD) BF6L 413F

Power: 160kW
Cushion pressure, max: 5kPa
Fans: Two VIM HCHB-031
Total flow: 18m³/s (at 6kPa)

CHINA, PEOPLE'S REPUBLIC

HEILONGJIANG WATER TRANSPORTATION SCIENTIFIC RESEARCH INSTITUTE

Two hoverbarges, converted from 300-ton and 600-ton deck barges, have been supplied to the Ministry of Communications. Between May 1981 and June 1982, they carried 6000 tonnes of cargo, travelled 24 000km and during trials recorded fuel savings, compared with conventional barges, of 20 to 30 per cent.

MARINE DESIGN AND RESEARCH INSTITUTE OF CHINA (MARIC)

346 Sichuan Road, Central, PO Box 3053, Shanghai, People's Republic of China

Telephone: 215044
Telex: 33029 MARIC CN
Cable: 5465

Liang Yun, *Deputy Chief Engineer, Director of Hovercraft Division*

MARIC Type 7301 platform

MARIC-designed Type 7301 air cushion platform built at the Dong Feng yard. An anti-spray skirt is fitted

DONG FENG SHIPYARD
Hangzhou

TYPE 7301

Designed by MARIC, the air cushion platform Type 7301 was completed in Dong Feng Shipyard in May 1987. The craft will undergo oil field trials and evaluation, operating in both offshore and onshore areas for transporting workers and equipment.

HULL: Main hull is built in welded marine steel construction, the superstructure is of aluminium alloy construction.

LIFT AND PROPULSION: Two Type 12180 four-stroke, water-cooled, turbocharged marine diesel engines rated at 800hp, driving two twin-air-inlet type centrifugal fans and two ducted air propellers.

CONTROLS: Directional control is by two sets of twin vertical aerodynamic rudders mounted on the rear of the propeller ducts.

DIMENSIONS
Length overall: 19·20m
Beam overall: 12·20m
Height overall: 6·90m

Draught, average, on cushion: 0·50m
 off cushion: 0·61m
WEIGHTS
Max weight: 80 tons
Payload: 35 tons
PERFORMANCE
Max calm water speed: 10km/h
Max ground speed: 10-20km/h
Endurance: 6 hours

FINLAND

OY WÄRTSILÄ AB

Helsinki Shipyard, PO Box 132, SF-00151 Helsinki 15, Finland

Telephone: 90 1941
Telex: 121246 WHT SF

Pekka Laine, *President, Shipbuilding Division*
Martin Saarikangas, *Senior Vice-President, Shipbuilding Division and Managing Director, Wärtsilä Helsinki Shipyard*
Robert Stenius, *President, Managing Director, Turku Shipyard*
Kaj Liljestrand, *Vice-President, Marketing, Sales and R & D, Helsinki Shipyard*

Towed amphibious barges and self-propelled amphibious lighters have been under development at Wärtsilä's Helsinki Shipyard since 1976. The vessels are designed to help transfer heavy cargoes from ship-to-shore in areas such as the Soviet Arctic regions where problems are created by the lack of harbour facilities, difficult ice conditions and shallow coastal waters.

The company's first self-propelled amphibious lighter, Vector 4, was introduced in 1983. Two larger derivatives, the Vector 75 and the Vector 200, with payloads of 75 tonnes and 200 tonnes respectively, were announced in 1984.

TAV 40

A contract for nine TAV (Towable Air-Cushion Vehicle) 40s was signed in Moscow early in 1981 and was followed by an order for a further five. The craft operate in conjunction with 14 SA-15 type 20 000-tonne, icebreaking, multi-purpose cargo ships designed by Wärtsilä. They were delivered during 1982 and 1983, newbuildings 446-459.

The overall dimensions of the TAV 40 and its self-propelled variants allow them to be carried in holds or on decks of SA-15 type icebreaking cargo ships.

The craft are based on a Soviet licence and are on long-term product development at Wärtsilä. Experience gained by Wärtsilä during the construction and testing of the TAV 40 will be shared with the Soviet organisation, Licensintorg.

TAV 40

The Soviet counterpart to the TAV 40 is the MPVP-40, a vehicle of similar overall design, construction, power and dimensions, described later in this section. The main difference between the two vehicles, both of which are intended for operation in Arctic conditions, is that the Soviet craft is designed for bow loading while the Finnish vehicle is designed for side loading.

TAV 40s can be equipped with a range of propulsion systems for operation in differing terrain and climatic conditions; systems tested and available to order include air and water screws, wheels, crawler track units, paddle wheels and screw rotors.

LIFT: One 590kW (790shp) marinised diesel mounted in an engine room at the bow drives two AB Finska Fläktfabriken centrifugal fans in two volutes, one each side of the elevated bridge aft.

HULL: Buoyancy raft-type structure in all-welded steel with light alloy superstructure.

SKIRT: Loop and segment type.

CONTROLS: All controls are in an elevated bridge on the centreline aft.

DIMENSIONS
Length overall: 20·7m (68ft)
Beam, max: 9·9m (32ft 6in)
Height, hull sides: 1m (3ft 3in)

WEIGHT
Useful load: 40 tons

PERFORMANCE
Speed (dependent on tow vehicle): Self-propelled variant achieves 5 knots in open waters and 15km/h (9-10mph) over land
Vertical obstacle clearance: 0·6m (2ft)

VECTOR 4

Derived from the TAV 40, Vector 4 is self-propelled and fitted with steerable outrigged crawler tractor units forward and aft. It is designed for carrying heavy cargoes on firm ground, swamps, across water, snow or ice. Accommodation is for a driver and an assistant. As with the TAV 40, larger versions are under development to carry loads of up to 100 tonnes.

DIMENSIONS
Length, overall: 27·0m
Length, waterline: 18·0m
Beam: 8·5m

PERFORMANCE
Speed across even ground: 20km/h
across calm water: 4 knots
Gradient capability: 6 degrees

VP-1

Wärtsilä VP-1 air cushion trailer for Arctic cargo handling as supplied to the USSR

VECTOR 75 (DESIGN)

A derivative of the Vector 4, Vector 75 is a self-propelled, year-round, heavy cargo transporter. It can be built in all-welded steel or aluminium and has a payload of 75 tonnes. The specification applies to the steel version.

LIFT AND PROPULSION: Motive power is supplied by two 625kW marinised diesels mounted transversely, one forward, one aft. Each drives two centrifugal fans mounted vertically on a common shaft and housed in two separate volutes. Power from the diesels is also transmitted to hydraulic pumps which drive outrigged crawler track-drive units forward and aft. Rubber wheels drive the crawler tracks. The pressure of the tracks on the supporting surface beneath is adjustable.

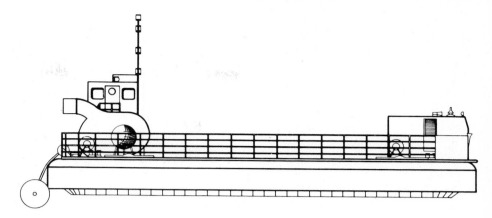

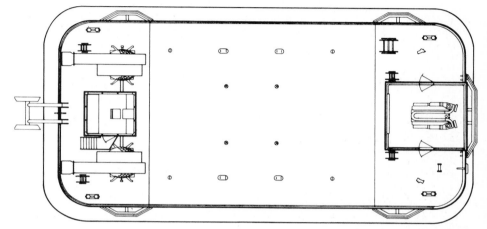

Profile and deck plan, TAV 40

TAV 40

Vector 4 showing forward tracked propulsion unit

CONTROLS: Craft heading is controlled by the forward track drive which is steerable.
DIMENSIONS
Length, on cushion: 37·5m
  hull: 28m
Beam, hull: 12m
WEIGHT
Payload: 75 tonnes
PERFORMANCE
Speed, even ground: 16·0km/h (10mph)
  open water: 3 knots
  astern: 3·2km/h (2mph)
Slope capacity, track drive: 8°
  towing winch: 15°

VECTOR 200 (DESIGN)

The layout of the Vector 200 is similar to that of the Vector 75, but the hardstructure is 10 metres longer and 8 metres have been added to the beam, giving overall hull dimensions of 38 × 20 metres. The vehicle is fitted with four 625kW diesels to cope with the additional structural weight and payload.

The brief specification at the end of this entry applies to the welded steel version.
LIFT AND PROPULSION, CONTROLS: Motive power is supplied by four 625kW diesels driving eight centrifugal lift fans and, via hydraulic pumps, outrigged crawler tracks as on the Vector 75.
HULL: Built in all-welded steel or aluminium.
DIMENSIONS
Length, on cushion: 48m
  hull: 38m
Beam, hull: 20m
WEIGHT
Payload: 200 tonnes
PERFORMANCE
Speed, even ground: 9·7km/h (6mph)
  open water: 2·5 knots
  astern: 3·2km/h (2mph)
Slope capacity, track drive: 3°
  towing winch: 5°

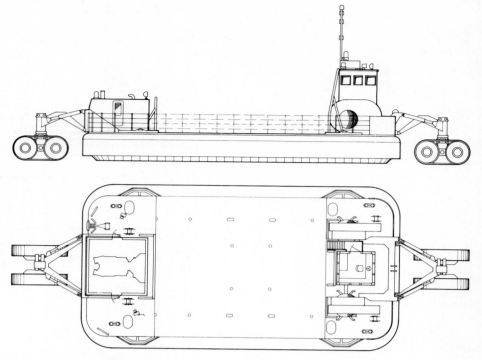

Profile and deck plan, Vector 4

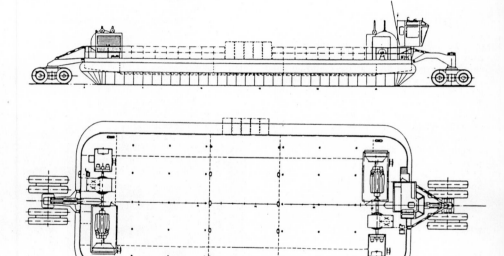

Vector 75 design

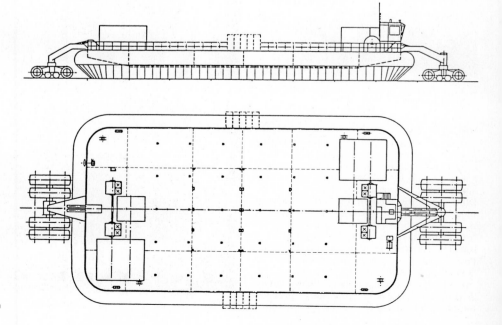

Vector 200 design

JAPAN

MITSUI ENGINEERING & SHIPBUILDING CO LTD

6-4, Tsukiji 5-chome, Chuo-ku, Tokyo 104, Japan

Telephone: (03) 544 3462
Telex: 22821/22924 J

Directors, see ACV section

SEP-1

A 310-ton hoverbarge for use in deep or shallow waters. A feature of the craft is the provision of jack-up legs similar to those employed on some offshore oil rigs. These enable the craft to be positioned above test or survey sites in shallow waters or in areas of marsh or tundra.

SEP-1 hoverbarge

UNION OF SOVIET SOCIALIST REPUBLICS

ALL-UNION OIL MACHINERY RESEARCH INSTITUTE, WEST SIBERIA (VNII neftmash)

Tyumen, USSR

A V Vladimirskii, *Director*
V A Shibanov, *Head of Air Cushion Vehicle Department*

Air cushion platforms with load capacities of up to 400 tonnes have been under development in the West Siberian lowlands since 1965. Eighty per cent of the gas and petroleum sites in this area are amid almost impassable swamps, salt marshes, taiga and stretches of water.

In the Tyumensk area, where deep wells are being drilled, more than 200 tonnes of support equipment are required at each site in addition to between 130 and 180 tons of drilling gear. In 1965 a group of ACV engineers and designers, headed by V A Shibanov, left the Urals for Tyumen to design a hover platform capable of carrying a complete oil rig across tundra and taiga, and also to design and construct an all-terrain vehicle for towing the drilling rig, on hover, to the drilling sites.

Small-scale models were used during the development stages, and several attempts were made before a completely satisfactory design was conceived.

The most successful arrangement, the BU-75-VP, is illustrated. It comprises a rectangular, all-metal buoyancy raft (the load carrying member), with side structures to carry a bag-type skirt. A derrick, derived from a standard BU-75 drilling rig, was mounted on the central raft, and the drilling pump, usually delivered to sites separately, was also installed on board. Apart from specialist items of oil drilling gear, the platform is equipped with lift fans and drilling engines which serve a dual purpose by driving the lift fans when the platform is changing location.

Two tractors are normally required to tow the platform in a fully loaded condition.

Transport and routeing problems are now greatly simplified as the need to detour virtually impassable lakes, marshes, and snow or water-filled ravines no longer arises. The rig has been employed in oilfields at Shaimskoye, Urai and Samotlor.

Two more multi-ton cargo-carrying ACV platforms have been completed at the Tyumen Ship Repair yard. One platform, which began service in 1974, has a load capacity of 203·2 tonnes.

A more recent design has been undergoing tests at the Strezhevoye workings at the Alexandrov field in the Tomsk region. Large ACV rigs with a capacity of several thousand tons are under development to aid the exploitation of oil and gas in Siberia and the Soviet far north.

The latest ACV product of the research institute is a 400-tonne oil pumping station ordered by the Sibkomplektmontazh Association for the Lyantorskoye oilfield, 200km north of Surgut, West Siberia. Cushion lift was supplied by two fans powered by two 800hp diesels. The skirt was made from 1500m² of rubberised fabric supplied by the Lisichansk Industrial Fabrics Plant, working in conjunction with the Rezinotekhnika Association which specialises in industrial rubber products and waterproofing fabrics. The skirt was attached directly to the body of the pumping unit, obviating the need for a platform.

The pumping station reached the Lyantorskoye field via two rivers, the Ob' and the shallower Pim. Throughout the journey it was towed by either a shallow draught tugboat or swamp tractor.

Builders, timber workers, geologists and other specialist workers in western Siberia are advocating the use of large air cushion platforms in the area as they would enable many rivers to be used in those areas which are too shallow for use by conventional displacement vessels.

BU-75-VP
DIMENSIONS
Length: 30m (98ft 5in)
Width: 20m (65ft 7in)
WEIGHT
Total: 170 tonnes
PERFORMANCE
Speed (depending on towing vehicle): About 10km/h (6mph)

ACV TRAILERS
Three ACV trailers have been developed by the organisation: a 6-ton platform; the PVP-40 with a

BU-75-VP oil rig mounted on air cushion platform

cargo capacity of 40 tonnes; and the PVP-60 with a capacity of 60 tonnes.

The PVP-40 is powered by a single diesel engine driving two centrifugal fans. Its 60-tonne counterpart is powered by a single gas turbine driving twin axial-flow fans. Discs or wheels fitted to swinging arms at the rear provide directional control when reversing. 'Trains' of ACV trailers can carry heavy loads and a further development is an articulated trailer, several times the length of platforms like the PVP-40, with one tractor forward and another at the rear.

A total of 550 PVP-40 and PVP-60 hover platforms had been put into service in Siberia, the Soviet far east and far north by the end of 1980. Another 560 were completed by the end of 1981. Total weight of the PVP-40 is 58 tonnes and the PVP-60, 84 tonnes. Total installed power for the PVP-40 is 305kW and the PVP-60, 390kW. Position of the lift fan/engine modules can be altered to suit load requirements.

UVP 400-TONNE CAPACITY, TRANS-PORTABLE HOVER PLATFORM

An all-purpose, towed air cushion platform for carrying extra-heavy loads has been built at Tyumen for the Sibkomplektmontazh Association. It differs from conventional air cushion platforms in that it is attached to the object to be carried.

During tests, which took place on the shore of the Ob' river, near Surgut, West Siberia, the 32-tonne vehicle was mounted on a 400-tonne high-pressure pumping station for pumping oil from a well into a pipeline. Its two diesel engines, each developing 800hp, and four fans lifted the station, and the whole structure, described as being as high as a three-storey building, was hauled by two tractors. Following trials, the equipment carried the pumping station from Surgut to the Lentorskoye oilfield, 220km to the north of Surgut. The platform and its tractors negotiated forests, marshes and rivers during the five-day operation.

To simplify transport, the platform breaks down into about six basic components, none of which weighs more than 6 tonnes. These can be carried to a site by truck, tractor, boat or helicopter.

It is claimed that the platform can be applied to even heavier loads, and it is proving successful in moving large fully-assembled units, particularly power station equipment, into areas without roads or technical facilities.

DIMENSIONS
Length: 36·21m
Width: 25·8m
Track width: 50m
WEIGHTS
Structure only: 32 tonnes
Load carrying capacity: 400 tonnes plus
PERFORMANCE
Towing speed: 10km/h
Clearance height: 0·2m

ACV TRACTORS

Towing requirements for the rigs and ACV trailers built in Tyumen were initially met by conventional GTT amphibious crawler tractors. Since these were unable to cope with very soft terrain, development of a true multi-terrain tractor was undertaken, and this led to the construction of the Tyumen I. This was the first of a completely new ACV type with combined crawler propulsion and air cushion lift. The first model, now in the Tyumen's ACV museum, carried a 2-tonne load at speeds up to 40km/h (25mph) in off-road conditions. It is described as a broad, squat vehicle on long narrow caterpillar tracks, with a flexible skirt between its crawlers. The second was the MVP-2 which was upgraded soon afterwards to the MVP-3 5-tonne capacity model. The MVP-3 uses extremely narrow crawler tracks for propulsion, steering and support on hard surfaces. As with the Bertin Terraplane series of wheel-assisted ACVs, the weight transfer to the crawler track is variable according to the nature of the terrain being crossed and the gradient. It is said

PVP-40 under tow across Siberian swamp

PVP-60 under tow

Towed PVP-60 cushion platform employed in Urengou area

6-ton capacity ACV trailer towed by 5-tonne capacity MVP-3 combined ACV/crawler tractor

to be capable of 80km/h (50mph) over swamps with 1m (40in) high hummocks, and cruises at 48km/h (30mph). At the time of its first demonstration to the Soviet press in July 1974, it had completed 96km (60 miles) over Siberian swamps.

Operation of the vehicle appears to be relatively simple. Main controls are an accelerator for the single engine, which has an automatic clutch, and two standard tracked vehicle steering levers which skid-steer through the differential use of the tracks.

The policy at Tyumen is to standardise on composite crawler ACV systems rather than air propeller or helicoidal-screw type propulsion.

MINISTRY OF THE MERCHANT MARINE, LENINGRAD CENTRAL DESIGN BUREAU

Leningrad, USSR

V Vladimirtsev, *Project Chief Designer*

LAISKI SHIPYARD
MPVP-40

During 1977-1980, the Leningrad Central Design Bureau, in conjunction with the Northern Shipping Line, undertook a research and development programme for the construction of a 40-tonne capacity seagoing hoverbarge to be employed as a lighter at landing points along the Northern Sea Route between Murmansk and Uelen.

Designated MPVP-40, the craft is intended to operate in conditions up to Sea State 4. Under normal conditions the craft is towed by tugs over water and by tractors over land. Provision has been made, however, for the craft to be propelled independently by air expelled through thrust nozzles which can be fitted aft of the fan casings. These provide a speed of 2·5 knots over calm water and ice and permit the craft to operate over stretches of shallow water.

The craft were to be produced at several Soviet shipyards and were intended primarily for operation from SA-15 type 20 000dwt, arctic multipurpose icebreaking cargo vessels, 28 of which are under construction for Soviet shipping operators at yards in Finland and the Soviet Union. Each is designed to carry two MPVP-40s or its Finnish-built counterpart, the TAV 40.

LIFT: Cushion air is supplied by a single 600hp (441kW) V2-800TK-S3 marine diesel driving, via a reduction gear, two VTsD-II fans, each of 1800m³/minute capacity. The engine compartment contains the essential accessories and pumps as well as a dc generator. Also included in the power pack are a PZhD-600 preheater and VTI-4 air filters. Engine cooling is of closed type, with radiator. Rotor of the VTsD-II fan, which is 1·1m in diameter and develops 5kPa static pressure, is built in welded stainless steel. Blades are in hollow stainless steel filled with foam plastic.

Fan transmission comprises a flexible coupling, friction clutch, reduction gear, neck bush and three jointed shafts.

CONTROLS: Rotating thrust ports control craft direction when operating independently of tugs and tractors. Twin metal wheels keep the platform on course during towing at sea or over ground.

HULL: Ribbed, carbon steel structure. Cargo deck and side plates, 4mm thick; deck and bottom, 3mm thick. Hull divided into three watertight compartments. The craft will remain afloat in the event of any one compartment flooding.

The engineer's cabin is on the port side in line with the engine. On the starboard side are the battery box and a heater used to preheat the lubricant and the liquid coolant during cold weather. A demountable signal mast is installed above the engineer's cabin. A deflection system protects the fan housing against spray. Both sides of the platform are enclosed by rope railings. At

MPVP-40 hover platform under tow

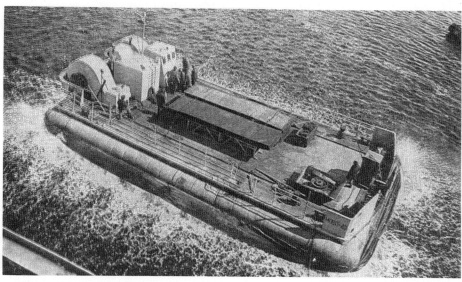
MPVP-40

the bow are anchor and ramp equipment, bollards, cable chocks, and mallets and pulleys for moving the load on the deck. The platform is equipped with a 50kg Matrosov anchor, two hand windlasses for weighing the anchor, lifting and lowering the ramps, and for mooring. Four separate ramps are fitted for cargo transhipment as well as the loading and offloading of wheeled and tracked vehicles.

SKIRT: Fingered bag type with transverse stability trunk and longitudinal stability keel in rear section. Cushion area, 14m².

DIMENSIONS
Length: 20·2m

Deck width: 8·5m
Structure height: 1m
Designed draught: 0·64m
WEIGHTS
Empty: 29 tonnes
Loaded: 69 tonnes
PERFORMANCE
Cruising endurance: 24 hours
Max permissible Sea State: 4
Max speed, independent air-jet propulsion: 2·5 knots

Please see Addenda for additional USSR air cushion platform developments.

UNITED KINGDOM

BRITISH HOVERCRAFT CORPORATION (BHC)

Now part of the Westland Aerospace Division of Westland plc, East Cowes, Isle of Wight, England

Telephone: (0983) 294101
Telex: 86761 G

Directors, see ACV section

HOVERBARGE (DESIGNS)

In recent years BHC has made several heavy-lift design studies including two for the US Army. The earliest of these studies considered a range of hoverbarges of the logistics-over-the-shore-operation (LOTS) type. More recently BHC has studied the use of SR.N4 and BH.7 components in craft to meet the lighter amphibious, heavy-lift LAMP(H) requirement. As a civil counterpart, SR.N4 pylons were sold to Sohio for a self-propelled air cushion barge project but which was not subsequently built.

BHC has completed for the CEGB a contract for the design of a towed air cushion barge, to be based on an existing dumb barge. For more general use it has designed a series of standard modules which can, in various combinations, be used to construct modular hoverbarges catering for a wide range of payloads.

Artist's impression of BHC air cushion barge design
for the UK Central Electricity Generating Board

UNITED STATES OF AMERICA

HOVER SYSTEMS INC

1500 Chester Pike, Eddystone, Pennsylvania 19013,
USA

Telephone: (215) 876 8241
Easylink telex: 62914561

James D Hake, *President & Treasurer*
Joseph J Nestel, *Vice President*
Frank W Hake II, *Vice President*

D-PAAC AMPHIBIOUS BARGE

In 1980 the company designed and built
D-PAAC, a 50-tonne payload, diesel-powered, air
cushion amphibious barge. Propulsion is provided
by a unique hydraulic drive unit operating a set of
eight fully articulated wheels outboard of the air
cushion. The wheel loading is controllable so that
traction can be maintained over almost any
terrain. Deep treads are provided on the wheels for
traction over land and paddle wheels cantilevered
laterally from the wheel hubs provide propulsion
over water. This craft successfully completed a
one-year test for the State of Alaska, Department
of Transportation operating on the Kuskokwim
River and adjacent areas.

During summer 1984 D-PAAC operated as
successfully over open water as it had during
winter conditions. The craft delivered fuel oil to
Eskimo villages (12 000 gallons from internal
tanks, pumped and metered to village storage
tanks), together with lumber and construction
material loaded on to the deck.

The average distance of a summer (or winter)
voyage was over 200 miles, servicing four villages
on three separate routes every three weeks. The
average continuous hover time each trip was 28
hours, with no shutdowns or overnight stops.

The paddle wheels provide a speed equivalent to
that of shallow draught Alaskan river tug-barges.
Two grounded barges and one tug were pulled to
safety during the annual low river water period in
August. The craft was subsequently sold to the US
Army and is in service at Fort Belvoir, Virginia.

FF-3

A 46-tonne capacity air cushion platform, non-
self-propelled.
POWERPLANT
Detroit Diesel 16V-71N
Fuel (5 hours): 1360kg
Fans: Alldays Peacock BA 1200 515W centrifugal

D-PAAC underway on paddle wheels on Kuskokwim river, Alaska

D-PAAC operating in Alaska

SKIRT
Depth: 1·22m
Cushion pressure: 10·29kN/m² (215lb/ft²)
DIMENSIONS
Length overall: 16·77m
Beam overall: 13·72m
Length, cushion: 13·41m
Beam, cushion: 10·37m
Cushion area: 131·83m²
Clear deck area: 127·7m²
WEIGHTS
Weight, empty: 93·35 tonnes
Payload, normal: 46 tonnes
Weight, max: 140 tonnes

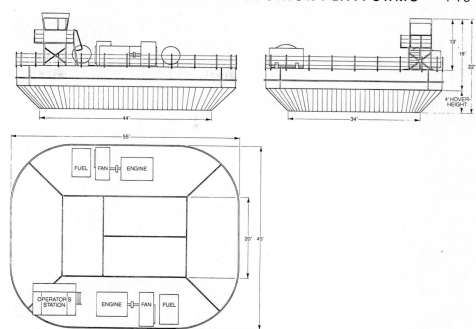

FF-3 46-tonne capacity air cushion platform

HYDROFOILS

AUSTRALIA

CARRINGTON SLIPWAYS PTY LIMITED

Old Punt Road, Tomago, New South Wales 2322, Australia

Telephone: (049) 648071
Telex: 28185 AA
Telefax: (049) 648316

D Laverick, *Managing Director*

RODRIQUEZ RHS 160F

An RHS 160F is to be built by Carrington Slipways Pty Ltd under licence from Rodriquez Cantieri Navali SpA for service with the Urban Transit Authority of New South Wales. Two sister vessels, the *Manly* and the *Sydney* were delivered by the Italian yard in 1984 and 1985 respectively, total outfitting of *Manly* having been carried out by Carrington Slipways. All three vessels seat 238 passengers. Please see the Rodriquez entry for details of the RHS 160F.

The 238-seat RHS-160F *Manly* (fitted out by Carrington Slipways Pty Ltd) passing the Sydney waterfront

BOLIVIA

HELMUT KOCK

44125 West Point Loma Blvd, Apartment 209, San Diego, California 92110, USA

Telephone: (619) 224 6657

Helmut Kock, designer of the Honald Albatross hydrofoil, which operated New York's first commercial hydrofoil service, and former chief engineer of International Hydrolines Inc, designed and built a 15·27m (50ft) hydrofoil ferry for Crillon Tours of La Paz, Bolivia. The craft, the *Bolivia Arrow*, was built during 1976 at Huatajata, on the shore of Lake Titicaca (3700m; 12 000ft) and entered service in February 1977.

All materials, equipment, engines, tools and machinery were imported from the USA. The entire craft is of welded aluminium and was built by Helmut Kock with the aid of a few Bolivian Indians who, in order to undertake the work, were taught how to use modern hand and electric tools and automatic welding techniques.

He has been responsible for modifying the three Sea World hydrofoils to improve their load capacity and performance.

ALBATROSS

Crillon Tours Ltd, La Paz, Bolivia, operates six of Helmut Kock's 20-seat Albatross craft on tourist routes across Lake Titicaca. The need to cope with increasing tourist traffic and to provide a craft capable of crossing the full length of the

Bolivia Arrow showing foil system

lake led to a decision by Darius Morgan, Crillon's chief executive, to build a craft tailored to the company's requirements on the shore of the lake. Construction of the first craft in Bolivia, *Bolivia Arrow*, began in December 1975 and it was launched in September 1976. The craft entered service in February 1977. It is designed for medium range fast ferry services on rivers, bays, lakes and sounds.

FOILS: Surface-piercing trapeze foil system with 'W' configuration pitch stability subfoil. Welded aluminium construction designed by Helmut Kock, US patent no 3, 651, 775.

POWERPLANT: Twin Cummins VT-8-370 diesels, each developing 350shp at sea level and oversize to compensate for loss of power due to altitude. Each engine drives its own propeller via an inclined shaft. Engine room is amidships, after the third row of seats.

ACCOMMODATION: Crew comprises a captain, deckhand and a tourist guide. The captain is accommodated forward in a raised wheelhouse. His seat is on the hull centreline with the wheel, engine controls and main instrumentation in front. Passengers are accommodated in a single saloon with seats for 40. Seats are arranged in ten rows of two abreast, separated by a central aisle. A washbasin/WC unit is provided and also a luggage compartment. All void spaces are filled with polyurethane foam.

DIMENSIONS
Length overall: 15·24m (50ft)
Hull beam: 3·55m (11ft 8in)
Width across foils: 5·79m (19ft)
Draught, hullborne: 2·28m (7ft 6in)
WEIGHT
Displacement fully loaded: 14 tons
PERFORMANCE
Cruising speed: 32 knots

Helmut Kock Albatross hydrofoil *Flecha Guarani* operating on Lake Itaipai, Paraguay   (Darius Morgan)

CHINA, PEOPLE'S REPUBLIC

HUTANG SHIPYARD

Shanghai, People's Republic of China

Hydrofoil torpedo boats of the 'Hu Chwan' (White Swan) class have been under construction at the Hutang Shipyard since about 1966. Some 120 are in service with the Chinese Navy and another 32 have been lent or leased to the Albanian Navy, six to Pakistan, four to Tanzania and six to Romania.

Twenty others, of a slightly modified design, have been built in Romania since 1973.

HU CHWAN (WHITE SWAN)

FOILS: The foil system comprises a bow subfoil to facilitate take-off and a main foil of trapeze or shallow V configuration set back approximately one-third of the hull length from the bow. At high speed in relatively calm conditions the greater part of the hull is raised clear of the water. The main foil and struts retract upwards when the craft is required to cruise in displacement condition.
HULL: High speed V-bottom hull in seawater resistant light alloy.
POWERPLANT: Three 1100hp M-50 type, water-cooled, supercharged 12-cylinder V-type diesels, each driving its own inclined propeller shaft.
ARMAMENT: Two 53cm (21in) torpedo tubes, plus four 15mm machine guns in two twin mountings.
DIMENSIONS (approx)
Length overall: 22m (72ft 2in)
Width across foils: 5·1m (16ft 9in)
Hull beam: 3·96m (13ft)
Draught hullborne: 1m (3ft 3in)
WEIGHT
Displacement full load: 40 tonnes
PERFORMANCE
Max speed foilborne calm conditions: 50-55 knots
Range: 100-150n miles

HEMA

A derivative of the 'Hegu' class FAC (missile) which is based on the Soviet Komar but has a steel hull. Hema differs from Hegu in that it is fitted with bow foils in a similar way to the Hu Chwan, Matka and Turya, it has a slightly longer hull and a second twin 25mm AA mount aft. The prototype was launched in 1970.
FOILS: Single main foil of surface-piercing configuration set back approximately one third of the hull length from the bow.

HULL: High-speed, V-bottom hull. Steel construction.
POWERPLANT: Four 1100hp M-50 type, water-cooled, supercharged 12-cylinder V-type light-weight marine diesels each driving an inclined propeller shaft.
ARMAMENT: Two SS-N-2A Styx missile launchers, one each side of the aft superstructure. Two twin 25mm AA mounts, one forward, one aft. Radar: Square Tie, IFF, High Pole A.
DIMENSIONS
Length overall: 29m (95ft 2in)
Beam, hull: 6·5m (21ft 4in)
WEIGHT
Displacement, full load: 95 tonnes
PERFORMANCE
Max speed, foilborne, calm conditions: 40-45 knots
Cruising speed, hullborne: 25 knots

Hu Chwan torpedo/fast attack hydrofoil of Chinese Navy

INDIA

VENKATAPATHY ENGINEERING (PTE) LIMITED

15 Khadar Nawazkhan Road, PO Box No 4533, Madras 600006, India

Telephone: 471412
Telex: 418198 COIN IN

Supramar Hydrofoils AG announced at the beginning of 1986 that Venkatapathy Engineering (Pte) Ltd had become a licensee for Supramar hydrofoil craft.

INDONESIA

PT PABRIK KAPAL INDONESIA (PERSERO) PT PAL INDONESIA

Head office: BPP Teknologi Building, 12th Floor, JL M H Thamrin No 8, Jakarta, Indonesia

Telephone: Lantai 12 323 774, 324 350
Telex: 61331 ATP JKT

Works: Ujung Surabaya, PO Box 134, Indonesia

Telephone: 24139, 291403
Telex: 31223 PAL SB

Prof Dr Ing B J Habibie, *President Director*
Suleman Wiriadidjaja, *Director of Technology*
Sukono, *Director of General Affairs*
Hariadi Soemarsono, *Director of Production*
Karsono, *Director of Maintenance*

M S M Harahap, *Assistant to President Director for Computer*
Pramono S, *Assistant to President Director for Programme*
Suparto S, *Assistant to President Director for Material*
Sunu Notodihardjo, *Assistant to President Director for Marketing*
Sion H S, *Assistant to President Director for Finance*
Parlin Napitupulu, *Assistant to President Director for Inspectorate*

With origins as a repair and maintenance facility for the navy in 1892, PT PAL now employs 6000 people, occupies an area of 150 hectares and has capacity for designing and building vessels from 60 tonnes to 30 000 tonnes.

Apart from the first Jetfoil 929-115 (*Bima Samudera I*) to be fitted out, two Jetfoil 929-119 are being fitted out and later, two 929-120 models.

Bima Samudera I fitted out by PT Pabrik Kapal Indonesia

ISRAEL

ISRAEL SHIPYARDS LIMITED

POB 1282, Haifa 31000, Israel

Telephone: 749111
Telex: 45132 YARD IL

Y Meivar, *Marketing Manager*

Israel negotiated with the US Government for the purchase of two Flagstaff multi-duty naval hydrofoils from Grumman Aerospace Corporation, together with the acquisition of a licence for the series production of these craft in Israel. The contract signed between Israel and Grumman permitted the construction of at least ten craft for the Israeli Navy without licence fees. Israeli-built

craft would also be made available for export. Israel Shipyards Limited has non-exclusive export rights to all countries except the USA and one Asian nation, but the US State Department has veto rights on all prospective Israeli export sales.

M161

In 1977 the US Government announced that

Craft built

Type	Name	Commissioned
M161	*Livnik*	1983
M161	*Snapirit*	1985

agreement had been reached on the joint development of hydrofoils by two countries and Grumman Aerospace Corporation stated it had 'received its first order for the Flagstaff from an overseas client'. Later, the Corporation confirmed that the country concerned was Israel. In May 1979 it was reported that two 105-tonne derivatives of the Flagstaff II, known by their Grumman design number M161, were under construction, one at Lantana Boatyard Inc, Florida, the other in Israel. The first craft to be completed, *Shimrit* (Guardian), was launched in May 1981, followed by equipment tests and sea trials in the Atlantic.

The first Israeli-built vessel, *Livnik* (Heron), followed six months behind the lead vessel. It is identical to the US-built craft and was launched during the latter half of 1982, beginning sea trials in July 1983.

A further hydrofoil, the *Snapirit*, was completed at Haifa in the first half of 1985. The original plan to construct 12 further M161 type hydrofoils has been dropped.

The M161 has been designed for a wide range of naval and military roles and can be fitted with a variety of weapons. Designs are available with differing payloads and endurances for applications including gunboat, troop transport, surveillance craft, missile boat, inshore ASW patrol, EEZ patrol and search and rescue.

FOIL SYSTEM: Fully-submerged system of conventional configuration, comprising twin inverted T-foils forward and single inverted T-foil aft. Approximately 70 per cent of the load is supported by two forward foils and 30 per cent by the aft foil. All three foils are subcavitating. They have an identical span of 5·23m, area of 4·97m² and aspect ratio of 5:5, and are machined from forged aluminium 6061-T652. All three foils are incidence-controlled and operated by Hamilton Standard automatic control system (ACS) employing electro-hydraulic actuators. Inputs are height, supplied by twin TRT radio altimeters in the bow, vertical acceleration, pitch and pitch rate, roll and roll rate and yaw rate. Pitch and roll attitudes are controlled by a vertical gyro. The system has an autopilot facility for heading hold. The stern foil power strut, together with the propeller, rotates ± 5 degrees for steering and all three foil/strut units retract completely clear of the water for hullborne manoeuvring. Break joints are incorporated on the two forward struts so that if either of them hit floating debris each would break clean at the point of its connection to its yoke. A shear bolt releases the aft strut permitting it to rotate rearwards and upwards aft of the transom.

HULL: Fabricated in 5086 and 5456 aluminium alloys. Frames and bulkheads are welded assemblies. Bottom, side and deck plating consists of large panels of wide-ribbed extrusions welded to the frames and bulkheads.

ACCOMMODATION: Size of the crew varies with the mission and weapons fitted. Minimum operating crew normally comprises three to four: helmsman, engineer, deck officer/navigator and, if necessary, a lookout. Stations and messing facilities for a crew of 15 on the Israeli craft. The pilothouse has three seats, the port position is occupied by the helmsman, the centre by the gunner operating the twin 30mm Emerlec cannon and the starboard by the commander, who sits in front of a radarscope. The CIC occupies the full width of the craft between hull frames 15 and 23. Stations are provided within the CIC for 13 of the 15 crew, all being involved in the operation of the weapon systems apart from the engineering officer who sits in front of an engineering operating station (EOS) which incorporates a one-person centralised and computerised engineering monitoring and control system (EMCS). All manned spaces are heated and air-conditioned by an Airscrew Howden system which comprises two Freon modules, each of 15-ton capacity. The

Snapirit, completed by Israel Shipyards Ltd in 1985

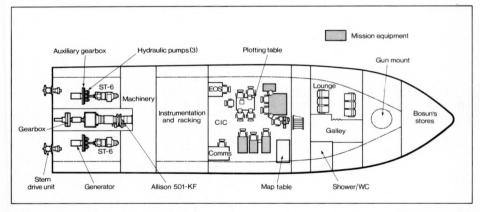

M161 deck plan   (Defence Attaché)

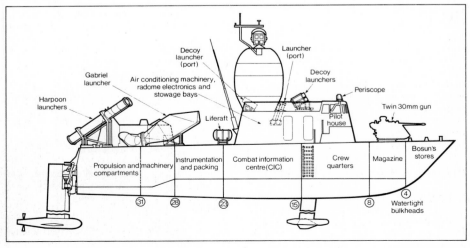

Inboard profile of M161   (Defence Attaché)

forward superstructure accommodates the bridge, which contains steering and engine control consoles and is elevated to give a 360-degree view. Entry to the deckhouse is via two 660mm × 1·52m (2ft 2in × 5ft) watertight doors, one port, one starboard. There is an emergency exit aft, behind the pilothouse on the weatherdeck. Escape hatches are provided in the living spaces.

POWERPLANT, FOILBORNE: A 5400hp Allison 501-KF marine gas turbine is installed. Power is transmitted to a 1·32m supercavitating four-bladed controllable-pitch propeller via a Western Gear transmission with a reduction ratio of 14:1 and a Grumman Z-drive transmission.

POWERPLANT, HULLBORNE: Twin 130hp Maritime Industries retractable and steerable outdrives. Three-bladed stainless steel 660mm (26in) fixed-pitch propellers driven through geared transmission by integrally-mounted Rexroth hydraulic motors.

FUEL: All installed prime movers operate on VP-5 or diesel No 2 or equivalent fuel. Maximum fuel tankage is 21 tonnes. Under way refuelling facilities can be provided.

SYSTEMS, ELECTRICAL: Two 200kW, 120/208V, 400Hz three-phase generators driven by two 660shp Pratt and Whitney ST-6 gas turbine APUs. Each generator is capable of supplying normal ship electrical load and can be operated in parallel during battle conditions.

HYDRAULICS: 3000 psi system driven by four pumps on both the hullborne and foilborne prime movers provides control power for hullborne and foilborne operation and turbine starting.

CONTROLS: An automatic control system stabilises the craft in foilborne operations. This comprises dual radar height sensors, an inertial sensor, a digital processor, displays and controls. Both flat or co-ordinated turns and platforming or contouring modes can be selected by the helmsman.

FIRE EXTINGUISHING: A Spectronix fire detection and suppression system is installed.

ARMAMENT: Typical armament kit comprises four McDonnell Douglas Harpoon ship-to-ship missiles in two pairs of launchers aft, and two IAI Gabriel Mk III ship-to-ship missiles immediately ahead of them. Anti-ship missile and aircraft defence is provided by a twin 30mm Emerlec remote-controlled cannon on the foredeck. Chaff launchers are mounted on the deckhouse roof.

ELECTRONICS: Large radome on deckhouse, built by Brunswick Corporation, houses the antenna of an Elta search radar. This is reported to employ horizontally polarised X-band for surface search and vertically-polarised S-band for air alert with selectable fast and slow rates of antenna rotation. Fire control radar: ECCM/ESM.

DIMENSIONS
Length, overall (hull moulded): 25·62m (84ft)
  between perpendiculars: 23·4m (76ft 9in)
  overall (foils retracted): 31·79m (104ft 4in)
  overall (foilborne): 29·81m (97ft 10in)
Beam, hull moulded: 7·32m (24ft)
  foils retracted (extreme): 12·95m (42ft 6in)
  foilborne (extreme): 12·45m (40ft 10in)
Draught (full load)
  foil system, retracted: 1·45m (4ft 9in)
  foil system, extended: 4·83m (15ft 10in)
  foilborne (nominal): 1·7m (5ft 7in)
Surface search radar height, hullborne: 9·99m (32ft 10in)
  foilborne: 12·13m (39ft 10in)

WEIGHTS
Light displacement: 71 tonnes
Full load displacement: 105 tonnes
Normal fuel load: 16 tonnes
Max fuel load: 21 tonnes

PERFORMANCE
Max intermittent speed: 52 knots
Most economical speed: 42 knots
Foilborne operating envelope (normal): 35-48 knots
Max hullborne speed: 9·5 knots
Range at 42 knots: 750-1150n miles
Specific range at 42 knots: 47-55n miles/tonne

ITALY

FINCANTIERI–CANTIERI NAVALI ITALIANI SpA

(Cantieri Navali Riuniti SpA was incorporated in Fincantieri in July 1984)
Head Office: Via Genova 1, I-34121 Trieste, Italy
Naval Shipbuilding Division: Via Cipro 11, 16129 Genoa, Italy

Telephone: 0039 10 59951
Telex: 216367 FINCGE I

Pietro Orlando, *Naval Shipbuilding Division Director*
Pasquale G Teodorani, *Director for Technical & Commercial Co-ordination*
Michele Diaz Satta, *Marketing & Sales Director*

The original Cantieri Navali Riuniti SpA took over the interests of Alinavi which was formed in 1964 to develop, manufacture and market advanced military marine systems.

Under the terms of a licensing agreement, Fincantieri has access to Boeing technology in the field of military fully-submerged foil hydrofoil craft.

In October 1970, the company was awarded a contract by the Italian Navy for the design and construction of the P420 Sparviero hydrofoil missilecraft. This is an improved version of the Boeing PGH-2 *Tucumcari*. The vessel, given the design name Sparviero, was delivered to the Italian Navy in July 1974. An order for a further six of this type was placed by the Italian Navy in February 1976.

Craft built	Commissioned
P420 Sparviero (class type)	1974
P421 *Nibbio*	1981
P422 *Falcone*	1982
P423 *Astore*	1982
P424 *Grifone*	1982
P425 *Gheppio*	1983
P426 *Condor*	1983

SPARVIERO

The Sparviero missile-launching hydrofoil gunboat displaces 60·5 tonnes and is designed for both offensive and defensive missions. Its combination of speed, firepower, and all-weather capability is unique in a ship of this class.

The vessel has fully-submerged foils arranged in canard configuration and an automatic control system. A gas turbine-powered waterjet system provides foilborne propulsion and a diesel-driven propeller outdrive provides hullborne propulsion. A typical crew comprises two officers and eight enlisted men.

Sparviero's advanced automatic control system considerably reduces the vertical and transverse acceleration normally experienced in rough seas. In Sea State 4 the maximum vertical acceleration likely to be found is in the order of 0·25g (rms), while the maximum roll angle is not likely to be greater than ± 2 degrees.

Three Sparviero hydrofoil missilecraft at Fincantieri yard at Muggiano

P420 Sparviero

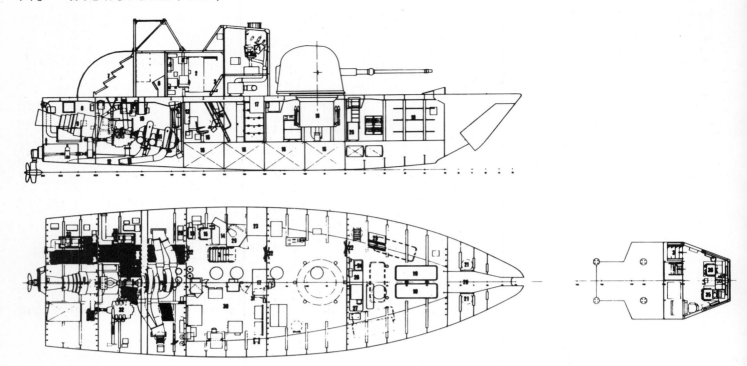

Inboard profile and deck plan of Sparviero: **(1)** helm/main control console **(2)** combat operations centre (COC) door **(3)** companionway ladders **(4)** COC electric power distribution panel **(5)** COC **(6)** air intake forward machinery room **(7)** filtering panels for combustion air **(8)** aft machinery room **(9)** gas turbine engine: foilborne propulsion **(10)** forward machinery room **(11)** waterjet pump **(12)** waterjet nozzle (P/S) **(13)** main electrical power distribution panel **(14)** engineer's console **(15)** engineer's station **(16)** fuel oil tanks **(17)** automatic control system **(18)** cannon revolving feeding machine **(19)** crew berths **(20)** forward hydrofoil retraction well **(21)** rope locker (P/S) **(22)** watertight doors **(23)** galley stores locker **(24)** lavatory **(25)** crew lockers **(26)** refrigerator **(27)** folding mess table with benches **(28)** main electrical switchboard **(29)** water closet **(30)** electronic equipment bay **(31)** gyrocompass **(32)** diesel engine: hullborne (unmanned) propulsion **(33)** turbine generator set **(34)** pump drive coupling **(35)** conning station **(36)** helm station

In the lower Sea States Sparviero class hydrofoils have a maximum continuous speed of 44 knots, decreasing to 40 knots in Sea State 4.

FOILS: Fully-submerged canard arrangement, with approximately one-third of the dynamic lift provided by the bow foil and two-thirds by the two aft foils. The aft foils retract sideways and the bow foil retracts forwards into a recess in the bow. Bow doors preserve the hull lines when the forward hydrofoil is either fully extended or retracted. Foils and struts are built in high resistance stainless steel.

Anhedral is incorporated in the aft foils to enhance the directional stability of the craft at shallow foil depths. In addition, the anhedral assures positive roll control by eliminating tip broaching during rough water manoeuvres.

CONTROLS: Automatic system incorporating two aircraft-type gyros, one to sense pitch and roll and the other to sense yaw, plus three accelerometers to sense vertical movements (heave) of the craft. Ultrasonic height sensors detect and maintain flying height above the water surface. Information from the sensors is sent to a hermetically-sealed solid-state computer, which calculates movement of the control surfaces necessary to maintain boat stability and/or pre-selected flying height, and sends appropriate commands to the servo-mechanisms that control trailing edge flaps on bow and stern foils.

FOILBORNE STEERING: Helm-commanded automatic control system controls hydraulic servo-actuated hydrofoil flaps and steerable forward hydrofoil strut to produce co-ordinated (banked) turns in design sea conditions. Forward foil strut is steerable through 10 degrees, port and starboard.

HULLBORNE STEERING: Helm-commanded steerable retractable outdrive unit driven by 160hp Isotta Fraschini diesel via toothed belt transmission. Outdrive unit can be steered through 360 degrees for maximum manoeuvrability when hullborne. Manual emergency hullborne steering is provided on the aft deck.

HULL: Hull and superstructure are built in corrosion-resistant aluminium, the hull being welded and the superstructure riveted and welded.

ACCOMMODATION: Ten berths are provided in the forward crew space. One toilet and one sink. A folding table with benches in the forward crew space.

Turning radius of Sparviero hydrofoils at 40 knots is under 125m

P421 *Nibbio*

POWERPLANT, FOILBORNE: Power for the waterjet is supplied by one 4500shp Rolls-Royce Proteus 15M/553 gas turbine.

Engine output is transferred to a single double-volute, double-suction, two impeller centrifugal pump. Water is taken in through inlets on the nose of each aft foil at the foil/strut intersection and passes up through the hollow interiors of the struts to the hull, where it is ducted to the pump. From the pump, the water is discharged through twin, fixed-area nozzles located beneath the hull under the pump.

POWERPLANT, HULLBORNE: An Isotta Fraschini ID 38 6VN marine diesel drives via a toothed belt a steerable propeller outdrive unit, which is mounted on the centreline of the transom. The unit is retractable and rotates through 360 degrees. Propeller is fixed-pitch. Continuous speed, hullborne, is 8 knots.

APUs: Two, each comprising a 150hp Solar T-62-T-32 gas turbine driving one 208V 400Hz three-phase 75kVA alternator, one 30V dc 200A starter generator and one hydraulic pump for ships services.

Craft may be refuelled through main deck connection at dock or at sea. The fuel tanks are equipped with fuel level indicators and vents.

ARMAMENT: A typical military payload consists of:

    one dual purpose 76mm/62-calibre automatic OTO Melara gun and 110 rounds of ammunition

    two fixed missile launchers and two ship-to-ship missiles, eg Sea Killers, Otomat or Exocet

    one Elsag NA 10 mod, 3 fire-control system

    one Orion 10X tracking radar

    one SMA MM SPQ 701 search and navigation radar

A variety of other payloads may be carried according to customer needs.

FIRE CONTROL SYSTEM: SPG 73 tracking radar, SXG 75 low light level tv and 2AC50C

P422 *Falcone*

console. Console includes tv monitor and 12in PPI screen for search radar video presentation.

DIMENSIONS

Length overall: 22·95m (75ft 4in)
    foils retracted: 24·6m (80ft 7in)
Width across foils: 10·8m (35ft 4in)
Deck beam, max: 7m (23ft)

WEIGHT

Max displacement: 60·5 tonnes

PERFORMANCE

Exact craft performance characteristics depend on the customer's choice of foilborne gas turbine and operating conditions which can affect the

quantity of fuel carried. Performance figures shown below, therefore, are representative.

Foilborne intermittent speed in calm water: 50 knots
    continuous speed in calm water: 44 knots
    continuous speed in Sea State 4: 38–40 knots
Hullborne continuous speed, foils down: 8 knots
Foilborne range at max continuous speed: Up to 400n miles
Hullborne range: Up to 1000n miles
Turning radius at 45 knots: Less than 150m
Rate of turn at max continuous speed, foilborne: 10 degrees/s

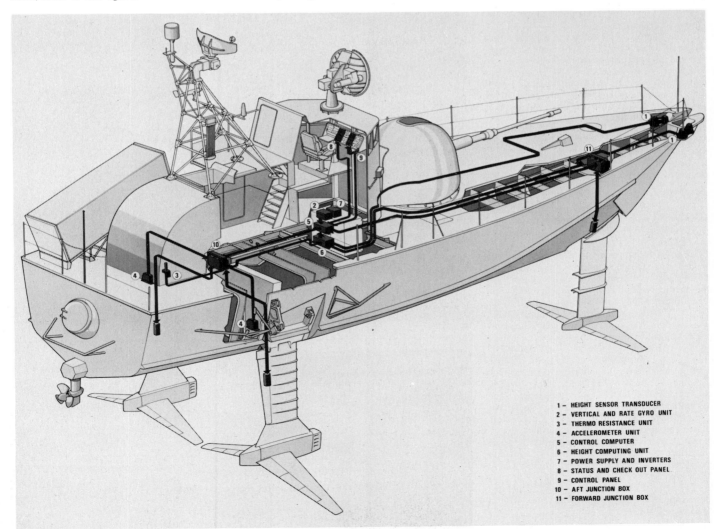

1 – HEIGHT SENSOR TRANSDUCER
2 – VERTICAL AND RATE GYRO UNIT
3 – THERMO RESISTANCE UNIT
4 – ACCELEROMETER UNIT
5 – CONTROL COMPUTER
6 – HEIGHT COMPUTING UNIT
7 – POWER SUPPLY AND INVERTERS
8 – STATUS AND CHECK OUT PANEL
9 – CONTROL PANEL
10 – AFT JUNCTION BOX
11 – FORWARD JUNCTION BOX

SEPA (Società di Elettronica per l'Automazione SpA) Automatic Attitude Control System (SEPA AN 700) as fitted to Sparviero class hydrofoil craft

RODRIQUEZ CANTIERI NAVALI SpA

Via S Raineri, 22-98100 Messina, Italy

Telephone: (090) 7765
Telex: 980030 RODRIK I
Telefax: (090) 717358

Cav del Lavoro Carlo Rodriquez, *Honorary President*
Dott Riccardo Rodriquez, *President*
Dott Gaetano Mobilia, *Vice-President*
Dott Ing Giovanni Falzea, *Technical Manager*

Rodriquez Cantieri Navali SpA, formerly known as Cantiere Navaltecnica SpA and as Leopoldo Rodriquez Shipyard, was the first company to produce hydrofoils in series, and is now the biggest hydrofoil builder outside the Soviet Union. On the initiative of the company's honorary president, Carlo Rodriquez, the Aliscafi Shipping Company was established in Sicily to operate the world's first scheduled seagoing hydrofoil service in August 1956 between Sicily and the Italian mainland.

The service was operated by the first Rodriquez-built Supramar PT 20, *Freccia del Sole*. Cutting down the port-to-port time from Messina to Reggio di Calabria to one-quarter of that of conventional ferry boats, and completing 22 daily crossings, the craft soon proved its commercial viability. With a seating capacity of 72 passengers the PT 20 carried between 800 and 900 passengers a day and conveyed a record number of some 31 000 in a single month.

Details of the PT 20 and PT 50 craft are given in the 1986 edition under the Supramar Hydrofoils Ltd entry.

Eight main types of hydrofoil have now been produced: PT 20, PT 50, RHS 70, RHS 110, RHS 140, RHS 150, RHS 160 and RHS 200. Many of the early craft built are still operating and the following table lists these craft built under Supramar licence.

In the summer of 1986 the company had four RHS 160Fs and one RHS 150 FL under construction and the hulls of two more 150 FLs were to be laid down. In the autumn of 1985 an order had been placed by the Italian Ministero dei Trasporti for a new series of hydrofoils for operation on Lake Como, Lake Garda and Lake Maggiore. A possible growth area for hydrofoils is in the offshore oil industry. Two Rodriquez hydrofoils have been in service with AGIP in the Adriatic for the past three years.

The RHS series are now fitted with a Rodriquez electronic Seakeeping Augmentation Controller.

RHS 70

This is a 32-ton coastal passenger ferry with seats for 71 passengers. Power is supplied by a single 1430hp MTU diesel and the cruising speed is 32·4 knots.
FOILS: Surface-piercing type in partly hollow welded steel. During operation the angle of the bow foil can be adjusted within narrow limits from the steering position by means of a hydraulic ram operating on a foil support across the hull.
HULL: V-bottom hull of riveted light metal alloy construction. Watertight compartments are below the passenger decks and in other parts of the hull.
POWERPLANT: A single MTU 12V 331 TC 82 diesel, developing 1430hp at 2340rpm, drives a three-bladed bronze aluminium propeller through a Zahnradfabrik W 800 H 20 gearbox.
ACCOMMODATION: 44 passengers are accommodated in the forward cabin, 19 in the rear compartment and 8 aft of the pilot's position, above the engine room, in the elevated wheelhouse. A wc/washbasin unit is provided in the aft passenger compartments. Emergency exits are provided in each passenger compartment. Cabin noise level is approx 76dBA.
SYSTEMS, ELECTRICAL: 24V generator driven by the main engine; batteries with a capacity of 350Ah.
HYDRAULICS: 120kg/cm³ pressure hydraulic system for rudder and bow foil incidence control.

Craft built (PT 3, PT 20) 1956 to 1971

Type	Name	Yard No	No of seats	Operated in	Date	Owner/Operator (1987/88)
PT 3	Hitachi PT 3	055	12	Japan	1957	—
PT 3	Supramar PT 3	056	12	Switzerland	1957	—
PT 20	*Freccia del Sole* (laid up 1986)	051	72	Italy	1956	Aliscafi SNAV SpA
PT 20	*Flying Fish*	052	72	USA	1957	—
PT 20	*Freccia delle Eolie*	053	72	Italy	1957	Aliscafi SNAV SpA
PT 20	*Freccia del Tirreno*	057	72	Italy	1957	Aliscafi SNAV SpA
PT 20	*Freccia del Garda*	058	80	Italy	1958	Navigazione Sul Lago di Garda
PT 20	*Flecha Mara*	060	72	Venezuela	1958	—
PT 20	*Flecha del Lago*	061	72	Venezuela	1958	—
PT 20	*Flecha del Zulia*	067	72	Venezuela	1959	—
PT 20	*Freccia delle Egadi*	068	72	Italy	1959	—
PT 20	*Alilauro III*	069	72	Italy	1960	—
PT 20	*Freccia dello Stretto*	070	72	Italy	1960	Aliscafi SNAV SpA
PT 20	*Alivit* (ex *Alinapoli*, 1984; ex *Ekspressen*, 1969)	071	72	Norway	1961	Alivit Due
PT 20	Hitachi PT 20	072	72	Japan	1960	—
PT 20	*Freccia del Peloro*	073	72	Italy	1961	Aliscafi SNAV SpA
PT 20	*Freccia di Reggio*	074	72	Italy	1961	Aliscafi SNAV SpA
PT 20	*Isola del Giglio* (ex *Fleche d'Or IV Le Corsaire*)	075	72	Italy	1962	—
PT 20	*Nefertiti*	082	72	Egypt	1962	—
PT 20	*Cleopatra*	083	72	Egypt	1963	—
PT 20	*Aligrado*	084	72	Italy	1962	—
PT 20	*Flecha Fluminense*	085	72	Brazil	1962	—
PT 20	*Freccia dell'Arcipelago*	086	72	Italy	1966	—
PT 20	*Freccia di Ustica*	087	72	Italy	1965	—
PT 20	*Hatshepsut*	094	72	Egypt	1964	—
PT 20	*Flecha de Cabimas*	095	72	Venezuela	1963	—
PT 20	*Flying Fish*	096	72	Philippines	1963	—
PT 20	*Enrique*	097	72	Philippines	1963	—
PT 20	*Manu-Wai*	098	72	New Zealand	1964	Ossie James, NZ
PT 20	*Coloane*	099	72	Hong Kong	1964	—
PT 20	*Flecha de Icarai* (ex *Flying Phoenix*)	100	85	Hong Kong	1964	TRANSTUR
PT 20	*Flecha de Ribeira* (ex *Flying Kingfisher*)	101	85	Hong Kong	1964	TRANSTUR
PT 20	*Flying Swift* (scrapped)	102	68	Hong Kong	1964	—
PT 20	*Freccia del Verbano*	103	72	Italy	1964	Navigazione Lago Maggiore
PT 20	*Freccia del Lario*	104	72	Italy	1964	Navigazione Lago di Como
PT 20	*Albatros*	105	72	Switzerland	1964	—
PT 20	*Flecha da Ribeira* (ex *Flying Heron*)	107	85	Hong Kong	1964	TRANSTUR
PAT 20	*Camiguin* (patrol duties) (laid up)	108	—	Philippines	1965	—
PAT 20	*Siquijor* (patrol duties) (laid up)	109	—	Philippines	1965	—
PT 20	*Freccia degli Ulivi*	110	72	Italy	1965	Navigazione Sul Lago di Garda
PT 20	*Flecha das Ilhas*	112	83	Brazil	1966	TRANSTUR
PT 20	*Sunda Karya I*	113	72	Indonesia	1965	—
PT 20	*Freccia del Vesuvio*	114	72	Italy	1966	Aliscafi SNAV SpA
PT 20	*Flecha de Rio*	115	83	Brazil	1969	TRANSTUR
PT 20	*Flecha de Niteroi*	116	83	Brazil	1970	TRANSTUR
PT 20	*Pinturicchio*	117	70	Italy	1968	SIREMAR
PT 20	*Freccia del Ticino*	127	72	Italy	1968	Navigazione Lago Maggiore
PT 20	*Porto Corsini*	130	32	Italy	1969	Agip/Aliscafi SNAV SpA
PT 20	*Angel*	149	71	South Korea	1971	Hanryeo Development Co Ltd
PT 20	*Freccia delle Azalee*	126	72	Italy	1969	Navigazione Lago di Como

PT 20 hydrofoil craft moored at the Messina works of Rodriquez Cantieri Navali SpA

DIMENSIONS
Length overall: 22m (72ft 2in)
Width across foils: 7·4m (24ft 3in)
Draught hullborne: 2·7m (8ft 10in)
  foilborne: 1·15m (3ft 9in)
WEIGHTS
Displacement fully loaded: 31·5 tons
Useful load: 6 tons
PERFORMANCE
Cruising speed, half loaded: 32·4 knots
Max speed, half loaded: 36·5 knots at 1400rpm

PT 50 *Freccia di Sorrento* built in 1959 and now in use by the Ministero dei Mercantile Marine for anti-pollution work

Forward foil arrangement of PT 50 *Freccia del Mediterraneo*

Craft built (PT 50) 1959 to 1970

Type	Name	Yard No	No of seats	Operated in	Date	Owner/Operator
PT 50	*Freccia di Messina**	059	125	Italy	1959	ex Aliscafi SNAV SpA
PT 50	*Freccia di Sorrento*	062	125	Italy	1959	Ministero dei Mercantile Marine
PT 50	*Freccia d'Oro*	063	130	Italy	1959	Aliscafi SNAV SpA
PT 50	*Freccia Atlantica*	064	125	Italy	1960	Aliscafi SNAV SpA
PT 50	*Freccia del Sud*	065	50 + 7t cargo	Italy	1960	Aliscafi SNAV SpA
PT 50	*Pisanello*	066	130	Italy	1961	SIREMAR
PT 50	*Queenfoil* (ex *Sleipner*)	076	125	Norway	1961	Transtour SA
PT 50	*Freccia di Lipari*	077	125	Italy	1961	Aliscafi SNAV SpA
PT 50	*Flecha de Buenos Aires*	078	125	Argentina	1962	Alimar SA
PT 50	*Flecha de Colonia* (ex *Flecha de Montevideo*)	079	125	Argentina	1962	Alimar SA
PT 50	*Flecha del Litoral***	080	125	Argentina	1963	Alimar SA
PT 50	*Freccia del Mediterraneo*	081	125	Italy	1963	Aliscafi SNAV SpA
PT 50	*Freccia di Sicilia*	088	125	Italy	1964	Aliscafi SNAV SpA
PT 50	*Nibbio*	089	125	Italy	1964	Adriatica di Navigazione SpA
PT 50	*Flying Albatross*	090	125	Hong Kong	1964	Hongkong Macao Hydrofoil Co Ltd
PT 50	*Flying Skimmer*	091	125	Hong Kong	1965	Hongkong Macao Hydrofoil Co Ltd

* destroyed by fire 12 June 1986, en route to Lipari
** destroyed by fire 1986

RHS 110

A 54-ton hydrofoil ferry, the RHS 110 was originally designed to carry a maximum of 110 passengers at a cruising speed of 37 knots.

FOILS: Surface-piercing type, in partly hollow welded steel. Hydraulically operated flaps, attached to the trailing edges of the bow and rear foils, are adjusted automatically by a Hamilton Standard stability augmentation system for the damping of heave, pitch and roll motions. The rear foil is rigidly attached to the transom, its incidence angle being determined during tests.

HULL: V-bottom of high-tensile riveted light metal alloy construction, using Peraluman plates and Anticorrodal profiles. The upper deck plates are in 3·5mm (0·137in) thick Peraluman. Removable deck sections permit the lifting out and replacement of the main engines. The superstructure, which has a removable roof, is in 2mm (0·078in) thick Peraluman plates, with L and C profile sections. Watertight compartments are below the passenger decks and other parts of the hull.

POWERPLANT: Power is supplied by two 12-cylinder supercharged MTU MB 12V 493 Ty 71 diesels, each with a maximum output of 1350hp at 1500rpm. Engine output is transferred to two three-bladed bronze-aluminium propellers through Zahnradfabrik W 800 H20 gearboxes. Each propeller shaft is 90mm (3·5in) in diameter and supported at three points by sea water-lubricated rubber bearings. Steel fuel tanks with a total capacity of 3600 litres (792 gallons) are aft of the engine room.

ACCOMMODATION: The wheelhouse/observation deck saloon seats 58 and the lower aft saloon seats 39. Additional passengers are accommodated in the lower forward saloon, which contains a bar.

In the wheelhouse, the pilot's position is on the port side, together with the radar screen. A second seat is provided for the chief engineer. Passenger seats are of lightweight aircraft type, floors are covered with woollen carpets and the walls and ceilings are clad in vinyl. Two toilets are provided, one in each of the lower saloons.

SYSTEMS, ELECTRICAL: Engine driven generators supply 220V, 50Hz, three-phase ac. Two groups of batteries for 24V dc circuit.

HYDRAULICS: Steering, variation of the foil flaps and the anchor windlass operation are all accomplished hydraulically from the wheelhouse. Plant comprises two Bosch pumps installed on the main engines which convey oil from a 60-litre (13-gallon) tank under pressure to the control cylinders of the rudder, foil flaps and anchor windlass.

FIREFIGHTING: Fixed CO_2 plant for the main engine room, portable CO_2 and foam fire extinguishers of 3kg (7lb) and 10-litre (2-gallon) capacity in the saloons, and one water firefighting plant.

DIMENSIONS
EXTERNAL
Length overall: 25·6m (84ft)
Width across foils: 9·2m (30ft 2¼in)
Deck beam, max: 5·95m (19ft 2in)
Draught hullborne: 3·3m (10ft 9⅘in)
    foilborne: 1·25m (4ft 1in)
WEIGHT
Displacement, fully loaded: 54 tons
PERFORMANCE
Max speed: 40 knots
Cruising speed: 37 knots
Range: 486km (300 miles)

RHS 140

This 65-ton hydrofoil passenger ferry seats up to 150 passengers and has a cruising speed of 32·5 knots.

FOILS: Surface-piercing V foils of hollow welded steel construction. Lift of the bow foil can be modified by hydraulically-operated trailing-edge flaps.

HULL: Riveted light metal alloy design framed on longitudinal and transverse formers.

ACCOMMODATION: Up to 150 passengers seated in three saloons. The belvedere saloon, on

Craft built (PT 50) 1959 to 1970 (contd)

Type	Name	Yard No	No of seats	Operated in	Date	Owner/Operator
PT 50	Svalan†	092	125	—	1965	ex Tarnan Line, Limassol, Cyprus
PT 50	Flying Condor	093	125	Hong Kong	1966	Hongkong Macao Hydrofoil Co Ltd
PT 50	Freccia delle Isole	111	125	Italy	1966	Aliscafi SNAV SpA
PT 50	Tarnan†	118	120	—	1966	ex Tarnan Line, Limassol, Cyprus
PT 50	Freccia Adriatica	119	125	Italy	1969	Aliscafi SNAV SpA
PT 50	Fairlight (laid up)	120	140	Australia	1966	Urban Transit Authority of New South Wales
PT 50	Flying Flamingo (scrapped)	121	125	—	1967	ex Hongkong Macao Hydrofoil Co Ltd
PT 50	Star Capricorn (ex Springeren)	122	117	Italy	1967	COVEMAR Eolie
PT 50	Stilprins (ex Teisten)	123	125	Norway	1970	Simon Møkster (ex Hardanger Sunnhordlandske Steamship Co)
PT 50	Long Reef (laid up)	124	140	Australia	1969	Urban Transit Authority of New South Wales
PT 50	Sun Arrow	125	125	Italy	1968	Aliscafi SNAV SpA
PT 50	Dee Why (laid up)	132	140	Australia	1970	Urban Transit Authority of New South Wales

† blown up by Israeli agents in Messina harbour 30 January 1986

RHS 70 *Shearwater 3*, sister vessel to three other RHS 70s delivered to Red Funnel Ferries

Craft built (RHS 70) 1972 to 1982

Type	Name	Yard No	No of seats	Operated in	Date	Owner/Operator
RHS 70	Shearwater 3	150	67	England	1972	Red Funnel Ferries
RHS 70	Shearwater 4	156	67	England	1973	Red Funnel Ferries
RHS 70	Freccia delle Betulle	185	71	Italy	1974	Navigazione Lago di Como
RHS 70	Freccia delle Camelie	186	71	Italy	1974	Navigazione Lago Maggiore
RHS 70	Freccia del Benaco	187	71	Italy	1974	Navigazione Sul Lago di Garda
RHS 70	Freccia delle Magnolie	188	71	Italy	1975	Navigazione Lago Maggiore
RHS 70	Freccia delle Gardenie	189	71	Italy	1976	Navigazione Lago di Como
RHS 70	Freccia dei Gerani	196	71	Italy	1977	Navigazione Sul Lago di Garda
RHS 70	Shearwater 5	197	67	England	1980	Red Funnel Ferries
RHS 70	Shearwater 6	221	67	England	1982	Red Funnel Ferries

Craft built (RHS 110) 1971 to 1973

Type	Name	Yard No	No of seats	Operated in	Date	Owner/Operator
RHS 110	Cacilhas	147	110	Hong Kong	1971	—
RHS 110	Flecha de Angra (ex Flying Phoenix)	148	140	Brazil	1970	TRANSTUR
RHS 110	Barca	157	122	Hong Kong	1972	—
RHS 110	Praia	158	111	Hong Kong	1973	—
RHS 110	Cerco	159	111	Hong Kong	1973	—

the main deck above the engine room, can be equipped with a bar. Wc washbasin units can be installed in the forward and aft saloons.
POWERPLANT: Power is provided by two MTU 12V 493 Ty 71 12-cylinder supercharged engines, each developing 1350hp at 1500 rpm. Engine output is transmitted to two, three-bladed 700mm diameter bronze propellers through Zahnradfabrik gearboxes.
SYSTEMS, ELECTRICAL: Two engine-driven generators supply 24V dc. Two battery sets each with 350Ah capacity.
HYDRAULICS: Steering and variation of foil flap incidence is accomplished hydraulically from the wheelhouse. Plant comprises two Bosch pumps installed on the main engines and conveying oil from a 70-litre (15·4-gallon) tank under pressure to the control cylinders of the rudder and foil flaps.
FIREFIGHTING: Fixed CO_2 plant for the engine room; portable CO_2 and foam fire extinguishers in the saloons. Water intake connected to bilge pump for fire hose connection in emergency.
DIMENSIONS
Length overall: 28·7m (94ft 1½in)
Width across foils: 10·72m (35ft 2¼in)
Draught hullborne: 3·5m (11ft 5¾in)
foilborne: 1·5m (4ft 11in)
WEIGHTS
Displacement, fully loaded: 65 tons
Carrying capacity, including 3 tons bunker, and 5 tons fresh water, lubricating oil and hydraulic system oil: 12·5 tons
PERFORMANCE
Max speed, half load: 36 knots
Cruising speed: 32·5 knots
Range at cruising speed: 550km (340 miles)

RHS 150

Combining features of both the RHS 140 and the RHS 160, the RHS 150 hydrofoil passenger ferry is powered by two 1430hp MTU supercharged 4-stroke diesels which give the craft a cruising speed of 32·5 knots and a cruising range of 130n miles.
FOILS: Surface-piercing W foils of hollow welded steel construction. Lift of the bow foil can be modified by hydraulically-operated trailing edge flaps.
HULL: Riveted light metal alloy design framed on longitudinal and transverse formers.
ACCOMMODATION: The standard model seats 150 in three saloons. High density model design originally for services on the Italian lakes seats 180: 63 in the aft saloon, 45 in the forward saloon and 72 in the belvedere. The forward and stern saloons each have a toilet/wc unit.
POWERPLANT: Motive power is furnished by two supercharged MTU MB 12V 331 TC 82 four-stroke diesels each developing 1430hp at 2140rpm continuous. Engine output is transmitted to two bronze propellers via two Zahnradfabrik BW 255L gearboxes.
SYSTEMS, ELECTRICAL: Two 1300W engine-driven generators supply 24V dc.
DIMENSIONS
Length overall: 28·7m (94ft 1½in)
Width across foils: 11m (36ft 1⅛in)
Draught hullborne: 3·1m (10ft 2in)
foilborne: 1·4m (4ft 7⅛in)
WEIGHT
Displacement, fully loaded: 65·5 tons
PERFORMANCE
Cruising speed, fully loaded: 32·5 knots
Cruising range: 240km (130n miles)

RHS 150 SL

This variant has been designed for inland navigation, particularly on the Great Lakes in Northern Italy. Because of the less severe conditions on such waters it has been possible to redesign the hull structure to allow for larger windows in the lower saloons and the superstructure, greatly increasing visibility for sightseeing. In addition, because the safety rules are less demanding than for open-water routes, there is a saving in weight in the design allowing an increase in passenger numbers, so that 200 may be carried, with lightweight seats fitted.

Craft built (RHS 140) 1971 to 1977

Type	Name	Yard No	No of seats	Operated in	Date	Owner/Operator
RHS 140	*Colonia del Sacramento* (ex *Condor*)	133	140	Uruguay	1971	Belt SA
RHS 140	*Flying Dragon*	134	140	Hong Kong	1971	Hongkong Macao Hydrofoil Co Ltd
RHS 140	*Flying Egret*	152	125	Hong Kong	1972	Hongkong Macao Hydrofoil Co Ltd
RHS 140	*Santa Maria del Buenos Aires* (ex *Tyrving*)	153	116	Uruguay	1972	Belt SA
RHS 140	*Farallón* (ex *Løberen*)	154	111	Denmark	1972	Belt SA
RHS 140	*Curl-Curl*	155	140	Australia	1972	Urban Transit Authority of New South Wales
RHS 140	*Viggen*	161	120	Sweden	1973	(ex A/S Dampskibs-selskabet Øresund)
RHS 140	*Flying Sandpiper*	180	125	Hong Kong	1972	Hongkong Macao Hydrofoil Co Ltd
RHS 140	*Flying Swift* (ex *Flying Goldfinch*)	180	125	Hong Kong	1973	Hongkong Macao Hydrofoil Co Ltd
RHS 140	*Flying Ibis*	182	125	Hong Kong	1975	Hongkong Macao Hydrofoil Co Ltd
RHS 140	*Condor 4*	184	136	England	1974	Condor Ltd
RHS 140	*Duccio* (ex *Fabricia*)	193	140	Italy	1977	TOREMAR SpA
RHS 140	*Albireo*	194	150	Italy	1977	CAREMAR SpA

Craft built (RHS 150) 1980

Type	Name	Yard No	No of seats	Operated in	Date	Owner/Operator
RHS 150	*Xel-Ha* (laid up)	203	151	Mexico	1980	Secretaria de Turismo, Mexico

Craft built (RHS 150 SL) 1979 to 1984

Type	Name	Yard No	No of seats	Operated in	Date	Owner/Operator
RHS 150 SL	*Freccia del Giardini*	204	190	Italy	1980	Navigazione Lago Maggiore
RHS 150 SL	*Freccia delle Valli*	199	190	Italy	1979	Navigazione Lago di Como
RHS 150 SL	*Freccia dei Gerani*	196	190	Italy	1980	Navigazione Lago Maggiore
RHS 150 SL	*Freccia delle Riviere*	206	190	Italy	1981	Navigazione Sul Lago di Garda
RHS 150 SL	*Galileo Galilei*	208	190	Italy	1982	Navigazione Sul Lago di Garda
RHS 150 SL	*Enrico Fermi*	220	190	Italy	1984	Navigazione Lago Maggiore
RHS 150 SL	*Guglielmo Marconi*	207	190	Italy	1983	Navigazione Lago di Como

RHS 150 SL *Galileo Galilei* delivered 1982 for service on Lake Garda, Italy

Craft built (RHS 150 F) 1984

Type	Name	Yard No	No of seats	Operated in	Date	Owner/Operator
RHS 150 F	*Dynasty*	210	161	Italy	1984	Aliscafi SNAV SpA

RHS 150 F

This variant has a wider deck and the superstructure volume has been increased to give a more aesthetic shape as well as greater volume for passengers, giving greater comfort. Improvements have also been incorporated in this variant increasing performance and reducing maintenance costs.

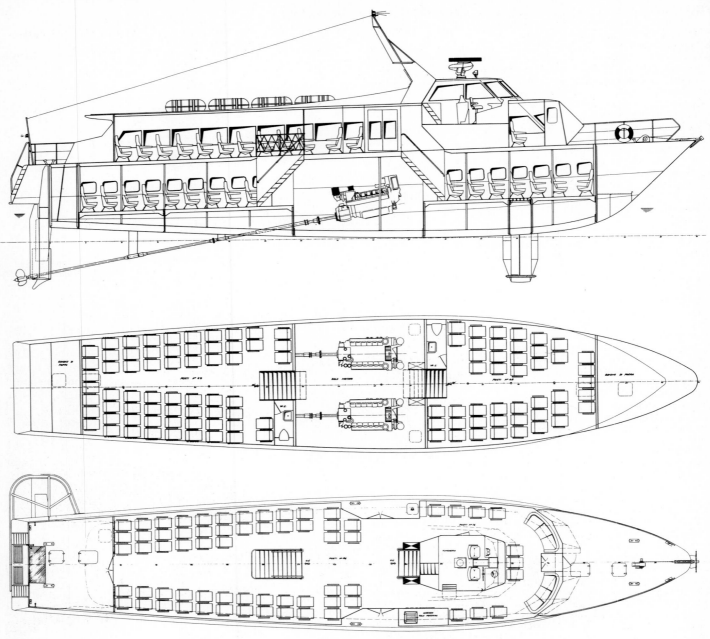

RHS 150

RHS 150 F *Dynasty* operated by Aliscafi SNAV SpA

RHS 160

A 95-tonne passenger ferry with seats for up to 180 passengers and a cruising speed of 32 knots.

In March and May 1986 two RHS 160s were used for oil spill clean-up trials.

Reference: Hydrofoil: High Speed Control and Clean up of Large Oil Spills by RADM Marcello Vacca-Torelli, Alberto L Geraci and Antonio Risitano. Dept of Civil Protection, Rome and University of Catania, Sicily, Italy, 1986.

FOILS: Surface-piercing W foils of hollow welded steel construction. Craft in this series feature a bow rudder for improved manoeuvrability in congested waters. The bow rudder works simultaneously with the aft rudders. Hydraulically-operated flaps, attached to the trailing edges of the bow and rear foils, are adjusted automatically by a Hamilton Standard electronic stability augmentation system, for the damping of heave, pitch and roll motions in heavy seas.

HULL: Riveted light metal alloy longitudinal structure, welded in parts using inert gas. The hull shape of the RHS 160 is similar to the RHS 140 series. In the manufacture of the hull, plates of aluminium and magnesium alloy of 4·4 per cent are used while angle bars are of a high-resistant aluminium, magnesium and silicon alloy.

ACCOMMODATION: 180 to 200 passengers seated in three saloons. 57 passengers are accommodated in the forward cabin, 63 in the rear compartment and 60 in the belvedere. Forward and aft saloons and belvedere have a toilet, each provided with wc washbasin units and the usual toilet accessories.

POWERPLANT: Power is provided by two supercharged MTU MB 12V 652 TB71 four-stroke diesel engines each with a maximum output of 1950hp at 1460rpm under normal operating conditions. Engine starting is accomplished by compressed air starters. Engine output is transmitted to two, three-bladed bronze propellers through two Zahnradfabrik 900 HS 15 gearboxes.

SYSTEMS, ELECTRICAL: Two 35kVA generating sets, 220V, 60Hz, three-phase. Three insulated cables for ventilation, air-conditioning and power. Two insulated cables for lighting,

Craft built (RHS 160) 1974 to 1986

Type	Name	Yard No	No of seats	Operated in	Date	Owner/Operator
RHS 160	Princess Zoe (ex Alijumbo Ustica, ex Lilau)	181	160	Italy Puerto Rico	1986 1974	Nautical Trading (St Kitts) Ltd
RHS 160	Diomedea	190	160	Italy	1975	Adriatica di Navigazione SpA
RHS 160	Condor 5	191	180	England	1976	Condor Ltd
RHS 160	Algol	195	180	Italy	1978	CAREMAR
RHS 160	May W Craig (ex Alijumbo)	198	180	Puerto Rico	1979	Nautical Trading (St Kitts) Ltd
RHS 160	Alioth	200	180	Italy	1979	CAREMAR
RHS 160	Botticelli	201	180	Italy	1980	SIREMAR
RHS 160	Donatello	202	180	Italy	1980	SIREMAR
RHS 160	Nicte-Ha	205	160	Mexico	1982	Secretaria de Turismo, Mexico

RHS 160 *Princess Zoe* engaged in anti-oil pollution trials

Aft foil arrangement of RHS 160 *Donatello*

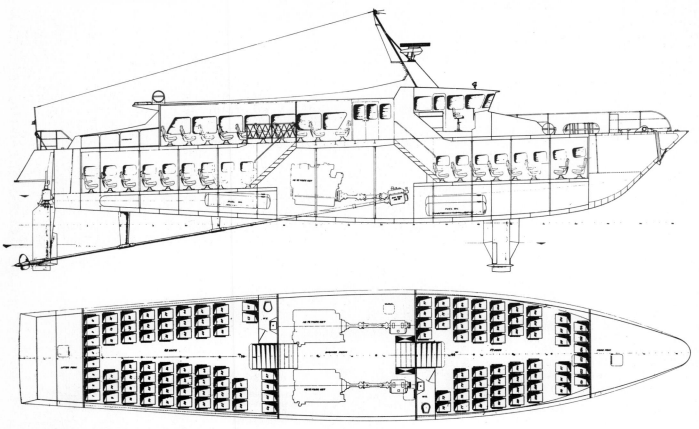

Inboard profile and lower deck plan of RHS 160

sockets and other appliances, 24V dc for emergency lighting, auxiliary engine starting and servocontrol. A battery for radio telephone supply is installed on the upper deck. Provision for battery recharge from ac line foreseen.

HYDRAULICS: Hydraulic steering from the wheelhouse. Plant comprises a Bosch pump installed on the main engines and conveying oil from a 45-litre (10-gallon) tank under pressure to the control cylinders of the rudder and anchor windlass, whilst a second hydraulic pump, which is also installed on the main engines, conveys oil under pressure to the flap control cylinders.

FIREFIGHTING: Fixed CO_2 plant of four CO_2 bottles of about 20kg each for the engine room and fuel tank space; portable extinguishers in various parts of the craft. Water intake is connected to fire pump for fire connection in emergency.

DIMENSIONS
Length overall: 30·95m
Width across foils: 12·6m
Beam, moulded: 6·20m
Draught hullborne: 3·7m
    foilborne: 1·35m

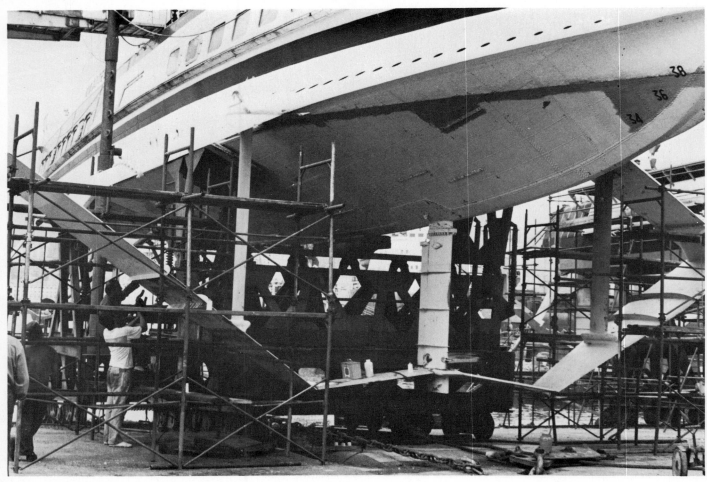

Forward foil arrangement of RHS 160 *Donatello*

WEIGHTS
Displacement, fully loaded: 95 tonnes
Payload, passengers and baggage: 13·5 tons
PERFORMANCE
Max speed: 36 knots
Cruising speed: 32 knots
Cruising range: 483km (300 miles)
Fuel consumption: 0·5 tonnes/h
Seakeeping capability in Sea State 4: Roll, less than 2° with electronic control; less than 3° without electronic control

RHS 160F

A recent addition to the Rodriquez range is the RHS 160F, a 91·5-ton passenger ferry with seats for up to 238 passengers and a cruising speed of 34·5 knots.

FOILS: Surface-piercing W foils of hollow welded steel construction. Craft in this series feature a bow rudder for improved manoeuvrability in congested waters. The bow rudder works simultaneously with the aft rudders. Hydraulically-operated flaps, attached to the trailing edges of the bow and rear foils, are adjusted automatically by a Hamilton Standard electronic stability augmentation system, for the damping of heave, pitch and roll motions in heavy seas.

HULL: Riveted light metal alloy longitudinal structure, welded in parts using inert gas. The hull shape of the RHS 160F is similar to the RHS 140 series. In the manufacture of the hull, plates of aluminium and magnesium alloy of 4·4 per cent are used while angle bars are of a high-resistant aluminium, magnesium and silicon alloy.

ACCOMMODATION: 210 passengers seated in three saloons. 58 passengers are accommodated in the forward cabin, 63 in the rear compartment and 89 in the belvedere. Forward and aft saloons and belvedere each have a toilet with wc washbasin units and toilet accessories.

POWERPLANT: Power is provided by two supercharged MTU 16V 396 TB83 four-stroke diesel engines each with a maximum output of 1400kW at 2000rpm under normal operating conditions. Engine starting is accomplished by compressed air starters. Engine output is transmitted to two, three-bladed bronze propellers through two Zahnradfabrik BW 7505 gearboxes, or, alternatively, through two Reintjes WVS 1032U gearboxes as fitted to the RHS 160F craft

RHS 160 *Donatello* arriving at Vulcano, October 1987

Craft built/being built (RHS 160F) 1984 to 1989

Type	Name	Yard No	No of seats	Operated in	Date	Owner/Operator
RHS 160F	*Manly*	211	238	Australia	1984	Urban Transit Authority of New South Wales
RHS 160F	*Sydney*	216	238	Australia	1985	Urban Transit Authority of New South Wales
RHS 160F	*Condor 7*	217	200	England	1985	Condor Ltd
RHS 160F	*Alijumbo Eolie*	218	220	Italy	1986	Aliscafi SNAV SpA
RHS 160F	*Alnilan*	227	210	Italy	1986	CAREMAR
RHS 160F	*Fabricia*	228	210	Italy	1987	TOREMAR
RHS 160F	001/160 (Malta yard)	—	210	Italy	1987	Aliscafi SNAV SpA
RHS 160F	*Aldebaran*	229	210	Italy	1987	CAREMAR
RHS 160F	*Masaccio*	230	210	Italy	1988	SIREMAR
RHS 160F	*Mantegna*	231	210	Italy	1989	SIREMAR
RHS 160F	—	236	210	Italy		
RHS 160F	—	239	210	Italy	1989	SIREMAR
RHS 160FL	—	240	210	Italy	1988	Navigazione Lago Maggiore
RHS 160FL	—	—	200	Italy	—	Navigazione Lago di Como
RHS 160FL	—	—	200	Italy	—	Navigazione Sul Lago di Garda

RHS 160F *Condor 7*

supplied to the Urban Transit Authority of NSW, Australia.

SYSTEMS, ELECTRICAL: Two 35kVA generating sets, 220V, 60Hz, three-phase. Three insulated cables for ventilation, air-conditioning and power. Two insulated cables for lighting, sockets and other appliances, 24V dc for emergency lighting, auxiliary engine starting and servocontrol. A battery for radio telephone supply is installed on the upper deck. Provision for battery recharge from ac line is foreseen.

HYDRAULICS: Hydraulic steering from the wheelhouse. Plant comprises a Bosch pump installed on the main engines and conveying oil from a 45-litre (10-gallon) tank under pressure to the control cylinders of the rudder and anchor windlass, whilst a second hydraulic pump, which is also installed on the main engines, conveys oil under pressure to the flap control cylinders.

FIREFIGHTING: Fixed CO_2 plant of four CO_2 bottles of about 20kg each for the engine room and fuel tank space; portable extinguishers in various parts of the craft. Water intake connected to fire pump for connection in emergency.

DIMENSIONS
Length overall: 31·2m
Length, waterline: 26·25m
Beam (hull), moulded: 6·70m
Depth (hull), moulded: 3·69m
Width across foils: 12·6m
Draught hullborne: 3·76m
  foilborne: 1·7m
WEIGHTS
Displacement, fully loaded: 91·5 tons
Payload, passengers and luggage: 17·8 tons
PERFORMANCE
Max speed: 38 knots
Cruising speed: 34·5 knots
Cruising range: 100n miles

RHS 200

Powered by two supercharged MTU MB 16V 652 TB 71 four-stroke diesel engines, the 254-seat RHS 200 has a cruising speed of 35 knots.

FOILS: Surface-piercing W foils of hollow welded steel construction. Craft in this series feature a bow rudder for improved manoeuvrability in congested waters. The bow rudder operates simultaneously with the aft rudders. An advantage of the W configuration bow foil is its relatively shallow draught requirement in relation to the vessel's overall size. Hydraulically-operated flaps are fitted to the trailing edge of the bow foil to balance out longitudinal load shifting, assist take-off and adjust the flying height. The craft can also be equipped with the Hamilton Standard electronic stability augmentation system, which employs sensors and servomechanisms to position flaps automatically on the bow and stern foils for the damping of heave, pitch and roll motions in heavy seas.

HULL: V-bottom hull of high tensile riveted light metal alloy construction, employing Peraluman plates and Anticorrodal frames. The rake of the stem is in galvanised steel.

ACCOMMODATION: Seats for up to 400 passengers, according to the route served. In typical configuration there are three main passenger saloons and a bar. The standard seating arrangement allows for 116 in the main deck saloon, 58 in the aft lower saloon and 66 in the bow passenger saloon. Seating is normally four abreast in two lines with a central aisle. The bar, at the forward end of the wheelhouse belvedere superstructure, has either an eight-seat sofa or 19 seats.

The wheelhouse, which is raised to provide a 360-degree view, is reached from the main deck belvedere saloon by a short companionway. Controls and instrumentation are attached to a panel on the forward bulkhead which extends the width of the wheelhouse. In the centre is the steering control and gyrocompass, on the starboard side are controls for the two engines, gearboxes and controllable-pitch propellers, and on the port side is the radar. Seats are provided for the captain, chief engineer and first mate. In the wheelhouse are a radio telephone and a chart table.

RHS 160F *Alijumbo Eolie* at Lipari, September 1987

Wheelhouse and main entrance of RHS 160F *Alijumbo Eolie*

Upper deck forward passenger cabin on RHS 160F *Alijumbo Eolie* showing the excellent forward visibility

Craft built (RHS 200) 1981 to 1984

Type	Name	Yard No	No of seats	Operated in	Date	Owner/Operator
RHS 200	*Superjumbo*	192	254	Italy	1981	Aliscafi SNAV SpA
RHS 200	*San Cristobal* (ex *Stretto di Messina*)	209	254	Puerto Rico	1984	Nautical Trading (St Kitts) Ltd
RHS 200	—	235 (under construction 1987)	—	—	—	—

POWERPLANT: Motive power is supplied by two supercharged MTU MB 16V 652 TB 71 4-stroke diesel engines, each with a maximum output of 2600hp at 1460rpm under normal operating conditions. Engine output is transferred to two supercavitating, controllable-pitch propellers.

SYSTEMS, ELECTRICAL: Two generating sets: one 220V, three-phase ac, for all consumer services, the second for charging 24V battery sets and operating firefighting and hydraulic pumps. Power distribution panel in wheelhouse for navigation light circuits, cabin lighting, radar, RDF, gyrocompass and emergency circuits.

FIREFIGHTING: Fixed CO_2 self-contained automatic systems for powerplant and fuel tank spaces, plus portable extinguishers for cabins and holds.

DIMENSIONS
Length overall: 35·8m (117ft 5in)
Width across foils: 14·5m (47ft 7in)
Draught hullborne: 4·55m (15ft 1¾in)
  foilborne: 2·05m (6ft 8⅓in)
WEIGHT
Displacement fully loaded: 130 tonnes
PERFORMANCE
Cruising speed: 35 knots
Max speed: 37 knots
Cruising range: 200n miles
Fuel consumption: 785kg/h

RHS ALIYACHT

A luxury hydrofoil yacht of light alloy construction, the RHS Aliyacht is derived from the RHS 110 passenger ferry. For detailed information please see *Jane's Surface Skimmers 1985* and earlier editions.

RHS 70 HYDROIL PORTO CORSINI

This name was given to an offshore crew/supply version of the RHS 70 which was delivered to the ENI Oil Corporation for use in the Adriatic. Full details are given in *Jane's Surface Skimmers 1985* and earlier editions.

PROJECT DESIGNS

Details of the following project designs are given in *Jane's Surface Skimmers 1985* and earlier editions: RHS 140 & 160 Hydroils, M-RHS 150 Search and Rescue, M-RHS 150 Patrol, M100, M150, M200 Patrol, M300 & 600 Fast Strike Craft.

Wheelhouse of RHS 200

Belvedere cabin of RHS 200

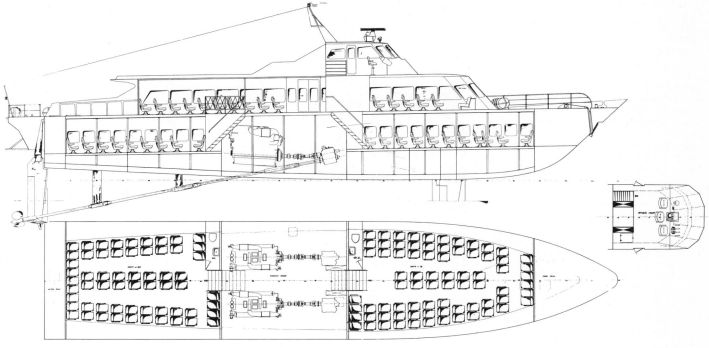
Inboard profile and lower deck arrangement of RHS 200

RHS 200 *Superjumbo*

JAPAN

HITACHI ZOSEN CORPORATION

Head Office: 6-14 Edobori 1-chome, Nishi-ku, Osaka, Japan

Telephone: (06) 443 8051
Telex: J 63376

Works: 4-1 Mizue-cho, Kawasaki-ku, Kawasaki, Kanagawa Pref, Japan

Telephone: (044) 288 1111
Telex: 3842524
Telefax: (044) 276 0022

Toshio Murayama, *President*
Shojiro Okada, *Executive Vice President*
Motohiro Yamaoka, *General Manager, Kanagawa Works*
T Shinoda, *Manager of Naval Ship Design, Kanagawa Works*

Hitachi Zosen, the Supramar licensee in Japan, has been building PT 20, PT 32 and PT 50 hydrofoils since 1961. By 1970 some 32 hydrofoils had been built and another ten by 1981. The majority of these have been built for fast passenger-ferry services across the Japanese Inland Sea, cutting across deep bays which road vehicles might take two to three hours to drive round, and out to offshore islands. Other PT 20s and 50s have been exported to Hong Kong, Australia and South Korea for ferry services.

Specifications of the PT 32 (*Jane's Surface Skimmers 1967-68*), PT 20 and PT 50 will be found under Supramar (Switzerland) (*Jane's Surface Skimmers 1985*). The Hitachi Zosen craft are identical apart from minor items.

In 1974 the company completed the first PT 50 Mk II to be built at its Kawasaki yard. The vessel, *Hikari No 2,* is powered by two licence-built MTU MB 820Db diesels, carries 123 passengers plus a crew of seven and cruises at 33 knots. It was delivered to Setonaikai Kisen KK of Hiroshima in March 1975. Hitachi Zosen has constructed 25 PT 50s and 17 PT 20s.

In conjunction with Supramar, Hitachi Zosen has developed a new roll stabilisation system for the PT 50. The first PT 50 to be equipped with this new system was completed in January 1983 and is now in service.

ROLL-STABILISED PTS 50 Mk II

Housho, the first PTS 50 Mk II to be equipped with this new system, was delivered to Hankyu Kisen KK on 19 January 1983 and is operating on the Kobe-Naruto route. The system, which was developed by Hitachi Zosen in conjunction with Supramar, reduces the PTS 50's rolling motion by between one-half and one-third.

The underside of the bow foil is fitted with two flapped fins to improve riding comfort. Operated by automatic sensors, the fins augment stability and provide side forces to dampen rolling and transverse motions.

PT 20 *Ryusei* operated by Ishizaki Kisen KK

PTS 50 Mk II *Housho*

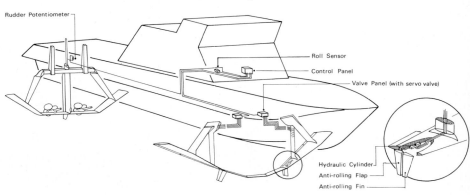

PT 50 Roll-Stabilizing System
Schematic Diagram

Rudder Potentiometer

Roll Sensor
Control Panel
Valve Panel (with servo valve)

Hydraulic Cylinder
Anti-rolling Flap
Anti-rolling Fin

PTS 50 Mk II roll-stabilising system as fitted to *Housho*

Housho is powered by two MTU 12V 331 TB82 marine diesels, each rated at 1380Ps at 2150rpm. It seats 123 passengers and has a maximum speed of about 38 knots.

DIMENSIONS
Length overall: 27·55m
Beam, hull: 5·84m
Width across foils: 10·8m
Draught hullborne: 3·5m
  foilborne: 1·4m
GRT: 128
WEIGHT
Displacement, loaded: 62 tonnes
PERFORMANCE
Max speed: About 38 knots

Hitachi hydrofoils believed to be currently in operation

Type	Name	Seats	Launched	Operator
Hitachi PT 20	*Hayate No 1*		April 1962	Showa Kaiun Co Ltd
Hitachi PT 20	*Kansei*		July 1962	Ishizaki Kisen KK
Hitachi PT 20	*Hibiki*		November 1966	Setonaikai Kisen KK
Hitachi PT 20	*Hibiki No 3*	66	March 1968	Setonaikai Kisen KK
Hitachi PT 20	*Shibuki No 2*		June 1969	Boyo Kisen Co Ltd
Hitachi PT 20	*Myojo*		June 1970	Ishizaki Kisen KK
Hitachi PT 20	*Kinsei*		July 1972	Ishizaki Kisen KK
Hitachi PT 20	*Ryusei*		March 1981	Ishizaki Kisen KK
Hitachi PT 50	*Ohtori*	113	January 1968	—
Hitachi PT 50	*Kosei*		February 1969	Ishizaki Kisen KK
Hitachi PT 50	*Ohtori No 2*	113	February 1970	Setonaikai Kisen KK
Hitachi PT 50	*Zuihoh*		December 1971	Hankyu Kisen KK
Hitachi PT 50	*Hoh'oh*		February 1972	Hankyu Kisen KK
Hitachi PT 50	*Condor*	121	June 1972	Setonaikai Kisen KK
Hitachi PT 50	*Ohtori No 3*		October 1972	Setonaikai Kisen KK
Hitachi PT 50	*Ohtori No 5*		May 1973	Setonaikai Kisen KK
Hitachi PT 50	*Shibuki No 3*		October 1973	Boyo Kisen Co Ltd
Hitachi PT 50	*Saisei*		March 1974	Ishizaki Kisen KK
Hitachi PT 50	*Condor No 2*	121	April 1974	Setonaikai Kisen KK
Hitachi PT 50	*Condor No 3*	100	August 1974	Setonaikai Kisen KK
Hitachi PT 50 Mk II	*Hikari No 2*	123	March 1975	Setonaikai Kisen KK
Hitachi PT 50 Mk II	*Shunsei* (ex *Kariyush I*)		June 1975	Ishizaki Kisen KK
Hitachi PTS 50 Mk II	*Housho*	123	January 1983	Hankyu Kisen KK

Flapped roll-stabilisation fin on *Housho*

KAWASAKI STEEL CORPORATION

Hibiya Kokusai Building, 2-3 Uchisaiwaicho 2-chome, Chiyoda-ku, Tokyo 100, Japan

In 1987 Kawasaki Steel Corporation was reported to have acquired a licence for the manufacture and marketing of Boeing Jetfoil hydrofoil craft.

KOREA, SOUTH

HYUNDAI HEAVY INDUSTRIES COMPANY LIMITED

Special and Naval Shipbuilding Division
1, Cheonha-Dong, Ulsan, Kyung-Nam, South Korea

Telephone: (0522) 32 1101/2161/2171
Telex: 53761 HYARD K
Telefax: (0522) 32 4007

RHS 70
   Builder of a RHS 70 hydrofoil, *Angel IX*, which entered service with Hanryeo Development Co Ltd, Seoul, in January 1985.
ACCOMMODATION: 71 passengers.
ENGINE: One MTU 12V 493, 1350bhp at 1500rpm.
DIMENSIONS
Length overall: 21·87m
Beam over deck: 4·80m
Width across foils: 7·78m
Draught, hullborne: 2·70m
Draught, on foils, cruising: 1·15m
WEIGHT
Displacement, fully loaded: 32·0 tonnes

Hyundai RHS 70 hydrofoil *Angel IX*   *(Hyundai)*

ROMANIA

The Romanian Navy operates about 20 Chinese-designed 'Hu Chwan' (White Swan) class hydrofoil torpedo boats. The first three were shipped from the Hutang Shipyard, Shanghai, complete, while the remaining craft were constructed locally under a building programme started in 1973.

Although the Romanian craft are identical outwardly in most respects to the imported models, there are minor differences in defensive armament and superstructure design.

FOILS: System comprises a bow subfoil to stabilise pitch and facilitate take-off and a main foil of trapeze or shallow V configuration set back approximately one-third of the hull length from the bow. At high speed in relatively calm conditions the greater part of the forward hull is raised clear of the water. The mainfoil and struts retract upwards when the craft cruises as a displacement vessel.

HULL: High speed V-bottom hull in sea water resistant light alloy.

POWERPLANT: Three 1100hp M50 or M401 watercooled, supercharged 12-cylinder, V-type diesels, each driving its own inclined propeller shaft.

ARMAMENT: Two 534mm (21in) torpedo

Romanian-built, Chinese-designed Hu Chwan hydrofoil torpedo boat

tubes, plus four 14·5mm cannon in two twin mounts.

DIMENSIONS (Approx)
Length overall: 21·8m (71ft 6½in)
Beam overall: 5·02m (16ft 6in)
Hull beam: 3·96m (13ft)
Draught, hullborne: 1m (3ft 3in)

WEIGHT
Displacement full load: 40 tons
PERFORMANCE
Max speed foilborne, calm conditions: 50-55 knots
Cruising speed: 30-35 knots
Range: 926km (500n miles) approx

SWITZERLAND

SUPRAMAR HYDROFOILS LIMITED
[PATENT HOLDING AND LICENSING ORGANISATION]
Ausserfeld 5, CH-6362 Stansstad, Switzerland

Telephone: (041) 613194
Telex: 78228 SUPR CH
Telefax: (041) 8142441

Dipl Ing Volkert Jost, *President*
Dipl Ing Harry Trevisani, *General Manager*
Dipl Ing Eugen Schatté, *Research and Development*
Dr Ing Herrmann de Witt, *Hydrodynamics*
Dipl Ing Otto Münch, *Stabilisation and Control*
Jürg Bally, *Board Member*

Supramar Hydrofoils Ltd and its predecessor Supramar Ltd (formed in 1952) developed on a commercial basis the hydrofoil system introduced by the Schertel-Sachsenberg Hydrofoil syndicate and its licensee, the Gebrüder Sachsenberg Shipyard. The development started in the 1930s and led to the realisation of a number of military hydrofoils of up to 80 tonnes displacement and 41 knots in speed.

The inherently stable, rigid surface-piercing V-foil system which is typical for the Supramar type craft was developed by the late Baron Hanns von Schertel.

In May 1953 the world's first passenger hydrofoil service started on Lake Maggiore in Italy with a Supramar type PT 10 craft *Freccia d'Oro*. She was later transferred to Lake Lucerne. A larger craft, the PT 20 was first built by Lürssen Shipyard in 1953 and named *Bremen Pioneer*. Since then many Supramar type hydrofoils have been built under licence from Supramar, mainly by Rodriquez, Hitachi and Westermoen. Full details of all Supramar designs are given in *Jane's Surface Skimmers 1985* and earlier editions.

Supramar Hydrofoils Ltd is also engaged in new designs of high-speed craft such as fast mono-hulls and catamarans as well as general engineering services. The company has recently completed the re-engining of Kometa type hydrofoils, which involved the substitution of the original Russian engines by MTU diesel engines.

PT 20 Mk II
Hydrofoil vessel for operation in coastal and sheltered waters. 74 passengers can be accommodated in three compartments.

Supramar PT 20 built by Hitachi Zosen

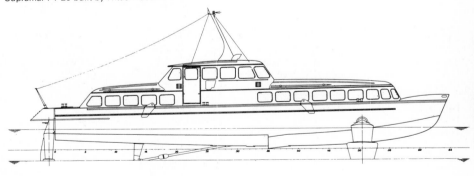

PT 20 Mk II

The hull is a combination of riveted and welded light metal alloy construction. The foils are made of structural steel. The vessel is powered by a single MTU 12V 396 TB83 diesel engine developing a maximum continuous output of 1045kW under tropical ambient conditions. The craft complies with international safety standards and can be classed by all major classification societies.

DIMENSIONS
Length overall: 20·75m
Beam, max: 4·99m

Width over foils: 8·07m
Draught hullborne: 3·08m
Draught foilborne: 1·40m
WEIGHTS/CAPACITIES
Displacement loaded: 33·0 tonnes
Disposable load: 8·40 tonnes
Passenger capacity: 74

PERFORMANCE
Speed cruising: 33 knots
Range: 250n miles

PT 20B Mk II

Similar to the PT 20 Mk II with regard to size and capacity, but different from the general configuration it accommodates up to 70 passengers in only two compartments.

The craft is of combined riveted and welded light metal alloy hull construction, the foils are made of structural steel. The engine is again the MTU 12V 396 TB83 but contrary to the PT 20 Mk II the shaft arrangement is straight and the engine room is situated below the forward upper passenger compartment. The design complies with the relevant safety standards and can be classed by the major classification societies.

DIMENSIONS
Length overall: 21·16m
Beam, max: 5·16m
Width over foils: 8·60m
Draught hullborne: 3·0m
Draught foilborne: 1·30m
WEIGHTS/CAPACITIES
Displacement loaded: 34·0 tonnes
Disposable load: 7·60 tonnes
Passenger capacity: 68-70
PERFORMANCE
Speed cruising: 33 knots
Range: 200n miles

PT 20B

UNION OF SOVIET SOCIALIST REPUBLICS

KRASNOYE SORMOVO A A ZHDANOV SHIPYARD

Head Office and Works: Gorki, USSR

M Yuriev, *Shipyard Director*
Ivan Yerlykin, *Chief Hydrofoil Designer*

Export enquiries: V/O Sudoimport USSR, Moscow 103006, Uspensky per 10, USSR

Telephone: 299 02 14
Telex: 411272/411387 SUDO SU

Krasnoye Sormovo is one of the oldest established shipyards in the Soviet Union. In addition to building displacement craft of many kinds for the Soviet River Fleet, the yard constructs the world's widest range of passenger hydrofoils, many of which are equipped with the Alexeyev shallow draught submerged foil system. The late Dr Alexeyev started work at the end of 1945 on the design of his foil system which had to be suitable for operation on smooth, but open and shallow rivers and canals. He succeeded in making use of the immersion depth effect, or surface effect, for stabilising the foil immersion in calm waters by the use of small lift coefficients.

The system comprises two main horizontal lifting surfaces, one forward and one aft, with little or no dihedral, each carrying approximately half the weight of the vessel. A submerged foil loses lift gradually as it approaches the surface from a submergence of about one chord. This effect prevents the submerged foils from rising completely to the surface. Means therefore had to be provided to assist take-off and prevent the vessel from sinking back to the displacement condition. The answer lay in the provision of planing subfoils of small aspect ratio in the vicinity of the

Principal hydrofoil craft built in the USSR

Civil

Type	Yard	No of seats	First launched
Raketa (produced in quantity and exported)		58	1957
Meteor (produced in quantity and exported)	Gorki	116	1960
Kometa (produced in quantity and exported)	Poti & Feodosiya	100	
Sputnik	Gorki	300	1961
Mir		92	1961
Strela (two built)		94	1962
Vikhr (seagoing version of Sputnik)		268	1962
Burevestnik (one built)		130-150	1964
Chaika	Gomel		1965
Byelorus			1965
Kometa-ME		116-120	1968
Typhoon (one built)	Leningrad	98-105	1969
Voskhod (produced in quantity and exported)	Gorki	71	1969
Delphin (Strela derivative)			pre 1968
Nevka (in production 1969-70)	Leningrad		1969
Volga		6	1972
Voskhod-2			1974
Kolkhida (exported to Greece, Italy and Yugoslavia) & Albatros (replacement for Kometas)	Poti	120	1980
Tsiklon (Cyclone)	Poti	270	1987
Polesye	Gomel	53	1985
Lastochka (replacement for Voskhod)		64	1986
Zenit			

Military

Type	Weight	In service
P8-Class (wooden hull)	—	retired
Pchela	75 tonnes	1968 or earlier
Turya	250 tonnes	1973 or earlier
Matka	260 tonnes	1977 or earlier
Sarancha (NATO code name)	330 tonnes	1977 or earlier
Babochka	400 tonnes	1978 or earlier

forward struts arranged so that when they are touching the water surface the main foils are submerged approximately to a depth of one chord.

The approach embodies characteristics of the Grunberg principle of inherent angle of attack variation, comprising a 'wing' and a stabiliser system. When the Alexeyev foils drop below the shallow draught zone, the craft converts momentarily to the Grunberg mode of operation, duplicating its configuration. The otherwise inactive sub-foils, coming into contact with the water surface, become the Grunberg stabilisers and cause the foils to climb up into the shallow draught zone where they resume normal operation in the Alexeyev mode.

The foils have good riding characteristics on inland waters and in sheltered waters.

The system was first tested on a small launch powered by a 77bhp converted car engine. Three more small craft were built to prove the idea, then work began on the yard's first multi-seat passenger craft, the Raketa, the first of which was launched in June 1957 and has completed more than 25 years of service.

The yard also co-operates with the Leningrad Water Transport Institute in the development of seagoing craft with fully submerged V-type and trapeze-type surface-piercing foils, similar in configuration to those of the Schertel-Sachsenberg system. Craft employing V or trapeze foils are generally described as being of the Strela-type, Strela being the first operational Soviet design to use trapeze foils. Seating 82 to 94 passengers, the vessel is powered by two M-50 diesels and in appearance is a cross between the PT 20 and the PT 50, though smaller than the latter. A military derivative, the Pchela (Bee), is employed by the Soviet frontier police for coastal patrol in the Baltic and Black Seas.

The first hydrofoil vessels to enter service with the Soviet Navy were the 75-ton 'P8' class, wooden-hulled torpedo boats which were equipped with bow foils and gas-turbine boost. These have now been retired. No new military hydrofoils have appeared since the Babochka in 1978.

Included in this entry are illustrations of the 260-tonne Matka (pre 1977), which was designed to replace the 25-year-old Osa missilecraft. Like the Turya (pre 1973) fast-attack torpedo craft, also based on an Osa hull, Matka has a bow foil only. Powered by three 5000hp radial-type diesels it has a top speed of 40 to 45 knots under calm conditions. Other military hydrofoil craft are a 330-tonne fast strike craft, known to NATO by the code name Sarancha, and the 400-tonne fast patrol boat known as Babochka. The Sarancha, armed with four SS-N-9 missiles is capable of speeds in excess of 50 knots. With an overall length of 50m (164ft) and a maximum weight of 400 tonnes, Babochka is the biggest military hydrofoil in operational service in the world.

Soviet passenger hydrofoils in production or being prepared for series production at yards on the Baltic and Black Seas are the Zenit, designed to replace Meteor and the Albatros and Kolkhida, Kometa replacements with seats for 120, stability augmentation and speeds of 36 knots. Smaller hydrofoils are also under development including the 50-seat Polesye at the river-craft shipyard at Gomel and Lastochka, which has been designed to supercede Voskhod.

Substantial numbers of Soviet hydrofoils have been exported, especially Kometas, Meteors, Raketas, Voskhods, Volgas and recently two Kolkhidas, which have been sold to a Greek operator. Countries in which they are being or have been operated include Austria, Bulgaria, Czechoslovakia, Finland, Yugoslavia, Italy, Iran, France, Cyprus, Greece, East Germany, Morocco, Spain, West Germany, the Philippines, Poland, Romania, the United Kingdom and the USA.

CIVIL CRAFT

RAKETA

The prototype Raketa was launched in 1957 and was the first multi-seat passenger hydrofoil to employ the Alexeyev shallow draught submerged

Raketa operating as fire tender in Leningrad   (J K Pemberton)

Bow foil and planing stabiliser foils of Raketa

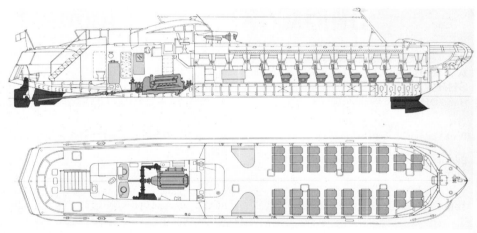

Inboard profile and plan view of standard 50-seat Raketa

foil system. Several hundred are now in service on all the major rivers of the Soviet Union.

In August 1982 it was announced that the prototype was still in service and has carried more than two million passengers. The distance travelled by the craft during the period was stated to be equal to '52 voyages around the equator'.

More than 300 Raketas are being operated on rivers and lakes in the Soviet Union, including 66 in service with the Volga United River Shipping Agency.

Variants include the standard non-tropicalised Raketa M, seating 64 passengers; the 58-seat Raketa T, which is both tropicalised and air-conditioned, and the Raketa TA, modified in London by Airavia Ltd and licensed by the UK Department of Trade to carry up to 100 passengers (58 seated) on high-density commuter and tourist routes on sheltered waters such as Westminster-Greenwich. On short-range commuter services additional passengers are seated around the promenade deck aft and others can stand.

A substantial number of Raketas have been

exported. Examples are in service in Austria, Bulgaria, Czechoslovakia, the Federal Republic of Germany, Hungary, Poland, Romania and Yugoslavia.

Production of the Raketa has now stopped and yards previously involved in their construction are building Voskhod and other designs.

The description that follows applies to the Raketa T, the standard export variant, powered by an M-401A diesel and with a cruising speed of about 58km/h (32 knots).

The vessel is designed for high-speed passenger ferry services during daylight hours on rivers, reservoirs and sheltered waters in tropical climates. It meets the requirements of the Soviet River Register Class 'O' with operation restricted to 0·8m (2ft 7in) waves when foilborne and up to 1·5m (4ft 11in) when hullborne.

The passenger saloon is provided with natural and induced ventilation and seats 58. The crew comprises a captain, engineer, deckhand and barman.

FOILS: The foil system comprises one bow foil,

one aft foil and two dart-like planing sub-foils, the tips of which are attached to the trailing edges of the outer bow foil struts. Foils, sub-foils and struts are in welded stainless steel. The bow foil, which incorporates sweepback, and the straight aft foil, are both supported by three vertical struts.

The base of the centre strut aft provides the end bearing for the propeller which is beneath the foil.
HULL: The hull is framed on longitudinal and transverse formers and all the main elements—plating, deck, partitions, bulkheads, platforms and wheelhouse—are in riveted duralumin. The stem is fabricated in interwelded steel strips. Below the freeboard deck the hull is divided into six watertight compartments employing web framing.
ACCOMMODATION: The passenger saloon seats 58 in aircraft-type, adjustable seats. At the aft end of the saloon is a bar. The saloon has one exit on each side leading to the promenade deck and one forward, leading to the forecastle. Aft of the saloon is the engine room, promenade deck with additional seats, two toilets, a storeroom and a companionway leading up to the wheelhouse.

The craft carries a full range of life-saving and firefighting equipment. There are 62 life jackets stowed in the passenger saloon and four for the crew in the wheelhouse and under the embarkation companionway. Two lifebelts are provided on the embarkation platform and two on the promenade deck. Firefighting equipment includes four foam and four CO_2 fire extinguishers, two fire axes, two fire buckets and two felt cloths.
POWERPLANT: Power is supplied by a single M-401A water-cooled, supercharged 12-cylinder V-type diesel, with a normal service output of 900hp. The engine drives, via a reverse gear and inclined stainless steel propeller shaft, a three-bladed cast bronze propeller. The fuel system comprises two fuel tanks with a total capacity of 1400kg, a fuel priming unit, and a hand fuel booster pump. A compressed air system, comprising a propeller shaft-driven air compressor and two 40-litre compressed air bottles, is provided for main engine starting, emergency stopping, operating the foghorn and scavenging the water intake.

The diesel generator unit comprises a Perkins P3.152 diesel engine employed in conjunction with a Stamford C20 alternator.
CONTROLS: The wheelhouse is equipped with a hydraulic remote control system for the engine, reverse gear and fuel supply. The balanced rudder, made in aluminium-magnesium alloy, is controlled hydraulically by turning the wheel. A hand tiller is employed in an emergency. Employment of gas exhaust as a side-thruster to assist mooring is permitted at 850rpm.
SYSTEMS, ELECTRICAL: A 3kW generator, rated at 27·5V and coupled to the main engine, is the main source of power while the vessel is under way. A 50Hz, 230V, 1500rpm three-phase alternator supplies ac power. Four 12V acid storage batteries, each with a 132Ah capacity and connected in series to give 24V, supply power during short stops.
HYDRAULICS: The hydraulic system for controlling the main engine, reverse gear and fuel supply, consists of control levers located in the

Raketa M

wheelhouse and on the main engine, power cylinders located on the engine, a filler tank, pipelines and fittings.
HEATING AND VENTILATION: Passenger saloon and wheelhouse are provided with natural ventilation, using ram inflow when the boat is in motion. Norris Warming air-conditioning is fitted for use in hot weather. One conditioner is installed in the wheelhouse and eight are installed in the passenger saloon and bar. The cooled air is distributed throughout the saloon by electric fans installed on the ceiling. One is provided in the wheelhouse. A radio-telephone with a range of about 30km (19 miles) is installed for ship-to-shore and ship-to-ship communication. The vessel also has a public address system and intercom speakers linking the engine room, wheelhouse and forecastle.
DIMENSIONS
Length overall: 26·96m (88ft 5in)
Beam amidships: 5m (16ft 5in)
Freeboard: 0·8m (2ft 7½in)
Height overall (excluding mast): 4·46m (14ft 8in)
Draught, hullborne: 1·8m (5ft 11in)
    foilborne: 1·1m (3ft 7¼in)

WEIGHTS
Displacement, fully loaded: 27·09 tonnes
    light: 20·31 tonnes
PERFORMANCE
Service speed: about 58km/h (32 knots)
Max wave height, foilborne: 0·8m (2ft 8in)
    hullborne: 1·5m (4ft 11in)
Turning diameter, hullborne: 3-4 boat lengths
    foilborne: 15-16 boat lengths

METEOR

Dr Alexeyev's Meteor made its maiden voyage from Gorki to Moscow in 1960, bringing high performance and unprecedented comfort to river boat fleets, and setting the pattern for a family of later designs.

The craft is intended for use in daylight hours on local and medium-range routes of up to 600km (373 miles) in length. It meets the requirements of Class O, experimental type, on the Register of River Shipping in the USSR.

Accommodation is provided for a crew of five and 116 passengers. Cruising speed at the full load displacement of 54·3 tonnes across calm water and

Meteor operating in Leningrad   (J K Pemberton)

Meteor

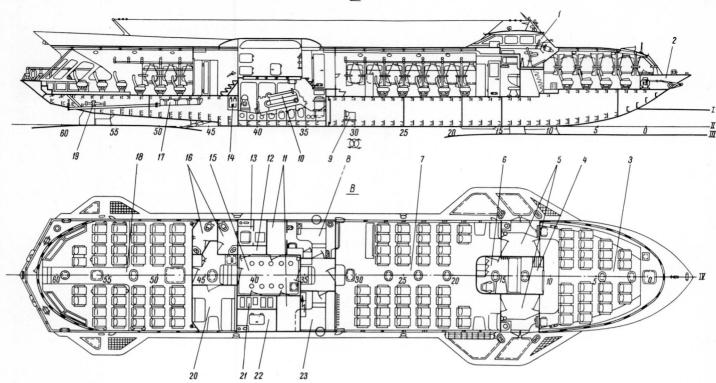

Meteor:
(A) inboard profile **(B)** main deck plan **(I)** waterline hullborne **(II)** hull base line **(III)** waterline foilborne **(IV)** longitudinal centreline **(1)** wheelhouse **(2)** anchor compartment **(3)** forward passenger saloon, 26 seats **(4)** luggage rack **(5)** embarkation companionway **(6)** crew duty room **(7)** midship passenger saloon, 42 seats **(8)** bar **(9)** refrigeration unit **(10)** engine room **(11)** pantry **(12)** boatswain's store **(13)** calorifier **(14)** fire fighting equipment **(15)** promenade deck **(16)** wcs **(17)** tank **(18)** aft passenger saloon, 44 seats **(19)** tiller gear **(20)** four-seat passenger cabin **(21)** storage batteries **(22)** hydraulic units **(23)** main switchboard

in winds of up to Beaufort Force 3 is about 65km/h (35 knots).

Outside the Soviet Union Meteors are operated in Bulgaria, Hungary, Poland and Yugoslavia.

FOILS: The foil arrangement comprises a bow foil and a stern foil, with the struts of the bow system carrying two additional planing sub-foils. The foils are attached to the struts, which are of split type, by flanges and bolts. The foils are in stainless steel, and the sub-foils in aluminium magnesium alloy. The foil incidence can be adjusted when necessary by the insertion of wedges between the flanges and the foils when the vessel is in dock.

HULL: With the exception of the small exposed areas fore and aft, the Meteor's hull and superstructure are built as an integral unit. The hull is framed on longitudinal and transverse formers and both hull and superstructure are of riveted duralumin construction with welded steel members. Below the main deck the hull is sub-divided longitudinally into eight compartments by seven bulkheads. Access to the compartments is via hatches in the main deck. The craft will remain afloat in the event of any two adjacent compartments forward of amidship flooding or any one compartment aft of midship. Frame spacing in the hull is about 500mm while that in the superstructure is 1000mm.

POWERPLANT: Power is supplied by two M-401A 12-cylinder, four-stroke, supercharged, water-cooled diesels with reversing clutches. Each engine has a normal service output of 1000hp at 1700rpm and a maximum output of 1100hp at 1800rpm. Specific consumption at rated output g/bhp/h is not more than 193, and oil, not more than 6. Guaranteed overhaul life is 1000 hours. Each engine drives its own inclined propeller shaft through a reverse clutch. Propeller shafts are in steel and the propellers, which are five-bladed, are in brass. The drives are contra-rotating.

Refuelling is via filler necks on each side of the hull. Fuel is carried in six tanks located in the engine room. Total fuel capacity is 3200kg. Lubricating oil, total capacity 370 litres, is carried in two service tanks and a storage tank located on the forward bulkhead in the engine room. Fuel and lubricating oil are sufficient for a cruising range, foilborne, of not less than 600km (373 miles).

AUXILIARY UNIT: 12hp diesel is fitted for generating 5·6kW electrical power when the craft is at its moorings, warming the main engines in cold weather and operating drainage pump.

Meteor hydrofoil in shipment on the *Zadonsk* from Ilyichevsk, near Odessa to Vladivostok

(Soviet Shipping)

CONTROLS: Control of the engines, reverse gear and fuel supply is effected remotely from the wheelhouse with the aid of a hydraulic system comprising transmitter cylinders in the wheelhouse, and actuators on the engine. The engines can also be controlled from the engine room.

Craft heading is controlled by two balanced rudders, the blades of which are in solid aluminium magnesium alloy. The rudders are operated hydraulically from the wheelhouse, the rudder angle being checked by an electric indicator in the wheelhouse. In an emergency, with the craft in hullborne conditions, the rudder is put over with the aid of a detachable hand tiller fitted to the rudder stock.

At low speed the craft can turn in its own length by pinwheeling—employing both engines with equal power in opposite directions—one ahead, the other astern.

Minimum diameter of the turning circle is approximately 250m (819ft) with the engines running at low speed (700-750rpm) and with the rudder put through an angle of 35 degrees. Turning circle diameter when operating foilborne with the rudder at an angle of 10 degrees is approximately 750m (2460ft).

The vessel takes off for foilborne flight in 120 to 140 seconds, ie within a distance of 25 to 28 lengths of its hull.

Landing run, with engines reversed, ranges from 1·5 to 2 hull lengths, while the braking distance without reversing the engines is within 3 to 4 lengths of the hull.

ACCOMMODATION: Passengers are accommodated in three compartments, a forward saloon seating 26, and central and aft saloons seating 46 and 44 passengers respectively. The central saloon has three exits, two forward leading to the embarkation platforms and one aft leading to the promenade deck above the engine room. On the port side of the central saloon, aft, is a small buffet/bar. Beneath the wheelhouse is a duty crew room and a luggage compartment which opens into the forward saloon.

The aft saloon has two exits, one leading to the promenade deck above the engine room and one to the weather deck aft. Forward and aft on both sides of the craft are sponsons to protect the foil systems during mooring. The forward pair are used as embarkation and disembarkation platforms.

SYSTEMS, ELECTRICAL: 24 to 28·5V dc from the vessel's power supply or 220V ac, 50Hz, from shore-to-ship supply sources.

RADIO: Ship-to-shore radio telephone operating on any of ten pre-selected fixed frequencies. Also passenger announcement system and crew intercom.

NAVIGATION: Magnetic compass.

COMPRESSED AIR: System comprises two 40-litre air storage bottles for starting the main engines, operating emergency stop mechanism, closing feed cocks of the fuel tanks, recharging the hydraulic system accumulator and the ship's siren.

FIREFIGHTING: Remote system for fighting outbreak in engine room, with automatic light and sound indicator operating in wheelhouse. Hand-operated foam and CO_2 extinguishers provided in passenger saloons and wheelhouse.

DIMENSIONS
Length overall: 34·6m
Beam overall: 9·5m
Height foilborne above water surface: 6·8m
Draught hullborne: 2·35m
     foilborne: 1·2m
WEIGHTS
Light displacement: 36·4 tonnes
Fully loaded: 53·4 tonnes
PERFORMANCE
Cruising speed, calm water: 65km/h (35 knots)
Endurance: 600km (325n miles)
Limiting Sea States, foilborne: Beaufort Force 3
     hullborne: Beaufort Force 4

SERGO ORDZHONIKIDZE SHIPYARD

KOMETA

Derived from the earlier Meteor, the Kometa was the first seagoing hydrofoil to be built in the Soviet Union. The prototype, seating 100 passengers, made its maiden voyage on the Black Sea in 1961, after which it was employed on various passenger routes on an experimental basis. Oper-

ating experience accumulated on these services led to the introduction of various modifications before the craft was put into series production.

Kometas are built mainly at the S. Ordzhonikidze Shipbuilding and Repair Yard at Poti on the Black Sea and the Feodosiya Yard.

Kometa operators outside the Soviet Union include Kompas Line, Yugoslavia; Empresa Nacional de Cabotage, Cuba; Alilauro Aliscafi del Tirreno SpA, Naples, Italy; and Transportes Touristiques Intercontinentaux, Morocco. Other vessels of this type have been supplied to Bulgaria, German Democratic Republic, Greece, Iran, Poland, Romania and Turkey. More than 60 have been exported.

Export orders have mainly been for the Kometa-ME, designed for service in countries with a moderate climate, which was introduced in 1968. Two distinguishing features of this model are the employment of new diesel engines, with increased operating hours between overhauls, and a completely revised surface-piercing foil system, with a trapeze bow foil instead of the former Alexeyev shallow draught submerged type.

A fully tropicalised and air-conditioned version is now in production and designated Kometa-MT.

The present standard production Kometa-ME seats 116 to 120. Because of the additional weight of the Kometa-MT's air-conditioning system and other refinements, the seating capacity is reduced in the interest of passenger comfort to 102.

Kometa under construction at Sergo Ordzhonikidze shipyard, Poti, in 1980

A kometa of Kompas Line, Yugoslavia, arriving at Venice, June 1986

Official designation of the Kometa in the USSR is Hydrofoil Type 342. The craft meets the requirements of the Rules of the Register of Shipping of the USSR and is constructed to Hydrofoil Class KM ★ 2 11 Passenger Class under the Register's technical supervision. IMCO recommendations on fire safety are taken into account and non-flammable basalt fibres are employed for sound and heat insulation and the engine room is clad with titanium plating. The craft is designed to operate during daylight hours on coastal routes up to 81km (50 miles) from ports of refuge under moderate climatic conditions.

The standard craft has proved to be exceptionally robust and has a good, all-round performance. On one charter, a Kometa-ME covered 5310km (3300 miles) by sea and river in 127 hours. It can operate foilborne in waves up to 1·7m (5ft 7in) and travel hullborne in waves up to 3·6m (11ft 10in).

One of the features of the more recent models is the relocation of the engine room aft to reduce the noise in the passenger saloons and the employment of a vee-drive instead of the existing inclined shaft. The arrangement is expected to be similar to that on the Voskhod-2. The revised deck configuration allows more seats to be fitted. These modifications are also incorporated in the recently announced Kometa derivative, the Kolkhida, which will be fitted with two 1500hp engines.

FOILS: Employment of a surface-piercing trapeze-type bow foil provides the Kometa-ME with improved seakeeping capability in waves. The foil system comprises a bow foil, aft foil, and two auxiliaries, one (termed 'stabiliser') located above the bow foil for pitch stability, the other sited amidship near the longitudinal centre of gravity to assist take-off. The foils are connected to the hull by struts and brackets. Middle and side struts of the bow foil are of the split type. The lower and upper components of each strut are connected by flanges and bolts. The upper sections are connected to the hull by the same means.

The bow and stern foils are of hollow welded stainless steel construction. The midship and pitch stability foils and the upper components of the foil struts are in aluminium-magnesium alloy.

HULL: Similar in shape to that of the earlier Meteor, the hull has a wedge-shaped bow, raked stem and a spoon-shaped stern. Hull and superstructure are built in AlMg-61 and AlM-6g alloys. Hull and superstructure are of all-welded construction using contact and argon arc welding. The hull is framed on longitudinal and transverse formers, the spacing throughout the length of the hull is 500mm and in the superstructure 1000mm.

Below the freeboard deck, the hull is divided by watertight bulkheads into thirteen compartments, which include the engine room, fuel compartments, and those containing the firefighting system, tiller gear and fuel transfer pump.

ACCOMMODATION: The Kometa-MT seats 102 passengers. It carries an operating crew of six, comprising captain, engineer, motorman, radio-operator, seaman, and one barman. Embarkation platforms immediately below the wheelhouse provide passenger and crew access.

The captain and engineer are accommodated in a raised wheelhouse located between the forward and main saloons, and equipped with two seats, a folding stool, chart table, sun shield and a locker for signal flags. The wheelhouse also contains a radar display and radio communications equipment.

Main engine controls are installed in both the wheelhouse and engine room.

Passengers are accommodated in three compartments, a forward saloon seating 22, and central and aft saloons seating 54 and 26 respectively. The central saloon has three exits, two forward, leading to the embarkation platforms, and one aft, leading to the promenade deck. This is located in the space above the engine room and is partially covered with a removable metallic awning.

In the current production model of the Kometa-ME, the forward saloon seats 24, the central saloon 56 and the aft saloon 36.

To the starboard side is a crew's off-duty cabin, hydraulic system pump room, bar store and bar,

Kometa craft built

Type	Name	Yard	Built	Operator/area in USSR
	10	—	1967	Sochi
	12	—	1967	Sochi
	13	Poti	1968	Odessa
	16	Poti	1969	Odessa
	17	Poti	1970	Yalta
Kometa	19	Poti	1973	Azov Shipping Co, Zhdanov
	20	Poti	1973	—
	21	Poti	1982	—
	21	Poti	1974	Caspian Shipping Co, Astrakan
	22	Poti	1974	Azov Shipping Co, Zhdanov
	23	Poti	1974	Yalta
	24	Poti	1975	Sochi
	25	Poti	1975	Murmansk
	27	Poti	1975	Black Sea Shipping Co
	28	Poti	1975	Caspian Shipping Co
	29	Poti	1976	—
	30	Poti	1976	Murmansk Shipping Co
	31	Poti	1977	—
	32	Poti	1977	Black Sea Shipping Co
	33	Poti	1976	Sochi
	34	Poti	1977	Soviet Danube Shipping Co, Izmail
Kometa	35	Poti	1978	Soviet Danube Shipping Co, Izmail
Kometa	36	Poti	1978	Soviet Danube Shipping Co, Izmail
	38	—	1978	USSR
	40	—	1979	Black Sea Shipping Co, Yalta
	41	—	1979	Black Sea Shipping Co, Odessa
	43	—	1980	—
	46	—	1980	—
	47	—	1980	—
	48	—	1981	—
	49	—	1981	—
	51	—	1981	—
	53	—	1982	—
	54	—	1982	—
	55	—	1982	—
	57	—	1983	—

Some of the above Kometas may have been exported. The following list shows Kometas operated outside the USSR:

Kometa craft built

Type	Name	Yard	Built	Operator/area
Kometa	1	—	1962	Navigation Maritime Bulgare (1977), Varna, Bulgaria
Kometa	2	Poti	1979	Navigation Maritime Bulgare
Kometa	2	Poti	1965	Navigation Maritime Bulgare
Kometa	3	—	1979	Navigation Maritime Bulgare
Kometa	Daria (ex 4)	Poti	1967	Zegluga Szczecinska, Poland (ex Navigation Maritime Bulgare)
Kometa	5	Poti	1970	Navigation Maritime Bulgare
Kometa	6	—	1972	Navigation Maritime Bulgare
Kometa	7	Poti	1974	Navigation Maritime Bulgare
Kometa	8	Poti	1974	Navigation Maritime Bulgare
Kometa	9	—	1974	Navigation Maritime Bulgare
Kometa	10	—	1975	Navigation Maritime Bulgare
Kometa	11	—	1975	Navigation Maritime Bulgare
Kometa	12	—	1976	Navigation Maritime Bulgare
Kometa-MT	18	Poti	1973	Empresa Nacional de Cabotage, Cuba
Kometa-MT	Scheherazade (ex 37)	Feodosiya	197?	Transtour SA, Morocco (ex Black Sea Shipping Co, Odessa)
Kometa-MT	Sindibad	—	1968	Transtour SA, Morocco
Kometa-MT	Aladin	—	1971	Transtour SA, Morocco
Kometa	Aliapollo 1984 (ex Alitunisi, ex Alispan Secondo, 1980, ex Atalanta, 1971)	Feodosiya	1970	Alilauro Aliscafi del Tirreno SpA
Kometa	Alieros (ex Aliconamar, 1984, ex Alibastea, 1982)	Poti	1973	Alivit Due
Kometa	Alivenere (ex Aligiglio)	Poti	1972	Alilauro Aliscafi del Tirreno SpA
Kometa	Alisaturno (ex Alielba)	Poti	1972	Alivit Due
Kometa	Alisorrento	—	—	Alilauro Aliscafi del Tirreno SpA
Kometa	Alivesuvio	—	—	Alilauro Aliscafi del Tirreno SpA
Kometa	Alivulcano 1977 (ex Alipan Primo, 1977, ex Lepa Vida, 1970)	Poti	1970	Alilauro Aliscafi del Tirreno SpA
Kometa	Freccia Pontina (ex Wera)	Poti	1978	Societa di Navigazione Basso Lazio srl, Gaeta, Italy
Kometa	Posei...	—	1970	Intreprinderea de Exploatare a Floti Maritime NAVROM, Galatz, Romania

and to the port are two toilets, boiler room, battery room and fire extinguishing equipment.

The aft saloon has two exits, one forward leading to the promenade deck, the other aft, leading to the weather deck, which is used for embarking and disembarking when the vessel is moored by the stern.

Floors of the passenger saloons, crew's cabins, bar and wheelhouse are covered in linoleum and the deckhead in the passenger saloons, as well as bulkheads and the sides above the lower edge of the windows, are finished in light coloured Pavinol. Panels of the saloons beneath the windows are covered with plastic.

Passenger saloons are fitted with upholstered chairs, racks for small hand luggage and pegs for clothing. The middle and aft saloons have niches for hand luggage and the former is fitted with cradles for babies. The bar is fully equipped with glass washers, an ice safe, an automatic Freon compressor, electric stove, etc.

SAFETY EQUIPMENT: A full range of lifesaving equipment is carried including five inflatable life rafts, each for 25 persons, 135 life jackets, and four circular life belts with life lines and self-igniting buoyant lights. There are two life rafts on the forward sponsons and two on the aft sponsons. When thrown into the water the life rafts inflate automatically. Life jackets are stowed under the seats in all saloons, and the circular life belts are stowed on the embarkation and promenade platforms. Kometas for export are provided with life jackets on the basis of 25 persons per raft.

FIREFIGHTING EQUIPMENT: An independent fluid firefighting system is provided for the engine room and fuel bay. An automatic light and sound system signals a fire outbreak. The firefighting system is put into operation manually from the control deck above the engine room door. Boat spaces are equipped with hand-operated foam and CO_2 fire extinguishers, felt cloths and fire axes.

POWERPLANT: Power is supplied by two M-401A water-cooled, supercharged 12-cylinder V-type diesels, each with a normal service output of 1000hp at 1550rpm and a maximum output of 1100hp at 1600rpm. Guaranteed service life of each engine before first overhaul is 2500 hours. Each engine drives via a reverse gear its own inclined shaft and the twin propellers are contra-rotating. The shafts are of steel and are parallel to the craft. Guaranteed service life of the M-401A before each overhaul is 2500 hours.

The propellers are of three-bladed design and made of brass.

Main engine controls and gauges are installed in both the wheelhouse and the engine room. A diesel-generator compressor-pump unit is provided for charging starter air bottles; supplying electric power when at rest; warming the main engines in cold weather and pumping warm air beneath the deck to dry the bilges.

Diesel oil tanks with a total capacity of 3000kg (6612lb) for the main engines and the auxiliary unit are located in the afterpeak. Two lubricating oil service tanks and one storage tank located at the fore bulkhead of the engine room have a total capacity of 250kg (551lb). Diesel and lubricating oil capacity ensures a range of 370km (230 miles).

CONTROLS: The wheelhouse is equipped with an electro-hydraulic remote control system for the engine reverse gear and fuel supply, fuel monitoring equipment, including electric speed counters, pressure gauges, lubricating and fuel oil gauges. The boat has a single, solid aluminium magnesium alloy balanced rudder, which is controlled through a hydraulic steering system or a hand-operated hydraulic drive. In an emergency, the rudder may be operated by a hand tiller. Maximum rudder angle is 35 degrees in hullborne conditions and 5·6 degrees foilborne. In the event of the steering gear failing the craft can be manoeuvred by differential use of the main engines, the rudder being locked on the centre line. The vessel can be pinwheeled in hullborne condition by setting one engine slow ahead, the other slow astern and turning the rudder hard over.

SYSTEMS, ELECTRICAL: Power supply is 24V dc. A 1kW dc generator is attached to each of the

Kometa craft built (contd)

Type	Name	Yard	Built	Operator/area
Kometa-M	*Flying Dolphin I*	Poti	1975	Ceres Flying Hydroways Ltd, Piraeus, Greece
Kometa-M	*Flying Dolphin II*	Poti	1975	Ceres Flying Hydroways Ltd, Piraeus, Greece
Kometa-M	*Flying Dolphin III*	Poti	1976	Ceres Flying Hydroways Ltd, Piraeus, Greece
Kometa-M	*Flying Dolphin IV*	Poti	1977	Ceres Flying Hydroways Ltd, Piraeus, Greece
Kometa-M	*Flying Dolphin V*	Poti	1976	Ceres Flying Hydroways Ltd, Piraeus, Greece
Kometa-M	*Flying Dolphin VI*	Poti	1976	Ceres Flying Hydroways Ltd, Piraeus, Greece
Kometa-M	*Flying Dolphin VII*	Poti	1976	Ceres Flying Hydroways Ltd, Piraeus, Greece
Kometa-M	*Flying Dolphin VIII*	Poti	1977	Ceres Flying Hydroways Ltd, Piraeus, Greece
Kometa-M	*Flying Dolphin IX*	Poti		
Kometa-M	*Flying Dolphin X*	Poti	1978	Ceres Flying Hydroways Ltd, Piraeus, Greece
Kometa-M	*Flying Dolphin XI*	Poti	1979	Ceres Flying Hydroways Ltd, Piraeus, Greece
Kometa-M	*Flying Dolphin XII*	Poti	1979	Ceres Flying Hydroways Ltd, Piraeus, Greece
Kometa-M	*Flying Dolphin XIV*	Poti	1981	Ceres Flying Hydroways Ltd, Piraeus, Greece
Kometa-M	*Flying Dolphin XV*	Poti	1981	Ceres Flying Hydroways Ltd, Piraeus, Greece
Kometa-M	*Flying Dolphin XVI*	Poti	1981	Ceres Flying Hydroways Ltd, Piraeus, Greece
Kometa	*Marilena*	—	1981	Nearchos Shipping Co, Greece
Kometa	*Gina*	—	1981	Nearchos Shipping Co, Greece
Kometa	*Poszum*	Poti	1973	Zegluga Gdanska, Gdansk, Poland
	Poweiw	Feodosiya	1973	Zegluga Gdanska, Gdansk, Poland
	Poryw	Poti	1976	Zegluga Gdanska, Gdansk, Poland
	Poswist	Poti	1975	Zegluga Gdanska, Gdansk, Poland
	Pogwizd	Poti	1977	Zegluga Gdanska, Gdansk, Poland
	Polot	Poti	1977	Zegluga Gdanska, Gdansk, Poland
Kometa	*Flying Dolphin*, 1983 (ex *Podmuch*, 1973)	—	—	Motion Shipping Co Ltd, Limassol, Cyprus
Kometa	*Stoertebeker I*	—	1974	Fahrgastechiffahrt Staisund, GDR
	Stoertebeker II	—	1974	Fahrgastechiffahrt Staisund, GDR
Kometa	*Stoertebeker III*	—	1974	Fahrgastechiffahrt Staisund, GDR
Kometa	*Alkyonis I*	Poti	1978	Alkyonis Speed Boats, Piraeus, Greece
Kometa	*Alkyonis II*	Poti	1978	Alkyonis Speed Boats, Piraeus, Greece
Kometa	*Wala*	—	1966	Zegluga Szczecinska, Poland
Kometa	*Lida*	—	1971	Zegluga Szczecinska, Poland
Kometa	*Kalina*	—	1973	Zegluga Szczecinska, Poland
Kometa	*Lena*	—	1975	Zegluga Szczecinska, Poland
Kometa	*Liwia*	—	1978	Zegluga Szczecinska, Poland
Kometa	—	—	1970	Vedettes Armoricaines, Brest, France
Kometa	*Iran Resalat*, 1980 (ex *Arya Ram*)	Feodosiya	1971	Islamic Republic of Iran Shipping Lines, Khorramshahr, Iran
Kometa	*Iran Taveeghat*, 1980 (ex *Arya Baz*, ex Kometa S-26)	Feodosiya	1969	Islamic Republic of Iran Shipping Lines, Khorramshahr, Iran
Kometa	*Krila Kornata*	Poti	1980	Kompas-Jugoslavija, Koper, Yugoslavia
Kometa	*Krila Kvarnera*	Poti	1970	Kompas-Jugoslavija, Koper, Yugoslavia
Kometa	*Krila Pirana*	Poti	1979	Kompas-Jugoslavija, Koper, Yugoslavia
Kometa	*Krila Primorske*	Poti	1980	Kompas-Jugoslavija, Koper, Yugoslavia
Kometa	*Krila Slovenije*	Poti	1977	Kompas-Jugoslavija, Koper, Yugoslavia

two engines and these supply power during operation. A 5·6kW generator is included in the auxiliary unit and supplies power when the craft is at rest. It can also be used when under way for supplying the heating plant or when the 1kW generators are inoperative. Four 12V acid storage batteries, each of 180Ah capacity and connected in series to provide 24V, supply power during short stops.

HYDRAULICS: The hydraulic system for controlling the main engines and reverse gear consists of control cylinders located in the wheelhouse, power cylinders located on the engines, a filler tank, pipe lines and fittings.

ANCHORS: The craft is equipped with two Matrosov anchors: a main anchor weighing 75kg (165lb) and a spare anchor weighing 50kg (110lb). The main anchor is raised by an electric winch located in the forepeak. The cable of the spare anchor can be heaved in manually and is wound over a drum fitted with a hand brake.

COMMUNICATIONS: A radio transmitter/receiver with r/t and w/t facilities is installed in the wheelhouse for ship-to-shore and inter-ship communications on SW and MW bands. A portable emergency radio and automatic distress signal transmitter are also installed in the wheelhouse. A broadcast system is fitted in the passenger saloons

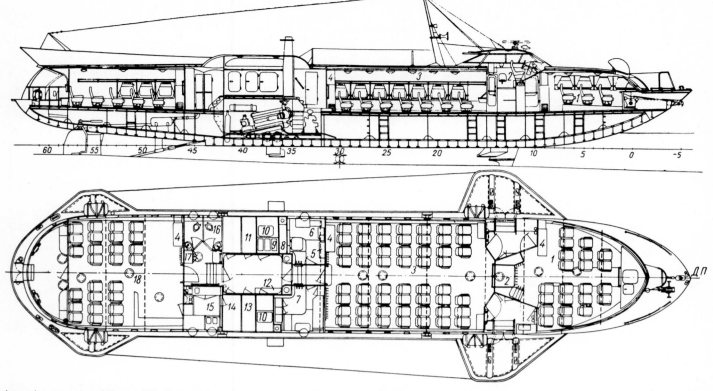

Internal arrangement of Kometa-MT, designed for tropical operation: **(1)** 22-seat forward passenger saloon **(2)** wheelhouse **(3)** 54-seat main passenger saloon **(4)** luggage rack **(5)** engine room door **(6)** control position **(7)** duty cabin **(8)** liquid fire extinguisher bay **(9)** battery room **(10)** engine room **(11)** boiler room **(12)** installation point for portable radio **(13)** store **(14)** provision store **(15)** bar **(16)** wc washbasin units **(17)** boatswain's store **(18)** 26-seat aft passenger saloon

and a two-way crew communications system is installed in the wheelhouse, engine room, anchor gear compartment and mooring stations.

NAVIGATION: The following navigation aids are standard: a gyrocompass, magnetic compass (reserve) and log.

KOMETA-ME
DIMENSIONS
Length overall: 35·1m (115ft 2in)
Beam overall: 11m (36ft 1in)
Height, foilborne from waterline to tip of mast: 9·2m
Draught, hullborne: 3·6m (11ft 9¾in)
  foilborne: 1·7m (5ft 6⅘in)
GRT: 142·1
WEIGHTS
Light displacement: 44·5 tonnes
Fully loaded displacement: 60 tonnes
PERFORMANCE
Max speed, intermittent: 66·8km/h (36 knots)
Cruising speed: 58km/h (32 knots)
Fuel consumption: 172g/hp/h
Oil consumption: 4·5g/hp/h
Max Sea State: Speed of the Kometa-M at full load displacement in Sea States 0-2 and wind conditions up to Force 3 is 32 knots. Under the worst permissible conditions under which the craft is able to navigate (Sea State 5, Wind Force 6) it will operate hullborne at 10 to 12 knots. Sea States up to 4 and wind conditions up to Force 5 are considered normal for Kometa operation.

KOMETA-MT
DIMENSIONS
Length overall: 35·1m (115ft 2in)
Beam: 11m (36ft 1in)
Height, foilborne, waterline to tip of mast: 9·2m (30ft 2¼in)
Draught, hullborne: 3·6m (11ft 9¾in)
  foilborne: 1·7m (5ft)
WEIGHTS
Light displacement: 45 tonnes
Fully loaded displacement: 58·9 tonnes
PERFORMANCE
Max speed: 61km/h (34 knots)
Service speed: 58km/h (32 knots)
Fuel consumption: 180g/hp/h
Oil consumption: 5g/hp/h
Range: 240km

Kometa-ME

Development of the Kometa is continuing. Current research is aimed at the introduction of a stability augmentation system employing either control flaps on the bow foil or air stabilisation on the stern foil and struts; the reduction of labour involved in construction; the introduction of design improvements through the use of grp and sandwich construction; noise reduction in the saloons and the extension of the cruising range.

SPUTNIK
The 100-ton Sputnik was the first of the Soviet Union's large hydrofoils. On its maiden voyage in November 1961, the prototype carried 300 passengers between Gorki and Moscow in 14 hours.

Although a heavy autumn storm was encountered en route the craft was able to continue under way at a cruising speed of 40 knots through several large reservoirs with waves running as high as 8ft.

Full details of the craft can be found in *Jane's Surface Skimmers 1984* and earlier editions.

STRELA
Developed from the Mir and intended for services across the Black Sea, the prototype Strela (Arrow) completed its acceptance trials towards the end of 1961. The craft, which was designed and built in Leningrad, was first put into regular passenger service between Odessa and Batumi, and later between Yalta and Sevastapol and

Prototype Strela during trials off Yalta coast

between Leningrad and Tallinn. It covers the latter distance in 4 hours, 90 minutes faster than the express train service connecting the two ports. Only two craft of this type have been built.

Two 970hp 12-cylinder V-type M-50 F3 diesels driving twin screws give the Strela a cruising speed of 75km/h (40 knots). The craft has trapeze type surface-piercing bow foils with a horizontal centre section between the main struts, and can operate in Sea State 4.

It carries 82 to 94 passengers in airliner-type seats.

DIMENSIONS
Length overall: 29·3m (96ft 1in)
Beam overall: 8·3m (26ft 4in)
Draught, hullborne: 2·25m (7ft 7in)
  foilborne: 1·2m (3ft 11in)
WEIGHT
Displacement, fully loaded: 46 tons
PERFORMANCE
Cruising speed: 40 knots
Sea State capability: 1·22m (4ft) waves
Range of operation: 740km (460 miles)
Time to reach service speed from stop: 130 seconds
Distance from full speed to stop: 234m (768ft)
Full speed ahead, to full speed astern: 117m (383ft)

VIKHR (WHIRLWIND)

Seagoing version of the 100-ton Sputnik, Vikhr employs the same hull and is one of the most powerful passenger hydrofoils operating today. Described as a 'Coastal liner', it is designed to operate during hours of daylight on inshore services on the Black Sea up to 50km (31 miles) from the coast. The craft was launched in 1962. It is understood that it is no longer in service. Full details can be found in *Jane's Surface Skimmers 1984* and earlier editions.

BUREVESTNIK

First Soviet gas turbine hydrofoil to be designed for series production, the Burevestnik has two 2700hp marinised aircraft gas turbines driving two two-stage waterjets. The prototype was launched

in April 1964 and it was intended to build two models: one for medium-range, non-stop inter-city services, seating 130 passengers, the other, for suburban services, seating 150.

After extensive trials and modifications, the prototype Burevestnik began operating on the Gorki-Kuibyshev route, about 700km (435 miles), in April 1968. It is understood that the vessel is no longer in service and has not entered production.

A full description of the Burevestnik can be found in *Jane's Surface Skimmers 1983* and earlier editions.

TYPHOON (Leningrad Yard)

The Typhoon, a gas-turbine powered fast ferry for 98 to 105 passengers, was launched in Leningrad in December 1969. During trials it completed the journey from Leningrad to Tallinn, the Estonian capital, in 4½ hours.

It is understood that the craft is no longer in service and has not entered production.

A full description can be found in *Jane's Surface Skimmers 1984* and earlier editions.

VOSKHOD-2

Designers of the Voskhod, which has been gradually replacing craft of the Raketa series, drew on engineering experience gained with the Raketa and also the more sophisticated Meteor and Kometa. Voskhod, in turn, was due to be succeeded by the new 50-seat Lastochka.

Among the basic requirements were that the Raketa's general characteristics should be preserved; foilborne operation should be possible in 1m (3ft 3in) high waves, with a 3 per cent safety factor; accommodation should be acceptable from health and safety viewpoints; noise levels should be significantly reduced, and the maximum use should be made of standard mechanical, electrical and other components and fittings proven on the Raketa.

In fact, the end product bears little resemblance to its predecessor. Visually the Voskhod is more

akin to a scaled-down Kometa with its engine room aft, replacing the rear passenger saloon.

In June 1974 Voskhod 2-01 began service on the Gorki-Kineshma route, across the vast Gorki reservoir which cannot be navigated by the Raketa because of its limited seaworthiness. It continued in service until the end of the 1974 navigation season. During this time it was demonstrated that its operating and technical performance was significantly superior to that of the Raketa.

Experience accumulated during this experimental service indicated the need for minor modifications which have been incorporated in the first series of production craft.

Voskhod 14 was launched in June 1980 and delivered to the Amur Line for summer services along the Amur river.

At the time of its inception, it was announced that the Voskhod would be available in a number of versions to suit local navigation and traffic requirements. Voskhod 3 will be powered by a gas turbine.

The vessel is designed for high-speed passenger ferry services during daylight hours on rivers, reservoirs, lakes and sheltered waters. It meets the requirements of Soviet River Register Class 'O' with the following wave restrictions (3% safety margin): foilborne, 1·3m (4ft 3in); hullborne, 2m (6ft 7in).

The passenger saloons are heated and provided with natural and induced ventilation. Full air-conditioning can be installed in craft required for service in tropical conditions. The crew comprises a captain, engineer, motorman and barman.

FOILS: Fixed foil system, comprising one bow foil with a pitch stability sub-foil immediately behind, one aft foil, plus an amidship foil to facilitate take-off. Bow and amidship foils appear to be of shallow V configuration and each has four vertical struts. The fully submerged stern foil has two side struts and is supported in the centre by the end bracket of the propeller shaft. The surface and lower parts of the foil struts and stabiliser are in Cr18Ni9Ti stainless steel, while the upper parts of

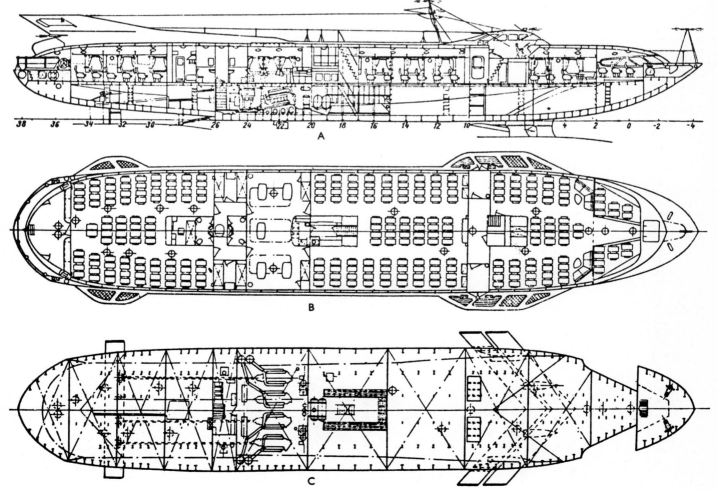

Internal arrangement of Vikhr. (**A**) profile (**B**) main deck (**C**) holds

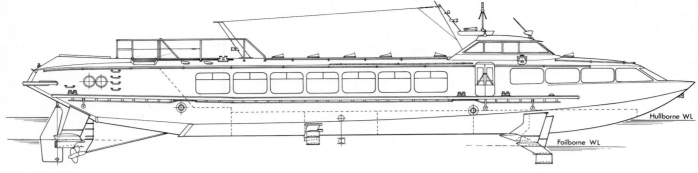

Voskhod-2, outboard profile

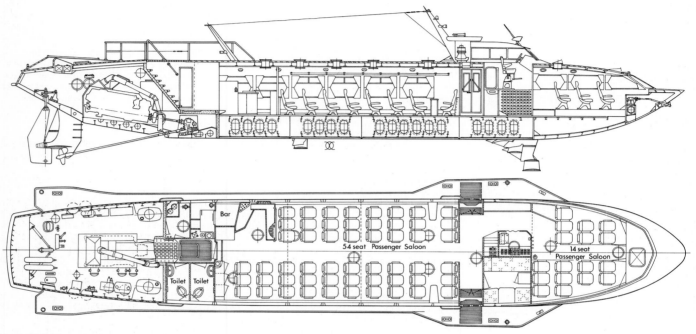

Voskhod-2, inboard profile and deck plan

the struts and stabiliser and also the amidship foil are in AlMg-61 plate alloy.

HULL: Similar in shape to the Kometa and earlier models of the Sormovo hydrofoil series, with a wedge-shaped bow, raked stem and spoon-shaped stern. A single step is provided to facilitate take-off. In fabricating the basic structure, which is largely in AlMg-61 aluminium magnesium alloy, extensive use has been made of arc and spot welding. The hull is framed on longitudinal and transverse formers. Below the deck it is divided into eight watertight compartments by transverse bulkheads. It will remain afloat with any one compartment or the machinery space flooded. Access to the forepeak, which houses the anchor

capstan, is via the forward passenger saloon and then through a rectangular hatch on the forecastle. Aft of the main passenger saloon is an area split into three compartments by two longitudinal bulkheads. The lower central space contains the reduction gear and V-drive, the starboard compartment contains the sanitary tank and the port compartment forms part of the double-bottom. Entrance to the engine compartment is via a door on the port side of the main deck. An emergency exit is provided starboard aft.

POWERPLANT: Power is supplied by a single M-401A four-stroke water-cooled, supercharged 12-cylinder V-type diesel, delivering 809·6kW (1100hp) at 1600rpm maximum and 736kW

(1000hp) at 1550rpm cruising. The engine, which has a variable-speed governor and a reversing clutch, is sited aft with its shaft inclined at 9 degrees. Output is transferred via a flexible coupling to a single six-bladed variable-pitch propeller via an R-21 vee-drive gearbox. Guaranteed service life of the engine before the first overhaul is 3000 hours. Specific fuel consumption, including attached units, is not more than 6g/ehp/h. Specific oil consumption is not more than 6g/ehp/h. The engine room is insulated with fire-retardant, heat and sound-insulating materials. Perforated aluminium alloy sheet is laid over the insulating materials.

CONTROLS: Single semi-balanced rudder in

Voskhod-2

AlMg plate provides directional control. Operation of the engine, rudder, reverse gear and fuel supply is effected hydraulically from the wheelhouse.

ACCOMMODATION: Voskhod-2 carries an operating crew of three, comprising captain, engineer and motorman, plus a barman. Embarkation platforms immediately below the wheelhouse provide passenger and crew access. Passengers can embark from both sides and from the stern.

The captain and engineer are accommodated in a raised wheelhouse located between the forward and main saloon. Main engine controls are in both the wheelhouse and the engine room.

Passengers are accommodated in two saloons, a forward compartment seating 17 and a main saloon seating 54. The main saloon has three exits, two forward, leading to the embarkation platforms, and one aft, leading to the stern embarkation area. Between the two saloons, on the starboard side, is a crew rest cabin. The saloons are fitted with upholstered seats, racks for small hand-luggage and coat pegs. Spacing between seats is 900mm and the central aisle is 800mm wide.

At the rear of the main saloon is a small buffet and bar and aft of the main saloon, at the foot of the rear embarkation steps, are two wc/washbasin units.

SYSTEMS, ELECTRICAL: Power supply is 24-27V dc. A 3kW generator is attached to the engine and supplies 27·5V while the craft is operating. Four 12V storage batteries, each of 180Ah capacity and connected in series-parallel to form a single bank, supply power during short stops. An auxiliary circuit can be connected to shore systems for 220V, single-phase, 50Hz ac supply.

FIREFIGHTING: Four carbon dioxide and four foam fire extinguishers for the passenger saloons and wheelhouse. Remote-controlled system employing '3·5' compound in the engine room.

HEATING AND VENTILATION: Heating in the saloons is provided by pipes circulating water from the internal cooling circuit of the engine. Ventilation is natural, using the dynamic pressure of the approaching air flow, and induced, by means of electric fans.

During the spring and autumn, the temperature of the ventilating air can be heated to 21°C.

DRINKING WATER: Hot and cold water supplies. An electric boiler supplies hot water for washbasins and the small kitchen behind the snackbar. Drinking water tank has a capacity of 138 litres.

BILGE WATER: System designed for bilge water removal by shore-based facilities or service vessels.

ANCHOR: Matrosov system, weighing 35kg (77lb), attached to an anchor cable 8·4mm (0·33in) in diameter and 80m (262ft) long, and operated by hand winch in the forepeak.

DIMENSIONS
EXTERNAL
Length overall: 27·6m (90ft 7in)
Hull length: 26·3m (86ft 3½in)
Beam overall: 6·2m (20ft 4in)
Height above mean water level, foilborne, including mast: 5·7m (18ft 8in)
Draught hullborne: 2m (6ft 6¾in)
  foilborne: 1·1m (3ft 7¼in)
INTERNAL
Deck area: 105m² (1130ft²)
  per passenger: 1·48m² (15·35ft²)
WEIGHTS
Displacement, fully loaded: 28 tonnes
Light displacement: 20 tonnes
Passengers per displacement tonne: 2·55
Payload, passengers and buffet/bar equipment: 5·9 tonnes
Payload/displacement: 21·2%
PERFORMANCE
Max speed, calm water, wind not in excess of Force 3,
  at 1550rpm (1000hp): 70km/h (37·8 knots)
  at 1450rpm: 60km/h (32·5 knots)
Turning circle diameter
  hullborne: 106m (348ft)
  foilborne: 380m (1246ft)

Range, based on normal fuel supply of 1400kg: 500km (310 miles)
Max wave height, with 3% safety margin
  hullborne: 2m (6ft 7in)
  foilborne: 1·3m (4ft 3in)

MOLNIA

This popular six-seat hydrofoil sports runabout was derived from Alexeyev's original test craft. Many hundreds are available for hire on Soviet lakes and rivers. In slightly modified form, and renamed Volga, the type is being exported to 44 countries. The craft is navigable in protected offshore water up to 2 miles from the land and has particular appeal for water-taxi and joy-ride operators.

Molnia is no longer in production, having been replaced by the Volga. Details of the Molnia can be found in *Jane's Surface Skimmers 1976-77* and earlier editions.

NEVKA (Leningrad Shipyard)

This light passenger ferry and sightseeing craft is in series production at a Leningrad shipyard and the first units have been supplied to Yalta for coastal services on the Black Sea. A multi-purpose runabout, it is intended to cope with a variety of duties including scheduled passenger services, sightseeing, VIP transport and crewboat. The standard version seats a driver and 14 passengers.

The craft, which is designed to operate in waves up to 1m (3ft 3in) high, is the first small hydrofoil in the Soviet Union to employ surface-piercing V

foils, and also the first to employ a diesel engine in conjunction with a Z-drive.

In December 1971 a waterjet-propelled variant made its first cruise along the Crimean coast. The 16-mile trip from Yalta to Alushta was made in half-an-hour.

FOILS: Bow and stern foils are of fixed V surface-piercing configuration and made of solid aluminium magnesium alloy.

HULL: Glassfibre reinforced plastic structure assembled in four basic sections. The outer hull is assembled with the transom, the deck with the rib of the windscreen, the cabin/cockpit with the engine air intakes and afterpeak, and the inner hull with the companionway at the aft of the cabin.

The lower hull is subdivided by watertight bulkheads into four compartments.

The hull contours are designed to facilitate easy transition from hull to foilborne mode and minimise structural loadings due to wave impact. Two transverse steps are incorporated.

ACCOMMODATION: The craft can be supplied with an open cockpit and folding canopy, as a cabin cruiser with a solid top or as a sightseeing craft with a transparent cabin roof. As a cabin cruiser, the craft is equipped with bunks, a galley and toilet. The driver's stand can be located either at the forward end of the cabin or in a raised position amidships.

POWERPLANT: Power is supplied by a single 3D20 four-cycle, six-cylinder diesel, developing 235hp at 2200rpm. The engine, located aft, drives a three-bladed propeller via a DK-300 Z-drive.

Nevka

Model of Nevka fitted with trapeze foils instead of V-foils which appear to be standard on export models

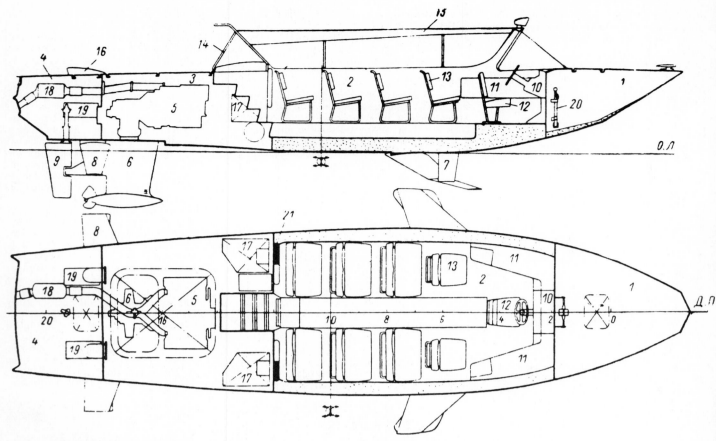

Inboard profile and deck plan of standard Nevka:
(**1**) forepeak (**2**) passenger cabin (**3**) engine bay (**4**) afterpeak (**5**) 235hp 3D20 four-cycle six-cylinder diesel (**6**) DK-300 Z-drive (**7**) bow foil (**8**) rear foil (**9**) rudder (**10**) control panel (**11**) lockers (**12**) driver's seat (**13**) passenger seat (**14**) guard rail (**15**) detachable awning (**16**) engine air intakes (**17**) fuel tank (**18**) silencer (**19**) storage batteries (**20**) anchor (**21**) lifebelt

CONTROLS: Craft heading is controlled by a single balanced rudder in solid aluminium alloy mounted aft of the rear foil main strut and operated by a steering wheel via a mechanical linkage. Other controls include a footpedal to control engine speed, and a reverse lever.

SYSTEMS, ELECTRICAL: Power is 24V dc. A 1kW engine-mounted generator supplies power while the craft is operating. Two 12V acid storage batteries, each of 180Ah capacity and connected in series to give 24V, supply power during stops.

FIREFIGHTING: An independent fluid fire-fighting system of aircraft type is installed in the engine bay and is operated remotely from the driving seat.

DIMENSIONS
Length overall: 10·9m (35ft 11in)
Hull beam: 2·7m (8ft 11in)
Beam overall: 4m (13ft 2in)
Draught, hullborne: 1·7m (5ft 3in)
    foilborne: 0·9m (2ft 9in)
WEIGHTS
Max take-off displacement: 5·9 tons
Displacement unloaded: 4·1 tons
Payload: 1·05 tons
PERFORMANCE
Cruising speed: 30 knots
Normal cruising range: 160 miles
Diameter of turn at max speed: 109m (357ft)
Take-off time: Approx 30 seconds
Max permissible wave height in foilborne mode: 1m (3ft 3in)
Fuel and lube oil endurance: 6 hours
Fuel consumption per hp at cruising rating: 178g/h

LASTOCHKA

In May 1981 it was announced that this craft was to be built to succeed the 71-seat Voskhod. Design speed is given as 90km/h (50 knots) and seating capacity 64. It has been reported that the first of the Lastochka class was launched in 1986.

ZENIT

Described as 'a second-generation fast passenger ferry', Zenit was reported in 1982 as being developed to replace Meteor. Design speed of the new craft is 90km/h (50 knots) compared with the 65km/h (35 knots) cruising speed of Meteor.

VOLGA 70

First export version of the Molnia sports hydrofoil, the Volga 70 incorporates various design refinements including a completely redesigned bow foil.

Powered by a 90hp Volvo Penta diesel engine it was introduced at the end of 1972. The cruising speed is 4km/h slower than that of the earlier model, but engine maintenance is easier and the acquisition of spares is simplified in many parts of the world. This model has been purchased by companies and individuals in the USA, West Germany, Sweden, Netherlands and Singapore.

A new export model of the Volga is due to be introduced. It will succeed both the Volga 70 and the Volga-275 described in *Jane's Surface Skimmers 1978*.

FOILS: The foil system consists of a bow foil with stabilising sub-foil and a rear foil assembly. The foils are of stainless steel.

HULL: Built in sheet and extruded light alloy, the hull is divided into three compartments by metal bulkheads. The forepeak is used for stores, the midship compartment is the open cockpit and the aft compartment houses the engine and gearbox.

ACCOMMODATION: Seats are provided for six: a driver and five passengers. The controls, instruments, magnetic compass and radio receiver are grouped on a panel ahead of the driver's seat. A full range of safety equipment is provided, including six life jackets, life line, fire extinguisher and distress flares. A folding awning can be supplied.

POWERPLANT: Power is supplied by a single Volvo Penta AQAD 32A/270TD diesel with a steerable outboard drive delivering 106hp at 4000rpm. Fuel capacity is 120 litres (26·4 gallons), sufficient for a range of 150 miles.

SYSTEMS, ELECTRICAL: 12V dc. Starting, instrument and navigation lights and siren, are provided by an engine-mounted generator and an acid stowage battery.

DIMENSIONS
Length overall: 8·55m (28ft 1in)
Beam: 2·1m (6ft 10⅜in)

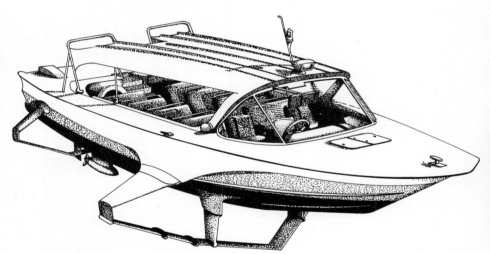

Perspective drawing of export model of Nevka showing foil details

Height above water when foilborne: 0·98m (3ft
  2⅜in)
Draught hullborne: 0·92m (3ft)
  foilborne: 0·52m (1ft 8½in)
WEIGHTS
Loaded displacement: 1930kg (4255lb)
Light displacement: 1350kg (2977lb)
PERFORMANCE
Max speed: 30 knots
Cruising speed: 28 knots
Range: 241km (150 miles)

Volga. Production is officially stated to have run
into 'several thousand'

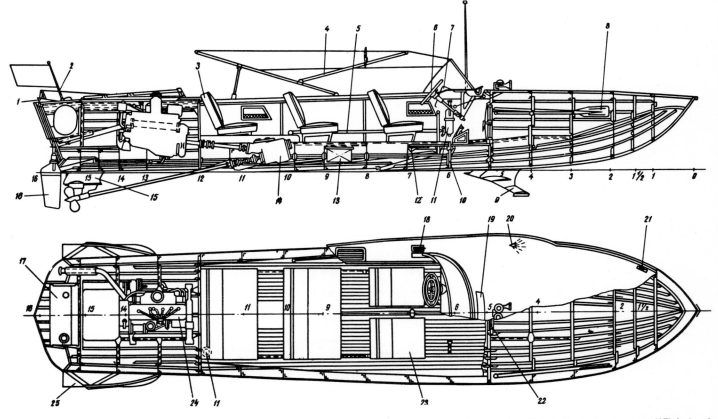

Inboard profile and plan of Volga 70:
(1) stern light **(2)** flag pole **(3)** bench seat **(4)** awning **(5)** dog hook **(6)** steering column **(7)** instrument panel **(8)** oar **(9)** bow foil assembly **(10)** anchor line **(11)** fire extinguisher OY-2 **(12)** anchor **(13)** storage battery **(14)** reduction and reverse gear **(15)** rear foil assembly **(16)** steering and rudder gear **(17)** fuel tank **(18)** cleat **(19)** air intake **(20)** side running light **(21)** fairlead **(22)** cover of first bulkhead hatch **(23)** seat **(24)** M652-Y six-cylinder automotive engine **(25)** foilguard

GOMEL YARD

Byelorussiya, USSR

BYELORUS

This craft was developed from the Raketa, via the Chaika, for fast passenger services on shallow winding rivers less than 1m (3ft 3in) deep and too shallow for conventional vessels.

It was put into series production at the river shipyard at Gomel, Byelorussiya in 1965. Byelorus was expected to be succeeded in service by the 53-seat Polesye.
FOILS: The shallow draught submerged foil system consists of one bow foil and one rear foil.
HULL: Hull and superstructure are built in aluminium magnesium alloy. The hull is of all-welded construction and the superstructure is riveted and welded.
ACCOMMODATION: Aircraft type seats for 40 passengers. The prototype seated only 30.
POWERPLANT: Power is supplied by an M-50 F-3 or M-400 diesel rated at 950hp maximum and with a normal service output of 600hp. The wheelhouse is fitted with an electro-hydraulic remote control system for the engine and fuel supply.

DIMENSIONS
Length overall: 18·55m (60ft 6in)
Hull beam: 4·64m (15ft 2in)
Height overall: 4·23m (13ft 11in)
Draught foilborne: 0·3m (1ft)
  hullborne: 0·9m (2ft 11in)
WEIGHTS
Light displacement: 9·6 tons
Take-off displacement: 14·5 tons
PERFORMANCE
Cruising speed: 60km/h (34 knots)

POLESYE

This shallow-draught hydrofoil craft is intended for the high-speed transportation of passengers and tourists during daylight hours in the upper reaches of major rivers, river tributaries and freshwater reservoirs in regions with temperate climate. The craft is classified ★R on the RSFSR Register of River Shipping and is suitable for use in conditions with a wave height of 0·5m when running on the hydrofoils, and with a wave height of up to 1·2m in the displacement mode.

Byelorus on Karakum Canal, Turkmenia

The craft has capacity for 53 passengers. The passengers are accommodated in a single lounge area in the midsection of the vessel. In calm waters with wind conditions up to Force 3, the vessel is capable of a speed of 65km/h. The vessel is capable of running on the hydrofoils on river channels with a radius of turn of up to 100-150m.

The time to accelerate from the stationary condition to becoming fully foilborne does not exceed 1·5 minutes. The distance from service speed to stop, with the propeller in reverse, is five to six boat lengths.

The hull is divided into five compartments by means of watertight bulkheads. The foils and side fenders are removable to facilitate overland transport. The vessel incorporates facilities for the prevention of environmental pollution and for the reduction of noise and vibration levels. The upholstered seats and wide windows in the lounge ensure that the passengers travel in comfort. The heating system for the vessel consists of water heating appliances and piping. The water is supplied from the internal circuit of the main engine. In the Autumn and Spring sailing periods, the air in the forced ventilation system is heated with a water heating appliance.

The vessel is powered by a 12-cylinder 'V' diesel engine with a maximum capacity of 810kW (1086bhp) at 1600rpm. The engine is installed at an angle of 12°30' to the horizontal and transmits power to the propeller via a direct-coupled reversing-gear unit.

Ship-to-shore communications are provided by an on-board fixed-frequency radio station, and for

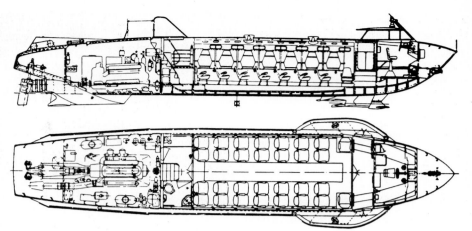

Profile and deck plan of Byelorus

public address and broadcasting purposes the vessel has a standard public-address and transmission broadcasting package. The vessel is supplied complete with supplies and spare parts in accordance with RSFSR River Register rules and with the boatbuilder's practice.

DIMENSIONS
Length, overall: 21·25m
Hull length, overall: 21·00m
Beam, overall: 5·0m
Hull width, overall: 3·60m
Hull height, midsection: 2·60m
Hull height, with deckhouse: 3·20m

Draught, extreme load (in displacement mode): 0·95m
Draught, extreme draught on hydrofoils: 0·40m
WEIGHTS
Displacement, light: 13·7 tonnes
Displacement, full load: 20·0 tonnes
PERFORMANCE
Range, full tanks: 400km
Endurance, full tanks: 8 hours
Speed, calm water, Beaufort Force 3: 35 knots (65km/h)
Sea State limits: Foilborne in waves up to 0·5m
Hullborne in waves up to 1·2m

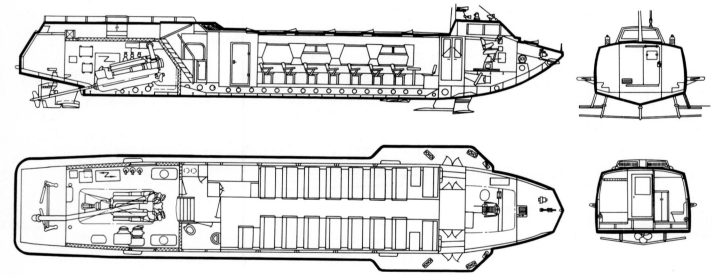

General Arrangement of Polesye

Polesye

Ś ORDZHONIKIDZE SHIP-BUILDING AND REPAIR YARD

Head Office and Yard: Poti, Georgia, USSR

Z N Archaidze, *Yard Director*
I Ye Malechanov, *Chief Designer*
Yu Golubkin, *Deputy Chief Designer*
B Pavlyuk, *Chief Engineer*
G A Terentyeb, *Manager, Sea Trials*

KOMETA

A large number of Kometas have been built at the Poti yard. Please see earlier entry in this section.

TSIKLON (CYCLONE)

An enlarged, double-deck derivative of the Kometa, the Cyclone seats 250 passengers and is propelled by waterjets driven by two 5000hp gas turbines, making it the most powerful Soviet commercial hydrofoil to date. Maximum speed is 45 to 50 knots and the cruising speed is 42 knots.

On completion of trials, the vessel was put into production at the S Ordzhonikidze Shipbuilding and Repair Yard at Poti.

The craft complies with the requirements of Class KM 2MA2 of the USSR Passenger Register. It also meets all the conditions of the Stability Specifications, USSR Shipping Register. It is designed to operate foilborne in waves up to 3m (9ft 10in) regardless of wave direction, and can operate hullborne in conditions up to Sea State 5. Foilborne range, fully-loaded, is 300n miles.
FOILS: Surface-piercing system of conventional configuration comprising two main foils, one at the bow and one at the stern; an amidship foil to assist take-off, a pitch stability sub-foil immediately aft of the bow foil, and the associated struts by which the foils are attached to the hull. A sonic/electronic autopilot system controls lift by operating trailing edge flaps on the central section of the bow foil and at both ends of the stern foil. Flap angles are variable in flight and provide a variation in the lift generated by the bow foil of ±35% and ±85% by the stern foil. The foil flaps are adjusted automatically to dampen heave, pitch, roll and yaw motions in heavy seas. A rudder is fitted to the central bow foil strut for improved manoeuvrability in congested waters. Main and stability foils are of welded construction. Bow and stern foil surfaces, flap tie-rods, the lower ends of the bow and stern foil struts, and the central bow foil strut are built in steel alloy. The amidship foil and struts, pitch stability foil and the upper sections of the bow and stern foil struts are in aluminium-magnesium alloy.
HULL: Twin-deck structure. All-welded construction, similar to that employed on Kometa series. Extensive use is made of pressed panels and rolled aluminium-magnesium alloy strip. Hull is framed on longitudinal and transverse formers. Below the main deck the hull is subdivided by 11 watertight bulkheads into 12 compartments. The craft will remain afloat with any two adjacent compartments flooded up to a total length of 9m—or 21% of the craft's overall length. To retard corrosion below the waterline, magnesium protectors are provided.

Kolkhida

POWERPLANT: Power for the waterjet propulsion system is supplied by two marinised gas turbines, each rated at 5000hp maximum and 4500hp continuous. Each unit has a gas-discharge device and the reduction gear rate of rotation at the power take-off shaft is 950rpm. The shafts of both gas turbines are each connected via flange couplings to the reduction gear of an axial-flow waterjet pump, each of the two pumps receiving water from a common intake. Fuel consumption per horsepower at continuous rating is 225g/h. Oil consumption of each gas turbine is 1·5kg/h and that of the reduction gear is 0·5kg/h. The service life of each gas turbine is 10 000 hours before the first overhaul.
ACCOMMODATION: Standard model is designed to carry a crew of 6 and 250 seated passengers. These saloons are provided on the main deck: a 46-seat bow saloon, a 66-seat amidships saloon and a 74-seat aft saloon. A further 64 are seated in a saloon on the top deck. A separate cabin is provided for the crew. Facilities include a luggage locker, a three-sided refreshment bar, a smaller bar and a promenade deck. Passenger saloons are fully air-conditioned and equipped with airliner-type seats arranged three abreast (32) and two abreast (77). Extensive use is made of heat, sound and vibration absorbing and insulation materials. Decks and serving spaces are overlaid with deep pile carpets. Captain and navigator are accommodated in a raised wheelhouse providing a 360-degree view. A remote control console in the wheelhouse is equipped with the necessary controls and instrumentation for the main and auxiliary engines, the autopilot system, manual steering and firefighting.
SYSTEMS, ELECTRICAL: APU drives two 14kW turbogenerators for 28·5V dc service and a 75kW diesel-generator set supplies alternating current at 230V and 50Hz. Two-wire, group-bus type distribution system.
HYDRAULICS: Three separate systems, the first for control of reversing gear, rudder and anchor winch; the second for control of the main engines and waterjet nozzles and the third for flap control.
COMMUNICATIONS: R/T simplex/duplex

single-band transceiver operating on 18 pre-selected frequencies in the 1·6 to 8·8MHz band and transmitting distress signals on 2182kHz and 3023·5kHz; VHF R/T transceiver operating on seven channels in the 156·3-156·8MHz band; portable lifeboat type radio, and a PA system.
NAVIGATION: Navigational radar, course indicating system with a steering repeater which automatically provides the course to be steered and transmits data to the repeater, magnetic compass, a log and an automatic steering and stabilisation system.
SAFETY EQUIPMENT: Ten 26-seat inflatable life rafts with provision for the automatic release of five (one side) at a time.
DIMENSIONS
Length overall: 49·9m (163ft 9in)
Width across foils: 13·2m (43ft 6in)
Hull beam: 8m (26ft 3in)
Height above water,
    foilborne (with folded mast): 9m (29ft 7in)
    hullborne: 6·4m (21ft)
Draught foilborne: 1·9m (6ft 3in)
    hullborne: 4·5m (14ft 9in)
WEIGHTS
Loaded displacement: 140 tonnes
Light displacement: 96·4 tonnes
Deadweight: 43·6 tonnes
PERFORMANCE
Max speed, foilborne: 45-50 knots
Cruising speed, foilborne: 42 knots
Endurance: 8 hours
Max wave height,
    foilborne: 3m (9ft 10in)
    hullborne: Sea State 5
Range: 300n miles

KOLKHIDA

Designed to replace the 20-year-old Kometa fast passenger ferry, Kolkhida is available in two versions: the Albatros, which will operate on domestic services within the Soviet Union, and the Kolkhida, intended for export. Keel for the prototype was laid at a ceremony attended by the First Secretary of the Central Committee of the Georgian Communist party in May 1980. The

Outboard profile of Cyclone

occasion also marked the entry of the craft into series production.

Kolkhida is faster than Kometa, seats more passengers, uses less fuel and can operate foilborne in higher Sea States. Among the various design innovations are a new foil system with automatic lift control, the use of new materials in the hull structure and a more rational cabin layout, permitting a substantial increase in seating capacity. The engine room is aft, as on the Voskhod, to reduce the noise level. Overall dimensions are almost identical to those of Kometa-M.

Trials of the Kolkhida prototype took place in the Baltic between March and June 1981 and the vessel has been in production since with sales being achieved in Greece, Italy and Yugoslavia. The craft meets the requirements of the Register of Shipping of the USSR and is constructed to Hydrofoil Class KM★ 2 A2 Passenger Class SPK under the Register's technical supervision. It complies fully with the IMO Code of Safety for Dynamically Supported Craft.

Kolkhida is designed to operate under tropical and moderate climates up to 50 miles from a port of refuge in open seas and up to 100 miles from a port of refuge in inland seas and large lakes, with a permissible distance between two ports of refuge of not more than 200 miles.

Foilborne, the craft can operate in waves up to 2m and winds up to Force 5; hullborne it can operate in waves up to 3m and winds up to Force 6. FOILS: The foil system, which is similar to that of Kometa, comprises a trapeze-type bow foil, an aft and an amidship foil, close to the longitudinal centre of gravity to assist take-off. The foils are connected to the hull by struts and brackets. A sonic/electronic autopilot controls lift by operating trailing edge flaps on the centre section of the bow foil and on the inner sections of the aft foil. The foil flaps are adjusted hydraulically to dampen heave, pitch, roll and yaw motions in heavy seas and provide co-ordinated turns. Bow and

Kolkhida

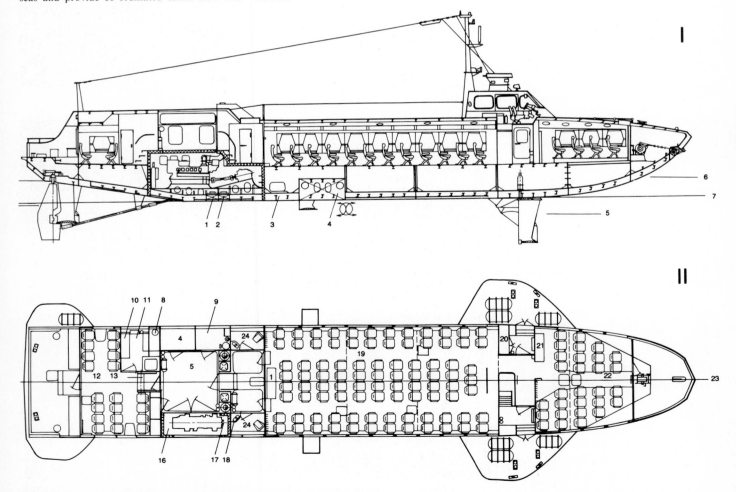

Kolkhida (area shown occupied by seats rows 12 and 13 is now a bar)
Longitudinal section: (1) waste oil collection tank (2) oil-containing water tank (3) sewage water tank (4) fuel tank (5) waterline when foilborne (6) waterline when hullborne (7) base line
Main deck plan: (8) hydraulic station (9) fuel and oil filling, waste water scavenging, fire-fighting station (10) conditioner (11) control post (12) 20-seat passenger saloon (13) VP (14) luggage room (15) promenade platform (16) auxiliary unit room (17) gas exhaust trunk (18) air intake trunk (19) 91-seat passenger saloon (20) Aggregate room (21) conditioner (22) 29-seat passenger saloon (23) central line (24) toilet

Kolkhida

stern foil surfaces and the lower ends of the bow
and stern foil struts are in steel alloy. The amidship
foil, struts, upper sections of the bow and stern foil
struts are in aluminium-magnesium alloy. A cast,
balanced rudder in 40mm thick aluminium-magnesium alloy is fitted. Total blade area is 2·75m².
Rudder movement is controlled hydraulically by
any one of three systems: push-button, manual or
via the autopilot.

HULL: Double-chine, V-bottom type, with raked
stern and streamlined superstructure. Hull and
superstructure are built in aluminium-magnesium
alloys. Framing is based on T and T-angle
webframes. Frame spacing is 600mm.
Longitudinal framing of the sides, decks and hull
bottom is based on stiffening ribs, keelson,
stringers and deck girders. Below the main deck

the hull is subdivided by watertight bulkheads into
nine compartments. The craft will remain afloat
with any two adjacent compartments flooded.

POWERPLANT: Power is supplied by two MTU
12V 396 TC82 water-cooled, supercharged 12-
cylinder V-type four-stroke marine diesels, each
with a normal service output of 960kW (1300hp),
1745rpm and 1050kW (1430hp), 1800rpm maximum. Guaranteed service life of each engine
before first major overhaul is 9000 hours; maximum service life is 12 years. Output is transferred
to twin 740mm diameter contra-rotating fixed-
pitch propellers through reversible gearboxes
which are remotely controlled from the
wheelhouse. The propeller shafts are inclined at 14
degrees and supported by rubber and metal
bearings.

Kolkhida forward starboard foils and struts

Kolkhida aft foil arrangement

Port double entrance doors on Kolkhida

Controls and instruments in Kolkhida wheelhouse

Interior of Kolkhida cabin

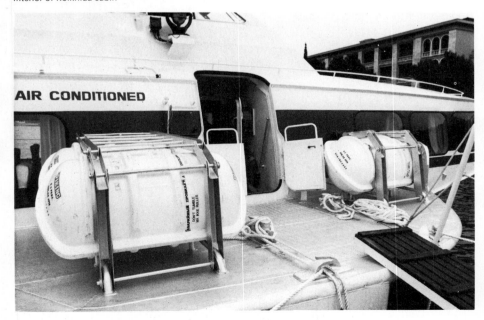

Liferaft installation on Kolkhida

ACCOMMODATION: Standard passenger-ferry version is designed to carry an operating crew of six and 120 passengers. A tourist sight-seeing version seats 150. Crew comprises a captain/engineer, two motormen, one seaman, one seaman/radio operator and a barman. On the tourist version, no barman is carried. Embark-ation platforms immediately below the wheelhouse provide access for passengers and crew. Captain and engineer are accommodated in a raised wheelhouse between the forward and main saloon.

The wheelhouse contains a radar display and radio-communications equipment. Main engine controls are installed in both the wheelhouse and engine room. Passengers are accommodated in three air-conditioned compartments, a forward saloon seating 29, a middle saloon seating 91 and an aft saloon with 20 seats. Facilities include two promenade decks, one immediately aft of the main saloon above the engine room, the other on the weather deck at the stern, toilets and a buffet/bar. Passenger saloons are equipped with airliner-type, reclining-back seats arranged four, three or two abreast. Extensive use is made of heat, sound and vibration absorbing and insulating materials. Decks in saloons and serving places are carpeted.

APU: Combined unit comprises a four-cylinder diesel engine rated at 33kW, a six-cylinder freon compressor, a 4·5kW 27·5 dc generator, a self-priming pump and a starting air compressor. Unit supplies electric power to shipboard consumers, operates air-conditioning system and replenishes starting bottles with compressed air.

SYSTEMS, ELECTRICAL: Engine-driven gen-erators supply power while the craft is operating. The 4·5kW generator included in the auxiliary unit supplies power when the craft is at rest. Acid storage batteries connected in series supply power during short stops.

ANCHOR: Single Matrosov 75kg main anchor and LGY 20 M1 hydraulic windlass. Also appro-priate mooring, towing and anchoring equipment.

COMMUNICATIONS: Radio transmitter/receiver with r/t and w/t facilities is installed in the wheelhouse for the ship-to-shore and inter-ship communications on SW and MW bands. Unified communications and relay equipment provides simplex command communication between wheelhouse, engine room, stern, control post, forward embarkation platforms and anchor winch compartment as well as relaying broadcasts and information announcements to the passenger saloons.

NAVIGATION: Gyrocompass, magnetic com-pass and log are standard.

AIR-CONDITIONING: Anton Kaiser-type module, comprising 33kW four-cylinder diesel, six-cylinder Freon compressor, a 27·5V, 4·5kW dc generator, self-priming circulating pump and start-ing compressor, all mounted on a single frame.

HYDRAULICS: System for operating rudder, foil flaps and windlass.

SAFETY EQUIPMENT: Six 25-seat inflatable life rafts in addition to life jackets, life belts, life lines and self-igniting buoyant lights. Chemical- and foam-type fire-extinguishing system installed throughout vessel.

DIMENSIONS
Length overall: 34·5m (113ft 3in)
Beam overall: 10·3m (33ft 10in)
  hull: 5·8m (19ft)
Height overall from water level, hullborne: 8·9m (29ft 3in)
  foilborne: 10·8m (35ft 10in)
Draught, hullborne: 3·5m (11ft 6in)
  foilborne: 1·9m (6ft 3in)
GRT: 143
WEIGHTS
Light displacement: 56·0 tonnes
Fully-loaded displacement: 72 tonnes
PERFORMANCE
Cruising speed, fully loaded: 34 knots
Take-off time: 20-40 seconds
Hullborne speed: 12 knots
Range, on foils: Over 150n miles
Specific fuel consumption: 215g/kW/h

MILITARY CRAFT
PCHELA (BEE)

This military derivative of the Strela is in service with the KGB for frontier patrol duties in the Baltic and Black Seas. Twenty-five were built between 1968 and 1972, but it is believed that only four remain in service.

POWERPLANT: One 4000bhp M-503 diesel.
ARMAMENT: Two twin 23mm AA mounts with remote optical director and two-to-four depth charges.
RADAR: Surface search and navigation, Pot Drum. IFF, High Pole B.
SONAR: Dipping type.
DIMENSIONS
Length overall: 27m (88ft 7in)
Hull beam: 6m (19ft 8in)
Width across foils: 8m (26ft 3in)
Draught, hull: 1m (3ft 4in)
  foils: 2·6m (8ft 7in)
WEIGHTS
Fully loaded: 75 tonnes
Standard: 60 tonnes
PERFORMANCE
Max speed: 42 knots

TURYA

Based on the well-proven Osa missile-firing FPB hull, Turya is equipped with a fixed, surface-piercing V or trapeze foil set back approximately one-third of the hull length from the bow. At 25 knots, in relatively calm conditions, the foil system generates sufficient lift to raise the forward hull clear of the water, providing a 'sprint' speed of 40 to 45 knots.

In addition to improving the maximum speed, the foils reduce the vessel's wave impact response, thus enhancing its performance as a weapon platform.

The installation of a dipping sonar on the transom suggests that the primary duty of Turya is anti-submarine patrol. The main armament appears to comprise four 53cm ASW or anti-ship

Craft built

Type	Name	Built	Operator
Kolkhida		1983	Black Sea Shipping Co, Odessa, USSR
Kolkhida	2	1984	Black Sea Shipping Co, Odessa, USSR
Kolkhida	3	1984	Black Sea Shipping Co, Odessa, USSR
Kolkhida	4	1984	Black Sea Shipping Co, Odessa, USSR
Kolkhida	5	1984	Black Sea Shipping Co, Odessa, USSR
Kolkhida	6	1985	Black Sea Shipping Co, Odessa, USSR
Kolkhida	*Magnolija*	1986	Kvarner Express, Yugoslavia
Kolkhida	*Kamelija*	1986	Kvarner Express, Yugoslavia
Kolkhida	*Mirta*	1986	Kvarner Express, Yugoslavia
Kolkhida	*Mimosa*	1986	Kvarner Express, Yugoslavia
Kolkhida	*Aliatlante*	June 1986	Alilauro Aliscafi del Tirreno SpA, Italy
Kolkhida	*Alieolo*	July 1986	Alilauro Aliscafi del Tirreno SpA, Italy
Kolkhida	*Flying Dolphin XVII*	1986	Ceres Flying Hydroways Ltd, Piraeus, Greece
Kolkhida	*Flying Dolphin XVIII*	1986	Ceres Flying Hydroways Ltd, Piraeus, Greece
Kolkhida	*Flying Dolphin XIX*	1986	Ceres Flying Hydroways Ltd, Piraeus, Greece
Kolkhida	*Aligea*	1986	Alivit Due, Italy

torpedoes in single fixed tubes, a forward 25mm twin mount and a twin 57mm AA mount aft.

The first of this class was launched in 1972. About 30 are in service. Eight have been supplied to the Cuban Navy.

Later versions are equipped with semi-retractable foils permitting the overall width to be reduced, thus enabling craft to be taken alongside conventional berthing facilities.

FOILS: Single main foil of trapeze configuration set back one-third of hull length from bow. Raises greater part of hull bottom clear of the water in calm conditions at speed of about 25 knots depending on sea conditions and loading. Similar system employed earlier on Soviet 'P8' class, now retired, and on the highly successful Chinese 'Hu Chwan' class.
HULL: Standard Osa hull, welded steel construction.

POWERPLANT: Three M-504 high performance radial-type diesels, each developing 5000hp and driving variable-pitch propellers through inclined shafts.
ARMAMENT: One twin 57mm dual-purpose gun with Muff Cob radar control and one remote optical director and one twin 25mm AA mount with local control. Mounts for SA-7 Grail light AA missile launcher and four 53cm ASW or anti-ship torpedoes. Latest variants fitted with twin 30mm fully-automatic dual purpose mount forward.
Navigation radar: Pot Drum
Fire-control radar: Muff Cob
Sonar: One dipping-type
ECM/ESM: One High Pole transponder and one Square Head interrogator.
DIMENSIONS
Length: 39·3m (128ft 11in)

Pchela

Turya

Beam: 7·7m (25ft 1in)
Width across foils: 12·3m (40ft 5in)
Draught, hull: 3m (9ft 11in)
    foils: 3·8m (12ft 6in)
WEIGHTS
Max loaded displacement: 250 tonnes
Standard: 200 tonnes
PERFORMANCE
Max speed foilborne: 40-45 knots

MATKA

A missile-equipped fast strike craft built at the Izhora Yard, Leningrad, Matka is designed to replace the 20-year-old Osa fast patrol boat and is based on the standard 39·3m Osa steel hull. A fixed surface-piercing trapeze foil is fitted at the bow to increase its speed in the lower sea states and reduce its wave impact response thereby improving its performance as a weapon platform. At a speed of between 24 to 28 knots, depending on sea conditions and loading, the bow foil generates sufficient lift to raise a substantial part of the forward hull clear of the water thus reducing hydrodynamic drag and providing a 'sprint' speed of 40 to 45 knots.

The Matka prototype was launched in 1977 and series production began in the spring of 1978. At least eight are in service.

FOILS: Single main foil of trapeze configuration, set back one-quarter of hull length from bow, raises much of the hull clear of the water in relatively calm conditions at speeds of 24 to 28 knots depending on sea conditions and loading. Similar to system proven on Chinese 'Hu Chwan' class and Soviet Turya. Latest version of Turya is equipped with semi-retractable foils, thereby reducing the overall width and enabling craft to be taken alongside conventional jetties, piers and other vessels without damaging the foil tips. Matka is likely to employ similar foil arrangement.

HULL: Standard Osa hull, welded steel construction.

POWERPLANT: Three 3700kW (5000hp) M-504 radial-type high-performance diesels, each driving a variable-pitch propeller through an inclined shaft.

ACCOMMODATION: Living, messing and berthing spaces for crew of 33.

ARMAMENT: Two SS-N-2C surface-to-surface missiles; one 76mm dual-purpose cannon; one six-barrelled ADMG-630 Gatling-type 30mm cannon for close-in AA defence and one mount for SA-7 Grail light AA missile launcher to counter attacks by low-flying subsonic aircraft.

CHAFF: Two 16-tube chaff launchers.
NAVIGATION RADAR: Cheese Cake.
SURFACE SEARCH: Plank Shave.
FIRE CONTROL: Bass Tilt.
ECM/ESM: One High Pole transponder and one Square Head interrogator.
COMMUNICATIONS: Cage Bear.
DIMENSIONS
Length: 39·3m (128ft 11in)
Hull beam: 7·7m (25ft 3in)
Width across foils: 12·3m (40ft 5in)
Draught, hull: 3m (9ft 10in)
    foils: 3·8m (12ft 6in)
WEIGHTS
Displacement, full load: 260 tonnes
    standard: 225 tonnes
PERFORMANCE
Max speed foilborne: 40-45 knots
Range: 750n miles at 24 knots

SARANCHA (NATO Code Name)

A fast strike missile craft, the 330-tonne Sarancha is one of the world's biggest naval hydrofoils. Designed and built at Petrovsky, Leningrad, in 1976 the craft is armed with four SS-N-9 anti-ship missiles, an SA-N-4 ship-to-air missile system and a 30mm Gatling-type rapid-fire cannon. The foil system is fully retractable to simplify slipping and docking. Autostabilisation equipment is fitted as well as an autopilot and the latest navigation, target detection and fire control systems.

Operational evaluation trials with the Soviet Navy began in the eastern Baltic in mid-1977.

Matka   (Danish Defence)

Matka on patrol in Baltic Sea   (Royal Swedish Air Force)

Matka in Baltic Sea

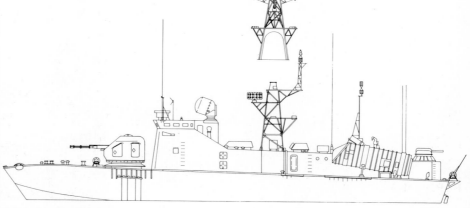

Outboard profile of Matka

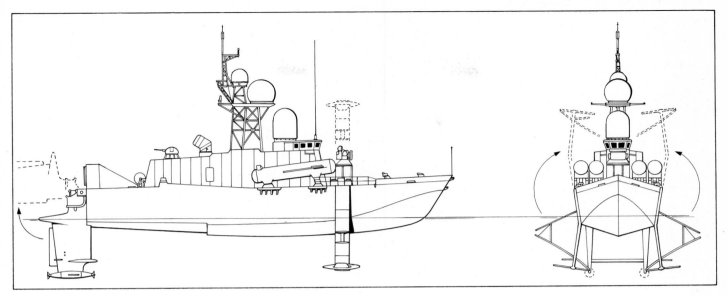

Provisional elevation and bow-on view of Sarancha

FOILS: Combined surface-piercing and submerged system. The bow foil, which provides the necessary transverse stability, is of split-V surface-piercing type and carries about 60% of the load and the single fully submerged rear foil supports the remaining 40%. The rear foil is supported by two vertical struts, each of which carries a twin propeller pod assembly at its base. The struts also carry the vertical shafts and second bevel gears of the Z-drive systems which transmit power from the gas turbines in the hull to the propellers. A sonic/electronic autopilot system controls lift by operating trailing edge flaps on the aft foil. Single rudders, which act individually for port or starboard turns, are fitted to the trailing edges of the aft foil struts. All three foil/strut units retract completely clear of the water, the two elements of the 'split V' bow foil sideways and the aft foil rearwards and upwards.

POWERPLANT: Foilborne power is believed to be provided by two NK-12MV marinised gas turbines, each delivering 12 to 15 000hp. Power is transmitted to the two propellers at the base of each strut through two sets of bevel gears and two vertical shafts to the nacelle. The central compartment of this contains the lower reduction gear which transmits power from the vertical shafts to the propeller shafts. The power transmission system is thought to have been derived from that employed on the Typhoon commercial hydrofoil, also built in Leningrad.

ARMAMENT: Four SS-N-9 Siren anti-ship missiles on four lightweight launchers amidship, one twin SA-N-4 surface-to-air missile launcher with 15 to 20 missiles on forward deck and one 30mm Gatling-type rapid-fire AA cannon aft. The SS-N-9s are activated by a Band Stand radar, the SA-N-4 launcher is controlled by a Pop Group radar and the 30mm cannon has a Bass Tilt fire control. The SA-N-4 may have limited surface-to-surface capability. The craft also carries Fish Bowl fire-control radar, a Band Stand radar for air search, one High Pole transponder and one Square Head interrogator for ECM/ESM. A new type of navigation and surface radar is carried.

DIMENSIONS
Length overall: 45m (147ft 8in)
Length, foils extended: 51m (167ft 4in)
Width, foils extended: 23m (75ft 6in)
Hull beam: 10m (32ft 9½in)
Width across foils: 24m (78ft 9in)
Draught hullborne, foils retracted: 2·5m (8ft 3in)
  foilborne: 3·5m (11ft 6in)
WEIGHT
Estimated normal take-off displacement: 330 tonnes
PERFORMANCE
Max speed foilborne: 50 knots plus

BABOCHKA

The world's largest and most powerful operational hydrofoil warship, this vessel is designed

Sarancha, 330-tonne missile armed fast attack craft (DpA)

Stern view of Babochka

Outboard profile of Babochka

for anti-submarine warfare. Motive power for its foilborne propulsion system appears to comprise three NK-12MV marinised aircraft gas turbines, each delivering between 12 000 to 15 000shp.

Combustion air for the three gas turbines is fed through a large inlet occupying the aft end of the

Babochka (Butterfly)

deckhouse. Exhaust discharge to atmosphere is via three angled funnels on the aft deck. If propeller driven, either V- or Z-drives are likely to have been employed so as to provide as great a clearance height as possible.

FOILS: Conventional configuration, with a surface-piercing bow foil and fully-submerged rear foil, and an automatic sonic/electronic control system operating trailing edge flaps on each foil.

ARMAMENT: Two six-barrelled 30mm Gatling-action guns for AA defence, activated by a Bass Tilt fire control radar or a remote optical director and eight 40cm AS torpedoes in two quadruple mounts immediately ahead of the superstructure between the deckhouse and the forward 30mm mount. Dipping sonar is also installed. Electronic

equipment includes High Pole B IFF, Square Head and Peel Cone radar.

DIMENSIONS
Length overall: 50m (164ft)

WEIGHTS
Normal take-off displacement: About 400 tonnes

PERFORMANCE
Max speed foilborne: 50 knots plus

UNITED STATES OF AMERICA

BOEING AEROSPACE COMPANY

Head Office: PO Box 3999, Seattle, Washington 98124, USA

Telephone: (206) 655 1414

Robert J Quinn, *Navy Systems*

The Boeing Company has conducted research, development, design, manufacture and the testing of high performance marine vehicles systems. Boeing's entry into the hydrofoil field was announced in June 1960, when the company was awarded a US $2 million contract for the construction of the US Navy's 120-ton PCH-1 *High Point*, a canard design which was the outcome of experiments with a similar arrangement in the US Navy test craft, Sea Legs.

Boeing also built a jet-driven hydroplane, the Hydrodynamic Test System (HTS), for testing foil models at full-scale velocity; the *Fresh-1*, a manned craft for testing superventilating or supercavitating foils at speeds between 60 and 100 knots, and a waterjet test vehicle, *Little Squirt*. Descriptions of *Fresh-1* and *Little Squirt* appear in *Jane's Surface Skimmers 1970-71* and earlier editions. The company also completed a highly successful waterjet-propelled gunboat, the PGH-2 *Tucumcari*, for the US Navy's Ship Systems Command. Its operational trials included several months of combat evaluation in Vietnam as part of the US Navy's coastal surveillance force. A full technical description of *Tucumcari* appeared in *Jane's Surface Skimmers 1974-75* and earlier editions. Data provided by the vessel assisted the design and development of the NATO/PHM, which is a 'scaled-up' *Tucumcari*, and the Jetfoil commercial hydrofoil.

High Point was modified by Boeing during 1972 to incorporate a new automatic control system, modified struts and foils, a new diesel for hullborne propulsion and a steerable forward strut for improved manoeuvrability. The craft was returned to the US Navy as Mod-1 configuration. In its revised form it was employed as a testbed for hydrofoil weapons compatibility.

In April 1975, the PCH was operated by the US Coast Guard for one month as part of a continuing research and development programme to evaluate high-speed water craft for the US Coast

PHM-2 USS *Hercules*

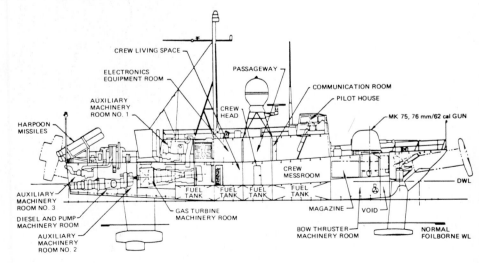

Inboard profile of PHM-3

Guard. Operating in Puget Sound and around San Francisco, the craft was employed on fisheries patrol, marine environmental protection and search and rescue missions.

In 1979 the PCH-1 was selected as the research and development vehicle for demonstrating the feasibility of the US Navy's Extended Performance Hydrofoil (EPH) project.

In January 1973 the keel was laid for the first 110-ton 250-seat Model 929-100 Jetfoil passenger ferry. The hull was assembled in a former 727 assembly building at Renton, Washington, and the first craft was launched in March 1974 on Lake Washington, which is adjacent to the plant. Ten Jetfoils of this type are in commercial service. Jetfoil 0011, which was launched in June 1978, is the first Jetfoil of improved design. This version, known as the Model 929-115, has improved performance, payload and reliability. By 30 June 1986, Jetfoils had logged 1700 million passenger miles during 295 000 under way hours, with a dispatch reliability of 99 per cent.

An order for the first fast patrol craft version of the Jetfoil was placed by the Royal Navy in 1978. This was a modified commercial Jetfoil, named HMS *Speedy*, and built on the commercial Jetfoil production line. Two Allison 501-K20A gas turbines are installed in this variant for foilborne operation and two Allison 8V-92T1 diesels for hullborne operation, giving added time on-station and increased endurance. HMS *Speedy* was commissioned by the Royal Navy in June 1980 but was subsequently decommissioned in April 1982 due to defence cuts.

In April 1973 US Naval Ship Systems Command awarded the company a US $42 602 384 contract for the design and development of the 235-tonne NATO/PHM missile-equipped patrol boat, under the terms of which Boeing was to build the lead craft for the US Navy for evaluation.

The PHM was the first US Navy craft to be designed on the basis of a co-operative technical interchange between the USA and its allies within NATO.

The first PHM, *Pegasus*, was launched in November 1974. Delivery to the US Navy took place in late 1976 and the craft completed its acceptance trials at Seattle in early June 1977.

In August 1977 it was announced by the US Defense Secretary that the US Navy would receive five more PHMs, the last of which was delivered in September 1982. The five production craft and *Pegasus* are assigned to a PHM squadron operating out of Key West, Florida.

In June 1985 Boeing announced a decision to focus sales efforts on the military hydrofoil market. Sales efforts for commercial passenger Jetfoils were suspended. Boeing continues to provide full service support to all existing hydrofoil operations and to market the PHM and Jetfoil derivatives for patrol and military roles. The decision reflected Boeing forecasts that commercial sales prospects did not warrant a continuing investment of management and resources to support both military and commercial lines. Both PAL of Indonesia and Kawasaki of Japan have been licensed for the production of Jetfoil craft.

Discussions between Boeing and the US Navy are continuing toward follow-on acquisitions of PHMs.

PCH-1 *HIGH POINT*

The PCH-1 *High Point* was accepted by the US Navy in August 1963 and used to evaluate the performance of an inshore hydrofoil ASW system. During April 1975 it was employed by the US Coast Guard in Puget Sound and off San Francisco. A full description of the craft can be found in *Jane's Surface Skimmers 1984* and earlier editions. *High Point* has been decommissioned but continues to be operated by Boeing for the David Taylor Naval Ship Research and Development Center (DTNSRDC) special trials unit.

PCH-1 *HIGH POINT* EPH FEASIBILITY DEMONSTRATOR PROJECT DESIGN

A description of this design investigation is given in *Jane's Surface Skimmers 1985* and earlier editions.

PGH-2 *TUCUMCARI*

A full technical description of this vessel appeared in *Jane's Surface Skimmers 1974-75* and earlier editions.

PHM-3 USS *Taurus*

Wheelhouse of PHM-3 USS *Taurus*

PHM-3 USS *Taurus*

NATO/PHM

Craft built	Commissioned
PHM-1 USS *Pegasus*	July 1977
PHM-2 USS *Hercules*	September 1982
PHM-3 USS *Taurus*	October 1981
PHM-4 USS *Aquila*	January 1982
PHM-5 USS *Aries*	May 1982
PHM-6 USS *Gemini*	13 November 1982

The NATO Hydrofoil Fast Patrol Ship Guided Missile (NATO/PHM) originated in mid-1969 when C-in-C South presented to NATO a requirement for a large number of fast patrol boats to combat the threat posed by missile-armed fast patrol boats in the Mediterranean.

The concept of a common fast patrol boat was studied, and in September 1970 it was decided that the submerged foil craft of 140 tons proposed by the US Navy was the vessel most suited to NATO mission requirements. In October 1971 the USA indicated that it would proceed at its own expense with the design of the vessel and share the results of the studies with those nations wishing to purchase PHMs. It also offered to conduct all aspects of design and development, contracting and management in co-operation with governments entering into project membership. Costs would be reimbursed only by those nations engaged in the project.

In November 1971 the US Navy awarded Boeing a US $5·6 million contract for the preliminary design of a 230-ton craft and the purchase of mechanical and electronic components for at least two PHMs. Seventeen months later, Boeing was awarded a US $42 607 384 contract for the design and development of the PHM for NATO navies. Under the terms of the contract the first craft, the *Pegasus*, was built for the US Navy.

Pegasus was launched in November 1974 and made its first foilborne flight in February 1975. It achieved its classified designed speed, completed the Navy-conducted phase of testing its weapons and then began operational evaluation in the San Diego area in autumn 1975.

It completed its acceptance trials during the first week of June 1977 and was commissioned into service in July 1977, becoming the first hydrofoil officially designated a United States Ship (USS *Pegasus*). Rear Admiral John Bulkeley, USN, President, Naval Board of Inspection and Survey, recorded that it had demonstrated 'superb reliability throughout her trial with no major or significant breakdowns or failures'.

The first squadron of PHMs consists of the USS *Pegasus* and its five sister ships, *Taurus*, *Aquila*, *Aries*, *Gemini* and *Hercules*, plus the PHM Mobile Logistic Support Group (MLSG) and the Squadron Commander's staff. An interim MLSG was established to support *Pegasus* and comprised one officer and 28 enlisted personnel operating from six standard 40ft (12·1m) containers and three roadable trailers fitted to provide shop, office and training space and stowage for spares and food stores. During the second phase of the squadron build-up a converted 1178 Class LST, to be known as a Hydrofoil Support Ship (AGHS), was to be made available. This would have provided all the facilities available from the van complex plus the basic fuel and other services now provided from ashore.

However, the AGHS has been deleted from the US Navy budget and a mobile complex comprising 2·4 × 2·4 × 6m (8 × 8 × 20ft) ISO standard vans has been procured and installed at Key West. The vans are equipped to provide maintenance, workshops, equipment stores, training classrooms and on-shore messing facilities.

All of the production craft are armed with a 75mm OTO Melara dual-purpose rapid-fire cannon and eight Harpoon anti-ship missiles in two four-tube lightweight canister launchers. Construction of PHM-2 *Hercules* began in May 1974 but was stopped in 1975, eventually being delivered in September 1982. All five craft were built by Boeing Marine Systems at its hydrofoil assembly plant at Renton, Washington, adjacent to Lake Washington. USS *Pegasus* was operationally assigned to the Atlantic Fleet at Key West, Florida in July 1980.

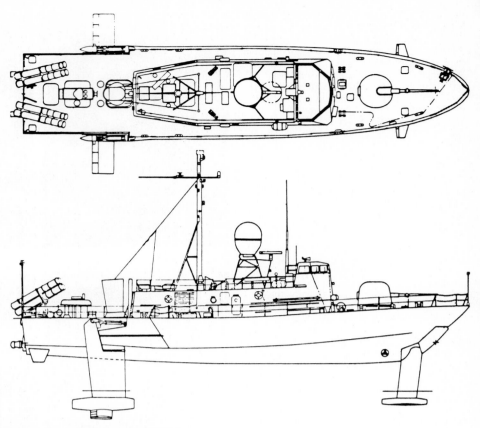

Outboard profile and deck plan of PHM-3

Boeing PHM-5 USS *Aries*

The PHM has sufficient design flexibility to allow for individual variations by any country. These variations will be primarily in the weapons systems installed, and the participating nations, current and future, can acquire the standard PHM carrying whatever combat equipment is determined necessary to meet national requirements.

PHM's potential in terms of strategic mobility was demonstrated between 30 September and 1 October 1975, when *Pegasus* completed the 1225 nautical miles from Seattle to San Diego in the record-breaking time of less than 34 hours, which included a refuelling stop at Eureka, California.

With the aid of midway refuelling the craft is capable of crossing oceans with fast carrier task groups, convoys of merchant ships and amphibious assault groups. With three under way refuellings, it can cross the Atlantic from Massachusetts to the United Kingdom at an average speed of 30 knots in 4·2 days, or it could cross from Norfolk, Virginia to Cadiz in 4·6 days with four under way refuellings.

PHM was designed to be self-supporting at sea for a period of five days although ten-day (and more) versions are routinely carried out. For extended periods, or during intensive operations, it is refuelled under way with either JP-5 or Naval Distillate (DFM) by oilers, major combatants and carriers.

PHM can be adapted for such roles as antisubmarine warfare, fisheries law enforcement and the protection of offshore resources.

The standard PHM is approximately 40·5m (132ft 10in) long, has a beam of 8·6m (28ft 2in) and a full load displacement of about 241 tonnes (238 tons). Foilborne range is in excess of 500n miles at speeds in excess of 40 knots in 2·4 to 3·6m (8 to 12ft) seas. The hull form and size, the major structural bulkheads and decks, foils and struts, waterjets, pumps, controls and main propulsion machinery are identical. The auxiliary equipment and arrangements, deckhouse and crew accommodation are also of standard design, but variations in the latter are possible to suit the manning requirements of individual countries.

FOILS: Fully-submerged canard arrangement

with approximately 31·8 per cent of the dynamic lift provided by the bow foil and 68·2 per cent by the aft foil. The aft foil retracts rearwards and the bow foil retracts forward into a recess in the bow. Bow doors preserve the hull lines when the forward foil is either fully extended or retracted. The foils and struts are in 17-4 PH martensitic, precipitation hardening stainless steel. Both forward and aft foils are welded assemblies consisting of spars, ribs, and skin. Flaps are fitted to the trailing edges to provide control and lift augmentation at take-off and during flight. The bow foil system incorporates a strut that rotates to provide directional control and reliable turning rates in heavy seas.

The shallow M or inverted double pi configuration of the aft foil is designed for improved hydroelastic and turning characteristics. The primary strut structure consists of spars, ribs and skin welded into watertight assemblies. The struts are designed as beam columns, and rigidly attached to the foil support structure at the hull.

The struts are attached to the hull with pivot pins that allow the foils to rotate clear of the water. Hydraulic actuators are used for retraction and extension, mechanical stops and position locks being employed to secure the foils in either position.

CONTROLS, FOILBORNE: The helm, throttle and an automatic control system (ACS) provide continuous dynamic control during take-off, foilborne operation and landing. Once take-off is complete, the ACS requires no attention by the crew. It controls the craft by sensing craft attitude, motion rates and acceleration, then comparing them electronically with desired values. Any deviations are processed by analogue control computer which generates electrical commands causing hydraulic actuators to reposition the control surfaces, thus minimising detected errors. The foilborne control surfaces are trailing edge flaps on each of the foils, plus the rotating bow foil strut which acts as the foilborne rudder.

Manual controls and displays for both hullborne and foilborne conditions are concentrated at the helm station and include the wheel, a foil-depth selector, a foil-depth indicator, a ship-heading indicator and a heading holding switch.

CONTROLS, HULLBORNE: Steering control in the hullborne mode is provided by steerable nozzles which rotate electro-hydraulically in response to the wheel. An automatic heading control, similar to that employed for foilborne operation, is incorporated, together with the necessary heading reference provided by the gyrocompass.

POWERPLANT, FOILBORNE: The foilborne propulsion system comprises a single 17 000shp, coaxial two-stage, two-speed waterjet, driven through two sets of reduction gears by a single General Electric LM 2500 marine gas turbine, developed from the GE TF39, which powers the US Air Force's C-5 transport and the DC-10 Trijet.

PHM-1 uses only 16 200hp from the engine while production craft use 17 000hp. Full use of the 30 000hp potential is possible in the future, although the gearbox will have to be redesigned to absorb this power.

Both the foilborne and hullborne propulsion systems were designed by Aerojet Liquid Rocket Company, Sacramento, California, under a Boeing contract.

The single foilborne propulsion pump is capable of handling 90 000 gallons/minute and the two hullborne pumps will each operate at approximately 30 000 gallons/minute.

Engine installation and removal for overhaul is accomplished through hatches in the main deck between the deckhouse and exhaust outlet.

Normal fuel is diesel oil MIL-F-16884 (NATO F-76) or JP-5 MIL-J-5624 (NATO F-44).

POWERPLANT, HULLBORNE: Twin Aerojet waterjet pumps powered by two 800hp Mercedes-Benz 8V331TC80 diesels propel the vessel when hullborne. Each waterjet propulsor has nozzle steering and reversing buckets. The hullborne system provides long-range cruising and slow-speed manoeuvring, while the gas turbine is

available when required for high-speed foilborne operation.

HULL: Hull and deckhouses are all-welded structures in AL 5456 alloy.

ACCOMMODATION: Crew will average 21 officers and men, but will vary according to the armament carried up to a total of 24. Accommodation on the US Navy version is provided for five officers—the commanding officer has a separate cabin—four chief petty officers and 15 enlisted men. The superstructure accommodates the bridge, which contains steering and engine control consoles and is elevated to provide a 360-degree view. A short ladder from the bridge leads down to the command and surveillance deckhouse that accommodates the fire-control, radar, communications and navigation equipment. The size of the deckhouse provides flexibility in accommodating various national equipment requirements. The space aft of the superstructure and forward of the foilborne engine exhaust is used to erect rigging for replenishment and refuelling.

Below the main deck, about one-third of the PHM's length is devoted to crew accommodation, the forward third is occupied by the primary gun, automatic loader mechanism, ammunition storage and forward foil, and the after third is occupied by the unmanned machinery spaces.

All manned spaces are equipped with a recirculating air conditioning system to give a maximum air temperature of 27°C at 55 per cent relative humidity in summer, and a minimum inside temperature of 18°C in winter. The officers' staterooms, crew quarters and lounge/messing area are fully air-conditioned, the temperature being controlled by individual thermostats in the spaces concerned.

SYSTEMS, ELECTRICAL: Ship's service electric plant comprises two AiResearch Ship Service Power Units (SSPUs), with ME831-800 gas turbines as prime movers driving 250kVA, 400Hz, 450V generators. Each SSPU also drives an attached centrifugal compressor for starting the LM 2500 engine and two hydraulic pumps for the ship's hydraulic system. One is capable of handling the entire electrical load, the second is provided as a standby. Through the use of static power conversion equipment, limited three-phase, 60Hz ac power and 28V dc is available for equipment requirements. In port, the craft can utilise shore power or use its own auxiliary power unit for this purpose, as well as battery charging and emergency use of navigation and radio equipment.

HYDRAULICS: 3000psi to actuate the hullborne and foilborne controls, foil retraction and hullborne engine starting. Dual hydraulic supply is provided to each service with sub-system isolation fore and aft in the event of major damage.

FIRE EXTINGUISHING: Dry chemical equipment throughout craft, and a fixed total flooding-type Freon 1301 system.

WEAPONS/FIRE CONTROL: Either WM-28 radar and weapons control system or US model, the Mk 92 (Mod 1). Both systems embody a combined fire control and search antenna system, mounted on a single stabilised platform and enclosed in a fibreglass radome. The Italian Argo system can also be installed.

TARGETING/MISSILE WARNING: Automatic classification ESM (electronic warfare support measures) set is installed for missile warning and over-the-horizon targeting of enemy surface units.

GUNS: Standard primary gun is the OTO Melara 76mm gun, which is unmanned and automatically controlled by the fire control system. The craft can also be delivered with secondary guns. If specified two Mk 20 Rh 202 20mm AA cannon can be provided, one each, port and starboard, adjacent to the fire control antenna structure.

MISSILES: The prototype carries eight Harpoon missiles in two four-tube lightweight canister launchers, but Exocet, Otomat, Tero or any smaller missile system can be installed. Space is provided aft to accommodate the four launchers, port and starboard, in parallel pairs. The launchers are deck-fixed in elevation and azimuth.

Armament of the standard US Navy version will be eight McDonnell Douglas RGM-84A Harpoon anti-ship missiles in lightweight container launchers; one Mk 75 76mm/62cal OTO Melara gun with 400 76mm rounds, and two Mk 135, Mod 0, 4·4in launchers, together with 24 Mk 171 chaff cartridges, small arms, ammunition and pyrotechnics.

COMMAND, CONTROL AND COMMUNICATIONS: True motion navigation radar; OMEGA navigation equipment; gyrocompass; dead reckoning tracer; Tactical and Navigation Collision Avoidance System (TANCAV); speed log; depth sounder/recorder; AN/SPA-25B repeater consoles (2); integrated intercom/ announcing/exterior communications system; HF, UHF and VHF communications (teletype and voice) IFF system, ESM system.

The basic PHM design allows for a growth of approximately 5 tons in full load displacement to enhance mission capability. Areas under consideration include sonar, torpedoes, improved surface-to-surface missiles and low-light-level TV, all of which appear to be feasible without having an adverse effect on its current capabilities.

The following details apply to the model under construction for the US Navy.

DIMENSIONS
Length overall,
  foils extended: 40·5m (132ft 10in)
  foils retracted: 44·3m (145ft 4in)
Beam max, deck: 8·6m (28ft 2in)
Max width across foils: 14·5m (47ft 6in)
Draught,
  hullborne, foils retracted: 1·9m (6ft 3in)
  hullborne, foils extended: 7·1m (23ft 2in)
  foilborne, normal: 2·5m (8ft 2in)
WEIGHT
Displacement, full load including margins: 241 tonnes
PERFORMANCE
Max speed foilborne: In excess of 50 knots
Cruising speed,
  foilborne, Sea State 0–5: In excess of 40 knots
  hullborne: 11 knots
Sea State: Can negotiate 10ft seas at speeds in excess of 40 knots
Range, foilborne: Not available
  hullborne: In excess of 1000n miles

JETFOIL 929-100

This is a 110-ton waterjet-propelled commercial hydrofoil for services in relatively rough waters. It employs a fully-submerged, automatically-controlled canard foil arrangement and is powered by two 3710hp Allison 501-K20A gas turbines. Normal foilborne cruising speed is 42 knots.

Typical interior arrangements include a commuter configuration with up to 350 seats and a tourist layout for 190 to 250 plus baggage.

Keel-laying of the first Jetfoil took place at the company's Renton, Washington, plant in January 1973 and the craft was launched in March 1974. After testing on Puget Sound and in the Pacific, the craft was delivered to Pacific Sea Transportation Ltd for inter-island services in Hawaii. High-speed foilborne tests began in Puget Sound in mid-July and it was reported that the vessel attained a speed of 48 knots during its runs.

During a rigorous testing programme to prove the boat's design and construction, Boeing No 0001 operated for 470 hours, including 237 hours foilborne. The latter phase of testing was conducted in the rough waters of the straits of Juan de Fuca and the Pacific Ocean, where it encountered wave swells as high as 9·1m (30ft), winds gusting up to 60 knots and wave chop averaging 1·8m (6ft) high.

The first operational Jetfoil service was successfully initiated in April 1975 by Far East Hydrofoil Co Ltd, of Hong Kong, with Jetfoil 002, *Madeira*. Before this, the Jetfoil received its ABS classification, was certificated by the Hong Kong Marine Department and passed US Coast Guard certification trials, although a US Coast Guard certificate was not completed as the craft would not be operating in US waters.

The first US service began in Hawaii in June

The 1976-launched *Acores* Jetfoil 929-100 in service on the Hong Kong to Macau route

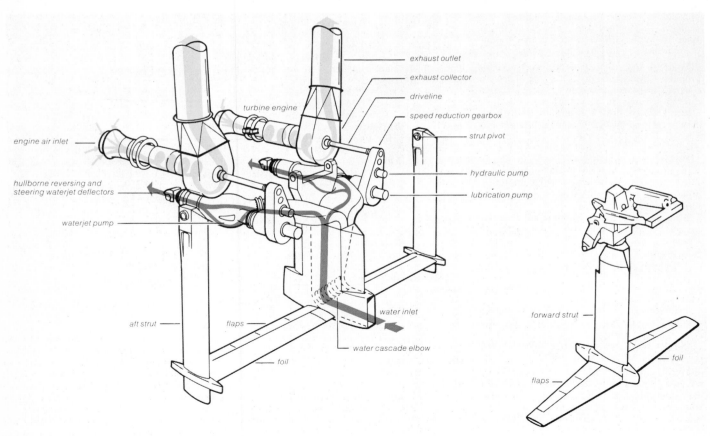

Principal elements of the Jetfoil propulsion and foil systems

1975 with the first of three Jetfoils, 003 *Kame-hameha,* starting inter-island runs. By the end of the summer all five Jetfoils were in service. The tenth Jetfoil was launched in May 1977.

FOILS: Fully-submerged canard arrangement with a single inverted T strut/foil forward and a three-strut, full-span foil aft. The forward foil assembly is rotated hydraulically through 7 degrees in either direction for steering. All foils have trailing-edge flaps for controlling pitch, roll and yaw and for take-off and landing. Hydraulically-driven foil flap actuators control the variation in flap positions through linkages between actuators and flap hinge points. Foils and struts retract hydraulically above the waterline, the bow foil forward, and the rear foil aft. All structural components of the foil/strut system are in 15·5PH corrosion resistant all-welded steel construction.

CONTROLS: The craft is controlled by a three-axis automatic system while it is foilborne and during take-off and landing. The system senses the motion and position of the craft by gyros, accelerometers and height sensors, signals from which are combined in the control computer with manual commands from the helm. The resulting computer outputs provide control-surface deflections through electro-hydraulic servo actuators. Lift control is by full-span trailing edge flaps on each foil. Forward and aft flaps operate differentially to provide pitch variation and height control. Aft flaps operate differentially to provide roll control for changes of direction.

The vessel banks inwardly into all turns to ensure maximum passenger comfort. The ACS introduces the correct amount of bank and steering to co-ordinate the turn in full. Turn rates of up to six degrees per second are attained within one second of providing a heading change command at the helm.

Three basic controls are required for foilborne operation: the throttle is employed to set the speed, the height command lever to set the required foil depth, and the helm to set the required heading. If a constant course is required, a 'heading hold' circuit accomplishes this automatically.

For take-off, the foil depth is set, the two throttles advanced, and the hull clears the water in about 60 seconds. Acceleration continues until the craft automatically stabilises at the command depth and the speed dictated by the throttle setting. The throttle setting is reduced for landing, the craft settling as the speed drops. The speed normally diminishes from 45 knots (cruising speed) to 15 knots in about 30 seconds. In emergencies more rapid landings can be made by the use of the height command lever to provide hull contact within two seconds.

HULL: Hull and deckhouse in marine aluminium. Aircraft assembly techniques are used, including high-speed mechanised welding processes.

POWERPLANT: Power for the waterjet propulsion system is supplied by two Allison 501-K20A free-power gas turbines, each rated at 3300shp at 27°C (80°F) at sea level. Each is connected to a Rocketdyne Powerjet 20 axial-flow pump through a gearbox drive train. The two turbine/pump systems are located in their own bays, port and starboard, separated by the slot in the hull into which the central water strut retracts for hullborne operation. The system propels the craft in both foilborne and hullborne modes. When foilborne, water enters through the inlet at the forward lower end of the aft centre foil strut. At the top of the duct, the water is split into two paths and enters into each of the two axial flow pumps. It is then discharged at high pressure through nozzles in the hull bottom.

The water path is the same during hullborne operations with the foils extended. When the foils are retracted, the water enters through a flush inlet located in the keel. Reversing and steering for hullborne operation only are accomplished by reverse-flow buckets located immediately aft of the water exit nozzles. A bow thruster is provided for positive steering control at low forward speeds.

A 15 140-litre (4000-gallon) integral fuel tank supplies the propulsion turbine and diesel engines. Recommended fuel is Diesel No 2. The tank is

Craft built (Jetfoil 929-100)

Name	Launched	Current Operator
Flores (ex *Kalakoua,* 1978) Boeing No (001)	29 March 1974	Far East Hydrofoil Co Ltd, Hong Kong
Madeira (002)	Oct 1974	Far East Hydrofoil Co Ltd, Hong Kong
Corvo (ex *Kamehameha*) (003)	Feb 1975	Far East Hydrofoil Co Ltd, Hong Kong
Santa Maria (005)	April 1975	Far East Hydrofoil Co Ltd, Hong Kong
Pico (ex *Kuhio*) (004)	June 1975	Far East Hydrofoil Co Ltd, Hong Kong
São Jorge (ex *Jet Caribe I*) (006)	Dec 1975	Far East Hydrofoil Co Ltd, Hong Kong
Acores (ex *Jet Caribe II*, 1980, ex *Oriente*, 1978) (008)	Nov 1976	Far East Hydrofoil Co Ltd, Hong Kong
Urzela (ex *Flying Princess*) (007)	May 1976	Far East Hydrofoil Co Ltd, Hong Kong
Ponta Delgada (ex *Flying Princess II*) (010)	May 1977	Far East Hydrofoil Co Ltd, Hong Kong
Okesa	Dec 1976	Sado Kisen Kaisha, Japan

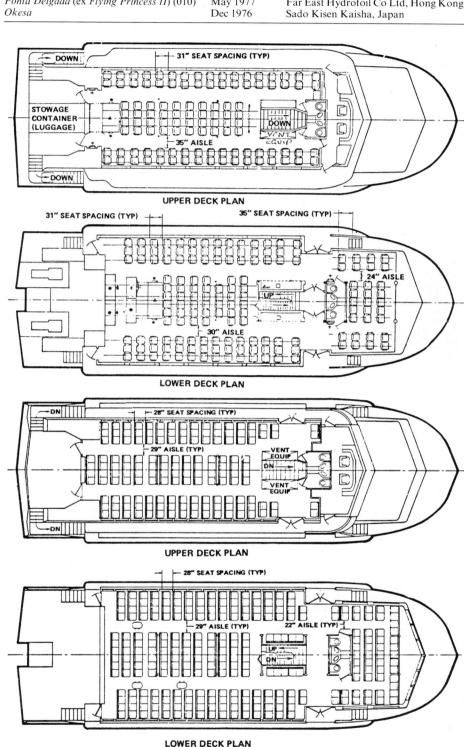

Jetfoil 929-100 interior arrangements

fitted with a 5cm (2in) diameter fill pipe and fittings compatible with dockside refuelling equipment. Coalescent-type water separating fuel filters and remote-controlled motor-operated fuel shut-off valves provide fire protection.

ACCOMMODATION: Air-conditioned passenger accommodation on two decks connected by a wide, enclosed stairway. Seats are track-mounted to facilitate spacing changes, removal or replacement. The cabins have 914mm (3ft) wide aisles and 2·06m (6ft 9in) headroom. In the commuter configuration 1·58m³ (56ft³) per passenger is provided and 1·87m³ (66ft³) in the tourist configuration. Floors are carpeted and 61cm (2ft) seats are provided. Lighting is indirect and adjustable from the wheelhouse. Interior noise is near conversation level (below 68dB SIL) and there is a public announcement system. Each deck level has two wc/washbasin units. There are drinking water dispensers on each passenger deck.

Quality of the ride in the craft is comparable with that of a Boeing 727 airliner. The vertical acceleration at the centre of gravity is very low and depends on Sea State. For example, at 2 metres significant wave height the vertical acceleration is only 0·05g RMS. Lateral acceleration is substantially less than vertical. Angles of pitch and roll are less than 1 degree RMS. A structural fuse is provided which limits deceleration to less than 0·4g longitudinally and 0·8g vertically. In the event of the craft striking a major item of floating debris at full speed, the structural fuse, when actuated, allows the foil and strut to rotate backwards, protecting the system from sustaining significant damage.

Crew comprises a captain and first officer plus cabin attendants.

SYSTEMS, ELECTRICAL: 60Hz, 440V ac electrical system, supplied by two diesel-driven generators each rated at 62·5kVA. Either is capable of supplying all vital electrical power. 90kVA capacity shore connection facilities provided, and equipment can accept 50Hz power. Transformer rectifier units for battery charging provide 28V dc from the ac system.

HYDRAULICS: 210·9kg/cm² (3000psi) system to actuate control surfaces. Each pump is connected to a separate system to provide split system redundancy in the event of a turbine, pump, distribution system or actuator malfunctioning.

EMERGENCY: Craft meets all applicable safety regulations of the US Coast Guard and SOLAS. Hull provides two-compartment sub-division and a high degree of stability. Life rafts and life jackets are provided.

NAVIGATION: Equipment includes radar. A low-light-level television system covering potential collision zone is available as an optional extra.

DIMENSIONS
Length overall, foils extended: 27·4m (90ft)
    foils retracted: 30·1m (99ft)
Beam overall, max: 9·5m (31ft)
Draught hullborne,
    foils retracted: 1·5m (4ft 10in)
    foils extended: 5m (16ft 4in)
WEIGHT
Displacement: 110 tons
PERFORMANCE
Max speed: 50 knots
Normal service speed: 42 knots
Turning radius at 45 knots: Less than 305m (1000ft)
Normal endurance at cruising speed: 4 hours
Max endurance: 8 hours
Max wave height foilborne: 3·65m (12ft)

JETFOIL 929-115

The last of the Jetfoil 929-100 series was the 010 *Flying Princess II*. The first of the improved 929-115 series. Jetfoil 011 *Mikado*, was launched at Renton, Washington in June 1978, and is operated by Sado Kisen in the Sea of Japan.

A number of detail changes have been made in order to comply with the international craft code, but most have been made as a result of operating experience with the earlier model. The improved model Jetfoil has a lighter structure allowing an increased payload, greater reliability and is easier to maintain. Some of the modifications are listed below.

FOILS: External stiffeners on the foil struts have been eliminated and the bow foil has been changed from constant section to tapered planform for improved performance. Stress levels have been reduced for extended life.

CONTROLS: Heading hold (autopilot) installed as basic equipment. Automatic control system 'Autotrim' is improved to reduce steady state pitch and depth errors to negligible values. This reduces or eliminates the need for foil angle of incidence adjustments. A higher thrust bow-thruster is fitted and the navigation radar is now installed on a pedestal between the captain and first officer so that it can be swivelled for viewing from either position.

HULL: The bow structure design has been simplified to provide equivalent strength with increased payload and bulkhead 2 has been revised for decreased stress levels. Based on a seven-

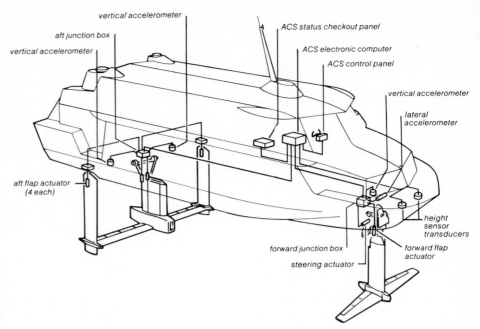

Principal elements of the Jetfoil autostabilisation system

Boeing Jetfoil 929-115 *Cu na Mara* now re-named *Ginga* and in service with Sado Kisen Kaisha

Craft built (Jetfoil 929-115 type and conversions)

Name	Launched	Owner
Mikado (011)	June 1978	Sado Kisen Kaisha, Japan
Ginga (ex *Cu na Mara*)	Nov 1979	Sado Kisen Kaisha, Japan
Terceira (ex *Normandy Princess*)	Jan 1979	Far East Hydrofoil Co Ltd, Hong Kong
Funchal (ex *Jetferry One*)	May 1979	Far East Hydrofoil Co Ltd, Hong Kong
Horta (ex *Jetferry Two*) (016)	March 1980	Far East Hydrofoil Co Ltd, Hong Kong
Princesa Guayarmia	Nov 1980	Compañia Transmediterranea SA, Spain
Princesa Guacimara	July 1981	Compañia Transmediterranea SA, Spain
Bima Samudera I (Boeing No 0022)	Oct 1981	PT PAL, Indonesia
Princesse Clementine	Feb 1981	Regie des Transports Maritimes, Belgium
Prinses Stephanie	April 1981	Regie des Transports Maritimes, Belgium
Jet 7 (ex *Spirit of Friendship*, ex *Aries*, ex *Montevideo Jet*)	Aug 1980	Kato Kisen Co Ltd/Kansai Kisen Co Ltd
Jet 8 (ex *Spirit of Discovery*)	April 1985	Kato Kisen Co Ltd/Kansai Kisen Co Ltd
— (modified to 929-119)	Aug 1984	Indonesian Government (Navy)
— (modified to 929-119)	Nov 1984	Indonesian Government
Speedy Princess (shipped 1986 to Hong Kong to be modified to type 929-320)	July 1979	Far East Hydrofoil Co Ltd (FEH), Hong Kong. (*Speedy Princess* (ex British Royal Navy, HMS *Speedy*) was purchased in September 1986 by FEH (departed UK, 16 Oct 1986) and will be converted to a commercial passenger vessel and renamed)
— (modified to 929-120)	Jan 1986	Indonesian Government
— (modified to 929-120)	June 1986	Indonesian Government

minute evacuation time in case of fire the following fire protection provisions have been made:

Fibreglass is used for thermal insulation where required throughout the passenger accommodation areas.

Aluminium ceiling panels and air conditioner sleeves are employed throughout, together with aluminium doors and frames.

One-half inch thick Marinite is employed in machinery spaces, with US Coast Guard-type felt added wherever required for insulation to comply with 30 minute fire test.

Carpet, seat fabrics and lining materials meet low flame spread, toxicity and smoke requirements of US Coast Guard and Department of Trade, United Kingdom.

POWERPLANT: The propulsion system has been uprated to operate at 2200 maximum intermittent pump rpm with an increase of 3 tons in maximum gross weight.

ACCOMMODATION: Seats of revised design are fitted; environmental control unit has been located forward to increase payload and aid servicing, stairway to upper deck has a round handrail for better grip.

SYSTEMS, ELECTRICAL: Dc system is now in the wheelhouse to comply with new dynamically-supported craft rules. Ac panels relocated to be closer to equipment served to reduce wire runs. Redundant power sources are provided from either diesel generator for services to 24V dc emergency loads and loads essential for foilborne operation. Emergency 24V dc lights have been added in lavatories and aft machinery areas. Daylight signalling lamps with self-contained batteries are provided.

HYDRAULICS: System is consolidated with one manifold and reduced piping.

AIR CONDITIONING: Machinery moved forward to space above the main stairway and forward machinery space to improve operation and servicing.

DIESEL FUEL SYSTEM: Separate fuel systems supply the propulsion engines and diesel generators. This allows alternate fuels to be used in the turbines and greatly simplifies the plumbing system.

Jetfoil 929-115 operated by Regie des Transports Maritimes, Belgium

SEA WATER SYSTEM: Cooling water for the propulsion system has been separated from the remainder of the system. This simplifies the system and improves its reliability.

MISCELLANEOUS: Originally the hull corrosion prevention system was based on the isolation of dissimilar metals and ship-to-shore grounding. The new approach uses dockside impressed current, resistance-controlled shorting of struts and foils to the hull, additional pod anodes and electrical isolation. Other changes include a changeover to titanium sea water piping, a change in sea water pump materials and protective painting added to the hydraulic system.

DIMENSIONS
Length overall, foils extended: 27·4m (90ft)
Beam, max: 9·5m (31ft)
Draught,
    foils extended: 5·2m (17ft)
    foils retracted: 1·7m (5ft 6in)
Height (without retractable mast),
    hullborne, above mean waterline: 12·8m (42ft)
    foilborne, at 2·4m (8ft) foil depth: 15·5m (51ft)
WEIGHT
Fully loaded displacement: 115 long tons

PERFORMANCE
Design cruising speed: 43 knots (80km/h; 50mph)

JETFOIL 929-117

Since 1985 Boeing has not manufactured any model of the Jetfoil. The 929-117 model, an updated version, is currently licensed for production outside the USA.

BOEING MODELS 929-119 & 929-120

Indonesia has reached agreement with Boeing Marine Systems for the purchase of four Boeing Jetfoil hydrofoils and has taken an option on six additional Jetfoils.

The initial contract, valued at approximately US$150 million, is for the purchase of four Jetfoils for coastal patrol. Boeing will assist P T Pabrik Kapal (PT PAL), the Indonesian national shipbuilding facility, in developing its capability for high technology hydrofoil manufacture. During these preparations Boeing will manufacture and supply to Indonesia components for the struts, foils and the automatic control system.

The rate of programme expansion will depend

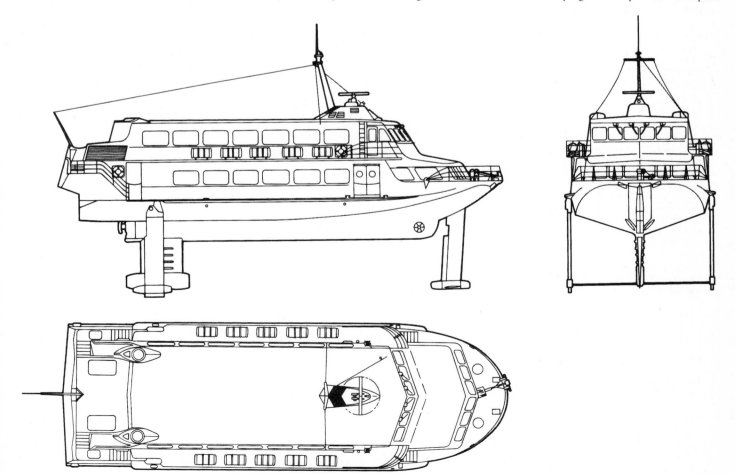

General Arrangement of Jetfoil Model 929-115 passenger ferry

on Indonesia's economic growth, which is moderate at present due to reduced world oil prices. If Indonesia takes up the option on a further six Jetfoils, the contract value to Boeing would total US$330 million.

The first two Jetfoils, Model 929-119s, were delivered in 1985 for use as personnel transport, followed by two Model 929-120 fast patrol boats in 1986. These will be structurally complete and PT PAL, Indonesia will fit them out.

A Boeing Jetfoil, *Bima Sumudera 1*, was purchased by Indonesia in 1981 and used to evaluate hydrofoil potential for coastal patrol and commercial applications. During evaluation the Jetfoil established several records, including a continuous foilborne operation of 11 hours 8 minutes.

The Indonesian trials covered nearly 10 000 nautical miles during 245 hours under way and proved the Jetfoil's stability and reliability. As a result, the Indonesian Navy has identified a long-term requirement for up to 47 Jetfoils. Commercial passenger-carrying Jetfoils would be in addition to that order.

JETFOIL 929-320
Craft built
Speedy Princess, ex HMS *Speedy*

The Jetfoil 929-320 was delivered to the Royal Navy in June 1980 for use in fisheries patrol in the North Sea. Named HMS *Speedy*, the craft was a modified Model 929-115 commercial Jetfoil and was built on the commercial Jetfoil production line. The craft was decommissioned by the Royal Navy in April 1982 and eventually sold to the Far East Hydrofoil Co Ltd (FEH) in the autumn of 1986. The craft is to be converted to passenger configuration and will operate on the Hong Kong to Macao route. This concept has evolved into a new projected version of the 929-320, incorporating the well-tested commercial Jetfoil systems into a basic military platform. Power for foilborne operation is provided by two Allison 501-K20A gas turbines and two Allison 8V-92T1 diesels are installed for hullborne operation, giving increased on-station time and endurance.

Externally the Model 929-320 resembles the projected Boeing Offshore Jetfoil, with the top passenger deck measuring 4·87 × 7·31m (16 × 24ft) which accommodates two semi-inflatable dinghies on davits. Light weapons will be carried. Displacement is 117 tons.
DIMENSIONS: As for Jetfoil Model 929-115.

WESTPORT SHIP YARD INC
PO Box 308, Westport, Washington 98595, USA

Telephone: (206) 268 0117

Randy Rust, *President*

WESTFOIL 25-METER
Design started on the Westfoil 25-meter fully-submerged hydrofoil in the autumn of 1986 with construction underway during the summer of 1987, the first boat being scheduled to be delivered in the spring of 1988. The hull lines come from Westport Ship Yard's latest mould, for a boat designed to meet the rigours of year-round commercial service. The submerged foil and automatic control system are based on 25 years of hydrofoil experience using the latest in proven technology to provide a ride which should be better than existing hydrofoils. The ducted air propellers will provide thrust at a low Mach number while the ducts will have acoustical treatment to reduce further sound.
ENGINES: Four DDA 12V-92 TA diesels with 145 type injectors, each 1080bhp max, at 2300rpm. Rpm limited to 2100.
PROPELLERS: Two ducted units by Pacific Propeller Inc with low-tip-speed variable-pitch propellers.
ACCOMMODATION
149 passengers at 81·3cm seat pitch
One galley
Four lavatories
Baggage allowance: 23kg/passenger
CAPACITIES
Fuel: 5677 litres (1500 US gallons)
Fresh water: 378 litres (100 US gallons)
ELECTRICAL POWER: One 30kW Northern Lights generator providing 110V ac power with 8kW back-up. Four alternators, one on each engine, providing 12V dc and 25V dc power and power for the automatic control system (ACS). Four 8D starting batteries for mains (24V). Six deep cycle 6V batteries wired for 12V lights. One 35A 24V charger and one 80A 12V charger. Long-life battery cluster for ACS system.
AUTOMATIC CONTROL SYSTEM (ACS): The ACS includes the flaps located at the trailing edges of both the fore and aft foils, the front strut rudder, the foil flap actuation system and the automatic stabilisation and control system. The foil flaps provide control of the craft in pitch, roll and yaw to provide a smooth ride in all seas up to design sea conditions, and for take off and landing. The foil flap actuators use input from the automatic stabilisation and control system to select the angle of the foil flaps so that the wave motions are counteracted. Flaps are moved in response to helm control to turn the boat in a banked attitude. The automatic stabilisation and control system employs a computer, motion sensors, a height sensor and gyroscopes to generate the commands sent to the actuators so that the foil flaps move to maintain the desired stable attitude and foil depth.
CONTROLS: The start, idle, power management and shut down, propeller pitch, boat direction, foilborne or hullborne mode selection and strut

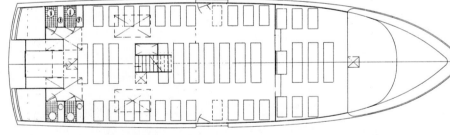

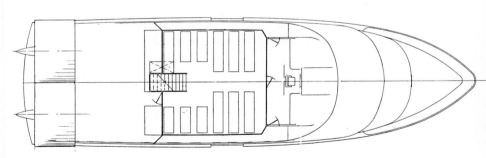

Provisional General Arrangement of Westfoil 25-meter

extension/retraction controls will be located for one-man operation in the wheelhouse. In addition, hullborne controls will be located on each bridge wing. Engine instrumentation is located in the wheelhouse.
FOILBORNE STEERING: Accomplished by actuating the aft flaps differentially (in response to helm commands) to roll the boat into a turn with appropriate front strut rudder setting to maintain a co-ordinated turn. The flaps and front strut rudder setting will be maintained by the ACS in response to helm commands and motion and height sensor feedback.

HULLBORNE STEERING: Utilises an Arneson drive system for hullborne steering and reversing. A bow thruster will be installed.
FOILS AND STRUTS: Nitronic 50 stainless steel and composite structure in a canard arrangement. The front and aft foil and strut systems can be retracted independently.
ENVIRONMENTAL SYSTEMS: Air-conditioning and heating is installed.
DIMENSIONS
Length, overall (struts included): 24·39m
Beam, moulded: 7·16m
Draught, struts retracted: 1·12m

Draught, struts extended, hullborne: 4·88m
GRT: Less than 100
WEIGHT
Displacement: 71·11 tonnes
PERFORMANCE
Speed: Estimated 42 knots in Sea State 5 at full
 weight
Cruise power: Approximately 750bhp each at full
 weight

Artist's impression of Westfoil 25-meter

SAILING HYDROFOILS
JAPAN

KANAZAWA INSTITUTE OF TECHNOLOGY

Department of Mechanical Engineering, 7-1 Ohgigaoka Nonoichi, Ishikawa 921, Japan

Telephone: (0762) 48 1100
Telex: 5122456 KITLC J
Telefax: (0762) 48 6189

Yutaka Masuyama, *Associate Professor*

The Hydrodynamic Department of Mechanical Engineering, Kanazawa Institute of Technology, has been studying sailing hydrofoil craft since 1975. Three experimental craft have been built. *Ichigo-Tei* was completed in 1975 and tested in 1976. Employing data obtained from this craft, *Hi-Trot II* was built and tested in 1977 and *Hi-Trot III* was tested in 1979.

ICHIGO-TEI

This is a basic test rig to investigate the man-oeuvrability, stability and balance of sails and foil systems. The *Ichigo-Tei* has a specially-designed catamaran hull, to which two surface-piercing bow foils and one stern foil are attached.

FOILS: The bow foils are of three-rung ladder configuration with removable outer rungs. The stern foil is of trapeze configuration with the rudder mounted immediately aft. Foil loading during a normal take-off is bow foils 60 per cent and stern foil 40 per cent. The foils, struts and rudder are in glassfibre and polyester resin. Foil section throughout is Göttinger 797, with 170mm (6·7in) chord.

HULL: Marine plywood sheathed with glassfibre and polyester resin.

SAIL: Sloop rig with a 10·2m² (110ft²) mainsail borrowed from the Hobie-cat 14, and a jib sail of 3·7m² (40ft²) borrowed from the Snipe.

DIMENSIONS
Length overall: 4·46m (14ft 8in)
 waterline: 4·2m (13ft 9in)
Hull beam: 2·2m (7ft 3in)
Width overall across foils: 4·3m (14ft 1in)
Draught afloat (fixed foils): 0·96m (3ft 2in)
 foilborne: 0·4-0·5m (1ft 4in-1ft 8in)
WEIGHT
Empty: 140kg (309lb)
PERFORMANCE
Take-off speed: 6 knots with 11-knot wind
Max speed foilborne: 9 knots with 14-knot wind

HI-TROT II

Employing data gathered during the test programme conducted with *Ichigo-Tei*, the Kanazawa Institute of Technology design team built the *Hi-Trot II*. The hull is longer than that of the earlier craft, but the chief difference, apart from the adoption of a simpler foil system, is the use of a rotating sail rig.

FOILS: The split bow foil is of surface-piercing V-type, with cantilevered extensions, set at 40 degrees dihedral, at the apex. The bow foil section is ogival, with 250mm (9·8in) chord and a 12 per cent thickness-to-chord ratio. The aft foil is of inverted T-type and the complete foil and strut assembly rotates for use as a rudder. About 80 per cent of the load is carried by the bow foils and the remaining 20 per cent by the stern foil. Foils, struts and rudder are in glassfibre, carbon fibre and epoxy resin.

HULL: Plywood structure sheathed with glass-fibre and epoxy resin.

SAIL: Comprises three sail panels, each 4·2m², mounted in parallel. An air rudder automatically adjusts the attack angle of the sails to the wind. Each panel has a wing section and, though the section is symmetrical, it can form a camber on either side by bending at 40 per cent chord length. The leading edge of each wing is covered with thin aluminium sheet while the trailing edges are

Ichigo-Tei

Hi-Trot II foilborne showing air rudder attached to central sail panel

Hi-Trot III during trials

covered with terylene cloth. Wing frames are of plywood and polystyrene foam sandwich and provide the necessary buoyancy to prevent the craft from capsizing should it turn on its side. The surface of each wing is spray painted with polyurethane paint.

DIMENSIONS
Length overall: 5·1m (16ft 9in)
   waterline: 4·95m (16ft 3in)
Hull beam: 2·68m (8ft 10in)
Beam, overall (fixed foils): 5·45m (17ft 11in)
Draught afloat (fixed foils): 1·1m (3ft 7in)
   foilborne: 0·4-0·55m (1ft 4in-1ft 10in)
WEIGHT
Empty: 250kg (551lb)
PERFORMANCE
Take-off speed: 7 knots with 15-knot wind
Max speed foilborne: 11 knots with 17-knot wind
SEA TEST: The craft has been tested in 10-20 knot winds. Due to mechanical problems, tests could not be undertaken in wind speeds exceeding 20 knots. Improvements are being made to remedy this.

HI-TROT III

During 1978 the Kanazawa Institute of Technology design team constructed and tested a third craft, *Hi-Trot III*. The major difference between it and *Hi-Trot II* is the use of two parallel soft wing sails.
FOILS: The split bow foil is of surface-piercing Y-type, and the aft foil is of inverted T-type as on the *Hi-Trot II*. Up to 90 per cent of the load is carried by the bow foils, and the remaining 10 per cent by the stern foil. Foils are of gfrp sandwich construction with polyurethane foam core and reinforced by carbonfibre.
HULL: Plywood structure sheathed with glass fibre and epoxy resin.
SAIL: Two parallel soft wing sails developed for *Hi-Trot III*, each 8m². Total sail area, 16m².
DIMENSIONS
Length overall: 5·08m (16ft 8in)
   waterline: 4·95m (16ft 3in)
Hull beam: 0·3m (1ft)
Beam overall, foils retracted: 3·74m (12ft 3in)
   foils extended: 6·84m (22ft 5in)

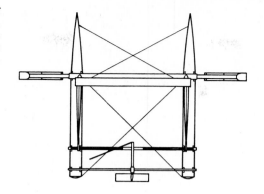

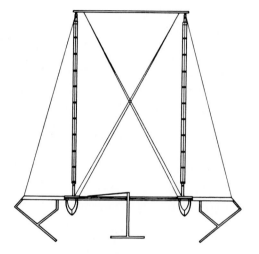

General Arrangement of *Hi-Trot III*

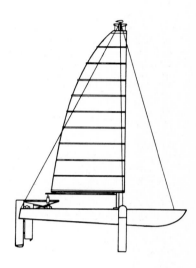

Draught afloat, foils retracted: 0·2m (8in)
   foils extended: 1m (3ft 3in)
Draught foilborne: 0·4m (1ft 4in)
WEIGHT
Empty: 255kg (562lb)

PERFORMANCE: *Hi-Trot III* takes-off at 8 knots in a 15-knot wind and accelerates to 15 knots rapidly. The maximum speed attained during trials was 21 knots in an 18-knot wind (1·2 times wind speed).

UNITED STATES OF AMERICA

DAK HYDROFOILS

PO Box 18041, 526 Third Avenue, San Francisco, California 94118, USA

Telephone: (415) 752 8748

David A Keiper, *Proprietor and Chief Designer*

Williwaw sailing in San Francisco Bay

Design of the 32ft *Williwaw*, the world's first seagoing sailing hydrofoil, began in 1963. Construction of the craft, which is based on a specially designed trimaran hull, began in May 1966 and tests started in November 1967.

After nearly three years of trials along the California coast, *Williwaw*, manned by David Keiper and one other crew member, successfully completed a 16-day passage between Sausalito, California and Kahului Harbour, Maui, Hawaii, in September 1970—the first ocean crossing by the hydrofoil sailboat.

Heavy seas and strong winds were encountered on the first two days of the voyage, during which the craft made 200 miles per day. At times the craft attained 25 knots, but light winds in mid-ocean prevented the craft from making the passage in record time.

The craft entered chartered sailing yacht service in March 1971, operating from Hanalei, Hawaii and, before returning to Sausalito, California, completed about 2000 miles of inter-island sailing around Hawaii, mainly in open sea conditions.

Williwaw was entered in the Pacific Multihull Association speed trials held in Los Angeles Harbour in May 1975. Average speed was determined over a 229m (250yd) course, planned so that the true wind was approximately 10 to 20 degrees aft of the beam. On one run, with a reasonably steady wind of 17 knots, *Williwaw* averaged 17·5 knots over the course. On another run, with a stronger wind of 24 knots, under gusty and turbulent conditions with 1·5ft (0·45m) very short wave chop, *Williwaw* averaged 18·5 knots.

The foils stabilised the craft perfectly. The bow kept up high in all runs, while various racing catamarans of 4·2 to 11·5m (14 to 38ft) experienced serious problems with bow burying.

Various modifications to the craft were undertaken during 1974-75, followed by a second series of sea trials in the summer of 1975, in the South Pacific.

Williwaw sailed to Hawaii again in June 1975. Wind was generally light until deep within the tradewind region. In heavy tradewind squalls with the boat running down steep 4·5m (15ft) seas, the foils stabilised perfectly and the bow was never submerged.

On a run from Hanalei, Hawaii to Whangaroa, New Zealand, made between November and December 1975, with stopovers in Samoa and Tonga, moderate trade winds were experienced during the first 2000 miles of the voyage and generally light winds during the last 2000 miles. During the first 12 days of the voyage, the foils were left set continuously. Over one ten-day period, the craft completed 1650 miles, including a doldrums crossing. Self-steering was used for most of the way, with the helm tied. Only the working sail area of 35·3m² (380ft²) was used.

The return trip from New Zealand to Hawaii was made via Rarotonga and Penrhyn in the Cook Islands. When the craft left New Zealand, a disturbed south west air stream was generating 35-knot squalls, day and night. Seas were very irregular and the boat would occasionally slam into walls of water at speeds in excess of 20 knots. About 500 miles from the New Zealand coast one freak wave encountered was 10·6 to 12m (35 to 40ft) high, and had a slope greater than 45 degrees. The trough was flat-bottomed, with no rounding between the slope and the trough. Descending the slope, the bow was well above the surface. After impact there was no tendency for the stern to lift. The bow remained under for about two seconds before it emerged and the boat started moving again. Waves such as this have been known to pitchpole yachts, mono-hull and multi-hull, but the hydrofoil trimaran showed no such tendency.

Williwaw operated sailing excursions from Hanalei, Hawaii, during the summers of 1971, 1975 and 1976. By the end of August 1976, it had completed 19 000 miles of sailing but was wrecked in 1977 while at anchorage.

In 1984, David Keiper was commissioned to design a 40ft hydrofoil trimaran for family cruising. His most recent craft is a 14ft hydrofoil trimaran, the *Stormy Petrel*, which can be carried on the roof of a small car.

WILLIWAW
Full details of this craft appeared in *Jane's Surface Skimmers 1985* and earlier editions.

PACIFIC EXPRESS 35 (PROJECT DESIGN)
Details of this project appeared in *Jane's Surface Skimmers 1985* and earlier editions.

STORMY PETREL
A 14-foot hydrofoil trimaran, *Stormy Petrel* is capable of 40 knots in ideal conditions and can be easily handled by a single occupant. It can be carried on the roof of a small car and erected and launched from a beach. The foils are retracted for sailing in light winds, in very shallow water, for beaching and for paddling against adverse tides in a calm.

When the wind is up, it can fly on its foils carrying one heavy occupant or two of medium weight. The helmsman sits on the aft deck and the second crew member, if carried, sits in a semi-protected cockpit.

The prototype was built in mid-1982 and tested during the 1982 and 1983 sailing season in all weathers. During sharp 30-knot wind gusts it accelerated to 25 knots. It has attained 30 knots in foggy 20-knot wind puffs and long sea swells in the Golden Gate region.

During tests, take-off has taken place on a close reach, with the boat accelerating increasingly as it was turned away from the wind. Its top speed was reached with the true wind on the quarter with the sails close-hauled and the boat tight against the apparent wind. In choppy waters the speed is reduced but the ride is smooth.

FOILS: The lateral foils have a two-inch chord and a 13-inch span, with six rungs on each ladder. Dihedral angles are 30 and 45 degrees. Clark Y section lifters are used and NACA 16012 section struts. The aluminium extrusions, joined with tapped screws and epoxy, are the same as used previously in DAK hydrofoil conversion kits.

ASSEMBLY: Four wingnuts clamp the crossarm unit to the main hull. Foil retraction is by rotating the crossarm through 180 degrees. For carrying on a car roof, the crossarm is laid parallel to the main hull.

MATERIALS: Plywood-epoxy hulls. Aluminium crossarm, mast, lateral foils and fittings.

SAIL AREA: 9·29m², including rotating mast area.

DIMENSIONS
Length, main hull deck: 4·27m
Beam overall: 4·27m
Hulls, length: 1·52m
Float max cross sectional area: 0·093m²
Draught, main hull: 20cm
  rudder, with foils retracted: 25cm
  foils: 61cm on both lateral foils and stern rudder foil
Main hull cross sectional area: 0·213m²

WEIGHTS
Rigged: 82kg
Main hull only: 32kg
Crossarm unit, including floats and lateral foils: 32kg

PERFORMANCE
Take-off speed and wind requirement: 10 knots in flat water or long swells. Increased by short wave chop, when main hull cannot completely clear tops of waves, although boat may still travel at high speed
Top speed: 40 knots in ideal conditions (limited by onset of cavitation)

PACIFIC EXPRESS 40 (DESIGN)
The Pacific Express 40 hydrofoil trimaran is designed to offer the ultimate in both sea worthiness and sailing speed performance, and also avoids many of the problems inherent in conventional trimarans, such as pounding, broaching, tunnel interference, quick motion, pitchpoling, poor control and poor self-steering in heavy seas.

This latest design from DAK Hydrofoils is a scale-up from the very successful hydrofoil trimaran *Williwaw*. Various improvements engineered into the design will result in greatly improved sailing performance. With the hydrofoil units achieving a greater lift-to-drag ratio, a more powerful sail rig, and the boat proportionately wider, the boat will be able to fly 100% foilborne close to the true wind. On many headings, the boat will be able to exceed true wind speed substantially. Proportionately deeper hydrofoil units will keep wave tops from slowing the boat as much as with previous designs. As before, the hydrofoils are easily retracted for light air sailing, for sailing in very shallow water, and for beaching. While designed for cruising, the same boat lightly laden can be successfully raced offshore against the fastest multi-hulls or mono-hulls.

Foils are set or retracted while the boat is stopped. Foil setting angles are fixed while flying, but can be readjusted for different wind, sea and load conditions. Boat automatically takes off with a bow-up trim of about 3 degrees to augment lift, and levels off at high speed to get optimum foil

Stormy Petrel with foils retracted, enabling craft to sail off beach. Note how lateral foils alternate with 30 and 45 degrees of dihedral to strengthen foil units

incidence angles. The boat can be safely operated with hydrofoils in all sea states and wave heights. Sails are reefed down in heavy conditions to maintain comfort, safety and ease of handling.
FOILS: The craft has four hydrofoil units, located at bow, stern and paired laterals projecting outboard of the float hulls. The deep-V dihedral surface-piercing bow foil spans the space between the float bows, with supporting struts to the main hull. The stern foil pivots for rudder action and is a semi-submerged ladder foil without dihedral. The lateral foils are dihedral ladder foils, less deep than the bow and stern foils. As the boat heels from sail side forces, the windward lateral foil comes out of the water, while the leeward lateral foil digs deeper and provides both righting forces and anti-leeway forces. When hard pressed, the leeward foil may be supporting ¾ of the boat's weight. In running downwind, both lateral foil units tend to be out of the water and the bow foil supplies ⅔ of the lift and the stern foil ⅓. Hydrofoil retraction is accomplished by removing pin bolts and swinging the foils up and out of the water using block and tackle.

HULL: Lightweight but strong monocoque trimaran, with foil support structures built-in. The thick wing section joining the hulls has modest deck area to minimise aerodynamic forces, and is made strong and rigid both by its shape and by a pair of main frames spanning the entire hull width. Each float hull has enough buoyancy to carry more than the weight of the entire boat. The floats provide stability that is important when the boat is moving slowly and accelerating to take-off. The hull is of marine ply sheathed in epoxy-glassfibre.

ACCOMMODATION: Double berths, port and starboard, in the wing sections. Wide single berth in the stern cabin. Single berth forward. In the main saloon, settees port and starboard of the aisle. Full standing head room. Between the cockpit and the main saloon, there is a galley to port, and dinette table to starboard. The marine toilet is forward. Provides considerable stowage space, both in lockers and various places in the main hull, wing section and floats.

PROPULSION: Wind power on the sails, primarily. A well, located beneath a cockpit seat, can take an outboard engine of from 5 to 20hp, to be used primarily with hydrofoils retracted.

HYDROFOILS: Aluminium extrusions, heavily anodised, 178mm chord length, joined together by tapped screws and epoxy. Lifters, NACA 16510 section; struts NACA 16007 section.

DIMENSIONS
Length along deck: 12·20m
Waterline length: 10·67m
Main hull waterline beam: 1·22m
Overall beam, hull: 7·32m (with foils set, lateral foils project an additional 152mm outboard)
Float hull length: 8·23m
Draught (stationary): 6·40m on main hull
Foil draught (stationary): 1·22m on lateral foil units
  1·83m on bow and stern foils
Mast height: 14·02m stepped on deck
Sail area: Rigged as a cutter, up to 88·26m², including roller-furling genoa jib; rigged as a sloop, 65·0m² of working sail, up to 75·2m² with roller-furling genoa jib

WEIGHTS
1814kg light. 2538kg offshore racing. 2720kg loaded for cruising

PERFORMANCE
Take-off speed and wind required: 12 knots in flat water or long swells
Top speed: 45 knots in ideal conditions (limited by cavitation)

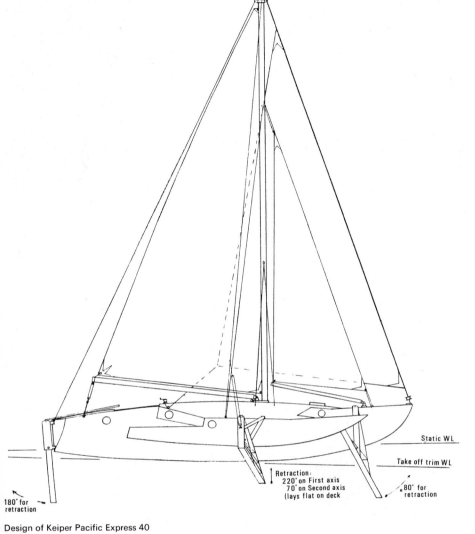

Design of Keiper Pacific Express 40

AIR BOATS AND HYDROCOPTERS

CANADA

ACTION AQUATICS INC

7680-134 Street, Surrey, British Columbia, Canada V3W 7T8

Telephone: (604) 596 5232
Telex: 04 55645

Fred David Cooper
Al Jenkins

AQUAVETTE

Development of the Aquavette air boat started in 1983 and it is now in production. The craft is unusual in that its deep-V variable-deadrise hull is supported by two sponsons. The hull is a grp moulding, hand laid and with compartmentations, filled with expanded foam.

ENGINE: Two cylinder, two cycle 40hp Rotax with 2:1 reduction drive, rpm max: 6400. Electric starter.
PROPELLER: Four-blade, 1·245m diameter.
BATTERY: 20Ah.
FUEL TANK: 22·75 litres (5 Imperial gallons).
CONTROLS: Twin air rudders (Morse rudder cables). Throttle.

Action Aquatics Aquavette

DIMENSIONS
Length: 4·27m
Beam: 2·29m
WEIGHT
Weight, empty: 190·5kg

PERFORMANCE
Speed: 48km/h (30mph, 26 knots)
PRICE (1986): Canadian $6700, in white; $75 for optional colours.

FINLAND

KONEPAJA NILS ERIKSSON KY

SF-21630, Lielax, Parainen (Pargas), Finland

Telephone: (921) 888 086

NE 3000 AMPHIBIAN

A six-seat hydrocopter fitted with road wheels for overland use on smooth surfaces. This craft may be powered by either a Ford or Rover V6 engine. These vehicles are in use in Finland, Norway and Sweden for private use and by pilots, the Coast Guard, the military and postal services.

When driving on snow or on ice hydraulic arms can raise the hull 27cm above the surface and the craft then runs on its skis. The wheel axles are spring-mounted and the wheels can be lowered for road transportation. The vehicle may be towed behind a car but it can also be driven with the assistance of its own engine. Over snow or ice the vehicle is steered with the help of the front skis and when in water by its air rudder.

The roof of the cabin is openable by electro-hydraulic actuators. The cabin is large enough to take two stretchers.
PRINCIPAL PARTICULARS
Length: 6·1m
Cabin length: 2·4m

The Nils Eriksson Amphibian

Cabin width: 1·47m
Seats: Six
Hull: Corrosion-resistant aluminium, 2-4mm thick

Buoyancy: Foam rubber-filled compartments
Speeds, over smooth ice: 100km/h
in heavy snow: 30-40km/h

Amphibian

Amphibian running over ice

SWEDEN

ALBIN JOHANSSON

Nåset, S-610 24 Vikibolandet, Sweden

Telephone: (0125) 20073/20464

ARKÖ SPECIAL HYDROCOPTER

The first hydrocopter was built by Albin Johansson in 1959 and since then over 300 have been built. The craft is powered by a 43hp ILO 2-stroke engine.

PRINCIPAL PARTICULARS
Length (excluding rudder): 3·75m
Width: 1·70m
Height (propeller horizontal): 1·55m
Propeller thrust: 97kp
Propeller rpm, max: 2200
Engine rpm, max: 6200
Fuel tank capacity: 23 litres
Fuel consumption: 8 to 12 litres/h
Accommodation: 2 seats

Albin Johansson Arkö Special Hydrocopter

Speed, over snow: about 150km/h
over water: about 20 knots

UNION OF SOVIET SOCIALIST REPUBLICS

A N TUPOLEV

TUPOLEV A-3 AMPHIBIOUS AEROSLEDGE

The provision of year-round transport in underdeveloped areas of the Soviet north, far east and Siberia would be impossible without the assistance of special vehicles. To reach communities in some of the more inaccessible regions means traversing deep snow, hummock ice, marshes that never freeze and natural waterways overgrown with reeds.

The diversity of the conditions in which transport has to operate, the demand for increased speed and the ability to cross all types of terrain complicates the development of a suitable vehicle.

In intermediate navigational seasons when the ice is melting and unsafe, during the winter freeze-up when large chunks of ice drift along rivers and when strips of unfrozen water abound in frozen or semi-frozen rivers, there is not, generally speaking, a single means of terrestrial transport which can provide reliable year-round communications.

One answer to the problem is the amphibious Aerosledge, which was designed under the direct control of one of the Soviet Union's best known aircraft designers, A N Tupolev. Employed for the carriage of mail, passengers, light freight, medical supplies and hospital cases, the craft has the appearance of a small speedboat powered by a radial engine driving an airscrew. It can carry a payload of half a ton over a distance of 300 to 500km (186 to 310 miles) at a cruising speed of 50 to 70km/h (31 to 43mph). At speed, when traversing snow, the slightly upturned bow of the hull,

Tupolev A-3

together with the difference of pressure between the upper and lower surfaces of the craft, generate an aerodynamic lifting force. At 80km/h (50mph) and above, aerodynamic lift reduces by almost one-third the pressure of the craft on snow. The depth of its furrow becomes negligible and resistance to the motion of the craft decreases accordingly. On water the large area of the hull bottom, with its small keel, makes it a stable, shallow-draught craft.

Additionally, the smooth lines of the hull's underside enable it to cross stretches of water overgrown with water weeds without difficulty and glide across areas of shallow water with a depth no greater than 50mm (2in). More than 200 vehicles of this type are in service with the Soviet Union, and many have been exported to Eastern Europe and elsewhere.

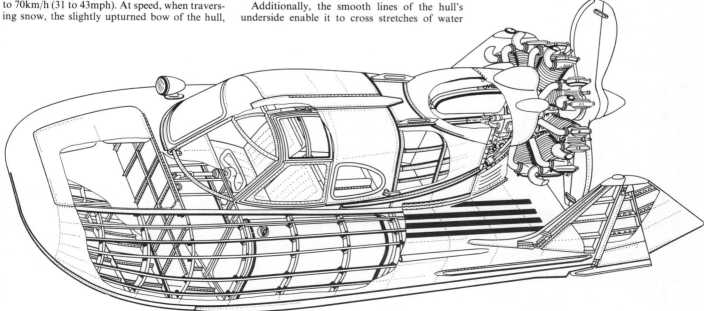

Cutaway showing basic structural components of Tupolev A-3

PROPULSION: Early production Aerosledges were fitted with a single 100hp, five-cylinder M-11 aircooled radial. This was replaced by the more powerful 260hp AI-14R radial. The engine is mounted aft on a tubular frame with shock-absorbers and drives a two-bladed wooden airscrew. The engine compartment is covered by an easily removable cowling. Above the compartment and beneath the cowling is the oil tank and pipes for the oil system. Fuel is carried in two tanks, concealed one on each side of the cabin. Filler caps are in wells in the decking.

CONTROLS: Craft direction is controlled by twin aerodynamic rudders aft operating in the propeller slipstream. For operation over snow or ice, positive control is obtained by steel runners fitted to the base of the rudders which maintain surface contact. When moving the rudder wheel to make a turn, upper (air) and lower sections of the rudder operate simultaneously. If the wheel is pulled towards the driver the rudders turn outwards to form a brake. If it is turned and drawn towards the driver only one rudder operates—the one on the inside of the turn. This assists turning when the Aerosledge is crossing expanses of water overgrown with reeds or weeds.

HULL: Riveted metal alloy construction employing 2mm D-16T plates and profiles. Ribs, stringers and plates are in D-16T duraluminium. A radial chine runs for 66 per cent of the overall length of the craft from the bow. Transverse bulkheads divide the hull into three watertight compartments. The craft will remain afloat in the event of any one compartment flooding. Double plating is employed on the hull bottom to strengthen it for crossing ice, snow mounds and ice hummocks. Low friction 3·5mm polyethylene is stuck to the bottom of the plates which are removable for replacement. Three stainless steel runners are fitted to the hull base, one on the central keel and one on each side. These ensure that the craft is able to hold a given course and prevent it from side-slipping on sheet ice when it is well heeled over.

ACCOMMODATION: In mail-carrying form the Aerosledge carries a driver, postman and mail weighing up to 650kg (1433lb) in winter and 300kg (661lb) in summer. Driver and passenger sit in swivelling armchairs. As a passenger vehicle, it carries a driver and up to four passengers. Ahead of the passenger cabin is a hermetically-sealed hatch providing access to a baggage compartment.

DIMENSIONS
Length overall: 6·11m (20ft 1in)
Hull length: 4·01m (13ft 2in)
Beam: 2·14m (7ft)
Cabin height: 1·35m (4ft 5in)
Airscrew diameter: 1·87m (6ft 2in)
WEIGHTS
Empty: 815kg (1797lb)
Payload: 650kg (1433lb)
PERFORMANCE
Max speed over snow: 120km/h (74·6mph)
    over water: 65km/h (40·4mph)
Max permitted wave height: 0·6m (2ft)

Tupolev A-3

Tupolev A-3

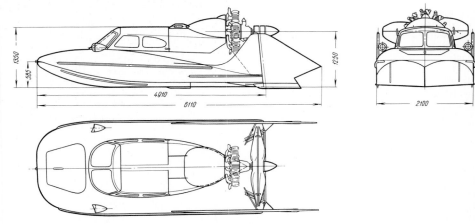

General Arrangement of Tupolev A-3

UNITED STATES OF AMERICA

THE PANTHER AIR BOAT CORPORATION

300 Wilson Avenue, Cocoa, Florida 32922, USA

Telephone: (305) 632 1722
Telex: 220883 TAUR

L A Bell, *President*
David L McClain, *International Sales Manager*

Panther Air Boat Corporation has developed a range of air boats capable of traversing snow, ice, rivers and swamps at speeds up to 88·5km/h (55mph). Thrust is provided by a large two-blade airscrew above the transom.

The company is concentrating on the construction of craft of 3·6 to 6m (12 to 20ft) long and 2·1 to 2·4m (7 to 8ft) wide, built in heavy duty 4·76mm (³⁄₁₆in) thick all-welded marine grade aluminium alloy. Craft of different dimensions and built in glassfibre can be made to order.

POWERPLANT: Modified and rebuilt General Motors automotive engines of 220hp (350in³) or 300hp (450in³) are normally fitted except on the 3·6m (12ft) models. Four- or six-cylinder Lycoming air-cooled aircraft engines are an optional alternative. Fuel consumption, depending on payload and horsepower, varies from 18·1 to 36·3 litres (4 to 8 gallons) per hour at cruising speed. Fuel capacity of the standard 35 US gallon aluminium tank provides an endurance of between 4½ and 9 hours and an operating range of 289·6 to 547·1km (180 to 340 miles).

CONTROLS: Heading controlled by single or twin rudders in the propeller slipstream. Standard instrument panel includes a tachometer, hour meter, ammeter, oil pressure and either water or oil temperature gauges. An electric starter, alternator, fuel pump, in-line fuel filter and a heavy duty 70-amp/hour battery are as standard.

WEIGHTS
Payload (according to model): 680-1474kg (1500-3250lb)

PERFORMANCE (according to model)
Max speed, normal load: 48-88km/h (30-55mph)
Cruising speed: 56-64km/h (35-40mph)

POWER PAC

A portable self-contained air drive system that bolts on to many types of small boat from flat bottom 'Jon' boats to Zodiac inflatables.

Engine: 40 or 50hp, 2-cycle
Weight: 78·2kg
Capability, depending upon hull
   payload: 270kg plus
   speed: 25mph plus
   draught: 2·5cm
Shipping dimensions: 1·95 × 1·63 × 1·63m

Panther Power Pac

Panther air boats

HIGH-SPEED CATAMARAN VESSELS

AUSTRALIA

BULL'S MARINE INDUSTRIES PTY LTD

PO Box 1, Gippsland Lakes, Metung, Victoria
3904, Australia

Telephone: (051) 56 2208

Robert Bull
Don Little
Owen Cropp

Completing builder of International Catamarans'
Thunderbird for Peels Tourist and Ferry Service
Pty Ltd, Metung, Victoria.

Craft built (In Cat)	Completed	Max speed	Seats	Operator	Operations
20·4m *Thunderbird*	December 1984	25 knots	190	Peels Tourist and Ferry Service Pty Ltd	Lakes Entrance to Paynesville, cruises

INTERNATIONAL CATAMARANS PTY LTD (IN CAT)

31 Evans Street, Hobart, Tasmania, Australia

Telephone: (002) 348355
Telex: 57076 INCAT AA
Telefax: (002) 349745

4 Help Street, Chatswood, New South Wales
2067, Australia

Telephone: (02) 4111725
Telex: 72710 INCAT AA
Telefax: (02) 349745

Philip Hercus, *Director*
Robert Clifford, *Director*

International Catamarans has been established
over eleven years and is privately owned by its two
directors; Philip Hercus undertakes the design and
marketing activities in Sydney and Robert
Clifford runs the manufacturing facilities in
Hobart. The company also has interests in some
ferry operations.

The company has around 70 craft built or being
built by In Cat or its licensees, mostly in the 20- to

Wheelhouse of *Our Lady Pamela*

Craft built and ordered	Yard No	Completed	Max speed	Seats	Operator	Route
18·0m *Derwent Explorer* (ex *Jeremiah Ryan*)		September 1977	26 knots	145		
18·0m *James Kelly I*		June 1979	28 knots	100	Scenic Gordon & Hells Gates Charters	Gordon River
20·0m *Fitzroy Flyer*		June 1981	28 knots		Fitzroy Island Resort	Cairns to Fitzroy
20·0m *Tangalooma*		December 1981	28 knots	170	Tangalooma Island Resort	Brisbane to Moreton Island
15·0m *Amaroo*		December 1981	12 knots	120		
20·0m *Green Islander*		June 1982	28 knots	220	Hayles Green Island Services	
20·0m *Quicksilver*		August 1982	28 knots	100	Outer Barrier Reef Cruises	Port Douglas to outer reef & St Crispin's Reef
29·0m *Spirit of Roylen*		December 1982	27 knots	240	McLeans Roylen Cruises Pty Ltd (ex Barrier Reef Holdings)	Mackay to Brampton Island
20·0m *Magnetic Northener* (ex *Keppel Cat 2*, ex *Trojan*)		1983			Hydrofoil Seaflight Services Pty Ltd	Rosslyn Bay, Yeppoon (Rockhampton) to Great Keppel Island
20·0m *Keppel Cat I*		September 1984		195	Hydrofoil Seaflight Services Pty Ltd	Rosslyn Bay, Yeppoon (Rockhampton) to Great Keppel Island
27·4m WPC* *Spirit of Victoria*		June 1985	28 knots	—	MBM Management Ltd	—
30·0m *Our Lady Patricia*		March 1986	31 knots	452	Sealink British Ferries Sealink UK Ltd	Portsmouth to Ryde, Isle of Wight, UK
30·0m *Our Lady Pamela*		July 1986	31 knots	452	Sealink British Ferries Sealink UK Ltd	Portsmouth to Ryde, Isle of Wight, UK
31·0m WPC* *Tassie Devil 2001*	017	December 1986	30 knots	—	In Cat Charters	—
22·80m *Genesis*	018	July 1987	35 knots	—	International Catamarans Pty Ltd	Research vessel
37·0m WPC* —	019	1988	27 knots	—	Quicksilver Connections Ltd	Barrier Reef operations
37·0m WPC* —	022	1988	27 knots	—	Quicksilver Connections Ltd	Barrier Reef operations
37·0m WPC* —	023	1988	27 knots	—	Quicksilver Connections Ltd	Barrier Reef operations
37·0m WPC* —	024	1989	27 knots	—	Quicksilver Connections Ltd	Barrier Reef operations

* Wave-piercing catamaran

30-metre range. The craft are generally of aluminium construction and the majority operate as fast passenger craft though a few of the larger ones have been built as oil rig crew/supply vessels, with a large clear deck aft.

A feature of some of the International Catamarans' vessels is the use of the company's own design of lifting rudder, which only enters the water when the helm is moved, hence reducing the resistance of the vessel. The craft also feature simple and rugged construction, as well as resiliently mounted superstructures giving the boats a high degree of reliability and comfort.

In July 1986 the 30m International Catamarans *Our Lady Pamela* undertook the longest delivery voyage of any high-speed catamaran ferry, from Hobart, Tasmania to Portsmouth, UK, a distance of over 13 987 miles, arriving at Portsmouth on 30 July, 41 days 7 hours 36 minutes after leaving Hobart. All but 10 days 18 hours were spent at sea. The longest single passage covered was 2397 miles. The total fuel used was 263 700 litres, although one refuelling contained 2000 litres of salt water. For the 2138-mile passage from Gibraltar to Yarmouth, UK, the vessel averaged more than 22 knots.

As well as building craft at its Hobart facilities, International Catamarans has licensed other builders in Australia, Singapore, New Zealand, Hong Kong, USA and Great Britain.

In 1983 In Cat constructed an 8·7m test vessel conceived as a wave-piercing catamaran. This craft, *Little Devil*, first underwent trials in 1984 and the results obtained allowed In Cat to proceed with a 28m wave-piercing catamaran, the *Spirit of Victoria*, which has been in commercial operation since mid-1985. This craft was followed by *Tassie Devel 2001* launched in December 1986, a 31m wave-piercing catamaran of similar construction to its predecessor but with enclosed side supports and improved appearance. She operated in the rough waters off Perth during the America's Cup races. These craft are capable of higher speeds and operation in bigger waves than the conventional catamarans. There are plans for 50m and larger versions of this new concept of vessel, with speeds in excess of 40 knots and with vehicle-carrying capacity.

Future catamaran development is seen to concentrate on the wave-piercer concept, in which great interest has been shown. The superior seakeeping and high performance of these craft are proving very attractive to passengers and operators alike. In January 1988 In Cat announced orders for four 37·2m wave-piercing catamarans for Australia and one for the USA (with more powerful engines), plus three orders for 31m versions, one for a 37m and one for a 43m. The yards in which these craft are to be built have not been specified.

30-METRE CATAMARAN
OUR LADY PATRICIA
OUR LADY PAMELA

CLASSIFICATION: Det norske Veritas + 1A1 Light Craft (CAT) R45 Passenger Ship EO UK DOT Class IV Partially Smooth Water Limits Passenger Vessel.

The first of these vessels entered service with Sealink British Ferries on 29 March 1986 and the second arrived on 30 July 1986.

HULL: Welded aluminium alloy construction (5083-H321 plating, 6061-T6 sections) with the superstructure on anti-vibration mountings. There are large gangway doors on the upper deck for embarkation and disembarkation at the existing Portsmouth and Ryde Pier berthing facilities.

ENGINES/GEARBOXES: Two MTU 16V 396 TC83 diesels of 1430kW each at 1845rpm continuous rating. Gearboxes are ZF BW 750, ratio 2·548:1.

PROPULSION: Two five-blade aluminium bronze fixed-pitch propellers.

AUXILIARY GENERATORS: Two Perkins 4108 diesels driving 26kVA alternators.

CONTROLS: International Catamarans patented hydraulically-operated lifting rudders.
NAVIGATION AND COMMUNICATIONS: Two radars, gyrocompass, two VHF radios, one echo sounder.
DIMENSIONS
Length overall: 29·60m
Length waterline: 25·50m
Beam overall (excluding fenders): 11·20m
Beam of single hull: 3·20m
Draught, loaded: 2·20m

WEIGHTS
Empty craft: 80·0 tonnes
Passengers and baggage: 37·5 tonnes
Crew and effects: 0·6 tonnes
Fresh water (500 litres): 0·5 tonnes
Fuel (two 2400-litre tanks): 4·0 tonnes
Baggage in containers: 2·4 tonnes
Total disposable load: 45·0 tonnes
PERFORMANCE
Trials speed (with disposable load of 22·5 tonnes): 31 knots

Our Lady Patricia departing Portsmouth harbour, UK

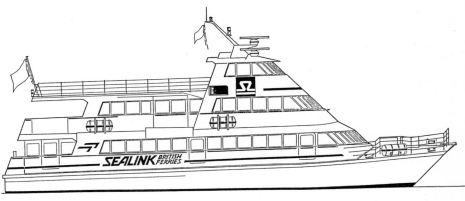

In Cat 30m catamaran as supplied to Sealink British Ferries

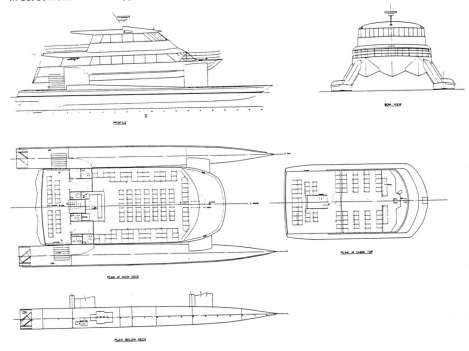

General Arrangement of *Spirit of Victoria*

International Catamarans wave-piercing catamaran ferry *Spirit of Victoria*

SPIRIT OF VICTORIA

This unusual 28-metre craft, Yard No 016, was launched in June 1985. The object of the design is to minimise the wave-following tendency as experienced by conventional semi-planing and planing hull craft; for this to be achieved a hull form that would cut through waves was envisaged. To explore the possibilities of this concept an 8·6-metre manned model, *Little Devil*, was constructed capable of carrying six people and powered by a 25hp outboard motor; extremely encouraging results were achieved, a speed of 16 knots being obtained at a scale displacement of 1·1 tonnes. This led to the decision to build a 28-metre version, *Spirit of Victoria*, with the backing of MBM Management Pty Ltd which was prepared to operate the boat under long term charter.

OWNER: In Cat Charters.
OPERATOR: MBM Management Pty Ltd, Melbourne, Australia.
HULL: Welded marine-grade aluminium. Materials: 5083 H321, and 6061 T6 alloys, 5086 H32.

SURVEY: Marine Board of Victoria, Class 1C.
CLASSIFICATION: DnV + 1A 2K Light Craft R15.
ENGINES: Two DDA GM 12V-92 TA, 650bhp each, at 1980rpm continuous rating.
PROPULSION: Two five-blade, 1000mm diameter Wageningen B series propellers.
GEARBOX: Two Reintjes WVS 532, ratio 2·452:1.
GENERATOR: Deutz S2L912 diesel-driven 17·5kVA alternator 415V, 3-phase, 50Hz ac or 240V, single-phase, 50Hz ac.
NAVIGATION: 24n mile JRC radar; Wagner Mk II autopilot.
COMMUNICATIONS: Codan 8121 SSB, GME VHF, Clarion PA.
ACCOMMODATION
219 seats; 115 in main cabin, 40 in upper cabin, 22 open main deck, 42 open upper deck
DIMENSIONS
Length overall: 27·40m
Length waterline: 25·0m
Beam overall: 13·02m

Beam, single hull: 2·22m
Draught: 1·74m
CAPACITIES
Fuel: Two 3500-litre tanks
Fresh water: One 300-litre tank
PERFORMANCE
Speed, light ship: 28 knots
Speed, full load: 26 knots

TASSIE DEVIL 2001

A developed version of *Spirit of Victoria* and the third wave-piercing catamaran to be built. The vessel is built under survey by Det norske Veritas Class + 1A1 Light Craft (CAT) R45. In addition the vessel is under survey by The Navigation and Survey Authority of Tasmania, Class ID, Partially Smooth Water Limits Passenger Vessel.
POWERPLANT: Two MWM 234 16V, 830kW each at 2265rpm (overload rating), 755kW each at 2200rpm (continuous light duty rating). Gearboxes ZF type BW 250, reduction ratio 3:1. Flexible couplings: Vulcan Rato S.

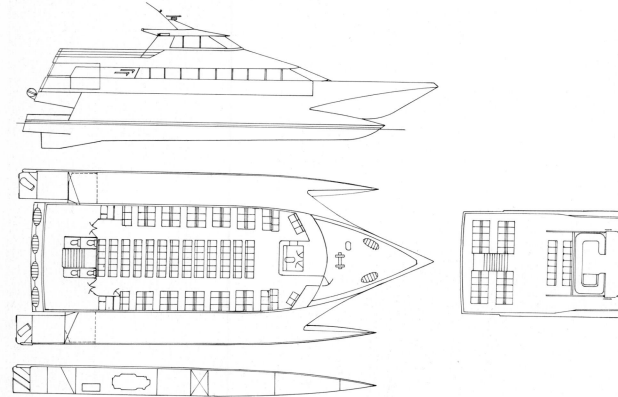

General Arrangement of *Tassie Devil 2001*

International Catamarans' *Tassie Devil 2001*

Tassie Devil 2001

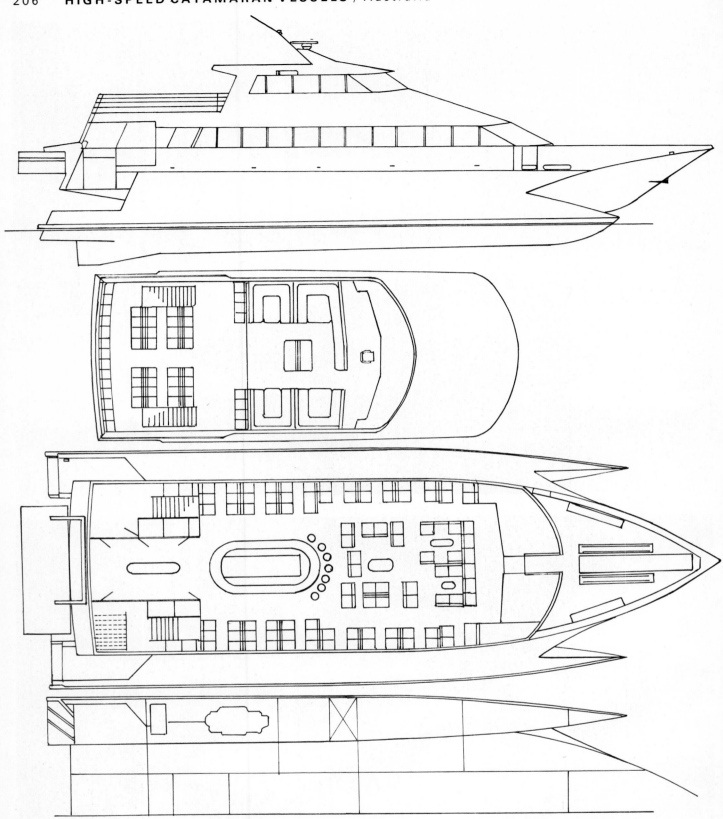

General Arrangement of 31·0m In Cat wave-piercing catamaran for Hamilton Island Enterprises

Tassie Devil 2001

PROPELLERS: 5-blade modified Troost 'B' type, aluminium bronze, 1383mm pitch, 1150mm diameter, blade-area ratio: 0·89.
ACCOMMODATION: 196 passengers.
NAVIGATION: Furuno 1700 radar, Mariner log.
COMMUNICATIONS: Codan 8121 HF, President Sea Eagle 55 VHF.
DIMENSIONS
Length: 30·45m
Length waterline (excluding trim tab): 25·00m
Beam (excluding fenders): 13·00m
Draught loaded: Approx 2·0m
PERFORMANCE
Speed, max: 31 knots

GENESIS

An In Cat development vessel launched August 1987 for development with waterjet systems, surface-drive systems and In Cat transom drive.
POWERPLANT: Two GM DDA 16V-92 TA, 930kW each at 2300rpm. Gearboxes: Niigata MGN 332X, ratio: 2·50:1.
PROPELLERS: Aluminium bronze surface-piercing types under development.
DIMENSIONS
Length: 22·80m
Length, waterline (excluding trim tab): 18·50m
Beam (excluding fenders): 8·20m
Draught, design waterline (excluding propeller): 0·88m
PERFORMANCE: On trials speeds up to 35 knots have been reached.

In Cat *Genesis*, a 22·8m development craft

Surface-piercing propeller development on In Cat *Genesis*

37·2-METRE WAVE-PIERCING CATAMARAN

Four of these vessels are on order for Quicksilver Connections Ltd, Port Douglas, Queensland.
SURVEY: Queensland Department of Harbours and Marine, Class 1G.
CONSTRUCTION: All-welded aluminium generally using alloys 5083 H321 and 6061 T6. Some light plates are 5086 H32.
POWER: Two GM diesel engines model 16V-149 TIB, each coupled to ZF gearbox model BU 460. Each engine will be rated 1230BkW at 1800rpm.
ACCOMMODATION: Interior seats will be individual armchairs with woollen upholstery. Exterior seats will be moulded polypropelene shells. A food service area will be fitted at the aft end of the lower cabin and a drinks bar will be fitted in the middle of the lower cabin. Passengers spaces will be air-conditioned.
WATERJETS: The vessel will be fitted with two KaMeWa waterjets model 63S 62/6.
ELECTRICAL SYSTEMS: Main services will be supplied by either of two diesel engine driven alternator sets. These will supply 415V 3ph and 240V 1ph 50Hz power. Engine starting, auxiliary and emergency services will be supplied from 24V dc battery banks.
DIMENSIONS
Length overall: 37·2m
Beam overall (excluding fenders): 15·6m
Beam hull: 2·6m
Draught (max): 1·3m
CAPACITIES
Passenger capacity: 340
Fuel capacity, normal: Two 2000-litre tanks
Fresh water capacity: 3000 litres
PERFORMANCE
Anticipated speed, loaded: 27 knots
light: 30 knots

A notable feature of these vessels is the decision to use waterjet propulsion. This is due to the addition of a new shallow draught service to the Quicksilver Connections' schedule and the company's desire to keep all vessels identical.

In addition to the Quicksilver order a USA operator has ordered a similar 37m wave-piercing catamaran for delivery in 1988. The only significant difference between this vessel and the Quicksilver craft will be the installation of more powerful engines in the USA vessel to give a service speed of approximately 32 knots fully loaded.

Further orders have been placed for three wave-piercers, one 31m, one 37m and one 43m. Two of these vessels are scheduled for completion in 1988 and the other in 1989.

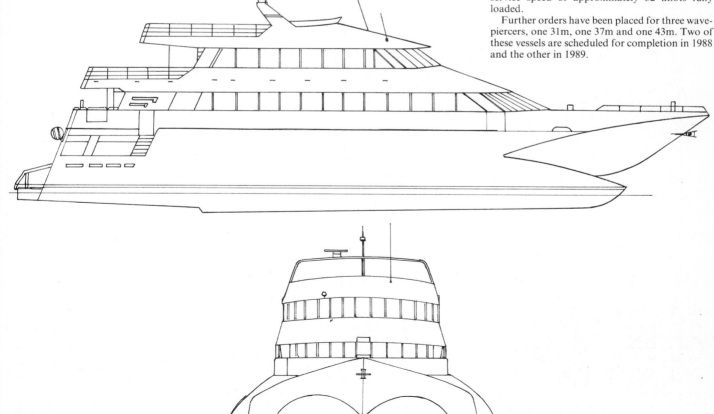

General Arrangement of 37·2m In Cat wave-piercing catamaran for Quicksilver Connections Ltd

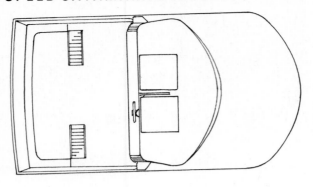

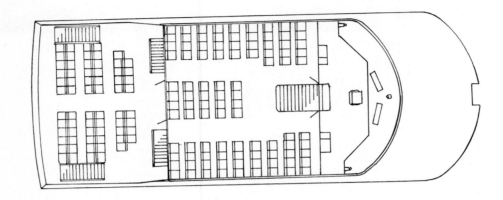

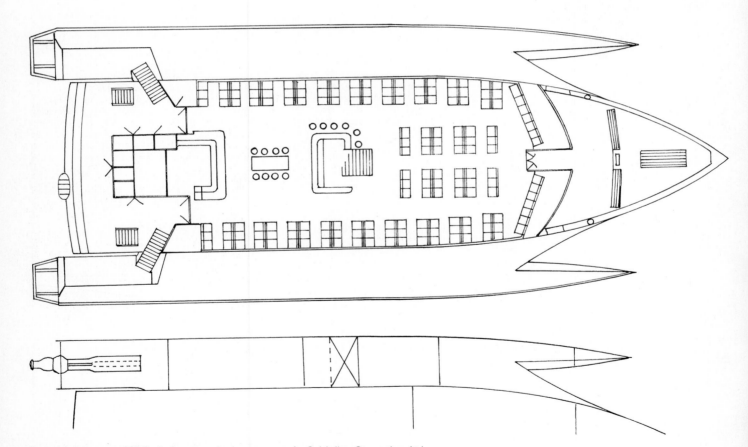

General Arrangement of 37·2m In Cat wave-piercing catamaran for Quicksilver Connections Ltd

BASS STRAIT FERRY (DESIGN)

The original wave-piercing catamaran concept was a large vessel capable of carrying 300-500 passengers and 60-80 cars at a service speed of 35-40 knots. Such a vessel would operate a ferry service across Bass Strait, the very rough waterway between Tasmania and the Australian mainland. With the establishment of the wave-piercing concept in smaller craft, attention has again turned to the Bass Strait vessel.

Preliminary details of an In Cat proposal for a Bass Strait wave-piercing ferry were released in early 1988:

All-aluminium construction with passenger spaces resiliently mounted to minimise noise and vibration, this feature being in common with conventional In Cat catamarans

Four engine, four waterjet propulsion to maximise reliability

Capacity for approximately 90 cars on a drive-through vehicle deck. The clear height on the vehicle deck is 2·2m at the sides and 3·5m at the centre to suit the perceived needs for the Bass Strait service. These heights can be easily increased if necessary at the cost of the small increase in weight and a small increase in

motion in the passenger spaces due to their greater height in vessel

Generous-sized passenger spaces due in part to the length of the crossing (about 4 hours) and in part to the ready availability of the required space. There are a number of survey and safety aspects which require special attention on this large wave-piercer:

The vessel has access stairs in each corner of the passenger deck. In Cat believe that the best evacuation proposal will be to provide exits in the cabin side adjacent to each of the stairs and to fit inflatable slides to give access from the passenger deck to inflatable rafts. Some small changes will have to be made to the passenger deck layout to provide space for the stowage of the slides and rafts

A fire detection system will be fitted in the vehicle deck, supported by a sprinkler system for fire extinguishing. Structural fire protection will be fitted to the underside of the passenger accommodation

As the vessel has no need for buoyant spaces above the vehicle deck it is intended that the vehicle deck will be open at the aft end to facilitate ventilation. This also means that adequate arrangements can be made to drain overboard any water which might find its way onto the vehicle deck. Consequently the vessel is not vulnerable to damage of the bow door; the door is only fitted to give weather protection to the vehicles.

No major problems are foreseen in attending to the above. It is believed that other aspects of safety, eg intact and damaged stability, lifesaving appliances, fire protection, etc can be readily and adequately covered by conventional regulations such as IMO Code A.373(X).

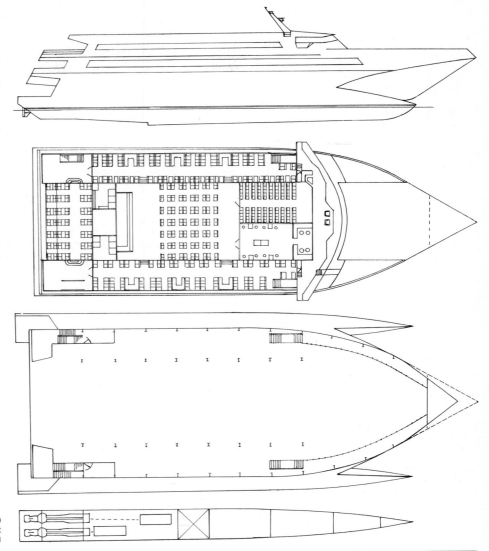

Preliminary In Cat design for a 60-80 car, 300-500 passenger wave-piercing catamaran for the Bass Strait crossing

NQEA AUSTRALIA PTY LTD

Buchan Street, PO Box 1105, Cairns, Queensland 4870, Australia

Telephone: 70 51 6600
Telex: 48087 AUS AA
Telefax: 70 51 5520

D G Fry, *Chief Executive*
S Grimley, *Managing Director*

G M Steene, *Executive Director, Marketing*
A Rankine, *Executive Director, Production*
R D Rookwood, *Senior Design Engineer*
A E G Mill, *Company Secretary*

NQEA started services in 1948 from the residence of its founder with a staff of three, the principal activity being the operation of general engineering agencies, leading to general engineering manufacture and in 1964 it entered the ship-

building industry with the construction of dumb barges. This was followed by work on many types of vessel, including Australian Navy patrol boats until in 1975 the first construction of vessels was undertaken. In 1977 NQEA was the successful tenderer for 14 'Freemantle' 42m class patrol craft, for the Australian Navy, the first having been built by Brooke Marine in England. Taking 85 weeks to construct the craft, NQEA was delivering at a rate of one every 14 weeks.

Craft built (In Cat)	Yard No	Delivered	Seats Class 1D	Seats Class 1C	Operator	Route
23·0m *Green Island Express*		June 1982	230	100	Hayles Green Island Services	Cairns to Green Island, Michaelmus Cay, Outer Barrier Reef
23·0m *Telford Reef*		October 1982		204	Telford South Molle Island Resort	
23·0m *Magnetic Express*		March 1983	240	100	Hayles Magnetic Island Pty Ltd	
29·2m *Telford Capricorn*		November 1983		326	Telford South Molle Island Resort	Whitsunday Island Group, North Queensland
23·0m *Cougar*		1984		200	Kalford Pty Ltd	Brisbane to Moreton Bay (Redcliffe)
23·0m *Reef Link**		1984	210	150	Reef Link Pty Ltd	Townsville to John Brewer Reef
24·0m *Quickcat I*		August 1984		145	Hamilton Island Enterprises	Shute Harbour to Hamilton plus Whitsunday and Great Barrier Reef cruises
24·0m *Quickcat II*		1985		195	Hamilton Island Enterprises	Shute Harbour to Hamilton plus Whitsunday and Great Barrier Reef cruises
30·0m *Reef Cat*		May 1986		305	Hayles Green Island Services	Cairns to Green Island and to Outer Barrier Reef
30·0m *Quicksilver*		October 1986		308	Low Island Cruises	Port Douglas to Agincourt Reef
24·0m *Supercat II*		October 1986		205	Fullers Captain Cook Cruises	Bay of Islands, New Zealand
30·0m *Reef Link 2*	147	February 1987		403	Reef Link Pty Ltd	Barrier Reef excursions
24·0m *Taupo Cat*	148	March 1987		205	Trout Line (The Jascar Group (NZ) Ltd)	Lake Taupo, New Zealand
30·0m *Quicksilver 2*		May 1987		300	Low Island Cruises	Port Douglas to Agincourt Reef
30·0m *Supercat III*	125	August 1987		390	Fullers Captain Cook Cruises	Auckland, New Zealand
24·0m *Roylen Sunbird*	151	August 1987		245	McLeans Roylen Cruises Pty Ltd	Mackay to Whitsunday Islands
30·0m *Reef King*	152	1988		—	Hayles Green Island Services	Queensland
24·0m —		1988		—	—	Queensland Fisheries Patrol

* Destroyed by fire, mid-1987

More recently NQEA has been building a number of high-speed catamarans, designed by International Catamarans of Sydney. Aircraft-type seating is fitted internally and moulded polypropylene shell seats externally.

23-METRE CATAMARAN

In Cat design with an all-welded aluminium hull. The superstructure is resiliently mounted to minimise noise and vibration.
SURVEYING AUTHORITY: Marine Board of Queensland, Partially Smooth Water (Class 1D), Restricted Offshore (Class 1C).
POWERPLANT: Two 800shp GM 12V-92 TA with Niigata MGN 80 reverse reduction gearbox 97:1.
PROPELLERS: Five-blade aluminium bronze.
ELECTRICAL POWER: 415V ac from shore power, or 35kVA Perkins diesel generator set 24V dc.
DIMENSIONS
Length overall: 23·0m
Length hull: 21·8m
Length waterline: 19·5m
Beam: 8·7m
Beam, single hull only: 2·5m
Draught loaded (max): 1·7m
Fuel capacity: Two 3000-litre tanks
PERFORMANCE
Speed, trial: 29 knots
Speed, cruising: 25 knots, loaded
Range: 1500 miles

28-METRE CATAMARAN

In Cat design with an all-welded aluminium hull and a resiliently mounted superstructure to minimise noise and vibration.
CLASSIFICATION: Queensland Marine Board, Class 1C, November 1983.
POWERPLANT: Two 1200shp GM 16V-92 TA high-speed diesels with ZF reverse/reduction gearbox 2·4:1.
PROPELLERS: Five-blade aluminium bronze.
ELECTRICAL POWER: 415V ac from shore power, or 80kVA GM diesel alternator set 24V dc.
DIMENSIONS
Length overall: 29·2m
Length hull: 28·0m
Length waterline: 25·0m
Beam: 11·2m
Air draught to cabin top: 8·7m
Draught loaded (max): 1·76m
Fuel capacity: Two 5000-litre tanks
GRT: 340·43

NQEA-built In Cat 23m *Telford Reef* showing the drop rudder configuration and stern hull shape

NQEA In Cat 24m *Supercat II*   *(Yon Ivanovic)*

An NQEA 24m catamaran on trials prior to export to New Zealand for operations on Lake Taupo   *(Yon Ivanovic)*

PERFORMANCE
Speed, trial: 29 knots
Speed, cruising: 26 knots

CHEETAH PATROL BOAT

NQEA has designed a patrol boat variant of the 23m commercial catamaran design. These boats will be identified as the Cheetah Class. One has been constructed for the Queensland Fisheries department and will be used for surveillance work in northern Australian waters. Normally operated by a six man crew, the craft has facilities to carry an additional 12-man landing party and has extended range cruising capabilities.

CREWBOAT PROJECT (DESIGN)

Another NQEA design variant based on an In Cat 29m hull arrangement and fitted with water-jet propulsion.

30·0m *Supercat III* being finished 23 August 1987 prior to delivery to New Zealand   (Yon Ivanovic)

Midway through the construction of a 30m catamaran in the under cover workshops of NQEA   (Yon Ivanovic)

PRECISION MARINE HOLDINGS PTY LTD

Cockburn Road, Jervoise Bay, Western Australia, Australia
PO Box 240, Hamilton Hill 6163, Western Australia, Australia

Telephone: 410 2222
Telex: 93517 PREMAR AA
Telefax: 410 2319

Robert Blom, *Managing Director*
John Baldock, *General Manager*

TROPIC SUNSEEKER

Built in 98 days from conception to first fare-paying passenger for Gibsea Pty Ltd, for Cairns to Townsville operation.

SURVEY: Western Australian Department of Marine and Harbours.
DESIGNER: Lock Crowther, Sydney, New South Wales, Australia.

Craft built	Seats	Delivered	Owner
33·40m *Tropic Sunseeker* (Yard No 787)	457	1985	Gibsea Pty Ltd
33·40m —	—	—	—
33·40m —	—	—	—
33·40m —	—	1986	—
33·40m —	—	1987	—
36·00m *Capricorn Reefseeker*	350	September 1987	Keppel Island Tourist Services
30·00m *Reef Adventurer II*	150	November 1987	P&O Australia

Precision Marine Holdings' *Tropic Sunseeker*, built in 98 days

HULL, DECK AND SUPERSTRUCTURE: Marine grade aluminium alloy, welded.
MAIN ENGINES: Two MWM TBD 604B V12, 1260kW each, at 1800rpm, fitted with ZF BW 460 2·025:1 ratio gearboxes.
ACCOMMODATION
Main deck: 225 aircraft-style seats
Upper deck: 139 couch seats
Aft deck: 93 aircraft-style seats
PROPELLERS: Stone Marine Singapore, five-blade, skewed.
SYSTEMS
Electrical: Two MWM D226 RTES generators, 55kVA each
Navigational equipment: Depth sounder. Koden CVS88 chromascope sounder; radar, Koden MDC 411 colour, satellite navigator, Navstar A300S; autopilot, Robertson AP40
Communications equipment: Radio, Codan HF8121, President Sea Eagle VHF, Uniden Seawasp and Philips UHF

DIMENSIONS
Length, overall: 33·40m
Length, waterline: 30·00m
Beam: 12·90m
Draught: 1·70m

WEIGHT
Displacement, approx, loaded: 170 tonnes
 empty: 67·0 tonnes

PERFORMANCE
Speed, max: 30 knots
Range: 700n miles
Fuel tanks capacity: 19 000 litres
Fresh water capacity: 7000 litres

CAPRICORN REEFSEEKER
Built in 18 weeks at a price of A\$3·0 million for day tripper/dive boat use with the Great Barrier Reef tourist trade.
DESIGNER: Lock Crowther.
MAIN ENGINES: Two MWM TBD 604B V12 driving through ZF BW 460 gearboxes.
ACCOMMODATION: 350 passengers.

The largest high-speed catamaran to be built in Australia (September 1987), the 36m Precision Marine *Capricorn Reefseeker*

DIMENSIONS
Length overall: 36·00m
Length waterline: 32·50m
Beam: 12·90m
Draught: 1·70m
WEIGHT
Lightship: 106 tonnes
CAPACITIES
Fuel tanks: 14 000 litres
Water tanks: 4000 litres
PERFORMANCE
Speed, max: 30 knots
Speed, continuous: 28 knots
Range, cruising: 750n miles

30·0-METRE CATAMARAN

A high-speed catamaran for service by a P&O company between Gladstone and Heron Island, Queensland. Cost A$2·5 million.
DESIGNER: Lock Crowther.
MAIN ENGINES: Two MWM TBD 604B V9 driving through ZF BW 255 gearboxes.
ACCOMMODATION: 150 passengers.
DIMENSIONS
Length overall: 30·00m
Length waterline: 27·75m
Beam: 10·00m
Draught: 1·30m
WEIGHT
Lightship: 50 tonnes
CAPACITIES
Fuel tanks: 12 000 litres
Water tanks: 2400 litres
PERFORMANCE
Speed, max: 30 knots
Range: 750n miles

38·0-METRE CATAMARAN

A new design offered in the autumn of 1987 with the first boat going to Chu Kong Shipping for August 1988 delivery.
CAPACITIES
Passengers: 280
Fuel capacity: 10 000 litres
Water capacity: 1500 litres
Sewage capacity: 800 litres
DIMENSIONS
Length overall: 38·00m
Length waterline: 35·50m
Beam: 12·90m
Draught: 1·30m

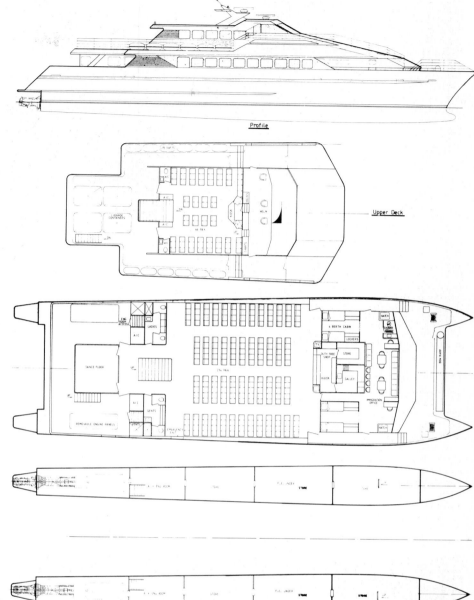

Precision Marine 38·0m catamaran

SBF ENGINEERING

Waters Edge, Lot 33 Cockburn Road, South Coogee, Western Australia 6166, Australia

Telephone: (09) 4102022/2244
Telefax: (09) 4101807

VICTORY III

Passenger ferry.
DESIGNER: Lock Crowther, Sydney.
OWNER: Great Keppel Island Tourist Services Pty Ltd, Rockhampton, Queensland, Australia.
LEGISLATING AUTHORITY: Queensland Marine and Harbours Department.
HULL: Catamaran hull and superstructure are constructed in all-welded marine grade aluminium alloy. Each bow has a streamlined bulb on the forefoot which increases waterline length and performance. Draught of hulls forward is slightly over 1m and the craft is designed to be beached by the bow to allow passengers to embark and disembark using an SBF designed telescopic ramp lowered from the foredeck.
MAIN ENGINES: Two MWM 16-cylinder marine diesels, each producing 807kW (1082bhp).
PROPULSION: Two right handed 970mm × 1760mm propellers.
ACCOMMODATION
Passenger capacity: 448
SYSTEMS
Electrical generator: One MWM 3-cylinder generator producing 33kVA

High-speed catamaran craft built	Seats	Operator	Route
33·0m *Victory III*	448	Great Keppel Island Tourist Services Ltd	
33·37m *Tropic Sunbird*	500 +	Sunseeker Cruises, Queensland, Australia	Cairns-Townsville-Dunk Island
33·37m *Quickcat*	500 +	Waiheke Shipping, Auckland, New Zealand	Auckland-Waiheke

SBF Engineering *Victory III* showing bulbous bows

Navigational equipment: JRC JMA 3425 colour radar; NWU 51 colour plotter; JAX2 Weatherfox; JLE 3850 satellite navigator; JFV 80 colour sounder

Communications: Codan 8121 SSB radio; Icom IC M80 VHF radio

Life saving: 450 coastal life jackets; 450 flotation rafts

Firefighting: Halon gas fire extinguishers

DIMENSIONS

Length overall: 33·0m

Beam: 10·0m

Draught: 1·40m

PERFORMANCE

Speed, max: 28 knots

Speed, fully loaded: 24 knots

TROPIC SUNBIRD

Passenger ferry, but first employed as a top press and spectator boat at the 1987 America's Cup.

DESIGNER: Lock Crowther, Sydney.

OWNER: Sunseeker Cruises, Cairns, Queensland.

LEGISLATION AUTHORITY: Department of Marine and Harbours, Western Australia.

HULL: Catamaran hull and superstructure are constructed in all-welded marine grade aluminium alloy. The hulls incorporate bulbous bows which reduce pitching through their extra buoyancy. This craft can carry up to 600 passengers (including its external seating) and has a very shallow draught of 1·36m.

ENGINES: Two Deutz-MWM TBD 604B V12.

GEARBOXES: Two ZF BW 455.

ELECTRONICS: Koden MDC 4105 Colour radar; Koden CVS 88 Colour echo sounder; Robertson AP-40 autopilot; Codan 8121 12V radio.

DIMENSIONS

Length overall: 33·37m

Length, design waterline: 30·01m

Beam: 13·00m

Draught: 1·36m

PERFORMANCE

Speed, max: 32 knots

Speed, cruise: 27 knots

QUICKCAT

Passenger ferry.

DESIGNER: Lock Crowther, Turramurra, NSW, Australia.

OWNER: Waiheke Shipping Co Ltd, Auckland, New Zealand.

LEGISLATION AUTHORITY: New Zealand Ministry of Transport.

ELECTRONICS: Koden 410 Colour radar; Raytheon echo sounder; Wagner SE autopilot; Codan 8121 24V radio.

PRINCIPAL PARTICULARS: As for *Tropic Sunbird* except that passenger cabin behind wheelhouse for *Quickcat* extends to the full width of the craft over its whole length.

The SBF catamaran *Tropic Sunbird*, another Lock Crowther bulbous-bow hull design

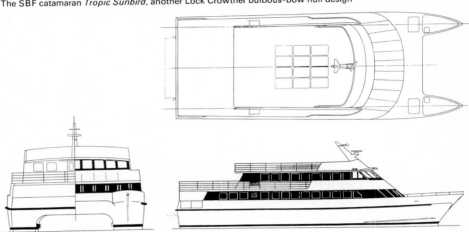

Tropic Sunbird General Arrangement

The SBF *Quickcat*, a sister vessel to *Tropic Sunbird*

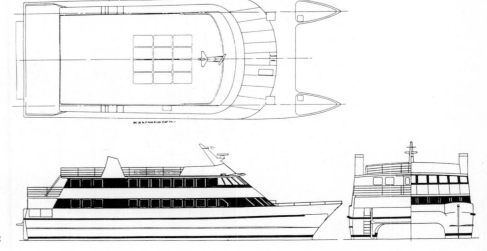

Quickcat General Arrangement

FINLAND

MXA-CONSULTING LTD OY [DESIGNERS]

It Pitkäkatu 3a D, Box 38, SF-20520 Turku, Finland

Telephone: (921) 333881
Telex: 62004 TURKU SF
Telefax: (921) 331934

Matti Ahtikari

MXA 1700

Designed by Matti Ahtikari, MXA-Consulting Ltd, Finland, the MXA 1700 is a 90-seat, shallow draught high-speed catamaran ferry built in marine grade aluminium. This is the first such vessel to employ an Arneson Surface Drive propulsion system. The vessel is classified by DnV, IAI-R45 EO Light Craft. Hull construction was undertaken by Waterman Oy.

The first vessel was completed in mid-1986.

POWERPLANT/PROPULSION: Two Isuzu UM 12 PB 1 TC diesels, each 340kW at 2300rpm, fitted with ZF BW 160 gearboxes driving Arneson Surface Drive systems, type ASD 14.

EQUIPMENT
Hydraulics: Vickers
Navigation: Radar 16n miles Vigil 2, depth sounder VDO, two-way radio Shipmate RS 8000 F, magnetic and electric compass
Steering gear: Electric
DIMENSIONS
Length overall: 17·0m
Beam: 6·4m
Draught, max: 0·9m
WEIGHT/CAPACITIES
Passengers: About 90
Crew: 2
Displacement, max: 24·0 tonnes
Fuel tank capacity: 2000 litres
PERFORMANCE
Speed, max: 30 knots
Speed, cruising: 24 to 26 knots
Range: 300n miles
Fuel consumption: 136 litres/h

VARIANTS

River and lake versions are planned, having lower freeboard and superstructure and waterjet units may be used instead of Arneson Surface Drive systems.

MXA 1700 showing its unusual bow form (Sept 1986)

Construction of MXA 1700

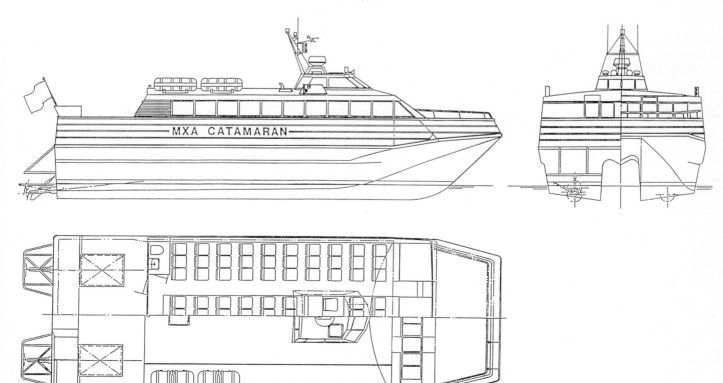
General Arrangement of MXA 1700

MXA 3300 II (DESIGN)
ENGINES: Two MTU 16V 396 TB83, 2095bhp
each.
DIMENSIONS
Length overall: 33·5m
Beam: 9·4m
Draught: 2·2m
PERFORMANCE
Speed: 25 to 28 knots
Passengers: 449

MXA 1700 high-speed catamaran ferry

FRANCE

CONSTRUCTIONS ALUMINIUM NAVALES sarl

47 Avenue Maurice Chevalier, 06150 Cannes La Bocca, France

Telephone: 93 47 30 30

VILLE DE TOULON III
A 200-passenger, 20-knot vessel (length 25m, beam 8m) launched in 1987. The superstructure is

of interest in that it is built up with tubular frames. Principal material of construction is aluminium AG 4 MC 5086. The craft is classified by Bureau Veritas.

Ville de Toulon III, one of three catamaran ferries built to a design by Constructions Aluminium Navales sarl

HONG KONG

A FAI ENGINEERS AND SHIPREPAIRERS LTD

861 Laichikok Road, Kowloon, Hong Kong

Telephone: 3-7410981/5
Telex: 45517 AFES HX
Telefax: 3-7419857

Vitus Szeto, *General Manager*

Builder of International Catamarans Pty Ltd catamarans.

Li Jiang, one of six International Catamarans 21m craft operated by People's Republic of China

Craft built (In Cat)	Completed	Seats	Speed	Operator	Route
21·0m *Mingzhu Hu*	January 1982	150	29 knots	Guangdong Province Hong Kong Macao Navigation, PRC	Hong Kong to Jiangmen
21·0m *Yin Zhou Hu*	March 1982	150	29 knots	Guangdong Province Hong Kong Macao Navigation, PRC	Hong Kong to Jiangmen
21·0m *Liuhua Hu*	September 1982	150	29 knots	Guangdong Province Hong Kong Macao Navigation, PRC	Hong Kong to Taiping
21·0m *Li Jiang*	June 1983	150	29 knots	Kwai Kong Shipping Co Ltd, Hong Kong	Hong Kong to Wuzhou
16·0m *Kwong Fai*	June 1984	40	21 knots	Castle Peak Power Co Ltd, Hong Kong	Hong Kong
21·0m *Yue Hai Chun*	October 1984	169	29 knots	Shen Zhen Shipping, PRC	Shekou to Zhuhai
21·0m *Shen Zhen Chun*	July 1985	169	29 knots	Shen Zhen Shipping, PRC	Shekou to Zhuhai
21·0m *Zhu Hai Chun*	December 1986	169	29 knots	Shen Zhen Shipping, PRC	Shekou to Zhuhai
22·0m (Patrol boat)	1987	—	33 knots	PRC	—
22·0m —	1988	—	—	—	—

ITALY

AZIMUT SpA

Corso M D'Azeglio 30, 10125 Turin, Italy

Telephone: (11) 650 21 91
Telex: 220450 AZITO I

Dr Paulo Vitelli, *President*
Dr Ing Giovanni Bianchi Anderloni, *Technical Manager*
Dr Massimo Perotti, *Export Sales*
Mrs Victoria Munsey, *Marketing Co-ordinator*

With an impressive background in the design and construction of high-speed mono-hull luxury yachts, patrol and surveillance craft (see High-speed mono-hull craft section), Azimut has a design proposal for a high-speed catamaran vessel, the AZ100.

AZ100 (DESIGN)

The AZ100 catamaran is projected in two versions, the Sea Plane for passenger transport (ferry) and the Sea Cargo for offshore platform support.

The following information relates to the Sea Plane version.

HULL: In grp, internal surfaces treated in fire resistant resin. Each hull has four structural bulkheads in grp and one in marine plywood. Deck areas in grp are reinforced with sandwich structures of balsa wood and polyurethane or divinycell. The superstructure may be in aluminium or grp.

MAIN ENGINES: Two MTU 16V 396 TB93, 2610shp each, max or two Isotta Fraschini PV 2012, 3040shp each, max.

PROPULSION: Fixed-pitch propellers.

ACCOMMODATION

Passengers: 308 covered decks
    94 sun deck
Crew: Up to 8
Cabins: 4

SYSTEMS

Electrical: Two 60kW diesel generators; batteries, engine starting 440Ah; general purpose 1200Ah; emergency radio 330Ah

Navigational equipment: One 72-mile radar; one 24-mile radar; one magnetic compass; one gyro-compass; one echo sounder

Communications equipment: One transceiver HF/SSB 400W; one transceiver VHF/FM 25W; one receiver MF/HF

DIMENSIONS

Length overall: 30·80m
Length waterline: 27·90m
Beam overall: 9·60m
Draught, max: About 1·90m

WEIGHTS

Displacement, full load: About 126 tonnes
Fuel: 6·5 tonnes
Fresh water: 2·0 tonnes

PERFORMANCE

Speed, max, full load: About 32·5 knots MTU engines; 35·0 knots IF engines
    continuous, full load: About 28·6 knots MTU engines; 31·5 knots IF engines
Range, continuous power: About 260n miles MTU engines; 230n miles IF engines

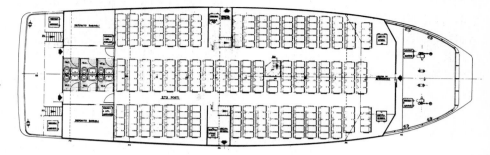

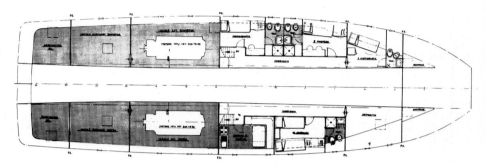

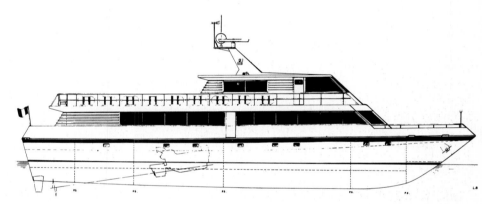

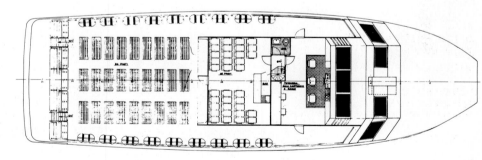

General Arrangement of the Azimut AZ100 catamaran project, Sea Plane passenger version

---

JAPAN

MITSUBISHI HEAVY INDUSTRIES

5-1, Maranouchi 2-chome, Chiyoda-ku, Tokyo, Japan

Telephone: (03) 212 3111
Telex: 22443 J

HI-STABLE CABIN CRAFT (HSCC)

See Addenda for illustration.

Announced by Mitsubishi in the autumn of 1987 this prototype catamaran craft features a passenger cabin mounted on hydraulically-actuated auto-stabilising rams. The cabin is centrally mounted on top of a 200mm diameter central hydraulic jack having a stroke of one metre. This supporting member is attached by a ball and socket joint to the hulls and positions the cabin completely clear of the hulls. Four other 85mm hydraulic rams, attached with shock absorbers, support the cabin's four corners.

When motion of the basic catamaran craft occurs in heave, yaw, surge or sway, all hydraulic rams are activated simultaneously by an on-board computer (a 16-bit personal computer) with a rapid response capability to monitoring sensors, thereby almost eliminating or minimising cabin motion. Trials have demonstrated reductions of cabin motion to one-third of the motion of the basic supporting catamaran structure.

The catamaran type was chosen as the basic vehicle because of its good stability characteristics and cabin width advantages. It is reported that the computer software required for the system was developed in a 5-year Y100m study programme initiated by MHI and supported by the semi-governmental Japan Foundation for Shipbuilding Advancement.

The prototype HSCC has the following characteristics:

Length: 12·70m
Accommodation: 12 passengers
Displacement: 17 tonnes

MITSUI ENGINEERING & SHIPBUILDING CO LTD

6-4, Tsukiji 5-chome, Chuo-ku, Tokyo 104, Japan

Telephone: (3) 544 3462
Telex: 22821 J, 22924 J

See ACV section for company officials

Under a licensing agreement concluded in 1973 with Westamarin A/S, Mandal, Norway, Mitsui built three Super Westamaran CP20s. The craft, which carries up to 182 passengers, has a cruising speed of about 25 knots, is comparable to the Norwegian-built Westamaran W86 and can operate in waves 1·2 to 1·5 metres high.

In 1978 Mitsui, employing its own design team, developed the Supermaran CP20HF, seating 195 passengers and with a cruising speed of about 30 knots. This craft has been redesigned for better seaworthiness and can operate in a maximum wave height of 2·5 metres when comfortable service can be provided with no loss of speed. Two were delivered, in March and June 1979.

The Supermaran CP30 was delivered to the Nankai Ferry Company Limited in Japan in July 1983. It carries 280 passengers at a cruising speed of 28 knots. Not only has this craft been improved for operational economy, with increased passenger capacity and comparatively less power, but also in seaworthiness. Maximum operable wave height is 3 metres and comfortable service is assured at a wave height of 2·5 metres or less with no loss of speed.

The Supermaran CP30 Mk II, *Marine Shuttle*, was introduced in service by the Tokushima Shuttle Line Co Ltd in February 1986. The vessel has a higher service speed than its predecessor the CP30, 32 knots against 28·1 knots.

A new type, the Supermaran CP10, *Marine Queen*, was delivered to the Sanzo Kigyo Co Ltd in April 1987, for cruising service in the Seto Inland Sea.

Two new 280-seat Supermaran CP30 Mk IIIs, *Blue Star* and *Sun Rise*, entered service later in 1987 with Tokushima Kosokusen Co Ltd to ply the route between Osaka and Tokushima. They have a service speed of 32 knots, and have improved seaworthiness and propulsive performance over the earlier CP20HF resulting from their greater dimensions. CP30 Mk IIIs are some of the largest high-speed catamarans built to date.

Craft built (CP types)	Yard No	Completed	Seats	Operator
26·46m CP20 Super Westamaran (ex *Blue Hawk*)		1975	162	Showa Kaiun Co Ltd
26·46m CP20 Super Westamaran (ex *Marine Star*)	02	1976	180	Setonaikai Kisen Co Ltd
26·40m CP20 Super Westamaran (ex *Sun Beam*)		1978	188	Tokushima Kosokusen Co Ltd
32·80m CP20HF Supermaran *Sun Shine*		March 1979	195	Tokushima Kosokusen Co Ltd
32·80m CP20HF Supermaran *Blue Sky*		June 1979	195	Tokushima Kosokusen Co Ltd
40·90m CP30 Supermaran *Marine Hawk*		July 1983	280	Nankai Ferry Co Ltd
41·00m CP30 Mk II Supermaran *Marine Shuttle*		February 1986	280	Tokushima Shuttle Line Co Ltd
21·67m CP10 Supermaran *Marine Queen*	1607	April 1987	88	Ueda Kaiun KK
41·00m CP30 Mk III Supermaran *Blue Star*	1605	June 1987	280	Tokushima Kosokusen Co Ltd
41·00m CP30 Mk III Supermaran *Sun Rise*	1606	July 1987	280	Tokushima Kosokusen Co Ltd

	Supermaran CP10	Super Westamaran CP20	Supermaran CP20HF	Supermaran CP30	Supermaran CP30 Mk II	Supermaran CP30 Mk III
Dimensions						
Length overall	21·67m	26·46m	32·8m	40·9m	41·0m	41·0m
Breadth	7·20m	8·8m	9·2m	10·8m mld	10·8m	10·8m
Draught	1·23m	1·18m	1·2m	1·37m full load	1·39m full load	1·39m full load
GRT, approx	80	192	275	283	268	270
Passengers	88	162 to 182	195	280	280	280
Crew	3	5	5	4	4	4
Main engines	Two GM 12V-92 TA	Two MTU 12V 331 TC82	Two Fuji Pielstick 16PA4V185-VG	Two Fuji Pielstick 16PA4V185-VG	Two Ikegai 16V 190 ATC	Two Fuji Pielstick 12 PA4V 200 VGA
Max continuous rating, each	825ps at 2170rpm	1240ps at 2270rpm	2540ps at 1475rpm	2540ps at 1475rpm	2750ps at 1450rpm	2630ps at 1475rpm
Continuous rating, each	660ps	1125ps at 2200rpm	2280ps at 1425rpm	2280ps at 1425rpm	2475ps at 1400rpm	2370ps at 1425rpm
Max speed	26·6 knots	28·5 knots	30·7 knots	approx 31·1 knots	approx 34 knots	approx 35·1 knots
Service speed, approx	21·8 knots	25 knots	30 knots	28·1 knots	32 knots	32 knots
Endurance, approx	20·0 hours	9 hours	9 hours	10 hours	8 hours	8 hours

Mitsui CP30 Mk II Supermaran *Marine Shuttle*

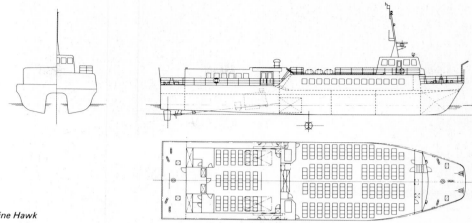

General Arrangement of Mitsui CP30 Supermaran *Marine Hawk*

SANUKI SHIP BUILDING & IRON WORKS CO LTD

Head Office: Postal code 769-11, 2112-17 Takuma, Mitoyo-gun, Kagawa-Pref, Japan

Telephone: (0875) 83-2550

Telex: 5827728 SANUKI J
Telefax: (0875) 83-6287

M Yoshikawa, *Manager, Planning Division*

The Sanuki Ship Building & Iron Works was established in February 1942. The yard has 8 berths and vessels of up to 3800 tons can be built. The company has built many kinds of aluminium high-speed passenger vessels and in 1987 launched a 30m high-speed catamaran craft very similar to the Marinteknik JC-F1 type. The Sanuki vessel is powered by two Deutz MWM TBD 604B V12 engines, 1260kW each at 1800rpm.

MALAYSIA

HONG LEONG-LÜRSSEN SHIPYARD BERHAD

4567 Jalan Chain Ferry, PO Box 43, 12700 Butterworth, PW, Malaysia

Telephone: (04) 347755
Telex: 40015 HLYARD MA

Telefax: (04) 342424

Kwek Hong P'ng, *Director*
G Lurssen, *Director*
Darwis bin Mohammed Daek, *Director*
Quek Leng Chan, *Director*
Klaus Jurges, *Director*

James Puthucheary, *Director*
Chuah Saik Ang, *Director*
Dr G F Kohler, *Director*
Mohammed Nasir bin Abdul Samad, *Director*
Roger Tan Kim Hock, *Director*
Chuah Chuan Yong, *Deputy General Manager*
Teh Choon Meng, *Financial Controller*

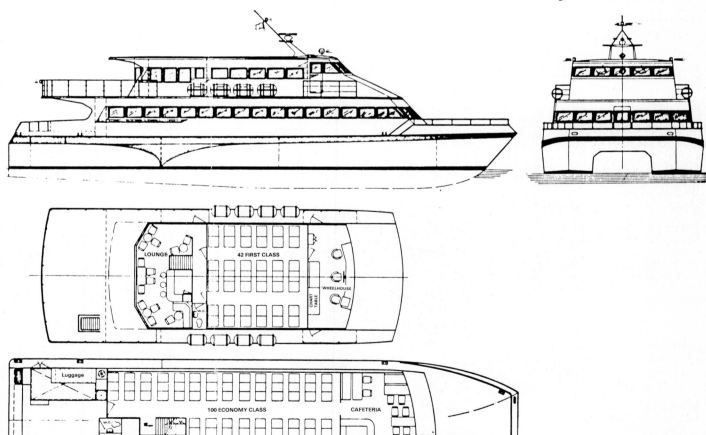

Hong Leong-Lürssen design for 28m catamaran, luxury cruise version, long range

Hong Leong-Lürssen-built *Zaharah*

Hong Leong-Lürssen was established in 1969 as a joint venture between Hong Leong Industries Bhd, Permodalan Nasional Bhd and Fr Lürssen Werft (GmbH & Co) of West Germany. The company engages in ship repair and shipbuilding of up to 2000-ton vessels.

ZAHARAH

This catamaran vessel (Hull No 1204) entered service in September 1984 for civil passenger transport.

HULL: Shipbuilding steel grade A. Longitudinal frames on web frames.
ACCOMMODATION: Crew 6, passengers 131. The vessel is air-conditioned.
POWERPLANT: Two MAN D 2542 MLE, each 625hp at 2300rpm. Fuel: Marine diesel oil, two fuel tanks, total capacity 2800 litres.
PROPELLERS: Stone Marine 850mm diameter Cunial.
SYSTEMS, ELECTRICAL: One generator, 23kW, 230V, single phase, 50Hz and 24V dc.

RADIO: One VHF Philips 828.
DIMENSIONS
Length overall: 21·75m
Beam overall: 8·0m
Draught max: 1·40m
WEIGHTS
Weight, empty: 48 tonnes
Max disposable load: 11 tonnes
PERFORMANCE
Speed, cruising: Approx 18 knots
Range: Approx 200n miles

28-METRE PASSENGER CATAMARAN (DESIGN)

Hong Leong-Lürssen Shipyard Berhad has developed its own high-speed catamaran design to meet the growing demand for high-speed craft in the Far East. Based on hard chine, symmetric hulls, the hull has been designed and tank-tested for operating speeds of 30 to 35 knots.

The basic platform is offered with various superstructure configurations depending on the role of the craft and is suitable for both propeller and waterjet propulsion.
CLASSIFICATION: DnV 1A1 R90.
POWERPLANT: Two MWM TBD 604B V12 1714hp each at 1800rpm*, speed 33 to 35 knots or Two MTU 12V 396 TB63 1330hp each at 1650 rpm*, speed 30 to 32 knots.
(* = derated for tropical conditions.)
DIMENSIONS
Length, overall: 28·00m
Length, waterline: 26·00m
Breadth: 9·00m
Depth: 2·90m
Draught (hull): 0·95m
PERFORMANCE
Payload: 18 tonnes (for high-speed operation)
Range (at 30 knots): 250n miles

NEW ZEALAND

INTERNATIONAL CATAMARANS (PACIFIC) LTD

Riverside Drive, Whangeri, New Zealand

Builder of two International Catamarans Pty Ltd craft.

Craft built	Completed	Speed	Seats	Operator
18·0m *Tiger Lily*	December 1979	22 knots	150	Mount Cook Line, New Zealand
18·0m *Tiger Lily II*	January 1981	22 knots	150	Mount Cook Line, New Zealand

WANGANUI BOATS NEW ZEALAND LTD

PO Box 8032, Wanganui, New Zealand
Shipyard: Heads Road

Telephone: 45 044
Telex: 3455 NZ

Douglas Wild, *Managing Director*
Chris Lendrum, *General Manager*

This company has built over 200 vessels of many types ranging from fishing vessels, workboats, dredges, tourist vessels, patrol boats, ocean-going yachts and more recently, high-speed catamaran ferries, designed by International Catamarans Pty Ltd of Sydney, Australia.

TIGER LILY III
POWERPLANT: Two MWM diesels, 660hp each, at 1900rpm.
Auxiliary power unit: MWM Markon 50kVA
ACCOMMODATION: 225 seats.
DIMENSIONS
Length, overall: 23·2m
Length, hulls: 22·0m
Beam: 8·7m
Draught, full load: 1·7m
PERFORMANCE
Speed, fully loaded: 22·5 knots at 1900rpm

Craft built	Completed	Speed	Seats	Operator
19·2m In Cat *Fiordland Flyer*	September 1985	22 knots	140	Fiordland Travel Ltd, New Zealand
23·2m In Cat *Tiger Lily III*	December 1985	21 knots	225	Mount Cook Line, New Zealand

Tiger Lily III (Wanganui Boats NZ Ltd)

FIORDLAND FLYER
POWERPLANT: Two MAN V10, 450hp each at 1800rpm.
Auxiliary power unit: MWM Markon 15kVA
ACCOMMODATION: 140 seats.
DIMENSIONS
Length, overall: 19·2m
Length, hull: 18·0m
Beam: 6·5m
Draught, full load: 1·6m
PERFORMANCE
Speed, fully loaded: 22 knots

Fiordland Flyer (Wanganui Boats NZ Ltd)

WHANGAREI ENGINEERING & CONSTRUCTION LTD (WECO)
PO Box 24, Port Road, Whangarei, New Zealand

Telephone: (089) 482 219
Telex: 21578 NZ
Telefax: (089) 487 845

Auckland office: 411 Great South Road, Penrose, New Zealand
PO Box 12496, Auckland 5, New Zealand

Telephone: (09) 599 512/593 941

Artist's impression of WECO design for 24m, 230-passenger catamaran ferry

NORWAY

BÅTSERVICE VERFT A/S
PO Box 113, N-4501 Mandal, Norway

Telephone: 43 61 011
Telex: 21862 YARD N
Telefax: 43 64 580

MXA 4200 II
In January 1988 it was announced that Båtservice Verft had reached agreement with MXA-Consulting Ltd Oy of Turku, Finland for co-operation with the intention of building MXA catamaran designs. The first design to be built may be the MXA 4200 II high-speed ferry.
CLASS: DnV 1A1 R150 EO light craft passenger ship.
ENGINES: Two MTU 16V 396 TB84, 2774hp each.
PROPELLERS: Levi Drive system.
DIMENSIONS
Length overall: 42·00m
Beam: 9·40m
Draught: 1·90m
WEIGHT
Payload: 324 passengers + 4 tonnes cargo
PERFORMANCE
Speed: About 36 knots

General Arrangement of MXA 4200 II

BRØDRENE AA BÅTBYGGERI A/S

N-6780 Hyen, Norway

Telephone: (5) 7 69 800
Telex: 42162 BRAA N

HYEN

A 25m catamaran ferry built in 1980 in glass-reinforced plastic for service with Fylkesbaatane i Sogn og Fjordane.

More recently Brødrene has built the surface-effect ships *Norcat*, *Ekwata* and *Ekwata II*; see the ACV section.

CLASSIFICATION: DnV +1 IA2 K Partly Sheltered Light Craft Catamaran.
POWERPLANT: Two MTU 12V 396 TC62, each 1200bhp at 1650rpm
Gearboxes: ZF type BW-455S, ratio 1:1·509
Auxiliary power: One Mercedes Benz OM314, 42bhp, Stamford generator 35kVA
ACCOMMODATION: 156 seats.
EQUIPMENT
Radar: Furuno FRM 60, reserve, Furuno FR 240 Mk II
Gyro: Robertson SKR-80
VHF: Sailor R143
DIMENSIONS
Length overall: 25·0m
Beam overall: 8·4m
Draught: 2·0m
GRT: 182
PERFORMANCE
Trial speed: 25·45 knots

Cirrus CIRR 27 R *Helgelandsekspressen* built by Brødrene Aa Båtbyggeri

HELGELANDSEKSPRESSEN

Delivered to Saltens Dampskibsselskab in July 1985. This Cirrus type CIRR 27 R catamaran is classified by Det norske Veritas +1 A1 R25 Light Craft. The vessel is of fibre-reinforced plastic/sandwich construction.
PROPULSION AND MACHINERY
Main engines: Two MTU 12V 396 TB83
Reduction gears: ZF BU 455
Auxiliary engines: Two Isuzu UM 4BBI
Generators: Two Stanford (29·5kVA, 220V, 50Hz)
Fire pumps: Vest Jet (electrical)
Bilge pumps: Six Dymatic Nova-Lens
Hydro pumps: Two Dymatic
Hydraulic gear for crane
ACCOMMODATION
Passenger lounge, 184 seats in 4 columns of 3 each at 85cm seat pitch
Luggage compartment aft in shelves
2·0m³ cargo room for mail and express cargo
4 toilets of which 1 for disabled and as nursery
Kiosk
Lobby for crew
Wheelhouse
DECK MACHINERY
Electrically operated anchor winch type Eurodrive
One 500lb Shpp anchor
One hydraulic deck-crane Tico 135 MSU
One searchlight type Noack
ELECTRICAL EQUIPMENT
220V/50Hz/3ph/two 29·5kVA. One set equipment on stand-by
24V emergency equipment
Shore-connection
Electrical equipment installed by Måløy Electro
HEATING AND VENTILATION
Interior has two 35kW heating capacity from main engine cooling-water, which heats fresh air

Ingøy built by Brødrene Aa Båtbyggeri,

sucked by two centrifugal fans with a capacity of 2700m³/h each
Four engine room fans
Wheelhouse has separate fresh air ventilation, electrically heated with a capacity of approximately 500m³/h
Electric heater for shore connection
ELECTRONICS
Decca radar RM 1070 with 4ft antenna; Decca radar 970 BT with 6ft antenna; gyrocompass Gyrostar NG 100; log JRC JLN 203; two VHF Sailor; mobile telephone (Cellnet) Panasonic Hand Free; econometer Ecomatic FC 10/20; fire alarm central board Autronic BX 11; two tv monitors for surveillance of engine rooms; intercom Phonico; control panel for bilging, Matre; radio/cassette-player; emergency transmitter Thron 1C
MISCELLANEOUS
Halon equipment for engine rooms, Heien-Larsen; magnet compass NOR 250; two hydraulic control systems for propellers and governor control, Hynautic; ten life-rafts, Viking 20K;

pick-up boat Zodiac, equipped for 25n miles open sea; crane for launching pick-up boat; sounding system, Soundfast 800-102
DIMENSIONS
Length overall: 27·0m
Length waterline: 24·50m
Beam: 9·0m
Depth to main deck: 2·80m
Draught, max: 1·92m
GRT: 197
CAPACITIES AND WEIGHTS
Cargo: 5 tonnes
Fuel oil: Two 3100-litre tanks
Potable water: 250 litres
Lubrication oil: 250 litres
PERFORMANCE
At 50% disposable load:
Contract speed at 80% MCR: 26 knots
Measured speed at 80% MCR: 30·2 knots
Measured speed at 100% MCR: 33·3 knots
100% MCR: Two engines at 1560hp
80% MCR: Two engines at 1250hp
Range, max, at service speed: 406n miles

FJELLSTRAND A/S

N-5632 Omastrand, Norway

Telephone: (5) 56 11 00
Telex: 42148 N
Telefax: (5) 56 12 44

Eirik Neverdal, *Managing Director*
Sverre O Arnesen, *Marketing Manager*

Craft built (25·5m Alumaran)

Yard No	Name	Completed	Operator
	Traena	1976	Helgeland Trafikkselskap A/S, Norway
1524	*Børtind*	1979	Compagnie Morbihamaise de Navigation, France (ex Saltens D/S)
	Manger	1979	Bergen-Nordhordland Rutelag A/S, Norway
	Biskopsbussen	1980	Fosen Trafikklag A/S, Norway

Kåre A Hamnes, *Technical Manager*
Leidolv Berge, *Financial Manager*

Fjellstrand of Omastrand was started in 1928 by Odd Oma. Wooden fishing boats were built first, then lifeboats in 1935, eventually in series production and from 1952 they were built in aluminium and later in grp. By 1962 boats up to 26m in length were being built. From 1964 Fjellstrand began to concentrate on aluminium boat building, first producing yachts, then fast workboats, ferries and other high-speed craft for the Scandinavian market, some of catamaran form.

At the beginning of the 1980s the potential of the export market was recognised in the fields of high-speed ferries and offshore crew/supply boats.

Following the delivery of nearly 400 aluminium vessels starting in 1952, Fjellstrand built its first catamaran (25·5m) in 1976, the Alumaran 165 type. A further four vessels of this size followed up to 1981, when the first 31·5m passenger catamaran was delivered to a Norwegian operator. Between 1981 and 1985 a further twelve 31·5m catamarans were delivered worldwide for passenger ferry work and crew/supply operations in the offshore oil industry. Design work on a larger 38·8m type started in 1983, and four of these vessels were sold in 1985 for delivery at the end of that year and early in 1986. By August 1987 a further fifteen 38·8m catamarans had been ordered, of which two were delivered in the second half of 1986 and five in the first half of 1987. The yard employs 175 people.

25·5-METRE CATAMARAN ALUMARAN 165 TYPE

An asymmetrical-hull, semi-planing catamaran fitted with either MTU 12V 339 TC62 or MTU 12V 493 TY70 engines. The following details are for *Børtind*.

Length overall: 25·67m
Beam, max: 9·28m
Draught: 1·20m
Approx GRT: 197
Seats: 194
Cargo capacity: 4 tonnes/5·5m³
Fuel capacity: 6000 litres
Classification: DnV +1A2-K- Partly Sheltered Light Craft Catamaran
Main engines: Two MTU 12V 493 TY70 each 1100hp at 1400 rpm
Speed, max: 26 knots
Auxiliary engines: Two Deutz F3L 952

31·5-METRE CATAMARAN

There are several versions of the 31·5-metre catamaran, ranging from a 400-seat passenger ferry to a crew/supply boat which can carry 96 people and, on the aft deck, 40 tonnes of cargo. Depending on the type of engines used, speeds of up to 32 knots can be attained.

HULL: Welded aluminium, with pointed V-frames at bow to reduce slamming and pitching stresses in rough seas. Hulls are divided into watertight compartments by transverse webs with longitudinal stiffeners. Main and superstructure decks are continuous and have transverse webs and longitudinal stiffeners. Tunnel height between the hulls at the bow is raised to increase buoyancy and to prevent waves from reaching the top of the tunnel.

NORSUL CATAMARA

Length overall: 31·5m
Beam: 9·4m
Depth: 3·5m
Draught (loaded): 1·85m
Approx GRT: 190
Seating: 96
Cargo capacity: 14 tonnes
Fuel capacity: 9800 litres
Fresh water capacity: 1000 litres
Service speed: 26 knots
Fuel consumption, full speed: 480 litres/h
Range, cruising speed: 510n miles
Main engines: Two MTU 12V 396 TB63 each 1300hp at 1650rpm
Auxiliary engines: Two MWM D226-6/Stamford

Craft built (31·5m)

Yard No	Name	Seats	Delivered	Operator/Owners
1544	*Lygra*	292	1981	A/S Bergen-Nordhordland Rutelag, Norway
1553	*Norsul Catamara*	96 + 14 tonnes cargo	1982	Norsul Offshore, Brazil
1557	*Anahitra*	161	1983	SURF et Cie (France), for Cameroon & Gabon
1558	*Helgeland*	160 + 8 tonnes cargo	September 1983	Helgeland Trafikkselskap A/S, Norway
1559	*Hjørungavåg*	228	1983	Møre og Romsdal Fylkesbåtar, Norway
1560	*Bei Xiu Hu*	291	1983	Chu Kong Shipping, China
1561	*Li Wan Hu*		March 1984	Chu Kong Shipping, China
1563	*Xiu Li Hu*		October 1984	Chu Kong Shipping, China
1564	*Qiong Zhou Yi Hao*		December 1984	Chu Kong Shipping, China
1562	*Asie III*	96 + 40 tonnes cargo	1984	Asie Crew Boat, Malaysia
1565	*Lian Hua Hu* (ex *Jasarina*)		1984	Chu Kong Shipping, China (ex Jahre Shah Shipping SDN BHD, Malaysia)
1566	*Yi Xian Hu*		March 1985	Zhen Hing Enterprises Co Ltd, China
1568	*Peng Lai Hu*		July 1985	Jiang Gang Passenger Transport Co, China

Lygra

Norsul Catamara, Fjellstrand 31·5m offshore catamaran

31·5m Fjellstrand *Xiu Li Hu* owned by Chu Kong Shipping, China

XIU LI HU

Length overall: 31·5m
Beam, max: 9·4m
Draught: 2·05m
Approx GRT: 299
Speed, max: 30 knots

Speed, cruising: 28 knots
Fuel capacity: 9000 litres
Engines: Two MTU 16V 396 TB83
Range, cruising: 350n miles
Fuel consumption, average: 750 litres/h

Fjellstrand *Victoria Clipper* serving Seattle and Vancouver

ASIE III

Class: DnV 1A2, Light Craft, R150, passenger
  catamaran
Length, overall: 31·5m
Beam, max: 9·4m
Depth: 3·5m
Cargo deck area: 100m²
Draught, max: 2·25m
Speed: 29·1 knots
Engines: Two MTU 16V 396 TB83, 1500kW
  (2010bhp) each, at 1940rpm
Gearboxes: Reintjes 2·5:1
Propellers: Liaaen/Helix controllable-pitch
Generators: MB/Stamford, 50kW each
Bow thrusters fitted to each hull

38·8-METRE CATAMARAN

This new type is based on a broadly similar
building specification to the 31·5m, but has design
features aimed at further improving performance,
economy, space and payload. Built in marine
grade aluminium alloy, designs include a ferry
version with 490 seats, and an offshore vessel with
a freight capacity of 40 tonnes. The hulls are of
symmetrical and slim design and tunnel height has
been increased to further improve seakeeping.
Speeds of up to 35 knots are claimed for the 38·8m
catamaran fitted with MTU 16V 396 TB83 engines.

Four 38·8m vessels were sold in 1985, two to
customers in China and the third to a Grand
Cayman Island registered company, for operations in Mexico.

Fjellstrand now offers both the 31·5m and
38·8m catamarans with KaMeWa waterjet propulsion as an alternative to Lips fixed-pitch
propellers, offering an increase in speed. The vessel
for Mexico was the first so equipped.

In May 1986 Fjellstrand announced the signing
of a contract for ten passenger catamarans for the
Istanbul Great City Municipality, Turkey. The
vessels are of the 38·8m type, five with two MTU
16V 396 TB83 engines, 1510kW (at 1940rpm)
each, and five with two MTU 12V 396 TB63,
1000kW (at 1800rpm) each, giving cruising speeds
fully loaded of 32 knots and 25 knots respectively.
The vessels will have seating for 449 passengers.
The value of the contract is given as between
NKr 250 and 300 million. The vessels will operate
in the Strait of Bosphorus transporting commuters from the Asian to the European side.

Anahitra, Fjellstrand 31·5m offshore catamaran

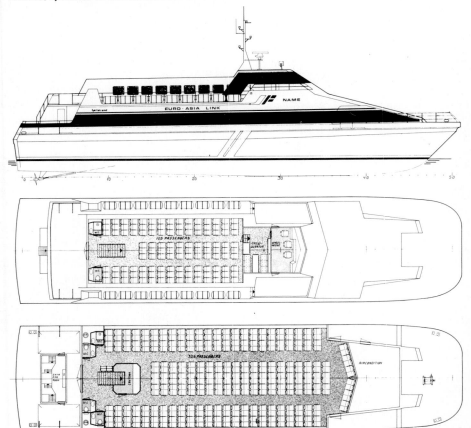

General Arrangement of Fjellstrand 38·8m catamaran
for the Istanbul Great City Municipality

MEXICO

The following specifications relate to the 38·8m *Mexico* which is fitted with waterjet units. The vessel has crew cabins fitted with bunks and has a shower facility.

ENGINES

Main engines: Two MTU 16V 396 TB83
Auxiliary engines: Two Mercedes Benz, 45kW each

DIMENSIONS

Length overall: 38·8m
Beam, max: 9·4m
Draught, loaded: 2·40m
GRT: 399

PERFORMANCE

Speed, max: 34 knots
Speed, cruising: 30 knots
Range, cruising: 360n miles
Passenger capacity: 370
Fuel capacity: 9000 litres
Fuel consumption, average: 700 litres/h

Please see *Jane's High-Speed Marine Craft and Air Cushion Vehicles 1987* for the General Arrangement drawing of *Mexico*.

THERMOLINER TYPE (38·8-METRE CATAMARAN)

ANNE LINE

On 9 July 1986 Fjellstrand A/S delivered a 480m³ cargo-carrying catamaran to the Norwegian company Gods-Trans A/S, the *Anne Line*. The vessel is equipped with cooling facilities for the transport of fish to customers in Europe and for onwards shipment to the United States and on return journeys the transport of fresh vegetables, fruit and fresh-cut flowers. For such changes of cargo, a cargo deck is provided facilitating easy and efficient cleaning. A Tico Marine 35 (3t) crane and electric fork lift truck are carried on the vessel for efficient goods handling.

The *Anne Line* has a very shallow draught enabling her to pick up cargo from any fish farm along the Norwegian coast. The 30-knot speed allows the vessel to go from Stavanger to Den Helder in the Netherlands in only 13 hours. This advanced slender-hull catamaran type of Fjellstrand offers good seakeeping qualities with favourable fuel economy and high speed.

Details specifically related to *Anne Line*. Other details as under 38·8m catamaran.

CLASSIFICATION: Det norske Veritas + 1A1, R 180, EO, Light Craft Catamaran.
ENGINES: Two MTU 16V 396 TB63, 1310kW (1780bhp) each at 1650rpm, ZF gears, BW 750S.
Auxiliary engines: Two 35kW Mercedes Benz/Stamford.
PROPULSION: Lips fixed-pitch propellers.
NAVIGATION: Two Furuno radars, gyrocompass, log, echosounder, autopilot and Decca navigator.
COMMUNICATION: Sailor SSB, Sailor VHF, intercom, 3 mobile telephones, internal TV control from bridge of engine rooms, hull sides and cargo hold.

DIMENSIONS

Depth: 3·97m
Draught, loaded: 2·45m
Temperature controlled space: 480m³
GRT: 380

WEIGHT/CAPACITIES

Deadweight: 65 tonnes
Fuel oil tanks: 15 000 litres
Fresh water tank: 1500 litres

PERFORMANCE

Speed, service (fully loaded): 29·0 knots
Range, at service speed: 720n miles

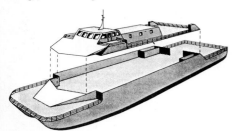

Exploded view of Thermoliner-type catamaran showing cargo deck area

Craft built (38·8m)

Yard No	Name	Completed	Seats	Operator
	Tian Lu Hu	September 1985	326	Zhen Hing Enterprises Co Ltd, China
1570	*Yong Xing*	November 1985	312	Ningbo Huagang Ltd, China
1571	*Mexico* (ex *Can Cun*)	January 1986	370	Cruceros Maritimos del Caribe SA, Mexico
1572	*Victoria Clipper*	May 1986	330*	Clipper Navigation Inc, USA
1573	*Anne Line*	July 1986	Freighter	Gods-Trans A/S, Norway
1574	*Caribbean Princess*	31 October 1986	310	Viking Express (Bahamas) Ltd, Bahamas
1575	*Bahamian Princess*	February 1987	310	Viking Express (Bahamas) Ltd, Bahamas
1576	*Caka Bey*	February 1987	449	Istanbul Great City Municipality, Turkey
1577	*Fjordprins*	September 1987	201	Fylkesbaatane i Sogn og Fjordane, Norway
1578	*Umur Bey*	May 1987	449	Istanbul Great City Municipality, Turkey
1579	*Yeditepe*	May 1987	449	Istanbul Great City Municipality, Turkey
1580	*Sognekongen*	December 1987	201	Fylkesbaatane i Sogn og Fjordane, Norway
1581	*Sarica Bay*	September 1987	449	Istanbul Great City Municipality, Turkey
1582	*Ulubatli Hasan*	October 1987	449	Istanbul Great City Municipality, Turkey
1583	*Uluc Ali Reis*	January 1988	449	Istanbul Great City Municipality, Turkey
1584	*Nurset*	March 1988	449	Istanbul Great City Municipality, Turkey
1585	*Karamursel Bey*	March 1988	449	Istanbul Great City Municipality, Turkey
1586	—	April 1988	249	A W Line Oy, Finland
1587	*Hezarifen Celebi*	September 1988	449	Istanbul Great City Municipality, Turkey
1588	*Cavil Bey*	September 1988	449	Istanbul Great City Municipality, Turkey

*of which 30 are external

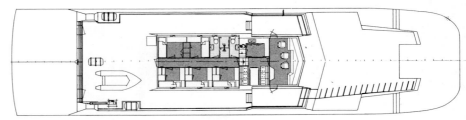

Crew quater - upper deck

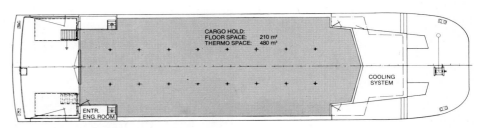

Cargo deck and crew quarters of *Anne Line*

VICTORIA CLIPPER

CLASSIFICATION: Det norske Veritas + 1A1 R150, Light craft, passenger catamaran.

ENGINES

Main engines: Two MTU 16V 396 TB83, 1499kW (2010bhp) each

Auxiliary engines: Two 60kW Mercedes Benz OM 352 A/Stamford

PROPULSION: Two KaMeWa waterjet, type 63S/62/6.

NAVIGATION: Two radars, gyrocompass, log, echosounder and autopilot.

COMMUNICATION: Sailor SSB, Sailor VHF, intercom/public address system, internal TV-control from the bridge to engine room, hull side and deck, public telephone.

DIMENSIONS

Length, overall: 38·80m

Beam: 9·40m

Depth: 3·97m

Draught, loaded: 1·51m

GRT: 420

PERFORMANCE

Passenger seats: 300 + 30 outside

Fuel consumption at service speed: 23·9 litres/ n mile

Range, at service speed: 920n miles

Fuel capacity: 22 000 litres

Fresh water capacity: 1500 litres

Speed, service, fully loaded: 31·5 knots

CARIBBEAN PRINCESS and BAHAMIAN PRINCESS

CLASSIFICATION: Det norske Veritas + 1A1 R45, Light craft, passenger catamaran.

ENGINES

Main engines: Two MTU 16V 396 TB83, 1430kW (1918bhp) each

Auxiliary engines: Two 60kW Mercedes Benz/ Stamford

PROPULSION: Two Lips fixed-pitch propellers driven via ZF BW 750 S gearboxes.

NAVIGATION: Aqua navigation lights, two Furuno radars, Furuno satellite nav, Anschatz gyrocompass, Ben log, Hondex echosounder and Robertson autopilot.

COMMUNICATION: Sailor MF radiotelephone, Sailor watchreceiver, two Sailor VHF radio-telephones, Skanti VHF emergency communication set. NTW PA/Intercom and Hitachi TV supervision system.

DIMENSIONS

Length, overall: 38·80m

Beam: 9·40m

Depth: 3·97m

GRT: 399

PERFORMANCE

Passenger seats: 310

Fuel capacity: Two 4500-litre tanks

Fresh water capacity: 1500 litres

Speed, service, with 31 500kg load: 32·0 knots

Range, at 32·0 knots service speed: 400n miles

Fjellstrand Thermoliner built for Gods-Trans A/S (480m³ cooled-cargo capacity)

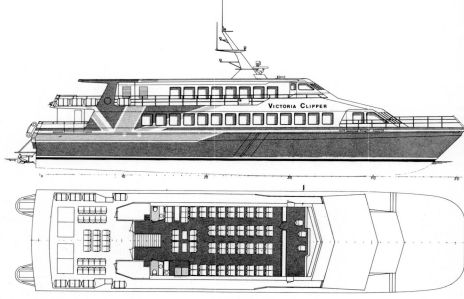

First class - upper deck

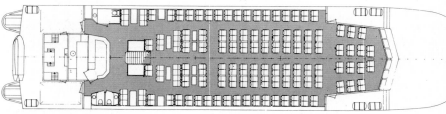

Layout of *Victoria Clipper*

Caribbean Princess

FJORDPRINS and SOGNEKONGEN

Two 38·8m catamarans embodying layout and facilities giving the highest priority to the passengers needs and activities. The interiors combine extreme quietness with a very high standard of decor in terms of design, colours, materials and finishes. Facilities include a TV/video saloon, grouped seating, reclining chairs, play areas for children and refreshment services from wagons and bar. The large windows provide excellent visibility for passengers.

CLASSIFICATION: Det norske Veritas + IAI Light Craft Catamaran, EO R5.

REGISTRATION: Norwegian flag.

YARD NO: 1577 and 1580, completed September 1987 and December 1987.

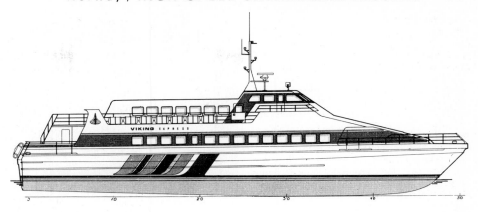

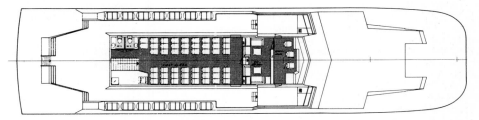

Viking class/VIP-saloon — upper deck

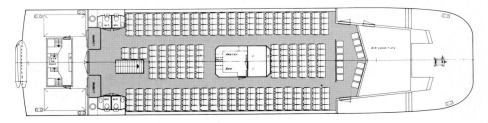

Layout of Caribbean Princess

Wheelhouse of Fjellstrand Fjordprins

FJORDPRINS

OWNER: Fylkesbaatane i Sogn og Fjordane, Norway. Trading area, west coast Norway.

ENGINES

Main engines: Two MTU 16V 396 TB84, each 2040kW at 1940rpm

Reduction gears: Two ZF marine gears BU 755

Auxiliary engines: Two Mercedes Benz OM 352A engines/two 38kW Stamford MSC 234 C generators

PROPULSION: Two KaMeWa 63 S62/6 water-jet units.

ACCOMMODATION: Passenger facilities include TV/video saloon, grouped seating, reclining chairs, good view through large windows, play areas for children, refreshment services from trolley and bar, telephone and an audio entertainment system. This system has three channels and outlets for stereo headphones are provided in 149 of the 201 seats.

NOISE LEVELS: In order to reduce the noise level in the vessel, a research programme was undertaken by Fjellstrand in co-operation with Det norske Veritas. At 38 knots service speed, the noise level in the wheelhouse is 58dBA, in the upper saloon 62dBA and amidships in the lower saloon 68dBA.

NAVIGATION: Tranberg navigation lights, two Decca radars, Robertson gyrocompass, Ben log, Robertson autopilot.

COMMUNICATION: Sailor VHF radiotelephones; NTW PA/Intercom and audio entertainment system, Hitachi TV-supervision system, Ericson mobil telephone.

DIMENSIONS

Length overall: 38·80m

Breadth: 9·40m

Depth: 3·97m

Draught loaded: 1·55m

Tonnage: Approx 406 GRT

CAPACITIES

Fuel oil tanks: Two 6000 litres each

Lubricating oil tank: 300 litres

Bilge water tank: 1000 litres

Fresh water tank: 1800 litres

PERFORMANCE

Service speed: 36·5 knots

Fjellstrand 38·8m *Fjordprins*

A section of the spacious interior of the Fjellstrand *Fjordprins*

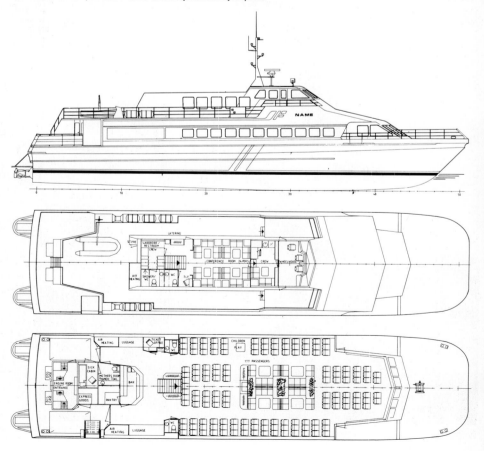

General Arrangement of 38·8m catamaran for Fylkesbaatane i Sogn og Fjordane, Norway

38·8-METRE CATAMARAN
(FOR A W LINE Oy, FINLAND)
CLASSIFICATION: Det norske Veritas + 1A1 R90, E-O Light Craft Passenger Catamaran.
REGISTRATION: Finnish flag.
YARD NO: 1586.
OWNERS: A W Line Oy. Trading area, Sweden to Åland, Finland.
ENGINES
Main engines: Two MTU 16V 396 TB84, each 2040kW at 1940rpm
Reduction gears: Two ZF marine gears BU 755
Auxiliary engines: Two Mercedes Benz OM 352A engines/two 38kW Stamford MSC 234 C generators
PROPULSION: Two KaMeWa 71 S62/6 waterjet units.
ACCOMMODATION: 249 seats, type Eknes (195 on main deck, 54 on second deck (conference room)), pantry/bar, luggage compartments, audio entertainment system, TV/video saloon, telephone, slot machines.
NAVIGATION: AQUA navigation lights, Furuno radars, Anshutz gyrocompass, Ben Athena log, Furuno echosounder, Sailor watchreceiver.
COMMUNICATION: Sailor MF radiotelephone, Robertson autopilot, Sailor VHF radiotelephones, NTW PA/Intercom and audio entertainment system, Hitachi TV-supervision system.
DIMENSIONS
Length overall: 38·80m
Breadth: 9·40m
Depth: 3·97m
Draught loaded: 1·55m (?)
Tonnage: Approx 400 GRT
CAPACITIES
Fuel oil tanks: Two 4500 litres each
Lubricating oil tank: 250 litres
Fresh water tank: 1800 litres
Sewage tank: Two 2000 litres
PERFORMANCE
Service speed: 34 knots

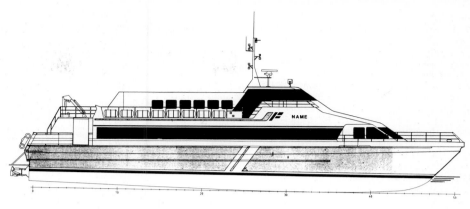

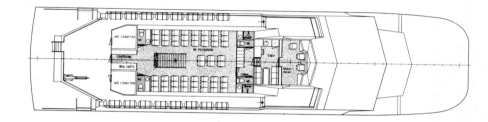

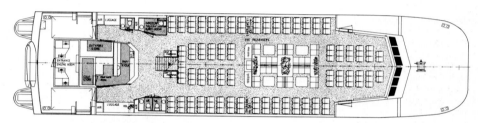

General Arrangement of 38·8m catamaran for A W Line Oy, Finland

WESTAMARIN A/S

PO Box 143, 4501 Mandal, Norway

Telephone: (43) 62222
Telex: 21514 WRIN N
Telefax: (43) 62302

Westamarin A/S is now part of the Swede Ship Invest AB group of companies which includes Oskarshamns Varv AB (Shipyard), Djupviks Varv AB (Shipyard) and an electrical contractor, Electro Swede AB. Westamarin A/S has an exclusive sales and production license for SES

craft from AB Karlskronavarvet in Sweden for the non-military market.

Westamarin A/S was established in 1961, under the name of Westermoen Hydrofoil A/S, to produce, develop, design and market high-speed vessels for commercial and military purposes. A

Craft built (W86)

Yard No	Name	Originally delivered	Seats	Operator	Route
21	Fjordglytt	June 1971	140	Fylkesbaatane i Sogn og Fjordane	Bergen-Årdalstangen
22	Belle De Dinard (ex Karmsund)	January 1972		Les Vedettes Blanches et Vertes, France	St Malo to Jersey
24	Fjordtroll	May 1972	140	Fylkesbaatane i Sogn og Fjordane	Bergen-Måløy-Bergen
25	Sauda	June 1972	148	Det Stavangerske Dampskibsselskab	Stavanger-Sauda-Jørpeland-Stavanger
26	Mayflower	October 1972	134	Stavangerske Westamarin A/S	Stavanger-Sanneid
27	Kongsbussen	April 1973		Fosen Trafikklag A/S	Trondheim-Sula-Trondheim
28	Hertugbussen	May 1973		Fosen Trafikklag A/S	Trondheim-Sula-Trondheim
29	Tedno	June 1973	140	Hardanger Sunnhordlandske Dampskibsselskap	Bergen-Tittelsnes-Bergen
32	Koegelwieck	September 1973		BV Terschellinger Stoomboot Mij, Netherlands	Terschelling-Harlingen
34	Olavsbussen	February 1974		Fosen Trafikklag A/S	Trondheim-Sula-Trondheim
35	Tjelden (ex Haugesund)	November 1973	94 + cargo	Hardanger Sunnhordlandske Dampskibsselskap	Os-Haugesund-Os
41	Fjordbris (ex Storesund)	September 1974	165	Det Stavangerske Dampskibsselskab	Stavanger area
42	Fjordkongen II	January 1975	140	Troms Fylkes Dampskibsselskap	Tromsø area
44	Brynilen	June 1975	94 (+6 tonnes freight)	Finnmark Fylkesrederi og Ruteselskap	Hammerfest-Loppa
45	Øygar	September 1975	140	Øygarden & Sotra Rutelag L/L	Rognøysund-Bergen
46	Fjorddronningen	January 1976	174	Troms Fylkes Dampskibsselskap	Harstad-Gryllefjord-Harstad
47	Trident 2 (ex Highland Seabird)	May 1976		Les Vedettes Blanches & Vertes	
48	Fjorddrott	June 1976	167	Det Stavangerske Dampskibsselskab	Stavanger-Sauda-Stavanger
49	Fjordprinsessen	March 1977	163	Troms Fylkes Dampskibsselskap	Jøkelfjord-Skjervøy-Tromsø-Gryllefjord
65	Bornholm Express (ex Steigtind)	June 1977	182	Bornholm Express	Allinge, Denmark to Simrishamn, Sweden
54	Mediteran	June 1978		Union Dalmacija-Oour Flota, Yugoslavia	
67	Marina I	July 1978		Union Dalmacija-Oour Flota, Yugoslavia	
66	Hornøy	October 1979	136	Finnmark Fylkesrederi og Ruteselskap	Måsøy-Hammerfest-Sørøysundbass

number of Supramar PT hydrofoil craft were built in the 1960s and a number are still in regular service.

In 1970 the Westamaran type was introduced, an asymmetric-hull catamaran based on a semi-planing hull of welded marine aluminium. This design was the first high-speed catamaran to enter ferry operations. Six versions, the Westamaran 86, 88, 95, 100, 120 and 160, have since been built totalling 47 vessels. Mono-hull vessels of type S75 and S80 have been built, as well as patrol boats for the Royal Norwegian Navy and Swedish Royal Navy.

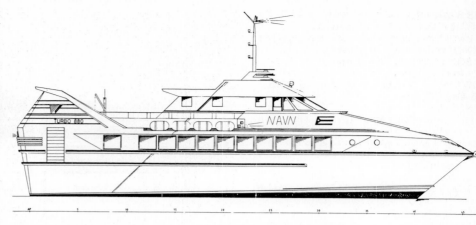

WESTAMARAN W86

Twenty-three Westamaran 86s were built up to 1979. Eighteen are in service in Norway, fitted out for up to 174 passengers. Three of the vessels operating in Norway are equipped to carry 94 to 100 passengers and up to 6 tonnes of freight. The main powerplants are two MTU 1100hp diesels.

DIMENSIONS
Length: 26·7m (89ft)
Beam: 9m (29ft)
Draught: 1·2m (4ft)
GRT: 200
NRT: 135
PERFORMANCE
Max speed: 28 knots
Range: 235n miles

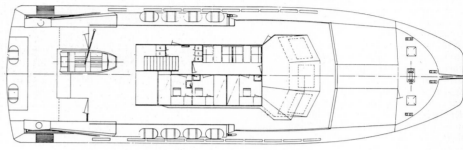

WESTAMARAN W95

This longer version of the W86 can carry up to 248 passengers. The standard version has been powered by two SACM AGO 195 V12C SHR 1800hp diesels giving the 29·1m vessel a maximum speed of 32 knots. Fourteen W95s have been built but the W95 is now replaced by the W100. In 1985, W95 Sunnhordland was fitted with MTU 12V 396 TB83 engines in place of the SACM engines and at the same time had its 0·84m diameter fixed-pitch propellers changed for 1·25m diameter controllable-pitch propellers. The gearboxes were changed from 1·103:1 to 2·54:1 ratio. Fuel consumption is 273 litres/hour.

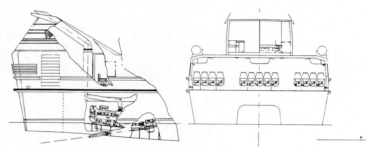

WESTAMARAN W88

A faster but slightly smaller capacity craft than the W86 or W95 and replacing the W86, four W88s have been sold the last, Fjordsol, being slightly longer at 29·4m. The hull and superstructure are constructed in marine grade aluminium, AA 5083. Skogøy, a W88 delivered in May 1985, is classified by DnV + 1A1, R-15, light craft with approval for operation in ice.
POWERPLANT AND PROPULSION: Two MTU 12V 396 TB83, each 1150kW (1560hp) at 1940rpm

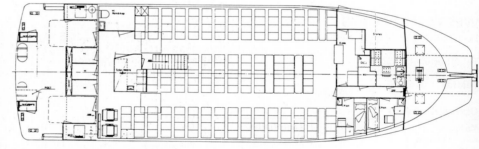

General Arrangement of Westamarin W88

Craft built (W95)

Yard No	Name	Delivered	Seats	Operator	Route
36	Vingtor	May 1974		Sameiet Flaggruten, Norway	Stavanger-Bergen-Stavanger
37	Sleipner	June 1974		Sameiet Flaggruten, Norway	Stavanger-Bergen-Stavanger
38	Sunnhordland	April 1975	180	Hardanger Sunnhordlandske Dampskipsselskap	Bergen-Ølen
39	Amarischia (ex Martini Bianco)	May 1975		Alilauro Aliscafi del Tirreno SpA, Italy	Naples-Ischia-Capri
43	Alisur Azul (ex Westjet) (W95T)	Dec 1976		(ex Alisur SA, Spain)	Spain
51	Draupner	April 1977		Sameiet Flaggruten	Stavanger-Bergen-Stavanger
52	Tunen	May 1977	180	A/S Dampskibsselskabet Øresund, Denmark	København-Malmø-København
50	Pegasus	June 1977		Service Maritime Carteret, France	Carteret-Jersey-France
53	Tranen	June 1978	180	A/S Dampskibsselskabet Øresund, Denmark	København-Malmø-København
68	Siken (ex Tumleren)	April 1979	180	A/S Dampskibsselskabet Øresund, Denmark	København-Malmø-København
79	Alisur Amarillo (W95D)	April 1981	218	Alisur SA, Spain	Canary Islands
80	Tromsprinsen	July 1981	210	Troms Fylkes Dampskibsselskap	Harstad-Tromsø
81	Celestina	June 1981	248	Alilauro Aliscafi del Tirreno SpA, Italy	Naples-Ischia
84	Trident I (ex Venture 84)	July 1982		Vedettes Blanches et Vertes, France	St Malo-St Helier

Craft built (W88)

Yard No	Name	Delivered	Seats	Operator	Route
78	Haugesund	March 1981	180	Det Stavangerske Dampskibsselskab	Haugesund-Stavanger
82	Midthordland	November 1981	170	Hardanger Sunnhordlandske Dampskipsselskap	
88	Skogøy	May 1985	132 + 10 tonnes cargo	Ofotens Dampskibsselskap	Narvik-Svolvær
91	Fjordsol	June 1986	202	Det Stavangerske Dampskibsselskab	Stavanger-Ryfylke

Reduction gearboxes: ZF type BW 455S, ratio 3·13:1

Propeller: Two three-blade Servogear controllable pitch

Auxiliary engines: Two Daimler Benz OM 314

Generators: Two Stamford, type MSC 234C or E, 3-phase, 230V, 50Hz

EQUIPMENT

Ventilation: Heating from main engines to all accommodation areas

Windlass: One electro-hydraulic anchor windlass

Navigation: Two radars, one gyrocompass, one magnetic compass, log and econometer

Communication: Two VHFs, intercom, mobile telephone, radio and music broadcast

Lifesaving equipment: Seven 20-person life rafts, one pick-up boat. Life preservers under seats

FACILITIES

Kiosk

Cabins for 4 crew

WCs: 3 for passengers, 1 for crew

DIMENSIONS

Length overall: 28·02m

Breadth moulded: 9·00m

Draught max: 2·20m

PERFORMANCE

Speed: 30 knots at 100% MCR

Range: 270n miles

Endurance: 9 hours at service speed

WESTAMARIN 3000

FJORDSOL

POWERPLANT: Two MTU 12V 396 TB83, 1150kW each at 1940rpm, ZF BW 455S gearboxes. Auxiliary engines: two Daimler Benz OM 352A driving Stamford MSC 234F generators, three 230V, 50 Hz.

HULL AND SUPERSTRUCTURE: Aluminium AA 5083.

DIMENSIONS

Length overall: 29·4m

Length, waterline: 25·4m

Breadth moulded: 9·0m

Draught max: 2·2m

GRT: 235·0

NRT: 75·0

CAPACITIES

Passengers: 202

Cargo: 10 tonnes, one hold of 52m³

Fuel oil: Two 2800-litre tanks

Fresh water: 600 litres

PERFORMANCE

Speed, service at 100% MCR, full payload: 30·0 knots

Range: 270n miles (9 hours at service speed)

Fuel consumption: 490kg/h at 100% MCR

WESTAMARAN W100

DIMENSIONS

Length overall: 32·9m

Breadth moulded: 9·8m

Draught max: 2·0m

PERFORMANCE

Main engines: Two MTU 16V 396 TB83 or similar

Speed: 30 knots fully loaded at MCR

Capacity: Up to 300 passengers

Westamarin W88 *Skogøy*

W88 *Fjordsol*

Craft built (W100)

Yard No	Name	Delivered	Operator
75	Gibline I (ex *Gimle Belle*, ex *Condor 6*)	April 1980	Gibline Ltd, Gibraltar
76	Independencia (ex *Gimle Bird*)	September 1981	Direccao Regieonal dos Portos da Madeira, Portugal
77	*Porec* (ex *Gimle Bay*)	January 1982	Splosna Plovba Piran, Yugoslavia
83	*Nearchos* (ex *Venture 83*)	May 1982	RENATOUR SA, Greece

Craft built (W3600, ex W120)

Yard No	Name	Seats	Delivered	Operator
89	*Zi Lang*	354	January 1987	Nantong Hi-Speed Passenger Ship Co, China

Craft built (W3600 SC)

Yard No	Name	Seats	Delivered	Owner
92	—	195 + 30m² cargo hold	April 1988	Saltens Dampskibsselskap
93	—	195 + 30m² cargo hold	May 1988	Ofotens Dampskibsselskap A/S

Craft built (W3700 S)

Yard No	Name	Seats	Delivered	Owner
95	—	300	1988	Gotlandslinjen (Nordstrøm & Thulin AB)

WESTAMARAN 3600 SC
(Yard No 92 and 93)
OPERATORS
Saltens Dampskibsselskap, 1988
Ofotens Dampskibsselskap, 1988
ACCOMMODATION
Passengers: 195
Cargo: 15 tonnes in hold of 60m³

DIMENSIONS
Length overall: 36·50m
Length waterline: 31·10m
Breadth moulded: 9·50m
Draught: 1·47m
CAPACITIES
Fuel oil: Two 4000-litre tanks
Fresh water: 600 litres

PERFORMANCE
Speed, service, full payload, at 100% MCR: 35 knots
Range: 280n miles
Endurance: 8 hours at service speed
Fuel consumption: 860kg/h at 100% MCR

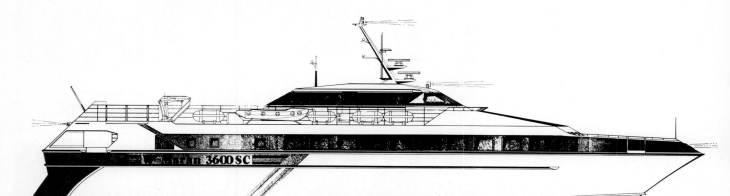

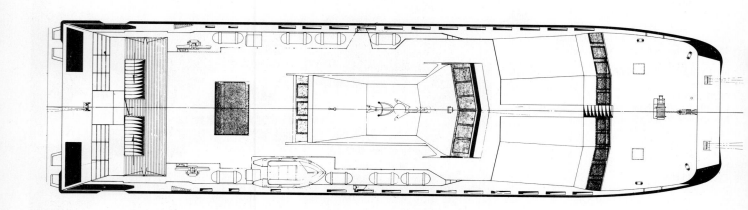

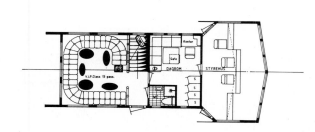

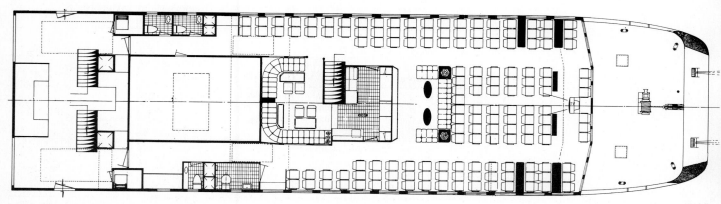

General Arrangement of Westamarin W-Maran 3600 SC

WESTAMARAN 3700 S
VINDILE (Yard No 95)

OPERATOR: Gotlandslinjen, 1988.

CLASSIFICATION: DnV 1A1-R45, Light Craft Passenger Vessel.

HULL: Hulls, superstructure and deckhouse with wheelhouse built in sea water corrosion resistant aluminium plates AA5083 (D54S ¼H), profiles in AA 6081 WP (B 51 SWP).

ENGINES: Two MTU 16V 396 TB84, 2040kW each, at 1940rpm.

PROPULSION: Two KaMeWa 63S waterjet units.

AUXILIARY POWER: Two Mercedes OM 352 driving Stamford MSC 234 E70kVA, 250V, 50Hz, 3-phase generators.

ACCOMMODATION
259 seats at 85 cm pitch
63 seats at 90cm pitch (VIP lounge)

DIMENSIONS
Length overall: 37·00m
Length waterline: 31·10m
Breadth moulded: 9·50m
Depth moulded: 3·56m
Draught: 1·47m

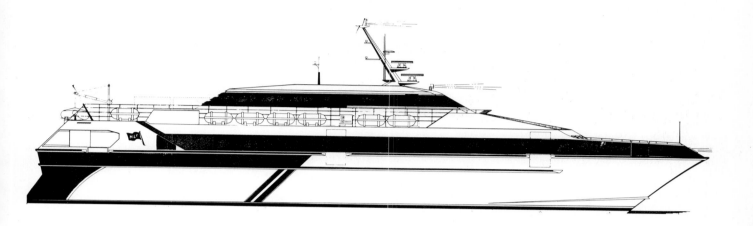

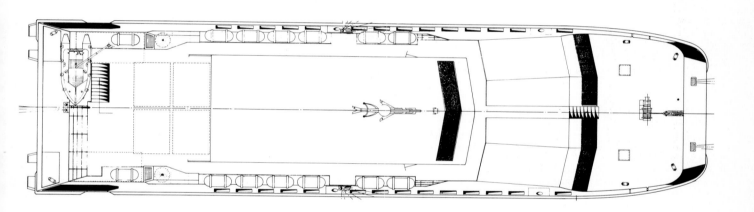

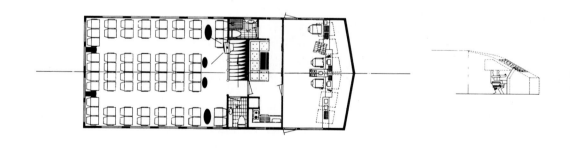

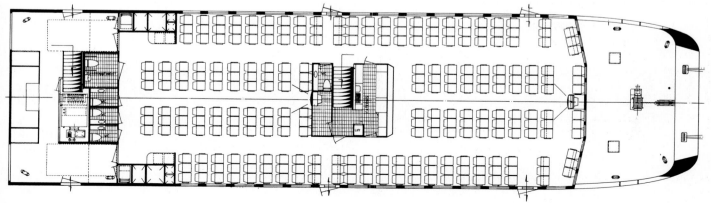

General Arrangement of Westamarin W-Maran 3700 S

Westamarin W3600 *Zi Lang* commissioned January 1987 for China

WESTAMARAN 3600 (ex W120)

ZI LANG

CLASS: DnV + 1A1, R45.
HULL AND SUPERSTRUCTURE: Aluminium AA5083.
ENGINES
Main engines: Two MTU 16V 396 TB83, each 1540kW at 1940rpm
Gearboxes: ZF BU 755S, ratio 3·07:1
Auxiliary engines: Two Mercedes OM 352 A
Generators: Two Stamford MSC 234F
ACCOMMODATION: 354 passengers, in two cabins.
DIMENSIONS
Length overall: 36·2m
Length waterline: 32·26m
Breadth moulded: 9·77m
Draught max: 2·20m
GRT/NRT: 378/140
PERFORMANCE
Speed: 25/27 knots fully loaded at MCR
Range: 270n miles
Fuel consumption: 650kg/h
Fuel capacity: Two 5000-litre tanks
Fresh water: 1200 litres

W-MARAN 5000

ANNE LISE

CLASSIFICATION: DnV 1A1 R 280 Light Craft-EO.

A 49·5m thermo-cargo catamaran delivered August 1987 to the Norwegian owner, Gods-Trans A/S, Hønefoss.

This vessel is the largest of its type, dimensioned for high regularity for North Sea operations. The cargo is placed on the main deck, which consists of one cooling room of 520m² and one freezing room of 276m². The main machinery consists of the first MTU 396 TB84 2040kW engines delivered to Norway. The propeller system (including reduction gear) is of a new type, called Speed-Z propulsion system, type HST 60/40-25, delivered from AM Liaaen in Ålesund, Norway. The solution is very similar to the different Azimuth thrusters (as the Compass thrusters made by

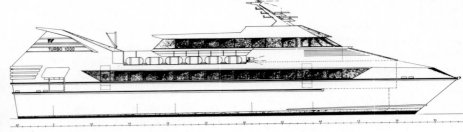

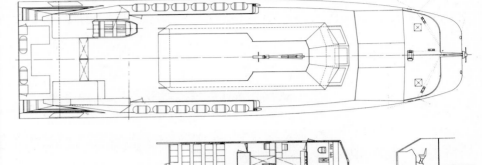

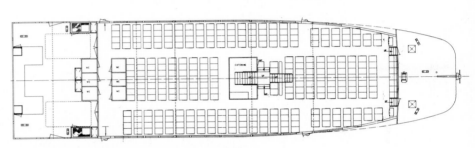

Outboard and inboard arrangement of Westamarin W3600

same). Windows are fitted for possible 369-seat ferry use.
HULL AND SUPERSTRUCTURE: Aluminium Aa 5083.
ENGINES: Two MTU 16V 396 TB84, 2040kW each, at 1940rpm.
REDUCTION GEARS: 2·52:1.
AUXILIARY ENGINES: Two Mercedes-Benz type OM 421, 116kW each at 1500rpm.
GENERATORS: Two Stamford type MSC 334 B.
DECK EQUIPMENT: Electro-hydraulic anchor windlass, 2600kp/3·5m.
COOLING SYSTEM
Refrigerator hold: Carrier type 5F30-C-644E, capacity: 34 kW

Freezer hold: Carrier type 5F30-C-644 K, capacity: 14 kW

NAVIGATION: Two radars, one gyrocompass, log and econometer, depth sounder, navigator.

COMMUNICATION: VHF, radio telephone, intercom, mobile telephone, TV monitoring of engine room, cargo space and hull sides.

LIFESAVING EQUIPMENT: Four 10-person inflatable life rafts, one pick-up boat.

CREW FACILITIES: 7 cabins, single with extra pullman berth, 2 WCs, washroom, 2 showers, provisions store, one pantry and mess/dayroom.

DIMENSIONS
Length overall: 49·45m

The world's largest high-speed catamaran, the 49·5m Westamaran 5000

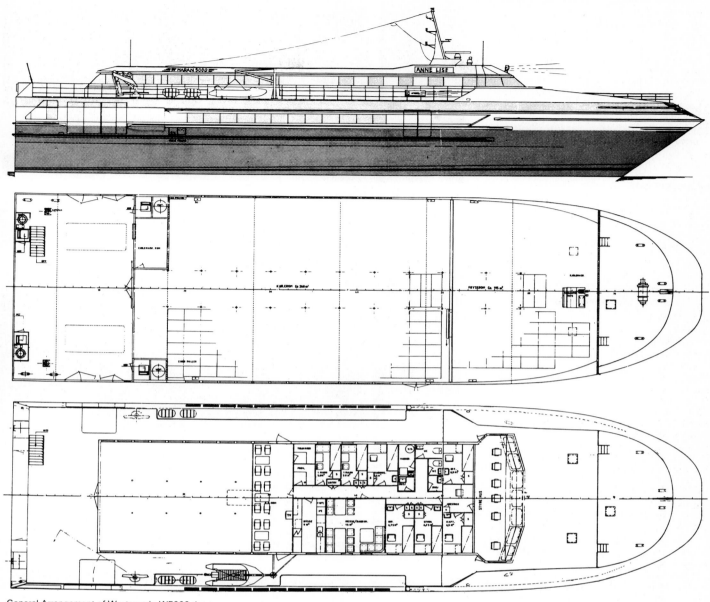

General Arrangement of Westamarin W5000 thermo-cargo catamaran

Length: 43·6m
Breadth: 14·0m
Draught, max: 2·60m excluding propellers
  3·10m including propellers
GRT: 1057

CAPACITIES
Cargo: 200 tons
Fuel: 70 000 litres
Deadweight: 285 tonnes
Cargo space: 520m³ ± 0°C

276m³ − 20°C
Fresh water: 2m³
Accommodation: 8 crew cabins
PERFORMANCE
Service speed: 26 knots depending on cargo load

SINGAPORE

MARINTEKNIK SHIPBUILDERS (S) PTE LTD

31 Tuas Road, Singapore 2263

Telephone: 8611706/7, 8616271/2/3
Telex: 86 53419 MARJET RS
Telefax: (65) 8614244

Denis Kerr, *Managing Director*
Part of Marinteknik International Ltd Group
  33/F New World Tower, 16-18 Queen's Road, Central, Hong Kong

Telephone: 5 218302/231054
Telex: 74493 HMHCO HX

David C H Liang, *Group Chairman*
John Warbey, *Managing Director*
Robert Liang, *Executive Director*
Mike McSorley, *Marketing Manager*

Marinteknik Shipbuilders (S) Pte Ltd was formed in 1984 by the parent company Marinteknik International Ltd of Hong Kong to build catamaran and mono-hull craft designed by Marinteknik Verkstads AB of Sweden.

HAKEEM

Designed by Marinteknik Verkstads AB of Sweden *Hakeem* is a Marinjet 34 CCB crew boat of catamaran form with symmetrical hulls with low-resistance, semi-planing characteristics. Construction of the craft in welded aluminium alloy follows the same principles as used in the Marinjet series of ferry craft. *Hakeem* has seating for 50 passengers and provision for a crew of 6.

CLASSIFICATION: Det norske Veritas R-60, Crew Boat, Light Craft.
PROPULSION
Two MTU 12V 396 TC 62 high-speed diesels, each giving 880kW at 1650rpm
Two KaMeWa 60/S62/6 waterjet units
OPERATOR: Ocean Tug Services, based at Belait, Brunei, delivered May 1985, for use by Shell Brunei.
DIMENSIONS
Length overall: 34·0m (hulls extended to provide side protection to waterjet units)

Craft built or ordered (high-speed catamarans)

Yard No	Type	Name	Delivery or ordered	Operator
101	34 CCB	*Hakeem*	May 1985	Ocean Tug Services
103	34 CCB*	*Layar Sentosa*	May 1987	Shell Sarawak
105	34 CCB	*Layar Sinar*	April 1987	Shell Sarawak
110	34 CPV	—	July 1987	Jiangmen Jiang Gang
111	35 CPV	—	July 1987	Hong Kong China Hydrofoil
112	33 CPV	*Shun De*	October 1987	Shun Gang
115	35 CPV	—	—	—

*Fitting out of Marinteknik, Sweden, Yard No 61

Beam overall: 9·4m
Draught full load: 1·1m
GRT: 243
NRT: 72
WEIGHTS
Disposable load: 19 tonnes
Cargo and supplies: 6·5 tonnes
Fuel capacity: 10 000 litres (8·5 tonnes)
Loaded displacement: 84·0 tonnes
PERFORMANCE
Speed cruise: 27 knots
Speed max: 30 knots
Fuel consumption: 440 litres/h
Range: 615n miles

LAYAR SINAR
The principal particulars are as follows:
ENGINES: Two MTU, 1180kW (1582bhp) each.
CLASSIFICATION: DnV R 150.
DIMENSIONS
Length overall: 34·0m
Beam: 9·4m
Draught: 1·2m
WEIGHTS
Freight: 23 tonnes
Displacement, loaded: 90 tonnes
PERFORMANCE
Speed, cruising: 30 knots
Passenger seats: 70 +

Marinteknik crew boat *Hakeem*

Layar Sinar

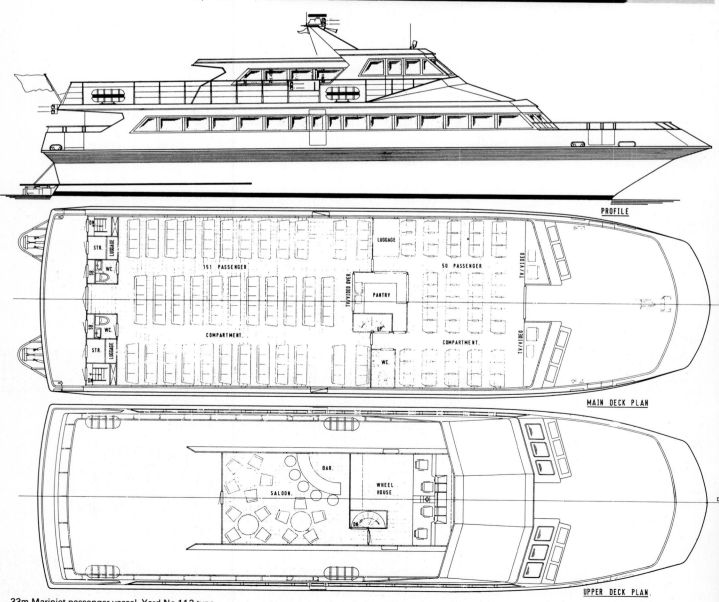

33m Marinjet passenger vessel, Yard No 112 type

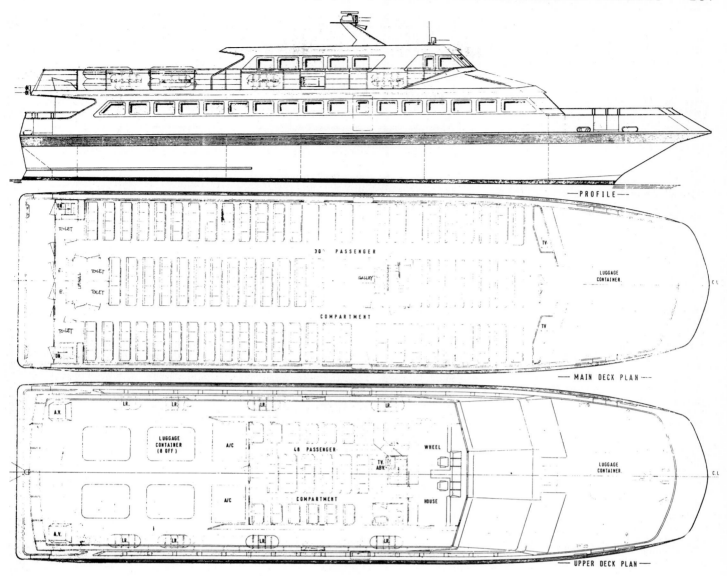

35m Marinjet passenger vessel, Yard No 111 type

SING KOON SENG

3 Benoi Road, Singapore 2262

Telephone: 861 0800
Telex: 23435 SKS RS

Builder of three International Catamarans Pty
Ltd catamarans with welded aluminium hulls.

IPO-IPO 3001

CLASSIFICATION: ABS +A1+AMS Unres-
tricted Service. Panamanian flag.
POWERPLANT: Two GM 16V 149 TI 1400bhp
each, at 1900 rpm.
GEARBOXES: ZF BW 455, ratio 2·529:1.
DIMENSIONS
Length overall: 30·2m
Beam (excluding fenders): 11·2m
Draught max loaded: 2·4m
Deck cargo area: 112m²
PERFORMANCE
Speed max: 27 knots
Seats: 15, aircraft type
Fire monitor: 150m³/h at 100m head

Craft built (In Cat)	Completed	Passengers	Operator
29·0m *Offshore Pioneer*	1983	15*	Singapore Navy, 1986 (ex Offshore Charters of Singapore)
29·0m *Offshore Pride*	1983	15*	Singapore Navy, 1986 (ex Offshore Charters of Singapore)
30·0m *Ipo-Ipo 3001*	May 1984	15*	(ex Zadco Productions, Abu Dhabi, UAE)

* plus cargo

Sing Koon Seng In Cat *Offshore Pioneer*

SWEDEN

MARINTEKNIK VERKSTADS AB

Varsvagen, Box 7, S-74071 Öregrund, Sweden

Telephone: (173) 30460
Telex: 76182 MARTAB S
Telefax: (173) 30976

Hans Ruppert, *Chairman*
Hans Eriksen, *Director*

Affiliated to Marinteknik International Ltd
Group, 33/F New World Tower, 16-18 Queen's
Road, Central, Hong Kong

Telephone: 5 218302/231054
Telex: 74493 HMHCO HX

During the 1970s Marinteknik Verkstads AB
was principally engaged in the design and building
of semi-planing 16- to 18-knot 300- to 400-passen-
ger ferries in welded aluminium. The yard was also
involved in the repair, modification, design and
building of other craft types in steel and aluminium up to 30m in length. In the period 1977/79
work proceeded on the design of a waterjet-
propelled catamaran vessel under the type name
Jetcat and construction started in November 1979.
The hulls of this catamaran were of symmetrical
form with a deep Vee forward leading to an almost
zero deadrise aft and with a hard chine developing
from the bow. Four similar boats were delivered to
the Hongkong Macao Hydrofoil Co in the period
1982/83 and since then another 11 catamarans
have been delivered or ordered, all employing
waterjet propulsion.

In addition mono-hull crew boats have been
delivered or ordered, also with waterjet propulsion. See High-speed mono-hull craft section.

MARINJET 33CPV (PV 2400)

A symmetrical-hull, semi-planing, waterjet-
propelled catamaran built in welded corrosion-
resistant aluminium alloy employing extrusions
for plating and frames.
MAIN ENGINES: Two MTU 12V 396 TB83,
1180kW, 1582bhp each at 1940rpm.
PROPULSION: Two KaMeWa 60/S62/6 water-
jet units driven via ZF gearboxes type BU 455,
2·025:1 ratio.
ACCOMMODATION: 218 to 276 passengers.
Three lavatories.
SYSTEMS
Fuel tank capacity: 7000 litres
Fresh water tank capacity: 500 litres
DIMENSIONS
Length overall: 33·0m
Beam overall: 9·40m
Draught, full load: 1·20m
WEIGHT
Payload: 20·5 tonnes (256 passengers)
PERFORMANCE
Speed, max: 35 knots
Speed, cruising: 32 knots
Range: 380n miles
Fuel consumption: 581 litres/h

MARINJET 34 CPV-D (formerly 33CPV DOUBLE DECK) (PV 3100)

CLASSIFICATION: Det norske Veritas 1A1,
R-45, EO Passenger.
HULL: Welded, corrosion resistant aluminium
alloy, employing extrusions for plating and
frames.
MAIN ENGINES: Two MTU 16V 396 TB83
diesels, 1540kW, 2065hp each, at 1940rpm.
PROPULSION: Two KaMeWa 63/S62/6 water-
jet units. ZF BU 750 gears.
ACCOMMODATION
210 passengers on main deck
25 passengers in a first class saloon on the upper
    deck
Cabin noise level, 70dBA approx to 66dBA in
    some areas
Air-conditioning, television and video, stereo
    sound and telephone facilities
Catering and duty-free shop facilities provided.

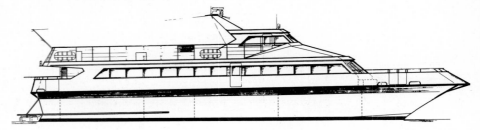

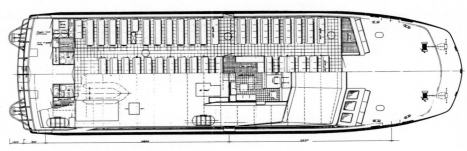

General Arrangement of Marinjet 33CPV (*Jetkat 1*, *Nettuno Jet* and *Giove Jet*)

Giove Jet departing from Ischia harbour

Bridge of Marinteknik 33CPV type

SYSTEMS
Fuel tank capacity: 9600 litres
DIMENSIONS
Length overall: 33·71m
Beam overall: 9·40m
Draught: 1·23m (summer freeboard)
GRT: 281
NRT: 100

WEIGHT
Lightship: 78·3 tonnes
PERFORMANCE
Speed, cruising at 85% MCR, fully laden: 32 knots
Speed, max (loaded): 36 knots
Range: 320n miles
Fuel consumption: 780 litres/h (554kg/h)
Wave height limit, at cruising speed: 2·1m

MARINJET 34 CPV

Two orders for this ferry type were received end of 1986, beginning 1987 for delivery to Aliscafi Alilauro del Tirreno SpA.

Launching of the Danish-registered Marinjet *Ørnen*

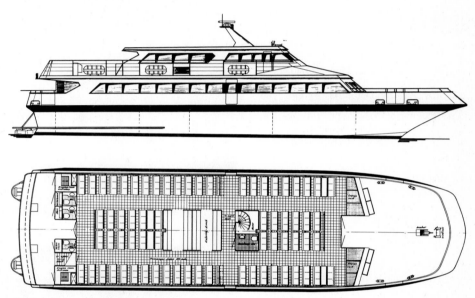

General Arrangement of Marinteknik 34 CPV-D (*Ørnen* and *Lommen*)

Craft built (high-speed catamarans)

Yard No	Type	Marinteknik Designations Old	New	Engines	Craft name	Cruise speed, full load, knots	Owner/operator	Originally delivered	Application	Seats	GRT/NRT	Loaded displacement, tonnes
42	29·0m	JC-F1	—	Two MTU 12V 396 TC 82, 1175kW	*Jaguar Prince* (ex *Jaguar*, ex *Mavi Haliç*)	27	Italy	Nov 1980	Ferry	197	251·00/173·00	85
46	29·0m	JC 3000	—	Two MTU 12V 396 TB 83, 1225kW	*Apollo Jet*	29	Hongkong Macao Hydrofoil Co Ltd	Jan 1982	Ferry	215	261·17/177·60	86
47	29·0m	JC 3000	—	Two MTU 12V 396 TB 83, 1225kW	*Hercules Jet*	29	Hongkong Macao Hydrofoil Co Ltd	1982	Ferry	215	261·17/177·60	86
48	29·0m	JC 3000	—	Two MTU 12V 396 TB 83, 1225kW	*Janus Jet*	29	Hongkong Macao Hydrofoil Co Ltd	Oct 1982	Ferry	215	261·17/177·60	86
50	29·0m	JC 3000	—	Two MTU 12V 396 TB 83, 1225kW	*Duan Zhou Hu* (ex *Triton Jet*)	29	Zhao Gang Steamer Navigation Co of China (ex Hongkong Macao Hydrofoil Co Ltd)	1983/ 23 Sept 1986	Ferry	215	261·17/177·60	86
51	33·71m	PV 2400	Marinjet 33CPV	Two MTU 12V 396 TB 83, 1225kW	*Nettuno Jet*		Alilauro Aliscafi del Tirreno SpA	May 1984	Ferry	218	260·00/75·00	86
54	33·71m	PV 2400	Marinjet 33CPV	Two MTU 12V 396 TB 83, 1225kW	*Jetkat 1*		SURF	1984	Ferry	233	269·00/95·00	93·67
55	33·71m	PV 2400	Marinjet 33CPV	Two MTU 12V 396 TB 83, 1225kW	*Giove Jet*		Alilauro Aliscafi del Tirreno SpA	1985	Ferry	276	269·00/95·00	96
56	34·0m	PV 3100 (Jumbo)	Marinjet 34 CPV-D	Two MTU 16V 396 TB 83, 1540kW	*Lommen*	32	Dampskibssellskabet Øresund A/S	Dec 1985	Ferry	235	281·00/100·00	97·58
59	34·1m	PV 3100	Marinjet 34 CPV-D	Two MTU 16V 396 TB 83, 1540kW	*Ørnen*	32	Dampskibssellskabet Øresund A/S	July 1986	Ferry	235	285·00/101·00	97·68
60	34·1m	CV 3400	Marinjet 34CCB	Two MTU 16V 396 TB 93, 1700kW	*Emeraude Express*		Chambon (SURF)	Jan 1986	Crew boat	—	288·00/103·00	99·80
61*	34·0m		Marinjet 34CCB	Two MTU 16V 396 TB 83, 1180kW	*Layar Sentosa*		On charter to Shell Sarawak	1986	Crew boat	—		
62	34·0m	—	Marinjet 34CPV	—	*Giunone Jet*		Alilauro Aliscafi del Tirreno SpA	—	Ferry			
70	34·0m	—	Marinjet 34CPV	—			Alilauro Italia	1988	Ferry	—	—	
74	41·0m	—	Marinjet 40CPV	Two MTU 16V 396 TB 84, 1935kW	—		Hongkong Macao Hydrofoil Co Ltd	Sept 1988	Ferry	406	—	

* Fitted out by Marinteknik Shipbuilders (S) Pte Ltd, Singapore

Marinteknik 34m 235-passenger catamaran ferry *Lommen* in service on the Copenhagen to Malmö route since July 1986

MARINJET 34CCB CREW BOAT
(CV 3400)

CLASSIFICATION: Det norske Veritas +1A1, R 50 EO.

MAIN ENGINES: Two MTU 16V 396 TB93 diesels, each 1700kW, 2280bhp MCR.

PROPULSION: Two KaMeWa 63/S62/6 water-jet units.

ACCOMMODATION

243 passengers
5 crew
Air-conditioned, video and stereo facilities

DIMENSIONS

Length overall: 34·10m
Beam overall: 9·40m
Draught: 1·20m

PERFORMANCE

Speed, max: 44 knots
Speed, cruising, full load: 40 knots

MARINJET 41-METRE BOAT

The largest Marinteknik high-speed catamaran at 41m overall length, the first of these vessels is to be delivered to Condor Ltd in 1988. Maximum payload is 32·5 tonnes (406 passengers). The vessel is air-conditioned.

CLASSIFICATION: DnV +1A1 R 25 Light Craft EO.

MAIN ENGINES: Two MTU 16V 396 TB84, 1935kW each at 1940rpm (MCR), sfc 220g/kWh.

AUXILIARY POWER: Two Mercedes OM type with Stamford generators, 380V, 3-phase, 50Hz.

PROPULSION: Two KaMeWa 71/S62/6 water-jet units driven via ZF gearboxes type BU 755 with disconnecting clutch.

CAPACITIES

Fuel: 7000 litres
Fresh water: 1000 litres
Lube oil: 500 litres
Hydraulic oil: 150 litres
Sewage: 1000 litres

ACCOMMODATION

First class (upper deck): 100 passengers
Economy class (main deck): 306 passengers
Crew: 11
Six lavatories
Noise level (max) in passenger saloons: 75dBA

DIMENSIONS

Length overall: 41·0m
Breadth moulded: 11·0m
Depth moulded: 3·5m
Draught loaded: 1·5m
Air draught, to mast top, light ship: 11·5m max

PERFORMANCE

Speed, cruising, 41·6 tonnes disposable load, 100% MCR, Beaufort 4: 36·5 knots

Passengers boarding the Marinteknik catamaran 34 CPV-D *Lommen* at the DSØ Copenhagen terminal

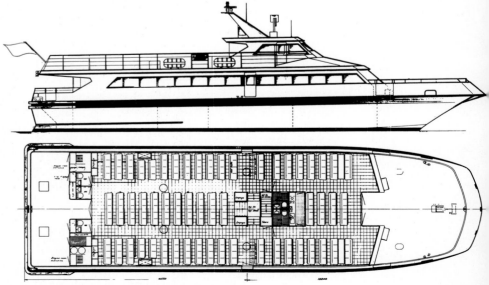

General Arrangement of Marinjet 34CCB crew boat

MARINJET 40-METRE CREW BOAT
(DESIGN)

Larger in beam and length than previous Marinteknik catamaran designs but otherwise of the same form of construction. This project is designed to have cargo carrying capacity of up to 30 tonnes.

MAIN ENGINES: Two MTU 16V 396 TB83, 1540kW each at 1940rpm.
PROPULSION: Two KaMeWa 63/S62/6 water-jet units.
SYSTEMS
Fuel tank capacity: 9600 litres
ACCOMMODATION
100 passengers (80kg each)
Cargo: Up to 30 tonnes
DIMENSIONS
Length overall: 40·0m
Beam overall: 11·0m
Draught, full load: 1·5m
PERFORMANCE
Speed, max: 43 knots
Speed, cruising: 40 knots
Range: 400n miles
Fuel consumption: 760 litres/h

Marinjet 34CCB crew boat *Emeraude Express*

Isometric drawing of Marinjet 40 CPV

THAILAND

TECHNAUTIC INTERTRADING CO LTD

44/13 Convent Road, Silom, Bangkok 10500, Thailand

Telephone: 234 0730/9368
Telex: 87650 TECO TH

Capt Nirun Chitanon, *Director and General Manager*

The Technautic shipyard employs 150 people, has a total area of 7944m², the main building occupying 2076m². Over 52 craft in the 8 to 26m range have been delivered, mainly patrol boats and work boats.

HYSUCAT 18

Designed by Hysucat Engineering, West Germany, an 18m patrol boat delivered to the Royal Thai Navy August/September 1986.
HULL AND SUPERSTRUCTURE: Kevlar and special grp with 'Airex' pvc foam core sandwich construction.
ENGINES: Two MWM TB 234 V12, each 822shp (continuous) marine diesels.
PROPULSION: Propellers.
DIMENSIONS
Length overall: 17·38m
Breadth, moulded: 6·57m
Depth, moulded: 3·11m
Draught, max (to keel): 1·15m
  max (to prop): 1·61m
Freeboard: 2·07m

Hysucat

WEIGHT
Displacement: 35 tonnes
PERFORMANCE
Speed, max: 38 knots
Speed, max continuous: 36 knots
Range, at max continuous rating: 500n miles
Fuel tank: 4170 litres

At Technautic Intertrading's expense the Hysucat concept was tested in one-tenth model scale form at the VWS Model Basin in July 1985. The form of construction is approved by Lloyds' Register of Shipping and the shipyard and associated equipment/facilities have been approved by Germanischer Lloyd.

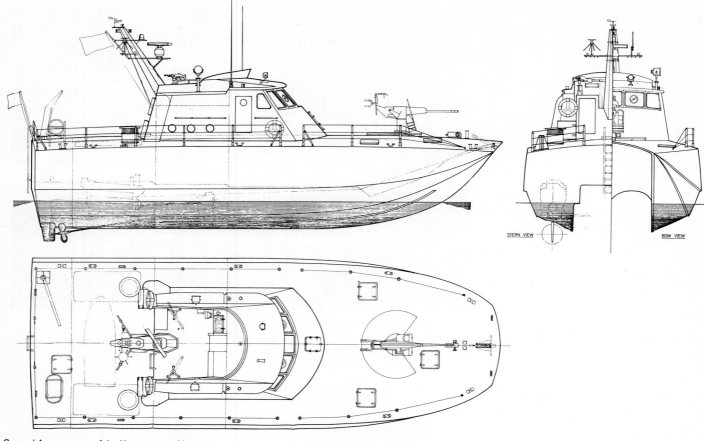

STERN VIEW   BOW VIEW

General Arrangement of the Hysucat patrol boat

UNITED KINGDOM

ALUMINIUM SHIPBUILDERS LTD (ASL)

Head Office: Guild House, Albert Road South, Southampton, Hampshire, England

Telephone: (0703) 30053
Telex: 265871 MONREF G, Attn: MMU 455
Telefax: (0703) 39241

P D P Kemp, *Chairman*
A Davies, *Managing Director*
W R Roberts, *Production Director*
D L Stock, *Commercial Director*

Aluminium Shipbuilders Ltd is a recently established manufacturing and consultancy company, with a management team and skilled workforce who have long experience in shipbuilding generally and aluminium work in particular.

The company has been appointed the licensee in the UK to build the range of fast catamarans to the designs of International Catamarans Pty Ltd, of Australia (qv).

ASL was involved with the sale to Sealink British Ferries of two 30m In Cat fast passenger ferries for the Portsmouth to Ryde service.

RIVER 50

In August 1987, the first of a series of lightweight, high-speed passenger catamarans was delivered to Thames Line plc for operation between Charing Cross Pier and West India Dock on the River Thames. The vessel is powered by twin Volvo Penta TAMD 71A engines driving Riva Calzoni waterjets.

Five further vessels have been ordered by Thames Line plc for delivery during 1988. These vessels are 17 metres long and have revised interior arrangements which allow for a spacious cabin for 70 passengers.
SURVEY: UK DOT Class V smooth water limits.

ENGINES: Volvo Penta TAMD 71A, 306bhp each at 2500rpm.
WATERJET UNITS: Riva Calzoni IRCL 39 D.
GEARBOXES: MPM IRM 301 PL-1.
CAPACITIES
Fuel capacity: Two 320-litre tanks
Fresh water capacity: 100 litres
DIMENSIONS
Length overall: 16·35m
Beam overall: 5·40m
Draught, full load: 0·60m
PERFORMANCE
Speed: 23-25 knots
The company has developed designs with its

licensor of military versions of the catamarans, which will take advantage of the craft's performance and stability characteristics and significant cost-effectiveness benefits.

As well as the catamarans, ASL has received orders from the Royal National Lifeboat Institution including the first two production 13-metre all-aluminium lifeboats; this is in addition to a number of aluminium superstructures for other lifeboats. It has also been involved with the building of 20-metre fast patrol boats and 55-knot patrol/interception vessels and hovercraft, including the production of API-88 hulls for British Hovercraft Corporation, including the recent Canadian Coast Guard craft, all in aluminium.

Aluminium Shipbuilders 51-seat River 50

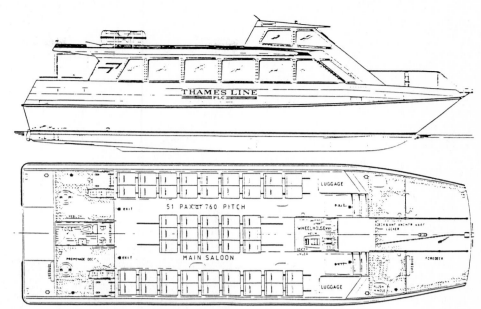

Aluminium Shipbuilders 16m InCat ferry

COUGAR HOLDINGS LIMITED

Cougar Quay, School Lane, Hamble, Hampshire
SO3 5JD, England

Telephone: (0703) 453513/4
Telex: 477229 COUGAR G
Telefax: (0703) 453513

N E Toleman, *Chairman*
C D Curtis, *Managing Director*
P Foster, *Director*
A S Hawkridge, *Director*
J P Sutcliffe, *Director Military Sales*
G P Wilson, *Director*
J W Walker, *Director*

Group Companies: Cougar Marine Ltd; Altech
Marine Ltd, Hamble, UK; Cougar Inc, Miami,
USA; Asiacraft Inc, Manila, Philippines; Cougar
Italia Srl, Viareggio, Italy
Cougar Holdings is part of the Toleman Group
of companies.

Founded in 1969 Cougar pioneered the
development of the catamaran hull form in circuit
racing power boats before moving into offshore
competitions and more recently high performance
production and commercial boat building. The
company was absorbed into the Toleman Group
of companies in 1980 and builds mono-hull and
catamaran craft up to 35 metres in wood, grp,
Kevlar, carbon composites and aluminium alloy.
Cougar's grp laminating plant is British Ministry
of Defence and Lloyds approved. Craft can be
built to Lloyds and similar authorities' classifications.

PEGASUS

Fast luxury motor yacht.
HULL AND SUPERSTRUCTURE BUILD-
ERS: Cougar Holdings Ltd.
FIT OUT: Commercial Marine Resources Inc,
19591 Bay F, North East 10th Avenue, North
Miami, Florida 33179, USA
Commercial Marine Resources commissioned
Cougar to design and build a pleasure yacht
capable of achieving speeds in excess of 100 knots.
A catamaran hull form was chosen and research
on the most suitable construction laminates was
carried out by Structural Polymer Systems Ltd,
Cowes, Isle of Wight, England. It is claimed that
the laminates used in the hull and superstructure
of the *Pegasus* have produced a saving of 3 tons
compared with building in Kevlar Aromat/grp
and 8 tons compared with a grp structure. Sea
trials were planned for mid-1987.
HULL: Superstructure and hull constructed in
epoxy-bonded Kevlar carbon composites, with
carbon-fibre glass stiffening.

Pegasus

Pegasus prior to shipment to USA

ENGINES: Two Avco Lycoming TF25 marine gas turbines, 2500shp each, at 15 100rpm. Two Perkins marine diesel engines for close manoeuvring.
PROPULSION: Two ASD 14 Arneson Surface Drives, with variable trim capability, coupled to specially designed Record surface-piercing titanium propellers. Separate shafts and propellers are fitted to the Perkins manoeuvring diesels.
CONTROLS: Power steering equipment.
CAPACITY
Fuel capacity: 9463 litres (2082 Imperial gallons)
ACCOMMODATION: Spacious master stateroom aft with heads, deck level saloon forward with two berths and galley. The wheelhouse and saloon forward are enclosed but fitted with a large sliding roof to take advantage of the sun. The large amount of deck area provides sunbathing space.
SYSTEMS
Auxiliary machinery: Auxiliary diesels fitted to provide electric power, compressed air and produce hydraulic power for bar thrusters
Air-conditioning: Fitted throughout
DIMENSIONS
Length overall: 17·37m
Length, waterline: 13·26m
Beam, max: 4·57m
Draught, max: 1·22m
WEIGHT
Displacement, max: 18 144kg
PERFORMANCE
Speed, max: 113 knots
Fuel consumption: 1745 litres/h (384 Imperial gallons/h)
Range at 112 knots: 600n miles

Virgin Atlantic Challenger (basis for CAT 2100 design)

CAT 2100 (DESIGN)

The CAT 2100 fast patrol boat design is based on Cougar's prototype 21-metre 50-knot Trans-Atlantic catamaran, *Virgin Atlantic Challenger*.
HULL: Option of grp or aluminium alloy construction.
MAIN ENGINES: Two MTU 12V 396 TB94 marine diesel engines each 2382bhp, operating through ZF 456, 1:1·3 reduction ratio gearboxes. Also one 250hp diesel engine linked to a 1066kg thrust PP waterjet mounted centrally in the tunnel top providing a loiter speed of 6 knots.
PROPULSION: Two five-blade surface-piercing propellers, or KaMeWa waterjets.
CONTROLS: Marinex steering system, control pistons wheelhouse and flying bridge.
CAPACITIES
Fuel, max capacity: 10·5 tonnes
Fresh water holding tank: 200 litres
Sewage holding tank: 200 litres
COMPLEMENT: Two officers, two senior ratings and six junior ratings.
ARMAMENT: One 20-25mm BMARC/ Oerlikon mounting forward, one 20mm mounting

Cougar CAT 2100 patrol boat design

aft, and two 12·7mm machine guns mounted on flying bridge.
SYSTEMS
Auxiliary machinery: Two G & M MDVWA4 diesel generators producing 24·2kVA
Navigational: Radar, data-true compass, magnetic compass, echo sounder, log, 1000W searchlight
Communications: VHF and SSB radios, crew intercom
Fresh water: 200-litre tank supplements a 750-litre/day osmosis plant
DIMENSIONS
Length overall: 21·25m

Length, waterline: 19·43m
Beam, max: 6·47m
Tunnel width, max: 1·82m
Draught, static max: 1·65m
WEIGHT
Displacement: 50·50 tonnes
PERFORMANCE
Speed, max, half load displacement in tropical climates, 2 hours in 12 hours: 40 knots
Speed, continuous, half load displacement in tropical climates: 35 knots
Speed, loiter: 6 knots
Sea State limitations: Craft can operate in weather conditions up to Sea State 5-6

FAIREY MARINTEKNIK (UK) LTD

Cowes Shipyard, Cowes, Isle of Wight PO31 7DL, England

Telephone: (0983) 297111
Telex: 86466 G

RTL HYDROCAT (DESIGN)

The Fairey RTL Hydrocat is a minimum-wash, waterjet-propelled high-speed catamaran vessel intended principally for use on rivers and lakes and is especially suited for shallow water operations. Conceived by Robert Trillo and developed in association with Fairey Marinteknik, traditional thinking in hull form has been avoided; two long and very slender hulls being employed enabling a high-speed displacement craft to be provided for relatively sheltered waters and offering negligible wash, low resistance and a smooth ride. Other advantages that arise from the configuration are very low water and air draughts (useful for shallow river operation with low bridges), rapid acceleration to cruise speed (necessary

for bus-stop type operations) and maximum immunity to debris collision effects. In addition the layout of the concept positions the passenger cabin well forward of the engine areas and in a separate structure thereby helping to provide a very quiet cabin as well as enhancing safety.

By using waterjet propulsion powerful manoeuvring control is available and in high winds the low side profile of the concept minimises unwanted side forces.

The first RTL Hydrocat design carries 50-55 passengers. Depending upon the choice of engine, cruising speeds will be in the range of 23 to 27 knots. Larger versions are already projected by Fairey Marinteknik for up to 135 passengers and speeds up to 30 knots.

The wash wave height (trough to crest) for the 55-passenger version is only 0·20m at 50m from the path of the craft.
POWERPLANT: Various 6-cylinder in-line, turbocharged, fresh water heat-exchanger-cooled engines may be used in the power range 167 to 250bhp, eg, Volvo TAMD 61 giving 187bhp continuous at 2200rpm or the TAMD 71A giving 250bhp continuous at 2200rpm.

PROPULSION: Two Hamilton waterjet units, Type 361.

ACCOMMODATION: 56 seats for passengers. Crew 2.

DIMENSIONS
Length overall: 24·95m
Length waterline: 23·00m
Height, above waterline: 3·82m
Length, superstructure: 13·85m
Beam: 5·90m
Draught, water, loaded: 0·62m
Draught, air: 3·20m
Saloon, internal size: 9·50 × 5·00m
Saloon, internal height: 2·10m (at centreline)
Control cab: 1·70 × 1·70m
Entrances: 1·81 × 1·00m

WEIGHT
Displacement, loaded: 17 tonnes

PERFORMANCE
Acceleration to 25 knots: 25s
Speed, full load, two Volvo TAMD 61: 23 knots
Fuel consumption, at 25 knots: 90 litres/h approx
Endurance: 13 hours approx

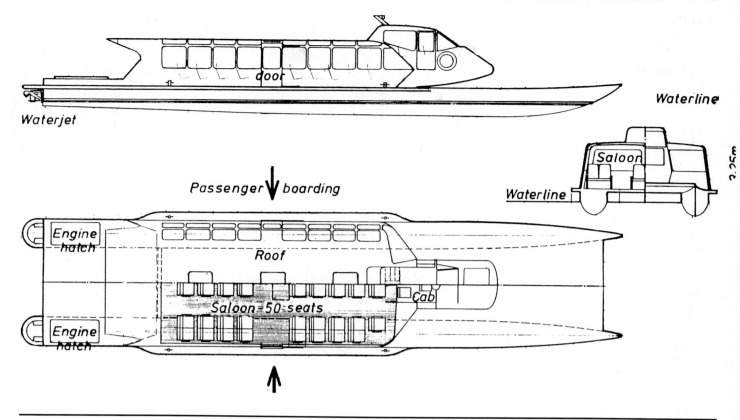

UNITED STATES OF AMERICA

ATLANTIC AND GULF BOAT BUILDING INC

PO Box 22947, Fort Lauderdale, Florida 33335, USA
1300 Eller Drive, Port Everglades, Florida 33316, USA

Telephone: (305) 763 8186
Telex: 264915 BARCO UR
Telefax: (305) 463 8128

Stan Joseph, *President*

Sub-licensed by Nichols Brothers Boat Builders Inc for the building of International Catamarans Pty Ltd range of catamaran craft.

BOTTOM TIME II

A 23·8m In Cat catamaran vessel delivered August 1986 to Bottom Time Adventurers of Fort Lauderdale, Florida, for diving expeditions throughout the Bahamas.
ENGINES: Two Perkins CV12 M 800, 597kW (800bhp) each, at 2100rpm.

PROPULSION: Two Columbian Bronze 5-blade propellers via ZF 2:1 gearboxes.
GENERATORS: Two 5kW Perkins 6.3544 (M) diesels.
ACCOMMODATION: 32 passengers in 16 staterooms.
SURVEY: USCG Sub-chapter T, Limited SOLAS.
PERFORMANCE
Speed, max: 30 knots
    cruising: 22 knots

ATLANTIC MARINE INC

PO Box 138, Ft George Island, Florida 32226, USA

Licensed in 1987 for the building of Fairey Marinteknik vessels.

COMMERCIAL MARINE RESOURCES INC

19591 Bay F, North East 10th Avenue, North Miami, Florida 33179, USA

Telephone: (305) 944 9144
Telex: 856276 CMR MIA

Michel J Meynard, *President*
Robert A Idoni, *General Manager*
W Harold Smith, *Project Co-ordinator*

PEGASUS

Commercial Marine Resources Inc were responsible for the above waterline design of this craft as well as the total fit out of the vessel, the hull and superstructure having been built by Cougar Marine Ltd, UK, to plastics design and specification carried out by Structural Polymer Systems Ltd, UK. Please see Cougar Marine entry for details of this craft.

GLADDING-HEARN SHIPBUILDING

The Duclos Corporation
PO Box 300-W, One Riverside Avenue, Somerset, Massachusetts 02726-0300, USA

Telephone: (617) 676 8596
Telefax: (612) 672 1873

George R Duclos, *President*

Sub-licensed by Nichols Brothers Boat Builders Inc for the building of International Catamarans Pty Ltd range of catamaran craft.

25-METRE IN CAT
MAKINAC EXPRESS

A 25m In Cat catamaran ferry built for the Arnold Transit Co for service from Upper and Lower Peninsulas of Michigan to the resort island in the Makinac Straits. The vessel is powered by two MWM 604B diesel engines.

The first In Cat catamaran built by Gladding-Hearn Shipbuilding, *Makinac Express*

DIMENSIONS
Length overall: 25·17m
Length, waterline: 21·50m

Beam, moulded: 8·70m
Beam of each hull: 2·50m
Draught, at design waterline: 2·10m

NATHAN I DANIEL

[PATENT HOLDER AND DEVELOPER]
948 Kailiu Place, Honolulu, Hawaii 96825, USA

Telephone: (808) 395 7373

Nathan I Daniel, *Inventor*
Howard E Daniel

SUPEROUTRIGGER

The essence of the SuperOutrigger invention is the provision of a craft with 'extended dimensions' in effective beam and length, aimed at permitting comfortable and economical operation in much rougher seas than possible with any current craft types. The efficiency of its long, thin main hull provides a substantial economic advantage over current fast craft, especially when viewed in conjunction with the SuperOutrigger's projected excellent seakeeping ability. The SuperOutrigger is aimed at combining comfortable motion, minimal speed loss in waves, good economics, simplicity and very shallow draught. There is no other craft type, mono-hull, catamaran, hydrofoil, hovercraft or SWATH, that appears to offer this combination of vital characteristics.

Following the principle of the outrigger canoe, the buoyancy of the craft is obtained from a single long, thin main hull, which supports the entire payload. The cabin (or deck) is centred atop an extremely strong, light and faired triangular truss structure, which carries it high above the low-freeboard main hull, well clear of wave crests. A similarly shaped but considerably smaller outrigger hull provides stability. The outrigger hull's relatively small size (about 20% of the volume of the main hull) makes it practical to place it far to the side of the main hull, permitting overall beam dimensions several times greater than those of catamarans. As a result, the SuperOutrigger's stability against roll is greater than that of corresponding catamaran craft. It is envisaged that whereas the main hull would be two-thirds submerged in normal full-load operating conditions, the stabilising outrigger hull would be only 50% submerged, so that the effects of beam seas would be balanced, ie, would not be initially biased toward either lifting or submerging the outrigger.

Preliminary investigations in the 20- to 30-knot speed range indicate that the SuperOutrigger's power requirements, in relation to its revenue-earning work capacity, will generally be less than those for current competitive craft types. In simple terms it can be seen that replacing the two hulls of a catamaran by a single hull of the same cross-section and twice the length will cut wave drag approximately in half. In addition, frictional resistance will also decrease about 10% because of the favourable effects of increasing hull length. These very significant reductions mean that the resistance of the much smaller outrigger hull will be more than offset, while at the same time making possible a craft of much greater effective length and beam, with greatly enhanced stability.

This increase in stability is obtained without recourse to either a deep draught configuration or autostabilisation systems. What has become the normally accepted limitation on size for ferry craft results from the matching of the product of speed and payload to the traffic on particular routes. This almost invariably results in craft which are too small for the higher sea states in which they are to operate. The SuperOutrigger alleviates this size problem, securing the benefits of the long, slender hull in low resistance, reduced motions and minimal speed loss in waves while avoiding the lack of roll stability and insufficient payload capacity that have prevented its use in mono-hull development.

17·68m demonstration model of the SuperOutrigger concept with Nathan I Daniel, inventor, at the controls in Honolulu harbour

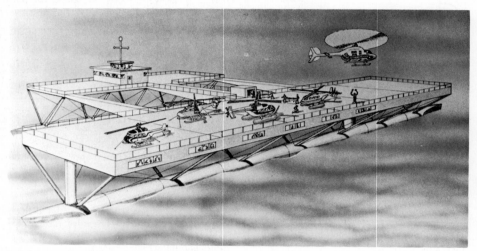

Artist's impression of the basic principles behind a helicopter application of the SuperOutrigger concept (fairings not shown)

The need to provide fast, economical and seakindly ferry service across Hawaii's rough inter-island channels was the stimulus for the SuperOutrigger invention. Widely patented by Nathan I Daniel, the concept was first tested in simple model form in 1979 to establish basic resistance and stability characteristics in the open sea. Ocean tests indicated that a 98m craft, with a roughly 30m span between the main and outrigger hulls, would neither pitch nor roll more than 5 degrees in low Sea State 6 (4m significant wave height). A 17·68m demonstration model was launched in 1986. Capable of carrying between 3600 and 4000kg on its open deck, or up to 50 passengers, this vessel has demonstrated in Hawaiian seas that the SuperOutrigger principle is extremely effective in reducing craft motions. Presentations to the press and other interested parties are continuing, and efforts are being actively pursued to find the funding needed to build and operate 90m, 35-knot, 300-passenger craft for the Honolulu-Maui and Honolulu-Kauai routes.

Aside from its wide potential application as a ferry, it is envisaged that SuperOutriggers could also be employed as helicopter carriers, coastal patrol/search and rescue craft, crew/work boats, fishing boats and pleasure craft. The benefits are expanded upon by Nathan I Daniel in the following text.

SuperOutrigger helicopter carriers, on coastal patrol or search and rescue duty, could head quickly toward a distress call while permitting the helicopters based onboard to stay out longer, cover a wider area and/or carry increasingly heavy loads as the vessel approached its objective.

SuperOutrigger crew/work boats, faster, smoother-riding and more efficient than mono-hulls, could take over many tasks presently performed at much greater cost by helicopters.

SuperOutrigger fishing boats could get to and from fishing grounds more quickly and cheaply than other craft, resulting in lower operating costs while also beating competing vessels in delivering the catch to market. Additionally, the Super-Outrigger's smooth ride could boost crew productivity by preventing the motion-induced fatigue fishermen generally experience on conventional craft.

SuperOutrigger pleasure craft would combine the speed of conventional motorboats with the comfort and deck-room of larger, slower, costlier and more sedate vessels. The SuperOutrigger's displacement hull would not be subject to the pounding generally experienced by conventional motorboats, which rely on planing hulls for speed.

NICHOLS BROTHERS BOAT BUILDERS INC

5400 S Cameron Road, Freeland, Whidbey Island, Washington 98249, USA

Telephone: (206) 321 5500

Telex: 821372
Telefax: (206) 221 7484

Matt Nichols, *President*

Builder of International Catamarans' designs.

22-METRE IN CAT
KLONDIKE

Christened 13 June 1984 at Langley, Washington. Vessel is fitted with a bow loading structure.
ENGINES: Two Caterpillar 3412 TA diesels, 700hp each.

GEARBOXES: Niigata MGN-80.
PROPELLERS: Coolidge 5-blade.
GENERATORS: Northern Lights 40kW.
RUDDERS: Curved dipping In Cat type.
DIMENSIONS
Length: 21·98m
Beam: 8·69m
Depth: 2·46m
CAPACITIES
Fuel tank capacity: 1000 US gallons
Water tank capacity: 1000 US gallons
PERFORMANCE
Seats: 210
Speed: 26 knots

SPIRIT OF ALDERBROOK
Main dimensions as for *Klondike*.
ENGINES: Two Detroit Diesel 12V-92 TA,
800bhp each.
GEARBOXES: Niigata MGN-80.
PROPELLERS: Coolidge 5-blade.
GENERATORS: Northern Lights 30kW.

26-METRE IN CAT
CATAMARIN & GOLD RUSH & EXPRESS (ex GLACIER EXPRESS, ex BAJA EXPRESS)
ENGINES: Two Deutz BAM 16M 816C diesels,
each 1346hp continuous at 1800rpm.
GEARBOXES: Reintjes WVS 832, ratio 1:2·29.
GENERATORS: Two John Deere 4275 engines
and Northern Lights 50kW generators. *Glacier
Express* has Pacific Diesel units.
PROPELLERS: Coolidge 5-blade, 1·169m ×
1·194m.
SYSTEMS
Steering: Wagner Engineering
Sound and entertainment system: Harris Electric
Heating, air-conditioning: Peter Kalby Company,
Seattle
DIMENSIONS
Length: 26·14m
Beam: 9·45m
Depth: 2·77m
Draught (full load): 2·39m
CAPACITIES
Fuel tank capacity: 5400 US gallons
Water tank capacity: 500 US gallons *Catamarin*,
400 US gallons *Gold Rush, Express*
PERFORMANCE
Speed: 28 knots

The In Cat 22m 210-seat *Klondike* built by Nichols Brothers

In Cat 22m 240-seat *Spirit of Alderbrook*

245-seat *Express* in service with Washington
State Ferries

EXECUTIVE EXPLORER

A 31·70m cruising catamaran, built 1986 for Alaskan and Hawaiian islands cruising. Beam is 11·20m, GRT 98, cruising speed 22 knots.

Forty-nine passengers are accommodated in 25 staterooms. A bow landing ramp is fitted.

Craft built (In Cat)	Delivered	Seats	Operator
22m In Cat *Klondike*	June 1984	210	Yukon River Cruises, Inc
22m In Cat *Spirit of Alderbrook*	1984	240	Wes Johnson, Seattle Harbor Tours
26m In Cat *Catamarin*	1985	400	Harbour Carriers Red and White Fleet (Crowley Maritime Corp)
26m In Cat *Express* (ex *Glacier Express* & *Baja Express*)	1985	245*	Washington State Department of Transportation
26m In Cat *Gold Rush*	September 1985	400	Harbour Carriers Blue and Gold Fleet
26m In Cat *Dolphin*	1986	400	Red and White Fleet
31m In Cat *Executive Explorer*	1986	49 passengers in 25 staterooms	Glacier Bay Yachts Tours, Inc Catamaran Cruise Lines, Hawaii
30m —	1987	—	Glacier Bay Yachts Tours, Inc

*400 total with outside seating

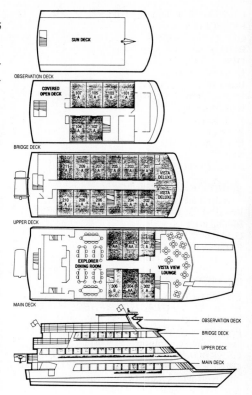

Layout of the four decks on the *Executive Explorer*, 22-knot cruise catamaran

SMALL-WATERPLANE-AREA TWIN-HULL (SWATH) VESSELS (SEMI-SUBMERGED CATAMARANS)

CANADA

EYRETECHNICS LIMITED

[CONSULTANTS/MARINE ENGINEERS]
Atlantic Region, Suite 207, 11 Morris Drive,
Dartmouth, Nova Scotia B3B 1M2, Canada

Telephone: (902) 466 7843

T Arnold P Eyre, *President*

SWATH SAR CUTTER (DESIGN)

In response to a particular Canadian Coast Guard operational requirement, Eyretechnics have developed a SWATH design for a CCG Type 500 Search and Rescue Cutter, primarily for operation in the choppy waters off Canada's west coast.

The 360-tonne all-aluminium vessel is arranged to facilitate handling and treatment of survivors by providing dedicated rescue zones, recessed into the port and starboard sides of the upper hulls. At each zone 15 square metres of deck space is provided leading to a triage area and treatment room amidships. Within the accommodation, seating and bunks are provided for up to 25 survivors. A helicopter landing pad is designed to enable landing and take-off of a Jet Ranger helicopter in up to Sea State 5 conditions. For ship external firefighting two monitors are located between the funnels with a capacity of 50% Fi-Fi1.

The vessel will be driven at 15 knots in Sea State 5 head seas by two medium speed diesels developing a total of 3600hp. The main engines are located within the main-deck structure with transfer of drive to controllable-pitch propellers via Kevlar reinforced drive belts.

Accommodation, all above main deck level, provides for mixed male and female 14 person

SWATH SAR cutter design by Eyretechnics Ltd

crew with officers forward and ratings aft. Stores, fuel and water requirements are designed for 15 days endurance at economical speed.

The design minimises development risks by employing standard, proven systems technology. The vessel will be built to Transport Canada regulations and classed with an international classification society.

DIMENSIONS
Length overall: 34·60m
Max beam: 15·50m
Draught (full load): 3·50m
WEIGHT
Displacement (full load): 360 tonnes
PERFORMANCE
Speed in Sea State 5: 15 knots

JAPAN

MITSUBISHI HEAVY INDUSTRIES

5-1, Marunouchi 2-chome, Chiyoda-ku, Tokyo, Japan

OHTORI

Built at the Kobe Shipyard and Engine Works of Mitsubishi Heavy Industries Ltd, the *Ohtori* was delivered to her owner, the Third District Port Construction Bureau in the Japanese Ministry of Transport on 25 March 1981. She was the first semi-submerged catamaran to be put into service.

Intended for surveying water and seabed conditions as part of a programme to purify the Seto Inland Sea, the vessel is equipped for the collection and analysis of seabed and water samples, the exploration of seabeds and the observation of sea and weather conditions.
PROPULSION: Two 1900hp diesels, 1475rpm, driving controllable-pitch propellers.
GENERATOR: 130kVA, 225V, 60Hz.
EQUIPMENT: Surveying crane, 0·99 tonne, 6·0m radius, two davits for surveying, box coner, piston coner, multi-cylinder sampler; water survey equipment (CSTD monitor, auto-analyser, turbidity meter); bottom survey equipment (ORP meter); depth and mud survey sounder (transducers);

Ohtori, sea condition survey vessel

position-finding equipment (microwave position finder, Loran C receiver); data processor.
DIMENSIONS
Length overall: 27·00m

Length bp: 24·00m
Breadth (upper deck) moulded: 12·50m
Depth, moulded: 5·10m
Draught, full load, moulded: 3·40m

GRT: 251·49
PERFORMANCE
Speed, max: 20·61 knots
Complement: 20

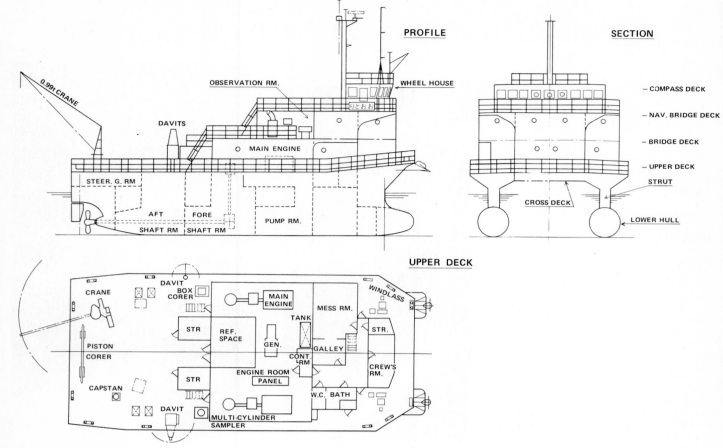

General Arrangement of *Ohtori*

MITSUI ENGINEERING & SHIPBUILDING CO LTD

6-4, Tsukiji 5-chome, Chuo-ku, Tokyo 104, Japan

Telephone: (03) 544-3462
Telex: 22821/22924 MITUIZOSEN J

Kazuo Maeda, *Chairman*
Isshi Suenaga, *President*
Jiro Hoshino, *Executive Managing Director*
Yoshio Yamashita, *General Manager, High-Speed Craft Division*
Tadashi Mabuchi, *Manager, High-Speed Craft Division*

Mitsui began its high-speed semi-submerged catamaran (SSC) development programme in 1970. Since 1976, the programme has been operated in conjunction with the Japanese Marine Machinery Development Association (JAMDA). In 1977 Mitsui built the experimental 18·37-tonne *Marine Ace* in order to obtain practical experience with this hull form. In 1979 the first SSC high-speed passenger vessel was launched under the provisional name *Mesa 80*. After extensive trials it was completed in 1981 and renamed *Seagull*. It has since been operated by Tokai Kisen Co Ltd on a passenger ferry service between Atami and Oshima island. It was only the second such vessel to be built, the first being the US Navy's SSP *Kaimalino* range support vessel, designed to operate in the rough seas off the Hawaiian islands.

The company has also developed and built a SSC hydrographic survey vessel, *Kotozaki*, for the Fourth District Port Construction Bureau of the Japanese Ministry of Transport. This vessel was completed in 1981.

Additionally, a support vessel for underwater experiments, the 61·55-metre *Kaiyo* was completed in 1985. This is a highly advanced semi-submerged catamaran and the largest of such

vessels in the world. It is not a high-speed vessel having a speed of 13·25 knots.

Semi-submerged catamarans can be built to suit a wide variety of applications from passenger ferries to offshore rig-support vessels.

As can be seen from the technical assistance contract concluded in 1985 by Mitsui with Lockheed Marine Systems Group shipyard for the

manufacture and marketing of SSCs, continued efforts are being made by Mitsui in opening overseas markets for this highly advanced shipbuilding technology.

MARINE ACE

Mitsui's first experimental SSC, *Marine Ace*, is built in marine-grade aluminium alloy and can

18·37-tonne *Marine Ace*, the first Mitsui SWATH, 1977

operate in Sea States 2 to 3. Its automatically-controlled fin stabilisers reduce ship motion in waves.

PROPULSION: Motive power for *Marine Ace* is supplied by two sets of V-type four-cycle petrol engines, each developing 200bhp at 3700rpm. Each drives, via a vertical intermediate transmission shaft and bevel gear, a three-bladed fixed-pitch propeller; one at the end of each of the two torpedo-like hulls.

TANK CAPACITIES
Ballast: 11·01m³ (2420 gallons)
Fuel oil: 1·45m³ (320 gallons)
AUTOMATIC MOTION CONTROL SYSTEM: Four sets of fin stabilisers, driven by hydraulic servo motors, reduce ship motion in heavy seas.
DIMENSIONS
Length overall: 12·35m (40ft 6in)
  registered: 11·95m (39ft 2in)
Beam max: 6·5m (21ft 4in)
  at load line: 5·8m (19ft)
Designed full load draught: 1·55m (5ft 1in)
GRT: 29·91 (*31·56)
WEIGHTS
Full load displacement: 18·37 tonnes (*about 22 tonnes)
PERFORMANCE
Speed, max cruising revolutions, full load
  draught: About 18 knots (*about 14 knots)
*after modification in 1978

SEAGULL

Developed jointly by Mitsui Engineering & Shipbuilding Co Ltd and the Japanese Marine Machinery Development Association (JAMDA), the 27-knot *Seagull* is the world's first commercial semi-submerged catamaran. *Seagull* is in service with Tokai Kisen on routes linking Tokyo, Oshima island, Atami and Nii-jima island. Despite its small size, the overall length is just under 36m (118ft), the vessel provides a stable ride in seas with 3·5m (11ft 6in) waves.

During the first ten-month long commercial run in a service between Atami and Oshima, *Seagull* established an operating record of 97 per cent. The incidence of seasick passengers was very low, 0·5 per cent or less, proving the exceptional riding comfort.

Craft built (SWATH)	Owner/operator	Delivered
Marine Ace 12·35m experimental SSC	Mitsui	October 1977
Seagull (ex *Mesa 80*) 35·90m ferry	Tokai Kisen Co Ltd	1979
Kotozaki 27·00m hydrographic survey	Japanese Ministry of Transport	March 1981
Kaiyo 61·55m underwater support vessel (low-speed)	Japan Marine Science and Technology Centre	May 1985
Marine Wave 15·10m pleasure cruiser	Toray Industries Inc	July 1985
Sun Marina 15·10m pleasure cruiser	San Marina Hotel	March 1987

Seagull

PROPULSION: Main engines are two Fuji-SEMT marine diesels, each developing 4050hp max continuous at 1475rpm. Each drives, via a vertical transmission shaft and bevel gear, a four-blade fixed-pitch propeller. Two 206·25kVA generators provide electrical power.
HULL: Built in marine grade aluminium alloy.
ACCOMMODATION: Crew of seven. Passenger seats provided for 446.
AUTOMATIC MOTION CONTROL SYSTEM: Four sets of fin stabilisers driven by hydraulic servo motors reduce ship motion in heavy seas.
DIMENSIONS
Length overall: 35·9m (117ft 9in)
Length, bp: 31·5m
Breadth, moulded: 17·1m (56ft 1in)
Depth, moulded: 5·84m (19ft 2in)
Designed draught: 3·15m (10ft 4in)
GRT: 672·08
PERFORMANCE
Max speed: about 27 knots

KOTOZAKI

The world's first hydrographic survey vessel of the SSC type, *Kotozaki* is operated by the Fourth District Port Construction Bureau of the Japanese Ministry of Transport. It was delivered in March 1981.

Kotozaki provides a stable platform from which data can be gathered and its rectangular decks allow ample space for hydrographic equipment, laboratory facilities, working and living accommodation.
PROPULSION: Main engines are two Fuji-12 PA 4V 185-V6 marine diesels, each developing 1900hp at 1475rpm. Each drives, via a vertical transmission shaft and bevel gear, a controllable pitch propeller type Kamome CPC-53F, diameter 1750mm, pitch 1400mm.
HULL: Steel catamaran hulls and aluminium alloy deck structure.
ACCOMMODATION: Complement of 20.
MOTION CONTROL SYSTEM: Controllable pitch propellers and manually-operated fin stabilisers.
DIMENSIONS
Length overall: 27m (88ft 6in)
Length, bp: 25·0m
Beam: 12·5m (41ft)
Depth: 4·6m (15ft 1in)
Designed draught: 3·2m (10ft 5in)
GRT: 253·67
PERFORMANCE
Max speed: About 20·5 knots

KAIYO

The first SSC type support vessel for underwater experiments, *Kaiyo* was delivered to the Japan Marine Science and Technology Centre in

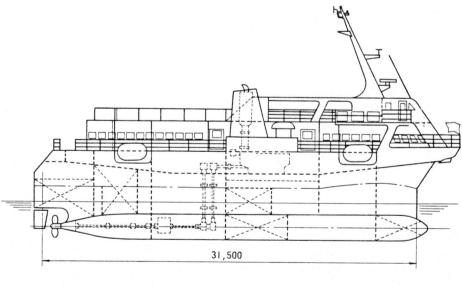

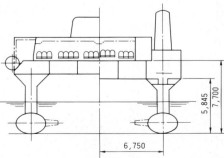

General Arrangement of *Seagull*

included here as it is one in the Mitsui series of SSC types and is the largest, most highly advanced semi-submerged catamaran vessel in the world.

The *Kaiyo* is fitted with a wide range of equipment including a deepsea diving system composing two submersible decompression chambers (SDC), a deck decompression chamber (DDC) and a dynamic positioning system (DPS).

The *Kaiyo* can function as an offshore testing base and is stable enough to maintain her position offshore for long periods. This stability characteristic facilitates research and development in the following areas: manned underwater work technology, deep ocean floor survey technology and new ocean monitoring systems, as well as preliminary research for manned subsea research vessels and group training and education on board.

HULL: High tensile steel for the main structure and mild steel for the superstructure.
ACCOMMODATION: Crew of 29, research personnel of 40 (limited to 50 persons on international voyages).
POWERPLANT: *Kaiyo* has a diesel-electric propulsion system.
Main generators: 1560kVA, 4 sets
Prime movers: High-speed marine diesel engines 1850hp, 4 sets
Main propulsive motors: 860kW, 4 sets
Propellers: Two 4-blade controllable-pitch
DIMENSIONS
Length overall: 61·55m
Breadth: 28·00m
Depth: 10·60m
Design full load draught: 6·30m
GRT: Approx 2800
PERFORMANCE
Cruising speed: Approx 13 knots
Range: 5100n miles

Kotozaki

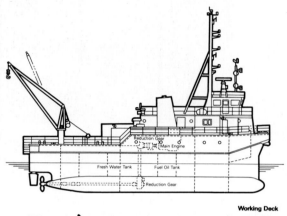
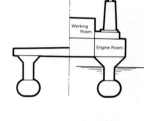
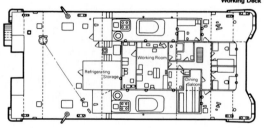

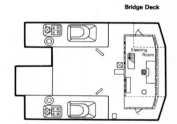

General Arrangement of *Kotozaki*

Mitsui *Kaiyo*, the largest SSC in the world

General Arrangement of Sea Saloon 15

SEA SALOON 15

MARINE WAVE

The first semi-submerged catamaran Sea Saloon 15 type cruiser *Marine Wave* built by MES for Toray Industries, Inc was delivered in July 1985.

Marine Wave, which is only about 15 metres in length, is relatively free from rolling and pitching by virtue of its SSC design which also allows a spacious deck to be provided and facilitates comfortable cruising. One of its most interesting features is the combination of its unusual shape with Toray's newly developed hull material incorporating carbon fibre composites. The Sea Saloon 15 has two sets of computer-controlled stabilising fins and two fixed fins.

Marine Wave is certificated by the Japan Craft Inspection Organisation for use in coastal waters. By August 1986 *Marine Wave* had operated over 860 hours including a voyage to West Japan in which she experienced waves up to 4·5m in height.
HULL: Glass reinforced plastic and carbon reinforced plastic.
ACCOMMODATION: Crew 2, luxury accommodation for 12 passengers plus 3 others.
POWERPLANT: Two high-speed marine diesel Ford Sabre 5950cc engines, 275hp each at 2500rpm, driving fixed-pitch propellers via Twin Disc MG 506 gearboxes, ratio 2·03:1.
TANKS
Fuel oil: 2000 litres
Fresh water: 300 litres
GENERATOR: Onan MDJJF-18R diesel unit.
DIMENSIONS
Length overall: 15·10m
Length, registered: 11·95m
Breadth, moulded: 6·20m
Depth, moulded: 2·74m
Draught, full load: 1·60m
GRT: 19
PERFORMANCE
Speed, max trial: About 18 knots
Speed, service: 16 knots
Endurance: About 20 hours

SUN MARINA

The second of Sea Saloon 15 series, *Sun Marina* was built by Mitsui for San Marina Hotel, opened as a grand resort hotel in Okinawa in March 1987.

Sun Marina has a large luxurious party cabin

Sea Saloon 15 interior arrangements

Mitsui SSC high-tech cruiser Sea Saloon 15 type, *Marine Wave* built in glass and carbon-reinforced plastic

Sun Marina

Guest saloon of *Sun Marina*

Mitsui SSC cruiser Sea Saloon 15 type *Sun Marina*

which can accommodate 30 guests of the Hotel, and sails round many coral reefs from the privately owned marina of the Hotel.
ACCOMMODATION: Passengers 30; crew 3.
POWERPLANT: Two 230hp marine diesel.
TANKS
Fuel oil tank: Two 900 litres

Fresh water: 400 litres
GENERATOR: 15kW.
DIMENSIONS
Length overall: 15·10m
Length registered: 11·925m
Breadth: 6·40m
Depth: 2·75m

Draught: 1·60m
WEIGHT
Gross tonnage: 19 tons
PERFORMANCE
Speed max: 20·5 knots
Speed service: 17 knots
Endurance: About 20 hours

KOREA, SOUTH

HYUNDAI HEAVY INDUSTRIES CO LTD

Head office: 1 Cheonha-Dong, Ulsan, South Korea
Seoul office: 140-2, Kye-Dong, Jongro-ku, Seoul, South Korea

Churl W Kim, *Director of Marketing and Business*

HYUNDAI SWATH (DESIGN)
DIMENSIONS
Length, bp: 23·60m
Length of strut: 24·60m
Breadth (max): 12·40m
Depth to main deck: 5·30m
Draught: 2·50m
WEIGHT
Displacement: 125 tonnes
PERFORMANCE
Speed: 25 knots
Passengers: 270

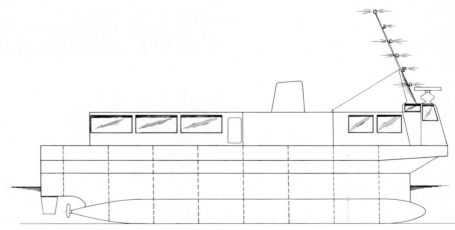

Preliminary design of Hyundai SWATH

UNITED KINGDOM

FAIREY MARINTEKNIK (UK) LIMITED

Member of the Marinteknik Group
Cowes Shipyard, Cowes, Isle of Wight PO31 7DL, England

Telephone: 0983 297111
Telex: 86466 CHEVTN G
Telefax: 0983 299813

Jack Barr, *Managing Director*
Gordon Dodd, *Manufacturing Director*
Mike McSorley, *Marketing Manager*
Robert Milner, *Regional Manager*
Patrick Methold, *Regional Manager*
Ian Campbell, *Regional Manager*
David Codd, *Commercial Manager*
Nigel Warren, *Chief Designer*

SWATH PATROL CRAFT (DESIGN)

Early in 1985 Fairey Marinteknik (UK) Ltd announced a proposal for a patrol craft employing the SWATH principle.

HULL: The catamaran hulls, main cross structure are of all-welded steel construction. Non-structural parts of the platform, saloon, wheelhouse

and casings are of all-welded marine grade aluminium alloy, BS 1470 and 1474, 5083 (N8).
MAIN ENGINES/GEARBOXES: Two MWM TBD D234 V16 marine diesels, heat exchange cooled, 900kW each at 2300rpm, at temperatures up to 27°C air, 27°C sea water.
    Gearboxes are Reintjes WVS 642, reverse, with 3·3:1 reduction.
PROPULSION: Monel K 500 shafts, 3-blade fixed-pitch propellers in nickel aluminium bronze BS 1400 AB2. Diameter 1300mm, pitch 1100mm, blade area ratio 0·65:1.
ACCOMMODATION: For crew of 12.
SYSTEMS
Auxiliary power: Two G & M 40 MPD4 diesel generators, 29kW 35kVA each (Lloyds unrestricted) supplying 220V ac, single phase 50Hz. Each engine is a Perkins 4.236 heat-exchanger cooled, 24V starting.
Dc supply: 24V
DIMENSIONS
Length, overall: 23·20m
Length, waterline: 21·0m
Beam, overall: 11·15m
Depth amidships: 5·40m
Draught (normal): 2·70m
WEIGHT
Displacement: 125 tonnes
PERFORMANCE
Speed, max (at full load): 20·5 knots
Range, at 14 knots: 1200n miles
    at 10 knots: 3000n miles
Periods of motion: Heave 4·6 seconds, pitch 7·0 seconds, roll 8·5 seconds

STORM MASTER FERRY (DESIGN)

This SWATH design was proposed by Fairey Marinteknik to provide a craft suitable for a ferry service in the rough waters between Kirkwall and the outlying Orkney islands. The hulls are des-

Design for a SWATH passenger/car and cattle ferry by Fairey Marine Ltd, now Fairey Marinteknik (UK) Ltd

igned with square cross-sections permitting the engines to be housed within them and providing sufficient room for servicing. To improve ride, twin fins are installed on the inside of each lower hull towards the stern and these fins are fitted with hydraulically operated variable flaps which enable trim adjustments to be made to suit loading and sea conditions. The flaps may also be linked to an autostabilising system to damp out vessel motions. Twin bow thrusters are positioned in the bow of each hull.

ACCOMMODATION: 100 passengers.
DIMENSIONS
Length: 35·7m
Beam: 15·0m
Depth: 5·8m
Draught: 2·7m
Hull cross-sections: 2·6m × 2·6m
WEIGHT
Displacement, loaded: 320 tonnes
PERFORMANCE
Speed: 14 knots

UNITED STATES OF AMERICA

JAMES BETTS ENTERPRISES

9495 Candida Street, San Diego, California 92126, USA

Telephone: (619) 578 8564/224 3422

James Betts
Paul Kotzebue

CHUBASCO

A new Ocean Systems Research Ltd project, *Chubasco* was built in 1986 for Leonard Friedman for drift fishing. The design and building is under patents of Dr Thomas G Lang of the Semi-Submerged Ship Corporation.

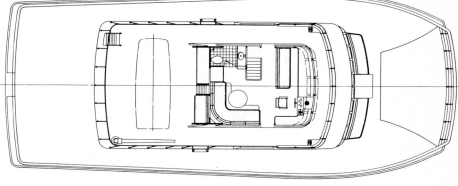

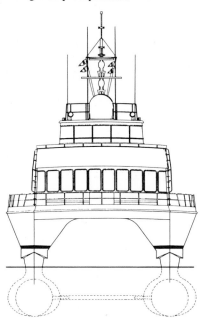

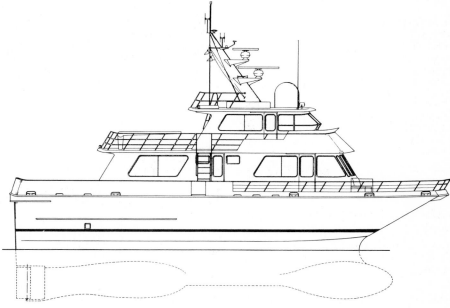

General Arrangement of *Chubasco*

HULL: Marine grade aluminium.

ENGINES: Two GM diesel, 750hp each, turbo-charged.

GENERATORS: Two 50kW Northern Light, one 7·5kW Northern Light.

TANKS: One 1135-litre macerator and holding tank, one 1890-litre potable water tank, four 4730-litre diesel fuel tanks with Delaval gauges, four bait tanks.

STABILISING FINS: Gyro-activated.

COMMUNICATIONS: Three VHS transceivers with ADF, two SSB radios, one Citizens Band radio, one Magnavox Satcom telephone.

NAVIGATION: One Magnavox Sat-Nav, one Furuno Loran unit, one Alden weatherfax, two Furuno 72-mile daylight radars, two Data Marine 305m (1000ft) fathometers, two Furuno colour fathometers, one Furuno 214m (700ft) sonar unit, two water speed indicators, one wind speed indicator, one wind direction indicator, one Sperry gyrocompass and automatic pilot.

CONTROLS: Steering station at stern, steering station at each wing outside pilot house, bow thruster and controls at three stations.

ACCOMMODATION: Sleeping accommodation for nine passengers on main deck in master stateroom, two guest staterooms, two sofa berths in saloon, plus one bunk. Pilot house berths three; all air-conditioned. Fully equipped galley.

DIMENSIONS
Length overall: 21·95m
Draught: 2·13m

PERFORMANCE
Speed, max: 28 knots
Speed, cruising, in 1·8m seas: 20 knots

Chubasco under construction, Sept 1986

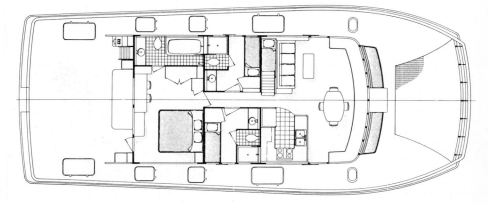

Main deck plan, *Chubasco*

Bow thruster on *Chubasco*

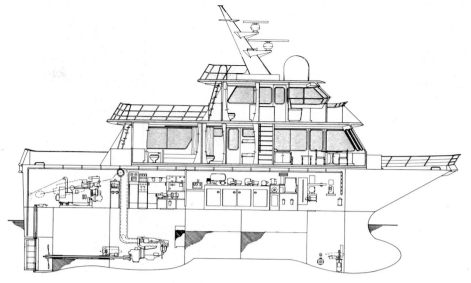

Chubasco machinery and equipment arrangements

INNERSPACE CORPORATION
Covina, California, USA

Calvin A Gongwer, *President*

SST *THEODOR VON KARMAN*
A new SWATH concept, with a central main

hull and two outer secondary hulls and is therefore really a semi-submerged trimaran. The vessel was constructed in 1986 as a research and development project.
DIMENSIONS
Length overall: 24·39m
Beam overall: 11·59m

Draught: 3·20m
WEIGHT
Displacement: 144 tonnes
PERFORMANCE
Speed, estimated max: Approx 18 knots
Range: 750n miles

LOCKHEED SHIPBUILDING COMPANY
2929 16th Avenue SW, Seattle, Washington 98134, USA

Joseph R Santosuosso, *President*
P J Mantle, *Director, Advanced Ship Business Development*

Lockheed and Mitsui have a licence agreement for the design and construction of SWATH ships for customers operating under the US flag. The US Navy is designing, with industry help including Lockheed's, a 3000-ton SWATH surveillance ship T-AGOS and a request for proposals was due in April 1986. This vessel is to be capable of towing submarine listening arrays into deep ocean areas.

The SWATH type vessel is under consideration as a new oceanographic ship for use by navy oceanographers and scientists from US oceanographic institutions. Lockheed is proposing a 3800-ton SWATH ship based on the Mitsui *Kaiyo* to meet this requirement, but this is not a high-speed vessel.

OCEAN SYSTEMS RESEARCH
San Diego, California, USA

BETSY (ex *SUAVE LINO*)
Completed in 1981 for Mr Friedman as a fishing boat *Betsy* was used more recently as a tender by the Sail America Syndicate during the America's Cup defence off Fremantle, Australia.

The vessel is constructed of aluminium with a single strut configuration for each hull. Two high-speed diesels of 425hp each, mounted at deck level drive fixed-pitch propellers through bevel gears. Automatic fin control is fitted.
DIMENSIONS
Length overall: 19·20m
Length bp: 16·80m

Breadth overall: 9·10m
Draught: 2·13m
Box clearance: 0·70m
WEIGHTS
Displacement: 53 tonnes
Payload: 14 tonnes
PERFORMANCE
Speed, max: 18 knots

PACIFIC MARINE ENGINEERING SCIENCE CO (PAMESCO)
[AN R & D CORPORATION FINANCING SWATH RESEARCH, SECURE PATENTS, MARKETING ORGANIZATION]
PO Box 29816, Honolulu, Hawaii 96820, USA

Telephone: (536) 7480

Steven C H Loui, *President*
Dr Ludwig H Seidl, *Vice President and Chief Naval Architect, Chief Scientist and Designer*
Dr Michael Schmicker, *Vice President, Business Development*

Technology for the development of the Pacific Marine SWATH came from Dr Ludwig Seidl, Professor of Ocean Engineering, University of Hawaii. In 1977 Pacific Marine (a private corporation founded in 1944 by the late Fred H M Loui) and Dr Seidl formed the Pacific Marine Engineering Science Co. In 1979 the company was granted patents (US Patent 4174671) covering its SWATH design.
One-tenth scale models of a series of PAMESCO SWATH designs were tested in commercial model boat basins in 1980 at the Schiffbautechnische Versuchsanstalt Wien in Vienna, Austria, and in 1981 at the University of California at Berkeley. In February and March 1987, Pacific Marine returned to Vienna to finalise

Artist's impression of the Pacific Marine 40·24m SWATH prototype the prototype design with a US$250 000 test effort. Close correlation was demonstrated between computer model predictions and actual model performance, leading to the company's decision to begin construction of the prototype. Pacific Marine invested US$2 million to build the vessel, the hull construction being subcontracted to Thompson Metal Fabricators, Vancouver, Washington.

The American naval architect/marine engineering firms of J Cameron McKernan and Raymond Richards have been retained as construction engineering consultants.

PACIFIC MARINE SWATH PROTOTYPE
CERTIFICATION: US Coast Guard (Subchapter T boat).
CLASSIFICATION: American Bureau of Shipping.
HULLS: Steel.
SUPERSTRUCTURE: Aluminium.
ENGINES: Two Deutz MWM 16V 816 CR diesels, 1350hp each.
REDUCTION GEARS: Ulstein Maritime 5·3:1 ratio.
PROPULSION: Controllable-pitch propellers.

CONTROL SYSTEM: Donald Higdon and Associates.
ACCOMMODATION: 500 (ferry/excursion); 300 (seated dinner cruise).
DIMENSIONS
Length: 40·24m
Beam: 16·16m
Draught: 2·44m to 3·66m (variable)
PERFORMANCE
Speed: 17 knots (up to 25 knots with more powerful engines)
Range, cruising: 1700n miles

RAINS
5145 Shore Drive South, St Augustine, Florida, USA

CHARWIN
A single strut SWATH vessel built by Mr Rains of St Augustine, Florida in 1983. *Charwin* was built as a fishing vessel but has also been used for trials by the Woods Hole Oceanographic Institution. In early 1987 she was laid up with the engines removed.
ENGINES: Two Caterpillar 3406.
DIMENSIONS
Length overall: 25·30m
Beam: 12·20m
Draught: 2·74m
WEIGHT
Displacement: 207 tonnes

NEWBUILDING
A new SWATH fishing vessels under construction early 1987 for Mr Rains.
ENGINES: 900 hp total.
DIMENSIONS
Length overall: 18·29m
Beam: 9·15m
Draught: 2·13m
Height, hull undersurface to water surface: 1·91m
Diameter of submerged hulls: 1·22m
WEIGHTS
Displacement: 61 tonnes
Payload: 5 tonnes
PERFORMANCE
Speed: 20 knots

SWATH fishing vessel *Charwin*

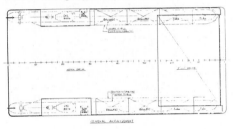

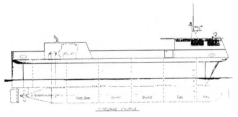

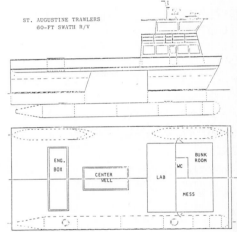

Layout of *Charwin*

Layout of new Rains 18·29m SWATH fishing vessel

RMI INC
(ceased trading 1986)

SD-60
HALCYON
RMI designed and built a 18·3m Small-Waterplane-Area Twin-Hull (SWATH) demonstrator boat, designated SD-60. *Halcyon* was launched in March 1985.

The SD-60 SWATH offers advantages over conventional craft in transporting passengers and cargo. For example, pitch and roll motions are significantly less than those of comparable small mono-hulls over the full range of anticipated sea conditions, and this will give an improved ride. Its increased speed performance in heavy seas enables it to maintain headway at design speed through and beyond Sea State 4; an important advantage in commercial service operations. The wide separation between its variable-pitch propellers allows precise manoeuvring within ports, channels and rivers, and positioning alongside ships or offshore oil platforms.

RMI SD-60 *Halcyon* operating in San Francisco Bay

The deckhouse has a galley, head and berthing accommodation for the crew of three and space for 20 passengers. The passenger space can be converted to living quarters for 9 additional crew members. The pilot house accommodates a full range of commercial communications and marine navigation systems. Microprocessor ship control systems and vessel management systems are fitted. Oceangoing ships or Lighter-Aboard-Ship (LASH) barges will be able to carry the boat on deck.

Propulsion power is by twin Caterpillar 3408 DITA marine diesels each driving, via a reduction gear and Eaton V-belt drive, a 45in diameter VPO FR-H Hundested variable-pitch propeller. The electric plant features twin Model 4.236M (25kW) Perkins marine diesel electric generator sets. The design meets USCG safety requirements and certification as a commercial passenger boat under 100 tons displacement, fully loaded.

DIMENSIONS
Length overall: 18·28m (60ft)
Max beam: 9·14m (30ft)
Navigational draught: 2·29m (7ft 6in)
Available cargo deck area: 54·71m² (589ft²)
WEIGHTS
Payload: 8 long tons
Full load displacement: 62 long tons
Light ship displacement: 52 long tons
PERFORMANCE
Max speed: 20 knots
Cruising: 18 knots
Cruising range (no fuel reserve and payload): Over 800n miles

SD-60 *Halcyon* SWATH under construction

SD-60 *Halcyon* SWATH hull nearing completion

SEMI-SUBMERGED SHIP CORPORATION (SSSCO)

[PATENT HOLDING AND DEVELOPMENT]
417 Loma Larga Drive, Solana Beach, California 92075, USA

Telephone: (619) 481 6417

Dr Thomas G Lang, *President*

SSSCO was founded by Dr Thomas G Lang, the inventor of the semi-submerged ship (S³). Basically, the S³ consists of two parallel torpedo-like hulls attached to which are two or more streamlined struts which pierce the water surface and support an above-water platform. Stabilising fins are attached near the after end of each hull and a pair of smaller fins are located near their forward ends.

Semi-submerged ship technology has been proved over the past ten years by the 190-ton SSP *Kaimalino*, a US Navy developed range-support vessel which has been operating in the rough seas off the Hawaiian islands since 1975. Following private development, Dr Lang introduced the concept into the US Navy in 1968 and holds several basic patents in the field. He led the Navy's first research work, and initiated and developed the hydrodynamic design for the stable semi-submerged platform (SSP), the world's first high-performance, open-ocean, semi-submerged ship.

The US Navy's present SWATH (Small-Waterplane-Area Twin-Hull) ship programme is based on the S³ concept. The performance features that distinguish S³s from conventional vessels are greatly reduced motions with sustained speed even in heavy seas, lower hydrodynamic drag and reduced power requirements at moderate to high speeds, and far superior course-keeping characteristics at all sea headings. S³s have excellent manoeuvrability at speed, when operating in confined harbours and when station-keeping.

The control surfaces of the S³ designs enable them to ride smoothly through the water. Con-trollable bow and stern fins can be operated collectively or differentially. Used together, the four fins control heave, pitch and roll. Twin rudders provide directional control at high speed. Twin screws and thrusters provide differential thrust at low speed, to help in delicate, close-in manoeuvres. The screws may have variable and reversible-pitch blades.

A number of applications of the S³ principle have been proposed by Dr Lang and these were described in *Jane's Surface Skimmers 1985* and earlier editions. These design proposals have included an offshore crew change vessel, a high-speed ferry, a rapid intervention vessel, supply and diving support vessels. Fishing vessel and cruise ship applications are also suggested.

KAIMALINO

Operated by the US Navy Ocean Systems Center at Hawaii the SSP *Kaimalino* has operated from near calm conditions to beyond Sea State 6 at speeds of up to 25 knots. Its motion is small relative to a conventional mono-hull either when at rest or under way. The SSP has made smooth transits in 4·57m (15ft) swells without any impacts; however, in short, steep 3·7m (12ft) waves, occasional bow impacts have occurred. No structural damage has occurred, even during storm

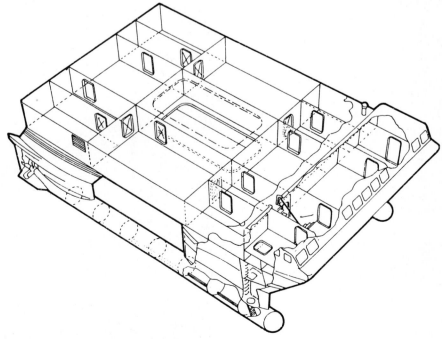
Cutaway showing basic hull configuration of SSP *Kaimalino*

conditions when 7·6 to 9·2m (25 to 30ft) high waves were encountered.

In February 1985 ten Woods Hole Oceanographic Institution scientists participated in a series of two- and three-day cruises off Hawaii on the SWATH vessel *Kaimalino* over a two-week period to test the suitability of the SWATH design for oceanographic research.

DIMENSIONS
Length: 27m (88ft)
Beam (at mid section): 14m (46ft)
Height: 9·7m (32ft)
WEIGHTS
Displacement: 217 tons
Max payload (including fuel): 50 tons
PERFORMANCE
Max speed: 25 knots
Range at max speed and payload: 400n miles
Reference: SSP Kaimalino; Conception, Development History, Hurdles and Success by Thomas G Lang. ASME, Paper 86-WA/HH-4. Presented at the Winter Annual Meeting Anaheim, California, 7-12 Dec 1986.

S³ OCEANOGRAPHIC RESEARCH SHIP PROJECT DESIGN (LOW SPEED)

A design prepared for Woods Hole Oceanographic Institution to have a payload carrying capability of 420 tons.

ACCOMMODATION/SPACE
60 people in 1- and 2-person staterooms
Deck space 1280m² on three levels
Scientific storage: 223m²
Laboratory area: 281m²
Several workshops
ELECTRIC POWER
4kW Caterpillar 3516 motor/generator
DIMENSIONS
Deck length: 66·46m
Beam length: 28·96m
Draught, full load: 7·32m
Draught, full load + ½ fuel: 5·88m
WEIGHT
2529 tonnes
PERFORMANCE
Max speed: 16·5 knots at 5027shp
Continuous speed: 15·9 knots at 4446shp
Cruise speed: 15·3 knots at 3779shp
Range: 11 400n miles at 15 knots
Endurance: 40 days
Normal work conditions: Through Sea State 6
Limited work conditions: Through Sea State 7

S³ MULTI-PURPOSE VESSEL PROJECT DESIGN (LOW SPEED)

A 19·5m semi-submerged ship design suitable for cruise, fishing, diving support, hydrographic survey, oceanography, crew transport and ferry work. Engines would be mounted on the lower hulls to provide more deck space and to reduce noise and vibration.

DIMENSIONS
Length: 19·51m
Beam: 10·76m
Draught: 2·16m
WEIGHT
59·85 tonnes
PERFORMANCE
Max speed full load: 15·8 knots
Speed, continuous power: 15 knots
Service speed: 14 knots at 85% max continuous bhp

SSP *Kaimalino*

Artist's impression of the 2529-tonne SSSCO S³ oceanographic research ship

Artist's impression of the RMI 19·5 m SSSCO S³ multi-purpose vessel

THOMPSON METAL FABRICATORS

Vancouver, Washington, USA

Builders of the Pacific Marine SWATH hull, see entry on page 257.

HIGH-SPEED MONO-HULL CRAFT

AUSTRALIA

AGNEW CLOUGH LIMITED

[PROJECT MANAGERS]
PO Box 61, North Fremantle, Western Australia,
Australia

Telephone: (09) 335 9855
Telex: 92588 AA

PROJECT 150
128 Great Eastern Highway, South Guildford,
Western Australia, Australia

Telephone: (09) 279 0011
Telex: 92012 AA

Project 150 comprises a consortium of Agnew
Clough Ltd, M G Kailis Group of Companies and
Wigmores Limited. The consortium was formed
to take a new approach to fishery protection
surveillance and to meet the needs of the Western
Australian Marine Services Association. The first
boat for Project 150, *Pioneer*, was designed by
Raymond Hunt Associates Inc.

PIONEER

Fishery protection patrol boat.
DESIGNER: C Raymond Hunt Associates Inc,
69 Long Wharf, Boston, Massachusetts 02110,
USA.
HULL: Grp/pvc foam sandwich, superstructure
aluminium alloy.
MAIN ENGINES: Two Caterpillar 3412, V-12
marine diesels totalling 1500hp (1120kW) at

Pioneer 25m fishery protection patrol boat

2100rpm coupled to Caterpillar 7221 reversing 2:1
ratio gearboxes.
CAPACITIES
Fuel capacity: 9200 litres
ACCOMMODATION: Master's cabin containing single berth and office facilities. Two twin-
berth cabins and one three-berth cabin. Two
heads, two showers and hand basins, galley and
crew mess accommodating eight persons.
DIMENSIONS
Length overall: 25·00m

Length waterline: 22·10m
Beam: 5·79m
Draught: 1·54m

WEIGHT
Displacement, half-load: 41 tonnes (approx)

PERFORMANCE
Speed, sprint: 26 knots
   continuous: 20 knots plus
Range at 12 knots: 1100n miles (approx)
   at 20 knots: 650n miles (approx)

AUSTRALIAN SHIPBUILDING INDUSTRIES (WA) PTY LIMITED (ASI)

Cockburn Road, South Coogee, Western Australia, Australia
PO Box 206, Hamilton Hill, Western Australia
6163, Australia

Telephone: (09) 410 1511
Telex: 93458 AA
Telefax: (09) 410 2056

ASI 315 PATROL BOAT
TORONGAU
VANUATU
DREGER

Australian Shipbuilding Industries won the
contract to build 13 patrol boats for the Pacific
Patrol Boat Project. Participating countries are
Papua New Guinea (4), Fiji (4), Vanuatu (1),
Western Samoa (1), Solomon Islands (1), Cook
Islands (1) and Tuvala (1). The first craft
HMPNGS *Torongau* was handed over in May
1987 to Papua New Guinea, the second for
Vanuatu was handed over in June 1987, and the
third *Dreger* was handed over to Papua New
Guinea in October 1987. The craft will undertake
surveillance and enforcement of the Exclusive
Economic Zones of the countries concerned.
HULL: Steel.
MAIN ENGINES: Two Caterpillar 3516 diesel
engines coupled to two ZF BW 465 gearboxes.
PROPULSION: Two 123·8mm propeller shafts
with 1200mm diameter propellers.
CONTROLS: Vickers Hydraulic steering gear
operating twin rudders, with twin pumps.
CAPACITIES/STORES
Fuel: 27·9 tonnes
Water: 6000 litres
Water making: 3000 litres/day
Fresh/frozen provisions: 10 days
Dry provisions: 21 days
Spares: 21 days

ACCOMMODATION/CREW
Complement: Captain and two officers, two senior
ratings and nine junior ratings
Layout: Captain's cabin, two-berth officer's cabin,
two-berth occasional officer's cabin, officer's
shower and heads, wardroom. Senior ratings
two-berth cabin and mess. Twelve-berth mess
deck for junior ratings plus two showers and two
heads, combined galley for total crew
SYSTEMS
Auxiliary machinery: Two Caterpillar 3304 (415V
3 phase and 240V single phase), harbour generator Lister HRW3 415V 3 phase, emergency
power 24V battery system; shore power connection 240V single phase, 415V 3 phase

Navigational: Tokyo Keiki ES11A gyrocompass
and repeats, Plaith Jupiter 73143 magnetic compass, Furuno 1011 radar with slave monitor,
Furuno FSN70 satellite navigation receiver with
gyro, log interface and data printer, Furuno
DS-70 Doppler log distance and speed indicator, Furuno FE881 echo sounder, Rubin SHC
20L searchlight

Communications: Sailor RT144C VHF, Collins
VHF (Aeronautcial Mobile), VHF 20A (118-
1136MHz, 20W), Collins AN/ARC UHF, Sailor
Auto Alarm 500kHz and Sailor 2182kHz
receiver distress sets, three VHF portables and
one HF portable

31·5m ASI patrol boat

Internal communications: Honeywell broadcast and alarm system, eight station intercoms

Life saving: Life rafts four 16-man RFD, life-jackets 60 RFD, lifebuoys 4, EPIRB 5, rescue boat 4·5m aluminium with two 30hp outboard motors plus Skanti TRP-1 hand-powered distress receiver

Ship services: Bilge pumps, two Gilkes; fuel system, one Gilkes; fresh water distribution ¾hp pressure system; ventilation, mechanical fan; grey water system, overboard discharge;

refrigerators five 150-litre built in cool and freezer rooms

Firefighting: Machinery space, Halon 1301 gas flooding system; magazine/lookers, water spray; throughout craft, hydrant and hose system; alarm system, heat and smoke detection; portable pump, Robin PTG 401; extinguishers, 5 BCF, 4 water, 6 foam

Desalinator: Osmotron 3000 (reverse osmosis)

DIMENSIONS

Length overall: 31·50m

Length waterline: 28·60m

Beam, max: 8·21m

Draught: 2·12m

WEIGHT

Displacement (full load): 165 tonnes

PERFORMANCE

Speed, max: 23 knots
 max sustained (full fuel): 21 knots
 economical: 12 knots
 minimum sustained: 7 knots

Range at 12 knots: 2500n miles

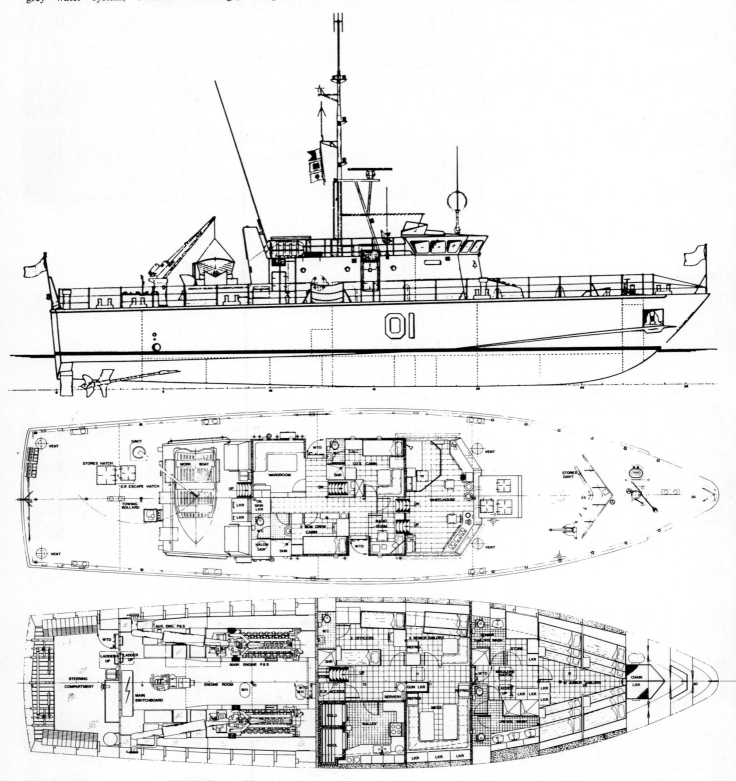

Profile and accommodation layout of ASI 31·5m patrol boat

OCEANFAST PTY LIMITED

26 St George's Terrace, GPO Box X2256, Perth, Western Australia, Australia

Telephone: (09) 325 8599
Telex: 94598 WACH AA
Telefax: (09) 325 6484

John Farrell, *Managing Director*

Oceanfast builds fast luxury motor yachts. The company is a division of Western Australia Capital Holding Limited. Over 250 people are employed and in 1986/87 the turnover exceeded A$20 million.

OCEANFAST 4000
PARTS VI
 Motor yacht.
DESIGNER: Phil Curran.
HULL: Hull and superstructure are constructed in aluminium.

Oceanfast 3000

MAIN ENGINES/GEARBOXES: Two MTU 12V 396 TB93, MCR 1200kW at 1975rpm, MR 1440kW at 2100rpm. One MTU 8V 396 TB93, MCR 800kW at 1975rpm, MR 960kW at 2100rpm.

PROPULSION: Three KaMeWa 63S 62/6 waterjet units.

ACCOMMODATION: Owner's stateroom on main deck; 4 guest staterooms on lower deck; crew's quarters on lower deck including captain's cabin and quarters for eight.

SYSTEMS

Auxiliary engines: Two Mercedes-Benz, driving 380V, 3-phase, 50Hz alternators at 68kVA each

Fuel capacity: 32 000 litres

Water capacity: 2000 litres supplemented by reserve-osmosis desalination capacity of 2000 litres/day

Navigational equipment: 100-mile variable range JRC colour radar, JRC auto direction finder, JRC satellite navigator, JRC automatic pilot and JRC echo sounder

Communications: 100W SSB radio with radio phone, Shipmate VHF radio with radio phone and JRC satellite communications system incorporating telephone, telex and facsimile

DIMENSIONS

Length overall: 46·69m

Length waterline: 37·47m

Beam: 8·20m

Draught: 1·20m

WEIGHT

Displacement, lightship: 140 tonnes

PERFORMANCE

Max speed, estimated: 30 knots

OCEANFAST 3000

NEVER SAY NEVER

Motor yacht. In use as a luxury charter vessel in the Carribean.

The Oceanfast 3000, a Phil Curran/Jon Bannenberg design

DESIGNER: Phil Curran.

HULL: Hull and superstructure are constructed in aluminium.

MAIN ENGINES: Two MTU 12V 396 TB83, 1960bhp each.

ACCOMMODATION: Owner's stateroom on main deck; 3 guest staterooms on lower deck; crew's quarters on lower deck including captain's cabin and separate quarters for 4 crew.

SYSTEMS

Fuel tank capacity: 16 000 litres

Water capacity: 2000-litre tank plus two desalinators producing 1000 litres each per 24 hours

Electrical generators: Two 47·50kVA, MWM 415V alternator sets

Oceanfast 4000 *Parts VI*

Navigational equipment: 100-mile variable range JRC colour radar, JRC auto direction finder, JRC satellite navigator, JRC automatic pilot and JRC echo sounder

Communications: 100W SSB radio with radio phone, Shipmate VHF radio with radio phone and JRC satellite communications system incorporating telephone, telex and facsimile

DIMENSIONS
Length overall: 33·40m
Beam: 7·0m
Draught, including propellers: 2·0m

WEIGHTS
Displacement: 75 tonnes

PERFORMANCE
Speed, cruise: 30 knots
  max: 34 knots

SUN PARADISE

A 94-seat passenger luxury fast ferry launched 1987 and delivered to Ansett Transport Industries.
DESIGNERS: Phil Curran and Jon Bannenberg.
HULL: Hull and superstructure are constructed in marine grade aluminium.
MAIN ENGINES: Two MTU 12V 396 TC82, 912kW each at 1745rpm.
PROPULSION: Two KaMeWa waterjet units, type 56S.

ACCOMMODATION
94 passengers
6 crew

CAPACITIES
Fuel: 15 500 litres
Fresh water: 2100 litres

DIMENSIONS
Length: 34·90m
Breadth: 7·45m
Draught: 1·00m

SPEED
Max: 25 knots

PRECISION MARINE HOLDINGS PTY LIMITED

Cockburn Road, Jervoise Bay, PO Box 240, Hamilton Hill 6163, Western Australia, Australia

Telephone: 410 2222
Telex: 93517 PREMAR AA
Telefax: 410 2319

Robert Blom, *Managing Director*
J Baldock, *General Manager*

The company was formed by the merger of Precision Marine, Star Boats WA, Westcoaster Pty Ltd (trading as Riverfront Boatbuilders) and Sea Chrome Electrics. Precision Marine operates with 200 employees and sub-contractors. The yard covers an area of 42 896m² and constructs commercial fishing craft, workboats, pilot and patrol vessels, large motor yachts, mono-hull and catamaran, pleasure cruisers and ferries in aluminium, grp, Kevlar and carbon fibre.

SUN GODDESS

Fast passenger ferry, operating along North Queensland coast.
DESIGNER: Phil Curran, Fremantle, Western Australia, Australia.
OWNER: Ansett Transport Industries (Operations) Pty Ltd.
CLASSIFICATION: Det norske Veritas.
HULL: Superstructure and hull constructed in marine grade aluminium alloy.
MAIN ENGINES: Two MTU 12V 396 TC82 diesel engines each developing 926kW at 1740rpm.

CAPACITIES
Fuel: 3000 litres (6000-litre long-range tank)
Water: 2000 litres

ACCOMMODATION/CREW: 200 passengers, 150 internal and 50 in rear cockpit. Accommodation is divided into three main passenger lounges,

with open areas on the after and upper sundecks. Main deck facilities include barbecue and bar area, and there is a second bar in the saloon. Crew consists of Captain, Engineer, and two crewmen.

SYSTEMS
Auxiliary engines: 50kVA MWM 425V alternator set
Navigational: 72-mile VR radar, auto direction finder, autopilot remote control steering, Elac Laz 70 echo sounder, gyrocompass and satellite navigator
Communications: 100W HF single side band

radio with headphone, VHF radio with headphone, 27 meg marine CB

DIMENSIONS
Length overall: 34·50m
Beam: 7·50m
Draught: 2·00m

WEIGHTS
Displacement, loaded (estimated): 75·0 tonnes
Displacement, dry (estimated): 50·0 tonnes

PERFORMANCE
Speed, max: 33 knots
Speed, cruising (laden): 27 knots

Sun Goddess wheelhouse

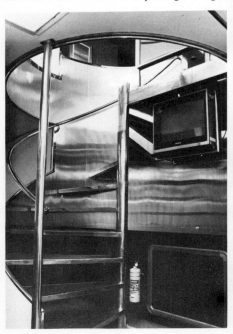

Circular staircase leading from the main saloon of *Sun Goddess* to the aft lounge

Sun Goddess forward passenger saloon

Sun Goddess 34m fast passenger ferry

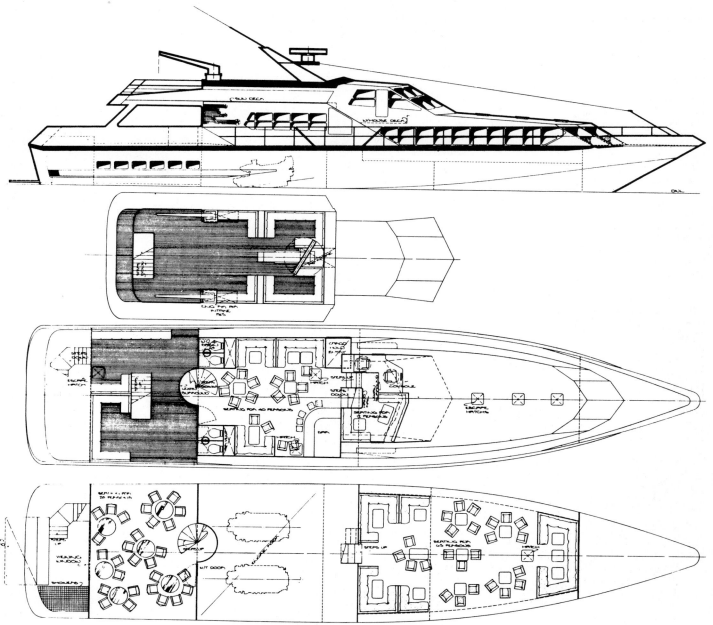

Layout of *Sun Goddess 2*, the second of this type to be built for Ansett Transport Industries

TROPIC SUNSEEKER

Fast passenger ferry operating between Cairns and Townsville, North Queensland.
MAIN ENGINES: Two 1715hp MWM marine diesels.
PROPULSION: Two five-bladed propellers.
CAPACITIES
Fuel: 6800 litres

ACCOMMODATION: Lounge seating 139 on upper deck, aircraft style seating for 225 on main deck and 93 on the aft deck.

DIMENSIONS
Length: 33·40m
Beam: 12·90m
Draught: 1·70m

PERFORMANCE
Speed: 30 knots
Range: 70n miles

SBF ENGINEERING

Waters Edge, Lot 33 Cockburn Road, South Coogee, Western Australia 6166, Australia

Telephone: (09) 410 2022/2244
Telex: 94110 AA
Telefax: (09) 410 1807

Don Dunbar, *Managing Director*

SBF Engineering builds high-speed aluminium crew boats and passenger ferries, designed to meet the operational needs of individual shipping companies. Apart from the vessels detailed below SBF Engineering have also built a 54-passenger, 35-knot, waterjet-propelled ferry, the *Fitzroy Reef Jet*.

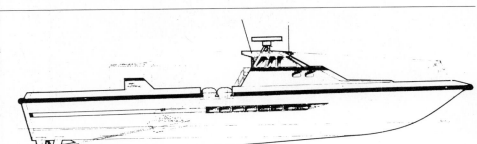

The Phil Curran-designed *Satrya Express* crew boat

SATRYA EXPRESS

A 30-knot crew boat built for the Indonesian company PT Satmarindo for operation in the Malacca Straits.
DESIGNER: Phil Curran, 2 Edward Street, Fremantle, Western Australia 6160, Australia.
CLASSIFICATION: Built to Det norske Veritas light craft regulations.
HULL: Hull and superstructure are constructed in marine grade aluminium.
MAIN ENGINES: Two MTU 12V 396 TB83 marine diesel engines producing 1260kW at 1900rpm.
CONTROLS: Vickers hydraulic steering gear.
ACCOMMODATION/CREW
Crew: 6
Passengers: 62
SYSTEMS
Fuel capacity: 12 000 litres
Electrical generators: Two 4-cylinder MWM generators producing 30kVA each
Navigational equipment: Two Furuno F240 radars, range 48 miles and Furuno FE400 echo sounder
Communications: Two AWA VHF Pilotphone 9 radios and Kodan 6801, 100W transceiver
DIMENSIONS
Length overall: 31·30m
Beam: 6·50m
Draught: 2·0m
PERFORMANCE
Speed, max: 30 knots plus
Range: 600n miles

SBF Engineering *Satrya Express*

SEA FLYTE

High-speed passenger ferry built in 1980, in service in Singapore.
DESIGNER: Phil Curran, East Fremantle.
LEGISLATING AUTHORITY: Harbour and Light Department of Western Australia, USL Code.
HULL: Hull and superstructure are constructed in marine grade aluminium.
MAIN ENGINES: Two MTU marine diesel engines developing 1050shp at 1840rpm.
PROPULSION: Two five-blade 980mm diameter, 1140mm pitch propellers by S & S Engineering, Kewdale, Western Australia.
ACCOMMODATION
Passenger capacity: 240
SYSTEMS
Electrical generators: One Ford diesel generator for air conditioning and bar refrigeration
Navigational equipment: Kodan radar
DIMENSIONS
Length overall: 31·30m
Length waterline: 27·50m
Beam: 6·50m
Draught: 0·80m

Sea Flyte

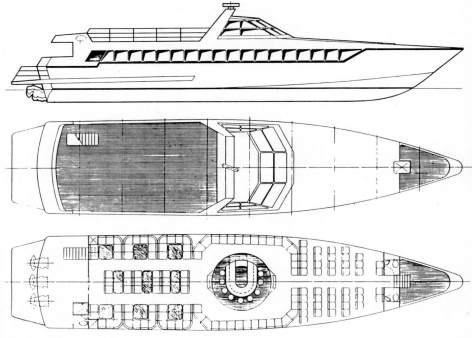

Sundancer V

SUNDANCER V

A triple-powered high-speed ferry for the route Port Douglas to Cooktown and owned by Dignum Pty Ltd, Perth, Western Australia.

CLASSIFICATION: Australian USL Class 1C.
DESIGNERS: Phil Curran and Don Dunbar.
HULL: Constructed in marine grade aluminium.
MAIN ENGINES: Three MWM TBD 234 V12.

Sundancer V

PROPULSION: Three Castoldi 07 Series waterjet units.
ACCOMMODATION: 160 passengers.
COMMUNICATIONS/NAVIGATION: Koden CVS 88 colour echo sounder, Koden MDC 410S 6ft colour radar, Robertson AP 40 autopilot, Codan 8121 12V radio.
DIMENSIONS
Length, overall: 27·5m
Length, design waterline: 23·4m
Beam: 6·30m
Draught: 0·80m
PERFORMANCE
Speed, max: 36 knots
Speed, service: 32 knots

JAMES KELLY II

A high-speed cruising vessel designed by Phil Curran of East Fremantle, owned by Scenic Gordon & Hells Gates Charters, PO Box 38, Strahan, Tasmania 7468, Australia.
CLASSIFICATION: Passenger ferry vessel class 1B—seagoing passenger vessel for use in all operational areas including offshore operations.
HULL: Hull and superstructure built in marine grade aluminium, plating 5083-H321, extrusions 6061-T6.
MAIN ENGINES/GEARBOXES: Two GM 12V 92 marine diesels fitted with Niigata 2·38:1 reduction gearboxes and one GM 16V 92 diesel engine rated at 1100hp.
PROPULSION: Two five-blade aluminium bronze propellers powered by GM 12V 92 engines, and one Castoldi 07 waterjet powered by GM 16V 92 engine.
ACCOMMODATION/CREW
Crew: 4
Passenger capacity: 200
SYSTEMS
Fuel tank capacity: 2000 litres
Fresh water tank capacity: 200 litres
Refrigeration space: 1·5m³
DIMENSIONS
Length overall: 27·67m
Length waterline: 23·50m
Beam: 6·40m
Draught (including propeller): 1·73m
WEIGHT
Design load displacement: 49·85 tonnes
PERFORMANCE
Max speed: 34 knots

WILDERNESS SEEKER

A high-speed cruising boat owned by Scenic Gordon & Hells Gates Charters. The craft was delivered in 1985.
DESIGNER: Phil Curran.
CLASSIFICATION: Vessel class 1D.
HULL: Constructed in marine grade aluminium.
MAIN ENGINES: Two MWM TBD 234 V12 diesels, 507kW each, at MCR.
PROPULSION: Two Castoldi 07 waterjet units.
ACCOMMODATION/CREW
Crew: 2
Passengers: 100
Upper-deck viewing for 50 passengers, with bar and catering facilities in main cabin
SYSTEMS
Electrical generators: One MWM 226-3 with 30kVA alternator

Wilderness Seeker, a 100-seat, 30-knot cruise boat operating in Tasmania

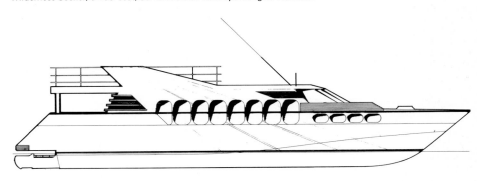

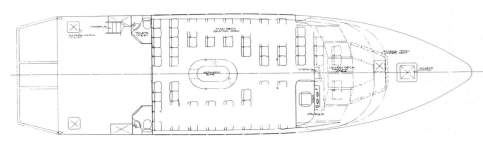

Layout of *Wilderness Seeker* designed by Phil Curran

James Kelly II

Fuel capacity: 5500 litres
Fresh water: 200 litres
Refrigeration space: 0·50m³
DIMENSIONS
Length overall: 22·50m

Length waterline: 19·95m
Beam: 6·20m
Draught: 0·75m
PERFORMANCE
Speed: 30 knots

WAVEMASTER INTERNATIONAL

115 Egmont Road, Henderson, Western Australia 6155, Australia

Telephone: 474 1497

The company specialises in designing and building high-speed luxury ferries, with a range of designs from 15 metres or even larger, if required, and in varying passenger and cargo configuration.

SEA RAIDER

Passenger ferry. This vessel holds the record for circumnavigation of Vancouver Island in 24 hours 47 minutes and 16 seconds, overcoming 6½m swells at full throttle. It is now offered in a patrol boat configuration with two DDA 8V-92 diesels for a top speed of 45-50 knots, lightship.
CLASSIFICATION: Det norske Veritas and other classifications at owner's option.
LEGISLATING AUTHORITY: Australian Uniform Shipping Laws (AUSL).
HULL: Hull construction is in aluminium. The bridge deck has the wheelhouse, and an enclosed and open lounge area. The upper deck consists of forward enclosed and aft open lounge areas divided by a snack bar/bar/servery. The main deck is fitted out with seating accommodation forward and aft.
MAIN ENGINES: Two MTU 8V 396 marine diesel engines driving twin screws.
ACCOMMODATION
Passengers: 250 to 1D (USL Code)
  200 to 1B (USC Code)
SYSTEMS
Electrical, generator: 35kVA alternator
Navigational equipment: 48-mile radar, echo sounder, autopilot
Communications: SSB radio, UHF radio, public address system
Firefighting: Halon engine room flooding system
DIMENSIONS
Length overall: 32·30m
Beam: 6·55m
Draught: 1·75m
WEIGHT
Displacement: 52 tonnes
PERFORMANCE
Speed, cruising: 26 knots
Range at 20 knots: 500 miles

Sea Raider 32m fast passenger ferry

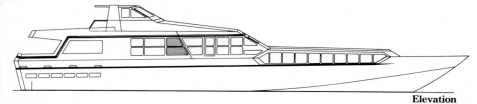

Elevation

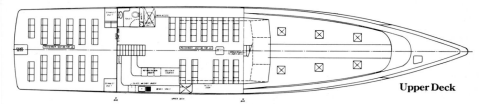

Upper Deck

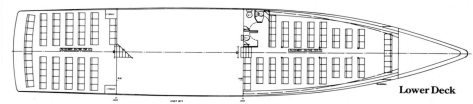

Lower Deck

Wavemaster International *Sea Raider*

Barbaros built by Wavemaster International Pty Ltd for Cyprus service

BARBAROS

CLASSIFICATION: Det norske Veritas + 1A1, R90, Light Craft, SF-LC, F-LC, NAUT C, NAUT B, EO-LC.

HULL: Monohedron planing type constructed in aluminium. The main deck consists of forward lounge, main lounge and aft lounge with an aft upper deck lounge and wheelhouse deck.

MAIN ENGINES: Two MTU 12V 396 TB83 marine diesels rated at 1075kW driving custom-designed 4-blade propellers via ZF 455 2:1 reverse reduction gearboxes.

AUXILIARY ENGINE: MWM 226-TD4 four cylinder marine diesel driving Stamford 47·5kVA 415 240V alternator.

CAPACITIES
Passengers: 245
Crew: 5
Fresh water: 1 tonne
Fuel: 9 tonnes in 3 fuel tanks
Cargo: 7 tonnes in palletised container system

NAVIGATION: Radar, Furuno 72 NM; VHF radio, Sailor 144C; HF radio, Sailor T124/R110; Watchkeeping receiver, Sailor R501; Autopilot, Wagner Mk IV.

DIMENSIONS
Length overall: 35m
Beam: 7·1m
Draught, max: 1·9m

WEIGHTS
Lightship: 58 tonnes
Full load: 84 tonnes

PERFORMANCE
Fully loaded cruising speed: 25 knots

Kita Express

KITA EXPRESS

Designed by Wavemaster to suit the demanding operational requirements in South East Asian waters this vessel has triple waterjet units and air-conditioned accommodation for 152 passengers.

SURVEY: Australian Uniform Shipping Laws Code 1C, restricted offshore service.

HULL: Monohedron planing form. Construction in aluminium. Wheelhouse forward on forward deck, lower main cabin with aft engine room.

MAIN ENGINES: Three MWM TBD 234 V12 marine diesels rated at 605kW at 2200rpm driving Hamilton 422 waterjets via cardan shafts.

AUXILIARY ENGINES: Two MWM D226-6 marine diesels driving Stamford 55kVA alternators for 100% redundancy.

CAPACITIES
Passengers: 152 in main cabin
Crew: 8
Cargo: 1 tonne in hold under wheelhouse
Hand luggage stowage areas in forward main cabin

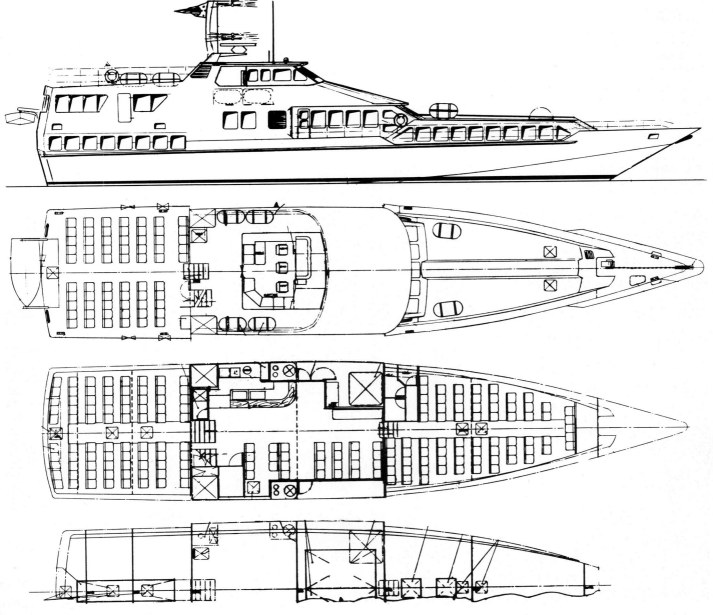

General Arrangement of *Barbaros*

Fresh water: 0·5 tonnes
Fuel: 3·2 tonnes
NAVIGATION: Radar, Furuno 24 NM range;
VHF radio, Uniden MC 610; HF radio, Codan
8525S; Autopilot, Wagner SE.
DIMENSIONS
Length overall: 30·5m
Beam: 6·2m
Draught: 0·8m
WEIGHTS
Lightship: 42 tonnes
Fully loaded, displacement: 60 tonnes
PERFORMANCE
Speed cruising, fully loaded: 28 knots
Speed, lightship: 33 knots

41-METRE HIGH-SPEED FERRY
(DESIGN)
CLASSIFICATION: Det norske Veritas + 1A1,
R90 Light Craft. SF-LC, F-LC, Naut C, Naut B,
ED-LG.
HULL: Monohedron planing form. Passenger
accommodation on three decks. The lower passenger cabin is forward with the engine room aft of
midships and cargo hold aft of engine room. The
main deck has a forward passenger cabin and
main cabin with a bar and bevery for all refresh-
ments aft. The wheelhouse deck has superior
passenger accommodation with a cocktail bar and
hardi grass area aft.
MAIN ENGINES: Two MTU 16V 396 TB
marine diesel engines rated at 1510kW MCR
driving custom-designed 4-blade propellers via ZF
BW 465 2·025:1 reverse reduction gearboxes.
AUXILIARY ENGINES: Two MWM TBD 226
6-cylinder marine diesels driving Stamford 85kVA
415/240V alternators.
ACCOMMODATION: 410 passengers.
CAPACITIES
Crew: 6
Fresh water: 2 tonnes
Fuel oil: 10 tonnes

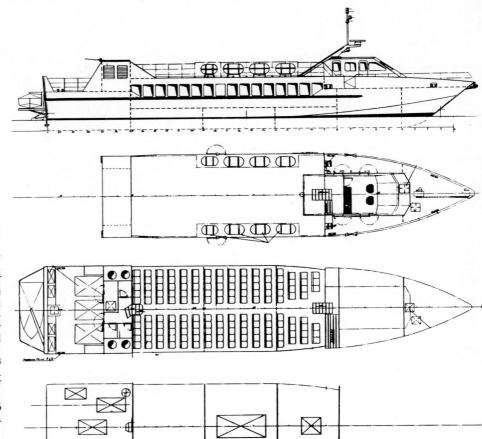
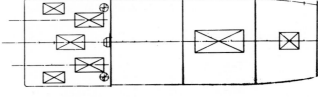

General Arrangement of *Kita Express*

CANADA

ADVANCED MARINE VEHICLES/ALBERNI ENGINEERING AND SHIPYARD LTD

3101 Bird Street, Port Alberni, British Columbia
V9Y 4B8, Canada

Telephone: (604) 723 7331/685 2527
Telex: 044 64511

Doug Blake, *President*
Conrad McCulloch, *General Manager*

Advanced Marine Vehicles are affiliated to the
Alberni Engineering and Shipyard Ltd, Port
Alberni, British Columbia.

EXPO 86 VOYAGER
Deep V offshore racing boat.
BUILDER: Alberni Engineering & Shipyard Ltd.
DESIGNER: Robert Allan Ltd.
HULL: Marine grade aluminium alloy.
MAIN ENGINES: Two Detroit Diesel Allison
6V-92 TA diesels total 950hp.
PROPULSION: Two Arneson Surface Drives
ASD 12, with Nibral propellers by Rolla, Switzer-
land.
CAPACITIES
Fuel, forward tanks: 1782 litres
    aft tanks: 1636 litres
Water: 272 litres
ACCOMMODATION: Sleeping accommod-
ation for 6.
DIMENSIONS
Length overall: 15·39m
Length waterline: 12·80m
Beam: 4·26m
Draught (max): 0·70m

Expo 86 Voyager 15m offshore racing boat

PERFORMANCE
Speed, max, light: 38 knots
Range at 33 knots: 500n miles

Expo 86 Voyager steering position

FINLAND

BÅTVARV HARRY ENGLUND

Pellinge, SF-07370, Finland

DIANA

Fast passenger ferry operating in vicinity of Helsinki.
DESIGNER: Båtvarv Harry Englund.
OWNER: Merimatkat Oy, Helsinki.
HULL: 15-degree deadrise monohedron planing hull constructed in aluminium.
MAIN ENGINES: Two MAN D 2840 10-cylinder MLE engines, 618hp each.
PROPULSION: Two Hamilton Model 421 waterjet units.
ACCOMMODATION: 120 passengers.
DIMENSIONS
Length: 18·04m
PERFORMANCE
Speed, max: 35 knots lightly laden

120-passenger ferry *Diana*

OY LAIVATEOLLISUUS AB

PO Box 152, 20101 Turku 10, Finland

Telephone: 21 401 444
Telex: 62174 LATE SF
Telefax: 21 401 578

Laivateollisuus Oy is a fully owned subsidiary of Wärtsilä Marine Industries Inc.

LOKKI CLASS PATROL CRAFT
(HULL NUMBERS: 364, 365 and 366)

TIIRA
KAJAVA

In July 1984 Laivateollisuus Oy received an order for three high-speed patrol craft from the Finnish Coast Guard. The first craft was delivered in early November 1985 and the others were delivered in 1986. The vessels will be used for patrol of Finnish territorial waters within the archipelago and open sea, perform search and rescue operations and act in anti-submarine defence and detection.

The hull of these craft is of a special hard-chine form developed through extensive tank testing at the Finnish Technical Research Centre. Great care has been taken in establishing the optimum long-itudinal centre of gravity position for minimum resistance and full-scale performance trials in the Baltic have confirmed the tank test results.

Kajava one of the Lokki class patrol boats for the Finnish Coast Guard   *(Oy Laivateollisuus Ab)*

Accommodation is to a high standard in keeping with the requirement for extended duration patrol duties.

HULL: Low-Vee section with hard chines, longitudinal framing in marine grade aluminium alloy.

MAIN ENGINES: Two MTU 8V 396 TB82 diesel engines, each 770kW continuous at 1940rpm, 840kW max at 2000rpm.

AUXILIARY ENGINES: Two 31kVA diesel generators, 220/380V, 50Hz, 24V, 12V.

TANKS
Fuel oil: 8m³
Fresh water: 2m³
Sewage tank
Bilge water tank
Lubrication and waste oil tanks

ACCOMMODATION
Below deck: Fore peak, accommodation compartment with six one-person cabins, one double cabin, washroom and toilet; aft peak, office, engine room, workshop and stores
In deckhouse: Messroom, galley, provisions, wheelhouse and stores
Above deckhouse: Open bridge

NAVIGATION AND COMMUNICATION EQUIPMENT: Magnetic compass, gyrocompass with repeaters, autopilot, radar, radio direction finder, doppler log, Decca navigator, sonar, searchlights, navigation lights, signalling typhons, VHF, HF, ship-to-air and portable radios.

DECK EQUIPMENT: Electric anchor windlass, electro-hydraulic deck crane, inflatable boat with outboard motor, three life rafts, portable suction pump for rescue operations and air-conditioning plant.

FIREFIGHTING: Smoke and temperature indicators in each compartment, alarm panel in the wheelhouse, Halon system in engine room, motor-driven water pumps and portable extinguishers.

DIMENSIONS
Length overall: 26·80m
Breadth, moulded: 5·50m
Depth, moulded: 3·0m
Draught: 1·85m

WEIGHT
Displacement, standard: 65 tonnes

PERFORMANCE
Speed: 25 knots plus

Laivateollisuus Oy have also introduced two new designs, their 20·9-metre patrol craft and their 30-metre fast motor yacht.

20·9-METRE PATROL CRAFT (DESIGN)

MAIN ENGINES: Two 1000kW engines.
PROPULSION: Choice of conventional propellers, waterjets, or surface-piercing propellers.

ACCOMMODATION
Complement: One officer, two senior ratings and six ratings

ARMAMENT: Two single 20mm guns.

DIMENSIONS
Length overall: 20·90m
Beam overall: 5·50m
Depth, moulded: 3·00m
Draught: 1·45m

PERFORMANCE
Speed: 40 knots

30-METRE MOTOR YACHT (DESIGN)

MAIN ENGINES: Two marine diesel engines Caterpillar or equivalent to suit customer speed requirements.

ACCOMMODATION: Owner's stateroom includes large double bed, private bathroom and WC. Two guest staterooms each with private showers and WC, double or twin beds. Sauna compartment incorporating sauna room, bathroom with whirlpool and showers, dressing room with bar and WC.

Facilities on main deck level include main saloon, dancing area and bar, cruising lounge adjacent to the wheelhouse with all-round view. Galley situated between main saloon and cruising lounge.

Crew accommodation consists of Captain's cabin with double bunk, and a crew cabin with two to four bunks, shower and WC.

SYSTEMS: Two 30kW generators, other equip-

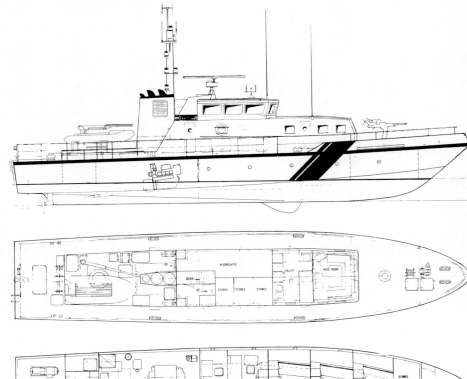

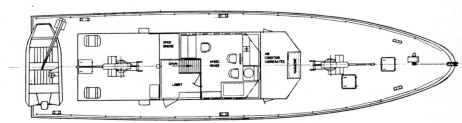

General Arrangement of Lokki class patrol boat

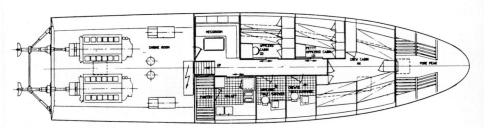

General Arrangement of 20·9m high-speed patrol boat design

ment includes deck machinery, navigational and communication sets and entertainment electronics.

DIMENSIONS
Length overall: 30·50m

Beam: 7·00m
Depth, moulded: 3·30m
Draught: 2·10m

PERFORMANCE
Speed: 20 knots plus

30m motor yacht design by Oy Laivateollisuus Ab

OY WÄRTSILÄ AB HELSINKI SHIPYARD

Box 132, SF-00151 Helsinki, Finland

Telephone: (90) 1941 (National); 358 0 1941 (International)
Telex: 121246 WHT SF

Wärtsilä Helsinki Shipyard have recently completed four fast attack craft for the Finnish Navy. The *Kotka* is the last unit of the series. These craft are designed to function as strike and patrol boats with seakeeping qualities for open-sea operation.

KOTKA

Fast attack craft.
MAIN ENGINES: Power output 8000kW.
ARMAMENT
One multi-purpose 57mm gun
Two twin 23mm anti-aircraft guns
Eight surface-to-surface missiles
An electronic fire control system
DIMENSIONS
Length overall: 45·00m
Beam overall: 9·00m
WEIGHT
Displacement: 280 tonnes
PERFORMANCE
Speed: 30 knots plus

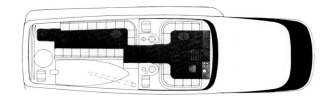

Wärtsilä 280-tonne fast attack craft

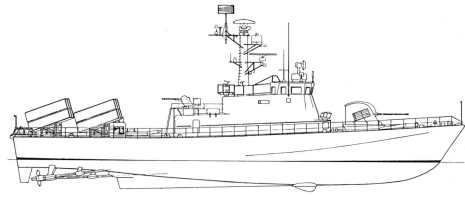

Wärtsilä *Kotka*, fast attack craft

FRANCE

CHANTIERS NAVALS DE L'ESTEREL SA

20/26 boulevard du Midi, Boite Postale 19, F-06321 Cannes la Bocca Cedex, France

Telephone: (93) 47 04 27
Telex: 470876 ESTEREL F
Telefax: (93) 47 21 06

Amiral de Laforcade, *President*
Pascal Chataignier, *Managing Director*
Alain Lecerf, *Sales Manager*
Raoul Tsalichis, *Technical Manager*

Created in 1945 the yard specialised for 40 years in the wooden construction of fast patrol boats, survey launches and luxury yachts. The yard is now in addition building in aluminium.

Esterel 26

The yard has an area of 14 000m² half of which is under cover. A 230-tonne capacity travelling gantry crane enables craft to be put into the water and to be lifted for dry docking very quickly.

By mid-1985 178 boats had been built with 109 exported to 24 countries. Eight types of fast patrol craft have been produced and the table on page 275 summarises their characteristics.

ESTEREL 26

Motor yacht.
HULL: Hull and superstructure built in triple planking glued construction, resin sheathed, or in aluminium.
MAIN ENGINES: Two GM 12V 71 TI marine diesels producing a total of 1300hp.
ACCOMMODATION/CREW
Number of cabins: 4 double berth (8 persons)
Crew: 3
SYSTEMS
Fuel capacity: 6000 litres
Water capacity: 2500 litres
DIMENSIONS
Length overall: 26·0m
Beam: 5·80m
Draught: 1·45m
WEIGHT
Displacement fully loaded: 53 tonnes
PERFORMANCE
Speed, max at half load: 23 knots
Speed, cruising: 15 to 18 knots
Range at 15 knots: 650 miles

ESTEREL 27

Motor yacht.
Similar to the Esterel 26 but powered by two MTU 8V 396 TB93 engines of 2600hp total, giving it a maximum speed of 32 knots.

ESTEREL 29

Motor yacht.
HULL: Hull and superstructure built in triple planking glued construction, sheathed with resin or aluminium.
MAIN ENGINES: Two MTU 8V 396 TB93 marine diesel engines, 1300hp each.
ACCOMMODATION/CREW
Number of cabins: 4 double berth (8 persons)
Crew: 3 to 5
SYSTEMS
Fuel capacity: 11 000 litres
Water capacity: 3000 litres
DIMENSIONS
Length overall: 29·20m
Beam: 7·0m
Draught: 1·80m
WEIGHT
Displacement fully loaded: 80 tonnes

Esterel 29

Esterel 34 de luxe fast yacht *Mes Amis*

PERFORMANCE
Speed, max at half load: 23 knots
Speed, cruising: 15 to 20 knots
Range at 15 knots: 650 miles

ESTEREL 34

Motor yacht *Mes Amis* delivered July 1985.
HULL: Hull and superstructure built in triple planking glued construction, sheathed in resin or aluminium.
MAIN ENGINES: Two MTU 16V 396 TB93 marine diesels, 2375hp each.

Type 21 Fast Patrol Boat

Type 27 Fast Patrol Boat

Type 28 Fast Patrol Boat

Type 30 Fast Patrol Boat

Type 32 Fast Patrol Boat

Type 32L Fast Patrol Boat

Type 42 Fast Patrol Boat

FAST PATROL BOAT

Type	21	27	28	30
In service with:	French Customs	French Customs French Navy other customs departments and navies	Guinean National Navy Indonesian Customs Nicaraguan Navy	French Customs French Sea Ministry
Length overall:	21·25m	26·80m	28·20m	30·30m
Beam overall:	4·80m	5·0m	5·20m	5·80m
Draught, max:	1·40m	1·55m	1·60m	1·70m
Displacement, full load:	32 tonnes	47 tonnes	57 tonnes	69 tonnes
Speed, max with two 490hp diesels:	25·0 knots	25·0 knots	two 800hp: 25 knots	two 1200hp: 29 knots
with two 750hp diesels:	28·5 knots	27·5 knots	980hp: 28 knots	two 1400hp: 31 knots
with two 980hp diesels:	—	30 knots	1305hp: 32 knots	two 1960hp: 34 knots
Range (1t 15 knots):	500n miles	700n miles	800n miles	1200n miles
Hull*: mahogany, glued triple planking,	32mm thick	35mm	35mm	36mm
Deck: marine plywood,	24mm thick	27mm	27mm	24mm with grp sheeting
Superstructure:	marine plywood	marine plywood	marine plywood	marine plywood
Complement:	one Commanding Officer one Petty Officer six ratings	one Commanding Officer one Petty Officer six ratings	one Commanding Officer one Petty Officer 4 or 6 ratings	one Commanding Officer three Petty Officers six ratings
Armament:	one 12·7mm MG	one 20mm Oerlikon gun	one 20mm gun on forecastle one 20mm gun on quarterdeck	one 20mm gun on forecastle one 20mm gun on quarterdeck

* protected with epoxy resin

Type	32	32L	42		Fast Strike Boat Design Type 42ME
In service with:	Customs departments and navies	French Navy and Cyprus Navy	Gabones National Navy		
Length overall:	32·0m	32·10m	42·13m	42·20m	42·0m
Beam overall:	5·75m	6·45m	7·15m	7·80m	7·80m
Draught, max:	1·60m	1·90m	1·90m	1·95m	2·0m
Displacement, full load:	80 tonnes	96 tonnes	150 tonnes	160 tonnes	190 tonnes
Speed, max with two 490hp diesels:	two 1305hp: 28 knots	two 1400hp: 27 knots	two 2380hp: 30 knots	29 knots	two 4080hp: 33 knots
with two 750hp diesels:	two 1960hp: 33 knots	two 1960hp: 30 knots	two 2900hp: 32 knots	31 knots	three 4080hp: 38 knots
with two 980hp diesels:		two 2380hp: 32 knots	two 4080hp: —	35 knots	
			two 4080hp: —	40 knots	
Range (at 15 knots):	1500n miles	1500n miles	1500n miles	1500n miles	1000n miles
Hull*: mahogany, glued triple planking,	40mm	40mm	45mm		45mm
Deck: marine plywood,	30mm	30mm	40mm		40mm
	marine plywood	marine plywood	marine plywood		marine plywood
Complement:	one Commanding Officer four Petty Officers 10 or 12 ratings	one Commanding Officer six Petty Officers 10 or 11 ratings	one Commanding Officer two Officers six Petty Officers 14 ratings		one Commanding Officer two Officers six Petty Officers 12 ratings
Armament:	one 20mm gun on forecastle one 40mm gun on quarterdeck	one 20mm gun on forecastle one 20mm gun on quarterdeck	one 40mm gun (or one twin 30mm gun) on forecastle one 40mm gun (or one twin 30mm gun) on quarterdeck two 20mm guns amidships one fire control system		one twin 40mm gun or one 57mm gun on forecastle one 30mm gun or one 40mm gun on quarterdeck 4 or 6 Exocet, type MM40 one fire control system Thomson Vega

* protected areas with epoxy resin or full aluminium construction

ACCOMMODATION/CREW
Number of cabins: 5 or 6 double cabins (10/12 persons)
Crew: 5 to 8
SYSTEMS
Fuel capacity: 16 000 litres
Water capacity: 5000 litres
DIMENSIONS
Length overall: 34·20m
Beam: 7·80m
Draught: 2·10m
WEIGHT
Full load displacement: 135 tonnes
PERFORMANCE
Speed, max at half load: 28 knots
Speed, cruising: 15 to 25 knots
Range at 15 knots: 800 miles

ESTEREL 42
Motor yacht *Acajou* delivered June 1982.
HULL: Hull and superstructure built in triple planking glued construction, sheathed with resin or aluminium.
MAIN ENGINES: Two MTU 16V 538 TB92 marine diesels, producing 3670hp each.
ACCOMMODATION/CREW
Number of cabins: 5 double berth (10 persons)
Crew: 7
SYSTEMS
Fuel capacity: 27 500 litres

Water capacity: 5000 litres
DIMENSIONS
Length overall: 42·0m
Beam: 7·80m
Draught, max: 2·10m
WEIGHT
Full load displacement: 165 tonnes
PERFORMANCE
Speed, max at half load: 34 knots
Speed, cruising: 15 to 20 knots
Range at 15 knots: 1500 miles

Esterel 42 prior to launching at Cannes la Bocca

Esterel 42 luxury fast yacht *Acajou*

CONSTRUCTIONS MÉCANIQUES DE NORMANDIE (CMN)

26 rue de Montevideo, 75116 Paris, France

Telephone: 45040877
Telex: 610097 F

ERRAID
A 27m customs patrol boat, launched 26 November 1987, for the Moroccan Customs Services. This vessel is identical to the six ships of the El Wacil class delivered by CMN to the Moroccan Navy in 1975 and 1976.
ENGINES: Two SACM diesels, 1270bhp each, at 1560rpm.
PROPELLERS: Two fixed-pitch.
DIMENSIONS
Length overall: 32·00m
Length waterline: 30·09m

Breadth, max, overall: 5·35m
Breadth, max, waterline: 4·92m
Depth, moulded, amidships: 3·00m
Draught, amidships at loaded displacement: 1·42m
WEIGHTS
Displacement, full load: 88·70 tonnes
Displacement, average: 81·35 tonnes
Displacement, light: 74·00 tonnes
PERFORMANCE
Speed: 27 knots

CONSTRUCTIONS NAVALES GUY COUACH

Gujan, France
Head office: 215 avenue Francis Tonner, 06150 Cannes la Bocca, France

Telephone: (93) 47 13 17
Telex: 470737 F
Telefax: (93) 48 03 66

Guy Couach are the successors to Couach Ltd who have been famous in yachting since 1897. They have been building motor yachts in glassfibre since 1962, and they were the first to build a large motor yacht in Kevlar. They now offer a range of 35 speed boats to luxury motor yachts of 6 to 30m. The following are models offered above 20m:

The Guy Couach 2400 *Nortada*

MODELS 2000 to 3000

Type	2000	2200	2400	2402	2600	2800	3000
DIMENSIONS (m)							
Length overall:	19·35	21·50	23·50	23·50	26·30	28·00	31·40
Length hull:	18·80	21·30	22·80	22·95	24·90	27·25	30·05
Beam overall:	5·40	5·40	5·40	6·30	6·30	6·30	6·30
Draught:	1·30	1·35	1·40	1·40	1·40	1·45	1·50
WEIGHTS (tonnes)							
Approx displacement,							
light:	24·00	30·00	32·50	35·00	43·00	45·00	48·00
full load:	31·20	37·50	39·20	42·00	54·00	56·00	62·00
MAIN ENGINES (largest installations)	Two GM 12V 92 TA 1080hp each	Two GM 12V 92 TA 1080hp each	Two GM 12V 92 TA 1080hp each	Two GM 12V 92 TA 1080hp each	Two MTU 12V 96 TB93 1960hp each	Two MTU 12V 96 TB93 1960hp each	Two MTU 12V 96 TB93 1960hp each
PERFORMANCE							
Speed, max (knots):	31/33	28/30	27/29	26/28	36/38	34/36	32/33
Range at 22 knots (n miles):	490	450	440	450	580	580	580
OPTIONS*	Kevlar + LDU	Kevlar + LDU	Kevlar + LDU	Kevlar + LDU	Kevlar + LDU	Kevlar + LDU	Kevlar + LDU
ACCOMMODATION							
Crew:	2	2	2	2	2/3	3	4
Passengers:	6	8	6/8	8	8	10	12
SYSTEMS							
Generators:	20kW	20kW	20kW	24kW	32kW	32kW	32kW
Battery charger:	60A	60A	60A	Two 40A	Two 40A	Two 40A	Two 40A
Starting battery:	190Ah	190Ah	190Ah	190Ah	190Ah	380Ah	380Ah
Servicing battery:	190Ah	190Ah	190Ah	190Ah	190Ah	380Ah	380Ah
Fuel tank capacity:	5800 litres	5800 litres	5800 litres	6000 litres	10 000 litres	10 000 litres	12 000 litres
Fresh water capacity:	1500 litres	1500 litres	1500 litres	1500 litres	2200 litres	2200 litres	3000 litres
Fresh water heater:	150 litres	150 litres	150 litres	200 litres	200 litres	250 litres	300 litres
Air-conditioning, BTU:	60 000	60 000	72 000	90 000	120 000	120 000	144 000

* Kevlar + Levi Drive Units can increase performance by 3/4 knots approx

---

SOCIÉTÉ BRETONNE DE CONSTRUCTION NAVALE (SBCN)

BP 20, Hent-Croas, 29125 Loctudy, Brittany, France

Telephone: 98 87 42 71
Telex: 941356 SBCN F

SBCN specialise in high-speed craft built in cold moulded plywood. The compound material is made up of very thin layers criss-crossed with hard mahogany fibres running in the same direction, vacuum-moulded in a matrix of epoxy resin. The resulting product is flexible, break-resistant and light, offers ease of maintenance and repair, good thermal and acoustic properties, avoidance of hull vibration and long term maintenance of shape. The yard has a workshop area of some 2500m². Craft delivered in 1986 and 1987 are summarised in the following paragraphs.

ATLANTE

This vessel is a high-speed passenger ferry launched in July 1985 for service with the Vedettes de L'Odet Ferry Co between Concarneau and the islands of Glénan, Brittany.

HULL: Cold moulded marine plywood.
ENGINES: Two MAN D2842 LE diesels, each 700hp.
PROPULSION: Two Hamilton Model 421 waterjet units.
PASSENGERS: 165.
DIMENSIONS
Length: 25·6m
Beam: 5·5m
Draught: 0·8m

PERFORMANCE
Speed, light, with 10% of permitted load: 30 knots at 31·6 tonnes displacement
fully laden: 24 knots

TOURVILLE (ex D'ILES D OR XVIII)

Passenger ferry, delivered 1986.
HULL: Cold moulded plywood.
MAIN ENGINES: Three MAN D 2840 LE marine diesels each 630hp.

The waterjet-propelled *Atlante*

PROPULSION: Three Hamilton 421 waterjet units.
PASSENGERS: 295.
DIMENSIONS
Length overall: 25·00m
Beam: 6·80m
PERFORMANCE
Speed, light, with 10% permitted load: 32 knots
fully laden: 24 knots

AMIRAL DE JOINVILLE
Passenger ferry, delivered 1986.

Amiral de Joinville, 25m passenger ferry

OWNERS: Société Anonyme Atlantic Armement, for service between Noirmontier and Yeu Islands.
HULL: Cold moulded plywood.
MAIN ENGINES: Two MAN D 2842 LE marine diesels each 750hp.
PROPULSION: Two Hamilton 421 waterjet units.
PASSENGERS: 195.
DIMENSIONS
Length: 25·00m
Beam: 6·70m

PERFORMANCE
Speed, light, with 10% permitted load: 31 knots
fully laden: 24 knots

NICOLAS BOUCHARD
32m fast passenger ferry. Delivered in September 1987.
OWNERS: Société Anonyme Atlantic Armement, for service between La Baule and Belle-Ile Island.
HULL: Cold moulded plywood.
MAIN ENGINES: Two MWM TBD 234 V16 marine diesels 1200hp each.
PROPULSION: Two Sauer Engineering SE 912 waterjet units.
PASSENGERS: 270.
DIMENSIONS
Length: 32·00m
Beam: 6·80m
PERFORMANCE
Designed speed, light: 37 knots
fully laden: 32 knots

PATRIOTE
38m patrol boat. Launched in November 1987.
OWNERS: Benin Navy.
HULL: Cold moulded plywood.
MAIN ENGINES: Three Baudouin 12P15-2 SR7 marine diesels 1200hp each.
PROPULSION: Three Sauer Engineering SE 912 waterjet units.
DIMENSIONS
Length: 38·00m
Beam: 6·90m
PERFORMANCE
Designed speed: 34 knots

SOCIÉTÉ FRANÇAISE DE CONSTRUCTIONS NAVALES (SFCN)

66 Quai Alfred Sisley, 92390 Villeneuve-la-Garenne, France

Telephone: (1) 47 94 64 46
Telex: 610998 FRANCONA F

Jeanne-Marie Baudron, *Chairman and General Manager*
Charles Baudron, *General Manager*
Paul Charcusset, *Sales Director*
Jérôme Gouffier, *Purchase Director*
Christian Gaudin, *Technical Director*

SFCN was founded in 1918 and for the past twenty years has specialised in the design and construction of sophisticated medium-tonnage boats (40/50m). The high performance of these conventional craft meet the demands of military applications such as light missile-launching corvettes and fast patrol boats.

To meet the demand for smaller craft with the same operational efficiency SFCN undertook hull design studies for their two new types of craft, the Espadon and Marlin class boats. The builder's claim that they have outstanding seaworthiness, perfect course and platform stability, exceptional manoeuvrability, less than 10 per cent speed loss in rough seas, low inboard diesel power, low operating cost, easy maintenance and are ideally suited for civilian and military applications.

ESPADON 28
High-speed sea-going passenger boat.
Length overall: 27·50m
Beam: 6·40m
Draught, max: 1·85m
Displacement, full load: 70 tonnes
light load: 50 tonnes
Engines: Two 1500hp
Max speed, full load: 25 knots
Speed cruising, with load: 22 knots
Range at 20 knots: 300 miles
Payload: 60 passengers + 7 tonnes freight
or 150 passengers + 1 tonne freight

ESPADON 33
High-speed sea-going passenger boat.
Length overall: 33·0m
Beam: 6·40m
Draught, max: 1·85m
Displacement, full load: 100 tonnes
light load: 75 tonnes
Engines: Two 1600hp
Max speed, full load: 25 knots
Speed cruising, with load: 22 knots
Range at 20 knots: 400 miles
Payload: 65 passengers + 15 tonnes freight
or 120 passengers + 5 tonnes freight

Model of SFCN Marlin class patrol boat design

ESPADON CLASS FAST PATROL BOAT DESIGNS

Type	Espadon 24	Espadon 29	Espadon 34
Hull:		hull constructed in steel, aluminium alloy superstructure	
Length overall:	24·50m	29·00m	34·00m
Beam, max:	5·80m	6·50m	7·10m
Draught, max:	1·60m	1·85m	1·85m
Full load displacement:	65 tonnes	90 tonnes	110 tonnes
Main engines:	two 1200kW	two 1650kW	two 1900kW
Propulsion:		two fixed-pitch propellers	
Continuous speed, full load:	30 knots	30 knots	30 knots
Range:	300n miles	500n miles	600n miles
Complement:	7/8	10/12	18
Armament:	two 20mm guns	one twin 30mm gun	one 40mm gun
		one 20mm gun	four MM40 missiles
		one optronic fire	one search radar
		control system	one fire control radar

SFCN CREW BOATS

Type	Marlin 30 Design	Marlin 35 *Angelica* and *Aida* hull and superstructure in aluminium alloy	Marlin 43 Design
Hull:			
Length overall:	30·00m	35·00m	43·00m
Beam, max:	6·50m	7·10m	9·10m
Draught, max:	1·10m	1·20m	1·50m
Full load displacement:	80 tonnes	95 tonnes	140 tonnes
Main engines:	two 1850kW	two 1850kW	two 1850kW
Propulsion:		two waterjets	
Weights:	15 tonnes: 150 passengers or 60 passengers plus 10 tonnes freight	23 tonnes: 250 passengers or 90 passengers plus 15 tonnes freight	32 tonnes: 400 passengers or 90 passengers plus 25 tonnes freight
Speed, continuous, full load:	40 knots	38 knots	27 knots
Range:	400n miles at 20 knots	350n miles at 20 knots	250n miles at 27 knots

Type	Espadon 24 Design	Espadon 28 steel hull with aluminium alloy superstructure	Espadon 34 Design
Hull:			
Length overall:	24·50m	27·50m	34·00m
Beam, max:	5·80m	6·40m	7·10m
Draught, max:	1·60m	1·85m	1·85m
Full load displacement:	65 tonnes	85 tonnes	110 tonnes
Main engines:	two 1200kW	two 1450kW	two 1900kW
Propulsion:		two fixed-pitch propellers	
Weights:	80 passengers	150 passengers	250 passengers
Speed, continuous, full load:	30 knots	30 knots	30 knots
Range:	350n miles at 20 knots	400n miles at 20 knots	40n miles at 20 knots

SEARCH AND RESCUE VESSEL DESIGNS

Model	SAR 150	SAR 200	SAR 300
Length overall:	38·60m	41·0m	52·20m
Beam:	6·20m	6·80m	7·15m
Max draught:	2·0m	2·10m	2·15m
Mean displacement:	150 tonnes	180 tonnes	270 tonnes
Max continuous speed (mean displacement):	with two 2200hp engines, 27 knots with two 3200hp engines, 30 knots	with two 2200hp engines, 25 knots with two 3200hp engines, 28 knots	with two 3200hp engines, 26 knots with two 5000hp engines, 30 knots
Range at 16 knots:	2000 miles	2000 miles	2000 miles
Complement (min/max):	3/5 officers 13/15 petty officers and ratings	5/7 officers 14/16 petty officers and ratings	5/7 officers 14/16 petty officers and ratings
Accommodation facilities:	12 rescued persons	15 rescued persons	20 rescued persons
Armament (optional):	one 20mm gun two 12·7mm machine guns	two 3mm twin guns two 12·7mm machine guns	one or two 20mm, 30mm or 40mm guns two 12·7mm machine guns

CREW BOATS (Yard Nos 841/1 and /2)

Two delivered March 1986.

Ordered by SURF & Cie in early 1985 for offshore transport from Pointe-Noire, Congo, and the offshore platforms or barges.

Length overall: 34·90m
  waterline: 28·0m
Breadth, moulded: 6·46m
Max draught, full load: 1·10m approx
Displacement: 88·70 tonnes
  light: 74·0 tonnes
Main engines: Two 1600hp
Speed: 27 knots
Passengers: 90
Crew: 5

SFCN Marlin class planing-hull fast patrol boat, type CGV 32

REGINA

Passenger launch, delivered July 1984.
OWNER: M Brudey, Pointe-à-Pitre.
HULL: Hull construction is in steel with aluminium alloy superstructure.
MAIN ENGINES: Two GM 16V 149 T diesel engines, max 1350hp each at 1850rpm.
ACCOMMODATION
Passenger capacity: 150 seated
DIMENSIONS
Length overall: 27·50m
Length waterline: 23·0m
Draught: 1·85m
WEIGHT
Full load displacement: 70 tonnes
PERFORMANCE
Speed, max: 25 knots
  cruise: 22 knots

CREW BOAT

Two built, delivered 1986.
OWNER: SURF & Cie.
CLASSIFICATION: Bureau Veritas I 3/3 service special-transport (coastal transport of personnel).
MAIN ENGINES: Two engines 1600hp each.
ACCOMMODATION/CREW
Crew: 5

Regina, Espadon 28 passenger ferry operating in the Antilles

Passengers: 90
DIMENSIONS
Length overall: 34·90m

Length waterline: 28·0m
Beam: 6·46m
Draught: 1·10m

Marlin 35 crew boats *Angelica* and *Aida* built for SURF & Cie operating off the Congo coast

WEIGHTS
Full load displacement: 88·70 tonnes
Light displacement: 74·0 tonnes
PERFORMANCE
Speed: 27 knots

FAST FERRY
  A 35m, aluminium alloy waterjet-propelled passenger boat delivered March 1988 for Société Anonyme d'Economie Mixte Maritime de Saint-Pierre et Miquelon.

SFCN SAR 150 design

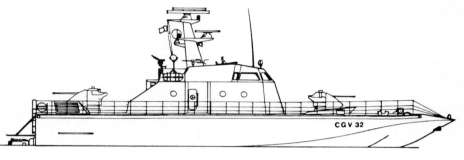

MARLIN CLASS FAST PATROL BOAT DESIGNS

Type	CGV 28	CGV 32	CGV 36
Length overall:	28·0m	32·0m	36·0m
Breadth, max:	6·0m	7·0m	8·0m
Draught, max:	1·65m	1·90m	1·10m
Hull:	light alloy	light alloy	light alloy
Speed:	with two 1200hp engines, 32 knots fixed-pitch propellers or waterjets or with two 1500hp engines, 35 knots variable-pitch propellers or waterjets	with two 2600hp engines, 36 knots variable-pitch propellers or waterjets	with two 3300hp engines, 36 knots variable-pitch propellers or waterjets
Range (at 16 knots):	1000n miles	1500n miles	2000n miles
Displacement:	55 tonnes	100 tonnes	120 tonnes
Complement:	2 officers 14 petty officers and ratings	3 officers 16 petty officers and ratings	3 officers 20 petty officers and ratings
Armament:	one Optronic fire control system one 20mm gun two 12·7mm machine guns	two 30mm Oerlikon guns two 12·7mm machine guns	one radar with MTI one fire control radar or Optronic fire control system one 57mm Bofors gun one twin 30mm Oerlikon gun 4 or 8 MM40 missiles one Sadral ship-to-air weapon system

Type	Marlin 26	Marlin 30	Marlin 35
Hull and superstructure:		aluminium alloy	
Length overall:	26·50m	30·00m	35·50m
Beam, max:	5·80m	6·50m	7·10m
Draught, max:	1·00m	1·10m	1·20m
Full load displacement:	50 tonnes	70 tonnes	95 tonnes
Main engines:	two 1250kW	two 1600kW	two 1935kW
Propulsion:		two waterjets	
Speed continuous, full load:	45 knots	42 knots	38 knots
Range:	600n miles	650n miles	700n miles
Complement:	7/8	10/12	18
Armament:	two 20mm guns	one twin 30mm gun one 20mm gun one Optronic fire control system	one 40mm gun four MM40 missiles one search radar one fire control radar

GERMANY, FEDERAL REPUBLIC

ABEKING AND RASMUSSEN SHIPYARD

An der Fähre 2, PO Box 1160, D-2874 Lemwerder, Federal Republic of Germany

Telephone: (0421) 6733-0
Telex: 245128 AR D
Telefax: (0421) 6733-112

SILVER SHALIS
  Yard No 6402, *Silver Shalis*, is a fast motor yacht driven by three KaMeWa waterjet units, one, type 271S62/6, absorbing 2720bhp and two, type 80S62/6, absorbing 2640bhp each.

F R LÜRSSEN WERFT (GmbH & Co)

Friedrich-Klippert-Strasse 1, 2820 Bremen 70, Federal Republic of Germany

Telephone: (0421) 6604-1
Telex: 0244484 AFLW D

Fast motor boats, motor cruisers and motor yachts have been built from the beginning of the company's history; in 1906 the motor boat *Donnerwetter* reached a speed of 65km/h against international competition, in 1926 the Lürssen Sedan cruiser won the Blue Ribbon of the Rhine and in 1927 a Lürssen racing boat reached the speed of 106·3km/h. These achievements were followed by a three-engine motor yacht *Oluka II* making 32 knots in 1928 and Gert Lürssen winning the world record for diesel-driven boats in 1939 with a speed of 37 knots. Recent construction includes fast attack craft, small corvettes, mine combat vessels, and fast yachts.

BERLIN and STEPPKE

Rescue craft.

First of class mothership/daughter rescue craft designed and built for the West German Sea Rescue Society.

MAIN ENGINES: One MTU 12V 396 TB93 marine diesel developing 1200kW and two MWM TBD 234 V12 wing engines each rated at 574kW.
PROPULSION: One 1200mm central propeller and two 950mm wing propellers (port and starboard).
CONTROLS: Steering gear is electro-hydraulic to the three rudders each having one emergency servo device.
CAPACITIES: 500 litres of fire extinguishant.
COMPLEMENT: Crew of 8.
DAUGHTER CRAFT: Launched down stern ramp and through a hinged flap on the transom. Length 7·50m, beam 2·29m, draught 0·60m, displacement 3·10 tonnes. Power BMW D190 diesel of 121kW output, driving a fixed-pitch propeller through reduction gearing, speed 15·0 knots.
SYSTEMS
Auxiliary machinery: Two Mercedes OM352 diesels connected to Kaick generators each set rated at 50kVA
Bow thruster: ZF Herion type 70/175/320 with an output of 75kW
Firefighting: Two monitors mounted at the after end of superstructure
DIMENSIONS
Length overall: 27·50m
Beam: 6·00m
Draught: 1·63m
WEIGHT
Displacement: 100 tonnes
PERFORMANCE
Cruising speed: 24 knots

GREECE

HELLENIC SHIPYARDS CO

Skaramanga Yard, Athens, Greece

Telephone: 5573426/5573350
Telex: (Athens office) 215123
(Skaramanga yard) 215293
Telefax: 5573359

Apart from the craft described in subsequent paragraphs the yard has built six missile-firing fast patrol boats based on the Combattante 111B for the Hellenic Navy.

29-METRE FAST PATROL BOAT

Hellenic Shipyards Co has built for the Greek Government a series of 10 fast patrol boats under licence from Abeking and Rasmussen of West Germany in the period 1977-79, to be used by coast guard, customs and other authorities.

Each boat is equipped with two MTU 12V 331 TC81 diesels 1360hp each giving a speed of about 27 knots. They have a steel hull and marine type aluminium alloy superstructure and a crew of 16. The hull form is round bilge semi-displacement. The standard armament of the vessel consists of two single 20mm naval guns on the main deck.
DIMENSIONS
Length overall: 29·00m
Length waterline: 27·00m
Beam at deck: 5·00m
Depth amidships: 2·56m
Max draught: 1·62m (approx)
WEIGHT
Design displacement: 71·00 tonnes (approx)

23-METRE FAST ATTACK BOAT

In the period 1980-81 Hellenic Shipyards Co has built two fast attack boats under licence from Panagopoulos Associates for the Hellenic Navy.

Each boat is equipped with two MTU 12V 331 TC92 diesels 1530hp each giving a speed of about 38 knots. Their structure is of all aluminium alloy and can take a crew of 6. They have a hard chine hull form with straight lines which were model tested in USA.
DIMENSIONS
Length overall: 23·00m
Length waterline: 21·00m
Beam at deck: 5·00m
Depth amidships: 2·90m
Max draught: 0·97m
WEIGHT
Design displacement: 35·00 tonnes

25-METRE FAST ATTACK CRAFT (FAC-25) (DESIGN)

MAIN ENGINES: Two MTU 12V 396 TB93 engines each rated at 1398kW max, and 1152kW continuous power.
PROPULSION: Two propellers.
COMPLEMENT: 11.

Hellenic Shipyards 29m fast patrol boat

ARMAMENT: One twin 30mm Oerlikon GCM-B01, two SSM launchers Penguin Mk 2, two 7·60mm light machine guns.
DIMENSIONS
Length overall: 25·00m
Breadth, moulded: 5·72m
Depth, amidships: 2·96m
Draught, full load (over propellers): 1·77m
WEIGHTS
Normal displacement (with half-filled tanks draught 1·70m): 62·90 tonnes

PERFORMANCE
Speed, sprint: 35 knots
Speed, cruising: 31 knots
Endurance: 580n miles at 30 knots, 800n miles at 20 knots

FAST ATTACK CRAFT (DESIGN)

MAIN ENGINES: Four MTU 16V TB94 each rated at 3500ps max driving through four reversible gearboxes.
PROPULSION: Four fixed-pitch propellers.

23m fast attack boat built by Hellenic Shipyards under licence from Panagopoulos Associates

COMPLEMENT: 25.
ARMAMENT: One Bofors type Mk 2 57mm gun, one Breda-Bofors 40L/70 40mm gun, four Exocet MM40 SSM launchers, two FFV/TP 43 × 0 400mm torpedo tubes, two Elma system depth charge racks, two Philips type 9CM/100 Chaff/IR decoy launchers.
DIMENSIONS
Length overall: 47·00m
Length, waterline: 43·50m
Beam, max: 7·80m (approx)
Beam at waterline: 7·00m
Depth, amidships: 4·60m
Draught, normal displacement: 2·10m
WEIGHTS
Displacement, full load: 280 tonnes (approx)
Displacement, half load: 260 tonnes (approx)
PERFORMANCE
Speed, max at half load displacement: 37·00 knots
Endurance: 1500n miles (approx) at 16 knots

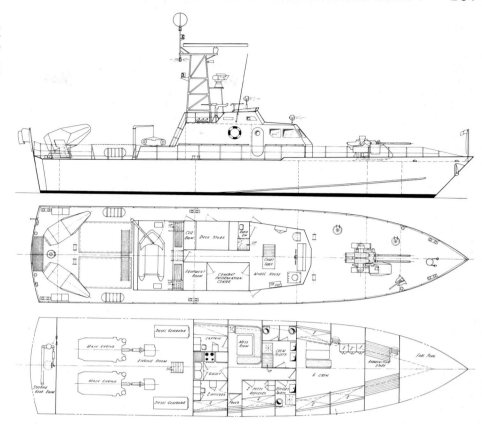

Hellenic Shipyards 25m fast attack craft design

HONG KONG

CHUNG WAH SHIPBUILDING & ENGINEERING COMPANY LIMITED

41 Yau Tong Marine Lot, Cha Kwo Ling Road, Kwun Tong, Kowloon, Hong Kong

Telephone: 3-7276333
Telex: 45803 WAHBU HX
Telefax: 3-7545144

Wong Wah Sang, *Chairman*
Philip J Carberry, *Vice Chairman*
Peter Man Kong Wong, *Managing Director*
Ronnie Man Chiu Wong, *Executive Director*
Cliff Thew, *Shipbuilding General Manager*
Geoffrey Robson, *Naval Architect*
Alan N Cowan, *Technical Consultant*
Alfred Pang, *Assistant General Manager*
Lau Kam Yuen, *Naval Architect*
C F Kwok, *Engineering Manager*

The company was established in 1940, and business covers shipbuilding, ship repairing, civil and mechanical engineering, steel structural construction, technical services and consultancy.

The shipbuilding and repair division employs a labour force of 2080 and has built 47 vessels and craft in steel ranging from salvage tugs, deck container vessels, fire boats to police patrol boats.

The company has recently completed an order for 15 King class steel police launches for the Royal Hong Kong Marine Police. These craft have been very successful due to the joint effort of Damen Shipyards, responsible for the basic design of the hull, and the Chung Wah Shipbuilding and Engineering Company.

'KING' CLASS

KING LAI
Police launch.
HULL: Constructed in steel.
MAIN ENGINES/GEARBOXES: Two MTU 12V 396 TB83 each delivering 1100kW through ZF gearboxes; one Kosan 424A engine, with ZF gearbox.

PL71, one of 15 Chung Wah-built high-speed launches for the Royal Hong Kong Marine Police

Flying bridge and coxswain console on PL71

PROPULSION: Two fixed-pitch propellers by SMM (MTU engines); one KaMeWa steerable waterjet (Kosan engine).

CONTROLS: Nautiservo BV electro-hydraulic steering gear.

ACCOMMODATION

Complement: 18 officers and crew

Air-conditioned

SYSTEMS

Electrical generators: Two Kosan 60kVA alternators

Navigational equipment: RM1226C 12in, with 9in slave radar and EMY1/C speed log repeater supplied by Racal Decca; one Sinrad echo sounder; one S G Brown 1000 gyrocompass and repeater

Search and rescue: One Avon sea rider launched or recovered by hydraulic crane operated from flying bridge

PERFORMANCE

Speed at operational displacement, with twin MTU engines: Over 24 knots
  with twin MTU engines and Kosan engine: Over 26 knots

Kosan engine loitering speed: 9 knots

Customs 6, one of three King class patrol boats for the Customs and Excise Department, Hong Kong

Wheelhouse: commander's and coxswain's position on King class *Customs 6*

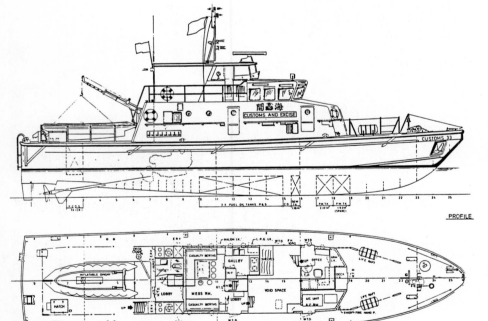

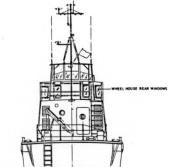

General Arrangement of King class patrol boats for the Customs and Excise Department, Hong Kong

INDONESIA

P T PABRIK KAPAL INDONESIA (PERSERO)
P T PAL INDONESIA

Jakarta office:
BPPT Building, 12th Floor, JL M H Thamrin No 8, Jakarta, Indonesia

Telephone: 323774/324350
Telex: 61331 ATP JKT

Surabaya office:
Ujung Surabaya, PO Box 134, Indonesia

Telephone: 291403/24139
Telex: 31223 PAL SB

The company produces patrol boats in wood and aluminium designed for customs, police, harbourmaster and naval duties. 6000 workers are employed on building and repair work.

FPB-28
Fast patrol boat.
HULL: Double planking hull construction, outer layer in teak and inner layer in red meranti. Hull frames and superstructure are in marine grade aluminium.
MAIN ENGINES: Two 1220hp diesel engines.
PROPULSION: Two three-blade fixed-pitch propellers.
SYSTEMS
Electrical generators: Two 18kVA 220/380V 50Hz 3ph generators

Batteries: 24V
Armament: One deck-mounted machine gun
Navigational equipment: One radar, one echo sounder and one magnetic compass
Communications: Internal and external
DIMENSIONS
Length overall: 28·0m
Length waterline: 26·0m
Beam: 5·40m
Draught: 1·84m
WEIGHTS
Light weight: 51·7 tonnes
Fuel displacement: 68·50 tonnes
PERFORMANCE
Max speed, continuous: 28·5 knots
  intermittent: 30·0 knots
Cruising speed: 15·0 knots
Range at 28·5 knots: 1100n miles

TJETTY MARINE

Tanjung Pinang, Indonesia

BIMA EXPRESS
A high-speed ferry built in glass-reinforced plastic for the Singapore to Tanjung Pinang route, approximately 63 miles and operated by Tjetty Marine.
ENGINES: Two GM 8V 92 TI, 570hp at 2300rpm.
PROPULSION: Two Hamilton Jet Model 421, Type 38 impeller, waterjet units.
DIMENSIONS
Length: 20·0m
Beam: 4·9m
Deadrise at stern: 13°
WEIGHTS
Light: 19·0 tonnes
Loaded: 24·0 tonnes

Tjetty Marine *Bima Express* propelled by two Hamilton waterjet units, type 421

PERFORMANCE
Speed, max, light: 32·0 knots
  loaded: 28·0 knots

ITALY

ALFA MARINE Srl

Via Della Scafa 135, 00054 Fiumicino, Italy

Telephone: (06) 645 3838/0355
Telex: 614580 ALFAMA I

ALFA 83 25-METRE FAST CRUISER
HULL: Built in grp with V-keel with longitudinal side fins.
ENGINES/GEARBOXES: Two MTU 8V 396 TB93, 1300hp each driving propellers through BW 255 gearboxes.
SYSTEMS
Electrical: Two diesel generators 16kW, central control and distribution panel 24V, batteries 500Ah, 24V
Fuel tank capacity: 6000 litres
Trim: Hydraulically actuated flaps for long-itudinal and transverse trim
Manoeuvring: Bow thruster

Alfa Marine 25m, 33-knot fast cruiser

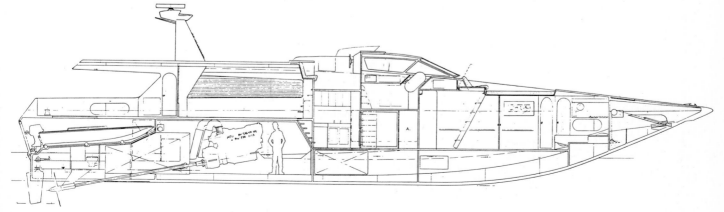

Interior Arrangement of Alfa 83 25m fast cruiser

Navigation: 40 mg radar, echo sounder with optical plotting, Loran C, automatic pilot
Communications: VHF 25W 60-channel, SSB 1 8-28m Hz 220W
ACCOMMODATION: Master cabin with bathroom and WC, four guest cabins, with bathroom and WC, kitchen, crew quarters, 2 bunkbeds, piloting cabin, 2 seats, fly deck controls, 3 seats, fly sun deck, poop deck, lounge with bar, aft deck. Air-conditioning fitted.
DIMENSIONS
Length overall: 25·0m
Beam: 6·0m
Air draught: 3·90m
Draught: 1·50m
WEIGHTS
Displacement, empty: 40·0 tonnes
Displacement, tanks half full: 43·75 tonnes
PERFORMANCE
Speed, max: 36 knots
   cruising: 33 knots

ALFA 84 (DESIGN)

Fast work and weapon systems carrier.
The Alfa 84 hull has been designed to carry out a variety of commercial and naval roles. Alter-native upper deck and accommodation layouts are available to meet individual operational requirements.
CLASSIFICATION: Built to ABS classification.
HULL: Grp and Kevlar hull with aluminium superstructure.
MAIN ENGINES: Two MTU 12V 396 TB93 marine diesels, 1900hp each, underwater exhaust discharge and hydrosilencers.
PROPULSION: Two waterjets, KaMeWa or Riva Calzoni Type IRC 41 DL.
CONTROLS: Pneumatic engine controls and hydraulic steering gear fitted in wheelhouse and flying bridge.
ACCOMMODATION: Living quarters for six to eight junior ratings, mess deck and heads, junior officer's three-berth cabin and commanding officer's living quarters.
ARMAMENT
Basic versions: One 20mm Oerlikon mounting forward
Gun boat version: Two 30mm Breda turrets fore and aft
Gun boat version B: Two 81mm coastal rocket launchers fore and aft
Patrol boat version: One 20mm Oerlikon mounting fore and aft, one RH60 rigid inflatable or two amphibious Gilettri Leopard 8 eight-wheel drive vehicles
Commando boat version: One 30mm Breda turret forward plus four semi-rigid inflatables capable of carrying 24 men in total
Mine-laying version: 20 anti-vessel Misar influence Manta ground mines (220kg each)
SYSTEMS
Auxiliary engines: Two 25kW diesel generators
Navigational: Automatic pilot, graphic and optic echo depth scanner, speed meterlog, radar and Loran
Communications: VHF SSB and telex
Air-conditioning: Fitted in living quarters
Searchlights: High Lux density searchlight, Galileo passive light intensification thermal telescope
DIMENSIONS
Length overall: 25·00m
Length, waterline: 20·00m
Beam: 6·00m
Draught: 1·20m
WEIGHT
Displacement: 60 tonnes
PERFORMANCE
Speed: 35 knots

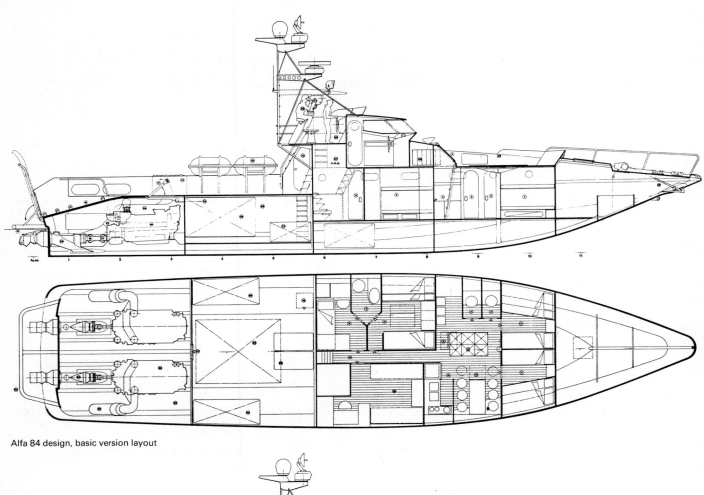

Alfa 84 design, basic version layout

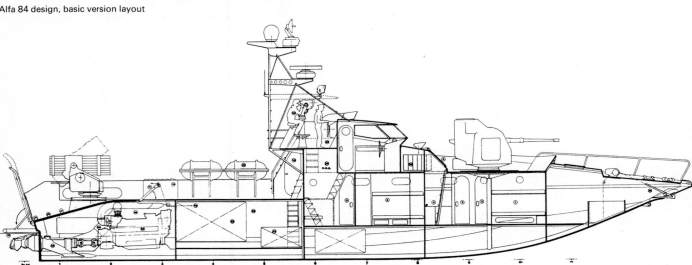

Alfa 84 design, gun boat version

Alfa 84 design, crew boat version

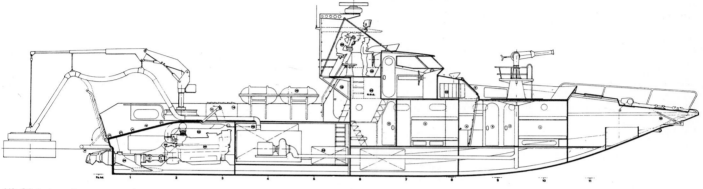

Alfa 84 design, oil recovery version

AZIMUT SpA

Corso M d'Azeglio 30, 10125 Turin, Italy

Telephone: (011) 650 21 91
Telex: 220450 AZITO I
Telefax: (011) 650 34 78

Dr Paolo Vitelli, *President*
Dr Ing Luciano Scaramuccia, *Technical Manager*
Dr Massimo Perotti, *Export Sales*
Mrs Victoria Munsey, *Marketing Co-ordinator*

The company was founded in 1969 and until recently concentrated on building motor yachts in glass reinforced plastic (grp). In September 1985 Azimut took control of the Fratelli Benetti yard at Viareggio. With the acquisition of the Benetti facility craft between 35 and 50 metres may also be built in aluminium or steel.

The Viareggio yard encompasses approximately 3000m², of which 2500m² is fully enclosed; the workforce is approximately 40. In addition there are two other grp fabrication yards employing 65 in total, and a fitting out yard for the small boat division employing 20 persons.

The company has recently expanded into the commercial and patrol boat markets offering a range of craft. There are patrol boat, fast passenger ferry, crew boat and fishing boat versions available.

AZ105 SEA HUNTER (DESIGN)

Patrol boat.
CLASSIFICATION: Craft can be built to Italian Naval Register (RINa), Lloyd's Register of Shipping, or Det norske Veritas.
HULL: Grp laminated hull with grp, balsa wood sandwich construction decks. Superstructure can be in grp or aluminium alloy.
MAIN ENGINES: Two MTU 16V 396 TB93 marine diesel engines each producing max power of 2610shp and continuous power of 2180shp.

An Allison gas turbine option is also available, with auxiliary engines.
PROPULSION: Fixed or controllable pitch propellers can be fitted.
ACCOMMODATION/CREW: Crew and accommodation layout dependent on choice of armament. Six different versions have been sug-

gested by the builders ranging from an armament of a single 30mm gun mounted forward and aft to one single 40/70 gun forward and one helicopter type Breda Hughes 500D or similar aft.
SYSTEMS
Fuel capacity: 14 285-17 857 litres
Fresh water capacity: 1000 litres
Stores: 1200kg
Weapons and ammunition: 7 tons
Electrical generation: Dependent on weapons and electronics fitted
Communications: One transceiver HF/SSB 100-150W; two MF/HF receivers; two VHF/AM 25W transceivers; one UHF/AM 20W trans-

ceiver; one FAC receiver; one IFF transponder; one broadcast system
Armament fire control: One fire control system, one surface and air search radar
Firefighting systems: Ammunition, water sprinkling with automatic controls; high pressure (7kg/cm²) sea water fire main; portable fire extinguishers in operations rooms and accommodation compartments
DIMENSIONS
Length overall: 30·80m
Length waterline: 26·0m
Beam: 6·80m
Draught: 1·90m

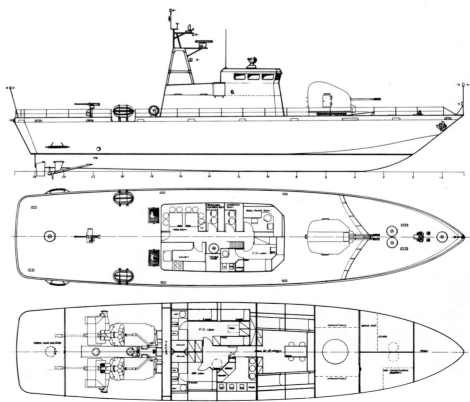

Azimut AZ105 Sea Hunter patrol boat design

WEIGHTS

Full load displacement (depending on fuel quantity and engines fitted): 81 to 95 tonnes

PERFORMANCE

With two MTU 16V 396 TB93 engines
Speed, max at full load: 31·8 knots
Speed, continuous at full load: 27·8 knots
Cruising range at continuous speed, full load: 467n miles

With Allison gas turbine
Speed max, full load: 45·2 knots
Speed, continuous at full load: 41·4 knots
Cruising range at continuous speed, full load: 378n miles

AZIMUT 60

Patrol boat.

HULL: Hull form is of hard chine full V-type with raked stern and raked radius transom. Construction of hull deck and superstructure is of hand-moulded sandwich grp with a polyurethane core. Internal surfaces are varnished with a self-extinguishing material.

MAIN ENGINES: Two MAN 12V 700hp marine diesels. Optional engines are also available.

PROPULSION: Two propellers.

ARMAMENT: Can be fitted out for a variety of roles: military intervention, tactical transport, water police, pollution control, search and rescue.

DIMENSIONS

Length overall: 18·30m

Model	66	71	76
Main engines	Two GM 12V 870hp	Two MTU 8V 1300hp	Two MTU 12Y 2600hp
Length overall	20·10m	21·45m	23·10m
Beam, max	5·10m	5·10m	6·00m
Draught	1·40m	1·50m	1·70m
Displacement, standard	26 tons	40 tons	50 tons
Speed, max	29 knots	35 knots	40 knots
Cruising, fast	27 knots	31 knots	36 knots

Beam, max: 5·10m
Draught: 1·35m

WEIGHT

Displacement, standard: 22 tonnes

PERFORMANCE

Speed, max: 27·0 knots
Fast cruising: 25·0 knots

AZIMUT 66, 71 and 76 (DESIGNS)

20-metre patrol boats.

The Azimut range of 20-, 21-, and 23-metre patrol boats are similar in construction to the Azimut 60 and can be fitted out for a variety of operational roles. Their dimensions and performance are summarised in the table above.

The Azimut 60 patrol boat

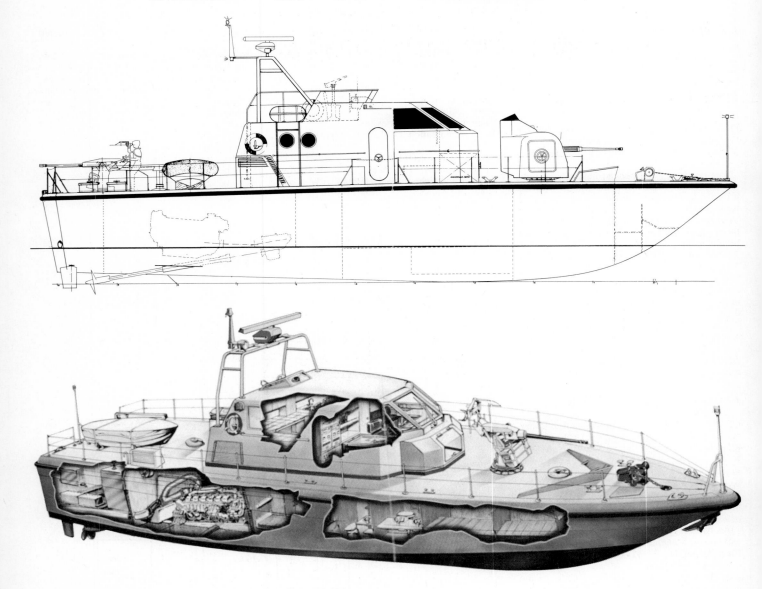

Azimut 20m patrol boat design

AZIMUT 30-METRE (DESIGN)

Patrol boat.
HULL: Constructed in grp.
MAIN ENGINES: Two marine diesels.
ARMAMENT: Can be fitted out as an offshore patrol vessel, fast attack craft or coastal patrol craft.
DIMENSIONS
Length overall: 31·00m
Beam: 6·80m
Draught: 1·80m
WEIGHT
Displacement: 100 tons (approx)
PERFORMANCE
Speed range: 28 to 40 knots

RIMA

Benetti 45 motor yacht.
MAIN ENGINES: Two marine diesel engines 3480hp each.
CAPACITIES
Fuel tank: 40m³
Fresh water: 8·0m³
ACCOMMODATION: Cabins for an owner's party of 14. Owner's suite consists of private bathroom, dressing room and lounge. There are six double-berth guest cabins. The galley serves a dining room seating 12 which adjoins the main saloon. There is also an upper deck saloon leading on to the after deck which has open-air dining facilities. Crew accommodation consists of eight

Azimut 30m naval vessel design

berths, double officer's cabin forward with the Captain's cabin and bathroom aft.
SYSTEMS: Desalinator plant producing 2150 litres/day.
DIMENSIONS
Length: 45·00m

Beam: 8·80m
Draught: 2·15m
PERFORMANCE
Speed, max: 27 knots
Speed, cruising: 24 knots
Range: 3000n miles

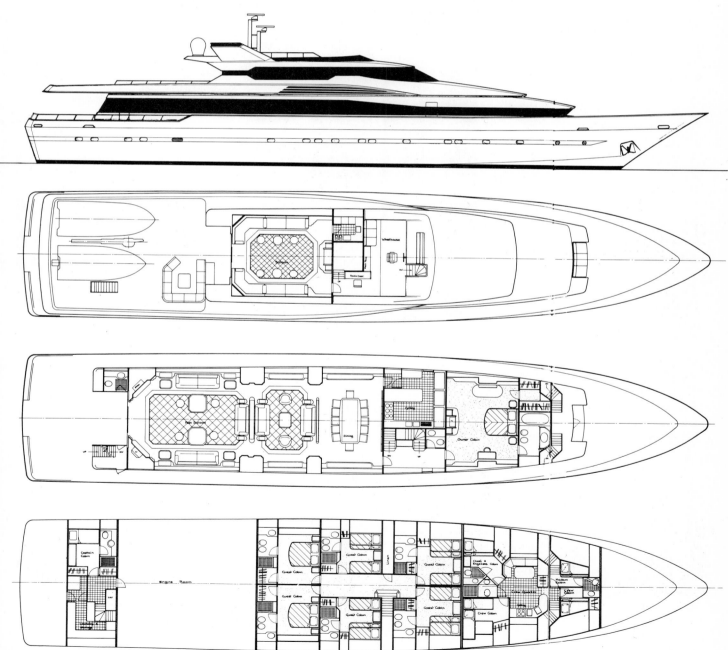

Profile and layout of the Benetti 45m motor yacht *Rima*

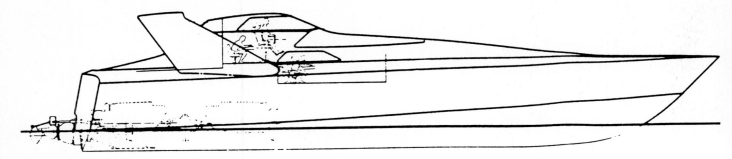

The Azimut *Atlantic Challenger* powered by four CRM BR 1/2000 diesel engines

ATLANTIC CHALLENGER

The Azimut *Atlantic Challenger* is being built to challenge the current record for a transatlantic crossing but without intermediate fuelling stops. The hull is being constructed at Azimut's Benetti yard in Viareggio, which was acquired by Azimut in 1985.

HULL: The hull form has a relatively shallow V aft moving gradually to a deeper V forward. Construction is in special corrosion-resistant aluminium.

MAIN ENGINES: Four CRM marine diesel engines, working in pairs, linked by means of two dual port reduction gears to two Riva Calzoni waterjet units.

Power: Four turbocharged, intercooled CRM BR 1/2000 diesel engines, maximum continuous power 1682hp at 2020rpm (Din/150) each, maximum sprint power 1850hp at 2075rpm (Din/150) each.

Transmission: Two reduction gears with dual ports, MAAG, ratio 1·853:1.

PROPULSION: Two Riva Calzoni type IRC DB2 DLX hydrojets, 1120rpm, continuous thrust at 45 knots, 6·4 tonnes each.

CAPACITIES: Seven structural, double-bottom fuel tanks fitted which will contain approximately 75 tons of diesel fuel. As the fuel is consumed a special open cell foam can be injected into the tanks to reduce fuel movement in the tanks in rough conditions.

ACCOMMODATION: The wheelhouse area has been designed to provide accommodation for six crew members and will include two helmsmen stations, a navigator and radio operator station.

DIMENSIONS
Length overall: 27·00m
Length, waterline: 24·07m
Beam, max: 7·50m
Beam, waterline: 7·10m
Height amidships: 3·55m
Deadrise aft: 13°

Deadline amidships: 22°
PERFORMANCE
Speed, max: 50 knots (approx)
Range: 3000 miles (approx)

AZ105
ATHINA R
Motor yacht.
Built 1985.
OWNER: Mme Onassis.
HULL: Hull construction is in grp.
MAIN ENGINES: Two MTU 12V TB93, 1960hp each.
ACCOMMODATION
Owner's suite: Three cabins and bathroom
Guests: Three double and one single cabins each with bathroom

Crew: Two 2-berth cabins, bathroom and crew lounge
Saloon: Formal dining for 12
SYSTEMS
Television: VCR/TV system with overhead projector, pull down screen, and stereo speakers
Communications: In addition to standard sets, telephone, telex and computer interface capabilities also fitted
Navigation: Standard equipment and a satellite navigation and communication system
DIMENSIONS
Length overall: 30·80m
Beam: 7·10m
Draught: 1·80m
PERFORMANCE
Speed, max: 27 to 31 knots

AZ105 *Athina R*

CANTIERI NAVALI BAGLIETTO SpA

Via di Villa Pepoli 23, 00153 Rome, Italy
and
Piazza Stefano Baglietto, 17019 Viarazze, Italy

Telephone: (06) 57 56 223
Telex: 625824 SAMI I
Telefax: (06) 57 82 709

A joint venture has been formed between Alucraft and Baglietto for the design and building of motor yachts. Alucraft Consulting Inc has co-ordinated the design and construction of large luxury motor yachts styled by Alberto Mercati. Built in steel or aluminium in Istanbul in a joint venture with Profilo Holding these vessels are built to Lloyds specifications. In 1985 a new project was announced by Alucraft-Baglietto, the 35m Seneca 'Megajet/Cruiser' motor yacht

with external design by Alberto Mercati and Baglietto shipyard handling the detailed hull, machinery and electrical plans and building at Viarazze.

Four versions of Seneca are proposed:
Version A with two MTU 12V 396 TB 93 engines with propellers
Version B with two MTU 12V 396 TB 93 engines with KaMeWa waterjet units
Version C with two MTU 12V 396 TB 94 engines with propellers
Version D with two MTU 12V 396 TB 94 engines with KaMeWa waterjet units

SENECA MEGAJET/CRUISER
Version B
Preliminary specification details.
HULL: Aluminium magnesium alloy.
ENGINES: Two MTU 12V 396 TB 93, derated for 32°C ambient air and 27°C sea, 1920hp (metric)

each at 2100rpm, intermittent rating, or 1600hp (metric) each at 1975rpm, max continuous rating.
Diesel generators, 75kVA.
CAPACITIES
Fuel tanks: 14 500 litres (can be increased to 38 000 litres)
Fresh water tanks: 4000 litres
(Fresh water daily production: Up to 1900 litres)
DIMENSIONS
Length overall: 35·0m
Length waterline (at standard displacement): 28·0m
Beam, max: 7·0m
Beam, max at chine: 5·10m
Depth amidships: 3·40m
Draught (at full load): 1·12m
WEIGHTS
Displacement, full load: 94·40 tonnes
Displacement, standard: 86·20 tonnes
Displacement, light and dry: 75·50 tonnes

PERFORMANCE
Speed, max: 28·50 knots
Speed, continuous: 26·0 knots
Range at 26 knots: 580n miles
   at 22 knots: 660n miles
   at 10 knots: 2900n miles (36 000 litres fuel)

ADLER
SENECA
CHATO
LADY ANFIMAR

  Three motor yachts, Yard nos 10076/11, 10079/

12 and 10080/13, were under construction in 1986, all driven by two 2130bhp KaMeWa waterjet units, type 63S62/6. A further motor yacht with the same power unit but fitted with KaMeWa type 50S62/6 waterjet units was also started in 1986, Yard no 10103/11 and named *Lady Anfimar*.

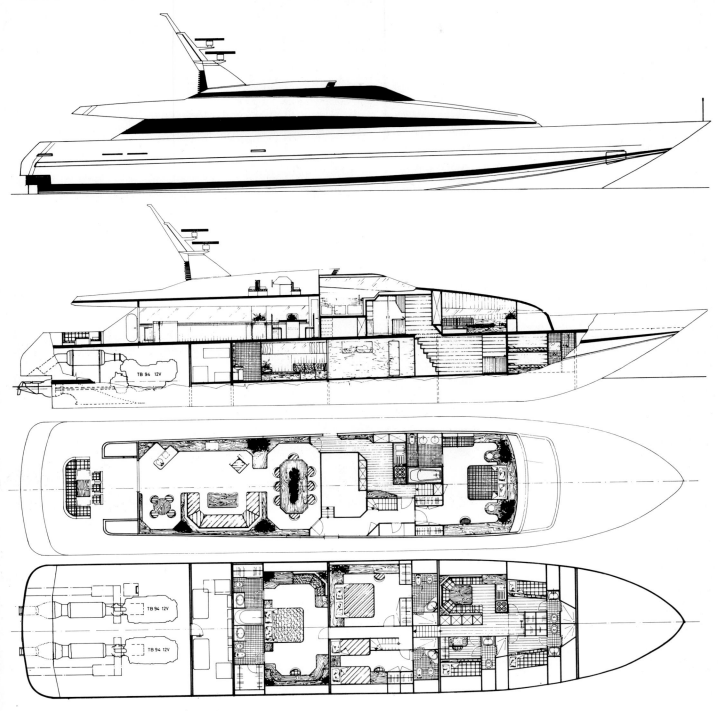

Alucraft-Baglietto 35m Seneca motor yacht

CANTIERI NAVALI ITALCRAFT
Srl

Head office: Via di Villa Emiliani 11, 00197 Rome, Italy

Telephone: (06) 802701/875377/870981/873650
Telex: 613054 ITCRAF I

  Italcraft, with a covered area of over 12 000m², has built more than 2500 craft since 1969. Its latest design is the M78, at 56 knots one of the world's fastest motor yachts, a development of its original 55-knot 'Drago' class. The M78 is available in three yacht layout variations including an 'open' version with limited accommodation. There are also patrol craft and 100-passenger, 45-knot ferry versions. The patrol boat has a maximum speed of 52 knots and the ferry 45 knots.

56-knot Italcraft M78

M78 AEROMARINA

Fast motor yacht.

HULL: Hull and deck constructed in grp with aramidic fibre (Kevlar 49 DuPont), impregnated with isophtalic resin. The superstructure consists of grp and isophtalic resin. Four transverse bulkheads subdivide the hull.

MAIN ENGINES: Two MTU 12V 331 TC92 diesel engines. Alternatively the craft can be powered with two CRM diesel engines, 1650hp each.

PROPULSION: Two reverse/reduction gearboxes are coupled by Aquamet 22 Armco shafts to two surface-piercing Nibral propellers.

CONTROLS: A dual station hydraulic steering system is coupled to special semi-intubated rudders, of Italcraft patent. Steering positions are in the wheelhouse and flying bridge.

ACCOMMODATION

Deckhouse: Wheelhouse, main saloon and galley
Between decks: Three double cabins
Owner's heads/shower
Guest heads/shower
Crew heads/shower
Double-berth crew cabin
All accommodation is air-conditioned

SYSTEMS

Auxiliary engines: One 12kW diesel generator, 220V ac 50Hz, alternative by electric equipment 60Hz standard USA
Navigational equipment: Furuno or Vigil radar, 48-mile range; Loran C; echo sounder; computerised electronic log
Communications equipment: V/HF, 55ch 25W; Navigraf radiotelephone, SSB 220W
Internal communications: Intercom between wheelhouse, flying bridge, forecastle and quarterdeck; intercom in cabins, saloon and bridge
Lifesaving: One inflatable life raft, life jackets and one semi-rigid pram dinghy with outboard
Firefighting: High pressure water pump for firefighting; portable fire extinguishers; automatic and remote control engine room fire extinguishing system

DIMENSIONS

Length overall: 21·0m
Beam: 5·45m
Draught: 1·20m
Moulded depth: 2·92m

WEIGHTS

Full load displacement: 37·0 tonnes
Half load displacement: 32·0 tonnes

PERFORMANCE

Speed, max at half load displacement: 56·0 knots
Speed, cruise continuous power: 45·0 knots
Speed, economical cruise: 37·0 knots
Range at 45 knots: 320 miles
Range at 37 knots: 350 miles

22-METRE COAST GUARD PATROL BOAT (DESIGN)

Fast patrol boat.

A recent addition to the range of craft offered by Italcraft is their 22-metre fast patrol craft which is capable of achieving a top speed of 52 knots. Two versions of this craft are available, both built in grp.

HULL: Constructed in grp.

DIMENSIONS

Length overall: 22·15m
Beam overall: 5·25m
Depth, moulded: 2·88m
Draught, at full load displacement
    Version A: 1·36m
    Version B: 1·29m

WEIGHTS

Full load displacement
    Version A: 43·50 tonnes
    Version B: 39·00 tonnes

PERFORMANCE

Speed, max
    Version A: 51·0 knots
    Version B: 52·0 knots
    high resistance
        Version A: 45·5 knots
        Version B: 45·5 knots
    cruise
        Version A: 28·0 knots
        Version B: 28·0 knots

Cockpit and saloon of the Italcraft M78

Wheelhouse of Italcraft M78 motor yacht

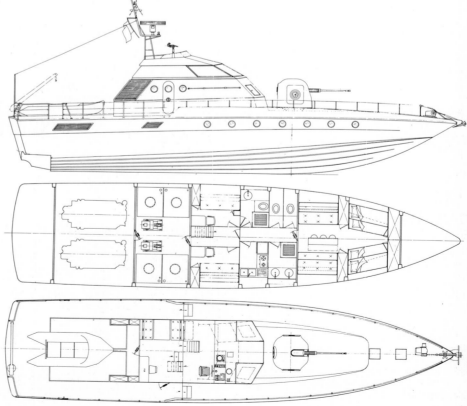

Italcraft 22m fast patrol boat design

MAIN ENGINES	**Version A**	**Version B**
Main power	Two MTU 12V 396 TB93	Two CRM 18/DSS
(1 hour every 12 hours):	1960hp at 2100rpm	1850hp at 2075rpm
Max continuous power:	1700hp at 2000rpm	1650hp at 2000rpm

CANTIERI NAVALI LIGURI

16037 Riva Trigoso (GE), Italy

Telephone: (0185) 44241
Telex: 270630 CARIVA PPCHV I

Dr Aldo Ceccarelli, *President*

Cantieri Navali Liguri assumed their present name in 1955 from the original company Cantieri Navali Liguri di Riva Trigoso. The yard special-ises in building steel-hulled craft.

CNL 35 (DESIGN)

Patrol boat.
HULL: All-welded steel hull divided into six watertight compartments, aluminium alloy super-structure.
COMPLEMENT: 20, including Commanding Officer, officers, senior and junior ratings.
ARMAMENT
Coast guard configuration: One twin 30mm gun mounting forward, two 12·5mm machine guns on upper deck

CNL 24 patrol boat design

Gun configuration: Two twin 30mm gun mount-ings forward and aft
Missile configuration: One twin 30mm gun mount-ing forward, two medium range ship-to-ship missiles in two launchers aft

DIMENSIONS
Length overall: 34·89m
Length waterline: 31·66m (130 tonnes displace-ment); 31·80m (160 tonnes displacement)
Beam: 8·30m

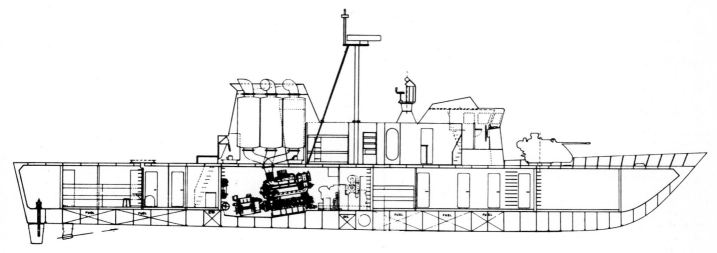

CNL 35 patrol boat design, coast guard version

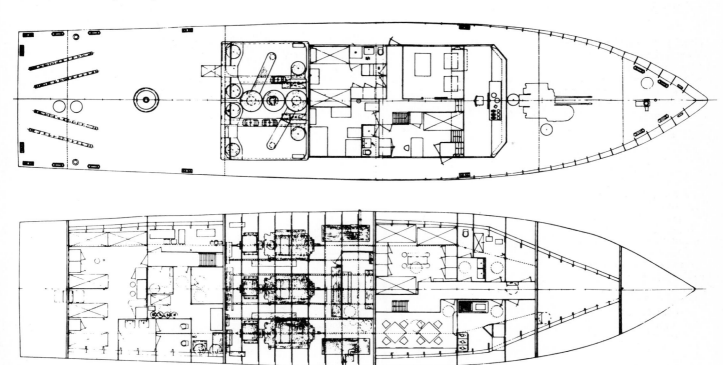

CNL 35 upper deck and lower deck accommodation layout

Draught: 2·40m
WEIGHT
Displacement: 130·0 tonnes to 160·0 tonnes
depending on armament
PERFORMANCE
Speed, max: up to 34 knots
max cruising: 28 knots
Endurance: 1·5 days at 28 knots, 3 days at
14 knots, 6 days at 12 knots

CNL 24 (DESIGN)
Patrol boat, designed for Middle East.
HULL: All-welded steel hull divided into six
watertight compartments, aluminium alloy super-
structure.
MAIN ENGINES: Two medium-speed diesels.
PROPULSION: Two fixed-pitch propellers.
CAPACITIES: Stores and supplies for 7 days at
sea.
COMPLEMENT: Crew of 10.
ARMAMENT: Two single 20mm guns.
DIMENSIONS
Length overall: 24·50m
Length waterline: 21·70m
Beam overall: 5·60m
Draught: 1·90m
WEIGHT
Displacement: 52·0 tonnes
PERFORMANCE
Speed, max: 26 knots
Speed, cruising: 24 knots
Endurance at 24 knots: 24 hours

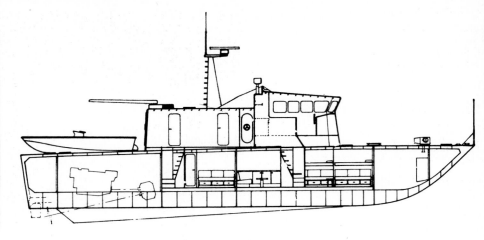

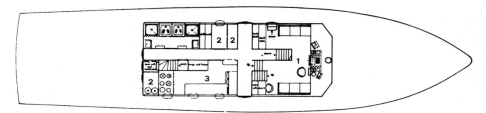

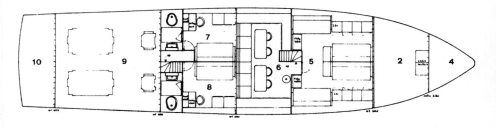

CNL 24 upper and lower deck accommodation layout

CANTIERI NAVALI PICCHIOTTI SpA

Darsena Italia 42, 55049 Viareggio, Italy

Telephone: (0584) 45345
Telex: 500328 PICCHT I
Telefax: (0584) 31273

Builder of fast patrol boats and high-speed
luxury motor yachts.

18-METRE DAY CRUISER
A recent 46-knot boat fitted with Riva Calzoni
waterjet propulsion, type IRC 47 DL. Range
approximately 400n miles at 39 knots.

Picchiotti 18m 46-knot day cruiser

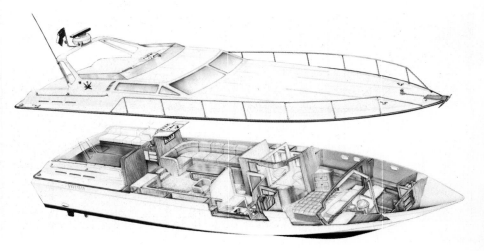

Interior of Picchiotti day cruiser

CANTIERI RIVA SpA

24067 Sarnico, Italy

Telephone: 35 910202
Telex: 300183 RIVA I

Riva, well known for their fast motor cruisers in the 9- to 13-metre range, have now increased the size of their production craft by introducing their Riva 60 Black Corsair and Cosaro series of craft. UK agents are Lewis Marine, 59-61 High Street, Wanstead, London E11 2AE. Telephone: 01-989 2265/6.

BLACK CORSAIR

Length: 18·71m.
Engines: Two 1300bhp diesels.
Speed: 39 knots.

Riva 60 Cosaro

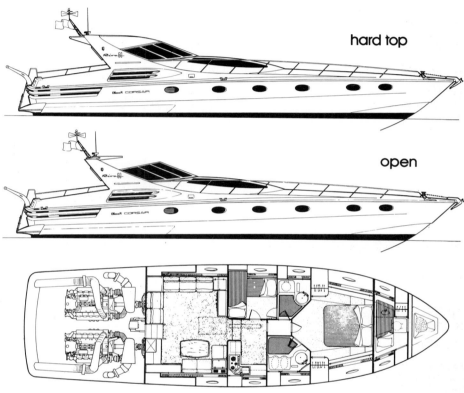

hard top

open

Black Corsair

Riva 60 Black Corsair

COSARO

Length: 18·68m.
Engines: Two 760bhp diesels.
Speed: 31 knots.

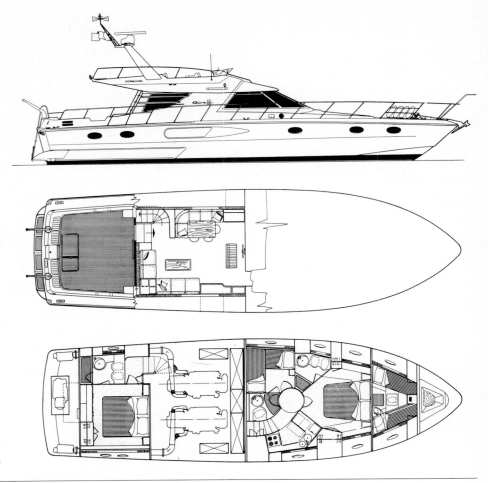

Cosaro

CRESTITALIA SpA

Via Armezzone, 19031 Ameglia (La Spezia), Italy

Telephone: (0187) 65 746/583/584
Telex: 283042 CRESTI I
Telefax: (0187) 65 282

Liaison offices: Via Gallarate 34-D, 20151 Milan, Italy

Telephone: (02) 32 71 873

Via Ottaviano 32, 00192 Rome, Italy

Telephone: (06) 31 85 94

Crestitalia started building grp craft in 1961 at Como and moved to a new slipyard at Ameglia

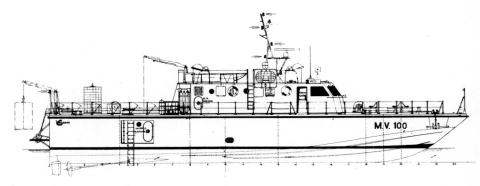

MV100 30m diving support and underwater exploration boat profile

MV100 30m diving support and underwater exploration boat

(La Spezia) in 1971. The company build craft in grp up to 40 metres in length and since 1961 have built approximately 20 000 craft 4 to 11m in length. The Ameglia yard has recently been equipped with a new launching deck and sheds capable of building five 40m craft simultaneously. Principal customers are the Italian Navy and Police, and overseas military and police forces.

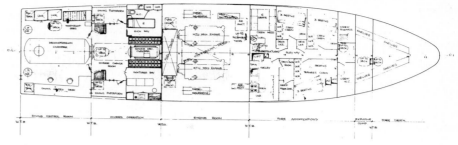

MV100 30m diving support and underwater exploration boat lower deck layout

MV100

Diving support and underwater exploration boat.

The MV100 is an enlarged version of the M85 (26m), the craft having a number of similarities in layout and equipment.

HULL: Semi-planing V-shaped hull in grp with a grp sandwich superstructure.

MAIN ENGINES: Two MTU 12V 396 TB93 marine diesels.

PROPULSION: Twin screw.

CONTROLS: Electric/hydraulic steering gear.

ACCOMMODATION: Two twin-berth officers' cabins, two crew cabins, three berths in each, and one trainee cabin with six berths.

ARMAMENT: One local control 30mm gun.

SYSTEMS

Auxiliary engines: Two Mercedes OM421 diesel generators providing 96kW each

Decompression chambers: Two, one three-person and one single Galeazzi chamber

Navigational: One magnetic compass and one Anschutz gyrocompass with two repeater compasses. One Sagem electro-magnetic log, one RN 770 Decca radar, one Noak long-range searchlight, Elac LAZ51AT/LSE 133 echo sounder, Zeiss Orion 80B night vision telescope, and Decca Navigator Mark 21

Air-conditioning: Full air-conditioning throughout

Underwater exploration equipment: Two Pluto RCVs equipped with search and identification sensors

DIMENSIONS

Length overall: 30·00m

Beam overall: 6·90m

Draught, light displacement: 0·96m

Draught, fully loaded: 1·05m

WEIGHTS

Displacement, full load: 95 tonnes

Max displacement with load on deck: 105 tonnes

PERFORMANCE

Max speed at full load: 27 knots (approx)

Endurance: Max range at 16·5 knots with full load, 560 miles

MV88 27m multi-purpose crew boat

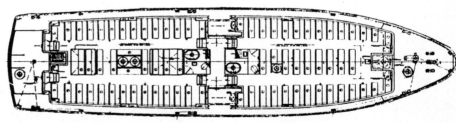

MV88 profile and interior layout

MV88

Multi-purpose crew boat and quick deployment forces transport.

HULL: Grp.

MAIN ENGINES: Two 1600hp marine diesels.

PROPULSION: Propellers or waterjets.

CAPACITIES

Fresh water: 2600 litres

ACCOMMODATION: 250 fully equipped military personnel.

CREW: 4.

DIMENSIONS

Length overall: 27·28m

Beam overall: 6·98m

Draught: 1·10m

WEIGHT

Displacement: 82 tonnes

PERFORMANCE

Speed, max: 28 knots
cruising: 23 knots

MV85

Fast patrol boat.

CLASSIFICATION: Registro Italiano Navale (RINa).

HULL: Grp.

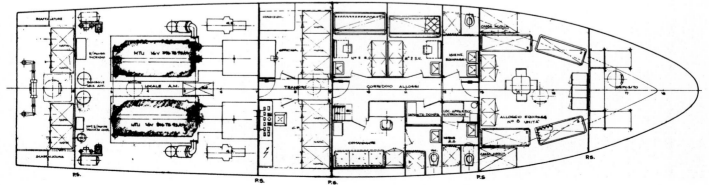

MV85 fast patrol boat, accommodation layout

MAIN ENGINES: Two MTU 16V 396 TB94 diesels.

Rating	Duration	rpm	Speed
Max:	one half hour		
	out of 6 hours	2100	45 knots
Overload:	two hours out		
	of 12 hours	2400	42 knots
Continuous:	24 hours over		
	24 hours	1975	40 knots

PROPULSION: Two three-bladed Nibral alloy propellers.

CONTROLS: Remote engine room controls from wheelhouse and flying bridge.

ACCOMMODATION/COMPLEMENT: Commanding Officer, four officers and eight ratings accommodated in single Commanding Officer's cabin, two double-berth officers' cabins and forward messdeck fitted with eight berths for ratings. Wardroom and galley situated in after part of wheelhouse structure.

ARMAMENT: One single 30mm Breda-Mauser mounting forward with remote FCS Elsag-Medusa control and two light machine guns on wings of flying bridge.

SYSTEMS

Auxiliary machinery: Two diesel generators of 50kW/50Hz output, each capable of providing normal full load requirements, one emergency diesel generator of 10kVA/380V

Navigational: One GEM 732 radar, one Anschutz

MV85 26m fast patrol boat max speed 45 knots

gyrocompass, one Sagem electronic data log, one echo sounder, and one ARPA radar

Communications: One complete radio station

Air-conditioning: Provided for all living areas

DIMENSIONS

Length overall: 26·40m
Beam overall: 6·95m
Moulded depth: 3·45m
Draught, light displacement: 0·92m
Draught, half load displacement: 1·00m

Draught, full load displacement: 1·02m

WEIGHTS

Displacement, light: 61·25 tonnes
Displacement, half load: 71·57 tonnes
Displacement, full load: 79·43 tonnes

PERFORMANCE

Speed, max: 45 knots
Speed, overload: 42 knots
Speed, continuous: 40 knots
Full load endurance at 18·5 knots: 1200n miles

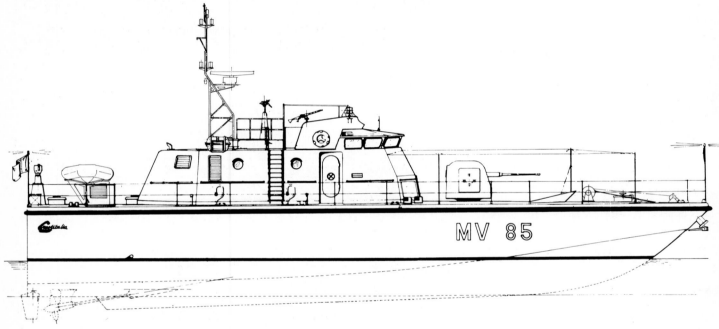

MV85 26m fast patrol boat profile

MV85 fast patrol boat

MV70

Fast patrol boat.
HULL: Grp.
MAIN ENGINES: Two 1400hp diesel engines.
PROPULSION: Two propellers.
CONTROLS: Mechanical remote controls to engines, hydraulic steering gear.
CREW: 12.
ARMAMENT: Twin Oerlikon 30mm.
SYSTEMS
Navigational: Radar and echo sounder
Communications: VHF-SSB-UHF
DIMENSIONS
Length overall: 21·10m
Beam overall: 5·30m
Draught: 0·90m
WEIGHT
Displacement: 40 tons
PERFORMANCE
Speed, max: 35 knots
Speed, continuous: 31 knots
Endurance at continuous speed: 17 hours

Crestitalia MV70 fast patrol boat

MV120 (DESIGN)

Coastal patrol boat.
HULL: Grp with aluminium alloy superstructure.
MAIN ENGINES: Three MTU 12V 331 TC92 marine diesel engines.
PROPULSION: Three propellers.
CAPACITIES
Fuel oil: 33 tonnes
CREW: 20.
ARMAMENT: Two Breda-Mauser single 30mm gun mountings.
SYSTEMS
Auxiliary machinery: Three 50kW/50Hz diesel generators
Navigational: One Decca 370 radar, one Anschutz gyrocompass, one Sagem log, one echo sounder
Communications: One HF/SSB Sailor 2000 and one VHF 25 Sailor
DIMENSIONS
Length overall: 36·00m
Beam overall: 6·60m
Draught, light displacement: 1·34m
Draught, full load displacement: 1·64m
WEIGHTS
Displacement, light: 98 tonnes approx
Displacement, full load: 145 tonnes
PERFORMANCE
Speed, max: 28 knots
Speed, continuous: 25 knots
Range at 25 knots: 1000n miles
Range at 15 knots: 1800n miles

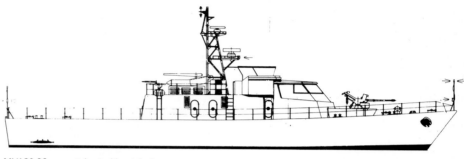

MV120 36m coastal patrol boat design

MV110 (DESIGN)

Coastal patrol boat.
HULL: Aluminium alloy superstructure and grp hull.
MAIN ENGINES: Two MTU 16V 396 TB04 marine diesel engines.
PROPULSION: Two three-bladed Nibral alloy propellers.
CREW: 20.
ARMAMENT: One surveillance/search radar Decca 2459 F/I, two twin Breda 30/40mm gun

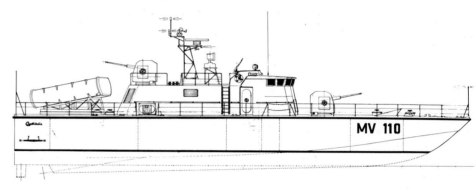

MV110 33m fast coastal patrol boat design

mountings, one multi-purpose chaff/rocket launcher, one Sadral launcher, one optronic/radar fire control system, one ESL system.
SYSTEMS
Auxiliary machinery: Two 150kW/50Hz diesel generators
Navigational: One Decca 370 radar, one Anschutz gyrocompass, one Sagem log, one echo sounder
Communications: One HF/SSB Sailor 2000 and one VHF 25 Sailor
Air-conditioning: Two Carrier units supplying air-conditioning to all living areas

DIMENSIONS
Length overall: 33·00m
Beam overall: 6·90m
Draught, light displacement: 0·90m
Draught, full load displacement: 1·10m
WEIGHTS
Displacement, light: 80 tonnes approx
Displacement, full load: 110 tonnes
PERFORMANCE
Speed, max: 40 knots
Speed, continuous: 36 knots
Range at 25 knots: 900n miles
Range at 18 knots: 1400n miles

INTERMARINE SpA

19038 Sarzana, La Spezia, Italy

Telephone: (0187) 671800
Telex: 271062 IMARIN I

23-METRE PATROL CRAFT

HULL: Constructed of grp, the hull is of soft round form with fine entry forward, running into a hard chine constant deadrise aft.
ENGINES: Two 1925kW diesels.
PROPULSION: Two three-blade, fixed-pitch propellers.
CREW: 11.
SYSTEMS
Generator: 43kVA
Navigation: Radar, log, echo sounder, gyrocompass
Communications: RTX VHF 60 Ch, RTX UHF, RTX HF/SSB 100W 16 Ch, RX MF/HF

Intermarine 27m patrol boat

Armament: One 30mm naval gun, two 7·62mm
    machine guns
DIMENSIONS
Length overall: 23·80m
Beam: 8·40m
Draught: 1·20m
WEIGHT
Displacement: 55·0 tonnes
PERFORMANCE
Speed, max: 40·0 knots
    max continuous: 35·0 knots
Range, at 30 knots: About 450n miles

27-METRE PATROL CRAFT
HULL: Of same material and form as the 23m
patrol craft.
ENGINES: Two 2575kW diesel engines.
PROPULSION: Two three-blade, fixed-pitch
propellers.
CREW: 15.
SYSTEMS
Generator: 76kVA
Armament: One 40/70 naval gun, optically stabil-
    ised fire control, one 20mm TB MG, optical
    sight
DIMENSIONS
Length overall: 27·27m
Beam: 6·80m
Draught: 2·10m
WEIGHT
Displacement: 85·0 tonnes
PERFORMANCE
Speed, max: 40·0 knots
    max continuous: 36·0 knots
Range, at 20 knots cruise: About 1000n miles

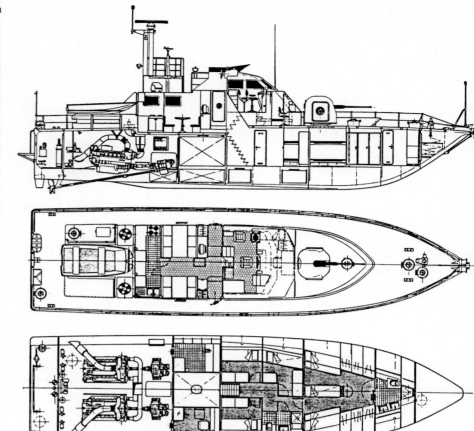

Intermarine 23m patrol boat

RODRIQUEZ CANTIERI NAVALI SpA

Via S Raineri 22, 98100 Messina, Italy

Telephone: (090) 7765
Telex: 980030 RODRIK I
Telefax: (090) 717358

Please see entry under Hydrofoils section for
company information.

MONOSTAB
This is a new patented concept for a stabilised
mono-hull vessel matching the characteristics of a
semi-planing hull with two automatically controlled surface-piercing foils, the object being to
achieve a better overall performance than obtain-
able with a pure mono-hull, especially at Froude
Numbers near unity.

If waterjet propulsion is used for a semi-planing
mono-hull it is almost inevitable that with engines
and auxiliary machinery being also at the stern,
the vessel will have a far aft centre of gravity with
subsequently large changes in centre of gravity
position from full load to light condition. Such
machinery location also allows however for a hull
shape with very fine entrance angles providing
reduction in bow wave generation and good
seakeeping performance especially in head seas.

Artist's impression of the
first Monostab

The Monostab concept reduces the difficulties
of an excessively rear centre of gravity position by
the provision of a pair of surface-piercing foils
connected to moving arms, manually- or automatically-controlled and positioned at the rear of
the craft. The effect is to allow for a true dynamic
relief of weight-load from abaft thereby reducing
the amount of craft weight supported by the
combined buoyant/planing lift of the hull and
effecting a planing trim reduction substantially
equivalent to a forward shifting of the craft centre

of gravity. This in turn is expected to lead to an
improvement of cruising performance because of
the higher efficiency of foils in relation to hull
efficiency in the range of speeds under consideration and because of the indirect advantage of
being able to trim the craft correctly for any load
condition. Further, with a considerable improvement in directional stability, with the dihedral
effect of the foils generating correct banking in
turns and the possibility of regulating the planing
trim angle of the craft in head seas to reduce

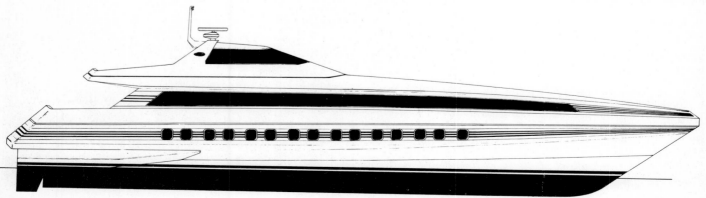

The new Rodriquez Monostab project

slamming, a large reduction of the hull bottom deadrise can be obtained, leading in turn to a better hydrodynamic efficiency of the hull.

Additional advantages of the concept, if trimmable foils are used, is that a strong roll and pitch damping effect is obtained together with an increase in the transverse stability of the basic hull. These effects allow for a reduction in the waterline beam, improving hydrodynamic efficiency and rough water performance. With automatic control

actuation of the moving arms a considerable increase in rough water performance can be obtained without involving unduly fast arm movements.

The first craft to be built according to the above principles is due to be launched in 1988.
ENGINES: Two MTU or Isotta Fraschini high-speed diesels.
PROPULSION: Two waterjet units.
ACCOMMODATION: 350.

DIMENSIONS
Length overall: 36·00m
Length waterline: 30·00m
Breadth, moulded: 7·50m
Draught: 0·90m
WEIGHTS
Displacement, fully loaded: 112 tonnes
Useful load: 35 tonnes
PERFORMANCE
Speed, cruising: 35 knots

TECNOMARINE SpA

Central Services, Via dei Pescatori 56, 55049 Viareggio, Italy

Telephone: (0584) 394466 (2 lines)/392029/391085
Telex: 500487 TECNO I

Ms Anna Maria Patini, *President*
Filippo Picchiotti, *Financial Manager*
Franco Klun, *Technical Manager*
Piero Picchiotti, *Production Manager*

Tecnomarine was established in 1973 as an independent branch of the Picchiotti shipyard, Viareggio, staffed with skilled labour and technicians from Picchiotti. The yard builds fast craft in wood, grp, and aluminium alloy from 14 to 36 metres and with speed ranges of 25 to 35 knots.

TECNOMARINE 118
Motor yacht.
HULL: Construction in aluminium alloy or grp.
MAIN ENGINES: Two MTU 16V 396 TB93, 2600hp at 2100rpm each.
CAPACITIES
Fuel: 14 000 litres
Fresh water: 4000 litres
DIMENSIONS
Length overall: 36·00m

Some Tecnomarine craft built up to the end of 1987

Length	Construction	Power	Max speed
19m	grp	two GM 870hp each	33·0 knots
24m	wood or grp	two GM 1080hp each	29·5 knots
28m	wood or grp	two MTU 1600hp each	30·0 knots
36m	light alloy or grp	two MTU 2610hp each	29-30 knots

T118 aluminium alloy hull under construction

Length waterline: 31·16m
Beam, max: 7·33m
Draught, max: 2·25m

PERFORMANCE
Speed, max: 29 to 30 knots
Range: 700n miles

T118 motor yacht, profile

T118 grp hull being removed from mould

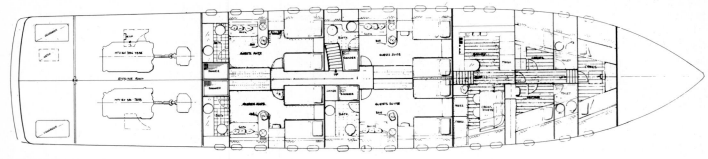

T118 accommodation layout

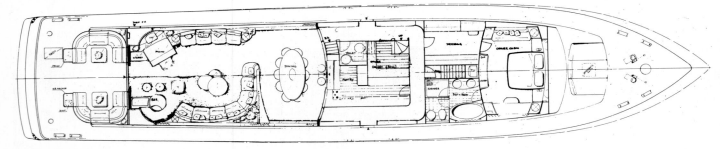

T118 upper deck layout

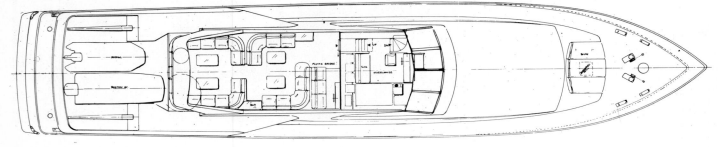

T118 sun deck layout

VERSILCRAFT Srl

Via dei Pescatori 64, Viareggio, Italy

Telephone: (0584) 390391-2
Telex: 624198 VERSIL I

Marketing
Versil Marine SA
Baarerstrasse 50, CH-6300 Zug, Switzerland

Telephone: (042) 418044
Telex: 865328 VEMA CH

Versil Marine France
64, La Croisette, Palais Mirimar, 06400 Cannes,
France

Telephone: (93) 435666
Telex: 970836 VERSIL F

73ft CHALLENGER
HULL: Grp.
MAIN ENGINES: Three GM 12V 92 TI.
ACCOMMODATION
Crew: 2 berths
Passengers: 6 to 8 berths
CAPACITIES
Fuel tank: 9988 litres
Water tank: 1614 litres
DIMENSIONS
Length, overall: 22·26m
Beam, overall: 6·10m
Draught: 1·83m
WEIGHTS
Displacement, normal load: 40 tonnes
Displacement, fully loaded: 45 tonnes
PERFORMANCE
Speed, normal displacement, max: 26 knots
Speed, normal displacement, cruising: 23 knots

FALCON
The latest craft produced by Versilcraft, built in
grp to ABS and RINa classification.
ENGINES: Two DDA 12V-71 TI, 870hp each.

Versil 73ft Challenger

Versil Falcon

FUEL TANK CAPACITY: 7500 litres.
DIMENSIONS
Length, overall: 22·25m
Beam, overall: 5·70m
WEIGHTS
Displacement, empty: 35·00 tonnes

Displacement, fully loaded: 45 tonnes
PERFORMANCE
Range: 600 miles
Cruising speed: 25 knots
Max speed: 28 knots
Auxiliary power: 25kW Oman generator

83ft SUPER CHALLENGER

MARCALEC
HULL: Grp.
MAIN ENGINES: Three GM 12V 92 TI diesel
engines.
ACCOMMODATION
Crew: 2 to 3
Guests/passengers: 6 to 8 berths
CAPACITIES
Fuel tank: 10 000 litres
Water tank: 1600 litres
DIMENSIONS
Length overall: 25·40m
Beam overall: 6·09m
Draught: 1·83m
Height above waterline to deck: 3·05m
WEIGHTS
Displacement, empty: 40·0 tons
   normal: 45·0 tons
   fully loaded: 50·0 tons
PERFORMANCE
Speed, max, normal displacement: 25·0 knots
   cruising, normal displacement: 22·0 knots
Range at economical speed: 572 miles

25-knot Versil motor yacht Super Challenger *Marcalec*

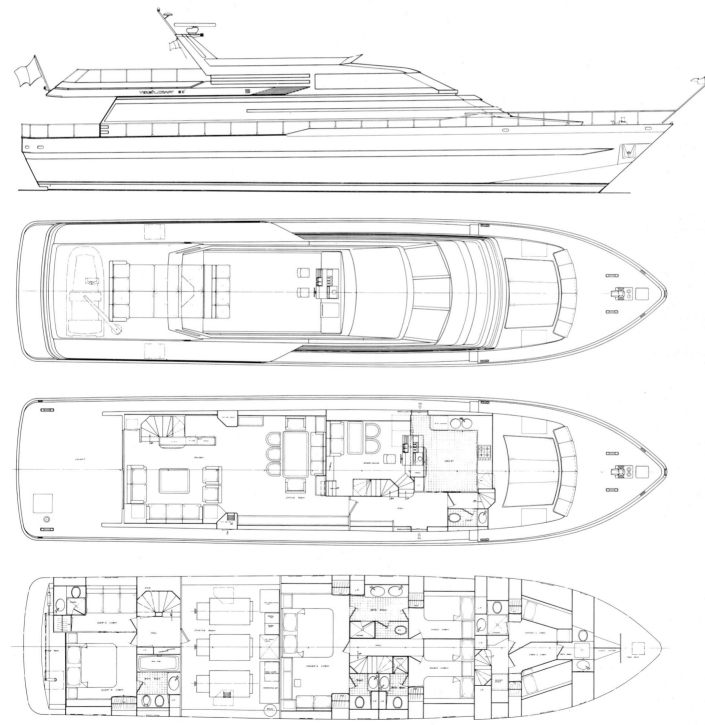

Versil 83ft Super Challenger

Super Challenger wheelhouse

JAPAN

MITSUBISHI HEAVY INDUSTRIES LTD (MHI)

5-1, Marunouchi 2-chome, Chiyoda-ku, Tokyo, Japan

Telephone: (212) 3111
Telex: 22443 J

SHIMONOSEKI SHIPYARD AND ENGINE WORKS

16-1 Enouni-cho, Hikoshima, Shimonoseki, Japan

Telephone: (66) 2111
Telex: 0682284 J

SUNLINE

This interesting vessel was first announced in October 1986. The *Sunline* high-speed passenger ship incorporates a new feature in naval architecture, a semi-submerged bow (SSB) designed to suppress intense pitching and rolling in rough weather. The aft part of the vessel is of conventional high-speed ship form. *Sunline* is owned by Nippon Koun Kaisha Ltd of Ehime Prefecture.
ENGINES: Two 1000hp, at 2170rpm.
DIMENSIONS
Length overall: 26·76m
Beam: 5·80m
Depth: 2·67m
PERFORMANCE
Passenger capacity: 70
Speed, max: 28·1 knots

See Addenda for General Arrangement drawing.

Semi-Submerged Bow (SSB) of the
Mitsubishi *Sunline*

HIGH-SPEED FISHING BOAT
NS2-10200

A 26·03-metre fishing boat capable of 30·6 knots.

ENGINES: Two GM DDA 16V-149 TI, MCR: 1675hp each at 1900rpm.

PROPULSION: Two 3-blade, fixed-pitch, 920mm diameter, 1180mm pitch, aluminium bronze.

COMPLEMENT: Nine.

DIMENSIONS

Length: 26·03m
Length, bp: 23·48m
Breadth, moulded: 5·73m
Depth, moulded: 2·84m
Draught, design: 1·05m
Draught, extreme: 1·09m
GRT: 56·0

Mitsubishi 70-passenger, 28-knot *Sunline*

PERFORMANCE

Fuel consumption: 160g/hph

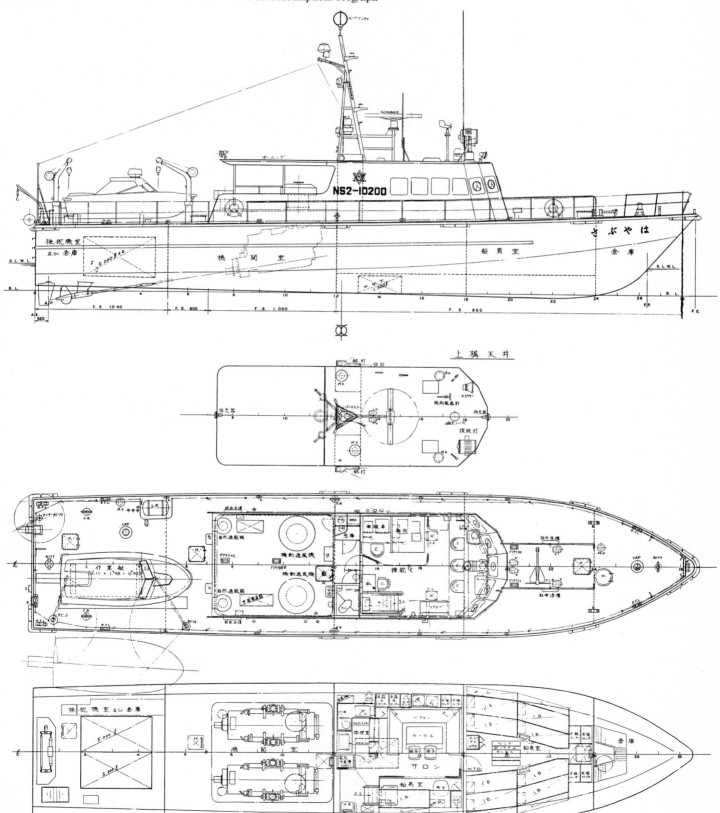

General Arrangement of Mitsubishi NS2-10200

Mitsubishi 30·6-knot fishing boat NS2-10200

MOKUBEI SHIPBUILDING COMPANY

Otsu, Biwa Lake, Japan

Dr M Ikeda, *Chief Naval Architect*

LANSING

A waterjet-propelled sightseeing tourist boat built in 1982 for operation by the Biwa Lake Sightseeing Co on the very shallow Biwa Lake. Built in aluminium, the vessel has seating for 86 passengers and 2 crew. The fully-laden power-to-weight ratio is 41·5hp/tonne.
POWERPLANT: Two MAN 254 MLE V12 diesels rated at 540hp each, at 2230rpm.
WATERJETS: Two Hamilton Model 421 type directly driven from engine flywheel via torsionally-flexible coupling and Cardan shaft.
AUXILIARY POWER/CONTROLS: The vessel is fitted with an auxiliary diesel ac generator which enables ac motor driven hydraulic powerpacks to be used for the waterjet unit controls. A tandem pump hydraulic powerpack is used for the reverse ducts while a single pump hydraulic powerpack operates the steering. At the helm, control for steering is via a wheel; the reverse is operated via a single electric joystick and two position indicators are fitted, one for the steering deflector angle and the other for the reverse duct position.
DIMENSIONS
Length overall: 22·0m
Length waterline: 19·80m
Beam: 4·0m
Draught: 0·55m
WEIGHT
Displacement, max: 26 tonnes
PERFORMANCE
Speed, max at 26 tonnes displacement: 27 knots
Speed, partially loaded: 30 knots

Mokubei 50-seat, 26·5-knot ferry

23·5-METRE FERRY

A twin-engine waterjet-propelled shallow draught craft.
DESIGNER: Dr M Ikeda.
ENGINES: Two Yanmar 6LAAM-UT1, 500hp each, at 1850rpm.
PROPULSION: Two Hamilton Jet 421 waterjet units.
ACCOMMODATION: 50 passengers.
DIMENSIONS
Length overall: 23·50m
Length waterline: 21·15m
Beam: 4·78m
Draught: 0·61m
WEIGHT
Weight, full load: 34·57 tonnes

PERFORMANCE
Speed, max: 26·50 knots
Speed, full load: 21·6 knots
Fuel tanks: Two 980-litre

ESCOURT BOAT

KAIYO

A 25·5-metre, 21·5-knot steel-hull firefighting boat equipped to carry foam liquid, launched 19 February 1986 and owned by Sanyo-kaiji Co Ltd and Nihon-kaiji-kogyo Co Ltd.
DESIGNER: Dr M Ikeda.
ENGINES: Two Yanmar 12LAAK-UT1, 1000hp each, at 1850rpm.
PROPULSION: Two fixed-pitch, 3-blade, aluminium bronze, 1000mm diameter, 1000mm

Stern of *Lansing* showing the Hamilton waterjet units   Mokubei *Lansing*

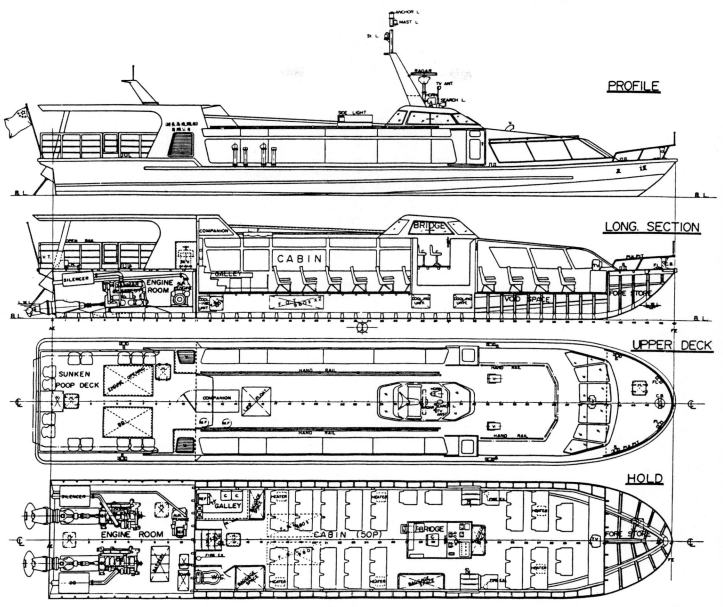

General Arrangement of Mokubei 50-seat ferry

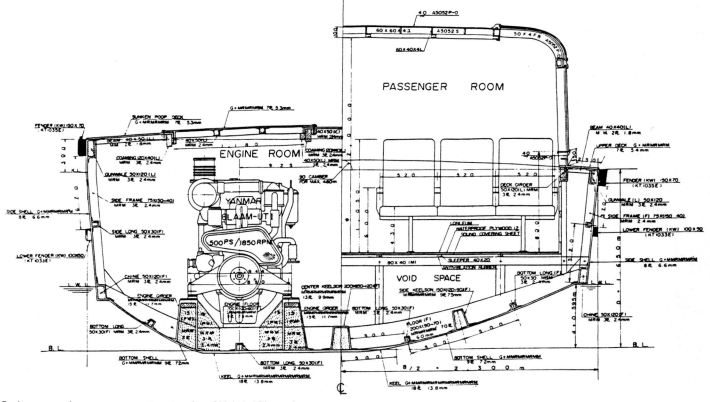

Engine room and passenger compartment section of Mokubei 50-seat ferry

pitch, developed blade-area ratio: 0·90. Propeller
shaft diameter: 99mm, length 6500mm.
REDUCTION GEAR: NICO-MGN 332, shaft
output MCR: 1000hp at 907rpm.
COMPLEMENT: Nine.
DIMENSIONS
Length overall: 25·50m
Breadth, moulded: 5·60m
Depth, moulded: 2·70m
Draught, design: 1·10m
WEIGHT
Lightweight: 54·85 tonnes
GRT: 49·0
PERFORMANCE
Fuel consumption: 165g/hph

Kaiyo

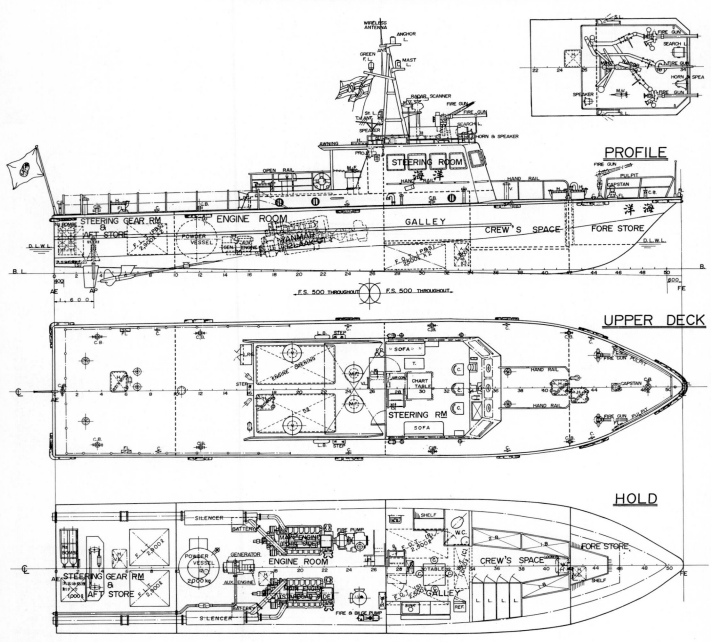

General Arrangement of *Kaiyo*

SHINJU SHIPBUILDING COMPANY

Kyushu Island, Japan

Telephone: (0944) 54 2117/9

TROPICAL QUEEN

A waterjet-propelled sightseeing tourist boat for
inter-island services from the island of Ishigaki,
Tropical Queen was delivered in July 1982. The
vessel was designed by the Yamaha Motor Co Ltd
and is built in glass-reinforced plastic sandwich
construction.
MAIN ENGINES: Two GM 12V 92 TI diesels,
730hp each at 2135rpm.
PROPULSION: Two Hamilton Model 421, type
56 impeller waterjet units.
CONTROLS: At the helm the steering is power
assisted and the reverse bucket is controlled by a
24V dc electric joystick switch. The hydraulic
powerpack for steering is belt-driven off one main
engine while separate 24V dc electro-hydraulic
powerpacks, activated by the single powerpack
switch, power-operate the reverse buckets.
DIMENSIONS
Length overall: 27·3m
Length waterline: 23·49m
Beam: 5·3m
Deadrise: 5°
WEIGHTS/CAPACITIES
Displacement, max: 37 tonnes
Fuel: 2000 litres

PERFORMANCE
Speed, fully laden, 37-tonne displacement: 27
  knots at 2000rpm, corresponding to 600hp
  input per engine
Speed, fully laden, max: 29 knots

150-passenger *Tropical Queen*

Tropical Queen

Tropical Queen

Interior of *Tropical Queen*

KARIUSHU

Passenger ferry.
HULL: Fibre-reinforced plastic.
MAIN ENGINES: Two GM 8V 71N, 395hp each at 2170rpm.
PROPULSION: Two ALBC$_3$ propellers.
ACCOMMODATION: Air-conditioned accommodation for 95 passengers and 3 crew.
SYSTEMS
Fuel tank capacity: 2000 litres
Electrical generator: One Mitsubishi M14H, 10hp at 2200rpm
DIMENSIONS
Length overall: 20·80m
Length, Japanese Registered: 19·50m
Breadth: 4·80m
Depth: 2·30m
GRT: 65
Japanese gross tonnage: 40
PERFORMANCE
Speed, max: 23·14 knots
    cruising: 19·0 knots

SEA ANGEL

Pleasure motor yacht.
HULL: Fibre-reinforced plastic.
MAIN ENGINES: Two MAN D 2542, 540hp each at 2170rpm.
PROPULSION: One ALBC$_3$ propeller.
ACCOMMODATION: Air-conditioned accommodation for 12 passengers and 8 crew.
SYSTEMS
Fuel tank capacity: 4000 litres
Electrical generator: One Oman MDEH-15R, 40hp at 1800rpm
Navigation: One 48-mile radar
DIMENSIONS
Length overall: 20·0m
Length, Japanese Registered: 19·24m
Breadth: 5·20m
Depth: 2·0m
GRT: 70
Japanese gross tonnage: 42
PERFORMANCE
Speed, max: 24·0 knots
    cruising: 22·0 knots

SHIMABARA

Passenger ferry.
HULL: Fibre-reinforced plastic.
MAIN ENGINES: Two GM 12V 92 TI, 700hp each, max continuous at 2170rpm.
PROPULSION: Two ALBC$_3$ propellers.
ACCOMMODATION: Air-conditioned, for 96 passengers and 3 crew.
SYSTEMS
Fuel tank capacity: 2400 litres
Navigation: One 48-mile radar
DIMENSIONS
Length overall: 23·80m
Length, Japanese Registered: 22·50m
Breadth: 4·80m
Depth: 2·30m
GRT: 80
Japanese gross tonnage: 51
PERFORMANCE
Speed, max: 28·0 knots
    cruising: 22·0 knots

YUKIKAZE 8

Fishing pleasure boat.
HULL: Fibre-reinforced plastic.
MAIN ENGINES: One Yanmar 12LAAK-DT, 800hp at 1800rpm.
PROPULSION: One ALBC$_3$ propeller.
ACCOMMODATION: Room for 12 passengers and 8 crew.
SYSTEMS
Fuel tank capacity: 4500 litres
Electrical generator: One Yanmar 3HMK, 27hp at 3200rpm
DIMENSIONS
Length overall: 19·79m
Length, Japanese Registered: 17·65m
Breadth: 4·0m
Depth: 1·80m
GRT: 32
Japanese gross tonnage: 19

Hamilton waterjets, model 421, type 56 impeller, on stern of *Tropical Queen*

Shinju *Kariushu* passenger ferry

Shinju *Sea Angel* motor yacht

Shinju *Shimabara* passenger ferry

Shinju *Yukikaze 8* fishing pleasure boat

KOREA, SOUTH

MIWON TRADING AND SHIPPING CO LTD

1-15, 2 KA Chung Hak-Dong, Yongdo-ku, Busan, South Korea

Telephone: 48 4411 4
Telex: 24592 MITRA K
Telefax: (02) 784 7857

28-METRE PASSENGER CRAFT

A sightseeing boat built in grp for the Jung Ahang Express Co. Four have been built, powered by DDA 12V-92 TI engines (850hp each, at 2300rpm), driving Hamilton Model 361 waterjet units. The fleet is to be based on Choong Joo Dam. The vessels can carry 128 passengers at 27 knots, the lightly laden top speed being over 31 knots.

Miwon Trading 27-knot sightseeing craft

NETHERLANDS

SCHEEPSWERF PORSIUS BV

Kruysbaken 10, 1505 HS Zaandam, Netherlands

Telephone: 075-158652
Telex: 19316 PORS NL

Scheepswerf Porsius is a yacht builder and in early 1986 had under construction a 33-metre aluminium motor yacht designed by MPS Engineering of Lemwerder, West Germany.

33-METRE MOTOR YACHT

HULL: Welded aluminium construction in marine grade aluminium AlMg 4·5Mn. All tanks are integrated in the bottom structure of the hull.

Three watertight bulkheads divide the engine room, owner's and guest area, crew area and foreship section.
MAIN ENGINES: Two MTU 12V 396 TB94 engines.
CONTROLS: Twin rudders, two stabilisers and one bow thruster hydraulically operated.
SYSTEMS
Auxiliary engines: Two generators, each delivering at least 50kW
Soundproofing: All machinery resiliently mounted. Main exhaust under water with sound dampened bypass above water for the idling condition
Sanitary system: US Coast Guard approved sewage plant connected to a vacuum system and holding tank
Air-conditioning: System installed to reach a

temperature difference outside to inside of 8°C and humidity difference of 35%
DIMENSIONS
Length overall: 32·90m
Length waterline: 28·20m
Beam overall: 7·40m
Max draught under rudder: 1·65m
Draught amidships: 1·40m
WEIGHTS
Full load weight incl max fuel capacity: 135·0 tonnes
Half load weight with 7·5 tonnes of fuel: 109·5 tonnes
Empty weight: 97·5 tonnes
PERFORMANCE
Max speed: 32 knots
Range: Approx 3000n miles with 30·50 tonnes of fuel and speed of 12 knots

32·90m MPS Engineering-designed motor yacht built by Scheepswerf Porsius

32-90m motor yacht built by Porsius

NORWAY

FJELLSTRAND A/S

N-5632 Omastrand, Norway
Telephone: (5) 56 11 00
Telex: 42148 N
Telefax: (5) 56 12 44

See entry in Catamaran section for company details.

The Fjellstrand company has built the following high-speed mono-hull ferry craft with speeds above 20 knots.

Craft built

Name	Length	Date built	Operator
Rødøyløven	26·0m	1977	Saltens Dampskibsselskap A/S
Rasa	26·0m	1979*	Helgeland Trafikkselskap A/S
Nefelin	26·0m	1980	Elkem-Spigerverket A/S
Veslestril	26·0m	1980	Simon Møkster
Tysfjord	23·0m	1981	Saltens Dampskibsselskap A/S
Øykongen	25·5m	1982	Saltens Dampskibsselskap A/S
Øgdronningen	25·5m	1982	Saltens Dampskibsselskap A/S

* Cargo and passengers

Veslestril

SINGAPORE

FAIREY MARINTEKNIK SHIPBUILDERS (S) PTE LIMITED

31 Tuas Road, Singapore 2263

Telephone: 8611706/7, 8616271/2/3
Telex: 53419 MARJET RS
Telefax: 8614244

Denis Kerr, *Managing Director*

Fairey Marinteknik Shipbuilders (S) Pte Ltd is part of Fairey Marinteknik International Ltd Group
33/F New World Tower, 16-18 Queen's Road, Central, Hong Kong

Telephone: 5 218302/231054
Telex: 74493 HMHCO HX

David C H Liang, *Group Chairman*
John Warbey, *Managing Director*
Robert Liang, *Executive Director*
Mike McSorley, *Marketing Manager*

As well as building catamaran ferries and crew boats to Marinteknik design, this yard has built a total of seven mono-hull ferries and crew boats. The hulls of two of the vessels completed have

Craft built (high-speed mono-hull)

Type	Designation	Yard No	Craft name	Owner/operator	Delivered	Engines	Classification	Payload	Speed
30·80m	30MCB (CV900)	102	*Hamidah**	Ocean Tug Service	1985	Two MTU 6V 396 TC62	DnV R-30 Crew boat, light craft	50 passengers + 6·8 tonnes	19 knots cruise
31·00m	31MCB	104	*Zakat*	Black Gold (M), Sdn Bhd, Malaysia	1986	Two MTU, 440kW each	GL + 100A2, 30 miles	38 passengers + 13·38 tonnes	37 knots
31·00m	31MCB	106	*Amal*	Black Gold (M), Sdn Bhd, Malaysia	1986	Two MTU, 440kW each	GL + 100A2, 30 miles	38 passengers + 13·38 tonnes	
35·00m	35MPV	107*	—	Discovery Bay Co	April 1987	Two MWM TBD 604B V8, 840kW each	HK Navy Dept, Cl2, Protected Waters	256 passengers	25 knots
35·00m	35MPV	108	—	Discovery Bay Co	May 1987	Two MWM TBD 604B V8, 840kW each	HK Navy Dept, Cl2, Protected Waters	256 passengers	25 knots
35·00m	35MPV	109	—	Discovery Bay Co	June 1987	Two MWM TBD 604B V8, 840kW each	HK Navy Dept, Cl2, Protected Waters	256 passengers	25 knots
35·00m	35MPV	110	*Wu Yi Hu*	Jiangmen Jiang Gang Passenger Traffic Co, China	1987	Two MTU 12V 396 TB83, 1180kW each		265 passengers + 3·12 tonnes	27 knots contract
35·00m	—	—	—	Alilauro Aliscafi del Tirreno SpA	1988	—	—		

*hull built by Marinteknik Verkstads AB, Sweden and fitted out by Fairey Marinteknik Shipbuilders (S) Pte Ltd, Singapore

been built in the Öregrund yard of Marinteknik Verkstads AB, Sweden.

35-METRE PASSENGER FERRY

A number of 35-metre passenger ferries have been built to differing operational requirements.
OWNER: Yuet Hing Marine Supplies.
CLASSIFICATION: Germinisher Lloyds + 100 A4K MCA and IMO code A373(×).
HULL: Deep V forward and flat V with flat chines aft. Constructed in marine grade aluminium T profile extrusions and plates welded by Robot MIG fully automatic welding machines. Provision is made for the main engines to be removed through two bolted access hatches.
MAIN ENGINES: Two MTU 12V 396 TB83 marine diesels, 1180kW at 1940rpm continuous each.
PROPULSION: Two KaMeWa type 63/S62/60 waterjet propulsion units.

CAPACITIES

Fuel: 6000 litres
Water: 1000 litres
Lube oil: 250 litres
Hydraulic oil: 150 litres
Sewage holding tank: 500 litres

ACCOMMODATION

Passengers: 265 and 3·12 tonnes of luggage
Complement: Officer/Crew 14

DIMENSIONS

Length overall: 35·00m
Beam, moulded: 7·70m
Depth, moulded: 2·84m
Draught, light: 1·05m (mean)
Draught, loaded: 1·25m (mean)

PERFORMANCE

Speed, max: 30 knots
Speed, cruising: 27 knots

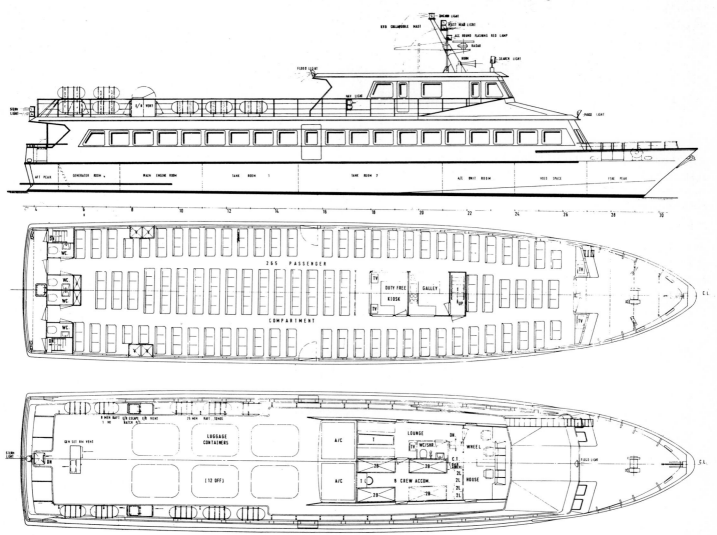

General Arrangement of the Fairey Marinteknik *Wu Yi Hu*

The 265-seat, 27-knot *Wu Yi Hu*

Discovery Bay 15 built by Fairey Marinteknik Shipbuilders (S) Pte Ltd

SINGAPORE SHIPBUILDING AND ENGINEERING LTD (SSE)

7 Benoi Road, Singapore 2262
Postal address: PO Box 138, Jurong Town Post Office, Singapore 9161

Telephone: 861 2244/6844
Telex: 21206 SINGA RS
Telefax: 861 3028

Shih Chih Chung, *Executive Director*
George Chow, *General Manager*
Boon Swan Foo, *Senior Manager (Design & Engineering)*
Heng Chiang Gnee, *Senior Manager (Operations & Repair)*
Wong Kin Hoong, *Senior Manager (International Marketing)*

Singapore Shipbuilding and Engineering Ltd (SSE) was established in 1968 as a specialist shipyard. Current areas of expertise include the building of specialised commercial vessels, military engineering equipment fabrication and the

Swift class patrol boat

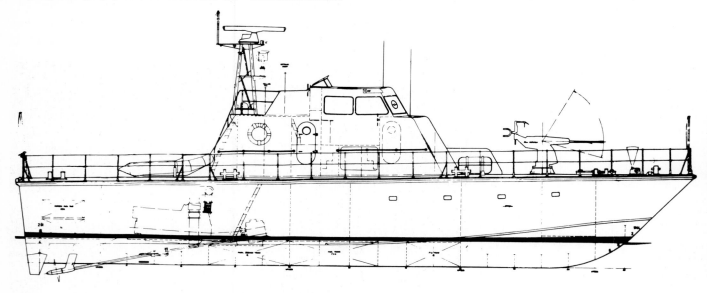

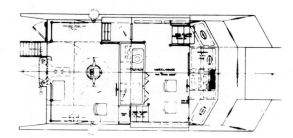

Layout of SSE Swift class patrol boat

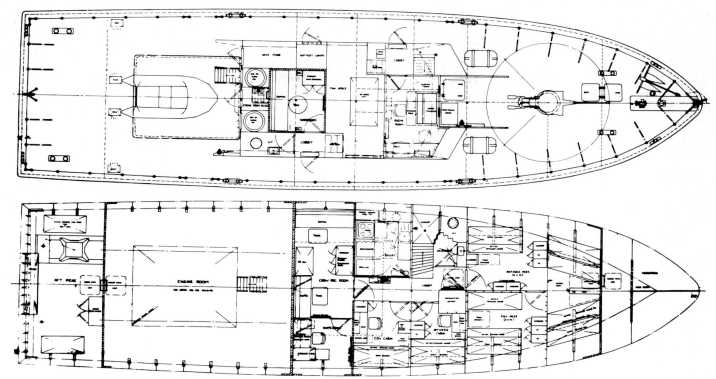

Layout of SSE Swift class patrol boat

reconstruction and modernisation of old vessels. SSE is located in a 30-acre site at the mouth of the Benoi Basin. In addition to the Swift class patrol boat described below SSE have built or have on order over 20 of their PT class patrol boats (14·54m, 30 knots), 11 for the Singapore Marine Police, two for Singapore Customs and Excise Dept and seven for the Royal Brunei Police Force, this latter order to be completed by the end of 1987.

SSE have also completed (1983) a luxury motor yacht, 14·13m, at present registered under SSE's name.

In 1986 SSE completed their first air cushion vehicle, an Air Vehicles Tiger 40.

SWIFT CLASS PATROL BOAT

A fast patrol boat, 12 of which were built over the period 1979 to 1980 (Yard Nos 152 to 163) for the Singapore Navy.

HULL: Hard chine planing form, welded aluminium.

ENGINES: Two Deutz SBA 16M 816 diesels, 1330hp each, at 2000rpm or two MTU 12V 331 TC92 diesels, 1475hp each, at 2300rpm.

AUXILIARY POWER: Two diesel generating sets, each 440V, 60Hz, 3-phase, can sustain 100% ship's load.

CAPACITIES

Main fuel tanks: 7000 litres
Reserve tanks: 1600 litres
Fresh water tank: 2000 litres

CREW: 12 (1 CO, 2 Officers, 3 Petty Ratings, 6 Ratings).

ARMAMENT: Two bridge wing general purpose machine guns or half-inch Browning guns. Missile system with two or three launchers aft depending on type of missile.

DIMENSIONS

Length overall: 22·70m
Length waterline: 20·00m
Beam, extreme: 6·20m
Depth, amidship: 3·00m
Draught, at design waterline: 1·60m

WEIGHTS

Displacement, half load (with missile): 47 tonnes
Displacement, half load (without missile): 43 tonnes

PERFORMANCE

Speed, max: 33 knots (Deutz), 35 knots (MTU)
Speed, max continuous: 31 knots (Deutz), 31 knots (MTU)
Range, at 10 knots: 900n miles
Range, at 20 knots: 550n miles

SWEDEN

DJUPVIKS VARV AB

S-440 64 Rönnäng, Sweden

Telephone: 304 62230
Telex: 21298 DVA S
Telefax: 304 62500

About two years ago Djupviks Varv became a member of the Swede Ship Group. The yard was founded in 1894 and since 1937 nearly all the Swedish Coast Guard vessels have been built by Djupviks Varv. The yard started building in aluminium in 1950 and have built about 100 craft in this material to date. During 1980 the building programme was extended to include deliveries of pilot boats, passenger vessels, high-speed catamarans and luxury yachts.

COAST GUARD 280 CLASS

Fast patrol boat. To date Djupviks Varv has delivered every craft in this class to the Swedish Coast Guard.

HULL: All-welded aluminium hull and superstructure.

MAIN ENGINES: Two Cummins marine diesels of 1100hp each.

SYSTEMS: Comprehensively equipped with navigational aids.

DIMENSIONS

Length overall: 21·00m
Beam: 5·00m

PERFORMANCE

Speed, max: 27 knots

Swedish Coast Guard 280 class patrol boat

MARINTEKNIK VERKSTADS AB

Varsvagen, Box 7, S-74071 Öregrund, Sweden

Telephone: 173 30460
Telex: 76182 MARTAB S
Telefax: 173 30976

Hans Ruppert, *Chairman*
Hans Erikson, *Managing Director*

Marinteknik Verkstads AB is affiliated with the Fairey Marinteknik International Ltd Group

Following the pioneering by Marinteknik of high-speed waterjet-propelled catamaran ferries, the same form of propulsion was applied to a mono-hull crew boat design. The first such craft were built at the company's yard at Öregrund and fitted out and delivered at the Marinteknik Singapore yard in 1985. Since then Marinteknik Verkstads AB have built a further four mono-hull craft for ferry operations in Hong Kong, Sweden and Italy.

Hamidah

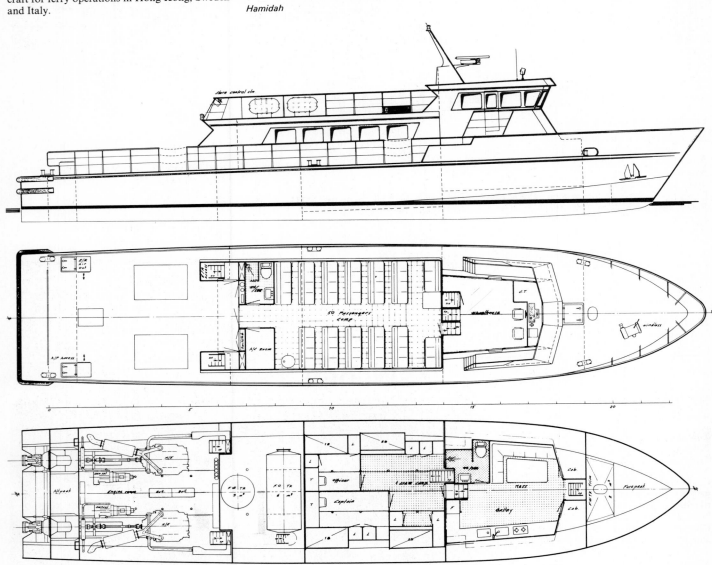

General Arrangement of Marinteknik Marinjet crew boat *Hamidah*

Craft built (high-speed mono-hull)

Type	Designation	Yard No	Craft name	Owner/Operator	Delivered	Engines	Payload	Speed
—	30 MCB (CV900)	58	*Hamidah**	Ocean Tug Service	1985	Two MTU 6V 396 TC82	50 passengers + 6·8 tonnes cargo	19 knots cruise
		64	*Discovery Bay 15*	Discovery Bay	April 1987			
41·90m	41 MPV	65	*Cinderella*	Rederi AB Marinteknik/ City Jet Line	1987	Four Scania DSI 14 300kW each	450 passengers	22 knots cruise
—	—	66	*Cosmopolitan Lady*	Private Cruise International I Ltd				
—	—	68	*Europa Jet*	Alilauro Italia	1987			
—	—	71	—	Alilauro 2000 Srl	1988			

*Fitted out by Fairey Marinteknik Shipbuilders (S) Pte Ltd, Singapore

Hamidah

Hamidah manoeuvring beside an oil rig

MARINJET 30MCB (CV900)

HAMIDAH

The Marinjet 30MCB is an all-aluminium semi-planing waterjet crew boat with a very shallow draught intended for coastal and inshore waters. Of deep-Vee form at the extreme bow the hard-chine lines lead to a flat-Vee deadrise at the stern. An aft steering control station situated on the roof of the passenger compartment offers an unobstructed view of the stern of the vessel for manoeuvring around platforms and barges.

CLASSIFICATION: Det norske Veritas R-30, Crew Boat, Light Craft.

HULL: Welded aluminium alloy, corrosion resistant with extrusions for plating and frames, a development by Marinteknik.

MAIN ENGINES: Two MTU 6V 396 TC62, cruise power 440kW, 590bhp each, at 1650rpm.

PROPULSION: Two KaMeWa 45/S65/6 waterjets.

ACCOMMODATION/PAYLOAD

50 passengers (80kg each)
Cargo and supplies: 6·8 tonnes

SYSTEMS

Fuel tank capacity: 6000 litres

DIMENSIONS

Length: 30·80m
Beam: 6·40m
Depth: 2·80m
Draught: 0·80m

WEIGHT

Disposable load, max: 16 tonnes

PERFORMANCE

Speed, max: 23 knots
    cruising: 19 knots
Range: 500n miles
Fuel consumption: 220 litres/h

Cinderella command position

CINDERELLA

A 41·9m fast passenger ferry/day cruise ship operating in Stockholm Archipelago.
OWNER: City Jet Line, Stockholm, Sweden.
CLASSIFICATION: Sjöfartsverket, Sweden.
HULL: Constructed in aluminium. Internal design by Lennart Janson.
MAIN ENGINES: Four Scania DSI 14 marine diesels, cruising power 300kW each at 1800rpm.
PROPULSION: Two Marinejet Power System waterjet units, belt driven.
CAPACITIES
Fuel: 6000 litres
ACCOMMODATION: Payload of 450 passengers, with 85-seat restaurant on the upper deck and a cafeteria in the main saloon.
SYSTEMS
Auxiliary engines: One Scania DN11 108kW generator and one Perkins 4236 25kW generator
Air-conditioning: Fitted throughout
DIMENSIONS
Length overall: 41·90m
Breadth: 7·70m
Draught, full load: 1·10m
PERFORMANCE
Speed, max: 25 knots
Speed, cruise (fully loaded): 22 knots
Range: 450n miles
Fuel consumption: 170 litres/h (tank: 7000 litres)

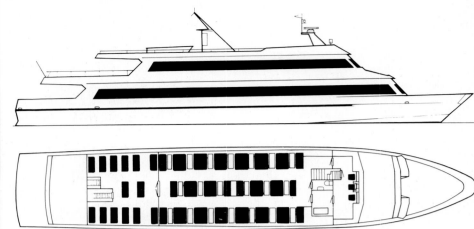

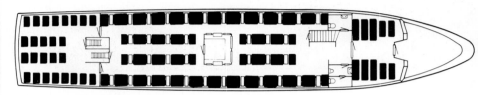

Layout of Marinteknik Verkstads *Cinderella*

Marinteknik *Cinderella* in service with City Jet Line, Stockholm, following launching on 15 May 1987

OSKARSHAMNS VARV AB

Box 2, S-57201 Oskarshamn, Sweden

Telephone: (0) 491 170 80
Telex: 4963 OSKYARD S

Parent company: Swede Ship Invest AB, 440 64 Rönnang, Sweden
Tel: (0) 304 622 20 **Telex:** 21298 DVA S
Telefax: (0) 304 625 00

Located on the east coast of Sweden, Oskarshamns Varv specialise in building aluminium and steel motor yachts and military craft. The company is part of the Swede Ship Group. Craft are built in construction halls 90 × 31·5m, 83 × 19·0m and 40 × 31·5m with overhead cranes, lifting capacity 80 metric tons. There are also machine shop and repair facilities with two floating docks for vessels up to 30 000 dwt. Number of employees is about 170.

24-METRE SPORT FISHERMAN

Fast motor yacht. The first of this class of motor yacht has been delivered.
CLASSIFICATION: Hull certificate, Det norske Veritas.
HULL: Construction of hull and superstructure is in aluminium.
MAIN ENGINES: Two MTU 12V 396 TB93 marine diesel engines 1600bhp each. Electrical trawling motors also fitted.
PROPULSION: Two CP propellers.
CAPACITIES
Fuel: 15 000 litres (approx)
Fresh water: 1000 litres (approx)

SYSTEMS
Auxiliary engines: Two G & M 60kW diesel generators
Navigational: Magnuavox Sat Nav system, Raytheon speed log and depth sounder, Foruno ADF, Decca colour radar, Loran C, Robertson autopilot and a Plath gyrocompass
Communications: Sailor SSB, Sailor VHF, Airphone intercom, Foruno Weatherfax Polaris Regency VHF back-up and Inmarsat satellite communications
DIMENSIONS
Length overall: 24·10m
Breadth: 7·20m
Draught: 1·75m
GRT: 75 tons (approx)
PERFORMANCE
Speed, service: 27 knots

Oskarshamns Varv 24m Sport Fisherman

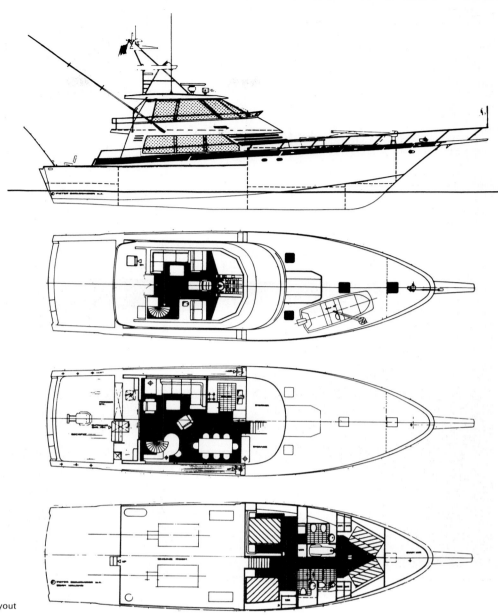

24m Sport Fisherman profile and accommodation layout

SMUGGLER MARINE AB

Sturegatan 24, 11436 Stockholm, Sweden

Telephone: 8-613799
Telex: 10651 NAVPROD S/15784 INTRADE S

Hans Lindgren, *Chief Executive*

Smuggler Marine AB has recently been formed by Intrade Invest AB following the merger of Naval Production and Smuggler Boats, two established Swedish companies that have been building power boats up to 35 metres in length for the past 25 years for the racing, commercial and military market sectors.

In co-operation with SP Systems of the Isle of Wight, England, Smuggler Marine have been working on the design of advanced composite production boats incorporating extensive use of carbon and aramid reinforcements in an epoxy matrix. Smuggler Marine claim that their first 13-metre prototype craft, the Smuggler 384, incorporating an integrated structure with the minimum of framing and novel construction techniques, has resulted in their craft being 40% lighter with more internal space than a conventional grp hull, while maintaining equivalent strength with increased stiffness. The Smuggler 384 (built by Green Marine (Lymington) Limited at Lymington, Hampshire, England) powered by a Saab-Scania 14-litre V8 marine diesel and driving a modified Hamilton 361 waterjet, can attain speeds up to 60 knots. This craft is currently being

Prototype of the Smuggler 384

evaluated by the Swedish Administration of Defence Materials and the Swedish Navy. Smuggler Marine intend to proceed with the construction of larger versions of the Smuggler 384.

TAIWAN

HI-STAR MARINE CO LIMITED

50, Ta Yeh S Road, Kaohsiung, Taiwan

Telephone: 7 8715286
Telex: 71826 HISTAR
Telefax: 7 8715280

Tim Juan, *Marketing Manager*

HI-STAR 66FT

A luxury motor yacht, the first 66ft will be delivered in August 1988 and the second around February 1989.
ENGINES: Two GM 8V-92 TA, 735bhp each at 2300rpm.
DIMENSIONS
Length overall: 20·12m
Length waterline: 17·45m
Beam: 5·64m

Draught: 1·17m
Freeboard, forward: 2·26m
Freeboard, aft: 1·96m
Design waterline to freeboard height: 4·80m
CAPACITIES
Fuel: 1200 to 1800 gallons
Water: 400 gallons
DISPLACEMENT: Approx 37·6 tonnes.
PERFORMANCE
Speed: 22 to 30 knots

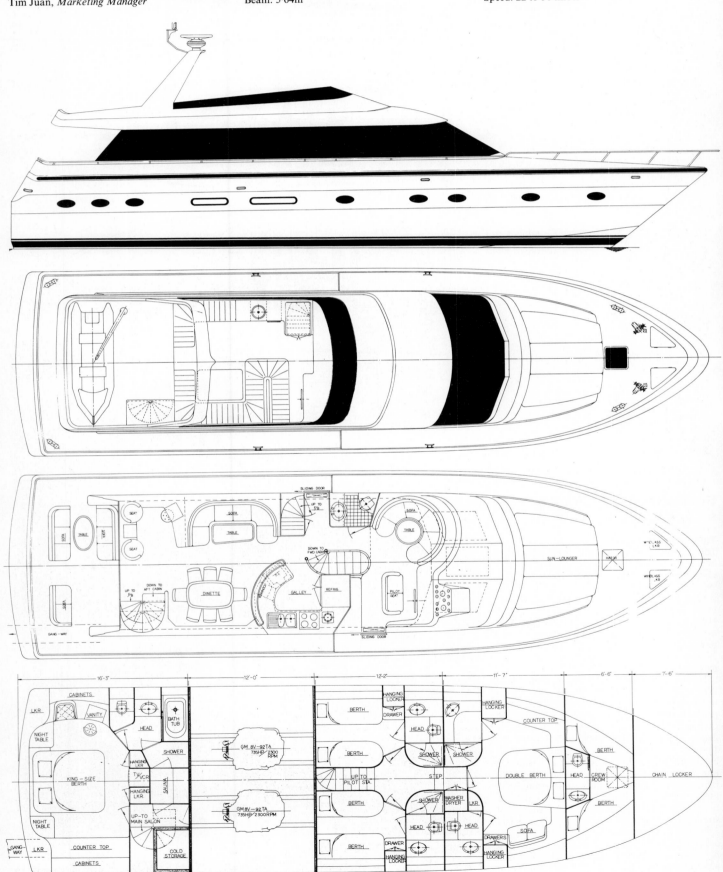

General Arrangement of Hi-Star 66ft motor yacht

THAILAND

ITALTHAI MARINE LIMITED

Italthai House, 11th Floor, 2013 New Petchburi Road, Bangkok, Thailand

Telephone: 314 6101-9/314 7578/314 7246
Telex: 21225 ITELECT TH
Telefax: 6602 3146385

Dr Chaijudh Karnasuta, *Chairman*
Angelo Gualtieri, *Managing Director*
Papit Gualtieri, *Executive Director*
Vice Admiral Chob Sirodom, *Assistant to Managing Director*
Suwit Khandawit, *Marketing Manager*

Italthai Marine was formed in 1978 by the amalgamation of the Italian-Thai Development Corporation, Italthai Holding Co Ltd, and Oriental Marine and Laminates Ltd. There are approximately 450 employees and the shipyard occupies about 56 000m² with workshops, fabrication shops and a shipway length of 190 metres with 250 metres in length of main building berths. There is also a floating dry dock of 100 metres with a lifting capacity of 6000 tons for repairing medium size sea-going vessels. The yard constructs and repairs small to medium size craft and vessels in steel, grp and aluminium.

50·14-METRE PATROL GUN BOAT

Built for the Royal Thai Navy.
HULL: Aluminium alloy/steel.
DIMENSIONS
Length overall: 50·14m
Breadth, moulded: 7·25m
Draught: 1·68m
WEIGHT
Load displacement: 300 tons
PERFORMANCE
Speed, max continuous: 24 knots

27·43-METRE PATROL BOAT

Built for Marine Police Division, Thai Police Department.
HULL: Aluminium alloy.
ENGINES: Deutz MWM SBA 16M 816 CR.
DIMENSIONS
Length overall: 27·43m
Beam: 5·60m
PERFORMANCE
Speed: 25 knots

19·59-METRE FAST PATROL CRAFT

Built for Royal Thai Navy.
HULL: Aluminium alloy.
DIMENSIONS
Length overall: 19·59m
Moulded breadth: 5·30m
Draught: 1·52m
WEIGHT
Displacement: 35·56 tonnes
PERFORMANCE
Max continuous speed: 25 knots

High-speed craft built

Year	Type	Length	Max speed	Main engines	Hull	No	Owner
1980-1981	Patrol Craft Fast (PCF)	19·59m	25 knots	MTU 6V 396 TC 82	Aluminium alloy	6	Royal Thai Navy
1982	Patrol Craft Fast (PCF)	20·80m	25 knots	MTU 6V 396 TC 82	Aluminium alloy	5	Royal Thai Navy
	Patrol Gun Boat (PGB)	50·14m	24 knots	MTU 16V 538 TB 91	Aluminium/steel	1	Royal Thai Navy
1983	Patrol Craft Fast (PCF)	20·80m	25 knots	MTU 6V 396 TC 82	Aluminium alloy	3	Royal Thai Navy
1984-1986	Patrol Boat	27·43m	25 knots	Deutz MWM SBA 16M 816 CR	Aluminium alloy	1	Police Department
	Patrol Gun Boat (PGB)	50·14m	24 knots	MTU 16V 538 TB 91	Aluminium/steel	5	Royal Thai Navy

Italthai 27·43m patrol boat delivered to Thai Marine Police

Italthai 50·14m patrol gun boat delivered to the Royal Thai Navy

Italthai 19·59m fast patrol boat, one of six delivered to Royal Thai Navy

TECHNAUTIC INTERTRADING CO LTD

44/13 Convent Road, Silom, Bangkok 10500, Thailand

Telephone: 234 0730/9368
Telex: 87650 TECO TH

Capt Nirun Chitanon, *Director and General Manager*

The Technautic shipyard employs 150 people, has a total area of 7944m², the main building occupying 2076m². Over 52 craft in the 8- to 26-metre range have been delivered, mainly patrol boats and work boats.

P86 (26-METRE PATROL BOAT)

Fast patrol boat.
DESIGNER: C Raymond Hunt Associates Inc, 69 Long Wharf, Boston, Massachusetts 02110, USA
Telephone: (617) 742 5669, Telex 294116 BOSTUX (Attn: Hunt Associates)
HULL: Grp sandwich with Airex pvc foam core.
MAIN ENGINES: Three Isotta Fraschini ID 36 8VSS, total 3150hp at 1900rpm.
PROPULSION: Three Castoldi 07 waterjets.

CAPACITIES
Fuel: 18 050 litres
Water: 2545 litres
ACCOMMODATION
Officers: Captain's cabin, 2 officers' cabins, heads, wardroom and galley
Ratings: Forward messdeck, accommodation for four ratings; after messdeck, accommodation for seven ratings, heads and washrooms
DIMENSIONS
Length overall: 26·20m
Length waterline: 22·60m
Beam: 6·30m
Draught: 1·10m

WEIGHTS
Displacement, light: 220 500kg
Displacement, half load: 264 600kg
Displacement, full load: 308 700kg

PERFORMANCE
Speed, max: 30 knots
    cruising: 27 knots

Technautic 26m fast patrol boat built to the C Raymond Hunt P86 design

UNION OF SOVIET SOCIALIST REPUBLICS

EVPATORIA

A passenger motor vessel announced in 1985 and designed for 40- to 50-mile coastal runs in the Black Sea. Considerable attention has been paid to reducing noise levels in the accommodation area.
HULL: Bulbous bow.
MAIN ENGINES: Two 3D6 diesel engines, 110kW each; one DRA-210B diesel engine, 735kW, gearbox reduction ratio 4·13:1. Reverse on side propeller drives only giving quick braking capability.
PROPULSION: Two side propellers and one central main propeller.
ACCOMMODATION: 294 passengers with plans to increase to between 350 and 380 passengers with a craft length increase of 4 to 5m. Heating in winter.
SYSTEMS
Electrical: Diesel engines give 3-phase, 230V at 16kW with generator also driven off propeller shaft in event of emergency. Two 28V 1·0kW constant-flow generators supply ancillary power to batteries, starters, lighting etc
Safety: Eight inflatable and fourteen life rafts
DIMENSIONS
Length: 37·6m
Width (at weather deck): 6·90m
Height of sides: 2·90m
Draught: 1·60m
WEIGHTS
Displacement, full load: 133·6 tonnes
Disposable load: 31·0 tonnes

Samantha Smith, an Evpatoria type 20-knot, 37·6m ferry   *(Soviet Shipping)*

PERFORMANCE
Speed: 17 knots (to be increased to 19 to 20 knots for developed version)
Full forward to full reverse in less than one minute
Crash stop distance: 100m

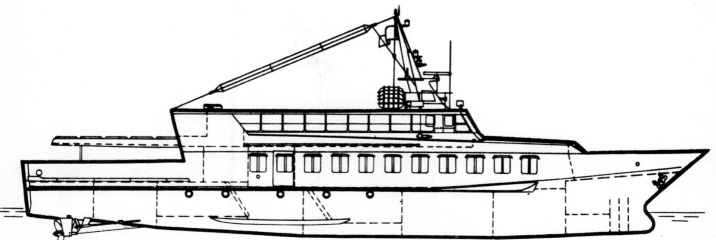

General Arrangement of Evpatoria showing bulbous bow

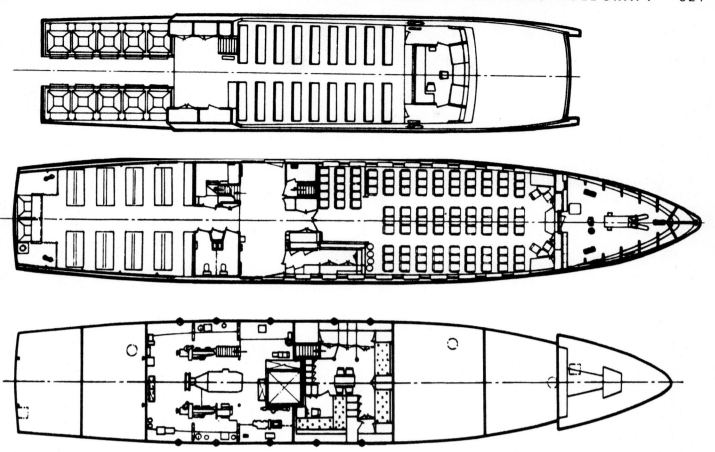

General Arrangement of Evpatoria

UNITED KINGDOM

AILSA-PERTH SHIPBUILDERS LIMITED

5-11 Lavington Street, London SE1, England

Telephone: 01-928 9266
Telex: 933640

Shipyard: Harbour Road, Troon, Ayrshire, Scotland DA10 6DN

Telephone: (0292) 311311
Telex: 778027 AILSA G

Gregory Copley, *Chairman*
Peter G Wayworth, *Managing Director*
Tom Jenkins, *Planning Director*

The Ailsa shipyard was privatised in February 1987 when it was taken over from British Shipbuilders by Ailsa-Perth. The yard has a covered building hall capable of constructing two vessels at a time of up to 114 metres in length with a beam of up to 20·50 metres. There are also two dry docks, fitting-out and repair jetties, also 5852 square metres of steel and outfit production shops. Ailsa-Perth have introduced three new naval designs, their 62-metre Highlander class corvette and the Cobra and Crescent class 34-metre patrol boats in addition to their 25-metre craft.

25-METRE PATROL BOAT (DESIGN)
Fast patrol boat.
DESIGNER: Alistair R Cameron, Camarc Ltd, Worthing, Sussex, England.
HULL: Superstructure and hull constructed in aluminium.
MAIN ENGINES: Two diesel engines varying in type up to 3000shp driving through U drive gearboxes or V drive units. Engine layout can incorporate a small waterjet for loiter use.
ARMAMENT: Dependent on operational requirements, typical layout would be 20/30mm cannon forward, two 7·20mm general purpose

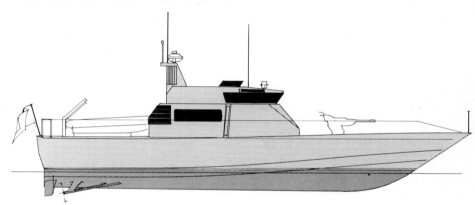

Profile of Ailsa-Perth 25m patrol boat design

machine guns mounted on bridge with a Sea Skua missile aft.
DIMENSIONS
Length overall: 25·00m
PERFORMANCE
Dependent on engine installation, payload and endurance requirements: 25 to 39 knots

CRESCENT AND COBRA CLASS
(DESIGN)
Patrol and general surveillance craft.
DESIGNER: Ailsa-Perth.
HULL: Steel.
MAIN ENGINES: Two Paxman Valenta 16cm each developing 2500kW at 1500rpm.

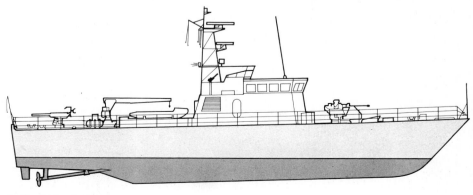

Profile of Ailsa-Perth Crescent and Cobra class designs

ARMAMENT: One 30mm Oerlikon twin mounting type GCMA 03-2 forward, one 20mm mounting aft, Cossor Naval Transponder Type IFF 2750, one Racal Decca Type 2459F surveillance radar.
COMPLEMENT: 21 consisting of commanding officer, two officers, nine senior ratings and nine junior ratings. The complement can be increased by a further three persons if required.

SYSTEMS
Electrics: 440V/3ph/60Hz, two main generator sets at 80kW per set
Navigational: Racal Decca type AC 1690/6 radar
DIMENSIONS
Length overall: 34·00m
Length, waterline: 30·90m
Breadth, moulded: 6·75m
Draught, moulded: 1·70m

WEIGHT
Displacement, half load: 146·25 tonnes
PERFORMANCE
Speed, sprint: 34 knots
Speed, max continuous: 29 knots
Range at 16 knots: 800km
Range at 14 knots: 1000km

BROOKE YACHTS INTERNATIONAL LIMITED

Heath Road, Lowestoft, Suffolk NR33 9LZ, England

Telephone: 0502 517151
Telex: 975665
Telefax: 0502 514663

Anthony de Kerdrel, *Managing Director*
David Semken, *Production Director*

VIRGIN ATLANTIC CHALLENGER II
DESIGNERS: Peter Birkett and Sonny Levi.
   The *Virgin Atlantic Challenger II* was designed and built in 21 weeks to break the Atlantic Blue Riband record set 34 years ago. The craft completed the 2949n mile passage from Ambrose Light to Bishop Rock on 29 June 1986 with a total run time of 3 days, 8 hours, 31 minutes and 35 seconds thus improving on the current Blue Riband time by 2 hours, 9 minutes and 35 seconds.
HULL: All-welded corrosion-resistant aluminium alloy. The wheelhouse is constructed separately and riveted and glued to the main frame.
ENGINES: Two MTU 12V 396 TB93 turbocharged diesels, each producing 2000hp at 2000rpm.
PROPULSION: Two Sonny Levi drive units driving Italian built surface-piercing five-bladed propellers.
SYSTEMS
Fuel tanks: Four Marston tanks mounted midships, 3·13 tonnes capacity each
Trim: One trimming tank of 1·20 tonnes in the bows
Safety: An Auto Marine buoyancy bag system is provided to prevent the boat from sinking in the event of major trouble
Navigation: Two Racal Decca 170 BT radars with enclosed randome scanners. The scanners can be connected to either radar display by means of switching connecting wires; two MNS 2000 Racal Decca, one Trimble combined Loran/GPS, one Lokata portable RDF working on MF frequencies, one Racal Decca CVP 3500 video plotter (the antenna on the two MNS 2000 are interchangeable between the receivers. Each MNS 2000 has a log and compass input. The colour plotter is connected to the main

Racal Decca MNS 2000), one Marine Data steering display, one Marine Data fluxgate compass, one Thomas Walker electromagnetic log, one Cetrek 7000 autopilot, one Cetrek fluxgate compass, two Ritchie high-speed magnetic compasses. (The Marine Data display has log and compass inputs as well as connection to the MNS 2000. The Cetrek autopilot is capable of obtaining heading information from either fluxgate compass)
Communication: Two Skanti HF SSB type TRP 8250 radios, one Sailor VHR radio type RT 2047 (Racal Decca supply), two Icom portable VHF radios on marine band, one Icom portable VHF radio on aircraft band, one Argos beacon, three Racal Decca EPIRBs
   All equipment operates directly from a 24V dc supply, and is fitted to absorb pounding at sea.
DIMENSIONS
Length overall: 22·02m
Beam, max: 5·82m
Cabin width: 4·0m
Cabin length: 5·0m
PERFORMANCE
Speed, max: In excess of 55 knots
Speed at full load, with 13·7 tonnes of fuel: 46·5 knots
Speed at half load: 51·6 knots

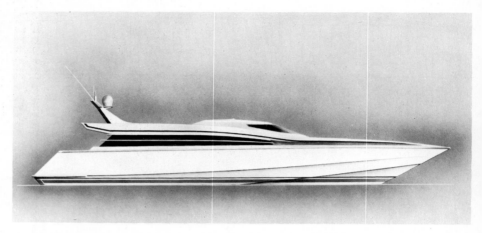

Don Shead design for Brooke Yachts 30m high-speed motor yacht (under construction 1987/88)

30-METRE HIGH-SPEED MOTOR YACHT
   Under construction 1987/88.
DESIGNER: Don Shead, 11 High Street, Fareham, Hampshire, England.
HULL: Aluminium alloy.
MAIN ENGINES: Two MTU 12V 396 TB94 marine diesel engines rated at 1920kW maximum power and 1600kW continuous power operating through ZF BW 465 gearboxes.
PROPULSION: Two KaMeWa waterjets type 63/S62/6.
CAPACITIES
Fuel: 10·00 tonnes
Fresh water: 1·50 tonnes
ACCOMMODATION: Four double cabins each with en suite heads and showers, Captain's cabin with en suite heads, and two double crew cabins with en suite heads.
SYSTEMS: Two diesel generators, 25kVA each.
DIMENSIONS
Length overall: 30·00m
Length waterline: 23·00m
Beam, max: 6·50m
Draught, max: 1·50m
Moulded depth: 4·30m
PERFORMANCE
Speed, max: 40 knots plus

Virgin Atlantic Challenger II

FAIREY MARINTEKNIK (UK) LIMITED

Cowes Shipyard, Cowes, Isle of Wight PO31 7DL, England

Telephone: 0983 297111
Telex: 86466 FAMBRO G
Telefax: 0983 299642

J Barr, *Managing Director*
B Peverley, *Financial Director*
Gordon Dodd, *Manufacturing Director*
David Codd, *Commercial Manager*
Mike McSorley, *Marketing Manager*
Robert Milner, *Regional Manager*
Nigel Warren, *Chief Designer*

Fairey Marinteknik (UK) Limited is part of Marinteknik International Ltd Group, Hong Kong

The company name was changed from Fairey Marine Ltd to Fairey Marinteknik (UK) Ltd on 31 March 1987. With expertise in the design and production of patrol boats, special service craft and lifeboats the acquisition of the company by Marinteknik International Ltd extends its capabilities into the field of advanced catamaran craft. A new project, the Fairey RTL Hydrocat high-speed minimum-wash craft was announced in March 1987.

'TRACKER' CLASS

Twenty-eight of these 20m patrol craft are in service with security forces and customs in eight countries.

HULL: The Tracker hull is of hard chine form with a fine entry and pronounced topside flare providing a dry, seakindly hull that will operate economically at high cruising speeds. A skeg enhances directional stability and gives some protection to the twin propellers and rudders.

Hull, deck and superstructure are of high quality hand lay-up grp. Hull and deck scantlings, construction and materials are approved by Lloyd's Register of Shipping and each hull is provided with a Lloyd's Construction Certificate.

The hull has close pitch transverse frames and deep full-length longitudinal engine girders. All fuel oil and fresh water is carried in integral centre-line tanks formed between the inner longitudinals. The deck and superstructure are of sandwich type construction.

Full cathodic protection by zinc anodes for minimum 1 year life.

MAIN ENGINES/GEARBOXES: Two Detroit Diesel GM 12V-71 TI, turbocharged, aftercooled, fresh water heat exchanger-cooled marine diesels with ZF BW190 2:1 reverse/reduction gearboxes. Each engine is maximum rated at 750shp (560kW) at 2300rpm.

PROPULSION: Monel K500 63·5mm diameter propeller shafts running in replaceable water-lubricated rubber bearings. Five-blade propellers and 'P' brackets are in nickel aluminium bronze.

CONTROLS: Two station hand hydraulic steering system operating twin balanced nickel aluminium bronze rudders. Emergency tiller provided.

ACCOMMODATION: Spacious accommodation is provided below decks for 6 crew and 2 petty officers forward of the engine room and for 2 officers and the captain aft. The accommodation is furnished and equipped, and is fully air-conditioned throughout. Watertight bulkheads divide the hull into 6 compartments: the forepeak (anchor chain locker); focsle with berths for 4 crew; forecabin with crew's mess area, berths for 2 crew, cabin for 2 petty officers, galley, dry food store and toilet/shower; engine room; aft cabin with wardroom, berths for 2 officers, captain's cabin and toilet/shower; aft peak (steering gear and general stowage).

Above decks, the enclosed wheelhouse has a centreline steering position together with separate navigator's and radio operator's stations. It is fully air-conditioned and large enough to be used as an operations room and to allow the installation of comprehensive navigation and communic-

Fairey Marinteknik 20m Tracker fast patrol boat

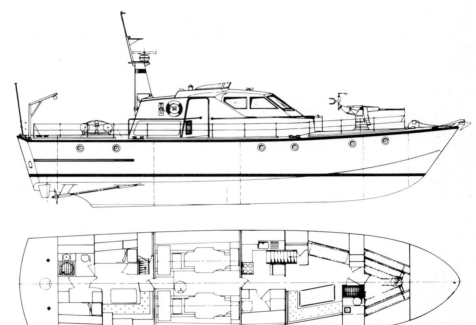

Fairey Marinteknik 20m Tracker fast patrol boat

ication systems. Aft of the wheelhouse is an open bridge deck equipped with a centreline steering position.

SYSTEMS

Electrical: 24V dc insulated return; 2 banks of batteries charged by main engine alternators and by transformer/rectifier from 240V ac system. 240V ac supplied by two 15kW diesel generators or shore supply and powering air-conditioning system, engine room fans, galley equipment, domestic water heater and main lighting

Bilge/fire: Electrically powered main bilge pump with suctions to each watertight compartment and piped to supply fire/deckwash hydrant in superstructure. Back-up manual bilge pump in main bilge circuit

ARMAMENT: A single 20mm cannon can be mounted on the foredeck and two 12·7mm machine guns on the bridge wings.

DIMENSIONS
Length, overall: 20·0m
Beam: 5·18m
Draught: 1·45m
Fuel capacity: 5460 litres
Fresh water capacity: 1365 litres
WEIGHT
Empty: 30 tonnes (approx)
PERFORMANCE
Speed, max: 25·5 knots
  continuous: 23·0 knots
Range at 20 knots: 450n miles

'PROTECTOR' CLASS

Three Protector 33m patrol boats were delivered to the Royal Bahamas Defence Force in 1986. These vessels were intended for long endurance patrol missions (fisheries protection and EEZ security duties).

HULL: The Protector hull is designed to combine good seakeeping with fuel efficiency at all operational speeds. The full-length topsides knuckle enhances stability and with the forward spray rail, gives a stable, dry and seakindly hull. Optional roll damping fins can replace the standard bilge keels.

The hull is divided into watertight compartments and meets strict one compartment flooded damage stability criteria.

The hull and major bulkheads are of all-welded mild steel construction with deep transverse frames and closed spaced longitudinals. Integral double bottom tanks are provided, 3 for fuel, 1 for fresh water. Deck and deckhouse are of all-welded marine aluminium with Kelocouple bi-metallic connection to hull at gunwale edge. All ladders, deck hatches, watertight and weathertight doors are of aluminium. Rectangular section plastic fendering around gunwale.

Full cathodic protection provided by zinc anodes for minimum 1 year life.

MAIN ENGINES/GEARBOXES: Two Paxman Valenta 8RP 200-1-CM fresh water heat exchanger-cooled marine diesel engines each maximum rated at 2000bhp (1492kW) at 1600rpm driving through ZF BWK 458 2:1 reverse/reduction gear-boxes.

Alternative machinery such as twin MTU 16V 396 or triple Detroit Diesel GM 16V-149 can be installed to suit particular requirements.

PROPULSION: Monel K500 115mm diameter propeller shafts running in replaceable water-lubricated rubber bearings in steel stern tubes and 'P' brackets. Twin, 3-blade fixed-pitch nickel aluminium bronze propellers.

CONTROLS: Two station hydraulic power-assisted steering system operating twin balanced hollow steel fabricated rudders. Hand hydraulic emergency steering position in aft peak.

ACCOMMODATION: Fully air-conditioned accommodation is provided for 19 permanent crew plus 7 spares. Two messes, one either side forward c/w berths, wardrobes, lockers, mess tables and seats, toilets and wash places house 14 ratings, with 4 spare berths and lockers further forward. Two cabins amidships accommodate 2 NCOs and 2 officers, each with one spare berth. Separate washplaces and toilets are provided. Adjacent is spacious wardroom for officers and NCOs and containing a spare settee berth. The CO's cabin is in the deckhouse aft of the wheel-house and includes a shower cubicle. The deck-house also houses the radio room and galley. The wheelhouse has fully equipped stations for the helmsman, OOW and navigator and has access aft to the open bridge with its second helmsman's station.

SYSTEMS

Electrical: 24V dc insulated return; 2 banks of batteries charged by main engine alternators and by transformer/rectifier from 240V ac sys-tem. Two 44kW diesel generators or shore supply provide 240/110V ac 60Hz single phase power for all major craft electrical power requirements including galley, laundry, air-conditioning and lighting
   Butyl insulated wiring with heat, oil resistant and flame retardant outer sheath to BS6883

Bilge/fire: Two electrically powered bilge/fire pumps discharge sea water to hydrants for fire-fighting and deck washing or bilge via a bilge manifold with suctions to each watertight com-partment. Fire detection and Halon 1301 extinguishing equipment is installed in machinery rooms

ARMAMENT: Foredeck deck ring for up to 30mm single gun mount. Spigots for GPMGs on bridge wings. Ammunition store below decks forward.

CAPACITIES

Fuel capacity: 16·0 tonnes

Fresh water capacity: 2·5 tonnes

DIMENSIONS

Length overall: 33·0m

Beam: 6·73m

Draught: 1·95m

WEIGHT

Empty: Approx 95 tonnes

PERFORMANCE

Speed, max: Up to 33 knots depending upon machinery installed

Range at 15 knots: 1200n miles

20-METRE PROTECTOR

Fast pilot cutter.

UK Customs and Excise Marine Branch has placed an order for three 26m Protector fast patrol cutters for entry into service during 1988. The craft are a development of the 33m Protector class, designed to meet the needs of HM Customs and Excise for operation anywhere round the coastline of Great Britain.

HULL: Hull, deck and superstructure in welded marine grade aluminium, with integral alloy fuel tanks.

MAIN ENGINES: Two Paxman 12 SET CW marine diesels of 1440bhp each with ZF BW 460S gearboxes, and one single Perkins T6.3544 marine diesel engine of 213shp driving a Hamilton 361 waterjet unit through a marine reverse-reduction gearbox.

PROPULSION: Two fixed-pitch propellers coupled to ZF BW 460S gearboxes via a V-drive, and one Hamilton 361 waterjet unit.

Fairey Marinteknik 33m Protector fast patrol boat; three delivered to the Royal Bahamas Defence Force, 1986

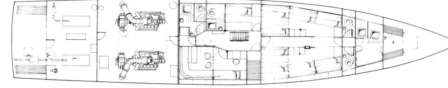

Fairey Marinteknik 33m Protector fast patrol boat

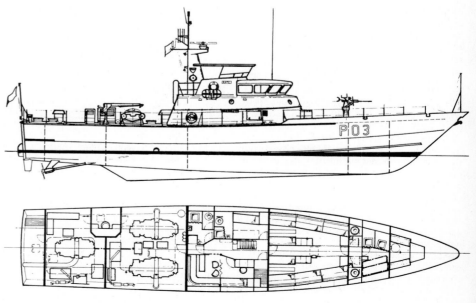

Three-engine layout for Protector

CONTROLS: Power-assisted hydraulic steering system operating twin-linked balanced aerofoil spade rudders.

ACCOMMODATION: Single cabins for commanding officer and seven crew.

SYSTEMS

Auxiliary engines: Two 30kW (continuous) diesel driven 240V single phase 50Hz generator sets and engine driven alternators

Electrical system: 24V dc and 240V, 50Hz single phase

Navigational: Equipment includes two navigational radars, one with ARPA plotter, gyro with repeaters, Decca Navigator Mk 53, direction finder, log, echo sounder and autopilot

Communications: VHF radio and internal communications system

Crane: An hydraulic knuckle boom crane mounted on main deck for launch and recovery of rigid inflatable boarding boat

DIMENSIONS

Length overall: 25·70m

Beam overall: 6·20m

Draught (approx): 1·70m

PERFORMANCE

Speed, max: In excess of 25 knots

Speed, loiter (waterjet only): 8 knots

Endurance: Several days at sea

41-METRE PASSENGER FERRY

Fast passenger ferry.

Presently under construction and due for delivery during summer 1988 this 41m passenger ferry will operate on the Naples/Capri route improving the service frequency by 50%.

DESIGNER: Fairey Marinteknik.

OWNERS: Navigazione Libera Del Golfo SpA, Italy.

CLASSIFICATION: Built to rules of the Code of Safety for Dynamically Supported Craft comparable to the SOLAS and Load Line Conventions, class notation RINa is *100-A (UL) 1.1-Nav. S-TP.

HULL: Superstructure and hull are built in welded marine grade aluminium, sub-divided into seven watertight compartments. A semi-planing hull with a deep-V forward progressing to a shallow-V aft with hard chines.

MAIN ENGINES: Two MTU 12V 396 TB83 marine diesels giving minimum 1180kW each at MCR, 1940rpm at ambient air temperature of 27°C and sea water temperature at 27°C. Engines are coupled to ZF marine reduction gearboxes.

PROPULSION: Two MJP waterjet units, steering deflection angle is 30 degrees port and starboard with an estimated reverse thrust of approximately half of the forward gross thrust.

CONTROLS: All controls and machinery instruments are within reach of the helmsman's seat. Steering and reversing buckets for the waterjets are controlled electro-hydraulically from the wheelhouse. A retractable bow thruster unit is fitted.

CAPACITIES

Fuel oil: 7000 litres

Lubrication oil: 200 litres

Fresh water: 1000 litres

ACCOMMODATION: Two passenger saloons can seat up to 480 passengers, with clearance to carry 350 passengers by the Italian classification authority Registro Italiano Navale on the Naples/Capri route. The main passenger saloons are air-conditioned and trimmed to a high level of

Guardian 21m fast patrol boat design

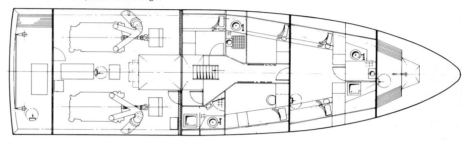

Guardian 21m accommodation layout between decks

comfort. Noise and vibration levels are low due to the waterjet propulsion system.

SYSTEMS

Auxiliary engines: Two diesel generators each driving a 30kVA alternator

Electrical supplies: 380V ac, 50Hz three phase, 220V ac, 50Hz single phase, 24V dc, shore supply connection

DIMENSIONS

Length overall: 41·00m

Beam: 7·80m

Draught: 1·10m

Typical disposable load: 35 tonnes

PERFORMANCE

Max cruising speed at a displacement of 100 tonnes: 28 knots

GUARDIAN FAST PATROL BOAT (DESIGN)

HULL: Hull, deck and deckhouse constructed in all welded marine aluminium alloy.

MAIN ENGINES: Two MTU 12V 396 TB93 fresh water-exchanger cooled marine diesels each maximum rated at 1756shp (1310kW) at 2100rpm driving through ZF BW 455S U drive 2:1 reverse/reduction gearboxes.

PROPULSION: Two Monel K500 100mm diameter propeller shafts running in replaceable water-lubricated rubber bearings in aluminium stern tubes and stainless steel 'P' brackets. Two, fixed-pitch nickel aluminium bronze propellers.

CONTROLS: Two station hand hydraulic steering system operates twin balanced stainless steel rudders. Emergency tiller provided.

CAPACITIES

Fuel: 8700 litres

Fresh water: 1137 litres

COMPLEMENT: Captain, four officers and four ratings.

ACCOMMODATION

Officers: Captain's cabin, two 2-berth officers' cabins, wash place with heads and showers. Wardroom and galley located in deckhouse abaft the wheelhouse

Ratings: Ratings mess, forward fitted with four bunks, lockers, and wardrobes, separate heads, showers and wash place

Wheelhouse: Contains fully equipped stations for helmsman, OOW/navigator, engineer and radio operator. Flying bridge situated on top of wheelhouse with second helmsman's station

SYSTEMS

Auxiliary machinery: 24V dc insulated return; 2 banks of batteries charged by main engine alternators and by transformer/rectifier from 220V ac systems. Two 34kW diesel generators or shore supply provide 220V ac 50Hz single-phase power for all major craft electrical power requirements

Air-conditioning: Accommodation is air-conditioned

ARMAMENT: Foredeck deck ring for 20mm single gun mounting. Spigots for GPMGs on bridge after guard rails.

DIMENSIONS

Length overall: 20·95m

Beam: 6·10m

Draught: 1·75m

PERFORMANCE

Speed, max: 38 knots

continuous: 34 knots

Endurance at 14 knots, UK trial conditions: 700n miles

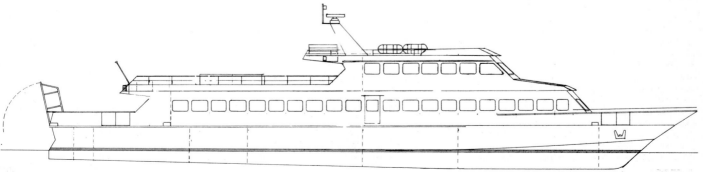

41m fast 350-passenger ferry under construction for Naples/Capri run

HALMATIC LIMITED

Havant, Hampshire PO9 1JR, England

Telephone: (0705) 486161
Telex: 86461 HALMAT G
Telefax: (0705) 453217

R H Hunting, *Chairman*

A G Hopkins, *Managing Director*
C G Dove, *Director*
P G Jones, *Director*

A member of Hunting Associated Industries, Halmatic build a range of commercial, leisure and patrol craft in grp. They also mould hulls for other builders to complete. Hulls are constructed under Lloyds Survey and can be completed to Lloyds, DTI, Bureau Veritas for France, RINa for Italy or equivalent classification. The company is also approved to the British Ministry of Defence Quality Assurance Standard 05/21.

HARGRAVE 85
MARIOLA

Designed by Jack Hargrave, the 85ft (25·91m) hull is a development of the Hargrave 64ft (19·51m) hull and uses the latest advances in grp design. The hull is of semi-displacement form designed for speeds up to 20 knots. Considerable hull volume is provided allowing comfortable coastal or world-wide operation.
DIMENSIONS
Length overall: 25·91m
waterline: 23·24m
Beam: 5·87m
Draught, max: 1·57m
WEIGHTS
Displacement: 70 to 80 tonnes
Hull weight: 13 607kg
PERFORMANCE
Speed, max: 20 knots

Mariola, a 20-knot motor yacht with Halmatic grp hull

SOUTER SHIPYARD LIMITED

Admiralty Gate, Thetis Road, Cowes, Isle of Wight PO31 7JD, England

Telephone: (0983) 294711
Telex: 86520 SOUTER G

W A Souter, *Chairman*
M A Souter, *Managing Director*
K Downer, *Director*
T C Chadwick, *Director*
J Tomlinson, *Financial Director*
P Willis, *Purchasing Manager*
G Truckell, *Production Manager*
T Collins, *Quality Manager*
J Willis, *Design Office Manager*

Founded in 1942 Souter Shipyard Ltd builds high-speed patrol craft, passenger carriers and VIP yachts. Construction is in glass reinforced plastic (grp), aluminium or steel from 5m to 35m in length. Affiliated companies are Souter Copland Composites Limited and Sims Fabrications Limited.

WASP 30-METRE PATROL CRAFT

Design began in early 1984 and trials of the first craft were completed in October 1985.

The hull is of semi-displacement soft chine form with raked stern and a flat, raked or vertical transom. The beam is slightly more than that of conventional craft of this size, which results in a slightly lower maximum top speed, but provides superior sea-going qualities with respect to crew fatigue and efficiency over a period of several days in bad weather. The craft is fully equipped with navigational aids and communication equipment. Accommodation layout is for a normal operational complement of three officers and six crew, enabling the craft to run on a continuous watch system.
HULL: The hull is constructed in grp and is subdivided by transverse bulkheads and frames. Scantlings are approved to Lloyds or similar marine standard agencies. The deck is of grp and

The Souter Wasp 30m patrol boat

integrally bonded to the hull. Superstructure is of marine grade aluminium alloy.
MAIN ENGINES/GEARBOXES: Two GM 16V-149 TI diesel engines, 1550shp each at 1900rpm with 2:1 ratio gearboxes.
PROPULSION: Two Lips Ltd, 1000mm diameter nickel aluminium bronze propellers.
CONTROLS: Hydraulic steering and engine controls.
ACCOMMODATION/CREW
Complement: 3 officers and six ratings
Crew spaces air-conditioned and ventilated
SYSTEMS
Auxiliary engines: Two G & M 47MDP4-63R marine diesel generators, 240V, 50Hz, single-phase giving a maximum output of 47kVA
Fuel tank capacities: Five aluminium tanks, total 17 200 litres
Refuelling points on main deck, port and starboard
Fresh water capacity: 2540 litres
Electrical: 240V ac and 24V dc
Navigational: Gyrocompass, autopilot Decca 450, Sat Nav Furuno FS70, Radar Furuno 1401, Video Plotter GD200
Communications: RT Sunair GSB900MF/HF, Motorola VHF/FM
Life saving: DOTI safety equipment
DIMENSIONS
Length overall: 30·0m
Length waterline: 27·0m
Beam overall: 6·70m
Draught, max including propellers: 1·70m
Air draught, max (waterline to highest mast/aerial): 12·0m
Air draught to cabin top: 7·0m
WEIGHTS
Empty weight (without fuel, crew, payload or provisions): 88 tonnes
Max disposable load (fuel, crew, payload and provisions): 17 tonnes
Design max displacement: 105 tonnes
PERFORMANCE
Speed, cruise: 22·0 knots
max: 25·0 knots
Range: 500n miles at 22 knots

VOSPER THORNYCROFT (UK) LIMITED

Head office: Victoria Road, Woolston, Southampton SO9 5GR, England

Telephone: 0703 445144
Telex: 47682 G

Vosper Thornycroft (UK) Limited continues the shipbuilding business established over a century ago by two separate companies, Vosper Limited and John I Thornycroft & Co Ltd.

These companies merged in 1966 and the organisation has continued the design and construction of warships from fast patrol boats to large frigates.

The company's main activities embrace the design and construction of warships, however hovercraft and hydrofoils have also been built and two 62-metre 27-knot fast passenger ferries were delivered to Hong Kong in early 1985.

Diversified engineering work is also undertaken including the design and manufacture of ship stabilisers and specialised electrical and electronic control equipment for marine and industrial use.

The current range of patrol craft designs extend from 30 to 56 metres in length and can be adapted to naval or coast guard roles.

34-METRE PATROL CRAFT (DESIGN)

Fast patrol boat.

The 34m patrol craft design has been produced for relatively inexperienced shipyards to build and develop their own technology. The craft has been designed under approval of Classification Society Rules thus offering assurance of quality and standards.
HULL: Construction of the hull is in all welded steel with longitudinal framing supported on deep

intermediate transverses and five watertight bulk-heads. The superstructure and machinery casing are constructed in marine grade aluminium alloy. Hull is a fine, well flared deep-V form forward matched to a straight line constant deadrise prismatic run to the transom ensuring good seakeeping, good course-keeping and manoeuvrability.

MAIN ENGINES: Two high-speed marine diesel engines each driving forward into a reverse/reduction gearbox via a cardion and universal joint in a U-drive configuration.

PROPULSION: Two fixed-pitch modern skew blade design propellers.

COMPLEMENT: Commanding Officer, two officers, six senior and six junior ratings.

ACCOMMODATION: Air-conditioned cabins and mess decks for 16 officers and ratings with a centralised galley for the whole complement. Superstructure contains the bridge, and adjacent operations room or CIC.

ARMAMENT: Two single 30mm mountings or one single 40mm automatic gun and one single 30mm gun.

SYSTEMS

Auxiliary engines: Three diesel-driven generator sets which provide ac and dc electrical power

Navigational: Racal S.1230 and Racal AC 1226C radars with interswitchable displays linked to a Racal CANE100 automatic navigational system

Air-conditioning: Provided in living spaces

Firefighting: A firefighting capability can be provided by the installation of two powerful water and foam generators supplied by an independently operated diesel engine-driven fire pump

Fresh water: Reverse Osmosis desalination plant provides continuous fresh water

DIMENSIONS

Length overall: 34·00m
Length waterline: 31·00m
Beam, max: 9·00m
Draught, amidships: 1·25m

PERFORMANCE

Speed, max: 37·5 knots
Speed, at max continuous power: 34·5 knots
Range: 1600n miles
Endurance: 6 days

30-METRE COASTAL PATROL
(DESIGN)

Fast patrol boat.

The 30m coastal patrol boat is designed for prolonged operation at speed in EEZ offshore conditons.

HULL: Construction of hull is in grp with marine grade aluminium superstructure. Hull shape is hard chine with a moderately high deadrise form with a fine entry forward and generous freeboard.

MAIN ENGINES: Two or three turbocharged marine diesels coupled to reverse reduction gearboxes.

PROPULSION: Two or three fixed-pitch propellers, waterjet propulsion optional.

COMPLEMENT: Commanding Officer, two officers, two senior ratings and eleven ratings.

ARMAMENT: One twin 30mm Oerlikon mounting forward and one single 20mm Oerlikon aft, two bridge mountings for GPMGs, one Wallop Stockade decoy launching system with two launchers, and four Wallop chemical smoke generators. Other weapon options available to meet operation requirements.

DIMENSIONS

Length overall: 30·45m
Length, between perpendicular: 26·55m
Breadth, moulded: 6·87m
Depth, moulded: 4·20m

WEIGHT

Displacement, half fuel and water: 95 tonnes

PERFORMANCE

Speed, max: 28 knots

33-METRE PATROL CRAFT

This is a long established design, with a displacement hull form, of which 24 have been built in the UK, and a further 15 have been under construction since 1986 by Bollinger Machine Shop and Shipyard, Inc, USA under licence for the US Coast Guard.

Model of 34m Vosper fast patrol design

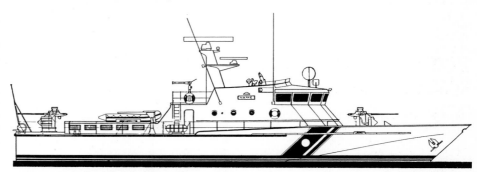

Profile of Vosper 34m fast patrol craft design

Model of Vosper 30m coastal patrol boat design

Vosper 30m coastal patrol boat design profile

DIMENSIONS

Length overall: 33·5m
Beam overall: 6·4m
Draught amidships: 1·9m

PERFORMANCE

With two 16-cylinder diesels, speed: 30 knots
Range: 1400n miles

CHEUNG KONG AND JU KONG

Two ferries have been built for Hong Kong owners Hi-Speed Ferries, and are operating over a 37n mile route between Hong Kong and Macau in competition with various types of high-speed ferry.

Each vessel was delivered with a layout for 659 seated passengers, plus four casino areas, and with a crew of 20.

The final design for the Hi-Speed Ferries is the culmination of several years of research and expertise. The overall philosophy for the project has been to provide the utmost in passenger comfort, entertainment and safety. Seating has been especially designed and manufactured in the UK, using the latest ergonomic concepts for maximum sea-going comfort. Additional care has been taken to ensure a minimum of noise and vibration, along with the installation of the latest in roll damping equipment. All accommodation spaces are fully air-conditioned, and food and beverage services are available on all three decks. The owners intend to fit a video TV system in three saloons; a fourth saloon is an observation lounge.

The vessels have been designed to meet the classification requirements of the American Bureau of Shipping. The passenger certificate has been issued by the Hong Kong Marine Department, the vessels are registered Class II Ships engaged in short international voyages primarily between Hong Kong and Macau.

PROPULSION AND CONTROL: Propulsive power for the vessels is provided by four Paxman Valenta 16RP 200M diesel engines each developing 3000shp. The engines are arranged in pairs, each pair driving a KaMeWa controllable-pitch

Cheung Kong on trials in the Solent

propeller via Renk combining/reduction gearboxes and forged hollow steel shafts.

The engine room and auxiliary machinery space are arranged with convenient access for operation and maintenance. Removal routes for main machinery are via the exhaust casing and also via portable panels in the decks. The vessels are designed and certified to operate with unmanned engine rooms, with all controls for starting, stopping, speed and directional control for main machinery and associated systems, located on the bridge.

Twin spade rudders are fitted outboard of the propeller centrelines actuated by a Wagner electro-hydraulic pack.

SYSTEMS

Electrical: Ship's service electrical power is provided by two diesel generator sets (Caterpillar diesels and Mawdsley alternators) producing 380V, 3ph, 3-wire, 50Hz. An emergency generator set of the same output but smaller capacity is also fitted. Transformers provide 220V, 1ph, 50Hz for primary lighting and general domestic services. An emergency dc

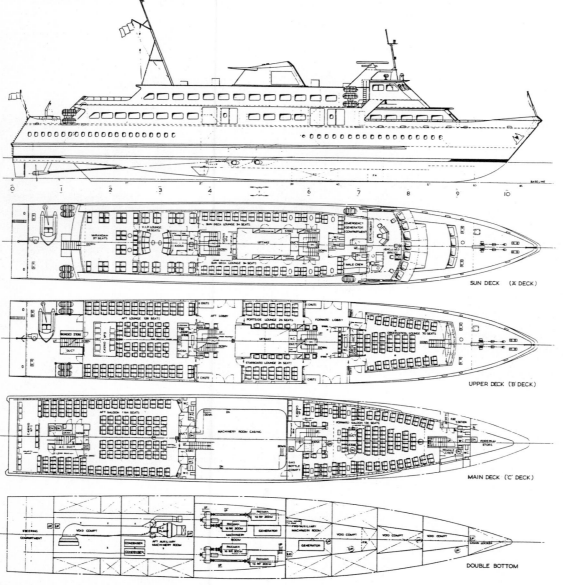

General Arrangement of Vosper ferries, *Cheung Kong* and *Ju Kong*

supply is provided for lighting and emergency communications equipment

Lifesaving: Modern lifesaving and passenger evacuation systems are installed. In an emergency, passenger evacuation is by way of an RFD Limited Marine Escape System Mk 5, comprising inflatable slides and platforms approved by the Department of Transport (UK) and Hong Kong Marine Department. Each vessel carries four escape systems supplemented by additional 42-person liferafts to give a total capacity in excess of the vessel's total occupancy. Each escape system consists of an inflatable platform and slide packed in a door stowage at the escape points in the lobbies at B deck level

CONSTRUCTION: Hull including B and C decks—welded mild steel. Superstructure including A deck—welded aluminium alloy.

MACHINERY

Main engines: Four 3000hp Paxman Valenta 16CM

Gearboxes: Two Renk 4:1 ratio, twin input, single output

Propellers: Two 2·3m diameter KaMeWa controllable-pitch

Generators: Two 3408 Caterpillar main generators; one 3304 Caterpillar emergency set

DIMENSIONS

Length overall: 62·5m
    on waterline: 58·3m
Beam moulded: 10·2m
Depth moulded: 4·3m
Draught, max: 3·2m

WEIGHT

Displacement: 500 tonnes
GRT: 1150

PERFORMANCE

Speed at full load and max continuous power: 27·5 knots
Service speed: 25 knots
Fuel consumption: 2·1 tonnes/h

ATLANTIC CHALLENGER III
    Challenger for Atlantic speed record.

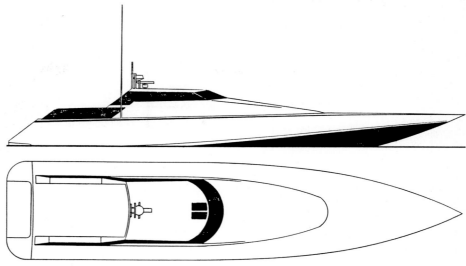

Preliminary lines of *Atlantic Challenger III*

OWNER: Tom Gentry, Honolulu, Hawaii.
DESIGN
Vessel: Peter Birkett
Engineering: Peter Dowie
Electrical: Ian Starr
LAUNCH: March 1988. See Addenda.
ATLANTIC CROSSING: Summer 1988.
HULL: V bottom, aluminium, fully welded with three watertight bulkheads. Wheelhouse has a welded framework with a rivet-bonded skin.
MAIN ENGINES: Two MTU 16V 396 TB94 sequentially turbocharged marine diesels 3480hp (2560kW) each at 2100rpm fitted with two ZF BU 755 1·87 reduction gearboxes.
PROPULSION: Two KaMeWa 63 waterjets incorporating steering and reversing gear.
CAPACITIES: Combination of double bottom tanks and flexible fuel cells with a total capacity of 45 tonnes.
ACCOMMODATION
Wheelhouse: Dual driving station including

engine and JPS controls, trim flap controls, magnetic and electronic compasses and autopilot, rpm, helm and log readouts. Navigation station including primary radar, electronic chart and navigators system, electronic compass and log repeaters, SSB and UHF radios. Engineer's station includes all engine instruments, fuel gauges and No 2 radar, switching for fuel valves and pumps. Off duty seating accommodation for 6
Below decks: Shower, heads, keyhole bunks for eight, access forward to foredeck
SYSTEMS
Firefighting: Manually operated Halon fire extinguisher system
Lifesaving: Argos beacon, two 8-man life rafts, survival suits, EPIRBs
DIMENSIONS
Length overall: 33·50m
Beam, max: 7·30m
Deadrise, aft: 18°

Ju Kong and *Cheung Kong* ready for shipment from the UK to Hong Kong

UNITED STATES OF AMERICA

ALUMINIUM BOATS INC

Crown Point, Louisiana, USA

77-FOOT ALUMINIUM FERRY BOAT

The first of these craft, to a design by J B Hargrave, Naval Architects, was built in 1979 and a sister vessel was completed in 1986. The vessels are operated by Sheplers Inc of Mackinaw City, Michigan, and operated on the Mackinaw City to Mackinac Island route. Two earlier fast ferries designed by J B Hargrave but built by Camcraft were the 18·3m *The Welcome* and the 17·1m *Felicity* with carrying capacities of 120 and 150 passengers respectively.

THE HOPE

ENGINES: Three GM 12V-71 TI diesels, V-drive induction gears.
ACCOMMODATION: 265 passengers.
DIMENSIONS
Length overall: 23·48m
waterline: 21·34m
Beam: 6·10m
Draught: 1·61m
PERFORMANCE
Speed, light: 24 knots
loaded: 20 knots

STERLING

Fast passenger ferry.
OWNERS: Boston Harbour Commuter Service.
The *Sterling* is a converted crew boat, ex *Sterling Fryou*, built in 1980 by Camcraft Inc for Bailey Marine service. The craft operates on 9·8 mile ferry run from Hingham Shipyard to Rowes Wharf, Boston.
MAIN ENGINES: Two Detroit Diesel 12V-71 TI diesel engines developing 510hp each at 2100rpm.
ACCOMMODATION: 150 passengers. Main cabin on the main deck seats 80 served by a small galley providing refreshments. Below the main deck there is seating for 39 plus lounge tables. The outer upper deck is certified for 100 passengers.
SYSTEMS
Auxiliary machinery: Two 40kW Detroit Diesel 371 engines with Delco generators
Navigational: Two radars
Communications: Crew boat communications sets retained
DIMENSIONS
Length: 30·48m
Beam: 7·31m
Draught: 1·52m
PERFORMANCE
Speed: 26 knots

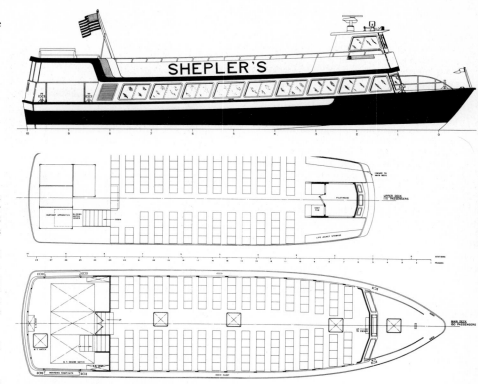

The Hope, a 265-seat 20-knot ferry

Sterling, a converted crew boat passenger ferry

BLOUNT MARINE CORPORATION

461 Water Street, Warren, Rhode Island 02885, USA

Telephone: (401) 245 8300

Luther H Blount, *President*
George Des Lauriers, *Chief Designer*
Ronald Baer, *Works Manager*
William Estrella, *Director of Marketing*

Blount Marine Corporation was formed in 1952 and as of August 1985 had designed and built 261 vessels ranging in size from 5 to 80m. Among the many types built has been the world's first small stern trawler and a significant number of all types of passenger/commuter vessels including mini-cruise ships, making Blount Marine one of the best known small passenger-boat builders in the USA. The Hitech composite hull was invented by Luther Blount.

HITECH EXPRESS

Hull No 251, Design No P452.
A multi-purpose craft design started in 1983 and built in 1984. The vessel has been granted USCG Certification for 149 passengers. Two smaller versions have been built.
Hitech Express has been engaged in demon-strating reliable, fast economical commuting service in the USA. It has made 5 runs to New York City from Warren, Rhode Island, a distance of 150 miles, in just over 5 hours (November 1984, May 1985, June 1985). It has made the run from the Battery, New York, to Staten Island fully loaded in 10 minutes, against 28 minutes via conventional ferry; also crossed the Hudson at mid-Manhattan in 2 minutes 46 seconds (in November 1984 and June 1985).
POWERPLANT: Two GM 12V-71 TI, 510shp at 2300rpm (each).
PROPELLERS: Two 711mm diameter, 622mm pitch Columbian Bronze bronze.
FUEL TANK: Integral 1923-litre.
FUEL: No 2 diesel.
CONTROLS: Throttle and clutch controls Morse MD-24 single lever type using sprockets, roller chain, ss cable, aluminium fairleads and Morse Instrument control unit mounted on each engine. Steering through Wagner hydraulic system. Trim tabs manually adjusted type.
HULL: Aluminium structural frames, bulkheads and decks with polyurethane foam sprayed over and a layed up glassfibre skin ¼" to ⅜" thick forming the outer hull covering.
ACCOMMODATION/CREW
Wheelhouse: Full-width console, engine instrument panel and engine alarm panel
Crew: One licensed operator and one deckhand

Passenger accommodation: Men's and women's toilet space, carpeting, or non-skid decking, fixed or movable seating, superstructure insulation, interior finish work, sound insulation, air-conditioning, heating, portable bar, and PA system optional. Cabin has aluminium framed and plated interior with fixed and sliding cabin windows and life preservers stowed in overhead racks. Ventilated through door and windows, air-conditioning and heat optional
SYSTEMS
Emergency exits and safety equipment: Life preservers, one ring buoy, one rescue ladder, flares, four fire extinguishers, one fire axe, 100ft fire hose, fire and bilge pump, first aid kit and anchor, all as required by USCG
Electrical: Two 60A alternators, one on each main engine providing 32V dc power throughout vessel. Engine room area available for optional generator
Communications and navigation: Radio: One Regency MT-5500 VHF or equal, standard equipment. Radar: One Furuno FR-240 or equal, standard equipment. Compass, horn and searchlight
DIMENSIONS
EXTERNAL
Length overall: 23·48m
Length waterline: 22·66m
Beam overall: 6·10m

Blount Marine *Hitech Express*

Draught (max, including propeller(s)): 1·12m
Air draught, max (waterline to highest mast or aerial): 7·16m
Air draught to cabin top: 3·05m
INTERNAL
Cabin, length: 15·24m
   max width: 5·64m
   max height: 2·11m
   floor area: 68·28m²
Doors, forward and aft: 0·91 × 1·98mm

Freight deck area, exterior aft: 27·87m²
WEIGHTS
Empty weight: 23·87 tonnes
Max payload: 15·00 tonnes
Max disposable load (fuel, crew, payload and provisions): 15·00 tonnes
Design max displacement: 56·39 tonnes
GRT: 65·59
PERFORMANCE (at max displacement)
Max speed, calm water (max power): 27·8 knots

Cruising (service) speed, calm water (max continuous power): 24·3 knots
Turning circle diameter starting at cruising speed: 60m
Rate of turn starting at cruising speed: Approx 15°/s
Crash stop, stopping distance: 24m
Time to accelerate to cruising speed: 15-20 seconds
Max permissible Sea State: 1·5m to 4-5 Beaufort
Range at cruising speed: 250/300 miles

BOLLINGER MACHINE SHOP & SHIPYARD INC

PO Box 250, Lockport, Louisiana 70374, USA

Telephone: (504) 532 2554
Telex: 58 4127

Donald G Bollinger, *Chairman*
Richard Bollinger, *President*
George Bollinger, *General Manager*
Donald T Bollinger, *Chief Executive Officer*

Founded in 1946 Bollinger expanded from a machine shop/repair facility to building offshore work boats for the oil industry. In August 1985 the company was awarded a contract to build 16 of the 'Island' class patrol boats for the US Coast Guard. The hull is the well proven 33·50m patrol boat design by Vosper Thornycroft (UK) Ltd and the superstructure has been adapted to meet US Coast Guard operational requirements. The twelfth craft of the 16 craft order was delivered in November 1986, and the remaining four were due for completion in early 1987.

'ISLAND' CLASS 33-METRE PATROL BOAT

FARALLON 1st boat
AQUIDNECK 9th boat
SANIBEL 12th boat
HULL: Designed by Vosper Thornycroft (UK) Ltd and built in steel with an aluminium superstructure.
MAIN ENGINES/GEARBOXES: Two Paxman Valenta 16RP 200M V type; 3000bhp at 1500rpm (max), 2910shp at 802rpm (max). Engines are coupled to Zahnradfabrik (ZF) gearboxes, ratio 1·87:1.
PROPULSION: Two Vosper Thornycroft five-blade (skewed) propellers, 1257mm diameter, 1066-1549mm pitch (0·7R)
CONTROLS: Vosper Thornycroft steering system. Paxman engine controls.
ACCOMMODATION
Complement: 18
SYSTEMS
Auxiliary engines: Two Caterpillar 3304T, 99kW generators
Fresh water tank capacity: 6661 litres
Fuel oil (95%) tank capacity: 39 295 litres
ARMAMENT: One 20mm Mk-16 gun and two M-60 machine guns.
DIMENSIONS
Length overall: 33·52m

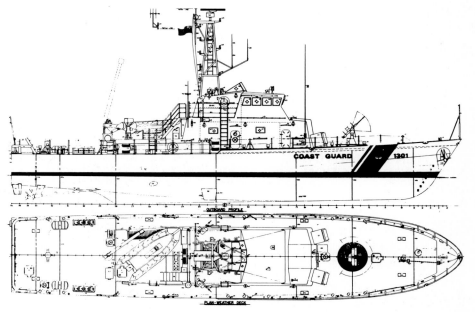

General Arrangement of *Farallon*

Bollinger built *Aquidneck*, the ninth of the 16 patrol boats to be built for the US Coast Guard

Beam overall: 6·40m
Depth, moulded, deck amidships: 3·35m
Draught, mean to design waterline: 1·98m
WEIGHTS
Design displacement: 167·76 tonnes
Displacement, light: 119·17 tonnes

PERFORMANCE
Speed, max sustained cruising: 26·0 knots (half load)
Speed, economical cruising: 12·80 knots
Speed, max: In excess of 26 knots
Max range at economical speed: 3380n miles

BREAUX'S BAY CRAFT INC

PO Box 306, Loreauville, Louisiana 70552, USA

Telephone: (318) 229 4246/7

Roy Breaux, Sr, *President*
Roy Breaux, Jr, *Vice-President*
Royce E Breaux, *Vice-President*
Jerry Lagrange, Sr, *Sales*
Hub Allums, *Sales*

AGATHE

Crew boat.
OWNER: Compagnie des Moyens de Surfaces Adaptes à L'Exploitation des Océans (SURF), serving ELF offshore Cameroun fields 5 times weekly since 1982.
CLASSIFICATION: Bureau Veritas I3/3 – Special Service – coastal waters.
HULL: Constructed in aluminium.
BUILT/LAUNCHED: 1979.
MAIN ENGINES: Three GM 16V-92 marine diesels, maximum rating 730hp each at 2150rpm; continuous 680hp at 2000rpm
PROPULSION: Three four-blade propellers.
ACCOMMODATION
Crew: Captain, engineer and seaman/cook
Passengers: Seating on deck level: 22
    Seating below deck: 43
SYSTEMS
Auxiliary engines: Two generators type Delco-GM 3L 71, 30kW
Fuel tank capacity: 1300 litres
Navigation equipment: Two radars, one autopilot and one echo sounder
Communications: One SSB radio and two VHF radios
Air-conditioning: Fully air-conditioned
Lifesaving: In accordance with Solas regulations. One Zodiac inflatable and outboard
DIMENSIONS
Length overall: 34·90m
Beam: 7·32m

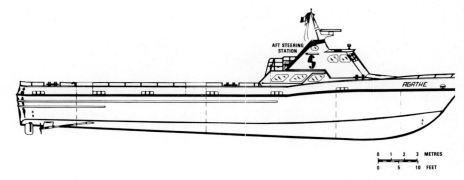

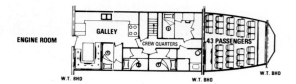

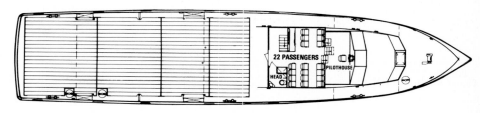

Agathe built by Breaux's Bay for SURF

Draught: 1·93m
Air draught, max: 7·62m
Air draught to cabin top: 6·10m
GRT: 190·72
NRT: 139·50
WEIGHTS
Empty weight: 65·0 tonnes

Payload: 25 tonnes on deck
Max disposable load: 33 tonnes
Designed max displacement: 100 tonnes
PERFORMANCE
Speed, max: 24 knots (light ship)
    cruising: 22 knots (half load)
Range at cruising speed: 1000n miles (48 hours)

CHRISTENSEN MOTOR YACHT CORPORATION

4400 Columbia Way, Vancouver, Washington 98661, USA

Telephone: (206) 695 7671
Telex: 754607 CHRISTENSEN
Telefax: (206) 695 6038

David H Christensen, *President*

The company builds production motor yachts of double Airex cored grp construction; Kevlar and carbon fibre materials are also used in areas of high stress. A standard mould is used for building hulls from 29m to 39m in length, which can be widened for different lengths and engine power requirements. Alternative superstructures are installed to meet individual owners' requirements. Unless otherwise specified Christensen yachts are built under ABS standard inspections.

Craft built and under construction

Craft	Speed	Delivered
37m Motor yacht	35 knots	December 1987
40m Motor yacht	22 knots	April 1988
40m Motor yacht	22 knots	July 1988
30m Motor yacht	22 knots	October 1988

CHRISTENSEN CXV

Pilot house motor yacht.
HULL: Double Airex cored grp and Kevlar construction.
MAIN ENGINES: Two Caterpillar 3412 marine diesel engines 605shp continuous rating at 1800rpm, 813shp intermittent at 2100rpm coupled to Twin Disc MG 514 marine gearboxes. Optional MTU, Cummins and GM engines available to attain speeds exceeding 35 knots.
CONTROLS: Hydraulic steering system and single lever air clutch and throttle controls fitted in pilot house.
CAPACITIES
Fuel: 26 495 litres
Motor oil: 416 litres
Used oil: 227 litres
Holding tank: 1892 litres
Fresh water: 3406 litres
Hot water: 250 litres
ACCOMMODATION: Owner's double cabin plus two separate bathrooms, galley, pantry, dining room and saloon are situated on the main deck. Three double guest cabins, two bathrooms and accommodation for Captain and crew of six with requisite heads and showers situated on lower deck. Alternative layout available for Captain's cabin to be fitted abaft the pilot house on the boat deck.
SYSTEMS
Auxiliary engines: Two Northern Lights 1800rpm 60kW generator sets
Bow thruster: Optional extra
Stabiliser system: Optional extra
Air-conditioning: Two-stage air-conditioning and heating system, Aqua-Air or equivalent
DIMENSIONS
Length overall: 36·57m
Length waterline: 32·30m
Beam: 8·15m
Draught: 1·82m
WEIGHTS
Displacement light: 88·30 tonnes
Displacement heavy: 120·31 tonnes
PERFORMANCE
Speed, max: 10 to 30 knots depending on hp of engines

CHRISTENSEN VC

Motor yacht.
HULL: Double Airex cored grp and Kevlar construction.
MAIN ENGINES: Two Caterpillar 3412 marine diesel engines 605shp continuous rating at 1800rpm, 813shp intermittent yacht rating at 2100rpm coupled to Twin Disc MG 514 marine gearboxes. Optional MTU, Cummins and GM engines available to attain speeds exceeding 35 knots.
CONTROLS: Hydraulic steering system and single lever air clutch and throttle controls fitted in pilot house.
CAPACITIES
Fuel: 26 495 litres
Motor oil: 416 litres
Used oil: 227 litres
Holding tank: 1892 litres
Fresh water: 3406 litres
Hot water: 250 litres

Finishing of a Christensen composite plastic hull

ACCOMMODATION: Owner's cabin and suite, two double guest cabins plus two separate bathrooms, Captain's cabin and crew accommodation in two double cabins situated on lower deck. Galley dining saloon, lounge area and pilot house are on the main deck with a seating area above on the boat deck.

SYSTEMS

Auxiliary engines: Two Northern Lights 1800rpm 60kW generator sets

Bow thruster: Optional extra
Stabiliser system: Optional extra
Air-conditioning: Two-stage air-conditioning and heating system, Aqua-air or equivalent

DIMENSIONS

Length overall: 30·48m
Length, waterline: 25·60m
Beam: 7·62m
Draught: 1·82m

WEIGHTS

Displacement, light: 77·18 tonnes
Displacement, heavy: 104·42 tonnes

PERFORMANCE

Speed, max: 10 to 30 knots depending on hp of engines fitted

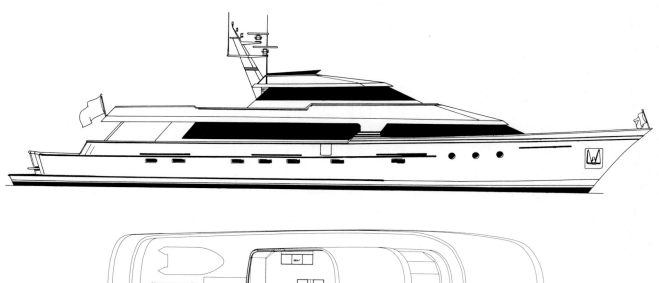

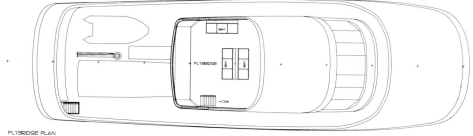

FLYBRIDGE PLAN

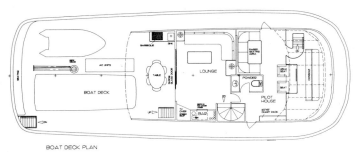

BOAT DECK PLAN

ALTERNATE BOAT DECK

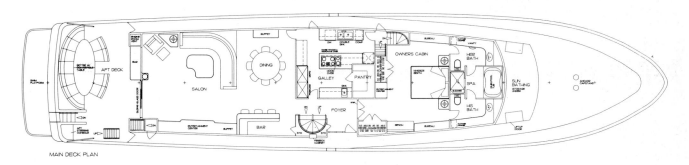

MAIN DECK PLAN

LOWER DECK PLAN

Christensen CXV 36·57m motor yacht

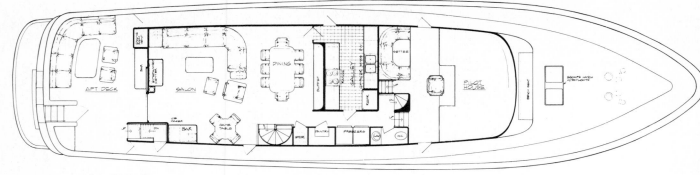

MAIN DECK PLAN

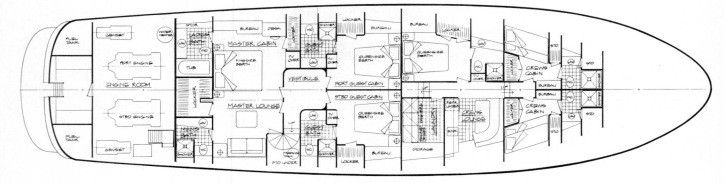

LOWER DECK PLAN

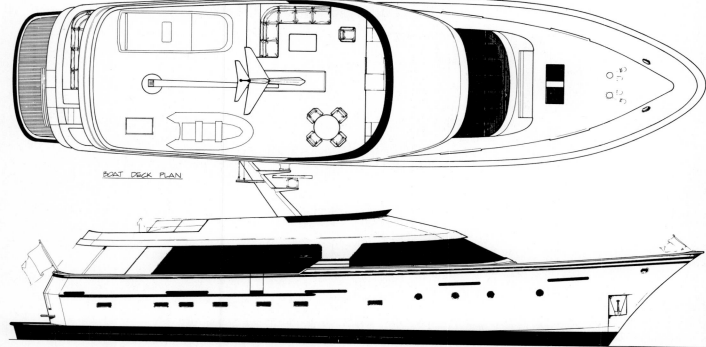

BOAT DECK PLAN

Christensen VC 30·46m motor yacht

DENISON MARINE INC

750 North East 7th Avenue, PO Box 805, Dania, Florida 33004, USA

Telephone: (305) 920 0622/4011
Telex: 316387 DENSHIP
Telefax: (305) 920 6553

Kit Denison, *President*
Joseph Langlois, *Vice President of Production*
Carl Bischoff, *Vice President of Production*

Denison Marine Inc specialises in the design and construction of aluminium motor yachts from 20 to 40m in length. At its inception in 1983, the company integrated modern automation technologies in shipbuilding with traditional craftmanship and attention to detail. Both conventional and modern yachts are manufactured in the US.

Denison Marine *Haggis II* driven by two Arneson Surface Drive units, type ASD 16

Denison Marine has pioneered the use of waterjet propulsion in yachts over 30·5m that exceed 34 knots. High performance hulls from 23·8 to 38·7m, capable of speeds beyond 50 knots, are presently under construction.

FOR YOUR EYES ONLY

Raised bridge motor yacht, built December 1985, hull No 103, fitted with trim tabs and bow thrusters.

HULL: Welded aluminium.

MAIN ENGINES: Two MTU 12V 396 TB93, 1931shp each, at 2100rpm, fitted with ZF BW 455, 2·27:1 reduction gears.

PROPULSION UNITS: Two KaMeWa type 63 waterjet units.

ACCOMMODATION/EQUIPMENT: Sleeps eight in four staterooms, four berths for crew. The three guest staterooms have twin or queen-size berths, hanging lockers, drawers and heads with showers. Flybridge lounge area has over 8m of seating, Mar Quipt hydraulic crane, 4·6m Bayliner tender with 85hp outboard, and lighted helicopter landing pad. Push-button, automatic fold-forward mast to clear helicopter rotor blades. Fully equipped galley.

ELECTRONICS: Anschutz autopilot; VHF, Standard USA; SSB Furuno/Skanti TRP-8258; Radar, Furuno FCR-1411 colour; Satnav, Furuno FSN-700; speed log, Datamarine 3000W/ S100KL Remote; two VHF ICOM 80C; CB, Cybernet CTX 40 + 4; Cellular Telephone, NEC M 5000 R; Loran, Northstar 800 Loran C; two depth sounders, Datamarine 3000W/3030 remote; Mentor Fuel Management Computer.

PERFORMANCE

Speed, cruising: over 30 knots

For Your Eyes Only built by Denison Marine

For Your Eyes Only

Denison motor yacht production in 1987

Hull No	Name	Length overall (m)	Beam (m)	Draught (m)	Type of motor yacht	Displacement half load (tonnes)	Engines	Propulsion units	Berths	Speed max (knots)
103	*For Your Eyes Only*	30·48	6·71	1·22	Raised bridge	92·5	Two MTU 12V 396 TB 93 1931shp each at 2100rpm	KaMeWa 63 waterjets	8 + 4 crew	34
112	*Nena VIII*	33·23	7·62	1·22	Raised bridge	114·8	Two MTU 16V 396 TB 93 2574shp each at 2100rpm	KaMeWa 71 waterjets	8 + 5 crew	38
114	*Quest*	33·54	6·71	1·75	Raised bridge	101·6	Two MTU 16V 396 TB 94 3432shp each at 2100rpm	KaMeWa 71 waterjets	8 + 5 crew	50 + †
116	*Thunderbolt*	31·40	6·71	1·75	Raised bridge cockpit	95·5	Two MTU 12V 396 TB 93 1931shp each at 2100rpm	KaMeWa 56 waterjets	10 + 4 crew	36
120	*Haggis II*	23·78	5·79	1·07	High-performance deep-Vee	40·64	Two MWM 604B 1938shp each at 1800rpm	Arneson Drive ASD 16	6 + 2 crew	45*

†Based on tank tests at Davidson Laboratory, Stevens Institute of Technology.
Haggis II, trials result, August 1987, reaching predicted value.

ROBERT E DERECKTOR OF RHODE ISLAND INC

There are three shipyards in the group and the craft covered in this entry will appear under the appropriate yard. The group have built over 260 boats up to 82 metres in length.

Robert E Derecktor, *President*

DERECKTOR SHIPYARD
(Rhode Island)

Coddington Cove, Middletown, Rhode Island 02840, USA

Telephone: (401) 847 9270
TWX: 710 387 6305
Telefax: (401) 846 1570

Geoff Prior, *Director of Marketing and Sales*

35-METRE PATROL BOAT (DESIGN)

HULL: All welded aluminium construction.
MAIN ENGINES
Standard: Two Paxman Valenta 12RP 200 marine diesels each developing 3000bhp at 1600rpm and coupled to ZF reduction gearboxes 2·03:1 ratio
Option: Two MTU 16V 538 TB92 marine diesels

each developing 4080bhp at 1900rpm and coupled to ZF reduction gearboxes 2·16:1 ratio
CAPACITIES
Fuel capacity: 20 tons
COMPLEMENT: 18.
DIMENSIONS
Length overall: 35·0m
Length, waterline: 32·60m

Beam: 6·50m
Depth, amidships: 3·50m
WEIGHT
Displacement: 152·40 tonnes
PERFORMANCE
Speed, max (fitted with standard engines): 29 knots
Speed, max (fitted with optional engines): 32 knots

Derecktor 35m patrol boat design

50-METRE PATROL BOAT
(DESIGN)
HULL: Aluminium construction.
MAIN ENGINES
Standard: Two MTU 16V 396 TB83 marine diesel engines each developing 2070bhp at 2000rpm. One Detroit Allison 571-K gas turbine developing 6830bhp at 10 500rpm
Option: Three Paxman Valenta 16RP 200CM marine diesel engines each developing 4000bhp at 1600rpm
PROPULSION: KaMeWa waterjets.
CAPACITIES
Fuel capacity: 38·10 tonnes
COMPLEMENT: 30.
DIMENSIONS
Length overall: 50·30m
Length, waterline: 47·71m
Beam: 8·42m
Depth, amidships: 4·12m
WEIGHT
Displacement: 269·24 tonnes
PERFORMANCE
Speed, max (fitted with standard engines): 45 knots
Speed, max (fitted with optional engines): 38 knots

DERECKTOR SHIPYARD
(New York)
311 E Boston Post Road, Mamaroneck, New York 10543, USA

Telephone: (914) 698 5020
TWX: 64 6904
Telefax: (914) 698 4641

Paul Derecktor, *President*

DERECKTOR 90 MOTOR YACHT
(DESIGN)
HULL: Constructed in aluminium.
MAIN ENGINES: Two MTU 12V 396 TB94 marine diesels.
PROPULSION: Two propellers.
CAPACITIES
Fuel: 22 710 litres
DIMENSIONS
Length overall: 27·61m
Beam: 6·70m
PERFORMANCE
Speed, max: 50 knots

FIRE ISLAND CLIPPER
Designed by Roper Associates, this vessel entered service 9 December 1979. She is built in 5086 aluminium alloy and powered by three GM 12V-71 diesel engines. The tunnel installed propellers are also protected by skegs. The craft has a length of 22·87m, beam 6·71m and a draught of 1·07m. A full passenger load of 350 can be carried.

Fire Island Clipper is believed to be the first all-aluminium high-capacity fast ferry to be built in the United States. There are nine sister vessels. *Fire Island Clipper* is owned by Wayfarer Leasing Corporation and is leased to Sayville Ferry Service, Inc, Long Island, New York.

See Operators' section for photograph of this vessel.

DERECKTOR GUNNELL, INC
(Florida)
775 Taylor Lane, Dania, Florida 33004, USA

Telephone: (305) 920 5756
TWX: 99 0116
Telefax: (305) 925 1146

Skip Gunnell, *Director*

Three high-performance luxury yacht designs are offered by this yard, the QED 50ft, 61ft and 70ft.

TRIDENT 105
A high-speed waterjet-propelled motor yacht under construction in early 1987, built to American Bureau of Shipping Maltese Cross A1 for Yachting Service.

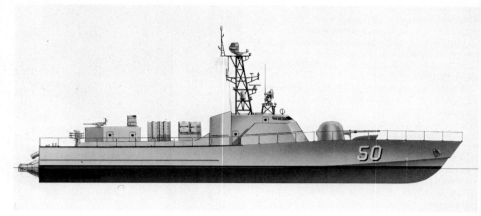

Derecktor 50m patrol boat design

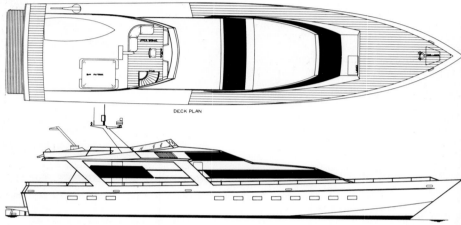

Derecktor 90ft 50-knot motor yacht design

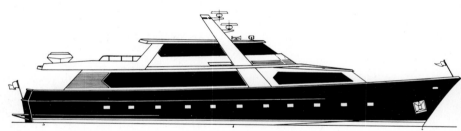

Trident 105 32m motor yacht

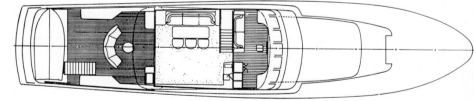

Trident 105 sun deck level

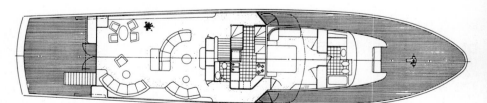

Trident 105 main deck

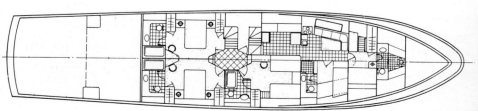

Trident 105 cabin plan

DESIGNERS: Sparkman & Stephens Inc, 79 Madison Avenue, New York, NY 10016, USA.

HULL: Aluminium alloy, 5086 series welded aluminium, 6061 aluminium extrusions, teak main deck and boat deck.

MAIN ENGINES: Two MTU 12V 396 TB93 diesel engines 1960hp each.

PROPULSION: Two KaMeWa series 63 water-jet units.

CAPACITIES
Fuel: 22 710 litres
Water: 6056 litres
Holding tanks (fibre glass): 2271 litres
Sump tanks (fibre glass): 378·5 litres

ACCOMMODATION
Sun deck: Pilothouse, saloon, boat deck with settees, seats and Jennaire electric barbecue

Main deck: Master state room and bathroom, entertainment centre with TV, VCR and radio, galley, main saloon entertainment centre

Lower deck: Two double-berth cabins and bathrooms, one cabin with two twin-size berths and bathroom. Captain's stateroom with double-berth and bathroom, double crew cabin with heads and shower, crews lounge and kitchenette

SYSTEMS
Auxiliary machinery: One 75kW Northern Lights generator and one 30kW slow speed Northern Lights night generator

Bow thrusters: Richfield 400mm retractable hydraulic bow thrusters with two control stations

Air-conditioning: Three 60 000Btu J D Nall water chiller units for air-conditioning throughout including engine room

Fresh water: Two Sea Recovery 2271 litres/day reverse osmosis water makers

Hot water: Two 170-litre hot water heaters with circulating pumps

Navigational: One Raytheon NGR and one Raytheon 3710 radar, one Raytheon SNA9-8 colour charting IBM PC planning terminal, one Furuno F5N-70 satnav system, one North Star 800X loran system, one Robertson-Shipmate Commander autopilot, one Raytheon weather fax system and Brookes and Gatehouse system instruments

Communications: VHF Incom Sailor, SSB Furuno Skanti TRP 82585, 250W, one Aiphone intercom system, Kenwood Bang & Olfson stereo system, and ACR-EPIRB

Tender: One Zodiac 5m hard bottom launch with 90hp Evinrude outboard

DIMENSIONS
Length overall: 32·00m
Length waterline: 27·66m
Beam: 7·01m
Draught: 1·22m

DERECKTOR 66

WICKED WITCH III
High-speed motor yacht.

OWNER: Donald Ford.

HULL: Aluminium alloy, stepped surface hull form, skeg on centreline.

MAIN ENGINES: Two GM 12V-71 T marine diesels 870hp each coupled to 195 ZF, V-drive gearboxes, propeller shaft angle: 7°.

DIMENSIONS
Length overall: 20·11m
Length waterline: 16·38m
Beam, max: 5·41m
Beam, waterline: 4·80m
Draught: 1·67m

WEIGHT
Displacement: 29·51 tonnes

PERFORMANCE
Speed, max: 33 knots

23-METRE PATROL BOAT

HULL: Aluminium alloy.

MAIN ENGINES: Two GM 12V-92 MTI marine diesels maximum rating 975bhp each at 2300rpm coupled to ZF reverse/reduction V-drive 2:1 ratio. Optional engines Mercedes-Benz MTU 331 maximum rating 1600bhp each at 2340rpm.

PROPULSION: Twin propellers.

CAPACITIES
Fuel: 15 140 litres
Fuel auxiliary (helicopter): 1890 litres

Fresh water: 756 litres

COMPLEMENT: 10.

SYSTEMS
Auxiliary machinery: Ac power provided by GM 2150 diesel generator 35kW 110/220V 3-phase powered by GM 2-71 diesel engine. Dc power provided by Constavolt La Marche A-5-60, 24V batteries six lead acid type, Surette 12V

Fresh water: Reverse osmosis fresh water maker

DIMENSIONS
Length overall: 23·44m
Length waterline: 21·35m
Beam, max: 4·88m
Depth, amidships: 3·05m
Draught, max: 1·93m

WEIGHTS
Displacement, light: 31·75 tonnes
Displacement: 43·09 tonnes

PERFORMANCE
Speed, max with GM 12V-92 MTI engines: 28·5 knots
    Range at 22 knots: 1100 miles
Speed, max with MTU 331 engines: 40 knots
    Range at max speed: 1000 miles

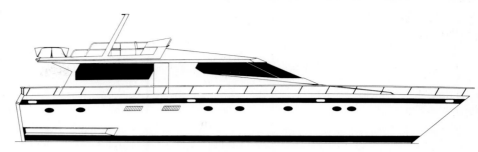

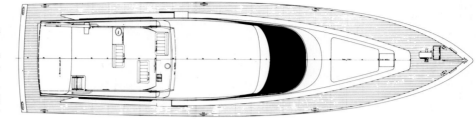

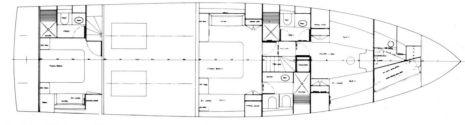

Derecktor 66, profile deck plan and accommodation

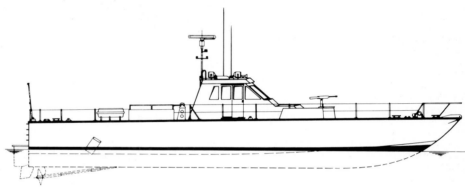

23m patrol boat outboard profile

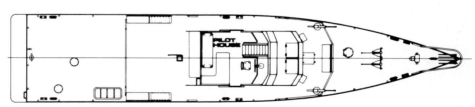

23m patrol boat deck plan

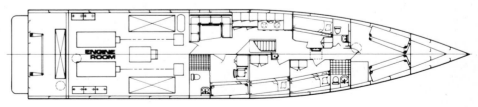

23m patrol boat interior plan

GLADDING-HEARN SHIPBUILDING

ie Duclos Corporation

One Riverside Avenue, Box 300, Somerset, Massachusetts 02706-0300, USA

Telephone: (617) 676 8596
Telefax: (617) 672 1873

George R Duclos, *President*

Sandy Hook 24-knot pilot boat, designed by C Raymond Hunt Associates

SANDY HOOK

Pilot boat for Port of New York.
DESIGNERS: C Raymond Hunt Associates Inc, 69 Long Wharf, Boston, Massachusetts 02110, USA
Telephone: (617) 742 5669
Telex: 294116 BOSTLX (Attn Hunt Associates).
OWNERS: Sandy Hook Pilots Association of New York and New Jersey.
HULL: Constructed in aluminium alloy.
MAIN ENGINES: Two MAN-B&W 12V D 2452 diesels developing 545bhp each at 1800rpm operating through L & S Marine reverse/reduction gearboxes with a ratio of 2:1.
PROPULSION: Twin Columbian Tetradyne propellers.
CAPACITIES
Fuel: 56 775 litres
Fresh water: 757 litres
Water ballast: 3785 litres
ACCOMMODATION/CREW
Complement: Six pilots and four crew
Accommodation: 12 recliner seats, a television and dinette in deckhouse. Below decks hull is divided into four watertight compartments, fore peak, galley/sleeping quarters, engine room, and steering Lazorette
SYSTEMS
Generators: Two Northern Lights diesel generators
Engine controls: Cobelt
Bow thruster: Hynautic
Navigation: Two Furuno radars, two depth sounders, Northstar Loran, a survey grade Raytheon for sounding docks and approaches
Communications: Three Shipmate VHF sets
DIMENSIONS
Length overall: 19·50m
Beam: 5·18m
Draught: 1·67m
PERFORMANCE
Speed, max: 24 knots
  cruising: 21 knots

Twin screw motor yacht *Silver Ghost*

SILVER GHOST

Flying bridge diesel yacht.
DESIGNER: C Raymond Hunt Associates Inc, 69 Long Wharf, Boston, Massachusetts 02110, USA
Telephone: (617) 742 5669
Telex: 294116 BOSTLX (Attn Hunt Associates).
HULL: Constructed in welded aluminium traditional style cruiser with a deep-V hull with work boat scantlings, watertight subdivisions and ABS grade collision tank.
MAIN ENGINES: Two GM Detroit 8V-92 TI marine diesels, each 585shp at 2300rpm coupled to Allison MH 1·97:1 reduction gearboxes.
PROPULSION: Two propellers.
CAPACITIES
Fuel: 4920 litres
Water: 1249 litres (plus water maker)
ACCOMMODATION: Large owners' state room forward with guest and crew cabins amidships. Saloon with galley and lower steering position over engine room, cockpit aft and flying bridge over saloon.
SYSTEMS
Auxiliary engines: One 20kW and one 8kW generator sets
DIMENSIONS
Length overall: 18·48m
Length waterline: 16·38m
Beam: 1·63m
Draught, hull: 0·99m
Draught, skeg: 1·53m

Stern of twin screw motor yacht *Silver Ghost*

Twin screw motor yacht *Chelonia*

WEIGHT
Displacement: 27·18 tonnes
PERFORMANCE
Speed, max: 25 knots
Speed, cruise: 20 knots
Range at 20 knots: 500n miles

CHELONIA
Twin screw motor yacht.
Multi-purpose yacht intended for ocean passages to Bermuda and Caribbean, sports fishing, diving and marine biological research trips. Equipped and constructed to commercial standards.
DESIGNER: C Raymond Hunt Associates Inc, 69 Long Wharf, Boston, Massachusetts 02110, USA
HULL: Welded aluminium.
MAIN ENGINES: Two GM Detroit 8V-92 TI marine diesels each developing 585shp at 2300rpm coupled to Allison MH 1·97:1 reduction gearboxes.
PROPULSION: Two propellers.
CAPACITIES
Fuel: 6813 litres (three tanks)
Water: 1135 litres (two tanks)
ACCOMMODATION: Cabin for two crew forward, guest cabin portside amidships with two berths, owner's cabin consists of double berth, heads and separate shower. Saloon consists of semi-enclosed galley, large desk, U-shaped dinette and lounge seating. After cockpit fitted with wide transom door/diving platform. Engine room is below the saloon situated in superstructure, enclosed bridge fitted above the saloon.
SYSTEMS
Auxiliary engines: One 20kW and one 8kW generator sets

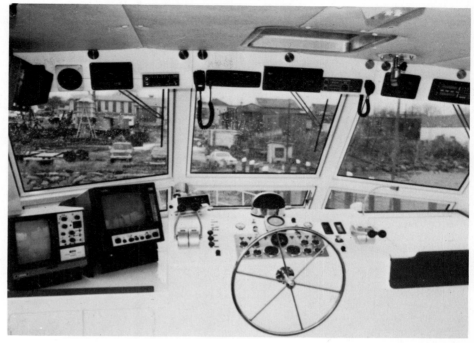

Chelonia enclosed bridge layout

DIMENSIONS
Length overall: 18·59m
Length waterline: 16·54m
Beam: 5·11m
Draught (hull): 0·99m
Draught (skeg): 1·52m

WEIGHT
Displacement: 27·18 tonnes

PERFORMANCE
Speed, max: 24 knots
Speed, cruise: 21 knots

GULF CRAFT INC

RR1 Box 395, Patterson, Louisiana 70392, USA

Telephone: (504) 395 5254/6259

R Scott Tibbs, *President*

Gulf Craft Inc is a builder of high-speed aluminium conventional hull passenger ferries and crew boats. The *Caleb McCall* is a 44-metre crew boat with a maximum speed of 27 knots. An interesting feature of this craft is that there are five engines which the owner claims gives better manoeuvrability and makes engine replacement or repair easier.

CALEB McCALL
Crew boat.
OWNER: McCall Boat Rental, Cameron, Louisiana, USA
CLASSIFICATION: USCG approved Gulf of Mexico, 200 miles offshore.

HULL: Superstructure and hull are built in aluminium. Hull plating is in 5086 grade, 15·8mm thick over the propellers, the remainder of the bottom is 12·7mm thick with 8·4mm side plating, superstructure is in 4·8mm plate.
MAIN ENGINES/GEARBOXES: Five Cummins KTA 19M diesel engines coupled to Twin Disc MG518, 2·5:1 reduction gearboxes.
PROPULSION: Five three-blade Columbian Bronze FP propellers.
CONTROLS: Orbitrol/Charlynn steering and Kobelt engine controls. Duplicate engine controls also fitted on the upper bridge allowing operator to face aft with a clear view while working cargo at rigs and oil platforms.
CAPACITIES
Passengers: 75
Diesel: 45 420 litres (12 000 US gallons)
Water: 75 700 litres (20 000 US gallons)
ACCOMMODATION: Three two-berth cabins, galley and mess room.

SYSTEMS
Auxiliaries: Two Cummins 6B5.8, 56kW generators
Deck equipment: McElroy windlass
Navigational equipment: Raytheon/JRC colour and Furuno FR 8100 radars, Si-Tex Koden Loran, Datamarine sounder, Decca 150 autopilot
Communications: Motorola Triton 20 SSB, Raytheon 53A VHF
DIMENSIONS
Length overall: 44·20m
Beam, moulded: 8·50m
Depth: 3·50m
Draught: 2·40m
Deck area (working): 25m × 7·3m
GRT: 70
NRT: 48
WEIGHT
Deck load: 150 tons
PERFORMANCE
Speed, light: 27 knots
Speed, loaded: 23 knots (approx)

HALTER MARINE INC

6600 Plaza Drive, Suite 500, New Orleans, Louisiana 70127, USA

Telephone: (504) 246 8900
Telex: 6821246 HALMAR

Jack Edwards, *President*
Archie Dunn, *President, Trinity Marketing*
Harvey Walpert, *Vice President, Contracts*
James Rivers, *Vice President, International Sales*
Ed Shearer, *Vice President, Business Development*
John Moreau, *Engineering Manager*
Barry Heaps, *Equitable/Halter, Yard Manager*

Formed in 1957, Halter Marine Inc has built over 1200 vessels since 1957 and has designed and built more high-speed vessels than any other shipyard in the USA. The yard specialises in aluminium and high strength Corten steel hulls. The parent company is Trinity Industries of Dallas, Texas and the sister company is Equitable Shipyard.

The following craft descriptions represent some of the principal types of high-speed craft designed and built by Halter Marine Inc, having lengths of approximately 20m or over with speeds of over 20 knots.

HALMAR 65 (CREW BOAT TYPE)
This is a crew boat design but is also available in the following variants: customs launch, tanker service launch, pilot boat, ferry, communications launch, work boat and ambulance launch. The

Halmar 65 20-knot crew boat, one of over 120 built

first of the type was designed and built in 1964 and by August 1985 112 had been built, with production continuing. The craft have been classified by various authorities including USCG, ABS and Lloyds. Most are in service with the offshore oil industry.

HULL: Corten steel, longitudinally framed; aluminium 5086, transverse framed.

MAIN ENGINE: Various options, the most popular being two GM 12V-71 TI, producing 510hp each at 2100rpm.

PROPULSION: Two Columbian Bronze propellers, 813mm diameter, in Nibral.

CONTROLS: Morse MD-24, manual, two stations. Steering hydraulic, 600lb/in².

ACCOMMODATION: 49 passengers and 2 crew (1 captain, 1 deckhand/engineer).

SYSTEMS

Fuel: One integral fuel tank: 3596 litres, diesel fuel No 2

Hydraulic: Steering and anchor windlass, 600lb/in², 41bar

Electrical: 110/220V ac, 60Hz, generator 2-71 GM, 20kW

DIMENSIONS

Length, moulded: 19·66m

Width, moulded: 5·90m

Draught, max: 1·12m

Air draught to cabin top: 3·66m

Air draught, max: 5·79m

Freight deck area: 4·57 × 6·10m

PERFORMANCE

Speed, max: 21 knots, aluminium hull
    18 knots, steel hull

Speed, cruising: 19 knots, aluminium hull
    16 knots, steel hull

Turning circle diameter: 49m

Crash stop distance: 30m

Time to accelerate to cruising speed: 50s

Max permissible Sea State for operation: 3 to 4

HALMAR 65 (PATROL BOAT TYPE)

Main particulars as for the Halmar 65 crew boat type but with the following differences:

MAIN ENGINES: Most popular, two GM 12V-71 TI, 675hp each at 2300rpm.

PROPULSION: Two Columbian Bronze propellers, 838mm diameter, in Nibral.

ACCOMMODATION: For captain, 2 officers and 4 crew.

SYSTEMS

Fuel: One integral tank containing 4546 litres, diesel fuel No 2

WEIGHT

Displacement at designed load waterline: 34·54 tonnes

PERFORMANCE

Speed, max: 26 knots, aluminium hull
    21 knots, steel hull

Speed, cruising: 22 knots, aluminium hull
    18 knots, steel hull

Time to accelerate to cruising speed: 45s

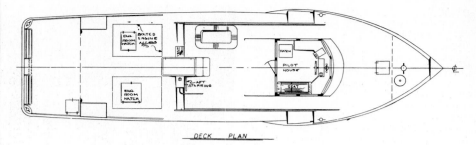

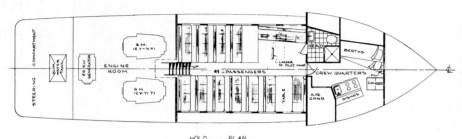

General Arrangement of Halmar 65 type crew boat

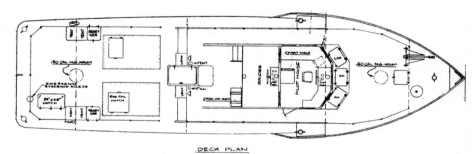

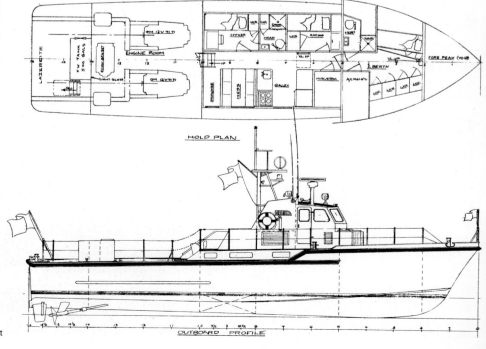

General Arrangement of Halmar 65 type patrol boat

HALMAR 78 (PATROL BOAT TYPE)

As for the Halmar 65 this design is built for various applications. The first Halmar 78 was completed in 1982 and 23 had been built by August 1985; Classification Lloyds Class 100 A-1, November 1982.

HULL: Corten steel, longitudinally framed.

MAIN ENGINES: Two GM 12V-71 TI, producing 675hp each at 2300rpm.

PROPULSION: Two Columbian Bronze propellers, 864mm diameter, in Nibral.

CONTROLS: Morse MD-24, manual, 2 stations.

ACCOMMODATION: For captain, 2 officers, 8 crew. Below the main deck there are 4 staterooms, 3 heads and a galley.

SYSTEMS

Fuel: Two integral tanks, total capacity of 10 607 litres, diesel fuel No 2

Hydraulic: Steering and windlass, 600lb/in², 41bar

Electrical: 220/440V ac, 50Hz, generator 2-71 GM, 20kW

Communications and navigation: Sailor RT-144 VHF and Decca 150 radar

DIMENSIONS

Length overall: 23·78m

Beam overall: 5·64m

Draught, max: 1·43m

Air draught to cabin top: 4·73m

Air draught, max: 7·0m

WEIGHTS

Empty: 42·67 tonnes

Max disposable load: 14·02 tonnes

PERFORMANCE

Speed, max: 22 knots

Speed, cruising: 20 knots

Turning circle diameter: 52m

Crash stop distance: 34m

Time to accelerate to cruising speed: 45s

Max permissible Sea State: 4 to 5

Range: 745n miles

Endurance: 38 hours

Halmar 65 type patrol boats

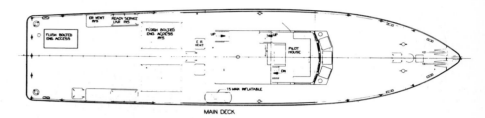

MAIN DECK

HOLD PLAN

OUTBOARD PROFILE

General Arrangement of Halmar 78 corten steel patrol boat

Halmar 78 crew boat *Oil Conveyor II*

HALMAR 101 (CREW BOAT TYPE)

A crew boat design available in a full range of variants. Designed and built first in 1977/78, 37 had been delivered by August 1985, classified either by USCG or ABS.

HULL: Aluminium 5086, transverse framed.

MAIN ENGINES/GEARBOXES: Three GM 12V-71 TI, 510hp each at 2100rpm, driving via twin disc 2·0:1 reduction gears.

PROPULSION: Three Columbian Bronze propellers, 864mm diameter, in Nibral (one vessel is fitted with three Rocketdyne waterjet units; two 406·4mm diameter driven by two GM 16V-92 TI diesel engines and one 609·6mm diameter driven by one Allison 501 gas turbine).

CONTROLS: Kobelt, pneumatic, 2 stations.

ACCOMMODATION/CREW

Passengers: 55

Crew: 6 (2 captains, 2 deckhands, 1 cook, 1 engineer)

SYSTEMS

Fuel: Two integral tanks, total 9092 litres

Hydraulic: Steering and anchor windlass, 600lb/in², 41bar

Electrical: Two generators, GM 3-71, 30kW each 110/220V ac, 60Hz

Communications and navigation: VHF, Sailor 144, SSB, Motorola, Radar, Decca D-150 36-mile range

Air-conditioning: Three units Freon, water-cooled

DIMENSIONS

Length overall: 31·0m

Beam overall: 6·48m

Draught, max: 1·68m

Air draught to cabin top: 4·67m

Air draught, max: 7·16m

Cargo deck (wood) area: 16·77 × 5·18m

GRT: Under 100

WEIGHTS

Empty: 55·88 tonnes

Payload: 30·48 tonnes

Disposable load: 40·43 tonnes

Deck load capacity: 30·48 tonnes

PERFORMANCE

Speed, max: 22 knots

Speed, cruising: 20 knots

Turning circle: 55m

Crash stop distance: 37m

Halmar 101 crew boat

Halmar 112 crew boat

Time to accelerate to cruising speed: 45s

Max permissible Sea State: 5

Range: 500n miles

Endurance: 24 hours

HALMAR 112 (CREW BOAT TYPE)

A crew boat design available in a full range of variants. Designed and built first in 1981, five had been delivered by August 1985, classified by the ABS, and are in service in the Middle East, India and the Far East.

HULL: Aluminium 5086, transverse framed.

MAIN ENGINES: Four GM 12V-71 TI, 510hp each at 2100rpm.

PROPULSION: Four Columbian Bronze propellers, 864mm diameter, in Nibral.

CONTROLS: Kobelt, pneumatic, 2 stations.

ACCOMMODATION: For 92 passengers and 5

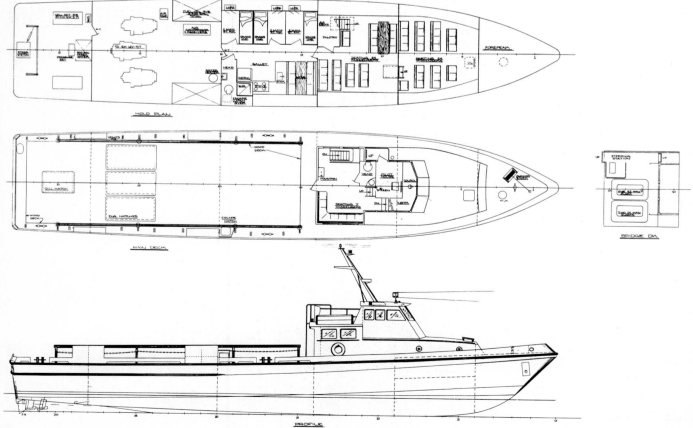

General Arrangement of Halmar 101

crew (2 captains, 1 engineer, 1 cook, 1 deckhand). Accommodation is air-conditioned and heated.

SYSTEMS

Fuel: Two integral tanks, total 28 413 litres, diesel No 2

Hydraulic: Steering and anchor windlass, 600lb/in², 41bar

Electrical: Two GM 3-71, 40kW generators 110/220V ac, 60Hz

Communications and navigation: VHF, Sailor, SSB, Motorola and Decca radar

DIMENSIONS

Length overall: 34·15m

Beam overall: 7·62m

Draught, max: 1·83m

Air draught to cabin top: 2·44m

Air draught, max: 7·72m

Cargo deck area: 17·38 × 6·10m

GRT: Under 100

WEIGHTS

Empty: 66·04 tonnes

Payload: 60·96 tonnes

Max disposable load: 62·48 tonnes

PERFORMANCE

Speed, max: 22 knots

cruising: 20 knots

Turning circle diameter: 55m

Crash stop distance: 40m

Time to accelerate to cruising speed: 45s

Max permissible Sea State: 5

Range: 1200n miles

Endurance: 54 hours

HALMAR 115 MOTOR YACHT

A high-speed motor yacht designed and built in 1984 to ABS Class.

HULL: Double chine, aluminium 5086, transverse framed.

MAIN ENGINES: Four GM 12V-92 MTI, 1000hp each at 2300rpm.

PROPULSION: Four Columbian Bronze propellers, 1016mm diameter, in Nibral.

CONTROLS: Kobelt, pneumatic, engine control, Bennett Trim, hydraulic.

ACCOMMODATION/CREW

Guests: 8

Crew: 5, captain, stewards, deckhands

Main deck: Pilot house, saloon, galley, bar

Lower deck: Crew's quarters, owner's cabin, 4 guest rooms, 6 heads, engine room, generator room

Flybridge: Flybridge station, jacuzzi, barbecue, boat deck lounge

Air-conditioned

Halmar 112 crew boat type Sea Shuttle

Halmar 115 32-knot motor yacht

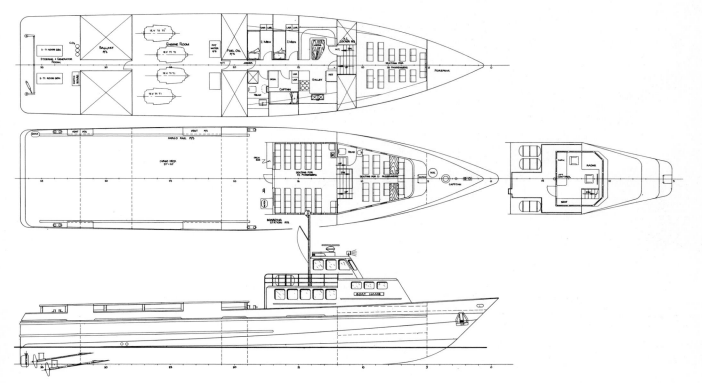
General Arrangement of Halmar 112

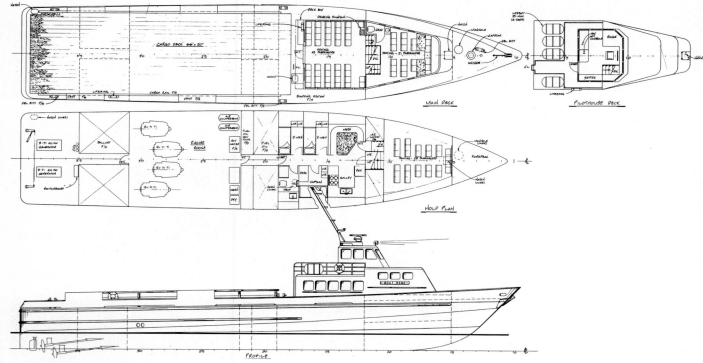

General Arrangement of Halmar 122

SYSTEMS
Fuel: Five integral tanks, total 43 566 litres, diesel No 2
Hydraulic: Boat crane, 1000lb/in², 68 bar. Bennett Trim
Electrical: Two 62·5kW generators, 220/440V ac, 50Hz
Communications and navigation: Two VHF Sailor, one SSB Sailor, two Decca radars, one satnav, one navigator, two fathometers, one autopilot
DIMENSIONS
Length overall: 35·06m
Beam overall: 7·62m
Draught, max: 1·60m
Air draught to cabin top: 5·18m

Air draught, max: 8·0m
WEIGHTS
Empty: 85·0 long tons
Max disposable load: 40·0 long tons
PERFORMANCE
Speed, max: 32 knots
        cruising: 29 knots
Turning circle: 56m
Crash stop distance: 30m
Time to accelerate to cruising speed: 35s
Max permissible Sea State: 5
Range: 2100n miles
Endurance: 65 hours

HALMAR 122 (CREW BOAT TYPE)
A large crew boat designed and completed in

1985 having a 70-ton cargo capacity. Built to ABS Class A1, this design, as for the Halmar crew boats, is available for a wide range of applications.
HULL: Aluminium 5086, transverse framed.
MAIN ENGINES: Four GM 12V-71 TI, 510hp each at 2100rpm.
PROPULSION: Four Columbian Bronze propellers, 864mm diameter, in Nibral.
CONTROLS: Kobelt, pneumatic, 2 stations.
ACCOMMODATION: For 92 passengers and 5 crew (2 captains, 1 engineer, 1 cook, 1 deckhand).
SYSTEMS
Fuel: Four integral tanks, total capacity of 4660 litres, No 2 diesel
Hydraulic: Steering, capstan and anchor windlass, 600lb/in², 41bar
Electrical: Two GM 3-71, 40kW generators 110/220V ac, 60Hz
Communications and navigation: One VHF, Sailor 144, one SSB, Motorola and one Decca D-150 36-mile range radar
Water, potable: 3714 litres
        ballast: 64 400 litres
DIMENSIONS
Length overall: 37·20m
Beam overall: 7·62m
Draught, max: 1·83m
Air draught to cabin top: 5·49m
Air draught, max: 7·72m
Cargo deck area: 20·12 × 6·10m
GRT: Under 100
WEIGHTS
Empty: 73·15 tonnes
Payload: 71·12 tonnes (deck load capacity)
Max disposable load: 75·65 tonnes
PERFORMANCE
Speed, max: 21 knots
Speed, cruising: 19 knots
Turning circle diameter: 56m
Crash stop distance: 41m
Time to accelerate to cruising speed: 45s
Max permissible Sea State: 5
Range: 1700n miles
Endurance: 88 hours

Halmar 122 deep-Vee hull crew boat

HUCKINS YACHT CORP INC

Florida, USA

HUCKINS 78
PRINCESS PAT
Motor yacht.
HULL: Grp/airex core construction.
MAIN ENGINES: Two MAN diesel engines

rated at 760shp at 2300rpm each connected to ZF 2·5:1 gearboxes.
PROPULSION: Two Arneson Surface Drives Model ASD 14, coupled to 1·07m diameter, four-bladed Nibral surface-piercing propellers.
DIMENSIONS
Length overall: 23·77m

Length waterline: 19·81m
Beam: 6·09m
Draught: 1·14m
WEIGHT
Displacement, full: 44·39 tonnes
PERFORMANCE
Designed speed: 23 knots

Huckins 78 23m aft cockpit motor yacht

KNIGHT AND CARVER YACHTS

3650 Hancock Street, San Diego, California 92110, USA

Telephone: (619) 295 3115

Joe Fole, *Designer*

SPORTS YACHT (DESIGN)
HULL: Composite.
MAIN ENGINES: Two MTU 12V 396 TB94 marine diesels, 2550hp each.
PROPULSION: Two KaMeWa 63 waterjets.
CAPACITIES
Fuel: 5565 litres
Water: 742 litres
ACCOMMODATION: Owner's suite, state room with bath, also lounge and galley, pilot station and after sunpad.
SYSTEMS
Auxiliary machinery: One 8kW generator
Communications: Radio telephone and telex, computer interface, television, VCR, TV and stereo

Navigation: Standard equipment
DIMENSIONS
Length overall: 21·34m
Beam: 5·79m
Draught: 0·67m
WEIGHTS
Displacement, dry: 23·58 tonnes
Displacement, full: 30·38 tonnes
PERFORMANCE
Speed, max, light load: 71 knots
Speed, max, full load: 62 knots

PANJANDRUM
Motor yacht under construction 1987.
HULL: Grp composite, coring material is Airex for the hull and Divinycell for the decks.
MAIN ENGINES: Two MTU 12V 396 TB94 diesel engines 2550hp each.
CAPACITIES
Fuel: 24 983 litres
Water: 2649 litres
ACCOMMODATION: Owner's suite includes two bathrooms, a jacuzzi, bar and desk area with a computer terminal. Two double guest staterooms each with a bath, saloon bar and film theatre, formal dining for eight and galley. Crews' quarters

consist of Captain's stateroom and bath, double cabin, crew bathroom, galley and lounge.
SYSTEMS
Auxiliary machinery: Two 33kW generators and one 12kW generator
Navigational: Standard equipment and a satellite navigation system
Communications: Standard telephone sets, telex, computer interface capability and satellite communications
Television: VCR/TV/electronic telescopes
Stabilisers: Koop rotary retractable stabilisers
DIMENSIONS
Length overall: 29·60m
Beam: 7·31m
Draught, full load: 0·88m
WEIGHTS
Displacement, dry: 45·80 tonnes
Displacement, half: 58·50 tonnes
Displacement, full: 71·20 tonnes
PERFORMANCE
Speed max, light load: 52 knots
Speed max, full load: 46 knots
Speed, continuous, light load: 35 knots
Speed, continuous, full load: 39 knots
Range at 12 knots approx: 3450 miles

Artist's impression of *Panjandrum* built by Knight and Carver Yachts

LANTANA BOATYARD INC

808 N Dixie Highway, Lantana, Florida 33462, USA

Telephone: (305) 585 9311
Telex: 513 480

Elliot R Donnelley, *Chairman of Board*
Alexander Stalker, *President*
David M Conway, *Chief Financial Officer & Treasurer*
Michael W Gore, *Director, International Sales*

Formed in 1965, Lantana Boatyard began construction of military boats in 1980. It is situated on a 10-acre site 12 miles south of the Port of Palm Beach.

GUARDIAN
Four of these 34-knot capability patrol boats have been built. The design was started in February 1982 and trials of the first boat completed in October 1983.
HULL: All-welded aluminium alloy 5086 construction longitudinally formed over transverse

bulkheads and web frames. Modified V hull with single hard chine.
MAIN ENGINES: Three MTU 8V 396 TB93, 1200shp each.
PROPULSION: Three Columbian Bronze propellers, 1067mm diameter, cast Nibral, fixed-pitch.
CONTROLS: Hydraulic power steering and pneumatic engine controls.
ACCOMMODATION: Enclosed wheelhouse forward with open bridge above. 19 crew. Commanding Officer's quarters on deck behind wheelhouse. Six officers below midships and twelve crew

below deck forward. All accommodation is air-conditioned.

SYSTEMS

Fuel tank capacity: 24 603 litres

Hydraulic: Steering, two pumps 81·6 bar, 1200lb/in²

Electrical: Two GM 4-71 diesel generators, 3-phase, 50kW each. 120/208V ac, 24V dc. Engine start with dc emergency power

Navigation and communication: Depth sounder, satnav, magnetic compass, Sperry gyrocompass, Sunaire SSB radio, VHF radio, Furuno radar

Lifesaving: One rigid/inflatable boat, two 10-person inflatable liferafts on deck

DIMENSIONS

Length overall: 32·32m

Length waterline: 30·49m

Freeboard, amidships: 1·96m

Beam overall: 6·25m

Draught, max: 2·10m

Air draught to cabin top: 5·49m

Air draught, max: 9·76m

WEIGHTS

Empty: 49 tonnes

Max disposable load: 27·2 tonnes

Design max displacement: 76·20 tonnes

PERFORMANCE

Speed, max: 34·0 knots

HMJS *Paul Bogle*, the Lantana built 30-knot-plus patrol craft of the Jamaica Defence Force Coast Guard commissioned September 1985

Speed, cruising: 30·0 knots

Turning circle diameter: 333m

Rate of turn, starting at cruising speed: 246°/minute

Crash stop distance: 115m

Time to accelerate to cruising speed: 137s

Max permissible Sea State for operation: Strong Gale Force 9

Range: 1200n miles

Endurance: 48 hours at 25 knots

MAGNUM MARINE CORPORATION

2900 Northeast 188th Street, North Miami Beach, Florida 33180, USA

Telephone: (305) 931 4292
Telex: 6811630

F M Theodoli, *President*
Mrs Katrin Theodoli, *Managing Director*

Magnum Marine specialises in the construction of high performance, offshore pleasure and patrol craft from 8m to just under 20m in length. In this range its standard designs are:

Magnum 27, an 8·33m grp fast coastal patrol boat

Magnum 38, an 11·58m grp flybridge patrol craft

Magnum 40, a 12·19m grp open patrol boat

Magnum 53, a 16·13m grp flybridge patrol boat

Magnum 63, a 19·20m grp/Kevlar patrol and pleasure craft

Magnum patrol craft are in service with the US Marine Patrol, US Customs, US Coast Guard and many other non-US agencies.

MAGNUM 63

This boat is built in accordance with the requirements of Lloyd's Register of Shipping or the American Bureau of Shipping. The first was completed in 1985 and by August 1986 a total of six had been built. A new version of the Magnum 63 was completed in 1987. In August 1987 the racing version won the 370-mile Miami-Nassau-Miami offshore race. The craft can be fitted out as

Magnum 63 flybridge

a patrol boat. A flybridge version was shipped to Japan in November 1987.

HULL: The boat is basically a four-piece construction consisting of a hull, deck, forward inner liner and cockpit liner, all laminated in grp or for additional weight saving the lamination can be of Dupont Kevlar. Interiors may be built of Kevlar and Nomex honeycomb composite materials. Deadrise aft is 24°.

ENGINES: Two GM 16V-92 TI, 1300hp each.

PROPULSION: Two Arneson Surface Drive SP2000 propeller units.

CAPACITIES

Fuel: 4320 litres

Fresh water: 720 litres

CREW: Nine.

SYSTEMS

Electrical: Eight 12V, 200Ah batteries, four for each engine; 60A engine driven alternators; 12V and 24V dc system; 100/220V 60Hz ac system; two automatic 60A converters; Oman diesel generator, 7·5kW

Firefighting: Manual and automatic firefighting equipment

DIMENSIONS

Length overall: 19·20m

Length waterline: 16·31m

Breadth overall: 5·28m

Draught, static: 0·91m (with Arneson Surface Drive)

PERFORMANCE

Speed, max: 52 knots

Range: 400 to 500n miles at continuous speed

MAGNUM 63 (1987 VERSION)
MALTESE MAGNUM

HULL: Constructed in Dupont Kevlar, superstructure to suit individual requirements.

MAIN ENGINES: Two CRM marine diesels, 1850hp each at 2075rpm coupled to two Arneson drives via 1·18:1 reduction gearboxes.

PROPULSION: Two five-blade Nibral propellers, 838mm dia, 1143mm pitch.

CAPACITIES

Fuel: 4542 litres

Fresh water: 946 litres

ACCOMMODATION: 6 to 10.

DIMENSIONS

Length overall: 19·20m

Beam, max: 5·18m

Draught, static: 0·91m

Draught, running: 0·46m

PERFORMANCE

Speed, max: 65·80 knots

1987 version of Magnum Marine 63, *Maltese Magnum*, winner of the 1987 Miami-Nassau-Miami Sea Race at an average of 51 knots over 314·77n miles

PACIFICA by KIPPER YACHTS

3595 Frankford Avenue, Panama City, Florida 32405, USA

Telephone: (904) 769 8976

Bill Jahn, *Production/Quality Manager*

PALMER JOHNSON INC

61 Michigan Street, Sturgeon Bay, Wisconsin 54235, USA

Robert Boler, *Vice President*
William Parsons, *Executive Vice President*

SWIFTSHIPS INC

PO Box 1908, Morgan City, Louisiana 70381, USA

Telephone: (504) 384 1700
Telex: 586453
TWX: 819 950 5700 SWIFT INC MGCY

Holding Company: UNC Resources, Falls Church, Virginia, USA.
Subsidiaries: Mangone Swiftships Inc, Houston and Champion-Swiftships, Pass Christion, Mississippi, USA.

Swiftships produces aluminium alloy craft up to 38 metres and steel vessels from 45 to 76 metres in length. Swiftships employs about 900 personnel and apart from their fast crew boats have supplied fast aluminium patrol craft ranging in size from 8 to 45 metres in length, in service with US armed forces, naval coastguard, and police forces in some 20 countries throughout the world.

65 PATROL BOAT

Patrol boats supplied to governments of Antigua, Dominica and St Lucia.
HULL: Superstructure and hull constructed in aluminium alloy.
MAIN ENGINES: Two GM 12V-71 TI marine diesel engines coupled to Twin Disc MG 514C reverse/reduction gearboxes.
PROPULSION: Two Columbian crew boat propellers.
CONTROLS
Engine controls: Ponish
Steering system: Vickers/Charlynn
CAPACITIES
Fuel: 4542 litres
Water: 1892 litres
SYSTEMS
Auxiliary machinery: 20kW Detroit Diesel/International Electric generator set
DIMENSIONS
Length overall: 19·81m
Beam: 5·56m
Draught, full load: 1·52m

115 CREW BOAT

Fast supply/crew boat.
CLASSIFICATION: USCG Sub-Charter T Requirements and certified for ocean service, limited to 200 miles offshore.
HULL: Superstructure and hull constructed in aluminium alloy.
MAIN ENGINES: Three MTU 8V 396 TC82 marine diesels providing 800shp each at 1845rpm through ZF BW 255 2:1 reduction gearboxes.
PROPULSION: 101mm diameter Aquamet 17 stainless steel shafts coupled to three four-bladed bronze 96mm × 1016mm Columbian propellers.
CONTROLS
Engine controls: Wabco air controls
Steering: Two Hydreco hydraulic pumps with Charlynn Orbitrols
CAPACITIES
Fuel: 14 004 litres
Industrial water (transferable): 49 432 litres

CONVINCER

Sport fishing, built in 1987.
HULL: Frp.
MAIN ENGINES: Two 1330bhp marine diesel engines.
PROPULSION: Two KaMeWa 50S62/6 waterjet units.

TIME

Built in 1986 for Atwood, Rockford, USA, this motor yacht is driven by two 2145bhp KaMeWa waterjet units, type 71S62/6.

DIMENSIONS
Length overall: 21·33m
Beam: 6·29m
Draught: 1·21m
WEIGHT
Displacement: 45 tonnes
PERFORMANCE
Speed: 34 knots

Swiftships 65 patrol boats

Ballast: 49 432 litres
Potable water: 3785 litres
Lube oil: 302 litres
Hydraulic oil: 151 litres
Sewage holding tank: 3406 litres
Transfer tank (fuel or water): 1324 litres
ACCOMMODATION
Crew: 6 persons in three double cabins

Passengers: Seats for 49 persons. Two heads and one shower
SYSTEMS
Auxiliary machinery: Two 30kW generators driven by Detroit Diesel 3-71 diesel engines at 1200rpm
Air compressors: Two Quincy F-325, two-stage type and driven by 5hp three-phase electric motors and 302-litre air receivers

Inboard Arrangement

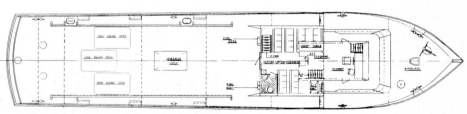

Main Deck Arrangement

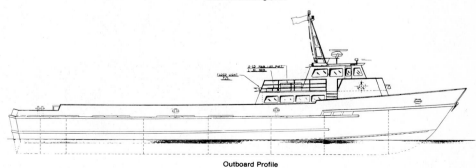

Outboard Profile

Swiftships 115 crew/supply boat profile, main deck and inboard layouts

Air-conditioning: Two central type cooling units servicing galley, staterooms, passenger spaces and pilot house. Heat provided by duct-mounted strip heaters

Firefighting: Two fire stations on main deck (port and starboard) with hoses and nozzles. Optional Akron Model No 508 fire monitor can be installed on top of main cabin

Transferable liquid system: Barnes Model 15CCE 76mm industrial water transfer pump driven by 7·5hp drip proof electric motor. Fuel transfer pump is a Barnes Model 15CCE 76mm, driven by a 7·5hp drip proof electric motor

Navigational: Danforth Constellation compass, two Perko 254mm searchlights, Konel Furuno FR-711 radar, Raytheon F720D fathometer, Loran C-Texas Instruments TI-9900, one EPIRB

Communications: Drake TRMI-SSB radio, and Drake MRT-55 UHF radio

Lifesaving: 54 life jackets, three ring buoys, three liferafts (two 25-man, one 10-man), fire extin-guishers, one fire axe and two hoses

DIMENSIONS
Length overall: 35·05m
Beam: 7·62m
Draught, max: 2·20m
Clear main deck area: 5·48m × 16·45m
WEIGHT
Deck cargo: 75·22 tonnes
PERFORMANCE
Speed, normal load: 23 knots
Range: 750n miles

WESTPORT SHIPYARD INC

PO Box 308, Westport, Washington 98595, USA

Telephone: (206) 268 0116

Randy Rust, *Proprietor*

Westport Shipyard was established in 1964 and sold to the present owners in 1977. The yard has a workforce of 60 and consists of 5110m² of covered building sheds and workshops plus 4 acres of fenced storage space. The range of craft built is from 10·4 to 36·6 metres in length. Hulls of the larger craft are built with a sandwich type construction of Airex pvc and grp, which the builder claims yields a tougher and lighter hull than an all-grp type. Hull moulds are adjustable for length and beam enabling craft to be built in the following length ranges: 16·15 to 19·80 metres, 19·80 to 29·0 metres and 27·4 to 36·6 metres. The company has built some 50 vessels to USCG 'S' classi-fication since 1977. From 1981 a further seven craft built to USCG 'L' classification have been delivered.

GLACIER SPIRIT
Fast ferry.
OWNERS: Stan Stephens Charters, USA.
DESIGNER: Jack Sarin, Bainbridge Island, Washington, USA.
HULL: Construction in grp/Airex foam core.
MAIN ENGINES/GEARBOXES: Twin Lugger L-8955A diesels 4 cycle, V-8 TA, 555hp each at 2100rpm coupled to Twin Disc MG-514 2·5:1 gearboxes.
PROPULSION: Two three-bladed 1016mm × 914mm Michigan propellers.
CONTROLS: Marol, MSSB electronic/hydraulic power steering system, with Marol autopilot.
CAPACITIES
Fuel: 5678 litres
Water: 757 litres
ACCOMMODATION: 150 passengers.
SYSTEMS: One Northern Lights, 20kW M-854 diesel generator and one Northern Lights, 10kW hydraulically powered generator, Wesmar bow thrusters.
DIMENSIONS
Length overall: 24·38m
Beam: 6·70m
Draught: 1·52m
WEIGHTS
Light: 45 tons
Loaded: 60 tons
PERFORMANCE
Speed, max: 22 knots

CATALINA EXPRESS
TWO HARBORS EXPRESS
Fast ferries.
OWNERS: Catalina Channel Express Lines, San Pedro, California, USA.
DESIGNERS
Hull lines: Edwin Monk Jr, Bainbridge Island, Washington, USA
Fit out: Jack Sarin, Bainbridge Island, Washington, USA
HULL: Construction in grp/Airex foam core.
MAIN ENGINES/GEARBOXES: *Catalina Express* has two DD 12V-92 TA water-cooled Pacific diesels developing 850shp each at 2100rpm, coupled to Twin Disc/Niigata MGN 80-1, 1:1·97 gearboxes. *Two Harbors Express* is fitted with Deutz MWM SBAM 12M 816 engines as for *Glacier Seas*.

Glacier Spirit

Catalina Express

Catalina Express passenger cabin

PROPULSION: Two Michigan Wheel 965mm × 864mm three-bladed Nibral propellers.
CONTROLS: Arnot pneumatic engine controls, and Wagner Engineering steering gear.
ACCOMMODATION: 149 passengers accommodated in main cabin, and VIP lounge fitted abaft the wheelhouse. The top deck features open seating.
SYSTEMS
Electrics: M843, 12kW Northern Lights diesel generator
Bow thruster: Wesmar 25hp
Hydraulic system: Spencer Fluid Power with Cessna 421 variable displacement pump
Stabilisers: Naiad Roll Control system
Navigational: Micrologic ML-3000 Loran C, Wagner Mk 4 autopilot, Wagner Rudaler Angle Indicator, Impulse 530 Depth Sounder, Impulse 580 SLT (speed/log/trim) indicator, Furuno FR360 Mk II radar, Furuno FR240 M3 radar, Ritchie Power damp compass
Communications: Horizon USA II standard VHF, Aiphone internal communications
Lifesaving: 9in Buoy liferings, Model 1280 automatic water lights, Model 1618 buoyant apparatus (4- and 16-person 'wafers')
Firefighting: Badger-Powhaton fire hydrant and hose
DIMENSIONS
Length overall: 27·43m
Beam: 6·40m
Draught: 1·37m
PERFORMANCE
Speed, max: 27 knots
   Subsequently two sister ships to the *Catalina Express* have been built fitted with two Deutz SBAM 12M 816 engines.

GLACIER SEAS
   Fast tour boat.
OWNERS: Chuck and Marguerite West, Traverse Pk, Alaska, USA.
DESIGNER: Jack Sarin, Bainbridge Island, Washington, USA.
HULL: Construction in Airex/frp.
MAIN ENGINES/GEARBOXES: Twin Deutz MWM SBAM 12M 816 marine diesel engines, 930hp at 1800rpm coupled to Reintjes reduction gearboxes.
PROPULSION: Two four-bladed Coolidge 1066·8mm × 914·4mm Nibral propellers.

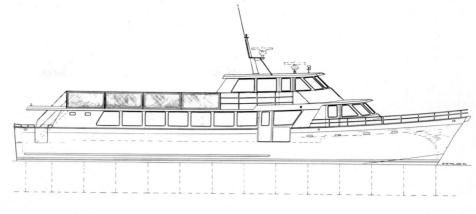
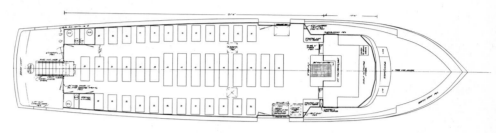

Catalina Express layout

ACCOMMODATION: Licensed to carry 130 passengers. The craft is equipped with bars on both enclosed decks and a galley for preparation of hot meals. Half of the seating is in dinette type benches and tables, the remainder consists of individual chairs.

SYSTEMS: 35hp Wesmar bow thruster.
DIMENSIONS
Length overall: 27·43m
Beam overall: 6·90m
PERFORMANCE
Speed, service: 21 knots

AIR-LUBRICATED-HULL CRAFT

AUSTRALIA

STOLKRAFT INTERNATIONAL PTY LIMITED

[PATENT HOLDERS, DESIGNERS AND DEVELOPERS]
Head Office: Suite E, 7th Floor, 445 Toorak Road, Toorak 3142, Australia

Telephone: (03) 241 8636
Telefax: (03) 241 7678

P G H Newton, *Chairman*
John A Leckey, *Managing Director*
Richard Jones, *Director*
Paul Van Epenhuysen, *Director*
Ben Lexcen, *Director*
Robert E Rees, *Director*
John A Lund, *Director*

North American Office:
Stolkraft High Speed Hulls Ltd, 3036, 11th Avenue, Vancouver, British Columbia, Canada V6K 2M6

Telephone: (604) 731 2790

Leo D Stolk's Stolkraft concept of optimising the benefits of air lubrication on a planing hull can be summarised as follows:

At speed an appreciable amount of aerodynamic lift is built up by a ram-air cushion at the bow and this creates a second ram-air cushion and lifts the craft so as to reduce frictional resistance.

A feature of the concept is the absence of trim variation. The craft rises bodily, parallel to the surface, and has no tendency to porpoise. At speed it creates neither bow-wash nor hull spray outward. The aerodynamic lift reduces fuel consumption.

Tests have been undertaken with a 2·4m (7ft 11in) model at the Netherlands Ship Model Basin (NSMB), Wageningen, Netherlands. The performance of this model was monitored in the high-speed tank and actual sea tests with 4·95m (16ft) and 8·45m (28ft) vessels provided additional data. During the tank tests speeds of up to 80 knots were simulated with no performance problems.

These and further NSMB tests in 1980 confirmed that the final design has a speed/power characteristic more favourable than the high-speed catamaran, planing craft and surface-piercing hydrofoils and in terms of total operating and capital costs, the Stolkraft is significantly more economical at higher speeds than air cushion vehicles and other high-speed vessels.

Details of the prototype Stolkraft, Inceptor II SK.16 Mk I and the Stolkraft Mk III 14-seat test craft are given in *Jane's High-Speed Marine Craft and Air Cushion Vehicles 1986, Jane's Surface Skimmers 1985* and earlier editions.

STOLKRAFT 10·3-METRE FAST FERRY

The first commercial order for Stolkraft was placed in 1986 for two 41-passenger, 10·3-metre fast ferries. These vessels entered service in January 1987 with the Gold Coast Water Bus Co at Australia's Gold Coast, south of Brisbane. Important factors for the ferry operator were high speed, minimal wash and wake and low capital and operating costs.
HULL: Glass-reinforced plastic in sandwich construction.
ENGINE: Volvo twin 270hp diesels with Hamilton waterjets (first boat) and Arneson surface drives (second boat).
ACCOMMODATION: 41 passengers.
DIMENSIONS
Length: 10·3m
Beam: 4·3m
Depth: 1·7m
Draught: 0·7m
PERFORMANCE
Operating speed: 30 knots

Stolkraft Inceptor II SK.16 Mk I

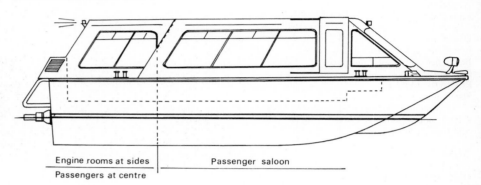
Engine rooms at sides
Passengers at centre
Passenger saloon

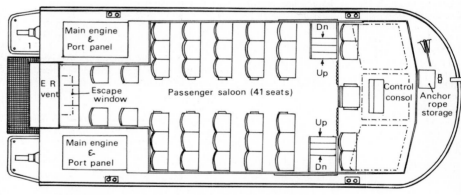
Layout of 10·3m Stolkraft fast ferries built for services in the Brisbane area

Hull form of 10·3m Stolkraft

10·3m Stolkraft waterbus in service at Gold Coast, Queensland

FUTURE DESIGNS

Stolkraft have proposed designs for several applications of the concept as follows:

Firefighting/rescue boat
  Length, overall: 18·00m
  Beam: 7·5m
  Draught: 1·0m
  5 monitors
  Speed: 40 to 45 knots

Passenger ferry
  Length, overall: 20·5m
  Beam: 8·5m
  Draught: 1·5m
  120 passengers
  Speed: 40 to 45 knots

Patrol boat
  Length, overall: 22·0m
  Beam: 8·0m
  Draught: 1·3m
  Speed: 45 to 50 knots

10·3m Stolkraft waterbus at speed

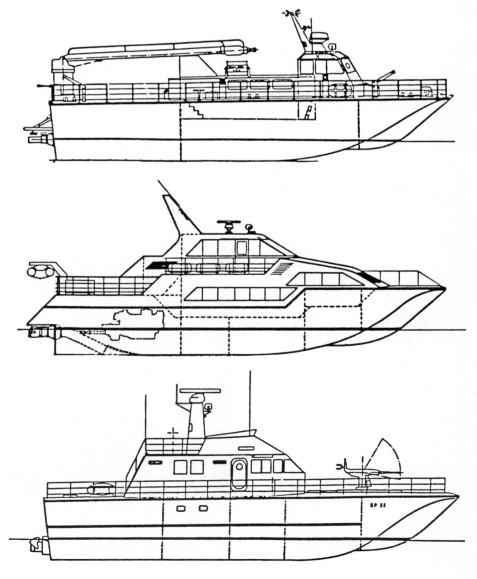

Three proposed Stolkraft designs

FRANCE

SOCIÉTÉ FRANÇAISE DE CONSTRUCTIONS NAVALES (SFCN)

66 Quai Alfred-Sisley, 92392 Villeneuve-la-Garenne, France

Telephone: (47) 94 6446
Telex: 610998 FRANCONA F

Directors: See entry for SFCN in the High-speed Mono-hull section

MARLIN 21 CLASS AIR-LUBRICATED HULL CRAFT

Details of these vessels in their basic form are given in the SFCN entry in the High-speed Mono-hull section. The Marlin design is now completed with an exclusive air lubrication system for the hull giving a considerable maximum speed increase. A French patent was applied for in October 1984.

The first vessel to be fitted with air lubrication, a Marlin 21, was launched 27 November 1986.
ENGINES: Two MWM TBD 234 V6, 489bhp each.
PROPULSION: Two Riva Calzoni waterjet units.
HULL: Aluminium alloy AG 4 MC.
DIMENSIONS
Length, overall: 21·75m
Beam, extreme: 4·10m
Draught: 0·65m
GRT: 39
WEIGHT
Displacement, full load: 15·10 tonnes
PERFORMANCE
Speed, without air lubrication: 33 knots
  with air lubrication: 40 knots

SFCN Marlin 21 class boat fitted with air lubrication system

HONG KONG

CHEOY LEE SHIPYARDS LTD

863-865 Lai Chi Kok Road, Kowloon, Hong Kong
PO Box 80040, Cheung Sha Wan, Kowloon, Hong Kong

Telephone: (3) 7437710
Telex: 56361 HX
Telefax: (3) 7455312

C H Elliott-Brown, *Technical Manager*

Several Air Ride designs are under development at Cheoy Lee Shipyards. Towards the end of 1987 a 25m Air Ride motor yacht was at an early stage of construction. Preliminary details of this craft are given under the Air Ride Craft Inc entry in this section. In addition mould tooling was in progress for a 23·8m passenger ferry. See Addenda.

UNION OF SOVIET SOCIALIST REPUBLICS

MOSCOW SHIPBUILDING AND SHIP REPAIR YARD (Ministry of the River Fleet)

Exporter: V/O Sudoimport, 10, Uspenski Per, 103006 Moscow, USSR

Telephone: 251 05 05/299 52 14
Telex: 411272/411387 SUDO SU

ZARIA (DAWN)

Experiments with high-speed waterbuses, capable of negotiating the many shallow waterways in the Soviet Union, began in 1961.

The object was to develop a vessel for services on shallow waters, with depths of only 0·5m (20in), at speeds of at least 21·5 knots. The prototype Zaria, called the Opytnye-1 (experimental), was put into experimental operation on the river Msta in 1963. During trials the craft attained a speed of 42km/h (26mph) and proved to have a turning radius of 40-70m (44-76 yards). The craft runs bow-on to any flat, sloping bank to embark passengers.

Built with a strong aluminium alloy hull and equipped with a well protected waterjet, the craft is unharmed by floating logs, even when they are encountered at full speed.

Variants include models with a flat load deck in place of the passenger cabin superstructure amidships, and used as light freight vessels. A total of 149 units of the first model of the Zaria were built.

Zaria

Zaria was designed by a team at the Central Design Office of the Ministry of the River Fleet, Gorki, working in conjunction with the Leningrad Water Transport Institute. Series production is under way at the Moscow Shipbuilding and Ship Repair Yard of the Ministry of the River Fleet.

Given the design prefix P83, Zaria conforms to Class P of the RSFSR River Register.

The latest model is distinguished by its trimaran bow configuration, which gives improved performance in waves and enables the craft to be routed on major waterways. Apart from the large number of Zarias in service in the USSR, a number have been supplied to Czechoslovakia, Poland and the German Democratic Republic.

PROPULSION: Power is provided by a single M401A-1 four-stroke, water-cooled, supercharged, 12-cylinder V-type diesel with a normal service output of 870-900hp at 1450-1500rpm and a maximum output of 1000hp. It has a service life of 3000 hours before the first overhaul. It has a variable-speed governor and reversing clutch and drives a single 0·7m (2ft 3½in) diameter variable-pitch, four-bladed waterjet impeller. Fuel consumption is 155kg/h. Lubricating oil consumption at continuous cruising speed is 5kg/h.

The waterjet is of single-stage type with a semi-submerged jet discharge. The brass four-blade, variable-pitch impeller, diameter 693mm, sucks in water through an intake duct which is covered by a protective grille. The discharged water flows around two balanced rudders which provide directional control. Two reversal shutters, interconnected by a rod and operated by cable shafting, reverse the craft or reduce the waterjet thrust when variations in speed are necessary.

A localised ram-air cushion, introduced by an upswept nose and contained on either side by shallow skegs, lifts the bow clear of the water as the craft picks up speed. The airflow also provides air/foam lubrication for the remainder of the flat-bottomed hull.

CONTROLS: Irrespective of load, the radius of turn is between 30 to 50m (98 to 164ft) with the rudder put hard over at an angle of 30 degrees. This turning radius can be decreased by throttling down the engine or closing the valves of the reversing system. At slow speed the craft is capable of pinwheeling. The time required to stop the vessel is 8 to 10 seconds, the coasting distance being between 50 and 60m. The craft is able to navigate small winding rivers with waterways of 12 to 15m wide with the radii of windings varying between 40 and 70m without slowing down.

The vessel can easily pull into shore without landing facilities, providing the river bed slope is no steeper than 3 degrees. The time required for pulling in, embarking passengers, then leaving, averages 1½ minutes. Steps for access are at the bow, port and starboard, and lowered by a control in the wheelhouse.

HULL: Hull and superstructure are of all-welded aluminium alloy plate construction, the constituent parts being joined by argon-shielded arc welding. Framing is of mixed type, with transverse framing at the sides and the main longitudinal elements within the hull bottom. The outside shell and bottom plating is 5mm thick, except for the

Zaria

base at the bow where it is 6mm thick. The wheelhouse is in moulded glass-reinforced plastic. The waterjet duct and nozzle are in grade Cr3 steel and are riveted to the hull.

ACCOMMODATION: Three transverse bulkheads and two recesses divide the hull into six compartments. Behind the forepeak and wheelhouse (frames 0-3) is the passenger cabin (frames 3-27) and aft of this is a compartment housing a small bar and toilet (frames 27-30). A soundproof cofferdam (frames 30-31) follows, aft of which is the engine room (frames 31-41) and steering compartment (frames 41 to stern). The raised wheelhouse, located at the bow, gives 360-degree visibility. The latest export model of the Zaria seats 63 in the passenger cabin, plus another four, without luggage, in two recesses. On routes of up to 45 minutes duration an additional 24 standing passengers can be carried. Life jackets for passengers are stowed in lockers in the baggage compartment and under seats at the rear of the cabin.

The crew off-duty room contains a sofa, table, wall-mounted cupboard, folding stool and a mirror. The toilet contains a wash basin, a bowl, mirror and soap tray.

The wheelhouse has rotating seats for the captain and engineer, two sun visors and there are two windscreen wipers.

The passenger cabin and wheelhouse are heated by warm air produced by hot water from the closed circuit main engine cooling system. Warm air is admitted into the passenger cabin and wheelhouse through a perforated chamber at the bulkhead. The engine room is heated by two 1·2kW electric heaters and the crew room by a 0·6kW electric heater.

SYSTEMS, ELECTRICAL: Main engine driven 3kW, 28V dc generator charges the storage bat-

teries and meets the demands of 24V circuits while the vessel is under way. Four lead-acid batteries type 6TCT-132 EMC 12V, 132Ah each are used to supply electric power for the lighting system, signal lights and radio equipment at anchorage as well as the priming unit and heater. The storage batteries are coupled to form a series-multiple connection yielding 24V and respective current intensity.

Current consumers operating at anchorage as well as the battery charger, electric water and oil heaters, heaters in the engine room and service spaces are fed single-phase ac 220V current.

FIREFIGHTING: Two tanks containing fire-extinguishing compound and hoses for fighting an outbreak in the engine room. System can be brought into operation either from the engine room or from the wheelhouse. Engine room is also provided with two portable carbon dioxide fire extinguishers. Another of the same type is provided in the wheelhouse and two foam fire extinguishers are standard equipment in the main cabin.

FUEL: Craft is refuelled through a filling hose and a neck on the port side of the superstructure. Fuel is fed to the main engine from a service tank with a capacity of 4·13m³, sufficient to enable a vessel to cruise for 8 hours without refuelling. In addition, there is a 400-litre storage tank which contains a two-hour reserve to be used in an emergency. The same tank supplies fuel to a water heater.

COMPRESSED AIR: Starting system for main engines comprising three 45-litre air-cylinders, valves (safety, shut-off, pressure reducing and starting) and piping. Pressure 75-150kgf/cm². Two cylinders in operation, one standby.

ACCOMMODATION
Seats in lounge: 63

Zaria

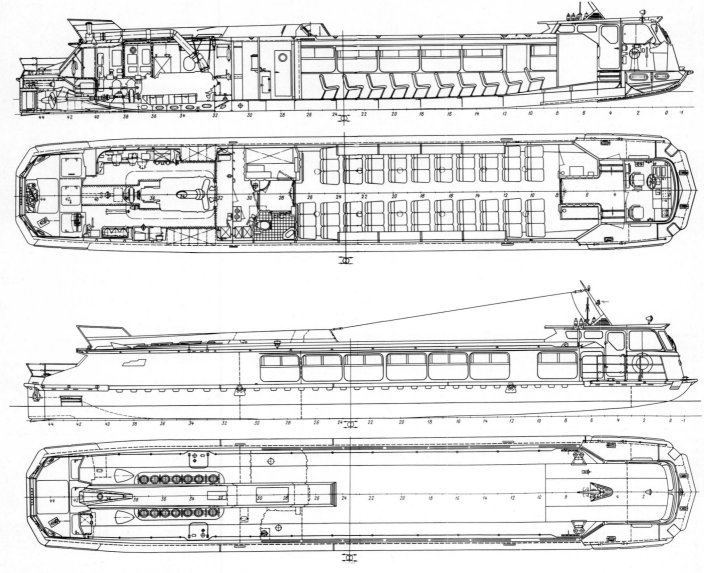

Inboard and outboard profiles and deck views of export model of Zaria

Seats in recesses (with luggage): 4
One washroom/WC
DIMENSIONS
Length overall: 23·9m (78ft 5in)
Beam overall: 4·13m (13ft 7in)
Freeboard up to undetachable parts at mean
draught of 0·44m (1ft 5½in): 3·2m (10ft 6in)
Depth: 1·20m

Mean draught, light: 0·44m (1ft 5½in)
loaded: 0·55m (1ft 9½in)
WEIGHTS
Empty: 16·68 tonnes
Weight with 60 passengers and stores for 8-hour
trip: 24·78 tonnes
Max weight of cargo stowed in luggage recesses: 1
tonne

Fuel capacity: 3·8 tonnes
PERFORMANCE
Speed (in channel of 0·8m depth): 40km/h, 21·6
knots
Range: Suitable for service distances of 150km
(93 miles) and above
Endurance at cruising speed: 8 hours
Max wave height, allowing full speed: 0·70m

UNITED KINGDOM

AIRMARAN LIMITED

[DESIGNERS AND DEVELOPERS]
Loxhill, Godalming, Surrey GU8 4BL, England

Telephone: (048649) 278

P F R Corson, *Director*
C K Corson, *Director*

Airmaran Limited is the design and sales organisation for the Airmaran air-lubricated catamaran. This craft is a medium-speed design, for
the 25- to 30-knot speed range, offering significantly lower fuel consumption compared with
conventional craft of the same work capacity; a
typical saving is of the order of 40 per cent.
Building costs are comparable to those for conventional vessels.
It is envisaged that craft up to approximately
1500 to 2000 tons can be built to the basic design
principles, but the first commercial application is
likely to be a class of 50-passenger Riverbuses for
service on the Thames. It is anticipated that the
operating cost of a Riverbus per passenger-mile

will be similar to that for a conventional river
ferry, but the Airmaran Riverbus will be nearly
twice as fast as the ferry and is thus likely to attract
considerably more traffic.

The design comprises an assymetric catamaran
hull form with air accelerated through the space
between the two hulls by fans. The energy transmitted to the air helps to raise the craft in the water

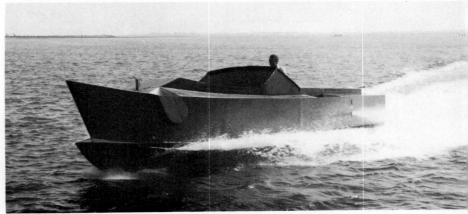

Airmaran test craft

and the air blast clears water from the underside of the hull. Wetted area and skin friction are reduced leading to an efficiency in terms of hp/payload ton-knot comparable to a sidewall hovercraft.

There are however important differences from sidewall hovercraft. No flexible skirt system is required with the Airmaran. The fact that the side members of the craft are substantial catamaran hulls rather than thin sidewalls greatly improves transverse stability. In addition, the lift generated by the hulls not only makes for a smoother ride but also results in a safer craft.

AIRMARAN 50-PASSENGER RIVER-BUS DESIGN

The waterjet propulsion gives very good man-oeuvrability. The craft can turn in its own length when stopped even when using only one jet. Almost total full thrust is available as soon as the throttles are opened, giving particularly marked acceleration, an important attribute on a route with a large number of calls. The system is well protected from floating debris and from grounding. The Riverbus will stop extremely quickly in an emergency. The boat simply drops in the water when the throttles are closed and decelerates rapidly but smoothly.

Construction will normally be of aluminium, allowing a greater variation of design to meet individual customer requirements than is possible with a grp hull.

Applications which have been discussed with potential operators include firefighting and rescue, police work, harbour service duties, inshore survey and fast passenger transport.

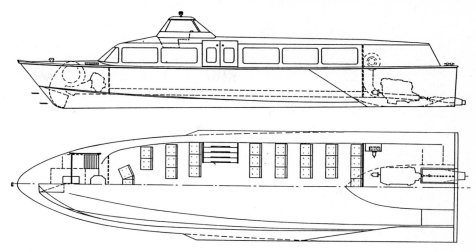

Airmaran 50-passenger Riverbus design

MACHINERY: Two 260hp Mermaid Turbo Plus diesels down-rated to 225hp each driving two PP 140 waterjet units and two hydraulic pumps powering two aft lift air fans.

One 36hp Mermaid Meteor diesel driving an Airscrew Howden 0·61m diameter Heba A centrifugal lift fan.

CABIN HEATING AND VENTILATION: Heating by warm air blower. Fresh air ventilation.

DIMENSIONS
Length overall: 18·90m
Beam: 4·57m

Draught, loaded, at rest: 0·69m forward, 0·60m aft
running: 0·21m forward, 0·45m aft
Air draught above waterline, at rest: 3·41m
running: 3·72m
Saloon inside: 9·76 × 3·81m
PERFORMANCE
Endurance, normal: 8 hours with 10% fuel remaining
Crew: 2
Passenger capacity: 50
Speed at full load, calm water: 27 knots
0·6m wave and 12-knot headwind: 22 knots

UNITED STATES OF AMERICA

AIR RIDE CRAFT INC

[PATENT HOLDERS, DESIGNERS AND DEVELOPERS]
15840 SW 84th Avenue, Miami, Florida 33157, USA

Telephone: (305) 233 4306
Telex: 990160 AIRIDE
Telefax: (305) 592 9655

Donald E Burg, *President*
James G Seat, *Vice President*

Inventor of the Air Ride concept is Donald E Burg, whose experience in high-speed marine craft includes work on the applications of Pratt & Whitney gas turbine-powered waterjets for US Navy hydrofoils and surface effect ships.

The Air Ride concept, developed by Burg since 1978, combines the appearance and simplicity of construction of conventional hulls with the low hydrodynamic drag of surface effect ships, but without heavily stressed structures. Originally the concept did not involve the use of flexible skirts but commercial requirements for higher speeds has led to the incorporation of a simple small flexible seal at the bow only of the new higher-speed Air Ride designs. This seal is normally comprised of several individual elements, each element removable by hand.

The hulls of the Air Ride vessels incorporate a long, shallow plenum chamber for pressurised air in the underside. Air is fed into the chamber by a fan and is retained by two shallow side walls and transverse frames fore and aft. Efficiency is claimed to be comparable to an SES or sidewall hovercraft. The ride is better than that of conventional boats at speed as there is less wetted hull impact area. In the same way as the bow of a conventional vessel shapes the waves, so does the structural bow of the Air Ride vehicle, permitting the use of a shallow air cushion. As Air Ride vehicles do not have a high centre of gravity, they do not need wide sidehull spacing for stability.

The company claims there is virtually no size restriction on craft employing the concept. Preliminary studies show that craft with lengths of 90 to 100m, and larger, are as effective in speed and economy as smaller craft.

Air Ride Craft Inc (previously known as Air Ride Marine Inc) was incorporated in 1979 as a technical services company to develop and market the design, making its invention available to users or qualified builders.

In October 1984 the company revealed that it was working in conjunction with Swiftships Inc, Morgan City, Louisiana, USA, on both commercial and military aluminium-hulled Air Ride designs of up to 60 metres, and also Lantana Boatyard, Lantana, Florida, USA, on similar craft of up to 40 metres and with speeds of up to 50 knots. The first major Air Ride design built, the *Air Ride Express* is described in the entry for its builders, Atlantic and Gulf Boat Building, Inc.

In 1987 building started at the Cheoy Lee Shipyards, Hong Kong of a 25m Air Ride design incorporating a bow flexible seal.

Air Ride Craft Inc has developed a rapid attachment docking system for which patents are pending. The system takes advantage of the elevation of the vessel possible through control over the volume of air in the pressurised air chamber beneath the vessel.

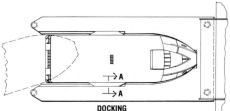

DOCKING

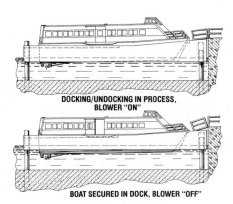

DOCKING/UNDOCKING IN PROCESS, BLOWER "ON"

BOAT SECURED IN DOCK, BLOWER "OFF"

Air Ride Rapid Attachment Docking arrangement

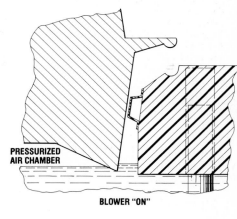

PRESSURIZED AIR CHAMBER

BLOWER "ON"

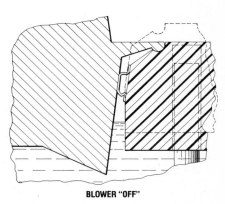

BLOWER "OFF"

CHEOY LEE SES 82 YACHT

This 25m Air Ride design adapted by Cheoy Lee for application as a high-speed yacht is under construction by Cheoy Lee Shipyards, Hong Kong using Airex-cored grp construction. The vessel is not a true SES or sidewall hovercraft but it does have a bow flexible seal, which with the aft hull design maintains an effective air cushion beneath the craft.

CLASSIFICATION: ABS.

NOISE REDUCTION: A special tuned venturi silencer is applied to the cushion fan inlet.

ENGINES

Propulsion: Two GM 12V-92TA, 1080bhp each

Lift: One GM 6V-92TA, 300bhp

PROPULSION: Two Arneson surface drive propellers.

DIMENSIONS

Length overall: 25·05m

Length waterline: 22·71m

Beam: 8·54m

Draught off cushion: 1·36m

Rise height: 0·9m

WEIGHTS/CAPACITIES

Displacement: 61·22 tonnes

Fuel capacity: 11 355 litres (3000 US gallons)

Water capacity: 2839 litres (750 US gallons)

PERFORMANCE

Speed, cruise: 38 knots

  max: 42 knots (estimated)

Range, at cruise speed: 1000n miles

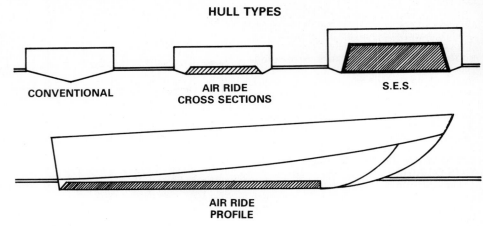

HULL TYPES

CONVENTIONAL

AIR RIDE
CROSS SECTIONS

S.E.S.

AIR RIDE
PROFILE

Air Ride hull profile

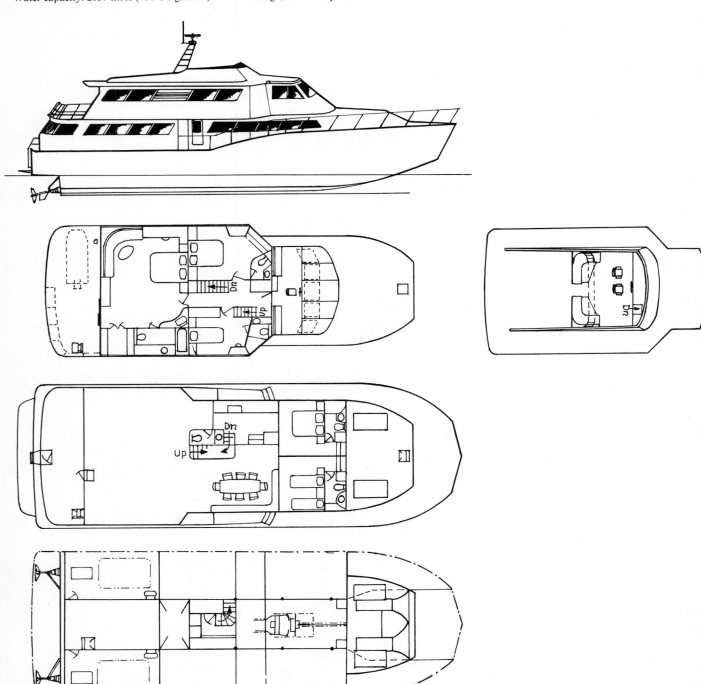

Preliminary General Arrangement of Air Ride SES 82 yacht

AIR RIDE 78 and 106 (DESIGNS)

Three new designs are currently proposed by Air Ride Craft; the 78, 106 and 128. The principal preliminary particulars of the 78 and 106 are as follows:

	AIR RIDE 78	AIR RIDE 106
Length	24·0m	32·3m
Beam	7·3m	9·8m
Displacement, lightship	33·66 tonnes	62·55 tonnes
Displacement, max	54·15 tonnes	100·20 tonnes
Payload plus fuel	20·49 tonnes	37·65 tonnes
Fuel capacity	4542 litres	6813 litres
Potable water capacity	625 litres	946 litres
Main engines	two DDA 12V-92TA	three DDA 16V-92TA
Air-lubrication fan engines	one DDA 6V-53T	one DDA 8V-92TA
Propulsion: Arneson Surface Drive	two ASD 14	three ASD 16
Speed, cruise, at 60% max payload	34 knots	38 knots
Fuel consumption	332 litres/h	590 litres/h
Range, at cruise speed	400n miles	400n miles
Draught, air lubrication fan off	1·53m*	1·59m*
Draught, air lubrication fan on	1·10m*	1·20m*

* These figures may be reduced by 0·30m if the Arneson Surface Drive is tilted up.

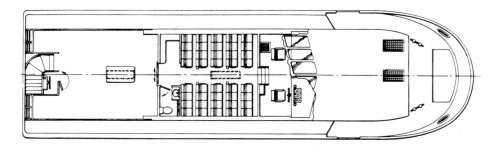

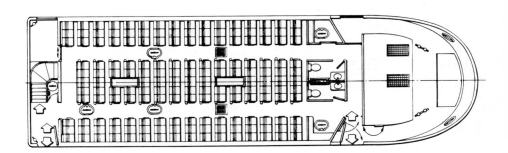

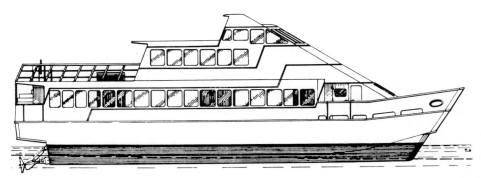

Commuter layout for the Air Ride 78 design

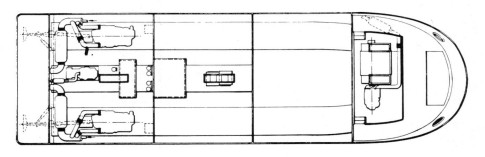

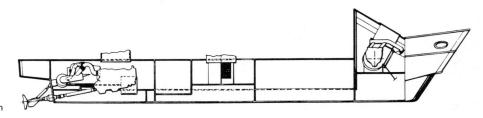

Machinery arrangements for the Air Ride 78 design

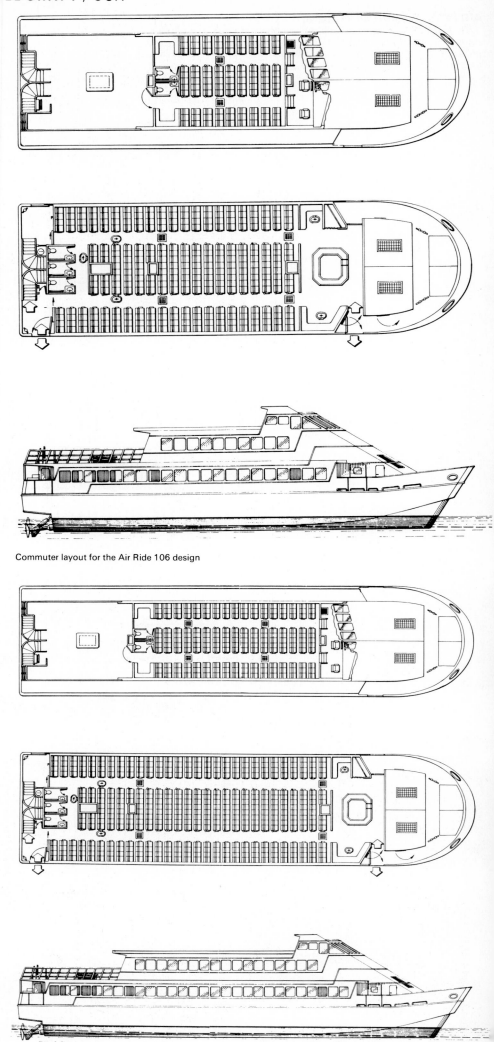

Commuter layout for the Air Ride 106 design

Commuter layout for the Air Ride 128 design

ALLEN JONES & WALTER A MUSCIANO

[PATENT HOLDERS, DESIGNERS AND DEVELOPERS]
5028 Lauderdale Avenue, Virginia Beach, Virginia 23455, USA
and
100 Church Street, Suite 1940, New York, NY 10007, USA

Telephone: (804) 464 0768/(212) 732 2800

Capt Allen Jones, Jr, *President, FASTCO, Fast American Ship Transportation Co, Virginia Beach, Virginia*
Walter Musciano, *Chief Designer, Consulting Chief Designer with Fast American Ship Transportation Co*

WAVE-FORMING KEEL HIGH-SPEED HULL DESIGN

The inventor of the Wave-Forming Keel (WFK) concept is Capt Allen Jones, USN (Rtd) who has been granted an original patent, US Patent No 4048939, believed to be the only original patent granted for hull design this century.

The WFK concept builds on the idea of the stepped planing hull by employing a novel method of introducing air to the step by using water to pump air to the planing surfaces to form a lubricating film of air and thereby reduce frictional resistance. This result is achieved by incorporating longitudinal V or flat-bottom V section, free-flooding, free-breathing, planing structures on the hull bottom, the wave-forming keels. Two or three of these longitudinal structures can be fitted. Each keel can in turn be divided into two or three sections, the spaces between the sections forming steps which function as mixed-fluid venturi pumps.

Originally the proposed designs for using the concept were based on rather conventional hulls but more advanced hull designs have now been developed expressly for use with Wave-Forming Keels. Tests have been conducted with a variety of WFK designs preparatory to turning over a manned test craft to the US Navy for testing and evaluation in early 1986. The craft selected will be operated and performance tested for speed and sea keeping ability with and without wave-forming keels. The principal objective of the proposed evaluation is to monitor operation of a craft equipped with wave-formers and collect sufficient performance data to evaluate its comparative

Wave-forming keel high-speed commuter ferry design with surface-piercing propellers

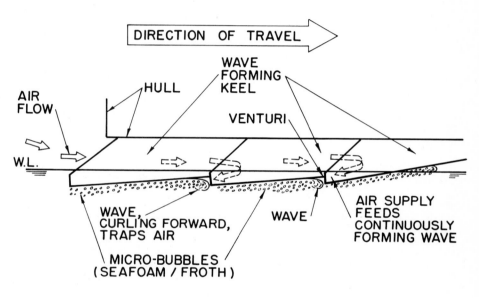
Principle of wave-forming keels providing air lubrication

Configuration of wave-forming keel (3 sections) on manned test craft

Underside of bow, looking aft, manned test craft

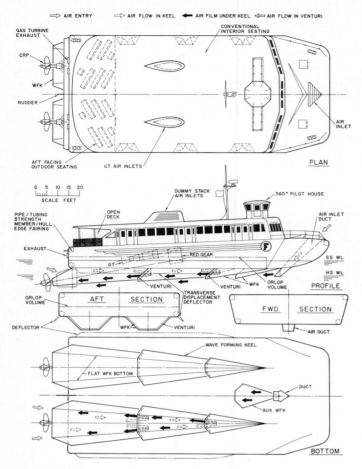

Wave-forming keel concept applied to a high-speed commuter ferry design

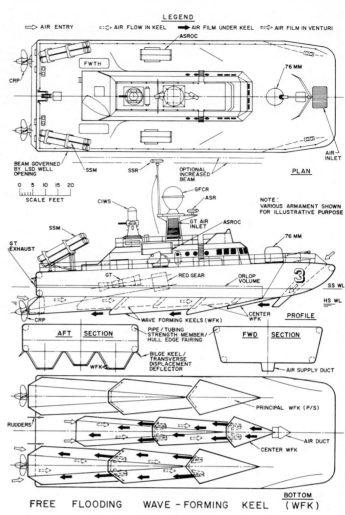

FREE FLOODING WAVE - FORMING KEEL (WFK)

Wave-forming keel concept applied to a fast-attack craft design

improvement over current state-of-the-art planing craft in the 50- to 100-knot speed range.

A fixed wave-former may be designed to be optimum for specific performance criteria or it may be designed for broader objectives or adjustable wave-formers may be applied.

For this project, three wave-former design variations will be applied to the same craft to demonstrate the broad range of performance that can be obtained from a single craft configuration and the ease with which the inherent speed and sea keeping characteristics of the same craft can be altered over a broad range.

The WFK is flooded when the craft is in its buoyant state (at rest or moving very slowly), therefore the resistance is very high at low speeds.

As speed increases, the craft begins to plane on the WFK and sea water begins to leave the flooded WFK. The mixed fluid pump action of the sea water on the venturi step then draws air into the WFK, via the rear opening. This air moves forward in the WFK, exits through the venturi openings and lubricates the WFK. Each design has specific speed ranges which allow for optimum operation of the venturi. As speed is reduced, the planing lift is reduced and the water flows into and fills the WFK as the craft returns to the buoyancy-supported condition.

The WFK increases the length of the trough built up aft of the hull, thus decreasing resistance by giving longer effective length to the Wave-Forming Keel. Typically, the merits of the WFK

are fully realised at speeds over 36 knots when about 75 per cent of buoyancy is replaced by dynamic lift at higher speeds.

The planing craft speed and ride quality are closely related and are determined by the WFK design, location and arrangement. Performance in a seaway can be expected to be superior to conventional planing hull craft because the impact area presented by the WFK is considerably less than a conventional planing hull craft.

Further refinements of the WFK concept have now been proposed by the developers. Hull and venturi forms optimised for calm sea use and for rough sea use are available as well as further detailed optimisation leading to improved efficiency.

ATLANTIC AND GULF BOAT BUILDING INC

PO Box 22947, Fort Lauderdale, Florida 33335, USA
1300 Eller Drive, Port Everglades, Florida 33316, USA

Telephone: (305) 763 8186
Telex: 264915 BARCO UR
Telefax: (305) 463 8128

Stan Joseph, *President*

Builder of the *Air Ride Express* air-lubricated hull boat.

AIR RIDE EXPRESS

This 19·8m crew/supply boat has been developed from a 12·8m aluminium-hulled prototype first tested in October 1980 to demonstrate the principles of Air Ride craft designs. Satisfactory test results led to the design of a

Air Ride Express

19·8m hull for the offshore industry. *Air Ride Express* was built for South Florida Offshore Services Ltd, Plantation, Florida, USA, and was operated by Gulf Crew Transport, Pensacola, Florida, first entering service in mid-1983.

It is understood that this vessel was sold in 1986 to be used as a high-speed passenger ferry, conversion being undertaken in the autumn of 1986.

LIFT AND PROPULSION: Power for the mixed-flow lift fan is supplied by a General Motors Detroit Diesel GM 6V-53T, capable of 265hp but only required to operate at 125hp at a constant setting. Power is transmitted directly to the fan through a simple flexible coupling. To ensure maximum operational life the fan is designed for 5g shock loadings although loadings in operation should not exceed 0·5g. The fan air inlet is an angled grille next to the stairway aft of the crew cabin. The main engines are two 590hp 12V-71TI General Motors Detroit Diesels each driving a single three-bladed Columbian Bronze Company bronze 36/44 crew boat propeller via a Twin Disc MG 514C 2·5:1 ratio gearbox. The main shafts are 3-inch diameter ARMCO Aquamet 17s. Standard fuel capacity is 4542 litres (1200 gallons).

CONTROLS: Hydraulically operated steering units at helm and stern. Morse single lever controls engine and each engine has a Murply low water monitor alarm that sounds in the pilothouse. A water ballast system trims uneven loads fore or aft, port or starboard. Ballast tanks, controlled from the pilothouse, have a total capacity of 9463 litres (2500 gallons).

HULL: All-welded aluminium structure.

ACCOMMODATION: Passenger cabin seats 32. Pilothouse equipped with heavy duty offshore captain's and mate's chairs. Carrier Transicold air-conditioning and heating. 3-ton marine commercial unit supplied by Thermo Air Inc, Miami. Full below deck living quarters for crew of 2 to 4, with 290ft² floor space and 6ft 8in headroom. Accommodation includes three bunks, stove, refrigerator, freezer, shower, colour television and storage for two weeks' provisions. Below deck area can be converted to seat 30 additional passengers. Potable water capacity, 1250 litres

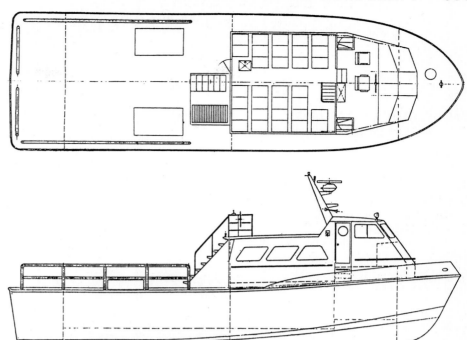

Air Ride Express

(275 gallons). Cargo deck area in excess of 450ft² (17ft 6in × 26ft). Design is certified by US Coast Guard for operations 100 miles offshore.

SYSTEMS, ELECTRONICS/NAVIGATION: Furuno FR 360 radar. Si-Tex/Koden 767 Loran C, Motorola Triton 55/75vhf. Raytheon 1210 SSB. Datamarine DL 2480 depth sounder.

DIMENSIONS
Length: 19·8m (65ft)
Beam, max: 6·4m (21ft)
Draught, hull only, lift fan on: 0·38m (1ft 3in)
lift fan off: 0·69m (2ft 3in)
Draught, including appendages, lift fan on: 1·37m (4ft 6in)
lift fan off: 1·67m (5ft 6in)

WEIGHTS
Displacement, light: 27 216kg (60 000lb)
Displacement, max: 43 092kg (95 000lb)
Payload and fuel: 15 876kg (35 000lb)
Fuel capacity: 4542kg (1200 US gallons)
Potable water capacity: 1040 litres (275 US gallons)
Ballast water capacity: 9463 litres (2500 US gallons)

PERFORMANCE
Speed, with 15 873kg disposable load: 27 knots
Fuel consumption at 26 knots, moderate load: 235 litres/h (62 gallons/h)
Range: 500n miles (927 km)
PRICE: Approximately US$700 000, fob (1983).

WING-IN-GROUND-EFFECT CRAFT

CHINA, PEOPLE'S REPUBLIC

CHINA SHIP SCIENTIFIC RESEARCH CENTRE

RAM-WING VEHICLE 902

A single-seat test vehicle. No details are available but development of the vehicle was proceeding in 1984.

MARINE DESIGN AND RESEARCH INSTITUTE OF CHINA (MARIC)

314 Sichuan Road, Central, PO Box 3053, Shanghai, People's Republic of China

Telephone: 215044
Telex: 33029 MARIC CN
Cable: 5465

Liang Yun, *Deputy Chief Engineer*

For further information on MARIC work please see Air Cushion Vehicles section.

PAR WIG TYPE 750

This two-seat experimental PAR/WIG craft was completed in 1987 and has been engaged in trials and tests in Shanghai.
HULL: Built in grp with aircraft construction techniques.
LIFT AND PROPULSION: Four 30hp piston engines driving four ducted propellers.
DIMENSIONS
Length overall: 8·47m
Beam overall: 4·80m

MARIC PAR WIG Type 750 coming ashore

Height overall: 2·30m
WEIGHTS
Max take-off weight: 745kg

Payload: 172kg
PERFORMANCE
Speed, max, calm water: 71·3 knots

MARIC PAR WIG Type 750 showing its considerable clearance height above the water

GERMANY, FEDERAL REPUBLIC

BOTEC ENGINEERING SOCIETY LTD

Odenwaldring 24, D-6101 Gros-Bieberau, Federal Republic of Germany

Telephone: (06162) 1013
Telex: 41994 12 BTEC D

Günther W Jörg, *Proprietor*

In 1987 Günther Jörg established this company for the design, development and construction of Airfoil-Flying Boats (aerodynamic ground-effect vehicles of all sizes). Construction was immediately put in hand with a small 2-seat craft,

the Sport-fly, and first trials started in the second week of December 1987. Serial production is planned.

A second company was also formed by Günther Jörg in 1987, **Airfoil Sales Company for Ground Effect Vehicles**, with the same address as above.

SPORT-FLY (JÖRG II, TAF VIII-1)

A two-seat craft designed to achieve 67 knots with a 64hp petrol engine, built in aluminium alloy and grp materials.
ENGINE: 2-cylinder, 2-cycle water-cooled, 64hp.
PROPELLER: 3-blade adjustable pitch, diameter 1·5m.

DIMENSIONS
Length: 8·30m
Width, max: 3·42m
Width for transporting: 2·25m (special trailer available)
WEIGHTS
Weight, empty: 450kg
Payload: 180kg
PERFORMANCE
Speed, take-off: 38 knots
Speed, cruising: 67·5 knots
Range: 108n miles with 25 litres (5·5 Imperial gallons) normal tank or 270n miles with additional tank
Surface clearance height: 0·2m to 0·3m
Buoyancy: Ten water-tight compartments

GÜNTHER W JÖRG

[DESIGNER, DEVELOPER AND PATENT HOLDER]
Odenwaldring 24, 6101 Gros-Bieberau, Federal Republic of Germany

Telephone: (06162) 3624/1013
Telex: 41994 12 BTEC D

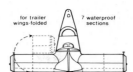

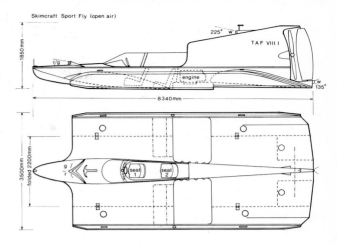

Skimcraft Sport Fly (open air)

Jörg Sport-fly

Günther W Jörg was for a number of years a constructor, works manager and development engineer for various West German vertical take-off and landing (VTOL) projects. He sees his Aerodynamic Ground Effect Craft (AGEC) concept as a means of providing fast, economical and comfortable long-distance travel. His experiments began in the 1960s with a series of radio-controlled models. Wind-tunnel tests were also undertaken and the results were checked by a computer. The first Günther Jörg ram wing, a two-seater powered by a modified Volkswagen engine, was designed in 1973, and first flew in 1974. After an extensive test programme, Jörg II was designed, performing its first flight in 1976. This incorporated more than 25 design improvements and has travelled more than 10 000km. During 1978 and 1979, Jörg designed a glassfibre-hulled four- to six-seater, Jörg III, which would have been put into series production in Poland had it not been for political tension. The first prototype was completed in 1980. Designs are being prepared for larger and faster craft capable of carrying heavier loads over greater distances.

Stabilisation about the pitch and roll axes and maintaining the flying height of the AGEC can be regulated independently by the ground/water surface reaction and therefore requires only a simple steering control for movement around the vertical axis. This basic requirement led to the development of a tandem wing configuration, the handling characteristics of which were first tested on models and then on two-seat research craft. Tests showed that the tandem wings had good aerodynamic qualities, even above turbulent water, with or without water contact.

AGEC's have ample buoyancy and are seaworthy, even while operating at low speed (cruising in displacement condition). After increasing speed the craft lifts off the surface of the water and the resulting air cushion reduces the effects of the waves. After losing water contact the boat starts its ram wing flight at a height of 4 to 8 per cent of the profile depth. A two-seater with a wingspan of 3·2m (10ft 6in) and a profile length of 3·05m (10ft) will have a flying height above the water surface of 102 to 203mm (4 to 8in) at a speed of 96·6km/h (60mph). The low power requirement of this type of craft is achieved through the improved lift/drag ratio of a wing-in-ground-effect as compared to free flight.

The exceptionally high lift/drag ratio of these craft keep the thrust requirements per kilogram of weight low, thus transport efficiency is high. The ratio of empty weight to payload for the test craft is 2:1, but calculations already show that it will be 1:1 with more advanced designs; large transport craft might be 1:2. A craft of more than 300 tons would have a wing chord of 36m and fly under ground effect conditions at between 3·5 and 7m. It would have a wing span of 40m and a length of 100m, requiring engine thrust of 55 000hp (40 000kW). Cruising speed would be 250km/h from 10 000hp (7350kW) and craft of this size could travel all-year-round over 90 per cent of the world's sea areas.

The main components of an Aerodynamic Ground Effect Craft are: forward main wing; aft wing; vertical stabiliser and rudder; longitudinal tip fence/float; fuselage for passengers and/or cargo and the powerplant. The latter comprises an engine with propeller or ducted propeller, which can be mounted as a pod on the rear wing or as a unit integrated with the rear fuselage.

Additional equipment might include a retractable undercarriage, which would enable the craft, under its own power, to run on to dry land or move from land to water for take-off. Towing connections can be provided for water-skiing and an electrically operated anchor winch can be fitted.

The following operational possibilities are foreseen:

INLAND WATERWAYS AND OFFSHORE AREAS: Suitable for rescue boats, customs, police, coast guard units, patrol boats, high-speed ferries, leisure craft.

COASTAL TRAFFIC: Large craft would be operated as fast passenger and passenger/car ferries and mixed-traffic freighters.

OVERLAND: Suitable for crossing swamps, flat sandy areas, snow and ice regions. Another pos-

The Jörg II-2, the production two-seat Sport-fly, 11 December 1987

sible application is as a high-speed tracked skimmer operating in conjunction with a guide carriage above a monorail.

Small craft, displacing 1 ton or more, can travel over the supporting surface at a height of 304mm (12in) or more at a speed of 96·6 to 144·8km/h (60 to 90mph).

Larger craft, weighing 10 to 50 tons will be able to fly at a height of 914mm to 1·98m (3ft to 6ft 6in) at a speed of 129 to 177km/h (80 to 110mph).

Coastal craft displacing more than 100 tons will fly at a height of 3·04m (10ft) or even higher.

The basic advantage of the AGEC is its ability to transport passengers and freight far quicker than conventional ship, rail or road transport. The ratio between empty weight and service load is about 2:1 but can certainly be improved. Fuel consumption is 80 to 85 per cent lower than that of a boat of similar construction.

JÖRG I
Total wingspan: 4·1m (13ft 6in)
Length overall: 6·2m (20ft 4in)
Wing profile length: 2·5m (8ft 2in)
Max take-off weight: 700kg (1543lb)
Passengers: 2
Cruising speed: 100km/h (62·1mph)
Installed power: 70hp
Average cruising height: 0·1m (4in)
Max flying height: 0·5m (20in)
Year of construction: 1973-74
Construction: Grp/wood
Range: 300km (186 miles)

JÖRG II SPORT-FLY
(PROTOTYPE)
A 2-seat test boat for series production, it was built in 1976 and is owned by Günther Jörg.
Total wingspan: 3·28m (10ft 9in)
Length overall: 8·3m (27ft 3in)
Wing profile length: 3m (9ft 10in)
Max take-off weight: 770kg (1700lb)
Passengers: 2
Cruising speed: 135km/h (84mph)
Installed power: 105hp
Average cruising height: 0·12m (4·75in)
Max flying height: 1m (3ft 3in)
Construction: Aluminium and fibreglass
Range: 500km (310 miles)
(with long-range tanks, more than 1000km (620 miles))

JÖRG II-2
TAF VIII-1
PRODUCTION VERSION OF JÖRG II
First flights of this craft were undertaken in December 1987.
Total wingspan: 3·42m
Length overall: 8·30m
Height, max: 1·90m
Weight, empty: 470kg
Payload: 180kg
Engine: 2-cylinder, 2-cycle water-cooled, 64hp
Propeller: 3-blade, adjustable pitch, 1·5m diameter
Speed, take-off: 38 knots
Speed, cruising: 67·5 knots
Fuel tank: 25 litres

Jörg II-2 at 130km/h (70 knots), 11 December 1987

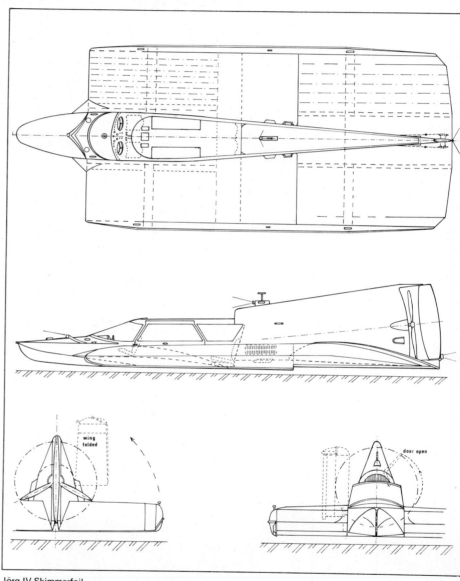
Jörg IV Skimmerfoil

Construction of TAF VIII-4S

TAF VIII-4S during ground test

Range: 108n miles
(with additional tank: 270n miles)
Cruising height over surface: 0·20 to 0·30m
over waves: higher
Hull: Aluminium and glassfibre, ten water-tight
sections
Trailer width, max: 2·25m

JÖRG III

A glassfibre 4- to 6-seater, 11·3m in length, built
in Poland in 1980.

JÖRG IV
Craft built
1st craft: Skimmerfoil
Owner: G Jörg held at University of Stellenbosch,
Cape Town, South Africa, built 1981
2nd craft:
Owner: FIGU AG, Schaffhausen, Switzerland,
built 1983
In March 1985 a Jörg IV achieved an average
speed of 158km/h over a distance of 145km at high
ambient air temperatures in the Arabian Gulf.
Total wingspan: 5m (16ft 5in)
Length overall: 11m (36ft 1in)
Wing profile length: 3·9m (12ft 10in)
Max take-off weight: 1500-1700kg (3300-3750lb)

TAF VIII-4S cockpit

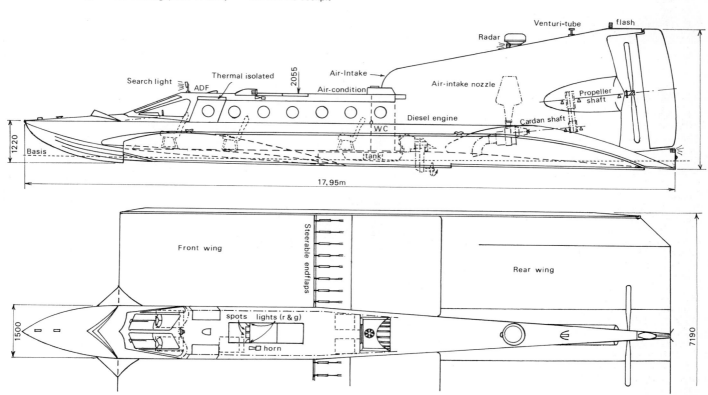

Layout of the Jörg Aerodynamic Ground Effect Craft TAF VIII-4S

Jörg V (TAF VIII-4S) on ground test, September 1986

Passengers: 4
Cruising speed: 127km/h (79mph)
Installed power: 220hp (3·5-litre BMW car engine)
Average cruising height (calm water): 0·17m (7in)
Max flying height: 1·2m (4ft) waves
Year of construction: 1981/1983
Construction: Aluminium
Range: 500-600km (310-370 miles)
Endurance: 4-4·75 hours

JÖRG V
TAF VIII-4S

This new Jörg craft underwent its first ground tests in September 1986. Open sea tests in the North Sea were due to start in March/April 1987.
Length overall: 17·95m
Speed: 80-165km/h (45-90 knots)
Passengers: 5-8

Jörg IV at 145km/h

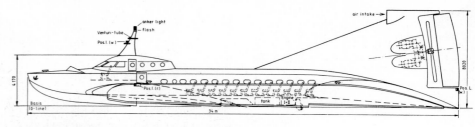

Jörg 34m Aerodynamic Ground Effect Craft for 1988/89 development

Weight: 3·5 tonnes
Flying height, calm water: 0·6m, higher over waves
Engines: One 650hp Textron Lycoming LTX 101 turboshaft with water-methanol injection available for 10 per cent power increase for take-off. One diesel engine driving a retractable marine propeller
Propeller: 4-blade, 2·9m diameter, cable/hydraulically controlled
Transmission: 9 V-belts (Optibelt, Höxter, W Germany)
Range: Up to 500km

PROJECT DESIGNS

Details of three project designs with passenger capacities of 15, 135 and 400 are given in *Jane's Surface Skimmers 1985*.
A new project design for 1988/89 development is for a 34m Aerodynamic Ground Effect Craft with a passenger capacity of 60.
Length: 34·00m
Beam (span): 14·32m
Height: 8·02m
Cruising height above surface: 0·5-2·0m
Weight: 28·50 tonnes
Draught: 0·5m
Engines: Two 1580hp plus diesel engine for harbour manoeuvring
Hull: Aluminium alloy

Reference: For further information on Jörg Aerodynamic Ground Effect Craft please see paper: *History and Development of the Aerodynamic Ground Effect Craft (AGEC) with Tandem Wings* by Dipl Ing G W Jörg. Proceedings of Ram Wing and Ground Effect Craft Symposium, Royal Aeronautical Society, London, 19 May 1987.

RHEIN-FLUGZEUGBAU GmbH (RFB)
(Subsidiary of Messerschmitt-Bölkow-Blohm)

Head Office and Main Works: Flugplatz, Postfach 408, D-4050 Mönchengladbach 1, Federal Republic of Germany

Telephone: (02161) 682-0
Telex: 08/52506 D
Telefax: (02161) 682200

Other Works: Flughafen Köln-Bonn, Halle 6, D-5050 Porz-Wahn, Federal Republic of Germany
Flugplatz, D-2401 Lübeck-Blankensee, Federal Republic of Germany

Dipl-Volkswirt Wolfgang Kutscher, *President*
Dipl-Ing Alfred Schneider, *President*

RFB is engaged in the development and construction of airframe structural components, with particular emphasis on wings and fuselages made entirely of glassfibre-reinforced resins. Research and design activities include studies for the Federal German Ministry of Defence.

Current manufacturing programmes include series and individual production of aircraft components and assemblies made of light alloy, steel and glassfibre-reinforced resin for aircraft in quantity production, as well as spare parts and ground equipment. The company is also active in the areas of shelter and container construction.

Under contract to the West German government, RFB services certain types of military aircraft and provides target-towing flights and other services with special aircraft.

The X-113 Am Aerofoil Boat was built and tested under the scientific direction of the late Dr A M Lippisch. Flight tests of the six- to seven-seat RFB X-114 have been successfully completed and after some hydrodynamic modifications, including the fitting of hydrofoils beneath the sponsons, it is undergoing a new series of tests.

In 1982, the company began an extensive weather survey to determine the potential sales for a production craft with dimensions similar to those of the X-114 and designed for operation in coastal regions.

RFB (LIPPISCH) X-113 Am AEROFOIL BOAT

The Aerofoil Boat was conceived in the USA by

RFB X-113 Am during flight demonstration over Wattenmeer

Dr A M Lippisch. The first wing-in-ground-effect machine built to Lippisch designs was the Collins X-112, which was employed by Lippisch to examine the stability problems likely to be encountered in the design of larger machines of this type.

Since 1967 further development of the concept has been undertaken by RFB with government backing. The single-seat X-113 has been built as a test craft to provide data for the design of larger craft of the same type.

The X-113 Am underwent its first airworthiness test from Lake Constance in October 1970.

During the first series of tests, the craft demonstrated its operating ability on water as well as flight capability at very low altitudes. These tests were followed, in autumn 1971, by a second series of trials during which performance measurements were taken. A cine camera built into the cockpit recorded instrument readings and a camera built into the lateral stabilisers took pictures of small threads on the upper wing surface for current flow analysis.

In November/December 1972 a third series of tests were conducted in the North Sea in the Weser estuary area.

Apart from various performance measurements, the aim of these trials was to investigate the machine's capabilities in roughish weather conditions. Although the machine was originally designed for only a brief general demonstration on calm water, it proved capable of take-offs and landings in a moderate sea.

Remarkably good sea behaviour was shown from the outset. Take-offs and landings in wave heights of about 0·75m (2ft 6in) presented no problem. Flights were made in the coastal region, and sometimes on the Wattenmeer, in wind forces of up to 25 knots, without any uncontrollable

flying tendencies being observed in low-level flight.

The flight performance measurements gave a gliding angle of 1 : 30, which cannot be greatly improved by enlarging the machine. The relatively thin outer laminate of the gfr wing sandwich, with a thickness of 0·4mm, stood up to the loads involved in taking off in a roughish sea and also remained watertight throughout the whole period of trials.

Towards the end of the trials, in order to reduce noise and give the airscrew better protection from spray, the machine was converted to pusher propulsion.

The company envisages a range of Aerofoil craft for a variety of civil and military purposes, from single-seat runabouts to cargo transporters with payloads of up to 10 tons. As transports they could be employed on coastal, inter-island and river services. Military variants could be used as assault craft, FPBs and ASW vessels.

Flight tests, including a series performed over rough water in the North Sea near Bremerhaven, have established that 50 per cent less power is required in ground effect, enabling operations in excess of 50-ton-miles per gallon of fuel at speeds in the 90- to 180-knot range.

RFB X-114 AND -114H AEROFOIL BOATS

Evolved from the X-113, the RFB X-114 six- to seven-seater has a maximum take-off weight of 1500kg and is fitted with a retractable wheel undercarriage, enabling it to operate from land or water.

Power is provided by a 200hp Lycoming IO-360 four-cylinder horizontally-opposed air-cooled engine driving a specially-designed Rhein-Flugzeugbau ducted fan. Range, with 100kg (220lb) of fuel, is more than 1000km (621 miles).

Operational speed is 75 to 200km/h (46 to 124mph).

An initial trials programme was successfully completed in 1977. A new series of trials was undertaken after hydrodynamic modifications that included the fitting of hydrofoils beneath the sponsons, raising maximum take-off weight to 1750kg. In this configuration it is known as the X-114H.

The vehicle is designed to operate over waves up to 1·5m (4ft 11in) in ground effect and can therefore be used without restriction during 80 per cent of the year in the Baltic Sea area and 60 per cent of the year in the North Sea. In high seas of more than 1·5m (4ft 11in), take-off and landing takes place in waters near the coast. Flying is virtually unrestricted, providing due allowance is made for the loss in economy.

Fuel consumption costs, while flying in ground effect, are lower than those for cars. RFB states that its economics cannot be matched by any other form of transport aircraft.

Although built primarily as a research craft to extend the experience gained with the X-113 Am single-seater, Aerofoil boats of the size of the X-114 are suitable for air-taxi work along coastlines, the supervision of restricted areas, patrol, customs and coastguard purposes, and search and rescue missions.

Without any significant new research the construction of a vehicle with a take-off weight of approximately 18 000kg is possible. On a vehicle of this size, the ratio of empty weight to take-off weight is less than 50 per cent.

DIMENSIONS
Length overall: 12·8m
Wing span: 7m
Height overall: 2·9m
WEIGHTS
Max take-off
 X-114: 1500kg
 X-114H: 1750kg
Payload: 500kg
PERFORMANCE
Max cruising speed: 200km/h (124mph)
Cruising speed in ground effect: 150km/h (93mph)
Max flight range: 2150km (1336 miles)

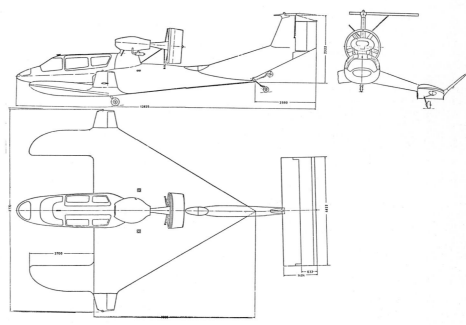

RFB X-114H Aerofoil boat with hydrofoils

General Arrangement of RFB X-114

RFB X-114 Aerofoil boat

UNION OF SOVIET SOCIALIST REPUBLICS

CENTRAL LABORATORY OF LIFESAVING TECHNOLOGY (CLST)
Moscow, USSR

Yury Makarov, *Chief Engineer*
A W Gremyatsky, *Project Leader*
Evgeniy P Grunin, *Designer*
N L Ivanov, *Designer*
S Chernyavsky
Y Gorbenko
A Kuzakov, *Consultant*
V Shavrov, *Consultant*
A Baluyev, *Director of Flight Trials*

The Central Laboratory of Lifesaving Technology (CLST), a division of the Rescue Organisation for Inland Waters (OSVOD), has designed a small aerodynamic ram-wing machine, capable of 140km/h (86mph), which will be used to answer distress calls on the Soviet lakes, rivers and canals.

The Ekranolyetny Spasatyelny Kater-Amphibya (ESKA) surface-effect amphibious lifeboat is available in several versions. It has been referred to as the Ekranolet and the Nizkolet (skimmer).

Apart from meeting emergency situations on waterways, the craft, which is amphibious, is capable of operating in deserts, tundra, arctic icefields and steppeland. Derivatives are to be employed as support vehicles for geologists, communications engineers and construction groups.

In Soviet publications emphasis has been given to the potential value of such craft in opening up the mineral wealth of Siberia, the Soviet far-east, far-north and other virgin territories.

As with the X-113 Am and other machines of this type, the vehicle operates on the principle that by flying in close proximity to the ground, the so-called image flow reduces induced drag by about 70 per cent. Flight-in-ground-effect inhibits the downwash induced by wing lift, thus suppressing the induced drag. Whereas an average aircraft at normal flight altitude carries about 4kg (9lb) per

hp of engine output, the wing-in-ground-effect machine, on its dynamic air cushion carries up to 20kg (44lb), an improvement of more than 400 per cent. 'Weight efficiency' of the craft (ratio of useful load to all-up weight) is 25 to 50 per cent depending on size.

At angles of attack of 2 to 8 degrees near the ground, its lift is 40 to 45 per cent greater than when flying out of ground effect. In addition the supporting surface hinders the vortex flow from the lower wing surface to the upper surface which decreases induced drag.

Control of the ESKA is said to be easy and pilots require no special training. Within ground effect it is no more complicated to control than a car.

The design, which has been strongly influenced by the Lippisch 'aerofoil boat' concept, employs an almost identical short span, low aspect ratio reversed delta wing with anhedral on the leading edge, dihedral tips and wing floats. A description of ESKA-1 follows, together with illustrations of other aerodynamic machines designed at the CLST, including the saucer-shaped E-120 single-seater; the An-2E, which incorporates the fuselage, engine and cabin of the Antonov An-2W seaplane, and a two-seater powered by a 210hp Walter Minor engine.

One of the Ekranoplan's designers has been quoted as saying: 'Craft of this type are destined to become, in the not-too-distant future, as popular as hydroplanes, hovercraft and helicopters'.

ESKA-1

Research on aerodynamic ram wings began at CLST during 1971. During 1971-72 a series of small scale models were built, followed by the construction of five different full-size craft, including one with a circular planform.

The initial design of the ESKA-1 was prepared by Evgeniy Grunin between September and December 1972. In December 1972 the CLST section specialising in the provision of transport rescue facilities gave the design its full approval and accepted it for construction without additions or alterations.

Several free-flying models of the design were built and tested. In February 1973, A Gremyatsky was nominated leader of the project, and test-flew the first prototype in August of that year. Flight tests were subsequently undertaken by A A Baluyev.

Keynotes of the design were low cost, the use of advanced technology wherever possible and overall reliability in operation. In addition the craft had to be easily broken down for storing and transport by road. Analysis of these and other requirements and conditions led to the decision to build the craft in wood, using 1mm thick aviation ply, plastic foam, glass fibre, glues and varnishes. The resulting machine operated for more than four years in various conditions.

The designers state that although the ESKA-1 is similar aerodynamically to the late Dr Alexander Lippisch's X-112, X-113 Am and X-114, the basis of ensuring longitudinal stability and the hydrodynamics at take-off differ. They add, 'In the absence of data on the results of tests for those designs, we relied on our own experience and used the results obtained in our own experiments with model ram wings'.

Practical help in the preparation of the initial design was given by A Kuzakov, designer of the MAK-15 glider, and the late V B Shavrov (1899-1976), designer of the Sh-2. Another well-known Soviet aircraft designer, V B Gribovsky acted as a consultant in solving the design problems presented by certain joints and structural members.

The basic aerodynamic design and construction of ESKA-1 has provided sufficient data for it to be recommended as a rescue/patrol and communications craft for certain national assignments. The test results show a case for continuing development work on two or three ESKA-1 prototypes, built with modern materials. It has shown considerable operational potential.

POWERPLANT: Single 32hp M-63 four-stroke two-cycle motorcycle engine drives, via a two-stage reduction gear, a wooden SDW-2 series 1·6m (5ft 3in) diameter constant pitch propeller. Engine is mounted on tubular steel tripod in dorsal position behind the cockpit. ST-4 electric starter mounted on engine block and driving the camshaft via a gear mounted on the extension shaft.

HULL: Built mainly of pinewood frames and longerons, with a box keel in plywood. Structure covered in aviation plywood with exterior clad in glass cloth saturated with ED-6 epoxy resin. Finished with white emulsion and synthetic varnish.

ACCOMMODATION: Cabin contains two aircraft seats in tandem with safety belts and space for parachutes. Rear seat for passenger or observer is placed close to centre of gravity so that no additional trimming is necessary when flying without a passenger.

WINGS: Cantilever shoulder-wing monoplane. Wooden monospar construction with leading edge covered in 1mm ply to form torque box. Dihedral tips each carry a wooden slotted aileron.

TAIL UNIT: Trapezium-shaped, strutted T-tail-

ESKA-1

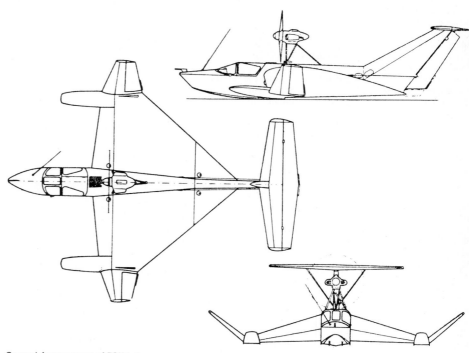

General Arrangement of ESKA-1

ESKA-1

plane mounted on top of fin by sheet metal fixtures. All-wooden single box spar structure. Fixed-incidence, single full-span elevator. Elevator and tailplane covered with AST-100 glass cloth. Wooden rudder secured to fin at two points.

LANDING GEAR: Wing-tip floats are made in pvc foam and covered with a single layer of ASTT3b/-S1 glass cloth. Each is attached to wing by four steel bolts.

CONTROLS: Single aircraft-type control column, incorporating engine throttle, located in the centre of cockpit ahead of pilot's seat. Conventional foot-operated bar to control rudder.

TESTING AND RECORDING EQUIPMENT: In addition to basic aircraft-type instrumentation,

the prototype ESKA-1 carried the following test equipment to record pitch and bank angles of up to 40 degrees: K12-51 oscilloscope; GS-6W equipment to measure pitch and angles of bank; synchronising equipment and an electrical supply pack, comprising an SAM28 27V battery and a PT-0.125-36/100 3F alternator.

RADIO: A modified portable 21 RTN-2-4M transmitter receiver provides a continuous radio link between ESKA-1 and the shore up to a distance of 2·5-3km (1·5-1·75 miles).

DIMENSIONS
Wing span overall: 6·9m (22ft 5⅜in)
Length: 7·55m (24ft 7in)
Height: 2·5m (8ft 2½in)

Wing area: 13·85m² (148·13ft²)
Tail area: 3m² (32·4ft²)
WEIGHTS
All-up weight: 450kg (992lb)
Empty: 230kg (507lb)
Useful load: 220kg (485lb)
Weight efficiency: 48·879%
PERFORMANCE
Speed, displacement condition: 30-40km/h (18-
   24mph)
   planing on water: 50-60km/h (31-37mph)
   ram flight at a height of 0·3-3m (11·75in-9ft
   10in): 100-140km/h (62-86mph)
   at altitude, 100-300m: 120-130km/h (74-80mph)
   take-off: 55km/h (34·17mph)
   landing: 50-55km/h (31-34mph)
Take-off run from water: 80-100m (260-300ft)
   from snow: 50-60m (162-195ft)
Landing run on water (without braking para-
   chute): 40m (131ft)
Most effective flying height in surface effect: 0·3-
   1·5m (1ft-4ft 11in)
Max altitude, with 50% load, for obstacle
   clearance: Up to 50m (164ft)
Range with full fuel supply: 300-350km (186-217
   miles)
Wing loading: 32·5kg/m² (6·67lb/ft²)
Power loading: 15kg/hp (33lb/hp)
Limiting weather conditions: Can operate in
   Force 5 winds

CLST ANTONOV An-2E

This adaptation of the An-2 multi-duty 12-seat
biplane was built in 1973 to the design of E P
Grunin. It incorporates several major components
of the Soviet-built floatplane version, the An-2W,
including the forward fuselage, cabin and engine—
a 1000hp Shvetsov ASh-621R nine-cylinder radial
air-cooled engine, driving a four-bladed variable-
pitch metal propeller.

The craft is intended for a range of utility
applications in addition to carrying passengers
and freight. Like the RFB X-114, which under-
went trials in the German Federal Republic, the
An-2E has a retractable wheeled undercarriage for
operation from land as well as rivers, lakes and
coastal waters.
DIMENSIONS
Span: 15·75m (51ft 8in)
Length: 18·65m (61ft 2in)
Height: 8·1m (26ft 7in)
Lift area: 94m² (1011ft²)
WEIGHT
All-up weight: 7000kg (15 435lb)

CLST EKRANOLET E-120

No technical details have been released concerning this circular planform WIG single-seater. One
of a number of experimental wing-in-ground-
effect machines designed by the CLST, it was built
in 1971.

PARAWING EKRANOPLANS

The originator of the idea of applying Rogallo-
type flexible delta wings to light ekranoplans is
Evgeniy Grunin, one of the designers of the
ESKA-1. The parawing is well known for its
outstanding aerodynamic qualities and stability
and is convenient for transport and storage.
Grunin, assisted by S Chernyavsky and N Ivanov,
fitted a flexible wing to the fuselage of the Czechoslovak Let L-13J Blanik, a powered version of the
well known two-seat, all-metal sailplane. Power is
supplied by a 42hp Jawa M-150 piston-engine
driving a 1·1m (3ft 7·25in) diameter Avia V210
propeller on a tripod mounting aft of the cockpit,
an arrangement almost identical to that employed
on ESKA-1. The craft was designated the E-0773
Shmiel (Bumblebee). Profiting from the encouraging results of the flight trials, the team has designed
a number of small ekranoplan projects incorporating flexible wings, including a modified
version of the An-2W, the floatplane version of the
Antonov An-2, single-engine general-purpose
biplane.

R-1001 MANTA

In 1974 the Central Laboratory of Lifesaving
Technology developed a two-seater ekranoplan

Cutaway of CLST ESKA adaptation of Antonov An-2W

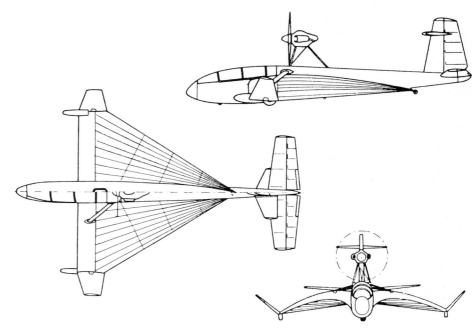

General Arrangement of E-0773 Bumblebee 1

R-1001 Manta

for light liaison duties with the Soviet fishing fleet.
Visually the craft shows the influence of the late Dr
Alexander Lippisch's design studies for a 300-ton
Aerofoil boat, a major departure from the Lippisch concept being the asymmetrically located
cabin jutting ahead of the broad aerofoil-shaped
hull on the port side. Reports suggest that in
building the wings and hull extensive use was

made of grp laminate reinforced with carbon fibres.

Power is supplied by a 210hp Walter Minor VI engine of Czechoslovak manufacture, and the craft has an all-up weight of 1460kg (3219lb).

Dynamic models were used to gather design data on stability, manoeuvrability and performance.

CLST ESKA EA-06

A developed version of ESKA-1, believed to be a four-seater, began trials in September 1973, one month after ESKA-1 made its first flight. Photographs of a radio-controlled model of the EA-06 indicate that its lines are similar to those of ESKA-1, major differences being a wider cabin with a full-view windscreen and an aft fuselage angled upwards to support the fin and high-mounted tailplane well clear of the water.

The dynamically similar model was built to ¼ scale and had a wing span of 1·75m (5ft 9in). Power was supplied by a two-cylinder motor, developing 1·8hp at 12 500rpm, and driving a 300mm (11·81in) diameter laminated airscrew. Laminated balsawood construction was employed.

OPERATORS

CIVIL OPERATORS OF HIGH-SPEED CRAFT

The following abbreviations are used in this section:

ALH	Air-lubricated hull craft
CAT	Catamaran vessel
HOV	Hovercraft, amphibious capability
HYD	Hydrofoil, surface piercing foils, fully immersed foils
MH	Mono-hull vessel*
SES	Surface effect ship or sidewall hovercraft (non-amphibious)
SWATH	Small-waterplane-area, twin-hull vessel
WPC	Wave-piercing catamaran

*Only craft exceeding 20m are covered.

ARGENTINA

Alimar SA

Avenida Cordoba 1801 (Esq Callao), Codigo Postal 1120, Buenos Aires, Argentina

Telephone: 41-6919, 41-5914
Telex: 0121510 ALMAR AR

High-speed craft operated

Type	Name	Seats	Delivered
HYD Rodriquez PT 50	*Flecha de Buenos Aires*	125	1962
HYD Rodriquez PT 50	*Flecha de Colonia*	125	1962
HYD Rodriquez PT 50	*Flecha del Litoral*	125	1963

Routes operated
Buenos Aires to Colonia, Uruguay (32n miles) and on by coach to Montevideo

AUSTRALIA

Ansett Transport Industries

Hayman Island, Queensland, Australia
Head Office: 501 Swanston Street, Melbourne, Victoria 3000, Australia

Telephone: (03) 6681334
Telex: 30085 AA

High-speed craft operated

Type	Name	Seats	Delivered
MH Wavemaster International Ltd 35m	*Sun Goddess Mk II*	60	1984

Brisbane Water Bus Company

North Quay, Brisbane, Queensland 4000, Australia

High-speed craft operated

Type	Seats	Delivered
ALH Stolkraft 10m	41	January 1987
ALH Stolkraft 10m	41	January 1987

Dignum Pty Ltd

Perth, Western Australia, Australia

High-speed craft operated

Type	Name	Seats	Delivered
MH SBF Engineering 27·50m	*Sundancer V*	160	1987

Fitzroy Island Resort

c/o Hayles Cairns Cruises, PO Box 898, Wharf Street, Cairns, Queensland 4870, Australia

Telephone: (070) 51 5644
Telex: 48284 AA

K L Reddicliffe, *Manager, Cruise Operations*
John Kerr, *Resort Manager*

High-speed craft operated

Type	Name	Delivered
CAT International Catamarans Pty Ltd (Hobart)	*Fitzroy Flyer*	June 1981

Routes operated
Cairns to Green Island and Fitzroy Island

International Catamarans Pty Ltd *Fitzroy Flyer* at Cairns, March 1983

Gibsea Pty Ltd

8 Elder Place, Fremantle, Western Australia, Australia

Telephone: (09) 430 4669

High-speed craft operated

Type	Name	Seats	Delivered
CAT Precision Marine 36m	*Tropic Sunseeker*	457	1985

Route operated
Cairns to Townsville

Gold Coast Water Bus Co Pty Ltd

12 Capri Commercial Centre, Isle of Capri, Gold Coast, Queensland 4217, Australia

Telephone: (075) 317951/920335

John Aitkenhead, *Managing Director*

High-speed craft operated

Type	Name	Seats	Delivered
ALH Stolkraft 10m	*Leo D Stolk*	41	January 1987
ALH Stolkraft 10m	*Lady Susan*	41	9 September 1987 (launched)

Routes operated
Shuttle service between Paradise Points and Nerang, Gold Coast, to be extended later to Brisbane via Sanctuary Cove

The first Stolkraft to enter service with the Gold Coast Water Bus Co

Great Keppel Island Tourist Services Limited

(previously operating as Hydrofoil Seaflight Services Pty Ltd)
168 Denison Street, Rockhampton, Queensland, Australia

Telephone: (079) 336744/272948

Claude Diehm, *Director*
Claude Diehm (Jr), *Director*
David Diehm, *Director*
Andrew Diehm, *Director*
Helen Jackson (Mrs), *Director/Secretary*

High-speed craft operated

Type	Name	Seats	Delivered
HYD Hitachi PT 20	ex *Manly**	72	
CAT SBF Engineering	*Victory III*	448	1985
MH SBF Engineering	*Aqua Jet*	48	1985
CAT Precision Marine 36m	*Capricorn Reefseeker*	350	1987

*Laid up

Routes operated

Rosslyn Bay (Yeppoon) to Great Keppel Island
Rosslyn Bay (Yeppoon) to Carricornia Section, Great Barrier Reef, 90 min

Hamilton Island Enterprises

CNR Broadwater Avenue, Shute Harbour, Shute, Queensland, Australia

Telephone: (079) 466858
Telex: 46793 AA

High-speed craft operated

Type	Name	Seats	Delivered
CAT NQEA InCat 24m	*Quickcat I*	145	August 1984
CAT NQEA InCat 24m	*Quickcat II*	195	1985
CAT InCat 30m WPC*	*Tassie Devil 2001*	—	April 1987
CAT InCat 31m WPC*	—	—	Early 1988

* Wave-piercing catamaran leased for 3 months from Easter 1987

Route operated

Shute Harbour to Hamilton Island

Hayles Green Island Services

Hayles Cairns Cruises, PO Box 898, Wharf Street, Cairns, North Queensland 4870, Australia

Telephone: (070) 51 5644
Telex: 48284 HAYLES AA
Telefax: (070) 51 7556

K L Reddicliffe, *General Manager*

High-speed craft operated

Type	Name	Delivered
CAT NQEA InCat 23m	*Green Island Express*	June 1982
CAT NQEA InCat 23m	*Magnetic Express*	March 1984
CAT NQEA InCat 30m	*Reef Cat*	June 1986

Routes operated

Cairns to Green Island
Cairns to Michaelmas Cay (via Green Island)
Cairns to Outer Barrier Reef-Norman Reef (via Green Island)

NQEA *Reef Cat* operating out of Cairns, Queensland

Hayles Magnetic Island Pty Ltd

PO Box 411, Townsville, Queensland 4810, Australia
Telephone: (071) 71 6927

High-speed craft operated

Type	Name	Delivered
CAT NQEA InCat 22m	*Magnetic Express*	March 1983

Route operated

Townsville to Magnetic Island

Stern view of NQEA *Magnetic Express*

Hovercraft Australia Pty Ltd

Operations terminated in 1987 and the Griffon 1500 TD was sold to Solomon Islands Navigation Services

Hover Mirage

91 Grafton Street, PO Box 6632, Cairns 4870, Queensland, Australia

Christopher Skase, *Chairman*
Michael Wright, *General Manager*

High-speed craft operated

Type	Name	Seats	In service
HOV NQEA AP1-88	*Hover Mirage*	70	15 August 1987
HOV NQEA AP1-88	*Hover Mirage II*	70	12 September 1987

Routes operated

Cairns International Airport to Port Douglas, 35n miles, 50 min, fare A$38·0
Tours from Port Douglas, A$38·0

Hover Mirage and *Hover Mirage II*   (Yon Ivanovic)

Hovertravel Australia Ltd

255 William Street, Melbourne, Victoria, Australia

John McEddie

High-speed craft operated

Type	Name	Seats	Launched
HOV NQEA AP1-88	Courier	84	7 December 1986, for disposal 1988

Route operated
Melbourne to Frankstone, Mornington (on the east side of Port Phillip Bay)

Courier which entered service with Hovertravel Australia Ltd in 1987

Incat Charters/MBM Management Pty Ltd

Melbourne, Victoria, Australia

High-speed craft operated

Type	Name	Seats	Delivered
CAT InCat (Hobart) 28m	Spirit of Victoria*	217	1985
CAT InCat (Hobart) 31m	Tassie Devil 2001*	200	1986
CAT NQEA InCat 18m	Incat II (ex James Kelly I)		1986
CAT NQEA InCat 20m	Tassie Devil (ex Keppel Cat I)		1986

*wave-piercing catamarans

Route operated
Hobart to Port Arthur
Tassie Devil 2001, first at Perth for the America's Cup 1986/87, then to Barrier Reef Island services

Kalford Pty Ltd

Redcliffe, Queensland, Australia

High-speed craft operated

Type	Name	Seats	Delivered
CAT NQEA InCat 22m	Cougar	200	1984

Route operated
Moreton Bay to Brisbane

Kilver Pte Ltd

Perth, Western Australia, Australia

High-speed craft operated

Type	Name	Seats	Delivered
MH SBF Engineering 31·30m	Seaflyte	224	1980

Operation
From 1986 *Seaflyte* was in use between Singapore and Batam

Low Island Cruises

Now operating under new company name: Quicksilver Connections Ltd. See entry on page 375.

McLeans Roylen Cruises Pty Ltd

Mackay Harbour, PO Box 169, Mackay 4740, Queensland, Australia

Telephone: (079) 553066
Telex: 48515 AA
Telefax: (079) 553186

Barry J Dean, *Manager*

High-speed craft operated

Type	Name	Seats	Delivered
CAT InCat (Hobart)	Spirit of Roylen	240	1982
CAT InCat (NQEA)	Roylen Sunbird	240	1987

Routes operated
Mackay to Great Barrier Reef (140km return)
Mackay to Hamilton Island (120km return)
Mackay to Lindeman Island (90km return)
Mackay to Brampton Island (40km return)

Tassie Devil 2001

(ZF AG)

Outer Barrier Reef Cruises

Port Douglas, Queensland, Australia
Telephone: Port Douglas 985373, Cairns 515547/518124

High-speed craft operated

Type	Name	Seats	Delivered
CAT InCat (Hobart) 20m	*Quicksilver*	100	August 1982

Routes operated

Port Douglas to Outer Reef
Port Douglas to St Crispin Reef

Peel's Tourist and Ferry Service Pty Ltd

3 Laura Street, Lakes Entrance 3909, Victoria, Australia

Telephone: (051) 551246/551527

Barrie Peel, *Proprietor*
Wayne Peel, *Proprietor*

High-speed craft operated

Type	Name	Seats	Delivered
CAT InCat (Hobart) } 20·4m Bulls Marine Pty Ltd }	*Thunderbird*	190	December 1984

Routes operated

Lakes Entrance to Paynesville and nearby lakes, channels and creeks

Peel's InCat *Thunderbird*

Queensland Ferries Pty Ltd

12 Creek Street, Brisbane, Queensland 4000, Australia

See Hover Mirage entry on page 373, the operating company for two NQEA AP1-88 hovercraft.

Quicksilver Connections Ltd

PO Box 171, Port Douglas, North Queensland, Australia 4871

Telephone: (070) 985373
Telex: 48969 LOWISL AA
Telefax: (070) 985772

Jim Wallace, *Managing Director*
Jo Wallace, *Managing Director*
W McNeil, *Marine Operations Manager*

High-speed craft operated

Type	Name	Seats	Delivered
CAT InCat (Hobart) 20·0m	*Low Isles Reef Express**	156	August 1982
CAT NQEA InCat 30·0m	*Quicksilver*†	300	June 1986
CAT NQEA InCat 30·0m	*Quicksilver II*†	300	June 1987
CAT InCat 37·2m WPC	—	340	1988
CAT InCat 37·2m WPC	—	340	1988
CAT InCat 37·2m WPC	—	340	1988
CAT InCat 37·2m WPC	—	340	1989

Routes operated

*Port Douglas to Low Isles
†Port Douglas to Agincourt Reef

Reef Link Pty Ltd

7 Tomlins Street, Townsville, Queensland 4810, Australia

Telephone: (077) 725733
Telex: 47381 REEFCT AA

Douglas Tarca, *Managing Director*

High-speed craft operated

Type	Name	Delivered
CAT NQEA InCat 30·0m	*Reef Link*	1983

Reef Link 2 was destroyed by fire in the middle of 1987

Route operated

Townsville to John Brewer Reef

Scenic Gordon & Hells Gates Charters

PO Box 38, Strahan, Tasmania 7468, Australia

Telephone: (004) 71 7187/7281
Telex: 59286 AA

Rex F Kearney, *Proprietor*
Julie A Kearney, *Proprietor*

High-speed craft operated

Type	Name	Seats	Delivered
MH SBF Engineering WA (Phil Curran)	*James Kelly II*	200	1983
MH SBF Engineering WA (Phil Curran) 19·95m	*Wilderness Seeker*	100	1986

Operations

High-speed cruising in Macquarie Harbour and Gordon River World Heritage area, 3½ hour trips
James Kelly II has been carrying 30 000 passengers annually to the Gordon River

James Kelly II

International Catamarans 30m vessels *Quicksilver* and *Quicksilver II* owned by Quicksilver Connections Ltd of Port Douglas

South Molle Island Resort
South Molle Island, Queensland, Australia

Telex: 48132 AA

S G McMullen, *General Manager*
Jock Collins, *Marine Manager*

High-speed craft operated

Type	Name	Seats	Delivered
CAT NQEA InCat 23·0m	*Telford Reef*	204	October 1982
CAT NQEA InCat 29·2m	*Telford Capricorn*	326	November 1983

Tadolan Pty Ltd
Cairns, Queensland, Australia

High-speed craft operated

Type	Name	Seats	Delivered
MH SBF Engineering 15·0m	*Fitzroy Reef Jet*	54	1987

Tangalooma Island Resort
Moreton Island, Queensland 4004, Australia

Telephone: (075) 482666
Telex: 43375 AA

High-speed craft operated

Type	Name	Delivered
CAT International Catamarans Pty Ltd (Hobart) 20·0m	*Tangalooma*	December 1981

Route operated
Brisbane to Moreton Island

Urban Transit Authority of New South Wales
Ferry Division, 6th Floor, 19 Pitt Street, Sydney, New South Wales 2000, Australia

Telephone: 2413734
Telex: 177609 AA
Telefax: 2514149

O P Eckford, *General Manager, Ferry Services*
L H Michaels, *Engineer Manager*

High-speed craft operated

Type	Name	Seats	Delivered
HYD Rodriquez PT 50	*Fairlight**	140	November 1966
HYD Rodriquez PT 50	*Long Reef*	140	1969
HYD Rodriquez PT 50	*Dee Why**	140	1970
HYD Rodriquez RHS 140	*Curl Curl*	140	January 1973
HYD Rodriquez RHS 160F	*Manly*	235	1984
HYD Rodriquez RHS 160F	*Sydney*	235	1985

*laid up

Route operated
Sydney (Circular Quay) to Manly (7n miles)

Long Reef approaching Manly terminal

Western Australia Ferry Operators Pty Ltd
Perth, Western Australia, Australia

High-speed craft operated

Type	Name	Seats
MH SBF Engineering (Phil Curran) 31·3m	*Seaflyte*	240

Operation
Perth to Rottnest Island

AUSTRIA

Donau-Dampfschiffahrts-Gesellschaft (DDSG)
Reisedienst, Handelskai 265, A-1021 Vienna, Austria

Telephone: (222) 266536
Telex: 131698 A

Hans Kreuzer, *Director*
Dr Helmut Zolles, *General Manager*
Dr Leopold Vavra, *General Manager*

High-speed craft operated

Type	Name	Seats	Delivered
SES Vosper Hovermarine HM 221	*Donaupfeil*	80	February 1986

Route operated
Vienna to Budapest (180n miles)

Vosper Hovermarine HM 221 80-seat *Donaupfeil*   (DDSG)

BAHRAIN, STATE OF
Coastguard Directorate
Ministry of the Interior, Public Security, PO Box 13, Bahrain

Telephone: 254021
Telex: 7707 CGD BN

Lt Col Abdul Aziz A Al-Khalifa, *Director*

High-speed craft operated
HOV Air Vehicles Tiger

Gray MacKenzie Marine Services EC
PO Box 26841, Bahrain

Telephone: 727084; 243296
Telex: 8926 GRAMAR BN

Disposed of all vessels in 1987 including the Vosper Hovermarine HM 221 *Grayspear*

BELGIUM
Eurosense Technologies NV
J Vander Vekenstraat 158, B-1810 Wemmel, Belgium

Telephone: (02) 460 7000
Telex: 26687 B
Telefax: (02) 460 4958

E Maes, *Managing Director*
A Grobben, *Assistant Managing Director*
P De Cant, *Director*

High-speed craft operated

Type	Name	Delivered
BHC SR.N6-1S (converted by Hoverwork to a survey craft)	Beasac* (ex Freedom)	April 1984

*BELFOTOP-Eurosense Acoustic Sounding Air Cushion Platform

Operation

BELFOTOP (Belgian Fotographic Topology) employs a Hoverwork-converted BHC SR.N6-1S for Belgian coast hydrographic survey and remote sensing work. The craft is based at Zeebrugge on behalf of the Ministry of Works.

Beasac hydrographic survey platform engaged in high-speed near-shore bathymetric surveys

Régie des Transports Maritimes (RTM)

Ministere des Communications, 30 Rue Belliard, B-1040 Brussels, Belgium

Telephone: (02) 2300180
Telex: 23851 REMATB B
Telefax: (02) 2311480

ir P Muyldermans, *General Director* (5 Natiënkaai, 8400 Ostend, Belgium)
F Anthonis, *Commercial Director* (30 Rue Belliard, 1040 Brussels, Belgium)

High-speed craft operated

Type	Name	Seats	Delivered
HYD Boeing Jetfoil 929-115	Princesse Clementine	316	May 1981
HYD Boeing Jetfoil 929-115	Princesse Stephanie	316	1981

Route operated

Ostend to Dover (64n miles, 1 hour 40min)

BOLIVIA

Crillon Tours SA

PO Box 4785, Avenida Camacho 1223, La Paz, Bolivia

Telephone: 350363; 374566/67; 372970
Telex: 2557 CRITUR BV

Darius Morgan, *President*
Elsa Morgan, *General Manager*
Helmut Kock, *Hydrofoil Designer and Consultant*

Crillon Tours SA was founded in 1959 by Darius Morgan and started its hydrofoil services on Lake Titicaca in 1966. Their first craft was the *Inca Arrow*, an Albatross type built by the Ludwig Honold Manufacturing Co. Three more hydrofoils were added in the next ten years, followed in 1976 by the first Bolivian hydrofoil, the *Bolivia Arrow*. A sister operation is undertaken on Lake Itaipu in Paraguay by Darius Morgan's other company, Aliscafos Itaipu SA.

High-speed craft operated

Type	Name	Delivered
HYD Ludwig Honold Manufacturing Co	Inca Arrow	1966
HYD Ludwig Honold Manufacturing Co	Bolivia Arrow	1976
HYD Ludwig Honold Manufacturing Co	Andes Arrow	
HYD Ludwig Honold Manufacturing Co	Copacabana Arrow	
HYD Ludwig Honold Manufacturing Co	Titicaca Arrow	
HYD Ludwig Honold Manufacturing Co	El Sol Arrow	
HYD Seaflight SpA H.57	Sun Arrow	1976

Route operated

Lake Titicaca, serving La Paz, Huatajata, Sun Island, Copacabana, Juli, Puno, Tiahuanacu, Guaqui, Pako

Five hydrofoils of the Crillon fleet on Lake Titicaca

Hovermarine Titikaka Transport

PO Box 3371, St Yanacocha No 300 of No 1, La Paz, Bolivia

Telephone: 343354/350339/352547/354945
Telex: 5490 BX

High-speed craft operated

Type	Name
SES Vosper Hovermarine HM 218	Rey del Titikaka
SES Vosper Hovermarine HM 218	Reina del Titikaka

Not operating since 1985

Route previously operated (Bolivia to Peru)
La Paz to Copancara to Sun Island to Juli to Puno

BRAZIL

Aerobarcos do Brasil, Transportes Maritimos e Turismo SA (TRANSTUR)

Avenida Amaral Peixoto 71, 11° Andar, Niterói 24020 RJ, Brazil

Telephone: 719 7070

Hamilton Amarante Carvalho, *Director President*
Luiz Paulo Amarante Carvalho, *Technical Director*
Vicente Oliveros Perez, *Financial Director*
Tse Min Hsu, *Administrative Director*

High-speed craft operated

Type	Name	Seats	Delivered
HYD Rodriquez PT 20	Flecha do Rio	83	1970
HYD Rodriquez PT 20	Flecha de Niterói	83	1971
HYD Rodriquez PT 20	Flecha das Ilhas	83	1972
HYD Rodriquez PT 20	Flecha de Itaipú	83	1972
HYD Rodriquez RHS 110	Flecha de Angra*	150	1976
SES Hovermarine HM 216	Gávea†	65	1976
SES Hovermarine HM 216	Gragoatá†	65	1976
SES Hovermarine HM 216	Guaratiba†	65	1976
HYD Rodriquez PT 20	Flecha de Ipanema	85	1978
HYD Rodriquez PT 20	Flecha de Icarai*	85	1978
HYD Rodriquez PT 20	Flecha da Ribeira*	85	1978

*These three craft are ex *Flying Phoenix*, ex *Flying Kingfisher* and ex *Flying Heron*, previously with Hongkong Macao Hydrofoil Co 1978.
†Only one believed to be operating.

Routes operated	Passengers in 1986
Rio de Janeiro-Niterói (5 mins, 2·8 miles)	2371 159
Rio de Janeiro-Ribeira (Ilha do Governador) (12 mins, 5·5 miles)	212 425*
Rio de Janeiro-Paquetá Island (20 mins, 9·2 miles)	216 678

* temporarily stopped

TRANSTUR RHS 110 *Flecha de Angra* ex Hongkong Macao Hydrofoil Co
(*TRANSTUR*)

TRANSTUR Rodriquez PT 20

Norsul Offshore SA

Av Augusto Severo 8, Rio de Janeiro, Brazil

Telephone: (021) 292 0122
Telex: (021) 22115

Delmas Abreu Penteado, *Managing Director*
Aristido Reichert, *Administrative/Financial Manager*
Julio Cesar G de Andrade, *Operations Manager*
Oswaldo Thielmann Jnr, *Contracts Manager*

High-speed craft operated

Type	Name	Seats	Delivered
MH Swiftships	*Parintins*	39	1972
MH Swiftships	*Parati*	39	1972
MH Swiftships	*Penedo*	39	1972
MH Breaux's Bay	*Palmares*	36	1975
MH Breaux's Bay	*Pelotas*	36	1975
MH Breaux's Bay	*Penalva*	36	1975
MH Breaux's Bay	*Piracicaba*	36	1975
CAT Fjellstrand	*Norsul Catamarã*	96 + 15 tonnes cargo	1982

Operation

Offshore support along Brazilian coast with bases in Macaé, Natal, Fortaleza, Aracajũ and Belẽm

BRUNEI

Brunei Shell Petroleum Company Sendirian Berhad

Seria, Negara Brunei Darussalam

Telephone: (037) 3999
Telex: 3313 BU

High-speed craft operated

Type	Name	Seats	Delivered
CAT Marinteknik Shipbuilders (S) Pte Ltd Marinjet CV 1800	*Hakeem*	50 (light cargo)	1985

Owner: Dart Marine Offshore SA
Charterer: Brunei Shell Petroleum Co Sdn Bhd
Operator: Ocean Tug Services (Sdn Bhd), Jasra Group

Operations

Delivered to the Brunei Shell Marine Department for a 5-year charter mainly for transportation services to the Fairley and Ampa offshore oil fields, *Hakeem* is based at Kuala Belait

Marinteknik Marinjet CV 1800 crew boat *Hakeem*

Fjellstrand *Norsul Catamarã* belonging to Norsul Offshore SA

BULGARIA

Navigation Maritime Bulgare (NAVIBULGAR)

Varna, Bulgaria

High-speed craft operated

Type	Name	GRT	Delivered
HYD S Ordzhonikidze	Kometa 1	127	1965
HYD S Ordzhonikidze	Kometa 2	127	1966
HYD Sormovo	Kometa 3	142	1966
HYD Sormovo	Kometa 6	136	1973
HYD S Ordzhonikidze	Kometa 7	142	1974
HYD S Ordzhonikidze	Kometa 8	142	1974
HYD Sormovo	Kometa 9	136	1975
HYD Sormovo	Kometa 10	142	1975
HYD Sormovo	Kometa 11	147	1975
HYD Sormovo	Kometa 12	142	1976

CAMEROON

SURF SA

See entry under France.

CANADA

Arctic Transportation Ltd (ATL)

Suite 1900, Esso Plaza, East Tower, 425 1st Street SW, Calgary, Alberta T2P 3L8, Canada

Telephone: (403) 234 7524
Telex: 03-824891 ARCTICTRSP CA
Telefax: (403) 264 9972

John G Wainwright, *Commercial Manager*

Arctic Transportation Ltd (ATL) of Calgary and Wärtsilä Arctic Inc of Vancouver formed a joint venture in 1985 to bring the Wärtsilä air cushion vehicle *Larus* into cold-weather-climate operation in Canadian and US western Arctic waters.

High-speed craft operated

Type	Name
HOV Wärtsilä PUC 22, CH-AHL	Larus

The *Larus* was constructed in 1981 at Wärtsilä's Helsinki, Finland, shipyard for the Department of Roads and Waterways, Government of Finland. Since delivery, it has operated as a ferry transporting vehicles and passengers to offshore islands within the Baltic Sea. The *Larus* has a payload of approximately 25 tonnes plus 48 passengers and a cruising speed, along calm water, level ice or terrain, of 20 knots. Among the many features of the *Larus* that make it particularly suited for Canadian Arctic operations, as a support, rather than a replacement, to present transportation systems in the Arctic, are: the fact that it was originally constructed for Arctic conditions and has since proven its capabilities in this environment in three years of operation in the Baltic Sea; four independent, rotatable, ducted propellers, each with controllable pitch, to enhance manoeuvrability; hydraulically controlled ramps at bow and stern to facilitate cargo transfer; large diameter propellers with relatively low tip speed to limit noise; and a full complement of navigation equipment and instrumentation.

ATL and Wärtsilä refurbished the *Larus* in Finland during May and June 1985. This refurbishing included installation of a new Arctic grade rubber skirt, upgrading of electronics and hydraulics, and replacement of an auxiliary diesel generator. The craft was laid up at Tuktoyaktuk, NWT, in 1986.

Operations

The *Larus* became available for charter commencing mid-September 1985 and was operated from ATL's base in Tuktoyaktuk, Northwest Territories. The vehicle was operated with a crew of three: pilot, navigator and loadmaster/engineer.

The joint venture foresees a number of applications for the *Larus* in the Canadian Arctic due to its ability to operate with cargoes beyond the current locales and environments of existing truck, helicopter, and icebreaking tug operations, including: transport of cargo and passengers to offshore islands and structures in the Beaufort Sea; transport of cargo and passengers along the shallow waters and tundra in the western Arctic; and shallow water seismic survey operations.

Canadian Coast Guard Hovercraft Units

The Canadian Coast Guard (CCG) operates two Hovercraft Units, administered from CCG Headquarters in Ottawa, with operational tasking controlled by the Region in which they are based.
Headquarters Administration: Fleet Aviation Office, Fleet Systems Directorate, Canadian Coast Guard, Tower A, Place de Ville, Ottawa, Ontario K1A 0N7, Canada

T F Melhuish, *Manager*

West Coast Canada
Canadian Coast Guard Hovercraft Unit: PO Box 23968, AMF, Vancouver International Airport, British Columbia V7N 1T9, Canada

Telephone: (604) 273-2556

J McGrath, *Officer in Charge*

This Unit also has a sub-base:
PO Box 2410, Parkesville, British Columbia V0R 2S0, Canada

Telephone: (604) 248-2724

J Palliser, *Officer in Charge*

The Canadian Coast Guard Hovercraft Unit in Vancouver was formed in 1968 for hovercraft evaluation in search and rescue and other coast guard duties.

High-speed craft operated

Type	Commissioned
HOV BHC SR.N6, serial No 039, CH-CGB, purchased from BHC	1977
HOV BHC SR.N6, serial No 031, CH-CGD, rebuilt by unit	1981
HOV BHC SR.N6, serial No 030, CH-CCG, rebuilt by unit	April 1986
(HOV BHC SR.N5, serial No 021 was retired and scrapped in April 1986)	

Operations

Patrol area is the Straits of Georgia and Gulf Islands (500 square miles), although search and rescue duties are undertaken outside this area. The average patrol distance is 80 miles.

The Unit commenced operations with SR.N5 021 in 1968 in the search and rescue role quickly establishing itself and within 5 years was responding to

Wärtsilä air cushion vehicle *Larus* at its Tuktoyaktuk base, Northwest Territories

(Ranson Photographers Ltd, Edmonton, Alberta)

Canadian Coast Guard SR.N6 (086) at Vancouver Airport, 2 October 1986

over 900 calls per year. The craft's speed and versatility made it ideal for other CCG roles, amongst which are light station servicing, buoy maintenance, ship inspections, shore patrols, pollution control, and emergency work with other agencies. In 1977, the additional work justified a second craft, and SR.N6 039 was purchased. Soon afterwards, new fishing fleet activities resulted in a northward extension of the SAR cover provided, and in 1980-81, the first of two old SR.N6 craft previously purchased was completely rebuilt and commissioned by Unit personnel, enabling a sub-base at Parkesville, some 90km north of Vancouver to be built and equipped with one SR.N6, becoming operational early 1982. By 1984, the SR.N5 was reaching the end of her economical life, and the second old SR.N6 began to be rebuilt, finally commissioning in April 1986, when 021 was retired.

All the craft are comprehensively equipped with sophisticated communications and navigation equipment, Night-sun searchlights (65 million candle power), auxiliary fuel tanks, firefighting equipment, and a full range of medical equipment, with stretchers, and oxygen equipment. The craft are on operational call 24 hours a day.

Eastern Canada
Laurentian Region ACV Unit
850, Nun's Island Boulevard, Nun's Island, Quebec H3E 1H2, Canada

Telephone: (514) 283 5841

G A More, *Officer in Charge*

High-speed craft operated
Type	Name	Commissioned
HOV BHC AP1-88/200, serial No 006, CH-CGC, serial No 201	*Waban-Aki*	Sept 1987
HOV Textron Marine Systems (ex Bell Aerospace) Voyageur, serial No 002, CH-CGA		1974

Operations
This Unit started operations by evaluating the potential of hovercraft in the Montreal District of the Laurentian Region, and in 1980 was integrated into the CCG Fleet operating in that region. In 1974-75, the Voyageur demonstrated remarkable capabilities for ice-breaking in the St Lawrence and its tributaries, and has been used extensively every winter to break and manage ice in shallow water, and for flood relief.

Equipped with a crane and winch, other tasks include shore-line construction and maintenance of beacons and towers; re-supply of lighthouses on islands with fuel, water and supplies; buoy moving and maintenance, and pollution control.

Voyageur was replaced in September 1987 with a BHC AP1-88/200 designed with a forward well-deck equipped with an easily removable crane, together with a hydraulic capstan and winch, and on-board accommodation for the crew.

Coastline HoverCraft Systems Inc
Vancouver, British Columbia, Canada

Telephone: (604) 731 7723

M Martin, *Proprietor*

Coastline HoverCraft Systems were operators of a Griffon Hovercraft Ltd 2500 TD during Expo '86 in Vancouver. The craft ran a service for the transport of visitors from Canada Place, near the Canada Pavillion to False Creek, the main site of Expo '86.

High-speed craft operated
Type	Name	Seats	In service
HOV Griffon Hovercraft Ltd 2500 TD	*Rain Dancer*	28	Summer 1986

(UK registration No GH 9454, Canadian registration No CH-FH1)

Route operated
Canada Place to False Creek, Vancouver. Journey time 30 min including 10 min harbour speed restrictions. Fare: $Can 10·0

Ice Control Enterprises Inc
40 Forest Avenue, Hamilton, Ontario L8N 1X1, Canada

Telephone: (416) 528 4283
Telefax: (416) 529 7097

D S Schroeder, *President*

and

Jones, Kirwan and Associates
Box 4406, Station D, Hamilton, Ontario L8V 4L8, Canada

These companies own the Air Trek Systems Ltd Air Trek 140 which has been used for commercial ice-breaking work during the winters of 1985/86 and 1986/87 in a number of locations in Ontario and Quebec.

North Coast Air Services Ltd
PO Box 610, Prince Rupert, British Columbia V8J 3R5, Canada

Telex: (047) 89214

Jack Anderson, *President*

High-speed craft operated
Type	Seats	In service
HOV British Hovercraft Corporation SR.N6 Mk I GH-2012*	38	April 1987

Route operated
From Prince Rupert to island 7n miles distant, providing passenger/freight service to Indian community centres
*Purchased from Hovertravel Ltd and shipped on 25 February 1987. This craft undertook the Amazon expedition in the 1960s. For disposal 1988

Ocean Craft Flight Hoverservices
1614, W 5th Street, Vancouver, British Columbia V6J 1N8, Canada

D Donald
R Sachowsky

High-speed craft operated
Type
HOV Air Vehicles Tiger (North American)

Operation
Fraser River passenger excursions

CHINA, PEOPLE'S REPUBLIC

Changjiang Shipping Administration Bureau
Shanghai, People's Republic of China

High-speed craft operated
Type	Delivered
SES Vosper Hovermarine HM 218, serial No 129*	1983
SES Vosper Hovermarine HM 218, serial No 130*	1983

*purchased from The Hong Kong & Yaumati Ferry Co Ltd

Routes operated
Pearl River and Aberdeen (Hong Kong) to Shekou (China)

Changqing Ship Transportation Co
People's Republic of China

High-speed craft operated
Type	Name	Seats	Delivered
SES Dong Feng MARIC 717 II	*Ming Jiang*	54 to 60	October 1984

China Air Cushion Technology Development Corporation (CACTEC)
Head Office: 9 Qi Xiang Nan Li, Binhu Road, Tianjin, People's Republic of China

Telephone: 331859/333339
Cable: 3333

Branch Office: 171 Gaoxion Road, Shanghai, People's Republic of China

Telex: 770539

Formed in 1984, CACTEC, subordinated to China State Shipbuilding Corporation (CSSC), is a specialised business corporation. Jointly with MARIC the corporation deals with a wide variety of applications of the air cushion principle, and lays emphasis on the research, development, design and production of both amphibious hovercraft and sidewall hovercraft.

High-speed craft operated

Type	Seats	Delivered
SES MARIC 7203	81	September 1982
SES MARIC 719	186	1984
HOV MARIC 716 II	32	1985

China Oriental Leasing Co (owner)

People's Republic of China

High-speed craft operated

Type	Name	Yard No	Seats	Delivered
CAT Westamarin W120	—	89	354	January 1987

Operation
Shanghai area

Chong-Qing Ferry Boat Co

People's Republic of China

High-speed craft operated

Type	Name	Seats	Delivered
SES Dong Feng MARIC 717 III	Chongqing	70	September 1984

Operation
Yangtze River rapids area

Chu Kong Shipping Co Ltd (CKS)

c/o 28 Connaught Road West, 7th floor, Hong Kong

High-speed craft operated

Type	Name	Seats	Delivered
CAT Fjellstrand 31·5m	Bei Xiu Hu	289	1983
CAT Fjellstrand 31·5m	Li Wan Hu	289	1984
CAT Fjellstrand 31·5m	Xiu Li Hu	291	1984
CAT Fjellstrand 31·5m	Qiong Zhou Ui Hao*	291	1984
CAT Fjellstrand 31·5m	Tian Lu Hu (ex Jasarina)		
CAT Fairey Marinteknik Pte Ltd			
CAT Fairey Marinteknik Pte Ltd			

Route operated
Kowloon (Hong Kong) to Guangzhou

*Hainando Island to Guangdong Province

Fjellstrand 31·5m *Xiu Li Hu*

Geophysical Surveys Inc (USA)

High-speed craft operated

Type	Delivered
HOV Griffon Hovercraft 1000 TD	1985
HOV Griffon Hovercraft 1000 TD	1985
HOV Griffon Hovercraft 1000 TD	1985

Operation
Three-year survey contract in China

Guangdong Province Hong Kong Macau Navigation Co

High-speed craft operated

Type	Name	Seats	Delivered
CAT A Fai Engineers and Shiprepairers InCat 21·9m	Mingzhu Hu	150	1982
CAT A Fai Engineers and Shiprepairers InCat 21·9m	Yin Zhou Hu	150	1982
CAT A Fai Engineers and Shiprepairers InCat 21·9m	Liuhua Hu	150	1982

Routes operated
Taiping and Jiangmen to Hong Kong

Guangdong San Fu Passenger and Cargo Transport Associate Co

High-speed craft operated

Type	Name	Seats	Delivered
CAT A Fai Engineers and Shiprepairers InCat 21·0m	Jin Shan Hu	150	September 1984

Jiang Gang Passengers Transport Co

c/o Chu Kong Shipping, 28 Connaught Road West, 7th floor, Hong Kong

High-speed craft operated

Type	Name	Seats	Delivered
CAT Fjellstrand 31·5m	Peng Lai Hu	291	1985

Route operated
Jiangmen to Kowloon (Hong Kong)

Jiangmen Jiang Gang Passenger Traffic Co

85 Dizhong Road, Jiangmen, Guangdong, People's Republic of China

Telephone: 32421/32438

Li Bai, *Manager*

High-speed craft operated

Type	Name	Seats	Delivered
MH Marinteknik Singapore, 35m (Yard No 110)	Wu Yi Hu	265	1987

Route operated
Jiangmen to Hong Kong (81n miles)

Nantong High Speed Passenger Ship Co

Nantong, People's Republic of China

High-speed craft operated

Type	Name	Seats	Delivered
CAT Westamarin 120 (ex W88)	Zi Lang	354	1987

Ningbo Huagang Ltd

No 2-2 86 Lane, Bai Sha Road, Ningbo, People's Republic of China

High-speed craft operated

Type	Name	Seats	Delivered
CAT Fjellstrand 38·8m	Yong Xing	312	November 1985

Route operated
Ningbo to Shanghai

Fjellstrand 38·8m *Yong Xing*

Sanfu Shipping China
People's Republic of China

High-speed craft operated

Type	Name	Seats	Delivered
CAT A Fai Engineers & Shiprepairers Ltd InCat 21·0m	Jin San Hu	150	1985

Shen Zhen Shipping
People's Republic of China

High-speed craft operated

Type	Name	Delivered
CAT A Fai Engineers and Shiprepairers InCat 21·0m	Yue Hai Chun	1984
CAT A Fai Engineers and Shiprepairers InCat 21·0m	Shen Zhen Chun	1985
CAT A Fai Engineers and Shiprepairers InCat 21·0m	Zhu Hai Chun	Dec 1986

Shenzou Transport Company
People's Republic of China

High-speed craft operated
Type
SES Hovermarine HM218

Shun Gang Passenger Corporation Co Ltd
c/o The Foreign Economics and Trading Committee of Shun De District, Shun De, Guangdong, People's Republic of China

High-speed craft operated

Type	Name	Delivered
CAT Marinteknik Singapore Marinjet 33CPV (Yard No 112)	Shun De	September 1987

Wuzhou Navigation Co

High-speed craft operated

Type	Name	Seats	Delivered
CAT A Fai Engineers & Shiprepairers Ltd InCat 21m	Lijiang	150	1983

Route operated
Wuzhou to Hong Kong

Zhao Gang Steamer Navigation Company
Harbour Building, Oong Nong Road North, Zhaoqing, Guangdong, People's Republic of China

High-speed craft operated

Type	Name	In service
CAT Marinteknik JC-3000	Duan Zhou Hu (ex Triton Jet)	September 1986

Route operated
Zhaoqing to Hong Kong, 143n miles, 5 hours. One single trip per day.

Zhen Hing Enterprises Co Ltd
c/o Chu Kong Shipping, 28 Connaught Road West, 7th floor, Hong Kong

High-speed craft operated

Type	Name	Seats	Delivered
CAT Fjellstrand 31·5m	Yi Xian Hu	291	1985
CAT Fjellstrand 38·8m	Tian Lu Hu		1985

Route operated
Zhong Shan to Kowloon (Hong Kong)

Fjellstrand 38·8m catamaran Tian Lu Hu

CUBA

Government

High-speed craft operated

Type	Delivered
HYD S Ordzhonikidze Kometa 18	1973

CYPRUS

Kibris Express
Cyprus

High-speed craft operated

Type	Name	Delivered
MH Wavemaster International	Barbaros	1987

CZECHOSLOVAKIA

Československá Plavba Dunajská (Czechoslovak Danube Navigation)
Ulica Cervenej Armády 35, 815 24 Bratislava, Czechoslovakia

Telephone: (7) 572 71
Telex: 93348 CSPD C

Ing Pavol Cibák, *Managing Director*
Ing Vojtech Skyva, *Deputy Manager*

High-speed craft operated
HYD Voskhod and Meteor hydrofoils

Routes operated
Vienna to Bratislava, 1 hr, fare 115 ATS (US$8·20)
Bratislava to Vienna, 1 hr 15 min, fare 115 ATS (US$8·20)
Bratislava to Budapest, 4 hr 30 min, 467 ATS (US$33·30)
Budapest to Bratislava, 4 hr 30 min, 467 ATS (US$33·30)

DENMARK

Bornholm Express
Nordbornholms Turistbureau, Hannershusvej 2, Sandvig, DK-3770 Allinge, Bornholm, Denmark

High-speed craft operated

Type	Name	Seats	In service
CAT Westamarin W86	Bornholm Express (ex Steigtind)	182	June-Aug 1986 June onwards 1987

*includes upper deck accommodation for 24

Route operated
Simrishamn (Sweden) to Allinge (Bornholm), Denmark, 1 hour

A/S Dampskibsselskabet Øresund (DSØ) Flyvebådene,
Havnegade 49, DK-1058 Copenhagen K, Denmark

Telephone: (01) 12 80 88
Telex: 27502 SUNDET DK

Flygbåtarna,
Skeppsbron 4, S-21120 Malmö, Sweden

Telephone: (040) 10 39 30
Telex: 32708 S

High-speed craft operated

Type	Name	Seats	Delivered
CAT Westamarin W95	Tunen (Yard No 52)	180	May 1977
CAT Westamarin W95	Tranen (Yard No 53)	180	June 1978
CAT Westamarin W95	Siken (ex Tumleren) (Yard No 68)	180	April 1978
CAT Marinteknik Marinjet	Lommen	235	December 1985
CAT Marinteknik Marinjet	Ørnen	235	1986

Marinteknik *Ørnen* operated by DSØ

(Paul Golombek)

Route operated

Copenhagen to Malmö (45 min, 17n miles). Ordinary single fare, economy class, DKr 66, SEK 60; 1st class, DKr 99, SEK 90, 1987 to April 1988, mostly hourly departures between 06.00 and 00.30 from Copenhagen, departures between 05.00 and 00.30 from Malmö, with some additional departures on the half hour on Saturdays and Sundays

A/S Dampskibsselskabet Øresund (DSØ)

Hovercraft Division
Postbox 150, 2770 Kastrup, Copenhagen, Denmark

Telephone: 01 521930/513111

Hermod Brenna-Lund, *Operation Manager*

Service introduced June 1984, craft leased to Scandinavian Airlines System (SAS).
Annual traffic: approx 200 000

High-speed craft operated

Type	Name	Seats	Delivered
HOV British Hovercraft Corporation AP1-88	*Liv Viking*	80	May 1984
HOV British Hovercraft Corporation AP1-88	*Freja Viking*	80	May 1984

Route operated

Copenhagen Airport, Kastrup to Malmö, Sweden (13n miles, 35 min)

AP1-88 *Freja Viking* at Malmö

DSØ service AP1-88 operated for SAS between Kastrup Airport, Copenhagen and Malmö, Sweden, crossing the Øresund during the very cold winter of 1984/85

JKL-Shipping A/S

See entry under Norway for company details

High-speed craft to be operated

Type	Name	Seats	To be delivered
SES Westamarin 3800 37·0m	—	450	Spring 1989
SES Westamarin 3800 37·0m	—	450	Spring 1989

Route to be operated

Copenhagen to Gothenburg

FINLAND

A W Line Oy

Norra Esplanaden 1A, 22100 Mariehamn, Åland, Finland

Telephone: 358 28 17271

High-speed craft operated

Type	Name	Seats	Delivered
CAT Fjellstrand 38·3m	—	249	April 1988

Route operated

Sweden to Åland (Finland)

Lake Saimaa Waterway Authority

Finnish National Board of Navigation, Helsinki, Finland

High-speed craft operated

Type	Delivered
HOV Finn-Leiju	1984

Operation

Trial operations began in 1984 with a Finn-Leiju 387 hovercraft for the maintenance and inspection of navigation lights and buoys in the Saimaa lake district. Two Finn-Leiju 387 hovercraft are now operated by the Lake Saimaa Waterway Authority

World Wildlife Fund Finland

Uudenmaankatu 40, 00120 Helsinki, Finland

Telephone: (90) 644 511

Lassi Karivalo, *Project Manager*

High-speed craft operated

Type	Delivered
HOV Finn-Leiju	1986

Operation

A Finn-Leiju FL387 hovercraft was purchased in 1986 and undertakes annual inspections on the whereabouts and size of the Saimaa seal population, Finland's most endangered mammal. The region covered extends to some 4460km^2 and the hovercraft is particularly valuable in the difficult conditions of late spring enabling the inventory period to be extended until melting of the final winter ice

Finn-Leiju FL387 in service with the World Wildlife Fund, Finland

FRANCE

Société Anonyme Atlantic Armement

8 rue de la Boetie, Paris 75008, France

Telephone: (1) 47 42 57 02
Telex: 280170

High-speed craft operated

Type	Name	Seats	Delivered
MH SBCN 25m	*Iles d'Or*	295	1986
MH SBCN 25m	*Amiral de Joinville*	195	1986
MH SBCN 32m	—	270	1987

Routes operated

Noirmoutier and Yeu Island (*Iles d'Or* and *Amiral de Joinville*).
La Baulle and Belle-Ile in 1987 using the new 32m SBCN craft

Chambon Group

See SURF SA

Société Anonyme d'Economie Mixte Maritime de Sainte-Pierre et Miquelon

France

High-speed craft operated

Type	Delivered
MH SFCN 35m	March 1988

IFREMER

Institut Français de Recherche Pour L'Exploitation de la Mer
Centre de Brest, BP 337, 29273 Brest Cedex, France

Telephone: (98) 22 40 40
Telex: 940627 OCEAN F
Telefax: (98) 05 04 73

Bertrand de Lagarde, *Chief of Department*

IFREMER has given financial and technical support for the development of the ADOC 12 which it owns.

High-speed craft operated

Type	Name	Delivered
HOV Aeroplast ADOC 12	*Jean-Pierre*	1985

Service Maritime de Carteret

Boite Postale 15, 50270 Barneville-Carteret, France

Telephone: (33) 538721
Telex: 170477 CARSEY F

High-speed craft operated

Type	Name	Seats	Delivered
CAT Westamarin W95 (Yard No 50)	*Pegasus* (ex *Gimletun* (1978), ex *Ta Yue Shan* (1977))	181	June 1977

Route operated

Carteret to Gorey, Jersey (30 min), March to November

Compagnie Morbihamaise de Navigation

France

High-speed craft operated

Type	Name	Max speed (knots)	Seats	Delivered
CAT Fjellstrand 25·5m	*Børtind*	26	194	1987

Westamarin W95 *Pegasus* in service with Service Maritime de Carteret

SURF SA
(Cie des Moyens de Surfaces Adaptes a l'Exploitation des Oceans)
148 rue Sainte, 13007 Marseilles, Boite Postale 48, 13262 Marseilles Cedex 7, France

Telephone: (91) 54 92 29
Telex: 401042 SURF F
Telefax: (91) 33 85 70

High-speed craft operated

Type	Name	Max speed (knots)	Seats	Delivered
MH Breaux 34·44m	*Agathe*	24	65	1979
CAT Fjellstrand 31·5m	*Anahitra**	30	161	1983
CAT Marinteknik 34CCB 34·1m	*Emeraude Express*	44	240	February 1986
MH SFCN 34·9m	*Aida*	31·5	90	April 1986
MH SFCN 34·9m	*Angelica*	31·5	90	April 1986
CAT Marinteknik Marinjet 33 CPV	*Jetkat 1*	—	233	1987
CAT Marinteknik Marinjet 33 CPV	*Nettuno Jet*	—	276	1987

*Transport to the Ekoundou and Kole oil fields

Operations
Offshore support, off Congo coast, Pointe Noir to Emeraude North and South oilfields and to the Likouala oilfield

SURF's *Angelica* crew boat   *(SURF)*

Agathe, built by Breaux for SURF   *(SURF)*

Vedettes Armoricaines
1er Eperon, Boite Postale 88, 56 rue d'Aiguillon, 29268 Brest Cedex, France

Telephone: (98) 80 70 15
Telex: 940210 NAVIPAM F

High-speed craft operated

Type	Name	Seats	Built
HYD S Ordzhonikidze	*Kometa 1*	—	1970
MH Tecimar	*Jaguar*	300	1980

Routes operated
Guernsey and Sark to St Helier, Jersey
St Helier to St Malo, Jersey (1 hour 25 min) and Granville

Les Vedettes Blanches
(Société Anonyme des Bateaux de la Côte d'Emeraude)
Gare Maritime de la Bourse, BP16, 35401 Saint Malo Cedex, France

Telephone: (99) 56 63 21
Telex: 740906 F

High-speed craft operated

Type	Name	Seats	Delivered
CAT Westamarin W95	*Trident* (ex *Venture 84*)	205	July 1982

Route operated
St Malo to St Helier, Jersey (1 hour 10 min)

Westamarin W95 *Trident* of Vedettes Blanches

Vedettes Blanches et Vertes
Gare Maritime de Carteret, 50270 Barneville-Carteret, France

Telephone: (33) 53 81 17
Telex: 170002 F

High-speed craft operated

Type	Name	Delivered
CAT Westamarin W86	*Belle de Dinard* (ex *Karmsund* 1976)	January 1972
CAT Westamarin W86	*Trident* (ex *Highland Seabird*)	May 1976

Route operated
Carteret to Gorey to St Peter Port (summer service only)

Vedettes de L'Odet Ferry Company
Concarneau, Brittany, France

High-speed craft operated

Type	Name	Seats	Delivered
MH Société Bretonne de Construction Navale	*Atlante*	165	July 1985

Route operated
Concarneau to Iles de Glénan

Vedettes Vertes Granvillaises
1-3 rue le Campion, 50400 Granville, France

Telephone: (33) 50 16 36
Telex: 170002 F

High-speed craft operated

Type	Name
CAT Westamarin W95	*Trident 2*

Route operated
Carteret to St Helier, Jersey (40 min)

Trident 2 (ex Highland Seabird) and Pegasus at Guernsey, May 1985 (A S Hands)

GABON

Gabon Ferry Services
Gabon

High-speed craft operated

Type	Name	Seats	Delivered
SES Brødrene Aa Båtbyggeri A/S CIRR 105P	Ekwata	290	September 1986
SES Brødrene Aa Båtbyggeri A/S CIRR 105P	Ekwata II	—	1988

Route operated
Libreville to Port Gentil, 85n miles

GERMANY, DEMOCRATIC REPUBLIC

Fahrgastechiffahrt Straisund
Democratic Republic of Germany

High-speed craft operated

Type	Name	Delivered
HYD S Ordzhonikidze Kometa	Stoertebeker I	1974
HYD S Ordzhonikidze Kometa	Stoertebeker II	1974
HYD S Ordzhonikidze Kometa	Stoertebeker III	1974

GERMANY, FEDERAL REPUBLIC

Köln-Düsseldorfer Deutsche Rheinschiffahrt AG (KD)
Frankenwerft 15, D-5000 Cologne 1, Federal Republic of Germany

Telephone: (0221) 20880
Telex: (08) 882 723

High-speed craft operated

Type	Name	Seats
HYD Sormovo Raketa	Rheinpfeil (Rhine Arrow)	64

Route operated
Cologne to Koblenz to Bingen to Mainz and many intermediate stops, April 4 to October 25

Raketa, Rheinpfeil, operated by Köln-Düsseldorfer (KD) German Rhine Line

GIBRALTAR

Gibline Ltd
9b George's Lane, PO Box 480, Gibraltar

Telephone: 76763
Telex: 2279 GIBLNE GK

Herman Bergshaven, *Chairman*
Joseph Gaggero, *Director*
Jan Lindberg, *Director*

General Sales Agents for Gibline Ltd:
Seagle Travel Ltd, 9b George's Lane, PO Box 480, Gibraltar

Telephone: 71415, 76763
Telex: 2279 GK

J A Vincent, *Director*
H L Llufrio, *General Manager*

High-speed craft operated

Type	Name	Seats†	Delivered*
CAT Westamarin 100D	Gibline 1 (ex Gimle Belle, ex Condor 6) (Yard No 75)	200/226	1985 (built 1981)

†16 reserved for Commodore Class on certain sailings
*to Gibline Ltd

Routes operated (22 April to 31 October 1987)
Gibraltar to Tangier (1 hour 10 min)
Gibraltar to M'Diq (1 hour 10 min) Wednesday only

Fares: Normal one way, £15·00, 3225 pesatas (1987); normal return, £26·00, 5600 pesatas (1987)

Westamarin 100D Gibline 1 at speed across the Strait of Gibraltar

GREECE

Alkyonis Speed Boats Limited

1, Har Trikoipi Street, Piraeus 185 36, Greece

Telex: 241289 ALKY GR

High-speed craft operated

Type	Name	Delivered
HYD S Ordzhonikidze Kometa	*Alkyonis 1*	1978
HYD S Ordzhonikidze Kometa	*Alkyonis 2*	1978

Routes operated

Patrai to Zakinthos to Argostolion
Mainland to Nisoi Islands of Zakinthos and Kefallinia

Ceres Flying Hydroways Limited

8 Akti Themistokleus, Freattys, Piraeus, Greece

Telephone: 45 31 716-17
Telex: 213606 SHPC GR; 212257 CHSE GR

Services started in 1977 with the Piraeus to Hydra route

High-speed craft operated

Type	Name	Delivered
HYD S Ordzhonikidze Kometa-M	*Flying Dolphin I*	1975
HYD S Ordzhonikidze Kometa-M	*Flying Dolphin II*	1975
HYD S Ordzhonikidze Kometa-M	*Flying Dolphin III*	1976
HYD S Ordzhonikidze Kometa-M	*Flying Dolphin V*	1976
HYD S Ordzhonikidze Kometa-M	*Flying Dolphin VI*	1976
HYD S Ordzhonikidze Kometa-M	*Flying Dolphin VII*	1976
HYD S Ordzhonikidze Kometa-M	*Flying Dolphin IV*	1977
HYD S Ordzhonikidze Kometa-M	*Flying Dolphin VIII*	1977
HYD S Ordzhonikidze Kometa-M	*Flying Dolphin IX*	
HYD S Ordzhonikidze Kometa-M	*Flying Dolphin X*	1978
HYD S Ordzhonikidze Kometa-M	*Flying Dolphin XI*	1979
HYD S Ordzhonikidze Kometa-M	*Flying Dolphin XII*	1979
HYD S Ordzhonikidze Kometa-M	*Flying Dolphin XIV*	1981
HYD S Ordzhonikidze Kometa-M	*Flying Dolphin XV*	1981
HYD S Ordzhonikidze Kometa-M	*Flying Dolphin XVI*	1981
HYD S Ordzhonikidze Kolkhida	*Flying Dolphin XVII*	1986
HYD S Ordzhonikidze Kolkhida	*Flying Dolphin XVIII*	1986
HYD S Ordzhonikidze Kolkhida	*Flying Dolphin XIX*	1986

(*Flying Dolphins IV, V* and *XII* are owned by Ceres Hydrofoils Shipping and Tourism SA. *Flying Dolphins IX, X* and *VIII* are owned by Ceres Hydrocomets Shipping and Tourism SA. *Flying Dolphins VI, VII* and *XI* are owned by Ceres Express Ways Shipping and Tourism SA. *Flying Dolphins XIV, XV, XVI* and *XVII* are owned by Ceres Hydrolines Shipping Co)

Routes operated

Aghios Konstantinos to Volos to Skiathos to Glossa to Skopelos to Aionissos
Piraeus (Zea) to Poros to Hydra to Eranioni to Spetsai to Porto Heli to Leonidi to Kiparissi to Monemvassia

Part of the Ceres 15-craft Kometa fleet   *(Page Beken Ltd/Wilson Walton)*

Nearchos Shipping Co

(ex Psiloritis Maritime)
56 El Venizelou, Athens 10678, Greece

Telex: 215284/219706 GR

High-speed craft operated

Type	Name	Delivered
HYD S Ordzhonikidze Kometa	*Marilena*	1981
HYD S Ordzhonikidze Kometa	*Tzina*	1981

Both certificated by ABS.

Rethimniaki Naftiliaki Touristiki (RENATOUR SA)

250 Arkadiou Rethymno, Crete, Greece

Telex: 291226 GR

High-speed craft operated

Type	Name	Seats	Delivered
CAT Westamarin W100D	*Nearchos* (ex *Venture 83*, launched as *Rosario*)	245	May 1982

Route operated

Réthimnon to Santorini (Thira)

GUADELOUPE

Brudey

Pointe-à-Pitre, Guadeloupe

High-speed craft operated

Type	Name	Seats	Delivered
MH Société Française de Constructions Navales (SFCN) 27·50m	*Regina*	150	July 1984

HONG KONG

Castle Peak Power Co Ltd

High-speed craft operated

Type	Name	Seats	Delivered
CAT A Fai Engineers and Shiprepairers Ltd InCat 16·0m	*Kwong Fai*	40	June 1984

Chu Kong Shipping

Hong Kong

High-speed craft operated

Type	Seats	Delivery
CAT Precision Marine 38·0m	280	August 1988

Customs and Excise Departments

8th Floor, Harbour Building, 38 Pier Road, Central, Hong Kong

High-speed craft operated

Type	Name
MH Chung Wah Shipbuilding and Engineering Co Ltd King Class Yard No 204	*Customs 6 Sea Glory*
MH Chung Wah Shipbuilding and Engineering Co Ltd King Class Yard No 205	*Customs 6 Sea Guardian*
MH Chung Wah Shipbuilding and Engineering Co Ltd King Class Yard No 206	*Customs 6 Sea Leader*

Hong Kong *Customs 6 Sea Glory* built by Chung Wah Shipbuilding and Engineering Co Ltd

Discovery Bay Transportation Services
Hong Kong

High-speed craft operated

Type	Yard No	Name	Seats	Originally delivered
SES Hovermarine HM 218	466	(ex *RTS 101*)		
SES Hovermarine HM 218	468	(ex *RTS 102*)		
SES Hovermarine HM 218	471	(ex *RTS 103*)		
SES Hovermarine HM 218 (HM 2 Mk IV)	446	(ex *HYF 108*)	92	1976
SES Hovermarine HM 218 (HM 2 Mk IV)	447	(ex *HYF 109*)	92	1979
SES Hovermarine HM 218 (HM 2 Mk IV)	448	(ex *HYF 110*)	92	1979
MH Marinteknik Sweden/Singapore 35m	64/107*	*Discovery Bay 12*	256	1987
MH Marinteknik Singapore 35m	108	*Discovery Bay 14*	256	1987
MH Marinteknik Singapore 35m	109	*Discovery Bay 15*	256	1987
CAT Fairey Marinteknik Singapore 35m	—	—	450	1988
CAT Fairey Marinteknik Singapore 35m	—	—	450	1988

* hull built in Sweden

Route operated
Discovery Bay, Lantau to Central, Hong Kong
The ex RTS Ltd HM 218s came into service in 1986

Hongkong China Hydrofoil Ltd
33/F New World Tower, 16-18 Queens Road, Central, Hong Kong

Telephone: (5) 218302
Telex: 74493 HMHCO HX

High-speed craft operated

Type	Seats	Entered service
CAT Marinteknik Verkstad 35m	215	June 1982

Hong Kong Hi-Speed Ferries Ltd (HSF)
13/F, V Heun Building, 138 Queens Road, Central, Hong Kong

Telephone: (5) 8152789
Telex: 89846 HKHPF HX
Telefax: (5) 430324

High-speed craft operated

Type	Name	Seats	Entered service
MH Vosper Thornycroft 62·5m	*Cheung Kong*	659*	May 1985
MH Vosper Thornycroft 62·5m	*Ju Kong*	659*	May 1985

* plus 30 external seats

Route operated
Hong Kong to Macau, HK$35 to 55 excluding tax

Hongkong Macao Hydrofoil Co Ltd (HMH)
New World Tower, 33rd floor, 16-18 Queen's Road, Central, Hong Kong

Telephone: (5) 218302
Telex: 74493 HMHCO HX

Kenny Tham, *Deputy General Manager*

This company started hydrofoil service in 1964 with two Rodriquez PT 20, 68-seat craft operating between Hong Kong and Macau. It now operates a fleet of 12 hydrofoil and waterjet catamaran ferries and is operating an additional route, Hong Kong to Zhuhai in China.

High-speed craft disposed of

Type	Name	Seats	Entered service	Status
HYD Rodriquez PT 20	*Flying Phoenix*	68	May 1964	Sold to Brazil 1978
HYD Rodriquez PT 20	*Flying Kingfisher*	68	May 1964	Sold to Brazil 1978
HYD Rodriquez PT 20	*Flying Swift*	68	Oct 1964	Scrapped
HYD Rodriquez PT 20	*Flying Heron*	68	Jan 1965	Sold to Brazil 1978
HYD Rodriquez PT 50	*Flying Flamingo*	125	March 1967	Scrapped 1982
CAT Marinteknik	*Triton Jet*	215	June 1983	Sold to Zhao Gang Steamer Navigation 1986

High-speed craft operated

Type	Name	Seats	Entered service
HYD Rodriquez PT 50	*Flying Albatross*	125	December 1964
HYD Rodriquez PT 50	*Flying Skimmer*	125	April 1965
HYD Rodriquez PT 50	*Flying Condor*	126	March 1966
HYD Rodriquez RHS 140	*Flying Dragon*	125	June 1971
HYD Rodriquez RHS 140	*Flying Egret*	125	February 1972
HYD Rodriquez RHS 140	*Flying Sandpiper*	125	January 1973
HYD Rodriquez RHS 140	*Flying Swift* (ex *Flying Goldfinch*)	125	December 1973
HYD Rodriquez RHS 140	*Flying Ibis*	125	December 1974
CAT Marinteknik Verkstads	*Apollo Jet*	215	January 1982
CAT Marinteknik Verkstads	*Hercules Jet*	215	June 1982
CAT Marinteknik Verkstads	*Janus Jet*	215	December 1982
CAT Marinteknik Verkstads 40 CPF	—	406	May 1988

The Marinteknik *Triton Jet* was sold in 1986 to the Zhao Gang Steamer Navigation Company and re-named *Duan Zhou Hu*

Routes operated
Of the 12 vessels in current operation, one Marinteknik catamaran, *Hercules Jet*, operates between Hong Kong and Zhuhai, a special economic zone in China on the Pearl Estuary, a route of 35n miles; two vessels operate between Kowloon and Macau and the remaining vessels between Hong Kong and Macau, a distance of 36n miles

HMH Rodriquez PT 50 *Flying Condor* (HMH Co Ltd)

Apollo Jet the first Marinteknik catamaran to enter regular service with the Hongkong Macao Hydrofoil Co Ltd (HMH Co Ltd)

Hong Kong Resort Company
2nd Floor, Connaught Centre, Central, Hong Kong

Telephone: (5) 263246
Telex: 65179 HKRCL HX

High-speed craft operated

Type	Yard No	Delivered
MH Marinteknik Singapore Marinjet 35MPV	108	May 1987
MH Marinteknik Singapore Marinjet 35MPV	109	June 1987

The Hong Kong & Yaumati Ferry Co Ltd
Central Harbour Services Pier, 1st Floor, Pier Road, Central District, Hong Kong

Telephone: (5) 423081
Telex: 83140 HYFCO HX
Telefax: CCITT G II & III (5) 423958

C K Lau, *Chairman*
Edmond T C Lau, *Managing Director*
Dominic W Wong, *General Manager*
Dennis K S Cheng, *Deputy General Manager*
David C S Ho, *Assistant General Manager, Operations*

The world's largest operator of sidewall hovercraft passenger ferries. See also entry for Sealink Ferries Ltd, Hong Kong.

High-speed craft operated

Type	Yard No	Name	Seats	Delivered
SES Hovermarine HM 216 (HM 2 Mk III)	328	*HYF 103*	74	1975
SES Hovermarine HM 216 (HM 2 Mk III)	329	*HYF 104**	60	1975
SES Hovermarine HM 218 (HM 2 Mk IV)	435	*HYF 105*	100	1976
SES Hovermarine HM 218 (HM 2 Mk IV)	443	*HYF 106*	100	1976
SES Hovermarine HM 218 (HM 2 Mk IV)	445	*HYF 107*	100	1976
SES Hovermarine HM 218 (HM 2 Mk IV)	457	*HYF 111*	100	1979
SES Hovermarine HM 218 (HM 2 Mk IV)	458	*HYF 112*	100	1979
SES Hovermarine HM 218 (HM 2 Mk IV)	459	*HYF 113*	100	1980
SES Hovermarine HM 218 (HM 2 Mk IV)	462	*HYF 114*	74	1980
SES Hovermarine HM 218 (HM 2 Mk IV)	463	*HYF 115*	100	1980
SES Hovermarine HM 218 (HM 2 Mk IV)	464	*HYF 116*	74	1980
SES Hovermarine HM 218 (HM 2 Mk IV)	469	*HYF 117*	100	1980
SES Hovermarine HM 218 (HM 2 Mk IV)	470	*HYF 118*	74	1980
SES Hovermarine HM 218 (HM 2 Mk IV)	473	*HYF 119*	74	1980
SES Hovermarine HM 218 (HM 2 Mk IV)	474	*HYF 120*	100	1980
SES Hovermarine HM 218 (HM 2 Mk IV)	475	*HYF 121*	74	1980
SES Hovermarine HM 218 (HM 2 Mk IV)	476	*HYF 122*	100	1980
SES Hovermarine HM 218 (HM 2 Mk IV)	477	*HYF 123*	74	1980
SES Hovermarine HM 218 (HM 2 Mk IV)	478	*HYF 124*	74	1980
SES Hovermarine HM 218 (HM 2 Mk IV)	479	*HYF 125*	100	1980
SES Hovermarine HM 218 (HM 2 Mk IV)	480	*HYF 126*	100	1980
SES Hovermarine HM 218 (HM 2 Mk IV)	481	*HYF 127*	100	1980
SES Hovermarine HM 218 (HM 2 Mk IV)	484	*HYF 130*	74	1980

*laid up

HYF 101, 108, 109, 110, 128 and *129* had been sold as of July 1986.
HYF 102 had been sold as of October 1986 to W & Y International Ltd, Hong Kong

Routes operated

	Annual traffic		
	1984	1985	1986
Hong Kong—Shekou, China 22·5n miles	173 000	163 910	178 754
Hong Kong—Whampoa, China 70n miles	55 000	59 796	36 857
Hong Kong—Zhoutoujui, China 80n miles	115 000	121 293	107 281

Kwai Kong Shipping Co Ltd

High-speed craft operated

Type	Name	Delivered
CAT A Fai Engineers and Shiprepairers InCat 21·0m	*Li Jiang*	June 1983

The Royal Hong Kong Police Force, Marine Region

25 Salisbury Road, Tsim Sha Tsui, Kowloon, Hong Kong

Telephone: (3) 692261
Telex: 65367 HX

R L J Macdonald, *Regional Commander, Assistant Commissioner*
R A Porter, *Deputy Regional Commander, Chief Superintendent*
M G F Prew, *Chief Staff Officer, Chief Superintendent*

High-speed craft operated

Type	Speed (knots)	Name
MH Vosper Thornycroft Singapore 23·8m	22	*PL 50 Sea Cat*
MH Vosper Thornycroft Singapore 23·8m	22	*PL 51 Sea Puma*
MH Vosper Thornycroft Singapore 23·8m	22	*PL 52 Sea Leopard*
MH Vosper Thornycroft Singapore 23·8m	22	*PL 53 Sea Eagle*
MH Vosper Thornycroft Singapore 23·8m	22	*PL 54 Sea Hawk*
MH Vosper Thornycroft Singapore 23·8m	22	*PL 55 Sea Lynx*
MH Vosper Thornycroft Singapore 23·8m	22	*PL 56 Sea Falcon*
MH Chung Wah Shipbuilding and Engineering Co Ltd 26·3m, Yard No 178, Mark II Patrol	25	*PL 57 Mercury*
MH Chung Wah Shipbuilding and Engineering Co Ltd 26·3m, Yard No 179, Mark II Patrol	25	*PL 58 Vulcan*
MH Chung Wah Shipbuilding and Engineering Co Ltd 26·3m, Yard No 180, Mark II Patrol	25	*PL 59 Ceres*
MH Chung Wah Shipbuilding and Engineering Co Ltd 26·5m, Yard No 166, Mark I Patrol	23	*PL 60 Aquarius*
MH Chung Wah Shipbuilding and Engineering Co Ltd 26·5m, Yard No 167, Mark I Patrol	23	*PL 61 Pisces*
MH Chung Wah Shipbuilding and Engineering Co Ltd 26·5m, Yard No 168, Mark I Patrol	23	*PL 62 Argo*
MH Chung Wah Shipbuilding and Engineering Co Ltd 26·5m, Yard No 169, Mark I Patrol	23	*PL 63 Carina*
MH Chung Wah Shipbuilding and Engineering Co Ltd 26·5m, Yard No 170, Mark I Patrol	23	*PL 64 Cetus*
MH Chung Wah Shipbuilding and Engineering Co Ltd 26·5m, Yard No 171, Mark I Patrol	23	*PL 65 Dorado*
MH Chung Wah Shipbuilding and Engineering Co Ltd 26·5m, Yard No 172, Mark I Patrol	23	*PL 66 Octans*
MH Chung Wah Shipbuilding and Engineering Co Ltd 26·5m, Yard No 173, Mark I Patrol	23	*PL 67 Vela*
MH Chung Wah Shipbuilding and Engineering Co Ltd 26·5m, Yard No 174, Mark I Patrol	23	*PL 68 Volans*
MH Chung Wah Shipbuilding and Engineering Co Ltd 26·5m, Yard No 189, Mark III Patrol	25	*PL 70 King Lai*
MH Chung Wah Shipbuilding and Engineering Co Ltd 26·5m, Yard No 190, Mark III Patrol	25	*PL 71 King Yee*
MH Chung Wah Shipbuilding and Engineering Co Ltd 26·5m, Yard No 191, Mark III Patrol	25	*PL 72 King Lim*
MH Chung Wah Shipbuilding and Engineering Co Ltd 26·5m, Yard No 192, Mark III Patrol	25	*PL 73 King Hau*
MH Chung Wah Shipbuilding and Engineering Co Ltd 26·5m, Yard No 193, Mark III Patrol	25	*PL 74 King Dai*
MH Chung Wah Shipbuilding and Engineering Co Ltd 26·5m, Yard No 194, Mark III Patrol	25	*PL 75 King Chung*
MH Chung Wah Shipbuilding and Engineering Co Ltd 26·5m, Yard No 195, Mark III Patrol	25	*PL 76 King Shun*
MH Chung Wah Shipbuilding and Engineering Co Ltd 26·5m, Yard No 196, Mark III Patrol	25	*PL 77 King Tak*
MH Chung Wah Shipbuilding and Engineering Co Ltd 26·5m, Yard No 197, Mark III Patrol	25	*PL 78 King Chi*
MH Chung Wah Shipbuilding and Engineering Co Ltd 26·5m, Yard No 198, Mark III Patrol	25	*PL 79 King Tai*
MH Chung Wah Shipbuilding and Engineering Co Ltd 26·5m, Yard No 199, Mark III Patrol	25	*PL 80 King Kwan*
MH Chung Wah Shipbuilding and Engineering Co Ltd 26·5m, Yard No 200, Mark III Patrol	25	*PL 81 King Mei*
MH Chung Wah Shipbuilding and Engineering Co Ltd 26·5m, Yard No 201, Mark III Patrol	25	*PL 82 King Yan*
MH Chung Wah Shipbuilding and Engineering Co Ltd 26·5m, Yard No 202, Mark III Patrol	25	*PL 83 King Yung*
MH Chung Wah Shipbuilding and Engineering Co Ltd 26·5m, Yard No 203, Mark III Patrol	25	*PL 84 King Kan*

Sealink Ferries Ltd

Central Harbour Services Pier, 1/F, Pier Road, Central District, Hong Kong

Telephone: (5) 423081/433298
Telex: 83140 HYFCO HX

This company was formed in 1981 to operate on the Kowloon-Macau route. Services began in September 1983 with four Vosper Hovermarine HM 527s. It became a wholly owned subsidiary of The Hong Kong & Yaumati Ferry Co Ltd on 30 June 1986.

High-speed craft operated

Type	Name	In service
SES Vosper Hovermarine HM 527 (501)	*Tejo*	September 1983
SES Vosper Hovermarine HM 527 (502)	*Douro*	1983
SES Vosper Hovermarine HM 527 (503)	*Sado*	1984
SES Vosper Hovermarine HM 527 (504)	*Mondego*	1984

Route operated

	Annual traffic	
	1984	1986
Kowloon to Macau, 1 hour 10 mins, 40n miles	550 000	850 000

One craft (503) has been leased for short periods to The Hong Kong & Yaumati Ferry Co for use on the route Kowloon to Canton.

Shun Tak Enterprises Corporation Ltd (STEC)

Penthouse, 39th Floor, Shun Tak Centre, 200 Connaught Road, Central, Hong Kong
(Previously under Far East Hydrofoil Co Ltd)

Telephone: (5) 8593111
Telex: 74200 SEDAM HX
Telefax: (5) 404997

Stanley Ho, *Managing Director*
David Hill, *General Manager*
Andrew Tse, *Manager, Financial Control*
Jenning Wang, *Engineering Manager*
Uwe G Willers, *Fleet Operations Manager*

The company started hydrofoil service in 1963 with a PT 20 and gradually built up to a total of 14 surface-piercing hydrofoils. It started the world's first commercial Jetfoil service in April 1975. Subsequently the Jetfoils took over the bulk of the traffic due to passenger demand and the surface-piercing hydrofoils were gradually phased out and additional Jetfoils purchased. All surface-piercing hydrofoils were removed from service by end 1983 and subsequently sold. In 1986 STEC Jetfoils carried 62·0% of all Hong Kong-Macau passenger traffic with 31 000 passages and 5·83 million passengers. STEC Jetfoils have carried a total of 46 726 850 passengers up to 30 June 1987.

High-speed craft operated

Type	Name	Entered service with STEC
HYD Boeing Jetfoil 929-100	*Madeira*	1975
HYD Boeing Jetfoil 929-100	*Santa Maria*	1975
HYD Boeing Jetfoil 929-100	*Flores* (ex *Kalakaua*)	1978
HYD Boeing Jetfoil 929-100	*Corvo* (ex *Kamehameha*)	1978
HYD Boeing Jetfoil 929-100	*Pico* (ex *Kuhio*)	1978
HYD Boeing Jetfoil 929-100	*São Jorge* (ex *Jet Caribe*)	1980
HYD Boeing Jetfoil 929-100	*Acores* (ex *Jet Caribe II*)	1980
HYD Boeing Jetfoil 929-100	*Ponta Delgada* (ex *Flying Princess II*)	1981
HYD Boeing Jetfoil 929-115	*Terceira* (ex *Normandy Princess*)	1981
HYD Boeing Jetfoil 929-100	*Urzela* (ex *Flying Princess*)	1981
HYD Boeing Jetfoil 929-115	*Funchal* (ex *Jetferry One*)	1983
HYD Boeing Jetfoil 929-115	*Horta* (ex *Jetferry Two*)	1983
HYD Boeing Jetfoil 929-115	*Ginga* (ex *Cu na Mara*)	1987
HYD Boeing Jetfoil 929-115*	*Lilau* (ex *HMS Speedy*)	1987

* converted 929-320

Routes operated

Hong Kong-Macau and Kowloon-Macau, distance 36-40n miles. Services 3 times per hour each way during daylight hours and 2 times per hour from sunset till midnight with the last departure at 2 am.

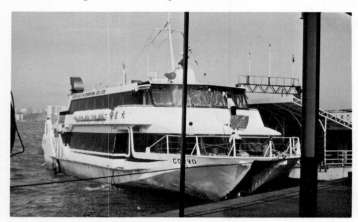

Corvo, Jetfoil Model 929-100, at the Hong Kong terminal

W & Y International Ltd

42-44 Granville Road, 8C, Kowloon, Hong Kong

High-speed craft operated

Type	Name
SES Hovermarine HM 216	ex HYF 102*

*purchased from The Hong Kong & Yaumati Ferry Co Ltd, 1987

HUNGARY

MAHART (Magyar Hajózási Részvénytársaság)

Apaczai Caere Janos utca 11, 1366 Budapest V, Pf58, Hungary

Telephone: 187-160
Telex: 225258 MAHART H

MAHART carries between 30 000 and 35 000 passengers a year. Total journeys come to 15 million passenger km/year.

High-speed craft operated

Type	Name	Seats	Built
HYD Sormovo Meteor	*Sólyom*	65	1971
HYD Sormovo Voskhod	*Vöcsök*	104	1976
HYD Sormovo Voskhod	*Vöcsök II*	—	1986
HYD Sormovo Voskhod	*Vöcsök III*	—	1987
HYD Sormovo Voskhod	*Vöcsök IV*	—	1987

Route operated

Budapest to Vienna, 282km, 5 hours, April to October

Sormovo Meteor *Sólyom* operated by MAHART

INDIA

Anklesaria

Bombay, India

High-speed craft operated
Type
SES Hovermarine HM 216

Operation
Crew boat

INDONESIA

PT Hover Maritim Semandera

Jalan Gondangdia Lama 26, Jakarta 10350, Indonesia

Telephone: 325608 (5 lines)
Telex: 45746 ESHARCO IA

Air Marshal (Rtd) Suharnoko Harbani, *Chairman*
H M Suharnoko MBA, MPA, *Vice Chairman*
Ir A W Suharnoko, *President Director*
First Admiral (Rtd) Kumoro Utojo, *Director Operations*

High-speed craft operated

Type	Name	Seats	Delivered
SES Vosper Hovermarine HM 218 Mk IV	*Semandera Satu*	78	1986
SES Vosper Hovermarine HM 218 Mk IV	*Semandera Dua*	78	1986

Routes operated

Tanjung Priok (Port of Jakarta) to Panjang (Port of Bandar Lampung), distance 110n miles, trip time 3 hours 40 min, service started March 1987, one return trip per day, weekdays only, departures: Jakarta 07:00, Bandar Lampung 12:30. Fare US$15·0 single.

Tanjung Priok to Seribu Islands (holiday resorts northwest of Jakarta), distance 40n miles, trip time 1 hour 20 min, service started February 1987, one, and occasionally three, return trips per day, major holidays and weekends only, departures: Jakarta 07:00, Seribu Islands 16:00. Fare US$21·0 return.

The craft that ran aground is now back in service after extensive repair completed in November 1987 under Lloyds' surveys.

Hover Maritim Semandera is also offering a two-day cruise package to the Ujung Kulon National Park from Jakarta, distance 135n miles, trip time 4 hours 25 min, service started September 1987, major holidays only, departures: 07:00 from Jakarta. Package fare US$250·0 per person

Vosper Hovermarine HM 218 Mk IV *Semandera Satu*

PT PELNI (Pelayaran Nasional Indonesia)/PT PAL Indonesia/P Seribu Paradise Travel Agent

Indonesia

High-speed craft operated

Type	Name	Seats	Delivered
HYD Boeing Jetfoil 929-115/0022	*Bima Samudera I*	255	1982
HYD Boeing Jetfoil 929-115	*Bininda II**		1986

*Navy owned

Routes operated

Tanjung Priok, Jakarta to Pandang, Lampung (Srengsan) on Mondays, Wednesdays and Saturdays. Fare US$42 single
Tanjung Priok, Jakarta to Palau Putri, P Seribu on Sundays

PT Satmarindo

Indonesia

High-speed craft operated

Type	Name	Seats	Delivered
MH SBF Engineering (Phil Curran design)	*Satrya Express*	62	1985

Crew boat with capacity for two 8-tonne deck containers.

Operation

Servicing of the Hudbay Oil Lalang oil and gas fields in the Strait of Malacca

Tjetty Marine

Tanjung Pinang, Indonesia

High-speed craft operated

Type	Name	Seats	Delivered
MH	*Bima Express*	75	July 1984

Route operated

Singapore to Tanjung Pinang (63 miles)

IRAN

Islamic Republic of Iran Shipping Lines

Khorramshahr and Bandar Abbas, Iran

High-speed craft operated

Type	Name
HYD USSR Feodosiya Shipyard Kometa	*Iran Resalat* (ex *Arya Ram*) Yard No S-34
HYD USSR Feodosiya Shipyard Kometa	*Iran Tareeghal* (ex *Arya Baz*, ex Kometa S-26)

ITALY

Adriatica di Navigazione SpA

Zattere 1411, Palazzo Sociale, 30123 Venice, Italy

Telephone: (041) 781611
Telex: 410045 ADRNAV I

High-speed craft operated

Type	Name	Seats	Delivered
HYD Rodriquez PT 50	*Nibbio*	125	1964
HYD Rodriquez RHS 160	*Diomedea*	160	1975
HYD Rodriquez RHS 160F	—		1988

Routes operated

1987 schedule April to September:
Nibbio: Ortona to Tremiti, 2 hours 10 min, fare 126 000 lira one way
Vasto to Tremiti, 1 hour 10 min, fare 8800 lira one way
Rodi Garganico to Tremiti, 40 min, fare 11 400 lira one way
Diomedea: Termoli to Tremiti, 45 min, fare 13 100 lira (13 June to 13 Sept): other times 6200 lira one way
Freccia: Peschici to Tremiti, 45 min, fare 13 700 lira one way

Agip SpA

S Donato Milanese, Milan, Italy

Telephone: 53531
Telex: 31246 ENI I

High-speed craft operated

HYD Rodriquez PT 20
HYD Rodriquez PT 50

Alilauro Aliscafi del Tirreno SpA

Head office: Via Caracciolo 11, 80 122 Naples, Italy

Telephone: (081) 684288
Telex: 720354 ALILAR I
Telefax: (081) 991990

Capt Salvatore Lauro, *President*

Subsidiary companies:
Alivit Srl
Alilauro 2000 Srl

High-speed craft operated

Type	Name	Seats	Delivered
HYD Rodriquez PT 50	*Alimarte* (ex *Alivit*)	140	1969
HYD Sormovo Kometa M	*Aliapollo*	116	1971
HYD Sormovo Kometa M	*Alivulcano*	116	1972
HYD Sormovo Kometa M	*Alivenere* (ex *Aligiglio*)*	116	1972
HYD Sormovo Kometa M	*Alisorrento**	116	1972
HYD Sormovo Kometa M	*Alivesuvio**	116	1973
HYD Sormovo Kometa M	*Alirug*	140	1969
CAT Westamarin W95	*Celestina*	248	June 1981
CAT Marinteknik Marinjet 33 CPV	*Giove Jet*	282	April 1985
HYD S Ordzhonikidze Kolkhida	*Aliatlante*	155	June 1986
HYD S Ordzhonikidze Kolkhida	*Alieolo*		July 1986
MH Marinteknik Marinjet 34 CPV	*Europa Jet*	300	September 1987
CAT Fairey Marinteknik Singapore Marinjet 34 CPV	—	300	1988

*These Kometas were fitted with MTU 8V 396 TB83 engines in the order shown in 1984, 1985 and 1986
Nettuno Jet was bought back by Marinteknik Verkstads AB and sold to SURF, France, 1987

Routes operated

Naples to Ischia Porto
Naples to Forio
Naples to Sorrento
Sorrento to Capri
Capri to Ischia
Salerno to Amalfi to Positano to Capri
Naples to Capri and the ports of the Cilento coast

The oldest craft in the Linee Lauro, the Rodriquez PT 50 hydrofoil *Alimarte*

Kometa *Alivenere* operated by Alilauro Aliscafi del Tirreno SpA

Aliscafi SNAV SpA
(Societa di Navigazione Alta Velocita)

Head Office: Cortina del Porto, Via San Raineri 22, 98100 Messina, Italy

Telephone: (90) 773722
Telex: 980030 RODRIK I

Terminal (main): Via Caracciolo 10, 80122 Naples, Italy

Telephone: (81) 660444
Telex: 720446 SNAVNA I

High-speed craft operated

Type	Name	Seats	Built
HYD Rodriquez PT 20 (laid up)	*Freccia del Sole*	72	1956
HYD Rodriquez PT 20	*Freccia delle Eolie*	72	1957
HYD Rodriquez PT 20	*Freccia del Tirreno*	72	1957
HYD Rodriquez PT 50	*Freccia d'Oro*	130	1959
HYD Rodriquez PT 50	*Freccia di Messina*	125	1959
HYD Rodriquez PT 20	*Freccia dello Stretto*	72	1960
HYD Rodriquez PT 20	*Freccia di Reggio*	72	1961
HYD Rodriquez PT 20	*Freccia del Peloro*	72	1961
HYD Rodriquez PT 50	*Freccia di Sicilia*	125	1964
HYD Rodriquez PT 20	*Freccia del Vesuvio*	72	1966

Four PT 20s approximately one sixth of the Aliscafi SNAV hydrofoil fleet at the Rodriquez Messina works

High-speed craft operated (contd)

Type	Name	Seats	Built
HYD Rodriquez PT 50	*Freccia delle Isole*	125	1966
HYD Rodriquez PT 50	*Freccia Atlantica*	125	
HYD Rodriquez PT 50	*Sun Arrow*	125	1968
HYD Rodriquez PT 50	*Freccia Adriatica*	125	1969
HYD Rodriquez PT 20	*Freccia dello Ionio*		
HYD Rodriquez PT 20	*Freccia di Posillipo*		
HYD Rodriquez PT 20	*Freccia di Procida*		
HYD Rodriquez PT 50	*Freccia del Sud*	105	
HYD Rodriquez RHS 160	*Alijumbo*	180	1979
HYD Rodriquez RHS 200	*Superjumbo*	254	1981
HYD Rodriquez RHS 150F	*Dynasty*	161	1984
HYD Westermoen Hydrofoil A/S PT 50	*Freccia del Lipari*		
HYD Westermoen Hydrofoil A/S PT 50	*Freccia del Mediteraneo*		
HYD Rodriquez RHS 160F	*Alijumbo Eolie*	220	1986
HYD Rodriquez RHS 150M			
HYD Rodriquez RHS 150M			

Routes operated (1987) for various periods in the year

Anzio to Ponza to Ventotene to Ischia to Naples
Reggio Calabria to Messina to Porto Levante to Lipari to Santa Marina to Panarea to Ginostra
Naples to Capri
Palermo to Cefalu to Filicudi to Rinella to Santa Marina Salina to Vulcano to Lipari
Naples to Ustica to Favignana to Trapani
Messina to Reggio Calabria to Messina to Vulcano to Lipari to Santa Marina Salina to Panarea to Stromboli
Rimella (Is Salina) to Santa Marina (Is Salina) to Lipari (Is Lipari) to Porto di Levante (Is Vulcano) to Lipari (Is Panarea) to Stromboli to Naples
Vibo Valenta to Stromboli to Panarea to Vulcano to Lipari to Vulcano

Rodriquez PT 20 *Freccia di Sorrento* in service with the Italian Ministero dei Mercantile Marine for anti-pollution work

Trapani to Pantelleria to Kelibia
Messina (Sicily) to Reggio Calabria to Messina to Stromboli to Panarea to Santa Marina Salina to Lipari to Vulcano
Capo d'Orlando (Sicily) to Vulcano to Lipari to Capo d'Orlando to Vulcano to Lipari
Milazzo (Sicily) to Is Vulcano to Lipari to Santa Marina (Is Salina) to Rimella (Is Salina) to Santa Marina to Is Panarea to Is Stromboli to Is Panarea to Is Filicudi to Is Alicudi to Is Filicudi to Rinella to Santa Marina (Salina) to Lipari to Vulcano to Milazzo
Casamicciola to Procida to Naples

Alivit Due Srl

Via Caracciolo 20, 80122 Naples, Italy

Telephone: (081) 668910
Telex: 720354 ALILAR I

Dott Ruggiero Vitobello, *Director*

High-speed craft operated

Type	Name	Seats	Built
HYD Sormovo Kometa-M	*Alisaturno*	116	1972
HYD Sormovo Kometa-M	*Alieros*	116	1973
HYD Rodriquez PT 20	*Alioceano*	60	1985
HYD Sormovo Kolkhida	*Aligea*	115	1987

Routes operated
Amalfi-Positano-Naples-Sorrento-Procida-Ischia
Naples-Capri-Positano-Amalfi-Salerno-Ports of Cilento coast

Aliscafi SNAV PT 50 (built in 1964) at the Lipari terminal, October 1987

CAREMAR
(Societa Compagnia Regionale Marittima SpA)
Molo Beverello 2, 80133 Naples, Italy

Telephone: (81) 315384
Telex: 720054 I

High-speed craft operated

Type	Name	Seats	Delivered
HYD Rodriquez RHS 140	*Albireo*	140	1977
HYD Rodriquez RHS 160	*Algol*	180	1978
HYD Rodriquez RHS 160	*Alioth*	180	1979
HYD Rodriquez RHS 160F	*Anilam*	210	1986
HYD Rodriquez RHS 160F	*Aldebaran*	—	1986

Routes operated
Naples to Capri
Naples to Ischia Porto
Naples to Procida

COVEMAR Eolie
Via Capp M Scala 21, Milazzo ME, Sicily, Italy

High-speed craft operated

Type	Name	Seats
HYD Rodriquez PT 50S	*Star Capricorn* (ex *Springeren*, 1967)	117
HYD Rodriquez PT 20	*Freccia della Salina*	—

Linea Navigazione del Tirreno SpA
Naples, Italy

High-speed craft operated

Type	Name	Delivered
CAT Marinteknik Verkstads JC-F1	— (ex *Jaguar*, ex *Jaguar Prince*, ex *Mavic Haliç*)	1987

Ministero dei Mercantile Marine

In 1987 a Rodriquez PT 50 hydrofoil was adapted for anti-pollution work. The vessel was previously operated by Aliscafi SNAV SpA.

High-speed craft operated

Type	Name	Built
HYD Rodriquez PT 50	*Freccia di Sorrento*	1959

Navigazione Libera del Golfo SpA
Italy

High-speed craft operated

Type	Seats	Delivered
MH Fairey Marinteknik (UK) 41·0m	350	mid-1988

Ministero dei Trasporti
Via L Ariosto 21, 20145 Milan, Italy

Telephone: (02) 48 120 86
Telex: 311294 NAVIGE I

Dott Ing Pietro Santini, *Government Manager*

The Italian Ministry of Transport has three subsidiary hydrofoil operating companies which run services on Lake Como, Lake Garda and Lake Maggiore as detailed below.

Navigazione Lago di Como
Via Rubini 22, 22100 Como, Italy

Telephone: 27 33 24/26 02 34

Dott Ing F Parigi, *Director*

High-speed craft operated

Type	Name	Seats	Built
Rodriquez PT 20	*Freccia del Lario*	80	1964
Rodriquez PT 20	*Freccia delle Azalee*	80	1967
Rodriquez RHS 70	*Freccia delle Betulle*	80	1974
Rodriquez RHS 70	*Freccia delle Gardenie*	80	1976
Rodriquez RHS 150SL	*Freccia delle Valli*	180	1981
Rodriquez RHS 150SL	*Guglielmo Marconi*	180	1983

Routes operated
Como-Argegno-Lenno-Tremezzo-Bellagio-Menaggio-Varenna-Bellano-Dongo-Gravedona-Domaso-Colico
Bellagio-Mandello-Lecco

Rodriquez RHS 150SL *Freccia delle Valli* departing from Bellagio, Lake Como

Rodriquez RHS 150SL en route on Lake Como   *(Ministero dei Trasporti)*

Navigazione Sul Lago di Garda
Piazza Matteotti 2, 25015 Desenzano del Garda, Italy

Telephone: (030) 914 1321/3
Telex: 303114 NAVIGA I

High-speed craft operated

Type	Name	Seats	Built
Rodriquez PT 20	*Freccia del Garda*	80	1958
Rodriquez PT 20	*Freccia degli Ulivi*	72	1965
Rodriquez RHS 70	*Freccia del Benaco*	71	1974
Rodriquez RHS 70	*Freccia del Gerani*	71	1976
Rodriquez RHS 150SL	*Freccia delle Riviere*	200	1981
Rodriquez RHS 150SL	*Galileo Galilei*	200	1982

Routes operated
Peschiera-Desenzano del G.-Sirmione-Bardolino-Garda-Salò-Gardone Riviera-Maderno-Torri del Benaco-Gargnano-Castelletto-Malcesine-Limone-Torbole-Riva del Garda

Rodriquez RHS 150SL

Navigazione Lago Maggiore

Viale F Baracca 1, 28041 Arona, Italy

Telephone: 0322 46651
Telex: 200248 NAVIMA I

Dott Ing Paolo De Pascale, *Director*

High-speed craft operated

Type	Name	Seats	Built
Rodriquez PT 20	*Freccia del Verbano*	80	1964
Rodriquez PT 20	*Freccia del Ticino*	80	1968
Rodriquez RHS 70	*Freccia delle Camelie*	80	1974
Rodriquez RHS 70	*Freccia delle Magnolie*	80	1975
Rodriquez RHS 150SL	*Freccia dei Giardini*	176 + 20	1981
Rodriquez RHS 150SL	*Freccia Enrico Fermi*	200	1984
Rodriquez RHS 150FL	*Goethe*	200	1987

Routes operated

Arona-Angera-Belgirate-Stresa-Baveno-Pallanza-Intra-Luino-Brissago-
Porto Ronco-Ascona-Locarno

SIREMAR
(Sicilia Regionale Marittima SpA)

Via Francesco Crispi 120, 90139 Palermo, Sicily, Italy

Telephone: 091 582688
Telex: 910135 SIRMAR I

High-speed craft operated

Type	Name	Seats	Built
Rodriquez PT 50	*Freccia Atlantica* (ex *Sirena*)	125	1960 leased from Aliscafi SNAV SpA
Rodriquez PT 50	*Pisanello*	130	1961
Rodriquez PT 20	*Pinturicchio*	70	1968
Rodriquez RHS 160	*Donatello*	180	1980
Rodriquez RHS 160	*Botticelli*	180	1980
Rodriquez RHS 160F	*Masaccio*		1987
Rodriquez RHS 160F	*Mantegna*		1989

Routes operated

Pisanello: Lipari-Salina-Filicudi-Alicudi
Lipari-Panarea-Stromboli
Freccia Atlantica: Palermo-Ustica
Donatello: Milazzo-Vulcano-Lipari
Botticelli: Trapani-Favignana-Levanzo-Marettimo
Pinturicchio: Marettimo-Levanzo-Favignana
Masaccio: Santa Marina Salina-Lipari-Vulcano-Milazzo

SIREMAR's RHS 160 *Donatello*

TOREMAR SpA
(Toscana Regionale Marittima SpA)

Scali del Corso 5, 57100 Leghorn, Italy

Telephone: (586) 22772
Telex: 590214 I

High-speed craft operated

Type	Name	Seats	Built
HYD Rodriquez RHS 140	*Fabricia*	140	1977
HYD Rodriquez RHS 160F	*Masaccio*		1987
HYD Rodriquez RHS 160F	*Duccio*		1988

Routes operated

Portoferraio to Cavo to Piombino (Elba to mainland)

Vetor srl

Italy

High-speed craft operated

Type	Name	Delivered
HYD Feodosiya Kometa	*Vetor 944*	1984

JAPAN

Awashima Kisen

Japan

High-speed craft operated

Type	Name	Speed	Seats	Delivered
MH Sumidagawa Zosen Co Ltd	*Iwayuri*	24 knots	144	May 1979

Route operated

Awashima to Iwafune

Biwako Kisen Co Ltd
(Biwa Lake Sightseeing Company)

1-5-24 Hama-Ohtsu, Ohtsu 520, Shiga Prefecture, Japan

High-speed craft operated

Type	Name	Speed	Seats	Delivered
MH Mokubei Shipbuilding Co Ikeda 22m (Hamilton Jet waterjet-propelled)	*Lansing*	27 knots	86	Aug 1982

Route operated

Biwa Lake, sightseeing

Designed by Dr M Ikeda, the Mokubei Shipbuilding Company waterjet-propelled *Lansing*

Boyo Kisen Co Ltd

134-6 Yanai-shi, Yamaguchi, Japan

High-speed craft operated

Type	Name	Speed	Seats	Delivered
HYD Hitachi Zosen PT 20	*Shibuki No 2*	32 knots	66	June 1969
HYD Hitachi Zosen PT 50	*Shibuki No 3*	34 knots	123	October 1973

Route operated

Yanai to Mitsuhama

Daitohmaru Kanko

Japan

High-speed craft operated

Type	Name	Speed	Seats	Delivered
MH New Japan Marine Co Ltd	*Daitohmaru No 12*	23 knots	56	December 1977

Route operated

Wadakano to Anagawa

Ehime Kisen

Japan

High-speed craft operated

Type	Name	Speed	Seats	Delivered
MH Miho Zosenjyo Co Ltd	*Kamome No 1*	25 knots	52	October 1973
MH Miho Zosenjyo Co Ltd	*Mishima No 2*	25 knots	75	August 1979

Route operated

Imabari to Takehara

Ena Kanko Kaihatsu

Japan

High-speed craft operated

Type	Name	Speed	Seats	Delivered
MH Kawai	*Hayabusa*	22 knots	50	April 1978

Routes operated

Around Enakyo
Nakatsugawa to Enakyo

Enoh Kisen

Japan

High-speed craft operated

Type	Name	Speed	Seats	Delivered
MH New Japan Marine Co Ltd	*Edajima No 2*	23·9 knots	60	February 1975
MH New Japan Marine Co Ltd	*Edajima No 3*	23·7 knots	60	January 1976
MH New Japan Marine Co Ltd	*Edajima No 5*	23·4 knots	74	November 1982

Route operated

Ujina to Fujinowaki

Ezaki Kisen

Japan

High-speed craft operated

Type	Name	Speed	Seats	Delivered
MH Garuda KK	*Garuda No 1*	23 knots	82	October 1972
MH Toei	*Garuda No 2*	23 knots	96	March 1976
MH Toei	*Garuda No 5*	23·9 knots	96	October 1979

Route operated

Ushifuka to Minamata

Fuke Kaiun Co Ltd

3500 Fuke, Misaki 599-03, Osaka Prefecture, Japan

An HM 216 purchased from Hovermarine Pacific Co Ltd in July 1981.

High-speed craft operated

Type	Name	Speed	Seats	Launched
SES Hovermarine Transport Ltd HM 216	*Sea Hope* (ex *Hovstar*)	33 knots	63	September 1976

Route operated

Fuke to Sumoto

Geibi Shosen

Japan

High-speed craft operated

Type	Name	Speed	Seats	Launched
MH Miho Zosenjyo Co Ltd	*Chidori No 5*	24 knots	70	March 1979

Route operated

Nakamachi to Ujina

Gotoh Ryokyakusen

Japan

High-speed craft operated

Type	Name	Speed	Seats	Launched
MH Nankai	*New Gotoh*	23 knots	170	May 1984

Route operated

Gohnokubi to Fukue

Habu Shosen

Japan

High-speed craft operated

Type	Name	Speed	Seats	Launched
MH Kiso Zosen Tekko Co Ltd	*Innoshima No 2*	25 knots	68	April 1976
MH Kiso Zosen Tekko Co Ltd	*Innoshima No 3*	26 knots	70	July 1979
MH Kiso Zosen Tekko Co Ltd	*Innoshima No 5*	26·5 knots	70	March 1981

Route operated

Habu to Mihara

Hankyu Kisen KK

45 Harcina-cho, Chuo-ku, Kobe, Hyogo Prefecture, Japan

Telephone: (78) 3315007

High-speed craft operated

Type	Name	Speed	Seats	Launched
HYD Hitachi Zosen PT 50	*Zuihoh*	35 knots	131	December 1971
HYD Hitachi Zosen PT 50	*Hoh'oh*	35 knots	131	February 1972
HYD Hitachi Zosen PT 50 Mk II	*Shunsei* (ex *Kariyush I*)	—	—	June 1975
HYD Hitachi Zosen PTS 50 Mk II	*Housho*	38 knots	123	January 1983

Routes operated

Kobe to Kameura
Kobe to Tokushima

Hayate Kaiun

Japan

High-speed craft operated

Type	Name	Speed	Seats	Delivered
MH Setouchi Craft Co Ltd	*Hayate No 11*	25 knots	70	March 1984

Route operated

Sarahama to Hirara

Hiroshima-Imabari Kohsokusen

Japan

High-speed craft operated

Type	Name	Speed	Seats	Delivered
MH Miho Zosenjyo Co Ltd	*Waka*	25 knots	84	July 1984
MH Miho Zosenjyo Co Ltd	*Seto*	25 knots	84	August 1984

Route operated

Ujina to Imabari

Horai Kisen

Japan

High-speed craft operated

Type	Name	Speed	Seats	Delivered
MH Fuji Yacht	*Hikari No 2*	23 knots	139	March 1978
MH Kanda Zosen	*Hikari No 3*	23 knots	69	November 1979

Route operated

Mihara to Setoda

Imabari Kohsokusen

Japan

High-speed craft operated

Type	Name	Speed	Seats	Delivered
MH Miho Zosenjyo Co Ltd	*Kamome No 2*	24 knots	52	November 1973
MH Miho Zosenjyo Co Ltd	*Kamome No 5*	25 knots	80	May 1976
MH Miho Zosenjyo Co Ltd	*Chidori No 7*	24 knots	70	January 1980
MH Miho Zosenjyo Co Ltd	*Kamome No 7*	25 knots	93	April 1982

Routes operated

Imabari to Iguchi
Imabari to Onomichi

Irabu Kaiun

Japan

High-speed craft operated

Type	Name	Speed	Seats	Delivered
MH Sunuki Zosen Co Ltd	*Kariushi No 3*	26 knots	200	October 1980
MH Superior Boat	*Kariushi No 5*	25 knots	78	October 1980

Route operated

Sarahama to Hirata

Iriomote Kanko Kaiun

Japan

High-speed craft operated

Type	Name	Speed	Seats	Delivered
MH Sumidagawa Zosen Co Ltd	*Marine Star*	24 knots	141	March 1979

Route operated

Ishigaki to Funaura

Ishizaki Kisen KK

1-4-9 Mistu, 1-chome, Matsuyama 791, Ehime Prefecture, Japan

Telephone: (899) 510 128

High-speed craft operated

Type	Name	Speed	Seats	Launched
HYD Hitachi Zosen PT 20	Kansei*	34 knots	66	1962
HYD Hitachi Zosen PT 50	Kosei	34 knots	125	1969
HYD Hitachi Zosen PT 20	Myojo	34 knots	66	1970
HYD Hitachi Zosen PT 20	Kinsei	34 knots	68	1972
HYD Hitachi Zosen PT 50	Saisei	34 knots	126	1974
HYD Hitachi Zosen PT 50	Shunsei	34 knots	123	1975
HYD Hitachi Zosen PT 20	Ryusei	34 knots	69	1981

*Spare craft

Routes operated

Matsuyama to Hiroshima (PT 50s)
Matsuyama to Onomichi (PT 20s)
Matsuyama to Mihara (PT 20s)

Iwakuni-Hashirashima Kaiun

Japan

High-speed craft operated

Type	Name	Speed	Seats	Delivered
MH Kiso Zosen Tekko Co Ltd	Suisei	22 knots	96	November 1982

Route operated

Iwakuni to Hashirashima

Izu-Hakone Railways Co Ltd

300 Ohba, Mishima 41, Shizuoka Prefecture, Japan

High-speed craft operated

Type	Name	Speed	Seats	Delivered
MH Sumidagawa Zosen Co Ltd	Cobalt Arrow 2	22 knots	132	March 1975
MH Sumidagawa Zosen Co Ltd	Cobalt Arrow 3	22 knots	144	December 1978

Route operated

Numazu to Matsuzaki

Japanese National Railways

Koko-tetsu Building, 1-6-5 Marunouchi 1-chome, Chiyoda-ku, Tokyo 100, Japan

Telephone: (03) 212 3587

High-speed craft operated

Type	Name	Speed	Seats	Launched
HOV Mitsui MV-PP5 Mk II	Tobiuo (Flying Fish)	45 knots	66	March 1980

Route operated

Uno to Takamatsu (11·34n miles, 23 min)

MV-PP5 Mk II *Tobiuo (Flying Fish)*, operated by Japanese National Railways

Kansai Express Ferry Co Ltd

1-3 Tamamo, Takamatsu 760, Kagawa Prefecture, Japan

High-speed craft operated

Type	Name	Speed	Seats	Delivered
MH Sunuki Zosen Co Ltd	Phoenix 1	23·27 knots	88	February 1975
MH Sunuki Zosen Co Ltd	Phoenix 2	23·00 knots	88	April 1975

Routes operated

Tonosho to Takamatsu
Takamatsu to Tonosho

Kasumigaura Jet Line KK

Japan

High-speed craft operated

Type	Name	Delivered
MH Yamaha Motor Co Ltd	Kasumi Jet	1984

Kato Kisen Co Ltd/Kansai Kisen Co Ltd

Japan

High-speed craft operated

Type	Name	Launched
HYD Boeing Jetfoil 929-115	Jet 7 (ex Spirit of Friendship)	August 1980
HYD Boeing Jetfoil 929-115	Jet 8 (ex Spirit of Discovery)	April 1985

Operation

Started 1987

Koshikijima Shosen Co Ltd (Koshiki Island Shipping Co)

181-2 Shinsei, Kushikino 896, Kagoshima Prefecture, Japan

High-speed craft operated

Type	Name	Speed	Seats	Launched
MH Mitsubishi	Sea Hawk	26·5 knots	290	January 1977

Route operated

Kushikino to Koshikijima

Kyodo Kisen Co Ltd (Kyodo Shipping Co)

1-5-24 Hama-Ohtsu, Ohtsu 520, Shiga Prefecture, Japan

High-speed craft operated

Type	Name	Speed	Seats	Delivered
MH Miho Zosenjyo Co Ltd	Hamakaze	25 knots	136	February 1976
MH Miho Zosenjyo Co Ltd	Shiokaze	25 knots	136	May 1977
MH Miho Zosenjyo Co Ltd	Asakaze	25 knots	135	August 1977
MH Miho Zosenjyo Co Ltd	Oikaze	25 knots	136	September 1978
MH Miho Zosenjyo Co Ltd	Sachikaze	25 knots	136	December 1978
MH Miho Zosenjyo Co Ltd	Urakaze	25 knots	136	November 1979

Routes operated

Osaka to Sumoto
Kobe to Sumoto

Kyushu Yusen Co Ltd

1-27 Kamiya, Hakata, Fukuoka 812, Japan

High-speed craft operated

Type	Name	Speed	Seats	Launched
MH Mitsubishi	Sea Ace	28 knots	231	May 1980

Route operated

Hakata to Iki

Maruto Kisen

Japan

High-speed craft operated

Type	Name	Speed	Seats	Delivered
MH Tohkai Boat Co Ltd	Queen Romance	27 knots	115	June 1976
MH Hayami Zosen Co Ltd	Queen Romance No 2	29 knots	126	April 1982

Route operated

Setoda to Mihara

Meitetsu Kaijo Kankosen Co Ltd (Meitetsu Maritime Sight-Seeing Passengerboat Co)

18-1 Sanbonmatsu, Atsuta, Nagoya 456, Japan

High-speed craft operated

Type	Name	Speed	Seats	Delivered
MH Sunuki Zosen Co Ltd	Ohtoki	22 knots	97	February 1981
MH Sunuki Zosen Co Ltd	Ohtoki 2	22 knots	97	July 1981
MH Sunuki Zosen Co Ltd	Ohtoki 3	22 knots	97	March 1982
MH Sunuki Zosen Co Ltd	Kaien 5	22 knots	61	March 1982
MH Sunuki Zosen Co Ltd	Kaien 6	22 knots	79	July 1982

Routes operated

Shinojima to Kohwa
Gamagohri to Toba

Mihara Kanko Kisen

Japan

High-speed craft operated

Type	Name	Speed	Seats	Delivered
MH Setouchi Craft Co Ltd	*Nishi Nikko No 3*	26 knots	150	October 1976
MH Setouchi Craft Co Ltd	*Nishi Nikko No 5*	26 knots	81	February 1981
MH Setouchi Craft Co Ltd	*Nishi Nikko No 8*	26 knots	81	October 1981

Route operated

Mihara to Setoda

Mikatagoko Yuransen

Japan

High-speed craft operated

Type	Name	Speed	Seats	Delivered
MH Ohtani	*Suisei No 3*	22 knots	50	July 1975
MH Ohtani	*Suisei No 5*	22 knots	50	July 1975
MH Ohtani	*Suisei No 6*	22 knots	50	August 1976
MH Ohtani	*Suisei No 7*	22 knots	50	August 1976
MH Ohtani	*Suisei No 8*	22 knots	50	May 1981

Route operated

Hayase to Mikatasanbashi

Ministry of Transportation

Maritime Safety Agency, Japan

High-speed craft operated

Type	Name	Delivered
MH Mitsubishi Heavy Industries Ltd 26·01m	*Iseyuki*	1975
MH Mitsubishi Heavy Industries Ltd 26·01m	*Hamazuki*	1976
MH Mitsubishi Heavy Industries Ltd 26·01m	*Hatagumo*	1976
MH Mitsubishi Heavy Industries Ltd 26·01m	*Isozuki*	1977
MH Mitsubishi Heavy Industries Ltd 30·99m	*Asagumo*	1978
MH Mitsubishi Heavy Industries Ltd 30·99m	*Hayagumo*	1979
MH Mitsubishi Heavy Industries Ltd 26·01m	*Hanayuki*	1981
MH Mitsubishi Heavy Industries Ltd 26·01m	*Awagiri*	1983
MH Mitsubishi Heavy Industries Ltd 30·99m	*Asagari*	1983

Operation

Patrol vessels

Third District Port Construction Bureau

Japan

High-speed craft operated

Type	Name	Delivered
SWATH Mitsubishi 27·01m	*Ohtori*	March 1981

Nankai Ferry Co Ltd

6-5 Chikkoh, Wakayama 640, Wakayama Prefecture, Japan

High-speed craft operated

Type	Name	Speed	Seats	Launched
CAT Mitsui CP30	*Marine Hawk*	28·5 knots	280	July 1983

National Institute of Polar Research

9-10 Kaga 1-chome, Itabashi-ku, Tokyo 173, Japan

Telex: 2723515 POLRSC J

N Murakoshi, *General Manager for Polar Research*

Designated polar terrain acv test craft, the Mitsui MV-PP05A air cushion vehicle was employed for expedition work in Antarctica.

High-speed craft operated

Type	Speed	Seats	Delivered
HOV Mitsui MV-PP05A	30 knots	3	1980

Nippon Koun Kaisha Ltd

Eime Prefecture, Japan

High-speed craft operated

Type	Name	Seats	Delivered
MH Mitsubishi Heavy Industries Ltd 26·76m	*Sunline*	70	September 1986

Nomicho Kotsu Office

Japan

High-speed craft operated

Type	Name	Speed	Seats	Delivered
MH Miho Zosenjyo Co Ltd	*Chidori No 6*	22 knots	76	June 1981

Route operated

Nakamachi to Ujina

Ohmi Marine

Japan

High-speed craft operated

Type	Name	Speed	Seats	Delivered
MH Mokubei	*Wakaayu*	22 knots	64	February 1972
MH Mokubei	*Wakaayu No 2*	22 knots	88	August 1973
MH Mokubei	*Wakaayu No 5*	24 knots	160	March 1983
MH Mokubei	*Wakaayu No 8*	24 knots	62	March 1984
MH Mokubei	*Wakaayu No 6*	24 knots	100	July 1984

Routes operated

Hikone to Chikubushima
Imazu to Chikubushima
Iiura to Chikubushima

Ohmishima Ferry

Japan

High-speed craft operated

Type	Name	Speed	Seats	Delivered
MH Miho Zosen Co Ltd	*Ohmishima No 3*	23·8 knots	70	May 1978

Route operated

Mihara to Iguchi

Oita Hover Ferry Co Ltd

1-14-1 Nishi-shinchi, Oita shi Oita ken, Japan

Telephone: (0975) 58 7180

Hiroshi Ono, *President*
Keiichiro Isayama, *Vice President*
Hiroshi Aizawa, *General Director*

Oita Hover Ferry Co Ltd was established in November 1970 and began operating in October 1971.
Annual traffic: approx 330 000

High-speed craft operated

Type	Name	Speed	Seats	Launched
HOV Mitsui MV-PP5 Mk 2	*Hakuchyo No 3*	45 knots	75	June 1970
HOV Mitsui MV-PP5 Mk 2	*Hobby No 1*	45 knots	75	May 1971
HOV Mitsui MV-PP5 Mk 2	*Hobby No 3*	45 knots	75	September 1971
HOV Mitsui MV-PP5	*Angel No 2*	45 knots	51	June 1972
HOV Mitsui MV-PP5 Mk 2	*Angel No 5*	45 knots	75	April 1975
HOV Mitsui MV-PP5	*Akatombo 51**		51	
HOV Mitsui MV-PP5	*Akatombo 52**		51	

*Reserve craft, 2nd hand

Routes operated

Oita to Oita Airport (15·6n miles, 24 min)
Beppu to Oita Airport (6·5n miles, 10 min)

National Institute of Polar Research MV-PP05A and icebreaker *Fiji* on fast ice near Syowa station, Antarctica

Oita Hover Ferry MV-PP5   *(K Isayama)*

Oki Kisen KK

Nakamachim, Saigo-cho, Okigun, Shimane Prefecture, Japan

Telephone: (85) 1221122
Telex: 628966 J

High-speed craft operated

Type	Name	Speed	Seats	Launched
CAT Mitsui Super Westamaran CP20	*Marine Star*	28 knots	351	December 1983

Route operated
Sakai to Oki

Ryobi Unyu

Japan

High-speed craft operated

Type	Name	Speed	Seats	Delivered
MH Miho Zosen	*Princess Olive*	24 knots	94	July 1981
MH Miho Zosen	*Queen Olive*	24 knots	94	October 1981

Route operated
Okayama to Tonosho

Sado Kisen Kaisha

1 00 9 Ban Bandaijima, Niigata 950, Japan

Telephone: 0252 (45) 2311

S Nakamura, *Jetfoil Manager*

Passengers carried in 1984: 465 000

High-speed craft operated

Type	Name	Speed	Seats	In service
HYD Boeing Jetfoil 929-100	*Okesa*	42 knots	282	May 1977
HYD Boeing Jetfoil 929-115	*Mikado*	42 knots	286	1978
HYD Boeing Jetfoil 929-115	*Ginga* (ex *Cu na Mara*)	42 knots		1986

Route operated
Niigata to Ryotsu, Sado Island (36·3n miles, 1 hour)

Sanyo Kisen Co Ltd

Japan

High-speed craft operated

Type	Name	Speed	Seats	Delivered
MH Sunuki Zosen Co Ltd	*Silver Star*	23 knots	90	March 1972
MH New Japan Marine Co Ltd	*New Sanyo*	22 knots	79	January 1973
MH Setouchi Craft Co Ltd	*Setoji*	24 knots	75	August 1982

Routes operated
Fukuyama to Marugame
Kasaoka to Sanagi

Sanyo Shosen Co Ltd

Japan

High-speed craft operated

Type	Name	Speed	Seats	Delivered
MH Miho Zosenjyo Co Ltd	*Hayabusa No 5*	24 knots	58	March 1975
MH Miho Zosenjyo Co Ltd	*Chidori No 3*	22 knots	52	June 1975
MH Miho Zosenjyo Co Ltd	*Hayabusa No 7*	24 knots	58	July 1975
MH Miho Zosenjyo Co Ltd	*Hayabusa No 8*	24 knots	58	April 1977
MH Miho Zosenjyo Co Ltd	*Hayabusa No 10*	24 knots	70	October 1977
MH Miho Zosenjyo Co Ltd	*Hayabusa No 11*	24 knots	70	March 1979

Routes operated
Nikata to Imabari
Mihara to Ohcho
Takehara to Namikata

Sanyu Kisen Co Ltd

Japan

High-speed craft operated

Type	Name	Speed	Seats	Delivered
MH New Japan Marine Co Ltd	*Wakamaru*	22·4 knots	60	March 1976

Route operated
Ujina to Akashi

Seiun Kisen Co Ltd

Japan

High-speed craft operated

Type	Name	Speed	Seats	Delivered
MH Miho Zosenjyo Co Ltd	*Chidori*	24 knots	46	September 1972
MH Miho Zosenjyo Co Ltd	*Hayakaze*	25 knots	52	July 1974
MH Miho Zosenjyo Co Ltd	*Shiokaze*	25 knots	80	February 1976

Route operated
Tsunoura to Uwajima

Setonaikai Kisen Co Ltd (Seto Inland Sea Lines)

1-12-23 Ujinakaigan, Minami-ku, Hiroshima 734, Japan

Telephone: (082) 255 3344
Telex: 653-625 STSHRM J
Telefax: (082) 251 6743

Toshihiro Yoshii, *Sales Director* (Hoshi Building 3F, 1-6-11 Kamiyacho, Nakaku, Hiroshima, Japan)

Setonaikai Kisen Co has been operating transport services linking the islands in the Inland Sea for many years and now has a fleet of 38 vessels, operating regular services along nine routes between Hiroshima and Shikoku, including a main route between Hiroshima and Matsuyama.

High-speed craft operated

Type	Name	Speed	Seats	Launched
HYD Hitachi Zosen PT 20	*Hibiki**	34 knots	66	November 1966
HYD Hitachi Zosen PT 20	*Hibiki No 3*	34 knots	66	March 1968
HYD Hitachi PT 20	*Ohtori No 2**	34 knots	113	February 1970
HYD Hitachi PT 20	*Ohtori No 3**	34 knots	113	October 1972
HYD Hitachi PT 20	*Hikari No 2**	34 knots	123	March 1975
HYD Hitachi Zosen PT 50	*Condor*	34 knots	121	June 1972
HYD Hitachi Zosen PT 50	*Ohtori No 5*	34 knots	113	May 1973
HYD Hitachi Zosen PT 50	*Condor No 2*	34 knots	121	April 1974
HYD Hitachi Zosen PT 50	*Condor No 3*	34 knots	121	August 1974
MH	*Marine Star 2*	24 knots	103	October 1970
MH	*Marine Star 3*	24 knots	120	January 1983
CAT Mitsui CP10 Supermaran	*Marine Queen*	—	88	April 1987

*spare craft

Routes operated
Ujina to Imabari and Hiroshima to Matsuyama *(Ohtori, Hikari No 2)*
Tomo to Onomichi to Imabari *(Ohtori No 2, Ohtori No 3)*
Miyajima to Hiroshima to Omishima Island (Port of Miyaura) to Setoda *(Ohtori No 5)*
Hiroshima to Matsuyama *(Condor, Condor No 2, Condor No 3)*
Mihara to Matsuyama *(Hibiki No 3)*
Mihara to Imabari *(Marine Star 2, Marine Star 3)*

PT 50 *Ohtori* operated by Setonaikai Kisen Co Ltd

Shikoku Ferry Company (Bridge Line)

Japan

High-speed craft operated

Type	Delivered
CAT Sanuki Shipbuilding and Iron Works 30m	1987

Shimabara Kanko Kisen

Japan

High-speed craft operated

Type	Name	Speed	Seats	Delivered
MH Shinju Zosen Kohgyo Co Ltd	*Hamayuu*	23 knots	86	January 1974
MH Toei	*Garuda No 3*	22 knots	83	September 1978

Route operated
Shimabara to Ohmuta

Shodoshima Kohsoku
Japan

High-speed craft operated

Type	Name	Speed	Seats	Delivered
MH Miho Zosenjyo	*Hikari*	25 knots	90	December 1974

Route operated
Takamatsu to Tonosho

Showa Kaiun Co Ltd
1-2 Katahora, Imabari 794, Ehime Prefecture, Japan

High-speed craft operated

Type	Name	Speed	Seats	Delivered
HYD Hitachi Zosen PT 20	*Hayate No 1*	33·5 knots	67	April 1962
CAT Mitsui Super Westamaran CP20	*Blue Hawk*	25 knots	162	

Routes operated
Matsuyama to Mihara (*Hayate No 1*)
Mihari to Imabari (*Blue Hawk*)

Taiyo Tokyo Shipping Co
Japan

High-speed craft operated

Type
SES Hovermarine HM 218

Tokai Kisen
1-9-15 Kaigan, Minato-ku, Tokyo 105, Japan

Telephone: 03-432-4551

High-speed craft operated

Type	Name	Speed	Seats	Launched
SWATH Mitsui	*Seagull* (ex *Mesa-80*)	25 knots	402	July 1979
MH Mitsubishi Heavy Industries Ltd	*Seahawk 2*	26·5 knots	401	February 1980

Routes operated
Seagull
Atami to Ohshima
Tokyo to Ohshima*
Tokyo to Niijima*
Ohshima to Tokyo
Seahawk 2
Inatori to Ohshima
Ito to Ohshima
Atami to Ohshima*
*summer services only

Tokushima Kosokusen Co Ltd (Tokushima High-speed Boat Co, Tokushima Shuttle Line Co)
3-11-8 Chikkoh, Minato, Osaka 552, Japan

Hiromu Harada, *President*

High-speed craft operated

Type	Name	Speed	Seats	Launched
CAT Mitsui Westamaran CP20HF	*Sun Shine**	30 knots	195	March 1979
CAT Mitsui Westamaran CP20HF	*Blue Sky**	30 knots	195	June 1979
CAT Mitsui Supermaran CP30 Mk II	*Marine Shuttle*	32 knots	280	February 1986
CAT Mitsui Supermaran CP30 Mk III	*Blue Star†*	32 knots	280	21 June 1987 (in service)
CAT Mitsui Supermaran CP30 Mk III	*Sun Rise†*	35·25 (max trial)	280	20 July 1987 (in service)

* replaced by the CP30 Mk IIIs

Routes operated
† Osaka to Tokushima, Shikoku Island
Wakayama to Tokushima, Shikoku Island

Mitsui Supermaran CP30 Mk III *Sun Rise*

Tokushin
Japan

High-speed craft operated

Type	Name	Speed	Seats	Delivered
MH Toei	*Cobalt No 1*	23 knots	95	January 1977
MH Toei	*Cobalt No 2*	23 knots	95	March 1977

Route operated
Hirato to Kashimae

Ueda Kaiun KK
Japan

Charterer of Mitsui Supermaran CP10 from KK Seto Naikai Cruising formed in 1987 as a joint venture of MES, the Chutetso Group and the Ueda Group.

High-speed craft operated

Type	Name	Seats	Delivered
CAT Mitsui CP10	*Marine Queen*	88	April 1987

Operation
Cruising on the Seto Inland Sea

Wakasawan Kanko
Japan

High-speed craft operated

Type	Name	Speed	Seats	Delivered
MH Obama Zosen	*Wakasa*	22 knots	180	April 1973

Route operated
Obama to Sodohmon

Yaeyama Kanko Ferry Co
1-3 Misaki-cho, Isigaki-shi, Okinawa, Japan

Telephone: 098082 5010
Telex: 792 681

High-speed craft operated

Type	Name	Speed	Seats	Delivered
MH Miho Zosenjyo Co Ltd	*Hayabusa*	27 knots	88	December 1974
MH Shinju Shipyard Co Ltd 27·3m	*Hirugi**	23·5 knots	80	July 1977
MH Shinju Shipyard Co Ltd 27·3m	*Tropical Queen*	30 knots	150	July 1982
MH Suzuki Zosen Co Ltd	*Hirugi 2*	28 knots	96	February 1986

*Laid up February 1986

Route operated
Ishigaki to surrounding islands

Model of *Tropical Queen* designed by Yamaha Motor Co

Yahatahama Unyu

Japan

High-speed craft operated

Type	Name	Speed	Seats	Delivered
MH Kiso Zosen Co Ltd	*Misaki*	23 knots	80	May 1977

Route operated
Yahatahama to Misaki

Yasuda Sangyo Kisen

Japan

High-speed craft operated

Type	Name	Speed	Seats	Delivered
MH Higashi Kyushu	*Ohmura*	23 knots	58	April 1976
MH (?)	*Ryuyo*	23 knots	55	August 1976
MH Shinju	*Ohmura 3*	23 knots	71	September 1976
MH Shinju	*Ohmura 5*	23 knots	71	December 1976
MH Shinju	*Ohmura 7*	23 knots	71	November 1977
MH Shinju	*Mishima*	23 knots	95	December 1979
MH Nankai	*Genkai 3*	23 knots	100	March 1982
MH Nankai	*Genkai 5*	25 knots	104	May 1983

Routes operated
Tokitsu to Nagasaki Airport
Tokitsu to Ohmura Speedboat Racing Stadium
Tokitsu to Ohmura

Yushima Shosen

Japan

High-speed craft operated

Type	Name	Speed	Seats	Delivered
MH Shinju Shipyard Co Ltd	*Kikumori-Maru*	22 knots	71	April 1979

Route operated
Yushima to Nishiariya

JORDAN

Port of Aquaba Authority

Aquaba, Jordan

High-speed craft operated
Type
SES Hovermarine HM 218

KOREA, SOUTH

Dong-Bu Co Ltd

Chongro 2 GA 9, Changro Gu, Seoul 110, South Korea

Telephone: (02) 720 6811/9

and

Chung-peong Lee 205-3, Puck-san meun, Chun Sung Kun, Kang-Won Doo, South Korea

Telephone: (0361) 2-6488

High-speed craft operated

Type	Name	Seats
SES Korea Tacoma Marine Industries Ltd 12m	*Que-Ryoung*	56

Route operated
Soyang River (Yang gu)-In jae

Dong-Hae Kosokchun Co

South Korea

High-speed craft operated

Type	Name	Seats
CAT Mitsui CP20	*Dong-hae Kosok 1*	182

Route operated
Imwon to Chodong

Ge-Jae Gaebal

5 Ga 16, Jung-Ang Dong, Jung Gu, Pusan City 600, South Korea (terminal)

Telephone: 463 0354

K S Kim, *President*

High-speed craft operated

Type	Name	Seats
SES Korea Tacoma Marine Industries Ltd 18m	*Phinex*	60

Route operated
Pusan to Gejae Island

Government

High-speed craft operated

Type	Name	Delivered
HOV Korea Tacoma Industries Ltd Turt IV type, 12m	*Eagle II*	1984

Hanryeo Development Co Ltd

9F Suhrin Building, 88 Suhrin Dong, Chongro-Gu, Seoul, South Korea

Telephone: (734) 5638/9
Telex: 24856 HANRYEO K
Telefax: (739) 4349

High-speed craft operated

Type	Name	Delivered
HYD Rodriquez PT 20	*Angel I*	
HYD Hitachi PT 20	*Angel III*	
HYD Rodriquez RHS 110	*Angel VII*	
HYD Hyundae PT 20	*Angel IX*	January 1985

Route operated
Busan to Yeosu

Sea trial of Hyundae PT 20 *Angel IX*, January 1985

Jung Ahang Express Company

South Korea

High-speed craft operated

Type	Seats	Delivered
MH Miwon Trading and Shipping Co 28m	20	August 1986
MH Miwon Trading and Shipping Co 28m	128	September 1986

Operation
A six-craft fleet operates on the man-made Choong Joo Dam where it is engaged in sightseeing tours

Korea Tacoma Marine Industries Ltd

974-15 Yangduk-dong, Masan, South Korea

Telephone: (0551) 55-1181/6
Telex: 53662 KOTAMAN K
Telefax: (0551) 94-9449

Chong-Su Lee, *President*
Sung-Jin Lee, *Executive Managing Director*
Chae-Woo Lee, *Director*

High-speed craft operated

Type	Name
SES Korea Tacoma Marine Industries Ltd 18m	*Tacoma II*

Route operated
Masan to Gejae Island

Sae-Chang Haewoon

5 Ga 16, Jung-Ang Dong, Jung Gu, Pusan City 600, South Korea

Telephone: 44 5994

J S Park, *President*

High-speed craft operated

Type	Name
SES Korea Tacoma Marine Industries Ltd 18m	*Air Ferry*

Route operated
Pusan to Gejae Island

Shin Young Shipbuilding & Engineering Co

789 Woodoo-ri, Tolsan-up, Yeochun Kun, Junnam, South Korea

Telephone: (0662) 2-1251-6
Telefax: (0662) 63-1256

Jang-Yeon Shin, *President*

High-speed craft operated

Type	Name	Seats
SES Korea Tacoma Marine Industries Ltd 26m	*Tacoma III*	158

Route operated
Yeosu to Gemun Island

Wha-Sung Haewoon

5 Ga 16, Jung-Ang Dong, Jung Gu, Pusan City 600, South Korea (terminal)

Telephone: 44 2063

W K Shin

High-speed craft operated

Type	Name	Seats
SES Korea Tacoma Marine Industries Ltd 18m	*Golden Star*	60

Route operated
Pusan to Gejae Island

Korea Tacoma 18m SES *Golden Star* entering Pusan Harbour

Young-Kwang Development Co Ltd

5 Ga 15, Jung-Ang Dong, Jung Gu, Pusan City 600, South Korea (terminal)

Telephone: Pusan 463-2255/7, Okpo 4-3560, Changsungpo 4-3561/2

K Y Sohn, *President*

High-speed craft operated

Type	Name	Seats
SES Korea Tacoma Marine Industries Ltd 23m	*Young-Kwang I*	158
SES Korea Tacoma Marine Industries Ltd 23m	*Young-Kwang II**	158

*modified 28m SES

Route operated
Pusan to Gejae Island (Okpo, Changsungpo and Dumo)

KUWAIT

Kuwait Public Transport Co

(ex Touristic Enterprises Company (KSC)
PO Box 23310 Safat, Kuwait)

Telephone: 412060
Telex: 22801 TENCO KT

High-speed craft operated

Type	Name	Seats	Delivered
SES Vosper Hovermarine HM 218	*Auhah*	82	February 1983
SES Vosper Hovermarine HM 218	*Umn Al Maradam*	82	1983
SES Vosper Hovermarine HM 218	*J/Kubbar*	82	1984

Route operated
Ras Al Ardh Terminal, Kuwait City to Failakai Island (10n miles, 25 min)

MADEIRA

See Portugal

MALAYSIA

Asie Crewboat Sdn Bhd

10th Floor Menara Apera ULG, 84 Jalan Raja Chulan, 50200 Kuala Lumpur, West Malaysia

Telephone: (03) 2610831/2610935
Telex: 30531 AMSB MA

Khalil Akasah, *Chairman*
Kamaruzaman Akasah, *Executive Director*
A Y Marshall, *Marketing Director*
Capt Mohd Nasir Ahmad, *Operations Manager*

High-speed craft operated

Type	Name	Seats	Delivered
MH Halter Marine Sea Shuttle 34·1m	*Asie I*	60 (+80 tons cargo)	1982
MH Halter Marine Sea Shuttle 34·1m	*Asie II*	60 (+80 tons cargo)	1982/83
CAT Fjellstrand 31·5m	*Asie III*	96 (+40 tons cargo)	March 1984
MH Halter Marine Sea Shuttle 31·0m	*Asie IV*	52 (+30 tons cargo)	February 1985
MH Halter Marine Sea Shuttle 31·0m	*Asie V*	52 (+30 tons cargo)	March 1985
MH Halter Marine Sea Shuttle 31·0m	*Asie VI*	52 (+30 tons cargo)	July 1985
MH Halter Marine Sea Shuttle 31·0m	*Asie VII*	52 (+30 tons cargo)	February 1985

Operation
For Esso Production Malaysia Inc (EMPI), Sarawak Shell Bhd, Union Oil of Thailand and others
Offshore support, Malaysia and Singapore, transport of cargo and passengers inter-fields offshore of Trengganu. Area of operation to include offshore Southern Thailand, Sabah & Sarawak waters

Associated Marine Sdn Bhd

Kuching, Sarawak, Malaysia

High-speed craft operated

Type	Yard No	Name	Seats	Originally delivered
SES Hovermarine HM 216 (HM2 Mk III)	326	(ex *HYF 101*)	60	1974

(laid up in Kuching, November 1986)

Black Gold (M) Sdn Bhd

151A Jalan Aminuddin Baki, Taman Tun Dr Ismail, Kuala Lumpur, Malaysia

High-speed craft operated

Type	Name	Delivered
CAT Fairey Marinteknik Shipbuilders (S) CCB 34m	*Amal*	1986
CAT Fairey Marinteknik Shipbuilders (S) CCB 34m	*Zakat*	1986

Hover Travel Sdn Bhd

1st Floor, 60 Market Place, Sibu, Sarawak, Malaysia

High-speed craft operated

Type	Name	Delivered
HOV Slingsby SAH 2200	*Challenger No 1*	1987

Kedah & Perlis Ferry Service Sdn Bhd

81 Dindong Kuah, Langkawi, Kedah, Malaysia

Telephone: (4) 749291

High-speed craft operated

Type	Name	Entered service
SES Vosper Hovermarine HM 218	*Kijang Mas*	February 1984

Route operated
Kuala Perlis to Langkawi Island (45 min)

Vosper Hovermarine HM 218 *Kijang Mas* operated by Kedah & Perlis Ferry Service Sdn Bhd

Malaysian Government

High-speed craft operated

Type	Name	Seats	Delivered
CAT Hong Leong-Lürssen Shipyard Bhd	*Zaharah*	131	September 1984

Malaysian International Shipping Corporation Bhd (MISC)/Amsbach Marine

2nd Floor, Wisma MISC, No 2 Jalan Conlay, 50450 Kuala Lumpur 04-09, Malaysia

Telephone: (03) 2428088
Telex: 30325 NALINE MA, 30428 MA, 31057 MA, 31058 MA

Arriffin Alias, *Managing Director*

High-speed craft operated

Type	Yard No	Name	Seats	Delivered
CAT Fairey Marinteknik Singapore, 34m crew boat	103/61*	*Layar Sentosa*	70 (+ 12 tons cargo)	June 1987
CAT Fairey Marinteknik Singapore, 34m crew boat	105	*Layar Sinar*	70 (+ 12 tons cargo)	June 1987

*hull built in Sweden

Operation
On time charter to a multinational oil company in coastal waters off Malaysia

Fairey Marinteknik Singapore crew boat *Layar Sentosa*

Pomas Sdn Bhd

Hovermarine Wharf, Bintawa, Kuching, Sarawak, Malaysia

High-speed craft operated

Type	Name	Seats	Entered service
SES Hovermarine HM 218	*Pomas No 1*	95	April 1986

Route operated
Kuching to Sarikei to Sibu (daily) (90n miles)

Rawa Safaris

Mersing Tourist Centre, Jalang Ismail, Mersing Jahore, Malaysia

Tengku Alang

High-speed craft operated

Type	Name	In service
HYD Vosper Singapore PT 20B Mk II	*Rawa Bird*	1987

Operation
Mersing, Pulau Rawa and Pulau Tioman (not in monsoon season)

MEXICO

Cruceros Maritimos del Caribe SA de CV

Calle 6 Nte No 14, Cozumel, Mexico

Telephone: (987) 21508/88

Venado 30, m18, SM 20, Cancún, Mexico

Telephone: 4 42 11/22 44

Jose Trinidad Molina Caceres, *Chairman of the Board*
Rogelio Molina Caceres, *General Manager*
Javier Guillermo Clausell, *Manager*

High-speed craft operated

Type	Name	Seats	Delivered
CAT Fjellstrand 38·8m	*Mexico*	390	February 1986

Operation
Mexican Caribbean area tourist service
Cancún to Cozumel, 43 miles, fare approx US$15·0, August 1987
Cozumel to Playa del Carmen, 9 miles, fare approx US$3·0, August 1987

Fjellstrand 38·8m *Mexico*

Secretaria de Turismo

Avenida Presidente Masarik 172, Mexico 5, DF, Mexico

Telephone: 250 8555

The Rodriquez hydrofoils, RHS 150 *Xel-Há* and RHS 160 *Nicte-Há*, operated by the Secretaria de Turismo, were laid up in 1986 in Veracruz.

MOROCCO

Cie Maritime des Hydrofoils Transtour (Transtour SA)

4 rue Jabha al Ouatania, Tangiers, Morocco

Telephone: 34004/5
Telex: 33608 M

High-speed craft operated

Type	Name	Seats	Delivered
HYD Sormovo Kometa	*Sindibad**	108	1968
HYD S Ordzhonikidze Kometa	*Aladin*	104	1971
HYD Feodosiya Kometa	*Scheherazade** (ex *Kometa 37*)	104	1973
HYD Rodriquez PT 50	*Queenfoil* (ex *Sleipner*)	125	1979

* Classification by Germanischer Lloyd + 100 A2 KLK + MC

Routes operated
Tangier to Tarifa, Spain
Tangier to Gibraltar

Kometa *Sindibad* operated by Transtour SA

NETHERLANDS

BV Rederij G Doeksen en Zonen

Terschelling, Netherlands

Telephone: (5620) 6111

Jan Doeksen, *Managing Director*
G Rombout, *Managing Director*

High-speed craft operated

Type	Name	Seats	Delivered
CAT Westamarin W86	*Koegelwieck*	176	1973

Route operated
Harlingen to West Terschelling (45 min)

Rotterdam Port Authority (Havenvan Rotterdam)

Galvanistraat 15, 3002 AP Rotterdam, Netherlands

Telephone: (010) 489 6911
Telex: 23077 ALGEMEEN

High-speed craft operated

Type	Name	Delivered
SES Vosper Hovermarine HM 2	*Havendienst 8*	1979
For disposal		
SES Vosper Hovermarine HM 2	*Havendienst 7*	1979
SES Vosper Hovermarine HM 2	*Havendienst 10*	1979
SES Vosper Hovermarine HM 2	*Havendienst 9*	1980

Operation
Port patrol duties in Rotterdam harbour area
Number in service not known

NEW ZEALAND

Fiordland Travel Ltd NZ

Milford and Doubtful Sounds, South Island, New Zealand

High-speed craft operated

Type	Name	Seats	Delivered
CAT Wanganui Boats (NZ) InCat 19·2m	*Fiordland Flyer*	140	September 1985

Fullers Captain Cook Cruises Ltd

Division of Fullers Corporation Ltd
PO Box 145, Maritime Building, Paihia, Bay of Islands, New Zealand

Telephone: 27421
Telex: 2613 NZ
Telefax: 27831

PO Box 448, Auckland, New Zealand

Telephone: 394901
Telefax: 370636

Harry L Julian, *Chairman*
Peter B Smith, *Joint Managing Director, Bay of Islands*
Lance Julian, *Joint Managing Director, Auckland*
Karl Andersen, *Director*

Paul van Dorsten, *Director*
Frederick Mills, *Director*
Barry Fenton, *Director*
John Kane, *General Manager, Group Marketing*
Niall Allock, *Company Secretary*

Well-established interests in the marine transport field were merged in 1986 to form the Fullers Captain Cook Group. Fullers vessels have plied the Bay of Islands water since 1886. A wide range of vessels and vehicles are involved in the company's operations including an 18-metre, 40-passenger underwater viewing craft. Their first high-speed vessels were acquired in 1986 and 1987.

High-speed craft operated

Type	Name	Seats	Delivered
CAT NQEA InCat 24·0m	*Supercat II*	250	October 1986
CAT NQEA InCat 30·0m	*Supercat III*	450	August 1987

Operation
Bay of Islands, Auckland Harbour, Kawau Harbour

Golden Sands Charter Cruises

Auckland, New Zealand

This organisation purchased the Auckland Airport SR.N6 rescue hovercraft in February 1986 for $NZ157 000. In February 1987 it was reported to be operating in the Hauraki Gulf area, North Island.

Gulf Ferries Ltd (Waiheke Shipping Co Ltd)

Endeans Building, PO Box 1346, Auckland, New Zealand

Douglas Hudson, *General Manager*

High-speed craft operated

Type	Name	Seats	Entered service
CAT SBF Engineering 33·37m	*Quickcat*	500 +	March 1987

Routes operated
Auckland to Waiheke Island, 30 min, Waiheke to Pakatoa Island, 1 hour

Hovercraft Adventures

PO Box 656, Queenstown, New Zealand

Telephone: 28034

Ewen J Mc Cammon, *Owner*

High-speed craft operated

Type	Delivered
HOV Hovercraft Manufacturers (NZ) Riverland Surveyor 8	1984

Operation
Half-hour tourist trips over mud flats, sand banks and river rapids in Queenstown area

Riverland Surveyor 8   *(E J Mc Cammon)*

The Mount Cook Group

Private Bag, Christchurch, New Zealand

High-speed craft operated

Type	Name	Delivered
CAT International Catamarans (Pacific) Ltd 18m	*Tiger Lily*	December 1979
CAT International Catamarans (Pacific) Ltd 19m	*Tiger Lily II*	January 1981
CAT Wanganui Boats New Zealand Ltd InCat 23·2m	*Tiger Lily III*	December 1985

Operation
Bay of Islands

Ossie James

Hamilton, New Zealand

The Rodriquez Supramar PT 20 hydrofoil *Manu-Wai*, originally delivered to Kerridge Odeon, New Zealand in 1964 as a 72-seat ferry and inactive since 1975, has been bought by Ossie James for conversion to a luxury hydrofoil yacht. For eight years from 1966 the craft was in service with North Shore Ferries in the run to Waiheke Island. The conversion includes fitting out to sleep six people, a shower, galley and couch seating. Normal passenger load will be 12 to 15 but the craft will be able to take up to 25. Executive charter work is anticipated for this craft following completion of work on the craft at Auckland.

Trout Line

The Jascar Group (NZ) Ltd
Lake Taupo, New Zealand

High-speed craft operated

Type	Name	Seats	Delivered
CAT NQEA InCat 24·0m	*Taupo Cat*	205	March 1987

Operation
Lake Taupo

Wanaka Lake Services Ltd

PO Box 20, Wanaka, New Zealand

Telephone: (02943) 7495
Telex: 5317

Bruce Miller, *Director*

High-speed craft operated
HOV Riverland Surveyor 8—originally operated by Airborne Hovercraft Services

Operation
Half-hour tourist trips over farm land and in river and lake areas of Lake Wanaka, Ram Island, Matukituki River and Glendhu Bay

NIGERIA

Federal Ministry of Transport (Ind)

19th floor, Western House, Broad Street, Lagos, Nigeria

High-speed craft laid up

Type	Name	Delivered
SES Vosper Hovermarine HM 218	*Innovator I*	1977
SES Vosper Hovermarine HM 218	*Innovator II*	1977
SES Vosper Hovermarine HM 218	*Innovator III*	1977

Police

High-speed craft operated

Type	Delivered
HOV Air Vehicles Ltd Tiger	1983

Operation
Lagos Harbour patrol duties

NORWAY

A/S Bergen Nordhordland Rutelag (BNR)

Olav Kyrresgt 7, PO Box 920, N-5001 Bergen, Norway

Telephone: (05) 318110
Telefax: (05) 317403

Thorolf Thunestvedt, *Commercial Director*

High-speed craft operated

Type	Name	Seats	Delivered
CAT Fjellstrand Aluminium Yachts Alumaran 165	*Manger*	189	1979
CAT Fjellstrand 31·5m	*Lygra*	292	1981

Route operated
Bergen to Frekhaug to Narvik to Frekhaug to Bergen. Round trip 1 hour 40 min to 1 hour 45 min

An early Fjellstrand catamaran *Manger* operated by Bergen Nordhordland Rutelag

Elkem-Spigerverket A/S

Lillebukt Stjernøy, N-9543 Stjernsund, Norway

Mr Martinsen, *Director*

High-speed craft operated

Type	Name	Seats	Delivered
MH Fjellstrand 26m	*Nefelin IV*	84 (+ 32m³ cargo)	1980

Fjellstrand *Nefelin IV* operated by Elkem-Spigerverket

Finnmark Fylkesrederi og Ruteselskap

Havnegt 3, N-9600 Hammerfest, Norway

Telephone: (084) 11655
Telex: 64257 N
Telefax: (084) 12773

Jan P Petersen, *Managing Director*

High-speed craft operated

Type	Name	Seats	Delivered
CAT Westamaran W86	*Brynilen* (Yard No 44)	94	June 1975
CAT Westamaran W86	*Hornøy* (Yard No 66)	136	October 1979
MH Brødrene Aa Båtbyggeri	*Tanahorn* (Yard No 182)	49	1986
CAT Brødrene Aa Båtbyggeri	*Ingøy* (Yard No 183)*	48 + cargo (incl 4 cars)	July 1987

Routes operated
Masøy to Hammerfest to Soroysundbass
*Masøy to Havøysund to Hammerfest

Cars being carried on *Ingøy*, owned by Finnmark Fylkesrederi og Ruteselskap on the most northerly high-speed ferry operation in the world

The passenger/car ferry *Ingøy* at speed

Fosen Trafikklag A/S

Fosenkaia, PO Box 512, N-2001 Trondheim, Norway

Telephone: (07) 525540

High-speed craft operated

Type	Name	Delivered
CAT Westamarin W86	*Kongsbussen* (Yard No 27)	April 1973
CAT Westamarin W86	*Hertugbussen* (Yard No 28)	May 1973
CAT Westamarin W86	*Olavbussen* (Yard No 34)	February 1974
CAT Fjellstrand Aluminium Yachts		
Alumaran 165	*Biskopsbussen**	March 1980

Routes operated
Trondheim to Brekstad to Storfosna to Hestvika to Fjellvoer to Fillan to Ansnes to Knarrlagsund to Sistranda to Mausundvoer to Vadsoysund to Bogoyvoer to Sula
*Trondheim to Vanvikan (25 min)

Fylkesbaatane i Sogn og Fjordane

Postbox 354, 6901 Florø, Norway
Strandavegen 354, 6900 Florø, Norway

Telephone: (057) 43 200
Telex: 42674
Telefax: (057) 43 760

Arne Dvergsdal, *Director*

High-speed craft operated

Type	Name	Seats	Delivered
CAT Westamarin W86	*Fjordglytt** (Yard No 21)	140	May 1971
CAT Westamarin W86	*Fjordtroll†* (Yard No 24)	140	May 1972
MH Westamarin S75	*Solundir*	80	1972
MH Brødrene Aa Båtbyggeri A/S	*Hyen*	156	1980
CAT Fjellstrand 38·8m	*Fjordprins*	201	October 1987
CAT Fjellstrand 38·8m	*Sognekongen*	201	December 1987

Routes operated
*Bergen to Årdalstangen
†Bergen to Måløy

Gods-Trans A/S

Hønefoss, Norway

High-speed craft operated

Type	Name	Cargo	Delivered
CAT Fjellstrand 38·8m	*Anne Line*	480m³ cooled volume	July 1986
CAT Westamarin W5000 49·5m	*Anne Lise*	950m³ cooled + refrigerated volume (270 tonnes)	August 1987

Operation
In 1986 *Anne Line* operated weekly trips linking Norway, England and the Netherlands, shipping salmon for eventual dispatch from London Airport to the USA. Return journeys were used to ship fruit and flowers to Norway. *Anne Lise* is involved in cod transport, Iceland to Holland, fruit and vegetable transport and can carry a payload of 300 tonnes at 26 knots service speed

Hardanger Sunnhordlandske Steamship Company (HSD)

PO Box 2005, N-5024 Nordnes, Bergen, Norway

Telephone: (05) 325070
Telex: 42607 HSD N
Telefax: (05) 324555

Johan Waage, *Managing Director*
Birger Skår, *Director, Shipowning Division*
See also Sameiet Flaggruten

High-speed craft operated

Type	Name	Seats	Originally delivered
HYD Rodriquez PT 50	*Teisten* (Yard No 123) laid up	128	April 1970
CAT Westamarin W86	*Tedno** (Yard No 29)	140	June 1973
CAT Westamarin W86	*Tjelden†* (Yard No 35) (ex *Haugesund*)	94 + cargo	November 1973
CAT Westamarin W95	*Sunnhordland‡* (Yard No 38)	180	April 1975
CAT Westamarin W86	*Øygar*	140	September 1975
CAT Westamarin W88	*Midthordland* (Yard No 82)	170	November 1981
MH Westamarin S80	*Vøringen* (Yard No 87)	103	March 1983

Routes operated
*Bergen to Tittelsnes
†to Haugesund
‡Bergen to Ølen

The Westamarin 103-seat S80 mono-hull ferry *Vøringen* owned by Hardanger Sunnhordlandske Steamship Company

The HSD Westamarin W88 *Midthordland*

Helgeland Trafikkselskap A/S

Helgelandsg 1, N-8800 Sandnessjøen, Norway

Telephone: (086) 40066

High-speed craft operated

Type	Name	Seats	Delivered
CAT Fjellstrand 31·5m	*Helgeland*	160 +8 tonnes cargo	1983
CAT Fjellstrand Aluminium Yachts Alumaran 165	*Traena*	119 passengers + cargo	1976
MH Fjellstrand Aluminium Yachts Alumaran 26m	*Rasa*		

Route operated
Sandnessjøen to Helgeland

Helgeland

Hovertransport A/S
PO Box 6, 1335 Snaroya, Norway

Jan Bjølgerud, *Administrative Director*

It was announced on 3 March 1987 that this company had leased a BHC AP1-88 hovercraft for 12 months from 1 March 1987 to operate in Oslo Fjord, linking Oslo, its satellite towns and Oslo's Fornebu Airport. The service was discontinued in November 1987 and the craft returned to British Hovercraft Corporation.

High-speed craft operated, 1987
Type	Name	Seats	In service
HOV AP1-88	(ex *Expo Spirit*)	82	22 April 1987 to November 1987

Route operated
Horten (base)-Tofte-Drøbak-Fornebu-Oslo
Reference: Hovertransport introduces Norwegian AP1-88 service. High-speed Surface Craft, Sept-Oct 1987.

JKL-Shipping A/S
PO Box 134, 1362 Billingstad, Norway
JKL Building, Stasjonsveien 18, Billingstad, Norway

Telephone: (02) 848590
Telex: 76113 JKL N
Telefax: (02) 848383

Jann K Lindberg, *Managing Director*

Please see entry under Denmark for details of proposed Copenhagen to Gothenburg SES operation.

Møre og Romsdal Fylkesbåtar
Fylkeshuset, N-6400 Molde, Norway

Telephone: (072) 52411
Telex: 40287 N

Johan Engja, *Commercial Director*
Havald Ekker, *Asst Director*
Olav Saumes, *Technical Manager*
Per Fjeld Gjetvik, *Maritime Manager*
Kåre Sandøy, *Nautical Personnel Manager*

High-speed craft operated
Type	Name	Seats	Delivered
CAT Fjellstrand 31·5m	*Hjørungavåg*	228	1983
CAT CIRR 265P Brødrene Aa Båtbyggeri	—	123	1987

Route operated
Ålesund to Hareid

Hjørungavåg

A/S Namsos Trafikkselskap
PO Box 128, D-S Kaia, N-7801 Namsos, Norway

Telephone: (77) 72433
Telex: 55492 NTS N
Telefax: (77) 72467

High-speed craft operated
Type	Name	Delivered
MH Westamarin S75	*Juvikingen*	June 1973

Route operated
Namsos to Kolvereid

A/S Ofotens Dampskibsselskap
PO Box 57, 8501 Narvik, Norway

Telephone: (082) 44090
Telex: 640 40

Per Bjerke, *Managing Director*

High-speed craft operated
Type	Name	Seats	Delivered
CAT Westamarin W88 (Yard No 88)	*Skogøy*	132 + 10 tonnes cargo	May 1985
CAT Westamarin W3600SC (Yard No 94)	—	195 + 30m² cargo hold	May 1988

Route operated
Narvik to Svolvaer

Oygarden og Sotra Rutelag A/S
5353 Straume, Norway

Telephone: (05) 33 0310

Bjørn Ove Børnes, *Managing Director*

This operator sold its Westamarin W86 *Øygar* at the end of 1986 to Hardanger Sunnhordlandske Dampskibsselskap. See 1987 edition, p 346

Saltens Dampskibsselskab
PO Box 312, N-8001 Bodø, Norway

Telephone: (081) 21020

High-speed craft operated
Type	Name	Seats	Delivered
MH Fjellstrand 26m	*Rødøyløven*		1977
MH Fjellstrand 23m			1981
MH Fjellstrand 25·5m	*Oykongen*		1982
MH Fjellstrand 25·5m	*Oydronningen*		1982
CAT Brødrene Aa Båtbyggeri CIRR 27P	*Helgelandsekspressen*	184	June 1985

Route operated
Bodø to Skutvik via Hellnessund, Nordskott, Holkestad and Bogøy

Sameiet Flaggruten
Owned by:
Det Stavangerske Dampskibsselskab (45%) with Sandnes Dampskibs-Aktieselskab (30%) and Hardanger Sunnhordlandske Dampskibsselskab (25%)

High-speed craft operated
Type	Name	Seats	Delivered
CAT Westamarin W95	*Vingtor*		May 1974
CAT Westamarin W95	*Sleipner*		June 1974
CAT Westamarin W95	*Draupner*		April 1977
SES Karlskronavarvet Jet Rider 3400	—	244	1988
SES Karlskronavarvet Jet Rider 3400	—	244	1988

Route operated
Stavanger to Bergen

Simon Møkster
PO Box 108, Skogstøstraen 37, N-4001 Stavanger, Norway

High-speed craft operated
Type	Name	Built
MH Fjellstrand 26m	*Veslestril*	1981
HYD Rodriquez PT50	*Stilprins* (ex *Teisten*)	1970

The 25-knot Fjellstrand *Veslestril* owned by Simon Møkster

Det Stavangerske Dampskibsselskab

Børehaugen 1, N-4001 Stavanger, Norway

Telephone: (04) 520020
Telex: 33032 N

Ansgar Johannssen, *Technical Superintendent*

High-speed craft operated

Type	Name	Seats	Delivered
CAT Westamarin W86	*Sauda* (Yard No 25)	148	June 1972
CAT Westamarin W86	*Mayflower*	134	October 1972
CAT Westamarin W95	*Vingtor* (Yard No 36)*		May 1974
CAT Westamarin W95	*Sleipner* (Yard No 37)*		June 1974
CAT Westamarin W86	*Fjordbris* (Yard No 41) (ex *Storesund*)	165	September 1974
CAT Westamarin W86	*Fjorddrott* (Yard No 48)	167	June 1976
CAT Westamarin W95	*Draupner* (Yard No 51)*		April 1977
CAT Westamarin W88	*Haugesund* (Yard No 78)	180	March 1981
CAT Westamarin W88	*Fjordsol* (Yard No 91)	202	June 1986

Routes operated

Stavanger to Judaberg to Jelsa *(Mayflower)*
Stavanger to Judaberg to Helgoysund to Eik to Nedstrand to Vikedal to Sandeid *(Fjorddrott)*
Stavanger to Judaberg to Jelsa to Hebnes to Marvik to Sand to Sauda *(Fjordsol)*
Stavanger to Sør-Bokn to Børey to Tuftene *(Fjordbris)*
Stavanger to Føresvik to Kopervik to Haugesund *(Haugesund)*
* operate the Sameiet Flaggruten service

A/S Torghatten Trafikkselskap

PO Box 85, N-8900 Brønnøysund, Norway

Telephone: (086) 20311
Telex: 55089 N
Telefax: (086) 21719

High-speed craft operated

Type	Name	Seats	Delivered
MH Brødrene Aa Båtbyggeri 27m	*Torgtind*	—	1981
CAT Brødrene Aa Båtbyggeri 25m	*Heilhorn*	48 + cargo (incl 4 cars)	1987

Routes operated

Brønnøysund to Vega to Tjøtta
Bindalsfjorden

Troms Fylkes Dampskibsselskap

Kirkegt 1, N-9000 Tromsø, Norway

Telephone: (083) 86088
Telex: 64 457
Telefax: (083) 88710

William Petersen, *Managing Director*
Jan M Leinebø, *Financial Manager*
Edvard Molund, *Technical Manager*
Karstein Jensen, *Operating Manager*

High-speed craft operated

Type	Name	Seats	Delivered
CAT Westamarin W86	*Fjorddronningen*	174	January 1976
CAT Westamarin W86	*Fjordprinsessen*	163	March 1977
CAT Westamarin W95	*Tromsprinsen*	210	June 1981
MH Brødrene Aa Båtbyggeri	*Gapøy*	43	June 1980
MH Djupviks Varv	*Reinfjord*	49	June 1984
SES Brødrene Aa Båtbyggeri CIRR 105P	*Fjordkongen*	268	1987

Operations

Fjordkongen, reserve craft
Fjorddronningen, Fjordprinsessen and *Gapøy* operate Hardstad area, *Tromsprinsen*, Tromso-Harstad, and *Reinfjord*, Skjervøy area

PAKISTAN

Pakistan Water and Power Development Authority

WPDA Offices Complex, Husseinabad, Giddu Road, Hyderabad, Pakistan

High-speed craft operated

Type	Name	Seats	Delivered
HOV Griffon Hovercraft Ltd 1000 TD-008 (GH 9456)	—	—	1987

Operation

Soil sampling in tidal areas (the craft is fitted with a sampling hatch in its underside)

Griffon Hovercraft 1000 TD (008) supplied to Pakistan WPDA

PANAMA, REPUBLIC OF

Chiriqui Hovercraft

Apartado 2615, Balboa, Ancon, Republic of Panama

Telephone: 28-3235
Telex: 3334 SERMAPAC

T H Little, *Manager, Chiriqui Hovercraft (Panama)*
Francisco Migoni, *Sales & Marketing Director (Mexico)*
Danilo Lopez P, *Sales Director (Guatemala)*

High-speed craft operated

Type	Name	Seats	Delivered
HOV Griffon Hovercraft Ltd 1500 TD	*C H Carolyn*	16	30 December 1985, laid up for disposal 1987

Operation

A Griffon 1500 TD was operated in 1986 for the Panama Canal Commission on Gatun Lake and in Cristóbal and Balboa harbours. The main function was transportation of canal pilots across the isthmus, including pilots boarding ships underway and at anchor. Line handlers, boarding officers and admeasurers evaluated the efficiency of the high-speed 1500 TD for their special needs. The test programme has been completed and was under evaluation October 1986. The main route distance was 27n miles and journey times varied from 58 min in flat calm to 1 hour 5 min in a small chop.

PARAGUAY

Aliscafos Itaipu SA

Yegros 690, Asunción, Paraguay

Telephone: 95-112
Telex: 264 IE PY

High-speed craft operated

Type	Name	Seats	Entered service
HYD Ludwig Honald Mfg Co Albatross	*Flecha Guarani**	22	June 1985
HYD Ludwig Honald Mfg Co	*Flecha de Itaipu*	22	June 1985

*built 1964, overhauled and re-engined in Miami

Operation

Tourist use on Itaipu Lake on the border between Brazil and Paraguay
Puerto Hernandarias-Puerto Guarani

One of the boarding points for Aliscafos Albatross hydrofoils operating on Lake Itaipu in Paraguay   *(Darius Morgan)*

PERU

Ministry of Health

Peru

The two Mark 3 River Rover craft used by the Joint Services Expedition to Peru in 1982, and working with the Amazon Trust River Medical Service based at San Francisco near Ayacucho, have been moved to other locations in Peru. This move was dictated by increased terrorist activity in the area and the withdrawal of the British funded Amazon Trust and the closure of the service.

River Rover 305 started operations in May 1984 at Puerto Bermudez on the River Pichis. Medical service involving doctor, nurse, health promoter and occasionally a dentist is provided to remote Campa Indian communities in the three rivers feeding the River Pichis. The rivers have extensive shallow areas making conventional boat travel slow, difficult and hazardous.

River Rover 303 is based at Iscozacin on the River Palcazu (an adjacent valley to the Pichis) and is also taking medical aid to remote Amuesha Indian communities as well as mixed race settlers in the area. The area is one of fast flowing, shallow rivers with many rocky outcrops and shingle banks. Boat transport is at best difficult, and in the dry season impossible in some areas. The medical team are reaching areas hitherto only visited on foot through the jungle.

Both craft are totally run, maintained and managed by the Peruvian Ministry of Health in conjunction with a Special Integrated Development Project of the Central Jungle.

PHILIPPINES

Bataan Manilla Ferry Services
Sea Express Services

Hoverferry Terminal, CCP Complex Rozas Boulevard, Metro-Manila, Philippines

Telephone: 8323653
Telex: 66927 SEA PN

High-speed craft operated

Type	Name
SES Vosper Hovermarine HM 216	Sea Express 101*
SES Vosper Hovermarine HM 216	Sea Express 102*
SES Vosper Hovermarine HM 216	Sea Express 103*

Route operated
Manila to Corregidor to Mariveles
*only one believed to be operational

POLAND

Przedsiebiorstwo Usiug Turystycznych "Pomerania"

Szczecin, Poland

High-speed craft operated

Type	Name	Built
HYD S Ordzhonikidze Meteor	Adriana	1973

Zegluga Gdanska

Ul Wartka 4, Gdansk, Poland

Telephone: 31-19-75

High-speed craft operated

Type	Name	Built
HYD Sormovo Kometa	Poszum	1973
HYD Sormovo Kometa	Poweiw	1973
HYD Sormovo Kometa	Poswist	1975
HYD Sormovo Kometa	Poryw	1976
HYD Sormovo Kometa	Pogwizd	1977
HYD Sormovo Kometa	Polot	1977

Routes operated
Gdynia to Hel (25 min)
Gdansk to Hel (55 min)
Gdynia to Jastarnia (25 min)
Sopot to Hel (25 min)
Gydnia to Sopot (10 min)
Gydnia to Hel to Wladyslawowo

Zegluga Szczecinska

Ul Energetyka 55, 70-952 Szczecin, Poland

Telephone: 455 61, 470 51
Telex: 0422158 PL

High-speed craft operated

Type	Name	Built
HYD Sormovo Kometa	Wala	1966
HYD Sormovo Kometa	Lida	1971
HYD Sormovo Kometa	Kalina	1973
HYD Sormovo Kometa	Daria (ex Kometa 4)	1975
HYD Sormovo Kometa	Lena	1975
HYD Sormovo Meteor	Iwona	1976
HYD Sormovo Kometa	Liwia	1978

Route operated
Szczecin to Swinoujscie (1 hour 15 min)

PORTUGAL

Direccao Regieonal dos Portos da Madeira

Av Arriaga No 50, 9000 Funchal, Madeira, Portugal

Telephone: 21041/2
Telex: 72290 DIPMAD P

High-speed craft operated

Type	Name	Seats	Delivered
CAT Westamarin W100	Independencia (Yard No 76) (ex Gimle Bird)	250	September 1981

Route operated
Funchal to Porto Santo Island, 44n miles

PUERTO RICO

Antilles Shipping Co & SNAV

San Juan, Puerto Rico

Telephone: (809) 724 2971/776 7787

Capt Giovanni Schironni (SNAV)

High-speed craft operated

Type	In service
HYD Rodriquez RHS 200	1986
HYD Rodriquez RHS 160	1986

Route operated
Round trip: San Juan, Puerto Rico (Crown Bay) and Charlotte Amelia, St Thomas, US Virgin Islands. One trip per day, four days per week, started May 1986. The service is operated and managed by SNAV
Journey time: Approx 2 hours, US$65.0 return

ROMANIA

Intreprinderea de Exploatare a Floti Maritime (NAVROM)

Galatz, Romania

High-speed craft operated

Type	Name	Delivered
HYD S Ordzhonikidze Kometa	Poseidon	1970

SAUDI ARABIA

Saudi Arabian Coastal and Frontier Guard

Ministry of the Interior, Airport Road, Riyadh, Saudi Arabia

High-speed craft operated

Type	Delivered
HOV BHC SR.N6 Mk 1	
HOV BHC SR.N6 Mk 1	
HOV BHC SR.N6 Mk 1	
HOV BHC SR.N6 Mk 1	
HOV BHC SR.N6 Mk 1	
HOV BHC SR.N6 Mk 1	
HOV BHC SR.N6 Mk 1	
HOV BHC SR.N6 Mk 8	1981
HOV BHC SR.N6 Mk 8	
HOV BHC SR.N6 Mk 8	
HOV BHC SR.N6 Mk 8	
HOV BHC SR.N6 Mk 8	
HOV BHC SR.N6 Mk 8	
HOV BHC SR.N6 Mk 8	1982
HOV BHC SR.N6 Mk 8	

Operation
Craft are based at Jeddah and Aziziyah for patrol, contraband control, search and rescue and liaison duties.

SINGAPORE

Dino Shipping Pte Ltd & Garuda Jaya Trading Co

Blk 334 Kreta Ayer Road No 02-08, Singapore 0208

Telephone: 2200555/27849
Telex: 33988 JAYACO RS
Telefax: 2250525

High-speed craft operated

Type	Name	Seats	Built
MH SBF Engineering	*Sea Flyte*	240	1980
MH Mitsui	*Bintan I*	80	—
MH Mitsui	*Bintan II*	80	—
MH Wavemaster International	*Sea Raider II*	200	—

Routes operated
Singapore to Tanjang Pinang (Bintan, Indonesia)
Singapore to Sekopang (Batam, Indonesia)

Shell Eastern Petroleum (Pte) Ltd

PO Box 1908, Pulau Bukom, Singapore 9038

Telephone: 229 4150
Telex: 21251 RS

Capt M J Whichelow, *Marine Manager*

Operator: **Straits Shipping Pte Ltd**
15 Hoe Chiang Road, Singapore

Telephone: 225 0788

High-speed craft operated

Type	Name	Seats	Entered service
SES Vosper Hovermarine 218	*Bukom Deras*	90	1983
SES Vosper Hovermarine 218	*Bukom Pantas*	90	1983
SES Vosper Hovermarine 218	*Bukom Lekas*	90	1983
SES Vosper Hovermarine 218	*Bukom Maju*	90	1983
SES Vosper Hovermarine 218	*Bukom Jaya*	90	1983

Route operated
Pasir Panjang to Pulau Bukom refinery

Yang Passenger Ferry Service

407 Jalan Besar, Singapore 0820

Telex: 56408 YANGFE RS

Yong Kian Chin, *Director*

High-speed craft operated

Type	Yard No	Name	Seats	Delivered
SES Vosper Hovermarine HM 218	472	*Auto Batam I*	78	1982

(previously owned by Auto-Shipping, Singapore and Union Hydraulic Jack (Pte) Ltd)

Type	Name
MH	*Auto Batam 2* —

Route operated
Singapore to Batam Island (Indonesia)

Vosper Hovermarine HM 218 *Auto Batam I*

Auto Batam 2

SOLOMON ISLANDS

Fisheries Protection

High-speed craft operated

Type	Delivered
MH Agnew Clough (C Raymond Hunt) 25m P-150	1981

Solomon Islands Navigation Services

PO Box 59, Honiara, Solomon Islands

Roy Clements, *Proprietor*

High-speed craft operated

Type	Seats	In service
HOV Griffon 1500 TD*	17	1987

*Previously operated in Australia

SPAIN

Alisur SA (Alisur Caribe)

La Esperanza 1-1 Dcha, Arrecife de Lanzarote, Canary Islands, Spain

Telephone: 81 42 72, 81 49 01
Telex: 96327 ALSR E

Bruno Hitz, *President*
Gennaro Doria, *Director*

The Westamarin W95T *Alisur Azul* was sold in June 1986.

High-speed craft operated

Type	Name	Delivered
CAT Westamarin W95D	*Alisur Amarillo* (Yard No 79)	April 1981

Route operated
St Maarten to St Barths 30 min, to Anguilla 30 min, to Saba 60 min, to Statia 75 min, to St Kitts 90 min (Netherlands Antilles)

Alisur Amarillo operating in the Netherlands Antilles

Compañia Trasmediterranea SA

Plaza Manuel Gómez Moreno s/n, Edificio Bronce-Centro Azca, Apartado de Correos 982, 28020 Madrid, Spain

Telephone: 4550049, 4560009
Telex: 27666 TRASM E

High-speed craft operated

Type	Name
HYD Boeing Jetfoil 929-115	*Princesa Guayarmina*
HYD Boeing Jetfoil 929-115	*Princesa Guacimara*

Route operated

Las Palmas, Grand Canaria to Santa Cruz de Tenerife (1 hour 20 min)

Boeing Jetfoil 929-115, *Princesa Guayarmina*, operated by Compañia Trasmediterranea

SWEDEN

Gotlandslinjen (Nordström & Thulin)

Sweden

High-speed craft operated

Type	Name	Seats	Delivered
CAT Westamarin W3700S	—	300	May 1988

Route operated

Oskarshamn to Gottland

Rederi AB Marinteknik

City Jet Line
PO Box 537, S-18500 Vaxholm, Sweden

Telephone: (0764) 32804/30882, (08) 606102

Capt Bjørn Justine

High-speed craft operated

Type	Name	Seats	Delivered	In service
MH Marinteknik Verkstads 42m	*Cinderella*	450	15 May 1987	12 June 1987

Route operated

Stockholm to Möjaström (60n miles) and outer islands

Marinteknik *Cinderella* in operation, Stockholm 1987

TURKEY

Istanbul Great City Municipality

Istanbul, Turkey

Ten Fjellstrand 38·8m, 449-passenger catamarans have been ordered to provide a ferry service for commuters across the Strait of Bosphorus. Five will have a 24-knot cruise speed capability and five, 32 knots. Yard Nos: 1576, 1578, 1579, 1581-5, 1587, 1588.

High-speed craft operated

Type	Name	Seats	Delivered
CAT Fjellstrand 38·8m (MTU 16V 396 TB83)	*Umur Bey*	449	April 1987
CAT Fjellstrand 38·8m (MTU 16V 396 TB83)	*Sarica Bey*	449	August 1987
CAT Fjellstrand 38·8m (MTU 16V 396 TB83)	*Ulic Ali Reis*	449	January 1988
CAT Fjellstrand 38·8m (MTU 16V 396 TB83)	*Nusret*	449	March 1988
CAT Fjellstrand 38·8m (MTU 16V 396 TB83)	*Hezarifen Celebi*	449	September 1988
CAT Fjellstrand 38·8m (MTU 12V 396 TB63)	*Caka Bey*	449	February 1987
CAT Fjellstrand 38·8m (MTU 12V 396 TB63)	*Yeditepe*	449	May 1987
CAT Fjellstrand 38·8m (MTU 12V 396 TB63)	*Ulubatli Hasan*	449	September 1987
CAT Fjellstrand 38·8m (MTU 12V 396 TB63)	*Karamursel Bey*	449	March 1988
CAT Fjellstrand 38·8m (MTU 12V 396 TB63)	*Cavli Bey*	449	September 1988

UNION OF SOVIET SOCIALIST REPUBLICS

Azcherryba

Taganrog, USSR

High-speed craft operated

Type	GRT	Delivered
HYD S Ordzhonikidze Kometa-*M*	142	1977

Azov Shipping Co

89, Admirala Lunina Pr, Zhdanov 341010, USSR

Telex: 412601/2, 115156

High-speed craft operated

Type	GRT	Delivered
HYD Kometa *19*	136	1973
HYD Kometa *22*	136	1974

Black Sea Shipping Company

1 Lastochkina Str, 270026 Odessa, USSR

Telex: 232711, 412677

High-speed craft operated

Type	GRT	Delivered
HYD S Ordzhonikidze Kometa *13*	127	1968 (Odessa)
HYD S Ordzhonikidze Kometa *16*	142	1969 (Odessa)
HYD S Ordzhonikidze Kometa *27*	136	1975 (Yalta)
HYD S Ordzhonikidze Kometa *32*	142	1977 (Yalta)
HYD S Ordzhonikidze Kometa *37*	142	1978 (Odessa)
HYD S Ordzhonikidze Kometa *40*	142	1979 (Yalta)
HYD S Ordzhonikidze Kometa *41*	142	1979 (Yalta)
SES Sosnovka, 30 delivered Rassvet	(80 seat)	
HYD — Tsiklon	250	November 1987

Routes operated

Daily services, Odessa to Ochakov, Kherson and Nikolaev
Black Sea Kometas carry over 1·5 million passengers a year and are mostly based in the ports of Sochi, Tuapse, Novorossiysk, Yalta, Odessa and Izmail

Kolkhida craft at Odessa

A Kometa taking on passengers at Novorossiysk on the Black Sea coast

Caspian Shipping Co

Astrakhan, USSR

D Gashumov, *President*

High-speed craft operated

Type	GRT	Delivered
HYD Kometa *21*	136	1974
HYD Kometa *28*	136	1975

Murmansk Shipping Co

Murmansk, USSR

High-speed craft operated

Type	GRT	Delivered
HYD Kometa *30*	142	1976

Soviet Danube Shipping Co

2, Pr Suvorova, Izmail 272630, USSR

Telex: 412699, 232817

High-speed craft operated

Type	GRT	Delivered
HYD Kometa *34*	142	1977
HYD Kometa *35*	142	1978
HYD Kometa *36*	142	1978

Volga-Don Shipping

In 1987 it was reported that 33 high-speed diesel-powered vessels were in the fleet comprising 40% of the passenger vessels. Of 29 in the Rostov sector, 14 are to be replaced. There are seven Meteors, seven Raketas, four Voskhod and two Zarya vessels, serving 12 routes.

Other Kometas delivered in the USSR

High-speed craft operated

Type	GRT	Delivered
Kometa *10*	127	1967 (Sochi)
Kometa *12*	127	1967 (Sochi)
Kometa *17*	127	1970 (Yalta)
Kometa *23*	136	1974 (Yalta)
Kometa *24*	136	1975 (Sochi)
Kometa *33*	142	1978 (Sochi)
Kometa *38*	142	1978
Kometa *1*	142	1980
Kometa *43*	142	1980
Kometa *46*	142	1980
Kometa *47*	142	1980
Kometa *48*	142	1981
Kometa *49*	142	1981
Kometa *51*	142	1981
Kometa *21*	142	1982
Kometa *53*	142	1982
Kometa *54*	142	1982
Kometa *55*	142	1982
Kometa *57*	142	1983

UNITED ARAB EMIRATES

Zadco Productions

Abu Dhabi, United Arab Emirates

High-speed craft operated

Type	Name	Seats	Delivered
CAT Sing Koon Seng Pte InCat 30m	*Ipo Ipo 3001*	15 + 60 tonnes cargo	1984

UNITED KINGDOM

Condor Ltd

Commodore House, Bulwer Avenue, St Sampson's, PO Box 10, Guernsey, Channel Islands, United Kingdom

Telephone: (0481) 46841
Telex: 4191289 CMDR G
Telefax: (0481) 49543

David Norman, *Managing Director*
Lionel Frampton, *Marine Superintendent*

Condor Ltd started in 1964 with *Condor 1*, a PT 50 and now has three hydrofoils, *Condor 4*, *Condor 5* and *Condor 7*. In June 1988 Condor was due to receive the first Marinteknik Verkstads 41m catamaran to be on charter until November 1988 when Condor will have a purchase option. This vessel will carry 406 passengers at 36·5 knots. The traffic is seasonal and the vessels are laid up from November to March at Marine and General Engineers' Shipyard in Guernsey.

Condor is the largest passenger carrier between the Channel Islands and the adjacent coast of France (St Malo) and carries over 300 000 passengers per annum.

High-speed craft operated

Type	Name	Seats	Built
HYD Rodriquez RHS 140	*Condor 4*	136	1974
HYD Rodriquez RHS 160	*Condor 5*	180	1976
HYD Rodriquez RHS 160F	*Condor 7*	200	1985
CAT Fairey Marinteknik Singapore 35 CPF	—	320	June 1988

Routes operated
St Malo, France to all the Channel Islands and an inter-island service between all the Channel Islands, serving St Malo, Jersey, Guernsey, Sark, Herm and Alderney from March to November
Jersey to Sark (27n miles, 45 min)
Guernsey to St Malo (56n miles, 1 hour 45 min)
In 1987, following a trial service in 1986, Condor initiated a new route from Jersey and Guernsey to Weymouth (70n miles, 2 hours). This service operates from 25 March to 19 October employing *Condor 7* and *Condor 5* from the beginning of May. Fares: £52 return adult, children half
The new Fairey Marinteknik 320-seat catamaran will operate between Jersey and St Malo and between Jersey and Sark/Guernsey
Between June 1 and September 23 the direct Weymouth to Jersey vessel calls at Alderney in each direction on Wednesdays, Fridays and Sundays

The 200-seat Rodriquez RHS 160F *Condor 7*

Hoverspeed Limited

The International Hoverport, Dover, Kent CT17 9TG, England

Telephone: (0304) 24010
Telex: 965915 G
Telefax: (0304) 240099

N J Tatham, *Chairman*
R W Wilkins, *Managing Director*
R S Adams, *General Sales Manager*
K S Hilditch, *Personnel Manager*

Hoverspeed SR.N4 Mk II *The Prince of Wales* with crew

C W Hunt, *Technical Manager*
P C Walker, *Company Secretary*
D Wise, *Operations Manager*

Hoverspeed was formed as a result of a merger between the two cross-Channel operators, British Rail Hovercraft Limited (Seaspeed) and Hoverlloyd. Operations began in October 1981. British Rail, former owner of Seaspeed, and the Brostrom Group, former owner of Hoverlloyd, each had a 50 per cent shareholding in the company. In February 1984 British Railways Board and Brostrom (UK) Limited both disposed of the whole of their investment in the company to a syndicate of new owners including a number of directors and executives of Hoverspeed.

In June 1986, Hoverspeed was sold to British Ferries Ltd, who are part of the Sea Containers Group. Hoverspeed will therefore benefit from the financial stability of being part of a large organisation, the increased marketing and sales exposure, joint purchasing power and the savings on re-routings.

A year-round service is operated between Dover and Boulogne/Calais. The city-link coach and rail services between London and major European cities are retained.

British Rail Hovercraft Limited was formed in March 1966 and launched its first commercial service in July 1966, between Southampton and Cowes. The cross-Channel service for passengers and cars between hovercraft terminals at Dover and Boulogne began in August 1968 using an SR.N4 *The Princess Margaret*. A year later the service was augmented by the introduction of a sister craft, *The Princess Anne* and in October 1970 a service began between Dover and Calais.

During 1978 the first of the two stretched SR.N4 Mk III craft came into operation. *The Princess Anne*, formerly a Mk 1 craft, had a 16·7m (55ft) midships section inserted at the British Hovercraft Corporation's factory at Cowes, Isle of Wight. The largest hovercraft in the world, it is driven by four uprated Marine Proteus gas turbine engines of 3800shp, each driving a fan unit and a 6·4m (21ft) propeller. Craft motion is considerably less than that experienced on the standard N4 and operating limitations have been extended to cope with waves of up to 3·5m. The car deck cabins have been incorporated into large, outward facing passenger decks. These widened compartments have been improved with the introduction of new overhead ventilation, underseat heating, improved hand luggage storage and lighting. An improved skirt design with lower pressure ratio, deeper fingers and increased air cushion depth at the bow, has improved passenger comfort and reduced crossing times in adverse weather. Seaspeed's second N4, *The Princess Margaret*, rejoined the Seaspeed fleet in May 1979, after being stretched.

Hoverspeed has not operated commercially from Ramsgate since summer 1982, current routes are Dover to Calais and Boulogne. The administration was transferred to Dover in October 1985 and the engineering facility (mainly used for craft overhauls) was also planned to move to Dover by the end of 1987. When complete it will end Hoverspeed's association with the hoverport at Pegwell Bay, Ramsgate which was built in 1968/69 by Hoverlloyd.

In 1985 Hoverspeed carried 238 000 vehicles and 1645 000 passengers and in 1986 Hoverspeed carried 257 000 vehicles and 1575 000 passengers. A freight express service was introduced in 1985 and has achieved continuous growth since then.

Further details of operations and terminal facilities are given in *Jane's Surface Skimmers 1985* and earlier editions.

Routes operated
Dover to Calais (23n miles)
Dover to Boulogne (27n miles)

Hoverspeed SR.N4 Mk II *Swift*   *(Hoverspeed Ltd)*

High-speed craft operated

Type	Name	First entered service	Payload
HOV BHC SR.N4 Mk I modified to Mk III in 1979	*The Princess Margaret* (GH 2006)	1968 Seaspeed	424 passengers 55 cars
HOV BHC SR.N4 Mk I modified to Mk III in 1978	*The Princess Anne* (GH 2007)	1969 Seaspeed	424 passengers 55 cars
HOV BHC SR.N4 Mk I modified to Mk II in 1973	*Swift* (GH 2004)	1969 Hoverlloyd	278 passengers 34 cars
HOV BHC SR.N4 Mk I modified to Mk II in 1974	*Sure* (GH 2005)	1969 Hoverlloyd (laid up)	278 passengers 34 cars
HOV BHC SR.N4 Mk I modified to Mk II in 1974	*Sir Christopher* (GH 2008)	1972 Hoverlloyd	278 passengers 34 cars
HOV BHC SR.N4 Mk II	*The Prince of Wales* (GH 2054)	1977 Hoverlloyd	278 passengers 34 cars

Vehicle/freight deck of SR.N4 Mk II   *(Hoverspeed Ltd)*

Flight deck of SR.N4 Mk II   *(Hoverspeed Ltd)*

Hovertravel Limited

Head office: 12 Lind Street, Isle of Wight, Hampshire PO33 2NR, England

Telephone: (0983) 65181
Telex: 86513 HOVERWORK G

Terminal offices: Quay Road, Ryde, Isle of Wight (Tel: 0983 65241); Clarence Pier, Southsea (Tel: 29988)

C D J Bland, *Chairman and Managing Director*
E W H Gifford, *Director*
J Gaggero, *Director*
A C Smith, *Director*
R G Clarke, *Director and General Manager*
G M Palin, *Company Secretary*

Hovertravel Limited was formed in 1965 to operate two SR.N6 Winchester hovercraft across the Solent between Ryde, Isle of Wight and Southsea and Gosport. The Gosport route was discontinued after a brief period.

Journey time is about 9 minutes on the Ryde to Southsea route. Approximately 450 000 passengers are carried each year on the route together with many tons of mail and freight parcel packages. By September 1986 the cumulative total number of passengers carried exceeded 9 million.

High-speed craft operated

Type	Name	Seats	Delivered
HOV BHC AP1-88 GH 2087	*Tenacity*	80	1983
HOV BHC AP1-88 GH 2088	*Resolution†*	80	1983
HOV BHC AP1-88 GH 2100	*Perseverance*	80	June 1985

Route operated

Portsmouth (Southsea Promenade) to Ryde (3·85n miles)
†See Hoverwork Ltd entry

Hoverwork Limited

12 Lind Street, Ryde, Isle of Wight, Hampshire PO33 2NR, England

Telephone: (0983) 65181
Telex: 86513 HOVERWORK G

C D J Bland, *Managing Director*
E W H Gifford, *Director*
A C Smith, *Director*
R G Clarke, *Director*
G M Palin, *Secretary*

Hoverwork Limited, a wholly-owned subsidiary of Hovertravel Ltd, was formed in 1966. The company provides crew training and charter facilities for all available types of ACVs, thus bridging the gap between the operators and manufacturers.

High-speed craft operated

Type	Name	Seats	Acquired
HOV BHC SR.N6 Mk 1 GH 2010		38	1968
HOV BHC AP1-88 GH 2088	*Resolution**	80	1983

*Hovertravel Ltd gave Hoverwork Ltd access to this craft for chartering. During 1986 and into 1987 *Resolution* continued in service with Textron Marine Systems and used for training US Navy crews. Sold to US Navy 1987.

SR.N6 Mk 1 GH 2012 was sold in 1987 to North Coast Air Services Ltd, Prince Rupert, British Columbia, Canada where it operated a passenger/freight service to Indian community centres.

Operations

The company has trained over 50 hovercraft captains and has received some 40 charter contracts, including film sequences and the operation of the SR.N6 craft for mineral surveys throughout the world. The company operated the hovercraft passenger service during Expo' 67 at Montreal and a service at the 1970 and 1976 Algiers Expositions.

Hoverwork is the largest international operator of hovercraft, having access to Hovertravel's SR.N6s, and its AP1-88 80-seat passenger craft. Hoverwork has undertaken operations in areas from the Arctic to the equator, including logistics exercises in the northern part of Svalbard and in equatorial parts of South America. To date Hoverwork has operated in the following areas: Canada, South America, Mexico, Brunei, Netherlands, Bahrain, Kuwait, the United Arab Emirates, Saudi Arabia, Algeria, Tunisia, English North Sea, Spitzbergen, Australia, Iraq and Egypt.

One of the SR.N6s has been based in the Middle East for the past 5 years.

Hovertravel's AP1-88/80 at Ryde terminal, Isle of Wight, showing low-water conditions and the Ryde pier head, half a mile from shore, used by displacement ferries

AP1-88-002 *Resolution*, employed in Florida to train US Navy personnel to operate hovercraft

Red Funnel Ferries

12 Bugle Street, Southampton, Hampshire SO9 4LJ, England

Telephone: 0703 333042
Telex: 47388 CHAMCON G

T E Thornycroft, *Managing Director*
D E L Archdeacon, *Secretary and Financial Director*
M E R Collis, *Commercial Manager*
J Day, *Group Chief Accountant*
R A Marshall, *Technical Manager*
Capt H Middleton, *Ferry Operations Manager*

Passengers carried in 1984: 411 000; 1985: 436 200; 1986: 466 700

High-speed craft operated

Type	Name	Seats	Delivered
HYD Rodriquez RHS 70	Shearwater 3	67	1972
HYD Rodriquez RHS 70	Shearwater 4	67	1973
HYD Rodriquez RHS 70	Shearwater 5	67	1980
HYD Rodriquez RHS 70	Shearwater 6	67	1982

Route operated
Southampton to West Cowes, Isle of Wight (10·8n miles, 20 min)

The Red Funnel *Shearwater 5*

Sealink British Ferries

Sea Containers House, 20 Upper Ground, London SE1 9PF, England

Telephone: 01-928 6969

Isle of Wight Services
Portsmouth Harbour, Portsmouth, Hampshire PO1 3EU, England

Telephone: 0705 812011

W E D Gibbons, *General Manager*
Maelor Jones, *Ship Manager*

High-speed craft operated

Type	Name	Seats	Delivered
CAT International Catamarans Pty Ltd (Hobart) 30·0m	Our Lady Patricia	450	March 1986
CAT International Catamarans Pty Ltd (Hobart) 30·0m	Our Lady Pamela	450	August 1986

Route operated
Portsmouth Harbour (Station) to Ryde Pier, Isle of Wight (15 min)
Single adult fare: £2.60 (1987)

The Sealink International Catamarans *Our Lady Patricia* passing Ryde pier at 30 knots

Thames Line plc

West India Pier, Cuba Street, London E14 8LB, England

Telephone: 01-987 0311
Telefax: 01-987 0291

R G Crouch, *Managing Director*
R M Mabbott, *Deputy Managing Director*

High-speed craft operated

Type	Name	Seats	Delivered
CAT Aluminium Shipbuilders Ltd InCat 16·35m River 50	Daily Telegraph	51	1987
CAT Aluminium Shipbuilders Ltd 17·5m River 50	—	—	1988
CAT Aluminium Shipbuilders Ltd 17·5m River 50	—	—	1988
CAT Aluminium Shipbuilders Ltd 17·5m River 50	—	—	1988
CAT Aluminium Shipbuilders Ltd 17·5m River 50	—	—	1988

Route operated
Thames, Charing Cross Pier to West India Dock

The Thames Line InCat *Daily Telegraph*

Torbay Seaways

5 Beacon Quay, Torquay, Devon, England

Telephone: 0803 214397
Telex: 42500 G

J G Thompson, *Managing Director*

The RHS Rodriquez PT 50S 117-seat hydrofoil *Star Capricorn* held the record for the fastest crossing, Torquay to Guernsey, 2 hours 7 mins. Operations started in May 1985, closing down for the winters, the vessel being sold in April 1987 to COVEMAR Eolie, Italy.

UNITED STATES OF AMERICA

Air Cushion Guides, Inc

6230 Dunbar Lane, Anchorage, Alaska 99504, USA

Telephone: (907) 338 1272

Kenneth C Lomax, *President*

Company founded 1983. As of late 1985 this company was the only privately owned commercial ACV company in Alaska. The company specialises in four areas: tour guides on local inland waterways; guided and un-guided waterfowl hunts; freight hauling and personnel transport for construction and oil companies; and ACV operator training (authorised by the USCG and licensed by the State of Alaska; designed to meet USCG requirements for a commercial ACV operation licence).

High-speed craft operated

Type	Seats
HOV Air Cushion Technologies International Inc Falcon III	5
HOV Air Cushion Technologies International Inc Corsair I	8
HOV Air Cushion Technologies International Inc Maverick	2

Operations
As above, on Knik River and Upper Cook Inlet, Alaska

Falcon III hovercraft on the Knik River, Alaska

Air Cushion Guides, Inc Corsair I hovercraft in the Upper Cook Inlet, Alaska

Alderbrook Marine Inc

Hood Canal, Washington, USA

High-speed craft operated

Type	Name	Seats	Delivered
CAT Nichols Bros Boat Bldrs InCat 22m	*Spirit of Alderbrook*	200	1984

Route operated

Catalina to San Pedro

Apostle Islands Outfitters, Inc

Bayfields, Wisconsin, USA

Operations started in 1982.

High-speed craft operated

Type	Name	Seats	Delivered
HYD Ludwig Honald Mfg Co	*Albatross*	21	1964

Route operated

Sightseeing trips through the Apostle Islands, Lake Superior

Arcorp Properties

Weehawken, New Jersey, USA

Arthur E Imperatore, *President*

High-speed craft operated

Type	Name	Seats	In service
MH Blount Marine Corporation	*Port Imperial*	149	1986

Route operated

Weehawken, New Jersey to 38th Street, Manhattan, every 20 min

Arnold Transit

Mackinac Island, Michigan, USA

High-speed craft operated

Type

CAT Gladding-Hearn InCat 25m

Blue and Gold Fleet

Box Z-2, Pier 39, San Francisco, California 94133, USA

Telephone: (415) 781 7890

Roger Murphy, *General Manager*

High-speed craft operated

Type	Name	Seats	Delivered
CAT Nichols Brothers Boat Builders InCat	*Gold Rush*	220	1985

Leased from EF Hutton Credit Corporation.

Routes operated

Cruise vessel for whale watching off Point Reyes, California, started 24 December 1985, a co-operative agreement between the Blue and Gold Fleet and The Oceanic Society.

Boat also performs 2-hour historical cruises in San Francisco Bay during summer months.

InCat 220-seat catamaran *Gold Rush* operated by Blue and Gold Fleet, San Francisco

Boston Harbor Commuter Service (BHCS)

One Range Road, Nahant, Massachusetts 01890, USA

Telephone: (617) 599 7620/740 1253

Dana Goodell, *President*

The BHCS operates under the aegis of the Massachusetts State Water Transportation System and the Massachusetts Bay Transit Authority.

High-speed craft operated

Type	Name	Seats	Delivered
MH Camcraft crew boat converted by Aluminium Boats Inc	*Chimera*		1984
MH Camcraft crew boat converted by Aluminium Boats Inc	*Sterling* (ex *Sterling Fryou*)	150	1986

plus two other low-speed ferries craft

Route operated

Hingham Shipyard to Rowes Wharf (9·8 miles, under 30 min)

Bottom Time Adventurers

Fort Lauderdale, Florida, USA

A J Bland, *Director*

High-speed craft operated

Type	Name	Seats	Delivered
CAT Atlantic & Gulf Boat Bldg 23·8m InCat	*Bottom Time II*	32 (16 staterooms)	August 1986

Operation

Diving expeditions throughout the Bahamas

Catalina Channel Express Lines

PO Box 1391, San Pedro (Berth 96), California 90733, USA

Telephone: (213) 519 1212/7971

Greg Bombard, *Vice President and General Manager*

High-speed craft operated

Type	Name	Seats	Delivered
MH Westport 56	*Channel Express*	60	1981
MH Westport 80	*Avalon Express*	80	1983
MH Westport Shipyard Inc 27·44m 90	*Catalina Express*	149	1984
MH Westport Shipyard Inc 27·44m 90	*Two Harbors Express*	149	1986
HYD Westport Shipyard Inc	*Catalina Foil*	149	1988

Route operated

San Pedro to Avalon, Santa Catalina Island, fare US$12·50, 1987

Two Harbors Express, of Catalina Channel Express Lines

Westport International 25m hydrofoil to be delivered to Catalina Channel Express Lines in 1988

Catamaran Cruise Lines

Please see entry for Glacier Bay Yacht Tours Inc

Clipper Navigation Inc

2701 Alaskan Way, Pier 69, Seattle, Washington 98121, USA

Telephone: (206) 443 2560
Telex: 4950497

PO Box 1663, Station E, Victoria, British Columbia V8W 2Y1, Canada

Telephone: (604) 382 8100
Telex: 329473 attn CLP-954
Telefax: (206) 443 2583

Philip Lepley, *President*
Merideth Tall, *Vice-President*
Darrell Bryan, *General Manager*

High-speed craft operated

Type	Name	Seats	Delivered
CAT Fjellstrand 38·8m	*Victoria Clipper*	310	April 1986

Vessel registered in the Netherlands Antilles

Route operated

Seattle to Victoria, British Columbia, Canada, from July 1986 (2 hours 30 min). Fare: US$35·0 single (1987) May 1-September 13, US$29·0 single (1987) September 14-April 3 1988

Victoria Clipper departing Seattle

Stern of Fjellstrand *Victoria Clipper*

Department of Transportation, United States Coast Guard

2100 Second Street SW, Washington DC 20593-0001, USA

Telephone: (202) 426 2997

G D Marsh, *Chief, Ship Design Branch Marine Technical and Hazardous Materials Division*

High-speed craft operated (Sea Bird class)

Type	Name	In service
SES Bell Halter Model 522A (110 Mk 1)	*Sea Hawk* (WSES-2)	October 1982
SES Bell Halter Model 522A (110 Mk 1)	*Shearwater* (WSES-3)	October 1982
SES Bell Halter Model 522A (110 Mk 1)	*Petrel* (WSES-4)	June 1983

Operations

Based at Key West, Florida and engaged in anti-drug smuggling patrols in the Caribbean Sea

Glacier Bay Yacht Tours Inc (Catamaran Cruise Lines)

Seattle ,USA

Robert Giersdorf, *President*
Bert Nordby, *Vice-President*

High-speed craft operated

Type	Name	Seats	In service
CAT Nichols Brothers Boat Builders InCat 30m	*Executive Explorer*	25 state-rooms*	October 1986
CAT Nichols Brothers Boat Builders InCat 30m	*Hawaii Express*	400	6 December 1986

*49 passengers

Operation

Summer months (June to mid-September): Alaska, based in Juneau, *Executive Explorer* calls at Skagway, Haines/Pt Chilkoot, Glacier Bay Lodge, Sitka and Ketchikan.
Hawaii Express operates one day excursions out of Maui's Maalaea harbour to Molokai and Lanai and to Molokini Island, started early 1987.

Golden Gate Ferry

Golden Gate Bridge, Highway and Transportation District, 101 East Sir Francis Drake Blvd, Larkspur, California 94939, USA

Telephone: (415) 457 8800

Gary T Giacomini, *President*
Carol Ruth Silver, *1st Vice President*
Richard D Spotswood, *2nd Vice President*
Carney J Campion, *General Manager*
Eric A Robinson, *Division Manager*
Carl D Harrington, *Operations/Maintenance Superintendent*

The Ferry Division was formed in 1970 to operate waterborne mass transit on San Francisco Bay, operating between Marin County and San Francisco. In 1976, service was expanded with three semi-planing, triple gas turbine, 25-knot, waterjet-propelled vessels. For economic reasons these three vessels have now been re-powered with twin diesel engines using conventional propellers and rudders and with a resulting speed of 20·5 knots. The last of the three vessels modified was delivered in its new form in October 1985. See High-speed mono-hull craft section.

High-speed craft operated

Type	Name	Seats	Originally entered service
MH Campbell Industries Spaulding S-165 50·3m	*Marin*	partially open deck 118 open deck 42 enclosed decks 372	December 1976
MH Campbell Industries Spaulding S-165 50·3m	*Sonoria*	partially open deck 118 open deck 42 enclosed decks 372	March 1977
MH Campbell Industries Spaulding S-165 50·3m	*San Francisco*	partially open deck 118 open deck 42 enclosed decks 372	September 1977

Route operated

San Francisco to Larkspur, Marin County. Time 42 to 43 min

The Golden Gate Ferry vessel *Sonoma*

Grundstad Marrietheim/Crown Cruise Line

2790 North Federal Highway, Boca Raton, Florida 33431-0900, USA

Telephone: (305) 394-7450
Telex: 159067 GO-GO
Telefax: (305) 392-5917

Lars-Johan Hagerup, *Vice President, Operations*

Owner of three Westamarin Supramar PT 150 hydrofoils. These three vessels have now been converted into luxury diving vessels and are due to be operated in the Caribbean. For details of the PT 150 hydrofoil, please see page 153 of the 1987 edition

High-speed craft operated

Type
HYD Westamarin PT 150 *Princess of the Waves* (ex *Princess of the Lakes* (1984), ex *Princess of the Waves* (1979))
HYD Westamarin PT 150 *Prince of Niagara* (ex *Prince of the Waves* (1979), ex *Norfoil* (1973), ex *Scandia* (1970), ex *Hydroliner* (1969), ex *Expressan* (1969))
HYD Westamarin PT 150 *Queen of Toronto* (ex *Queen of the Waves* (1979))

PT 150, one of three converted into luxury diving craft

Maryland Natural Resources Police

Tawes State Office Building, Annapolis, Maryland 21401, USA

Telephone: (301) 974 3170/3187
Telefax: (301) 974 3189

High-speed craft operated

Type	Seats	Delivered
Slingsby Aviation Hovercraft SAH 2200	16	August 1987

Operation

The craft is used on a multi-mission basis to include law enforcement patrol, emergency medical transport, search and rescue and icebreaking. In addition, the unit is called upon to perform all other missions that are difficult or impossible for conventional patrol craft or light aircraft. This includes search and rescue during inclement weather and transport of US Coast Guard personnel over pack ice to service aids to navigation as needed.

A Griffon 1500 TD was operated in excess of 1300 hours between April 1984 and December 1986. During this period the craft was operated over all types of waterfront terrain and weather conditions which included operating in 50-knot winds and 2m seas and breaking ice 15cm thick to clear harbours. The craft was also demonstrated to thousands of people and rides given to more than 5000 people. Although this programme was very successful (with operational cost and fuel consumption of 4·5 US gallons per hour), the programme with this craft ended in December 1986, when Hover Systems Inc was not the low bidder to supply this agency with a larger craft.

The Slingsby 2200 became fully operational in September 1987. It is being used on a multi-mission basis to include law enforcement patrol, emergency medical transport, search and rescue and icebreaking. In addition, the unit may be called upon to perform all other missions that are difficult or impossible for conventional patrol craft or light aircraft. This includes search and rescue during inclement weather and transport of personnel over pack ice. A primary mission of this craft is the provision of emergency medical services and medical transport. For these purposes the craft will be staffed with Emergency Medical Technicians and a Cardiac Rescue Technician with all the necessary equipment to meet the requirements of an advanced life support unit. This pilot programme has an operational target date of May 1988 and will be tested and evaluated for one year to determine its feasibility for expansion or deletion.

Slingsby Aviation SAH 2200 in service with the Maryland Natural Resources Police

Ramada Inns Inc

USA

High-speed craft operated

Type
SES Hovermarine International HM 216

Red and White Fleet, Crowley Maritime Corporation

Pier 41, San Francisco, California 94133, USA

Telephone: (415) 546 2800

David Pence, *General Manager*
Barry Yap, *Marketing Manager*
Shirley Kohlwes, *Operations Manager*

High-speed craft operated

Type	Name	Seats	Delivered
CAT Nichols Brothers InCat 26m	*Catamarin*	274	1985
CAT Nichols Brothers InCat 26m	*Dolphin*	274	1986

Operation

Marin County area commuter and cruise services
Catamarin and *Dolphin* operating (1986) ferry services between San Francisco and Sausalito, Tiburon, and Vallejo on San Francisco Bay. Also used on cruise service to Marineworld Africa USA in Vallejo from San Francisco

Saltair Marina

Salt Lake City, Utah, USA

Operation started 1983.

High-speed craft operated

Type	Name	Seats	Built
HYD Ludwig Honald Mfg Co	*Albatross* (ex *Victory II*)	21	1964

Routes operated

20-min sightseeing trips: from south shore of the Great Salt Lake, tour of Salt Lake City and the lake. Variable schedule.

Sayville Ferry Service Inc

River Road, PO Box 626, Sayville, Long Island, New York 11782, USA

Telephone: (516) 589 0810

Capt Kenneth Stein, *President*

Sayville Ferry Service have a total fleet of 10 vessels with passenger capacity from 6 to 350. Most of them are operated at between 15 and 20 knots but the *Fire Island Clipper* can cruise at 26 knots at full load.

High-speed craft operated

Type	Name	Seats	Built
MH Derecktor Shipyard	*Fire Island Clipper*	350	1979

Operation

Sayville, Long Island (South Shore) to Fire Island, 5n miles, serving two summer communities

Sayville Ferry Services *Fire Island Clipper*

Sea World of California

1720 South Shores Road, Mission Bay, San Diego, California 92109, USA

Telephone: (619) 222 6363

Jan Schultz, *President*
Don Hall, *Vice President of Operations*

High-speed craft operated

Type	Name	Seats
HYD Ludwig Honald Mfg Co Albatross	*Sea World II*	28
HYD Ludwig Honald Mfg Co Albatross	*Sea World III*	28
HYD Ludwig Honald Mfg Co Albatross	*Sea World IV*	28

craft modified 1981 by Helmut Kock and Sprague Engineering Co

Operation

Sightseeing tours around Mission Bay, San Diego

Sea World II operated on sightseeing tours by Sea World of California, San Diego

Shepler's Inc

Mackinaw City, Michigan, USA

High-speed craft operated

Type	Name	Seats	In service
MH Camcraft Boats Inc (Hargrave) 18·30m	*The Welcome*	120	
MH Camcraft Boats Inc (Hargrave) 17·10m	*Felicity*	150	
MH Aluminium Boats Inc (Hargrave) 23·78m	*Captain Shepler*	265	1986

Route operated

St Ignace (Upper Peninsula) to Mackinaw City (Lower Peninsula) and Mackinac Island, Michigan

Tidewater Marine Service Inc

1440 Canal Street, Suite 2100, New Orleans, Louisiana 70112, USA

Telephone: (504) 568 1010
Telex: 0460050

Richard M Currence, *President, Tidewater Marine Service Inc*
John P Laborde, *Chairman and Chief Executive Officer, Tidewater Inc*

In November 1985 it was announced by Tidewater Inc that its subsidiary, Tidewater Marine Service Inc, had taken delivery of the Bell Halter Model 212B 110 Mk II *Speed Tide* on a long-term charter with a purchase option from the owner, Bell Halter Inc of New Orleans.

With the addition of *Speed Tide*, the Tidewater fleet numbered 268 vessels of all major classes in worldwide service. Of these, April 1985 listing showed 16 to be crew boats, a number of which would be in the high-speed category.

High-speed craft operated

Type	Name	Seats	Delivered
SES Bell Halter 212B, 110 Mk II	*Speed Tide*	119	November 1986

Operation

The vessel is working in the Gulf of Suez, for the Gulf of Suez Petroleum Company, a venture of Egypt's national oil company and Amoco, delivering support crews and supplies to drilling rigs and production facilities located within a 50-mile radius in the Gulf of Suez.

Bell Halter Model 212B (110 Mk II) *Speed Tide* on long term charter with Tidewater Marine Service Inc   *(Donlen)*

United New York-New Jersey Sandy Hook Pilots Association

Sandy Hook, New Jersey, USA

High-speed craft operated

Type	Name	Delivered
MH Gladding-Hearn Ship Building Corp (C Raymond Hunt) 19·51m	*Sandy Hook*	1985

Viking Express Inc

World Trade Building, Fort Lauderdale, Florida, USA

High-speed craft operated

Type	Name	Seats	Delivered
CAT Fjellstrand A/S 38·8m	*Caribbean Princess*	310	October 1986
CAT Fjellstrand A/S 38·8m	*Bahamian Prince*	310	February 1987

Route operated

Fort Lauderdale to Freeport, Grand Bahama Island *(Caribbean Princess)*, 2 hours 30 min daily service. Overnight packages from US$79

Washington State Ferries

Colman Dock, Pier 52, Seattle, Washington 98104, USA

Telephone: (206) 464 7800

The catamaran *Express* made her inaugural voyage on 30 December 1985 in Elliott Bay. The *Express* is the fifth such catamaran built by Nichols Brothers Boatbuilders since the programme began in 1984.

Prior to being purchased by the Washington State Department of Transportation (WSDOT), the *Express* was owned and operated by Glacier Bay Yacht Tours. The vessel's schedule called for six months service in Alaska as the *Glacier Express*, providing commuter and excursion trips out of Juneau to Glacier Bay and Tracy Arm Fjord. For the alternate six months of the year, the vessel, then to be called the *Baja Express*, was to have provided dinner/excursion service between San Diego and Ensenada in Baja, California.

Now named the *Express*, the vessel will be part of a 10-months demonstration of a high-speed passenger-only ferry service being conducted by WSDOT. The purchase price of the vessel was US$2·5 million less US$1·6 million provided by a grant from UMTA (Urban Mass Transportation Administration) funding. Sea trials and an independent marine survey were conducted prior to finalising the purchase. The contract was signed 15 September 1986, the same day Washington State Ferries took possession of the vessel. This particular vessel was chosen because of research which indicates the catamaran hull design to be a proven high-speed passenger ferry. Additional research conducted for the Washington State Ferries Long Range Plan indicates likely success for passenger-only service on the Seattle-Bremerton and Vashon-downtown Seattle routes. If the demonstration is successful, Washington State Ferries expects to have four high-speed passenger-only vessels in the fleet by 1993. (For details of *Express* please see High-Speed Catamaran Vessels section.)

High-speed craft operated

Type	Name	Delivered
CAT Nichols Bros InCat	*Express* (ex *Glacier Express*, ex *Baja Express*)	15 Sept 1986

Route operated

Seattle-Bremerton, approx 35 min, weekdays only

Nichols Bros InCat *Express* in service with Washington State Ferries

Yukon River Cruises, Inc

Anchorage, Alaska, USA

High-speed craft operated

Type	Name	Seats
CAT·22m Nichols Bros InCat	*Klondike*	210

URUGUAY

Belt SA

Rio Negro 1356 bis, Montevideo, Uruguay

Telephone: (90) 5128/5063/7892
Telex: 22133 BELT UY

Juan Carlos Deicas, *Managing Director*

Annual traffic: 180 000 to 200 000 passengers

High-speed craft operated

Type	Name	Acquired
HYD Rodriquez RHS 140	*Tyrving*	1979
HYD Rodriquez RHS 140	*Colonia del Sacramento* (ex *Condor*)	1979
HYD Rodriquez RHS 140	*Farallón* (ex *Løberon*)	1984

Routes operated
Colonia to Buenos Aires
Montevideo to Colonia to Buenos Aires

VENEZUELA

Inversiones Turisticas Margarita CA (INTUMACA)

Coracrevi, Apartado Postal 101, Caracas, Venezuela

High-speed craft operated

Type	Name	Speed	Seats	Delivered
MH Swiftships 38·0m	*Gran Cacique I*	28 knots	300	1978
MH Swiftships 38·0m	*Gran Cacique II*	28 knots	300	1980
MH Swiftships 38·0m	*Gran Cacique III*	28 knots	300	1980

Route operated
Puerto La Cruz to Margarita Island

Gran Cacique I operating off the Venezuelan coast

Maraven SA

Apartado 809, Caracas 1010-A, Venezuela

Telex: 23535/23536/23227 CCAR

Rafael Pardo, *Director*
Carlos Borregales, *Exploration and Production Manager*
Hans Krause, *Exploration and Production Manager*

High-speed craft operated

Type	Yard no	Name	Seats	Delivered
SES Vosper Hovermarine HM 218	454	*Zumbador*	70	1979
SES Vosper Hovermarine HM 218	455	*Zumaya*	70	1980
SES Vosper Hovermarine HM 218		*Barroso*	70	1980

Operation
Support duties for oil production platforms on Lake Maracaibo

VIRGIN ISLANDS (US)

Nautical Trading (St Kitts) Ltd

St Kitts, US Virgin Islands

High-speed craft operated

Type	Name	Seats	In service
HYD Rodriquez RHS 200	*San Cristobal*	254	1986
HYD Rodriquez RHS 160	*May W Craig* (ex *Alijumbo*)	180	1986

Routes operated
Puerto Rico-St Thomas-St Croix

Transportation Services of St John

St John, US Virgin Islands

High-speed craft operated

Type	Name	Seats	Delivered
ALH Atlantic & Gulf Boatbuilding Air Ride 65	*Caribe Air Ride* (ex *Air Ride Express*)	149	1987*

*Launched March 1983, originally delivered to South Florida Offshore Services Ltd, Plantation, Florida

Route operated
St John to St Thomas airport

YUGOSLAVIA

Atlas Pogon Hidrokrilnih Brodova

5001 Dubrovnik, Pile 1, Yugoslavia

Telex: 27515 YU

Operator of Kometa hydrofoils

Kompas-Jugoslavija

International Tourism, PO Box 307/IV, Pražakova 4, 61001 Ljubljana, Yugoslavia

Telex: 31209/32183 KOMPAS YU

High-speed craft operated

Type	Name	Delivered
HYD S Ordzhonikidze Kometa	*Krila Slovenije*	1977
HYD S Ordzhonikidze Kometa	*Krila Kvarnera*	1978
HYD S Ordzhonikidze Kometa	*Krila Pirana*	1979
HYD S Ordzhonikidze Kometa	*Krila Kornata*	1980
HYD S Ordzhonikidze Kometa	*Krila Primorske*	1980

Routes operated
Poreč to Pula, Poreč to Umag, Poreč to Rovinj, Poreč to Portoroz
Venice to Istria

A Kompas Kometa at Venice, 1986

Kvarner Express

Maršala Tita 186, 51410 Opatija, PO Box 92, Yugoslavia

Telephone: (51) 711 111
Telex: 24174 OPATUR YU/24379 KVEX YU

Radomir Premuš, *Managing Director*
Aldo Simper, *Assistant Managing Director*

In 1985 Kvarner Express introduced high-speed daily ferry services from Opatija to the Island of Rab and to Venice. The company now operates a fleet of four 35-knot Kolkhida hydrofoil craft.

High-speed craft operated

Type	Name	Seats	Delivered
HYD S Ordzhonikidze Kolkhida	*Magnolija*	145	1985
HYD S Ordzhonikidze Kolkhida	*Kamelija*	145	1985
HYD S Ordzhonikidze Kolkhida	*Mirta*	145	1986
HYD S Ordzhonikidze Kolkhida	*Mimoza*	145	1986

Routes operated
Opatija to Rab, 50n miles
Opatija to Venice and in spring 1987 to Ancona and Rimini

S Ordzhonikidze Kolkhida *Magnolija*, one of four in service with Kvarner Express, Yugoslavia

Splosna Plovba Piran

Yugoslavia

High-speed craft operated

Type	Name	Delivered
CAT Westamarin W100	*Porec*	January 1982

Union Dalmacija

Oour Flota, Kupalisni prilaz 12, 58000 Split, Yugoslavia

Telephone: (58) 513-066
Telex: 26102 DALTUR YU

High-speed craft operated

Type	Name	Delivered
CAT Westamarin W86	*Mediteran*	June 1978
CAT Westamarin W86	*Marina I*	July 1978

Operation
Dalmatian coast

OPERATORS OF LOW-SPEED AIR CUSHION PLATFORMS

CANADA

TRANSPORT CANADA
Canadian Coast Guard (CCG)

Tower A(7th fl), Place de Ville, Ottawa, Ontario
K1A 0N7, Canada

Telephone: (613) 998 1602

Transportation Development Centre (TDC)

Complex Guy Favreau, 200 Dorchester West,
Suite 601, West Tower, Montreal, Quebec H2Z
1X4, Canada

Telephone: (514) 283 0033

T F Melhuish, *Manager, Fleet Aviation, CCG*
Jacque E Laframboise, *Senior Development
Officer, TDC*

AIR CUSHION ICEBREAKING BOW (ACIB)

The Air Cushion Icebreaking Bow (ACIB) is a
technology that has been under development in
Canada since 1971. Trials have indicated that the
use of low-speed, non-self-propelled hovercraft in
conjunction with vessels offers significant savings
in fuel consumption and icebreaking time. The
Canadian Coast Guard has been operating air
cushion icebreakers since 1975 with the Bell
Aerospace Voyageur hovercraft and with the
ACIB. Details of early air cushion icebreaking
work by Transport Canada are given in *Jane's
Surface Skimmers 1985* (ACT 100/Iceeater 1).

The Canadian Coast Guard air cushion icebreaking bow was designed and constructed by
Hoverlift Systems Limited (HSL) in Calgary to
CCG specifications. It was moved from Calgary to
Thunder Bay in autumn 1981 and erected at the
Port Arthur Shipbuilding Company following
which limited tests were carried out late in winter
1981/82. These tests achieved a performance similar to that of the earlier icebreaking platform,
ACT-100, and also revealed a number of deficiencies.

Late in 1982 a contract was placed for repairs,
modifications and further testing with the tug
Thunder Cape and the CCGS *Alexander Henry*. A
mild season permitted the modification and maintenance to be done but restricted the scope of the
trials. Nevertheless, a lot of information was
obtained and experience gained.

Very late in 1983 a further contract was placed
for repairs, modifications and engineering support
for the ACIB during ice management operations
by the CCG. The host ship was to be the CCGS
Alexander Henry but it was intended also to
conduct trials with the tug *Thunder Cape* to
explore the limits of its capability. Due to the
lateness of the contract, the ACIB was not ready
for operations until February 1984 but after that
successful ice management tasks were conducted
until April 1984 when the Master of the *Alexander
Henry* was satisfied that the ACIB was no longer
required.

Problems were experienced with damage to the
skirt and, particularly, to notch segments. This
was the result of a number of circumstances:
deterioration of the material, poor quality control,
design deficiencies and inability to adjust cushion
pressure and speed to ice conditions. Also, the
ACIB was operated in some situations where the
Alexander Henry alone would have been equally
effective, in very thin ice and in broken ice.

The CCG *Alexander Henry* using the ACIB to open a slipway, March 1984

The tug *Thunder Cape* pushing the ACIB over 0·60m of ice at a speed of 4 knots

Circumstances did not permit the proposed trials with the *Thunder Cape* to be performed but the ACIB/*Alexander Henry* combination was used in a test concerning breaking out slips between elevators (Manitoba Pool No 1). This was very successful in spite of the caution dictated by the nature of the test. The entire slip, with ice thicknesses of up to 90cm, was broken out in a matter of minutes, with no undesirable loads on the dock structure.

The HSL 533 ACIB was declared surplus during 1985 and turned over to Crown Assets for disposal. This decision was taken when a new ship entered service at Thunder Bay for CCG. This more powerful ship replaced the CCGS *Alexander Henry*; it was felt that this ship could manage the local icebreaking tasks without the ACIB.

The HSL 533 design was rather simple, due to the funding constraints placed on the supplier. A design review was carried out by TDC in 1985 to define an ACIB that would not have the limitations forced on the HSL craft. Characteristics felt to be desirable for such a vehicle were, among others, the provision of liquid ballast so that the ACIB weight could be adjusted to suit local ice conditions and the possibility to change skirt segments over water. While the ACIB could operate with a number of damaged segments, prudence dictated a return to base whenever damage was observed, thus limiting severely the operating range.

Within their operating theatre the two ACIBs in CCG service demonstrated a technical icebreaking efficiency in excess of that of conventional icebreakers. However, ACIBs have yet to be integrated into the operational inventory of the Canadian Coast Guard.

References: Please see Bibliography Section for extensive references to technical papers on Canadian air cushion platform developments

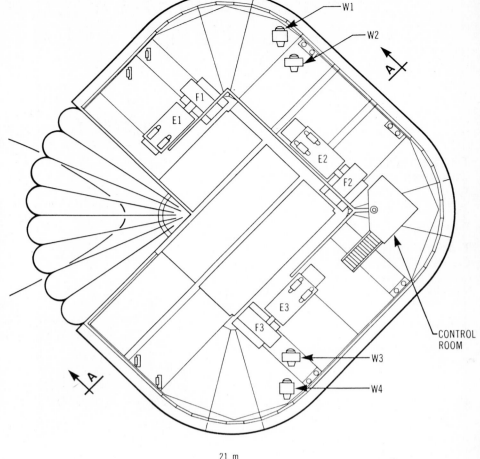

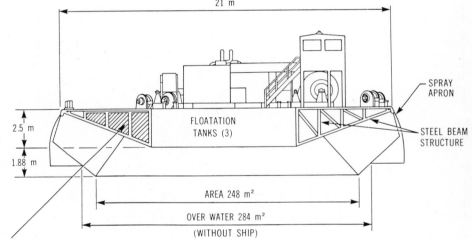

Layout of HSL 533 Air Cushion Icebreaking Bow

UNION OF SOVIET SOCIALIST REPUBLICS

NORTHERN SHIPPING LINE & THE NORTHERN DEPARTMENT OF TsNIIMFa

Arkhangel'sk, USSR

These organisations operate the MPVP-40 type hover platform, details of which are given in the Low-Speed Air Cushion Platforms section.

The MPVP-40 platform is in use with the Northern Shipping Line for cargo transfer to areas of undeveloped coastline. Research carried out by the Northern Department of the TsNIIMFa in the regions of the White, Bering and Karskoye Seas led to standards and recommendations for cargo operations using the Soviet MPVP and Finnish VP air cushion platforms. As with all operations of air cushion platforms, difficulties have been experienced due to the severe northern conditions, the very conditions that demand the capabilities of air cushion platforms. The platform is not yet therefore in series production. The Merchant Marine Ministry (Minmorflot) are engaged in the development of a reliable towing craft capable,

Operations with the Laiski MPVP-40 air cushion platform

with the MPVP, of successfully overcoming choppy conditions in shallow coastal waters.

In 1985 the MPVP-40, No 3, shipped a total of 3890 tonnes. Considerable attention is being paid to improving the effectiveness of the platforms and their utilisation.

The Northern Shipping Line has six air cushion platforms and three amphibious tugs. Four of the platforms were built by the Wärtsilä Yard in Finland, with participation of Leningrad designers, and two by the Soviet Lajskij Ship Repair Yard. These platforms have empty weights ranging from 36 to 42 tonnes with carrying capacities from 38 to 40 tonnes. With the aid of amphibious tugs they may be propelled in water at speeds up to 3·5 knots. Experience with these air cushion platforms over a period of more than four years has shown that the productivity of an amphibious complex (two platforms and one tug) is two to three times greater than the productivity which is achieved using conventional technology barges and pontoons, daily transhipment of 400 tonnes being possible with the amphibious units. Such air cushion platforms were operated experimentally in the extreme north of the USSR from 1982 to 1984 and in full practical use from 1985 onwards. By the beginning of 1987 more than 20 000 tonnes of various goods had been delivered to destinations on the White and Barents Sea. It is considered that until an effective, reliable and sufficiently operational simple self-propelled air cushion cargo ship has been created, towing will continue to be necessary. The design bureau of the Northern and Murmansk Shipping Lines have created and tested their own models for self-propelled air cushion platforms but no new vehicles are yet developed. For some time, it is anticipated that amphibious tugs will be integral elements in the operation of air cushion platforms.
Reference: V Khmurin, Northern Section of the Central Research Institute for Mercantile Marine, Soviet Shipping Journal

A heavily-loaded air cushion platform of the Wärtsilä TAV 40 type in operation with the Soviet Northern Shipping Line

Operations with the Laiski MPVP-40 air cushion platform

UNITED STATES OF AMERICA

GLOBAL MARINE DEVELOPMENT INC (GMDI)

777 W Eldridge, PO Box 4577, Houston, Texas 77210, USA

Telephone: (713) 596 5900
Telex: 76 5558
Telefax: (713) 531 1260

G L Kott, *President*
F C Newton, *Vice President, Sales*
S B Wetmore, *Director, Engineering Technology*

Associated Company:
Veco Inc, Anchorage, Alaska, USA

Global Marine Development Inc owns the Canadian-built ACT-100 which was completed in 1971, an air cushion platform with a 100-ton payload capability. Specification details and details of its operations in the 1970s are given in *Jane's Surface Skimmers 1985* and earlier editions.

All personnel of Global Marine Development

Inc have been integrated into the parent subsidiary, Global Marine Drilling Company.

In the winter of 1979 the ACT-100 was moved to Prudhoe Bay, Alaska and after several trials it was used by the Sohio Alaska Petroleum Company to establish the drag of an air cushion platform over different surfaces and to demonstrate the operational capability on a year-round basis. The following extracts from a paper by J T Walden of Sohio and D F Dickens of D F Dickens Associates give some interesting information on these operations.

'The first series of tests were held in October 1981 in which an ice-strengthened tug pushed the ACT-100 through a 36cm level ice sheet. Acting as an icebreaker (the ACT-100 can break up to 75cm of ice), the tug-hoverbarge combination traversed a distance of about 25 miles over a 4-day span through areas of level ice, rafted ice and refrozen tracks. Speeds of up to 3 knots were attained. These tests confirmed the fact that icebreaking imposes the highest drag on an air-cushion vehicle, and that propulsion requirements will be dictated by this condition. Minimising the cushion

pressure and hence the icebreaking ability of the craft is critical to lowering the capital cost and horsepower requirements of the propulsion system.

'In April 1982 the ACT-100 was towed by a Rolligon and an Archimedean Screw tractor over 1·8m thick flat ice and rubble using an instrumented tow cable. These tests showed that while rough ice drag is not as severe as icebreaking, it is significantly higher than that over a smooth ice profile. It therefore may be cost-effective (from a fuel consumption viewpoint) to avoid rough ice areas, even if it may mean travelling over greater distances. The tests also documented the fact that a groomed surface, such as an existing ice road, imposes the minimum drag of all conditions encountered offshore.

'The final set of tests with the ACT-100 were conducted in June 1982 when the craft was towed with a 183m tow line by a Vertol 107 twin-rotor helicopter just prior to ice breakup. In this demonstration the hoverbarge was towed to a Sohio drill site 45 miles from Prudhoe Bay, where it was loaded with 50 tons of cargo for its return trip.

Although the surface was covered with melt pools, no icebreaking occurred and vehicle drag was less than that encountered during freezeup. These trials proved that while helicopter towing is possible, its marginal thrust capability makes it undesirable operationally, although it could perform adequately in an emergency.'

In 1984 Sohio of Alaska contracted the ACT-100 to move 2000 tons of drilling equipment from its 'Mukluk' Gravel Island project in Harrison Bay, Alaska. Excellent results were achieved and loads in excess of 100 tons were carried safely during this move. The ACT-100 is at present stationed at Prudhoe Bay, Alaska.

Boeing Vertol 107 Helicopter towing ACT-100 hoverbarge from Prudhoe Bay, Alaska to Alaska Island, June 1982. Towing altitude: 6 to 15m, average speed 5 knots, one trip distance 42n miles   *(William Bacon Productions)*

PRINCIPAL ENGINEERING COMPONENTS FOR HIGH-SPEED CRAFT

ENGINES

CANADA

PRATT & WHITNEY CANADA

1000 Marie-Victorian Blvd, Longueuil, Quebec
J4G 1A1, Canada

Telephone: (514) 677 9411

E L Smith, *Chairman*
L D Caplan, *President and Chief Executive Officer*
R F Steers, *Vice President, Finance*
G P Ouimet Sr, *Vice President, Operations*
C J Pascoe, *Vice President, Counsel*
R C Abraham, *Vice President, Production*
J B Haworth, *Vice President, Industrial and Marine Division*
R M Sachs, *Director of Marketing, Industrial and Marine Division*

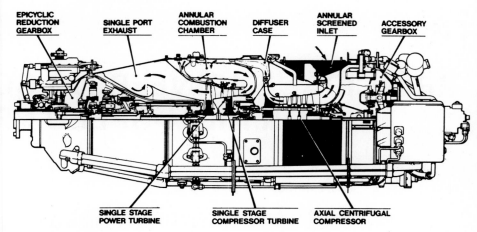

Main components of ST6

In addition to its wide range of small aircraft turbines (for example the PT6A turboprop, PT6B, PT6T and T400 turboshafts, and JT15D turbofan), Pratt & Whitney Canada also manufactures a marine derivative of the PT6, the ST6 series of turboshafts. These engines are rated at 550shp and upwards and are installed in a number of ACV and hydrofoil vessels. Two ST6T-75 Twin-Pac® turbines powered the Bell Aerospace Canada Voy-

ageur hovercraft. Larger Voyageurs for the US Army, designated LACV-30, and built by Textron Marine Systems are powered by ST6T-76 engines.

Including aero-engine installations, over 25 000 of this series of gas turbines have been delivered. Between them they have accumulated running experience in excess of 126 million hours.

ST6 MARINE GAS TURBINE

ST6 marine gas turbines are designed and manufactured by Pratt & Whitney Canada. Details of the engine specifications are given below:

TYPE: All ST6 engines are of the simple cycle, free turbine type with a single spool gas generator and a multi-stage compressor driven by a single-stage turbine. Burner section has an annular combustion chamber with downstream injection. The single- or two-stage free turbine may provide a direct high-speed drive or may drive through a reduction gearbox.

The ST6T-76 Twin-Pac® is a dual engine with two power sections mounted side-by-side and coupled to a twinning reduction gear.

AIR INTAKE: Annular air intakes are located at rear of engine with an intake screen.

COMPRESSOR: All ST6 models feature compressors with three axial-flow stages, plus a single centrifugal stage. The single-sided centrifugal stage typically has 26 vanes, made from a titanium forging. Axial rotors are of the disc-drum type with titanium stator and rotor blades. Stator vanes are brazed in their casings. The rotor blades are dove-tailed to discs. Discs through-bolted with the centrifugal compressor to the shaft. One-piece stainless steel casing and radial diffuser.

ST6 gas turbine

ST6 and SPW 100 SERIES ENGINE DATA SUMMARY
Sea Level Standard Pressure at 15°C (59°F) Inlet Temperature

IMPERIAL MEASURE

Model	Maximum		Intermediate		Normal		Output	Length	Width	Height	Weight
	shp	sfc*	shp	sfc*	shp	sfc*	rpm (max)	(in)	(in)	(in)	(lb)
ST6L-77	811	0·59	—	—	654	0·62	33 000	52·2	19	19	306
ST6J-77	750	0·61	650	0·63	550	0·66	2200	62	19	19	379
ST6K-77	690	0·62	620	0·64	550	0·66	6230	60	19	19	350
ST6L-81	1065	0·58	955	0·6	840	0·62	30 000	59·4	19	19	360
ST6T-76	1850	0·615	1645	0·63	1440	0·65	6600	66·4	44·4	31·6	730
SPW-124	2810	0·476	—	—	2400	0·492	20 000	60	26	33	740

METRIC MEASURE

Model	Maximum		Intermediate		Normal		Output	Length	Width	Height	Weight
	kW	sfc*	kW	sfc*	kW	sfc*	rpm (max)	(mm)	(mm)	(mm)	(kg)
ST6L-77	605	0·358	—	—	488	0·377	33 000	1326	483	483	139
ST6J-77	560	0·371	485	0·384	410	0·401	2200	1575	483	483	172
ST6K-77	515	0·377	463	0·389	410	0·401	6230	1524	483	483	159
ST6L-81	794	0·353	712	0·365	627	0·377	30 000	1509	483	483	164
ST6T-76	1380	0·374	1227	0·381	1074	0·395	6600	1687	1128	803	332
SPW-124	2096	0·289	—	—	1790	0·299	20 000	1624	660	838	336

*sfc = lb/hph (imperial)
    = kg/kWh (metric)

COMBUSTION CHAMBER: Annular reverse-flow type of stainless steel construction, with 14 Simplex burners. Two spark plug igniters.
GAS GENERATOR TURBINE: Single-stage axial. Rotor blades of sulphidation-resistant material mounted by fir tree roots. Cooled vanes in some models.
POWER TURBINE: Single- or dual-stage axial. Rotor blades mounted by fir tree roots.
BEARINGS: Gas generator and power turbine each supported by one ball bearing and one roller bearing.
SHAFT DRIVE: Single- or two-stage planetary reduction gear or direct drive, depending on engine model. Torque measuring system incorporated with reduction gearing.
FUEL GRADE: Diesel Nos 1 and 2 and Navy diesel or aviation turbine fuel.
JET PIPE: Single port exhaust discharging vertically upwards or at 30, 60 or 90 degrees port or starboard of vertical. Models available with twin ports discharging horizontally.
ACCESSORY DRIVES: Mounting pads on accessory case including for starter or starter-generator and tacho-generator. Also tacho-generator drive on power section.

LUBRICATION SYSTEM: One pressure and three scavenge gear type pumps driven by gas generator rotor. Integral oil tank.
OIL SPECIFICATIONS: Type 2 synthetic lube oil PWA-521 MIL-L-23699.

SPW-124

This engine is an industrial and marine version of the PW-124 turboprop engine, one of the most powerful and efficient Pratt & Whitney Canada engines. The SPW-124 is a twin-spool free-turbine engine with two centrifugal compressor stages.

CHINA, PEOPLE'S REPUBLIC

Please see United Technologies International Inc entry regarding forthcoming production of 24 609kW FT8 marine gas turbine in China.

FRANCE

MOTEURS BAUDOUIN

165 Boulevard de Pont-de-Vivaux, BP 32, 13362 Marseilles Cedex 10, France

Telephone: (91) 79 90 91
Telex: 410 944 MOBOD F
Telefax: (91) 79 09 38

12 P 15.2 SR7

Fitted to the SBCN 38-metre patrol boat.
TYPE: A four-stroke direct injection diesel engine.
CYLINDERS: 12 cylinders, V-form, rigid wet type cylinder liners.
ASPIRATION: Turbocharged with air cooler.
COOLING: By water from closed circuit with fresh water/raw water heat exchanger integrated with engine.
LUBRICATION: Gear pump with full flow cartridge type oil filters.
INJECTION: Monoblock injection pump with mechanical governor.
TECHNICAL DATA
Swept volume: 31·8 litres
Compression ratio: 14·0:1
Max rating: 1030kW (1381bhp) at 2000rpm
Mean effective pressure: 19·44 bar at 2000rpm
Fuel consumption: 265 litres/h
Dry weight, without gearbox: 3000kg

	A mm	B mm	C mm	D mm	E mm	Approx weight in kg without water or oil
12 P 15.2 SR7						3000
12 P 15.2 SRC IRS	355	1229	340	1084	165	3970
12 P 15.2 SRC IRX	488	1839	460	1356	226	5105
12 P 15.2 SRC RHS	355	1611	340	1084	165	3965
12 P 15.2 SRC RHX	488	2071	460	1356	226	5105

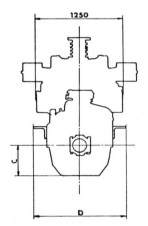
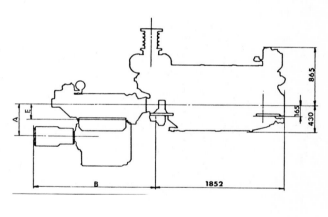

Dimensions of Baudouin Series 12 P 15.2 SR7 engines/gearboxes

Baudouin 12 P 15.2 SR7 marine diesel engine

GERMANY, FEDERAL REPUBLIC

DEUTZ (KLOCKNER-HUMBOLDT-DEUTZ AG)

Deutz Muehleimer Str 111, Postfach 80 0509, D-5000 Cologne 80, Federal Republic of Germany

Group companies:
Motoren-Werke Mannheim AG and MWM Diesel und Gastechnik GmbH, PO Box 1563, D-6800 Mannheim 1, Federal Republic of Germany

KHD Great Britain Limited, Riverside Road, London SW17 0UT, England

Telephone: 01-946 9161
Telex: 8954136 KHDLON G
Telefax: 01-947 6380

KHD Deutz air-cooled engines of the 413F series have been in large-scale production for many years. Comprising 5- and 6-cylinder in-line and 6-, 8-, 10- and 12-cylinder 'V' engines, these naturally aspirated engines cover outputs ranging from 118kW (158bhp) to 282kW (378bhp).

The 513 series is a further development of the 413F engine. The main feature of this new engine family is a completely re-designed combustion system. Other advantages include reduced exhaust gas emissions, electronically controlled cooling blower, and higher torque. In addition the same maximum power at 200rpm lower engine speed provides higher power at medium engine speeds and lower fuel consumption. Engines of the 513 series are available as 6-, 8-, 10- and 12-cylinder 'V' type, in naturally aspirated versions as well as 6-cylinder in-line and 8-, 10- and 12-cylinder 'V' type turbocharged or turbocharged/after-cooled versions. The power developed by this engine family covers a range from 141kW (189bhp) to 386kW (518bhp), and for some applications extends up to 441kW (591bhp) flywheel net. The turbocharged/after-cooled 12-cylinder automotive version of the design offers the best power to weight ratio for that application.

KHD Deutz engines are installed in the following hovercraft:- Griffon Hovercraft Ltd 1000 TD and 1500 TD powered by single BF6L 913C diesels, the 2500 TD by two BF6L 913Cs and the 4000 TD design by two BF8L 513s; Air Vehicles Ltd Tiger 16, Holland Hovercraft Kolibrie 2000 and Slingsby Aviation Ltd SAH 2200 are powered by single BF6L 913Cs. Both Griffon Hovercraft Ltd and Air Vehicles Ltd have further models planned, using Deutz air-cooled engines. Four Deutz BF12L 513CP diesels are installed in the BHC AP1-88 general purpose hovercraft, two for lift and two for propulsion.

BF6/8/10/12L 513C
TYPE: Air-cooled four-stroke diesel with direct fuel injection naturally aspirated or turbocharged; BF12L 513C with air-charge cooling system.
CYLINDERS: Individually removable cylinders made in grey cast iron alloy, each with one inlet and one exhaust valve, overhead type. The valves are controlled via tappets and pushrods by a camshaft running in three metal bearings in the upper part of the crankcase. Camshaft is crankshaft driven via helical spur gears arranged at the flywheel end of the engine. Crankcase is grey cast iron. The main journals are supported after each throw in three metal bearings, one of which is designed as a locating bearing.
PISTONS: Each is equipped with two compression rings and one oil control ring and are force oil-cooled.
COOLING SYSTEM: Air-cooled, mechanically

Deutz BF12L 513C as fitted to BHC and NQEA AP1-88 hovercraft

driven axial type cooling air blower with optional load-dependent, electronic control.
LUBRICATION: Force feed by gear type pump. Oil is cleaned by full-flow paper filters. A centrifugal filter is installed in the hub as a high efficiency secondary flow filter.

BF12L 513C
Power, max (intermittent duty): 386kW at 2300rpm
Number of cylinders: 12
Bore/stroke: 125/130mm
Capacity: 19·144 litres
Compression ratio: 15·8:1
Rotational speed: 2300rpm
Mean piston speed: 9·96m/s
Specific fuel consumption (automotive rating flywheel net at max torque): 205g/kWh (0·336lb/hph)
Shipping volume: 3·16m³
DIMENSIONS
Length: 1582mm
Height: 1243mm
Width: 1196mm
USER: British Hovercraft Corporation AP1-88.

BF12L 513CP
This engine is a variant of the turbocharged and inter-cooled V12 which, by utilising a remotely mounted air-to-air inter-cooler raises the intermittent power to 441kW (591bhp) at 2300rpm.
This is used by BHC on their latest, well-deck version of the AP1-88 for lift and propulsion.

BF6L 913C
Built to the same specification as the 513, this 6-cylinder in-line engine is also available for hovercraft applications. It is fitted with an exhaust turbocharger and charge air-cooler.
Max (intermittent duty) power: 141kW at 2500rpm
Number of cylinders: 6
Bore/stroke: 102/125mm
Capacity: 6·128 litres
Compression ratio: 15·5 : 1
Rotational speed: 2500rpm
Mean piston speed: 10·4m/s

Specific fuel consumption (automotive rating at max torque): 214g/kWh
Shipping volume: 0·8m³
DIMENSIONS
Length: 1245mm
Height: 991mm
Width: 711mm
Weight: 510kg
USERS: Griffon Hovercraft Ltd 1000 TD, 1500 TD and 2500 TD, Air Vehicles Ltd Tiger 16, Slingsby Aviation Ltd SAH 2200. The BF6L 913 also powers the MARIC type 7210 and three are used in the MARIC type 716 II.

Please see MWM entry for details of Deutz MWM 234, 816 and 604B type engines.

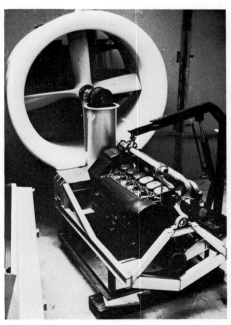
Deutz BF6L 913C engine driving a Robert Trillo ducted propeller for Griffon Hovercraft 1000, 1500 and 2500 TD installations

DEUTZ MWM
Motoren-Werke Mannheim AG
Carl-Benz Strasse, PO Box 1563, D-6800 Mannheim 1, Federal Republic of Germany

Telephone: (0621) 384-1
Telex: 462341 D
Telefax: 221 822 3698

Following the merger in 1985 of Motoren-Werke Mannheim AG and Klockner-Humboldt-Deutz AG, the company now offers a combined range of water-cooled medium-sized and large engines from 100 to 7250kW (134 to 9722bhp).
The principal engine ranges suitable for high-speed surface craft and hovercraft are as follows:

TBD 234
The 234 series is a modern high-power, high-speed engine design offering decisive advantages in power/weight ratio, power/space ratio, durability and fuel consumption. The engine is available in 60° V 6-, 8-, 12- and 16-cylinder versions, either turbocharged and inter-cooled or naturally aspirated. Power outputs are available

Installation of one of the MWM TBD 604B V12 diesels in the Precision Marine *Tropic Sunseeker*

from 105kW (141hp) at 1500rpm up to 900kW (1207bhp) at 2300rpm. Examples of their application include a new series of Spanish built 14-metre customs launches, with a maximum speed in excess of 55 knots. Each is driven by twin TBD 234 V12 engines rated at 735kW at 2300rpm direct coupled to Riva Calzoni waterjet units. Another application is the International Catamarans Pty 31-metre wave-piercing catamaran *Tassie Devil 2001*, which is driven by two TBD 234 V16 engines each rated continuous at 755kW at 2200rpm.

BAM 816

The 816 series is a compact, low profile design. The engine is available in in-line 6 and 8 cylinders, together with 120° V 12- and 16-cylinder versions. The power range available is from 100kW (131bhp) at 1000rpm to 1270kW (1703bhp) at 2000rpm. Examples of their application include the Westamarin W88 catamaran ferry *Haugesund* powered by twin BAM 16M 816 each rated at 865kW (1160bhp) at 2000rpm.

TBD 604B

Developed from the existing 603/604 engine family, the new series 604B engine type is a compact high-speed diesel engine incorporating the very latest technology to give excellent power/weight ratios and a very favourable fuel consumption of only 190g/kWh. The engine is a four-stroke, as are all Deutz MWM water-cooled diesel engines, and is turbocharged and inter-cooled. To give a power spread of 420kW (563bhp) at 1000rpm up to 1930kW (2588bhp) at 1800rpm, the engine is available with an in-line 6-cylinder, together with 90° V 8-, 12- and 16-cylinder variants. The engine is fitted with a novel system –

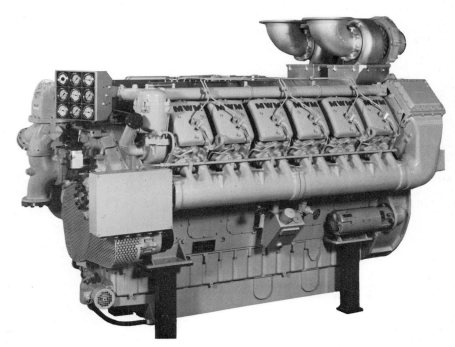

Deutz MWM TBD 604B V12 diesel engine, 1440kW (1931bhp) at 1800rpm

the HALLO swirl – allowing optimum combustion even under idling and other low load conditions. Typical applications include the Fairey Marinteknik (S) Pte Ltd 35m mono-hull ferries for Hong Kong, using twin TBD 604B V8 with an mcr of 840kW at 1800rpm, to give a service speed of 25 knots. Also operating are various units for International Catamarans Pty and a 47-knot SES built by Brodrene Aå in Norway, using two TBD 604B V12 at 1260kW (1690bhp) at 1800rpm. A larger SES vessel is being built by the same company using TBD 604B V16 engines rated at 1690kW and with lift engines of type TBD 604B L6 rated at 295kW.

MAN

MAN Nutzfahrzeuge GmbH

Nuremberg Works, PO Box 44 01 00, Frankenstrasse 15, 8500 Nürnberg 44, Federal Republic of Germany

Telephone: (0911) 18-0
Telex: 622 914-0 MN D
Telefax: (0911) 44 65 22

MAN GHH (Great Britain) Ltd, 4-5 Grosvenor Place, Hyde Park Corner, London SW1X 7DG, England
Telephone: 01-235 5011
MAN High Performance Diesels, 160 Van Brunt Street, Brooklyn, NY 11231, USA
Telephone: 718 935 1900
MAN GHH Australia Pty Ltd, MAN-Building, 275 Alfred Street, North Sydney, NSW 2060, Australia
Telephone: 2 922 7745
MAN B & W Diesel (Singapore) Pte Ltd, 29 Tuas Avenue 2, Singapore 2263, Singapore
Telephone: 862 1401

MAN marine diesel engines are blocked for different marine applications, rating 1 for displacement hulls, rating 2 for displacement and semi-displacement hulls and rating 3 for planing hulls. The kW or ps/hp rating given for the engine models featured in subsequent paragraphs is for rating 3.

D 0226 MLE

TYPE: Four-stroke diesel engine, 6-cylinder vertical in-line water-cooled with turbocharger and inter-cooler. Direct injection system. High unit output, low noise level and quiet running with low fuel consumption. Long service life and low upkeep and all ports to be serviced are readily accessible.
CRANKCASE AND CRANK ASSEMBLY: Cylinder block of grey cast iron, seven bearing crankshaft with integral forged balance weights, three layer type bearings and die forged connecting rods.
CYLINDER HEAD AND VALVE TRAIN: Double cylinder heads of grey cast iron, overhead valves, one inlet and one exhaust valve per cylinder, valve actuation via tappets, pushrods and rocker arms, four bearing camshafts.
LUBRICATION: Forced-feed lubrication-by-gear pump, oil-to-water oil-cooler, full-flow oil filter, changeover type optional.
FUEL SYSTEM: Bosch in-line injection pump with mechanical speed governor, fuel supply pump, fuel filter, changeover type optional.
INTAKE AND EXHAUST SYSTEM: Viscous air filter, water-cooled exhaust, manifold connected in engine cooling circuit.
SUPERCHARGING: Water-cooled exhaust turbocharger, seawater-cooled inter-cooler.
ELECTRICAL SYSTEM: Two-pole starter, 4kW, 24V and two pole alternator 28V, 35A.
APPLICATIONS: Work boats, customs and police patrol boats, yachts.
TECHNICAL DATA
Bore/stroke: 102/116mm
Swept volume: 5·691 litres
Compression ratio: 17:1
Rotation locking on flywheel: Anti-clockwise
Flywheel housing: SAE 3
Weight of engine dry, with cooling system: 545kg
Max rating 3: 154kW/207bhp at 2800rpm
Mean effective pressure: 11·6 bar at 2800rpm
Torque: 525Nm at 2800rpm
Mean specific fuel consumption (+5%) at 2800rpm: 225g/kWh at 2800rpm

Model Summary

Model	No of cylinders/ configuration	Bore/ stroke in mm	Displacement in litres	Dry weight kg	Speed rpm	Rating ①		Rating ②		Rating ③	
						kW	ps/hp	kW	ps/hp	kW	ps/hp
D 0226 ME	6	102/116	5·69	520	1800	60	82	66	90	—	—
					2100	70	95	77	105	—	—
					2400	79	107	83	113	—	—
					2800	87	118	95	130	—	—
					3000	—	—	—	—	100	136
D 0226 MTE (T)	6	102/116	5·69	530	2600	110	150	121	165	—	—
					2800	—	—	125	170	135	184
D 0226 MLE (L)	6	102/116	5·69	545	2600	125	170	125	170	—	—
					2800	—	—	147	200	154	210
D 2866 E	6	128/155	11·97	985	1500	125	170	132	180	—	—
					1800	151	205	162	220	—	—
					2100	165	224	178	242	—	—
					2200	—	—	—	—	185	252
D 2866 TE (T)	6	128/155	11·97	1000	1800	190	258	206	280	—	—
					2100	—	—	227	300	—	—
					2200	—	—	—	—	235	320
D 2866 LE (L)	6	128/155	11·97	1035	1800	246	326	—	—	—	—
					2100	—	—	260	354	—	—
					2200	—	—	280	380	300	408
D 2848 LE	8	128/142	14·62	1200	2300	—	—	—	—	375	510
D 2840 LE (L)*	10	128/142	18·27	1350	1800	346	470	365	496	—	—
					2300	—	—	—	—	—	—
D 2842 LE (L)*	12	128/142	21·93	1550	1800	420	571	441	600	—	—
					2300	—	—	—	—	559	760

T = Turbocharged model
L = Turbocharged and intercoded model
*From August 1987 the D 2840 LE will be uprated from 635hp to 820hp and will be known as the D 2840 LXE. Similarly, the D 2842 LE will be uprated from 760hp to 900hp and will be designated D 2842 LXE. The existing models will be maintained in the sales programme. The dry weight of the D 2842 LXE is 1580kg.

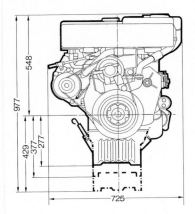
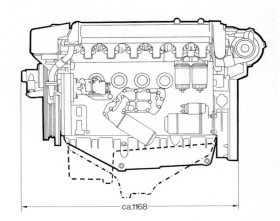

MAN Model D 0226 MLE, dimensions (mm)

MAN Model D 0226 MLE marine diesel

D 2866 LE

TYPE: Four-stroke, direct injection.
CYLINDERS: 6 cylinder in-line, wet replaceable cylinder liners.
ASPIRATION: Turbocharged inter-cooled.
COOLING: Water circulation by centrifugal pump fitted on engine.
LUBRICATION: Forced-feed lubrication by gear pump, lubrication oil cooler in cooling water circuit of engine.
GENERATOR: Bosch three-phase generator with rectifier and transistorised governor type K1, 28V, 35A.
STARTER MOTOR: Bosch solenoid operated starter type KB, 24V, 5·4kW.
TECHNICAL DATA
Bore/stroke: 128/155mm
Volume: 11·97 litres
Compression ratio: 15·5:1
Max rating 3: 300kW/402bhp at 2200rpm
Mean effective pressure: 13·7 bar at 2200rpm
Torque: 1302Nm at 2200rpm
Fuel consumption (+5% tolerance) at max rating 3: 214g/kWh at 2200rpm

D 2848 LE

TYPE: Four-stroke, direct injection.
CYLINDERS: 8 cylinders, V-form, wet replaceable cylinder liners.
ASPIRATION: Turbocharged, inter-cooled.
COOLING: Water circulation by centrifugal pump fitted on engine.
LUBRICATION: Force-feed lubrication by gear pump, lubrication oil cooler in cooling water circuit of engine.
INJECTION: Bosch in-line pump with mechanical Bosch speed governor fitted.
GENERATOR: Bosch three-phase generator with rectifier and transistorised governor type K1, 28V, 35A.
STARTER MOTOR: Bosch solenoid-operated starter, type KB, 24V, 6·5kW.
TECHNICAL DATA
Bore/stroke: 128/142mm
Volume: 14·62 litres
Compression ratio: 15·5:1
Max rating 3: 375kW/503bhp at 2300rpm
Mean effective pressure: 13·4 bar at 2300rpm
Torque: 1559Nm at 2300rpm
Fuel consumption (+5% tolerance): 215g/kWh at 2300rpm

D 2840 LXE

(Supercedes D 2840 LE)
FEATURES: Four-stroke marine diesel engine, 10-cylinder, V-form, water-cooled with turbocharger and inter-cooler. Direct injection system.
CRANKCASE AND CRANK ASSEMBLY: Grey cast iron cylinder block, 6-bearing crankshaft with screwed-on balance weights, three-layer type bearings, die forged connecting rods. Replaceable wet-type cylinder liners.
CYLINDER HEADS AND VALVE TRAIN: Individual cylinder heads of grey cast iron, overhead valves, one intake and one exhaust valve per cylinder, valve actuation via tappets, push rods and rocker arms. Six-bearing camshaft, shrunk-fit valve seat inserts.
LUBRICATION SYSTEM: Force-feed lubrication by gear pump, oil-to-water oil cooler, full-flow oil filter, changeover type optionally.
FUEL SYSTEM: Bosch in-line injection pump with mechanical speed governor, fuel supply pump, fuel filter, changeover type optionally.
INTAKE AND EXHAUST SYSTEM: Viscous air filter, water-cooled exhaust manifold connected in engine cooling circuit.
SUPERCHARGING: Turbochargers, water-cooled in fresh water circuit, sea water-cooled inter-cooler.
ELECTRICAL SYSTEM: Two-pole starter, 6·5kW, 24V, two-pole alternator 28V, 120A, additional alternator 28V available with 35A, 55A or 120A on request.
APPLICATIONS: Yachts, customs and police patrol boats.
TECHNICAL DATA
Bore/stroke: 128/142mm
Volume: 18·271 litres

MAN Model D 2866 LE marine diesel

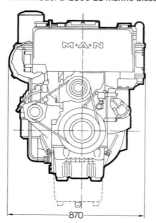
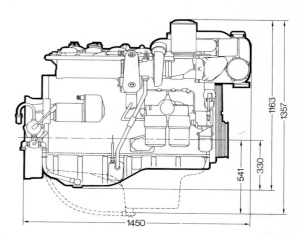

MAN Model D 2866 LE, dimensions (mm)

MAN Model D 2848 LE

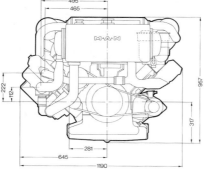

MAN Model D 2848 LE, dimensions (mm)

Compression ratio: 13·5:1
Rotation locking on flywheel: Anti-clockwise
Weight of engine, dry with cooling system: 1380kg
Speed: 2300rpm
Duty 3, max rating: 603kW/820hp
Mean effective pressure: 17·2 bar
Torque: 2504Nm
Mean specific fuel consumption (+ 5%): 220g/kWh

D 2842 LXE

(Supercedes D 2842 LE)
FEATURES: Four-stroke marine diesel engine, 12-cylinder, V-form, water-cooled with turbo-charger and inter-cooler. Direct injection system.
CRANKCASE AND CRANK ASSEMBLY: Cylinder block of grey cast iron. Replaceable wet-type cylinder liners. Seven-bearing crankshaft with screwed-on balance weights, 3-layer type bearings, die-forged connecting rods.
CYLINDER HEADS AND VALVE TRAIN: Individual cylinder heads of grey cast iron, over-head valves, one intake and one exhaust valve per cylinder, valve actuation via tappets, push rods and rocker arms. Seven-bearing camshaft, shrunk-fit valve seat inserts.
LUBRICATION SYSTEM: Force-feed lubric-ation by gear pump, oil-to-water oil cooler, full flow oil filter, changeover type optionally.
FUEL SYSTEM: Bosch in-line injection pump with mechanical speed governor, fuel supply pump, fuel filter, changeover type optionally.
INTAKE AND EXHAUST SYSTEM: Viscous air filter, water-cooled exhaust manifold con-nected in engine cooling circuit.
SUPERCHARGING: Turbochargers, water-cooled in fresh water circuit, sea water-cooled inter-cooler.
ELECTRICAL SYSTEM: Two-pole starter, 6·5kW, 24V, two-pole alternator 28V, 120A, additional alternator 28V with 35A, 55A or 120A on request.
APPLICATIONS: Yachts, customs and police boats.
TECHNICAL DATA
Bore/stroke: 128/142mm
Volume: 21·931 litres
Compression ratio: 13·5:1
Rotation locking on flywheel: Anti-clockwise
Weight of engine, dry with cooling system: Approx 1580kg
Speed: 2300rpm
Duty 3, max rating: 662kW/900hp
Mean effective pressure: 15·7 bar
Torque: 2749Nm
Mean specific fuel consumption (+ 5%): 220g/kWh

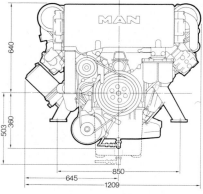
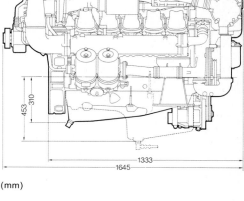

MAN Model D 2840 LXE, marine diesel, dimensions (mm)

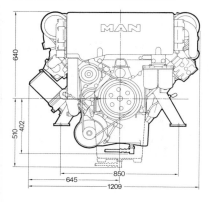

MAN Model D 2842 LXE marine diesel

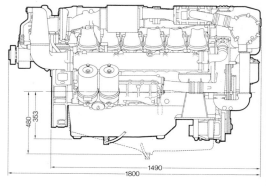

MAN Model D 2842 LXE, dimensions (mm)

MTU

Motoren-und Turbinen-Union Friedrichshafen GmbH

Olgastrasse 75, Postfach 2040, 7990 Friedrichshafen 1, Federal Republic of Germany

Telephone: (07541) 291
Telex: 734280-0 MT D

Dr Ing Hans Dinger, *President*
Hubert Dunkler, *Executive Vice President*
Dr Ing Peter Beer, *Senior Vice President*
Prof Dr Ing Wolfgang Heilmann, *Senior Vice President*
Dr Ing Wolfgang Hansen, *Senior Vice President*
Günther Welsch, *Senior Vice President*

The MTU group consists of MTU München and MTU Friedrichshafen.

MTU Friedrichshafen comprises the two plants of the former Maybach Mercedes-Benz Motoren-bau GmbH at Friedrichshafen and is owned by MTU München. MTU München in turn is owned by Daimler-Benz AG.

MTU diesel engines for catamaran, hydrofoil and hovercraft propulsion and similar high-speed craft

Engine model		Engine speed rpm	Fuel stop power Overload power		Engine dry weight (basic engine)	
			kW	hp (metric)	kg	lb
6V 183 AA 91	(OM 421)*	2300	154	209	852	1879
8V 183 AA 91	(OM 422)*	2300	200	272	1018	2245
10V 183 AA 91	(OM 423)*	2300	254	345	1178	2597
12V 183 AA 91	(OM 424)*	2300	301	409	1338	2950
12V 183 TA 91	(OM 424A)*	2300	380	517	1388	2950
12V 183 TC 91	(OM 424LA)*	2300	441	600	1444	3184
6V 396 TB 83		2000	630	855	2060	4540
8V 396 TB 83		2000	840	1140	2570	5670
12V 396 TB 83		2000	1260	1710	3570	7880
12V 396 TB 84		2000	1680	2285	4000	8830
16V 396 TB 83		2000	1680	2285	4800	10 600
16V 396 TB 84		2000	2240	3045	5200	11 480
12V 1163 TB 83		1200	3600	4900	13 900	30 680
16V 1163 TB 83		1200	4800	6530	17 050	37 640
20V 1163 TB 83		1200	6000	8160	20 500	45 255

* original Mercedes-Benz designation on which types the corresponding MTU engines are based

The areas of activity of the two MTU companies are as follows:

MTU München:

Development, production and support of lightweight, advanced-technology gas turbines mainly for aircraft applications.

MTU Friedrichshafen:

Development, production and application of high-performance diesel engines.

MTU Friedrichshafen is the development and production centre for high-performance diesel engines of Maybach and Mercedes-Benz origin and embodies the experience of these companies in diesel engine technology. In addition to diesel engines, MTU Friedrichshafen is responsible for industrial and marine gas turbine sales and application engineering.

In the field of hydrofoils, surface effect ships, catamarans and other high-speed craft MTU can draw from decades of experience with 230 engines having been supplied for the propulsion of hydrofoils starting as early as 1955 when an MB 820 engine was delivered for the first PT 20 hydrofoil built by Cantiere Navale Rodriquez (nowadays Rodriquez Cantieri Navali SpA) in Messina.

Currently the 183, 396 and 1163 engine families are offered for propulsion of these special types of craft. These engines cover a wide range of power. In the accompanying table the standard power outputs are listed; these, however, may have to be adjusted depending on the application, the power demand and the operating profile. The outputs are based on ambient conditions of 27°C air intake temperature and 27°C sea water temperature.

In addition to the delivery of the propulsion engine MTU can lay-out, design and deliver complete propulsion packages including the interface engineering and the technical assistance during installation and the start-up phase. An example is the re-engining task of the Kometa type hydrofoils where the original engines have been substituted by a powerpack consisting of two 8V 396 TB 83 engines with ZF gears.

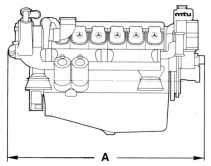
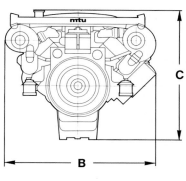

Engine model		A	B	C
6V 183 AA 91	(OM 421)*	1150	1180	1080
8V 183 AA 91	(OM 422)*	1310	1180	1055
10V 183 AA 91	(OM 423)*	1480	1180	1120
12V 183 AA 91	(OM 424)*	1630	1180	1135
12V 183 TA 91	(OM 424A)*	1660	1280	1170
12V 183 TC 91	(OM 424LA)*	1670	1280	1170

Main dimensions (mm) for Series 183 engine family

MTU 16V 396 TB 84

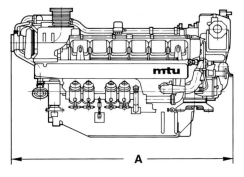
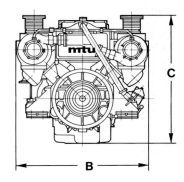

Engine model	A	B	C
6V 396 TB 83	1720	1460	1420
8V 396 TB 83	1950	1440	1420
12V 396 TB 83	2550	1510	1510
12V 396 TB 84	2970	1420	1780
16V 396 TB 83	3020	1580	1700
16V 396 TB 84	3445	1420	1840

Main dimensions (mm) for Series 396 engine family

Engine model	A	B	C
12V 1163 TB 83	3720	1660	2720
16V 1163 TB 83	4410	1660	2810
20V 1163 TB 83	5100	1660	2905

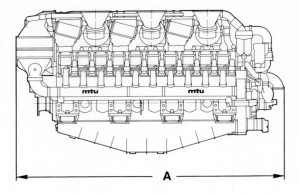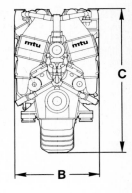

Main dimensions (mm) for Series 1163 engine family

ITALY

CRM MOTORI MARINI SpA

Head Office: Via Manzoni 12, 20121 Milan, Italy

Telephone: (02) 708 326/327 and 784 118
Telex: 334382 CREMME I
Telefax: 796 052

Works: 21053 Castellanza, Via Marnate 41, Italy

Telephone: (0331) 501548

G Mariani, *Director*
Ing B Piccoletti, *Director*
Ing S Rastelli, *Director*
Ing G Venturini, *Director*

CRM has specialised in building lightweight diesel engines for more than 30 years. The company's engines are used in large numbers of motor torpedo boats, coastal patrol craft and privately-owned motor yachts. The engines have also been installed in hydrofoils (*Tehi*).

During the 1960s the company undertook the development and manufacture of a family of 12- to 18-cylinder diesel engines of lightweight high-speed design, providing a power coverage of 600 to 1335kW.

These comprise the 12-cylinder 12 D/S and 12 D/SS and the 18-cylinder 18 D/S, 18 D/SS and BR-1. All are turbocharged with different supercharging ratios. The 12 cylinders are arranged in two banks of six and the 18 cylinders are set out in an unusual 'W' arrangement of three banks of six.

All engines are available in non-magnetic versions; the perturbation field is reduced to insignificant amounts when compensated with the antidipole method.

CRM 18-CYLINDER

First in CRM's series of low weight, high-speed diesel engines, the CRM 18-cylinder is arranged in a 'W' form. Maximum power is 993kW at 2075rpm for the 18 D/S; 1213kW at 2075rpm for the 18 D/SS and 1335kW at 2075rpm for the BR-1. Four 18 D/SS-BR-1 engines, each producing 1850hp at 2020rpm, are being fitted in the Azimut 27m *Atlantic Challenger* in an attempt to break the Atlantic Blue Riband record. The engines will be linked in pairs to two Riva Calzoni waterjets. The attempt at the record will take place in July 1988. The following description relates to 18 D/S, 18 D/SS and BR-1.

TYPE: 18-cylinder in-line W type, four-stroke, water-cooled, turbocharged with different supercharging ratios: 2·1 (18 D/S); 2·4 (18 D/SS) and 2·6 (BR-1).

CYLINDERS: Bore 150mm (5·91in). Stroke 180mm (7·09in). Swept volume 3·18 litres (194·166in³) per cylinder. Total swept volume 57·3 litres (3495in³). Compression ratio 14 : 1.

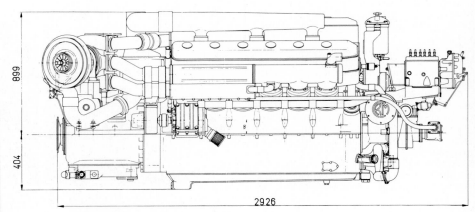

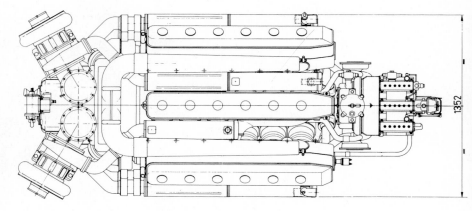

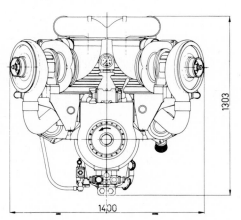

CRM 18 D/SS-BR-1

Separate pressed-steel cylinder frame side members are surrounded by gas-welded sheet metal water cooling jacket treated and pressure-coated internally to prevent corrosion. Cylinders are closed at top by a steel plate integral with side wall

to complete combustion chamber. Lower half of cylinder is ringed by a drilled flange for bolting to crankcase. Cylinder top also houses a spherical-shaped pre-combustion chamber as well as inlet and exhaust valve seats. Pre-combustion chamber is in high-strength, heat and corrosion resistant steel. A single cast light alloy head, carrying valve guides, pre-combustion chambers and camshaft bearings bridges each bank of cylinders. Head is attached to cylinder bank by multiple studs.

PISTONS: Light alloy forgings with four rings, top ring being chrome-plated and bottom ring acting as oil scraper. Piston crowns shaped to withstand high temperatures especially in vicinity of pre-combustion chamber outlet ports.

CONNECTING RODS: Comprise main and secondary articulated rods, all rods being completely machined I-section steel forgings. Big-end of each main rod is bolted to ribbed cap by six studs. Big-end bearings are white metal lined steel shells. Each secondary rod anchored at its lower end to a pivot pin inserted in two lugs protruding from big-end of main connecting rod. Both ends of all secondary rods and small ends of main rods have bronze bushes.

CRANKSHAFTS: One-piece hollow shaft in nitrided alloy steel, with six throws equi-spaced at 120 degrees. Seven main bearings with white metal lined steel shells. 12 balancing counterweights.

CRANKCASE: Cast light alloy crankcase bolted to bed plate by studs and tie bolts. Multiple integral reinforced ribs provide robust structure. Both sides of each casting braced by seven cross ribs incorporating crankshaft bearing supports. Protruding sides of crankcase ribbed throughout length.

VALVE GEAR: Hollow sodium-cooled valves of each bank of cylinders actuated by twin camshafts and six cams on each shaft. Two inlet and two outlet valves per cylinder and one rocker for each valve. End of stem and facing of exhaust valves fitted with Stellite inserts. Valve cooling water forced through passage formed by specially-shaped plate welded to top of cylinder.

FUEL INJECTION: Pumps fitted with variable speed control and pilot injection nozzle.

PRESSURE CHARGER: Two turbochargers Holset type on 18 D/S, and Brown Boveri on the 18 D/SS and BR-1.

ACCESSORIES: Standard accessories include oil and fresh water heat exchangers; fresh water tank; oil and fresh water thermostats; oil filters, fresh water, salt water and fuel hand pumps; fresh water and oil temperature gauges; engine, reverse gear and reduction gear oil gauges; pre-lubrication, electric pump and engine rpm counter. Optional accessories include engine oil and water pre-heater, and warning and pressure switches.

COOLING SYSTEM: Fresh water.

FUEL: Fuel oil having specific gravity of 0·83 to 0·84.

LUBRICATION SYSTEM: Pressure type with gear pump.

OIL: Mineral oil to SAE 40 HD, MIL-L-2104C.

OIL COOLING: By salt water circulating through heat exchanger.

STARTING: 24V 15hp electric motor and 85A, 24V alternator for battery charge, or compressed air.

MOUNTING: At any transverse or longitudinal angle tilt to 20 degrees.

REVERSE GEAR: Bevel crown gear wheels with hydraulically-controlled hand brake.

REDUCTION GEAR: Optional fitting with spur gears giving reduction ratios of 0·561 : 1, 0·730 : 1 and 0·846 : 1. Overdrive ratio 1·18 : 1.

PROPELLER THRUST BEARING: Incorporated in reduction gear. Axial thrust from 29·5kN to 39·5kN (3000 to 4000kgf).

	18 D/S	18 D/SS	BR-1
DIMENSIONS			
Length:	2305mm (90·74in)	2305mm (90·74in)	2305mm (90·74in)
Width:	1352mm (53·22in)	1400mm (55·11in)	1400mm (55·11in)
Height:	1303mm (51·29in)	1303mm (51·29in)	1303mm (51·29in)
Reverse gear:	621mm (24·44in)	621mm (24·44in)	621mm (24·44in)
WEIGHTS			
Engine dry:	1735kg (3845lb)	1760kg (3880lb)	1760kg (3880lb)
Reverse gear:	340kg (750·5lb)	340kg (750·5lb)	340kg (750·5lb)
Reduction gear:	150 to 300kg	150 to 300kg	150 to 300kg
RATINGS (metric)			
Max power:	993kW (1350hp) at 2075rpm	1213kW (1650hp) at 2075rpm	1335kW (1815hp) at 2075rpm
Continuous rating:	919kW (1250hp) at 2020rpm	1103kW (1500hp) at 2020rpm	1213kW (1650hp) at 2020rpm
Specific fuel consumption:	0·238 ± 5% kg/kWh (0·175kg/hph)	0·224 ± 5% kg/kWh (0·165kg/hph)	0·23 ± 5% kg/kWh (0·169kg/hph)
Specific oil consumption:	0·004 ± 5% kg/kWh	0·004 ± 5% kg/kWh	0·004 ± 5% kg/kWh

CRM 18 D/SS-BR-1

End view of CRM 18 D/SS-BR-1

CRM 12-CYLINDER

Second in the CRM series of low weight diesels, the CRM 12-cylinder is a unit with two blocks of six cylinders set at 60 degrees to form a V assembly. The bore and stroke are the same as in the CRM 18 series and many of the components are interchangeable including the crankshaft, bed-plate, cylinders and pistons. The crankcase and connecting rod-assemblies are necessarily of modified design; the secondary rod is anchored at its lower end to a pivot pin inserted on two lugs protruding from the big-end of the main connecting rod. The fuel injection pump is modified to single block housing all 12 pumping elements located between the cylinder banks.

TYPE: 12-cylinder V type, four-stroke, water-cooled, turbo-supercharged with medium super-charging ratio (2·15 for 12 D/S) and light super-charging ratio (2·85 for 12 D/SS).

PRESSURE CHARGER: Two Holset type on 12 D/S and Brown Boveri type on 12 D/SS.

	12 D/S	12 D/SS
DIMENSIONS		
Length:	1909mm (75·15in)	2147mm (84·52in)
Width:	1210mm (47·63in)	1210mm (47·63in)
Height:	1204mm (47·4in)	1310mm (51·57in)
Reverse gear:	621mm (24·44in)	621mm (25·44in)
WEIGHTS, dry		
Engine:	1380kg (2891lb)	1560kg (3443lb)
Reverse gear:	340kg (750lb)	340kg (750lb)
Reduction gear:	150 to 300kg (331 to 662lb)	150 to 300kg (331 to 662lb)
PERFORMANCE RATINGS		
Max power:	687kW (935hp) at 2075rpm	1010kW (1374hp) at 2075rpm
Continuous rating:	625kW (850hp) at 2010rpm	918kW (1248hp) at 2020rpm
Fuel consumption:	0·227kg/kWh ± 5% (0·167kg/hph)	0·238kg/kWh ± 5% (0·175kg/hph)
Oil consumption:	0·004kg/kWh	0·004kg/kWh

FIAT AVIAZIONE SpA

Marine & Industrial Products Department, Via Nizza 312, Turin, Italy

Telephone: (011) 3302543
Telex: 221320 FIATAV I

The LM500 gas turbine is a compact high performance marine and industrial power unit in the 3000 to 6000 shaft horsepower class. General Electric's Marine and Industrial Engine Division and Fiat Aviazione SpA, in a co-operative undertaking, initiated the design programme in July 1978. In January 1980 the first engine began full load testing and the LM500 went into production.

The LM500 is a simple-cycle, two-shaft gas turbine engine with a free power turbine. It incorporates a variable stator compressor, with excellent stall margin capability, driven by an air-cooled, two-stage turbine. It is derived from the TF34 high bypass turbofan aircraft engine which was designed for marine operation in the US Navy's S-3A aircraft and later incorporated in the US Air Force's A-10 aircraft, with the same materials and marine corrosion protection as employed in the very successful LM2500 marine gas turbine. The LM500 incorporates the latest in proven design technology and corrosion-resistant materials to provide a mature design with maximum reliability, component life and time between inspections and overhaul. The LM500 demonstrates higher efficiency than currently available gas turbines in its class and is suited for marine applications requiring low weight and fuel economy.

General Electric Company and Fiat Aviazione SpA have designed the LM500 gas turbine to produce power for marine applications requiring significant fuel economy, compactness, light weight, minimum maintenance, high tolerance to

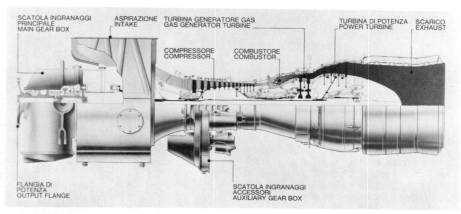

Cutaway of LM500

fouling/deposits, and reliable operation. Such applications include military land craft, hydro-foils, air cushion vehicles, fast patrol boats, cruise power propulsion and on-board electric power generators.

LM500

The LM500 is a simple-cycle, two-shaft gas turbine engine. The single shaft gas generator consists of a 14-stage high pressure compressor with variable inlet guide vanes and variable stator vanes in the first five stages, an annular machined ring combustor with 18 externally mounted fuel injectors and an air-cooled, two-stage HP gas generator turbine. The free power turbine has four stages and the output shaft connecting flange is at the air inlet end of the engine.

AIR INTAKE: The LM500 offers, as optional equipment, an air inlet collector to guide the inlet air from the customer's intake ducting into the engine. The inlet duct is made from aluminium

and provides the structural connection for the forward engine mounts or for the reduction gearbox containing the forward mounts.

An off-engine inlet screen is also offered to prevent objects from entering the compressor.

COMPRESSOR: The compressor is identical to the TF34 and consists of the front frame, accessory drive assembly, compressor rotor and case/vane assembly. The front frame is an uncomplicated four strut aluminium casting and is designed to provide the compressor inlet flowpath, the forward structural support for the engine, support the forward bearings and seals for the gas generator and power turbine rotors, and support the accessory gearbox.

COMBUSTOR: The LM500 combustor is of the TF34 flight engine design. It is an annular through-flow combustor using a machined ring liner construction for long life. Metered fuel is distributed and introduced through 18 central, individually replaceable injectors.

HIGH PRESSURE TURBINE: The LM500 high pressure turbine is a two-stage, fully air-cooled design, identical to the TF34 turbine except for minor changes to improve performance and meet the requirements for marine and industrial applications.

POWER TURBINE: The LM500 power turbine is a four-stage, uncooled, high performance design incorporating aerodynamic and mechanical features and materials identical to the TF34 low pressure turbine. The power turbine rotor structural components are made of inconel 718 material. The four turbine discs carry tip shrouded turbine blades that are attached to the discs with single tang dovetails. The blades are made of René 77 material with the first stage Codep coated. The durability of René 77 alleviates the need for coatings on the other stages. At operating gas temperatures 111°C (200°F) less than the TF34, the LM500 blades have virtually infinite stress rupture life. The structural integrity of the power turbine rotor has been demonstrated to a speed of 9030rpm, 29 per cent over the normal rated speed of the LM500 engine.

LM500

LUBRICATION: The LM500 lubricating oil system provides the following functions: lubricates and cools the gas turbine main bearings; supplies hydraulic fluid for the variable geometry actuation system and fuel metering valve actuator.

The main engine bearings are lubricated from an accessory gearbox-driven lube pump. The scavenge circuit is based on a dry sump system and each bearing sump is scavenged by a separate pump or pump elements driven off the accessory gearbox. All scavenge oil is filtered (coarse screens) prior to entry into the pump elements.

FUEL: The LM500 is designed to operate with marine diesel, diesel, and JP fuels. The fuel system consists of on- and off-engine components. Filtered fuel is supplied by the customer to the fuel pump, which is mounted on the accessory gearbox, where the fuel pressure is increased by a centrifugal boost element and then ported externally to an on-engine last chance fuel filter. From the filter the fuel is routed to an off-engine fuel regulating assembly (FRA) which meters the engine fuel flow according to signals received from the off-engine main electronic control assembly (MECA). Also included in the FRA are two fuel shut-off valves mounted in series for redundancy which are used to shut off the fuel to the engine during normal shutdowns and automatic shut-downs. Fuel is then routed to the on-engine fuel distributor which divides the fuel through separate hose assemblies to 18 fuel injectors.

SPECIFICATION
BASIC ENGINE:
Length overall: 2184mm (86in)
Width: 864mm (34in)
Weight: 580kg (1276lb)
WITH OPTIONAL INLET AND AXIAL EXHAUST DUCT, STARTER KIT AND OUTPUT GEARBOX:
Length overall: 3307mm (130·2in)
Width: 1179mm (46·4in)
Weight: 1031kg (2269lb)

ISOTTA FRASCHINI SpA
Via Milano 7, 21047 Saronno, Italy

Telephone: (02) 9617.1
Telex: 332403 BRIF I

Isotta Fraschini SpA is a company belonging to the Group Iri Fincantieri and owns two factories, one located at Saronno, 15 km north of Milan, and one at Bari. About 1000 people are now employed. Diesel engines are produced in the range of 200 to over 2500hp.

Current high-speed marine diesel engines are the Series ID 36 (6, 8, 12 and 16 cylinders), Series ID 38 (6 cylinders) and Series ID 32 (6 cylinders).

The engine type notation is defined as follows:
N naturally aspirated engine
S turbocharged engine
SS turbocharged and inter-cooled engine
6, 8, 12 and 16 Six, eight, twelve and sixteen cylinders respectively
V vee
P flat
L in-line
M special

ID 32 SERIES
Marine diesel.
CYLINDER NUMBER AND ARRANGEMENT: 6 in-line.
VERSION: Vertical (L).
INJECTION TYPE: Direct.
STROKE/BORE: 126/128mm.
DISPLACEMENT: 9·60 litres.
VALVES PER CYLINDER: 2.
MAIN BEARINGS: 7.
AIR FEEDING OPTIONS: N, S or SS.
COMPRESSION RATIO: 1:16·4 (N); 1:16·6 (S, SS).

ID 32 6L (Vertical Engine)

Engine type	Outputs according to ISO 3046/1						Weights ±5% kg
	A 2700rpm		B 3000rpm		C 3000rpm		
	kW	cv/hp	kW	cv/hp	kW	cv/hp	
ID 32 N 6L	132	180	154	210	162	220	705
ID 32 S 6L	176	240	198	270	213	290	725
ID 32 SS 6L	206	280	247	335	257	350	750

ID 32 SS 6LM (Vertical Engine)

Engine type	Outputs according to ISO 3046/1						Weights ±5% kg
	A 2800rpm		B 3000rpm		C 3000rpm		
	kW	cv/hp	kW	cv/hp	kW	cv/hp	
ID 32 SS 6LM	228	310	266	362	294	400	750

Note:
A = Continuous output for workboats
B = Continuous output for fast boats
C = Engine max nominal output

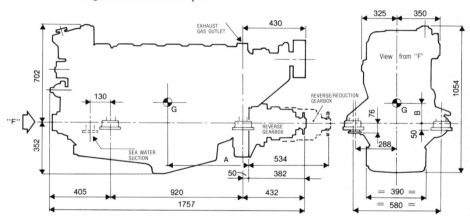

ID 32 diesel engines overall dimensions (mm)

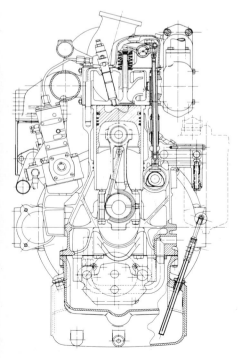

ID 32 SS 6L engine cross-section

ID 32 marine diesel engine

DIRECTION OF ROTATION: Clockwise or anti-clockwise.
FUEL: A.S.T.M. No 2 (class A according to BSS)
LUBRICATION OIL: SAE 30 or 40 – HD suppl. 3.
STARTING: Electric 24V dc.
COOLING: Water-cooling by means of heat exchangers.
OIL SUMP CONTENTS: 20kg.
ANGLE OF MAX TILT, REAR OR FRONT DOWN: 15°.

ID 36 SERIES

Marine diesel.

The ID 36 series are four-stroke direct injection diesels. There are 6- to 16-cylinder versions of this engine.

CRANKCASE: Single block cast iron.
CYLINDERS: Incorporated into the crankcase with wet type removable and replaceable centrifugal cast iron liners.
HEADS: Single type for each cylinder, in special cast iron with four valves (two intake and two exhaust) and inserted valve seats.
CRANKSHAFT: Alloy steel forged, normalised and hardened with nitrided journals and crank pins.
MAIN BEARINGS: Special steel coated with anti-friction alloy layer.
CONNECTING RODS AND CON-ROD BEARINGS: Side-by-side con-rod in high resistance alloy steel, special steel bushing coated with an anti-friction alloy layer, big-end bearings made of steel bushing coated with nickel-treated bronze.
PISTON: Light alloy type, oil-jet cooled.
TIMING SYSTEM: Gear driven and transmitted by means of satellites to various components (crankshaft, water pump, oil pump, injection pump etc).
INJECTION PUMP: Single block-type with variable delivery pumping elements driven by a mechanical speed governor. Feeding by gear pump.
LUBRICATION: Engine driven force-feed lubrication by means of two gear pumps. Each pump is equipped with a safety valve inside the engine.
WATER-COOLING: By means of gear driven centrifugal pump. The circuit is set to have an entry and an exit from the exchanger.
TURBOCHARGING AND INTER-COOLING: By means of two turbochargers activated by exhaust gases and two heat exchangers.

In the hp/rpm table below, light duty refers to passenger craft, hydrofoil speed boats, supply vessels and light tug boats. Heavy duty refers to tugs, fishing vessels and dredgers.

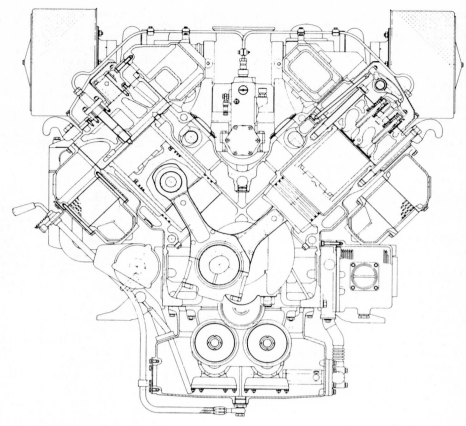

ID 36 series cross section

Engine type	Workboats hp/rpm light duty	heavy duty	Pleasure craft hp/rpm	Dimensions (mm) A	B	C
ID 36 N 6 V	300/1650	300/1650	—			
ID 36 SS 6 V	660/1800	540/1800	800/1900	1400	1200	1467
ID 36 N 8 V	400/1650	400/1650	—			
ID 36 SS 8 V	880/1800	720/1800	1050/1900	1605	1200	1478
ID 36 N 10 V	500/1650	500/1650	—			
ID 36 SS 10 V	1100/1800	900/1800	1300/1900	1865	1200	1478
ID 36 N 12 V	600/1650	600/1650	—			
ID 36 SS 12 V	1320/1800	1080/1800	1600/1900	2285	1200	1529
ID 36 N 16 V	800/1650	800/1650	—			
ID 36 SS 16 V	1760/1800	1440/1800	2100/1900	3090	1380	1695

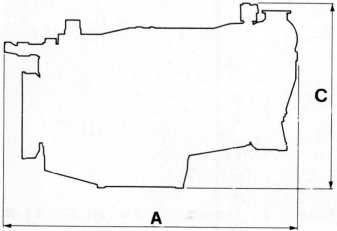
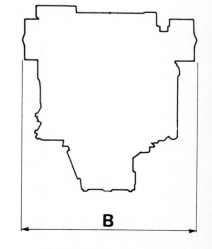

ID 36 series outline dimensions (mm)

ID 38 SERIES

Marine diesel.
TYPE: ID 38 6V.
CYLINDER NUMBER AND ARRANGE-
MENT: 6 V 90°.
INJECTION TYPE: Direct.
STROKE/BORE: 126/128mm.
DISPLACEMENT: 9·73 litres.
VALVES PER CYLINDER: 2.
MAIN BEARINGS: 4.
AIR FEEDING: N, S or SS.
COMPRESSION RATIO: 1:16·4 (N); 1:15·6 (S, SS).
DIRECTION OF ROTATION: Clockwise or anti-clockwise.
FUEL: A.S.T.M. No 2D (class A according to BSS).
LUBRICATING OIL: SAE 30 or 40 - HD suppl. 3.
STARTING: Electric 24V dc or by compressed air.
COOLING: Water cooling by means of radiator or heat exchangers.
OIL SUMP CONTENTS: 20kg.
ANGLE OF MAX TILT, REAR OR FRONT DOWN: 30°.
DRY WEIGHT: 780kg.

N-S-SS type engines

CRANKCASE: High tensile cast iron.
CYLINDER HEADS: 2 high quality cast iron.
PISTONS: Aluminium.
CONNECTING RODS: High tensile alloy steel.
FUEL INJECTION PUMP: Block type.
FUEL FEEDING PUMP: Diaphragm type.
OIL PUMP: Gear type.
OIL FILTER: 1 cartridge type.
AIR CLEANER: Dry type.
SPEED GOVERNOR: Mechanical type.
STARTING MOTOR: 1-6hp, 24V dc.
ENGINE WATER COOLING: By heat exchanger or radiator.
LUBRICATION: By oil-to-water heat exchanger.
ENGINE WATER PUMP: Belt driven type.
THERMOSTATIC VALVES: 2.
EXHAUST GAS MANIFOLDS: Water-cooled type.

S-SS type engines only

AIR CHARGING: By means of 2 turbochargers.

SS type engines only

CHARGING AIR INTER-COOLING: By means of air-to-water heat exchangers.

Optional equipment

Engine anti-vibration mountings
Flywheel housing
Instruments panel
Battery charger – 700W, 24V dc
Compressed air starting device
Sea water pump

ID 36 series marine diesel

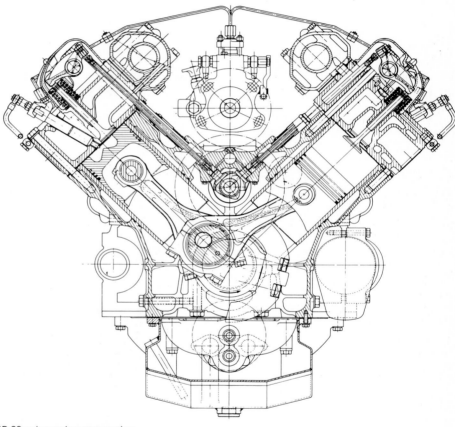

ID 38 series engine cross section

ID 38 series marine diesel

Notes
Types of service
C = Continuous unlimited service with blocked output.
D = Continuous service for fast military and pleasure craft without overload.
CONDITIONS
For continuous service C and D:-
  Ambient air temperature: 27°C
  Sea water temperature at heat exchanger inlet: 32°C
  Relative humidity: 60%
DERATING
For air temperatures of 40°C consider a 6% derating.

	Outputs according to ISO 3046/1							
	Work C				Pleasure and Military D		Racing Applications	
Engine type	2700rpm		2900rpm		3000rpm		3150rpm	
	kW	hp	kW	hp	kW	hp	kW	hp
ID 38 N 6 V	132	180	143	195	331	450		
ID 38 SS 6 V	257	350	294	400				
Examples of application	Works and fishing boats, tugs and ferries				Fast craft, catamarans, hydrofoils, motor yachts and patrol boats			
ID 38 SS 6V SA							588	800

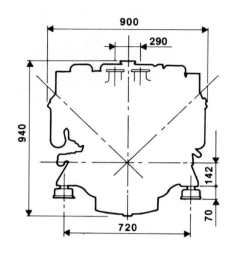
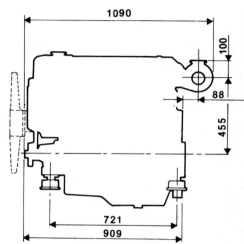

ID 38 series engine and gearbox dimensions (mm)

ID 38 SS 6V SA, 800hp at 3150rpm, for offshore racing applications

SWEDEN

SAAB-SCANIA

Scania Division: S-15187 Södertälje, Sweden

Telephone: 755 81000
Telex: 13479 SCANMOTS
Telefax: 755 83180

Scania marine diesels cover a range of 112kW (152hp) to 252kW (343hp). Power test codes are ISO 3406, DIN 6271, BS 5514 and SAE J 1349.

The manufacturers claim that as a result of extensive controlled tests, their engines consistently show low consumption of fuel and oil. Fuel consumption is commonly found to be 10% below that of comparable engines of other makes, and in some cases even lower. One of the reasons for good economy in lube oil, and the elimination of coking in piston ring grooves is that Keystone type piston rings are fitted. An additional advantage of Keystone rings is that, in conjunction with other design features, they enable full load to be assumed on starting without jeopardising engine life. Scania also claim that their patented two-stage cyclone/centrifugal oil cleaner is an important factor effecting clean lube oil, engine efficiency and serviceability.

Marine diesel engines
RATINGS

Engine type	Turbo	Inter-cooled	Displace-ment dm³	Config-uration	Continuous uninterrupted service[1] kW (hp) rpm	Propulsion Duty Medium duty commercial service[2] kW (hp) rpm	Light duty commercial service[3] kW (hp) rpm	Specific fuel consumption[1] at 1500rpm g/kWh (g/hph)
Heat exchanger								
DN 11 (171)	—	—	11·0	6 L	112(152)2000	—(—)—	126(171)2200	222(163)
DN 11 (215)	—	—	11·0	6 L	134(182)2000	—(—)—	158(215)2200	220(162)
DS 11 (285)	T	—	11·0	6 L	—	—	—	
DS 11 (317)	T	—	11·0	6 L	188(256)1800	218(296)1800	233(317)2100	208(153)
DSI 11 (350)	T	I	11·0	6 L	214(291)1800	238(324)1800	257(350)2100	209(154)
DS 14 (412)	T	—	14·2	V 8	252(343)1800	282(383)1800	303(412)2100	206(152)
DSI 14 (450)	T	I	14·2	V 8	279(379)1800	310(421)1800	332(450)2100	204(150)
Keel cooling								
DN 9 (174)	—	—	8·5	6 L	104(141)1900	—(—)—	128(174)2200	219(161)
DS 9 (226)	T	—	8·5	6 L	140(190)1900	158(215)1900	166(226)2200	207(152)
DS 9 (252)	T	—	8·5	6 L	154(209)1900	176(239)1900	185(252)2200	205(151)
DN 11 (215)	—	—	11·0	6 L	134(182)2000	—(—)—	158(215)2200	220(162)
DS 11 (317)	T	—	11·0	6 L	188(256)1800	218(296)1800	233(317)2100	208(153)
DS 14 (412)	T	—	14·2	V 8	252(343)1800	282(383)1800	303(412)2100	206(152)

WEIGHTS[5]

Engine type	Length	Max dimensions (mm) Width	Height	Weight dry (kg)
with heat exchanger				
DN 11	1574	756	1097	1085
DS 11	1732	756	1097	1110
DSI 11	1732	756	1106	1135
DS 14	1314	1202	1165	1250
DSI 14	1314	1202	1197	1325
for keel cooling				
DN 9	1332	775	1123	845
DS 9	1360	755	1072	860
DN 11	1388	692	1090	985
DS 11	1546	702	1090	1010
DS 14	1314	1152	1165	1180

[1] **Continuous uninterrupted service.** No limitations on load factor or running hours.

[2] **Medium-duty commercial service.** Limited to 8h per 24h or continuous running max 2000h/year.

[3] **Light-duty commercial service.** Intermittent service. Full power 1h in 6h. No limitation on annual running hours; or (turbocharged engines only) full power 1h in 2h and running time max 1000h/year.

[4] **Power conditions:** Prime power for continuous operation under varying load factors, with 10% overload capacity for 1h in 12h. Speed variations as per ISO 3046/IV, class A1.

[5] **Weights and dimensions.** Quoted are purely a guide; there are variations for each engine type. Weights exclude oil and water.

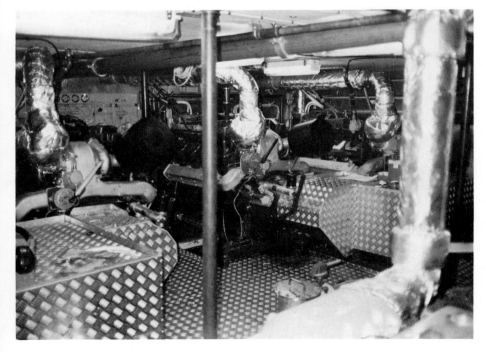

Installation of four Saab-Scania DSI 14 diesels in Marinteknik Verkstads 41·9m *Cinderella*

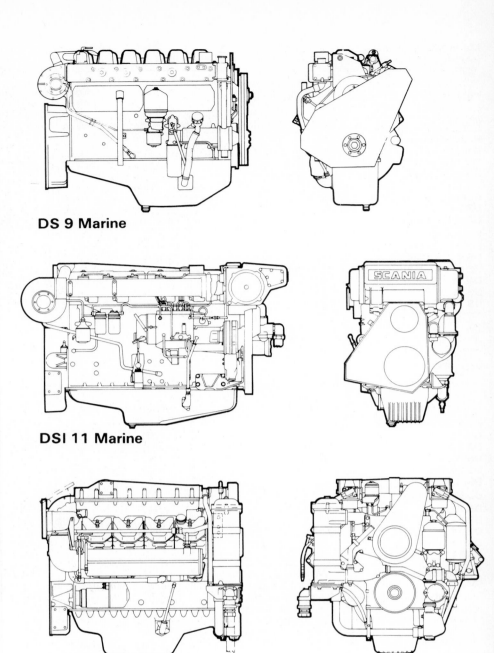

DS 9 Marine

DSI 11 Marine

Saab-Scania marine diesel engines

DSI 14 Marine

AB VOLVO PENTA

S-405 08 Gothenburg, Sweden

Telephone: (31) 235460
Telex: 20755 PENTA S
Telefax: (31) 510595

Pehr G Gyllenhammer, *Chairman*
Bo Nyhlen, *President*
Ole Johansson, *Director*
Ernst Knappe, *Director*
Anders Lindström, *Director*
Hans Eric Odin, *Director*
Union Group: Bengt Segeheden
    Sven Timm

AB Volvo Penta designs, manufactures and markets engines, transmissions, accessories and equipment for marine and industrial use.

Part of the Volvo Group, the sales of Volvo Penta engines account for around 4 per cent of sales within the transport equipment sector. The engines are used in ferries, pilot vessels, fishing boats and all types of leisure craft, as well as for industrial propulsion or power generation applications.

Production facilities are in the USA, Brazil and Mexico plus four locations in Sweden. Volvo Penta products are sold in 130 countries worldwide. Approximately 2600 people are employed either directly or indirectly by Volvo Penta.

Volvo Penta TAMD 31 direct injection 3-litre engine

Volvo Penta diesels for commercial craft can provide over 420hp. The company has updated the entire engine range covering two-, three- and four-cylinder commercially rated diesels as well as the in-line six series.

New to the range are the 31 and 41 series, 3- and 4-litre models, plus the 61/71 series 6- and 7-litre engines developing up to 357hp light duty.

All eight units in the 31 and 41 series feature direct injection which reduces thermal stress, heat and pressure loss resulting in lower fuel consumption and longer life expectancy. Fuel consumption is around 15% less than with the equivalent pre-chamber ignition diesels. The new turbocharger is fresh water-cooled, and the pistons are oil-cooled to increase engine life.

Further up the power range are the 6- and 7-litre models TAMD 61 and TAMD 71. Both are turbocharged, after-cooled in-line, six diesels for which the latest three-dimensional computer techniques have been used as a means towards reducing engine weight and providing optimum rigidity. Increased power has been achieved by refining the direct fuel injection system and modifying the turbocharging and after-cooling operations. A newly designed anti-vibration mounting helps to reduce noise and vibration; it also facilitates easier installation. Further improvements include a new cylinder head with flame barrier to increase gas test life; a revised method for tightening head bolts to give better sealing; and new intake/exhaust channels giving identical swirl in each cylinder to reduce smoke and increase fuel economy.

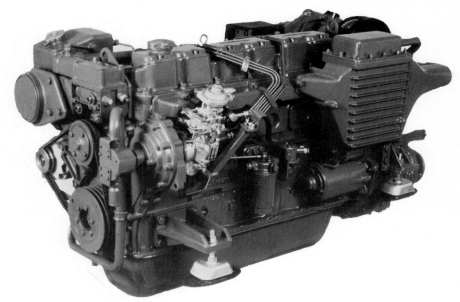

Volvo Penta TAMD 41 (ex 41A)

Volvo Penta TAMD 61 (ex 61A), in-line, six turbocharged and after-cooled 6-litre engine

VOLVO PENTA 3- TO 12-LITRE MARINE PROPULSION ENGINES

TAMD 31	hp	kW	rpm
Flywheel output,			
light duty:	130	96	3800
medium duty:	110	81	3250

Weight: 385kg including MS4 gearbox
Displacement: 2·39 litres

TAMD 41	hp	kW	rpm
Flywheel output,			
light duty:	200	147	3800
medium duty:	170	125	3250

Weight: 465kg including MS4 gearbox
Displacement: 3·59 litres

TAMD 61	hp	kW	rpm
Flywheel output,			
light duty:	306	225	2800
medium duty:	228	168	2500
heavy duty:	187	140	2200

Weight: 680kg excluding gearbox
Displacement: 5·48 litres

TAMD 71	hp	kW	rpm
Flywheel output,			
light duty:	357	263	2500
medium duty:	292	213	2500
heavy duty:	222	163	2000

Weight: 810kg excluding gearbox
Displacement: 6·73 litres

TMD 100	hp	kW	rpm
Flywheel output,			
light duty:	272	200	2000
medium duty:	258	190	1800
heavy duty:	238	175	1800

Weight: 1180kg excluding gearbox
Displacement: 9·6 litres

TAMD 121	hp	kW	rpm
Flywheel output,			
light duty:	422	310	2000
medium duty:	387	285	1900
heavy duty:	367	270	1800

Weight: 1360kg excluding gearbox
Displacement: 11·98 litres

The following definitions define the duty ratings given in the accompanying table.

LD: Light Duty

Engines with this power setting are for applications where rated power for rated speed is utilised

Volvo Penta TAMD 71A, in-line, six turbocharged and after-cooled 7-litre engine, now TAMD 71

for short periods only, followed by cruising at reduced speed; also when operating time is short and does not exceed 500 hours per year.
Examples: Certain patrol boats, fireboats, rescue boats and charter craft.

MD: Medium Duty

Engines with this power setting are intended for applications where rated power at rated speed is utilised during part of the operating time only (up to ⅓), followed by cruising at reduced speed. Operating time should not exceed 2000 hours per year, or on average, one shift per working day.

Examples: Patrol boats, pilot boats, police boats and certain fishing vessels.

HD: Heavy Duty

Engines with this power setting are intended for applications where neither PD, LD nor MD applies and rated power at rated speed could be needed continuously. No interruption or load cycling is expected other than for service and maintenance.
Examples: Tugboats, ferries, fishing boats and most commercial applications in displacement vessels.

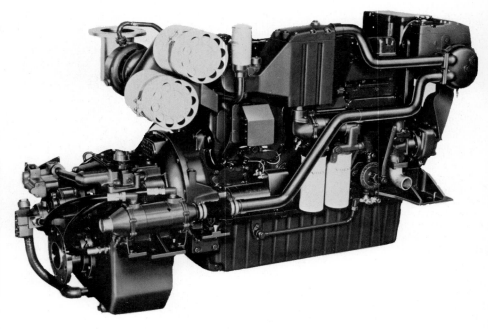

Volvo Penta TAMD 121C

Volvo Penta TMD 100 (ex TMD 100C)

UNION OF SOVIET SOCIALIST REPUBLICS

A IVCHENKO (AI)

This design team, which was headed by the late A Ivchenko, is based in a factory at Zaporojie in the Ukraine, where all prototypes and pre-production engines bearing the 'AI' prefix are developed and built. Chief designer is Lotarev and chief engineer, Tichienko. The production director is M Omeltchenko.

First engine with which Ivchenko was associated officially was the 55hp AI-4G piston engine used in the Kamov Ka-10 ultra-light helicopter. He later progressed via the widely used AI-14 and AI-26 piston engines, to become one of the Soviet Union's leading designers of gas turbine engines.

Two AI-20s in de-rated, marinised form and driving two three-stage waterjets power the Burevestnik, the first Soviet gas-turbine hydrofoil to go into series production, and a single AI-24 drives the integrated lift/propulsion system of the Sormovich 50-passenger ACV. Two AI-20s, each rated at about 3600shp continuous, are also thought to power the Lebed amphibious assault landing craft.

IVCHENKO AI-20

The Ivchenko design bureau is responsible for the AI-20 turboprop engine which powers the Antonov An-10, An-12 and Ilyushin Il-18 airliners and the Beriev M-12 Tchaika amphibian.

Six production series of this engine had been built by the spring of 1966. The first four series, of which manufacture started in 1957, were variants of the basic AI-20 version. They were followed by two major production versions, as follows:
AI-20K. Rated at 3945ehp. Used in Il-18V, An-10A and An-12.

AI-20M. Uprated version with T-O rating of 4190ehp (4250ch e). Used in Il-18D/E, An-10A and An-12.

Conversion of the turboprop as a marine power unit for hydrofoil waterjet propulsion (as on the Burevestnik) involved a number of changes to the engine. In particular it was necessary to hold engine rpm at a constant level during conditions of varying load from the waterjet pump. It was also

1750hp Ivchenko AI-23-CI marine gas turbine

necessary to be able to vary the thrust from the waterjet unit from zero to forward or rearwards thrust to facilitate engine starting and vessel manoeuvring.

Constant speed under variable load was achieved by replacing the engine's normal high pressure fuel pump with a special fuel regulator pump. The waterjet pump was modified to have a variable exit area and was fitted with an air valve enabling a variable amount of air to be passed into the intake just ahead of the pump rotor. With less air passing through the waterjet, unit load on the engine increased, and vice versa if the air flow was increased by opening the air valve.

The fuel regulator pump was designed to maintain engine rpm constant and to regulate output while the AI-20 was driving the waterjet unit. Steady running conditions were shown to be satisfactorily maintained by the engine under all operating conditions—and rpm and turbine temperature were held within the limits laid down for the aircraft turboprop version. Engine rpm did not fluctuate outside ±2·5% of its set speed when loading or unloading the waterjet unit.

During development of the marinised AI-20, the normal aircraft propeller and speed governor were removed and the turboprop was bench tested over the full range of its operating conditions. This demonstrated stable engine performance throughout, from slow running to normal rpm. These tests were run initially using aviation kerosene Type TS-1 fuel, and then diesel fuels Types L and DS.

Following satisfactory results on the bench, the test engine was mounted on a self-propelled floating test bed equipped with a waterjet propulsion unit. Further tests with this configuration were also satisfactorily concluded, including starting checks with varying degrees of submersion of the pump section of the waterjet unit.

Electrical starting of the engine up to slow running speed (equal to approximately 25% of rated rpm) was shown to take 70 to 85 seconds. For starting and ignition at ambient conditions below 10°C, fuel pre-heating is employed and modified igniters are fitted. With this equipment, starts have been achieved down to minus 12°C.

Based on this experience, the marinised AI-20 for the twin-engined Burevestnik was rated at 2700hp at 13 200rpm. At this power output, the hydrofoil achieved speeds of up to 97km/h (60mph). Specific fuel consumption was 320-330g (0·71-0·73lb)/hph.

Testing with the Burevestnik revealed a number of operating characteristics: when the two AI-20s were running while the vessel was moored or manoeuvring, residual exhaust thrust from the turbines occurred and this is required to be balanced by a negative or reverse thrust from the waterjet by partially closing the unit's nozzle flaps. This increased the load on the engine, however, and caused a rise in fuel consumption.

Experience showed that with a normal start following a series of wet starts, any fuel which had accumulated in the jet pipe ignited. This resulted in a sharp rise in turbine temperature and back pressure, and flame emerged from the ejection apertures into the engine compartment and exhaust nozzle. To circumvent this, the ejection apertures were covered with a metal grid, and a spray of water is provided at the exhaust nozzle prior to starting.

Based on an overhaul life for the turboprop AI-20 of several thousand hours, special techniques have been applied to the marinised version to increase its service life. These include: the use of high quality assembly procedures for the engine; efficient design of the air intake and exhaust duct; adoption of appropriate procedures for starting and on-loading of the main and auxiliary turbines at all ambient temperature conditions; utilisation of highly-skilled servicing methods of the installation during operation.

The AI-20 is a single-spool turboprop, with a ten-stage axial-flow compressor, cannular combustion chamber with ten flame tubes, and a three-stage turbine, of which the first two stages are cooled. Planetary reduction gearing, with a ratio of 0·08732 : 1, is mounted forward of the annular air intake. The fixed nozzle contains a central bullet fairing. All engine-driven accessories are mounted on the forward part of the compressor casing, which is of magnesium alloy.

The AI-20 was designed to operate reliably in all temperatures from −60°C to +55°C at heights up to 10 000m (33 000ft). It is a constant speed engine, the rotor speed being maintained at 21 300rpm by automatic variation of propeller pitch. Gas temperature after turbine is 560°C in both current versions. TBO of the AI-20K was 4000 hours in the spring of 1966.

WEIGHTS
DRY
AI-20K: 1080kg (2380lb)
AI-20M: 1039kg (2290lb)

PERFORMANCE RATINGS
Max T-O:
AI-20K: 4000ch e (3945ehp)
AI-20M: 4250ch e (4190ehp)
Cruise rating at 630km/h (390mph) at 8000m (26 000ft):
AI-20K: 2250ch e (2220ehp)
AI-20M: 2700ch e (2663ehp)

SPECIFIC FUEL CONSUMPTION
At cruise rating:
AI-20K: 215g (0·472lb)/hph
AI-20M: 197g (0·434lb)/hph

OIL CONSUMPTION
Normal: 1 litre/h (1·75 pints/h)

IVCHENKO AI-24

In general configuration this single-spool turboprop engine, which powers the An-24 transport aircraft, is very similar to the earlier and larger AI-20. Production began in 1960 and the following data refers to engines of the second series, which were in production in the spring of 1966.

A single marinised version, developing 1800shp, drives the integrated lift/propulsion system of the Sormovich 50-passenger ACV.

An annular ram air intake surrounds the cast light alloy casing for the planetary reduction gear, which has a ratio of 0·08255 : 1. The cast magnesium alloy compressor casing carries a row of inlet guide vanes and the compressor stator vanes and provides mountings for the engine-driven accessories. These include fuel, hydraulic and oil pumps, tacho-generator and propeller governor.

The ten-stage axial-flow compressor is driven by a three-stage axial-flow turbine, of which the first two stages are cooled. An annular combustion chamber is used, with eight injectors and two igniters.

The engine is flat-rated to maintain its nominal output to 3500m (11 500ft). TBO was 3000 hours in the spring of 1966.

LENGTH (overall): 2435mm (95·87in)

WEIGHT
Dry: 499kg (1100lb)

PERFORMANCE RATING
Max T-O with water injection: 2859ch e (2820ehp)

KUZNETSOV
KUZNETSOV

NK-12M

The NK-12M, which powers the Aist amphibious assault ACV and is thought to power the Babochka and Sarancha hydrofoils, is the world's most powerful turboprop engine. In its original form it developed 8948kW (12 000ehp). The later NK-12MV is rated at 11 033kW (14 795ehp) and powers the Tupolev Tu-114 transport, driving four-blade, contra-rotating propellers of 5·6m (18ft 4in) diameter. As the NK-12MA, rated at 11 185kW (15 000shp), it powers the Antonov AN-22 military transport, with propellers of 6·2m (20ft 4in) diameter.

The NK-12M has a single 14-stage axial-flow compressor. Compression ratio varies from 9:1 to 13:1 and variable inlet guide vanes and blow-off valves are necessary. A can-annular-type combustion system is used. Each flame tube is mounted centrally on a downstream injector, but all tubes merge at their maximum diameter to form an annular secondary region. The single turbine is a five-stage axial. Mass flow is 65kg (143lb)/s.

The casing is made in four portions from sheet steel, precision welded. An electric control for variation of propeller pitch is incorporated to maintain constant engine speed.

NK-12MV

(Aviation International, Paris)

DIMENSIONS
Length: 6000mm (236⅛in)
Diameter: 1150mm (45¼in)
WEIGHT
Dry: 2350kg (5181lb)

PERFORMANCE RATINGS
T-O: 11 033kW (14 795ehp)
Nominal power: 8826kW (11 836ehp) at 8300rpm
Idling speed: 6600rpm

SOLOVIEV

P A Soloviev, *Designer in Charge of Bureau*

SOLOVIEV D-30

This two-spool turbofan, in marinised form, was believed to provide the thrust for a power-augmented ram-wing project. It powers the Tu-134 twin-engined airliner and is derived from the D-20. Major portions of the core and carcass are similar, but the complete powerplant is larger, more powerful and efficient than the D-20.
TYPE: Two-shaft turbofan (by-pass turbojet).
AIR INTAKE: Titanium alloy assembly, incorporating air bleed anti-icing of centre bullet and radial struts.

D-30KU turbofan

FAN: Four-stage axial (LP compressor). First stage has shrouded titanium blades held in disc by pinned joints. Pressure ratio (T-O rating, 7700rpm, S/L, static), 2·65:1. Mass flow, 125kg (265lb)/s. By-pass ratio, 1:1.
COMPRESSOR: Ten-stage axial (HP compressor). Drum and disc construction largely of titanium. Pressure ratio (T-O rating, 11 600rpm, S/L static), 7·1:1. Overall pressure ratio, 17·4:1.
COMBUSTION CHAMBER: Can-annular, with 12 flame tubes fitted with duplex burners.
FUEL GRADE: T-1 and TS-1 to GOST 10227-62 (equivalent to DERD. 2494 or MIL-F-5616).
TURBINE: Two-stage HP turbine. First stage has cooled blades in both stator and rotor. LP turbine also has two stages. All discs air-cooled on both sides, and all blades shrouded to improve efficiency and reduce vibration. All shaft bearings shock-mounted.
JET PIPE: Sub-sonic fixed-area type, incorporating main and by-pass flow mixer with curvilinear ducts of optimum shape. D-30-2 engine of Tu-134A fitted with twin-clamshell (Rolls-type) reverser.
LUBRICATION: Open type, with oil returned to tank.
OIL GRADE: Mineral oil MK-8 or MK-8P to GOST 6457-66 (equivalent to DERD. 2490 or MIL-0-6081B). Consumption in flight is not more than 1kg/h.
ACCESSORIES: Automatic ice-protection system, fire extinguishing for core and by-pass flows, vibration detectors on casings, oil chip detectors and automatic limitation of exhaust gas temperature to 620°C at take-off or when starting and to 630°C in flight (five minute limit). Shaft-driven accessories driven via radial bevel-gear shafts in centre casing, mainly off HP spool, accessory gearboxes being provided above and below centre casing and fan duct. D-30-2 carries constant-speed drives for alternators.
STARTING: Electric dc starting system with STG-12TVMO starter/generators.
DIMENSIONS
Overall length: 3983mm (156⅔in)
Base diameter of inlet casing: 1050mm (41¼in)
WEIGHT
Dry: 1550kg (3417lb)
PERFORMANCE RATINGS
T-O: 66·68kN (14 990lb)
Long-range cruise rating: 11 000m (36 000ft)
Mach 0·75: 12·75kN (2866lb)
SPECIFIC FUEL CONSUMPTION
T-O: 17·56mg/Ns (0·62lb/h/lb)
Cruise as above: 21·81mg/Ns (0·77lb/h/lb)

SUDOIMPORT

5 Kaliayevskaya Str, Moscow 103006, USSR

Telephone: 251 05 05/299 52 14
Telex: 411272/387 SUDO SU

Soviet industry has developed a variety of marine diesel engines, selected models of which have been installed in the Krasnoye Sormovo series of hydrofoil craft. Most popular of these are the 1100hp M401 powering the Kometa hydrofoil, and the 1200hp M50 powering the Byelorus, Chaika, Meteor, Mir, Raketa, Sputnik, Strela and Vikhr hydrofoils. A third marine diesel engine is the 3D12 with a continuous rating of 300hp. A version of this engine is installed in the Nevka hydrofoil.

These and other marine diesels are available through Sudoimport, the USSR marine export, import and repair organisation.

TYPE M400

TYPE: Water-cooled, 12-cylinder, V-type four-stroke supercharged marine diesel engine.
CYLINDERS: Two banks of six cylinders set at 30 degrees, each bank comprising cast aluminium alloy monobloc with integral head. Pressed-in liner with spiral cooling passages comprises inner alloy steel sleeve with nitrided working surface, and outer carbon steel sleeve. Each monobloc retained on crankcase by 14 holding-down studs. Bore 180mm (7·09in). Stroke 200mm (7·87in). Cubic capacity 62·4 litres (3810in³). Compression ratio 13·5 : 1.
SUPERCHARGING: Single-stage centrifugal supercharger, mechanically driven and providing supercharging pressure of at least 1·55kg/cm² (22lb/in²) at rated power.
CRANKCASE: Two-part cast aluminium alloy case with upper half carrying cylinder monoblocs, and transmitting all engine loads.
CYLINDER HEADS: Integral with cylinder monoblocs.
CRANKSHAFT: Six-crank seven-bearing crankshaft in nitrided alloy steel with split steel shells, lead bronze lined with lead-tin alloy bearing surface. Spring damper at rear end reduces torsional vibrations.
CONNECTING RODS: Master and articulated rods, with master connected to crankshaft by split big-end with lead bronze lining. Articulated rods connected by pin pressed into eye of master rods.
PISTONS: Forged aluminium alloy with four rings, upper two of which are of trapeziform cross-section. Alloy steel floating gudgeon pin. Piston head specially shaped to form combustion chamber with spherical cylinder head.
CAMSHAFTS: Two camshafts acting direct on valve stems.

VALVES: Four valves in each cylinder, two inlet and two exhaust. Each valve retained on seat by three coil springs.
COOLING: Forced circulation system using fresh water with 1 to 1·1% potassium dichromate added. Fresh water pump mounted on forward part of engine. Fresh water and lubricating oil leaving the engine are cooled by water-to-water and water-to-oil coolers, in turn cooled by sea water circulated by engine-mounted sea water pump.
SUPERCHARGING: Single-stage centrifugal supercharger, mechanically driven and providing

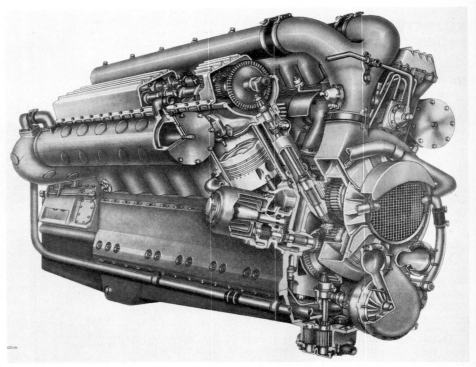

M400

supercharging pressure of at least 1·55kg/cm² (22lb/in²) at rated power.

LUBRICATION: Comprises delivery pump together with full-flow centrifuge; twin-suction scavenge pump, double gauze-type strainers at inlet and outlet to oil system; and electrically-driven priming pump to prime engine with oil and fuel.

FUEL INJECTION: Closed-type fuel injection with hydraulically-operated valves, giving initial pressure of 200kg/cm² (2845lb/in²). Each injector has eight spray orifices forming 140-degree conical spray. High pressure 12-plunger fuel injection pump with primary gear pump. Two filters in parallel filter oil to HP pump.

STARTING: Compressed air system with starting cylinder operating at 75 to 150kg/cm² (1067 to 2134lb/in²) two disc-type air distributors and 12 starting valves.

GOVERNOR: Multi-range indirect-action engine speed governor with resilient gear drive from pump camshaft. Governor designed to maintain preset rpm throughout full speed range from minimum to maximum.

EXHAUST SYSTEM: Fresh water-cooled exhaust manifolds fastened to exterior of cylinder blocs. Provision made for fitting thermocouple or piezometer.

REVERSING: Hydraulically-operated reversing clutch fitted to enable propshaft to run forwards, idle or reverse with constant direction of crankshaft rotation.

MOUNTING: Supports fitted to upper half of crankcase for attaching engine to bedplate.

DIMENSIONS
Length: 2600mm (102½₀in)
Width: 1220mm (48½in)
Height: 1250mm (49⅛in)

PERFORMANCE RATINGS
Max: 1100hp at 1800rpm
Continuous: 1000hp at 1700rpm

FUEL CONSUMPTION
At continuous rating: Not over 193g (0·425lb)/hph

OIL CONSUMPTION
At continuous rating: Not over 6g (0·013lb)/hph

TYPE 3D12

TYPE: Water-cooled, 12-cylinder, V-type, four-stroke marine diesel engine.

CYLINDERS: Two banks of six cylinders in jacketed blocks with pressed-in steel liners. Bore 150mm (5·9in). Stroke 180mm (7·09in). Cubic capacity 38·8 litres (2370in³). Compression ratio 14 to 15 : 1.

CRANKCASE: Two-part cast aluminium alloy case with upper half accommodating seven main bearings of steel shell, lead bronze lined type. Lower half carries oil pump, water circulating pump and fuel feed pump.

CYLINDER HEADS: Provided with six recesses to accommodate combustion chambers. Each chamber is connected via channel to inlet and outlet ports of cylinder bloc.

CRANKSHAFT: Alloy steel forging with seven journals and six crankpins. Pendulum anti-vibration dampers fitted on first two webs to reduce torsional vibration.

CONNECTING RODS: Master and articulated rods of double-T section forged in alloy steel. Master rod big-end bearings have steel shells, lead bronze lined. Small-end bearings of master rods and both bearings of articulated rods have bronze bushes.

PISTONS: Aluminium alloy.

CAMSHAFTS: Carbon steel camshafts with cams and journals hardened by high frequency electrical current.

COOLING: Closed water, forced circulation type incorporating centrifugal pump, self suction sea water pump and tubular water cooler.

LUBRICATION: Forced circulation type with dry sump, incorporating three-section gear pump, oil feed pump, wire-mesh strainer with fine cardboard filtering element and tubular oil cooler.

FUEL INJECTION: Rotary fuel feed pump, twin felt filter, plunger fuel pump with device to stop engine in event of oil pressure drop in main line. Closed-type fuel injectors with slotted filters.

3D12

Plunger pump carries variable-speed centrifugal governor for crankshaft rpm.

STARTING: Main electrical starting system, with compressed air reverse system.

REVERSE-REDUCTION GEAR: Non-coaxial type with twin-disc friction clutch and gear-type reduction gear giving optional ratios, forwards, of 2·95 : 1, 2·04 : 1 or 1·33 : 1 and 2·18 : 1 astern.

DIMENSIONS
Length: 2464mm (97·0in)
Width: 1052mm (41⅖in)
Height: 1159mm (45⅜in)

WEIGHT
Dry fully equipped: 1900kg (4189lb)

PERFORMANCE RATING
Continuous: 300hp at 1500rpm

FUEL CONSUMPTION
At continuous rated power: 176g (0·388lb)/hph

OIL CONSUMPTION
At continuous rated power: Not over 9g (0·02lb)/hph

M401A

The M401A, fitted to the Voskhod and the latest variants of the Kometa and Raketa, is based on the M50. The new engine is more reliable than its predecessor and its development involved the redesigning of a number of units and parts, as well as the manufacturing of components with a higher degree of accuracy, which necessitated the employment of the latest engineering techniques.

The engine is manufactured in left- and right-hand models. These differ by the arrangement on the engine housing of the fresh water pump drive and the power take-off for the shipboard compressor.

TYPE: Water-cooled, 12-cylinder, V-type four-stroke supercharged marine diesel.

CYLINDERS: Two banks of six cylinders set at 60 degrees. Monobloc is a solid aluminium casting. Pressed into monobloc are six steel sleeves with spiral grooves on the outer surface for the circulation of cooling water. Bore 180mm (7·09in). Stroke 200mm (7·87in). Compression ratio 13·5 : 0·5.

CRANKCASE: Two-piece cast aluminium alloy case with upper half carrying cylinder monoblocs and transmitting all engine loads.

CYLINDER HEADS: Integral with cylinder monobloc.

CRANKSHAFT: Six-crank, seven bearing crankshaft in nitrided alloy steel with split steel shells, lead-tin bronze lined with lead tin alloy bearing surface.

CONNECTING RODS: Master and articulated rods, with master connected to the crankshaft by split big-end, lined with lead tin bronze. Articulated rod connected to crankshaft by a pin pressed into its eye ring.

PISTONS: Forged aluminium alloy with five rings. Top two steel rings, one cast iron of rectangular section and the two bottom rings, in cast iron and steel, are oil control rings fitted in a common groove.

CAMSHAFTS: Two, acting directly on valve stems.

VALVES: Four in each cylinder, two inlet and two exhaust. Each retained on seat by three coil springs.

SUPERCHARGING: Two, Type TK-18H superchargers, each comprising an axial-flow turbine and a centrifugal compressor mounted on a common shaft with a vane diffuser and volute. A silencer can be installed on the compressor air inlet. Turbine casing cooled with fresh water from the diesel engine cooling system.

GOVERNOR: Multi-range indirect action engine speed governor with resilient gear drive from pump camshaft. Designed to maintain preset rpm throughout full speed range.

LUBRICATION: Delivery pump with full-flow centrifuge, scavenge pump, double gauge strainers and electrically driven priming pump to power engine with oil and fuel.

COOLING: Double-circuit forced circulation system using fresh water with 1 to 1·1% potassium dichromate to GOST 2652-71. Fresh water pump mounted on engine. Fresh water and lubricating oil leaving engine are cooled by water-to-water and water-to-oil coolers in turn cooled by sea water circulated by engine-mounted sea water pump.

STARTING: Compressed air system with two disc-type air distributors and twelve starting valves.

REVERSING: Hydraulically operated reversing clutch to enable propeller shaft to run forwards, idle or reverse. Manual control available in emergency.

PERFORMANCE RATING

Rated power at ahead running under normal atmospheric conditions and at rated rpm: 1000hp

Rated rpm at ahead running: 1550

Max hourly power at max rpm: 1100hp

Max rpm at ahead running: 1600

Max power at astern running: 250hp

Minimum rpm at astern running (with the diesel engine control lever at reverse stop): 750

Max specific fuel consumption at rated power (with operating generator, hydraulic pump and the power take-off for compressor): 172g/ehp/h + 5%

Max specific oil burning losses at rated power: 5g/ehp/h

FUEL

Diesel fuel Grade (GOST 4749—49) Oil MC-20 (GOST 4749—49) with additive (GOST 8312-57) 3% in weight

DIMENSIONS
Length: (with muffler at intake) 2825mm (111⅒in)
Length: (without muffler at intake) 2720mm (107in)
Width: 1252mm
Height: 1250mm

WEIGHT
Weight (dry) with all units and pipe lines mounted: 2000kg (4409lb)

PERFORMANCE
Sense of power take-off flange rotation (if viewed from turbo-supercharger)
of right-hand diesel engine: Clockwise
of left-hand diesel engine: Counter-clockwise
Operating life (until major overhaul): 2500 hours

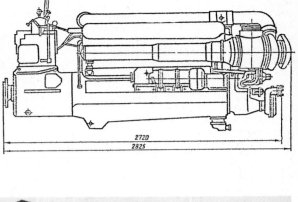

M401A

M503A AND M504
The M503A is a multi-cylinder radial-type diesel which was introduced on the Osa missile fast-attack craft in the late 1950s and subsequently installed in the Shershen and probably the Pchela hydrofoil.

It is radically different from any other marine diesel in use today because of its radial or 'star' configuration, peculiar to aero-engines, and also because of the number of cylinders incorporated in the design.

The M503A has 42 cylinders in six seven-cylinder blocks, but a more powerful version, the M504, has 56 cylinders in eight seven-cylinder blocks. M504, which develops 5000hp at 2000rpm, powers the Osa II, Turya, Matka and Stenka.

A tropicalised version of the M504, derated to 4000hp, is installed in export Osa IIs and other craft designed for these engines and destined to operate in warm climates. Designation of the tropicalised M504 is M504T.

A twin-pack version, employing two M504s with a common gearbox driving a single shaft, is employed in the Nanuchka missile corvette. Nanuchka has three M504 twin-packs, each developing 10 000hp, giving a total maximum output of 30 000hp.

On the M504 the drive and reduction gear is mounted directly on the engine, enabling the propeller shaft to run forwards or in reverse. Lubricating and water-cooling systems are cooled by sea water circulated under ram pressure when making headway and pumped in when going astern or when stopped. A supercharger is mounted on the forward end of the engine and can be powered either by drive from a main turbine or mechanical transmission from the crankshaft.

The most economical operation of the engine is attained at 1400 to 1700rpm, at which point the specific fuel consumption is 160 to 165g/hph. Economy at low power is achieved by cutting out some of the cylinders. Running hours between overhaul should be 1500 provided that the engine is operated at maximum output for only 10 per cent of that time.

The following details apply to the M504 only:
PERFORMANCE RATING
Max output: 5000hp at 2000rpm
CYLINDERS: Total 56, mounted in eight banks of seven.
Cylinder diameter: 16mm
PISTON STROKE: 17mm
WEIGHT (including gearbox and drive): 7200kg
POWER TO WEIGHT RATIO: 1·44kg/hp
DIMENSIONS
Length: 4·4m
Width: 1·65m
Height: 1·64m

M503

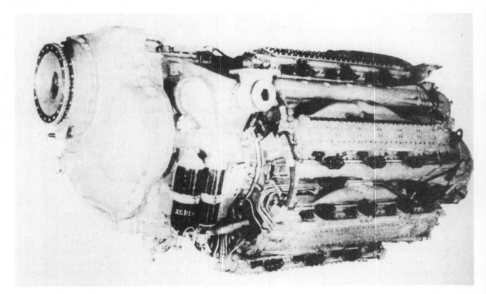

M503

UNITED KINGDOM

PAXMAN DIESELS LIMITED
(a management company of GEC Diesels Limited)
Paxman Works, Hythe Hill, Colchester, Essex CO1 2HW, England

Telephone: (0206) 575151

Telex: 98151 GENERAL G
Telefax: (0206) 577869

VALENTA RP200-2-CM
(Previously the Mk 2)
TYPE: Direct injection, V-form, 8-, 12-, 16- and 18-cylinder, turbocharged and water-cooled, four-stroke engine.

OUTPUT: 1000-5000bhp, 1000-1600rpm.
BORE AND STROKE: 197 × 216mm (7·75 × 8·5in).
SWEPT VOLUME (per cylinder): 6·57 litres (401in³).
HOUSING: High quality SG iron.
CRANKSHAFT AND MAIN BEARINGS: Fully nitrided shaft carried in aluminium tin pre-

finished steel-backed main bearings. Engine fully balanced against primary and secondary forces.

CONNECTING RODS: Fork and blade type with steel-backed, aluminium tin-lined large end (forked rod) and steel-backed, lead bronze-lined, lead tin flashed bearings (blade rod).

PISTONS: Two-piece pistons, forged steel crown and forged aluminium skirt. Three compression rings in steel crown; one oil control in skirt.

CYLINDER HEAD: High grade casting carrying four-valve direct injection system.

LINERS: Wet type seamless steel tube, chrome plated bore and water side surface honeycombed for surface oil retention.

FUEL INJECTION: Single unit pumps. Pump plungers and camshaft lubricated from main engine pressure system. Feed and injection pump driven from engine drive and gear train; a fuel reservoir and air bleed system fitted. Multi-hole injectors spray fuel into the toroidal cavity in the top of piston. Injectors retained by clamp. Sleeved connection inside cover (Valenta).

GOVERNOR: Standard hydraulic 'Regulateurs Europa' unit with self-contained lubricating oil system; mechanical, electrical or pneumatic controls. Alternative makes available.

PRESSURE CHARGING AND INTER-COOLING: Water-cooled exhaust-gas-driven turboblowers mounted above engine. Air-to-water inter-cooler.

LUBRICATION: Pressure lubrication to all bearing surfaces; single pump system. Oil coolers mounted externally and integral with engine; sea water cooled (Valenta). Full flow single or duplex oil filter can be supplied.

FRESH WATER COOLING: Single pump at free end, shaft-driven from drive end gear train. Thermostatic control valve mounted above pump, giving quick warm-up and even temperature control of water; oil thermostat.

EXHAUST: Single outlet from turboblower; water-cooled manifolds.

STARTING: Air, electric or hydraulic starting.

FUEL: Gas oil to BS.2869/1983 Class A1 and A2 or equivalent, and certain gas turbine fuels. Other classes of fuel subject to specification being made available.

LUBRICATING OIL: Oils certified to MIL-L-46152 (with a TBN of not less than nine).

OPTIONAL EXTRA EQUIPMENT: Gearboxes, starting control systems, and all associated engine ancillary equipment necessary for marine applications.

Applications

Recent applications of Valenta diesels in high-speed craft include the following:

Valenta 8RP200-1-CM Limbongan T patrol boat for Malaysian MoE

Valenta 12RP200-1-CM Brooke Marine patrol boat for Malaysian Customs

Valenta 12RP200-1-CM Brooke Marine patrol boat for Barbados

Valenta 16RP200-1-CM Karlskrona patrol boat for Trinidad and Tobago

Valenta 16RP200-1-CM Penang Yard patrol boat for Malaysian Police

Valenta 16RP200-1-CM MSE Yard patrol boat for Malaysian Customs

Valenta 16RP200-1-CM two Vosper Thornycroft

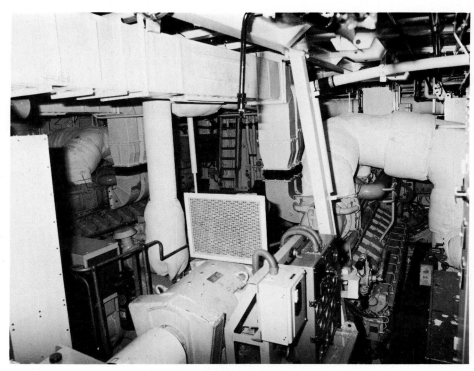

Valenta 18RP200-1-CM installation in Province Class fast missile attack craft

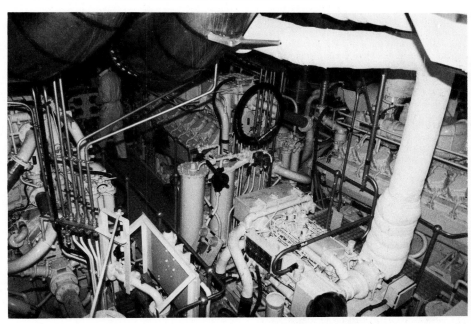

Valenta 16RP200-1-CM installations in Vosper Thornycroft ferries for Shun Tak Shipping, Hong Kong

ferries for Shun Tak Shipping (High Speed Ferries)

Valenta 16RP200-1-CM Picchiotti patrol boat for Seychelles

Valenta 16RP200-1-CM Bollinger Shipyard Island Class for United States Coast Guard

Valenta 18RP200-1-CM Vosper Thornycroft

Province Class for the Sultanate of Oman

Valenta 18RP200-1-CM Vosper Thornycroft for fast strike craft

12 SET CWM Sheng Hsing Shipbuilding Taiwan for Dragin Shipping Co

12 SET CWM Fairey Marinteknik Protector fast patrol boat for HM Customs and Excise

---

PERKINS ENGINES (SHREWSBURY) LTD

Sentinel Works, Shrewsbury, Shropshire SY1 4DP, England

Telephone: 0743 52262
Telex: 35171 ROYCAR G

J F Davaney, *Managing Director*
B M Parsisson, *Director and General Manager, Sales*

Perkins marine diesel engines are built at the former Rolls-Royce diesel engine factory at Shrewsbury following its purchase in 1984.

CV 12 M 800

A 12-cylinder, 800bhp turbocharged, charge-cooled marine diesel engine suitable for a wide variety of purposes. One application has been in the British Royal Navy Training Boats (20·0m, 32 tonnes standard displacement) for which they are rated at 611kW (820hp). More recently, a pair have been installed in the InCat *Bottom Time II*.

TYPE: 12 cylinders in 60° 'V' form, water-cooled.
BORE: 135mm.
STROKE: 152mm.
COMPRESSION RATIO: 14·5:1.
CAPACITY: 26·11 litres.
INDUCTION: Turbocharged, charge cooled.

ROTATION: Anti-clockwise viewed on flywheel.
NET DRY WEIGHT: 2800kg with Twin Disc MGN 332-1.

STANDARD FEATURES

Thermostatically controlled, pressurised, closed circuit coolant system with gear driven centrifugal fresh water pump

Fresh water heat-exchanger cooling with 'Gilmec' self-priming raw water pump

Fresh water-cooled exhaust manifolds and turbochargers

Charge-air coolers integral with induction manifolds

Dry type air-cleaners

Perkins CV 12 M 800

Fresh water-cooled lubricating oil cooler, integral with three full-flow, spin-on element lubricating oil filters

Twin engine mounted fuel filters with spin-on elements

Fuel line water separator (loose)

Front and rear engine mounting brackets

Front power take-off facility

SAE No 0 Flywheel Housing

Flywheel suitable for marine reverse/reduction gears to SAE J 620d size 18

24V, insulated return marine electrics with 35A alternator and associated electrical equipment, including battery master switch and start button

Instrumentation includes: Tachometer, ammeter, coolant temperature gauge, engine oil pressure gauge, oil pressure switch, coolant temperature switch, and engine hours counter

CV 8 M 536

A new 8-cylinder 536bhp turbocharged, charge-cooled marine diesel engine introduced in 1985 and used to provide auxiliary power for the British Royal Navy Type 23 Frigate.

Perkins CV 8 M 536

POWER RATINGS

	Max power	rpm	Fuel consumption
Pleasure:	600kW	2100	162·3 litres/h
Light dry commercial:	550kW	2100	149·1 litres/h
Heavy duty commercial:	455kW	1800	115·9 litres/h

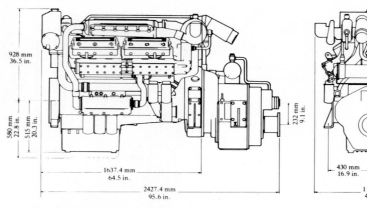

Perkins CV 12 M 800

TYPE: Eight cylinders in 90° 'V' form, liquid cooled.

BORE: 135mm.

STROKE: 152mm.

COMPRESSION RATIO: 14·5:1.

CAPACITY: 17·41 litres.

INDUCTION: Turbocharged, charge cooled.

ROTATION: Anti-clockwise viewed on flywheel.

NET DRY WEIGHT: 1425kg.

STANDARD FEATURES

Thermostatically controlled, closed circuit coolant system with gear driven centrifugal fresh water pump

Fresh water heat-exchanger cooling

Self-priming raw water pump

Fresh water-cooled exhaust manifolds

Raw water-cooled charge air coolers

Dry type air-cleaners

Fresh water-cooled lubricating oil system with spin-on lubricating oil filters

SAE 1 flywheel housing

Flywheel suitable for marine reverse/reduction gears

24V insulated return marine electrics

Instrumentation

Closed circuit breather system

Front and rear engine mountings

Front power take-off facility

Low lubricating oil pressure switch

High coolant temperature warning switch

Low coolant level warning switch

POWER RATINGS

	Max power	rpm	sfc
Pleasure:	400kW	2100	222g/kWh
Light dry commercial:	343kW	1900	
Heavy duty commercial:	298kW	1800	207g/kWh

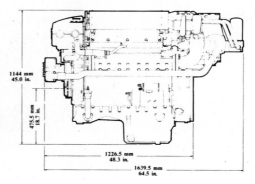 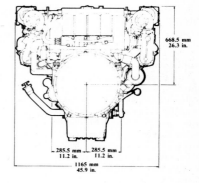

Perkins CV 8 M 536

ROLLS-ROYCE plc
(Industrial & Marine)

Ansty, Coventry, West Midlands CV7 9JR, England

Telephone: 0203 624000
Telex: 31636 G

Frank Turner, *Director, Industrial and Marine*
Robin Bussell, *Head of Marine Business*

In April 1967 Rolls-Royce plc formed a new division merging the former industrial and marine gas turbine activities of Rolls-Royce and Bristol Siddeley. The new division was known as the Industrial & Marine Gas Turbine Division of Rolls-Royce.

In May 1971, Rolls-Royce (1971) Limited was formed combining all the gas turbine interests of the former Rolls-Royce company, and in 1987

the company, now called Rolls-Royce plc, was returned to the private sector.

Rolls-Royce plc offers a wider range of industrial and marine gas turbines based on aero-engine gas generators than any other manufacturer in the world. Marinised gas turbines at present being produced or on offer include the Tyne, Olympus and Spey.

Over 2350 marine and industrial engines are in service or have been ordered for operation around the world. Twenty-five navies and nine civil operators have selected the company's marine gas turbines to power naval craft, following the initial orders from the Royal Navy in the late 1950s.

HYDROFOILS: Proteus 15M/553 gas turbines power the seven Sparviero class hydrofoil craft of the Italian Navy.

HOVERCRAFT: The Gnome powers the BHC SR.N5 and SR.N6. The Proteus powers the SR.N4 and the BH.7.

MARINE GNOME

TYPE: Gas turbine, free-turbine turboshaft.

AIR INTAKE: Annular 15°C.

COMBUSTION CHAMBER: Annular.

FUEL GRADE

DERD 2494 Avtur/50 Kerosene.

DERD 2482 Avtur/40 Kerosene.

Diesel fuel: BSS 2869 Class A, DEF 1402 or NATO F75.

TURBINE: Two-stage axial-flow generator turbine and a single-stage axial-flow free power turbine.

BEARINGS: Compressor rotor has a roller bearing at the front and a ball bearing at the rear. Gas generator turbine is supported at the front by the compressor rear bearings, and at the rear by a roller bearing.

Single-stage power turbine is supported by a roller bearing behind the turbine disc and by a ball bearing towards the rear of the turbine shaft.

JET PIPE: Exhaust duct to suit installation.

ACCESSORY DRIVES: Accessory gearbox provides a drive for : the fuel pump, the hydro-mechanical governor in the flow control unit, the centrifugal fuel filter, the dual tachometer and the engine oil pump.

LUBRICATION SYSTEM: Dry sump.

OIL SPECIFICATION: DERD 2487.

MOUNTING

Front: Three pads on the front frame casing, one on top, one on each side

Rear: Without reduction gearbox, mounting point is the rear flange of the exhaust duct centre-body. With reduction gearbox, mounting points are provided by two machined faces on the reduction gearbox

STARTING: Electric.

DIMENSIONS

Length: 1666mm (65⅜in)

Width: 462mm (18⅛in)

Height: 518mm (20⅓in)

PERFORMANCE RATINGS

Max: 1435bhp

Ratings are at max power-turbine speed, 19 500rpm. A reduction gearbox is available giving an output speed of 6650rpm.

SPECIFIC FUEL CONSUMPTION

Max: 271g (0·597lb)/bhp

OIL CONSUMPTION

0·67 litres (1·2 pints)/h

Power turbine: 0·84 litres (1·5 pints)/h

MARINE PROTEUS

TYPE: Gas turbine, free-turbine turboprop.

AIR INTAKE: Radial between the compressor and turbine sections of the engine. 15°C.

COMBUSTION CHAMBERS: Eight, positioned around the compressor casing.

FUEL GRADE: DEF 2402—Distillate diesel fuel.

TURBINE: Four stages coupled in mechanically independent pairs. The first coupled pair drives the compressor, the second pair forms the free power turbine which drives the output shaft.

BEARINGS: HP end of compressor rotor is carried by roller bearing, the rear end by a duplex ball bearing. Compressor turbine rotor shaft is located by a ball thrust bearing, as is the power turbine rotor.

JET PIPE: Exhaust duct to suit installation.

ACCESSORY DRIVES: All accessories are driven by the compressor or power turbine systems. Compressor driven accessories are: compressor tachometer generator, fuel pump and centrifugal oil separator for the breather. The power turbine tachometer generator and governor are driven by the power turbine. The main oil pressure pump and also the main and auxiliary scavenge pumps are driven by both the compressor and power turbines through a differential gear.

LUBRICATION SYSTEM: The engine is lubricated by a single gear type pump connected by a differential drive to both the compressor and power turbine systems.

OIL SPECIFICATION: OEP 71. DERD 2479/1 or DERD 2487 (OX 38).

MOUNTING: Three attachment points comprise two main trunnions, one on each side of the engine close to the diffuser casing, and a steady bearing located beneath the engine immediately aft of the air intake. Engines are supplied with integrally-mounted reduction gears giving maximum output shaft speeds of 5240, 1500 or 1000rpm depending on the gearbox selected.

DIMENSIONS

Length: 3147mm (123¾in)

Diameter: 1067mm (42in)

WEIGHT

Dry: 1414kg (3118lb)

PERFORMANCE RATINGS

Sprint: 5000bhp

Max: 4500bhp

SPECIFIC FUEL CONSUMPTION

At max rating: 256g (0·566lb)/bhp

OIL CONSUMPTION

Average: 0·28 litres (0·5 pints)/h

MARINE SPEY (SM2 and SM3)

Rolls-Royce produces two versions of the SM series of marine propulsion units based on the Spey, a high performance fully marinised machine derived from the Spey aero gas turbine.

The two types are available for light craft, offering high thermal efficiency (in excess of 35 per cent) and up to date features. They were designed to bridge the gap in the range of current marine gas turbines and to provide high-speed or cruising power for a wide range of present and future designs of warships.

For strike missile craft, corvettes or surface effect ships, a lightweight version, designated the SM2 is available.

A second variant, suitable for small craft, SWATH ships and hydrofoils is designated the SM3.

Following development of the SM series of marine gas turbine in a programme sponsored by the British Ministry of Defence, the engine is in production for three navies.

TYPE: Marine gas turbine incorporating two independently-driven compressors and a purpose-designed smoke free power turbine.

GAS GENERATOR CHARACTERISTICS

AIR INTAKE: Direct entry, fixed, without intake guides.

LP COMPRESSOR: 5 axial stages.

HP COMPRESSOR: 11 axial stages.

COMBUSTION SYSTEM: Turbo-annular type with ten interconnected straight flow flame tubes.

TURBINES: Impulse reaction, axial-type. Two HP and two LP stages.

EXHAUST: Fixed volume.

STARTING: Air/gas starter motor.

FUEL SYSTEM: Hydromechanical high pressure system with automatic acceleration and speed control.

FUEL GRADE: Diesel fuel Grade 'A'. DEF 2402 or NATO F75.

LUBRICATION SYSTEM: Self-contained gear pump filters and chip detectors.

POWER TURBINE: Two-stage free axial-flow turbine.

DIMENSIONS

SM2 UNIT

Length: 6·096m (20ft)

Width: 2·286m (7ft 6in)

Height: 2·294m (9ft 2in)

SM3 UNIT

Length: 6·544m (21ft 5in)

Width: 2·069m (6ft 8in)

Height: 2·352m (7 ft 7in)

WEIGHTS (Estimated) dry

SM2 UNIT: 12 273kg (27 000lb)

SM3 UNIT: 8295kg (18 287lb)

GAS GENERATOR CHANGE UNIT: 1732kg (3818lb)

NOMINAL PERFORMANCE

Sprint rating: 14mW (18 800bhp)

Max rating: 12·75mW (17 100bhp)

*Specific fuel consumption (Sprint rating): 0·235kg/kWh (0·386lb/bhph)

*Based on LCV of fuel of 43 125kJ/kg (18 540btu/lb)

No power take-offs

No intake or exhaust duct losses

Ambient air temperature of 15°C (59°F) and an atmospheric pressure of 101·3kPa (14·7lbf/in²)

UPRATED MARINE SPEY

Work is well advanced on an uprated version of the Marine Spey, giving maximum output of 19 500kW (26 139bhp) and cruise power of 18 000kW (24 129bhp).

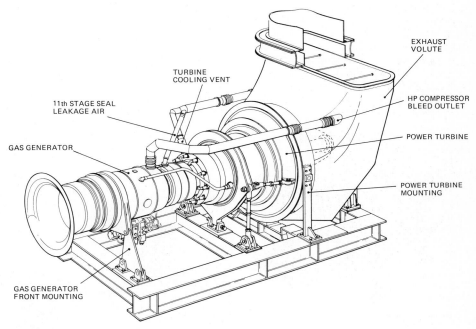

Spey SM2

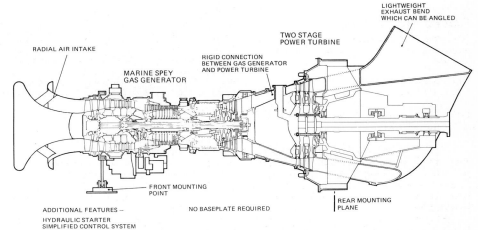

Spey SM3

UNITED STATES OF AMERICA

ALLISON GAS TURBINE DIVISION
(General Motors Corporation)
General Offices: PO Box 420 SCU6, Indianapolis, Indiana 46206-0420, USA

Telephone: (317) 242 4151
Telex: 276400

Allison Gas Turbines has been active in the development of gas turbines for aircraft, industrial and marine use for many years. Production of the first Allison gas turbine began in the 1940s, when the company built the powerplant for the P-39, the first jet-powered aircraft to fly in the United States.

Later, the Allison T56 turboprop aircraft engine was developed. It demonstrated outstanding reliability and the same basic design has been adapted for industrial and marine applications. In the early 1960s, the first Allison 501-K gas turbine-powered electric powerplant went into service. Today, in excess of 1100 501-K industrial series engines are used not only in electric powerplants but also in industrial and marine applications. The two-shaft marine engine powers the Boeing Jetfoil and is installed in the Israeli Shipyards Ltd M161 hydrofoil craft for primary propulsion.

ALLISON 501-K SERIES

The Allison 501-K series industrial gas turbine incorporates a 14-stage axial-flow compressor, with bleed valves to compensate for compressor surge.

Of modular design, it comprises three main sections: the compressor, combustor and turbine. Each section can be readily separated from the other. Modular design provides ease in handling and servicing of the engine.

The first stage of the four-stage turbine section is air-cooled, permitting the engine to be operated at higher than normal turbine inlet temperatures.

The combustor section of the 501-K consists of six combustion chambers of the through-flow type, assembled within a single annular chamber. This multiple provides even temperature distribution at the turbine inlet, thus eliminating the danger of hot spots.

The 501-K series engines are available in single-shaft or free turbine design.

The lightweight, compact size of the 501-K lends itself to multiple engines driving a single shaft through a common gearbox, or as a gas generator driving a customer-furnished power turbine.

The engine can be operated on a wide range of liquid fuels. Designation of the marine model is 501-KF, a brief specification for which follows. Dimensions are shown on the accompanying general arrangement drawing.
Exhaust gas temperature: 535°C (994°F)
Inlet air flow: 26 000cfm
Exhaust air flow: 81 000cfm
Engine jacket heat rejection: 6000 Btu/min
Lube heat rejection (Gasifier): 1270 Btu/min
Max liquid fuel flow: 6365 litres (360ghp)
Liquid fuel: DF-1, DF-2 per Allison EMS66
Lubricant: Synthetic oil per Allison EMS35 and 53
Specific fuel consumption: 0·24 litre (0·503lb)/hph
Required auxiliaries:
25hp starter
20-29V dc electrical power
Power take-off shaft and couplings
Temperature and speed controls from engine-furnished signals
Oil cooler
Auxiliary lube pump
Compressor inlet sensor
Gauge panel, meters and associated components
Engine exhaust diffusing tailpipe

ALLISON 570-K

A 7000hp gas turbine designed as a prime mover in the industrial and marine fields, the 570 series is a front drive, two-shaft gas turbine. It entered

Allison 501-KF

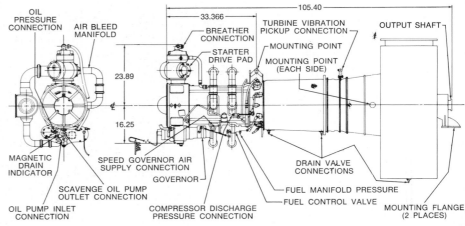

General Arrangement of Allison 501-KF

Side view of Allison 501-KF

production in 1978 and is in full operation. The model 570 represents General Motors' newest entry in the industrial and marine markets and is a derivative of the US Army's heavy lift helicopter (HLH) engine.

The 570 engine uses a variable geometry, 13-stage, axial flow compressor with a compression ratio of 12·1:1; the inlet guide vanes and the first five stages of stators are variable. The compressor is directly coupled to a two-stage axial flow turbine

and the vanes and blades of both stages are air-cooled. A power turbine drives the output shaft at the front end of the engine through a torque senser assembly located on the engine's centreline. The air foils of the power turbine are solid and do not require air cooling.

The 570 is operated by a full authority electronic control which features automatic starting sequence, speed governing, turbine temperature limiting, vibration sensing etc.

All production 570 engines are fully marinised using materials and coatings selected after more than ¼ million hours of marine experience with Boeing Jetfoils and DD 963 'Spruance' class destroyers.

The 570-K engine incorporates many technological advances and these have resulted in the unit having the lowest specific fuel consumption (sfc) of any turbine in its hp class. At maximum rated power of 7170hp, the engine's sfc is 0·46lb/hph. This low level is maintained over a wide range of output power and speed; at 50 per cent power the sfc increases by only 7 per cent.

The Allison 571, a larger version, designated the model 571-KF, entered production in mid-1985. A three-stage power turbine is used and the unit has a maximum power rating of 8288hp with an sfc of 246kg/kWh (0·405lb/hph). The engine is installed in the Swedish Stockholm Class fast patrol boats, yachts, and is awaiting installation in Canada's DDH-280 Trump destroyer programme as the cruise engine.

570-KF (two-stage) and 571-KF (three-stage) Gas Turbines

	Maximum		Continuous	
	570-KF	*571-KF*	*570-KF*	*571-KF*
Power shp (kW)				
15°C (59°F)	7170 (5347)	8288 (6180)	6445 (4806)	7694 (5738)
26·7°C (80°F)	6610 (4929)	7602 (5669)	5890 (4392)	6908 (5151)
Fuel consumption 15°C (59°F)				
g/kWh	282	246	280	249
lb/hph	0·462	0·405	0·46	0·408
Power turbine temperature				
°C	850	835	803	803
°F	1562	1535	1477	1477
Compression ratio	12·1	12·8	11·3	12·3
Corrected airflow				
kg/s	19·4	20·1	18·1	19·6
lb/s	42·8	44·2	40	43·3
Power turbine speed (rpm)	11 500	11 500	11 500	11 500
Weight				
kg	612	733	612	733
lb	1350	1615	1350	1615
Length				
metres	1·83	1·87	1·83	1·87
inches	72	74	72	74

Allison 570-KF

354163

BRIGGS AND STRATTON CORPORATION

PO Box 702, Milwaukee, Wisconsin 53201, USA

Frederick P Stratton Jr, *President and Chief Executive Officer*
Laverne J Socks, *Executive Vice President*
L William Dewey Jr, *Executive Vice President*
George A Senn, *Executive Vice President*
Robert K Catterson, *Vice President, Engineering and Research*
J Byron Smith, *Vice President of Production*
James F Sullivan, *Vice President, Sales*
Michael D Hamilton, *Vice President, International*

Sales Representative and Central Service Distributor for Great Britain and Ireland:
Autocar Electrical Equipment Company Limited, 640 Ripple Road, Barking, Essex IG11 0RU, England

Briggs and Stratton Corporation is a major supplier of small two- and four-stroke petrol engines manufactured in the USA and at the Farymann Diesel factory in West Germany. Uses range from lawn and garden equipment to industrial and agricultural machinery. In accordance with US government regulations, Briggs and Stratton has introduced a range of 'quiet' engines

and most recently an electric start system with a brake function to stop the engine when the operator leaves the controls. For industrial and other heavy-use applications, the I/C series was designed for prolonged life, low maintenance and general heavy-duty use.

With over 4·4 million square feet of manufacturing facilities and a new service parts distribution centre, Briggs and Stratton can produce custom-designed engines to more than 50 000 specifications. Central service distributors provide parts and technical training to 25 000 dealers around the world. Briggs and Stratton is one of the largest manufacturers of small engines in the world (more than 140 million since 1953).

Engines offered by Briggs and Stratton Corporation

Series No	Displacement in³/cc	hp	Net weight lb	Series No	Displacement in³/cc	hp	Net weight lb
Four-cycle aluminium alloy engines				132200	12·57/206	5	29·75
90700	9·02/147·9	3·5	20·75	130900	12·57/206	5	20·25
91700	9·02/147·9	3·5	21·75	132900	12·57/206	5	20·25
92900	9·02/147·9	3·5	19·75	132400	12·57/206	5	31·75
94500	9·02/147·9	3	20·25	170400	16·79/275·1	7	44
94900	9·02/147·9	3·5	20·75	171400	16·79/275·1	7	44
110700	11·39/186·7	4	22	190400	19·44/318·5	8	44·5
111700	11·39/186·7	4	22·5	195400	19·44/318·5	8	44·5
110900	11·39/186·77	4	21	170700	16·79/275·1	7	43
114900	11·39/186·7	4	24·75	190700	19·44/318·5	8	43·5
112200	11·39/186·7	4	25·5	191700	19·44/318·5	8	48·5
113900	11·39/186·7	4	21·5	221430	22·04/361·2	10	62
130200	12·57/206	5	29·75	220700	22·04/361·2	10	55

Engines offered by Briggs and Stratton Corporation (contd)

Series No	Displacement in³/cc	hp	Net weight lb	Series No	Displacement in³/cc	hp	Net weight lb
Four-cycle aluminium alloy engines				402707 (ducted)	40/656	16	98·25
252410	24·36/399·2	11	63·25	422437	42·33/694	18	87·25
252700	24·36/399·2	11	59·25	422437 (ducted)	42·33/694	18	100·75
253700	24·36/399·2	11	59·25	422707 (ducted)	42·33/694	18	98·25
253410 (non-ducted)	24·36/399·2	11	63·5				
253410 (ducted)	24·36/399·2	11	68·5	**Cast-iron cylinder series**			
				233400	22·94/376·5	9	92
Four-cycle cast iron engines				243430	23·94/392·3	10	96
233400	22·94/376·5	9	92	326430	32·4/530·9	16	106·5
243430	29·94/392·3	10	96				
326430	32·4/530·9	16	106·5	**Industrial/commercial series**			
				Vertical crankshaft			
Four-cycle twin-cylinder engines				131922	12·57/206	5	30·25
402707	40/656	16	98·25	192700	19·44/319	8	48·5
402417 (non-ducted)	40/656	16	86·25	193700	19·44/319	8	48·5
402437 (non-ducted)	40/656	16	87·25	402707	40/656	16	98·25
402417 (ducted)	40/656	16	99·75	422707	42·33/694	18	98·25
402437 (ducted)	40/656	16	100·75				
402707 (ducted)	40/656	16	98·25	Horizontal crankshaft			
422437 (non-ducted)	42·33/694	18	87·25	81232	7·75/127	3	24·5
422437 (ducted)	42·33/694	18	100·75	131232	12·57/206	5	30
422707 (ducted)	42·33/694	18	98·25	195432	19·44/318·5	8	46·5
				221432	22·04/361·3	10	63·25
Twin cylinder				233431	22·94/376·5	9	92
402417	40/656	16	86·25	243431	23·94/392·3	10	96
402417 (ducted)	40/656	16	99·75	326431	32·4/530·9	16	106·5
402437	40/656	16	87·25	402437	40/656	16	100·75
402437 (ducted)	40/656	16	100·75	422437	42·33/694	18	100·75

CUMMINS ENGINE COMPANY INC

Box 3005, Columbus, Indiana 47202-3005, USA

Telephone: (812) 377 5000

W L Erfmeier, *Marine Marketing Manager*

Formed in 1919 in Columbus, Indiana, the Cummins Engine Company produces a wide range of marine diesel engines which are now manufactured and distributed internationally. In addition to manufacturing plants in the United States, the company also produces diesel engines in Brazil, India, Japan, Mexico, China and the United Kingdom. All these plants build engines to the same specifications thus ensuring interchangeability of parts and the same quality standards. These standards meet design approvals for world-wide agency certification.

VTA-903-M

TYPE: Four-stroke cycle, turbocharged, aftercooled V-8 diesel engine.
AFTERCOOLER: Large capacity aftercooler plumbed for raw water cooling.
BEARINGS: Replaceable, precision type, steel-backed inserts. Five main bearings, 95mm (3·75in) diameter. Connecting rod bearings, 79mm (3·12in) diameter.
CAMSHAFT: Single camshaft precisely controls valve and injector timing. Lobes are induction hardened for long life. Five replaceable precision type bushings, 63mm (2·5in) diameter.
CAMSHAFT FOLLOWERS: Induction hardened, roller type for long cam and follower life.
CONNECTING RODS: Drop forged, I-beam section 208mm (8·2in) centre to centre length. Rifle drilled for pressure lubrication of piston pin. Rod tapered on piston pin end to reduce unit pressures.
COOLING SYSTEMS: Gear-driven centrifugal engine coolant pump. Large volume water passages provide even flow of coolant around cylinder liners, valves, and injectors. Modulating by-pass thermostat regulates coolant temperature. Spin-on corrosion resistor checks rust and corrosion, controls acidity and removes impurities.
CRANKSHAFT: Fully counterweighted and spin balanced high tensile strength steel forging with induction hardened fillets.

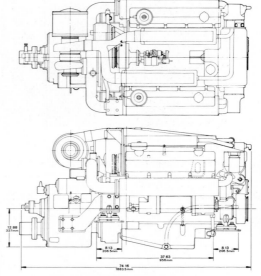

Cummins VTA-903-M turbocharged diesel engine

CYLINDER BLOCK: Alloy cast iron with removable wet liners. Cross bolt support to main bearing cap provides extra strength and stability.
CYLINDER HEADS: Alloy cast iron. Each head serves four cylinders. Drilled fuel supply and return lines. Valve seats are replaceable corrosion-resistant inserts. Valve guides and cross head guides are replaceable inserts.
CYLINDER LINERS: Replaceable wet liners dissipate heat faster than dry liners and are easily replaced without reboring the block.
FUEL SYSTEM: Low pressure system with wear compensating pump and integral dual flyweight governor. Camshaft actuated fuel injectors give accurate metering and precise timing. Fuel lines are internal drilled passages in cylinder heads. Spin-on fuel filter.
GEAR TRAIN: Timing gears and accessory drive gears are induction hardened. Spur gears driven from crankshaft and located at rear of block.
LUBRICATION: Large capacity gear pump provides pressure lubrication to all bearings. Oil cooler and full-flow filters maintain oil condition and maximise oil and engine life.
PISTONS: Aluminium alloy, cam ground and

barrel-shaped to compensate for thermal expansion, ensures precise fit at operating temperatures. One oil and two compression rings.
PISTON PINS: Full floating, tubular steel retained by snap rings, 44mm (1·75in) diameter.
TURBOCHARGER: Exhaust gas-driven turbocharger mounted at rear of engine. Turbocharging provides more power, improved fuel economy, and lower smoke and noise levels.
VALVES: Dual 48mm (1·87in) diameter poppet-type intake and exhaust valves. Wear resistant face on exhaust valves.
POWER RATINGS
High output: 336kW (450bhp)
Rated rpm: 2600
Medium continuous: 283kW (380bhp)
Rated rpm: 2600
Continuous duty: 239kW (320bhp)
Rated rpm: 2300
Bore and stroke: 140 × 121mm (5½ × 4¾in)
Displacement: 14·8 litres (903in³)
Oil pan capacity: 19 litres (5 US gallons)
Net weight, dry*: 1660kg (3650lb)
*With selected accessories and Capitol HY-22000 marine gear.

6BT5.9-M

This engine is now replacing the VT-555-M type. Its compact size provides for ease of installation and easy access for routine maintenance. Fewer parts enables less inventory, faster maintenance and repair, and enables engines to be serviced and repaired with ordinary hand tools.

TYPE: Four-stroke cycle, turbocharged, direct injection, in-line, 6-cylinder diesel engine.

SKIRTED BLOCK: Cast iron with main bearing supports between each cylinder, for maximum strength and rigidity, low weight and optimum crankshaft support.

FUEL INJECTION SYSTEM: Direct, with high swirl intake ports for thorough mixing of air and fuel to provide low fuel consumption.

CRANKSHAFT: Forged steel with integral counterweights, allowing high power output from a compact size.

CONNECTING RODS: Forged steel, I-beam cross section, with angle split cap-to-rod interface and capscrew attachment for maximum structural strength and ease of service.

CAMSHAFT: Side-mounted gear drive for low engine height and minimum maintenance.

ALTERNATOR AND WATER PUMP DRIVE: Single-belt with self-tensioning idler for minimum belt maintenance.

CYLINDER HEAD: Single piece cross flow for short length and maximum structural stiffness of the block/head assembly and for fewer head gasket problems.

VALVES PER CYLINDER: Two with single valve springs for fewer parts.

TURBOCHARGER: Water-cooled exhaust manifold and water-cooled turbocharger can be configured for top-out or rear-out exhaust for added flexibility.

POWER RATINGS
High output: 157kW (210bhp)
Rated rpm: 2600
Medium continuous: 134kW (180bhp)
Rated rpm: 2500
Bore and stroke: 102 × 120mm
Displacement: 5·9 litres
Oil pan capacity: 14·2 litres
Net weight, dry: 579kg*
*Heat-exchanger-cooled and MG-502 marine gear.

6BTA5.9-M

As for 6BT5.9-M except:
TYPE: Four-stroke cycle, turbocharged, after-cooled, direct injection, in-line, 6-cylinder diesel engine.

JACKET WATER AFTERCOOLER: Mounted on top of intake manifold.

TURBOCHARGER: Water-cooled exhaust manifold and water-cooled turbocharger, configured for rear-out exhaust for lower profile.

POWER RATINGS
High output: 186kW (250bhp)
Rated rpm: 2600
Medium continuous: 164kW (220bhp)
Rated rpm: 2500
Bore and stroke: 102 × 120mm
Displacement: 5·9 litres
Oil pan capacity: 14·2 litres
Net weight, dry: 613kg*
*Heat-exchanger-cooled and MG-506A marine gear.

KTA19-M

TYPE: Four-stroke cycle, turbocharged, after-cooled diesel.

AFTERCOOLER: Large capacity aftercooler results in cooler, denser intake air for more efficient combustion and reduced internal stresses for longer life. Aftercooler is located in engine coolant system, eliminating need for special plumbing.

BEARINGS: Replaceable, precision type, steel backed inserts. Seven main bearings, 140mm in diameter. Connecting rod bearings 102mm in diameter.

CAMSHAFT: Single camshaft precisely controls valve and injector timing. Lobes are induction hardened for long life. Seven replaceable precision type bushings 76mm in diameter.

CAMSHAFT FOLLOWERS: Induction hardened, roller type for long cam and follower life.

CONNECTING RODS: Drop forged, I-beam section 290mm centre to centre length. Rifle drilled for pressure lubrication of piston pin. Rod is tapered on piston pin end to reduce unit pressures.

COOLING SYSTEM: Gear driven centrifugal pump. Large volume water passages provide even flow of coolant around cylinder liners, valves and injectors. Modulating by-pass thermostats regulate coolant temperature. Spin-on corrosion resistor checks rust and corrosion, controls acidity and removes impurities.

CRANKSHAFT: High tensile strength steel forging with induction hardened fillets and journals. Fully counterweighted and dynamically balanced.

CYLINDER BLOCK: Alloy cast iron with removable wet liners. Cross bolt support to main bearing cap provides extra strength and stability.

CYLINDER HEADS: Alloy cast iron. Each head serves one cylinder. Drilled fuel supply and return lines. Valve seats are replaceable corrosion resistant inserts. Valve guides and cross head guides are replaceable inserts.

CYLINDER LINERS: Replaceable wet liners dissipate heat faster than dry liners and are easily replaced without reboring the block.

FUEL SYSTEM: Cummins PT self adjusting system. Integral dual flyweight governor provides overspeed protection independent of main engine governor. Camshaft actuated fuel injectors give accurate metering and timing. Fuel lines are internal drilled passages in cylinder heads. Spin-on fuel filters.

GEAR TRAIN: Timing gears and accessory drive gears are induction hardened helical gears driven from crankshaft and located at front of block.

LUBRICATION: Large capacity gear pump provides pressure lubrication to all bearings and oil supply for piston cooling. All pressure lines are internal drilled passages in block and heads. Oil cooler, full-flow filters and by-pass filters maintain oil condition and maximise oil and engine life.

PISTONS: Aluminium alloy, cam ground and barrel shaped to compensate for thermal expansion assures precise fit at operating temperatures. CeCorr grooved skirt finish provides superior lubrication. Oil cooled for rapid heat dissipation. Two compression and one oil ring.

PISTON PINS: Full floating, tubular steel retained by snap rings, 61mm in diameter.

TURBOCHARGER: AiResearch exhaust gas driven turbocharger mounted on right side of engine. Turbocharging provides more power, improved fuel economy, altitude compensation, and lower smoke and noise levels.

VALVES: Dual 56mm diameter poppet type intake and exhaust valves. Wear resistant face on exhaust valves.

POWER RATINGS
Continuous duty: 373kW (500bhp)
Rated rpm: 1800
Intermittent duty: 507·3kW (680bhp)
Rated rpm: 2100
Bore and stroke: 159 × 159mm
Displacement: 19 litres
Oil pan capacity: 38 litres
Net weight, dry: 3084kg*
*Heat-exchanger-cooled and MG-502 marine gear.

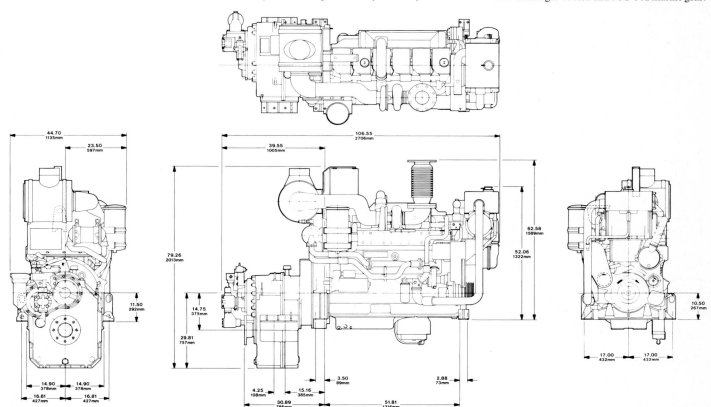

Cummins KTA19-M turbocharged after-cooled diesel engine

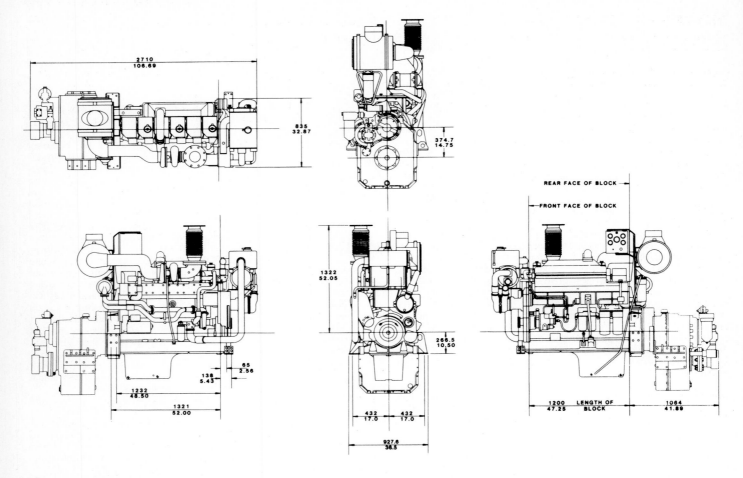

Cummins KTA19-M W/MG 518 deep case, keel cooled/Twin Disc MG-518 gear

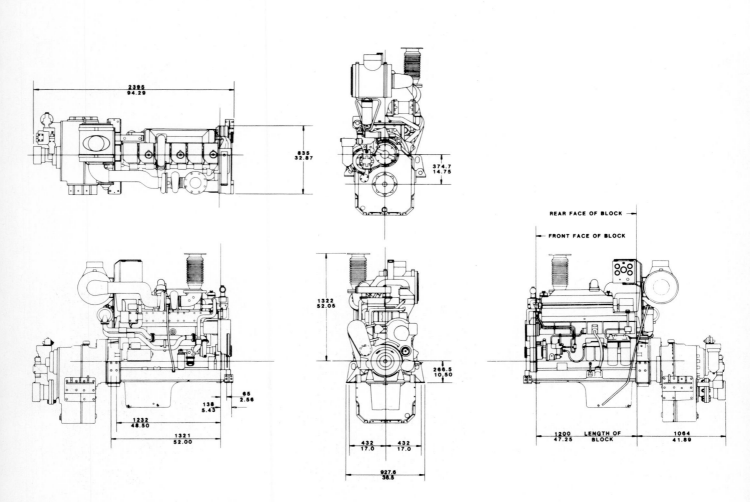

Cummins KTA19-M W/MG 518 deep case, heat-exchanger cooled/Twin Disc MG-518 gear

CUYUNA ENGINE COMPANY

1st Street SW, PO Box 116, Crosby, Minnesota
56441, USA

Telephone: (218) 546 8313
Telex: 757996 CUYUNA ENG UD

Roger P Worth, *President*

The company manufactures a range of axial-fan-cooled single- and twin-cylinder engines, developing 20 to 40hp.

The engines are serviced through a network of 2000 independent service outlets and central distributors throughout the USA and Canada.

CUYUNA AXIAL-FAN SINGLE- AND TWIN-CYLINDER ENGINES

Models 215, 340 and 440

Features of this range include a standard mounting for all models to ease installation; low engine profile with built-in shrouding; lightweight construction to reduce overall vehicle weight and high interchangeability of all parts. Crankshafts, crankcases, blower assemblies, magnetos, recoil starters and hardware items are fully interchangeable, thus reducing spare parts inventory requirements and lowering maintenance costs. Specifications for the six standard productions are given in the accompanying table. Models 250LC, 430LC and 500LC are the marine engines.

Single- and Twin-cylinder Axial-fan-cooled Engines

Model	215	340	440
Bore	67·51mm (2·658in)	60·00mm (2·632in)	67·51mm (2·658in)
Stroke	60·00mm (2·362in)	60·00mm (2·362in)	60·00mm (2·362in)
Displacement	214cc	339cc	428cc
Compression ratio		12·5 : 1	
Brake hp/rpm	20hp	32hp	40hp
	6500/7000rpm	6500/7000rpm	6500/7000rpm
Base mounting hole thread		⁷⁄₁₆—14 UNC	
Cylinder		Aluminium with cast iron sleeve	
Connecting rod bearing upper		Needle	
Connecting rod bearing lower		Needle	
Connecting rod material		Forged steel	
Main bearings		2 heavy duty ball bearings (double row, PTO end)	
Lighting coil		12V, 150W	
Ignition setting before TDC		0·102in to 0·112in (cam fully advanced)	
Spark plug thread		14 × 1·25mm (0·75in) reach	
Gap		0·016in to 0·02in	
Type		Champion N-3	
Rotation		Counter-clockwise viewed from PTO end	
Fuel-oil mixture		40:1 (1 pint to 5 gallons)	
Lubrication		Premium Gasoline & Cuyuna 2 Cycle Engine Oil	
Starter		Rewind type, standard; electric, optional	
Rope material		Nylon	
Weight	86kg	137kg	137kg

Single- and Twin-cylinder Liquid-cooled Marine Engines

Model	250LC	430LC	500LC
Type	Single-cylinder	Twin-cylinder	Twin-cylinder
Bore		67·50mm (2·658in)	
Stroke		60·00mm (2·362in)	
Displacement	214cc (13in³)	428cc (26·10in³)	
Brake hp/rpm	25hp	40hp	50hp
	6500rpm	6250rpm	6500rpm
Power take-off shaft		30mm dia—10:1 Taper—½—20UNF	
Base mounting hole thread		4—⁷⁄₁₆—14 UNC	
Cylinder		Aluminium with cast iron sleeve	
Connecting rod bearings		Needle	
Connecting rod and crankshaft material		Forged steel	
Main bearings		Heavy duty ball bearings (double row, PTO end)	
Number of main bearings		4	
Ignition		Capacitor discharge (CDI)	
Alternator		12V, 150W ac output	
Carburettor		Downdraft with USCG approved flame arrestor	
Exhaust		Liquid-cooled manifold, elbow and tuning chamber	
Spark plug		Champion N3C or NGK BR8ES	
Cooling		Liquid—external supply	
Rotation		Counter-clockwise viewed from PTO end	
Fuel-oil mixture		40:1 (1 pint to 5 gallons)	
Starter		Electric	
Weight		28 to 30·87kg	

Horsepower ratings established in accordance with specifications SAE-J607.

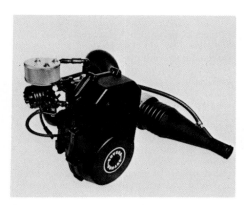

Cuyuna Model 250LC 214cc 25hp liquid-cooled marine engine

Cuyuna Model 430LC 428cc 40hp liquid-cooled marine engine

Cuyuna Model 500LC 428cc 50hp liquid-cooled marine engine

DETROIT DIESEL ALLISON
Division of General Motors

13400 Outer Drive West, Detroit, Michigan
48239-4001, USA

Telephone: (313) 592 5000

A range of marine diesel engines is available ranging in maximum shp from 92 to 1745. The following table gives the maximum marine ratings for these engines:

Type	shp	rpm
3-53	92	2800
4-53	128	2800
4-71	160	2300
6V-53	197	2800
6V-71	240	2300
6-71	240	2300
6-71M	257	2300
6V-92	280	2300
6V-53T	292	2800
8V-71	325	2300
6V-71TA	365	2300
8V-92	375	2300
8V-71TI	450	2300
6V-92TA	458	2300
6V-92TA	465	2300
12V-71	480	2300
8V-92TI	585	2300
8V-92TI	625	2300
16V-71	640	2300
12V-71TI	650	2300
12V-71TI	720	2300
16V-92	725	2100
12V-149	770	1900
12V-71TI	840	2300
8V-149TI	870	1900
12V-149T	1019	1900
16V-149	1025	1900
12V-149TI	1165	1900
16V-149T	1340	1900
16V-149TI	1745	1900

These ratings are applicable to installations in pleasure craft, fast patrol craft and fast ferries. The most powerful engines are in the 16V-149 series (1745shp max); two 16V-149TI diesel engines propel the Bell Halter Model 730A surface effect ship, USS *Jaeger*.

Basic Engine	16V-149	16V-149T	16V-149TI
Model:	9162-7000	9162-7300	9162-7301
Description:	naturally aspirated	turbocharged	turbocharged inter-cooled
Number of cylinders:	16	16	16
Bore and stroke:	146 × 146mm	146 × 146mm	146 × 146mm
Displacement:	39·18 litres	39·18 litres	39·18 litres
Compression ratio:	17 : 1	16 : 1	16 : 1
Net weight (dry):	7258kg	5330kg*	5421kg*
Continuous,			
injectors:	120	140	140
rated gross power:	694kW at 1800rpm†	907kW at 1800rpm†	955kW at 1800rpm†
rated net power:	671kW at 1800rpm†	877kW at 1800rpm†	927kW at 1800rpm†
Intermittent,			
injectors:	130	140	150
rated gross power:	791kW at 1900rpm†	940kW at 1900rpm†	1130kW at 1900rpm†
rated net power:	765kW at 1900rpm†	910kW at 1900rpm†	1094kW at 1900rpm†
Max,			
injectors:	130	145	190
rated gross power:	791kW at 1900rpm†	1033kW at 1900rpm†	‡1343kW at 1900rpm†
rated net power:	765kW at 1900rpm†	1000kW at 1900rpm†	1302kW at 1900rpm†

* Weights shown are without marine gear
† Rating conditions of SAE: 77°F (25°C) air inlet temperature and 29·31 in Hg (99 kPa) Barometer (Dry)
‡ Preliminary data

Model 9162-7000   **16V-149**

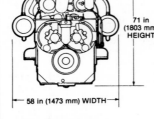

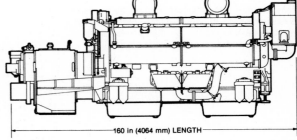

Model 9162-7300   **16V-149T**

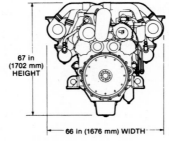

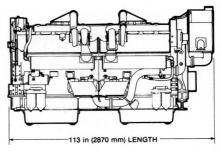

Model 9162-7301   **16V-149TI**

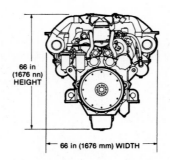

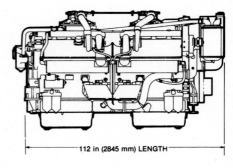

Principal dimensions of DDA 16V-149, 149T & 149TI series engines

---

GENERAL ELECTRIC COMPANY
Aircraft Engine Business Group

1 Neumann Way, PO Box 156301, Mail Drop N35, Cincinnati (Evendale), Ohio 45215-6301, USA

Telephone: (513) 243 2000

Brian H Rowe, *Senior Vice President and Group Executive*
W R Phillips, *Counsel*

The General Electric Company's Dr Sanford A Moss operated the first gas turbine in the United States in 1903 and produced the aircraft turbo-supercharger, first flown in 1919 and mass-produced in the Second World War for US fighters and bombers.

The company built its first aircraft gas turbine in 1941, when it began development of a Whittle-type turbojet, under an arrangement between the British and American governments.

Since then General Electric has produced over 82 000 aircraft gas turbines for military and commercial aircraft, as well as aircraft derivative gas turbines for marine and industrial uses. Six General Electric gas turbines have been marinised: the LM1500, the LM2500, the LM100, the LM500, the LM1600 and the LM5000. The LM2500 has been specified to power various classes of ships in 17 navies; the LM500 has been specified for the Danish Navy Stanflex 300 fast multi-mission patrol craft. In the 1960s 17 LM100 turbines powered Bell Aerosystems SK-5 hover-craft used by the US Navy, US Army and Oakland Port Authority.

LM2500

The LM2500 marine gas turbine is a two-shaft, simple-cycle, high-efficiency engine derived from the General Electric military TF39 and the commercial CF6 high by-pass turbofan engines for the US Air Force C-5 Galaxy transport and DC-10, Boeing 747 and A300 commercial jets. The compressor, combuster and turbine are designed to give maximum progression in reliability, parts life and time between overhaul. The engine has a simple-cycle efficiency of more than 36 per cent, which is due to advanced cycle pressures, temperatures and component efficiencies.

The LM2500 marine gas turbine provides foil-borne power for the US Navy PHM hydrofoils. The six PHM 'Pegasus' class vessels were built by the Boeing Company, Seattle, Washington. In addition the LM2500 has been combined with diesels to power several classes of high-speed patrol boats, providing top speeds in excess of 40 knots.

Total operating time of LM2500 engines in all marine service is more than two million hours.

TYPE: Two-shaft, axial flow, simple cycle.
AIR INTAKE: Axial, inlet bellmouth or duct can be customised to installation.
COMBUSTION CHAMBER: Annular.
FUEL GRADE: Kerosene, JP4, JP5, Diesel, heavy distillate fuels and natural gas.
TURBINE: Two-stage gas generator, six-stage power.
JET PIPE: Vertical or customised to fit installation.
OIL SPECIFICATION: Synthetic Turbine Oil (MIL-L-23699) or equal.
MOUNTING: At power turbine and compressor front frame.
STARTING: Pneumatic, hydraulic.
DIMENSIONS
Length: 6530mm (257in)
Width: 2240mm (88in)
PERFORMANCE RATINGS: 30 000shp at 15°C (59°F) at sea level
SPECIFIC FUEL CONSUMPTION: 0·171kg (0·376lb)/hph

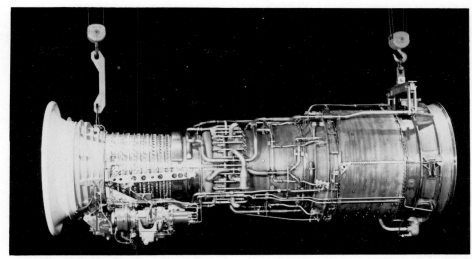
LM2500

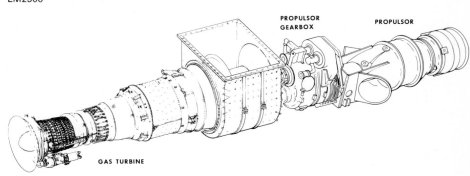
LM2500 installation aboard PHM 'Pegasus' class hydrofoil

PROPULSOR GEARBOX   PROPULSOR   GAS TURBINE

TEXTRON LYCOMING
(previously Avco Lycoming)

550 Main Street, Stratford, Connecticut 06497, USA

Telephone: (203) 385 2000
Telex: 964242

John R Myers, *Vice President and General Manager, Lycoming Division*
Richard Ainsworth, *Vice President, Engineering*

Textron Lycoming, Stratford, is the turbine engine manufacturing subsidiary of Textron.

Textron Lycoming manufactures a wide range of gas turbine engines for helicopters, commuter jets, tanks and tracked vehicles, as well as for marine and industrial applications. Marine versions of the large turboshaft and turbofan T55 family are designated the TF25 and TF40. The latest addition to the range is the TF15, a marine version of the AGT 1500.

TF25

The current production version of the TF25 is a high-speed shaft-turbine engine, with output shaft speed equal to power turbine speed. Integral oil tank and cooling system. An earlier TF25 powered the Vosper Thornycroft VT1, the Coastal Patrol Interdiction Craft (CPIC-X) and the Mitsui MV-PP15 155-seat hover ferry. Two are installed in the 36-tonne CHACONSA VCA-36 amphibious assault landing craft under sea trials for the Spanish Navy.

AIR INTAKE: Side inlet casting of aluminium alloy supporting optional reduction gearbox and front main bearings. Provision for intake screens.
COMPRESSOR: Seven axial stages followed by a single centrifugal stage. Two-piece aluminium alloy stator casing with one row of inlet guide vanes, and seven rows of steel stator blades, bolted to steel alloy diffuser casing to which combustion chamber casing is attached. Rotor comprises seven stainless steel discs and one titanium impeller mounted on shaft supported in forward thrust ball bearings and rear roller bearing. TF25 pressure ratio is 6:1.
COMBUSTION CHAMBER: Annular reverse flow type. Steel outer shell and inner liner. 28 fuel nozzles with downstream injection.

FUEL SYSTEM: Woodward fuel control system. Gear-type fuel pump, with gas producer and power shaft governors, flow control and shut-off valve.
FUEL GRADE: MIL-J-5624 grade JP-4, JP-5, MIL-F-46005 or marine diesel standard and wide-cut kerosene.
TURBINE: Two mechanically-independent axial-flow turbines. First turbine with single-stage drives compressor, has cored-out cast steel blades and is flange-bolted to outer coaxial drive shaft. Second, two-stage turbine drives output shaft, has solid steel blades and is mounted on inner coaxial drive shaft.
EXHAUST UNIT: Fixed area nozzle, with inner cone, supported by six radial struts.

ACCESSORIES: Electric, air or hydraulic starter. High-energy ignition unit; four igniter plugs.
LUBRICATION: Recirculating type. Integral oil tank and cooler.
OIL GRADE: MIL-L-17808, MIL-L-23699.
DIMENSIONS
Length: 1·27m
Width: 0·87m
Height: 1·11m
WEIGHT
Dry: 600kg (1324lb)
PERFORMANCE RATINGS
Max intermittent (peak): 3000shp
Max continuous (normal): 2500shp
FUEL CONSUMPTION
At max continuous rating: 0·62sfc 198 US gallons/h

TF25

TF40 and TF40B

The TF40 engine is a scaled-up TF25 with higher mass flow and a four-stage turbine section.

Both the JEFF(A) (Aerojet-General) and JEFF(B) (Textron Marine Systems) AALCs employ earlier model TF40s. JEFF(A) employs six, each developing 3350shp continuous. Four drive individual, steerable ducted propellers, and the remaining two drive separate centrifugal lift fans. In the case of JEFF(B), the six engines are arranged in two groups of three, located port and starboard. Each trio drives a single propeller and lift system through integrated gears.

An uprated version, the TF40B, is in production and provides the lift and propulsive power for the US Navy's Landing Craft, Air Cushion (LCAC) built by Textron Marine Systems. The machinery arrangement is similar to that of JEFF(B) apart from the use of four engines instead of six.

AIR INTAKE: Side inlet casting of aluminium alloy housing internal gearing and supporting power producer section and output drive shaft. Integral or separately mounted gears are optional. Provision for intake filters and/or silencers. Integral water-wash nozzles are provided.

COMPRESSOR: Seven axial stages followed by a single centrifugal stage. Two-piece aluminium alloy stator casing, with seven rows of steel stator blades bolted to steel alloy casing diffuser, to which combustion chamber casing is attached. Rotor comprises seven stainless steel discs and one titanium impeller mounted on shaft supported in forward thrust ball bearing and rear roller bearing. TF40 pressure ratio is 8·4:1.

COMBUSTION CHAMBER: Annular reverse flow type. Steel outer shell and inner liner. Twenty-eight fuel nozzles with downstream injection.

FUEL SYSTEM: Woodward fuel control system. Gear-type fuel pump, with gas producer and power shaft governors, flow control and shut-off valve.

FUEL GRADE: MIL-T-5624, JP-4, JP-5; MIL-F-16884 diesel, standard and wide-cut kerosene.

TURBINE: Two mechanically-independent axial-flow turbines. First turbine, with two stages, drives compressor. It has cored-out cast blades and is flange-bolted to outer coaxial drive shaft. Second two-stage turbine drives output shaft. It has solid blades and is mounted on inner coaxial drive shaft. (Other features include: integral cast cooled first turbine nozzle, cooled turbine blades in both first and second stages, second turbine vane cooling, and second turbine disc and blade cooling.)

EXHAUST UNIT: Fixed area nozzle, with inner cone, supported by six radial struts.

ACCESSORIES: Electric, air or hydraulic starter. High-energy ignition unit; four igniter plugs.

LUBRICATION: Recirculating type. Integral oil tank and cooler.

OIL GRADE: Synthetic base oils.

DIMENSIONS
Length: 1·32m
Width: 0·88m
Height: 1·11m

PERFORMANCE RATINGS
Max intermittent (at 15°C (59°F)—sea level): 4600shp
Max continuous (at 15°C (59°F)—sea level): 4000shp

FUEL CONSUMPTION
At max continuous rating: 0·54sfc 255 US gallons/h
OIL CONSUMPTION: 0·5pint/h

TF15

The marine version of the AGT 1500 is rated at 1500shp. It comprises a two-speed compressor with a single can combustor which delivers combustion gas to two single-stage compressor drive turbines. A two-stage power turbine further expands the gases to deliver the output power at 3000rpm at the rear of the engine. A multi-wave plate recuperator minimises fuel consumption throughout the speed range.

The TF15 is approximately half the weight of a diesel engine of similar rating and significantly smaller. It burns several grades of diesel fuel as

Cutaway of TF40 marine/industrial gas turbine rated at 4000shp continuous, 4600shp 'boost' power

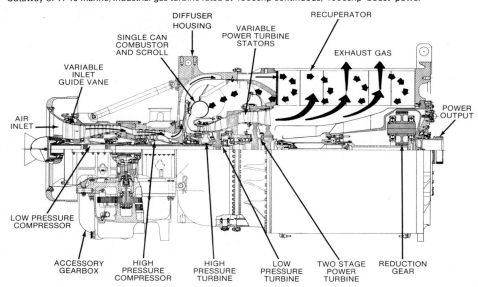

TF15 cutaway

TF15 marine gas turbine

well as aviation kerosene.

POWER RATINGS
Output power: 1500shp

Output shaft rotational speed (100%): 3000rpm
LP compressor rotational speed (100%): 33 500rpm

HP compressor rotational speed (100%):
43 500rpm
OPERATING ENVELOPE
Engine inlet air temperature: $-70°F$ ($-57°C$) to
$+130°F$ ($54°C$)
Altitude: 0-2500m (8000ft)

FUEL: DF-2, DF-1, DF-A, JP-4, JP-5.
LUBRICATING OIL: MIL-L-23699, MIL-L-7808
Consumption: Less than 0·38 litre/h (0·1 gallon/h)
Tank capacity: 9·5 litres (2·5 gallons)
Smoke emission: A1A smoke No 30 (non-visible)

DIMENSIONS
Length: 168·5cm
Width: 99·1cm
Height: 84·6cm
WEIGHT
Net: 1137kg (2500lb)

UNITED TECHNOLOGIES INTERNATIONAL INC

Turbo Power and Marine Systems Inc (TPM)

308 Farmington Avenue, Farmington, Connecticut 06032, USA

Telephone: (203) 678 9000
Telex: 221432 TPM UTC

F L Bruno, *General Manager and Chief Operating Officer*
W H Day, *Director Industrial Gas Turbine Programmes*
R L Wheeler, *Director, Marketing/Sales*

United Technologies Power Systems Division (Turbo Power and Marine Systems Inc) designs and builds industrial and marine gas turbine powerplants and related systems employing the FT4 Modular Industrial Turbine. It also provides a systems support for each of its installations.

Canadian sales of the FT4 are handled by Pratt & Whitney Canada (qv) which also manufactures and sells the ST6 marine gas turbine.

Turbo Power and Marine efforts have resulted in over 1200 Modular Industrial Turbines supplied or on order in the USA and in 28 other countries. The turbines will supply more than 35 million hp for electric power generation, gas transmission and industrial drives as well as for marine propulsion.

FT4 MARINE GAS TURBINES

UTI's FT4 marine gas turbines were first used for boost power in military vessels, including two Royal Danish Navy frigates, 12 US Coast Guard 'Hamilton' class high endurance cutters and four Canadian Armed Forces DDH-280 'Iroquois' class destroyers. Another boost power application of the FT4 is in the Fast Escort and ASW vessel *Bras d'Or* also built for the Canadian Armed Forces. Another application is for two new 12 000-ton Arctic icebreakers for the US Coast Guard. With three FT4 marine gas turbines, these vessels are capable of maintaining a continuous speed of 3 knots through ice 1·8m thick, and are able to ram through ice 6·4m thick.

UTI's marine gas turbines are used for both the main and boost propulsion in the four Canadian DDH-280 destroyers. These are the first military combatant vessels to be designed for complete reliance on gas turbine power.

FT4 gas turbines were also used initially as the main propulsion unit in the *Finnjet*, a high-speed Finnlines passenger liner which cut the Baltic crossing time in half, routinely maintaining 30 knots, with an engine availability over 99 per cent.

FT4 POWER PAC

Each FT4 Power Pac is built upon a rigid mounting frame and includes a housing and gas turbine mounting system, together with controls, accessory equipment, wiring and piping. A remote control system is also provided. Installation is simple. Since all the equipment is pre-tested at the factory before shipment, time required for checkout after installation is minimised.

The gas generator portion of the gas turbine is easily removed for servicing. With a spare gas generator to replace the one removed for servicing, the ship's powerplant can be changed in a matter of hours.

The FT4 gas turbine comprises the gas generator and the power (free) turbine. The independent power turbine accepts the kinetic energy of the gas generator and converts it to mechanical energy through a shaft which extends through the exhaust duct elbow.

Production model of FT4 with 38 600shp base load

UTI/PSD marine power pac with FT4 modular industrial turbine

PERFORMANCE DATA: FT4 MARINE GAS TURBINE

Rating	Power Output *(1)*	Specific Fuel Consumption *(2)*
Max intermittent	36 018kW (48 300shp)	264g/kWh (0·435lb/hph)
Max continuous	32 662kW (43 800shp)	268g/kWh (0·440lb/hph)
Normal	28 784kW (38 600shp)	274g/kWh (0·450lb/hph)

(1)   all ratings at 3600rpm shaft speed, 15°C (59°F) and sea level
(2)   Based on fuel with LHV of 18 500 Btu/lb

GAS GENERATOR

TYPE: Simple-cycle two-spool turbine. A low pressure compressor is driven by a two-stage turbine and a high pressure compressor is driven by a single turbine. The burner section has eight burner cans which are equipped with duplex fuel nozzles.

AIR INTAKE: Cast steel casing with 18 radial struts supporting the front compressor bearing and equipped with a bleed air anti-icing system.

LOW PRESSURE COMPRESSOR: Nine-stage axial flow on inner of two concentric shafts driven by two-stage turbine and supported on ball and roller bearings.

HIGH PRESSURE COMPRESSOR: Seven-stage axial flow on outer hollow shaft driven by single-stage turbine and running on ball and roller bearings.

COMBUSTION CHAMBER: Eight burner cans located in an annular arrangement and enclosed in a one piece steel casing. Each burner has six duplex fuel nozzles.

TURBINES: Steel casing with hollow guide vanes. Turbine wheels are bolted to the compressor shafts and are supported on ball and roller bearings. A single-stage turbine drives the high compressor and a two-stage turbine drives the low compressor.

POWER TURBINE: The gas turbine is available with either clockwise or counter-clockwise rotation of the power turbine. Desired direction of rotation specified by customer. Power turbine housing is bolted to gas generator turbine housing. The three-stage turbine shaft assembly is straddle mounted and supported on ball and roller bearings. The output shaft is bolted to the hub of the power turbine rotor and extends through the exhaust duct.

BEARINGS: Anti-friction ball and roller bearings.

ACCESSORY DRIVE: Starter, fluid power pump, tachometer drives for low compressor, high compressor and free turbine.

LUBRICATION SYSTEM: Return system and scavenge pumps with internal pressure, 3·09kg/cm².

LUBRICATING OIL SPECIFICATIONS: Type 2 synthetic lube oil PWA-521.

MARINE APPLICATIONS: Meets installation, high shock and ships seaway motion requirements.

STARTING: Pneumatic or hydraulic.

DIMENSIONS
Length: 8788mm
Width: 2438mm
Height: 2794mm

FT4C-3F gas turbine

FUEL SPECIFICATIONS
Light Distillate (Naptha): PWA-532(1)
Aviation Grade Kerosene: PWA-522(1)
Marine Diesel: PWA-527(1)
Heavy Distillate: PWA-539
(1) Covered by TPM-FR-1 for series engine
Treated crude and residual oil refer to manufacturer.

FT8 MARINE GAS TURBINE

United Technologies have recently introduced a new model, the FT8 marine gas turbine based on their JT8D aircraft engine, which will be available in 1990. The nominal 24 609kW, 33 000hp (33 462 metric hp) size of the FT8 is expected to fit naval applications.

Derived from the Pratt and Whitney JT8D aircraft engine and the TPM FT4 industrial gas turbine, the FT8 has been launched with a collaboration programme between TPM and the China National Aerotechnology Import-Export Corporation (CATIC) of the People's Republic of China. Under this agreement, CATIC will purchase 37 FT8 gas turbines over a 10-year period and will produce some parts of the gas generator, the complete power turbine and some of the package components for the worldwide market.

The first gas generator is expected to be ready for testing at Pratt and Whitney in 1988 and the first complete FT8 gas turbine to be tested in China in 1989.

Reference: FT8: A High Performance Industrial and Marine Gas Turbine Derived from the JT8D Aircraft Engine, by William H Day, ASME Paper No 87-GT-242 presented at the Gas Turbine Conference and Exhibition, Anaheim, California, 31 May-4 June 1987.

SUMMARY OF PROPULSION ENGINE APPLICATIONS IN HIGH-SPEED CRAFT

ALH	Air-lubricated-hull craft
CAT	Catamaran
HOV	Amphibious hovercraft
HYD	Hydrofoil
MH	Mono-hull
SES	Surface-effect ship/sidewall hovercraft
SWATH	Small-waterplane-area twin-hull
WIGE	Wing-in-ground-effect craft

Engine manufacturer, engine principal designation, craft builder	Craft	Engine secondary designation	Craft name	Craft type
ALLISON GAS TURBINE DIVISION **General Motors Corporation** **501-K**				
Israel Shipyards Ltd	M161	F	—	HYD
Boeing Aerospace Company	Jetfoil 929-100	20A	—	HYD
Boeing Aerospace Company	Jetfoil 929-115	—	—	HYD
Boeing Aerospace Company	Jetfoil 929-115 Patrol	20A	—	HYD
570-KA				
F R Lürssen Werft (GmbH & Co)	46·60m yacht	—	—	MH
MOTEURS BAUDOUIN **12 F 11 SRM**				
International Catamarans Pty Ltd	20m	—	—	CAT
12 P 15.2 SR7				
Société Bretonne de Construction Navale (SBCN)	38m Patrol boat	—	—	MH
CATERPILLAR TRACTOR COMPANY, ENGINE DIVISION **3208**				
Jones Kirwan & Associates	Air Trek 140	—	—	HOV
Tjetty Marine	—	TA	*Jalesveva*	MH
3408				
RMI Inc	SD-60	DITA	*Halcyon*	SWATH
3412				
International Catamarans Pty Ltd	22m	TA	*Klondike*	CAT
CHINA, PEOPLE'S REPUBLIC **12V 150 C**				
	Type 717			
12150 CZ				
China Dagu Shipyard	Type 7203	—	—	SES
12180				
China Wuhu Shipyard	Type 719	—	—	SES
M50				
Hutang Shipyard	—	—	—	HYD
CRM MOTORI MARINI SpA **CRM 18 D/SS-BR-1**				
Azimut SpA	27m	—	*Atlantic Challenger*	MH
CUMMINS ENGINE COMPANY INC **KTA-50-M** (16 cylinder)				
Gulf Craft Inc		—	*Paula McCall*	MH
V-555-M (8 cylinder)				
Vosper Hovermarine	HM 216	—	—	SES
VT-8-370				
Helmut Kock		—	*Bolivia Arrow*	HYD
DETROIT DIESEL ALLISON (GENERAL MOTORS) **Division of General Motors** **6V-92**				
Vosper Hovermarine Ltd	HM 221	TI	—	SES
Cheoy Lee	Air Ride 82	TA	—	ALH
8V-71				
Shinju Shipbuilding Co	—	N	*Kariushu*	MH
8V-92				
Vosper Hovermarine	HM 221	MTI	—	SES
Bell Halter	Model 720A	N	*Rodolph*	SES
Bell Halter	Model 212B	—	—	SES
International Catamarans Pty Ltd	20m	TI	—	
International Catamarans Pty Ltd	18m	TI	—	CAT
International Catamarans Pty Ltd	18m	TA	—	
Tjetty Marine	—	—	*Bima Express*	MH
Azimut SpA	AZ60	TI	—	MH
Vosper Hovermarine	HM 218	TI	—	SES
Boeing Aerospace Company	Jetfoil 929-320	TI	—	HYD

Engine manufacturer, engine principal designation, craft builder	Craft	Engine secondary designation	Craft name	Craft type
12V-71				
Korea Tacoma Marine Industries Ltd	21m	TI	—	SES
Chantiers Navals de l'Esterel SA	Esterel 26	TI	—	MH
Fairey Marinteknik (UK) Ltd	Tracker	TI	—	MH
Aluminium Boats Inc	Hargrave 23·78m	TI	The Hope	MH
Halter Marine Inc	Halmar 65	TI	—	MH
Halter Marine Inc	Halmar 101	TI	—	MH
Halter Marine Inc	Halmar 112	TI	—	MH
Halter Marine Inc	Halmar 122	TI	—	MH
12V-92 (with 145 type injection)				
Westport Shipyard Inc	Westfoil 80	TA	—	HYD
NQEA International Catamarans Pty Ltd	28m, 23m, 22m InCat	TA	Spirit of Victoria/ Spirit of Alderbrook	CAT
SBF Engineering	—	—	James Kelly II	MH
Shinju Shipbuilding Co	—	TI	Tropical Queen	MH
Shinju Shipbuilding Co	—	TI	Shimabara	MH
Halter Marine Inc	Halmar 115	MTI	—	MH
Halter Marine Inc	—	—	Sportsfisher	SES
Precision Marine Holdings Pty Ltd	33m	TA	Motive Explorer	CAT
International Catamarans Pty Ltd	23m	—	—	CAT
Miwon Trading & Shipping Co Ltd	28m	—	—	MH
International Catamarans Pty Ltd	20m	TA	—	CAT
Cheoy Lee	Air Ride 82	TA	—	ALH
16V-92				
NQEA	InCat 28m/29m	TA	—	
NQEA	InCat 24m	TI	—	
Breaux's Bay Craft Inc	—	—	Agathe	MH
Magnum Marine Corp	Magnum 63	TI	—	MH
International Catamarans Pty Ltd	28m	TA	—	CAT
16V-149				
Brødrene Aa Båtbyggeri A/S	CIRR 105P Norcat	TIB	—	SES
Bell Halter Inc	212B	TIB	—	SES
Société Française de Constructions Navales (SFCN)	—	T	Regina	MH
Souter Shipyard Ltd	Wasp	TI	—	MH
Campbell Industries	Spalding 165	TI	—	MH
Sing Koon Seng	InCat	TI	Ipo-Ipo 3001	CAT
Bell Halter Inc	730A (SES-200)	TI	Jaeger	SES
International Catamarans Pty Ltd	37·2m	TIB	—	CAT
Mitsubishi Heavy Industries Ltd	26·03m	TI	—	MH
DEUTZ (KHD)				
BF6L 912				
Dong Feng Shipyard	Type 7210	—	—	HOV
BF6L 913				
Air Cushion Enterprises Pty Ltd	Surveyor 12 D	C	—	HOV
Air Vehicles Ltd	Tiger 16	C	—	HOV
Air Vehicles Ltd	Tiger 40	C	—	HOV
Griffon Hovercraft Ltd	1000 TD	C	—	HOV
Griffon Hovercraft Ltd	1500 TD	C	—	HOV
Griffon Hovercraft Ltd	2500 TD	C	—	HOV
Dong Feng Shipyard	Type 7210	—	—	HOV
Holland Hovercraft vof	Kolibrie 2000	C	Capricorn 1	HOV
Slingsby Aviation Ltd	SAH 2200	C	—	HOV
BF10L 413F				
Korea Tacoma Marine Industries	Turt IV	FC	—	HOV
BF12L 413				
Shanghai Hu Dong Yard	Type 716 II	FC	—	HOV
Korea Tacoma Marine Industries	Turt IV	FC	—	HOV
BF12L 513				
British Hovercraft Corporation plc	AP1-88/200 well-deck version	CP	—	HOV
NQEA	AP1-88	C	—	HOV
British Hovercraft Corporation plc	AP1-88	C	—	HOV
DEUTZ MWM				
TBD 234 V6				
Société Française de Constructions Navales (SFCN)	Marlin 21	—	—	MH
TBD 234 V12				
NQEA	22·0m, 24·0m	—	—	CAT
TBD 234 V16				
Fairey Marinteknik (UK) Ltd	28·8m	—	—	MH
International Catamarans Pty Ltd	30·0m	—	—	CAT
TBD 603 V16				
Vosper Private Ltd	—	—	Jubail Fireboat	MH
SBF Engineering	—	—	Victory III	CAT
TBD 604B V8				
Fairey Marinteknik Shipbuilders (S) Pte Ltd	35 MPV	—	—	MH
International Catamarans Pty Ltd	29m	—	—	CAT
TBD 604B V12				
NQEA	30·0m InCat	—	—	CAT
Brødrene Aa Båtbyggeri	—	—	Ekwata	SES
Fjellstrand A/S	38·8m	—	—	CAT
Precision Marine Holdings Pty Ltd	33·4m	—	Tropic Sunseeker	CAT

Engine manufacturer, engine principal designation, craft builder	Craft	Engine secondary designation	Craft name	Craft type
TBD 604B V16				
Fjellstrand A/S	38·8m	—	—	CAT
International Catamarans Pty Ltd	—	—	Tassie Devil 2001	CAT
Brødrene Aa Båtbyggeri	—	—	Ekwata II	SES
BAM 16M 816				
Nichols Brothers Boat Building Inc	InCat	C	Catamarin	CAT
Westamarin A/S	W88	—	Haugesund	CAT
International Catamarans Pty Ltd	26m	—	—	CAT
Italthai Marine Ltd	27·4m	CR	—	MH
SBAM 12M 816				
Westport Shipyard Inc	27·4m	—	—	MH
SBA 16M 816				
Singapore Shipbuilding and Engineering Ltd	Patrol boat 22·7m	—	—	MH
FUJI PIELSTICK				
12 PA 4V 200 VGA				
Mitsui Engineering & Shipbuilding Co Ltd	CP30 Mk III	—	—	CAT
16 PA 4V 185-VG				
Mitsui Engineering & Shipbuilding Co Ltd	CP20HF	—	—	CAT
Mitsui Engineering & Shipbuilding Co Ltd	CP30	—	—	CAT
Mitsui Engineering & Shipbuilding Co Ltd	—	—	Kotozaki	SWATH
GENERAL ELECTRIC COMPANY				
LM100				
Textron Marine Systems (formerly Bell Aerospace Canada Textron)	Voyageur 001	—	—	HOV
LM500				
Danish Navy Stanflex 300	Multi-mission Patrol	—	—	MH
LM2500				
Boeing Marine Systems	PHM	—	—	HYD
IKEGAI CORPORATION				
16V 190 ATC				
Mitsui Engineering & Shipbuilding Co Ltd	CP30 Mk III	—	—	CAT
Ikegai MAN 254 MLE V12				
Shinju Shipbuilding Co	—	—	Lansing	MH
ISHIKAWAJIMA-HARIMA HEAVY INDUSTRIES				
IM-100 (GE LM-100)				
Mitsui Engineering & Shipbuilding Co Ltd	MV-PP5	—	—	HOV
ISOTTA FRASCHINI SpA				
ID 32 SS 6				
A Fai Engineers & Shiprepairers Ltd	InCat 16m	LM	—	CAT
ID 36 6V				
Cantieri Navali Picchiotti 75	22·86m	SS	—	MH
Cantieri Navicelli	23·00m	SS	—	MH
A Fai Engineers & Shiprepairers Ltd	InCat 21m	SS	—	CAT
Oy Wärtsilä AB	PUC 22	S	—	HOV
ID 36 12V				
Feodosiya	Kometa	SS	—	HYD
Cantieri Navali Baglietto SpA	23m	—	—	MH
Navalmeccanica Belletti	27m	—	—	MH
Cantieri di Lavagna	32m	—	—	MH
ID 38 6V				
Fincantieri-Cantieri Navali Italiani SpA	Sparviero (auxiliary engine)	N	—	HYD
MAN NUTZFAHRZEUGE GmbH				
D 2540				
Wanganui	18m InCat	MLE	—	CAT
D 2542				
Hong Leong-Lürssen Shipyard Bhd	—	MLE	Zaharah	CAT
Versil Marine SA	—	—	Challenger	MH
Seaconstruct Pte Ltd	—	MLE	Jetwise, ex Mariam	MH
Gladding-Hearn Shipbuilding	19·15m C Raymond Hunt	—	Sandy Hook	MH
Shinju Shipbuilding Co	—	—	Sea Angel	MH
D 2840 (10 cylinder)				
Société Bretonne de Construction Navale (SBCN)	25m	LE	Iles D'or XVIII	MH
D 2842 (12 cylinder)				
Société Bretonne de Construction Navale (SBCN)	—	LE	Atlante	MH
Société Bretonne de Construction Navale (SBCN)	25m	LE	Amiral de Joinville	MH
MTU				
12V 93 TY 70				
Fjellstrand A/S	25·5m	—	—	CAT
8V 331				
Boeing Aerospace Company	PHM	TC 80	—	HYD
12V 331				
Rodriquez Cantieri Navali SpA	RHS 70	TC 82	—	HYD
Rodriquez Cantieri Navali SpA	RHS 150	TC 82	—	HYD
Hitachi Zosen	PTS 50 Mk II	TB 82	—	HYD
Cantieri Navali Italcraft Srl	M78	TC 82	—	MH
Vosper Private Ltd	SNV SEEB	TC 92	—	MH

Engine manufacturer, engine principal designation, craft builder	Craft	Engine secondary designation	Craft name	Craft type
12V 331 (contd)				
Mitsui Engineering & Shipbuilding Co Ltd	CP20	TC 82	—	CAT
Swiftships Inc	125ft	TC 71	—	MH
12V 339				
Fjellstrand A/S	Alumaran 165 25·5m	TC 62	—	CAT
6V 396				
Marinteknik Verkstads AB	30MCB (CV900)	TC 82	—	MH
8V 396				
Korea Tacoma Marine Industries	26m	TB 83	—	SES
Wavemaster International Pty Ltd	Sea Raider	—	—	MH
Valmet Oy	Patrol craft 364-366	TB 83	—	MH
Westamarin A/S	S80	TB 83	Vøringen	MH
Oceanfast Pty Ltd	4000	TB 93	—	MH
Lantana Boatyard	Guardian	TB 93	—	MH
NQEA	22/23m InCat	TC 82	—	CAT
12V 396				
Marinteknik Verkstads AB	JC-F1	TC 82	—	CAT
Marinteknik Verkstads AB	JC 3000	TB 83	—	CAT
Marinteknik Verkstads AB	Marinjet 33CPV (PV 2400)	TB 83	—	CAT
Marinteknik Verkstads AB	Marinjet 34CCB	TC 82	—	CAT
Vosper Hovermarine Ltd	HM 527 Series 1	TB 83	—	SES
USSR S Ordzhonikidze Shipbuilding & Repair Yard	Kolkhida	TC 82	—	HYD
Brødrene Aa Båtbyggeri A/S	25m	TC 62	Hyen	HYD
Fairey Marinteknik Shipbuilders (S) Pte Ltd	Marinjet 34CCB	TC 62	Hakeem	CAT
F R Lürssen Werft (GmbH & Co)	—	TB 83	Shergar	MH
Chung Wah Shipbuilding & Engineering Co Ltd	King Class	TB 83	—	MH
Scheepswerf Porsius BV	33m	TB 94	—	MH
Watercraft Ltd	P2000	TB 93	—	MH
Westamarin A/S	W88	TB 83	—	CAT
Fjellstrand A/S	31·5m	TB 63	—	CAT
Brooke Yachts Ltd	—	TB 93	Virgin Atlantic Challenger II	MH
Cantieri Navali Baglietto SpA	Seneca Megajet	TB 93	—	MH
16V 396				
SBF Engineering	—	TB 83	—	MH
Fjellstrand A/S	38·8m	TB 83	—	CAT
Marinteknik Verkstads AB	Marinjet 33CPV-D (PV 3100)	TB 83	—	CAT
Marinteknik Verkstads AB	Marinjet 34CCR (CV 3400)	TB 93	—	CAT
International Catamarans Pty Ltd	29·6m	TC 82	—	CAT
Fjellstrand A/S	38·8m	TB 63	—	CAT
Fjellstrand A/S	49·5m	TB 94	—	CAT
International Catamarans Pty Ltd	30·0m	TC 83	—	CAT
Sing Koon Seng Pte Ltd	InCat 29·0m	TB 63	—	CAT
Vosper Thornycroft Ltd	33·5m	TB 94	Atlantic Challenger III	MH
Westamarin A/S	W5000	TB 84	Anne Lise	CAT
12V 493				
Rodriquez Cantieri Navali SpA	RHS 110	Ty 71	—	HYD
Rodriquez Cantieri Navali SpA	RHS 140	Ty 71	—	HYD
Rodriquez Cantieri Navali SpA	RHS 70	—	—	HYD
Rodriquez Cantieri Navali SpA	PT 50	Ty 71	—	HYD
Fjellstrand A/S	Alumaran 165 25·5m	Ty 70	—	CAT
Westamarin A/S	W86	Ty 70	—	CAT
Vosper Singapore Pte Ltd	PT 20B Mk II	Ty 70	—	HYD
Rodriquez Cantieri Navali SpA	PT 50 SL	Ty 70	—	HYD
16V 538				
Chantiers Navals de l'Esterel SA	Esterel 29 & 42	TB 92	—	MH
Italthai Marine Ltd	PGB 50·14m	TB 91	—	MH
12V 652				
Rodriquez Cantieri Navali SpA	RHS 200	TB 71	—	HYD
Supramar Hydrofoils Ltd	PTS 75 Mk III	—	—	HYD
Vosper	PT 75	—	—	HYD
12V 1163				
Westermoen Hydrofoil A/S, now Westamarin A/S	PTS 150 Mk III	TB 83	—	HYD

PAXMAN DIESELS LTD

8RP 200-1-CM				
Fairey Marinteknik (UK) Ltd	33m Protector Class	—	—	MH
16RP 200-1-CM				
Vosper Thornycroft (UK) Ltd	62·5m	—	Cheung Kong	MH
	62·5m	—	Ju Kong	MH
Bollinger Machine Shop and Shipyard Inc	33·0m Island Class	—	—	MH
Vosper Thornycroft (UK) Ltd	56m Province Class	—	—	MH
Vosper Thornycroft (UK) Ltd	Fast strike craft	—	—	MH
12 SET CWM				
Sheng Hsing Shipbuilding, Taiwan	Fast ferry	—	—	MH
Fairey Marinteknik (UK) Ltd	Protector fast patrol boat	—	—	MH

PERKINS ENGINES (SHREWSBURY) LTD

CV 12 M 800				
Atlantic and Gulf Boat Builder Inc	24m InCat	—	—	CAT
T6				
Aluminium Shipbuilders Ltd	19m InCat	—	—	CAT

Engine manufacturer, engine principal designation, craft builder	Craft	Engine secondary designation	Craft name	Craft type
PRATT & WHITNEY CANADA				
ST6T				
Textron Marine Systems (formerly Bell Aerospace Canada Textron)	Model 7467 LACV-30	—	—	HOV
ST6T-76 Twin Pac				
Textron Marine Systems (formerly Bell Aerospace Canada Textron)	Voyageur 002 LACV-30	—	—	HOV
ROLLS-ROYCE plc				
Marine Gnome GN 1301				
British Hovercraft Corporation plc	SR.N6 Mk 6	—	—	HOV
Marine Proteus				
Fincantieri-Cantieri Navali Italiani SpA	Sparviero	15M/553	—	HYD
British Hovercraft Corporation plc	SR.N4 Mk 3 (ex Mk 1)	15M/529	—	HOV
British Hovercraft Corporation plc	BH.7 Mk 5A	15M/549	—	HOV
SAAB-SCANIA				
Scania Division				
DSI 14				
Marinteknik Verkstads AB	41·9m	—	Cinderella	MH
Wico Boat, Finland	21·8m	—	—	MH
TEXTRON LYCOMING				
TF25				
Mitsui Engineering & Shipbuilding Co Ltd	MV-PP15	—	—	HOV
CHACONSA	VCA-36	—	—	HOV
Cougar Holdings Ltd/Commercial Marine Resources		—	Pegasus	CAT
TF40				
Textron Marine Systems	LCAC	B	—	HOV
Westamarin A/S	W100T	S	—	CAT
LTX101				
Günther W Jörg	18·0m Jörg V	—	—	WIGE
VOLVO PENTA				
AQAD 40/280B				
Korea Tacoma Marine Industries Ltd	12m	—	—	SES
MD 40A				
Korea Tacoma Marine Industries Ltd	12m	—	—	SES
TAMD 71				
Aluminium Shipbuilders Ltd	16·35m	—	Daily Telegraph	CAT
YANMAR				
6 LAAM				
Mokubei Shipbuilding Co	23·5m	UT 1	—	MH
12 LAAK				
Mokubei Shipbuilding Co	25·5m	UT 1	Kaiyo	MH

GEARBOXES

BELGIUM

TWIN DISC INTERNATIONAL SA

Chaussée de Namur 54, 1400 Nivelles, Belgium

Telephone: (067) 21 49 41
Telex: 57414 TWINSA B
Telefax: (067) 21 95 77

Ph Pécriaux, *Managing Director and Technical Director*
Ph Bronselaer, *Director, Finance and Administration*
K Sethi, *Marketing Director*
J Pierquain, *Marine Product Sales Manager*

During the Second World War Twin Disc Inc started manufacturing marine gears for landing craft. After the war production and development continued with marine gears for engine manufacturers and private boat builders. Twin Disc has manufacturing facilities in Racine, USA and Nivelles, Belgium.

The gearboxes types MG 5111 series and MG 5091 series have recently gone into production and in the next year Twin Disc will start production of a new model every three to four months.

Range of standard gearboxes produced
Planing craft ratings

		MG 502-1	MG 506A	MG 506-1	MG 5061A	MG 5061SC	MG 507A-1	MG 507-1	MG 507A-2	MG 507-2	MG 5090A	MG 5091SC	MG 5111A	MG 5111SC
Pleasure craft rating	hp	270	320	320	400	400	420	420	500	500	600	600	800	800
	rpm	@ 2800	@ 2800	@ 2800	@ 2800	@ 2800	@ 2300	@ 2300	@ 2300	@ 2300	@ 2300	@ 2300	@ 2300	@ 2300
Ratios		1·5	1·1	1·1	1·1	1·1	1·1	1·1	1·1	1·1	1·5	1·5	1·5	1·5
		2·0	1·5	1·5	1·5	1·5	1·5	1·5	1·5	1·5	2·0	2·0	2·0	2·0
			2·0	2·0	2·0	2·0	2·0	2·0	1·77	1·77	2·5	2·5	2·5	2·5
			2·5	2·5	2·5	2·5	2·5	2·5				3·0		3·0
			3·0	3·0		3·0	3·0	3·0						
Input housing		3	1, 2, 3	1, 2, 3	2, 3	2, 3	1, 2, 3	1, 2, 3	1, 2, 3	1, 2, 3	1, 2	1, 2	1, 2	1, 2
Down angle or centre drop		10°	10°	Co-axial	7°	144mm	7°	Co-axial	7°	Co-axial	7°	173mm	7°	190mm
V-drive		√			√						√		√	
Power take-off					√	√					√	√	√	√
Cruise control			√	√	√		√	√	√	√	√		√	
Weight (kg)		70	100	100	95	95	160	160	160	160	200	225	245	250

Twin Disc MG 507A-1 gearbox

Twin Disc MG 5111A gearbox

GERMANY, FEDERAL REPUBLIC

LOHMANN & STOLTERFOHT GmbH

Postfach 1860, D-5810 Witten, Federal Republic of Germany

Telephone: (2302) 176-1
Telex: 8 229005
Telefax: (2302) 88148

Lohmann and Stolterfoht manufacture a range of gearboxes for torques ranging from 5kNm to 3580kNm for marine propeller transmissions.

Type	Torque	Reduction ratios available
Navilus GUU	5 to 16kNm	1·5 to 6·5:1·0
Navilus GUS	8·4 to 49kNm	2·0 to 6·0:1·0
Navilus GWC	15·5 to 190kNm	2·0 to 6·0:1·0
Navilus GCS/GUC	39·0 to 2200kNm	1·5 to 6·0:1·0
Navilus GUT	570·0 to 3580kNm	1·5 to 12·0:1·0
Navilus GVA/GVE	50·0 to 1620kNm	2·0 to 6·0:1·0
Navilus GVG	690 to 3580kNm	2·0 to 6·0:1·0

REINTJES

Eisenwerke Reintjes GmbH
Postfach 567, 3250 Hameln 1, Federal Republic of Germany

Telephone: (05151) 104-0
Telefax: (05151) 104-300

UK representative: European Marine and Machinery Agencies, 22-26 Gore Road, New Milton, Hampshire BH25 6RX

Telephone: (0425) 618704
Telex: 417170

Reintjes have specialised in the manufacture of marine gears for harbour craft and sea-going vessels for more than 50 years. The company has produced over 60 000 gearboxes.

WVS GEARBOX

The WVS gearbox is specifically developed for operational requirements that have weight saving as a priority. The manufacturers claim that this has been achieved with high efficiency, an aluminium housing giving a low power to weight ratio, and smooth control with optimum quietness when operating.

The gear range covers several sizes with a maximum input torque of 51 600Nm at a power/speed ratio between 0·09 and 4·411kW/rpm for the offset version of the WVS gearbox. The torque values for co-axial lightweight gears lie between 25 000Nm and 70 000Nm.

Gearboxes are fitted with a three-shaft arrangement. The output shaft is vertically offset below the input shaft, the intermediate shaft is laterally offset between both shafts. Clutch wheels on the input and intermediate shafts are continually washed. Both shafts have reduction pinions driving the wheel mounted on the main shaft. Full power can be transmitted in both directions, ahead and astern, thus identical engines in multi-engine layouts with contra-rotating propellers can be used.

All WVS gearboxes can be supplied with trailing oil pumps, loiter drives, and power take-offs.

Applications

WVS 110 P: Installed in landing craft, input power 300kW at 2800rpm, reduction ratio 2·28:1·0.
WVS 2232 P: Installed in motor yachts, input power 3460kW at 1850rpm, reduction ratio 3·95:1·0.
WAV 4942 SO: This gearbox has been installed in the Peacock class of patrol boats built by Hall Russell of Aberdeen, Great Britain. Input power is 5220kW at 1000rpm.

WATERJET DRIVES

Reintjes have developed a new gear design for waterjets. The gear unit can be used with either vertical or horizontally offset shafts rotating left- or right-handed. The reduction ratios meet the requirements for waterjets as they have a tolerance of ±3%. These drives can also be fitted with a secondary drive for an hydraulic pump.

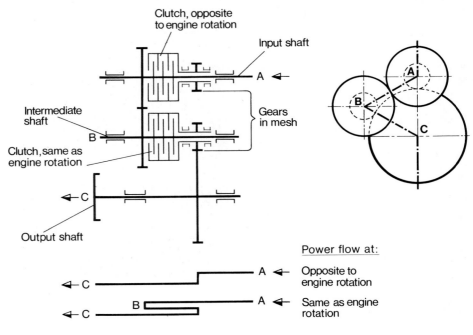

Power flow diagram for Reintjes WVS gearbox

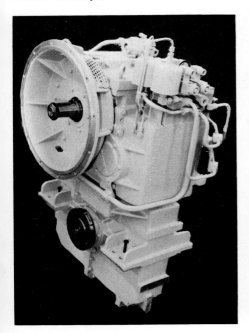

Reintjes WVS 110 P gearbox

Reintjes WVS 2232 U gearbox

Reintjes WAV 4942 SO gearbox

RENK AKTIENGESELLSCHAFT

Postfach 10 00 53, D-8900 Augsburg 1, Gögginger
Strasse 73, Federal Republic of Germany

Telephone: (0821) 5700-0
Telex: 53781
Telefax: (0821) 5700460

PLS AND PWS GEARBOXES

Renk Tacke's marine planetary gear units (PLS
and PWS series) have been specifically developed
for use in fast ships such as corvettes, speedboats,
minesweepers, minelayers, OPVs and IPVs.
Designed for a performance range between 800
and 10 000kW, they cover a very wide range of
applications. The specific characteristics and

Planetary marine gears

Type	Size	Reduction ratio (i)	kW/rpm	A i ≤ 2·8	A i > 2·8	B	C	D
PLS	12·5	1·5-4·8	1·7	850	750	730	890	400
PWS	12·5	1·5-4·8	1·7	970	870	730	900	400
PLS	18	1·5-4·8	2·4	900	800	820	920	450
PWS	18	1·5-4·8	2·4	1050	930	820	940	450
PLS	25	1·5-4·8	3·5	950	850	890	950	500
PWS	25	1·5-4·8	3·5	1130	1030	890	1000	500
PLS	35·5	1·5-4·8	5	1130	1050	1060	1040	580
PWS	35·5	1·5-4·8	5	1280	1150	1060	1100	580
PLS	50	1·5-4·8	7	1200	1100	1170	1140	650
PWS	50	1·5-4·8	7	1400	1250	1170	1150	650
PLS	60	1·5-4·8	8·4	1250	1150	1230	1150	690
PWS	60	1·5-4·8	8·4	1550	1400	1230	1180	690
PLS	71	1·5-4·8	10	1300	1100	1300	1200	710
PWS	71	1·5-4·8	10	1600	1500	1300	1200	710

Renk planetary gear unit during assembly

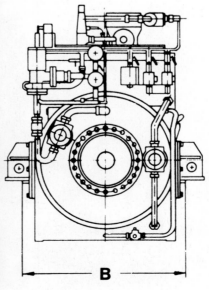

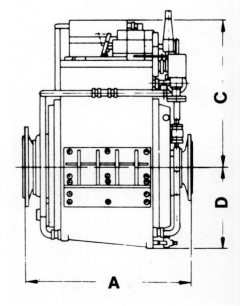

Renk PLS and PWS series gearboxes

advantages of disconnectable planetary gear units (PLS) and planetary reversing gear units (PWS) are:

ratios 1·5 to 4·8

PWS series efficiencies 97·5 to 98%

PLS series efficiencies 98·5 to 99%

compact design, permitting favourable engine room concepts

low power-to-weight ratio of less than 0·5kg/kW

co-axial input and output shafts for optimum powerplant layouts

high shock resistance due to planetary design

insensitivity of transmission elements to hull distortion, providing high operational reliability even under extreme service conditions

high efficiency due to epicyclic concept

starboard and port gear units offer identical connection interfaces and with PWS units this means completely identical starboard and port gear units, even for multi-propeller ships

forward and reverse gears of PWS units are both designed for 100% loads, engines can therefore

operate with the same direction of rotation without affecting the gear unit

on request, these gear units can be built under the supervision of any classification society. Anti-magnetic versions are available

high reliability

suitable for use with gas turbines

if required, low-speed gear can be provided

special design with vertically offset shafts for V drives

ZF

Zahnradfabrik Friedrichshafen AG
Postfach 2520, Löwentaler Strasse 100, D-7990 Friedrichshafen 1, Federal Republic of Germany

Telephone: (07541) 77-0
Telex: 734207-0 ZF D
Telefax: (07541) 772158

H Marschner, *Head, Marine Department*

ZF produces about 5000 marine gears annually, including about 1000 at their main plant in Friedrichshafen, 2500 in Padua, Italy and 1500 in São Paulo, Brazil. Their range of reduction and reversing gears is from 75 to 4500kW for high-speed craft and 75 to 1000kW for work boats. All gears can be supplied with classification approval. ZF gears have been fitted in a large number of high performance, naval, commercial and leisure craft throughout the world.

TYPE BW 450

A three-shaft reversing and reduction gearbox with offset input and output shafts, with one clutch on the input shaft and one on the reversing shaft. These gearboxes are suitable for fast leisure craft.

TYPE BW 190

A three-shaft marine reversing and reduction gearbox with offset input and output shafts, with one clutch on the input shaft and one on the reversing shaft. Suitable for fast crew boats.

TYPE BW 452

A reversing gearbox with a front-mounted spur gear reduction stage. The output shaft of the spur gear reduction stage is the input shaft of the reverse reduction stage. A multi-disc clutch is fitted to the input shaft and the reverse shaft. Suitable for heavy-duty work boats and fishing craft.

TYPE BW 1500

A three-shaft reversing and reduction gearbox with dual clutch on the input shaft. Fitted in fast patrol and strike craft.

TYPE MS 1000

A marine 15°-V reduction gearbox for high output installations with a gas turbine as the prime mover. Fitted in high-speed strike craft.

TYPE BW 250

A three-shaft reversing and reduction gearbox with dual clutch on the input shaft. Fitted in patrol boats, fast pilot cutters and fast lifeboats.

TYPE BW 451

A three-shaft reversing and reduction gearbox with offset input and output shafts, with one clutch on input shaft and one on the reversing shaft. Typical applications include hydrofoils, catamarans, mono-hull and sidewall fast ferries.

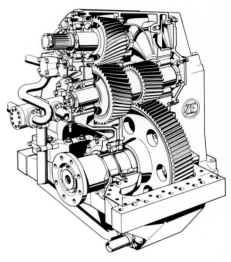

Type MS 1000 ZF gearbox

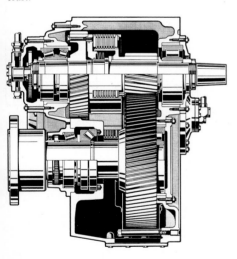

Type BW 450 ZF gearbox

Type BW 250 ZF gearbox

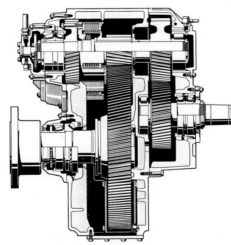

Type BW 452 ZF gearbox

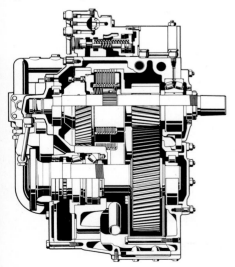

Type BW 190 ZF gearbox

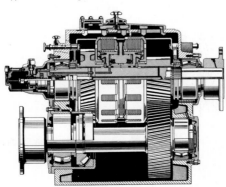

Type BW 1500 ZF gearbox

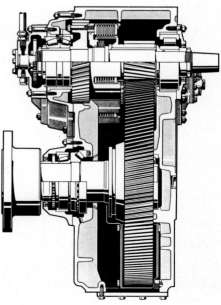

Type BW 451 ZF gearbox

MARINE RANGE

Details of the marine range of gearboxes for high-speed diesel engines are contained in the accompanying tables for power ratings of between 150 and 5800kW.

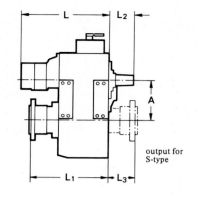
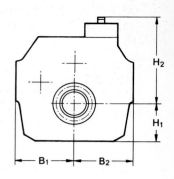

output for standard type

output for S-type

Type	Dimensions (mm)									Mass approx. kg
	A	B_1	B_2	H_1	H_2	L	L_1	L_2	L_3	
BW 120	170	255	255	155	381	539	507	110	—	249
BW 120 S							—		94	253
BW 121	278	350	350	275	489	539	508	110	—	383
BW 160	200	305	305	200	487	505	385	99	—	260
BW 160 S							—		95	250
BW 165	200	305	305	200	487	505	385	99	—	267
BW 165 S							—		95	252
BW 161	365	355	355	340	652	505	390	99	—	568
BW 190	220	340	340	250	522	506	445	132	—	320
BW 190 S							—		100	325
BW 195	220	340	340	250	522	506	445	132	—	322
BW 195 S							—		100	330
BW 191	390	400	400	365	692	506	435	132	—	680
BW 250	235	340	340	250	572	570	565	151	—	430
BW 250 S							—		100	455
BW 255	235	340	340	250	572	570	565	151	—	433
BW 255 S							—		100	468
BW 251	360	375	375	395	697	570	625	151	—	870
BW 450 - 1	310	445	445	316	649	655	565	162	—	667
BW 450 - 1 S							—		144	733
BW 460	310	445	445	316	649	655	565	162	—	672
BW 460 S							—		144	738
BW 465	310	445	445	316	649	655	565	162	—	677
BW 465 S							—		144	743
BW 451 - 1	460	465	465	439	799	655	638	162	—	1254
BW 461										1259
BW 750	340	500	500	348	694	759	600	146	—	880
BW 750 S							—		120	910
BW 755	340	500	500	348	694	759	600	146	—	885
BW 755 S							—		120	915

Main installation dimensions and weights for ZF gearboxes BW 120 to BW 755S (subject to technical modifications and valid for basic design of gearbox)

Types and capacities of ZF marine gearboxes

Type	kW range				
	1000	2000	3000	4000	5000
BW 120	▮				
BW 160	▬				
BW 190	▬▬				
BW 250	▬▬				
BW 450	▬▬				
BW 750	▬▬				
BW 1200		▬▬▬			
BW 1500/2000			▬▬▬▬		

Types and capacities of ZF marine gearboxes

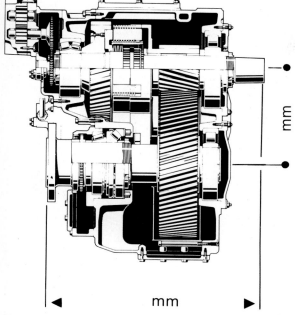

ZF marine gearbox range

Type	Possible ratios	Input torque max. Nm continuous*	Input torque max. Nm intermittent*	Input speed may. min⁻¹	Length mm ◄ ►	Center distance ● mm ●
			Marine Gears			
BW 120	1.1 – 3.0	1220	1320	2600	617	170
BW 121	2.6 – 5.6	1220	–	2600	618	278
BW 160	1.1 – 3.0	1850	2100	2600	484	200
BW 165	1.1 – 2.5	–	2500	2600	484	200
BW 161	3.0 – 6.5	1850	–	2600	489	365
BW 190	1.1 – 3.0	2400	2800	2600	577	220
BW 195	1.1 – 2.5	–	3300	2600	577	220
BW 191	3.0 – 6.5	2400	–	2600	557	390
BW 250	1.1 – 3.5	3300	3750	2500	716	235
BW 255	1.1 – 2.75	–	4600	2500	716	235
BW 251	3.2 – 6.0	3300	–	2500	776	360
BW 460	1.2 – 3.5	5750	–	2500	727	310
BW 465	1.2 – 3.5	–	8250	2500	727	310
BW 451	3.5 – 5.6	4750	–	2000	800	460
BW 461	3.5 – 5.6	5750	–	2000	800	460
BW 750	1.2 – 3.2	7900	9400	2300	746	340
BW 755	1.2 – 3.2	–	11500	2300	746	340
BW 1200	1.1 – 2.2	–	16000	1900	1085	320
BW 1201	1.9 – 3.6	–	16000	1900	1085	450
BW 1203	3.3 – 5.6	–	16000	1900	1565	320
BW 1500	1.1 – 1.9	–	20000	1900	1085	320
BW 1501	1.6 – 3.2	–	20000	1900	1085	450
BW 1503	2.8 – 5.6	–	20000	1900	1565	320
BW 2000	Range on request					
*T max not applicable for entire reduction range.						

ITALY

MPM

Meccanica Padana Monteverde SpA
Viale dell'Industria 48, 35100 Padova, Italy

Telephone: 807 1020/77390
Telex: 430320 MPM PD I

E Rasera, *Commercial Director*

Manufacturer of gearboxes for over 50 years.
MPM is now a full member of the ZF Group.

Type	Nominal ratio	Continuous 1800rpm bhp (kW)	Continuous 2100rpm bhp (kW)	Duty service classification Intermediate duty 2100rpm bhp (kW)	Duty service classification Intermediate duty 2800rpm bhp (kW)	Pleasure 2400rpm bhp (kW)	Pleasure 2800rpm bhp (kW)	Max input rpm
IRM-220 A/V	1·23	130 (97)s	152 (114)s	197 (147)	263 (196)	257 (192)	300 (224)	4500●
	1·53	94 (70)s	108 (81)s	175 (131)	233 (175)	257 (192)	300 (224)	4500●
	2·05	94 (70)s	108 (81)s	175 (131)	233 (175)	257 (192)	300 (224)	4500●
	2·45	94 (70)s	108 (81)s	147 (110)	196 (147)	187 (140)	218 (163)	4500●
IRM-220	2·62	161 (120)s	188 (140)s	222 (166)	300 (224)	—	—	3200
	3·13	149 (111)s	174 (129)s	216 (161)	288 (215)	—	—	3200
	3·55	135 (101)s	157 (118)s	196 (146)	261 (195)	—	—	3200
	3·96	123 (92)s	143 (107)s	181 (135)	241 (180)	—	—	3200
	4·64	111 (83)s	129 (97)s	155 (116)	207 (155)	—	—	3200
IRM-301 AL-1	1·19/1·52	164 (122)	191 (142)	251 (187)	335 (250)	380 (284)	444 (331)	3000+
	2·00/2·90	164 (122)	191 (142)	251 (187)	335 (250)	380 (284)	444 (331)	3000+
IRM-301 PL-1	1·10/1·41	179 (133)	209 (155)	303 (223)	405 (298)	413 (309)	482 (360)	3000+
	1·86/2·69	179 (133)	209 (155)	269 (201)	359 (268)	413 (309)	482 (360)	3000+
IRM-301-1	3·13/3·55	229 (171)	267 (199)	346 (258)	461 (344)	—	—	2600
	3·96/4·64	194 (145)	226 (169)	295 (220)	393 (293)	—	—	2600
	5·0	169 (126)	197 (147)	270 (202)	360 (269)	—	—	2600
		1800rpm	2100rpm	2100rpm	2400rpm	2400rpm	2800rpm	
IRM-320 A	1·59	322 (240)	376 (280)	463 (345)	529 (394)	645 (481)	—	3000◆
	2·08	322 (240)	376 (280)	463 (345)	529 (394)	645 (481)	—	3000◆
	2·58	322 (240)	376 (280)	405 (302)	463 (345)	512 (382)	—	3000◆
IRM-320 PL	1·05/1·48	322 (240)	376 (280)	463 (345)	529 (394)	645 (481)	—	3000◆
	2·19	322 (240)	376 (280)	463 (345)	529 (394)	645 (481)	—	3000◆
	2·53	322 (240)	376 (280)	405 (302)	463 (345)	512 (382)	—	3000◆
IRM-320	3·03	322 (240)	376 (280)	463 (345)	—	—	—	2100
	4·14	273 (203)	318 (237)	463 (345)	—	—	—	2100
	5·06	236 (176)	275 (205)	338 (252)	—	—	—	2100
IRM-400	2·07/2·49	446 (333)	521 (388)	622 (464)	—	—	—	2200
	3·02/3·60	446 (333)	521 (388)	622 (464)□	—	—	—	2200
	4·16/4·96	446 (333)	521 (388)	—	—	—	—	2200
	5·95	402 (300)°	469 (349)	—	—	—	—	2200
	6·74	347 (259)	405 (302)	—	—	—	—	2200
BW-161	3·61+, 4·00	468 (349)	546 (407)	563 (420)	643 (480)	—	—	2600
	4·53+, 5·14	468 (349)	546 (407)	563 (420)	643 (480)	—	—	2600
	5·59+, 6·12	468 (349)	546 (407)	—	—	—	—	2600
	6·48	468 (349)	546 (407)	—	—	—	—	2600

+ IRM-301AL/PL-1   Max continuous duty speed limit is 2600rpm
◆ IRM-320 A/PL   Max continuous duty speed limit is 2100rpm
● IRM-220/A/V   Diesel engine speed limit 4000rpm, and for gasolene engines – 4500rpm
□ IRM-400   Max allowable reduction ratio 3·02:1 for light duty
° IRM-400   312kW 1800rpm with a high elastic coupling
s IRM-220   Max continuous duty speed limit is 3200rpm

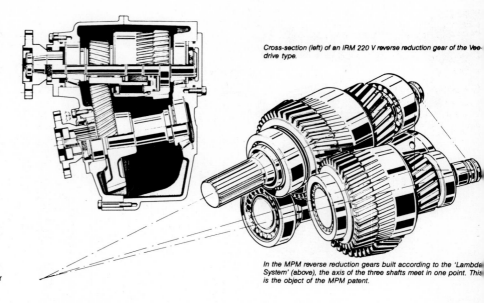

Cross-section (left) of an IRM 220 V reverse reduction gear of the Vee-drive type.

In the MPM reverse reduction gears built according to the 'Lambda System' (above), the axis of the three shafts meet in one point. This is the object of the MPM patent.

MPM IRM 220 V reverse reduction gear

NORWAY

Servogear produce lightweight gears to their own design which have in-built servo systems for controllable-pitch propellers and hydraulic shaft clutches. Servogear gearboxes are specifically designed for high-speed craft where low weight and small size are particularly important.

SERVOGEAR A/S

5420 Rubbestadneset, Norway

Telephone: (054) 27380
Telex: 40909 N
Telefax: (054) 27783

Servogear gearboxes for high-speed craft

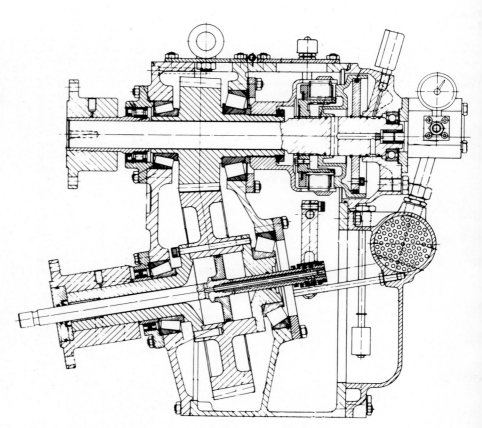

Section through a Servogear gearbox

UNITED KINGDOM

NEI-APE LTD ALLEN GEARS

Atlas Works, Pershore, Worcestershire WR10 2BZ, England

Telephone: (0386) 552211
Telex: 337488
Telefax: (0386) 554491

D H Evans, *General Manager*
D E Yates, *Technical Manager*
H I Grant, *Sales and Marketing Manager*

Allen Gears first became associated with high-speed surface craft in the early 1950s when the Royal Navy commissioned two Vosper prototype

aluminium hull vessels. Each triple-screw craft was powered by three Rolls-Royce Proteus gas turbines driving fixed-pitch propellers. The turbines had a rating of 3500hp at a speed of 11 600rpm, and an Allen epicyclic gear was incorporated to reduce engine speed to 5000rpm. The secondary reduction Allen gearbox consisted of bevel gears for a shaft angle of 15 degrees, driving into a double-train epicyclic reversing section. Since their introduction and subsequent uprating to 4250hp, over 260 primary gear sets have been supplied by Allen Gears to many of the world's navies.

C FORM GEARBOX

In 1978 Allen Gears fitted their C form gearboxes in a Don Shead-designed 29-metre, 45-knot luxury yacht. The yacht cruises on two wing, diesel engine-driven jets and a gas turbine provides power for maximum speed. The turbine is a Textron Lycoming Super TF40 which produces 4600hp at 15 400rpm and drives a Rocketdyne jet pump running at 1664rpm. The gearbox has a C drive configuration, both input and output shafts are at the aft end, and consists of a primary epicyclic train with a single helical parallel-shaft secondary train. An idler is required to cover the necessary centre distance from the gas turbine to the Rocketdyne jet pump and also matches their standard rotations. The jet pump houses the main thrust bearing, therefore secondary gearbox bearings need only accommodate the thrust imposed by single helical gearing. A caliper disc brake is fitted to the free end of the secondary pinion enabling the main jet pump to be held stationary when using wing engine propulsion.

FIVE-SHAFT C FORM DRIVE GEARBOX

As a follow-on from uprated gears for the Royal Navy, Allen Gears constructed a combined epicyclic and parallel-shaft C drive gearbox for a 46-metre, 45-knot luxury yacht built by Fr Lürssen Werft, Federal Republic of Germany. The yacht was powered by two Allison 570 gas turbines driving a KaMeWa waterjet. In addition there were two wing engines driving small waterjets of 1500hp. Total available power was 17 500hp. The gas turbines were positioned aft, driving forward into the gearbox. Each of the turbines has a maximum input of 7250hp at 12 000rpm giving an output speed to the waterjet unit from gearbox of 681rpm. A five-shaft configuration gearbox was adopted to accommodate the centre distance between the gas turbines and the output shaft. The input is taken from the primary epicyclic train through quill-shafts, within the secondary pinion, to SSS self-synchronising clutches at the forward end of the gear case. This arrangement permits the second gas turbine to be introduced to the drive line or to be disconnected without interruption of power.

The Allen five-shaft C form 12 000 to 681rpm reduction gearbox as fitted to an Fr Lürssen Werft luxury yacht, two 5406kW, 7250hp gas turbines

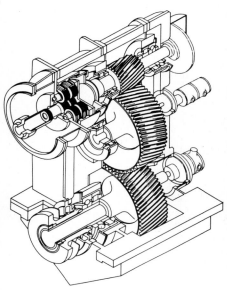

A section view of the Allen C form drive gearbox showing first and second stage reduction gears

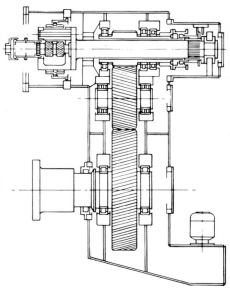

Sectional view of one drive line of the five-shaft C form reduction gearbox

Allen pylon and splitter gearboxes on test before fitting in the CHACONSA VCA-36. Input 14 500rpm, output 1011 and 1080rpm to propellers and lift fans respectively

PYLON GEARBOXES

Another major assignment for Allen Gears has been the development of main splitter and pylon gearboxes for a 60-knot multi-purpose amphibious hovercraft designed by the Spanish company CHACONSA. Power is provided by two Textron Lycoming gas turbines with input speed of 14 500rpm and power of 3000hp. Through the specially-designed gearboxes 1100hp is taken at 1080rpm to drive the lift fans and 1900hp at 1988rpm, further reduced in the pylon gearboxes to 1011rpm, to drive the propellers.

The fastest craft with which Allen Gears is associated has a projected speed of over 100 knots, a power boat for the Pegasus project by Commercial Marine Resources Inc. Two Textron Lycoming 2500hp gas turbines each drive 6000rpm surface-piercing propellers through two Allen parallel shaft gearboxes.

Design and development work is continually being undertaken, in particular for gas turbine-driven propulsion and lift fan drives for a non-integrated air cushion vehicle transmission system incorporating the latest gear technology based upon aircraft experience.

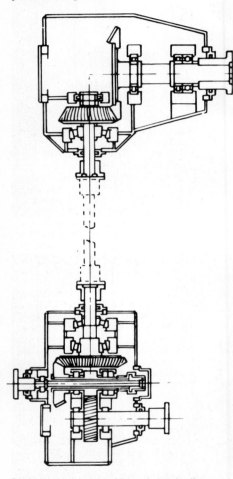

Sectional view showing Allen pylon and splitter gearboxes

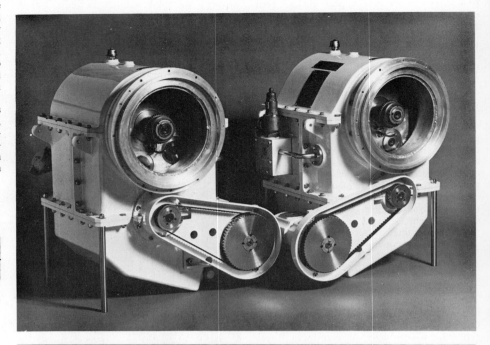

Allen reduction gears (left- and right-handed) for the Commercial Marine Resources Pegasus project (two Textron Lycoming TF25 gas turbines, 2500hp each)

UNITED STATES OF AMERICA

THE CINCINNATI GEAR COMPANY

5657 Wooster Pike, Cincinnati, Ohio 45227, USA

Telephone: 513 271 7700
Telex: 21-4568

D R Bardill, *Marketing Manager*

The Cincinnati Gear Company was founded in 1907. Since the 1950s it has specialised in epicyclic gearing with installations in the Boeing Jetfoil craft series, and the Textron Marine LCAC assault craft.

TWIN DISC INC

Racine, Wisconsin 53403, USA

See entry under Twin Disc International SA, Belgium.

AIR PROPELLERS

FRANCE

RATIER FIGEAC

46100 Figeac, France

Telephone: (65) 34 04 30/34 06 30
Telex: 531977 F

Manufacture of propellers for air cushion vehicles has now ceased.

GERMANY, FEDERAL REPUBLIC

HOFFMANN PROPELLER GmbH & Co KG

Postfach 265, Küpferlingstrasse 9, D-8200 Rosenheim 2, Federal Republic of Germany

Telephone: (08031) 32011
Telex: 525811 HOCO D

Richard Wurm, *Chairman*
Johann Sterr, *Managing Director*

Hoffmann Propeller GmbH & Co KG was founded in 1955 by Dipl-Ing Ludwig Hoffmann and Ing Richard Wurm and now employs about 70 people, divided into 15 clerical, 5 design, 5 inspectors and 45 in production. Of the three design engineers, one is a licensed test pilot.

The company covers the following certification: LBA I-EC 2 for design and development of aircraft propellers; LBA I-C 14 for production of aircraft propellers and equipment; LBA II-A 35 for repair of aircraft propellers and governors not of Hoffmann manufacture; FAA 810-3 F for repair and overhaul of aircraft propellers and accessories licensed by the US airworthiness authority; CAA Hovercraft Approval for design and production of hovercraft propellers.

The total space is about 2600m² and this year the factory will be enlarged with about 1800m² for wood working and composite materials production.

Hoffmann Propeller has been involved in research and development for the German Ministry of Research and Technology, the Ministry of Transportation, the Ministry of Defence as well as

for major aircraft companies such as Messerschmitt-Bölkow-Blohm, Dornier and others.

Propellers have been designed, constructed, tested and produced from 6 to 6000shp. In the latter case Hoffmann blades were installed in an original British Aerospace Dynamics hub on the German Military transport aircraft C-160 Transall. The propeller received military certification. Other developments were, for instance, the 5-bladed shrouded propeller for the MBB/RFB Fantrainer, this aircraft being produced under licence in Thailand. Besides aircraft propellers, blades for wind energy converters, blowers and large fan blades for windtunnel application in the automotive industry are in current production. Propeller overhaul and service is provided for all types of general aviation propellers and different manufacturers.

Special hovercraft propellers have been manufactured as well as propellers for airboats. The reason for this was the excellent erosion resistant features of the composite materials which are superior to aluminium alloy.

Recent installations (Hovercraft and Airboat Propellers)

1960 Since 1960 smaller fixed-pitch and some ground-adjustable and variable-pitch propellers were constantly built for air-propeller driven boats, snow sledges and Hovercraft.
The Manx Hovercat and earlier Scorpion were the first hovercrafts for which Hoffmann built fixed-pitch propellers and electrically controlled variable and reversing pitch propellers. The electric-controlled propeller was, however, too slow in pitch change.

ca. 1970 CHACONSA, VCA-2/3 small craft, 2 propellers, free, driven by about 150kW, 2-bladed, ground adjustable, 2m diameter. Propellers have been overhauled after 1000 hours in good condition, replacements have been delivered.

1981 Wärtsilä *Larus*, 4 propellers, ducted, driven by about 550kW, 4-bladed, for-

ward and reversing, 3m diameter, hydraulically controlled by control valve. This craft is currently with Arctic Transportation Ltd, Tuktoyaktuk, Northwest Territories, Canada.

1982 BHC AP1-88, 2 propellers per craft, ducted, driven by approx 370kW, 4-blade, ground adjustable, 2·75m diameter. Experience with these propellers is increasing and the first propellers are close to 5000 hours time since new. A special polyurethane outer coating and additional leading-edge protection gives a service time for the blade between 1000 and 2000 operating hours before overhaul is considered necessary. The craft are in service between Portsmouth and the Isle of Wight, UK, between Denmark and Sweden (Copenhagen to Malmö) and in Australia.

1982 CHACONSA, VCA-36, 2 propellers, free, one lefthand, one righthand rotation, 1100kW, 5-blade, controllable and reversing pitch propellers, 4m diameter, hydraulically controlled by control valve.

1985 BHC AP1-88, 2 propellers, shrouded, driven by approx 370kW, 4-blade, controllable and reversing, 2·75m diameter. Blade design as for ground adjustable propellers. Craft is in service in USA.

1985 Slingsby, Tropimere 6, 2 propellers, ducted, 3-blade ground adjustable, 1·10m diameter.

1985 Slingsby SAH 2200 (ex 1500), 1 propeller, ducted, 3-blade, 1·50m diameter, reversing.

1986 Marineswift Thunderbolt 30, 1 propeller, ducted, driven by approx 200kW, 5-blade, 1·12m diameter, ground adjustable.

1987 USSR: 2 propellers, ducted, 4-blade, 257kW, 3m diameter, hydraulically controlled.
In development: 5-blade hovercraft propeller, ducted, 2600kW, 4m diameter, hydraulically controlled.

Ducted Hoffmann 2·75m diameter propeller on the Canadian Coast Guard BHC AP1-88

Wärtsilä *Larus* propelled by Hoffmann HO-V194 ducted propellers operating in the Canadian Arctic 1986 *(Hoffmann)*

MT-PROPELLER ENTWICKLUNG GmbH & Co KG

Postfach 0720, D-8440 Straubing, Federal Republic of Germany

Telephone: 094 29 1201/8111

Telex: 65599 MTPRO D
Telefax: 094 29 8432

Gerd Mühlbauer, *President*

This company was formed in 1982 and is mainly involved in the production of propellers for air-

craft. It has developed a range of electric variable-pitch propellers and hydraulic constant-speed propellers. Some of the propellers are LBA approved. The largest diameter propeller built by the end of 1986 was 2·9m, for 800shp, but designs can be undertaken up to 3·5m, 2000shp, and above.

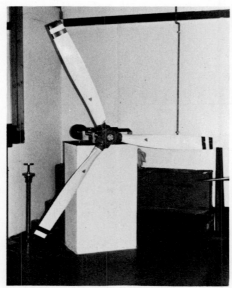  

Examples of recent MT-Propeller Entwicklung propellers

UNITED KINGDOM

AIR VEHICLES LIMITED

Head Office and Factory: Unit 4, Three Gates Road, Cowes, Isle of Wight, Hampshire, England

Telephone: 0983 293194
Telex: 86513 HVWORK G
Telefax: 0983 294704

C D J Bland, *Director*
C B Eden, *Director*
A Moseley, *Director*

Air Vehicles Limited has been involved in hovercraft since 1968 and have manufactured centrifugal fans and propellers of various sizes for their own craft and others.
PROPELLERS: These are of the four-bladed, fixed-pitch, laminated-mahogany type and incor-

porate stainless steel leading-edge protection. Sizes from 0·61m to 1·83m diameter are manufactured. Associated propeller ducts are also produced and ducted propeller systems using propellers up to 2·03m diameter have been built.
FANS: Aluminium centrifugal fans of various sizes up to 0·915m are produced. They are of the reverse aerofoil type, using fabricated or extruded blades in marine aluminium giving a robust fan with a good fatigue life.

  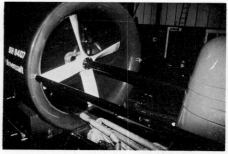

Air Vehicles duct installation fitted to an SR.N6 military craft

0·76m diameter aluminium fan produced by Air Vehicles Ltd

Air Vehicles-built, Robert Trillo-designed propeller on an AV Tiger 16

BRITISH AEROSPACE PLC

Manor Road, Hatfield, Hertfordshire AL10 9LL, England

Telephone: 07072 62300
Telex: 22324/5 G
Telefax: 07072 61915

For over 50 years de Havilland Propellers Ltd, now part of British Aerospace, has been designing, developing and manufacturing propellers with their ancilliaries and control systems. British Aerospace has been responsible for providing the largest propellers for air cushion vehicles.

Recent installations (Air cushion vehicles)
British Hovercraft Corporation BH.7, 6·40m diameter, 4-blade, hydraulic pitch control with reversing, single propeller installation

SEDAM N 500, 6·40m diameter, 4-blade, hydraulic pitch control with reversing, triple propeller installation
British Hovercraft Corporation SR.N4, 5·76m diameter, 4-blade, hydraulic pitch control with reversing, four propeller installation
British Hovercraft Corporation SR.N4 Super 4, 6·40m diameter, 4-blade, hydraulic pitch control with reversing, four propeller installation, swivelling
These propellers have the following design and construction features:
PROPELLER HUB: This is similar for both the 5·76m and 6·4m propellers, comprising a split barrel and a spider to which the blades are fitted and retained by lips on the barrel. Centrifugal loads are taken by single roller thrust bearings between the blade root flanges and the barrel lips. The spider mounts onto a modified SBAC splined

engine shaft and is retained on the shaft by split front and rear cones and a retaining nut.
The hub is protected against the corrosive effects of salt water by epoxy type paint. The ingress of water is prevented by rubber water excluders around the blade shanks, a glassfibre excluder around the pitch change dome/barrel opening and by brushing sealant over all joint faces and fastenings.
The propeller blades on the 5·76m propeller are conventional aluminium alloy suitably anodised and protected against erosion by rubber leading edge sheaths. The 6·4m propeller has composite construction blades consisting of an aluminium alloy spar, with a root end similar to the 5·76m and with a glassfibre blade shell. The shell is made by laminating glassfibre on a former having the specified shape and aerofoil section using a wet lay up process. The shell is then cured in an oven and

One of the four composite-material blade propellers on the BHC SR.N4 Super 4 hovercraft

bonded to the anodic protected spar. Foam is then introduced into the hollow cavities of the blade and the inboard end of the blade is sealed by glass-fibre fairings. The leading edge of the blade is protected by an electro-formed nickel sheath and rubber erosion strip. The finished blade is then sprayed with special polyurethane paint.

PITCH CHANGE MECHANISM: Hydraulic oil is transmitted to the front or rear of a piston depending upon the requirement to alter the pitch angle of the blades. Motion of the piston is transmitted to the blade shank bevel gear by fixed rotating cylindrical cams. The piston and cams are housed in a dome which is fitted onto the front of the propeller hub and held by the dome retaining nut. The rate of change of blade angle is nominally 10° per second. The available range of blade angle can be altered to suit an application within the range − 30° to + 45° (at the 1·83m station on the blade) and with a feather angle of + 90° nominal if desired.

PROPELLER CONTROL SYSTEMS: The Division has produced both analogue and digital electronic control systems and the choice between these methods will depend upon the requirements of a particular application. A typical system is that provided for a large car/passenger carrying hover-craft.

In this hovercraft system the signal demanding blade pitch angle required by the pilot to carry out a particular manoeuvre is put into digital form and is then compared by standard mathematical tech-niques with the existing blade angle which is measured by an optical shaft encoder. The error signal so produced is modified by digital methods to obtain the required overall system response characteristics. The power stage of the electronics drives a stepper motor which controls the position of a single stage hydraulic control valve. Accord-ing to the position of the valve, oil is directed through the bush and sleeve of a pitch control unit to the oil tubes which connect to the front and rear of the pitch change piston. The pitch control unit is mounted on a rear face of the propeller/engine gearbox and a mechanical blade angle feedback is provided through the movement of the oil tubes which is sensed by the shaft encoder previously mentioned.

The ability to feather the propeller is indepen-dent of the control system, so that when a solenoid valve is energised a feathering pump moves oil to push the control valve spindle into the feather position, which in turn directs oil to the pitch change mechanism. A transmitter gives an output

Erosion damage protection sheath, 0·914m length, for fitting to a 3·05m long glassfibre propeller blade

signal to an instrument on the flight deck indi-cating pitch angle and feather position.

WEIGHTS
6·4m diameter propeller (comprising hub, pitch change mechanism and blades): 812·83kg*
Oil in propeller: 33·11kg
Total 'on shaft' wet weight: 846kg
*Total weight subject to a production tolerance of + 2·5%.
Polar moment of inertia: 998·7kg/m²

EROSION/DAMAGE PROTECTION SYS-TEM: The experience gained over many years of servicing glassfibre bladed 6·4m propellers on hovercraft in very severe operational and environ-mental conditions has enabled an Erosion/Damage Protection System (EDPS) to be devel-oped and patented for blade leading edges. This system can be applied to any shape of component within the overall dimensions of a cylinder 2·44m long and 0·6m in diameter.

The breakthrough in technology which the EDP system offers, is the ability to plate a resilient substrate material with erosion-resistant nickel so that an integral molecular bond is formed which withstands erosion and impact or implosion damage. A further characteristic is that any cracks so caused to the nickel plating do not diminish the erosion properties of the system and neither do the cracks propogate to the main structure being protected. Experience in service, at rotational tip speeds of approximately 220m/s, has proved that the nickel plating, even though severely damaged, does not peel away from the substrate material.

The EDP system can be designed to give a predictable erosion life by varying the thickness of the substrate material and, more importantly, by changing the thickness of the nickel deposit locally, to adjust for varying erosion rates over the surface shape of the component being protected.

Shell:- Fibreglass rein-forced plastic with environmental pro-tection of electro-formed nickel sheath and rubber type leading edge erosion strips plus polyurethane paint over remaining area.

Electro-formed leading edge nickel sheath.

Root end enclosure.

Shell ending.

Steel thrust rings.

Neoprene and polyurethane strips.   Bond   Low density foam fill.

Section AA   Spar   Shell   Bond

Low density foam fill.   Spar   Bond

Section BB   Nickel leading edge sheath.   Shell

British Aerospace composite blade construction

DOWTY ROTOL LIMITED

Cheltenham Road, Gloucester GL2 9QH, England

Telephone: 0452 712424/711815
Telex: 43246 G
Telefax: 0452 713821

D G M Davis, *Technical Director*
J D Kemp, *Engineering Manager, Propulsion*
D H Soley, *Project Engineer, Propulsion*
M B Kelly, *Sales and Marketing Director*
D S Russell, *Executive Director, Sales*
R J Willcox, *Sales and Marketing Manager*

Dowty Rotol has been designing and manufac-turing propellers for aircraft since 1937 and for over 25 years has been actively engaged in propul-sion systems for air cushion vehicles.

The company is at present engaged in the production of propellers for the Textron Marine Systems LCAC vehicles and in December 1987 was awarded a further US$8 million contract for propellers and spares, 15 sets in all, 9 for Textron Marine Systems and 6 for Lockheed Shipbuilding Co.

There is a repair, overhaul and assembly plant in the USA: Dowty Rotol Inc, PO Box 5000, Sully Road, Staverton West, Stirling, Virginia 22170.

Telephone: 703 450 5930
Telex: 64269 (International), 824459 (Domestic)

Recent installations (Air cushion vehicles)
British Hovercraft Corporation SR.N5, SR.N6, 2·744m diameter, 4-blade hydraulic pitch con-trol with reversing, single propeller installation, produced in aluminium alloy and composite material construction
British Hovercraft Corporation SR.N6 Mk 6, 3·049m diameter, 4-blade, hydraulic pitch con-trol with reversing, 2-propeller installation, aluminium alloy blades

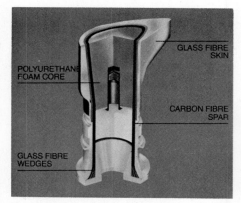

Dowty Rotol blade root retention features

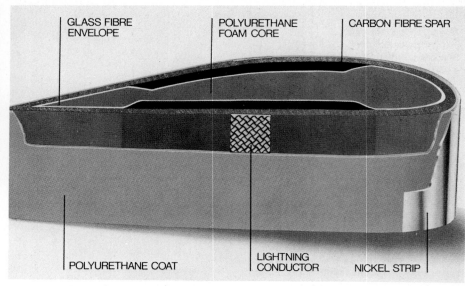

Dowty Rotol composite-material blade construction

Mitsui PP15 3·201m diameter, 4-blade, hydraulic pitch control with reversing, single-propeller installation, aluminium alloy blades

Vosper Thornycroft VT 2 4·116m diameter, 7-blade, 2-propeller installation (ducted), composite-material blades

Textron Marine Systems LCAC 3·582m diameter, 4-blade, 2-propeller installation (ducted) composite material blades

This craft is also built by the Lockheed Shipbuilding Co.

The extensive corrosion and erosion problems associated with air cushion vehicles led Dowty Rotol to develop composite blades with all-over erosion protection. These blades, the latest of which incorporate advanced technology aerofoil sections unique to Dowty Rotol, offer the following advantages: low weight combined with high strength, internal carbon fibre spars for high integrity, freedom from corrosion, easily repairable.

Dowty Rotol propellers for air cushion vehicles are designed to combine simple construction with safe operation. Techniques proven on ACVs have in turn been applied to and certificated on new generation general aviation, executive and commuter aircraft.

Installation of Dowty Rotol propeller on Textron Marine Systems LCAC

Dowty Rotol composite-material blade propeller for Textron Marine Systems LCAC

UNITED STATES OF AMERICA

ADVANCE RATIO DESIGN COMPANY, INC (ARDCO)

2540 Green Street, JEN Industrial Campus, Chester, Pennsylvania 19013, USA

Telephone: (215) 494 3200

David F Thompson, *President*

ARDCO specialises in lightweight, high strength, rotating airfoil blading of all kinds. It has designed and produced all-composite blades for turboprops, ducted propulsion fans, hovercraft compressors and helicopter main rotors. Blades are made of glassfibre, graphite and/or Kevlar/epoxy oriented-linear-filament reinforced materials, compression-moulded with low density cores of honeycomb or foam plastic and flush co-bonded metal leading edge erosion strips. ARDCO also builds special heat-resistant blading for working environments over 300°F. The company produces blades to fit existing hubs, or complete rotor assemblies, as required. Advanced composite finite element analysis and dynamic/aeroelastic analyses are applied as required, using specialist analytical services.

Some propeller blade forms produced by ARDCO

PACIFIC PROPELLER INC (PPI)

(Subsidiary of IMC Magnetics Corp)
5802 S 228th St, Kent, Washington 98032, USA

Telephone: (206) 872-7767
Telex: 32-0368
Telefax: (206) 872-7221

Charles W Johnson, *President*
Dennis Patrick, *Director of Engineering*
Roger Pearson, *Sales Manager*

Pacific Propeller manufactures, overhauls and sells propeller systems for aircraft and hovercraft use, having been in this business since 1946. PPI has manufactured over 10 000 metal propeller blades for single and multi-engine installations and is the current supplier of propellers for the Canadian Coast Guard SR.N5, SR.N6 and Voyageur hovercraft. In addition, PPI's designed and manufactured propeller blades are the only current production units approved for installation on the US Army LACV-30 hovercraft. As a further extension of the development work performed on hovercraft, PPI has entered into an R&D contract with the US Army to provide a ducted, low-speed propulsion system to retrofit on the LACV-30.

HC200-1S PROPELLER BLADE

This is a solid aluminum derivative of the AG-series blades manufactured for aircraft use. It is designed to be tougher and more erosion resistant to the effects of salt and sand spray. Typical hovercraft installations use the 3-bladed HSP 43D50 hub coupled to the P&W ST6 TwinPac or the Rolls Royce Gnome turbine engines. Propeller diameter is 2·72m (8ft 11 inches). This configuration has been tested in excess of 1600 input hp and is safe for operation up to 2300rpm. Each blade weighs 22·22kg (49lb) and can be overhauled using standard propeller overhaul facilities.

LOW-SPEED AIRFOIL DESIGN

Efforts are currently under way to develop military and commercial applications of Pacific Propeller's proprietary low-speed airfoil technology. This includes work for the US Army on the PPI 1300 blade design for application on the LACV-30 and a similar commercial adaptation for the Westfoil 25-metre hydrofoil craft. Other low-speed design projects in the preliminary stage of investigation include installation on large capacity airships.

Technicians preparing an instrumented PPI propeller for testing on Canadian Coast Guard Voyageur

An experimental hovercraft blade, model PPI 1300

MARINE PROPELLERS

AUSTRALIA

SS ENGINEERING (1984) PTY LIMITED

10 Ballantyne Road, Kewdale, Western Australia 6105, Australia
PO Box 5, Cloverdale, Western Australia, Australia

Telephone: (09) 3578388
Telex: 92044 PROPSS AA

Telefax: (09) 4586539

Dennis Wade, *Manager*

Manufacturer of propellers from 250mm diameter to 2550mm in three-, four- or five-blade designs. Materials include 88/10/2 gunmetal, CX3 manganese bronze, AB2 aluminium bronze or CMAI bronze.

A recent installation of SS E and F propellers was on the 190-seat, 25-knot International Catamarans *Thunderbird* built by Bulls Marine Industries at Metung, New South Wales. The propellers are 864mm in diameter, 812mm in pitch. They are also installed on the International Catamarans wave-piercing catamaran *Spirit of Victoria*.

Propellers can be supplied with up to 5, 6 or 7 blades and finished to ISO 484/2-1981 (E) to Class 2, 1 or S standards as required.

DENMARK

HUNDESTED MOTOR & PROPELLER FABRIK A/S

Skansevej 1, DK-3390 Hundested, Denmark

Telephone: (02) 337117
Telex: 40245 HMF DK
Telefax: (02) 339902

Designers and manufacturers of controllable-pitch propellers since 1929. The 20-knot RMI SD-60 *Halcyon* SWATH vessel is fitted with Hundested 1143mm diameter fully-reversible (type FR-H) propellers.

Hundested type FR-H controllable-pitch propeller system as fitted to the RMI *Halcyon*

GERMANY, FEDERAL REPUBLIC

SCHOTTEL WERFT
Josef Becker GmbH & Co KG
D-5401 Spay/Rhein, Federal Republic of Germany

Telephone: (02628) 61
Telex: (17) 262891 SWSPAY D
Telefax: (02628) 61 300

RUDDERPROPELLER SRP 105/105

A contract in 1980 for the Water Police Auth-
ority Rheinland-Pfalz in Mainz included two Police boats to be built to the same specification but one fitted with twin Rudderpropellers and the other with twin shafts, conventional stern gear and rudders. The Rudderpropeller high-speed propulsion system is showing less resistance than conventional shaft layouts in comparison trials, tests of the SRP 105/105-driven police patrol boat WSP 1 being undertaken at the Berlin Institute and optimum configurations tested in a self-propulsion mode at the Tank Test Institute, Duisburg. The resulting lower gear unit proved cavitation

free up to 30 knots and had a surface area of 0·62m² which compared very favourably with the conventional layout which had a surface area (in addition to the hull surface) of 0·94m² (52% increase). Schottel were particularly encouraged by these results as the resistance of lower gear housings in a twin installation at a speed of 26 knots (48km/h), although lower than a conventional layout, still accounted for some 22% of the overall resistance during a series of tests.

The ultimate test was when the two Water Police Mainz vessels underwent trials under

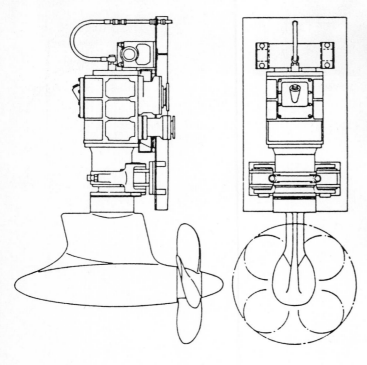

Test craft for Schottel low-resistance Rudderpropeller SRP 105/105

The Schottel low-resistance Rudderpropeller SRP 105/105 cavitation free up to 30 knots

the same conditions. In fact the Rudderpropeller variant (WSP 1) was reported to be at some disadvantage as its final displacement at 12·20m³ was some 0·4m³ more than the conventional vessel (WSP 6). Despite this difference both vessels reached exactly the same speed of 48km/h (26 knots). Both vessels were fitted with twin MAN D 2566 MTE engines each developing 221kW at 2200rpm but apparently the Rudderpropeller only absorbed 170kW at 2200rpm. Schottel have

therefore proposed that the Rudderpropeller boat achieved the 26 knots with 25% less power.

Schottel has also suggested a number of additional advantages such as unsurpassed manoeuvrability, particularly at low speed and even with only one engine; and also considerably less noise due to the ability of the thruster unit and engine to be easily installed on flexible mountings. A noise level of 70dB was measured compared with 74dB on the conventional vessel.

	WSP 6	WSP 1
Length overall	14·00m	14·20m
Length waterline	12·60m	12·70m
Beam overall	3·70m	3·80m
Draught	0·95m	0·95m
Displacement	11·80m³	12·20m³
Power	two 221kW	two 221kW
Speed	48km/h	48km/h

ITALY

COCO MOTORI

Via Aurelia Sud 137, 55044 Marina di Pietrasanta (Lucca), Italy

Telephone: (0584) 21611

Mario P Coco, *Proprietor*

Producer of Deltaprop® 406mm diameter propellers for high-performance planing craft powered by Volvo Penta and BMW engines.

MARINE DRIVE UNITS (MDU)
(LEVI DRIVE UNITS)

Piazza S Ambrogio n16, Milan 20123, Italy

Telephone: (02) 8057795
Telex: 380283 I
Telefax: 31 852376

Ambrogio Caccia Dominioni, *Director*
Renato Levi, *Director*

LEVI DRIVE UNITS

The Levi Drive Units are designed by Renato Levi, a designer of fast power boats over the past 30 years, a pioneer of the Deep-V hull and the Delta configuration. He sought to avoid appendage drag and towards the end of the 1960s he produced his Step-Drive system of propulsion which was first adopted on the 13·1m *Drago*, the world's fastest diesel production cruiser at that time. Since then he has designed over 50 craft employing the Step-Drive system. In seeking to improve this system he evolved the Levi Drive Unit offering the advantages of the conventional 'Z' drive with the increased performance of surface propulsion.

The engine may be fitted amidships or right aft without the added complication of a costly V-drive and transmission shaft. The tunnel rudders over the top half of the propellers have been employed to overcome some of the disadvantages of conventional rudders or propeller power steering. The two vertical rudder blades which are a continuation of the shroud act as side-walls, and, operating below the hull, give positive control as required as well as protecting the propeller in shallow water.

To enhance the reverse thrust capabilities of a fixed-pitch propeller Levi has devised a new blade section profile, giving on the back of the blade a concave area towards the trailing edge, producing improved section lift coefficients and hence thrust when in reverse rotation. The propeller incorporating this profile is called the Diamond Back® superface propeller and overcomes the poor astern thrust associated with surface propellers.

The present complement of Levi Drive Units covers a range from 50 to 2000hp. MDU Marine

Drive are however conducting tests on two further models, the 3000 and 4000, designed to transmit 3000 and 4000hp respectively.

Summary of features
Body of LDU: Monocoque structure in 316 stainless steel, welded and heat treated
Rudder: Of semi-circular design together with reinforcing plate and stock of 316 stainless steel plate and bar respectively

Rudder linkage: Consisting of yoke, dummy tiller and tie rod terminals in cast 316 stainless steel, or nickel-aluminium-bronze
Propeller shaft: Armco Aquamet 17-18-22 or monel k 500
Surface propeller: Four-bladed with Diamond Back sections cast in nickel-aluminium-bronze (NAB). For the Model 2000 and above the propellers are five-bladed
Shaft bearings: Water-lubricated in synthetic fibre

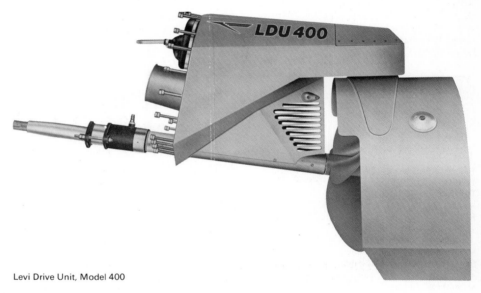

Levi Drive Unit, Model 400

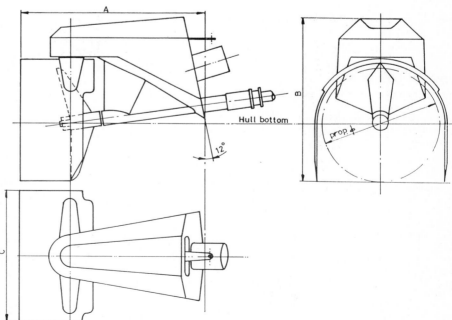

Levi Drive Unit dimensions, see table

Diamond Back® superface propeller

LDU Model data

Model	50	50PL	200	200PL	400	800	800PL	2000
Max torque, shaft, kg/m:	26	45	72	105	205	360	550	850
Rpm/hp indicative limits:	52hp at 1465rpm to 128hp at 3605rpm	120hp at 1950rpm to 292hp at 4760rpm	152hp at 1560rpm to 240hp at 2470rpm	280hp at 1920rpm to 438hp at 3010rpm	438hp at 1540rpm to 700hp at 2460rpm	650hp at 1330rpm to 1000hp at 2040rpm	1200hp at 1600rpm to 1650hp at 2200rpm	1630hp at 1400rpm to 2330hp at 2000rpm
Max torque, rudder stock, kg/m:	30	30	75	75	150	250	250	500
Exhaust, outside dia, mm:	100	100	130	75	160	200	200	300
Fitting to transom (studs):	22	22	20	22	22	24	24	24
Lubrication, linkage:				molybdenum grease				
Lubrication, shaft:				water				
Dimensions: A, mm:	806	806	878	878	1117	1356	1356	1596
B, mm:	670	670	805	805	1019	1231	1231	1450
C, mm:	526	526	635	635	798	952	952	1120
Weight, excluding propeller, kg:	66	70	130	140	265	500	540	1000

OFFICINE E RADICE

Frazione Bettola-Via Valtellina 43, 20093 Cinisello Balsamo, Milan, Italy

Telephone: 02 6182548
Telex: 332352 RADIPRO I

Alfredo Ridici
Carlo Ridici

Manufacture of fixed-pitch propellers for high-speed craft. Early Hovermarine HM2 craft were fitted with Ridici propellers in stainless steel.

JAPAN

KAMOME PROPELLER CO LTD

690 Kamiyabe-cho, Totsuka-ku, Yokohama 245, Japan

Telephone: (045) 811 2461
Telex: 3822315 KAMOME J

Design and manufacture of a wide range of controllable-pitch propellers from 300 to 15 000hp. Recent installations have included 1750mm diameter, 1400mm pitch CPC-53F propellers on the Mitsui 20·5-knot *Kotozaki*, a 27m SWATH vessel.

NETHERLANDS

LIPS BV

PO Box 6, 5150 BB Drunen, Netherlands

Telephone: 4163 88115
Telex: 35185 LIPS NL
Telefax: 4163 73162

F Bult

Lips was established in 1934 and are world leaders in the field of marine propellers, covering fixed-pitch, controllable-pitch, side-thruster and systems to their own design. Five hundred people are employed in the Netherlands company.

Lips provide a dealer network for Riva Calzoni. The company has provided propellers for a number of high-speed craft including Fjellstrand catamarans.

Lips transcavitating CP propeller that was designed for the US Navy SES *Sea Viking*

NORWAY

LIAAEN HELIX A/S

Kjøpmannsgt 23, N-6025 Aalesund, Norway

Telephone: (071) 21191/25838
Telex: 42581 HELIX N
Telefax: (071) 28561

J Aurdal

Designers and manufacturers of controllable-pitch propellers, tunnel thrusters, compass thrusters and the newly developed Speed-Z Propulsion System. Recent high-speed applications have included a controllable-pitch installation on the Fjellstrand high-speed catamaran, *Asie III*, and two Liaaen Speed-Z 4-blade propulsion units, Type CPZ, for the Westamarin W5000 *Anne Lise*, 49·5m high-speed thermo-cargo catamaran, delivered June/July 1987. These units each absorb 2040kW (2736hp) and position the propellers in undisturbed free-stream flow. In comparison with conventional propeller systems an efficiency gain of 10% is claimed. The system

Layout of the Liaaen Speed-Z Propulsion System Type CPZ

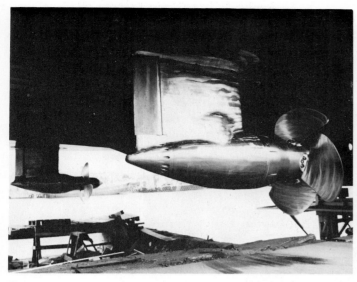 

Liaaen Helix Speed-Z Propulsion Systems Type CPZ 60/40-125 fitted to the Westamarin 5000 *Anne Lise,* 28-knot thermo-cargo catamaran

combines propulsion and steering functions. Other advantages of the Speed-Z propulsion system are reduced vibration and noise onboard, a cost efficient compact installation, effective load control for protection of the drive motors and good manoeuvring capability.

Since Speed-Z is a traction (pulling) propeller there are no appendages in front of it and therefore the propeller acts in a homogeneous velocity field. These are ideal conditions for efficiency and avoidance of damaging cavitation. This has been substantiated by cavitation tests and prototypes in operation which produce no noticeable noise or vibration in the hull.

Another major advantage is the right-angle drive which allows the propeller to be installed in line with the water flow. A conventional propeller installation is always a compromise between keeping the shaft angle low to avoid harmful root cavitation and ensuring sufficient clearance between the propeller and the hull to avoid noise and vibration from the high pressure pulses created by the propeller. The Speed-Z unit has, as mentioned, the best possible conditions of flow to the propeller giving stable cavitation conditions and minimal fluctuating forces.

A comparison has been made, based on model test tank results with the Speed-Z unit, with a conventional installation with sloping shaft, brackets and rudder. The propeller on the conventional installation had a diameter of 1·6m with a maximum speed of 525rpm, while the Speed-Z unit has a diameter of 1·25m at 769rpm. Even though the Speed-Z unit is higher loaded, that is the power per unit area is greater, the propeller efficiency is 76% at an engine output of 2040kW and ship speed of 28 knots. The corresponding efficiency of a conventional installation is about 72%. When the resistance of the appendages was taken into account the improvement in efficiency was even more significant. The result of the model tests showed that the overall propulsive efficiency of the model fitted with the Speed-Z was 66% at 28 knots which compared with 58% for the conventional system as described above. In this case the new Speed-Z gave an improvement in efficiency of 8%, that is to say a saving in installed power of 13·8% to achieve the same speed.

Liaaen Helix Speed-Z Propulsion Unit showing the top reduction gear with clutch and the lower 90° reduction gear with rudder flap and propeller mounting

SERVOGEAR A/S
N-5420 Rubbestadneset, Norway

Telephone: (054) 27380
Telex: 40909 N
Telefax: (054) 27783

Leif M Endresen, *Technical Manager*

Designers and manufacturers of controllable-pitch propellers (up to 2000hp) and drive systems. Servogear propellers are on a number of high-speed craft including the Westamarin S80 mono-hull vessel *Vóringen* and the Westamarin W95 *Sunnhordland.*

A new V-drive system, Type VD 250A, specifically for high-speed craft was announced in 1986. This unit has a built-in clutch and a servo for controllable-pitch propellers. The gearbox has the following characteristics:
  max continuous power input: 590kW at 2300rpm
  reduction ratio: 1·96:1
  torque: 2500N
  dry weight: 160kg
Servogear propellers are manufactured in manganese bronze for the bosses and nickel-aluminium bronze for the blades, but other materials can be used if requested.

SWEDEN

J W BERG
S-43090 Öckerö, Gothenburg, Sweden

Telephone: (31) 781220
Telex: 89200868 S

Telefax: (31) 783716

Design and manufacture of special types of propellers for high-speed craft.

KAMEWA AB
Box 1010, S-68101 Kristinehamn, Sweden

Telephone: 0550 84000
Telex: 66050 KAMEWA S
Telefax: 0550 18190

KaMeWa has accumulated experience from over 40 years of activity in the marine field. The company is also the only manufacturer of controllable-pitch propellers to possess a cavitation laboratory with comprehensive facilities for advanced testing of the various forms of marine propulsion device.

The KaMeWa design and manufacture of propellers for high-speed craft covers super-cavitating designs, super-cavitating designs modified to meet quiet and high-efficiency cruising conditions, wide-blade designs for these conditions, skewed wide-blade propellers for extremely quiet cruising and the same designs incorporating ventilated blades. These propellers are manufactured in either stainless steel or nickel-aluminium bronze.

The smallest propeller in the range is 710mm in diameter and is designed to absorb about 1200shp. Weighing 75kg these propellers are installed in fast patrol craft with maximum speeds of up to 43 knots.

The waterjet unit is becoming an ever increasing alternative for high-speed craft propulsion. KaMeWa is leading also in this field; please see KaMeWa entry in Waterjet Unit Manufacturers section.

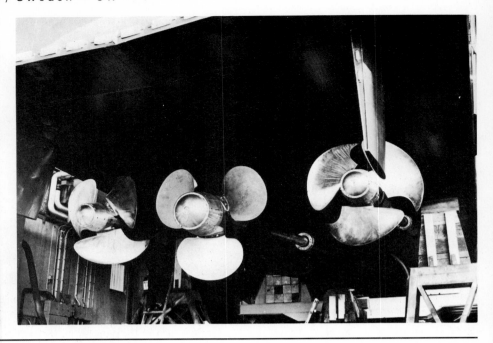

KaMeWa propeller installation on HMS *Stockholm*. The super-cavitating centre propeller is used as a booster, the highly-skewed wing propellers are for quiet running and cruising economy

SWITZERLAND

ROLLA SP PROPELLERS SA

Via Silva 5, PO Box 251, Balerna 6830, Switzerland

Telephone: 091 439361
Telex: 842448 CH
Telefax: 091 430653

Philip Rolla, *Proprietor & Managing Director*

The company was founded in 1962 by Philip Rolla. Surface-piercing and fully submerged propellers are produced to any required geometry and with up to eight blades. In general, propellers are produced in high-tensile stainless steel for very high-speed craft and Nibral for commercial, military and pleasure boats up to 65 knots. Recent applications have included:

Magnum, all of their production boats
Hatteras, all of their high-speed Fisherman
Denison, a 45-knot version with Arneson drives
Pegasus, a 100-knot project built by Cougar Marine and fitted out by Commercial Marine Resources
Lloyd's Ships *Awesome*

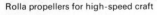

Rolla propellers for high-speed craft

UNITED KINGDOM

BRUNTON'S PROPELLERS LIMITED

Station Road, Sudbury, Suffolk CO10 6ST, England

Telephone: 0787 73611
Telex: 98400 PROPS G

Brunton 5-blade propeller for twin-propeller 33·5m patrol boat

1·0m diameter propellers (Dr Kruppa design) for HM5 surface effect ship

Brunton's Propellers Ltd is a specialist in the design and manufacture of propellers for high performance craft such as patrol boats, surface effect ships, hydrofoils, catamarans etc, where the propellers have to work in very exacting conditions. The design requirements in such cases can be extremely critical and manufacturing to very close tolerances is required, ISO 484 Class 'S' and better. Brunton's parent company is Stone Manganese Ltd, designers and manufacturers of ship propellers.

As well as meeting commercial requirements, Brunton's Propellers Ltd supplies the British MoD and navies around the world.

Propellers may be manufactured in high-tensile manganese bronze, nickel-aluminium bronze, Novostron (a manganese-aluminium bronze alloy), Superstron 70 and gunmetal, though this last material is now seldom used.

Brunton's associated company, Stone Propellers Ltd, manufactures extremely accurate model propellers for test and research work in test tanks and cavitation tunnels.

STONE MANGANESE MARINE LIMITED

Dock Road, Birkenhead, Merseyside L41 1DT, England

Telephone: (051) 652 2372
Telex: 629270 SMMBH G

A member of the Langham Industries group

J M Langham, *Chairman*
J R Wilson, *Managing Director*
W J Teasdale, *Director*
B N Preston, *Director*
G Patience, *Technical Director*

Stone Manganese Marine Ltd KCA design propellers for high-speed craft

Stone Manganese Marine has been manufacturing propellers for more than 100 years. The company and its associates operate ten manufacturing units throughout the world and the product range covers all sizes of fixed-pitch marine propellers for all types of ships, including high-speed marine craft.

The main factory is at Birkenhead, which includes the technical department, offering a comprehensive technical service to customers and the preparation of the company's proprietary Meridian design.

The company has a long established connection with the University of Newcastle upon Tyne, collaborating in the operation of the cavitation tunnel where the KCA design, specifically to suit high-speed craft, was developed and tested. The KCA design has been adopted for high-speed marine applications worldwide.

TEIGNBRIDGE PROPELLERS LIMITED

Decoy Industrial Estate, Newton Abbot, Devon TQ12 5NB, England

Telephone: (0626) 69751
Telex: 42976 TEPROP G

D A Duncan, *Director*
D A Hunt, *Sales Director*
F R Phillips, *Director*

J Haines, *Engineering Manager*

The Teignbridge Propulsion Group comprises three separate manufacturing companies under one ownership. The companies, Teignbridge Propellers, Hamble Propellers and New Age Propulsion, combine to offer a comprehensive range of standard and special propellers. The Group specialise in designing and manufacturing propellers for high-speed craft such as catamarans, hydrofoils, surface effect ships and patrol boats. The design parameters for propellers used on such vessels are extremely close, usually ISO 484 Class 'S'.

All Hi-Definition propellers manufactured by the Group are dynamically balanced and are manufactured from the materials to the highest specification, usually nickel aluminium bronze.

The Group also manufacture stern gear, rudders, shaft brackets, etc, offering craft builders a complete equipment package to the specialist field of high-speed propulsion.

Teignbridge propeller for a hydrofoil with MTU engines, 1530kW each at 2000rpm, gear ratio 2·028:1

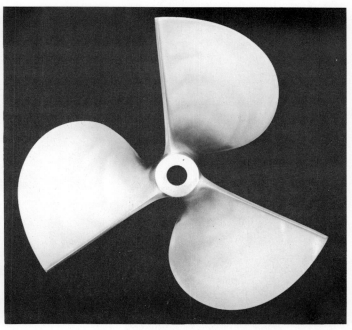

A Teignbridge surface-piercing propeller fitted to a Bellamy surface drive, operating at speeds above 40 knots

UNITED STATES OF AMERICA

ARNESON MARINE INC

15 Koch Road, Unit E, Corte Madera, California
94925, USA

Telephone: (415) 927 1500
Telex: 171242 ARNESON DRIVE
Telefax: (415) 927 1937

Craig W Dorsey, *President*

The Arneson Surface Drive system combines
surface-piercing propeller technology with
hydraulically actuated steering and trim control
effected through angular displacement of the
propeller shaft. There is minimal underwater drag
as drag of shafts, struts and rudders is eliminated.

A selection of surface-piercing propeller designs
are available, manufactured in Nibral, stainless
steel and manganese bronze.

Distributors have been appointed in Australia,
Brazil, Japan, Kuwait, Scandinavia, Switzerland,
Taiwan and Turkey. The Eastern Regional office
is in North Miami Beach, Florida. The office
which oversees Europe, the Middle East and
Africa is in Viareggio, Italy.

Arneson Surface Drives combine proven surface-piercing propulsion technology with directed
thrust, providing greater propulsion and manoeuvring effectiveness. In most applications, the
elimination of the underwater drag of shafts,
struts and rudders results in a marked improvement in vessel performance and efficiency.

The concept allows complete flexibility of engine
location, weight placement and effective reduction
of noise and vibration. With the hydraulic steering
and propeller depth control, manoeuvrability is
outstanding, and shallow water capability becomes
limited only by the draught of the vessel itself.

AMI currently manufactures fourteen models
of Arneson Surface Drives, serving the commercial, military and pleasure craft market. Differen-
tiated by torque capacity, production ASD units
are available for use with petrol, diesel and gas
turbine engines up to approximately 5000hp.

Included among the many projects completed in
the past year are the supply of Arneson Surface
Drives for a 17m passenger catamaran in Finland,
a 12m patrol boat for Japan and a 16m high-
performance offshore vessel for Canada, as well as
numerous other pleasure and commercial installations in the United States and overseas.

Recent applications of the larger Arneson Drive
Units have included the following craft:
Huckins 78, 23·78m motor yacht *Princess Pat*, two

Arneson ASD 10 in-line unit

ASD 14 units, 21 knots
Magnum Marine 19·21m pleasure yacht *Maltese
Magnum*, two ASD 14 units, with two 18-cylin-
der CRM diesels giving an average speed of 51·0
knots when winning the Miami-Nassau-Miami
sea race, 11 July 1987
Denison Marine 24·39m pleasure yacht *Haggis II*,
two ASD 16 units, 45 knots

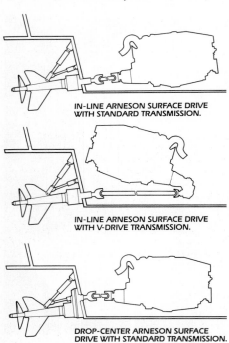

IN-LINE ARNESON SURFACE DRIVE
WITH STANDARD TRANSMISSION.

IN-LINE ARNESON SURFACE DRIVE
WITH V-DRIVE TRANSMISSION.

DROP-CENTER ARNESON SURFACE
DRIVE WITH STANDARD TRANSMISSION.

Three possible layouts for Arneson Surface Drives

An Arneson Surface Drive installation

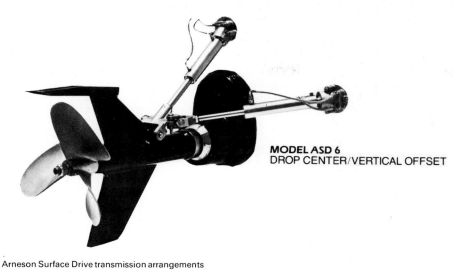

MODEL ASD 6
DROP CENTER/VERTICAL OFFSET

Arneson Surface Drive transmission arrangements

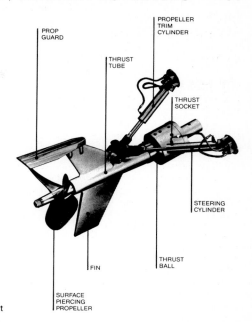

PROP
GUARD

PROPELLER
TRIM
CYLINDER

THRUST
TUBE

THRUST
SOCKET

STEERING
CYLINDER

THRUST
BALL

FIN

SURFACE
PIERCING
PROPELLER

Components of Arneson ASD 6 in-line unit

Model	ASD 6	ASD 7	ASD 8	ASD 10	ASD 12	ASD 14	ASD 16	ASD 18
Horsepower acceptance								
petrol:	to 450-550	to 730	to 1200		to be determined			
diesel:	to 235-300				to 3500 (subject to application)			
Unit weight, dry, with								
hydraulic cylinders (in-line):	61kg		129kg	189kg			900kg A	1769kg A
(drop centre):	72kg	147kg	220kg	272kg	352kg	515kg	1150kg B	2268kg B
Overall external length:	914-991mm	1114mm	1067mm	1270mm	1638mm	1805mm	2184mm	2896mm
Steering angle:	40°	40°	40°	40°	40°	40°	36°	36°
Trim angle (max travel inclusive):	15°	15°	15°	15°	15°	15°	15°	13°
Materials								
socket:	A or B	A or B	B	B	B	B	A or B	A or B
thrust tube:	A or B	A or B	B	B	B	B	A or B	A or B
ball:	B	B	B	B	B	B	A or B	A or B
propeller shaft:				Aquamet 17 stainless steel				

A—aluminium alloy
B—manganese bronze
C—stainless steel

BIRD-JOHNSON COMPANY
Pascagoula Operations
3719 Industrial Road, Pascagoula, Mississippi 39567, USA

Telephone: (601) 762 0728
Telex: 589938
Telefax: (601) 769 7048

James W Elliot Jr, *Manager*

110 Norfolk Street, Walpole, Massachusetts 02081, USA
Telephone: (617) 668 9610
Telex: 6817294
Telefax: (617) 668 5638

Charles A Orem, *Chief Executive Officer and President*
Donald E Ridley, *Vice President, Regional Operations*

Gary W Dayton, *Director, Marine Marketing and Services*

Bird-Johnson Company is a leading supplier of fixed-pitch and controllable-pitch propeller systems for naval application. In-house capabilities include design, foundry, hand and NC finishing, assembly, test and repair. All products are backed by logistic support including a 24-hour emergency service network.

COOLIDGE PROPELLER GULF COAST

Now Bird-Johnson Company, Pascagoula Operations (see preceding entry).

COLUMBIAN BRONZE CORPORATION

216 N Main Street, Freeport, New York 11520-2295, USA

Telephone: (516) 378 0470
Telex: 144550

Bill Bailey, *President*
Peter J Lapp, *Naval Architect*
William Thompson, *Chief Engineer*
James Burns, *Sales Engineer*

Designer and manufacturer of fixed-pitch propellers since 1901 in various alloys including manganese bronze, Nibral and stainless steel from 0·2m to 3·05m diameter (8in to 10ft). Standard catalogue styles are available in a wide range of sizes including the high-blade-area Crewboat/Mako style proven successful on many high-speed craft. Custom propellers also available to either in-house or customer design. Capability exists to manufacture to all tolerance levels and to dynamically balance up to 4·90m (16ft) diameter. Recent applications include: custom 5-blade Nibral propellers for Nichols Bros *Hawaiian*

Express and Gladding-Hearn *Mackinac Express* high-speed catamarans; 1·07m (42in) 4-blade Nibral and stainless steel crewboat propellers for 36·6m (120ft) Lantana Boat 30-knot patrol craft; custom 1·016m (40in) 3-blade Nibral 1·00 BAR propellers for US Coast Guard SES craft; custom 0·914m (36in) 4-blade Nibral props for 35-knot plus *Donzi*, 19·82m (65ft) Sportfisherman and 40-knot plus Lydia Yacht 27·44m (90ft) Sportfisherman *That My Hon*; 4-blade Mako style propellers for world class Burger Boat and Broward Marine yachts.

KAHLENBERG BROS CO
Two Rivers, Wisconsin, USA

Telephone: (414) 793 4507

K W Kahlenberg, *Proprietor*

Kahlenberg Bros Co was one of the pioneer internal combustion engine builders in the US and at the turn of the century it produced its first steel propellers. Of today's production of fixed-pitch propellers, 85% are in stainless steel but if re-

quested, propellers may also be cast in manganese bronze, cast iron or other alloys. Custom-built propellers up to 2·59m diameter and adjustable-pitch propellers can be supplied.

490MARINE PROPELLERS / USA

MICHIGAN WHEEL CORPORATION

1501 Buchanan Avenue SW, Grand Rapids, Michigan 49507, USA

Telephone: (616) 452 6941

Telex: 6877077 MIMOT UW
Telefax: (616) 452 6941

William Herrick, *Director/Marketing Services*

Established in 1903, Michigan Wheel produces a wide range of fixed-pitch propellers, including the Machined-Pitch type, diameter up to 2·44m, the Dyna-Foil type, diameter up to 2·44m, the Star, diameter up to 1·83m and the Super Crew Boat type, diameter up to 1·02m. These propellers can be made in manganese bronze alloy, nickle-bronze, aluminium bronze and stainless steel.

WATERJET UNITS

ITALY

CASTOLDI SpA

Viale Mazzini 161, 20081 Abbiategrasso, Milan,
Italy

Telephone: (02) 94821
Telex: 330236 CAST I
Telefax: (02) 9460800

Dr Eng Andrea Tonti, *Export Sales Manager*

Castoldi SpA is associated with BCS SpA, the
leading European manufacturer of self-propelled
agricultural machines, and MOSA SpA, manufacturer of mobile electric welding machines.
Development of Castoldi waterjet units started in
1958 and units are now available for fast craft in
the range of 4 to 28m. Several Australian high-
speed ferries have been fitted with Castoldi waterjet units including the SBF Engineering's *Wilderness Seeker, Aquajet* and *James Kelly II*.

Castoldi manufactures a range of axial-flow
waterjet units, the JET 03 for powers up to
40·5kW (55hp), the JET 05 for up to 130kW
(170hp), the Turbodrive 238 for up to 184kW
(250hp), the JET 06 for up to 266kW (350hp) and
the JET 07 for up to 883kW (1200hp).

All the Castoldi units feature a single stage
axial-flow impeller; the casings are built in lightweight aluminium alloy which becomes very durable being hard anodised up to 80 microns. The
impeller, the impeller shaft and many other parts
are made in stainless steel.

The Castoldi drives (except for the JET 03) have
several features that make them stand out from
other waterjet units; a built-in gearbox for adapt-
ing the power and rpm characteristics of the
engine to the Jet Drive, a positive clutch for
engaging and disengaging the impeller, a remote-
operated movable weed rake for cleaning the
water intake, and other refinements. The Castoldi
waterjet units are equipped with especially designed mechanical or electronic/hydraulic controls
which make them extremely easy to operate.

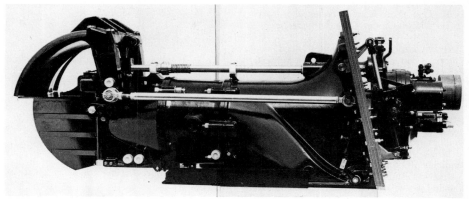

Castoldi JET 07

Castoldi Turbodrive TD 238

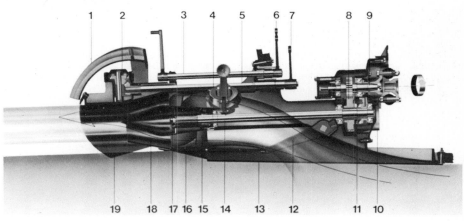

Components of a Castoldi JET 05 waterjet unit
(1) Deflector (2) Rudder control gears (3) Deflector control shaft (4) Inspection port (5) Rudder control shaft
(6) Deflector control lever (7) Rudder control lever (8) Gear coupling (9) Primary shaft (10) Transmission box
flange (11) Dog clutch (12) Movable grill (13) Body of unit (14) Impeller shaft (15) Impeller (16) Impeller shell
(17) Impeller retaining bolt (18) Nozzle (19) Rudders

Two Castoldi JET 06 units powered by two Iveco/Aifo
8361 SRM 10, 320hp engines drive the Novamarine
RH1250 R.I.B. at 35 knots

RIVA CALZONI SpA

Via Stendhal 34, 20144 Milan, Italy

Telephone: (02) 41461
Telex: 332292 RIVAT I
Telefax: (02) 425749-G3/E2

Dr Ing Piero del Pesco, *General Manager*
Dr Ing Gianfranco Bianchi, *Technical Manager*
Dr Ing Andrea Gasparri, *Sales Manager*

Riva Calzoni is a long-established major European designer and manufacturer with extensive experience of hydraulic machinery covering large water turbines, pumps, pump-turbines, governors for water and steam turbines, waterjet propulsion units, various types of hydraulic equipment, valves, gates and penstocks. Design techniques as well as laboratory and manufacturing facilities are being continually improved in order to cope with the increasingly demanding requirements of modern installations.

Riva was established in 1861, Calzoni in 1830. The first partnership between the two companies dates from 1922 and they merged in 1966 to form Riva Calzoni, which is privately owned and employs some 1200 personnel.

RIVA CALZONI WATERJETS

The very first waterjet, rated at 75kW, was designed, manufactured and tested by Riva Calzoni in 1932. Today Riva Calzoni is one of the leading manufacturers of waterjet propulsion units in the world, with a power range extending from 200 to over 20 000kW.

A recent order by Spanish Customs for patrol boats was met by Rodman Shipyards which delivered seven 14-metre craft fitted with Riva Calzoni IRC 41 DL waterjet units. These boats were powered by twin MWM diesels, rated at 735kW each, at 2300rpm, and can reach maximum speeds in excess of 55 knots which is believed to be the highest speed ever reached by waterjet-propelled patrol boats.

Riva Calzoni waterjets are high quality, high performance units with the following characteristics:

are optimised for each installation, for best performances;

are equipped with pumps of sure and well-known reliability, with high efficiency and excellent anticavitating characteristics, deriving from extensive experience in this field;

are fabricated from AISI 316L stainless steel for low weight, high strength and corrosion resistance;

are normally equipped with a complete intake

Riva Calzoni IRC 41 DL units

A twin Riva Calzoni IRC 67 installation

duct, including a protective grid, for easy installation on board;

upon request, they can be provided with a manually or hydraulically operated movable cleaning device for the grid;

are equipped with an external thrust bearing for easy inspection;

can be completely overhauled without dry-docking the boat;

are controlled by a hydraulic control system,

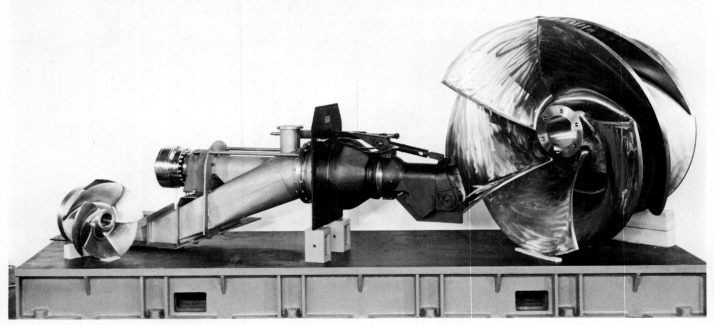

Left to right: Impeller for Riva Calzoni IRC 64 DL; waterjet unit IRC 41 DL, complete with disconnecting clutch, impeller for waterjet unit IRC 190 DL, maximum input power 15 000kW which can be supplied as complete package with the waterjets;

are available in two different basic configurations, which can be optimised to suit each application:
IRC series, with conventional steering and reversing system;
IDRC series, with 360-degree rotating vectored thrust.

Two models of a special disconnecting clutch, hydraulically operated, are available for direct drive installations. The clutch can be installed on the waterjet and is operated by the electro-hydraulic control system.

The latest Riva Calzoni waterjet model is the IRCL 39 D type built in anodised light alloy and designed principally for low-speed river vessels.

Riva Calzoni waterjets, with their specific characteristics, permit the full exploitation of the advantages of waterjet propulsion, such as:
elimination of all external underwater appendages when using flush type intakes (lower drag values, shallow water operation, higher safety at sea);
active manoeuvring system, not submerged, incorporated in the propulsor (excellent manoeuvrability at any speed and also with only one waterjet in operation);
high overall propulsive efficiency in a wide speed range;
very good acceleration and deceleration (also possibility of emergency crash stops);
elimination of pressure peaks in the stern area of the craft;
better control of the flow entering the impeller (absence of induced vibrations);
freer choice of location of propulsion machinery;
elimination of long and complex transmission lines;
elimination of reverse gear; reduction gear gen-

Riva Calzoni IDRC 26 DL waterjet unit with 360° rotating vectored thrust capability

erally avoided with associated saving in prime cost and weight;
possibility of single waterjet operation without external torsional effects on the hull and without appreciable lateral thrust;
absence of additional resistance of free running

propellers in case of operation with reduced number of engines, in multi-shaft configurations (pump inlets not in use can be blanked, if necessary);
high reliability and easy maintenance (eliminating necessity of dry docking);

Delivery in	Craft type	Delivered to	Number of units	Type	Shaft power kW	bhp	Shaft rpm	Engine
1932	Test boat	Italy	1	Prototype	70	95	1440	Petrol engine
1976	Motor yacht	Italy	2	IRC 28 D	235	320	2890	Isotta Fraschini ID 32 SS 6/L
1976	Motor yacht	Monte Carlo	2	IRC 38 D	495	675	2340	MTU 6V 331TC80
1976	Motor yacht	Italy	2	IRC 28 D	235	320	2890	Isotta Fraschini ID 32 SS 6/L
1979	Patrol boat	Italian Navy	2	IRC 28 D	235	320	2890	Isotta Fraschini ID 32 SS 6/L
1980	Motor yacht	Italy	2	IRC 38 D	478	650	2300	GM 8V 92 MTI
1980	Patrol boat	Italian Police	2	IRC 28 D	265	360	2900	Isotta Fraschini ID 32 SS 6/LM
1980	Patrol boat	Italian Police	2	IRC 28 D	265	360	2900	Isotta Fraschini ID 32 SS 6/LM
1981	Work boat	Italy	2	IDRC 38 D	160	215	1590	FIAT AIFO 8210M
1981	Motor boat	Arabian Gulf	2	IRC 47 DL	920	1250	2100	MTU 8V 396 TB93
1981	Patrol boat	Italian Police	2	IRC 28 D	265	360	2900	Isotta Fraschini ID 32 SS 6/LM
1981	Patrol boat	Italian Police	2	IRC 28 D	265	360	2900	Isotta Fraschini ID 32 SS 6/LM
1981	Patrol boat	Italian Police	2	IRC 28 D	265	360	2900	Isotta Fraschini ID 32 SS 6/LM
1981	Patrol boat	Italian Police	2	IRC 28 D	265	360	2900	Isotta Fraschini ID 32 SS 6/LM
1981	Patrol boat	Italian Navy	2	IRC 32 DL	330	450	2800	BPM V.12/570
1982	Patrol boat	Italian Police	2	IRC 28 D	265	360	2900	Isotta Fraschini ID 32 SS 6/LM
1982	Frigate	Model testing	2	IRC 15 DL	Variable			Electric motor
1983	Patrol boat	Italian Coast Guard	2	IRC 43 DL	548	745	1950	Isotta Fraschini ID 36 SS 6V
1983	Patrol boat	Italian Coast Guard	2	IRC 43 DL	548	745	1950	Isotta Fraschini ID 36 SS 6V
1984	Patrol boat	Italian Coast Guard	2	IRC 43 DL	662	900	2075	CRM 12 DS/2
1984	Patrol boat	Spanish Customs	2	IRC 36 DL	320	435	2300	GM 6V 71 TA
1984	Motor yacht	Italy	2	IRC 38 D	515	700	2300	MAN D2542 MLE
1985	Patrol boat	Italian Navy	2	IRC 39 D	367	500	2140	BPM V.12/570
1985	Supply vessel	Italy	2	IRC 43 DL	283	385	1485	AIFO 8281 SRM
1985	Patrol boat	Spanish Customs	2	IRC 41 DL	720	980	2300	MWM TBD 234 V12
1985	Patrol boat	Spanish Customs	2	IRC 41 DL	720	980	2300	MWM TBD 234 V12
1985	Patrol boat	Spanish Customs	2	IRC 41 DL	720	980	2300	MWM TBD 234 V12
1985	Patrol boat	Spanish Customs	2	IRC 41 DL	720	980	2300	MWM TBD 234 V12
1985	Patrol boat	Spanish Customs	2	IRC 41 DL	720	980	2300	MWM TBD 234 V12
1985	Patrol boat	Spanish Customs	2	IRC 41 DL	720	980	2300	MWM TBD 234 V12
1985	Patrol boat	Spanish Customs	2	IRC 41 DL	720	980	2300	MWM TBD 234 V12
1986	Supply vessel	France	2	IRC 36 DL	359	489	2300	MWM TBD 234 V6
1986	Patrol boat	Italian Navy	2	IRC 39 D	367	500	2140	BPM V.12/570
1986	Patrol boat	Italian Navy	2	IRC 39 D	367	500	2140	BPM V.12/570
1986	Amphibious vessel	Italy	1	IRDCL 26 DL	110	150	2750	FIAT 8062
1986	Amphibious vessel	Italy	1	IRDCL 26 DL	110	150	2750	FIAT 8062
1986	Amphibious vessel	Italy	1	IRDCL 26 DL	110	150	2750	FIAT 8062
1987	Patrol boat	Spanish Customs	2	IRC 41 DL	720	980	2300	MWM TBD 234 V12
1987	Patrol boat	Spanish Customs	2	IRC 41 DL	720	980	2300	MWM TBD 234 V12
1987	Patrol boat	Spanish Customs	2	IRC 41 DL	720	980	2300	MWM TBD 234 V12
1987	Patrol boat	Spanish Customs	2	IRC 41 DL	720	980	2300	MWM TBD 234 V12
1987	Motor yacht	Spain	2	IRC 41 DL	660	900	2300	MAN D2842 LXE
1987	Thames River Bus	England	2	IRCL 39 D	226	300	1785	Volvo Penta TAMD
1987	Patrol boat	Italian Coast Guard	2	IRC 43 DL	548	745	1950	Isotta Fraschini ID 36 SS 6V
1987	Patrol boat	Italian Coast Guard	2	IRC 43 DL	548	745	1950	Isotta Fraschini ID 36 SS 6V
1987	Patrol boat	Italian Coast Guard	2	IRC 43 DL	662	900	2075	CRM 12 DS/2
1987	Patrol boat	Italian Coast Guard	2	IRC 43 DL	662	900	2075	CRM 12 DS/2
1987	Corvette	Model testing	2	IRC 19 DL	Variable			Electric motor
1987	Thames River Bus	England	2	IRC 39 D	226	300	1785	Volvo Penta TAMD
1987	Thames River Bus	England	2	IRC 39 D	226	300	1785	Volvo Penta TAMD
1987	Thames River Bus	England	2	IRC 39 D	226	300	1785	Volvo Penta TAMD
1987	Thames River Bus	England	2	IRC 39 D	226	300	1785	Volvo Penta TAMD
1987	Thames River Bus	England	2	IRC 39 D	226	300	1785	Volvo Penta TAMD
1987	Passenger ferry	France	3	IRC 76 DLX	1492	2030	1092	GM 16V 149 TI
1987	Motor yacht	Italy	2	IRC 82 DLX	2640	3590	1160	2xCRM 18D/SS
1987	Passenger ferry	Italy	2	IRC 82 DLX	1865	2537	1050	MWM TBD 604 16V
1987	Patrol boat	Spanish Customs	2	IRC 41 DL	720	980	2300	MWM TBD 234 12V
1987	Patrol boat	Spanish Customs	2	IRC 41 DL	720	980	2300	MWM TBD 234 12V

Total Number of Waterjets—113
Total Absorbed Power (kW)—60 036

cubic law power absorption, virtually independent
of craft speed (engines not overloaded, full power
always available, longer engine life);
good recovery of boundary layer (positive
influence on frictional resistance of displacement
and semi-displacement ships);
easy control of cavitation in all working conditions;
low underwater noise.

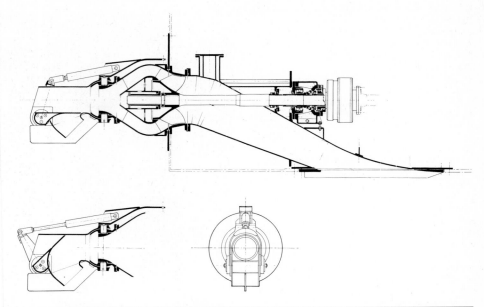

Riva Calzoni IRC type waterjet unit

NEW ZEALAND

CWF HAMILTON AND COMPANY LIMITED

Annex Road, PO Box 709, Christchurch, New
Zealand

Telephone: (3) 488 849
Telex: 4244 HAMJET NZ
Telefax: (3) 480 725

Designers and manufacturers of waterjets since
the mid-1950s, the company now offers models
capable of absorbing up to 1119kW (1500shp). A
large number of units have been installed around
the world in many types of craft such as high-
speed passenger ferries, police patrol craft, naval
troop carriers, fishing boats, crew boats, rescue
craft, pleasure cruises and fire boats. Current
Hamilton waterjet models in production are the
770 Series, 1031, 271, 291, 361, 421 and 422.

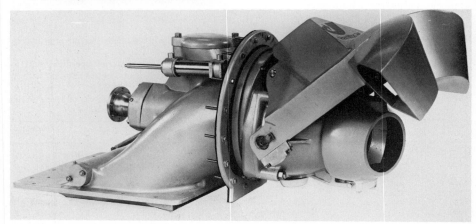

The new Hamilton Jet Model 271

MODEL 271

A smaller model of the proven 291 unit suitable
for engine power levels between 150 and 240kW in
small planing craft. In production from May 1987.
Impeller dia (9 configuration options): 270mm
Unit weight, less controls: 114kg
Thrust example
    max bollard pull: 1315kg at 225kW
    at 30 knots: 767kg at 225kW
Standard coupling: 120mm dia driveshaft flange
Intake screen: Heavy duty aluminium bar
Rotation: Clockwise looking aft

MODEL 291

Suitable for most high-speed marine diesel
engines up to 300kW/3000rpm.
Impeller dia (6 configuration options): 290mm
Configuration: Single stage, axial flow
Thrust, max: 1300kgf
Casing material: LM6 aluminium alloy
Mainshaft: T316 stainless steel
Weight: 175kg
Steering: T3 single conical deflector with inboard
    tiller
Reverse: Twin duct deflector and HERC electro-
    hydraulic system

TYPICAL SINGLE 291 JET APPLICATION
Vessel: 10·4m aluminium fishing boat *Wiebbe
    Hayes*
Weight: 7 tonnes
Speed: 30 knots
Engine/propulsion: One Caterpillar 3208 TA
    directly driving jet unit 330shp (after ancillary
    pumps etc)
Owner: Phil McAuley, Geraldton, Western Aus-
    tralia

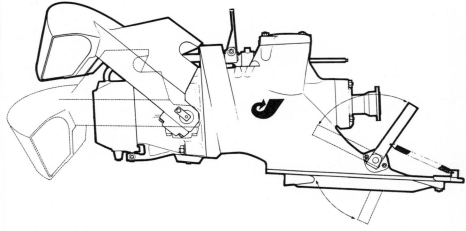

Side view of Model 271

8·8m *Rebel III* crayfishing boat (NZ) fitted with two Hamilton Jet 271 waterjet units giving 33 knots at 4·1 tonnes

TYPICAL TWIN 291 JET APPLICATION
Vessels: Fleet of nine 11·35m Meriuisko assault
  troop carriers
Weight: 6·8 tonnes (light)
Speed: 37 knots
Engines: Two Volvo TAMD70E producing 221kW
  (300hp) at 2500rpm
Owner: Finnish Navy

TYPICAL TRIPLE 291 JET APPLICATION
Vessel: 20m VIP passenger launch *Jalesveva*
Weight: 20 tonnes
Speed: 26 knots (3 jets operating); 20 knots (2 jets
  operating); 12 knots (1 jet operating)
Engines/propulsion: Three Caterpillar 3208 TA
  directly driving jet units
Owner: Indonesian Navy

MODEL 361

The first of the new Hamilton Model 361
waterjets was completed in April 1986. The 360mm
diameter single-stage axial flow jets incorporate all
the latest technological features such as: electronic
reverse control (HERC) system, twin duct reverse
deflector and T3 single piece steering deflector.
These features combined give sensitive finger-tip
control for in-harbour manoeuvrability. By working the reverse and steering deflectors in unison a
resultant waterflow can be obtained in any direction giving a craft 360-degree thrusting.

A complete range of CAD (computer-assisted
design) impellers are available for matching the
361 jet to a wide range of high-speed marine diesel
engines from 300kW (2000rpm) up to 500kW
(2300rpm). The performance of the 361 jet with
various impeller options has been thoroughly
tested and evaluated on Hamilton's water tunnel
test facility. Precise performance and thrust data
available from these tests enable accurate speed
predictions to be made by comparing the 361 jet
thrust with craft hull resistance data.

The versatility of the 361 jet and the absence of
engine overloading (power demand depends on
throttle opening only and is virtually independent
of craft speed) makes them ideal for multiple speed
craft. They can be used in conjunction with
propeller drive systems or other waterjets, for
either high-speed or loiter-speed operation. The
flush-mounted 361 waterjet offers no drag when
not driving and can contribute useful thrust at any
speed.

An innovative feature of the 361 jet is the
adjustable steering system which can be rotated 15
degrees to either port or starboard, allowing the
361 jet to be utilised for single, twin or triple
installations in hulls with deadrise angles of up to
30 degrees. Installation kits supplied with each jet
are available to suit aluminium, steel, grp and
wooden hulls.

Typically a single 361 jet is designed for efficient
propulsion of planing craft of up to 12 tonnes, and
with limited input power, displacement craft up to
20 tonnes. Twin 361 jets are suitable for planing
craft up to 26 tonnes and displacement craft up to
45 tonnes and triple 361 jets for craft up to 42
tonnes and 90 tonnes respectively.

Supplied as a complete factory tested package,
the 361 jet includes integral steering and reverse
systems. Installation is simple with no complicated
alignment of components. With a minimum of
preparation to the hull, the unit is simply lowered
into place, bolted in, and steering, reverse controls
and driveshaft coupled up. Installation studies of
similarly sized Hamilton jet packages have shown
savings of up to 40% in installation time when
compared to the multiple job of installing a
conventional propeller drive system of equivalent
power.

Steering control supplied is a heavy duty manual hydraulic system complete with a stainless
steel helm. Standard equipment with the 361 jet is
Hamilton's latest HERC system which includes
control lever, 12V or 24V dc hydraulic power unit,
electronic control box, senders and hoses. The
HERC system allows extremely fine control of the
twin duct reverse deflector for excellent slow speed
manoeuvrability. Each 361 jet package is assembled to order with an impeller and nozzle combination finely matched to the engine selection.

One of nine Finnish Meriuisko troop carriers fitted with Hamilton Jet 291 units

Hamilton Jet 291

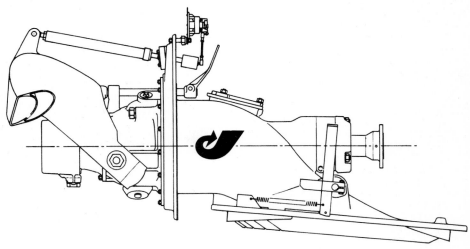

Hamilton Jet 291

Hamilton Jet 361

Other standard items with 361 jet include: transom seal assembly, intake block installation kit, all necessary nuts, bolts and fastenings, cathodic protection with anodes, coupling flange, water offtake for engine cooling system or wash down hose, owners manual, HERC manual and special tools kit. Optional accessories available to order with the 361 are: single lever reverse/throttle control, dual station steering and reverse controls, twin and triple jet reverse controls and an inspection hatch overflow preventer.

Impeller diameter (6 options): 360mm
Configuration: Single stage, axial flow
Thrust, max: 2100kgf
Casing material: LM6 aluminium alloy
Mainshaft: T316 stainless steel
Weight: 303kg
Steering: T3 single conical deflector with manual hydraulic cylinder and helm
Reverse: Twin duct deflector and HERC electro-hydraulic system
Certification available to: ABS, Lloyds, NKK

TYPICAL PLANING CRAFT
APPLICATIONS FOR 361 JET UNITS
Single 361 Jet – Max 12 tonnes
Twin 361 Jets – Max 26 tonnes
Triple 361 Jets — Max 42 tonnes

MODEL 421
Suitable for most high-speed marine diesel engines up to 650kW (870hp), 2400rpm.
Impeller diameter (6 options): 400mm
Configuration: Single stage, axial flow
Thrust, max: 2750kgf
Casing material: LM6 aluminium alloy
Mainshaft: T316 stainless steel
Unit weight: 535kg
Steering: Twin balanced deflectors
Reverse: Twin duct deflector and HERC electro-hydraulic system
Certification available to: ABS, Lloyds, NKK

TYPICAL SINGLE 421 JET APPLICATION
(Loiter Propulsion)
Vessel: 26m patrol craft
Weight: 80 tonnes
Speed (main propulsion): 24 knots
Speed, loiter propulsion (jet only): 7 knots
Engine driving 421 Jet: Mercedes OM402 145kW (195hp) at 2200rpm
Owner: Hong Kong Marine Police
Benefits of waterjet unit for secondary propulsion:
no drag at speed;
unloads main propulsion system;
360 degree thrusting ability for excellent slow speed manoeuvrability;
boosts top speed;
increases acceleration

TYPICAL TWIN 421 JET APPLICATIONS
A
Vessel: 25·6m high-speed passenger ferry *Atlante*
Weight: 31·6 tonnes (light)
Speed: 30 knots
Engines: Two MAN D 2842 LE each developing 700hp
Owner: Vedettes de L'Odet Ferry Company, France

B
Vessel: 18·4m passenger ferry
Weight: 30 tonnes
Propulsion: Twin Hamilton Model 421 waterjets
Engines: Two V10 MAN 2840 MLE diesels, each producing 618hp
Top speed: 35 knots
Owner: Vainio Fleet, Helsinki

C
Vessels: Four new 28m passenger ferries – Choong Joo Dam Korea (Commissioned 20/8/86)
Weight: 35 tonnes
Propulsion: Two Hamilton Model 421 waterjets
Engines: Two GM 12V-71TI marine diesels each producing 870hp at 2300rpm (Int); 730hp at 2180rpm (cont rating)
Top speed: 28 knots
Owner: Jung Ahang Express Company, South Korea

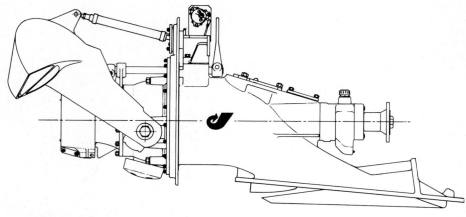

Hamilton Jet 361

12·8m Smuggler 384 (Sweden), one Hamilton Jet Model 361 giving 40 knots with Scania V8 DS 114

Hamilton Jet 421

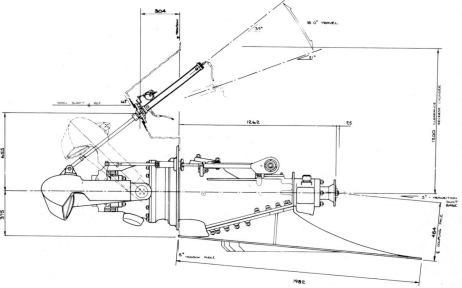

Hamilton Jet 421

D
Vessel: 22m passenger ferry – Brittany, France
Weight: 45 tonnes laden
    37 tonnes light
Speed: 26 knots (light)
Propulsion: Two Hamilton Model 421 waterjets
Engines: Two MAN D 2842 LE marine diesels,
    each producing 760hp at 2300rpm
Builder: Société Bretonne de Construction Navale,
    France

TYPICAL TRIPLE 421 JET APPLICATIONS
A
Vessel: 25·62m rescue/firefighting craft *Jetwise*, ex
    Miriam
Weight: 40 tonnes
Speed: 26 knots
Engines: Three MAN 12V D 2542 MLE marine
    diesel engines each producing 500hp at 2230rpm
Owner: Wijsmuller Salvage BV, Holland

B
Vessel: 25·6m high-speed passenger ferry
Weight: 54 tonnes (laden)
    42 tonnes (light)
Speed, light: 29·5 knots
Propulsion: Three Hamilton Model 421 waterjets
Engines: Three MAN D 2840 LE each producing
    630hp at 2300rpm
Builder: Société Bretonne de Construction Navale,
    France

MODEL 422
Impeller: 4- or 5-blade cast CF8M stainless steel
Unit weight, dry: 550kg
Entrained water weight: 110kg
Transition duct weight, steel: 300kg
    other materials: 140kg
Casings: Cast LM6 aluminium alloy
Standard coupling: GWB 587/50 250mm univer-
    sal driveshaft
Rotation: Clockwise looking aft
Thrust example: 3175kg at 1118kW at 40 knots
Astern thrust: Up to 55% of ahead thrust

18m JMSA patrol boat fitted with two Hamilton Model 421 waterjet units giving 22 knots at 26·5 tonnes

26·2m Royal Hong Kong patrol boat, one Hamilton
Jet Model 421 for loiter propulsion

SWEDEN

KAMEWA AB
PO Box 1010, S-68101 Kristinehamn, Sweden

Telephone: (550) 84000
Telex: 66050 S
Telefax: (550) 84049

Since the beginning of this century KaMeWa in Sweden has designed and manufactured hydroturbines and large pumps of various types. In the 1930s the first KaMeWa propeller of controllable pitch type was delivered. A vast amount of experience in the marine propulsion field has since then been collected at KaMeWa. In the last two decades KaMeWa has been a major supplier of controllable pitch propellers and thrusters. The company uses a well developed international network for sales and after sales service.

In the mid-1960s KaMeWa built two prototype jet-propulsion systems for small craft. The first larger units, however, were delivered in 1980 and since then KaMeWa has systematically established itself as the dominant producer of larger systems for waterjet propulsion.

An appreciable amount of research and development in hydrodynamics, mechanics and electronics constitutes the basis for the KaMeWa Jet-Propulsion System. Significant benefits for vessels with KaMeWa Jet-Propulsion Systems are high propulsive efficiency, even at part load; insensitivity to floating debris; suitability for shallow draught operation; good manoeuvrability; low hydro-acoustic and vibration levels; and low magnetic signature.

These features make waterjet propulsion suitable for example in medium and high-speed vessels such as corvettes, patrol boats, landing craft, passenger ferries, motor yachts and work boats.

DESIGN: Principally the waterjet consists of an inlet duct leading the water to the impeller, a pump casing and an outlet nozzle, forming the jet. Steering is accomplished by a steering nozzle, directing the jet ± 30 degrees which re-directs the jet of water issuing from the nozzle. Astern thrust is achieved by a reversing bucket incorporated in the steering nozzle.

The most effective propulsion will be with the jet just above the dynamic waterline. However, to secure priming of the pump at start-up, the pump shaft centre must not be higher than the waterline at rest.

INLET DUCT: In order to improve efficiency and to avoid excessive cavitation in the pump (the impeller and its casing), the velocity head of the inlet flow must be used to the largest possible extent. Thus, the inlet channel should lead the water to the pump with only small losses. Unsuitable inlet shapes not only cause losses but also result in choking, which can disturb the pump.

To be able to meet these demands, tests at correct cavitation numbers have been made in the KaMeWa Marine Laboratory with models of various inlet designs. Based upon these model tests the inlet duct can be given an efficiency of about 75-80% in relation to the inlet velocity head.

The inlet duct is preferably integrated into the

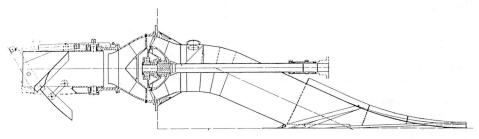

KaMeWa waterjet system, basic form

hull and normally built by the shipyard according to KaMeWa drawings. The inlet at the hull surface is well rounded to avoid vortices entering the pump at low speeds. Debris is prevented from entering the inlet by a grid. Should the pump get clogged it can be cleaned through the inspection openings in front of the impeller. The inlet duct ends at the transom with a connecting flange for the pump.

PUMP: The pump is of the mixed flow type and the 6-blade impeller is bolted to a stub shaft carried in the stator hub by one radial and one axial roller bearing. The bearings are spherical with the same centre of sphere, so that they are unaffected by minor deviations from the theoretically correct centre line of the pump shaft. Movements of an elastically-mounted prime mover will thus not affect the bearings.

The pump unit also contains the stationary guide vanes and the outlet nozzle forming the jet.

The thrust of the pump unit is taken up and transferred to the transom of the vessel.

The impeller hub is filled with oil to lubricate and cool the bearings. The thrust bearing also acts as a centrifugal pump circulating the oil within the hub. The temperature of the oil is thus kept within about 20°C above the water temperature without any extra oil cooler. To minimise the risk of water leakage into the hub, the oil pressure is kept above the water pressure by a gravity tank. For larger units the lubrication oil is slowly circulated from the hub into the tank and back by a small electric driven pump. In this way a continuous monitoring of the oil with regard to flow and temperature is possible.

The pump unit as well as the pump shaft and the steering/reversing gear are made of acid-proof steel. Sacrificial zinc anodes are fitted within the space between the impeller chamber and the conical aft part of the inlet duct to protect the hull and inlet.

STEERING AND REVERSING GEAR: Steering forces are achieved by deflecting the jet sideways by turning the steering nozzle 30° port or starboard. The steering nozzle also incorporates the reversing device. Jet reversal is obtained by

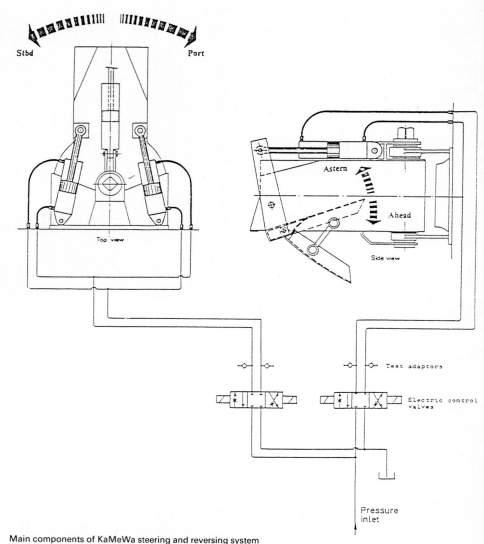

Main components of KaMeWa steering and reversing system

Installation of KaMeWa 63S62/6 waterjet units on the Marinteknik 33 CPV *Ørnen*, in service with DSØ

Size	A	B	C	D	E	øF	G	H	øJ	K	L min	M min
40	1095	(2830)	440	300	20	75	415	480	790	(900)	480	2000
45	1400	(3350)	493	350	20	80	410	640	840	(1220)	540	2200
50	1520	(3750)	550	375	25	100	635	695	945	(1350)	600	2200
56	1670	(4200)	620	395	35	110	835	760	1030	(1510)	670	2500
63	1900	(4700)	695	465	35	120	675	860	1120	(1700)	760	2600
71	2115	(5300)	772	535	35	130	745	965	1280	(1900)	850	2900
80	2395	(5970)	875	535	40	140	810	1085	1450	(2140)	960	3300
90	2615	(6720)	972	630	30	165	1030	1185	1610	(2410)	1080	3500
100	3000	(7470)	1100	670	50	180	1020	1360	1820	(2680)	1200	4130
112	3360	(8360)	1230	750	60	200	1140	1520	2030	(3000)	1350	3620
125	3750	(9330)	1370	840	65	220	1270	1700	2270	(3350)	1500	5160

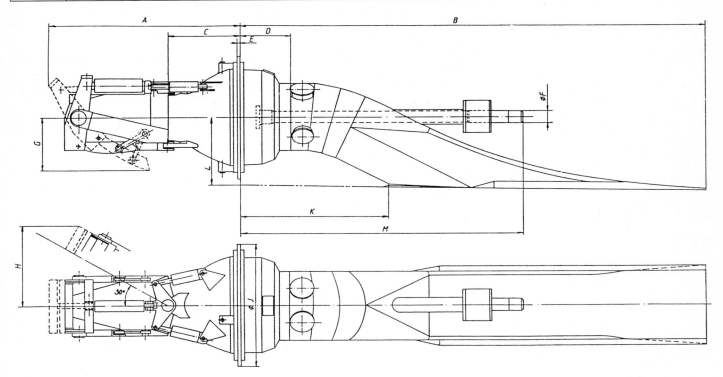

Size options for KaMeWa Type 62 waterjet units

turning the bucket under the nozzle. It gradually enters the jet from below and finally gives full reverse thrust. By setting the bucket in intermediate positions the thrust can be continuously and smoothly varied from zero to maximum ahead and astern.

The fact that the bucket is coming from under the jet means that a very low vibration level is achieved on the gear since only that part of the jet which needs to be deflected is affected while the remaining part of the jet is undisturbed.

The bearings for the steering as well as for the reversing bucket are of self-lubricating type. On top of the steering nozzle are two supports for the pivoted hydraulic cylinders for steering. The reversing bucket consists of an upper and a bottom part linked together by bearings at the aft end. The movement of the two parts is controlled by a yoke welded to the upper part and journalled in the steering nozzle. The bottom part is coupled to the steering nozzle by one link on each side of the nozzle. The yoke is connected to the pivoted hydraulic cylinder for reversing positioned on top of the steering nozzle. When reversing, the upper part closes the steering nozzle and deflects the jet down to the bottom part which further changes the jet direction to forward/down, resulting in astern thrust.

For feed-back and position indication, there are cables connected to the steering nozzle and to the reversing bucket. The cables are drawn through the transom and connected to potentiometers.

HYDRAULIC AND LUBRICATING SYSTEM: A separate hydraulic powerpack for each unit is used for manoeuvring. Normally the load compensated main pump is PTO-driven and for start and stand-by a small electric motor driven pump is used. The control valves are mounted on top of the powerpack.

For larger units, size 60 and above, a separate lubrication oil pack is delivered for each unit. A small electric motor driven pump is used for

The Marinteknik *Hamidah* crew boat turning at zero speed with KaMeWa waterjet units

circulating the oil as well as to maintain a pressure higher than the waterhead outside the seal. The pack should be positioned above the waterline in order to keep a static head at stand still.

For smaller jet units only a gravity tank is used.

REMOTE CONTROL SYSTEM: Two standard electronic remote control systems are normally used. Either a steering wheel and one combined lever for control of engine speed and reversing bucket, or one combined lever for control of steering, engine speed and reversing bucket.

The two systems can be extended to include additional control stations, back-up control and electric shaft system.

Advantages and some installations

The KaMeWa waterjet units have the following advantages and characteristics:

Designed to give high performance at high ship speeds as well as at low cruising speed. The efficiency has been verified in a number of full scale installations.

For medium speed vessels, top speed 25-30 knots, the fuel economy is in general competitive with that achieved with propellers.

For fast patrol boats fuel economy may be improved compared with fixed-pitch propeller installation from top speed down to the 10-15 knots region.

The water inlets have a very low drag when idling during cruising which makes the KaMeWa waterjet units attractive as booster units, also in combination with propellers.

The thrust/weight ratios of the KaMeWa waterjet units are optimised for most common hull forms, ie planing and semiplaning hulls, catamarans and sidewall hovercraft (SES).

KaMeWa's modern Marine Laboratory provides the testing facility required for inlet design, cavitation and performance studies.

Fixed geometry inlets can be designed to operate satisfactorily at full engine load from low cruising speeds (when running on a reduced number of shafts) up to the top speed of the vessel.

The pump shaft speed is practically independent of ship speed at constant power output. This means that the waterjet unit will never overload a diesel engine as the power absorption always is approximately proportional to rpm³. Reduced maintenance costs due to prolonged MTBO for the diesels may be achieved in certain installations.

Due to the absence of appendages and the rugged design of the KaMeWa waterjet units the costs for maintenance and off-hire time due to damages from floating debris can be reduced.

In multi-shaft installations CODAG/CODAD propulsion is possible without complex gearing and control systems. Full diesel power is always available irrespective of increased ship resistance due to bad weather, fouling etc or at extreme light displacements. This means increased top speed of the vessel.

The KaMeWa waterjet units are designed to simplify maintenance and overhaul. The units can be mounted and dismounted from outside the ship without docking of the vessel.

The KaMeWa waterjet installations are characterised by low noise and vibration levels.

Excellent manoeuvrability over the whole speed range of the vessel. Full engine torque is always

Comparison of KaMeWa impellers from Marinteknik *Apollo Jet* after 15 000 hours service with a new impeller, shown in the foreground

available for manoeuvring and acceleration.

Years of operating in the debris-laden waters of the Hong Kong area have proven that the units are very reliable and insensitive to sand and floating debris in the water.

Sixteen units of 1645bhp each have been sold to catamaran ferries, of which eight are operating in Hong Kong. The vessels have a cruising speed of 30-34 knots depending on displacement. The first units delivered in 1980 to Hong Kong have been in daily service without any mechanical and hydro-dynamic problems and are absolutely free from cavitation erosion.

A 77-tonne, 3-shaft planing craft uses two KaMeWa waterjet units for cruising. At full diesel power the cruising speed is about 25-26 knots. The wing units are also used in combination with a booster centre unit at about 50 knots. The units were delivered in 1981 and have functioned very satisfactorily.

The most powerful KaMeWa waterjet unit,

absorbing about 10 000kW, was delivered to Fr Lürssen Werft NB 13503. The 230-tonne, 3-shaft vessel went on successful trials during July 1983. The vessel has two KaMeWa waterjet wing units, driven by diesel engines for cruising at about 15-16 knots. The centre KaMeWa waterjet unit is driven by two gas turbines (totalling 10 000kW). The top speed of the vessel is above 45 knots with all three waterjet units running. The diesel engines can deliver full power both at 15 and 45 knots without overload/overspeed.

APPLICATIONS: Following the first 250 and 480shp experimental units, KaMeWa delivered in 1980 two 1575bhp units for the first Marinteknik Jetcat JC-F1 catamaran ferry and the first such craft to use waterjet units. This installation represented a major move by KaMeWa into the field of waterjet propulsion, a step which has led to continuing orders for waterjet units in the 400 to 4500shp range and one of 13 900shp. The following table summarises these applications.

KaMeWa Jet-Propulsion Systems

Delivery in	Name of ship	Type of ship	Owner	Shipyard	Yard No	Number of units	bhp/shaft	kW/shaft	Size of unit
1980	Jaguar Prince (ex Mavi Halic, ex Jaguar)	Catamaran	Italy	Marinteknik AB Öregrund, Sweden	42	2	1575	1160	60S62
1981	Apollo Jet	Catamaran	Hongkong Macao Hydrofoil Co Ltd	Marinteknik AB Öregrund, Sweden	46	2	1645	1210	60S62
1981	Hercules Jet	Catamaran	Hongkong Macao Hydrofoil Co Ltd	Marinteknik AB Öregrund, Sweden	47	2	1645	1210	60S62
1982	Janus Jet	Catamaran	Hongkong Macao Hydrofoil Co Ltd	Marinteknik AB Öregrund, Sweden	48	2	1645	1210	60S62
1981	Fortuna	Motor yacht	Patrimonio Nacional, Spain	Retrofit	—	2	1330	980	60S62
1983	Shergar	Motor yacht	—	Fr Lürssen Werft Bremen, West Germany	13503	1	13 900	10 220	112S62
						2	1440	1060	63S62
1983	Duan Zhou Hu (ex Triton Jet)	Catamaran	Zhao Gang Steamer Navigation, Hong Kong	Marinteknik AB Öregrund, Sweden	50	2	1645	1210	60S62
1983	Nettuno Jet	Catamaran	Alilauro Aliscafi del Tirreno SpA Naples, Italy	Marinteknik AB Öregrund, Sweden	51	2	1645	1210	60S62
1983		Work boat	Finnish Navy	Rauma Repola Oy, Savolinna, Finland	461	2	550	400	40S62
1983		Work boat	Finnish Navy	Rauma Repola Oy, Savolinna, Finland	462	2	550	400	40S62
1984	Jetcat 1	Passenger catamaran	Marinteknik AB, Öregrund, Sweden	Marinteknik AB Öregrund, Sweden	54	2	1645	1210	60S62
1984	Giove Jet	Passenger catamaran	Alilauro Aliscafi del Tirreno SpA	Marinteknik AB Öregrund, Sweden	55	2	1645	1210	60S62
1984	PL 70 King Lai	Patrol craft	Hong Kong Police	Chung Wah Shipbuilding, Hong Kong	189	1	465	340	45S62
1984	PL 71 King Lee	Patrol craft	Hong Kong Police	Chung Wah Shipbuilding, Hong Kong	190	1	465	340	45S62
1984	PL 72 King Lim	Patrol craft	Hong Kong Police	Chung Wah Shipbuilding, Hong Kong	191	1	465	340	45S62
1984	PL 73 King Hau	Patrol craft	Hong Kong Police	Chung Wah Shipbuilding, Hong Kong	192	1	465	340	45S62
1984	PL 74 King Dai	Patrol craft	Hong Kong Police	Chung Wah Shipbuilding, Hong Kong	193	1	465	340	45S62
1984	PL 75 King Chung	Patrol craft	Hong Kong Police	Chung Wah Shipbuilding, Hong Kong	194	1	465	340	45S62
1984	PL 76 King Shun	Patrol craft	Hong Kong Police	Chung Wah Shipbuilding, Hong Kong	195	1	465	340	45S62
1984	PL 77 King Tak	Patrol craft	Hong Kong Police	Chung Wah Shipbuilding, Hong Kong	196	1	465	340	45S62
1984	PL 78 King Chi	Patrol craft	Hong Kong Police	Chung Wah Shipbuilding, Hong Kong	197	1	465	340	45S62
1984	PL 79 King Tai	Patrol craft	Hong Kong Police	Chung Wah Shipbuilding, Hong Kong	198	1	465	340	45S62
1984	PL 80 King Kwan	Patrol craft	Hong Kong Police	Chung Wah Shipbuilding, Hong Kong	199	1	465	340	45S62
1984	PL 81 King Mei	Patrol craft	Hong Kong Police	Chung Wah Shipbuilding, Hong Kong	200	1	465	340	45S62
1984	PL 82 King Yan	Patrol craft	Hong Kong Police	Chung Wah Shipbuilding, Hong Kong	201	1	465	340	45S62
1984	PL 83 King Yang	Patrol craft	Hong Kong Police	Chung Wah Shipbuilding, Hong Kong	202	1	465	340	45S62
1984	PL 84 King Kan	Patrol craft	Hong Kong Police	Chung Wah Shipbuilding, Hong Kong	203	1	465	340	45S62

KaMeWa Jet-Propulsion Systems (continued)

Delivery in	Name of ship	Type of ship	Owner	Shipyard	Yard No	Number of units	bhp/ shaft	kW/ shaft	Size of unit
1984	T.B.A.	River tug	—	La Meuse et Sambre SA, Benz, Belgium	—	2	190	140	32S62
1984	Island Explorer	Mini cruise liner	—	Seaconstruct Private Limited, Singapore	037	2	821	600	63S62
1984	Haakem	Crew boat (catamaran)	Shell Brunei	Marinjet Shipbuilders (Singapore) Singapore	101	2	880	650	60S62
1984	Kasumi Jet	Passenger vessel	Kasumigaura Jet Line KK, Japan	Yamaha Motor Co Ltd, Gamagori Shipyard, Japan	208	2	700	515	40S62
1984	Hamidah	Crew boat	Ocean Tug Services, Brunei	Marinteknik Verkstads AB Öregrund, Sweden	B58	2	600	440	45S62
1985	TRPB S85	Transport vessel	—	Marinvarvet, Fårösund, Sweden	—	3	450	330	45S62
1985	Kalamoun	Motor yacht	—	Fr Lürssen Werft Bremen, West Germany	—	2	3050	2240	71S62
1985	Norcat	S.E.S. conversion	—	Brödrene Aa Båtbyggeri A/S Hyen, Norway	—	2	1600	1175	60S62
1985	Silver Shalis	Motor yacht	—	Abeking & Rasmussen Lemwerder, West Germany	6402	1 / 2	2640 / 2130	2000	71B / 80S
1985	Lommen	Passenger catamaran	DSØ, Öresund A/S, Dampskibsellskabet Copenhagen, Denmark	Marinteknik Verkstads AB, Öregrund, Sweden	B56	2	2090	1535	63S62
1985	Baltrum IV	Ferry	Baltrum Linie GmbH Co KG, Nordseebad Baltrum, West Germany	Julius Diedrich Schiffwerft GmbH, Moormerland, West Germany	—	2	390	285	40S62
1985	Emeraude Express	Crew boat (catamaran)	SURF, France	Marinteknik Verkstads AB, Öregrund, Sweden	B60	2	2090	1535	63S62
1985	For Your Eyes Only	Motor yacht	—	Denison Marine Florida, USA	103	2	1630	1200	63S62
1985	Angelica	Crew boat	SURF, France	SFCN Villeneuve la Garenne, France	—	2	1600	1175	63S62
1985	Aida	Crew boat	SURF, France	SFCN Villeneuve la Garenne, France	—	2	1600	1175	63S62
1986		Patrol craft	—	Hollming Ltd Rauma, Finland	264	2	4250	3125	90S62
1986	Ørnen	Passenger catamaran	DSØ, Öresund A/S, Dampskibsellskabet Copenhagen, Denmark	Marinteknik Verkstads AB, Öregrund, Sweden	B59	2	2090	1535	63S62
1986	Mexico	Passenger catamaran	Transportes Maritimos de Yucatan y del Caribe, Mexico	A/S Fjellstrand Omastrand, Norway	1571	2	1779	1310	63S62
1986	Parts VI	Motor yacht	—	Oceanfast Pty Ltd Perth, Western Australia	—	1 / 2	1088 / 1632	800 / 1200	63S62
1986	Nena VIII	Motor yacht	—	Denison Marine Inc Florida, USA	112	2	2176	1600	71S62
1986	Quest	Motor yacht	—	Denison Marine Inc Florida, USA	114	2	2176	1600	71S62
1986	Sun Liner IX	Motor yacht	—	SIAR SpA Spantarelli Industria Arredamenti Fano, Italy	—	2	2150	1580	63S62
1986	Adler	Motor yacht	—	Baglietto Shipyard SpA Varazze, Italy	10076/11	2	2130	1565	63S62
1986	Seneca	Motor yacht	—	Baglietto Shipyard SpA Varazze, Italy	10080/13	2	2130	1565	63S62
1986	Chato	Motor yacht	—	Baglietto Shipyard SpA Varazze, Italy	10079/12	2	2130	1565	63S62
1986	Amal	Crew boat	Black Gold Sdn Bhd, Malaysia	Marinteknik Shipbuilders (S) Pte Ltd, Singapore	M104	2	592	435	45S62
1986	Zakat	Crew boat	Black Gold Sdn Bhd, Malaysia	Marinteknik Shipbuilders (S) Pte Ltd, Singapore	M106	2	592	435	45S62
1986	Victoria Clipper	Passenger catamaran	Clipper Navigation Co, USA	A/S Fjellstrand Omastrand, Norway	1572	2	2010	1480	63S62
1986	Time	Motor yacht	Atwood, Rockford, USA	Palmer Johnson Inc Sturgeon Bay, USA	—	2	2145	1575	71S62
1986	Ekwata	SES ferry	Gabon Ferry Services, Gabon	Brödrene Aa Båtbyggeri AS, Hyen, Norway	184	2	1628	1195	56S62
1986		Motor yacht	Ter Haak Marine Amsterdam, Netherlands	van Mill Marine Service, Netherlands	146	2	2200	1855	80S62
1986	Panjandrum	Motor yacht	—	Knight & Carver Custom Yachts San Diego, USA	—	2			56S
1986	Sun Goddess II	Motor yacht	—	Oceanfast Pty Ltd Perth, Western Australia	—	2		910	56S
1986	Layar Senar	Crew boat (catamaran)	Amsbach Marine, Malaysia	Marinteknik Shipbuilders (S) Pte Ltd, Singapore	103	2		1175	63S
1986	Layar Sentosa	Crew boat (catamaran)	Amsbach Marine, Malaysia	Marinteknik Shipbuilders (S) Pte Ltd, Singapore	105	2		1175	63S
1986	—	Motor yacht	—	Construzioni Navali Lavagna srl Lavagna, Italy	—	2		1605	63S
1986	Lady Anfimar	Motor yacht	—	Baglietto Shipyard SpA Varazze, Italy	10103/11	2		1565	50S
1986	Convincer	Sport-fisherman	—	Pacifica by Klipper Yachts Florida, USA	—	2		980	50S
1986	Brownies III	Motor yacht	—	AB Nya Oskarshamns Varv Oskarshamn, Sweden	—	2		1200	90S
1986	—	Lifeboat	KNZHRM, Netherlands	W de Vries Lentch Bureau voor Scheepsbouw BV Amsterdam, Netherlands	—	2		365	40S
1986	—	Motor yacht	—	Christensen Motor Yacht Corporation, USA	—	2		1605	63S
1987	—	Coastal-corvette	Swedish Navy	Karlskronavarvet AB Karlskrona, Sweden	422	3		2130	80S
1987	—	Coastal-corvette	Swedish Navy	Karlskronavarvet AB Karlskrona, Sweden	423	3		2130	80S
1987	—	River tug	Belgian Army	SA La Meuse et Sambre Benz, Belgium		25 × 2		140	32S
1987	—	Passenger catamaran	A/S Torghatten Trafikkselskap, Norway	Brödrene Aa Båtbyggeri AS, Hyen, Norway	187	2		1175	50S
1987	Discovery Bay 12	Ferry	Discovery Bay Hong Kong	Marinteknik Shipbuilders (S) Pte Ltd, Singapore	107	2		840	50S
1987	Discovery Bay 14	Ferry	Discovery Bay Hong Kong	Marinteknik Shipbuilders (S) Pte Ltd, Singapore	108	2		840	50S
1987	Discovery Bay 15	Ferry	Discovery Bay Hong Kong	Marinteknik Shipbuilders (S) Pte Ltd, Singapore	109	2		840	50S
1987	Octopussy	Motor yacht		Heesen Shipyard BV, Oss, The Netherlands	7038	2 / 1		2130 / 2130	63S / 63B
1987	—	Passenger catamaran	Finnmark Fylkesrederi, Norway	Brödrene Aa Båtbyggeri AS, Hyen, Norway	183	2		845	50S
1987	—	Motor yacht	—	Oceanfast Pty Ltd Perth, Western Australia	3000 :02	2		1200	63S
1987	Sleipner	Passsenger-SES	Det Stavangerske D/S, Hardanger Sunnhordlanske D/S, Sandnes D/S, Norway	Westamarin A/S Norway	427	2		1540	63S
1987	Draupner	Passsenger-SES	Det Stavangerske D/S, Hardanger Sunnhordlanske D/S, Sandnes D/S, Norway	Westamarin A/S Norway	428	2		1540	63S
1987	Storm	Patrol craft	Norwegian Navy	Bergens Mekaniske Verksteder, Norway	—	2		2650	80S
1987	Lady Margaret	Motor yacht	—	Robert E Derecktor of Rhode Island Inc, USA	—	2		1200	63S
1987	—	Patrol craft	—	Fast Craft Florida, USA	—	2		1200	45S

KaMeWa Jet-Propulsion Systems (continued)

Delivery in	Name of ship	Type of ship	Owner	Shipyard	Yard No	Number of units	bhp/ shaft	kW/ shaft	Size of unit
1987	*Thunderbolt*	Motor yacht	—	Denison Marine, Florida, USA	116	2		1200	56S
1987	—	Passenger catamaran	Shikoku Ferry, Japan	Sanuki Zosen, Japan	103 A	2		1260	63S
1987	*Wu Yi Hu*	Ferry	Jiang Gang Traffic Co, Hong Kong	Marinteknik Shipbuilders (S) Pte Ltd, Singapore	110	2		1180	63S
1987	*Shun De*	Catamaran ferry	Shun Gang, People's Republic of China	Marinteknik Shipbuilders (S) Pte Ltd, Singapore	111	2		1935	71S
1987	—	Catamaran ferry		Marinteknik Shipbuilders (S) Pte Ltd, Singapore	112	2		1180	63S
1987	*Ekwata II*	SES	Gabon Ferry Services, Gabon	Brödrene Aa Båtbyggeri, AS, Hyen, Norway	—	2		1760	56S
1987	*Europa Jet*	Ferry	—	Marinteknik Verkstads AB, Öregrund, Sweden	68	2		770	56S
1987	—	SES	—	Alfa/Naval, La Seyne sur Mer, France		2		1070	50S
1987	—	Motor yacht	—	Oceanfast Pty Ltd, Perth, Western Australia	91	3		Two 2130 One 1200	80S
1987	—	Ferry	—	Marinteknik Shipbuilders (S) Pte Ltd, Singapore	113	2		1180	63S
1987	—	Ferry	—	Marinteknik Shipbuilders (S) Pte Ltd, Singapore	—	2		1935	71S
1987	—	Passenger catamaran	Fylke, Norway	A/S Fjellstrand Aluminium Yachts, Omastrand, Norway	1577	2		1836	63S
1987	—	Passenger catamaran	Fylke, Norway	A/S Fjellstrand Aluminium Yachts, Omastrand, Norway	1580	2		1836	63S
1987	—	Patrol craft	—	Precision Marine Holdings Pty Ltd, Western Australia	825	2		740	45S
1987	—	Ferry	Société Anonyme d'Economie Mixte Maritime de Sainte-Pierre et Miquelon, France	SFCN, Paris, France	—	2		1287	63S
1987	*Atlantic Challenger III*	Atlantic racing boat	The Gentry Companies, Hawaii, USA	Vosper Thornycroft, UK	AC III	2		2560	63S
1987	—	Motor yacht	Sven Jönsson, Norsborg, Sweden	Retrofit	"MY EDI"	2		1000	45S
1988	—	Coastal-corvette	Swedish Navy	Karlskronavarvet AB Karlskrona, Sweden	424	3		2130	80S
1988	—	Coastal-corvette	Swedish Navy	Karlskronavarvet AB Karlskrona, Sweden	425	3		2130	80S
1988	—	Catamaran ferry	Saltens Dampskibsselskab, Bodö, Norway	Westamarin A/S, Norway	93	2		2040	63S
1988	—	Catamaran ferry	Ofoten, Norway	Westamarin A/S, Norway	94	2		2040	63S
1988	—	Catamaran ferry	Nordstöm-Thulin, Sweden	Westamarin A/S, Norway	95	2		2040	63S
1988	—	Motor yacht	—	Heesen Shipyard BV, Oss, The Netherlands	—	2		1600	80S
1988	—	Motor yacht	—	Oceanfast Pty Ltd, Jandakot, Western Australia	92	2		980	66S
1988	—	Motor yacht	—	MCP, Brasilien	—	2		1090	63S
1988	—	Patrol craft	MSA, Japan	MHI Shimonoseki Shipyard, Shimonoseki, Japan	—	1		1839	80S
1988	—	Passenger catamaran	—	A/S Fjellstrand Aluminium Yachts, Omastrand, Norway	1586	2		2040	71S
1988	—	Passenger catamaran	Fylkes, Norway	Brödrene Aa Båtbyggeri, Hyen, Norway	196 E	2		1175	50S
1988	—	SES	—	Brödrene Aa Båtbyggeri, Hyen, Norway	199	2		1600	63S
1988	—	SES	—	Brödrene Aa Båtbyggeri, Hyen, Norway	200	2		1600	63S
1988	—	SES	—	Brödrene Aa Båtbyggeri, Hyen, Norway	201	2		1600	63S
1988	—	SES	—	Brödrene Aa Båtbyggeri, Hyen, Norway	202	2		1600	63S
1988	—	SES	—	Alfa Naval, La Seyne, France	27-02	2		1500	56S
1988	—	SES	—	Alfa Naval, La Seyne, France	27-03	2		1500	56S
1988	—	SES	—	Alfa Naval, La Seyne, France	27-04	2		1600	58S
1988	—	Passenger catamaran	—	A/S Fjellstrand Aluminium Yachts, Omastrand, Norway	1594	2		2040	71S
1988	—	Passenger catamaran	Yuet Hing, Hong Kong	Precision Marine Holdings Pty Ltd, Jervoise Bay, WA, Australia	863	2		1680	71S
1988	—	Passenger catamaran	—	NQEA Australia Pty Ltd, Cairns, Australia	156	2		725	50S
1988	—	Passenger catamaran	—	NQEA Australia Pty Ltd, Cairns, Australia	157	2		725	50S
1988	—	Passenger catamaran	—	Bätutrustning A/S, Rubbestadneset, Norway	87	2 / 1		730 / 730	40S / 40S
1988	—	Passenger catamaran	Quicksilver Connections Ltd, Australia	NQEA Australia Pty Ltd, Cairns, Australia	—	2		1650	63S
1988	—	Passenger catamaran	Quicksilver Connections Ltd, Australia	NQEA Australia Pty Ltd, Cairns, Australia	—	2		1650	63S
1988	—	Passenger catamaran	Quicksilver Connections Ltd, Australia	NQEA Australia Pty Ltd, Cairns, Australia	—	2		1650	63S
1989	—	Passenger catamaran	Quicksilver Connections Ltd, Australia	NQEA Australia Pty Ltd, Cairns, Australia	—	2		1650	63S

MJP MARINE JET POWER AB

S-74063 Österbybruk, Sweden

Telephone: (0295) 20785
Telex: 76229 FAGSTA S
Telefax: (0295) 20777

Gerard Törneman, *Managing Director*
Gunilla Törneman, *Director*

Marine Jet Power AB is a new company combining technical know-how, modern engineering and experience, set up to create advanced propulsion systems for commercial operation in vessels of various types and sizes, especially for high-speed surface craft such as mono-hulls, catamarans and SES.

During 1986 a series of advanced waterjets were developed, covering engine sizes from 300kW up to 3500kW and for cruising speeds from 15 knots to 60 knots.

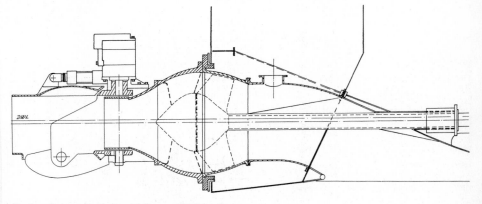

Sectioned view of a Marine Jet Power waterjet unit

MANOEUVRING CAPABILITY: The system includes jet propulsors, steering/reversing units, electro-hydraulic controls and a computerised remote control system (RMC) which is claimed to be the first digital control system in this field. With the computerised RMC the crews' learning period

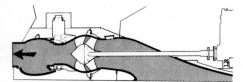
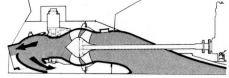
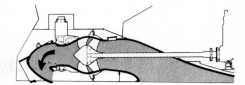

MJP waterjet forward to reverse thrust variation

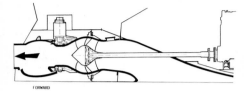

FORWARD

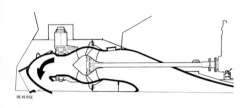

NEUTRAL

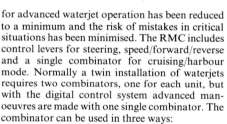

REVERSE

Mechanism of flow re-direction on MJP waterjet units

The Marine Jet Power AB J650R waterjet unit

for advanced waterjet operation has been reduced to a minimum and the risk of mistakes in critical situations has been minimised. The RMC includes control levers for steering, speed/forward/reverse and a single combinator for cruising/harbour mode. Normally a twin installation of waterjets requires two combinators, one for each unit, but with the digital control system advanced manoeuvres are made with one single combinator. The combinator can be used in three ways:

1) at cruising for different speed setting on each unit, in harbour mode
2) lateral movement of the vessel without the need of bow thrusters
3) rotation around the vessel's centre of flotation.

The different settings of the waterjets ie forward/neutral/reverse, outward/inward inclination and speed are controlled by the computer and can be adjusted for different vessels and loading conditions by the crew.

For steering purposes hydraulic rotary actuators are used which allow full nozzle turning from one side to the other within 2·5 seconds. The feedback to the electro-hydraulic controls and the inclination to the mimic panel in the wheelhouse are done through double built-in electrical transmitters in the hydraulic actuators.

The complete steering and reversing unit is made of stainless steel castings and the reverser is positively balanced, which allows a stepless re-direction of the jetflow from full speed ahead to full speed astern.

EFFICIENCY: To achieve predicted efficiency and speed a new type of mixed-flow pump was developed. The blade-to-blade flow analysis was carried out on a computer together with the finite element strength analysis of the impeller. This design technique ensures low drag and high freedom from cavitation.

To increase further the efficiency a new type of impeller bearing was designed including a continuous bearing monitoring system. This careful design also increases vessel comfort due to freedom from vibration of impeller and shaft.

OPERATING RELIABILITY: Many of today's

One of the two MJP J650R installations on the Marinteknik catamaran ferry *Gione Jet*

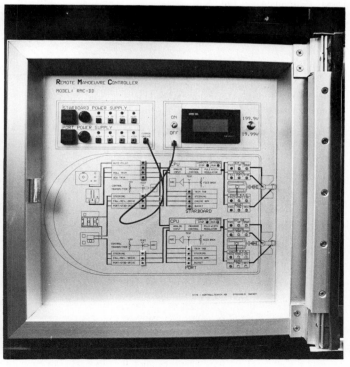

MJP waterjet propulsion Remote Control System

Basic form of MJP J650R waterjet propulsion system

high-speed surface craft are constructed in light alloy plate, and therefore a new type of intake including plastic parts was designed to avoid corrosion problems by insulating the stainless steel pump unit from the hull. All other components and materials are also chosen to avoid corrosion and mechanical wear in the demanding marine environment.

The monitoring system for the RMC has built-in measuring points which give fast fault indication and in addition considerably shortens the servicing time.

The first four systems of this new design were delivered in 1987 to Marinteknik Verkstads AB in Sweden, for use in their 41m mono-hull ferries and their 34m catamarans with engine sizes up to 2000kW and maximum speed of 45 knots.

MJP J450R, J550R, J650R and J750R

Four types of complete propulsion systems, single or double, including waterjets, hydraulics and computerised remote control system.
Output: 200-3500kW per unit
Speed range: 18-60 knots

Assembly of MJP hub unit and impeller

Material: Stainless steel in waterjets
Weight: 600-2000kg
Manoeuvring: Electro-hydraulic servo system
Remote control: Computerised control including combinator for lateral movement and rotation

UNITED KINGDOM

DOWTY HYDRAULIC UNITS LTD (DHU)

Arle Court, Cheltenham, Gloucester GL51 0TP, England

Telephone: (0242) 529422
Telex: 43176 G
Telefax: (0242) 533004

DHU is part of the Dowty Group of companies, the UK-based high technology engineering group, with overseas representation in USA and Canada.

Dowty Group:
Lord Harroby, *Chairman*
A N Thatcher, *Chief Executive*
A C Buckmaster, *Managing Director, Industrial Division*
Dowty Hydraulic Units Ltd:
C E Davies, *Managing Director*
R J Scarborough, *Sales Director*
C R G Ellis, *Sales Manager*

The product range of DHU includes waterjets, developed over 30 years' involvement in the marine field, starting with the Dowty Turbocraft jet boats of the 1950s. The current products, known as the Dowty Hydrojets are among the most numerous in the world.

Hydrojets have been produced for defence markets and are principally designed to produce very high thrust at relatively low speed, without suffering from cavitation.

The basic component of the Hydrojet is an axial-flow impeller (single- or two-stage) made of stainless steel, set within a 300mm diameter stainless steel reaction casing. The intake and outlet ducts are of cast aluminium.

The control mechanisms are simple and are designed to be robust and reliable. Both the steering and reversing actuator arms penetrate the transom plate and are readily adapted to match the boat's control systems. The zero thrust condition is achieved by the downward vectoring of the jet.

The control of the unit is identical to conventional rudder practice, requiring no retraining of crew. The jet can be directed 33° either side of the central position and the pivot arrangement ensures a high level of flow efficiency, in all conditions.

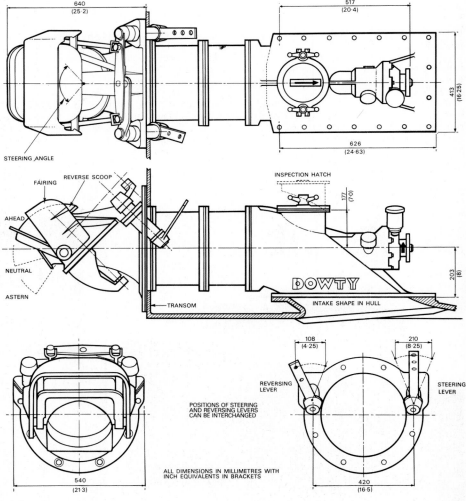

Dowty Hydrojet 300

The components are all made from high quality materials and require minimal maintenance. Ingested debris can be cleared from within the boat by means of an access hatch, or simply discharged by back-flushing the unit.

The Hydrojet 300 is installed in over 400 craft,

including combat support boats for the USA, British, Greek, other NATO and Far Eastern armies. Versions of the basic unit have also been installed in army amphibious vehicles, where space constraints have dictated changes to the unit's layout.

The Dowty Hydrojet also has applications in the field of auxiliary or loitering propulsion for larger craft, such as patrol boats, where good manoeuvrability and slow speed economy are required.

Dowty is undertaking continuous development work on waterjet units and a new Hydrojet outlet arrangement has been developed. This is the rotating nozzle jet which is capable of being directed through 360°.

Dowty offers purpose-built Hydrojets to meet customer requirements. It has produced 330mm and 400mm diameter units, capable of absorbing up to 600bhp and is prepared to investigate other sizes and powers to suit special applications. Development is proceeding into higher thrust output Hydrojets.

PERFORMANCE
Single-stage units:
  At max quoted power levels:
    Bollard pull, 110shp, 685kg
    Thrust at 20 knots, 137shp, 400kg
    Thrust at 30 knots, 150shp, 285kg
Two-stage units:
  At max quoted power levels:
    Bollard pull, 230shp, 1000kg
    Thrust at 20 knots, 255shp, 680kg
    Thrust at 30 knots, 285shp, 550kg

Rotating nozzle version of Dowty Hydrojet unit

PP JETS

R G PARKER (ENGINEERING) LTD

Units 5-7 Ailwin Road, Moreton Hall, Bury St Edmunds, Suffolk IP32 6DS, England

Telephone: 0284 701568
Telex: 817670 ASABSE G
Telefax: 0284 706410

R G Parker, *Managing Director*
H E Parker, *Secretary*

PP Jets offer a range of jet units up to their model PP 250 of 635mm impeller diameter suitable for powers up to 1500kW (2000hp).

PP Jets have for a number of years successfully used glass-reinforced plastic for the major fixed components of their waterjet units. The range of jet units from model PP 115 upwards is now being built with a mixture of glassfibre, Kevlar and carbonfibre reinforcement. These materials are totally corrosion resistant and give excellent structural properties. All metal parts exposed to the water can be made in stainless steel or, for special applications, in more exotic materials eliminating problems associated with dissimilar metals in contact with salt water.

The method of construction allows the form of the jet to be made to match the hull contour with comparatively simple additions to the mould. Further, the moulded surface presents a highly polished finish for the water flow.

An adjustable trim facility is available on all models, except the PP 90, giving up and down nozzle movement of ± 10°.

Canadian Coast Guard rescue boat *Hurricane* fitted with twin PP 140 waterjet units, driven by Caterpillar 375hp engines

PP 140
PERFORMANCE EXAMPLES
At max quoted power levels:
  Thrust at 10 knots, 400shp, 1517kg
  Thrust at 20 knots, 400shp, 1245kg
  Thrust at 40 knots, 400shp, 725kg

PP 140 units are fitted to the prototype Airmaran, an air-lubricated-hull craft of catamaran form, a possible predecessor of Thames Riverside passenger craft.

PP type number	65	90 90G	115	140	170	210	250
Engine size (hp)							
Petrol	40-200	60-350	—	—	—	—	—
Diesel	10-50	40-250	70-400	100-600	200-900	400-3000	600-2000
Impeller dia at inlet (mm)	165	229	292	356	431	533	635
Materials							
Jet unit body		Aluminium LM25 hard anodised (PP 90G—GRP)		Composite materials			
Impeller		Aluminium bronze		Stainless 316			
Weight (kg)	30	60 (PP 90G—70)	125	200	300	500	700

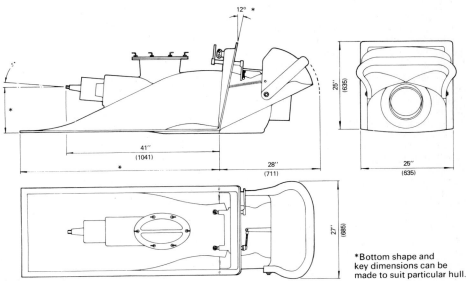

12° *

25″ (635)

41″ (1041)

28″ (711)

25″ (635)

27″ (685)

*Bottom shape and key dimensions can be made to suit particular hull.

Model PP 140 waterjet unit

UNITED STATES OF AMERICA

AEROJET TECHSYSTEMS COMPANY

MARINE AND INDUSTRIAL SYSTEMS
PO Box 13222, Sacramento, California 95813, USA

Telephone: (916) 355 3011
Telex: 377-409 ALRCSAC

Aerojet Techsystems is no longer involved in waterjet manufacture. Details of waterjet units,

built for example for the six Boeing Marine Systems PHM patrol hydrofoils, are given in *Jane's Surface Skimmers 1985* and previous editions.

NORTH AMERICAN MARINE JET INC

216 E Sevier, PO Box 1232, Benton, Arkansas 72015, USA

Telephone: (501) 778-4151
Telex: 536433 AIDC LRK

Len Hill, *President*
Paul Brunette, *Director of Marketing*

North American Marine Jet Inc purchased in 1984 the entire inventory of the Jacuzzi Marine Jet Division waterjet systems.

Four principal waterjet units are offered: the Nomera 12, 14, 20 and 12Y HT.

NOMERA 12

Designed for engines in the 140 to 350shp range this unit has an installed dry weight of 181kg. The major castings of the unit are of cast 356-T6 aluminium, hard anodised to resist corrosion but the unit is not designed for continuous salt-water operation. All fittings are of stainless steel. The shaft is of precision machined stainless steel with 1⅜ inch 10 spline.
PERFORMANCE
At max quoted power levels:
Bollard pull, 400shp, 700kg
Thrust at 20 knots, 400shp, 738kg
Thrust at 40 knots, 400shp, 635kg

NOMERA 14

Designed for engines in the 160 to 350hp range this unit has an installed dry weight of 290kg. The major castings of the unit are of nickel alloy cast iron type 2 Ni Resist, this material being suitable for salt-water operation.
PERFORMANCE
At max quoted power levels:
Bollard pull, continuous, 140shp, 762kg
Thrust at 20 knots, 300shp, 862kg
Thrust at 40 knots, 300shp, 531kg

NOMERA 20

Designed for engines in the 250 to 700hp range this unit has an installed dry weight of 499kg. Materials of construction are as for the Nomera 14.
PERFORMANCE
At max quoted power levels:
Bollard pull, continuous, 280shp, 1442kg
Thrust at 20 knots, continuous, 550shp, 1633kg
Thrust at 40 knots, 700shp, 1306kg

NOMERA 12Y HT

The new Nomera 12Y high thrust has been developed especially for use in light commercial craft which require high initial thrust and have engines that operate primarily in the 3000 to 4000hp range.
ESTIMATED PERFORMANCE
At max quoted power levels:
Bollard pull, 100shp, 590kg
Thrust at 20 knots, 350shp, 950kg
Thrust at 40 knots, 350shp, 700kg

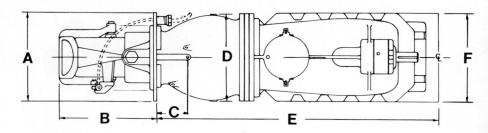

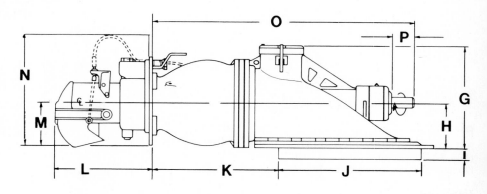

MODEL	A	B	C	D	E	F	G	H	I	J	K	L	M	N	O	P
NOMERA 12	15 38.1	—	4.5 11.4	12 30.5	—	7.7 19.7	15.5 39.4	—	1.3 3.2	20 50.8	—	—	—	—	14.5 36.8	3 7.6
NOMERA 14	19 48.3	16 40.6	5.5 14	15 38.1	47 119.4	15.3 38.7	17.5 44.5	7.6 19.4	2 5.1	24 60.9	21 53.3	16 40.6	7.3 18.4	22.5 57.2	43.8 111.1	3.5 8.9
NOMERA 20	25 63.5	23 58.4	8.3 20.9	20 50.8	61.5 156.2	17.8 45.1	21 53.3	10 25.4	2 5.1	34 86.4	27.5 69.9	23 58.4	10 25.4	25 63.5	56.5 143.5	6 15.2

North American Marine Jet Inc waterjet units (dimensions given in inches and centimetres)

Nomera 20

Nomera 12Y HT

ROCKWELL INTERNATIONAL CORPORATION

ROCKETDYNE DIVISION

6633 Canoga Avenue, Canoga Park, California 91304, USA

Telex: 698478 ROCKETDYN CNPK

The Rocketdyne Division of Rockwell is no longer involved in waterjet production. Details of waterjet units, built for example for the Boeing Jetfoil hydrofoil craft, are given in *Jane's Surface Skimmers 1985* and earlier editions.

AIR CUSHION SKIRT SYSTEMS

FRANCE

KLEBER INDUSTRIE

4 rue Lesage-Maille, BP No 22, 76320 Caudebec les Elbeuf, France

Telephone: (35) 81 00 99
Telex: 770438 KLEBER F

Michel Magnan, *Commercial Director*

Kleber is one of Europe's major producers of coated fabrics and a principal supplier to inflatable boat and life raft manufacturers which involves conforming to rigorous technical standards. In addition fabrics are produced for the construction of various forms of hovercraft skirt. Coatings are available in hypalon, neoprene and natural rubbers. Dependent upon the specification, a range of colours can be supplied. Materials are available in weights (total) ranging from 170g/m² to 1500g/m².

Kleber materials have been used in the UK on hovercraft produced by Air Vehicles Ltd and Griffon Hovercraft Ltd.

PENNEL & FLIPO

384 Rue d'Alger, 59052 Roubaix Cedex 1, France

Telephone: 20 36 92 60
Telex: 820373 F

Pennel & Flipo, a subsidiary of Prouvost SA,

employs 450 people. Sales in 1986 reached Fr280 million. This 60-year-old company has concentrated its considerable experience to develop a diverse range of products and coatings based on calendering and laminating of rubber, pvc and polyurethane.

Hypalon rubber-coated fabrics are produced for inflatable boats, either on a polyamide base enka nylon or on a high-tenacity polyester trevira. A whole range of neoprene-coated fabrics have been produced for general use including hovercraft skirt applications. Finished weights for the various materials are in the range of 950g/m² to 2500g/m².

SPAIN

NEUMAR SA

Head Office: La Rinconada, B-6, 28023-Madrid, Spain

Telephone: (1) 2071998/4582982

J M Isidro, *President*
M de la Cruz, *Technical Director*
J A Barbeta, *Manufacturing Manager*

Neumar SA specialises in research, development and design of air cushion lift systems, and in the manufacture of flexible structures for hovercraft. The company was formed to bring together a group of engineers and technicians all of whom had previous experience in hovercraft technology; of this previous experience it is worth mentioning the research and development, design and manufacture of the hovercraft lift system and skirt for the company CHACONSA under a contract for the Spanish Ministry of Defence.

Neumar has developed a hovercraft lift system that offers very high stability with low power requirements and reduced manufacturing and maintenance costs. It has been called an Automatic Transversal Air Distribution or ATAD lift system because of the main function it performs. Several two-dimensional models and a prototype have been built and tested, with which the viability of this new lift system has already been demonstrated. The ATAD lift system is described in detail in the ACV Builders section under the Neumar SA entry.

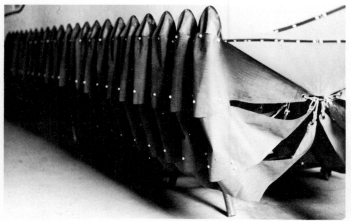

Two views of the Neumar skirt system developed to secure high stability with low power requirements

UNION OF SOVIET SOCIALIST REPUBLICS

LISICHANSK INDUSTRIAL FABRICS PLANT

Lisichansk, Ukraine, USSR

Suppliers of rubberised fabric for Soviet air cushion oil rig platforms. The materials were developed in conjunction with the Rezinotekhnika Association which specialises in industrial rubber products and waterproofing fabrics.

UNITED KINGDOM

AIR CUSHION EQUIPMENT (1976) LIMITED

15/35 Randolph Street, Shirley, Southampton SO1 3HD, England

Telephone: 0703 776468
Telex: 477537 G

J D Hake, *Chairman (USA)*
R C Gilbert, *General Manager*
R R Henvist, *Factory Manager*

Air Cushion Equipment (ACE) specialises in the manufacture of flexible structures, mainly for the hovercraft industry. The company produces skirts for UK and US hovercraft manufacturers, for craft ranging from small two-seaters to large hoverbarges.

Because hovercraft skirts are an integral part of a system, the ACE design contribution varies from skirt design to full-scale development of the craft manufacturer's own design. In all cases, templates are produced and held by ACE. As a result of the company's long period of involvement with the hovercraft industry, it is able to advise on material suitability, manufacturing techniques and assembly methods.

The ACE factory in Southampton has equipment capable of making hot bonded (vulcanised) seams up to 5·18m long and bonding areas up to 2·44 × 1·22m in one operation. The workshops are fitted with an extraction system which allows large areas to be safely coated with adhesives associated with cold bonding. The company also possesses long-arm sewing machines and HF welding equipment. This equipment is in continuous use for the manufacture of flexible water tanks, mainly for sailing craft.

Stocks of material varying in weight from 170g/m² to 3388g/m² coated with pvc, hypalon, neoprene, natural rubber, polyurethane and nitrile/pvc, are held at the factory.

AVON INDUSTRIAL POLYMERS LIMITED (AIP)

Bumpers Way, Bristol Road, Chippenham, Wiltshire SN14 6NF, England

Telephone: (0249) 656241
Telex: 444557 G
Telefax: (0249) 660678

S J Willcox, *Managing Director*
M Gillespie, *General Manager AIP Chippenham, Vice President Bell Avon*
P D Miller, *General Manager Bell Avon*
A J Bridger, *Commercial Manager*
P Inch, *Technical Manager*
K D Smith, *Production Manager*
B J Stables, *Management Accountant*
T J Dove, *Quality Assurance Manager*

Operating from its purpose-built factory in Chippenham, England, Avon Industrial Polymers (AIP) has facilities to provide comprehensive design, development, manufacture and material supply services to craft manufacturers and operators. Throughout its long involvement in this field, AIP has built up a world-wide reputation based on its quality of service and on the strength of its bonded materials. Avon is able to offer a wide range of coating weights, which in conjunction with particular weave types make skirts in these materials highly resistant to delamination.

Applications of Avon skirt materials include the following:

SR.N4 Mk II (BHC)

Avon has been sole supplier of fingers for the four SR.N4 Mk II craft, now operated by Hoverspeed, having first supplied to Hoverspeed's predecessors (Hoverlloyd and Seaspeed) in 1972. Avon also supplied and developed fingers for Hoverlloyd and Seaspeed SR.N4 Mk I craft dating back to 1969.

Avon's involvement over the years has led to major increases in finger life and has provided a high throughput test bed for the development of improved coated fabric materials and bonding systems.

Avon has also supplied the material to BHC for the loop sections since 1973 and has manufactured finger attachment flaps, cones and loop sections since 1978.

SR.N4 Mk III (BHC)

Avon has been sole supplier of fingers to Hoverspeed for the SR.N4 Mk III since two craft were 'stretched' from the original Mark II craft in 1978. Avon was involved in the detailed design study for these components in 1976 and is involved in the continuing specification and manufacture of development fingers for these craft. In addition to fingers, Avon supplies the material for loop sections, has designed and supplied finger attachment flaps and has supplied cones for the rear trunk, stability trunk and 'bookend' cones, and inner loop walls.

Avon Industrial Polymers bow skirt on the Bell Halter Model 730A, the US Navy SES-200

LCAC (Textron Marine Systems)

Avon is the only approved supplier of materials for the skirt system on this craft and has been heavily involved in the development of components for ship sets 1 to 6. Involvement started in 1980, at which time Avon had also carried out design studies for Rohr Marine Inc as an alternative prime LCAC contractor.

HM5/HM2 (Hovermarine International)

Avon developed the bow and stern seals for the four HM5 SES craft now operating on the route between Hong Kong and Macau. It also designed and manufactured a special rear seal for the HM2 craft, a seal which required no separate fan air supply.

LACV-30 (Textron Marine Systems)

In 1983 Avon manufactured a prototype spray suppression skirt as a direct contract for the US Army Meradcom. Avon has also supplied materials for these craft since 1979.

BH 110 SES—Bell Halter (now Textron Marine Systems)

Avon has been sole supplier of bow and stern seals for Bell Halter's BH 110 craft since development craft went into production in 1981 and has also been manufacturing and developing components for the prototype since 1979. Two craft are on charter from Bell Halter for Egyptian offshore

operations and a further three are operated by the US Coast Guard at Key West. In 1984 the US Coast Guard awarded Avon further contracts for the refurbishment of fingers.

CIRR 105P SES (Brødrene Aa Båtbyggeri A/S)

Detailed design and manufacture of the prototype bow and stern skirt systems for Cirrus A/S in 1983-84 and has since supplied components as replacements and for further craft for this designer.

AP1-88 (BHC)

Avon has supplied all materials for BHC for this craft since 1982.

JET RIDER (Karlskronavarvet)

Avon was awarded a contract in 1987 for design and supply of the skirt system for this craft.

Avon Industrial Polymers Limited wish to correct a statement contained in its last entry in *Jane's High-Speed Marine Craft and Air Cushion Vehicles* regarding the supply of skirt materials and/or components to Hovermarine International for the HM2 craft. Avon Industrial Polymers Limited wish to make clear that it is a joint supplier of these materials with Northern Rubber Company Limited and apologise for the error in the entry.

BRITISH HOVERCRAFT CORPORATION LIMITED (BHC)

East Cowes, Isle of Wight, Hampshire PO32 6RH, England

Telephone: 0983 294101
Telex: 86761 BHC G

For Directors see BHC entry in ACV Builders section

BHC has produced more than 90 hovercraft in various sizes covering seven basic types. These have together accumulated over 500 000 hours of operation, and have involved a great deal of research particularly in the design and manufacture of flexible skirts. BHC has designed and manufactured skirts for other craft builders as well as for its own hovercraft. The result has been a progressive improvement in skirt performance,

BHC skirt fitted to Textron Marine Systems LCAC-1

life and reliability and the build-up of experience and expertise. Much of this knowledge has been gained under extreme conditions in Scandinavia, the Middle East and Northern Canada.

In 1963, BHC granted a licence to Bell Aerospace (now Textron Marine Systems) and has, since then, been closely involved with that company's ACV programme. BHC was responsible

BHC peripheral skirt on the SR.N4 Mk 3 *The Princess Anne*

for design and manufacture of the skirt for the Bell SKMR-1 and for the Bell Aerospace Canada Viking. The company was also retained to carry out research and development work for the skirt of the ARPA SEV designs, co-operated with Bell in the design of the 2K SES project skirt, and was consultant for the design of the JEFF(B) skirt. BHC also designed and manufactured skirts for LACV-30. The LCAC skirt was designed by BHC, and the company continues to be the major manufacturer of skirt systems under this programme having now fabricated the first 12 craft sets.

As well as its unrivalled design experience, BHC has been continually improving its manufacturing techniques. The hot bonding process now used produces excellent integration. In the case of the LCAC skirt, bond strength has, under test, been proved to equal coating adhesion. Excellent flexibility is also achieved, giving the benefit of better fatigue life. Bonding adhesives are generally proprietary, being manufactured by FPT, a sister company of BHC, within the Westland Group.

A comprehensive description of BHC skirt production methods was given in the contributed paper of the 1986 edition of *High-Speed Marine Craft and Air Cushion Vehicles*.

A section of the LCAC skirt

Stern corner of BHC SR.N4 skirt

GREENGATE POLYMER COATINGS LIMITED (GPC)

Greengate Works, Manchester M3 7WS, England

Telephone: (061) 834 5652
Telex: 666706 G
Telefax: (061) 834 1497

John Rogers, *Director and General Manager*
E J Thomas, *Sales Director*
R Wisner, *Manufacturing Manager*
R W Collier, *Technical Manager*
A Yorke-Robinson, *Technical Sales Manager*

GPC manufactures many high-performance fabrics for hovercraft uses including buoyancy tubes, skirt, finger (segment) and ancillary applications.

Example materials:

GPC quality	Composition	Total weight (g/m²)	Breaking strength (kg/50mm)	Tear strength (kg)
1188	Neoprene/Nylon	375	100	7·5
6816	Natural rubber/Nylon	620	250	20
2026	Neoprene/Nylon	1040	275	20
3144	Neoprene/Nylon	1200	450	35
3504	Hypalon/Nylon	1300	300	25

Tiger 4 hovercraft with GPC skirt

THE NORTHERN RUBBER COMPANY LIMITED

Mechanical Division, Victoria Works, Retford, Nottinghamshire DN22 6HH, England

Telephone: (0777) 706731
Telex: 56417 RUBBER G
Telefax: (0777) 709739

D E P Owen, *Managing Director*
W J Newbold, *Technical Director*
M J Thompson, *Sales and Marketing Director*
K D Bacon, *Commercial Manager and Overseas Sales*
S G Kenney, *National Sales Manager*
I L Gilchrist, *Assistant Commercial Manager and Marketing*
H T Brown, *Textile Division Production Manager*
G Surtees, *Sales*
D S Offord, *Business Development Manager*

The Northern Rubber Company has worked in co-operation with many major constructors of hovercraft around the world, supplying skirt materials, components and complete fabrications for lightweight sport vehicles to some of the largest craft currently in service.

Experience gained during initial development of skirt fabrics in the UK, together with continuing development closely matched to the requirements of constructors and operators, has led to an established range of materials used for the complete requirements of skirt structures, including fingers (segments), cones, loops, doublers, spray suppressors, anti-bounce webs etc.

Recent applications for Northern Rubber's materials include:

SR.N4 Series British Hovercraft Corporation (BHC)

Northern Rubber supplies materials used extensively on the above series, having been closely involved with BHC during the development of the skirt system for the SR.N4 Mk1 which came into service in 1969. Hoverspeed as operators continue to use Northern Rubber materials in the maintenance of these skirts.

SR.N6 Series (BHC)

Both civil and military variants of this series have incorporated skirt materials from the Northern Rubber range. The abilities of the materials to withstand the most rigorous operating conditions has contributed to the development of the SR.N6 Mk6 which features significantly enhanced all-weather performance and improved manoeuv-

rability partly due to skirt construction in which Northern Rubber materials feature.

AP1-88 (BHC)

Northern Rubber currently supplies skirt component materials to the UK and overseas constructors and operators of the AP1-88.

HM5/HM2 Series (Hovermarine International)

Many of these craft are in service in the Far East with the Hong Kong and Yaumati Ferry Company on routes to Macao and China, where Northern Rubber skirt fabrics perform under conditions of high utilisation.

Properties of Northern Rubber Skirt Materials

Number Reference	Materials Description	Total Weight/Unit Area (oz/yd²)	(g/m²)	Typical Use
NR-11310	Nylon coated both sides with equal weight of neoprene compound	8	271	Skirt and finger segments for use on sporting hovercraft. Segments for use on lower hover pellets
NR-11520	Nylon coated both sides 67% reverse 33% neoprene compound by weight	12	407	Skirt and finger segments for use on two- and four-seat hovercraft
NR-11846	Nylon coated both sides with equal weight of neoprene compound	18	600	Skirt and finger segments for use on lightweight hovercraft
NR-11323	Nylon coated both sides with equal weight of neoprene compound	28	950	Segment fabric for hovertrailers, also inflatable craft
NR-11111	Nylon coated both sides with equal weight of neoprene compound	40	1360	Finger segments for use on sidewall hovercraft
NR-C11569	Nylon coated both sides with equal weight of neoprene compound	40	1360	Skirt segments for hovercraft, water skates and heavy load trailers
NR-C11533	Nylon coated both sides with equal weight of neoprene compound	60	2040	Finger segments for sidewall hovercraft, also segments for water skates
NR-C10863	Nylon coated both sides with equal weight of neoprene compound	74	2515	Skirt and finger fabric for commercial passenger carrying vehicles
NR-11843	Nylon coated both sides with equal weight of natural rubber compound	83	2800	Skirt and finger fabric for commercial passenger carrying vehicles
NR-C11184	Nylon coated both sides with equal weight of neoprene compound	85	2890	Skirt and segment fabric for heavy-load transporters and passenger carrying vehicles
NR-C11828	Nylon coated both sides with equal weight of natural rubber compound	90	3000	Skirt and segment fabric for heavy-load transporters and passenger carrying vehicles
NR-C11748	Nylon coated both sides with equal weight of neoprene compound	95	3220	Segments for heavy-load transporters and passenger carrying vehicles
NR-C11549	Nylon coated both sides with equal weight of natural rubber compound	100	3400	Segments for heavy-load transporters and passenger carrying vehicles
NR-C11580	Nylon coated both sides with equal weight of natural rubber compound	110	3740	Segments for heavy-load transporters and passenger carrying vehicles

PUC 22 *(LARUS)* (Wärtsilä)

The complete skirt system for *Larus* was fabricated by Northern Rubber, and completed in a restricted period to schedule. On transfer to Canada, the craft underwent modification to allow operation in temperatures down to −50°C, temperatures which caused no detrimental effects on the skirt or the flexibility and integrity of its materials.

Other applications have included BHC BH.7, Maxcat, Finn-Leijo 378 and River Rover.

Two River Rover craft were used by the Joint Services Expedition to Nepal, where the turbulent white water along a 60-mile stretch of the Kali Gandaki River offered a severe test for both vehicles and their skirt systems, fabricated entirely from Northern Rubber materials. Originally constructed in 1978 one of the craft still operates in these arduous conditions.

MATERIALS: The range of composite flexible materials are manufactured in combinations of natural rubber or neoprene polymer and nylon substrates. All materials are tested in accordance with the highest standards covered by BS 4F100, but to demonstrate properly the adhesive properties of the hovercraft materials, Northern Rubber has developed a system of testing the materials which gives results related to closely monitored representative conditions.

Neoprene composite materials have outstanding oil and ozone resistance, and good low temperature flexibility down to −30°C. Natural rubber composite materials combine excellent abrasion resistance and lower temperature flexibility down to −51°C.

Craft employing Northern Rubber skirt materials: SR.N6 Mk6, BHC SR.N4 Mk3 and River Rover

UNITED STATES OF AMERICA

BELL AVON INC

1200 Martin Luther King Jr Blvd, Picayune, Mississippi 39466, USA

Telephone: (601) 799 1217
Telex: 6711729 BELAVON
Telefax: (601) 799 1360

Malcolm Gillespie, *Vice President, Operations*
P David Miller, *General Manager*
Vivian H Smith, *Sales Administrator*
P Gene Smith, *Production Manager*
Russell C McDermid, *Technical Superintendent*

Bell Avon Inc is the Avon Industrial Polymers rubber fabrications company in the USA and is a joint venture with Textron Inc. Bell Avon was formed to meet the growing demand in the USA and Canada for high quality rubber-coated fabrics and hovercraft skirts. Backed by the parent company, Avon, it provides a comprehensive design, development and manufacturing service to several North American craft manufacturers and operations.

Bell Avon started operations in its new purpose-built, fully air-conditioned facility in Mississippi in April 1985, using specialised equipment and procedures identical to those developed over the last two decades by Avon in England. Bell Avon is managed and operated by Avon-trained technical, process and managerial personnel. The plant is currently undertaking ambitious expansion plans and expects to employ more than 100 personnel in a facility of 7435m² by 1990.

BONDING SYSTEMS AND MATERIALS

Bell Avon offers both cold- and hot-bonding techniques. Cold-bonding utilises air-drying cold adhesives, and is not generally appropriate for the harsh environments facing ACV and SES skirts. Hot-bonding is accomplished using a range of specialised, proprietary hot-vulcanised Avon adhesives, which are not usually available to unaffiliated companies. After appropriate surface preparation, the adhesive is applied to the surfaces to be bonded. The surfaces are then joined under high pressure and temperature conditions. This process results in an extremely well-integrated composite structure, and the very thin adhesive layer provides considerably better flexural fatigue than hot-bond tapes or adhesives available from rubber companies for less demanding applications.

Bell Avon offers customers the full range of Avon coated fabrics, both as rolls of coated fabric and fabricated for hovercraft skirts and other applications. The ten major types of rubber-coated fabric are stocked at the company's Mississippi location, offering North American customers significantly reduced lead times. Special run or non-stock fabrics can normally be obtained in 10-15 weeks, depending on the type required.

DESIGN CAPABILITY

Bell Avon maintains an in-house pre-production engineering capability, which is coupled with a continuous value engineering input to offer customers major benefits in terms of both improved cost and enhanced operational skirt performance.

Typically, design engineers employed by SES and ACV manufacturers are insufficiently familiar with the range of advanced polymer fabrication techniques to be able to assess the practicability and cost implications inherent in particular facets of a required skirt configuration. Bell Avon's programme team works with a customer's design engineers to obtain an acceptable compromise between theoretical design and final cost. In one major ACV programme, this approach cut 50% and almost $200 000 from the final cost of the skirt assembly.

This detail design input is utilised by customers for virtually every original equipment proposal or contract received by Bell Avon. On less frequent occasions, customers may require major design engineering input, and Bell Avon will usually request service of this type from the British parent company, Avon Industrial Polymers Ltd. Avon's design capability has included full skirt design, involving stress analysis, design appraisal and reduced- or full-scale model testing.

REFURBISHMENTS

Traditionally, many ACV and SES craft operators have accomplished skirt repairs using crude 'bolt-on' patches. Avon initially developed a simple panel-replacement system for SES bow fingers, and subsequently became the sole source of supply for this service to Bell Halter and their SES customers such as the Coast Guard.

Bell Avon's US location has permitted the company to extend this service to other SES craft, and refurbishment has now been accomplished on SES skirts used by the US Coast Guard, the US Army Corps of Engineers, the US Navy, and Tidewater Marine Service Inc.

More significantly, Bell Avon now offers an unparalleled skirt repair and refurbishment capability for the more complicated ACV skirts. Such skirt components as LCAC keel systems, spray suppressors and even an entire craft set, have been inspected and rebuilt to operational condition in the Mississippi facility. This repair work is carried out to factory standards at a small fraction of the cost of providing new components. This service begins with a thorough inspection of all seams and doubler areas. A report is then issued to the client showing damage or abrasion. An important bonus to this approach has been that a significant and reliable database of common repair types has been accumulated, highlighting areas for possible redesign. Bell Avon's report also indicates the likely failure mode, the proposed repair, and a firm cost proposal for accomplishing the repair. The company's repair proposals assess both the financial and structural viability of such work, pointing out key parameters the client might consider in deciding whether to proceed with refurbishment.

LCAC SKIRT SYSTEMS

The LCAC skirt comprises more than 80 different components, and is supplied to the craft manufacturers as assembled segments for ease of installation. The skirt is developed from the now-

Avon bow skirt on Bell Halter US Coast Guard vessel *Dorado* (WSES 1)

Textron Marine Systems Landing Craft, Air Cushion (LCAC) for which Bell Avon has now become a major supplier of skirt systems and components

Textron Marine Systems LACV-30 for which Bell Avon have developed a new stern seal skirt configuration

conventional bag-and-finger design, using lock-bolts to facilitate the changing of worn or damaged components. The skirt design uses seven different weights of rubber-coated fabrics and calendered sheet to arrive at the optimum combination of weight, flexibility and operational life. The coated fabric weights vary between 1390g/m² and 3050g/m², and both natural and synthetic types of rubber are used, compounded and processed to meet the unusual environmental and operating conditions which will face this craft.

Bell Avon has rapidly become a major supplier for the LCAC programme. The company's first LCAC contract was received when Bell Avon's new plant had been open less than two weeks. In October 1985, Bell Avon received contracts worth more than $1 million for the supply of COSAL (Coordinated Shipboard Allowance) spares for the US Navy's West Coast operating base. At press time, Bell Avon was bidding for a similar quantity of spares for the Navy's East Coast base to be completed early in 1988. Bell Avon has received orders from Textron Marine Systems for three craft sets (LCAC-15, -16 and -17) and from Lockheed Shipbuilding Company for their two craft (LCAC-18 and -21). At press time, the US Navy had awarded Lockheed seven further craft and Textron ten further craft, and Bell Avon was bidding both companies for these requirements. Bell Avon has quickly become the major supplier of operational spares for the LCAC programme.

Bell Avon's increasing involvement has enabled the company to offer full service to LCAC craft manufacturers and the US Navy. Many spares requirements are now met from Bell Avon stock. When this is not possible, the company offers a flexible rapid response scheduling service to meet customer requirements, quoting a maximum four weeks lead time for routine requirements. The company has also refurbished many LCAC skirt components and sub-systems worn or damaged in use.

LACV-30 SKIRT SYSTEMS

In summer 1986, the US Army was carrying out testing of a new air cushion spray suppressor system for the LACV-30 craft. The spray skirt was manufactured by Bell Avon's parent company, Avon Industrial Polymers Ltd, UK.

In October 1986, Bell Avon completed manufacture of a new prototype stern seal system for LACV-30. Prior to starting manufacture, Bell Avon had been involved with Textron Marine Systems in the development of detail designs for the craft for about two years. The new prototype stern seal is of the bag-and-finger type, replacing the lateral keel-and-cone system used by LACV-30 in common with other craft of similar vintage such as SR.N6. The new skirt is expected to give improved lift with reduced air loss.

BELL HALTER SES CRAFT SKIRT SYSTEMS

The surface effect ship (SES) concept utilises full height bow fingers, some facets of which are patented by Bell Halter. The stern seal of this craft is a well-proven two-lobe system, giving excellent operational life. Several different weights of coated fabric are used, varying between 2375g/m² for small craft up to 4340g/m² on some parts of the larger craft. All craft currently utilise synthetic rubber compounds, specially developed for abrasion, flexural and environmental resistance.

Bell Avon is now jointly, with Avon, the supplier of skirts for SES craft. Bow finger and stern seal components manufactured and assembled by Bell Avon have been installed on Bell Halter commercial craft in Egypt, on US Coast Guard craft in Key West, Florida, on the US Navy's SES 200 and on the US Army Corps of Engineers survey boat, *Rodolph*.

OTHER HOVERCRAFT PROGRAMMES

Bell Avon is actively developing contacts with other US and Canadian hovercraft operators and manufacturers. Small numbers of skirt components have been supplied to Air Cushion Technologies Inc (for their Falcon and Corsair craft) and to the Canadian Coast Guard (Vancouver and Montreal). One further ACV and two SES programmes are also in the development stages.

SERVICES

MARINE CRAFT REGULATORY AUTHORITIES

ARGENTINA
Prefectura Naval Argentina
Avenida Madero 235,
Buenos Aires,
Argentina

AUSTRALIA
ACVs and Hydrofoils
*Covers interstate and international voyages.
Smaller craft come under jurisdiction of state or
local authorities.*
Department of Transport and Communications
Maritime Safety Division,
GPO Box 594,
Civic Square,
ACT 2601,
Australia
Telephone: 062 687111
Telex: 62018 AA
Telefax: 062 572505

New South Wales
The Maritime Services Board of NSW
Circular Quay West,
Sydney,
New South Wales 2001,
Australia
or
PO Box 32 GPO,
Sydney,
New South Wales 2001,
Australia
Telephone: (02) 240 2111
Telex: 24944 MSBSY AA
Telefax: (02) 251 2364

Northern Territory
Department of Transport and Works
Marine Branch,
GPO Box 2520,
Darwin,
Northern Territory 5794,
Australia
Telephone: (089) 81 6701
Telex: 85605 AA

Queensland
Department of Harbours and Marine
PO Box 2595,
Mineral House,
Corner George Street and Margaret Street,
Brisbane,
Queensland 4000,
Australia
Telephone: 224 8794
Telex: 40760 HARBRS AA
Telefax: 229 5914

South Australia
Department of Marine and Harbours
PO Box 19,
Port Adelaide,
South Australia 5015,
Australia
Telephone: (08) 47 0611
Telex: 82525 AA
Telefax: (08) 47 0605

Tasmania
Navigation and Survey Authority of
Tasmania
1 Franklin Wharf,
GPO Box 202B,
Hobart,
Tasmania 7001,
Australia
Telephone: (002) 34 7122
Telex: 58319 AA
Telefax: (002) 31 0693

Victoria
The Port of Melbourne Authority
World Trade Centre,
GPO Box 4721,
Melbourne,
Victoria 3001,
Australia
Telephone: (03) 611 1777
Telex: 34211 AA
Telefax: (03) 611 1905

Western Australia
Department of Marine and Harbours
1 Essex Street,
PO Box 402,
Fremantle,
Western Australia 6160,
Australia
Telephone: 09 335 0888
Telex: 94784 AA
J M Jenkin, *Executive Director*

BELGIUM
Ministry of Communications
Administration de la Marine et de la Navigation
Intérieure,
rue d'Arlon 104-B3,
B-1040 Brussels,
Belgium
Telephone: 02/233 12 11
Telex: 61880 VERTRA B

CANADA
Transport Canada, Special Ships Division
Canadian Coast Guard,
Tower A,
Place de Ville,
Ottawa,
Ontario K1A 0N7,
Canada
Telephone: (613) 998 0660
R G Wade, *Superintendent*
Design approval and safety certification of all
craft covered by the IMO Code of Safety for
Dynamically Supported Craft and licensing of
their maintenance personnel.

DENMARK
Government Ships Inspection Service
Snorresgade 19,
DK-2300 Copenhagen S,
Denmark
Telephone: (1) 547131
Telex: 31141 SOFART DK

EGYPT
ACVs
The Arab General Organisation for Air Transport
11 Emad El Din Street,
Cairo,
Egypt

FIJI
Director of Marine
Marine Department,
PO Box 326,
Suva,
Fiji

FINLAND
Board of Navigation
Vuorimiehenkatu 1,
PO Box 158,
SF-00141 Helsinki,
Finland
Telex: 12-1471

FRANCE
Secrétariat d'Etat auprès du Ministre des Transports, Chargé de la Mer
3 Place de Fontenoy,
75700 Paris,
France
Telephone: 273 55 05
Telex: 250 823 (Mimer Paris) F

THE GAMBIA
Gambia Ports Authority
Wellington Street,
PO Box 617,
Banjul,
The Gambia,
West Africa

GERMANY, FEDERAL REPUBLIC
See-Berufsgenossenschaft
Ships Safety Department,
Reimerstwiete 2,
2000 Hamburg 11,
Federal Republic of Germany

GHANA
The Shipping Commissioner
Ministry of Transport and Communications,
PO Box M.38,
Accra,
Ghana

GREECE
Ministry of Mercantile Marine
Merchant Ships Inspectorate,
Palaiologou 1 str,
Piraeus 185 35,
Greece
Telephone: 411 1214
Telex: 212581 GR

HONG KONG
Director of Marine
Marine Department,
Harbour Building,
38 Pier Road,
GPO Box 4155,
Hong Kong
Telephone: 5-8523001
Telex: 64553 MARHQ HX
Telefax: 5-423199

HUNGARY
General Director
General Inspection of Transport,
PO Box 102,
1389 Budapest 62,
Hungary
Telephone: 122-800/124-290

ICELAND
Directorate of Shipping
PO Box 7200,
Hringbraut 121,
IS-127 Reykjavik,
Iceland
Telex: 2307

INDIA
Directorate General of Shipping
Bombay,
India

INDONESIA
Department of Transport, Communications and
Tourism
8 Medan Merdelka Barat,
Jakarta-Pusat,
Indonesia

IRELAND
Department of the Marine
  Leeson Lane,
  Dublin 2,
  Ireland
Telephone: 785444
Telex: 90253

ISRAEL
Ministry of Transport
  Administration of Shipping and Ports,
  102 Ha'atzmauth Road,
  PO Box 33993,
  Haifa,
  Israel

ITALY
Ministero della Marina Mercantile
  Ispettorato Tecnico,
  Viale Asia,
  00100 Rome,
  Italy

IVORY COAST
Ministère des Travaux Publics et des Transports
  BP V6,
  Abidjan,
  Ivory Coast

JAMAICA
The Marine Board
  c/o The Port Authority,
  15-17 Duke Street,
  Kingston,
  Jamaica
Telephone: 92 20290/8

JAPAN
Japanese Ministry of Transportation
  2-1-3 Kasumigaseki,
  Chiyoda-ku,
  Tokyo,
  Japan

KOREA, SOUTH
Bureau of Marine Transportation
  Ministry of Transportation,
  1 3 Do Dong,
  Choong-ka,
  Seoul,
  South Korea

KUWAIT
Marine Affairs Department
  General Administration for Transport Affairs,
  Ministry of Communications,
  PO Box 318,
  Safat,
  State of Kuwait
Telephone: 4814371/2
Telex: 22197 US PTT KT

LEBANON
Ministère des Travaux Publics
  Direction des Transports,
  Beirut,
  Lebanon

LUXEMBOURG
Service de la Navigation
  Ministère des Transports,
  19-21 boulevard Royal,
  L-2910 Luxembourg
Telephone: 4794-336
Telex: 1465 CIVAIR LU

MADAGASCAR
Ministère de l'Amina
  Jement du Territoire,
  Anosy,
  Antananarivo,
  Madagascar

MALAWI
Ministry of Transport and Communications
  Private Bag 322,
  Capital City,
  Lilongwe 3,
  Malawi
Telephone: 730122

MALAYSIA
The Ministry of Transport
  Wisma Perdana,
  Jalan Dungun,
  Damansara Heights,
  Kuala Lumpur,
  Malaysia
Telephone: 948122
Telex: 30999 MA

MEXICO
Departamento de Licencias
  Direction de Marina Mercante,
  SCT,
  Luerpo A,
  2 Piso,
  Mexico 12,
  Mexico

MOROCCO
Ministère de l'Equipement
  Direction des Affaires Techniques,
  Rabat-Chellah,
  Morocco

NETHERLANDS
Ministerie van Verkeer en Waterstaat
  Directoraat-Generaal Scheepvaart en Maritieme
  Zaken,
  Bordewijkstraat 4,
  Postbus 5817,
  2280 HV Rijswijk,
  Netherlands

NEW ZEALAND
Ministry of Transport
  Marine Division,
  Private Bag,
  Aurora House,
  62 The Terrace,
  Wellington 1,
  New Zealand
Telephone: 721 253
Telex: 31524 NZ
  Hovercraft regulations currently being drafted. Among other things these will require hovercraft over a certain size to be licensed for commercial operation. The administration of all legislation for hovercraft and hydrofoils is the responsibility of the above.

NORWAY
Sjøfartsdirektoratet
  Norwegian Maritime Directorate,
  Thv Meyersgt 7,
  PO Box 8123-Dep,
  0032 Oslo 1,
  Norway
Telephone: 02-35 02 50
Telex: 76997 SIDR N

SOUTH AFRICA
Department of Transport
  Private Bag X193,
  Pretoria 0001,
  South Africa

SPAIN
Dirección General de la Marina Mercante
  Ruiz de Alacron No 1,
  Madrid 14,
  Spain

SWEDEN
The National Swedish Administration of Shipping and Navigation
  Sjöfartsverket,
  Centralförvaltningen,
  S-601 78 Norrköping,
  Sweden

SWITZERLAND
Lake Constance
Schiffahrtskontrolle des Kantons Thurgau
  Bleichestrasse 42,
  CH-8280 Kreuzlingen,
  Switzerland
Telephone: 072 753232/2222
Strassenverkehrs und Schiffahrtsamt des Kantons
St Gallen
  Abr. Schiffahrt,
  9400 Rorschach,
  Switzerland
Telephone: 071 411474
Kantonale Schiffahrtskontrolle
  Rosengasse 8,
  CH-8200 Schaffhausen,
  Switzerland
Telephone: 053 80601

Lake Geneva
Departement de Justice et Police Service de
la Navigation
  6 rue du 31-Décembre,
  CH-1207 Geneva,
  Switzerland

Lake Lucerne
Strassenverkehrsamt des Kantons Luzern
  Schiffsinspektorat,
  Arsenalstr 45,
  6010 Kriens,
  Switzerland

Lake Lugano and Lake Locarno
Ufficio Cantonale della Circolazione
  Servizio Navigazione,
  CH-6528 Camorino,
  Switzerland

Lake Neuchatel
Departement de Police
  CH-2000 Neuchatel,
  Switzerland

Lake Thoune, Lake Brienz and Lake Biel
Strassenverkehrs-und Schiffahrtsamt
des Kantons Bern
  Schermenweg 5,
  Postfach 2681,
  3001 Bern,
  Switzerland
Telephone: 031-402111
Telex: 911520 SABE CH

Lake Zürich
Seepolizei Gewässerschutz-Schiffahrtskontrolle-
Hafenverwaltung der Stadt Zürich
  Bellerivestrasse 260,
  CH-8034 Zürich,
  Switzerland
Telephone: (1) 216 73 61

TURKEY
T C Ulastirma Bakanligi
  Deniz Ulaştirmasi Genel Müdürlügü,
  Ankara,
  Turkey
T C Ulastirma Bakanligi
  Marmara Bolgesi Liman ve Denizisleri
  Müdürlügü,
  Karaköy-Istanbul,
  Turkey

UNITED KINGDOM
Civil Aviation Authority
Hovercraft—Certification, Issue of Type, Safety, Experimental and Export Certificates. Approval of persons or organisations from whom the CAA may accept reports on the design, construction, maintenance or repair of hovercraft or elements thereof. Approval of hovercraft items and equipment.
Publication of 'British Hovercraft Safety Requirements'

Technical enquiries to:
A C G Seal,
  Head,
  Hovercraft Department,
  CAA Safety Regulation Group,
  Aviation House,
  South Area,
  Gatwick Airport,
  Gatwick
  West Sussex RH6 0YR
  England
  Telephone: 0293 567171
  Telex: 87853
  Telefax: 0293 573999

Publications:
Civil Aviation Authority
  Printing and Publication Services,
  Greville House,
  37 Gratton Road,
  Cheltenham,
  Gloucestershire GL50 2BN,
  England
  Telefax: 0242 584139

Department of Transport
Hovercraft Operating Permits, Registration and Hydrofoil Passenger Certificates
Department of Transport
  Marine Directorate,
  Room 2/33,
  Sunley House,
  90 High Holborn,
  London WC1V 6LP,
  England
  Telephone: 01 405 6911
  Telex: 264084 MARBOT G

UNITED STATES OF AMERICA
Cdr R B Meyer
Department of Transportation
Commandant (G-MTH-4/13)
  US Coast Guard,
  Washington DC 20593-0001,
  USA
Telephone: (202) 267 2997

VENEZUELA
Ministerio de Transporte y Comunicaciones
  Dirección General Sectorial de Transporte Acuatico Dirreccion de Navegacion Acuatico,
  Caracas,
  Venezuela

YUGOSLAVIA
Yugoslav Federal Economic Secretariat
  Transport Department,
  Bulevar AVNOJ-a 104,
  Belgrade,
  Yugoslavia

body page

CONSULTANTS AND DESIGNERS

AUSTRALIA

CROWTHER MULTIHULLS
PO Box 35, Turramurra (Sydney), NSW 2074, Australia

Telephone: (02) 997 4599
Telefax: (02) 997 5841

Lock Crowther, *Proprietor*

Lock Crowther is a long-established designer of multi-hull sail, motor and motor/sail craft.

The Crowther design office is an Australian Government-approved research organisation and manufacturers are eligible for Government grants (in Australia) on research and development work carried out by the office.

Designs of recent years from the Crowther office have included:
R V SUNBIRD. A 46ft (14m) marine biological research catamaran motor sailer (design no 69) for The Great Barrier Reef Lizard Island Research Station.
DMB. A 74ft (22·4m) ketch rigged pearling/diving catamaran (design no 73) of exceptional performance under sail and power.

TAFUA. Four 60ft (18m) luxury charter motor sailers (design no 58).
SOUTHERN SPIRIT. A 98ft (29·9m) luxury motor sailer/yacht (design no 96 Mk II).
OCEAN SPIRIT. A 105ft (32m) tourist motor sailer yacht (design no 126).
SUNBIRD, SUNSEEKER and *QUICKCAT.* Three 110ft (34m) high-speed passenger ferries (designs nos 109, 117 and 132).
MOTIVE EXPLORER. A 110ft (34m) mini passenger liner catamaran (design no 120).

PHIL CURRAN DESIGN
Philip E Curran Pty Ltd
2 Edward Street, Fremantle 6160, Western Australia, Australia

Telephone: (09) 335 9966
Telex: 94110 FILCO AA
Telefax: (09) 430 4032

Phil Curran, *Director, Naval Architect*
Jackie Bouter, *Director, Administrative Manager*

Phil Curran designs range from 6-metre dinghies to high-speed private luxury yachts of over 65 metres, nearly 400 designs having been produced since first starting business some 10 years ago.

Commercial and pleasure craft are designed in all forms of construction, Phil Curran Design specialising in modern 'high-tech' construction materials such as aluminium, foam sandwich and Kevlar.

Recent designs have included the following craft:
BENSON-BROWN. A 19·2m, 38-knot, 15-tonne displacement vessel with waterjet propulsion.
CONTRACTOR. An 8·36m, 38-knot, 1·8-tonne displacement tender support craft with waterjet propulsion for the New Zealand America's Cup Challenge 1986/87.
VULTURE and *BUZZARD.* A 12·255m, 45-knot, 5·4-tonne displacement high-speed tender support for the Parry Task Force '87 defence of the America's Cup.
PM 17. Built by Precision Marine Holdings Pty Ltd. This 17m power boat design has received over 20 orders and has won the '1986 Power Boat of the Year' award and the Australian Design Award. With a 24-tonne displacement the boat is capable of 40 knots.

OCEANFAST 4000 PARTS VI. A 46·69m, 30-knot, 150 tonnes (light ship) luxury motor yacht used by the Royal Perth Yacht Club as their flagship during the 1986/87 America's Cup Regatta in Fremantle, Western Australia.

OCEANFAST 3000 NEVER SAY NEVER. A 33·3m, 30-knot luxury charter vessel now operating in the Caribbean.

SUN GODDESS. A 200-seat, 34·0m, 25-knot ferry, the second to be built for Ansett Transport Industries, Hayman Island, Queensland, Australia.

SUNDANCER. A 145-seat, 27·5m, 34-knot ferry with waterjet propulsion built by SBF Engineering.

WILDERNESS SEEKER. A 100-seat, 19·95m, 30-knot ferry with waterjet propulsion, built for Gordon River operations in Tasmania.

CANADA

DF DICKINS ASSOCIATES LIMITED
3732 West Broadway, Vancouver, British Columbia V6R 2C1, Canada

Telephone: (604) 224 4124
Telex: 04 54247 CA

D F Dickins, *President*

DF Dickins Associates Ltd is actively involved in Arctic marine transportation studies. The company provides route evaluation, conceptual, design and testing for Arctic air cushion vehicles. DF Dickins offers a range of consulting expertise through affiliations with specialists in hovercraft skirt systems, naval architecture and propeller design.

From 1981 to 1984 Dickins Associates provided technical direction of Sohio Petroleum Company's hovercraft research. This involved the co-ordination of an international design team to develop the concept for a 1000-ton ACV. In the last year of the Sohio programme, Dickins Associates directed the testing of the 200-ton JEFF(A) at Prudhoe Bay.

A recently completed project for Gulf Canada Resources involved the conceptual design of a series of large self-propelled hovercraft up to 845 tonnes gross weight. The project included a complete economic evaluation of capital and operating costs in comparison with a Boeing 234 helicopter, and existing hovercraft capable of operating over rough ice with obstacles over 2·5m in height.

Current programmes include the evaluation of air cushion vehicles as high-speed platforms for spraying chemical dispersants on oil slicks at sea. The Canadian Coast Guard Vancouver Search and Rescue base provided an SR.N6 for preliminary trials during the summer of 1986.

Recent publications are included in the bibliography section of this edition. David Dickins is currently preparing a chapter entitled Arctic Transportation to be included in a new book, *Technology, Economics and Applications of Hovercraft* (Ed R Amyot, Elsevier Science Publishers).

FINLAND

MXA-CONSULTING LTD OY
It Pikäkatu 3a D, SF-20520 Turku, Finland

Telephone: (921) 333881

Telex: 62004 TURKU SF
Telefax: (921) 331934

Matti Ahtikari

Designer of the MXA 1700, MXA 3300 II and MXA 4200 II high-speed catamaran ferry types.

FRANCE

SOCIÉTÉ BERTIN & CIE
BP 3, 78373 Plaisir Cedex, France

Telephone: (30) 56 2500
Telex: 696231 F

Eric Barsalou, *President, Director General*
Georges Mordchelles-Regnier, *Director General*

Société Bertin & Cie has been engaged in developing the Bertin principle of separately fed multiple plenum chambers surrounded by flexible skirts since 1956. A research and design organisation, the company employs a staff of more than 500, mainly scientists and design engineers who are involved in many areas of industrial research, including air cushion techniques and applications.

SEDAM was originally responsible for developing the Naviplane and Terraplane vehicles but this responsibility has now passed to IFREMER (see following entry). The Bertin principle of multiple air cushions has also led to the development of the Aérotrain high-speed tracked transport system and to numerous applications in the area of industrial handling and aeronautics. These applications, developed by Bertin, are described in the sections devoted to *Air Cushion Applicators, Conveyors and Pallets* and *Air Cushion Landing Systems* in *Jane's Surface Skimmers 1980* and earlier editions.

INSTITUT FRANÇAIS DE RECHERCHE POUR L'EXPLOITATION DE LA MER (IFREMER)

Centre de Brest, BP 337, 29273 Brest Cedex, France

Telephone: (98) 224040
Telex: 940627 OCEAN F

Bertrand de Lagarde

IFREMER was formed in 1984 from the merger between CNEXO (National Centre for Sea Development) and ISTPM, Scientific and Technical Institute for Sea Fisheries. IFREMER is commissioned by the French Government to conduct studies for the evaluation of unconventional ships, eg amphibious hovercraft, surface effect ships, hydrofoil craft, catamarans and SWATH vessels and may participate in any development of these concepts. Test facilities are located at Brest in Brittany. The largest part of the unconventional ship research programme of IFREMER is concerned with air cushion technology and the relevant patents have been acquired from the former SEDAM company. In 1986 IFREMER was involved in three designs: the ADOC 12 amphibious hovercraft, a surface effect ship and the Aerobac, a track-propelled air cushion vehicle under development by the Transportation Development Centre of Transport Canada.

ADOC 12

Full details of this 14-seat craft are given in the Société Aeroplast entry in the main Air Cushion Vehicles section of this edition. In 1986 IFREMER conducted complete performance tests on the craft from their establishment at Brest.

NES 24

A 22m surface-effect ship project which is being studied in collaboration with French shipyards (see DCN entry in Air Cushion Vehicles section).

AEROBAC AB-7

Aerobac AB-7 is a concept developed by the Transportation Development Centre of Canada, in collaboration with VRV Inc. The Aerobac combines an air cushion platform with muskeg tractor tracks. (See Transport Canada, Transportation Development Centre entry in Air Cushion Vehicles section.)

THE NETHERLANDS

WIJSMULLER ENGINEERING BV

Sluisplein 34, 19 75 AG Ijmuiden, The Netherlands
PO Box 510, 1970 AM Ijmuiden, The Netherlands

Telephone: (02550) 62666
Telex: 41110 WIJSM NL

Telefax: (02550) 18695

Feasibility studies, conceptual and final design, writing of tender specifications, bid evaluation, contract negotiations, building supervision, surveys, maintenance and repair co-ordination, training and development of marine management information systems.

NORWAY

CIRRUS A/S

Kanalveien 54, PO Box 223, N-5032 Minde, Bergen, Norway

Telephone: (0) 5 29 79 01
Telex: 40422 CIRR N

Dick Vinkler, *General Manager*

Cirrus A/S was responsible for the design of the CIRR 105P Norcat SES, for operation on inter-city passenger ferry services in Norway and is also undertaking the marketing and sales of further vessels of this type. For a description of the Norcat, which was built by Brødrene Aa Båtbyggeri A/S, see Air Cushion Vehicles section.

OTTO L SCHEEN A/S

Holterteigveien 5, N-1440 Drøbak, Norway

Designers of high-speed mono-hull vessels for a wide variety of applications, many in the range of 15 to 20m.

TEKNISK MODELL-SENTER A/S

6780 Hyen, Nordfjord, Norway

Telephone: (057) 69805

Ola Lilloe-Olsen, *Proprietor*

Design consultants with towing-tank facility, established 1979. Designers of a large number of high-speed mono-hull ferries.

SINGAPORE

VOSPER-QAF PTE LTD

232 Tanjong Rhu Road, Singapore 1543

Telephone: 344 4144
Telex: 21219 RS
Telefax: 344 6642

UK Office: Hamble Point Marina, Southampton SO3 5NB, England

T T Durai, *Managing Director*
W R Harvey, *Technical Director*
R N Cooper, *Marketing & Sales Manager*
M J Beales, *Logistic Support Manager*
D L K Lim, *Project Operations Manager*

With experience going back to 1923, the company specialises in the design and construction of high performance naval craft up to 95 metres in length, special duty craft such as patrol vessels for Coast Guard and Customs, high-speed firefighting boats and VIP yachts. In 1986, the ownership of Vosper Private Limited was transferred to QAF Limited, a large and diversified Singapore-based group and the company was renamed Vosper-QAF Pte Ltd.

The company specialises in the following fields: naval ship design and construction; specialist commercial ship design and construction; refit and repair; transfer of naval technology; logistic support and supply; planned maintenance systems; international procurement; shipyard and naval base design and consultancy; management services; research and development; and surveying and consultancy.

The uniqueness of Vosper-QAF is seen in its recent decentralisation of its shipbuilding activities which offer clients well-balanced and effective options for cost, delivery, supervision and quality considerations. A ship order may be directed to one of Vosper-QAF's contracted shipyards in or outside Singapore. The shipyards are continuously and comprehensively assessed by Vosper-QAF to ensure that they are technically qualified and adequately equipped for the construction of naval vessels.

Technology transfer forms a substantial portion of the business, involving the supply of design and production technology to overseas shipyards for the construction of Vosper-QAF-designed vessels. Three recent contracts have involved the placing of Vosper management and technical staff within foreign shipyards to oversee production and advise on quality, production and trials procedures.

Since their acquisition, Vosper-QAF have continued to market successfully high-quality naval technology with orders including two 46-metre OPVs for the Brazilian Navy, two 54-metre landing craft transport for a Middle East Navy, six 32-metre inshore/offshore anti-submarine and harbour defence patrol boats for a Far Eastern Navy and a naval damage control and firefighting simulator for Brunei. Additionally the logistics division supports naval and maritime authorities in the Middle and Far East, supplying spares and technical support for many different vessels, including those constructed by Vosper.

SWITZERLAND

DR ING E G FABER

Gratstrasse 20, CH-8472 Seuzach, Switzerland

Telephone: (052) 53 30 40
Telex: 78670 DATAG CH

Consultant in marine engine plant planning, marine engineering and marine technology, with special emphasis on high-speed and hydrofoil craft, feasibility studies, cost estimates, specifications, plant descriptions, speed estimates and hydrodynamic problems.

DIPL ING E SCHATTÉ

Amlehnstrasse 33, CH-6010 Kriens (Luzern), Switzerland

Telephone: 041 41 27 94

Consulting in hydrodynamics, aerodynamics and marine technology, especially high-speed craft.

SUPRAMAR HYDROFOILS AG

Ausserfeld 5, CH-6362 Stansstad, Switzerland

Telephone: (041) 61 31 94
Telex: 866274 SUPR CH
Telefax: 814 24 41

Dipl Ing Volkert Jost, *President*

Dipl Ing Harry Trevisani, *General Manager*
Dipl Ing Eugen Schatté, *Research and Development*
Dr Ing Herrmann de Witt, *Hydrodynamics*
Dr Ing Otto Münch, *Stabilisation and Control*
Jürg Bally, *Board Member*

Supramar was founded in Switzerland in 1952 to develop on a commercial basis the hydrofoil system introduced by the Schertel-Sachsenberg

Hydrofoil Syndicate and its licensee, the Gebrüder Sachsenberg Shipyard.

Since its foundation, Supramar has provided a world-wide consultancy service, covering not only its hydrofoil vessels but also other aspects of fast marine transport. Its scientists have delivered papers to most of the world's leading professional bodies.

The company has been under contract to many governments and military services.

UNITED KINGDOM

AIR CUSHION EQUIPMENT (1976) LIMITED

15-35 Randolph Street, Shirley, Southampton, Hampshire SO1 3HD, England

Telephone: 0703 776468
Telex: 477537 G

J D Hake, *Chairman*
R C Gilbert, *General Manager*
R R Henvest, *Works Manager*

Air Cushion Equipment (1976) Limited offers its services as design engineers and technical consultants for air cushion and water cushion systems. Past experience has involved investigations into systems using both water and air as the cushion fluid.

AIR VEHICLES LIMITED

Head Office and Factory: Unit 4, Three Gates Road, Cowes, Isle of Wight, Hampshire, England

Telephone: 0983 293194
Telex: 86513 HVWORK G
Telefax: 0983 294704

C D J Bland, *Director*
C B Eden, *Director*
A Moseley, *Director*

Air Vehicles Limited, formed in 1968, has a wide experience of all types of hovercraft and hovercraft operation and can offer a full range of services as consultants. Particular fields where Air Vehicles Limited has specialised knowledge are in the design and manufacture of small, up to 40-seat, hovercraft and in their operation in many countries. In addition Air Vehicles has expertise in the manufacture of ducted propellers with sizes ranging from 1·3m diameter on the Tiger 12 to 2·7m diameter ducts for a US military contract.

Approved by the Civil Aviation Authority, the company can design and undertake modifications

to larger craft. Typical of this work is the conversion of SR.N5 and SR.N6 to flat deck layout for logistic operations, the addition of high speed, dunking hydrographic equipment to SR.N6 and Tiger 12 craft and various modifications for seismic surveying operations. The company also has Tiger 12 and 16 hovercraft available for charter.

Air Vehicles Limited also undertakes feasibility studies and was responsible for an original design concept leading to the AP1-88, 80-passenger diesel craft operated by Hovertravel Limited and undertook the detail design for this craft.

A G BLYTH

2 Aubrey Villas, Green Lane, Warsash, Southampton SO3 6JJ, England

Telephone: (04895) 4432
Telefax: (04895) 5965

Andrew G Blyth, *Principal*

Design, evaluation and feasibility studies for high-speed marine vehicles, especially surface effect ships, mono-hulls and catamarans, from a

background of practical shipyard design experience allied to experimental and theoretical research and development work.

Consultant to EEL Ltd (Test Facilities) (UK) for technical direction of a major research programme into the ultimate stability boundaries of surface effect ships, funded by the UK Department of Transport and the United States Coast Guard. This six-year-long fundamental research project has established a new and more comprehensive understanding of the on-cushion stability limitations of this type of vessel.

Consultant to Civil Aviation Authority (UK), for developing theoretical methods of evaluating

the on-cushion roll stability of surface effect ships, and determining suitable criteria for safe operation, in a seaway and in high-speed turns.

Consultant to SSPA Maritime Consulting AB (Sweden) for surface effect ship design, development and experimental evaluation and techniques.

Particular expertise in parametric comparative studies, powering and performance predictions including model testing, SES lift and skirt system development, design and execution of complete theoretical and experimental investigations in the field of high-speed vessel naval architecture, as well as conducting conventional conceptual and production design work.

HOVERCRAFT CONSULTANTS LIMITED (HCL)

Chinook, Nash Road, Dibden Purlieu, Southampton, Hampshire SO4 5RS, England

Telephone: (0703) 843178
Telex: 477580 HOVCON G
Telefax: (0703) 843711

J E Rapson, *Managing Director*
M J Cox, *Director*
J P Towndrow, *Director*
S M Rapson, *Secretary and Director*

Hovercraft Consultants Limited (HCL) offers a comprehensive advisory service to the hovercraft

and related industries. Since HCL has no affiliation with any manufacturer or operator, it is able to provide unbiased appraisals of existing and projected craft. The suitability of such craft for particular routes and duties is assessed both technically and economically. The company keeps extensive and up to date records of both the technical and commercial aspects of high-speed, waterborne transport. This information, which includes details of craft, operations, manufacturers, routes and traffic, can be made available to its clients.

HCL specialises in the design of cushion and skirt systems and has designed skirts for a hover-platform to carry payloads of 300 tons in the Arctic for the Sohio Petroleum Company. This programme involved extensive model work over

water and simulated ice surfaces as well as the construction of a full scale box test rig in conjunction with Avon Industrial Polymers operating at pressures greater than the full scale cushion pressure. HCL has been involved with the design of several passenger-carrying amphibious craft for use in coastal waters, carrying from 4 to 100 persons at speeds up to 50 knots, a complete cushion system for a 55-knot sidewall hovercraft including the fitting of the skirt and management of the trials programme, a small hover platform to carry 0·6 tons of payload for building site operations and a series of air cushion icebreaking bows for use with conventional ships.

The company has recently been involved in the design of an amphibious hovercraft to be built in Asia. For this contract HCL was required to design and construct a 2·5m model which was tested in a wind tunnel and a testing tank and was then converted for radio controlled tests on open water.

HCL has built on its existing experience in skirt design and has completed twelve full-scale skirt designs, covering all sizes of craft, since 1982. It has carried out independent technical and commercial evaluations of various types of hovercraft and other forms of high-speed water transport. The company also undertakes research and development in connection with improving the economics and the general efficiency and controllability of all types of hovercraft.

HCL is headed by John Rapson, who has been involved with hovercraft technology since 1956. Formerly with Hovercraft Development Limited as Technical Director and Chief Engineer, he has advised government departments and official committees on design, operational requirements and safety of hovercraft.

HOVERCRAFT SALES AND MARKETING (HOVSAM)

PO Box 7, Sarisbury Green, Southampton SO3 6YS, England

Telephone: (042 121) 3547
Telex: 477164 HOVSAM G

G A Gifford, *Managing Director*

Hovercraft Sales and Marketing (HOVSAM) undertakes general hovercraft consultancy work, specialising in the recommendation of various amphibious and non-amphibious hovercraft for particular routes and applications. In the 1- to 4-tonne payload range of hovercraft, HOVSAM represents Griffon Hovercraft Ltd. The company

also represents Hovermarine International Ltd and Graham Gifford has been responsible for placing many of these non-amphibious surface effect ships into operation around the world.

HOVSAM undertakes several overseas sales visits each year and advises on route feasibility and economics, and the suitability of both commercial and military hovercraft for particular areas and applications.

HOVERWORK LIMITED

12 Lind Street, Ryde, Isle of Wight, Hampshire PO33 2NR, England

Telephone: (0983) 65181
Telex: 86513 (A/B Hoverwork Ryde)
Telefax: (0983) 65181

C D J Bland, *Managing Director*

E W H Gifford, *Director*
A C Smith, *Director*
R G Clarke, *Director*
G M Palin, *Secretary*

Hoverwork Limited, formed in early 1966, is a wholly owned subsidiary of Hovertravel, the Solent ferry company, which has been operating hovercraft longer than any other company in the world. In addition to its fleet of SR.N6 type craft it

now has access to Hovertravel's new, much larger, AP1-88, also fully amphibious and with approximately the same performance capability.

The company specialises in chartering craft for seismic and other survey work, crew change operations and other related operations within the oil industry in shallow water areas and terrain difficult for other forms of transport.

The company also offers a route feasibility investigation service.

P N STRUCTURES LIMITED
Marine and Engineering Division

5 Vigo Street, Piccadilly, London W1X 1AH, England

Telephone: 01-734 2578
Telex: 884392 G
Telefax: 01-434 3465

Theo Pellinkhof, *Chairman*
Karin M Adeler, *Director*
Henk J Wimmers, *Associate (The Netherlands)*
Dolf Le Comte, *Associate (The Netherlands and USA)*
David J Rimmer, *Secretary*

Consultancy in the fields of marine transport systems for: economic commercial use, effective surveillance duties, and leisure.

Consultancy includes selection of hydrofoils, air cushion vehicles or any other type of surface effect ships and the full range of the more conventional craft varying from the planing hull to the full displacement type.

Consultancy also covers marine engineering and materials handling (air cushion platforms).

A wide area of industrial and technological resources will be made available to clients.

R A SHAW

(*Managing Director* Hoverprojects Limited)
Fell Brow, Silecroft, Millom, Cumbria LA18 5LS, England

Telephone: 0657 2022

R A Shaw, *Managing Director*
L M James
M A Shaw

With a background in flying boat research and the management of research aircraft, advice is offered on proposed new designs and applications. Experience with hovercraft dates back to 1957 when the first study contract was placed with Saunders Roe and the prototype SR.N1 was built.

Studies have been made of proposed fast ferry services, assessing the economic and operating problems of both hydrofoils and hovercraft. Latterly these have been directed to a fast ferry service proposed on the Thames in London. Here it has been found that ferry craft designed on the Airmaran principle have distinct advantages, both

in their economics and operating characteristics, over rival hovercraft, hydrofoils and conventional catamarans.

The opportunity to use large simple hovercraft for passenger and freight operations over long distances on rivers has not so far been exploited. A design for a 30-knot, 1000-ton amphibious hovercraft suitable for such operations has been prepared. Designed for assembly on site from components which would be shipped, trucked or flown in, an assessment of the economics of its operation looks very favourable.

SKIMA HOVERCRAFT LIMITED

6 Hamble Close, Warsash, Hampshire SO3 6GT, England

Telephone: 04895 3210

M A Pinder, *Director*

In 1972 Pindair Limited was set up by M A Pinder who developed the Skima range of inflatable and semi-inflatable hovercraft which the company manufactured and sold to 70 countries. In 1982 Skima Hovercraft Limited was formed as a separate development company with Pindair Ltd concentrating on manufacturing and marketing. In 1983 it was decided to subcontract or licence

manufacture and Pindair Limited was wound up. The Skima 4 hovercraft is now marketed by Air Vehicles Ltd. Skima Hovercraft Limited is continuing the design and development programme on this craft. Details of Skima hovercraft types are given in *Jane's High-Speed Marine Craft and Air Cushion Vehicles* 1986.

ROBERT TRILLO LIMITED (RTL)

28a St Thomas St, Lymington, Hampshire SO4 9NE, England

Telephone: 0590 75098/22220
Telex: 47674 MATCOM G
Telefax: 0590 72720

Robert L Trillo, *Managing Director*
Ann U Alexander, *Director and Secretary*

An independent firm formed in 1969, since when consultancy has been undertaken in many countries. RTL is engaged principally in consultancy and design work on all forms of high-speed waterborne transport, amphibious vehicles and low-speed aerodynamics. Specific areas include: conceptual studies, propulsion (water, amphibious, air) with extensive expertise in the design of ducted air propellers, eight hovercraft types now employing RTL designs; noise, in particular propeller noise; design of air cushion vehicles; feasibility studies and appraisals of projects for development financing; high-speed craft marketing, technology, economics and aesthetics.

Continuing investigations have also been undertaken in airship propulsion and resistance. Thrust devices have been designed for amphibious vehicle swamp propulsion.

Work has continued on the new RTL concept, a minimum-wash, high-speed ferry craft specially conceived and optimised for relatively calm and shallow-water operations in city and urban transport areas. This concept has been taken up by Fairey Marinteknik (UK) Ltd as the Fairey RTL Hydrocat.

UNITED STATES OF AMERICA

AEROPHYSICS COMPANY

3500 Connecticut Avenue NW, Washington DC 20008, USA

Telephone: (202) 244 7502

Dr Gabriel D Boehler, *Chairman*

Carl W Messinger Jr, *President*
William F Foshag, *Chief Engineer*

Founded in 1957, Aerophysics Company has undertaken research and development work in all phases of ACV design. Dr Boehler had previously performed feasibility studies with ACV pioneer Melville Beardsley. Although still interested in the complete vehicle, Aerophysics has recently concentrated on lift systems. Termination of the US Navy's 3K SES halted Aerophysics' full-scale fan development.

DAI INC

451 Hungerford Drive, Suite 700, Rockville, Maryland 20850, USA

Telephone: (301) 424 0270

William B Humphrey, *President and Technical Director*

Ronald G Bryant, *Vice President and Controller*

Dai Inc, formerly Doty Associates, is a privately-owned, small business firm founded in 1968. The firm specialises in financial management, project control, weapons system analysis, test planning and evaluation, operations research, cost and economic analyses for Department of Defense and other government and state agencies.

Since its foundation, the firm has provided engineering services to the US Navy on a number of high technology programmes. These programmes include both the 2K and 3K Surface Effect Ship (SES) designs, the PHM hydrofoil, the Sea Control Ship and the Vertical Support Ship (VSS). In addition, the firm has been involved in Naval V/STOL aviation studies.

FRYCO

7107 Silver Leaf Lane, Houston, Texas 77088, USA

Telephone: (713) 931-8932
Telex: 493-7128 FRYCO
Telefax: (713) 931-5168

Edward D Fry, *Principal*

Edward Fry established FRYCO in 1978 after 22 years building experience. Fry has supervised the design and construction of over 700 commercial, military and pleasure craft including: US Navy high-speed combatants for Navy SEAL Teams, catamarans for commercial and US Army use, mono-hull yachts up to 50 knots, and rig service vessels up to 30-knot speed. He has also conducted scale model tests at various institutions and has data available for design study, designed equipment and wrote training manuals for oil pollution recovery equipment at five major ports and supervised Middle East licensee shipyard for US builder for 4 years.

FRYCO designs vessels up to 50 metres and specialises in high-speed craft. Experienced in gas turbine engine packaging and installation as well as diesel and petrol engines. Computer models are used for speed prediction and hydrostatics. Hulls are created with computer graphics making fully developed offsets available to the builder for automatic CAD/CAM cutting. Fry's building background assures practical, economic designs with emphasis placed on reliability and serviceability.

Recent projects

1986 Design, scale model test, styling model, specifications for 50-knot, gas turbine powered 31·10m high-speed yacht.
1986 Design, computer modelling and construction details for 19·82m passenger catamaran, diesel powered, USCG certified, 30-knot speed in Sea State 4.
1987 Design, computer modelling, computer lines and offsets for 35·06m rig service vessel, diesel powered, 30-knot service speed in Sea State 3.

GIBBS & COX

119 West 31st Street, New York, New York 10001, USA

Telephone: (212) 613 1300

Arlington Office: 1235 Jefferson Davis Highway, Arlington, Virginia 22202, USA

Telephone: (703) 979 1240

Newport News Office: Rouse Tower, 6060 Jefferson Avenue, Newport, Virginia 23605, USA

Telephone: (804) 380 5800

Project management, co-ordination and consultation on conceptual and preliminary designs, contract drawings and specifications and construction drawings for commercial or naval ships of the SES/ACV or submerged hydrofoil systems, destroyers, escorts, frigates, corvettes and VTOL/Helo carriers.

KINETICS GROUP INC (KGI)

PO Box 1071, Mercer Island, Washington 98040, USA
&
1315 NW Mall Street, Suite C, Issaquah, Washington 98027, USA

Telephone: (206) 392 7267

J F Sladky, *Principal*
P M Ressler, *Principal*

Kinetics Group Inc has been established to engage in the management of technology development with particular expertise being available in marine vehicle design, combustion processes, signature reduction and propulsion systems. KGI is interested in bringing about technology transfer and helping negotiate technical teaming and co-operative agreements.

TIMOTHY GRAUL MARINE DESIGN

211 North Third Avenue, PO Box 290, Sturgeon Bay, Wisconsin 54235, USA

Telephone: (414) 743 5092

Timothy Graul, *Principal*

Timothy Graul Marine Design was established in 1981 to provide naval architecture, consulting and design services to owners, builders and vessel operators. The firm now has six full-time employees. The principal, Timothy Graul, has 25 years' experience in design of patrol boats, ferries, tugs, fireboats, military vessels, research boats, passenger craft and river towboats and barges. Graul is a graduate of the University of Michigan and previously worked for Grafton Boat Co Inc and Peterson Builders Inc. The firm has as clients several premier vessel builders and is a consultant to the George G Sharp naval architecture firm. Graul is a charter member of the Small Craft Committee of SNAME and a member of both the SC-1 (Power Craft) Panel and the RINA. He is the author of numerous papers and articles on planing craft, steering systems and aluminium boat construction.

Timothy Graul Marine Design is qualified and capable to design fast craft up to about 40 metres in length. Graul staff are experienced in vessel construction and operation as well as design, and as such emphasise practical solutions to design problems. The firm is conversant with modern design techniques and practices, and applies these whenever feasible, but only within the context of reliability and production constraints. Timothy Graul Marine Design stresses practical, serviceable vessels which perform efficiently and at minimum cost and highest levels of dispatch availability.

Timothy Graul Marine Design has been heavily involved in the design of passenger vessels, ferries and yachts over the past year. Deliveries in 1987 included the 30·8m (101ft) passenger/vehicle ferry *Endeavor* for Neuman Boat Line of Sandusky, Ohio, and the 19·8m (65ft) fast passenger vessel *Island Clipper* for Voight Marine Service of Gills Rock, Wisconsin. The firm also did detail engineering and working plans to support the construction of a 38·4m (126ft) aluminium fast luxury yacht which is powered by waterjets. The yacht was designed by Tom Fexas Yacht Design Inc, and built by Palmer Johnson Inc, of Sturgeon Bay, Wisconsin. Other designs now on the boards at Timothy Graul Marine Design include a 27·4m (90ft) passenger/vehicle ferry, a 30·5m (100ft) ice-service ferry, a 25·9m (85ft) aluminium dinner/excursion boat, a 19·8m (65ft) excursion boat, an 11·6m (38ft) motor vessel and several fast craft in the preliminary design phase.

J B HARGRAVE NAVAL ARCHITECTS INC

205½ Sixth Street, West Palm Beach, Florida 33401, USA

Telephone: (305) 833 8567
Telefax: (305) 833 7791

Cable: HARGRAVE

Dudley A Dawson, *Vice President*

Designers of a range of medium- to high-speed mono-hull ferry boats. A recent example was completed by Aluminium Boats Inc in the summer of 1986 for Shepler's Inc. This 20-knot, 23·8m vessel *Capt Shepler* was the fifth design by J B Hargrave for the Shepler fleet and the third passenger vessel built in 1986 to a Hargrave design.

J B Hargrave have been designing a wide variety of passenger vessels, commercial vessels and yachts for nearly 30 years ranging from 5·5m runabouts to a 190·5m chemical tanker.

HOVER INC

4112 Victoria Blvd, Hampton, Virginia 23669, USA

Telephone: (804) 722 6994

Ronald Gorton, *President*
Simon T Gorton, *Vice-President*
Steven G Doleac, *Project Manager*

Hover Inc has been established to aid in the development of the market for air cushion tech-nology. As a service company, it performs consult-ing, marketing and sales functions for various industry participants. The company utilises a marketing approach rather than the traditional engineering approach and serves suppliers, manu-facturers, sellers, resellers and buyers within the industry. Each of these participants have separate identifiable needs which Hover Inc addresses.

Hover Inc offers suppliers and manufacturers: new product analysis; market analysis and evalu-ation; and advertising and promotional pro-grammes for new or existing products. Hover Inc provides support system programmes to resellers of this technology. Such programmes are similar to those listed above but are tailored to meet the needs of the seller rather than the manufacturer.

The company also serves the needs of buyer groups interested in air cushion technology. It provides information about products available from the industry along with the associated reg-ulations. Hover Inc also puts together buyer and seller of this technology recommending manufac-turers and/or craft for various applications and markets.

C RAYMOND HUNT ASSOCIATES INC

69 Long Wharf, Boston, Massachusetts 02110, USA

Telephone: (617) 742 5669
Telex: 294116 BOSTLX (Attn: Hunt Associates)

John H Deknatel, *President*
Winn Williard, *Manager Commercial and Military Projects*
Peter S Boyce
John C Kiley

Stephen M Weld
Amy B Tichnor
Rollinson C Tait
Craig J Obara

C Raymond Hunt Associates created the deep-V hull design in 1959 and have been refining the concept since. Specialising in the design of deep-V fast yachts and commercial and military craft, Hunt Associates' in-house capabilities include the full range of design and engineering services. The present staff of eight includes naval architects and engineers with expertise in all construction materials and methods of propulsion. Recent commercial applications of the Hunt deep-V fast pilot and patrol boat designs include:
SANDY HOOK. A 20m, 24-knot, aluminium pilot boat for Port of New York-New Jersey built by Gladding-Hearn Shipbuilding Corp.
P-150. A 25m 27-knot frp patrol vessel for Wes-tern Australia syndicate, now a fisheries patrol vessel in the Solomon Islands.
TPB-86. A 26m, 30-knot frp waterjet patrol vessel built in Thailand by Technautic Co Ltd.

M ROSENBLATT & SON INC

350 Broadway, New York, New York 10013, USA

Telephone: (212) 431 6900

Lester Rosenblatt, *Chairman and Chief Executive Officer*
P W Nelson, *President*
A M Stein, *Vice President, Operations*
S Halpern, *Vice President and Manager, Western Division*
N M Maniar, *Vice President and Technical Direc-tor*
Z Awer, *Vice President and Head, Mechanical Section*
D M Krepchin, *Vice President and Manager, San Diego Branch*
A Baki, *Vice President and Manager, Washington DC Area Branch*

M Rosenblatt & Son Inc is an established naval architectural and marine engineering firm with over 40 years of proven experience in all phases of ship and marine vehicle design.

With offices in 12 US cities and abroad, the firm is close to the entire shipbuilding community and has a thorough understanding of its problems and needs. Its experience covers programme man-agement and inspection of construction, as well as design.

A major portion of the company's design activities has been and is for the US Navy. Completed assignments are of the broadest pos-sible variety covering research and development, feasibility studies, and conceptual and detail design for all classes of major combatants, aux-iliaries, and high performance craft. In addition, the company has provided extensive design services for the conversion, overhaul and repair of naval combatants, auxiliaries, submarines, amphibious warfare supply and landing craft.

The service to the maritime industry includes a wide variety of tasks covering the new and modification design of oceanographic ships, con-tainerships, tankers, general cargo ships, dredges, bulk carriers, drilling platforms and ships, survey vessels, pipe-laying barges, and a great variety of supporting craft.

Typical ACV assignments have included:

ARPA Advanced Surface Effect Vehicles
Conceptual studies, parametric studies and propulsion machinery analysis for phase 'O' studies of Advanced Surface Effect Vehicles for Advanced Research Project Agency. Work per-formed for American Machine and Foundry Company.

JSESPO Surface Effect Ship Test Craft
Conceptual and feasibility design studies of candidate SES vehicles for the JSESPO sizing study for second generation SES test craft in the 1000- to 3000-ton range. The work included studies of various candidate versions of SES to identify and evaluate their unique operational and design capabilities; technological assessment of various structural materials and systems; prepar-ation of a proposed development programme with required supporting research and development. Work performed for Joint Surface Effect Ship Program office.

SRI INTERNATIONAL
(formerly the Stanford Research Institute)
333 Ravenswood Avenue, Menlo Park, California 94025, USA

Telephone: (415) 326 6200

William F Miller, *President and Chief Executive Officer*

SRI employs about 3000 staff in offices and laboratories in North America, Europe, East Asia and the Middle East. Each year it undertakes several hundred research projects for the public and private sectors on a wide variety of interests and issues. Overall, SRI's research operations divide into four programme groupings: man-agement and economics, the sciences, engineering and world business.

STEVENS INSTITUTE OF TECHNOLOGY DAVIDSON LABORATORY

Castle Point Station, Hoboken, New Jersey 07030, USA

Telephone: (201) 420 5345

Dr D Savitsky, *Director*

Organised in 1935 as the Experimental Towing Tank, the Laboratory is active in basic and applied hydrodynamic research, including smooth water performance and manoeuvrability, seakeeping, propulsion and control of marine vehicles includ-ing ACV, SES, hydrofoil craft, planing craft etc. Special model test facilities are available to inves-tigate the dynamic behaviour of all types of vessels and platforms in smooth water and waves.

TRACOR HYDRONAUTICS INC

7210 Pindell School Road, Howard County, Laurel, Maryland 20707, USA

Telephone: (301) 776 7454
Telex: 87585
Telefax: (301) 953 1895

William M Pugh, *President*
Eugene R Miller Jr, *Technical Director*
Stephen D Clark, CPA, *Treasurer and Contracting Officer*

The company was founded in July 1959, and has undertaken research, development and design of air cushion vehicles, hydrofoil craft and other high-speed marine vehicles as well as advanced propulsion systems, under US Government and industrial contacts. Tracor Hydronautics has its own ship model basin and high-speed water channel suitable for the evaluation of air cushion vehicles and hydrofoils.

WHEELER INDUSTRIES INC

Corporate Headquarters and Systems Research Center: 2611 Jefferson Davis Highway, Suite 1200, Arlington, Virginia 22202, USA

Telephone: (703) 892 1500
Telex: 90 40 84
Telefax: (703) 685 1897

Executive Offices: 110 Marter Avenue, Moorestown, New Jersey 08057, USA
Telephone: (609) 778 7161

1816 Old Mobile Highway, PO Box 126, Pascagoula, Mississippi 39567, USA
Telephone: (601) 769 6321

72 Front Street, Room 1, Bath, Maine 04530, USA
Telephone: (207) 443-9033

PO Box 433, Wayland, Massachusetts 01778, USA
Telephone: (617) 358-2721

350 North Lantana, Suite 214, Camarillo, California 93010, USA
Telephone: (805) 388-8818

Fred L Thomas, *Chairman and Chief Executive Officer*
E Joseph Wheeler Jr, *President and Chief Operating Officer*
Roy G Shults, *Senior Vice President and Director of Operations*
James F Lillis, *Vice President, Accounting and Administration*
Bernard Moulton, *Manager, Advanced Craft Programmes*

Wheeler Industries Inc is a privately-owned, small disadvantaged business firm which was founded in 1966 and specialises in systems engineering for ship, air, electronic and deep ocean systems, as well as oceanographic and environmental research. Since its establishment the company has continuously provided technical, engineering and management support, primarily in the ship acquisition areas, to the US Navy. This support has encompassed a wide range including top level management plans; ship acquisition plans; technology assessments and forecasts; subsystem analysis and trade-offs; development and acquisition requirements and specifications; programme budgeting; development of hydrofoil design data; and hydrofoil strut/foil hydrodynamic load criteria and data. The company employs experienced professionals capable of providing engineering, technical, design and management services associated with hydrofoils, air cushion vehicles and surface effect ships.

The technical and operational functions and capabilities are co-ordinated by the Director of Operations. Permanently assigned Project Managers (for ship, electronic and oceanographic systems) form engineering task teams for the duration of a contract or included task(s). They are assisted as necessary by technical support (clerical, graphics, editorial and reproduction) personnel. This approach allows maximum management visibility and control over each task, and provides optimum response to customers while minimising costs.

ASSOCIATIONS AND CLUBS
INVOLVED WITH HIGH-SPEED CRAFT

AUSTRALIA

HOVER CLUB OF AUSTRALIA

GPO Box 1882, Brisbane, Queensland 4001, Australia
H B Standen, *Hon Secretary*

BELGIUM

HOVERCLUB AND ASSOCIATION OF BELGIUM

Bld St Michel 78, 1040 Brussels, Belgium

CANADA

CANADIAN AIR CUSHION TECHNOLOGY SOCIETY (CACTS)

Canadian Aeronautics and Space Institute
222 Somerset Street West, Suite 601, Ottawa, Ontario K2P 2G3, Canada

Telephone: (613) 234 0191

R MacEwen, *Chairman*
A J S Timmins, *Executive Director*
J E Laframboise

The Canadian Air Cushion Technology Society (CACTS) is a constituent society of the Canadian Aeronautics and Space Institute (CASI). It is devoted to the development and application of air cushion technology, principally with regard to the transportation domain, but also in industry and in other fields where this technology may be of benefit. The goal of the society is to keep its members abreast of developments in the field through information dissemination and exchange. This is done through periodic conferences to which participants from various countries involved in air cushion technology and hovercraft are invited.

EUROPE

EUROPEAN HOVERCRAFT FEDERATION

24 Rue Louis Dardenne, 92170 France

Franz Berndt, Senior (Germany), *President*
Louis Le Chevalier (France), *Secretary*
Francois Porot (France), *Treasurer*

This is a Federation of all the European National Governing bodies for the sport of hovercraft. The Federation has an annual delegate meeting for the formation of regulations and its prime objective is to promote the annual European Hovercraft Racing Championships. This consists of a series of race meetings held in some of the participating countries.

Present Members of the Federation
Hoverclub of CSSR
Ing Villiam Teply
Jesenskeho 12, 81102 Bratislava, Czechoslovakia
Federation Francaise des Clubs d'Aeroglisseurs
Louis Le Chevalier
12 rue Beranger, F-92100 Boulogne BT, France

Hoverclub von Deutschland
Frantz Berndt Senior
Lechfeldstrasse 2, 8905 Mering, Federal Republic of Germany
Hoverclub of Great Britain
HCGB, 12 Mount Pleasant, Bishops Itchington, Warwickshire CV33 0QE, England
Nederlandse Hovercraft Club
Hans Peerenboom
Uiterdijksehof 5-1394 JK, Nederhorst Den Berg, Netherlands
Italian Hoverclub
Sandro Scanavino
Via Medail 87, 10052 Bardonecchir, Torino, Italy
The Hover Club of Sweden
Manfred Schneider
Ollonvagen 17, 18400 Akersberga, Sweden

FRANCE

FÉDÉRATION FRANÇAISE DES CLUBS D'AEROGLISSEURS

12 rue Béranger, 92100 Boulogne Billancourt, France

J Beaudequin, *Founder and Honorary President*
Gabriel J Vernier, *President*
Louis Le Chevalier, *Secretary*

Member Clubs:

AERO-CLUB DE L'OISE
15 place des Hortensias, 60610 La Croix St Ouen, France
B Raynal, *President*

AERO-CREATION
5, 7 rue LN Nordman, 92250 La Garenne Colombes, France
P Gachelin, *President*

AEROGLISSEURS BERRY CLUB
26b rue des Petits Champs, 8320 Jouet S/L'Aubois, France
B Vrinat, *President*

AEROGLISSEURS D'AQUITAINE
Les 3 Fontaines, Ste-Eulalie, 33560 Carbon Blanc, France
P Dalongeville, *President*
Saint Ciers de Canesse, 33710 Bourg/Gironde, France

AEROGLISSEURS D'ILE DE FRANCE
15 rue de Vaugirard, 75291 Paris Cedex 06, France
10 bis avenue P Semard, 91700 Ste Genevieve des Bois, France
M Soulabail, *President*

AEROGLISSEURS D'OC
Aeroplast Creux Redon du Cantadou, 34400 Lunel, France
B Tirlet, *President*
Chemin des Surveillants, 34400 Lunel, France

AEROGLISSEURS PARIS EST
4 Allee d'Orgemont, Le Clos, 77200 Torcy, France
J P Noel, *President*

AEROGLISSEURS VAL DE METZ
18 rue des Prés, Argancy, 57640 Vigy, France
M Lallier, *President*

AERO LOIRE
Bar "Av bon accueil", 16 rue St Nicolas 45110, Chateauneuf, France
and
8 rue Jeanne d'Arc, St Péravy la Colombe, 45310 Patay, France
P Barry, *President*

ANJOU AEROGLISSEURS
La Grosse Pierre, 49220 Le Lion D'Angers, France
J P Godicheau, *President*

CLUB AEROGLISSEURS DE TOURAINE
Clos du Puits Cangey, 37530 Amboise, France
J Lallemand, *President*

GRECA SECTION AEROGLISSEURS
Aerodrome de Rouen, 76520 Boos, France
P Cannone, *President*
2 rue Emile Eliot, 76360 Barentin, France

RHONE ALPES AEROGLISSEURS
Lot La Richardiere Berland, 38380 St Christophe S/Guiers, France
Ph. Cussot, *President*

GERMANY, FEDERAL REPUBLIC

HOVERCLUB OF GERMANY

c/o Helgrel Ruft, AM Clockenbach 10, D-8000, Munich, Federal Republic of Germany

JAPAN

HOVER CLUB OF JAPAN

Information from Masahiro Mino, Senior Director, Aerodynamics Section, Nihon University at Narashino, 7-1591 Narashinodai, Funabashi, Chiba-Ken, Japan

NEW ZEALAND

HOVERCRAFT CLUB OF NEW ZEALAND

22 Puriri Road, Manurewa, Auckland, New Zealand
Tel: 2669188
H Stockley, *President*
R Armstrong, *Hon Secretary*

SWEDEN

SWEDISH HOVERCLUB

(Svenska Svävarklubben)
PO Box 1436, S-751 44 Uppsala, Sweden
Tel: 01046 18322632
Lars Gullberg, *President*

Ollonvägen 17, S-184 00 Åkersberga, Sweden
Tel: 0764 23431
Manfred Schneider, *Treasurer*

UNITED KINGDOM

THE HOVERCLUB OF GREAT BRITAIN LIMITED

The National Organisation for Amateur Hovercraft
10 Long Acre, Bingham, Nottinghamshire, England

Mrs B Kemp, 10 Long Acre, Bingham, Nottingham, *Secretary*
Mrs D Naylor, 12 Mount Pleasant, Bishops Itchington, Leamington Spa, Warwickshire (Tel: 0926 613180)
J Kemp, 10 Long Acre, Bingham, Nottingham, *Chairman*
(Tel: 0949 37294)
A Bliault, Askeveien 3, Lura, 4300 Sandnes, Norway, *Chief Scrutineer*
(Tel: 4 678343)

As Britain's national organisation for light hovercraft, the Hoverclub exists to encourage the construction and operation of light, recreational hovercraft by private individuals, schools, colleges, universities and other youth groups. The main role of the Club over the last few years has been the organisation of a series of race meetings, at sites throughout Britain for a National Championship. At these events, which are held at stately homes or lakes and pastures, craft will race over a land and water course. It is possible that up to 100 racing hovercraft may attend the meetings. The Hoverclub is a founding member of the European Hovercraft Federation, which organises an International Race series every year.

A growing activity within the Hoverclub has been the development of recreational use in the form of organised river and coastline cruises and also Hover Holidays where members meet for a weeks' camping in an area where there is plenty of opportunity to use their craft. One such event is held in the Loire region of France every year.

The Hoverclub provides a technical advice service for members through a Scrutineering Committee and can arrange insurance for racing and recreational use.

PUBLICATIONS
Light Hovercraft A monthly magazine for Club members with race reports, news, comment, technical articles and childrens pages.
Light Hovercraft Handbook The prime reference book for the design and construction of small recreational and competition hovercraft.
Guide to Model Hovercraft An introduction to small models ranging from rubber band to radio controlled.
Design, Construction and Safety Requirements for:
  Racing Hovercraft
  Cruising Hovercraft
  Utility Hovercraft
Three separate and detailed regulations governing how a craft should be built. Compliance to these regulations is checked by scrutineers at events.
Competition Rules These are regulations used for the running of all National and International races.
CHILTERNS
K Dymond,
Hillside, Akeley, Nr Buckingham, Buckinghamshire
Tel: 02806 209

EAST ANGLIA
B Hill,
10 Fenland Road, Reffley Estate, Kings Lynn, Norfolk
MIDLAND HOVERCLUB
Mrs B Kemp,
10 Long Acre, Bingham, Nottingham
Tel: 0949 37294

NORTH WEST
Rev W G Spedding,
26 Milverton Close, Lostock, Bolton BL6 4RR
Tel: 0204 41248
SOUTH EASTERN HOVERCLUB
G L Parson, *Secretary,*
64 Hawthorn Avenue, Rainham Mark, Gillingham, Kent MF8 6TS
Tel: 0634 35197
SOUTHERN HOVERCLUB
R Henvist,
37 Fox Hills, Totton, Southampton, Hampshire
Tel: 042129 2521
WELSH
Robert Lansdown,
13 Dovedale Close, Lady Mary Estate, Cyncoed, Cardiff
Tel: 0222 484788

INDEPENDENT CLUB
ESSEX
E W Sangster,
53 Elm View Road, Benfleet, Essex SS7 5AR

THE HOVERCRAFT SOCIETY (THS)

24 Jellicoe Avenue, Alverstoke, Gosport, Hampshire PO12 2PE, England

Sir Christopher Cockerell, *President*
R L Wheeler, *Vice President*
J E Rapson, *Vice President*
W F S Woodford, *Vice President*
M A Pinder, *Chairman*
Jill Walker, *Secretary*
B J Russell, *Editor, Hovercraft Bulletin*

Formed in 1971, the Hovercraft Society was the UK constituent member of the 'International Air Cushion Engineering Society'. Membership is open to persons engaged in hovercraft related fields and to those having a bona fide interest in hovercraft in the UK and overseas. Current membership is drawn from ACV manufacturers, ferry operators, design groups, government departments and agencies, financial and insurance organisations, consultants, journalists and universities.

THS organises regular meetings at which talks are given on the technical, commercial and military, design and operating aspects of hovercraft and air cushion devices. Many of these lectures have been taken from proceedings written for THS and are available to members. THS also produces a monthly *Hovercraft Bulletin* containing the latest information on hovercraft activities throughout the world. Occasionally, THS arranges visits and social events for its members.

A collection of books, periodicals, papers and reports on the subject of hovercraft have been accumulated by the Society. These are housed in Southampton University Library and can be freely consulted by members.

HOVERMAIL COLLECTORS' CLUB

Highlights, Down Road, Tavistock, Devon PL19 9AQ, England

John L Hobbs, *Chairman*
J K Pemberton, *Editor, Slipstream*

The Hovermail Collectors' Club arranges and provides first day covers for collectors and organises occasional auctions. *Slipstream*, a monthly newsletter, advises members on new material available and provides details of new developments in the hovercraft transport industry.

UNITED STATES OF AMERICA

THE HOVERCLUB OF AMERICA INC

Box 216, Clinton, Indiana 47842-0216, USA

Ralph Weas, *President*
Ralph Garner, *Vice President*
Sara Mahler, *Secretary and Treasurer*
Al Mahler, *Editor, Hovernews*

Membership of the Hoverclub of America Inc costs $15 for new members and $25 for renewals, US dollars only, per annum.

Following a general meeting of the members of the American Hovercraft Association in May 1976, it was agreed to reorganise the Association into the Hoverclub of America Inc. The Hoverclub of America was incorporated under the State Laws of Indiana in 1976.

In the USA the Hoverclub of America Inc organises rallies and other events for members and also publishes a newsletter, *Hovernews*.

To locate other Club members and/or Chapters in your region please contact the Hoverclub at the above address. The Hoverclub of America Inc holds the North American Rally during the month of June in the midwestern United States.

THE INTERNATIONAL HYDROFOIL SOCIETY
North American Association (NAA)
PO Box 2100, Gaithersburg, Maryland 20879, USA

NAA Board of Directors:

1985-88	1986-89
Ronald Adler	William Stolgitis
Mark Bebar	Juanita Kalerghi
Raymond Hoop	James Schuler, *President*
John W King, Jr	John Meyer, *Vice President*

1987-90
William Ellsworth
George Jenkins
Robert Johnston
Michael Eames
Patsy N Jackson, *Recording Secretary*

Officers, elected by the Board, serve for one year and are installed at the Annual Meeting held each year in conjunction with American Society of Naval Engineers Day, in Washington DC, USA.

BIBLIOGRAPHY

In general, only papers specifically concerned with high-speed marine craft and air cushion platforms are included in this bibliography. In a few instances some of the papers listed may not be available in published form.

All papers prior to 1980 have been deleted from this edition (186 in all) but may be referred to in the 1987 edition.

Section 1 contains references in the order in which they appeared in the 1985 edition of *Jane's Surface Skimmers*, together with additional titles that have since become available.

Section 2 contains references of papers given at conferences, some of which have been published in bound proceedings.

Section 3 covers reference publications, books and periodicals.

Key to principal coverage

ALH	Air-lubricated-hull craft
CAT	Catamaran
DISP	Displacement hull vessel
GEN	Generally applicable
HOV	Amphibious hovercraft
HYB	Hybrid craft
HYD	Hydrofoil craft
LSACP	Low-speed air-cushion platform
PAR	Power-augmented ram-wing craft
PLA	Planing craft
SES	Surface effect ship (sidewall hovercraft)
SHYD	Sailing hydrofoil
SWATH	Small-waterplane-area twin-hull vessel
WIGE	Wing-in-ground-effect craft

SECTION 1

AP.1-88 Logistic Support Craft—Arctic Variant, R L Wheeler, BHC. Canadian Air Cushion Technology Society, 1984.

Canadian Coast Guard Air Cushion Icebreaking, 1982-83 Trials, P de L Markham (German & Milne Inc, Ottawa), J E Laframboise (Transportation Development Centre, Montreal) and M A Ball (Fleet Aviation, Canadian Coast Guard). Seventeenth Canadian Symposium on Air Cushion Technology, October 1983.

High-Speed Air Cushion Icebreaking, Membrane Ice Sheet Model, M J Hinchey (Memorial University of Newfoundland). Seventeenth Canadian Symposium on Air Cushion Technology, October 1983.

The Integration of the Hovercraft into the Modern Coast Guard Service, Terence F Melhuish (Manager, Fleet Aviation, Canadian Coast Guard, Ottawa). Third International Hovercraft Conference, Southampton, November 1981.

The Jeff(A) Test Programme, D Dickins, Canadian Air Cushion Technology Society, 1984.

The Light-Footed Giants, Howard S Fowler (Head of Engine Laboratory, Division of Mechanical Engineering, National Research Council, Canada). 1981 Lord Sempill Memorial Paper, Institution of Production Engineers, November 1981.

A New Design for ACIB Icebreaking, P Markham, J E Laframboise and D B Colbourne. Canadian Air Cushion Technology Society, 1984.

West Coast Update—Canadian Coast Guard, J McGrath, Canadian Coast Guard. Canadian Air Cushion Technology Symposium, 1982.

Design of an Air Cushion Transporter for Arctic Operations, J T Walden and D F Dickens. Fourteenth Annual Offshore Technology Conference, Houston, May 1982.

The Drag and Roll/Pitch Stability of Hoverferries at Low Speed over Water, H S Fowler (NRC of Canada). High-Speed Surface Craft Conference, Brighton, June 1980.

Hoverbarges, R Wheeler, BHC. Canadian Air Cushion Technology Society, 1984.

Initial Experience with a Three-Plenum Air Cushion Equipment Transporter, R W Helm (Bell Aerospace Canada Textron). Seventeenth Canadian Symposium on Air Cushion Technology, October 1983.

The Segmented Air Track Amphibious All-Purpose All-Terrain Vehicle, William R Bertelsen (Bertelsen Inc). Seventeenth Canadian Symposium on Air Cushion Technology, October 1983.

Air Cushion Vehicle Demonstration in Bethel, Alaska: Costs, Performance and Impact. US Department of Transportation, Urban Mass Transportation Administration, Washington DC 20590, March 1982.

Commercial Applications of Advanced Marine Vehicles for Express Shipping, George Luedeke Jr, Robert B Farnham. *Naval Engineers' Journal,* May 1983.

Commercial Hovercraft Operations—A New Perspective into Profitability, A Curtis (British Rail Hovercraft Limited). Third International Hovercraft Conference, Southampton, November 1981.

Ferry Management—Fact or Fiction, E Lau (General Manager, Hong Kong & Yaumati Ferry Co Limited). Seventh Annual Conference, International Marine Transit Association, San Francisco, November 1982.

Habitability as the Passenger Sees It, J E Chaplin (Vice President Engineering, Bell Halter Inc). Seventh Annual Conference, International Marine Transit Association, San Francisco, November 1982.

The Hong Kong & Yaumati Ferry Company HM.2 Operations, E Lau (Hong Kong & Yaumati Ferry Co Limited). Third International Hovercraft Conference, Southampton, November 1981.

Hovercraft in the Canadian Coast Guard, T F Melhuish (Canadian Coast Guard). High-Speed Surface Craft Conference, Brighton, June 1980.

Large Passenger Hovercraft—Is There a Commercial Future? J Cumberland (Managing Director, Hoverspeed (UK) Limited). Third International Hovercraft Conference, Southampton, November 1981.

A New Generation 80-Passenger Hovercraft, R Wheeler (British Hovercraft Corporation). Canadian Air Cushion Technology Symposium, 1982.

US Government Survey and Analysis of High-Speed Waterborne Transportation Services Worldwide—A Progress Report, P Cass (US Department of Transportation/UMTA, Washington DC) and W G Wohleking (Advanced Marine Systems Associates, Huntingdon, New York). High-Speed Surface Craft Conference, London, May 1983.

Why Sidewall Hovercraft in Rotterdam? And the Experience to Date, J Wernsing (Port of Rotterdam Authority). Third International Hovercraft Conference, Southampton, November 1981.

BH.7 To The Year 2000—The BH.7 Mk 20, D J Hardy (Deputy Chief Engineer, British Hovercraft Corporation Limited). High-Speed Surface Craft Conference, London, May 1983.

AERODYNAMICS	AIR LUBRICATION	ARCTIC, ANTARCTIC APPLICATIONS	COMMERCIAL APPLICATIONS/OPERATIONS	DESIGN	DEVELOPMENT	DYNAMICS/SEAKEEPING	ECONOMICS	ENVIRONMENTAL ASPECTS	FANS	HYDRODYNAMICS	ICE BREAKING	LEGISLATION	LIFT-AIR SYSTEMS	MILITARY/NAVAL APPLICATIONS/OPERATIONS	PERFORMANCE/DRAG	POWER PLANTS	POWER TRANSMISSION	PRODUCTION	PROPULSION	SAFETY	SKIRTS/SEALS	STABILITY AND CONTROL	STRUCTURE/MATERIALS	TEST FACILITIES	TRIALS
		HOV		HOV																					
											HOV														
											HOV														
			HOV																						
		HOV																							
				HOV																					
											HOV														
			HOV																	HOV					
		LSACP		LSACP																					
															HOV							HOV			
				LSACP																					
				LSACP										LSACP											
				HYB																					
			HOV																						
			HOV SES																						
							HOV																		
			SES																						
								HOV SES																	
			SES																						
			HOV																	HOV					
			HOV																						
				HOV																					
			GEN																						
			SES																						
				HOV										HOV											

Maintenance by Design, D J Vitale (NSSC). High-Speed Surface Craft Conference, Brighton, June 1980.

Turning Technology into Fleet Capability, J Benson and R Kennefick (NSRDC). High-Speed Surface Craft Conference, Brighton, June 1980.

An Update on Large SES Progress, G E Rich (Lockheed). High-Speed Surface Craft Conference, Brighton, June 1980.

AP.1-88, J C Leonard (Deputy Chief Engineer, British Hovercraft Corporation Limited). High-Speed Surface Craft Conference, London, May 1983.

Design Aspects and Trials of the HM 5 Prototype, E G Tattersall (Vosper Hovermarine Limited). Canadian Air Cushion Technology Symposium, 1982.

The Design of the Griffon 1000 TD, a One-Tonne Capacity Diesel-Engined Workboat, D R Robertson and E W Gifford (Gifford and Partners). High-Speed Surface Craft Conference, London, May 1983.

HM.5 Development—Concept to Prototype Launch, E G Tattersall, H Shattock and A J English (Vosper Hovermarine Limited). Third International Hovercraft Conference, Southampton, November 1981.

Heave Control of Amphibious Hovercraft, P A T Christopher, K F Man, Yan-nan Cheng and E W Osbourn (Cranfield Institute of Technology). High-Speed Surface Craft Conference, London, May 1983.

Hovercraft—Towards the Second Quarter Century, G H Elsley and D J Hardy (British Hovercraft Corporation Limited). Third International Hovercraft Conference, Southampton, November 1981.

Non-Dimensional Comparison of Amphibious Hovercraft, M de la Cruz and J Mowinckel (Neumar SA, Madrid). High-Speed Surface Craft Conference, London, May 1983.

Surface Effect Ship (SES) Amphibious Assault Ship (LSES) Feasibility Study, M Stoiko and Isidor Patapis. *Naval Engineers' Journal,* June 1982.

Variants of the Vosper Hovermarine SES Designs, E G Tattersall (Vosper Hovermarine Limited). High-Speed Surface Craft Conference, London, May 1983.

Canadian Potential for Non-Recreational Small Hovercraft, M A Pinder (Pindair Limited). Canadian Air Cushion Technology Symposium, 1982.

Light Hovercraft Development, H S Fowler. Canadian Air Cushion Technology Society, 1984.

Who Needs Small Hovercraft? M Pinder (Pindair Limited). Third International Hovercraft Conference, Southampton, November 1981.

Advanced Concept Ships for US Navy Underway Replenishment, H D Kaysen, Raytheon Service Company, Ventura, California. AIAA Sixth Marine Systems Conference, September 1981. Paper AIAA-81-2075.

Amphibious Assault Landing Craft JEFF(A), E F Davison (Aerojet-General) and M D Fink (NSRDC). High-Speed Surface Craft Conference, Brighton, June 1980.

Combat Damage—A Unique Element, D J Vitale (US Naval Sea Systems Command). Canadian Air Cushion Technology Symposium, 1982.

Demonstrated Performance of the Amphibious Assault Landing Craft JEFF(B), A Coles (Bell) and M Kidd (NSRDC). High-Speed Surface Craft Conference, Brighton, June 1980.

Hovercraft in Mine Counter Measures, C M Plumb and D K Brown (DG Ships, MOD). High-Speed Surface Craft Conference, Brighton, June 1980.

Operational Characteristics Comparison (ACV and SES), F W Wilson and P R Viars (David W Taylor Naval Ship Research and Development Center, Bethesda, Maryland). AIAA Sixth Marine Systems Conference, September 1981. Paper AIAA-81-2064.

Operational Deployment of the Air Cushion Vehicle, R W Helm (Bell Aerospace Canada Textron). Canadian Air Cushion Technology Symposium, 1982.

The Potential for Military Hovercraft on NATO's Northern Flank, J S Dibbern (US Army). Canadian Air Cushion Technology Symposium, 1982.

The Power-Augmented-Ram Wing-In-Ground-Effect Concept as an Airborne Amphibious Quick Reaction Force, C E Heber (David W Taylor Naval Ship Research and Development Center, Bethesda, Maryland). AIAA Sixth Marine Systems Conference, September 1981. Paper AIAA-81-2077.

Test Evaluation and Cost Effectiveness of an Air Cushion Vehicle in a Logistics Support Role for the US Army, F D DeFilippis (MERDC). High-Speed Surface Craft Conference, Brighton, June 1980.

Canadian Air Cushion Vehicle Safety Standards, R G Wade (Canadian Coast Guard, Ottawa). Seventeenth Canadian Symposium on Air Cushion Technology, October 1983.

Hovercraft Contracts and the Law, R R C Wilkins (Vosper Hovermarine Limited). The Hovercraft Society, January 1982.

AERODYNAMICS	AIR LUBRICATION	ARCTIC, ANTARCTIC APPLICATIONS	COMMERCIAL APPLICATIONS/OPERATIONS	CONTRACTS	DESIGN	DEVELOPMENT	DYNAMICS/SEAKEEPING	ECONOMICS	ENVIRONMENTAL ASPECTS	FANS	HYDRODYNAMICS	ICE BREAKING	LEGISLATION	LIFT-AIR SYSTEMS	MILITARY/NAVAL APPLICATIONS/OPERATIONS	PERFORMANCE/DRAG	POWER PLANTS	POWER TRANSMISSION	PRODUCTION	PROPULSION	SAFETY	SKIRTS/SEALS	STABILITY AND CONTROL	STRUCTURE/MATERIALS	TEST FACILITIES	TRIALS
					HOV SES																					
															SES											
															SES											
					HOV																					
					SES																					SES
					HOV																					
						SES																			SES	
							HOV																			
					HOV	HOV																				
															HOV											
					SES										SES											
					SES																					
			HOV																							
					HOV	HOV																				
			HOV																							
															SES											
															HOV											
															HOV SES											
															HOV	HOV										
															HOV											
															HOV SES											
			HOV												HOV											
															HOV											
															PAR											
															HOV											
														HOV							HOV					
		SES												SES												

Hovercraft Noise. The Noise Advisory Council, London, 1980.

The Avco Lycoming TF40B Marine Gas Turbine for the US Navy LCAC, S Silver and T B Lauriat (Avco Lycoming). High-Speed Surface Craft Conference, London, May 1983.

Design Performance and Operational Features of the LM500, Dr H E Fogg and Dr L Maccaferri. High-Speed Surface Craft Conference, Brighton, June 1980.

Epicyclic Gearboxes for High-Speed Marine Craft, R Hicks. publ The Hovercraft Society, London, 1980.

New Concept in Hovercraft Design, Diesel Engines versus Gas Turbines, D E Emmas (Deutz Engines Limited). Canadian Air Cushion Technology Symposium, 1982.

LCAC—From Test Craft To Production Design, V B Paxhia (Bell Aerospace Textron, New Orleans). AIAA/SNAME/ASNE, Seventh Marine Sys·.r.1s Conference, February 1983.

Application of System Identification Flight Analysis Techniques to Pitch-Heave Dynamics of an ACV, P A Sullivan and T A Graham (University of Toronto). Canadian Air Cushion Technology Symposium, 1982.

Development of the Aerobac, P F Alepin (SNC Group) and J E Laframboise (Transport Development Centre, Transport Canada). Canadian Air Cushion Technology Symposium, 1982.

Development of Hovercraft 140, D Jones (Jones, Kirwan and Associates) and J De Konig (Airtrek Limited). Seventeenth Canadian Symposium on Air Cushion Technology, October 1983.

The Development of the Modern Propeller, R Bass (Dowty Rotol Limited). Hovercraft Society Meeting, University of Southampton, December 1982.

The Development of New Hovercraft Engineering, P Winter (Air Vehicles Limited). Third International Hovercraft Conference, Southampton, November 1981.

Dynamics of SES Bow Seal Fingers, A Malakhoff and S Davis (Naval Sea Systems Command (PMS 304) Bethesda, Maryland). AIAA Sixth Marine Systems Conference, September 1981. Paper AIAA-81-2087.

An Experiment on Active Control of Air Cushion Heave Dynamics, J R Amyot and H S Fowler (National Research Council of Canada). Seventeenth Canadian Symposium on Air Cushion Technology, October 1983.

Heave Stability of the Canadian Coast Guard ACIB, M Hinchey and P A Sullivan. Canadian Air Cushion Technology Society, 1985.

Hovercraft Noise, three papers presented at a symposium organised by the Hovercraft Society and The Royal Aeronautical Society, London. The Hovercraft Society, 1980.

Hovercraft Research on the Cranfield Whirling Arm Facility, P A T Christopher and K H Lim (Cranfield Institute). High-Speed Surface Craft Conference, Brighton, June 1980.

How to Improve Air Cushion Performance with VUMP-Equipped Wave-Forming Keel, A Jones Jr (Fast American Ship Transportation Company). Canadian Air Cushion Symposium, 1982.

Measurement of Unsteady Forces and Moments on ACV Sidewalls in Regular Waves, M Guilbaud (University of Poitiers, France). High-Speed Surface Craft Conference, May 1983.

Operational Evaluation of the Bell Halter 110-ft Surface Effect Ship by the US Coast Guard, K G Zimmerman (US Coast Guard). Canadian Air Cushion Technology Symposium, 1982.

Power-Augmented-Ram Landing Craft, F H Krause (DTNSRDC). High-Speed Surface Craft Conference, Brighton, June 1980.

Proportional Control Experiment on Lift System, J R Amyot. Canadian Air Cushion Technology Society, 1984.

R & D on a Tangential Blower System for ACVs, J S Mitchell and R E Stevens. Canadian Air Cushion Technology Society, 1984.

SEDAM Research Survey on Amphibious Hovercraft, M Herrouin, M Lafont, M Rabier, M Sablayrolles, Miss Morelle (SEDAM) and M Bonnat (Bertin & Cie). High-Speed Surface Craft Conference, London, May 1983.

Simulated Dynamics of the AALC Jeff(B) Craft over Waves, C W Lin (Ori Inc) and E Zarnick and D D Moran (David Taylor Naval Ship Research and Development Center). Canadian Air Cushion Technology Symposium, 1982.

Simulation of Air Cushion Heave Dynamics with Vent Valve Relay Control, J R Amyot (National Research Council of Canada). Seventeenth Canadian Symposium on Air Cushion Technology, October 1983.

Seaway Performance Assessment for Marine Vehicles, P Maudel (David W Taylor Naval Ship Research and Development Center, Bethesda, Maryland). AIAA Sixth Marine Systems Conference, September 1981. Paper AIAA-81-2081.

AERODYNAMICS	AIR LUBRICATION	ARCTIC, ANTARCTIC APPLICATIONS	COMMERCIAL APPLICATIONS/OPERATIONS	DESIGN	DEVELOPMENT	DYNAMICS/SEAKEEPING	ECONOMICS	ENVIRONMENTAL ASPECTS	FANS	HYDRODYNAMICS	ICE BREAKING	LEGISLATION	LIFT-AIR SYSTEMS	MILITARY/NAVAL APPLICATIONS/OPERATIONS	PERFORMANCE/DRAG	POWER PLANTS	POWER TRANSMISSION	PRODUCTION	PROPULSION	SAFETY	SKIRTS/SEALS	STABILITY AND CONTROL	STRUCTURE/MATERIALS	TEST FACILITIES	TRIALS
								HOV				HOV													
																HOV									
																GEN									
																	GEN								
																HOV									
														HOV											
						HOV																			
					HYB																				
				HOV	HOV																				
																			HOV						
					HOV																				
						SES															SES				
					HOV																				
						LSACP					LSACP														
								HOV SES																	
						HOV																			HOV
	GEN																								
						SES																SES			
			SES																SES						SES
														PAR											
						HOV							HOV												
								HOV																	
															HOV										
						HOV																			
						HOV																			
						GEN																			

Setting Vent Valve Controller Parameters for ACV Heave Attenuation, J R Amyot (National Research Council of Canada). Canadian Air Cushion Technology Symposium, 1982.

Technical Aspects of the Aerobac AB-7, D Gawish (The SNC Group), J Boudreault (Bombardier Limited) and G Herrouin (SEDAM). Canadian Air Cushion Technology Symposium, 1982.

Techniques of Model Testing Hovercraft, B Clarke (BHC). *The Hovercraft Proceedings,* Vol 1, 1980. The Hovercraft Society, London.

UTIAS Research on the Dynamic Stability of Air Cushion Vehicles, M J Hinchey (University of Toronto). Canadian Air Cushion Technology Symposium, 1982.

Development of Stability Standards for Dynamically-Supported Craft—A Progress Report, D R Lavis (Band Lavis). High-Speed Surface Craft Conference, Brighton, June 1980.

ACV Lift Fans—More Puff For Less Power, H S Fowler (National Research Council of Canada). Canadian Air Cushion Technology Symposium, 1982.

Effect of Fabric Structure on Flex-fatigue of Skirt Materials, M M Schoppes, M M Toney, J Skelton and W Klemens. Canadian Air Cushion Technology Society, 1984.

Hovercraft Control, B J Russell (AMTE). High-Speed Surface Craft Conference, Brighton, June 1980.

Latest Developments in Hovercraft Skirt Materials, Dr E Gardner and J Morris (Avon Industrial Polymers Limited). Third International Hovercraft Conference, Southampton, November 1981.

On the Development of an Experimental Hovercraft for the Antarctic, R Murao, N Murakoshi, K Moriwaki, Y Daimon and M Inaba. Canadian Air Cushion Technology Society, 1984.

Responsive Hovercraft Skirts, J Rapson (Hovercraft Consultants Limited). Third International Hovercraft Conference, Southampton, November 1981.

Ride Improvement Systems for Sidewall Hovercraft, M Barnesley and J Ruler. publ The Hovercraft Society, London, 1980.

Skirt Design and Development on the Naviplane, G Herrouin and A Lafant (Dubigeon Normandie/SEDAM). High-Speed Surface Craft Conference, Brighton, June 1980.

Applications of Surface Effect Ships, Lt Cdr P Lindley (Vosper Hovermarine). High-Speed Surface Craft Conference, Brighton, June 1980.

Bell Halter Surface Effect Ship Development, J B Chaplin (Bell Halter Inc, New Orleans, Louisiana). AIAA Sixth Marine Systems Conference, September 1981. Paper AIAA-81-2072.

The History of SES Technology in the USA, A Ford (David W Taylor Naval Ship Research and Development Center, Bethesda, Maryland). Third International Hovercraft Conference, Southampton, November 1981.

The Series 2 HM 527, E G Tattersall. Canadian Air Cushion Technology Society, 1984.

The Surface Effect Catamaran—A Sea Capable Small Ship, F W Wilson and P R Viars (David W Taylor Naval Ship Research and Development Center, Bethesda, Maryland). AIAA Sixth Marine Systems Conference, September 1981. Paper AIAA-81-2076.

The Surface Effect Catamaran—Progress in Concept Assessment, F W Wilson, Philip R Viars and John D Adams. *Naval Engineers' Journal,* May 1983.

Technical Evaluation of the SES-200 High Length-to-Beam Surface Effect Ship, John D Adams, Walter F Beverly III. *Naval Engineers' Journal,* May 1984.

High-Speed Catamarans, Their Characteristics and Roles in Modern Warfare, C D Curtis and J P Sutcliffe (Cougar Marine). High-Speed Surface Craft Conference, London, May 1983.

Choice of Hydrofoil Propulsion, Dr D Di Blasi (Rodriquez Cantieri Navali). High-Speed Surface Craft Conference, Brighton, June 1980.

Extended Performance Hydrofoils, J R Meyer (David W Taylor Naval Ship Research and Development Center, Bethesda, Maryland). AIAA Sixth Marine Systems Conference, Seattle, Washington, September 1981. Paper AIAA-81-2067.

HYCAT Hybrid Hydrofoil Catamaran Concept, D E Calkins (University of Washington, Seattle, Washington). AIAA Sixth Marine Systems Conference, September 1981. Paper AIAA-81-2079.

After HMS Speedy—The Military Mission, G R Meyers (Boeing Marine Systems, Seattle, Washington). AIAA Sixth Marine Systems Conference, September 1981, Paper AIAA-81-2080.

Mission Applications of Military Hydrofoils, Lt Cdr W C Stolgitis (US Navy) and R E Adler (R E Adler Consultants). High-Speed Surface Craft Conference, Brighton, June 1980.

AERODYNAMICS	AIR LUBRICATION	ARCTIC, ANTARCTIC APPLICATIONS	COMMERCIAL APPLICATIONS/OPERATIONS	DESIGN	DEVELOPMENT	DYNAMICS/SEAKEEPING	ECONOMICS	ENVIRONMENTAL ASPECTS	FANS	HYDRODYNAMICS	ICE BREAKING	LEGISLATION	LIFT-AIR SYSTEMS	MILITARY/NAVAL APPLICATIONS/OPERATIONS	PERFORMANCE/DRAG	POWER PLANTS	POWER TRANSMISSION	PRODUCTION	PROPULSION	SAFETY	SKIRTS/SEALS	STABILITY AND CONTROL	STRUCTURE/MATERIALS	TEST FACILITIES	TRIALS
						HOV							HOV												
				HYB																					
																								HOV	
						HOV																		HOV	
																					GEN				
									HOV																
																					HOV				
																					HOV				
																					HOV SES				
		HOV																							
						HOV															HOV				
						SES																			
					HOV																HOV				
			SES											SES											
					SES																				
					SES																				
				SES																					
				CAT																					
				CAT																					
														SES											SES
														CAT											
																			HYD						
					HYD										HYD										
				CAT																					
														HYD											
														HYD											

Examining the Pitch, Heave and Accelerations of Planing Craft Operations in a Seaway, M Haggard and M Jones (Naval Sea Systems Command). High-Speed Surface Craft Conference, Brighton, June 1980.

Experimental Analysis on a Surface-Piercing Hydrofoil at Sea, Prof R Tedeschi, Dott Ing S Martellini and D G Mazzeo. High-Speed Surface Craft Conference, Brighton, June 1980.

Importance of Rudder and Hull Influence on Cavitation Tests of High-Speed Propellers, O Rutgersson (Swedish Maritime Research Centre). High-Speed Surface Craft Conference, Brighton, June 1980.

Life Saving Systems for High-speed Surface Craft, D V Edwards, A J Burgess and M D Martin (RFD Inflatables). High-Speed Surface Craft Conference, Brighton, June 1980.

A Simulation of Hydrofoil Motions, N Bose and R C McGregor. High-Speed Surface Craft Conference, London, May 1983.

Waterjet Propulsion in High-Speed Surface Craft, G Venturini. High-Speed Surface Craft Conference, Brighton, June 1980.

Jetfoil Variant for Offshore Transportation, H F Turner and P R Gill (Boeing Marine Systems, Seattle, Washington). AIAA Sixth Marine Systems Conference, September 1981. Paper AIAA-81-2070.

A Method of Predicting Foilborne Performance Characteristics of Hydrofoil Craft in Calm Seas, Li Bai-Qi (China Ship Scientific Research Centre). High-Speed Surface Craft Conference, London, May 1983.

A Study of Novel Hydrofoil Craft for The Yangtze, B J Zhang, D X Zhang, S X Lan and R F Chen (China Ship Scientific Research Centre, Wuxi, China). High-Speed Surface Craft Conference, London, May 1983.

A Record of Progress Made on a Purpose-built Hydrofoil Supported Sailing Trimaran, N Bose and R C McGregor (Glasgow University). High-Speed Surface Craft Conference, Brighton, June 1980.

A Sculling Hydrofoil Development, J Grogono. High-Speed Surface Craft Conference, Brighton, June 1980.

Surface Piercing vs Fully Submerged Foils for Sailing Hydrofoils: The Design and Development of Two Small Sailing Hydrofoils, D R Pattison and J B Wynne. High-Speed Surface Craft Conference, Brighton, June 1980.

Seakeeping Assessment and Criteria of Naval Combatant SWATH Vehicles, B Chilo and R T C Santos (CETENA Italian Ship Research Centre, Genoa). High-Speed Surface Craft Conference, May 1983.

Arctic Marine Shipping Route Evaluations, D F Dickins. Meeting of The Society of Naval Architects and Marine Engineers, Ottawa, Canada, 17-19 June 1981.

Bibliography: High-Speed Waterborne Passenger Operations and Craft, Urban Mass Transportation Administration report No UMTA-IT-32-0001-84-2, August 1984. UMTA, Office of Technical Assistance, Washington DC 20590 (contains over 1200 references prior to September 1982).

Design of an Air Cushion Transporter for Arctic Operations, D F Dickins and T Walden. Annual Offshore Technology Conference, Houston, Texas, USA, 3-6 May 1982.

Design and Testing of a High-Performance Waterjet Propulsion Unit, K Haglund, R Svensson and O Bjorheden (KaMeWa AB, Kristinehamn, Sweden). Symposium on Small Fast Warships and Security Vessels, The Royal Institute of Naval Architects, London, 1982.

Review of an Air Cushion Vehicle Program for Offshore Arctic Operations, J T Walden, Sohio Petroleum Company and D F Dickins, D F Dickins Associates Ltd. Paper presented at The Seventh International Conference on Port and Ocean Engineering under Arctic Conditions, POAC 83, 5-9 April 1983, Helsinki, Finland.

Lateral Stability of Semi-Displacement Craft at High Speeds, B P Wakeling, J L Sproston and A Millward, University of Liverpool (UK). Paper presented at the International Conference on Design Considerations for Small Craft, Copenhagen, Denmark, 7-9 September 1983.

Design and Construction of a 25m High-Speed Aluminium Motor Yacht, P A Lalangas and P L Yannoulis (Hellenic Shipyards Co, Athens, Greece). Presented at Annual Meeting, New York, USA, November 1983 of The Society of Naval Architects and Marine Engineers, SNAME Trans Vol 191, 1983, pp 89-124.

On the Heave Dynamics of Large Air Cushion Platforms, M J Hinchey, P A Sullivan and A D Dupuis, Institute of Aerospace Studies, University of Toronto, UTIAS Reprint No 482. Journal of Sound and Vibration, 96 (4), 1984.

AP.1-88 Logistic Support Craft—Arctic Variant, R L Wheeler. Proc CACTS International Conference on Air Cushion Technology, Vancouver, Canada, September 1984.

The JEFF (A) Arctic Test Program, D F Dickins. Proc CACTS International Conference on Air Cushion Technology, Vancouver, Canada, September 1984.

Arctic Hovercraft: Lessons Learned and Future Prospects, D F Dickins Associates Ltd, Vancouver, BC. Paper presented at the Arctic Offshore Technology Conference, 3-5 September 1985, Anchorage, Alaska.

AERODYNAMICS	AIR LUBRICATION	ARCTIC, ANTARCTIC APPLICATIONS	COMMERCIAL APPLICATIONS/OPERATIONS	DESIGN	DEVELOPMENT	DYNAMICS/SEAKEEPING	ECONOMICS	ENVIRONMENTAL ASPECTS	FANS	HYDRODYNAMICS	ICE BREAKING	LEGISLATION	LIFT-AIR SYSTEMS	MILITARY/NAVAL APPLICATIONS/OPERATIONS	PERFORMANCE/DRAG	POWER PLANTS	POWER TRANSMISSION	PRODUCTION	PROPULSION	SAFETY	SKIRTS/SEALS	STABILITY AND CONTROL	STRUCTURE/MATERIALS	TEST FACILITIES	TRIALS
						PLA																			
						HYD																			HYD
										HYD									GEN						
																			GEN						
						HYD																			
																			GEN						
		HYD																							
															HYD										
		HYD	HYD																						
				SHYD																					
				SHYD																					
			SHYD	SHYD																			SHYD		
						SWATH								SWATH											
		GEN																							
			GEN				GEN																		
		HOV		HOV																					
																		GEN							
		HOV																							
																						PLA DISP			
				MH PLA																			MH PLA		
						HOV LSACP																			
		HOV		HOV																					
		HOV																							HOV
		HOV																							

An Air Cushion Vehicle for the Western Canadian Arctic, J G Wainwright and E Makinen. Proc Arctic Opportunities 85, Edmonton, Alberta, Canada, June 1985.

The Larus Air Cushion Vehicle in the Beaufort Sea, E Makinen and J Wainwright. Proc Arctic Offshore Technology Conference, Anchorage, Alaska, September 1985.

Design Studies for an Arctic Heavy Lift Air Cushion Vehicle, Robert F Tangren and D F Dickins Associates Ltd. Accepted for presentation at the Offshore Mechanics and Arctic Engineering Symposium, Tokyo, Japan, April 1986.

The Design, Construction and Operation of Light Air Cushion Vehicles, H S Fowler. Canadian Air Cushion Technology Society, Ottawa, Canada, 1982.

A Review of Selected High-Speed Waterborne Operations Worldwide, US Department of Transportation, August 1984. UMTA-IT-32-0001-4.

Study of High-Speed Waterborne Transportation Services Worldwide, US Department of Transportation, August 1984. Report to Congress. Prepared by Advanced Marine Systems Associates Inc with Peat, Marwick Mitchell & Co.

An Assessment of High-Speed Waterborne Vessels and Their Builders, US Department of Transportation, August 1984. UMTA-IT-32-0001-5.

A Guide for Implementing High-Speed Waterborne Passenger Transportation Services, US Department of Transportation, September 1984. Prepared by Advanced Marine Systems Associates Inc with Peat, Marwick Mitchell & Co.

Existing and Former High-Speed Waterborne Passenger Transportation Operations in the United States, US Department of Transportation, August 1984. UMTA-IT-32-0001-84-3.

An Assessment of the Potential for High-Speed Waterborne Passenger Services in Selected United States Sites, US Department of Transportation, UMTA Technical Assistance Program, 1984.

Progetto Preliminare Dell'Elica di un Mezzo Navale Tipo SWATH, L Grossi, Genoa, 1982. CETENA SpA, Genoa, Italy, report No 1488.

LEIN No 42: Risultati Delle Prove Alla Vasca Eseguite Con un Modello di Catamarano Semisommerso (SWATH), Genoa, April 1983. CETENA SpA, Genoa, Italy, report No 1742.

Calcolo Approssimato Delle Forze Eccitanti D'onda di un Veicolo SWATH Avente un "Body" Schematizzabile da un Rettangolo, R Santos, Genoa, September 1983. CETENA SpA, Genoa, Italy, report No 1854.

Approximate Motions of Small Waterplane Area Twin Hull Ship (SWATH), B Chilo and R Santos, Genoa, February 1984. CETENA SpA, Genoa, Italy, report No 1974.

Non-Linear Oscillations of a Simple Flexible Skirt Air-Cushion, P A Sullivan, J E Byrne and M J Hinchey (Institute for Aerospace Studies, University of Toronto), UTIAS Reprint No 498. Journal of Sound and Vibration 102(2), 1985, pp 269-283.

Small Water Area Twin Hull (SWATH) Vessels For Offshore, A Eyres (Eyretechnics Ltd, Dartmouth, Nova Scotia). Canadian Offshore Resources Exposition Conference, Halifax, Nova Scotia, 7-9 October 1986.

A New Methodology Developed by CETENA to Assess the Seakeeping Behaviour of Marine Vessels, B Chilo, B Della Loggia, G Sartori and R Santos, Genova, July 1983, presented at the Shanghai Convention, September 1983. CETENA Rapporto No 1837 (Viale IV Novembre 6, 16121 Genova, Italy).

Design and Hydrodynamic Aspects of a "SWATH" Car/Passenger Ferry, G Polydorou and R Santos, Genova, March 1984, presented at the IMAEM Convention, Athens, May 1984. CETENA Rapporto No 2027 (Viale IV Novembre 6, 16121 Genova, Italy).

On the Vertical Plane Stability of Small Waterplane Area Twin Hull Ships, R Santos and G Sartori, Genova, March 1984, presented at the IMAEM Convention, Athens, May 1984. CETENA Rapporto No 2029 (Viale IV Novembre 6, 16121 Genova, Italy).

Comparacion Adimensional de Aerodeslizadores Anfibios (Non-dimensional comparison of amphibious hovercraft). Paper presented at High-Speed Surface Craft Conference, London, May 1983. Pub: Ingenieria Naval, Vol 53 No 597, March 1985.

El Vehiculo de Colchon de Aire (ANFINAVE) (The Air-Cushion Vehicle), P Ruiz de Azcarate (Captain, Spanish Navy). Pub: Ingenieria Naval, No 564, June 1982.

Distribucion de Presiones Bajo un Vehiculo de Colchon de Aire (Pressure distribution beneath an air-cushion vehicle), J Fernandez de Palencia (Empresa Nacional Bazan). Pub: Ingenieria Naval, No 595, January 1985.

AERODYNAMICS	AIR LUBRICATION	ARCTIC, ANTARCTIC APPLICATIONS	COMMERCIAL APPLICATIONS/OPERATIONS	DESIGN	DEVELOPMENT	DYNAMICS/SEAKEEPING	ECONOMICS	ENVIRONMENTAL ASPECTS	FANS	HYDRODYNAMICS	ICE BREAKING	LEGISLATION	LIFT-AIR SYSTEMS	MILITARY/NAVAL APPLICATIONS/OPERATIONS	PERFORMANCE/DRAG	POWER PLANTS	POWER TRANSMISSION	PRODUCTION	PROPULSION	SAFETY	SKIRTS/SEALS	STABILITY AND CONTROL	STRUCTURE/MATERIALS	TEST FACILITIES	TRIALS
		HOV																							
		HOV																							
		LSACP		LSACP																					
				HOV																			HOV		
			GEN																						
			GEN																						
			GEN																						
			GEN																						
			GEN																						
			GEN																						
														SWATH											
																									SWATH
						SWATH																			
						SWATH																			
						HOV															HOV				
				SWATH																					
					GEN																				
				SWATH						SWATH															
																						SWATH			
															HOV										
														HOV											
													HOV	HOV											

Resistencia de Formacion de Olas de un SES (Wave resistance of an SES (Surface Effect Ship)), J Fernandez de Palencia (Empresa Nacional Bazan). Pub: Ingenieria Naval, No 605, November 1985.

Hydrofoil Performance Control Introducing Tangential Liquid Jet, P Kozhukharov, V Hadjimikhalev, V Mikuta and L Maltzev. ASME International Symposium on Jets and Cavities, Miami Beach, Florida, 1985.

Computer-Aided Geometrical Design of Hull Lines and Lifting Surfaces of High-Speed Marine Vehicles, P Bogdanov and S Kovachev. ICCAS '85, Trieste, 1985.

Some Dynamical Effects on Bow Relative Motion of Semi-Displacement High-Speed Ships in Waves, R Kishev and P Hadjimikhalev. 12th Scientific and Methodological Seminar on Ship Hydrodynamics, Bulgarian Ship Hydrodynamics Centre, Varna, 1983.

High-Speed Semi-Displacement Ships With Cavitating Screw Propellers: Performance Prediction Based on Model Test Results, V Hadjimikhalev, P Kozhukharov and A Minchev. National Symposium on Ship Hydrodynamics, Galatz, Bulgaria, October 1982.

Cavitating Propeller Characteristics and their Use in Propeller Design, P Kozhukharov and Z Z Zlatev. High-Speed Surface Craft Conference, London, 9-12 May 1983.

Recent Developments in Waterjet Propulsion, R Svensson (KaMeWa AB, Sweden). Shipbuilding Technology International, 1986. Sterling Publications Ltd, London.

SWATH Developments and Comparisons with Other Craft, T G Lang and J E Sloggett (Semi-Submerged Ship Corporation, Solana Beach, California, USA). RINA International Conference on SWATH Ships and Advanced Multi-Hulled Vessels, London, April 1985.

Replacement of the University Research Fleet and a 2500-Ton SWATH Ship Candidate, R P Dinsmore and T G Lang. AIAA 8th Advanced Marine Systems Conference, San Diego, California, USA, 22-24 September 1986.

SSP *Kaimalino*: **Conception, Development, Hurdles, Success,** T G Lang. ASME Winter Annual Meeting, Anaheim, California, USA, 9 December 1986.

Influence of the Moment of Equilibrium on the Powering Characteristics of Planing Craft including Hydrofoils, F Van Walree and E Stierman (Maritime Research Institute, Netherlands). RINA Warship '86 Symposium, London, 19-22 May 1986.

Air-Cushion Vehicles for Amphibious Assault — The Next Generation, D R Lavis and E Band (Band, Lavis Associates Inc, New York). RINA Warship 86 Symposium, London, 19-22 May 1986.

Development of the Turt 4 Diesel-Powered Amphibious Hovercraft, S Lee, C Lee and S Kim (Korea Tacoma Marine Industries Ltd). RINA Warship 86 Symposium, London, 19-22 May 1986.

Diesel Engines Specially Designed for Fast Patrol Boats, B Gondouin (Alsthom Groupe Diesel). RINA Warship 86 Symposium, London, 19-22 May 1986.

The Use of Amphibious Hovercraft for Assault Purposes, G Elsey (British Hovercraft Corporation). RINA Warship 86 Symposium, London, 19-22 May 1986.

New Developments in Amphibious Warfare Vessels and Equipment of the US Navy, A Preston. RINA Warship 86 Symposium, London, 19-22 May 1986.

Design, Construction and Operational Experience of High-Speed Aluminium Patrol Craft for the Finnish Coastguard, O Ostring (Valmetin Laivateollisuus OY, Finland). RINA Warship 86 Symposium, London, 19-22 May 1986.

Diesel Engine Design, MTU Motoren und Turbinen-Union Friedrichshafen GmbH (West Germany). RINA Warship 86 Symposium, London, 19-22 May 1986.

Catamarans versus Single-Hull Concepts. A Study of Stability, Powering and Seakeeping Qualities for Small Warships, O Rutgersson (SSPA Maritime Consulting AB, Sweden). RINA Warship 86 Symposium, London, 19-22 May 1986.

Pitch and Roll Hydrodynamics of a Pericell Hovercraft, D D Moran (David Taylor Naval Ship Research and Development Center, Bethesda, Maryland, USA). Canadian Aeronautics and Space Journal Vol 32, No 4, December 1986, pp 314-320.

Research Plan for the Investigation of Dynamic Instability of Small High-Speed Craft, S H Cohen and D L Blount. Presented at the SNAME Annual Meeting, New York, 19-22 November 1986.

A Bulbous Bow Design Methodology for High-Speed Ships, J W Hoyle, B H Cheng, B Hays, B Johnson and B Nehrling. Presented at the SNAME Annual Meeting, New York, 19-22 November 1986.

Vessel Construction Contracts and Specifications, E D Fry. Presented at Work Boat Show '83 Technical Session, 4 February 1983.

AERODYNAMICS	AIR LUBRICATION	ARCTIC, ANTARCTIC APPLICATIONS	COMMERCIAL APPLICATIONS/OPERATIONS	CONTRACTS	DESIGN	DEVELOPMENT	DYNAMICS/SEAKEEPING	ECONOMICS	ENVIRONMENTAL ASPECTS	FANS	HYDRODYNAMICS	ICE BREAKING	LEGISLATION	LIFT-AIR SYSTEMS	MILITARY/NAVAL APPLICATIONS/OPERATIONS	PERFORMANCE/DRAG	POWER PLANTS	POWER TRANSMISSION	PRODUCTION	PROPULSION	SAFETY	SKIRTS/SEALS	STABILITY AND CONTROL	STRUCTURE/MATERIALS	TEST FACILITIES	TRIALS
											SES					SES										
											HYD															
					GEN																					
							PLA / DISP																			
																PLA / DISP										
																		GEN								
																		GEN								
							SWATH																			
			SWATH																							
					SWATH	SWATH																				
																PLA / HYD										
											HOV															
						HOV																	HOV			
																PLA										
											HOV															
											HOV															
			PLA		PLA																		PLA			
																GEN										
							CAT								CAT											
											HOV												HOV			
							PLA																			
					DISP						DISP															
				PLA / GEN																						

Further Discussions on the Dynamic Instability of Small High-Speed Craft, S H Cohen, D L Blount and J Zseleczky. Presented at the SNAME 1987 Power Boat Symposium.

Design of Cored Laminates for Chines in FRP Boat Hulls, J J Seidler and R P Reichard. Presented at the SNAME 1987 Power Boat Symposium.

Experimental Investigation of Hydrofoil with Jet Control of Circulation, P A Bogdanov, V H Hadjimikhalev, P G Kozhukharov, L I Maltzev and V I Mikuta. International Symposium on Ship Hydrodynamics and Energy Saving, Madrid, September 1983.

Investigation on Cavitating Screw Propellers Operating in Oblique Flow, P G Kozhukharov, Y M Sadovnikov and V A Frolov. 2nd International Conference on Cavitation, Institution of Mechanical Engineers, Edinburgh, Scotland, September 1983.

Investigation of Tip Clearance Effect on Supercavitating Propeller Performance Characteristics, P G Kozhukharov and K Y Yosifov. Written contribution to Cavitation Committee Report (17 ITTC, Gothenburg, Sweden), 1984.

An Approach to Computer-Aided High-Speed Propeller Design, P G Kozhukharov and V H Hadjimikhalev. International Symposium on Propellers and Cavitation, China, 1986.

Tests of a Skimmer with the BSHC High-Speed Towing Carriage, P Kozhukharov, N Draganov, Tz Tzvetanov and L Bekyarov. 14th Scientific and Methodological Seminar on Ship Hydrodynamics, Bulgarian Ship Hydrodynamics Centre, Varna, 1985.

Hydrofoil with Jet-Controlled Performance under Free Surface, P Kozhukharov, L Maltzev and V Mikuta. 14th Scientific and Methodological Seminar on Ship Hydrodynamics, Bulgarian Ship Hydrodynamics Centre, Varna, 1985.

The BH-7 MK.20 Amphibious Hovercraft in the MCM Role, R L Wheeler (British Hovercraft Corporation Ltd). International Symposium on Mine Warfare Vessels and Systems, London, 12-15 June 1984, The Royal Institution of Naval Architects.

The Application of Air Cushion Technology to Mine Countermeasures in the United States of America, J B Chaplin (Bell Aerospace Textron). International Symposium on Mine Warfare Vessels and Systems, London, 12-15 June 1984, The Royal Institution of Naval Architects.

Notes on the Propulsion of Fast Craft and CRM Engines, G Venturini (CRM Motori Marini). Milan, Italy, 1986.

Development of the BR — 1/2000 High-Speed Marine Diesel Engine, G Venturini (CRM Motori Marini). Milan, Italy, 1986.

Planing-Hull Resistance, G Venturini (CRM Motori Marini). Milan, Italy, 1986.

SWATH Design: Summary of CETENA Activity
Design and Hydrodynamic Aspects of a SWATH Passenger Car Ferry, G Polydorou and R Santos.
On the Vertical Plane Stability of Small Waterplane Area Twin Hull Ships, R Santos and G Sartori. CETENA Quaderno No 60 (Viale IV Novembre 6, 16121 Genova, Italy).

Preliminary Fast Ship Design Based on Experimental Data Banks. A Design Method for Fast Twin-Screw Ship Based on a Statistical Approach, C Camporese, B Della Loggia and L Doria (CETENA). Presented at the IMAEM Convention, Athens, May 1984. CETENA Quaderno No 66 (Viale IV Novembre 6, 16121 Genova, Italy).

An Example of Dynamic Wave Loads Assessment for Non-Conventional Vehicle (SWATH) in Mediterranean Waters, R Santos and G Sartori, Genova, July 1981. CETENA Rapporto No 1290 (Viale IV Novembre 6, 16121 Genova, Italy).

Forze Eccitanti D'Onda Agenti su uno SWATH, B Chilo and R Santos, Genova, November 1981. CETENA Rapporto No 1362 (Viale IV Novembre 6, Genova, Italy).

Progetto Preliminare Dell'Elica de un Mezzo Navale Tipo SWATH, L Grossi, Genova, August 1982. CETENA Rapporto No 1488 (Viale IV Novembre 6, 16121 Genova, Italy).

Un Metodo di Calcolo Rapido per Valutare le Forze Eccitanti D'Onda ed i Moti Agenti su un Veicolo SWATH, B Chilo and R Santos, Genova, September 1982. CETENA Rapporto No 1580 (Viale IV Novembre 6, 16121 Genova, Italy).

Seakeeping Assessment and Criteria of Naval Combatant SWATH Vehicles, B Chilo and R T C Santos, Genova, January 1983. CETENA Rapporto No 1617 (Viale IV Novembre 6, 16121 Genova, Italy).

Stability and Control of Hovercraft: Notes for Commanders, UK Department of Industry, Ship & Marine Technology Requirements Board, London, 1980.

Design and Testing of a High-Performance Waterjet Propulsion Unit, K Haglund, R Svensson and O Bjorheden (KaMeWa AB, Sweden). Presented at the RINA Symposium on Small Fast Warships and Security Vessels, 1982. Paper No 17.

A Method for Estimating the Resistance of Catamarans, Huang Wulin and Zhang Surong. Ship Engineering No 1, 1987, The Chinese Society of Naval Architecture and Marine Engineering.

AERODYNAMICS	AIR LUBRICATION	ARCTIC, ANTARCTIC APPLICATIONS	COMMERCIAL APPLICATIONS/OPERATIONS	DESIGN	DEVELOPMENT	DYNAMICS/SEAKEEPING	ECONOMICS	ENVIRONMENTAL ASPECTS	FANS	HYDRODYNAMICS	ICE BREAKING	LEGISLATION	LIFT-AIR SYSTEMS	MILITARY/NAVAL APPLICATIONS/OPERATIONS	PERFORMANCE/DRAG	POWER PLANTS	POWER TRANSMISSION	PRODUCTION	PROPULSION	SAFETY	SKIRTS/SEALS	STABILITY AND CONTROL	STRUCTURE/MATERIALS	TEST FACILITIES	TRIALS
						PLA																			
																							PLA		
						HYD																			
																			GEN						
																			GEN						
																			GEN						
										PLA														PLA	
										HYD															
														HOV											
														HOV											
																GEN									
																GEN									
										PLA					PLA										
			SWATH							SWATH															
				GEN																					
						SWATH																			
						SWATH																			
														SWATH											
						SWATH																			
						SWATH								SWATH											
																						HOV			
																			GEN						
															CAT										

The Solent Seakeeping Experiments: Some Results and their Comparisons with Computer Predictions, A P A Hawes and M J Stevens. RINA Symposium on Small Fast Warships and Security Vessels, 1982. Paper No 2.

Amphibious Assault Hovercraft, R L Wheeler (British Hovercraft Corporation). RINA Warship Symposium 86, London, 19-22 May 1986.

The Take-Off Characteristics of Hydrofoil Craft Calculated by Means of a Newly Developed Prediction Method, F van Walree (Maritime Research Institute, Netherlands). RINA Warship Symposium 86, London, 19-22 May 1986.

The Equation of Cushion Pressure for Air-Cushion System, He Zhifei and Xing Shengde (China Ship Scientific Research Centre, China). RINA Warship Symposium 86, London, 19-22 May 1986.

Design Trends in Aluminium Patrol Craft, T Graul (Timothy Graul Design). The Port & Coastal Services Conference 1980, USA. Paper No 5.

Motion Characteristics of the Kaiyo, M Saeki (Japan Marine Science and Technology Center) and H Nakamura (Mitsui Engineering & Shipbuilding Co Ltd). Presented at OCEANS '86, Washington DC, USA, 23-25 September 1986.

Technical Evaluation of the SES-200 High Length-to-Beam Surface Effect Ship, J D Adams and W F Beverly. *Naval Engineers Journal*, May 1984, pp 77-93.

An Example of the Selection of Types of High-Speed Passenger Ferries From Economical Point of View in Comparison with Land Transportation, Y Kaneko, Chief Naval Architect, and M Muto, Project Manager, Mitsubishi Heavy Industries Inc, Japan. Papers presented at the 9th Annual Conference of the International Marine Transit Association (IMTA), New York, October 1984.

Resistance Predictions and Parametric Studies for High-Speed Displacement Hulls, Siu C Fung. *Naval Engineers Journal*, Vol 99, No 2, March 1987.

Views from the Bridge, ed, J L Schuler (US Naval Sea Systems Command). *Naval Engineers Journal*, Vol 97, No 2, February 1985 (American Society of Naval Engineers).

Introducing New Vehicles, P J Mantle (Lockheed Shipbuilding Company). *Naval Engineers Journal*, Vol 97, No 2, February 1985 (American Society of Naval Engineers).

Ship-to-Shore Surfaceborne Mobility, Dr A L Slafkosky (Scientific Advisor, US Marine Corps). *Naval Engineers Journal*, Vol 97, No 2, February 1985 (American Society of Naval Engineers).

US Army Watercraft, Dr J Hein (US Army). *Naval Engineers Journal*, Vol 97, No 2, February 1985 (American Society of Naval Engineers).

Coast Guard Vessels to do the Job, Capt G Moritz (US Coast Guard). *Naval Engineers Journal*, Vol 97, No 2, February 1985 (American Society of Naval Engineers).

An Economic Analysis of High-Speed Ferry Service, Patricia Cass (US Urban Mass Transportation Administration). *Naval Engineers Journal*, Vol 97, No 2, February 1985 (American Society of Naval Engineers).

Future Naval Surface Ships, M C Eames (Canadian Defense Research Establishment Atlantic). *Naval Engineers Journal*, Vol 97, No 2, February 1985 (American Society of Naval Engineers).

The Modern Mono-Hull, Captain C Graham (US Navy). *Naval Engineers Journal*, Vol 97, No 2, February 1985 (American Society of Naval Engineers).

SWATH Ships, ed, J L Gore (David Taylor Naval Ship R&D Center). *Naval Engineers Journal*, Vol 97, No 2, February 1985 (American Society of Naval Engineers).

Planing Craft, ed, Dr D Savitsky (Davidson Laboratory, Stevens Institute of Technology). *Naval Engineers Journal*, Vol 97, No 2, February 1985 (American Society of Naval Engineers).

Hydrofoils, ed, Capt R J Johnston (Advanced Marine Systems Associates Inc). *Naval Engineers Journal*, Vol 97, No 2, February 1985 (American Society of Naval Engineers).

Air-Cushion Craft, D Lavis (Band, Lavis & Associates Inc). *Naval Engineers Journal*, Vol 97, No 2, February 1985 (American Society of Naval Engineers).

The Surface Effect Ship, ed, E A Butler (US Naval Sea Systems Command). *Naval Engineers Journal*, Vol 97, No 2, February 1985 (American Society of Naval Engineers).

Inspection and Evaluation of the Canadian Coast Guard Air-Cushion Icebreaking Bow, C Carter (German & Milne Inc, Montreal), 1984. Publ Transportation Development Centre, Montreal, TP 5079E.

A Mathematical Analysis of Dynamic Ice Rupture by Hovercraft, Final Report, M Shinbrot, 1983. Publ Transportation Development Centre, Montreal, TP 4235E.

Mise au Point de la Technique de Deglacage par Plateforme a Coussin d'Air (Icebreaking with an air-cushion platform) 1975-1978, A A Hope, J Udell and M Tapiero (TDC) 1980. Publ Transportation Development Centre, Montreal, TP 1924.

AERODYNAMICS	AIR LUBRICATION	ARCTIC, ANTARCTIC APPLICATIONS	COMMERCIAL APPLICATIONS/OPERATIONS	DESIGN	DEVELOPMENT	DYNAMICS/SEAKEEPING	ECONOMICS	ENVIRONMENTAL ASPECTS	FANS	HYDRODYNAMICS	ICE BREAKING	LEGISLATION	LIFT-AIR SYSTEMS	MILITARY/NAVAL APPLICATIONS/OPERATIONS	PERFORMANCE/DRAG	POWER PLANTS	POWER TRANSMISSION	PRODUCTION	PROPULSION	SAFETY	SKIRTS/SEALS	STABILITY AND CONTROL	STRUCTURE/MATERIALS	TEST FACILITIES	TRIALS
						GEN																			GEN
														HOV											
															HYD										
													HOV		HOV										
				PLA																			PLA		
						SWATH																			
																									SES
			GEN																						
															DISP										
			GEN											GEN											
			GEN											GEN											
														GEN											
														GEN											
			GEN																						
			GEN																						
						GEN								GEN											
				DISP										DISP											
				SWATH		SWATH																			
			PLA	PLA			PLA			PLA					PLA				PLA						
			HYD	HYD		HYD								HYD	HYD				HYD				HYD		
		HOV	HOV	HOV				HOV	HOV					HOV		HOV			HOV	HOV	HOV	HOV	HOV		
				SES CAT WIGE		SES			SES					SES	SES				SES		SES	SES	SES		
											LSACP														
											HOV														
											LSACP														

Nickel Plating of Voyageur ACV Propeller Blades to Improve Their Erosion Resistance, G A Malone (Bell Aerospace Canada) 1981. Publ Transportation Development Centre, Montreal, TP 3147.

A Preliminary Analysis of Dynamic Ice Rupture by Hovercraft, M Shinbrot (University of Montreal) 1980. Publ Transportation Development Centre, Montreal, TP 2461.

Small Waterplane Area Twin Hulled (SWATH) Vessel Ice Tests, J E Carter and B Colbourne (German & Milne Inc) 1985. Publ Transportation Development Centre, Montreal, TP 6681E.

SSACV Icebreaking LNG Tanker Feasibility Study, Final Report, D Dadachanji and P de L Markham (German & Milne Inc) 1982. Publ Transportation Development Centre, Montreal, TP 3423.

1981/82 ACIB Evaluation: Data Collection and Analysis, D Dubois et al (Arctec Canada Ltd) 1983. Publ Transportation Development Centre, Montreal, TP 4086E.

Application of Harmonic Capstan to Air-Cushion Platform, Wong Huilin. Ship Engineering, The Chinese Society of Naval Architecture and Marine Engineering, No 1, 1988.

High-Speed Marine Diesel Engines, B Feurer, MTU Friedrichshafen GmbH, West Germany. Shipbuilding Technology International Review, 1988.

High-Speed Marine Engines for Naval and Commercial Vessels, W J Gardner, Caterpillar Inc. Shipbuilding Technology International Review, 1988 (Sterling Publications, London).

Waterjet Propulsion for Ferries, R Svensson (KaMeWa AB, Sweden). Shipbuilding Technology International Review, 1988 (Sterling Publications, London).

The Hamilton Waterjet Concept for Work Boats, G H Davison (C W F Hamilton & Co Ltd, New Zealand). Shipbuilding Technology International Review, 1988 (Sterling Publications, London).

The Surface Effect Ship – Ride Control, *Naval Engineers Journal,* Special Edition on Modern Ships and Craft edited by E A Butler, American Society of Naval Engineers, February 1985, pp 220-222.

Marinjet – A Waterjet Catamaran, PetroAsia, June 1984, pp 68-70.

Hydrodynamics of High-Speed Small Craft, L J Doctors (University of Michigan). Department of Naval Architecture and Marine Engineering (University of Michigan), Report No 292, January 1985.

Noise Control Program for the USCG 100-Foot Patrol Boats – A Case History, R W Fischer. Paper presented at the SNAME Spring Meeting/Star Symposium, May 1987, USA.

Why the GNI Doesn't Plane – Computer-Aided Diagnosis, P S Glandt. Paper presented at the SNAME Spring Meeting/Star Symposium, 27-30 May 1987, Philadelphia, USA.

The Viability of Naval SWATH Ships, Combat Craft, September/October 1985.

A Status Report on Design and Operational Experiences with the Semi-Submerged Catamaran (SSC) Vessel, T Mabuchi, Y Kunitake and H Nakamura. RINA International Conference on SWATH Ships and Advanced Multi-Hulled Vessels, London, 17-19 April 1985. Paper No 3.

Test and Evaluation of the Ocean Systems Research 64' SWATH Demonstration Craft, M P Jones (Naval Sea Systems Command, Norfolk, VA, USA). Report No 6660-95, October 1982.

RMI's Prototype SWATH on Sea Trials at San Diego, Combat Craft, May/June 1985.

Ride Quality Tests of Various High-Speed Water Craft, Boeing Marine Systems, Seattle, WA, USA. January 1985.

Research Plan for the Investigation of Dynamic Instability of Small High-Speed Craft, S H Cohen (US Coast Guard Headquarters, Washington, DC) and D L Blount (Naval Sea Combat Systems Engineering Station, Norfolk, VA, USA). SNAME Annual Meeting, New York, 19-22 November 1986. Paper No 7.

SSP *Kaimalino*: Conception, Developmental History, Hurdles and Success, T G Lang (Semi-Submerged Ship Corporation, Solana Beach, CA, USA). ASME Winter Annual Meeting, Anaheim, California, 7-12 December 1986.

Adaptation of Crew Performance, Stress and Mood Aboard a SWATH and Monohull Vessel, S F Wiker and R L Pepper (US Coast Guard). USCG Report CG-D-18-81, February 1981.

Side by Side Buoy Tender Evaluation Seakeeping and Manoeuvering Comparisons of the USCGC *Mallow* (WLB-396) and SSP *Kaimalino* (Semi-Submersible Platform), T J Coe (US Coast Guard). USCG R&D Center, Groton, CT, USA. February 1983.

SWATH: Calm Seas for Oceanography, V Kaharl. The Oceanography Report, EOS Vol 66 No 36, pp 626-7, American Geophysical Union 0096-3941/6636-0625, September 1985.

AERODYNAMICS	AIR LUBRICATION	ARCTIC, ANTARCTIC APPLICATIONS	COMMERCIAL APPLICATIONS/OPERATIONS	DESIGN	DEVELOPMENT	DYNAMICS/SEAKEEPING	ECONOMICS	ENVIRONMENTAL ASPECTS	FANS	HYDRODYNAMICS	ICE BREAKING	LEGISLATION	LIFT-AIR SYSTEMS	MILITARY/NAVAL APPLICATIONS/OPERATIONS	PERFORMANCE/DRAG	POWER PLANTS	POWER TRANSMISSION	PRODUCTION	PROPULSION	SAFETY	SKIRTS/SEALS	STABILITY AND CONTROL	STRUCTURE/MATERIALS	TEST FACILITIES	TRIALS
								HOV											HOV						
											HOV														
								SWATH																	
											SWATH														
											LSACP														LSACP
			HOV																						
																GEN									
																GEN									
																			GEN						
																			GEN						
						SES																			
				CAT																					
										GEN															
								PLA																	
										PLA															
														SWATH											
			SWATH	SWATH																					
																									SWATH
																									SWATH
						GEN																			
						GEN																			
				SWATH	SWATH																				
								SWATH																	
								PLA																	
						SWATH																			
			SWATH																						

SWATH Developments and Comparisons with Other Craft, T G Lang and J E Sloggett. RINA International Conference on SWATH Ships and Advanced Multi-Hulled Vessels, London, 17-19 April 1985. Paper No 1.

Replacement of the University Research Fleet and a 2500 ton SWATH Ship Candidate, R P Dinsmore and T G Lang. AIAA 8th Advanced Marine Systems Conference, San Diego, CA, 22-24 Sept 1986.

Standardization Trials of the Stable Semi-Submerged Platform, SSP *Kaimalino*, with a Modified Buoyancy Configuration, E L Woo and J L Mauck. DTNSRDC-80/049, April 1980.

Aerodynamic and Hydrodynamic Aspects of High-Speed Water Surface Craft, Dr R K Nangia (Consulting Engineer, Bristol, England). Paper No 1500, *Aeronautical Journal*, Vol 91 No 906, June/July 1987. Paper based on a lecture given to the Aeromarine Group of The Royal Aeronautical Society, The Royal Institution of Naval Architects and the Society for Underwater Technology, 19 March 1985, London.

Study of Aerobac AB-7 Vehicle for Airport Rescue in Difficult Terrain, P F Alepin, B Gauthier and R N Yong (Intercan Logistical Services Ltd) 1983. Publ Transportation Development Centre, Montreal, TP 5116E.

ACV Propeller Blade Erosion: A Study of Protection Methods for CCG Hovercraft, Hanson Materials Engineering (Western) Ltd, 1980. Publ Transportation Development Centre, Montreal, TP 2566.

Advanced ACIB Concepts Design Study, B Colbourne (German & Milne Inc, Montreal) 1984. Publ Transportation Development Centre, Montreal, TP 5653E.

Air-Cushion Icebreaking Bow (ACIB) Operations Report 1983/84, J A Tarzwell, P de L Markham and T Anderson (German & Milne Inc, Montreal) 1984. Publ Transportation Development Centre, Montreal, TP 5497E.

Air-Cushion Icebreaking Bow (ACIB) Trials Report 1982/83, Final Report, J A Tarzwell, P de L Markham and C W Carter (German & Milne Inc, Montreal) 1983. Publ Transportation Development Centre, Montreal, TP 4446E.

Air-Cushion Icebreaking Bow Development Program, 1975-1978, Summary Report, A A Hope, J Udell and M Tapiero (TDC), 1980. Publ Transportation Development Centre, Montreal, TP 1924.

Air Trek 140 – 1985 Trials: Tests on the Air Trek Type 140 Hovercraft Carried Out at Quatsino Sound, British Columbia, D Jones (Omnitech Steel Works) 1985. Publ Transportation Development Centre, Montreal, TP 6215E.

Concepts for the Integration of a Fluid Cushion into the Bow of a Ship, N Dadachanji and P Markham (German & Milne Inc) 1982. Publ Transportation Development Centre, Montreal, TP 3407E.

Design Review and Conceptual Design of Interim Notch Seal – Air-Cushion Icebreaking Bow HSL-533, Final Report, G R Tothill and A Y Simpson (Bell Aerospace Canada Ltd) 1981. Publ Transportation Development Centre, Montreal, TP 3332E.

Etudes de Concepts: Proue Brise-Glace a Coussin d'Air (Design Study: Air-Cushion Icebreaking Bow), B Colbourne (German & Milne Inc) 1984. Publ Transportation Development Centre, Montreal, TP 6014F.

The Seakeeping Characteristics of a Small Waterplane Area, Twin-Hull (SWATH) Ship, J A Fein, M D Ochi and K K McCreight. ONR/National Academy of Sciences/Shipbuilding Research Association of Japan 13th Symposium on Naval Hydrodynamics, Tokyo, Paper V-4, 6-10 October 1980.

Seakeeping and Motion Control Trials of SSP *Kaimalino* in Sea States 4 and 5, J A Fein. DTNSRDC-81/015. February 1981.

Comparison of Full-Scale and Rigid Vinyl Model Structural Responses for a Small Waterplane Area Twin-Hull Craft (SSP *Kaimalino*), W H Hay. DTNSRDC-81/058, August 1981.

Comparative Ship Performance Sea Trials for the US Coast Guard Cutters *Mellon* and *Cape Corwin* and the US Navy Small Waterplane Area Twin-Hull Ship *Kaimalino*, D A Woolaver and J B Peters. DTNSRDC-80/037, March 1980.

A Vessel Class Comparison of Physiological, Affective State and Psychomotor Performance Changes in Men at Sea, S F Wiker, R L Pepper and M E McCauley. US Coast Guard Report CG-D-07-81, August 1980.

On a Programme for the Study of Dynamic Ice Rupture by Hovercraft, M Shinbrot (M Shinbrot Mathematical Consulting Inc). Transport Canada Transportation Development Centre, TP 7857E, 1986.

SWATH Feasibility Study, T W Edwards, D J Hussey and J F Mitchell (Eyretechnics Ltd). Transport Canada Transportation Development Centre, TP 7419E, 1986.

Parameters Analysis of Air-Cushion Vehicle Responsive Skirt Characteristics, Zhou Weilin. Ship Engineering (Chinese SNAME) No 5, 1987.

A Simulation Study on Sway-Roll-Yaw Coupled Instability of Semi-Displacement Type High-Speed Craft, E Baba, S Asai and N Toki. 2nd International Conference on the Stability of Ships and Ocean Vehicles, Tokyo, Japan, October 1982.

Transverse Dynamic Stability of Planing Craft, F Wellicome and S Campbell. University of Southampton, England, Ship Science Report No 12, January 1984.

AERODYNAMICS	AIR LUBRICATION	ARCTIC, ANTARCTIC APPLICATIONS	COMMERCIAL APPLICATIONS/OPERATIONS	DESIGN	DEVELOPMENT	DYNAMICS/SEAKEEPING	ECONOMICS	ENVIRONMENTAL ASPECTS	FANS	HYDRODYNAMICS	ICE BREAKING	LEGISLATION	LIFT-AIR SYSTEMS	MILITARY/NAVAL APPLICATIONS/OPERATIONS	PERFORMANCE/DRAG	POWER PLANTS	POWER TRANSMISSION	PRODUCTION	PROPULSION	SAFETY	SKIRTS/SEALS	STABILITY AND CONTROL	STRUCTURE/MATERIALS	TEST FACILITIES	TRIALS
				SWATH																					
				SWATH																					
																									SWATH
GEN PLA						GEN PLA				PLA										GEN	GEN				
			HYB																						
								HOV											HOV						
											LSACP														
											LSACP														
											LSACP														
											LSACP														
																									HOV
											LSACP														
				LSACP					LSACP																
											LSACP														
						SWATH																			
						SWATH																			
						SWATH																	SWATH		
						SWATH																			SWATH
								GEN																	
											HOV														
				SWATH																					
						HOV															HOV				
						PLA DISP																			
						PLA																			

Dynamic Instability of a High-Speed Planing Craft – An Approach to the Problem, S H Cohen. SNAME Power Boat Symposium, Miami, Florida, February 1985.

A Case Study of Dynamic Instability in a Planing Hull, L Codega and E Lewis. SNAME, Hampton Roads Section, USA, April 1986.

Stability of Sidewall Hovercraft, A G Blyth. The Naval Architect, November 1983.

Recent Research into the Ultimate Stability of Surface Effect Ships, A G Blyth. RINA International Conference on Ship Stability and Safety, London, June 1986.

The Roll Stability of an SES in a Seaway, A G Blyth. 4th International Hovercraft Conference, Southampton, May 1987.

The Contribution of the Progetto Finalizzato Trasporti in the Field of the Sea Transport, L Bianco (Progetto Finalizzato Trasporti, Consiglio Nazionale delle Ricerche, Italy) 1987.

Design Studies for a Diesel-Powered Heavy Lift Vehicle, D Dickins. 5th International Offshore Mechanics and Arctic Engineering Symposium, Tokyo, April 1986.

Arctic Hovercraft: Lessons Learned and Future Prospects, D Dickins. Arctic Offshore Technology Conference, Anchorage, Alaska, September 1985.

Development of the BR-1/2000 High-Speed Marine Diesel Engine, G Venturini (CRM, Milan) 1987.

Hovercraft, Waterborne Ambulance for the Future, Lt Col H C Cook (Maryland Natural Resources Police, USA) 1987.

Stability Analysis and Prediction of Performance for a Hydrofoil Sailing Boat Part 1. Equilibrium Sailing State Analysis, Y Masuyama (Kanazawa Institute of Technology, Ishikawa, Japan). International Shipbuilding Progress, Vol 33, No 384, August 1986.

Stability Analysis and Prediction of Performance for a Hydrofoil Sailing Boat Part 2. Dynamic Stability Analysis, Y Masuyama (Kanazawa Institute of Technology, Ishikawa, Japan). International Shipbuilding Progress, Vol 34, No 390, February 1987.

Motion of a Hydrofoil System in Waves, Y Masuyama. Journal of the Kansai Society of Naval Architects (in Japanese), Japan, No 196, 1985.

Stability of Hydrofoil Sailing Boat in Calm Water and Regular Wave Condition, Y Masuyama (Kanazawa Institute of Technology, Ishikawa, Japan). 3rd International Conference on Stability of Ships and Ocean Vehicles, STAB '86, Gdansk, Poland, September 1986. Paper 4.7.

Hydrofoil: High-Speed Control and Cleanup of Large Oil Spills, M Vacca-Torelli (Italian Navy, Ret, Operational Center for Emergency at Sea, Department of Civil Protection, Rome) and A L Geraci and A Risitano (Machinery Institute, Department of Engineering, University of Catania, Italy) 1987. Publ Rodriquez Cantieri Navali, Messina, Italy.

The Evolution of Round Bilge Fast Attack Craft Hull Forms, A Steven Toby (Princeton University, USA). *Naval Engineers Journal,* November 1987.

The High-Speed Displacement Ship Systematic Series Hull Forms – Seakeeping Characteristics, J J Block and W Beukelman. SNAME Transactions, New York, 1984.

A New Generation of High-Performance Planing Craft, O P Jons, J Koelbel and R Sheldon. *Naval Engineers Journal,* May 1985.

Air-Cushion Transport Technology in Brazil – The "Projecto VCA" Experience, M H de Souza Oliveira, M A de Rezende Veiga, P J Bandeira de Mello and R R de Araujo (University of Brasilia, Brazil). International Society for Terrain Vehicle Systems 9th International Conference, Barcelona, Spain, 31 August-4 September 1987.

Recent Developments of 4-Stroke Medium and High-Speed Engines for Marine Applications, V Drei (Diesel Ricerche, Italy). CETENA International Symposium on Advanced Research for Ships and Shipping in the Nineties, Genoa, Italy, 1-3 October 1987.

Advanced Marine Vehicles: A Critical Review, P van Oossanen (MARIN, The Netherlands). CETENA International Symposium on Advanced Research for Ships and Shipping in the Nineties, Genoa, Italy, 1-3 October 1987.

Deep V Hull-Form Design. A Model Experimental Investigation on Resistance and Propulsive Performances, A Colombo, I Elice, A Coscia and M Parodi (Fincantieri CNI, Italy). CETENA International Symposium on Advanced Research for Ships and Shipping in the Nineties, Genoa, Italy, 1-3 October 1987.

Wave Loads Experienced by SWATHs in Waves, W G Price, P Temarel and Tongshu Wu (Brunel University, UK). CETENA International Symposium on Advanced Research for Ships and Shipping in the Nineties, Genoa, Italy, 1-3 October 1987.

NES 200L – The French SES Programme, Yann Pivet (Constructions Mecaniques de Normandie, Cherbourg, France). 6th WEMT Symposium, Lubeck-Travemunde, West Germany, 2-5 June 1987.

Optimisation of a CRM 18D/SS BR-1 Engine and Waterjet Package for a 1200kW Propulsion System, G Venturini (CRM Motori Marini, Milan, Italy). 6th WEMT Symposium, Lubeck-Travemunde, West Germany, 2-5 June 1987.

Overview of Surface Effect Ships Structural Loads Test Program, A Malakhoff. 18th ASNE Annual Technical Symposium, 1981.

AERODYNAMICS	AIR LUBRICATION	ARCTIC, ANTARCTIC APPLICATIONS	COMMERCIAL APPLICATIONS/OPERATIONS	DESIGN	DEVELOPMENT	DYNAMICS/SEAKEEPING	ECONOMICS	ENVIRONMENTAL ASPECTS	FANS	HYDRODYNAMICS	ICE BREAKING	LEGISLATION	LIFT-AIR SYSTEMS	MILITARY/NAVAL APPLICATIONS/OPERATIONS	PERFORMANCE/DRAG	POWER PLANTS	POWER TRANSMISSION	PRODUCTION	PROPULSION	SAFETY	SKIRTS/SEALS	STABILITY AND CONTROL	STRUCTURE/MATERIALS	TEST FACILITIES	TRIALS
						PLA																			
						PLA																			
																						SES			
						SES																SES			
						SES																SES			
			GEN																						
				HOV																					
		HOV																							
																GEN									
		HOV																							
															SHYD							SHYD			
															SHYD							SHYD			
						HYD																			
						SHYD																SHYD			
			HYD																						
										PLA															
										DISP															
				PLA																					
				HOV																					
																GEN									
				GEN																					
										PLA					PLA										
						SWATH																			
				SES																					
																GEN			GEN						
																							SES		

Planing Craft, D Savitsky. *Naval Engineers Journal*, Vol 97, No 2, February 1985.

Effects of a Bow Bulb and Various Stern Wedges on the EHP of FFG-7 Class Frigates, J Zseleczky and B Johnson. US Naval Academy Report EW-6-84, February 1984.

FFG-7 Model Powering Test With and Without a Stern Wedge, J Zseleczky and B Hays. US Naval Academy Report EW-28-84, December 1984.

Air-Cushion Vehicles: Any Potential for Canada?, J E Laframboise, Transport Canada, Transportation Development Centre. Canadian Aeronautics and Space Journal Vol 33 No 3, September 1987.

Investigations of the Dynamics of Large Air Cushions, P A Sullivan, M J Hinchey, T A Graham, J E Byrne, A Dupuis, N Milligan and C Walsh (Institute for Aerospace Studies, University of Toronto). TP 7560E, August 1986. Prepared for Transport Canada.

Fifteen Years Experience with Composite Propeller Blades, R McCarthy (Dowty Rotol Ltd, UK). European Chapter SAMPE Intercontinental Conference on Advanced Technology in Materials Engineering, Cannes, France, 12-14 January 1981.

Project "Frigonav" Hovercraft Type 140 Operating Experience, February-March 1987, D Jones (Ice Control Enterprises Inc, Hamilton, Ontario). Report (with French summary) prepared for Transport Development Centre, Montreal, TP 8432E, April 1987.

Experimental Study of Wing-in-Ground-Effects in the Afit 5-foot Tunnel, L C Edwards (Air Force Flight Dynamics Laboratory, Wright-Patterson Air Force Base, Ohio) 1987.

FT8: A High-Performance Industrial and Marine Gas Turbine Derived from the JT8D Aircraft Engine, W H Day (Turbo Power and Marine Systems Inc, Farmington, USA). Presented at the Gas Turbine Conference, Anaheim, California, 31 May-4 June 1987. Publ The American Society of Mechanical Engineers, New York. 87-GT-242.

Design and Operation of ACV Lightering Barges, S V Yakonovsky (Leningrad Central Project and Design Bureau, USSR). Paper presented at 1987 CACTS International Conference on Air-Cushion Technology, Canada.

Rotating Stall in Centrifugal Fans – A Cure in Sight, A N Bolton (Fluids Division, National Engineering Laboratory, East Kilbride, Glasgow, Scotland). CME, January 1988.

Compact Gas Turbine Power for Fast Ships, T B Lauriat (AVCO Lycoming Textron). SAE Technical Paper 861211, 1986.

Non-Conventional Propulsion for Air-Cushion Vehicles, J F Sladky, Jr (University of Washington, Seattle). AIAA/SAE/ASME/ASEE 21st Joint Propulsion Conference, 8-10 July 1985, Monterey, California. AIAA-85-1450.

Investigations of the Dynamics of Large Air Cushions, P A Sullivan, M J Hinchey, T A Graham, J E Byrne, A Dupuis, N Milligan and C Walsh (University of Toronto Institute for Aerospace Studies). Prepared for Transportation Development Centre. TP 7560E, August 1986.

SECTION 2

PAPERS PRESENTED AT CONFERENCES SPECIFICALLY COVERING HIGH-SPEED CRAFT AND INCLUDING SOME LOW-SPEED AIR CUSHION VEHICLES, 1984 TO 1988

Papers presented at the High Performance Vehicle Design Sub-committee of the Ship Design Academic Committee of the Chinese Society of Naval Architecture and Marine Engineering Second National Conference on High-speed Craft 1984.

Development of Hovercraft at Home and Abroad During the Last Decade, Yun Liang (Marine Design and Research Institute of China).

Technical Development of Amphibious Hovercraft and its Power Plant Selection, Zheng Ren-tao and Jiang Xian-ping (Marine Design and Research Institute of China).

Stability Analysis of Amphibious Hovercraft, Zhou Wei-lin, Hua Yi and Gu Xiong (Marine Design and Research Institute of China).

SES Roll Stability Investigation (Part II), Li Gen-lin, Yun Liang and Lin Shu Gwang (Marine Design and Research Institute of China).

SES Roll Stability —its Test and Calculation, Xing Sheng-de and He Zhi-fei (China Ship Scientific Research Center).

Design Analysis of Water Propeller for SES, Sheng Yong-chuan and Min-tong (Marine Design Research Institute of China).

Some Points regarding the Design of Sidewall Hovercraft, Cai Tian-Kai (Shanghai Ship and Shipping Research Institute).

The Concept of High Length-to-Beam Ratio for Application to Inland Waterway Sidewall Hovercraft, Ji Liang-min (Communication Department of Anhui Province).

Design, Reconstruction and Trial Testing of the SES 'Shen Xiang', Xu Yun-chu (Marine Design and Research Institute of China).

AERODYNAMICS	AIR LUBRICATION	ARCTIC, ANTARCTIC APPLICATIONS	COMMERCIAL APPLICATIONS/OPERATIONS	DESIGN	DEVELOPMENT	DYNAMICS/SEAKEEPING	ECONOMICS	ENVIRONMENTAL ASPECTS	FANS	HYDRODYNAMICS	ICE BREAKING	LEGISLATION	LIFT-AIR SYSTEMS	MILITARY/NAVAL APPLICATIONS/OPERATIONS	PERFORMANCE/DRAG	POWER PLANTS	POWER TRANSMISSION	PRODUCTION	PROPULSION	SAFETY	SKIRTS/SEALS	STABILITY AND CONTROL	STRUCTURE/MATERIALS	TEST FACILITIES	TRIALS
										DISP PLA															
										PLA															
										PLA															
			HOV																						
						HOV																			
																			HOV						
											HOV														
WIGE																									
																GEN									
		LSACP	LSACP																						
									GEN																
																GEN									
																			HOV						
						HOV																			
			HOV SES																						
			HOV													HOV									
																							HOV		
																							SES		
																							SES		
																			SES						
			SES																						
			SES																						
			SES																						SES

The Development of 'Flying Dragon'—the Sidewall Pleasure Hovercraft on Song Hua River, Yuan Shu-chen (Heilongjiang Research Institute of Water Transportation Science).

Adaptation of a Patrol Boat's Axial Waterjet Pump to Sidewall Hovercraft, Zhang Zi-ping (Communication Science Research Institute of Anhui Province).

The Use of Tube Shape Sandwich Structure for GRP Sidewall Hovercraft Construction, Cheng Zhu-yu and Dai Ling (Communication Science Research Institute of Anhui Province).

The Research and Design of Air Cushion Drilling Platform for Beach Oil Exploration, Gu Xiong (Marine Design and Research Institute of China).

Structural Design and Construction of the Single-crew Ram-wing Vehicle 902, Xu Gui-sheng and Ji Fu-liang (China Ship Scientific Research Center).

The New Trend of Hydrofoil Design and Research—on the Promotion of the Use of Hydrofoil in China, Zhong Ben-ji (China Ship Scientific Research Center).

Design Feature and Test Analysis of the Appendages of the Yangtze Hydrofoil No 2, Shen Zhou-zhong and Tang Chong-gao (Marine Design and Research Institute of China).

The Selection of Main Parameter for Hydrofoil Waterjet Propulsion System with Ram Inlet, Ren Chao-hai (China Ship Scientific Research Center).

An Effective Way of Significantly Reducing the Resistance of Stepless Planing Craft—an Example of Applying the Additional Two Wedges to Full-scale Craft, Zhang Ji-meng (Marine Design and Research Institute of China).

Application of Fluid Dynamic Lifting Force for Interim Operation of High-speed Craft, Zhang Cheng-xia (Hudong Shipyard).

Shallow Water Resistance Calculation for Planing Craft, Dong Tsu-sun (Naval Engineering Institute).

Experimental Investigation of Planing Craft Resistance Reduction by Means of 'Induced Air Cushion', Yang Su-Zhen, Han Hong-shong and Zhang Min-guo (Huazhong Engineering Institute of China).

Development of SWATH Type Vessels in China and Abroad, Cao Yong-qing (Marine Design and Research Institute of China).

A High-performance Hull—High-speed Catamaran, Jin Ping-zhong and Shen Zhon-zhong (Marine Design and Research Institute of China).

Analysis of Model Test Method as Applied to High-speed Craft, He Zhi-fei and Zing Sheng-de (China Ship Scientific Research Center).

Experimental Investigation of Resistance of High-speed Displacement Vessel with Wider Transom Stern, Dou Shang-zin, Cheng Bin, Wang Yun-cai and Shao-ming (Shanghai Jiao Tong University).

Shallow Water Waves due to Moving Disturbance in Transcritical Region, Wu De-ming (Harbin Shipbuilding Engineering Institute).

Experimental Investigation into the Flow Pattern of a Waterjet Unit in Wind Tunnel, Wu Min-quan, Ren Chao-hai, Ha Bi-xiao, Liu Hai (China Ship Scientific Research Center).

Structural Design of High-speed Craft, Chen Yuan-han (Wuhan Ship Research and Design Institute).

Criterion of Material Selection for High-speed GRP Craft and Methods of Structural Design, Yang Chen-ye, Xu Shen-pan and Jia Guan-lin (Shanghai Ship and Shipping Research Institute).

Light, Corrosion-resistant and Weldable Aluminium Magnesium is an Ideal Material for the Construction of High Performance Craft, Lu Er-kang (Marine Design and Research Institute of China).

The Development of Heilongjiang Hoverbarge and its Experiment, Operation and Prospect, Fan Hong-ji (Heilongjiang Water Transportation Scientific Research Institute).

Research of the Design of Air-supported Ships, Zhang Xiao-chen and Lu Yong-chang (Heilongjiang Research Institute of Water Transportation Science).

Experimental Investigation of Characteristics of Hoverbarge, Su Yong-chang, Tian Yong-an and Huang Xi-rong (Harbin Shipbuilding Engineering Institute).

The Application of Sidewall Hovercraft to Water Passenger Transportation Systems and Sandwich GRP Structure, Chen Guo-yu and Ni-Bu-you (Shanghai Ship and Shipping Research Institute).

AERODYNAMICS	AIR LUBRICATION	ARCTIC, ANTARCTIC APPLICATIONS	COMMERCIAL APPLICATIONS/OPERATIONS	DESIGN	DEVELOPMENT	DYNAMICS/SEAKEEPING	ECONOMICS	ENVIRONMENTAL ASPECTS	FANS	HYDRODYNAMICS	ICE BREAKING	LEGISLATION	LIFT-AIR SYSTEMS	MILITARY/NAVAL APPLICATIONS/OPERATIONS	PERFORMANCE/DRAG	POWER PLANTS	POWER TRANSMISSION	PRODUCTION	PROPULSION	SAFETY	SKIRTS/SEALS	STABILITY AND CONTROL	STRUCTURE/MATERIALS	TEST FACILITIES	TRIALS
					SES																				
																			SES						
																							SES		
				LSACP																					
				WIGE																			WIGE		
			HYD																						
										HYD															
																			HYD						
															PLA										
										GEN															
															PLA										
	PLA														PLA										
					SWATH																				
				CAT																					
										GEN															
										DISP															
										HYD															
																			GEN						
				GEN																			GEN		
																							GEN		
																							GEN		
			LSACP																						
					GEN																				
															LSACP										
			SES																				SES		

Papers presented at the Royal Institution of Naval Architects International Symposium on SWATH Ships and Advanced Multi-hulled Vessels, London, April 1985.

SWATH Developments and Performance Comparisons with other Craft, Dr T G Lang (Semi-Submerged Ship Corporation, California, USA) and J E Sloggett (Jolyon Associates, UK).

Application of Multi-variable Control Techniques to the Active Motion Control of SWATH Craft, Dr F L A Caldeira-Saraiva and Dr D Clarke, (British Ship Research Association, UK).

Application of the SWATH Principle to Passenger Vessels, T Routa (Wärtsilä Helsinki Shipyard, Finland).

Seakeeping Evaluation in SWATH Ship Design, R Hosoda and Y Kunitake (University of Osaka Prefecture and Mitsui Engineering & Shipbuilding Co Ltd, Japan).

A Status Report on Design and Operational Experiences with the Semi-Submerged Catamaran (SSC) Vessels, T Mabuchi, Y Kunitake and H Nakamura (Mitsui Engineering & Shipbuilding Co Ltd, Japan).

SWATH Ship Design Trends, C G Kennell (Naval Sea Systems Command, USA).

Asset/SWATH—A Computer-based Model for SWATH Ships, R D Mulligan (Ministry of Defence, UK) and LCDR J N Edkins (David Taylor Naval Ship R & D Center, USA).

SWATH Model Resistance Experiments, A Koops (Netherland Ship Model Basin, MARIN) and W C E Nethercote (Defence Research Establishment Atlantic).

The RMI SD-60 SWATH Demonstration Project, G Luedeke, Jnr, J Montague, H Posnansky and Q Lewis (RMI Inc, USA).

Some Motion and Resistance Aspects of SWATH-Ship Design, D B Seren, N S Miller, A M Ferguson and R C McGregor (Department of Naval Architecture and Ocean Engineering, University of Glasgow, UK).

The Effect of Tilt and Interference on the Hydrodynamic Coefficients of SWATH-type Sections, M Atlar, D B Seren and J Validakis (Hydrodynamics Laboratory, Department of Naval Architecture and Ocean Engineering, University of Glasgow, UK).

Structural Responses of a SWATH or Multi-hull Vessel Travelling in Waves, W G Price, P Temarel and Wu Yousheng (Brunel University, UK).

SWATH Technology Development at the Naval Ocean Systems Center, J D Hightower, L A Parnell, A T Strickland and P L Warnhuis (Naval Ocean Systems Center, USA).

Mission Related Preliminary Design Solutions for Small SWATH Ocean Patrol Vessels, F Fernandez-Gonzalez (E N Bazan, Madrid, Spain).

Design of a Wave-piercing Catamaran, P Hercus (International Catamarans, Australia).

Papers presented at the Canadian Air Cushion Technology Society and US Hovercraft Society Joint International Conference on Air Cushion Technology, Rockville, Maryland, USA, September 1985.

Nonlinear Dynamics of a Segmented Skirt Air Cushion, T A Graham and P A Sullivan (University of Toronto, Canada).

Air Cushion Vehicle Skirt Systems, C Payne (Hovercraft Fabrics Ltd, Canada).

Effect of a Responsive Skirt on Air Cushion Vehicle Seakeeping, W L Zhou and T Ma (Marine Design and Research Institute of China, China).

Aerodynamic Characteristics of a Bag-Cone Skirt, N Zheng and T Ma (Marine Design and Research Institute of China, China).

Calculations of the Static Forces Acting on ACV Bag-Finger Skirts, Y N Xie and Y Hua (Marine Design and Research Institute of China, China).

Practical Problems Relating to the Hovercraft Application of Marine Gas Turbines, Z J Zhang (Marine Design and Research Institute of China, China).

Stretching the HM200 Series SES, E G Tattersall and N Gee (Vosper Hovermarine, UK).

Development of the Air Cushion Equipment Transporter (ACET), R Helm (Bell Aerospace Canada Textron).

Prevention of Propeller Foreign Object Damage, Theory and Practice, D J Vitale (US Hovercraft Society) and C Payne (Hovercraft Fabrics Ltd, Canada).

Air Propellers and their Environmental Problems on ACVs, D Soley (Dowty Rotol Ltd, UK).

Assessing ACV Navigation, D Wetherell and H R Graham (US Naval Sea Systems Command).

AERODYNAMICS	AIR LUBRICATION	ARCTIC, ANTARCTIC APPLICATIONS	COMMERCIAL APPLICATIONS/OPERATIONS	DESIGN	DEVELOPMENT	DYNAMICS/SEAKEEPING	ECONOMICS	ENVIRONMENTAL ASPECTS	FANS	HYDRODYNAMICS	ICE BREAKING	LEGISLATION	LIFT-AIR SYSTEMS	MILITARY/NAVAL APPLICATIONS/OPERATIONS	PERFORMANCE/DRAG	POWER PLANTS	POWER TRANSMISSION	PRODUCTION	PROPULSION	SAFETY	SKIRTS/SEALS	STABILITY AND CONTROL	STRUCTURE/MATERIALS	TEST FACILITIES	TRIALS
															SWATH GEN										
						SWATH																			
			SWATH																						
						SWATH																			
				SWATH																					SWATH
				SWATH																					
				SWATH																					
															SWATH										
				SWATH																					
						SWATH									SWATH										
															SWATH										
						SWATH																			
					SWATH																				
														SWATH											
				CAT																					
						HOV															HOV				
																					HOV				
						HOV															HOV				
HOV																					HOV				
							HOV														HOV				
															HOV										
					SES																				
					LSACP									LSACP											
							HOV												HOV	HOV					
							HOV												HOV						
														HOV SES											

SES and ACV Applicability to Naval Missions, K Spaulding (US Naval Sea Systems Command).

Hovercraft in Law Enforcement, H C Cook (Department of Natural Resources, State of Maryland, USA).

Managing the LCAC Program in an Evolving Acquisition Environment, R W Kenefick (US Naval Sea Systems Command).

On the Manoeuvring Simulation of an Antarctic Hovercraft, R Murao (Aoyama Gakuin University, Japan) and T Noziri (Mitsui Engineering & Shipbuilding Co Ltd, Japan).

Pitch and Roll Hydrodynamics of a Pericell Hovercraft, D D Moran (David Taylor Naval Ship Research & Development Center, USA).

Computer-Aided Conceptual Design of Air Cushion Vehicles, E G U Band and D R Lavis (Band, Lavis and Associates Inc, USA).

The Use of Model Test Data for Predicting Full-Scale ACV Resistance, B G Forstell (Band, Lavis and Associates Inc, USA) and C W Harry (David Taylor Naval Ship Research & Development Center, USA).

Passive Control of Air Cushion Heave Dynamics, J R Amyot (National Research Council of Canada, Ottawa, Canada).

Papers presented at the American Society of Naval Engineers (Flagship Section) and US Coast Guard Technical Symposium Patrol Boats 86, Arlington, Virginia, USA, 13-14 March 1986.

Development of a Hydrofoil Combatant, Preliminary Design, D S Olling.

The Combat Patrol Boat, Topside Design, P E Law, Jr, S Kuniyoshi and T Morgan.

US Coast Guard Conceptual Design of an Offshore Patrol Boat, S Cohen.

A Patrol Boat Hybrid Concept for the Coast Guard, J R Meyer.

Nasty Patrol Boats, J Stebbins.

AMPB—Advanced Multi-Mission Patrol Boat, L R Sheldon and T Sauer.

Patrol Boat Design Considerations, H Winters.

USN Sea Viking Design Development Highlights, C M Lee.

Compact Diesel Engines for Patrol Boats, V Jost.

Gas Turbines for Patrol Boat Power, J E Roberts.

Design, Development and Application of Diesel Engines for High Performance Patrol Craft, K Hosking.

Papers presented at the Royal Institution of Naval Architects International Symposium on Coastal Defence and Assault Vessels and Systems, Warship 86, London, 19-22 May 1986.

Influence of the Moment of Equilibrium on the Powering Characteristics of Planing Craft Including Hydrofoils, F Van Walree and E Stierman (Maritime Research Institute, Netherlands).

Air Cushion Vehicles for Amphibious Assault—The Next Generation, D R Lavis and E Band (Band, Lavis Associates Inc, USA).

Development of the Turt 4, Diesel Powered Amphibious Hovercraft for the Amphibious Warfare Role, S Lee, C Lee and S Kim (Korea Tacoma Marine Industries Ltd, Korea).

Diesel Engines Specially Designed for Fast Patrol Boats, B Gondouin (Alsthom Groupe Diesel, France).

The Use of Amphibious Hovercraft for Assault Purposes, G Elsley, UK.

Design, Construction and Operational Experience of High-Speed Aluminium Patrol Craft for the Finnish Coast Guard, O Ostring (Valmetin Laivateollisuus OY, Finland).

Diesel Engine Design, MTU (Motoren und Turbinen-Union Friedrichshafen GmbH), Federal Republic of Germany.

Catamarans Versus Single-Hull Concepts. A Study of Stability, Powering and Seakeeping Qualities, O Rutgersson (SSPA Maritime Consulting AB, Sweden).

The Dynamic Response of Surface-Effect-Ships in Regular Head Seas using Model Simulations, B R Clayton and R Webb (Dept of Mechanical Engineering, University College, London).

AERODYNAMICS	AIR LUBRICATION	ARCTIC, ANTARCTIC APPLICATIONS	COMMERCIAL APPLICATIONS/OPERATIONS	DESIGN	DEVELOPMENT	DYNAMICS/SEAKEEPING	ECONOMICS	ENVIRONMENTAL ASPECTS	FANS	HYDRODYNAMICS	ICE BREAKING	LEGISLATION	LIFT-AIR SYSTEMS	MILITARY/NAVAL APPLICATIONS/OPERATIONS	PERFORMANCE/DRAG	POWER PLANTS	POWER TRANSMISSION	PRODUCTION	PROPULSION	SAFETY	SKIRTS/SEALS	STABILITY AND CONTROL	STRUCTURE/MATERIALS	TEST FACILITIES	TRIALS
														HOV SES											
			HOV																						
														HOV											
		HOV																				HOV			
																						HOV			
				HOV																					
														HOV SES											
						HOV																			
					HYD									HYD											
														PLA											
			PLA																						
			PLA																						
				PLA										PLA											
														PLA											
				PLA										PLA											
														SES											
																PLA									
																PLA									
																PLA									
															PLA HYD										
														HOV											
														HOV											
																PLA									
														HOV											
														PLA											
																	GEN								
						CAT GEN								CAT GEN								CAT GEN			
						SES																			

Papers presented at the High-Speed Surface Craft and Shipping News International 5th International High-Speed Surface Craft Conference, Southampton, England, 7-8 May 1986.

Meeting the Channel Tunnel Challenge, D Meredith (Hoverspeed).

Regression Analysis of Gawn-Burrill Series for Application in Computer-Aided High-Speed Propeller Design, Dr P G Kozhukharov (Bulgarian Ship Hydrodynamics Centre).

ADOC 12: A Light Utility Air Cushion Vehicle, B de Lagarde (IFREMER).

SWATH Seakeeping in the Presence of Control Fins, Dr J -Y Wu and Dr R C McGregor (Department of Naval Architecture and Ocean Engineering, University of Glasgow).

Successful High-Speed Fleets Prove Viability of Waterjet Propulsion, J Seastrom (North American Marine Jet).

Experience with Jet-Propulsion Systems in Various Types of Craft, R Svensson (KaMeWa AB).

Fast Ferry Potential in the United States, W Wohleking (Advanced Marine Systems Associates).

A Numerical Method for Calculating Hydrodynamic Characteristics of a Hydrofoil with Arbitrary Planform, L Baiqi (China Ship Scientific Research Center).

The Development of the Wave-Piercing Catamaran, P Hercus (International Catamarans).

Hovercraft Design with an Automatic Transversal Air Distribution Lift System, M de la Cruz and J M Berbiela (Neumar).

Advanced Composite Structures for High-Speed Surface Craft, A Marchant (Marchant Filer Dixon).

Papers presented at 'On a Cushion of Air—A Review of Hovercraft Technology' symposium, organised by the British Association for the Advancement of Science and The Hovercraft Society, London, 11 December 1985.

Review of the first 25 years of Hovercraft, J Rapson (Hovercraft Consultants Ltd).

Large Amphibious Hovercraft, R Wheeler (British Hovercraft Corporation).

Small Amphibious Hovercraft, Introduction and Overview, B Russell (Editor, Hovercraft Bulletin).

Small Amphibious Hovercraft, Recent Developments, C Eden (Air Vehicles Ltd).

Surface Effect Ships, E G Tattersall (Vosper Hovermarine).

Moving Loads on a Cushion of Air, G Westerling-Norris (Air Cushion Equipment Ltd).

Papers presented at the Urban Waterborne Mass Transportation Symposium, Miami, Florida, 26 April 1986, sponsored by The Marine Council and The Southeast Section, The Society of Naval Architects and Marine Engineering.

Development of a Series of Fast Passenger Catamarans in Australia, Mathew Nichols.

Surface-Piercing Hydrofoil Application to Ferry Missions, Trial Program, James H King and John R Meyer.

A Total Approach to Rapid Waterborne Transportation, Donald E Burg.

Three Years of Coast Guard Operation Experience in Relation to Mass Transportation Needs, Cmdr Paul C Jackson.

The Operations and Economics of Marine Transit: Comparative Studies by Computer, Edward C Hagemann.

Assessing the Market and Financial Feasibility of Waterborne Transportation Systems, John F DiRenzo.

Papers presented at the 1986 CACTS International Conference on Air Cushion Technology, arranged by the Canadian Air Cushion Technology Society of the Canadian Aeronautics and Space Institute in co-operation with The Hovercraft Society and the US Hovercraft Society. Held in Toronto, Ontario, 16-18 September 1986.

Design Criteria for Light High Speed Desert Air Cushion Vehicle, B E Abulnaga (McGill University, Montreal, Canada).

Preliminary Testing of Linear Propellers over Water, C Ives (Hudex International Consultants Ltd, Montreal, Canada).

Some Tests at IMD on High-Speed Hovercraft Icebreaking, J Whitten, M Hinchey (Memorial University of Newfoundland) and B Hill, S Jones (Institute of Marine Dynamics, St John's, Newfoundland).

Flow Visualization and Ducted Propellers on the LACV 30, P E Robertson (X-Aero, USA).

AERODYNAMICS	AIR LUBRICATION	ARCTIC, ANTARCTIC APPLICATIONS	COMMERCIAL APPLICATIONS/OPERATIONS	DESIGN	DEVELOPMENT	DYNAMICS/SEAKEEPING	ECONOMICS	ENVIRONMENTAL ASPECTS	FANS	HYDRODYNAMICS	ICE BREAKING	LEGISLATION	LIFT-AIR SYSTEMS	MILITARY/NAVAL APPLICATIONS/OPERATIONS	PERFORMANCE/DRAG	POWER PLANTS	POWER TRANSMISSION	PRODUCTION	PROPULSION	SAFETY	SKIRTS/SEALS	STABILITY AND CONTROL	STRUCTURE/MATERIALS	TEST FACILITIES	TRIALS
			HOV																						
																			GEN						
				HOV																					
						SWATH																			
																			GEN						
																			GEN						
			GEN																						
										HYD															
					CAT																				
													HOV												HOV
																							GEN		
				HOV	HOV																				
				SES	SES																				
				HOV																					
				HOV																					
				HOV																					
				SES																					
				LSACP																					
					CAT																				
			HYD																						
	ALH		ALH				ALH																		
			SES																						
							GEN																		
							GEN																		
				HOV																					
																			GEN						
											HOV														
																			HOV						

Bertelsen Research on Sliding Seals for an Air Cushion Crawler Tractor, W R Bertelsen (Bertelsen Inc, USA).

The High Speed Performance Vehicle in Anti-Submarine Warfare, M Reid (Defence Programs, External Affairs, Canada).

Diesel Engine Concepts for Hovercraft, H Evans (InTech International Inc, Spokane, Washington, USA).

Propagation of an ACIB Air Cavity Under a Floating Ice Sheet, M J Hinchey (Memorial University of Newfoundland).

Performance Criteria for Air-Cushion Heave Dynamics, J R Amyot (National Research Council of Canada, Ottawa).

A Proposed Laboratory Method to Determine Propeller Foreign Object Damage, D J Vitale (US Naval Sea Systems Command).

The Experimental Investigation of the Bounce Characteristics of an ACV Responsive Skirt, W L Zhou and T Ma (Marine Design and Research Institute of China).

The Improvement of the ACV Skirt Test Facilities, N Zheng and Y Hua (Marine Design and Research Institute of China).

Hovercraft in Law Enforcement — Part 2, H C Cook (Department of Natural Resources, State of Maryland, USA).

The LACV 30 in Service, R G Helm (Bell Aerospace Textron, USA).

Papers presented at the AIAA 8th Advanced Marine Systems Conference, San Diego, California, USA, 22-24 September 1986.

Ride Quality Criteria of Assessment for Advanced Marine Vehicles, W E Farris (Boeing Marine Systems, Seattle, Washington, USA). Paper AIAA-86-2360.

Linear Analysis of Heave Dynamics of a Bag and Finger ACV Skirt, T Mar and P A Sullivan (University of Toronto, Canada). AIAA-86-2361.

Analysis and Prediction of Flat Bottom Slamming Impact of Advanced Marine Vehicles in Waves, P Kaplan (Virginia Polytechnic Institute and State University, Blacksburg, Virginia, USA). AIAA-86-2362.

Innovation in SWATH, T A Schmidt (Lockheed Advanced Marine Systems, Santa Clara, California, USA). AIAA-86-2363.

Progress in the Development of the Surface Effect Catamaran Hull Form, J M Durkin and N M Paraskevas (David W Taylor Naval Ship R&D Center, Bethesda, Maryland, USA). AIAA-86-2364.

Ram Air Catamaran (RAC) Vehicle Concepts, R W Gallington (Science Applications International Corp, Seattle, Washington, USA). AIAA-86-2365.

Worldwide Study on High Speed Waterborne Transportation, W G Wohleking (Advanced Marine Systems Associates, Gaithersburg, Maryland, USA). AIAA-86-2366.

High Speed Catamarans, M Nichols (Nichols Boat Builders, Freeland, Washington, USA). AIAA-86-2367.

The Mitsui Sea Saloon 15 *Marine Wave*, K Nishimura (Mitsui Engineering & Shipbuilding Co Ltd, Tokyo), H Nakamura (Mitsui Engineering & Shipbuilding Co Ltd, Ichihara, Japan) and M Komoto (Mitsui Zosen (USA) Inc, New York). AIAA-86-2368.

Hydrofoil Operations, L Rodriquez (Rodriquez Cantieri Navali, Messina, Italy). AIAA-86-2369.

The SWATH Ship *Halcyon* Operations, R Cramb (RMI Inc, National City, California, USA). AIAA-86-2370.

A High Productivity Waterborne Rapid Transport System, D E Burg (Air Ride Craft Inc, Miami, Florida, USA). AIAA-86-2371.

The Surface Effect Ship Special Warfare Craft (SWCM), C Lee (RMI Inc, National City, California, USA). AIAA-86-2372.

The Arctic ACV Program, J Koleser (Naval Sea Systems Command, Washington DC, USA). AIAA-86-2375.

Preliminary Design of an Air-Cushion Crash Rescue Vehicle (ACCRV), R Brown (AFWAL/FIEMB Wright-Patterson Air Force Base, Ohio) and R Thom (Bell Aerospace Textron, Buffalo, New York, USA). AIAA-86-2377.

Replacement of the University Research Fleet and a SWATH Ship Candidate, R P Dinsmore (Woods Hole Oceanographic Institution, Woods Hole, Massachusetts, USA) and T G Lang (Semi-Submerged Ship Corp, Solana Beach, California, USA). AIAA-86-2378.

Arctic Operations of *Larus*, E Makinen (Wärtsilä Arctic Inc, Vancouver BC, Canada). AIAA-86-2380.

Development of HYCAT, D E Calkins (University of Washington, Seattle, Washington, USA). AIAA-86-2381.

New Small Waterplane Area Ship Concept, W C O'Neill (Newton Square, Pennsylvania, USA). AIAA-86-2382.

AERODYNAMICS	AIR LUBRICATION	ARCTIC, ANTARCTIC APPLICATIONS	COMMERCIAL APPLICATIONS/OPERATIONS	DESIGN	DEVELOPMENT	DYNAMICS/SEAKEEPING	ECONOMICS	ENVIRONMENTAL ASPECTS	FANS	HYDRODYNAMICS	ICE BREAKING	LEGISLATION	LIFT-AIR SYSTEMS	MILITARY/NAVAL APPLICATIONS/OPERATIONS	PERFORMANCE/DRAG	POWER PLANTS	POWER TRANSMISSION	PRODUCTION	PROPULSION	SAFETY	SKIRTS/SEALS	STABILITY AND CONTROL	STRUCTURE/MATERIALS	TEST FACILITIES	TRIALS
																					HYB		HYB		
														GEN											
															HOV										
											LSACP														
						HOV																			
								HOV											HOV						
						HOV															HOV				
																					HOV			HOV	
			HOV																						
														HOV											
						GEN																			
						HOV															HOV				
						GEN																			
				SWATH	SWATH																				
					CAT																				
				CAT																					
			GEN																						
				CAT	CAT																				
				SWATH																					
				HYD																					
				SWATH																					
				ALH																					
														SES											
		HOV																							
				HYB																					
			SWATH																						
		HOV																							
					CAT																				
					HYD																				
				SWATH	SWATH																				

The Wavestrider Family of Planing Boats, P Payne (Ketron Inc, Annapolis, Maryland, USA). AIAA-86-2383.

SWATH T-AGOS: A Producible Design, P M Covich (Naval Sea Systems Command, Washington DC, USA). AIAA-86-2384.

Large SWATHs: A Discussion of the Diminishing Returns of Increasing SWATH Ship Size, C B McKesson and T R Cannon (NAVSEA, Baltimore, Maryland, USA). AIAA-86-2385.

Air-Cushion Equipment Transporter (ACET), G R Wyen (AFWAL Wright-Patterson Air Force Base, Ohio, USA) and R Helm (Bell Aerospace Textron, Buffalo, New York, USA). AIAA-86-2386.

Papers presented at The Hovercraft Society Fourth International Hovercraft Conference, Southampton, England, 6-7 May 1987.

The Development of the Current Range of Griffon Hovercraft, J Gifford (Griffon Hovercraft Ltd, UK).

The Tiger 40 Hovercraft, C B Eden (Air Vehicles Ltd, UK).

AP1-88 Operating Experience, M D Mant (British Hovercraft Corporation, UK).

The United Kingdom Trials of the SES 200, B J W Pingree, B J Russell and J B Willcox.

The Roll Stability of an SES in a Seaway, A G Blyth (UK).

Coupled Roll and Heave Motions of Surface Effect Ship in Beam Seas, L Yun, T F Wu and Y N Cheng (Shanghai, China).

Experimental Investigation of Bounce Feature of ACV Bi-Bag Skirt, W L Zhou and T Ma (Marine Design and Research Institute of China).

The Hovercraft Doctor Service, M Cole.

The Static Formation Calculation of ACV Bi-Bag Skirts on the Water Surface, N Zheng, T F Wu and Y Hua (Marine Design and Research Institute of China).

ACVPP – A Computer Application for Air-Cushion Vehicle Power Prediction, F J Steele, Jr (University of Michigan, Ann Arbor, USA).

The Deep Cushion SES Concept, E G Tattersall (Hovermarine International Ltd, UK).

The Use of Hovercraft in the Defence of the Home Base, B J Russell (Ministry of Defence, UK).

Papers presented at The Royal Aeronautical Society, London, Ram Wing and Ground Effect Craft Symposium, 19 May 1987.

Taking Advantage of Surface Proximity Effects with Aero-Marine Vehicles, Robert L Trillo (Robert Trillo Limited, Lymington, Hampshire).

Ram Wings – A Future? J M L Reeves (Naval Air Development Center, USA).

Power Augmentation of Ram Wings, R W Gallington (Science Applications International Corporation, USA).

History and Development of the "Aerodynamic Ground Effect Craft" (AGEC) with Tandem Wings, G W Jorg (West Germany).

On the Design of Stable Ram Wing Vehicles, R W Staufenbiel (Institute of Aerospace Engineering, West Germany).

A Possible Maritime Future for Surface Effect Craft in the UK, C B Betts and B R Clayton (University College, London).

Papers presented at the American Society of Naval Engineers ASNE Day 1987 and published in the Naval Engineers Journal (ASNE) Vol 99 No 3, May 1987, USA.

The Effect of Stern Wedges on Ship Powering Performance, G Karafiath and S Fisher.

The Deep-Vee Hull Form – Improves Seakeeping and Combat System Performance, J W Kehoe, Jr (USN, Ret), K S Brower and E H Serter.

The History of Aluminium as a Deckhouse Material, R A Sielski.

T-AGOS 19: An Innovative Program for an Innovative Design, P Covich.

AERODYNAMICS	AIR LUBRICATION	ARCTIC, ANTARCTIC APPLICATIONS	COMMERCIAL APPLICATIONS/OPERATIONS	DESIGN	DEVELOPMENT	DYNAMICS/SEAKEEPING	ECONOMICS	ENVIRONMENTAL ASPECTS	FANS	HYDRODYNAMICS	ICE BREAKING	LEGISLATION	LIFT-AIR SYSTEMS	MILITARY/NAVAL APPLICATIONS/OPERATIONS	PERFORMANCE/DRAG	POWER PLANTS	POWER TRANSMISSION	PRODUCTION	PROPULSION	SAFETY	SKIRTS/SEALS	STABILITY AND CONTROL	STRUCTURE/MATERIALS	TEST FACILITIES	TRIALS
				PLA		PLA																			
																		SWATH							
				SWATH																					
														LSACP											
				HOV	HOV																				
				HOV																					
			HOV																						
														SES											
																						SES			
						SES																			
					HOV																HOV				
			HOV																						
																					HOV				
														HOV											
						SES																			
														SES HOV											
ACV WIGE			GEN WIGE																						
			WIGE																						
WIGE															WIGE										
															WIGE										
					WIGE																	WIGE			
														SES											
										PLA					PLA										
										PLA				PLA											
																							GEN		
				SWATH																					

Papers presented at the 1987 CACTS International Conference on Air-Cushion Technology, Montreal, Canada, 22-24 September 1987. Sponsored by Transportation Development Centre, Transport Canada. Presented by the Canadian Air-Cushion Technology Society with the co-operation of the US Hovercraft Society and The Hovercraft Society.

Planning Surface Transportation in Northern Canada, V Hume (Indian and Northern Affairs, Canada).

Tractive Requirements for Off-Road ACVs, R N Young and P Bonsinsuk (McGill University, Montreal).

Air-Cushion Assisted Airport Rescue Vehicle, D J Perez (Wright-Patterson Air Force Base, USA).

GPC: A Device for Easy Control of a Small ACV, B de Lagarde (IFREMER, France).

Development of Hovercraft Skirt for Desert Operation, B E Abulnaga (American University, Cairo, Egypt).

Industrial Applications of Air-Cushion and Fluid Jets by Bertin & Cie, J Cayla (Bertin & Cie, France).

Ice Management Chicoutimi Harbour with an ACV, G Desgagnes (Chicoutimi Port) and D Jones (Ice Control Enterprises, Canada).

Critical Speed Data for a Floating Model Ice Sheet, M J Hinchey (Memorial University of Newfoundland, Canada).

Requirements for ACV Operations in Antarctica, J S Dibbern (US Army, Charlotteville, VA, USA).

Design and Operation of ACV Lightering Barges, V A Galistsky (Leningrad Central Project and Design Bureau, USSR).

Specification and Acquisition of AP1.88 by the CCG, T F Melhuish (Canadian Coast Guard).

Design of Canadian Coast Guard AP1.88, J Leonard (British Hovercraft Corporation, UK).

Initial Operating Experience with the CCG AP1.88, G Moore (ACV Base, Canadian Coast Guard, Montreal).

Operational Costs and Requirements for the AP1.88, D Marshall (SRO-KMA Consultants Inc, Montreal).

Engineering Development and Service Experience of the Amphibious ACV *Gepard*, I A Martynov (Neptun Central Design Bureau, Moscow, USSR).

Hovercraft Water/Land Ambulance Service, H Cook (Maryland Natural Resources Police, USA).

Design and Test Results of Air-Cushion Vehicles Built by A M Gorki Institute, S F Kirkin (Mariiskiy Polytechnic Institute A M Gorki, USSR).

Design Criteria for Hovercraft Propellers: US Army LACV-30 Case Study, R J Gornstein (Pacific Propeller Inc, Kent, WA, USA).

Horizontal Launch System for Transatmospheric Vehicles, M D Chawla (Wright-Patterson Air Force Base, USA).

Hovercraft Dynamics Modeling: A Review of Current Techniques, P Taylor (US Navy Ocean Engineering, MIT) and D D Moran (David Taylor Naval Ship R&D Center, USA).

Papers presented at the 12th Annual Conference of the International Marine Transit Association, Taormina, Sicily, 28-30 September 1987.

Possible Improvements in Semi-Conventional Fast Marine Craft, A Magazzu (Palermo University, Italy).

The Competitivity of the Offer on the Market of Fast Ships, C Sicard (Organisation Claude Sicard).

The future for Composite Materials in Marine Transportation, A Marchant (Marchant Filer Dixon, UK).

Development of High Velocity Marine Vehicles for Passenger Transportation in Mediterranean Area, B Della Loggia (CETENA, Italy).

Self Propulsion Tests with Waterjets, V Ruggiero (University of Genoa) and G Venturini (CRM, Milan, Italy).

AP1.88 Operating Experience, M D Mant (British Hovercraft Corporation, UK).

AERODYNAMICS	AIR LUBRICATION	ARCTIC, ANTARCTIC APPLICATIONS	COMMERCIAL APPLICATIONS/OPERATIONS	DESIGN	DEVELOPMENT	DYNAMICS/SEAKEEPING	ECONOMICS	ENVIRONMENTAL ASPECTS	FANS	HYDRODYNAMICS	ICE BREAKING	LEGISLATION	LIFT-AIR SYSTEMS	MILITARY/NAVAL APPLICATIONS/OPERATIONS	PERFORMANCE/DRAG	POWER PLANTS	POWER TRANSMISSION	PRODUCTION	PROPULSION	SAFETY	SKIRTS/SEALS	STABILITY AND CONTROL	STRUCTURE/MATERIALS	TEST FACILITIES	TRIALS
		GEN																							
															HOV HYB										
			HOV HYB																						
																						HOV			
								HOV													HOV				
GEN										GEN															
										HOV															
										HOV															
		HOV																							
		HOV	HOV																						
				HOV																					
				HOV																					
			HOV																						
			HOV				HOV																		
			HOV	HOV	HOV																				
			HOV																						
				HOV											HOV										HOV
																			HOV						
WIGE																									
						HOV																		HOV	
										GEN					GEN										
			GEN																						
																							GEN		
			GEN		GEN																				
																			GEN						
			HOV																						

Papers presented at IMAEM '87, IV Congress of the Bulgarian Ship Hydrodynamics Centre, Varna, Bulgaria, 25-30 May 1987.

Influence of Skirt Parameters on Hovercraft Transverse Stability Characteristics, E Brzoska, L Kobwlinski and M Krezelewski (Ship Research Institute, Technical University of Gdansk, Poland).

Some Features of Computerized High-Speed Propeller Design Based on Data from Systematic Tests of Cavitating Propeller Series, P Kozhukharov and V Dimitrov (Bulgarian Ship Hydrodynamics Centre, Varna).

Experimental Investigation of Propulsive Characteristics of Ships with Waterjet Propulsion Systems, S Lazarov (Bulgarian Ship Hydrodynamics Centre) and K Varsamov (Higher Institute of Machine and Electrical Engineering, Sofia, Bulgaria).

Papers presented at the 6th International High-Speed Surface Craft Conference, London, 14-15 January 1988. Proceedings published by Hawkedon International Ltd, Chipping Norton, England. ISBN 1 869894 08 1.

Fast River Ferries, R M Mabbott (Thames Line, England).

The Design and Construction of a Stolkraft High-Speed Passenger Ferry, J A Lund (Stolkraft International, Australia).

The Servogear High Performance Propulsion System, L M Endresen (Servogear A/S, Norway).

The Influence of Shaft Inclination on the Relative Merits of Propellers and Waterjets, A G Blyth (Consultant, UK).

The Development of SES Jet Rider, O Gullberg (Karlskronavarvet AB, Sweden).

Model Tests – A Powerful Design Tool in SES Development, L Ronnquist (SSPA Maritime Consulting, Sweden).

Evaluation of a Ride Control System for SES, B R Clayton and R Webb (University College, London).

The Role for Composite Materials in Future Marine Transportation, A Marchant (Marchant Filer Dixon, UK) and R F Pinzelli (Du Pont de Nemours, Switzerland).

Flexural Fatigue Properties of Advanced Marine Composites, R J Rymill and J E Course (Lloyd's Register of Shipping) and R F Pinzelli (Du Pont de Nemours, Switzerland).

High Performance Composites and their Effectiveness in Sandwich Panels, H G Allen and K Raybould (Southampton University, UK).

The Powering Characteristics of Hydrofoil Craft, F van Walree (Maritime Research Institute, Netherlands).

A New Generation of Marine Engines with Very Low Mass/Power Ratios and Their Application on Fast Craft, G Venturini (CRM Design Office) and V Ruggiero (Genoa University, Italy).

The Influence of High-Speed Powerboat Design on Commercial and Military Operations, J P Sutcliffe (Cougar Holdings Ltd, UK).

Drag Estimation for Hovercraft, Y Wang (Dalian Institute of Technology, China).

On the Design Technology of SWATH Ship for High-Speed Coastal Passenger Vessel, K-Y Lee and D-K Lee (Korea Institute of Machinery and Metals) and E-S Kim, J-G Kim and J-H Kim (Hyundai Heavy Industries, Korea).

Wigfoil Interface Craft Concept, Y Manor (Manor Engineering Products, Israel).

SECTION 3

REFERENCE PUBLICATIONS, BOOKS AND PERIODICALS

LEGISLATION

INTERNATIONAL
Code of Safety for Dynamically Supported Craft, London 1978, Resolution A 373(X), International Maritime Organisation.

CANADA
Standards relating to Design, Construction and Operational Safety of Dynamically Supported Craft in Canada, Vol 1, Air Cushion Vehicles; Vol 2, Registration and Certification of Dynamically Supported Craft and Dynamically Supported Craft Operations, Transport Canada, Ship Design and Construction Division, Ship Safety Branch, Canadian Coast Guard, Ottawa, December 1985.

NORWAY
Rules for Classification of High-Speed Light Craft, 1985, Det norske Veritas (Veritasveien 1, N-1322 Norway).

UK
British Hovercraft Safety Requirements, CAA Safety Regulation Group (Aviation House, South Area, Gatwick Airport, Gatwick, West Sussex RH6 0YR, UK).

BIBLIOGRAPHIES AND GLOSSARIES
Glossary for High-Speed Surface Craft, The Society of Naval Architects and Marine Engineers (1 World Trade Center, Suite 1369, New York, NY 10048, USA).

ITTC Dictionary of Ship Hydrodynamics, Maritime Technology Monograph No 6, 1978. The Royal Institution of Naval Architects, London, August 1978.

Bibliography and Proposed Symbols on Hydrodynamic Technology as Related to Model Tests of High-Speed Marine Vehicles, SSPA Public Research Report No 101, 1984. (SSPA, PO Box 24001, S-40022, Gothenburg, Sweden.)

High-Speed Waterborne Passenger Operations and Craft: Bibliography, US Department of Transportation, Urban Mass Transportation Administration, Washington DC, USA. UMTA-IT-32-0001-84-2, August 1984.

Jane's High-Speed Marine Craft and Air Cushion Vehicles 1987. Contains a bibliography of 186 papers prior to 1980. ISBN 0 7106 0837 3.

GENERAL INTEREST BOOKS
Hovercraft and Hydrofoils, Roy McLeavy. Blandford Press Ltd.

Hovercraft and Hydrofoils, Jane's Pocket Book 21, Roy McLeavy. Jane's Publishing Company.

The Interservice Hovercraft (Trials) Unit, B J Russell. Hover Publications, 1979, ISBN 0 9506 4700 4.

The Law of Hovercraft, L J Kovats. Lloyd's of London Press Ltd, 1975.

Amazon Task Force, Peter Dixon. Hodder and Stoughton, London, UK, 1981, ISBN 0 3403 2713 8 and 0 3403 4578 0 Pbk.

Hydrofoils and Hovercraft, Bill Gunston. Aldous Books, London, UK, 1969, ISBN 4900 0135 1 and 4900 0136 X.

An Introduction to Hovercraft and Hoverports, Cross & O'Flaherty. Pitman Publishing/Juanita Kalerghi.

Light Hovercraft Handbook, (ed) Neil MacDonald. Hoverclub of Great Britain Ltd (available from 45 St Andrews Road, Lower Bemerton, Salisbury, Wilts), 1976.

Hover Craft, Angela Croome, 4th edition, 1984. Hodder and Stoughton Ltd, ISBN 0 3403 3201 8, ISBN 0 3403 3054 6 Pbk.

Twin Deliveries, J Fogagnolo. International Catamarans Pty Ltd, Hobart, Tasmania. Paperback, 1986.

Ships and Shipping of Tomorrow, Rolf Schonknecht, Jurgen Lusch, Manfred Schelzel, Hans Obenaus, Faculty of Maritime Transport Economics, Wilhelm-Pieck University, Rostock, German Democratic Republic. MacGregor Publications Ltd, Hounslow, England, 240pp, 1987.

TECHNICAL BOOKS
Jane's Surface Skimmers (annual 1967-1985) (ed) Roy McLeavy. Jane's Publishing Company.

Jane's High-Speed Marine Craft and Air Cushion Vehicles (annual, 1986 onwards) (ed) Robert L Trillo, Jane's Transport Press.

Hovercraft Design and Construction, Elsley & Devereux. David & Charles, Newton Abbot, UK, 1968.

Dynamics of Marine Vehicles, Rameswar Bhattacharyya (US Naval Academy, Annapolis, Maryland, USA). John Wiley & Sons, 1978. ISBN 0 4710 7206 0.

Air Cushion Craft Development (First Revision), P J Mantle (Mantle Engineering Co, Inc, Alexandria, Virginia, USA); David W Taylor, (Naval Ship Research and Development Center) DTNSRDC-80/012, January 1980.

Transport Ships on Hydrofoils, Blumin, Massejef and Ivanof Isdatelstvo Transport, Basmannij Tupik, D 6a, Moskowsaja Tipografija Nr 33, Glawpoligrafproma, Moscow, USSR, 1964.

Marine Hovercraft Technology, Robert L Trillo, 1971. ISBN 0 2494 4036 9. Available from Robert Trillo Ltd, Lymington, Hampshire, UK.

Resistance and Propulsion of Ships, Sv Aa Harvald (The Technical University of Denmark). John Wiley and Sons, 1983. ISBN 0275 8741.

Industrial Fans – Aerodynamic Design, Papers presented at a seminar organised by the Fluid Machinery Committee of the Power Industries Division of the IMechE, held London, 9 April 1987. Published: MEP Ltd.

Global Wave Statistics, N Hogben (British Maritime Technology Ltd). Unwin Brothers Ltd, Woking, UK, 1987. 656pp, £295.

Fibre Reinforced Composites 1986, Institution of Mechanical Engineers publication 1986. ISBN 0 8529 8589 4/297, 262pp.

PERIODICALS
High-Speed Surface Craft, (bi-monthly) High-Speed Surface Craft Publishing Associates, 69 Kings Road, Kingston upon Thames, Surrey KT2 5JB, England.

Hovercraft Bulletin, (monthly) The Hovercraft Society, Rochester House, 66 Little Ealing Lane, London W5 4XX, England.

Light Hovercraft, (monthly) The Hoverclub of Great Britain Ltd, 45 St Andrews Road, Lower Bemerton, Salisbury, Wilts, England.

Work and Patrol Boat World, (monthly) Baird Publications Pte Ltd, 190 Middle Road, Unit 15-07 Fortune Centre, Singapore 0718
and
PO Box 460, South Yarra 3141, Australia.

Ship and Boat International, (ten times a year) 16 Lower Marsh, London SE1 7RJ, England.

Small Ships, (bi-monthly) International Trade Publications Ltd, Queensway House, 2 Queensway, Redhill, Surrey RH1 1QS, England.

ADDENDA
AUSTRALIA

DOEN JET MARKETING INTERNATIONAL PTY LTD

6/3 Industrial Complex, Gibbs Street, Labrador, Queensland 4215, Australia

Telephone: (075) 371799
Telefax: (075) 372019

This company has a range of waterjet units available for power levels between 30 and 400hp and designs available for higher power levels up to 2000hp. Some of their early models have now been in trouble-free service for six years.

Doen Jet model range

Doen Jet model	Impeller diameter millimetres (inches)	Nozzle diameter millimetres (inches)	Power range horsepower (kilowatts)	Rpm range	Static thrust pounds-force (newtons)	Construction housing
DJ 60	152·4mm (6in)	88·9-92·0mm (3½-3⅝in)	30-90hp (22-67kW)	3000-5500rpm	200-700lbf (890-3100N)	Alloy/stainless steel
DJ 80	203·2mm (8in)	114·3-120·7mm (4½-4¾in)	100-350hp (75-260kW)	3500-4500rpm	1000-1600lbf (4450-7100N)	Alloy-stainless steel
DJ 100	254·0mm (10in)	152·4mm (6in)	100-400hp (75-298kW)	3000-3500rpm	1200-1800lbf (5350-8000N)	Alloy-stainless steel
DJ 140	355·6mm (14in)	To specification	200-900hp (149-671kW)	2250-2500rpm	3000-4000lbf (13350-17800N)	Alloy or complete stainless steel
DJ 200	508·0mm (20in)	To specification	500-2000hp (373-1491kW)	1700-2000rpm	7000-9000lbf (31000-40000N)	Alloy or complete stainless steel

W A LIGHT HOVERCRAFT COMPANY

281 Main Street, Balcatta 6021, Western Australia, Australia

M Dixon, *Proprietor*
T Dixon, *Proprietor*

The proprietors of this company have been building hovercraft for almost ten years and in 1985 the partnership was formed to offer plans and components for small hovercraft. Services include repair work and sales of Yamaha motors and plans for Simple Cyclone hovercraft.

BEACHCOMBER

In 1986 the partnership went into production of the Beachcomber, a two-seat fibreglass craft for the pleasure and sport market with agricultural uses as well. Beachcomber is available as a bare hull, in assembly-kit form, or completed craft. The craft features quiet operation, low spray and good performance. Several craft have been sold to customers in the far north of Western Australia and have operated in some very diverse and harsh conditions, from waterless desert in 45°F heat to plains flooded by monsoonal rains. This craft has also operated in the huge tidal areas of King Sound, where the tide ranges up to 10m, and has made a trip down the Fitzroy River.

HULL: Gel-coated chopped strand mat, hand laid-up in a monocoque construction with buoyancy foam an integral part of the construction. The seat is a motorcycle type with the tank built-in and engine bearers moulded into cockpit floor.
ENGINE: Yamaha PE 485 twin-cylinder two-stroke developing 51bhp at 6500rpm, driving a 740mm diameter fan through timing belt reduction and tapered roller bearing fan hub.

SKIRT: Sixty-five separate segments of pvc-coated nylon.
STEERING: Handle-bar type with twist-grip throttle control.
DIMENSIONS
Length: 3·4m
Width: 1·94m
Ground clearance: 230mm
WEIGHTS/CAPACITIES
Fuel capacity: 20 litres
Total weight: 150kg
Payload: 200kg
PERFORMANCE
Speed, max: 100km/h (calm conditions)
Gradient, max (standing start): 25° (driver only)
Fuel consumption, approx: 8 litres/h
PRICES (Feb 1988)
Bare hull: A$1000
Assembly kit: A$6450
Completed craft: A$8750

Beachcomber

Beachcomber

CHINA, PEOPLE'S REPUBLIC

CHINA SHIP SCIENTIFIC RESEARCH CENTRE

People's Republic of China

WIG CRAFT 902
Built 1984/85.
ENGINES: Two 15kW.
DIMENSIONS
Length: 9·55m
Width: 5·85m
Height: 2·32m
WEIGHTS
Weight, empty: 285kg
Weight, loaded: 385kg
PERFORMANCE
Speed: 110 to 120km/h
Clearance height: 0·6 to 1·0m
Crew: 1

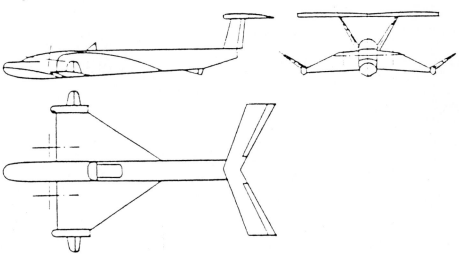

Wing-in-ground-effect craft built by China Ship Scientific Research Centre

FINLAND

WICO-BOAT

07955 Tessjö, Finland

FAST SUPPLY BOAT

A fast supply boat for evaluation by the Swedish Coastal Defence Corps.

HULL: Sandwich glass-reinforced plastics construction with Divynicell core.

ENGINES: Two Scania DS 114 diesels, 485hp each.

PROPULSION: Levi LDU 800 cowled propellers driven via ZF 1·2:1 gearboxes.

DIMENSIONS

Length: 21·8m

WEIGHTS/CAPACITIES

Displacement, empty: 20·0 tonnes

Load capacity, max: 15·0 tonnes

Liquid cargo capacity, water: 4000 litres

fuel: 2000 litres

PERFORMANCE

Speed, lightship: 23·5 knots

Speed, 5-tonne load: 18·0 knots

The Scania-powered Wico-built Swedish defence supply boat

HONG KONG

CHEOY LEE SHIPYARDS LTD

863-865 Lai Chi Kok Road, Hong Kong

Telephone: (3) 743 7710
Telefax: (3) 745 5312

CHEOY LEE 78 FERRY

This 215-passenger Air Ride vessel is now under construction in cored grp. The vessel is powered by two DDA 16V-92 TA diesels, 950hp each, driving Arneson ASD 14 units. The lift-air centrifugal fans are driven by a single DDA 8V-92 TA delivering 350hp.

AIR RIDE SES 82

Mould tooling for Cheoy Lee Air Ride SES 82 motor yacht

Air Ride SES 82 motor yacht

HONG KONG HI-SPEED FERRIES LTD

13/F, V Heun Building, 138 Queen's Road, Central, Hong Kong

Telephone: (5) 8152789
Telex: 89846 HKHPF HX
Telefax: (5) 430324

Dr Stanley Ho, *Executive Chairman & Managing Director*

Capt P N Parashar, *General Manager*

Traffic carried on the Hong Kong to Macau route by the two Vosper Thornycroft ferries *Cheung Kong* and *Ju Kong* was approximately 1·15 million passengers in 1987 and this figure is expected to rise to 1·25 million in 1988. Journey time is 90 minutes with speeds up to 28 knots for the 650-seat vessels. One-way fare, economy class, is HK$35 and first class, HK$55; children under two are free. Hong Kong departure fare, HK$15 for all adults.

Vosper Thornycroft 650-seat, 28-knot ferry *Cheung Kong*, operated by Hong Kong Hi-Speed Ferries Ltd

JAPAN

MITSUBISHI HEAVY INDUSTRIES LTD

5-1, Marunouchi 2-chome, Chiyoda-ku, Tokyo, Japan

Telephone: (212) 3111
Telex: 22443 J

SHIMONOSEKI SHIPYARD AND ENGINE WORKS

16-1 Enouni-cho, Hikoshima, Shimonoseki, Japan

Telephone: (66) 2111
Telex: 0682284 J

SUNLINE
See p 302 for details of this vessel.

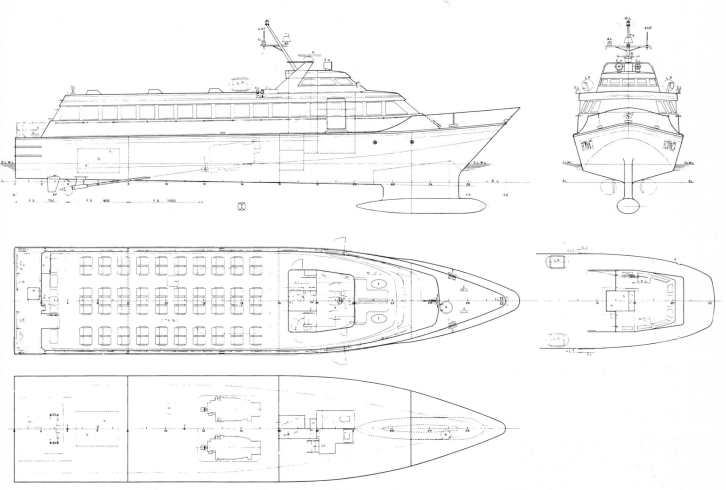

General Arrangement of the Mitsubishi 70-passenger *Sunline* semi-submerged-bow high-speed ferry

HI-STABLE CABIN CRAFT (HSCC)
See p 217 for details of this vessel.

The Mitsubishi HSCC at sea

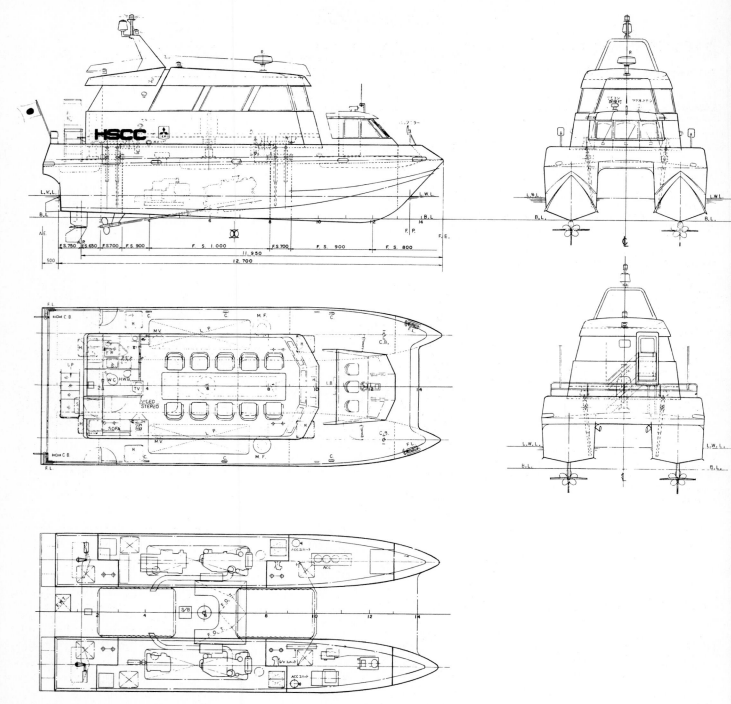

General Arrangement of the Mitsubishi Hi-Stable Cabin Craft (HSCC), a research vessel designed to explore the possibilities for cabin auto-stabilisation

---

MITSUI ENGINEERING AND SHIPBUILDING CO LTD (MES)

6-4 Tsukiji 5-chome, Chuo-ku, Tokyo 104, Japan

Telephone: 544 3462
Telex: 22821/22924 J

Kazuo Maeda, *Chairman*
Isshi Suenaga, *President*
Yoshio Yamashita, *General Manager, High-Speed Craft Division*

SEABULLET 27-M

A revolutionary Seabullet hull form for planing craft has been developed by Mitsui Engineering & Shipbuilding Co Ltd, designed to achieve a combination of high-speed performance and riding comfort. Unlike conventional mono-hull planing craft, the Seabullet has a triple-support hull form with three planing surfaces, a form previously used only in racing boats. This hull form, adapted for commercial purposes, makes the Seabullet a

high-performance craft with not only high-speed stability and high seaworthiness but also an unprecedented ability to withstand impacts.

The Seabullet 27-M has been built to take full advantage of this new hull form. With a new, aesthetically attractive streamlined shape, she is designed as a pleasure boat or sightseeing craft.

Taking advantage of the excellent characteristics of the Seabullet hull form, MES plans to produce a series of diverse pleasure boat models, and to market them actively for both commercial and recreational uses.

The Seabullet was jointly developed by MES and the Japan Marine Machinery Development Association (JAMDA) with financial support from the Japan Shipbuilding Industry Foundation.

Features claimed by MES for the Seabullet hull form are:

The planing surface is divided into three parts and three-point support is maintained even at high-speeds; the craft can run smoothly and stably in its entire speed range.

Even during high-speed running, the Seabullet boat is unusually immune to impacts from

waves; riding comfort is thereby doubly ensured.

Highly seaworthy, she excells both in wave-plowing and wave-riding performance.

The vessel is less susceptible to side skidding and is superior in turning performance and manoeuvrability.

As the hull form allows greater breadth, a correspondingly larger deck area can be secured.

HULL MATERIAL: Frp.
ENGINE AND DRIVING SYSTEM: Gasoline engine, stand drive. Engine output: Two 200hp engines.
DIMENSIONS
Length overall: 7·95m
Breadth: 3·2m
Height overall: About 3·4m (excluding mast)
Depth: 1·3m
PERFORMANCE
Plying limit and route: Limited coastal waters
Speed: 35 knots
Fuel oil tanks: Two 180-litre tanks
Max complement: 13 persons
Equipped with toilet and basin, and air-conditioned

KOREA, SOUTH

DAE WON FERRY LTD

South Korea

High-speed craft to be operated

Type	Delivery
CAT Fjellstrand 38·8m	Late 1988

Route to be operated
Pohang to Ullung-Do island, 85n miles (on east coast)

THE NETHERLANDS

HOLLAND HOVERCRAFT vof

Industrieweg 2, 2921 LB Krimpen a/d IJssel, The Netherlands
PO Box 733, 2920 CA Krimpen a/d IJssel, The Netherlands

Telephone: (01807) 15975
Telex: 21571 HOCON NL
Telefax: (01807) 19956

Wim Mv Poelgeest, *Managing Director*
Tom H van der Linden, *Technical Director*

KOLIBRIE 2000
CAPRICORN 1

Please see p 26 for basic details of this craft. The first Kolibrie 2000 was demonstrated to the press on 18 March 1988. The craft platform structure is built in welded marine grade aluminium alloy and the superstructure in grp mouldings. The side deck structures can be folded for easy road transport. The centrifugal fans for the cushion air supply are mounted beneath the side decks and are driven hydraulically. Considerable attention has been paid in the design of the craft to reducing noise both externally and in the cabin, the craft being particularly quiet in arrival and departure manoeuvres.

Holland Hovercraft Kolibrie 2000 *Capricorn 1*

Capricorn 1 is fitted out and finished to a very high standard. Full instrumentation is fitted along with radio and radar. Cabin air-conditioning is provided, specifically designed for the craft.

Fabric-covered bench seating is fitted along the sides of the cabin and across the back. The skirt is the conventional loop and segment type, constructed in neoprene-coated nylon fabric.

NORWAY

FJELLSTRAND A/S

N-5632 Omastrand, Norway

Telephone: (5) 561100
(after office hours: (94) 67062/68309/65902)
Telex: 42148 FBOAT N
Telefax: (5) 561244

Erik Neverdal, *Managing Director*
Sverre O Arnesen, *Marketing Manager*
Kåre A Hamnes, *Technical Manager*
Leidolv Berge, *Financial Manager*

38·8-METRE CATAMARAN FOR SOUTH KOREA

On 4 March 1988 Fjellstrand A/S announced the signing of an order for a 396-passenger, 33-knot (service speed) catamaran for Dae Won Ferry Ltd, South Korea, the first newbuilding order ever won by a Norwegian yard from a Korean owner. The vessel is waterjet-propelled.

This order brings the total number of Fjellstrand 38·8m Advanced Slender Catamarans sold to 21, valued at some NKr660 million.

SWEDEN

MARINTEKNIK VERKSTADS AB

Varsvagen, Box 7, S-74071 Öregrund, Sweden

Telephone: (173) 30460
Telex: 76182 MARTAB S
Telefax: (173) 30976

Hans Ruppert, *Chairman*
Hans Erikson, *Managing Director*

MINI CRUISE-SHIP

Newbuilding 88 on order for Private Cruise International 1 Ltd. Keel laid January 1988. Length overall: 38·0m; length waterline: 35·0m; speed, max: 24 knots.

Marinteknik Verkstads 38·0m mini cruise-ship building for 1988 delivery

CHIVALRY UNIVERSAL COMPANY

PO Box 36-48, Taipei, Taiwan

TAIWAN

CY-6 Mk IV
See p 45 for details of this craft.

Chivalry Universal CY-6 Mk IV hovercraft

UNION OF SOVIET SOCIALIST REPUBLICS

LENINGRAD CENTRAL DESIGN & PROJECT BUREAU (LCPKB) MINISTRY OF MERCHANT MARINE OF THE USSR

Krasnoy Konnitsy Str 6, 193015 Leningrad, USSR

In a paper given to the Canadian Air Cushion Technology Society in Montreal, September 1987 written by S V Yakonovsky, Chief Designer of the Leningrad Central Design and Project Bureau, details were given of a number of ACV lightering barges. In the late 1970s and early 1980s the Ministry of Merchant Marine ordered 18 hover-barges, four built in the USSR to the designs of the LCPKB and 14 designed and built by Wärtsilä in Finland which purchased a licence for the design and construction of hoverbarges using LCPKB documentation. The various designs are similar, fan location being the main difference.

PROJECT 10352

The following description is an extract from the above mentioned paper:

'The hoverbarge is a towed pontoon with a skirt attached along its perimeter, the powerplant and control station being arranged aft. The midship and fore parts of the deck remain free and are used for the carriage of cargo. Cargo to be transported on the marine hoverbarge can be up to 12m long, 8·1m wide and up to 35 tonnes, as well as vehicles, containers and bulk cargo.

The service area is restricted to area of navigation III (according to the Rules of the USSR Register of Shipping). The barge may proceed not more than 10 miles from the shore or the ship at Sea State up to 4. Stability meets the requirements of the USSR Register Rules.

The marine hoverbarge remains afloat with any one compartment flooded.

The skirt may be of two types: bag or segmented. Attached to the external surface of the skirt is an apron. The skirt material is a rubberised fabric which is frost-resistant down to −40°C. The barge has an all-welded hull with longitudinal framing, the thickness of sides and bottom is 3mm, of deck 4mm, with local thicknesses increased to 6mm.

Anchor arrangements consist of one high-holding-power anchor of 100kg weight and a special mooring capstan with electrical and manual drives.

Mooring and towing arrangements include four mooring bollards installed in the bulwark in the hull corners, two mooring capstans in the forward part and two towing eyebolts welded into the deck.

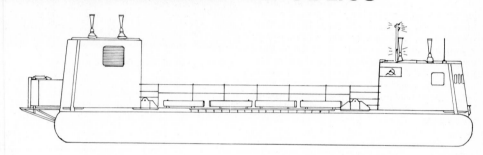

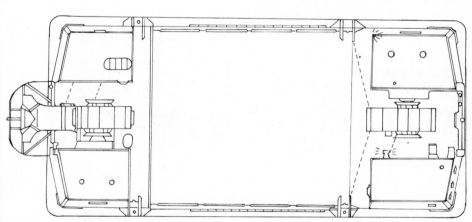

Project 10351 marine hoverbarge

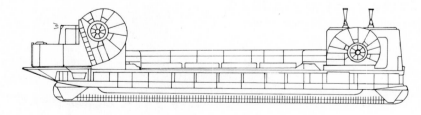

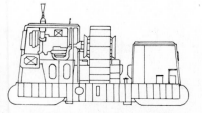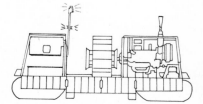

Project 10351 longitudinal and transverse sections

A ramp is constructed as four separate girders each 320 × 3700mm in size and of 132kg weight with a permissible concentrated load of 40kN.

Life-saving appliances include 6-man liferaft in a container with a launching device and individual life-saving appliances.

The powerplant consists of a 220kW, four-cycle, non-reversible V-engine driving through a jaw clutch a centrifugal lift-air supply fan having a capacity of 33m³/s at a pressure of 0·0054MPa, and an ac diesel generator with a power output of 20kW.

Provision is made for a ballast (heeling) system and a water fire-main system serviced by an electrically driven pump having a capacity of 10m³/h at a head of 40mwg.

The barge is non-self-propelled. Special towing means are used for its water and land surface movement.

The craft is to be carried on board and thus be compatible with the existing ships. Therefore due to the limitations of the barge dimensions and mass, the development of a self-propelled ACV would result in a reduction of payload and hence impair economic indices.

Operation of hoverbarges under real conditions of the Arctic began in 1980. Initially non-amphibious towing vehicles had been employed, namely 70kW tug boats for towing in water and land tractors of the same power for overground movement. In so doing, two or more tractors have been required to overcome slopes of more than 4-5°. Such operational schemes, however, do not permit the full realisation of all the advantages of the hoverbarge as an amphibious craft. The transfer of the towing rope from the tug boat to the tractor and vice versa involves delays and it is inconvenient to operate with two or more tractors simultaneously.

In this connection, a need appeared to create a special amphibious towing vehicle to tow a hover-barge from the ship to the storehouse. Using running gear of one of the tracked vehicles as a basis, a design was developed and three amphib-ious towing vehicles were constructed in 1981-82.

The main requirements for a new amphibious towing vehicle are: pressure on the ground not in excess of 0·4kg/cm²; slope to be overcome with a towed hoverbarge of about 80 tonnes at a speed of 1·5-2·0km/h, up to 15°; maximum speed of hover-barge towing in water, 5·0 knots; fuel endurance, about 24 hours; restricted area of navigation with a distance from the shore or a ship equal to 10 miles; operation is to be ensured in ambient air temperatures from −25°C to 35°C, and of water from −1°C to 20°C; winter stay at temperatures down to −50°C; provision is to be made for a towing winch with a pull of about 350kN (35 tonnes) and a drum having a capacity of about 100m of wire rope.

Main particulars of marine hoverbarges built in the USSR

	Project 10351	Project 10352
Length overall		
in displacement mode	19·85m	18·29m
on air cushion, with bag skirt	19·95m	18·41m
Breadth, extreme		
in displacement mode	9·20m	9·10m
on air cushion, with bag skirt	9·20m	9·91m
on air cushion, with segmented skirt	—	9·91m
Depth	1·00m	1·10m
Draught, design	0·64m	0·66m
Displacement, fully loaded	71·80 tonnes	74·70 tonnes
Displacement, light	40·50 tonnes	38·00 tonnes
Cargo areas		
length	8·80m	12·00m
breadth	8·10m	8·10m
Clearance height	0·70m	0·55m
Air cushion pressure	4860Pa	4860Pa
	(495kg/m²)	(495kg/m²)
Air cushion area	146m²	151m²
Air cushion pattern	one-chamber	two-chamber
Payload	28·4 tonnes	35·00 tonnes
Crew	2	2
Gross tonnage	47·20	36·00

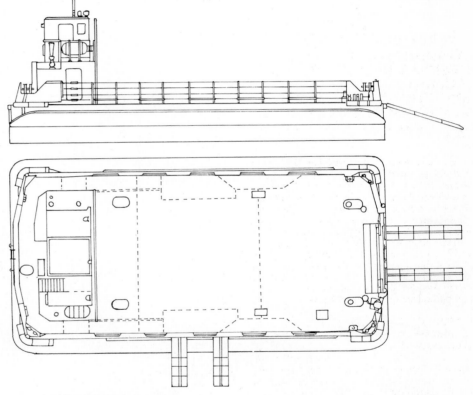

Project 10352 marine hoverbarge

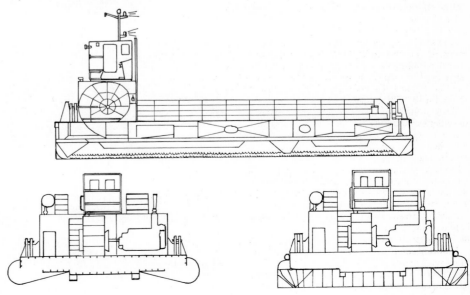

Project 10352 longitudinal and transverse sections

Main particulars of amphibious towing vehicle

Length, design: 11·80m
Breadth: 3·90m
Depth: 2·14m
Draught: 1·10m
Displacement, fully loaded: 27·40 tonnes
Displacement, light: 25·00 tonnes
Main engine: Diesel engine
Engine output: 280kW (380hp)
Number of propellers: 2
Number of gears: 3
Speed
  in water: About 5 knots
  over land: About 30·0km/h
Bollard pull: 24·5kN (25 tonnes)
Pull when moved over land surface using first gear
  (at a speed about 5km/h: 122·2kN (12·5 tonnes)

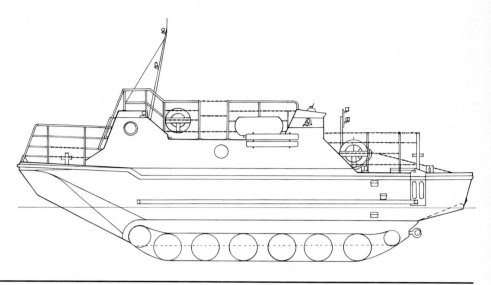

Amphibious towing vehicle for marine hoverbarges

UNITED KINGDOM

VOSPER THORNYCROFT (UK) LIMITED

Paulsgrove, Portsmouth PO6 4QA, England

Telephone: (0705) 379481
Telex: 88115 VTPSTH G
Telefax: (0705) 381124

ATLANTIC CHALLENGER III
See p 329 for details of this vessel.

Atlantic Challenger III under construction, January 1988

Gentry Eagle

UNITED STATES OF AMERICA

AIR RIDE CRAFT INC

15840 SW 84th Avenue, Miami, Florida 33157,
USA

Telephone: (305) 233 4306
Telex: 990160 AIRIDE
Telefax: (305) 592 9655

AIR RIDE 102

Early in 1988 Air Ride Craft Inc announced
that a contract had been placed for an Air Ride
102 passenger ferry in the southern United States.
The contract includes the patent-pending Air Ride
rapid attachment docking system. The detailed
structural, mechanical and electrical designs for
this vessel have been undertaken by RPM Marine
Systems Inc, St Rose, Louisiana. Classification
will be USCG, construction in 5086 marine
aluminium. The vessel is due to enter service in
May 1988.

MAIN ENGINES: Three Deutz MWM 16V 234,
950hp each.

AIR-LUBRICATION FAN ENGINES: One
MWM 8V 234, 450hp.

PROPULSION: Arneson Surface Drive.

ACCOMMODATION: 356 passengers.

DIMENSIONS
Length: 31·07m
Beam: 9·04m

WEIGHTS/CAPACITIES
Displacement, lightship: 90·40 tonnes
Displacement, max: 132·08 tonnes
Fuel capacity: 12 490 litres
Potable water capacity: 1514 litres

PERFORMANCE
Speed: 36 to 44 knots
Range, at 38 knots: 875n miles

Air Ride Craft Inc offer the Maritime Dynamics
Inc ride-control system as standard on their large
passenger ferry designs.

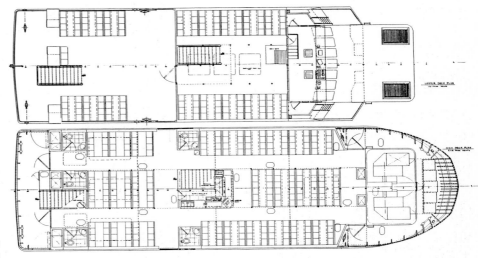

The Air Ride 102 for which a contract has now been placed in the southern United States

ROBERT E DERECKTOR OF RHODE ISLAND INC

Coddington Cove, Middletown, Rhode Island
02840, USA

Telephone: (401) 847 9270
TWX: 710 387 6305
Telefax: (401) 846 1570

Robert E Derecktor, *President*

CATAMARAN 100 (DESIGN)

A 200-seat high-speed catamaran passenger
ferry design, hull in aluminium alloy, 5086 series,
welded.
MAIN ENGINES: Two MTU 2300hp each.
DIMENSIONS
Length overall: 30·49m
Beam: 10·37m
Draught: 1·83m
WEIGHT: 98 tonnes.
PERFORMANCE
Speed, max: 33 knots

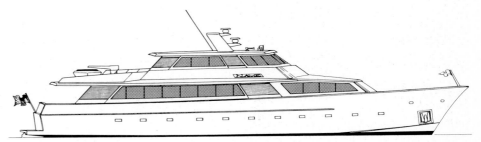

Derecktor Trident 105 high-speed yacht, revised profile

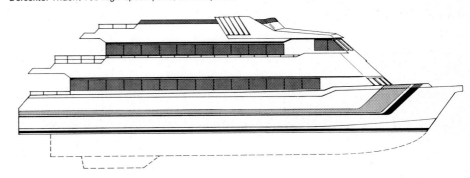

Derecktor 100 high-speed catamaran ferry design

HOVER SYSTEMS INC

1500 Chester Pike, Eddystone, Pennsylvania
19013, USA

Telephone: (215) 876 9292
Telex: 62914561 (Easylink)

James D Hake, *President*
Joseph J Nestel, *Executive Vice President*
Frank W Hake II, *Vice President*

A US built Husky G1500 TD has been purchased by the National Science Foundation for
service in the Antarctic by ITT Antarctic Services

Inc. Special design features were incorporated in
the craft, along with careful selection of equipment and materials, in order to meet the low
temperature and hostile environment of Antarctic
operations. The craft was delivered in early
February 1988 after completing acceptance tests
on the Delaware River and over-ice trials have

been completed in the McMurdo Sound area of the Antarctic.

The craft will operate over sea ice as a support vehicle for scientists. It will also complement helicopter operations and relieve shuttle services to William Field during periods of soft ice surface conditions.

The Husky G1500 TD can be loaded into a single C-130 aircraft and further over-ice applications are being evaluated.

Hover Systems Husky G1500 TD operating in McMurdo Sound

TEXTRON MARINE SYSTEMS (TMS)

Division of Textron Inc

6800 Plaza Drive, New Orleans, Louisiana 70127-2596, USA

Telephone: (504) 245 6600

John J Kelly, *President*

Textron Inc and Trinity Industries Inc announced 2 March 1988 that Textron has purchased all of the shares of Bell Halter Inc owned by Halter Marine Inc, a wholly owned subsidiary of Trinity Industries. Textron now owns all of the outstanding shares of Bell Halter Inc. Price and terms were not disclosed.

Bell Halter Inc was formed in 1980 as a joint venture of Textron Inc and Halter Marine Inc for the purpose of constructing surface effect ships and air cushion vehicles. Bell Halter, which is located in New Orleans, Louisiana, will continue to be managed by the Textron Marine Systems Division of Textron Inc.

Textron Marine Systems delivered LCAC-12 at the end of 1987. The first six were delivered by TMS in 1986. The current TMS building programme is for a total of 24, the US Navy planning additional procurement for a total of 90, including Lockheed-built craft.

INDEX OF ORGANISATIONS

INDEX OF CRAFT TYPES

INDEX OF ENGINE TYPES

INDEX OF CRAFT NAMES

Printed and made in the United Kingdom by Netherwood Dalton & Co. Ltd., Huddersfield